20TH CENTURY PAINTERS AND SCULPTORS

Frontispiece: STANLEY SPENCER, 1891-1959. *'Shipbuilding on the Clyde — Furnaces'*, 1946. 70¼ in. x 50½ in.
Imperial War Museum.

20th Century
PAINTERS
and Sculptors

by Frances Spalding

Assistant Editor Judith Collins

ANTIQUE COLLECTORS' CLUB

ISBN 1 85149 106 6

Published for the Antique Collectors' Club
by the Antique Collectors' Club Ltd.

British Library CIP Data

Spalding, Frances
    The dictionary of British 20th century painters and sculptors
    1. Great Britain. Visual arts — Biographies — Collections
    I. Title   II. Collins, Judith
    709.22

Endpaper illustration: DOROTHY COKE, 1897-1979. *'The Garden Party'*, 1929.
28in. x 36in. Private Collection.

Printed in England by the Antique Collectors' Club Ltd.
5 Church Street, Woodbridge, Suffolk

Antique Collectors' Club

The Antique Collectors' Club was formed in 1966 and now has a five figure membership spread throughout the world. It publishes the only independently run monthly antiques magazine *Antique Collecting* which caters for those collectors who are interested in widening their knowledge of antiques, both by greater awareness of quality and by discussion of the factors which influence the price that is likely to be asked. The Antique Collectors' Club pioneered the provision of information on prices for collectors and the magazine still leads in the provision of detailed articles on a variety of subjects.

It was in response to the enormous demand for information on "what to pay" that the price guide series was introduced in 1968 with the first edition of *The Price Guide to Antique Furniture* (completely revised, 1978 and 1989), a book which broke new ground by illustrating the more common types of antique furniture, the sort that collectors could buy in shops and at auctions rather than the rare museum pieces which had previously been used (and still to a large extent are used) to make up the limited amount of illustrations in books published by commercial publishers. Many other price guides have followed, all copiously illustrated, and greatly appreciated by collectors for the valuable information they contain, quite apart from prices. The Antique Collectors' Club also publishes other books on antiques, including horology and art reference works, and a full book list is available.

Club membership, which is open to all collectors, costs £17.50 per annum. Members receive free of charge *Antique Collecting,* the Club's magazine (published ten times a year), which contains well-illustrated articles dealing with the practical aspects of collecting not normally dealt with by magazines. Prices, features of value, investment potential, fakes and forgeries are all given prominence in the magazine.

Among other facilities available to members are private buying and selling facilities, the longest list of "For Sales" of any antiques magazine, an annual ceramics conference and the opportunity to meet other collectors at their local antique collectors' clubs. There are over eighty in Britain and more than a dozen overseas. Members may also buy the Club's publications at special pre-publication prices.

As its motto implies, the Club is an amateur organisation designed to help collectors get the most out of their hobby: it is informal and friendly and gives enormous enjoyment to all concerned.

For Collectors — By Collectors — About Collecting

The Antique Collectors' Club, 5 Church Street, Woodbridge, Suffolk

Contents

Colour Plates

Colour Plates *continued*

Acknowledgements

We are grateful to many for assistance with the compilation of this book, particularly to those artists, dealers, arts administrators and gallery or museum curators who have responded so readily to our requests for information or for material for reproduction; their generosity has made a significant contribution. This dictionary, however, would not have been possible without access to the Tate Gallery Library's unique collection of exhibition catalogues, and we wish to express especial thanks to Beth Houghton and her staff, Lizz Beardshaw, Elizabeth Bell, Krzysztof Cieskowski and Meg Duff. Our thanks go also to the staff of the Tate Gallery Archives, the Arts Council of Great Britain, the Scottish and Welsh Arts Councils, and the Federation of British Artists. Emma Shackleton acted as Research Assistant during a critical period in the book's progress, and at regular intervals Maureen Daly and David Rose provided help with typing. It has been a pleasure to work with Pam Henderson, Jill Champion, Diana McMillan and Peter Ling at the Antique Collectors' Club, and in general we have been continually encouraged by the enthusiasm with which this project has been received. Its greatest supporter has been our publisher, John Steel, who conceived the idea and, with ebullience and far-sightedness, remained the prime motivating force behind its production.

Abbreviations

A	Associate	**OBE**	Officer (of the Order) of the British Empire
AIA	Artists' International Association	**P**	President
ATS	Auxiliary Territorial Service	**POW**	prisoner of war
b.	born	**RA**	Royal Academy, Royal Academician
BA	Bachelor of Arts	**RAF**	Royal Air Force
CAS	Contemporary Art Society	**RAMC**	Royal Army Medical Corps
cat.	catalogue	**RBA**	Royal Society of British Artists
CBE	Commander (of the Order) of the British Empire	**RBS**	Royal Society of British Sculptors
CND	Campaign for Nuclear Disarmament	**RCA**	Royal College of Art
d.	died	**RE**	Royal Society of Painter-Etchers and Engravers
DBE	Dame Commander (of the Order) of the British Empire	**RHA**	Royal Hibernian Academy
		RI	Royal Institute of Painters in Water Colours
DOE	Department of the Environment	**RIBA**	Royal Institute of British Architects
DSO	(Companion of the) Distinguished Service Order	**ROI**	Royal Institute of Oil Painters
exh.	exhibitor, exhibited	**RP**	Royal Society of Portrait Painters
F	Fellow	**RS**	Royal Society
GHQ	General Headquarters	**RSA**	Royal Scottish Academy
GI	Glasgow Institute of the Fine Arts	**RSBA**	Royal Society of Artists, Birmingham
GLA	Greater London Arts	**RSW**	Royal Scottish Society of Painters in Water Colours
GLC	Greater London Council	**RWEA**	Royal West of England Academy
GPO	General Post Office	**RWS**	Royal Society of Painters in Water Colours
ICA	Institute of Contemporary Arts	**SSA**	Society of Scottish Artists
IS	International Society of Sculptors, Painters and Gravers	**SWA**	Society of Women Artists
		UCL	University College, London
KCVO	Knight Commander of the Royal Victorian Order	**UCLA**	University of California at Los Angeles
LAA	London Artists' Association	**V&A**	Victoria & Albert Museum
LCC	London County Council	**VP**	Vice President
LG	London Group	**WAAF**	Women's Auxiliary Air Force
MA	Master of Arts	**WHO**	World Heath Organisation
MC	Military Cross	**WIAC**	Women's International Art Club
MOMA	Museum of Modern Art	**WRAC**	Women's Royal Army Corps
NEAC	New English Art Club	**WRNS**	Women's Royal Naval Service

Note: All pictures are oil on canvas unless otherwise stated. Measurements are given height by width. * An asterisk against an artist's name in the biographical entries indicates a separate entry in the relevant alphabetical section.

Publisher's Preface

Now that we are in the last decade of the twentieth century the absence of a dictionary of British painters and artists working since 1900 is a very obvious gap in the literature of British art. The question may well be asked why in the competitive world of publishing such an obvious deficiency has been allowed to continue for so long.

The comment once made in another connection, that 'journalism is the first rough draft of history', though not revelant to the professionalism of the author, provides a clue, for the task of assembling information about the thousands of artists (many more than in Victorian Britain) who have worked and are still working, is a formidable one. To provide information on the development of their art as Frances Spalding has done, complicates the task significantly. What could well have defeated a less determined authority was to keep this gargantuan task in touch with the multitude of diverse directions and intellectual concepts into which art has increasingly become divided as the twentieth century progresses. Commentators on Victorian art could summarise their chapters into understandable groupings like genre, historical, nudes, fairies, and neoclassical painters, etc., but such convenient compartmentalisations are not revelant today.

Against such difficulties the problems of copyright of works of art and photographs of works of art — unique to works of this century — has been a mere irritant.

Interest in twentieth century painting and sculpture has reached a level not seen since Victorian England. Over the last fifteen to twenty years interest in painting has moved forward to the point where 'Modern British Art' has become a principal collecting subject even to the detriment of the Victorian artists, whose work held the popular interest during the 1960s and 1970s.

What is not perhaps generally recognised are the sheer numbers of artists who have worked over the last hundred years. *The Dictionary of British Artists 1880-1940* was compiled on the basis of the exhibitions held at forty-seven of the main galleries and institutions during that period. The compiler turned up an astonishing 41,000 artists and no doubt there were ten or twenty thousand more who chose not to exhibit or were rejected. Frances Spalding has therefore had the added problem of selecting some 7,000 (a physical limit imposed by the size of one volume) whose work she feels justifies inclusion on the grounds of their artistic contribution. While there is no argument against the inclusion of the better known artists, there is huge room for disagreement as one descends the listing. Any author's judgement, no matter how professional, is bound to contain an element of subjectivity, while the mammoth task of assembly makes it almost inevitable that some artists have been omitted. It is clear that within four to five years a second edition of this book will be needed, for quite apart from any omissions or the correction of inaccuracies, new artists will emerge, some careers will end and new directions will be followed.

It would be of constructive assistance if those artists (or their surviving relatives), who feel that their exclusion has been unjustified or that they have been under-acknowledged, would see this work as seminal and not definitive, and would assist by providing details in the form set out in the dictionary.

Preface

The excitement generated by the making of this book has grown out of the need to acknowledge a greater diversity of style, content, medium and method than is found in the art of any previous century. Our intention was catholic: to reflect a wide spectrum of tastes and interests; to incorporate names associated with mainstream as well as outsider art, traditionalists, populists and the avant-garde. We have attempted to take account of the consensus, not just of art historians, critics and administrators, but also of the saleroom, minority groups and public taste. Inevitably, in order to make this dictionary viable certain limitations have been imposed. Illustrators, who are already served by a dictionary of their own, have been excluded, except in those instances where, as in the case of Ronald Searle, the distinctiveness and originality of their work has earned them a Fine Art status. Though installations, in that they are an extension of sculpture, come within our realm, performance art, because it requires the extra dimension of time, does not. Both it and photography are specialist disciplines that lie outside the brief suggested by our title. There is, of course, no clear dividing line here as several artists included in this book have ventured into performance activities, whilst still more have made use of photography or worked in the field of illustration. Nevertheless the tighter focus obtained by concentrating primarily on painters and sculptors can be seen to be less conservative than forward-looking. For despite all that new technology offers the artist, painting and sculpture still today have undiminished vitality and are the means by which artists choose to affirm the intransigence of the British imagination.

What this book cannot be expected to provide is the same sense of fixity that previous dictionaries in the series have had. This century is still unfinished and many reputations have yet to stand the test of time's levelling effect. Selection is here more deliberate when dealing with artists who worked during the early decades of this century. At the other end of the time scale, the ever-increasing number of practising artists, accompanied by the mushrooming of private galleries specialising in contemporary art, has presented us with a daunting task. Here selection has been influenced by solo exhibitions which, at the very least, attest to an artist's visibility. Equally difficult has been the recovery of artists' dates. We can boast that certain women artists have been persuaded to disclose dates of birth which have previously been withheld from catalogues. But, as cataloguers at the Tate Gallery have also found, dates of death can prove equally difficult. The situation has not been helped by the fire that destroyed many of the Federation of British Artists' records.

Bibliographical entries, for reasons of space, have been confined to the most useful and accessible items. These have often been chosen because of the bibliographies they contain. Also, if a major retrospective is mentioned in the main entry, it seemed unnecessary to list its catalogue, unless it remains the most significant publication available on that particular artist.

In order to prevent this book from becoming a mere dictionary of names it has been necessary to retain a certain editorial independence. For this reason, we have made only limited use of artists' registers. Inevitably artists of merit will have slipped through our net and our lacunae will in time make a second edition necessary; but for the immediate future this dictionary, in its range and content, provides what no other has yet attempted.

Introduction

It is easy to forget, amid the hubbub of interest that currently surrounds British art, that this century had an uneasy start. Traditions were stagnant; innovation hard to find. The Royal Academy, which had wielded such enormous influence during the second half of the nineteenth century, was in decline. Insular and conservative, it was attacked in the press for its administration of the Chantrey Bequest which enabled work to be bought each year from the Summer Exhibition for the nation. Equally unassertive was the New English Art Club, originally founded in 1886 to promote French-influenced art and as an exhibiting body that would offer a challenging alternative to the Academy. By 1900, however, it had become little more than a nursery to the older institution, for many of its members had either gravitated towards the Academy or exhibited at both institutions. One of its founder-members, Walter Sickert, sadly observed that by 1910 it had developed an over-insistence on two motifs: 'The one the august-site motif, and the other the smartened-up-young-person motif.' This descent to the pleasing and picturesque had resulted in a loss of direction that affected both painting and sculpture. Admittedly sculptors were enjoying a very fertile relationship with architects at this time, but the adverse side to this was that it left them in a subservient role. For many sculptors during the first decade of this century the job in hand was either decorative or commemorative. Ezra Pound, looking back on this period, declared that sculptors had been 'engaged wholly in making gas fittings and ornaments for electric light globes', or hard at work on 'large, identical ladies in night-gowns holding up symbols of Empire or Commerce or Righteousness'. This latter remark referred to the mass production of Queen Victoria statues which today solemnly preside over many a park and town square.

Pound's remarks, however, overstate the case and reflect in part on his allegiance to Henri Gaudier-Brzeska, one of the sculptors who successfully broke with the conventions restricting the Edwardian era. Nowadays Edwardian sculpture is seen to represent a final hothouse flowering of Renaissance ideals, classical themes and sources. Still working within this period were the four great late Victorians — Sir Thomas Brock, Sir George Frampton, Sir William Hamo Thornycroft and Alfred Gilbert. The last of these was perhaps the most typical in that his sculpture is highly wrought, fabulously eclectic and intricately detailed. Gilbert often worked with a variety of materials, for he brought to his art the skills of jeweller and silversmith as well as those of the sculptor. He also achieved colouristic effects in his bronzes through use of oriental alloys and pickles. The impulse in both his monuments and smaller statues constantly to embellish is related to his failure to complete major commissions. Throughout much of the Edwardian era Gilbert was bankrupt, dishonoured and in exile in Bruges. It was an ironic twist of fate that brought about his return to England in 1926, his completion of the Duke of Clarence tomb, reconciliation with the Royal Family and his knighthood in 1932.

Plate 2. WALTER SICKERT, 1860-1942. *'The Siesta'*. 15in. x 18in. Private Collection, U.K. Photograph: Thomas Agnew & Sons Ltd.

A high level of craftsmanship is equally a characteristic of Edwardian painting. In certain quarters there was an attempt to revive the techniques of the Old Masters. Charles Ricketts and Charles Shannon were influential figures in this development, setting high standards as well in the field of book production with their Vale Press. More widespread was the insistence on tonal harmony, the chief legacy of Whistler who died in 1903 at the height of his reputation. The binding effect of tone can be found in the work of Gwen John, at one time Whistler's pupil, in the elegant beach scenes by Charles Conder, and in the work of the 'Glasgow Boys' — John Lavery, James Guthrie and E.A. Walton among them — who revered Whistler and whose influence in this city was affirmed when the Glasgow Corporation acquired his portrait of Carlyle. In addition Whistler had a small circle of friends and followers who imitated his carefully selective vision. One of these was Theodore Roussel whose marine paintings, like Whistler's, distil the essence of the sea with a few broad sweeps of fluid paint and on which distant ships are registered with delicate brevity. Roussel taught another admirer of Whistler, the hunchback, Paul Maitland, who divided most of

Plate 3. MALCOLM DRUMMOND, 1880-1945. *'19 Fitzroy Street'*. 28in. x 20in. Tyne & Wear Museums Service.

SIR ALFRED GILBERT, 1854-1934. *'Perseus Arming'*. Height 14¼ in.
The Fine Art Society, London.

his short life between the Chelsea Embankment, where he lived, and Kensington Gardens, his best-loved subject. Human activity, when it occurs in his scenes, is seen at a distance and often through a barrier of trees and empty chairs or a fence. Using a sequence of low, subtle tones, softly graduated, Maitland registers atmospheric subtlety and a fine, Whistlerian sense of interval.

Such tonal acuity helped keep the influence of the French Impressionists at bay. Whistler had deprecated their 'screaming blues and violets and greens', and when the dealer, Durand-Ruel, brought a large exhibition of French Impressionist art to London in 1905, it was treated scornfully in the press and few pictures sold. The British Impressionism that had developed in the 1880s had not imitated the analytical methods or chromatic divisionism of Monet, Sisley, Renoir and Pissarro, but had taken as its starting point the work of Jules Bastien-Lepage who painted peasant subjects in the village where he lived and favoured the steady grey light created by an overcast sky. This very mild form of Impressionism had slipped easily into the anecdotal vocabulary of late Victorian art; it was, as Quentin Bell has remarked, 'an Impressionism from which the colour had been removed and to which a high moral tone had been added'.

Bastien-Lepage's chief apologist in Britain was George Clausen. He praised the Frenchman's 'studied impartiality' towards his subject, which it was felt artists could only achieve if, like Bastien-Lepage, they lived and worked among their subjects. As a result the late nineteenth century had seen the development of artists' colonies, at Newlyn and St. Ives in Cornwall, Staithes in Yorkshire and at Brig O'Turk and Cockburnspath in Scotland. Certain of these remained significant outposts well into the twentieth century, attracting a younger generation of artists, such as Ernest and Dod Prockter, Laura Knight and Billie Waters, among others. The finest examples of British Impressionism may belong to the 1880s, but the habit of painting *en plein air* became a lasting one and in the hands of Algernon Talmage or Harry Watson, for example, encouraged a lively rendering of naturalistic effects, of sunshine, air and breeze.

The Edwardian era is also celebrated as the last great period of society portraiture, which celebrated a social and economic order soon to be destroyed by the First World War. The acclaim that was attached to portraiture at this period meant that certain young artists, Augustus John and William Orpen, for example, made it their chosen path to success. Portrait drawing was the means by which William Rothenstein moved among the great and the good, as he later recounted in his richly illuminating three-volume autobiography. Sir John Lavery, Sir William Nicholson and Sir Oswald Birley were among the foremost practitioners of the day, but none surpassed the reputation that clung to John Singer Sargent whose portraits have helped stamp the luxury and elegance of this period on popular imagination.

Born in Florence, of American parents, Sargent, a cosmopolitan by upbringing, studied painting in Paris under Carolus-Duran who taught the construction of form, not through the use of outline but alterations in tone. When Sargent arrived in London in 1886 he was regarded at first as a suspicious foreigner. To a nation bred on the Pre-Raphaelites, for whom painting was a matter of coloured drawing, Sargent's ability to suggest a hand emerging from a sleeve with a few flicks of the brush had a daring insolence. But after the success of his *Lady Agnew* (National Gallery of Scotland), with its breathtaking chic, commissions poured in, at such a rate that his interest in portraiture gradually curdled into dislike. Nevertheless with his painterly nonchalance he successfully gave to the Edwardian plutocracy what many of them lacked through birth: a suggestion of aristocratic ease. His bravura manner was much imitated, though never quite with the same ringmaster's flash of the whip, and this degeneration into a fashionable mannerism led Sickert to talk of 'the wriggle-and-chiffon school of portraiture'.

Plate 4. GWEN JOHN, 1876-1939. *'The Student'*, 1903. 22⅛in. x 13in.
Manchester City Art Galleries.

Plate 5. PAUL F. MAITLAND, 1863-1909. *'Kensington Gardens'*. Ashmolean Museum, Oxford.

Sickert, himself, had been abroad when the century began, dividing his time between Dieppe and Venice. On his return to England in 1905 he swiftly assumed a position of leadership. He took rooms in Mornington Crescent in Camden, a once fine area which had been dramatically altered by the arrival of the railway and the building of the three termini, Euston, St. Pancras and King's Cross. Here, in its battered streets, music halls and seedy lodging-house interiors, Sickert found the kind of subjects that suited his love of low-toned, mellow colour harmonies. His capricious wit, knowledge and experience, all of which fed his many articles and exhibition reviews, gave him a magnetism that drew other artists into his vicinity. In 1907 he formed the Fitzroy Street Group which took rooms in a house opposite his Fitzroy Street studio and there held 'at homes' on Saturday afternoons. Each artist donated an easel on which one of his or her paintings would be displayed, whilst others could be pulled out from the stacks behind. Very little formality prevailed and membership was never fixed, but the eight artists originally associated with this venture were Sickert, Spencer Gore, Harold Gilman, Nan Hudson, Ethel Sands, Walter Russell, William Rothenstein and his brother Albert, who later changed his name to Rutherston.

The Fitzroy Street Group is the first of various artist collectives which throughout this century have challenged the status quo with their search for a contemporary style or method. Sickert's intention in founding this Group was to promote work of 'a modern character'. Following his apprenticeship to Whistler, he had responded to the influence of Degas, in particular the French artist's ability to discern interest in a momentary configuration. Like Degas, he achieved apparently casual effects through carefully studied means; he built up his oils in the studio from annotated drawings, but gave to his pictures the immediacy of a snapshot through the use of unexpected cropping. Though the Fitzroy Street Group never developed a cohesive manifesto or style, it encouraged a move towards a vocabulary of subjects which became more pronounced in 1911, when Sickert's venture evolved into the Camden Town Group which began organising public exhibitions. Harold Gilman, in an attempt to create a tighter more rigorous body and to reduce the number of Sickert's lady-friends, insisted that women should be excluded. This cut out artists of talent — Sylvia Gosse, Nan Hudson and Ethel Sands — but did increase the emphasis on London subjects, its streets, squares and gardens, on humble figure subjects and portraits of costermongers. All were treated with a selective but dispassionate accuracy. Though certain of these artists, among them Robert Bevan, Charles Ginner, Gilman and Gore, began using unmodulated colour, often high-keyed, their work retained a very British sobriety.

A brighter, stronger, palette was not confined to the Camden Town Group. The Scottish Colourists — F.C.B. Cadell, J.D. Ferguson, Leslie Hunter and S.J. Peploe — had also begun using colour, not as the mere consequence of reflected light, but as a building block in a picture's design. The Scottish tradition of bypassing London for Paris gave these artists a closer link with the Parisian avant-garde than most British artists at this date, with the exception of Phelan Gibb, who was familiar with the circle of artists around Gertrude Stein, and Roderic O'Conor, an Irish artist domiciled in Paris. The Scottish Colourists assimilated various influences, from Monet, Manet, Chabaud and the Fauves, and began using pure colour and simplified drawing with panache and a marvellous feeling for the quality of paint.

In England a post-impressionist style of painting did not begin to appear until the first of the Roger Fry's two famous exhibitions. 'Manet and the Post-Impressionists' opened at the Grafton Galleries on November 5, 1910, and was dominated by the work of Cézanne, Gauguin and Van Gogh. To an audience familiar with the skilled illusionism that Sir Edward Poynter or Sir Lawrence Alma-Tadema brought to their domestic scenes set in ancient Greece or Rome, Post-Impressionist paintings seemed brash in colour, ineptly drawn and spatially unconvincing. The critics denounced these French artists as 'bunglers' and 'lunatics', their paintings, the product of incompetence or insanity. But the fury aroused went beyond aesthetics. The public vaguely sensed that the affront caused by these paintings was related to potential violence elsewhere: to the contemporaneous Welsh coal-miners' strike which was broken up by troops; to the programme of disruption which the Suffragettes had embarked upon; to the demand for Home Rule in Ireland and the fear of German invasion. It was this wider context that lay behind the critic Robert Ross's remark: this exhibition, he said, which opened on November 5, revealed 'the experience of a widespread plot to destroy the whole fabric of European painting'.

Roger Fry was convinced it had done no such thing. He saw in the work of the Post-Impressionists a call to order, to the formal principles of design discoverable in great art of the past but lost sight of in the Impressionist's attempt to convey the fleeting and evanescent effects of light. Fry was a very recent convert to French Post-Impressionism, but for more than a decade he had been regretting publicly the lack of structural design in the work of many of his contemporaries. Invited to sit on the New English Art Club jury in 1900, he had found himself trying to reject impressionist paintings which his colleagues thought the vanguard of fashion. D.S. MacColl, the critic and painter, labelled Fry at this time 'a pastichist of the ancients and opponent of modern French painting', little realising that he would later become a leading avant-garde figure and the man who introduced England to modern art.

'Manet and the Post-Impressionists' was followed by 'The Second Post-Impressionist Exhibition', again held at the Grafton Galleries, in the winter of 1912-13. This time Matisse and Picasso were the two artists who dominated the show. Together, both exhibitions introduced the British public, in the space of just two years, to developments in art that had taken place in France over the last thirty. The impact on artists was sudden and dramatic. The two Bloomsbury painters closely associated with Fry — Vanessa Bell and Duncan Grant — began experimenting with mosaic-like patches of colour and radically simplified methods of representation. With their help, Roger Fry founded the Omega Workshops in 1913, in an attempt to introduce a post-impressionist sense of design and colour into the field of applied arts. He also wanted to give part-time work to artists in need of an income and had attracted into this venture Wyndham Lewis, Frederick Etchells, Cuthbert Hamilton and Edward Wadsworth, among others. These four artists suddenly departed when Wyndham Lewis had a disagreement with Fry which Lewis made public by means of a round robin letter. He and his contingent left the Omega and set up, in competition, the Rebel Art Centre. More importantly, their departure led directly to the creation of Vorticism.

Of all the various avant-garde developments that followed after the two Post-Impressionist exhibitions, Vorticism was the most far-reaching. Wyndham Lewis was its chief protagonist, the author of the Vorticist Manifesto which he published in his magazine *Blast* in the summer of 1914. This movement is associated with a spare, architectonic style, abstract or near abstract in content. It employed the formal sobriety of Cubism but was not confined to the Cubists' repertoire of traditional subjects. It shared the Italian Futurists' interest in the machine and urban, industrial life but, unlike the Futurists, it did not attempt to represent speed. Instead Wyndham Lewis often arranged his abstract or near abstract designs around a central nugget of interest (the still centre of a vortex). Though much dispute has arisen as to who or what was Vorticist, the main figures associated with this group were David Bomberg, William Roberts, Jacob Epstein and Gaudier-Brzeska.

The Vorticists were fortunate in having two writers as their spokesmen — Ezra Pound and T.E. Hulme. Pound's interest in Imagist poetry, with its paring away of detail to a few essentials, helped reinforce the Vorticist interest in the steady compression of an idea into a severely reduced, near abstract statement, such as is found in David Bomberg's *The Mud Bath* (Tate Gallery). Hulme, on the other hand, praised the hard and durable, arguing that artists should imitate the principles and economy that govern machinery. He took a particular interest in the work of the sculptor, Epstein, and began writing a book on him. Hulme's theoretical interests may have directed Epstein towards the making of his *Rock-Drill,* in which a robot-like creature was found seated upon an actual drill capable of operating with shattering force. But what might have been a triumphant image of the machine age became ambivalent in Epstein's hands; by giving his figure a hooded gaze and an amputated arm he suggests the worker's limited control over the machine he operates.

Nevertheless Vorticism, with its aggressive emphasis on the non-organic, the terse and clean-cut, later came to be seen as in some way prophetic of war. Yet only one artist, the sole English Futurist, C.R.W. Nevinson, actively welcomed the onset of battle. Ill health prevented him from becoming a soldier, but the moment hostilities began he joined the Red Cross and crossed to Dunkirk. 'When a month had passed,' he later wrote, 'I felt I had been born in the nightmare. I had seen sights so revolting that man seldom conceives them in his mind...' By 1915 he was in such a poor state that he was sent home, still, however, convinced that war was 'a violent incentive to Futurism' and that there could be 'no beauty except in strife, and no masterpiece without aggressiveness'. He began making a visual record of the scenes he had experienced, bringing to his pictures of troops marching or resting a clipped, semi-cubist faceting of form that successfully evoked the anonymity and rigour of modern warfare. But it was a style he could not sustain. When in July 1917 he was sent back to France as an Official War

Plate 6. HARRY WATSON, 1871-1936. *'Holidays'*, 1922. 40 ½ in. x 61in.
The Bridgeman Art Library, City of Bristol Museum and Art Gallery.

Artist for the British Government, he adopted a more naturalistic documentary style, his former radicalism giving way to the more urgent need to record accurately and tellingly on what he saw.

The First World War effectively terminated avant-garde developments in Britain. Wyndham Lewis and William Roberts had been called up; Henri Gaudier-Brzeska and T.E. Hulme were killed in the trenches. Commissions given to artists by the British Government or the Canadian War Memorials Fund further demoralised progressive endeavour for the emphasis on the need to 'record' meant that a style had to be used that would be readily understood. Though there remained a few who still practised in an avant-garde manner, they were isolated figures such as Phelan Gibb whose 1917 exhibition at the Alpine Club Gallery was entirely non-figurative. Another was Jacob Kramer, who continued to use a radically simplified method of drawing for his paintings of Jewish devotional subjects, the greatest of which is his *The Day of Atonement* in Leeds City Art Gallery. These individuals could do little to prevail against the mood of retrenchment that had set in by the end of the war. Even Wyndham Lewis admitted of the post-war period: 'The geometrics which had interested me so exclusively before I now found bleak and empty. They wanted *filling*.'

Thus the 1920s began with a return to order and native traditions. There was some attempt to reawaken interest in developments abroad, notably an exhibition of modern French art mounted at Heal's in London, in 1919, by Osbert

Plate 7. DUNCAN GRANT, 1885-1975. *'The Vase'*, 1915. 10in. x 14in. Sandra Lummis Fine Art, London.

and Sacheverell Sitwell. But on the whole London in the 1920s displayed very little interest in what was happening abroad and not until 1926 did the Tate Gallery (originally entitled the National Gallery of British Art) begin to display contemporary European art. English artists were, for the most part, left to their own devices.

One important development at this time was the revival of interest in the art of printmaking. Though the great boom in etching did not really begin until 1924, at the start of this decade it was a popular medium at Goldsmiths' College. It was taught by Malcolm Osborne who, when he moved on to the Royal College in 1925, was replaced by Stanley Anderson. Among the star pupils at Goldsmiths' who specialised in etching were Paul Drury, Graham Sutherland and Robin Tanner. All admired the work of F.L. Griggs, especially his *Highways and Byways* illustrations which set a standard of excellence that a younger generation was to emulate. But interest in this medium was further enhanced in the mid-1920s by the rediscovery of Samuel Palmer. His example can immediately be felt in the etchings of the young Graham Sutherland and which in 1925 earned him associate membership of the Royal Society of Painter-Etchers and Engravers, an exhibiting body founded in 1880 by Whistler's brother-in-law, Seymour Haden and which during the 1920s was presided over by Sir Frank Short.

Running parallel with the etching revival was the renewed interest in the less flexible and more strenuous medium of wood-engraving. A key figure here was Noel Rooke who taught at Central School of Art and Crafts. Together with his pupil Robert Gibbings, later to become the proprietor of the Golden Cockerell Press, Rooke founded the Society of Wood-Engravers in 1920 and which attracted into its ranks the master-engraver, Eric Gill, as well as Lucien Pissarro, Paul and John Nash, Eric Ravilious and David Jones, among others. But from its inception it was riddled with dispute and in 1926 Leon Underwood, Blair Hughes-Stanton and Gertrude Hermes split off to form the English Wood-Engraving Society. Much of the work produced by both societies was fed into a number of flourishing private presses which produced illustrated books in limited editions, inspired by the ideals of the Arts and Crafts movement and in particular by William Morris's Kelmscott Press. To some extent this development had a reactionary bias, for it was fuelled by a dislike of modern photographic production. Most of these artists also looked back to the unsurpassed master of wood-engraving, Thomas Bewick, who had worked in the late eighteenth century. But though his example can be felt behind much 1920s wood-engraving, it nevertheless displays a crispness, a surface tension that is modern.

One artist who excelled in this medium was Eric Ravilious. His designs, with their careful balancing of dark and light, have a satisfying density and compactness that is nevertheless also airy and light. He is often associated with Edward Bawden whom he met in the Design School of the Royal College of Art and where both were taught by Paul Nash. Both adopted Nash's use of a relatively starved brush for watercolour painting, often using it to create hatching that allows the white of the paper to show through with crystalline effect. This technique can be found in Bawden's Essex scenes, with their severe outlines and patterned fields, and which uphold his interest not in atmosphere but in the surfaces of things.

Bawden and Ravilious first came to the fore in 1928 when, with Charles Mahoney, they executed mural decorations at Morley College, a commission that had in part been fostered by the success of Rex Whistler's murals for the tea rooms (now the restaurant) at the Tate Gallery. The creative, competitive friendship between Bawden and Ravilious continued until 1942 when Ravilious, employed as an Official War Artist in Iceland, took off on a reconnaissance flight that never returned. The versatility that had characterised Ravilious's output proved also to be the making of Bawden's long career. The need to earn his living kept him in the field of commercial art and he turned his hand to illustrations for the Curwen Press, the Folio Society, Chatto and Windus, Penguin Books and *The Listener,* which had become renowned for the high quality of its graphic art; he also designed wallpapers with John Aldridge and produced advertisement material for Fortnum and Mason, Midland Bank, Twining's Tea and the Saffron Walden division of the Labour Party, among many others. With his adaptability and unerring skill, he remained a model of professionalism for many artists practising in the field of graphic design. And like many others he benefited from enlightened patronage with regard to poster design, producing work for Jack Beddingham at Shell, Frank Pick and London Transport and for St. John Woods, artistic director for Ealing Studios.

For those artists whose livelihood did not depend on obtaining the next commission, the return of peace brought an opportunity to travel abroad. This had an especial allure for painters interested in landscape as a warmer climate meant escape from British weather. In the 1920s Matthew Smith, Duncan Grant and Vanessa Bell set up second homes in France, Edward Wadsworth spent much time touring in France and Italy and Edward Burra discovered the bars in Toulon and Marseilles. David Bomberg, with help from the Zionist Organisation, travelled to Palestine and there began to develop his expressionist approach to landscape painting which he brought to fulfilment in Spain.

Landscape, in all its various interpretations, had a particular place in 1920s art, partly because it assisted the flight from the machine age and partly because it was a suitable vehicle for the discovery of 'significant form'.

This phrase, which became a catchword in the 1920s, had originally been promoted by Clive Bell in his book *Art,* initially published in 1914 and which was several times reprinted. It had developed out of the aesthetic theories that Roger Fry had put forward to justify Post-Impressionism and it directed attention to the formal or aesthetic content in a work of art. As a touchstone in art it brought both advantages and disadvantages: it encouraged in artists an awareness of the language of paint or sculpture, but it also downgraded literary or poetic content as well as art's role as a social document.

Evidence of this concern with 'significant form' could be seen in the still lifes and views through a window that peppered the annual exhibitions of the London Group. When this was first founded in 1914 it had incorporated the Camden Town Group along with other avant-garde factions. By the 1920s however, it still maintained a decent professionalism but lacked a capacity to startle or shock. In general, it represented an attempt to consolidate the legacy of Post-Impressionism with more traditional approaches to picture-making. There was a fairly widespread respect for the virtues of Cézanne whose importance was further underlined by Roger Fry's monograph on this artist, published in 1927. London Group exhibitions also avoided the staleness and sentimentality that gave to the Royal Academy Summer Exhibitions an unavoidable air of mediocrity.

Wyndham Lewis was not the only avant-garde artist to return to figuration after the war. In William Roberts's work a brittle angularity lingered on into the early 1920s but it gradually gave way to a smooth rotundity, a bluntness that suited his love of everyday scenes. The impersonal regularity that informs his tubular figures helped bring out the rhythmic nature of their movements. No matter how busy or crowded his pictures are, they display the deliberation of a formal frieze, each clearly stated form being well-knit into the overall design. Both Roberts and Stanley Spencer successfully revived the Victorian love of story-telling in modern terms. Spencer's masterpiece is his decorations for the Burghclere Chapel which he worked on between 1923 and 1932, and which drew upon his marvellous sympathy with human activity and his conviction that 'all ordinary acts such as the sewing on of a button are religious things'. Behind his career as a whole lies a consistent religious purpose: the desire to see 'the wholeness of things', to unite spirit with body, the sacred with the profane.

Visionary intensity can also be found in the Brittany paintings which Christopher Wood produced during the last few months of his short life. A lyrical colourist with a concise touch, he learnt much from his friendship with the retired Cornish fisherman, Alfred Wallis, whom he and Ben Nicholson discovered in 1928. Wallis had begun painting at the age of seventy, after the death of his wife, and used as his materials odd bits of cardboard that he obtained from the greengrocer. He adjusted the rhythm and design of his pictures to suit the irregular outlines of his format. He also had an innate feeling for paint and for the movement of boats on water. Both Wood and Nicholson saw in Wallis's small gems confirmation of their own search for a *faux-naif* style, which, with its apparently child-like directness of statement would challenge the tired verisimilitude found elsewhere.

Nicholson became a key figure within the 7 & 5 Society, originally founded in 1919 with seven painters and five sculptors. With hindsight its most significant founder-member was Ivon Hitchens, though it was not until the 1940s that he evolved a distinctively personal style, producing swathes of colour with a broad, full brush on a double-square format. His inventive and highly original interpretation of the English landscape enabled him to suggest seasonal moods, the shimmer of light in the sky or on water, the passage of the eye through space

Plate 8. JACOB KRAMER, 1892-1962. *'The Day of Atonement'*, 1919. 39in. x 48in. Leeds City Art Galleries.

or the movement of wind. His musical paintings, planned in phrases and movements, evolved after the bombing of his studio caused his move to Sussex. He took with him his familiarity with the work of Braque and Matisse, and the inspiration gained from his friendship with Ben and Winifred Nicholson, especially the latter.

Owing to the work of the Nicholsons, Hitchens, Wood and others, the 7 & 5 Society, by the late 1920s, had become associated with a painterly lyricism and a 'primitivism' which allowed an aesthetic sophistication to be concealed behind a simplicity and directness of touch. Cedric Morris became a member of this society in 1927. All his life he continued to paint with unhesitating honesty, with thick, opaque paint, in a style that cold-shouldered the more usual conventions. In keeping with his scorn for artistic fashions, he left London for Suffolk in the 1930s and there, with his lifelong associate, Arthur Lett-Haines, set up the East Anglian School of Painting and Drawing.

In 7 & 5 Society painting of the late 1920s the nature of paint is never disguised. The notion of 'truth to materials' was equally important in the field of

Plate 9. DAVID JONES, 1895-1974. *'Sussex Haven'*, 1927. Watercolour with pencil. 15⅛ in. x 22¼ in. Austin/Desmond Fine Art, London.

Plate 10. ERIC RAVILIOUS, 1903-1943. *'Downs in Winter'*, 1936. Watercolour on paper. 70½ in. x 21½ in. Towner Art Gallery, Eastbourne.

sculpture at this time, particularly in the work of Henry Moore and Barbara Hepworth as they began to supersede Epstein and Frank Dobson as the two most significant sculptors of the inter-war period. Both built upon the return to carving that Epstein, Gaudier-Brzeska and Gill had pioneered. Both gained ideas from European and non-European sources, blending these into a modern language in which rhythmic, plastic and tactile relationships are predominant. In Moore's art the influence of Mexican art informed his view of carving and began his interest in the reclining figure, a motif which he continued to rework throughout his career, with great versatility and a profound range of expression. He was also aware of an analogy between the reclining figure and landscape, the rise and fall of the body creating hills, arches, slopes and plateaux. As he refined upon this theme, he reintroduced to sculpture some of the nobility and seriousness that he had admired in the art of far distant periods and cultures.

Whilst studying in Italy on a scholarship Hepworth had met and married the sculptor, John Skeaping and for a while aligned her ideas with his. But after she became familiar with Ben Nicholson, whom she later married, she began to respond more to European modernism and by the mid-1930s her work had become completely abstract. Hepworth, Nicholson and Moore were all working in the Mall Studios, off Parkhill Road, Hampstead, in the 1930s, where the critic Herbert Read also lived and worked, as did the painter Cecil Stephenson. When Mondrian fled Paris for England in 1938, a studio was found for him nearby. His presence and that of other refugee artists, architects and designers helped make Hampstead in the late 1930s a centre for internationalism.

An avant-garde impetus had revived a few years earlier, in 1933, when Paul Nash got together the group, Unit One, and announced its existence in *The Times*. For the past few years he had been supplementing his income as an artist by writing art criticism for the *Weekend Review* and *The Listener*. His familiarity with developments at home and abroad left him aware of one definite weakness in English art — 'the lack of structural purpose'. His desire to bring together artists and designers whose work would be expressive of 'a truly contemporary spirit' led to Unit One, which made its headquarters the Mayor Gallery in London's Cork Street, published a book entitled *Unit One* but, owing to disputes among members, had a lifespan of little more than one year.

Unit One occurred just as the avant-garde in Britain was to split into two groups: constructivists and surrealists. Encouraged by his meeting with Mondrian and certain French artists, and by his association with the Paris-based exhibiting society, Abstraction-Création, Nicholson had moved into abstraction in the early 1930s and in 1934 proposed that the 7 & 5 Society should retitle itself the 'Seven and Five Abstract Group' and that its 1935 exhibition should consist solely of abstracts. This successfully antagonised a number of artists and brought about the society's demise: its 1935 exhibition, at which only eight artists were represented, was its last.

The following year Nicolete Gray organised the exhibition 'Abstract and Concrete', in which Nicholson's white reliefs, honed to purity in their use of a few geometrical shapes, were shown alongside work by Mondrian, Moholy-Nagy, Helion, Léger, Miró and other key figures in the development of European Modernism. The Russian Constructivist, Naum Gabo, was one of these, and, having recently settled in London, he became friendly with Nicholson and the architect, Leslie Martin. These three men edited the book *Circle* in 1937, a collection of essays and photographs intended to promote a 'constructive' attitude to art and life and thereby create 'a new cultural unity'. Nicholson, Hepworth and others began calling themselves 'constructivists' and shared in the search for universal beauty, discoverable in the structure of a leaf as much as in art and architecture, and which through its display of harmony and balance was, by implication, intended to make the viewer critical of the disorder in everyday life.

This idealist and somewhat high-brow development found its exact counterpart in Surrealists. The Surrealists, far from believing in an underlying order and unity, challenged belief in man's capacity to be in control, of himself or others. They mocked at bourgeois values and accepted conventions and produced objects and images intended to jar the viewer out of habitual ways of seeing. 'Do not judge this movement kindly,' wrote Herbert Read. 'It is not just another amusing stunt. It is defiant — the desperate act of man too profoundly convinced of the rottenness of our civilisation to want to save a shred of its respectability.' Surrealist art appealed not to the rational mind but to the subconscious which it attempted to tap by means of automatic writing, dream imagery and unexpected conjunctions.

Two men — the artist Roland Penrose and the poet David Gascoyne — were responsible for bringing this movement to England. When they met in Paris in 1935 both were already friends of several leading Surrealists. They returned to London to gather support for the movement and in 1936 mounted the International Surrealist Exhibition in which genuine Surrealist work was mixed with the surreal productions of children, mental patients and tribesmen.

Though the Paris-based Surrealists did have links with the proletarian cause and thus with the concept of revolution, their English counterparts were less politically motivated and concerned only to liberate the imagination. Therefore though various Surrealist activities took place in London after the 1936 exhibition, the movement remained little more than an affiliation of like-minded friends. When André Breton tried to extract from his British counterparts greater political allegiance, he met with resistance which was further intensified when these artists were asked not to exhibit or publish except as Surrealists.

Constructivism and Surrealism represent two extreme wings of the avant-garde in the 1930s. It was perhaps inevitable that before long a reaction would set in which in Britain took the form of a return to realism. In 1937 William Coldstream, Claude Rogers and Graham Bell, later joined by Victor Pasmore, founded the Euston Road School, in an attempt to re-establish communication between artists and the public and as a protest against the élitism of much art that was thought to be artistically revolutionary. The aim of the Euston Road School was low key; it sought to teach, not style or theory, but observation and a return to a measured, objective approach to representational painting. Inspiration was drawn, not from leading Modernists, but from Sickert's choice of subject matter, Degas's delicately hatched brushstrokes and Cézanne's searching analysis. Euston Road School painting can be dull but it never lacks integrity. And though the School itself lasted less than two years owing to the onset of war, several of its leading figures joined the staff of Camberwell School of Art and Crafts during or after the war and there sustained the quiet realism and objective appraisal of appearance associated with Euston Road painting. Under William Johnstone, its Principal, Camberwell became one of the liveliest art schools in England after the war, and a whole generation of painting students, many of them on ex-service grants, acquired a sober, well-trained, realist mode. When these same students moved on to other art schools, this approach was further disseminated. In addition William Coldstream moved from Camberwell to become professor at the Slade and there upheld the importance of 'measuring', which had been a key word at the Euston Road School.

The approach and onset of war fuelled nostalgic and patriotic sentiment. John Piper, whose paintings of the mid-1930s had been abstract, returned to landscape painting in 1938, giving special attention to scenes of particular topographical or architectural interest, because, as he has said, the worsening situation in Europe 'made the whole pattern and structure of thousands of English sites more precious as they became likely to disappear'. No other artist has so successfully revived the picturesque for Piper brought to his work a vigorous romantic handling, frequently making heavy use of black and at times scratching into his paint so that the dark background shows through with sombre effect. This rough treatment also enabled him to suggest the ravages of weather on stone, the sparkle of light or the movement of wind. His interest in architecture also fed his work for the *Architectural Review;* with its editor, J.M. Richards, he travelled England, sketching, taking photographs and making notes, not just of famous monuments, but also pubs, lighthouses, harbours, forts and standing stones. Friendship with John Betjeman further encouraged his ability to find appeal in nondescript places; his Shell guide to Oxfordshire took as its model Betjeman's *Cornwall.* The approach of both men was committed but irreverent. 'It was a lark in those days,' Betjeman observed. 'There were no scholars.'

Whilst Piper was reviving interest in our architectural heritage, a subject that became still more dramatic once the Blitz began, Graham Sutherland was independently discovering ways in which the English landscape tradition could be extended and renewed. On a visit to Pembrokeshire in 1934 he had been struck by the 'exultant strangeness' of the landscape and began sketching objects and motifs which, in the quieter environs of Kent where he lived, helped sustain the oils he produced based on his memory of the Welsh landscape. Each year he returned to Wales to experience afresh the combination of elation and disquiet that the countryside aroused in him. In his reconstruction of it he frequently employed the kind of spatial elisions also found in the art of Samuel Palmer and which help make distant hills seem close, thereby bringing them into more dramatic relationship with the foreground. The intensity of the scene was further enhanced by his use of non-naturalistic colour and, as in Piper's work, heavy use of black.

By the early 1940s Sutherland had become all the rage. For his first solo exhibition at the Rosenberg Gallery, London in 1938, Kenneth Clark had written the foreword to the catalogue. The press was enthusiastic and a second exhibition followed in 1941. The effect of both, combined with the publication of his 'Welsh Sketch Book' letter in *Horizon* in 1942, as well as the fact that discerning collectors such as Clark and the arts patron, Peter Watson, had bought his work, was to make Sutherland an inspiration to younger artists in search of romantic solutions. Keith Vaughan, John Minton and John Craxton all took their direction from Sutherland in the early 1940s.

Wartime conditions fostered a desire to escape into a world of private mystery and refuge; and in the landscapes these three younger artists drew or painted the terrain is often that of the imagination rather than reality. Though inspired by specific locations, the work of these artists conveys an elegiac melancholy that distances the scene and suggests a world apart.

Much of their wartime work was done not in oil but watercolour and pen and ink. The neo-romantics, concerned as they were with the fragility of the passing moment, favoured those media that allowed them to work fast. They were also aware that Sutherland was using pen and ink, wax crayon and coloured wash for his wartime paintings of Cornish tin-mines, open-cast quarries, steel foundries and scenes of devastation. Henry Moore adopted similar means for his famous 'Shelter' drawings that developed from his observation of people sheltering from air-raids in the Underground. Many Second World War artists also chose to use more graphic media than oils, in their rendering of fugitive moments caught within the impersonal mechanism of war. Such work was facilitated by the War Artists' Advisory Committee set up by the Ministry of Information and chaired by Sir Kenneth Clark. Under the WAAC's auspices, an artist was either employed for a fixed period of time or commissioned to produce a certain number of pictures for a fixed sum. All kinds of artists, ranging from the avant-garde, such as Paul Nash, to traditionalists such as Frank Wootton and Charles Cundall,

Plate 11. BEN NICHOLSON, 1894-1982. *'Milk and Plain Chocolate'*, 1933. 53in. x 32in.
Private Collection.

were employed. By 1946 nearly 6,000 pictures had been accumulated. They were distributed to public art galleries, at home and abroad, but by far the largest collection was deposited with the Imperial War Museum.

Very little Second World War art rises to the level of a masterpiece. This is partly because refinements in warfare meant that battles were mostly fought at long range. In addition many commissions ensured that artists were removed from the fighting; most only ever saw the home front. As a result what is lacking in Second World War art is any record of human suffering. It was photography and film that first brought home the atrocities associated with concentration camps and the effects of the atom bomb. The legacy of the war rested more importantly in the art of the future, in representations of the human figure that are no longer noble and consoling but the product of 'angst', or which convey an underlying pessimism.

What startled the public in April 1945 was the appearance in a mixed show at the Lefevre Gallery of Francis Bacon's *Three Studies for Figures at the Base of a Crucifixion*. These maimed, bandaged and howling figures, half animal, half human, were unlike anything that had previously been seen in British art. The triptych gains in savagery because it is not an indictment of human bestiality, merely an excoriating statement of it. Gradually over the next few years Bacon began to emerge as the colossus in Britain. His twisted and distorted figures, found alone in bare settings or in the act of coupling with another, suggest extreme situations, of isolation or despair. The ingredients in his art are theatrical, the language he uses that of rhetoric, but the feelings he deals with are those of unescapable reality. They range, as Helen Lessore has commented, from helpless fury to sullen resentment at inescapable doom.

Bacon remains an isolated figure within the history of twentieth century British art. More typical of the post-1945 period was the figurative expressionism found in the work of Prunella Clough, Robert Colquhoun, Robert MacBryde and John Minton. In the winter of 1945-6 the Victoria and Albert Museum had mounted a Matisse and Picasso exhibition. It was Picasso who made the most impact. His ability to paraphrase appearances strengthened the decorative impact of his scenes. His terse, often aggressive stylisation helped banish the elegiac melancholy and nostalgia that had characterised neo-romanticism. Picasso's example encouraged artists in Britain to work on a larger scale and with more forthright design; from now on, however deep the perspective in a picture, its shapes and colours had to be held in tense relation with the picture surface.

Picasso's influence had to some extent been preceded by that of the Polish painter, Jankel Adler, who, like another of his compatriots, Josef Herman, arrived in Scotland with the remnants of the Polish Army in 1940. He soon became a central figure within an artistic community in Glasgow which the former publisher and entrepreneur, David Archer, helped to create. For a short period Glasgow hummed with excitement, but around 1943 an exodus to London began, Jankel Adler moving south that year and soon settling into a studio at 77 Bedford Gardens. In another studio in the same building lived Colquhoun, MacBryde and Minton, all of whom fell under Adler's spell for with his experience of persecution, his familiarity with Klee, Picasso and other European Modernists, and with his love of Armagnac, he quickly became the *grand seigneur* of Bedford Gardens, his love of deep, rich colours and tessellated patterning directing others in the search for a new decorative strength.

Though the artists domiciled at Bedford Gardens were well served by the nearby pub, the Windsor Castle, they were also drawn to Soho which during the war had proved a hospitable refuge for many artists and writers. No history of twentieth century British art would be complete without acknowledgement of the role Soho has played in the lives of many artists since the war. One of its most notorious haunts was the Colony Room, a private drinking club in a first floor room in Dean Street which was presided over by the formidable Muriel Belcher. Her rudeness is legendary, her foul language made memorable by her upper-class voice. In this upside-down world, where the drawn curtains shut out the time of day and male customers were addressed as 'Miss', Muriel Belcher created a freeing atmosphere which artists welcomed. Francis Bacon, Lucian Freud, John Minton, Michael Andrews and Frank Auerbach, are some of the best known names to have been numbered among her clientele.

If figurative art held sway in the late 1940s and early 1950s, it was steadily being undermined by a swelling tide of interest in abstraction. Artists like John Minton found themselves attacked on both sides: by Alfred Munnings, President of the Royal Academy, who in 1948 made a vituperative speech against all forms of modern art at a Royal Academy dinner, and, on the other hand, by those who saw abstraction as the way forward. In 1948 Victor Pasmore began making abstract collages and from these moved on through a series of abstract oils to the making of reliefs. He did so convinced by Charles Biederman's book, *Art as the Evolution of Visual Knowledge,* that the next logical step for artists to take was from illusionism to actuality, from the use of flat surfaces to real materials in real space. Others followed Pasmore, notably Kenneth and Mary Martin, and they became known as Constructionists, a label derived from Biederman's talk of 'constructionism', a movement that attempted not to imitate the appearance of nature but to derive structural processes from it. A constructionist relief usually consists of geometric units composed in horizontal and vertical formations, the parts held in a taut, asymmetrical balance. Some of these artists, in particular Mary Martin, hoped that Constructionists would be able to collaborate with architects and thus infiltrate the environment with their sense of order and measure. As a movement, Constructionism inspired a devoted following and remained a viable way of working for many years.

The original Constructionists were momentarily allied with the St. Ives abstract painters when Adrian Heath in 1953 held a weekend exhibition in his studio. Two Constructionists — Anthony Hill and Kenneth Martin — were also represented in Lawrence Alloway's small book, *Nine Abstract Artists,* published in 1954, and in which it became clear he preferred the concrete and figurative-based art of the Constructionists to the St. Ives abstracts which took their inspiration from nature. 'In St. Ives,' he remarked, 'they combine non-figurative theory with the practice of abstraction because the landscape is so nice nobody can quite bring themselves to leave it out of their art.'

St. Ives had been an artists' haunt since the 1880s. One of the attractions was a light which, reflected off the sea on three sides of the small town, gives to it an unusual clarity. In addition, the sail-lofts, left empty by the declining fishing industry, made excellent studios. By the 1920s artists at St. Ives were sending enough paintings to the Royal Academy each year to fill an entire railway carriage. For many years the artistic scene had changed little. Then, in 1939, Ben Nicholson and Barbara Hepworth and their triplets moved down a week before war broke out. They were soon followed by Naum Gabo. The presence of these three artists had transformed St. Ives into a vital centre of modern art and set a standard of professionalism that a younger generation was to emulate. Gabo's influence, in particular his fusion of internal and external space, can be felt in Wilhelmina Barns-Graham's glacier paintings, also in the early work of Peter Lanyon and that of John Wells. After the war, artists began to migrate to St. Ives in large numbers during the summer. Among these were Terry Frost, Roger Hilton, Patrick Heron, William Scott, Bryan Winter and Alan Davie. All began in their different ways to evolve abstract or near abstract work which, though locally inspired, placed as much emphasis on the artist's gut response to the subject and his or her interaction with the materials used. A Terry Frost abstract might be based on the rocking movement of boats in harbour. For Peter Lanyon, the starting point was the rugged ingredients of the Cornish landscape,

Plate 12. HENRY MOORE, 1898-1986. *'Reclining Figure'*, 1929. Leeds City Art Galleries.

with its slate greys, acid greens, his awareness of the buried shafts of the tin mines and of the dramatic meeting between the sea and rocks. Though each artist brought to his or her work a different set of interests and no group style evolved, there are certain shared characteristics to be found in their art: lines and marks are often terse and abrasive; full, hulk-like shapes recur; and, as in St. Ives itself, the impression is gained of something rugged, wind-swept and on edge.

A similar move towards abstraction can be found in British sculpture of the late 1940s and '50s. In the aftermath of war the monumentality and humanism of Henry Moore's sculpture had less interest to a younger generation of artists than the etiolated figures and quivering outlines of Giacometti's stick-like figures. With images of Auschwitz, Belsen and Buchenwald now a part of human consciousness, it no longer seemed possible to assert in art the Renaissance ideal of man as the centre of the universe, noble, dignified and in control. In Giacometti's hands the human figure suggested anguish, doubt and vulnerability. His mature work began to receive attention at the same time that Existentialism became dominant in Paris, and two of its key figures, Jean-Paul Sartre and Simone de Beauvoir, espoused his art, finding in it an expression of their own concerns. Photographs of Giacometti's work reached London in the form of magazine illustrations. But he was also promoted by the critic, David Sylvester, and given a retrospective in Britain in 1955.

Plate 13. FRANCIS BACON, b.1909. *'Self Portrait'*, 1970. 59⅞in. x 58in. Private Collection.

A sense of the fragility of human life, of menace and despair persistently recurs in post-1945 sculpture. Elisabeth Frink produced a series of dead or wingless birds. Bernard Meadows began making pieces that evolve their claws and scuttling movement from the image of the crab. And George Fullard, who had been severely wounded in the battle of Cassino, constructed assemblages in which found objects are wittily transformed into something else, an infant St. George is found mounted on a table which becomes his horse, its head, the open drawer, its mane, a row of clothes pegs. The playful element in his work echoes that of the child's battle games. But the recurrence of the tank gun motif introduces a note of terror.

Three other sculptors who came to the fore at this time were Kenneth Armitage, Reg Butler and Lynn Chadwick. Armitage made a series of sculptures entitled 'People in the Wind' in which the figures merge into an organic group. Composed on the slant, they suggest flight and urgency and were seen to be expressive of the human predicament. Chadwick, likewise, brought to his representation of the figure a sense of the momentary. In order to explore sensations of weight and balance, he often rested the bulk of his figures on spindly legs and sometimes merged the concept of a human with that of a bird. As a result his sculptures sometimes have the impression that they have merely alighted on the plinth and will at any moment take off again. Butler, in the early 1950s, produced welded iron sculptures in which the human figure is reduced to a taut arrangement of linear abstract shapes. His prize-winning maquette for the 1952 competition for a monument to the Unknown Political Prisoner has a similar spareness, its linear framework carrying allusions to the cross, cage, scaffold, watch tower and guillotine.

As the 1950s progressed, and post-war austerity was replaced by growing confidence in an expanding economy, a lighter and more optimistic mood began to make itself felt. New York took over from Paris as the main centre of artistic innovation. Then in 1956 the exhibition 'Modern Art in the United States' opened at the Tate Gallery. The final room was devoted to Abstract Expressionism and included work by Gorky, Kline, de Kooning, Motherwell, Pollock and Rothko. Its sheer scale, its radical simplicity and space-creating use of colour, its authority and professionalism made much British art seem parochial and dilettante. Art students abandoned the advice of their tutors and experimented with large scale abstraction. One student at the Royal College of Art, William Green, became famous for the space of a few weeks when the press heard that he was using a bicycle wheel to move the paint around his picture. When press photographers turned up to investigate, he obligingly bicycled across the piece of hardboard on which he was working and jokes about the bicycle in art superseded those that *Punch* and other magazines had extracted from Moore and Hepworth's introduction of the hole into sculpture.

At a more serious level the impact of American Abstract Expressionism had far-reaching effect. It struck a death blow at the idea that the making of art depended on the acquiring of skills: the notion that an art student could be 'trained' was replaced by an emphasis on personal endeavour, the discovery of personal interests and expression. The study of life drawing gradually dwindled and in some places for a period died out, for whilst the urge to imitate the daring economy and energy of the Americans lasted, there was no need for a student to develop his or her powers of observation. A groundswell of interest in abstraction had begun in the early 1950s but with the 1956 Tate exhibition, followed by another in 1959 devoted entirely to Abstract Expressionism, the theory and practice of abstract art became dominant.

In 1957 the Redfern Gallery in London mounted 'Metavisual Tachiste and Abstract Painting in England', the first exhibition in Britain to register English response to the American example. More specifically American in inspiration, however, were the two 'Situation' exhibitions of 1960 and 1961 which were organised by artists, with Robyn Denny acting as Secretary. These excluded the nature-based abstraction of the St. Ives artists as the concern was to promote wholly non-representational art, also to bypass the dealer system. Many of the artists who co-operated had recently begun working on a large scale in an attempt to create canvases which, like those of the Abstract Expressionists, make an almost physical impact on the spectator and create their own environment. Among those who co-operated with one or both of the two exhibitions were Gillian Ayres, Bernard Cohen, John Hoyland, Gwyther Irwin and Richard Smith.

Smith also became aligned with Pop Art owing to his interest in the brash colours and patterns used in the packaging of consumer goods. These he reinterpreted in abstract terms on a scale reminiscent of advertising hoardings. Smith was a fellow student with Peter Blake and Joe Tilson at the Royal College of Art and with them formed the second wave of Pop artists in England. An earlier manifestation had been stimulated by the Independent Group which met intermittently at the ICA between 1952 and 1955. It brought together a wide range of intellectuals all of whom were interested in understanding the implications of modern technology and mass-media culture. Some of its members organised the 1956 'This is Tomorrow' exhibition which used, as catalogue illustration and poster, Richard Hamilton's famous collage, *Just what is it that makes today's homes so different, so appealing?* In this details from magazine illustrations and advertisements are juxtaposed to create an environment that half-humorously celebrates the latest advancements in twentieth century life.

Hamilton can retrospectively be seen as the father of Pop Art in England. Of all the artists associated with this development he was the one who made the most teasing and ironical use of 'ad-mass' material. He dissected the banal ingredients upon which the glamour of advertising rests, and recomposed details into pictures that trigger various allusions. Abstract shapes challenge figurative passages, in the same way that authorial marks or dripped paint question the illusionistic representation achieved through the use of photographic silkscreen. Hamilton delighted in pre-coded imagery and the slippages of meaning that the alteration of medium within a single work could introduce. He upheld the Independent Group's belief that notions of 'high' and 'low' art should be abolished and all should be regarded as part of a continuum. In a letter to the architects, Peter and Alison Smithson, written in 1957, Hamilton outlined what 'Pop' art should be: 'Popular (designed for a mass audience), Transient (short-term solution), Expendable (easily forgotten), Low cost, Mass-produced, Young (aimed at Youth), Witty, Sexy, Gimmicky, Glamorous, Big Business.'

To an extent Pop Art was a reaction against the high seriousness of abstract art. It reinforced figuration and with its interests in films and film stars, records and pop singers, it helped create an expansionist aesthetic and broadened the audience for art. Moreover some British Pop artists enjoyed a similar kind of publicity to that given to pop stars.

Attention began to focus on David Hockney while he was still a student at the Royal College of Art. One of the third wave of Pop artists, he was a contemporary at the RCA with Derek Boshier, R.B. Kitaj, Peter Phillips, Allan Jones and Patrick Caulfield. Like others, Hockney found that friendship with Kitaj acted as a catalyst in his development. It was Kitaj who made the simple but earth-shaking suggestion that he should paint what interested him. From then on Hockney's work became unashamedly autobiographical. He 'came out' on canvas, scribbling messages to his boyfriends in a style reminiscent of the agonised urgency of graffiti. But the various influences at work in Hockney's early style gradually gave way to clearer, more coherent methods of representation. As his work became more and more naturalistic, he relied more on the camera for information. Though his work has no obvious Pop Art ingredient, its coolness, deadpan humour and chic has made it extremely popular. Its demotic appeal justifies the Pop label.

Britain's economic resurgence in the 1960s was accompanied by a mood of optimism and confidence in the arts. Alongside Pop Art developed the Op art movement. Whereas much abstract painting of this period explored the flatness of the picture surface, Op Art explored the destruction of that surface by illusion. Patterns and colours were composed in such a way as to set up reactions in the

Plate 14. JOHN HOYLAND, b.1934. '10.7.89'. Acrylic on cotton duck. 100in. x 93in. Waddington Galleries.

viewer's retina so that the image on the canvas seemed to buzz or move. Bridget Riley was the leading exponent of this style. She first confined her work to black and white but then moved through greys to the introduction of colour. Working, until recently, solely with stripes, her paintings set up vibrations and cross-rhythms that accumulate with exhilarating effect.

Colour was a major concern of the 1960s, not only in painting but also sculpture. Anthony Caro began using a single hue for each of his sculptures made out of prefabricated steel, bolted and welded together. With scrapyard elements he explored relationships of shape and outline, the full complexity of

Plate 15. R.B. KITAJ, b.1932. *'Germania (The Audience)'*, 1989. 48½ in. x 60¼ in. Marlborough Fine Art (London) Ltd.

which is only discoverable when the work is viewed from several angles. Though abstract, his art explores familiar sensations for it is built upon the language of physical gesture; each unit leans against, weighs upon or supports another, as well as describing movement in space. The accessibility of his work was enhanced by his insistence that it should be placed in the spectator's space, on the floor and not on a pedestal. Colour acted as a psychological pedestal, unifying the work and often heightening its mood or expression.

Caro had been an assistant to Henry Moore, on a part-time basis, between 1951 and 1953. Though a meeting with the American critic, Clement Greenberg, followed by a visit to the United States in 1960, had caused him to turn away from the modelling of figures, his subsequent sculpture is not as antipathetic to Moore's example as is often stressed. In both artists' work is often found an insistent horizontality, also an alert sensitivity to rhythm and balance and a dread of the inert. Caro occupied a two-day-a-week teaching post at St. Martin's School of Art until 1974. His presence there helped turn the sculpture department into a forum for new ideas, and owing to his example a group of artists emerged from this school who worked with clear, simple, geometric shapes, often in steel, and who were given the label 'New Generation' sculptors after an exhibition of that title held at the Whitechapel Art Gallery in 1965. Those associated with this development are David Annesley, Michael Bolus, Phillip King, Tim Scott, William Tucker and Isaac Witkin. William Turnbull, the sculptor and painter, is also associated with this group, even though he had no connection with St. Martin's.

To an extent New Generation sculpture was inspired by gestalt psychology and its concern with wholeness. Much of their sculpture is, unlike Caro's, extremely explicit and can be perceived at a glance, understood from any angle. Again, in reaction against the 'truth to materials' ethos that had dominated the work of Hepworth and Moore, the nature of the material used was disguised by a layer of paint, sprayed on to give the work an impersonal, factory-like finish. Retrospectively, this sculpture seems very much of its period, optimistic, buoyant and concerned with surface appearance. Some of the artists associated with this group gave up or for a period stopped producing once the decade was over, though Caro and King continued to work with steel in this vein, gradually complicating their art throughout the next decade and dropping the use of colour.

During the 1960s and early '70s the chase after the new meant that little attention was given to native traditions. Sheila Fell continued to make the landscape of West Cumbria, where she had been born and brought up, her sole subject, but after the closure of her dealer Helen Lessore's Beaux Arts Gallery she had no solo exhibition in London for fifteen years, and for much of the time all that was seen of her work in this city were the six paintings she sent each year to the RA Summer Exhibition. Her case is not untypical. For many artists whose work did not conform to the avant-garde concerns of the day, this period was one of doubt and exclusion. Possibly this was in the long run to their advantage. For the need to go on, without encouragement in an artistic climate lead by dogma, may have obliged many to cling even more tenaciously to their particular concerns. Those of Sheila Fell's generation, such as Frank Auerbach, Leon Kossoff, Michael Andrews and Howard Hodgkin, who re-emerged in the late 1970s, did so as artists of much greater stature than those who had responded to the more fashionable trends in artistic theory.

For an art student in the late 1960s it was hard to resist the various 'isms' that were promoted by the art market and discussed in such glossy magazines as *Studio International, Art International* and *Art Forum.* These and other periodicals helped foster the British determination to escape provincialism and insularity and instead to produce art that would take its place within an international framework.

A concern with Modernism took on a more fanatic outlook as a result of the ideas promoted by the American critic, Clement Greenberg. According to him the primary concern of art was its dialogue with its inherent material attributes: a painting should be about itself. This justified the move from Abstract Expressionism into Post Painterly Abstraction which cut out the more expressive aspects of Abstract Expressionism in its more impersonal pursuit of purely formal relationships. Much abstract painting of the 1960s took as its starting point the ineluctable flatness of the picture surface. This aesthetic of exclusion encouraged a 'minimalist' approach which though it never became a recognisable movement in the way that Minimalism did in America, produced work that was dead-pan, autonomous and which required a plenitude of theory to explain its emptiness. It was an art that looked at its best in galleries, or in rooms painted white and admitting only the minimum of streamlined furniture.

The sheer scale of this painting or sculpture, much of it now relegated by subsequent developments to the storerooms of public art galleries, eventually began to stimulate a revolt against its emphasis on material presence. For a late 1960s generation of art students, living through a period of political crisis, there was also the realisation that however radical the art produced it was rapidly assimilated by the art market which turned artists into mere pawns within the capitalist system. The result was the rise of Conceptualism, a move away from the making of art objects to an emphasis on concepts. Conceptual art could take any conceivable form. It was primarily concerned with ideas and information and only secondarily with visual presentation. Art & Language, a group of artists and writers, sought to investigate 'those fraudulent conceptualisations by means of which normal art was supported and entrenched'. The group's primary practice was 'conversation, discussion and conceptualisation'. The subjects they pursued were published in the magazine *Art-Language,* the first volume of which appeared in May 1969. They also found representation in galleries by exhibiting filing cabinets containing indexes filled with the outcome of Art & Language's debates.

Other practitioners of Conceptualism turned deliberately to depersonalised media — photographs, video, maps, diagrams and typewritten texts. A key figure was Victor Burgin who, like Art & Language, succeeded in taking art out of the visual court entirely by reducing the work of art to a written description, which could be constructed imaginatively in the reader's head. He went on to make written statements, cross-referenced and capable of multiple interpretations, but soon abandoned these for the combination of photography and text in which the information provided by the words clashes with and subverts the initial reading offered by the photograph.

Emphasis on concept licensed a range of activities that expanded the parameters of art. Richard Long turned his walks through landscape into a work of art by exhibiting in galleries maps, photographs and brief texts that record the terrain he had covered and the time it had taken him to do so. He was one of several students at St. Martin's School of Art who rebelled against the orthodoxy in the sculpture department that had accrued around the practice of making abstract steel sculpture. Bruce McLean has described how he began to find the postures adopted by St. Martin's tutors during seminars more involving than the work they were discussing. As a result he began to enact performances that satirised pose. Gilbert and George, also students in the St. Martin's sculpture department, decided to turn themselves into 'living sculptures' and have continued ever since to turn their joint lives into a continuous work of art.

Inevitably, Conceptualism itself aroused a reaction and the second half of the 1970s saw a revival of interest in the traditional modes of painting and sculpture. A number of artists who had for some years been underrated now came to the fore, amongst them Paula Rego, Ken Kiff, Howard Hodgkin and John Bellany. Figuration returned, and with it an interest in narrative, symbolism and myths. Painting, which during the conceptual period had been regarded as a self-limiting medium, began to broaden and deepen as an art form. Abstracts grew richer and multi-coloured, with, in Gillian Ayres' art, exuberant effect. Lucian Freud became the artist who, par excellence, proved the continuing vitality of the realist tradition. Sculpture, likewise, began to proliferate in various directions, enjoying a return to the traditional materials of wood and stone at the same time as it extended into new practices, with Tony Cragg and Bill Woodrow reclaiming materials that have been rejected, in order to make art that is formally exciting yet also contains an implicit critique of consumer society and the issues of the day.

Many factors have contributed to the richly complex nature of art in Britain today. Feminist artists continue to uncover new ways to subvert dominant ideologies and ways of seeing. The post-modernist debate, with its insistence on the failure of 'master-narratives', its licensing of pastiche, parody, and the ransacking of the past for visual quotations, has helped create an anarchic climate in which old issues of figurative versus abstraction or form versus content become redundant. Meanwhile black artists in Britain continue to explore a wide range of expression, from optimism and love to anger, in art that

Plate 16. BARRY FLANAGAN, b.1941. *'The Cricketer'*, 1989. Bronze, edition 1/5. 186in. x 72in. x 72in.
Waddington Galleries Ltd., London.

Plate 17. JOYCE CAIRNS, b.1947. *'The Last Supper in Footdee',* 1987-8. 7ft. x 8ft. (two panels 7ft. x 4ft.) Private Collection.

frequently deals with their complex position within British society, a position which seems to generate a binding creative energy.

It has been argued that the central achievement of post-1945 British art is the figurative art of Bacon, Freud, Auerbach and Kossoff. Viewed from another angle it can be argued that the strength and vitality of British art in the last decade of the twentieth century lies less in the work of the few than in the activity of the many. Its ability to perform a multiplicity of tasks, to sustain wide-ranging interests, to be both stubbornly traditional and also challengingly innovative, has led to the formation of a broad river of communication that attracts many audiences. And it was with this multiple audience in mind that this dictionary was composed.

EDWIN AUSTIN ABBEY, 1852-1911. 'Sylvia'. William A. Clark Collection, Corcoran Gallery, Washington D.C.

ABBEY, Edwin Austin   1852-1911
Painter, illustrator. Born Philadelphia, USA and studied
at the local Academy of Fine Arts. Employed as illustrator
by the magazine *Harper's*. Left for England in 1878 and,
after a brief return to the United States in 1880, settled
permanently in London. Made his reputation as a painter
of historical subjects and in 1896 was commissioned to
paint the coronation picture of Edward VII. With Sargent*
and Puvis de Chavannes, he contributed to the mural
decoration of McKim's Boston Public Library. Exhibited
at RA from 1885. Elected ARA 1896 and RA 1898. Has
been called the last of the great Anglo-American history
painters, in the tradition of Sir Joshua Reynolds, John
Singleton Copley and Washington Allston.

Bibl: *Edwin Austin Abbey,* Yale University Art Gallery, 1974.

ABBOTT, John   1884-1956
Painter. Self-taught and only practised as a painter after
his retirement from the Indian Civil Service in 1932.
Exhibited at the RA, the NEAC, the ROI and elsewhere.

ABBOTT, John   b.1948
Painter. Born Manchester. Studied at Liverpool College of
Art, West of England College of Art, Bristol and RCA.
Taught for a year at South Devon Technical College and
now subsidises his painting through occasional labouring
jobs. His paintings and drawings are mostly small, often
intricately textured and, in the relationship of the figures
to each other and their setting, suggest narratives.

JANE ACKROYD, b.1957. 'The Witness', 1988. Waxed mild steel. 100in. x 66in. x 29in. Anderson O'Day Fine Art, London.

ABELL, Roy   b.1931
Painter. Studied at Birmingham College of Art and RCA. Taught at Birmingham College of Art (subsequently Birmingham Polytechnic), becoming Head of the School of Painting in 1974 and later Director of the BA Fine Art Course. Retired from teaching in 1982. Has exhibited regularly since 1956 and has had several one-artist exhibitions in the Birmingham area. Specialises in landscape, in watercolour and oils.

ABERCROMBIE, Douglas   b.1934
Painter. Born Glasgow, Scotland. Studied at Glasgow School of Art, 1952-6, winning Carnegie Travelling Scholarhip in 1956. From 1958-63 worked as a painter/designer at the Citizens Theatre, Glasgow. 1964 moved to London and worked at the Royal Opera House, Covent Garden. 1965-7 lived and painted in Spain. First one-person show at 57 Gallery, Edinburgh, 1958.

ABLETE, Thomas Robert   d.1945
Painter. Born London. Founder member of the Royal Drawing Society in 1888. Specialised in landscapes and figure subjects and exhibited at RA and elsewhere.

ABRAHAMS, Ivor   b.1935
Sculptor. Born Wigan, Lancashire. 1952-4 studied at St. Martin's School of Art and in 1954 at Camberwell School of Art. 1954-6 worked as an apprentice at the Fiorini Bronze Factory, London and in 1956 worked as a display artist. From 1960, visiting lecturer in sculpture at Birmingham, Coventry and Hull College of Art and Goldsmiths' College, London. First one-person show at Gallery One, London, 1962. Many solo exhibitions in Europe and at the Mayor Gallery, London. Makes polychromed sculpture, his concern with gardens giving way in recent years to an interest in the human figure.

ACHESON, Anne   1882-1962
Sculptor. Born Portadown, Northern Ireland. Studied at RCA. Exhibited at RA and abroad. 1938 received the Gleichen Memorial Award.

ACKERMANN, Gerald   1876-1960
Painter of land and townscapes, in oil and watercolour. Born Blackheath, London. Studied at Heatherley's and

NORMAN ACKROYD, b.1938. 'Little Skellig', 1987. Monotype and watercolour. 35 ½ in. x 25 ¼ in. Anderson O'Day Fine Art, London.

RA Schools where he won the Creswick Prize and Landseer Scholarship. Exhibited at RA, RI and had one-artist shows at the Leicester Galleries and the Fine Art Society. Painted widely in Britain, but became associated with north Norfolk after he settled at Blakeney.

ACKLING, Roger   b.1946
Sculptor. Born Isleworth, London. Studied at St. Martin's School of Art. Since 1974 has made sculpture by scorching marks into the surface of recycled wood using the sun's rays gathered through the lens of a magnifying glass. Solo exhibitions at Lisson Gallery 1981 and 1984, Bradbury and Birch Fine Art 1984, Françoise Lambert Gallery, Milan, 1984, and others in London, Paris, New York and Japan.

Bibl: *Roger Ackling: Works from Norfolk,* Annely Juda Fine Art, London, 1990.

ACKROYD, Jane   b.1957
Sculptor. Born London. Studied at St. Martin's School of Art, 1979-82, and RCA, 1982-3. 1984, artist-in-residence, Leicestershire. First solo exhibition held at Kingsgate Workshops Gallery, 1984. Now represented by Anderson O'Day, London.

ACKROYD, Norman   b.1938
Printmaker. Born Leeds, Yorkshire. Studied at Leeds College of Art and RCA. Has taught printmaking at Manchester College of Art and Design and acted as visiting lecturer in Britain and abroad. Has exhibited regularly and has work in many public collections. 1989 elected ARA. Represented by Anderson O'Day, London.

ADAMS, Bernard   d.1965
Painter. Born London. Studied at Westminster School of Art and at the Antwerp Academy. Exhibited in London and the provinces and specialised in landscapes and portraits.

ADAMS, Christine   b.1947
Landscape painter. Studied at Burnley Municipal School of Art and Slade, winning the Steer Landscape prize and the Tonks drawing prize. Part-time lecturer at Heatherley's, Hartlepool College of Art, then Preston Polytechnic. One-artist exhibitions in Newcastle, Preston and London (William Darby).

ADAMS, Danton F.   b.1904
Painter. Born Eastbourne, Sussex. Studied at Putney School of Art and Chelsea School of Art. Exhibited at RA, RWS, ROI, the Paris Salon, and elsewhere.

ADAMS, Harry William   1868-1947
Painter. Born Worcester. Employed by the Royal Worcester Porcelain Factory for eight years as a decorative artist before he began studying art in Paris, 1895. From 1896 exhibited at RA and 1912 elected RBA. Associated with the Worcester area where he lived, painted and taught. President of the Birmingham Art Circle. Work in the Tate Gallery collection.

ADAMS, Hervey   b.1903
Landscape and portrait painter, in oil and watercolour. Born Kensington, London. Studied languages and singing in France and Spain. 1928-30 studied art under Bernard Adams.* Lived in the Cotswolds, 1929-37 and during this time was elected member of the RSBA and held his first one-artist show at Fine Art Society. 1937 published *The Student's Approach to Landscape Painting*. 1940-63 art-master at Tonbridge School. Continued to paint and publish and, on his retirement, returned to the Cotswolds. Exhibited RA, NS, RSBA.

ADAMS, Norman   b.1927
Painter. Born Walthamstow, London. Studied at Harrow School of Art, 1940-6. Imprisoned in Wormwood Scrubs as conscientious objector, 1946. 1948-51 studied at RCA, and had his first one-artist exhibition at Gimpel Fils, 1952. Regular exhibitions with Roland, Browse and Delbanco since 1955. 1962-71 Head of Painting, Manchester College of Art. 1956 began to exhibit at RA. 1957 elected ARA. 1959 became member of the London Group. A large body of his work is concerned with religious and mystical experience, but landscape and nature has also provided important stimulus. Has executed many commissions, for illustrations to the Old Testament (OUP), murals (St. Anselm's Church, Kennington and for Harry Taylor's, Ltd.), ceramic reliefs (Church of Our Lady of Lourdes, Milton Keynes). 1981 appointed Professor of Fine Art at the University of Newcastle. 1986 elected Keeper, Royal Academy Schools.

Bibl: *A Decade of Painting 1971-1981*, Third Eye Centre, Glasgow, 1981; *Norman Adams: Colour Chart of a Way*, Royal Academy, London, 1988.

ADAMS, Robert   1917-1984
Sculptor. Born Northampton. Studied at Northampton School of Art. Employed as an engineer for a while, then served as instructor at the Central School of Art, 1949-59. Exhibited a work in the 1951 Festival of Britain exhibition on the South Bank. 1960s showed at the Venice Biennale, and the Sao Paulo Biennale, where he won first prize in the print award. 1961 produced metal sculptures for the liners *Canberra* and *Transvaal Castle;* 1966 sculpture for the BP Building in London; 1967 sculpture for the New Customs House at Heathrow Airport. Represented in Tate Gallery, Arts Council, British Council, MOMA New York, Hirshhorn Museum and Sculpture Garden, Washington, and Albright-Knox Art Gallery, Buffalo.

ADAMS, Tony   b.1936
Painter. Educated at Rugby, Lower School, before going into foundry management. 1954 served in RAF. Studied at Chelsea School of Art, 1956 and at University of Bristol, 1961. At times since has taught art, art history and complementary studies, and travelled extensively. First solo exhibition held at Arthur Tooth and Sons, 1976.

ADAMS, W. Dacres   1864-1951
Painter of architectural subjects in oil and watercolour. Educated at Exeter College, Oxford and briefly articled to a solicitor before taking up painting. Studied at Birmingham School of Art, Herkomer School, Bushey and at Munich. Exhibited at RA, ROI, Fine Art Society and Leicester Galleries. His pictures are mostly small in scale, reserved in colour, and meticulously crafted.

ADAMSON, Crawfurd   b.1953
Painter. Born Edinburgh, Scotland. Studied at Duncan of Jordanstone College of Art, Dundee, 1971-6. Awards include a travelling scholarship from the Scottish Education Department, 1974 and a scholarship to work in South West France, 1976-7. 1984 first exhibited at the Cylinder Gallery, London, followed by a second exhibition there in 1985. Included in the collection of the Wiltshire Education Department. Figurative artist, using abrupt definition and expressionist colour. Recent exhibitions include one at the Scottish Gallery, London, 1989.

ADENEY, Bernard   1878-1966
Painter and textile designer. Born London. Studied at RA Schools, 1892-7, and at Académie Julian, Paris, 1897 and at the Slade, 1912. Married the painter, Noel Gilford. 1898 began exhibiting at the RA. 1911 assisted Roger Fry* and others with the decoration of a room in the Borough Polytechnic. Had work included in the 1912 Post-Impressionist exhibition, and continued to paint in a style of Post-Impressionism that was primarily indebted to Cézanne. In the 1920s was made president of the London Group, but during his period of office, it was his friend and mentor, Roger Fry, who remained the real power behind the throne. His second wife was Thérèse Lessore,* who taught at Central School from 1903 and was head of its textile department, 1930-47. Memorial exhibition held at Dulwich College, 1966. Adeney's work has yet to be reassessed.

ADENEY, Noel (née Gilford)
Painter. Studied at Slade School. Married Bernard Adeney* and exhibited with the London Group and elsewhere.

ADLER, Jankel   1895-1949
Painter. Born Tuszyn, near Lódź, Poland. Studied at the Barmen School of Arts and Crafts in Germany and at the Akademie der Kunst, Düsseldorf. During the First World War was conscripted into the Russian Army, returning

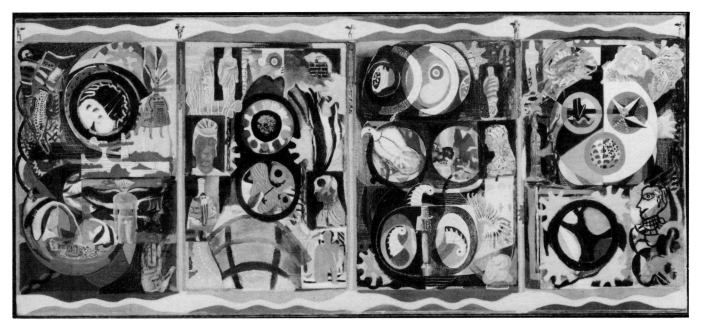

EILEEN AGAR, b.1904. *'Autobiography of an Embryo'*, 1933-4. 35 ½ in. x 84in. Tate Gallery.

after the war to Germany. Lectured at Akademie der Kunst, Düsseldorf and had his work declared 'degenerate' by the Nazis in 1933. 1933-40 he was in France, where he worked with Stanley William Hayter and travelled extensively. 1940 enlisted in the Polish Free Army and was evacuated to Scotland with the Polish Artillery. 1943 settled in London where he influenced a number of younger artists with his European Expressionism, including Robert Colquhoun* and Robert MacBryde.* He combined the spirit of European modernism with a humanistic approach, creating images expressive of a melancholy acceptance of fate.

Bibl: *Jankel Adler,* Tel Aviv Museum, 1985.

ADLER, Valerie
Painter. Born South Africa. Came to Great Britain at the age of seventeen. Twelve years later she went to live and work in Israel. Studied history of art at the Hebrew University of Jerusalem. On her return to Great Britain in 1982 she studied at Chelsea School of Art. First solo exhibition at Galleria Spazia Nuovo, Venice, 1986, followed by an exhibition at the Solomon Gallery, London, 1987. Continues to visit Israel frequently.

ADSHEAD, Mary　b.1904
Painter and muralist. Born London. Studied at the Slade School of Fine Art under Tonks, 1921-4, and executed there her first mural commission with Rex Whistler.* Commissioned to paint murals for the home of Lord Beaverbrook, and advertisement murals at Bank Underground Station, 1928. First solo exhibition at the Goupil Gallery, London, 1930. Designed a series of stamps for the GPO for their first pictorial issues, 1949. Studied art at Ravenna and Sicily and also the techniques of Italian mosaic at Kingston Art School, 1962. Included in the collection of Graves Art Gallery, Sheffield. Married the painter, Stephen Bone.*

ADZAK, Roy　b.1927
Born Reading, Berkshire. 1949 emigrated to Australia and studied at Sydney Art School. 1957 returned to Europe, and has since lived and worked in Scandinavia, Paris and London. First one-person exhibition at the Cultural Centre, New Delhi, 1956. Represented in the following collections: Tate Gallery; Stedelijk Museum, Amsterdam; Toronto Museum; Kunst Museum, Boros, Sweden; Stadtische Galerie, Munich.

AGAR, Eileen　b.1900
Painter. Born Buenos Aires, Argentina, of British parents. Came to England when a child. Studied under Leon Underwood* in 1924 and 1925-6 at the Slade. 1928-30 in Paris. 1934 became a member of the London Group. 1936 associated with the surrealist manifestations that accompanied the International Surrealist Exhibition held in London. 1937 visited Picasso at Mougins with Paul Eluard, Penrose and Man Ray. She has exhibited at the Redfern, Leger, Hanover, Obelisk, and Brook Street Galleries in London and at New Art Centre, and elsewhere.

Bibl: Eileen Agar, *A Look at My Life,* Methuen, London, 1988.

AIKEN, John Macdonald　1880-1961
Painter. Born Aberdeen, Scotland. Studied at Gray's School of Art, Aberdeen, at RCA and in Florence. Head of Gray's School of Art, 1911-14, before serving for four years in the First World War. Elected an associate of the RSA, 1923 and a full member, 1935.

AINSLEY, Sam　b.1950
Tapestry artist. Born North Shields, Tyne and Wear. Studied at Jacob Kramer College of Arts, Leeds, 1972-3, and Newcastle Polytechnic, 1974-7. 1975 spent six weeks in Japan studying Sukiya architecture; the use of natural

AINSWORTH, Mark

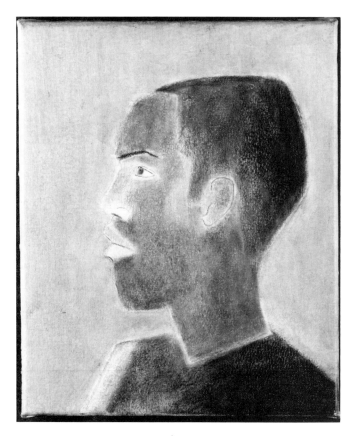

CRAIGIE AITCHISON, b.1926. *'Portrait of Bruce Marcus'*, 1986-7. 12in. x 10in. Albemarle Gallery.

materials in Japanese art affected her wall hangings of the late 1970s which incorporate canvas, cotton bindings and wood, in a way suggestive of Japanese costumes. 1977 she studied tapestry at Edinburgh College of Art, and began using brighter colours and abstract shapes. 1983 she produced a 30ft. long tapestry for General Accident Headquarters in Perth. 1984 made banners for the newly sited Scottish National Gallery of Modern Art. Recent work has signalled a political concern with the role of women in contemporary society. 1986 held a solo exhibition at Third Eye Centre, Glasgow.

AINSWORTH, Mark   b.1954
Painter. Studed at Blackpool College of Art, Ravensbourne and RCA. Exhibited in group shows since 1974 and has work in the Arts Council collection.

AIRY, Anna   1881-1964
Painter. Born London. Studied at Slade, 1899 and won Melville Nettleship Prize, 1901. Exhibited RA, RS Painter-Etcher, RIOP and elected RI, ROI, RE. 1918 was commissioned to paint munitions factions for the Imperial War Museum. 1945 elected President of the Ipswich Art Club. Exhibited at RA and elsewhere. One of the leading women artists of her generation in her mid-thirties. Published *Making a Start in Art,* 1951. Her academic approach to drawing and painting matched her business-like presentation of her work.

Bibl: *Anna Airy,* Ipswich Art Club, 1985.

AITCHISON, Craigie   b.1926
Painter. Born Scotland. Studied law at Middle Temple, but abandoned it to paint. Studied at Slade School of Art, 1952-4. His childhood memories of the Dunbartonshire countryside and the Isle of Arran helped form his art, as did his family's involvement with the Church. 1955 he studied in Italy on a British Council Scholarship and was profoundly affected by the light, the landscape, and early Italian art. Soon after this formulated his personal style, employing radically simplified description, and a few jewel-like, unmodulated colours. 1959 held first solo exhibition at Beaux Arts Gallery, London. Since 1963 has also produced portraits in this pared down manner. Recently he has executed a series of crucifixions and nativities.

Bibl: *Craigie Aitchison,* Serpentine Gallery, London, 1981.

AITKIN, John Earnest   1881-1957
Painter. Born Liverpool. Studied under his father, a marine painter, and at Manchester, Liverpool and Wallasey Schools of Art. Exhibited at RA, RSA, RSW and elsewhere. Specialised in landscapes and coastal scenes and travelled widely. Member of the Liverpool Academy of Art and the Manchester Academy of Fine Arts.

AIVALIOTIS, Sharon   b.1951
Printmaker. Born Trinidad, West Indies. Studied at St. Martin's School of Art, 1975-9 and at the Slade School, 1979-81. First solo exhibition, 'Twelve Mezzotints a Year', at the Grafitti Gallery, London, 1982. Since this date she had also exhibited in group exhibitions in Europe, Australia and the United States. Her work is included in the collections of the V & A, The British Council, Whitworth Gallery, Manchester, Bradford and Leeds City Art Galleries, Graves Art Gallery, Sheffield, Duncroon Arts Centre, Wigan, Wakefield Art Gallery, Dudley Art Gallery, Ferens Art Gallery, Hull, the Bedford and Wiltshire Education Authorities and the Library of Congress, USA.

AKERBLADH, Alexander   b.1866
Painter. Studied architecture at Glasgow School of Art and was apprenticed as an architect for seven years. Retrained as a painter at St. John's Wood Art School. Exhibited at RA, NEAC, and elsewhere and held a solo exhibition at the Fine Art Society, London, 1929.

ALDIN, Cecil   1870-1935
Painter of animal, sporting and topographical subjects, mostly in watercolour. Studed at RCA under W. Frank Calderon. Contributed illustrations to a number of books and magazines; his first contribution to *The Graphic* appearing in 1891. 1894-5 illustrated Kipling's *Jungle Stories* for the *Pall Mall Budget.* Published *Dogs of Character,* 1927, *The Romance of the Road,* 1928 and *An Artist's Models,* 1930.

ALDRIDGE, Eileen   b.1916
Painter in oil and watercolour. Studied at Kingston School of Art and London Polytechnic. Has exhibited with NEAC, RA, the London Group, the Women's International Art Club, and elsewhere. Has written and illustrated children's books for the Medici Society.

JOHN ALDRIDGE, 1905-1983. 'Aberayron Evening', 1954. 20in. x 30in. Tate Gallery.

ALDRIDGE, John   1905-1983

Landscape painter and book illustrator. Born Woolwich, London. Classical Scholar at Corpus Christi, Oxford. No formal art training but drew and painted since early childhood. 1928 settled in Chiswick with Norman Cameron. Made excursions to Paris, Rome, Germany and Tenerife, and to Majorca at the invitation of Robert Graves and Laura Riding. Exhibited with the Leicester Galleries in 1931, 1933, 1936, 1940 and 1947, also with the 7 and 5 Society, on Ben Nicholson's* request. 1933 moved to Great Bardfield in Essex where he lived ever afterwards, except for war service 1941-5. Elected ARA 1954 and RA 1964. Joined the staff at the Slade 1949, at William Coldstream's request. His paintings have a sober, resolute quality that reflects his profound study of nature. Of particular importance were the illustrations he provided for publication by the Seizin Press, edited by Robert Graves and Laura Riding. His portrait of Graves is in the National Portrait Gallery. He is also represented in the Tate Gallery, and in public galleries in Aberdeen, Leeds, Manchester, Newport and Northampton, among other places.

ALEXANDER, Edwin   1870-1926

Painter. Born Edinburgh, Scotland, the son of the painter, Robert Alexander. 1887 visited Tangier in the company of his father and Joseph Crawhall* whose influence can be detected in Alexander's work. Studied at Royal Institution, Edinburgh, 1887-8, and under Fremiet in Paris, 1891. 1892-6 visited Egypt and lived on a houseboat on the Nile and in a tent in the desert. 1904 settled at Inveresk, Midlothian. Best known as an animal and bird painter, but also produced landscapes of his native country. 1902 elected an associate of RSA, and 1913 a full member.

ALEXANDER, Harry   b.1905

Painter of landscapes and abstracts. Graduated from Trinity College, Cambridge. Worked abroad, in West Africa and Canada before becoming a farmer in England. Met Hugh Griffiths, a teacher who stimulated his interest in abstraction, drawn from the patterns of landscape, seasonal change and man's relationship with the natural elements.

ALEXANDER, Herbert   1874-1946

Painter. Born London. Studied under Herkomer at Bushey and at the Slade School. Served in India and Mesopotamia during the First World War. Associated with Cranbrook in Kent where he lived for many years. 1905 elected an associate of the RWS, and 1927 a full member.

ALEXANDER, Norman   b.1915

Self-taught painter. Manual labourer at Smithfield Market, Truman's Brewery and elsewhere. One-artist shows at Redfern Gallery, 1954 and 1958. Has also shown at RA, NEAC, and at Leicester Galleries. Work in Transport House, London.

ALEXANDER, Robert   1875-1945
Watercolourist, specialising in animals and landscapes. Entered his family's business, an export merchant's office, but attended evening classes at Hornsey School of Art and, later, at the Slade. He was encouraged by Mark Fisher* and George Clausen* and was also influenced through his wife by her teacher, Hercules Brabazon Brabazon. Exhibited at RA and NEAC and has work in V & A, Fitzwilliam Museum, Cambridge, British Museum and elsewhere.

ALFORD, John   1929-1960
Painter. Born Tunbridge Wells, Kent. Studied at Camberwell School of Art. Specialised in landscapes and portraiture and exhibited in London and the provinces.

ALISON, David   1882-1955
Painter. Born Dysart, Scotland. Studied at Glasgow School of Art, and in Paris and Italy, after receiving the Haldane and Carnegie Travelling Scholarships. 1916 elected an associate of the RSA, and 1922 a full member. Represented in several public collections.

ALLAN, Julian Phelps   b.1892
Sculptor. Born Southampton, Hampshire. Served in France from 1917-19. Began training as a domestic science teacher but switched to art, studying at the Westminster School of Art, the RA Schools, 1922-5 and then in Florence. 1929 changed her name from Eva Dorothy to Julian Phelps. 1938-45 served in the ATS, and became first president of the ATS War Office Selection Board. Awarded the OBE. Executed bas-reliefs at Lambeth and Maudsley Hospitals and elsewhere. Since 1947 has carried out many ecclesiastical commissions. 1937 made ARBS and 1947 FRBS. Work in the Tate Gallery collections.

ALLAN, Richard   b.1933
Constructivist. Born Worcester. Studied at Worcester School of Art, and Bath Academy. 1960 received an Italian Government Scholarship. 1966 became Commonwealth Scholar in India. One-artist exhibitions in London (Angela Flowers, 1971) and abroad. 1967 Fellowship in Art, University of Sussex. Works in series, in geometric units.

ALLAN, Robert Weir   1852-1942
Painter. Born Glasgow, Scotland. Studied at Académie Julian in Paris, 1875-81, and 1882 settled in London. A founder-member of the NEAC, which was sympathetic to his *plein-air* landscapes and seascapes. He only exhibited there twice, 1886 and 1887. Made many trips abroad but is best known for his Scottish coastal scenes.

ALLAN, Rosemary   b.1911
Painter. Born Bromley, Kent. Studied at Slade School. Exhibited at RA, NEAC, and with the London Group. 1937 married Allan Gwynne-Jones.*

ALLARD, Geoffrey   b.1947
Painter. Born Chester, Cheshire. Studied at Regional College of Art, Liverpool, 1966-9. 1969 on a John Moore scholarship travelled in Germany and France. First one-artist show, 'London Today', held at the Fine Art Society, London, 1972.

ALLCOTT, Walter Herbert   1880-1951
Painter. Born Ladywood, Birmingham, West Midlands. Studied at Birmingham School of Art. 1898 began exhibiting and 1919 settled at Chipping Camden in Gloucestershire, where he painted landscapes in watercolour. Made regular visits abroad and exhibited at RA and elsewhere.

ALLEN, Alistair   b.1947
Born Sussex. Studied at Chelsea School of Art. Maker of pop art objects. 1969 first one person exhibition held at the Galerie Aesthetica, Stockholm, and 1970 in London, at the Hulton Gallery. Included in Art Spectrum Exhibition, London, 1972.

ALLEN, Colin   b.1926
Painter. Born Cardiff, Wales. Studied at Cardiff College of Art and RCA. Has exhibited widely, in John Berger's 'Looking Forward' exhibition, at the RA, the RSA, at the Piccadilly Gallery, London, and elsewhere. Work in various public collections, including the Glynn Vivian Art Gallery, Swansea. Became Head of the Department of Fine Art, Carlisle College of Art.

ALLEN, Eddie
Painter. Born Nottingham. Trained at Bath Academy. Lives in London and at Torino and exhibits in Venice, Torino and Milan.

ALLEN, Frank Humphrey   b.1896
Painter. Born London. Studied at Chelsea School of Art, 1933-5. Exhibited with the London Group and elsewhere.

ALLEN, George Warner   1916-1988
Painter. Born Paris, the only son of wine expert, Herbert Warner Allen. Studied at the Byam Shaw School of Art, 1933-9, where he befriended an older student Brian Thomas. Influenced by the work and thought of Charles Ricketts.* Worked in the Directorate of Camouflage at Leamington Spa during the Second World War, then taught at the Byam Shaw School. Held a successful one man exhibition at Walker's Galleries, London, 1952, followed by another at Reading Art Gallery, 1953. Worked in oils and tempera, grinding his own pigments. Produced large complex paintings which dealt with mythological and religious subjects. Tried to live the life of an artist of the 16th century Venetian school, eschewing 20th century developments. He found it difficult to paint during the later 1950s but began again in 1962. Worked in isolation and seclusion in Oxfordshire. He was received into the Roman Catholic church, 1973. His work was rediscovered in the mid-1980s and included in the Late Romantics exhibition at the Barbican Gallery, 1989.

ALLEN, Georgina   b.1954
Painter. Born Bonn, West Germany. Studied at Chelsea School of Art, London, 1982-7. 1986 represented in a group exhibition, 'London Institute Class of '86'; 1987 represented in 'CAS Market' at Smith's Gallery, Covent Garden, followed by joint exhibition with John Devane* at

the Paton Gallery, London, 1988, showing new abstract paintings whose subdued tonality suggest a debt to Morandi and Gwen John.*

ALLEN, Harry E.   1894-1958

Painter. Born Sheffield, Yorkshire, son of a craftsman mask-maker. Employed in Arthur Balfour's steelworks after leaving school. Enlisted in the army 1915 and wounded at the front in 1917, losing a leg. Returned to Balfour's, and became private secretary to Arthur Balfour, who was created the first Lord Riverdale in 1935. 1930s began painting full-time and was associated with the 'School of Sheffield', a group of painters inspired by Ruskin's legacy to the city. Allen specialised in scenes of Derbyshire, particularly the White Peak area around Buxton. He painted mostly in tempera, allowing its clarity to contribute to the fixity of his compositions, in which a search for rhythm and design predominated.

Bibl: Janet Barnes, *The Decorative Paintings of Harry E. Allen,* Sheffield Arts Department, 1986.

ALLEN, James

Painter and printmaker. Born Lurgan, Northern Ireland. Studied at Belfast College of Art, 1961-5, and Brighton College of Art, 1965-7. 1967-70 worked as a part-time lecturer in etching at Goldsmiths' College of Art. 1972 taught part-time at Ravensbourne College of Art. 1968 first one-person show at the Arts Council of Northern Ireland Gallery, Belfast. 1972 one of seven artists at the Serpentine Gallery. Represented in the following collections: Arts Council of Northern Ireland, County Museum of Armagh, and Educational Committees in Ireland and England, Arts Council of Great Britain.

ALLEN, John Edsall   1861-1944

Painter. Born London. Studied at Charterhouse School of Art and at RCA. Principal of St. Martin's School of Art, 1892-1927. Exhibited at RA and elsewhere.

ALLEN, Kathleen   b.1906

Painter. Born Acton, London. Due to childhood bovine tuberculosis, was educated at home until the age of fourteen. Studied at RCA and afterwards taught art in various schools. 1935-8 painted murals in various schools in Kent and Warwickshire. 1936 returned to London and set up a studio in the City. 1936-7 studied at the Slade. 1939 appointed war artist and seconded from teaching one day a week to record the work of war industries. 1941 studio in Fetter Lane bombed and much early work destroyed. 1938-48 member of the AIA committee and exhibition secretary. Elected member of the Society of Industrial Artists. 1946 appointed Senior Lecturer at Goldsmiths' College. 1954 elected a member of the Worshipful Company of Painters and Stainers. 1966 retired from teaching and painted full-time. Responded to the idiom of the period and to the transformations occurring in London during the war and post-war period.

Bibl: *Kathleen Allen. A retrospective exhibition,* South London Art Gallery, 1983.

ALLEN, Trevor   b.1939

Printmaker. Born Portsmouth, Hampshire. Studied at Camberwell. Has taught in various art colleges and exhibited in many group exhibitions. An exhibition of his relief prints was shown at Thumb Gallery, London, 1982.

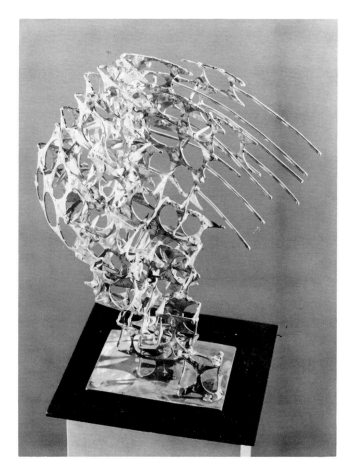

ANTHEA ALLEY, b.1927. *'Spatial Form',* 1962-3. Metal sculpture. 13¼ in. high. Tate Gallery.

ALLEY, Anthea   b.1927

Sculptor. Born Malawi, East Africa. During the Second World War she lived in Australia and South Africa. 1944 came to England with her family. Studied painting and design at the Regent Street Polytechnic, Chelsea School of Art and the RCA. 1957 began to make assemblage paintings and welded sculptures. 1960 first one-person exhibition at the Molton Gallery. 1961 awarded a prize for painting in the John Moores exhibition, Liverpool. Experimented with kinetic sculpture, and with works incorporating light and water. Represented in Tate Gallery, Arts Council, Birmingham City Art Gallery.

ALLIN, John   b.1934

Painter. Born Hackney, London. Self-taught. Began painting whilst working as a lorry driver. First solo exhibition held at Portal Gallery, London, 1969. Has exhibited in Holland, Germany, France and the United States, and, annually, in Switzerland where he won the Prix Suisse de Peinture Naive, 1979. 1974 his book *Say Goodbye,* with text by Arnold Wesker (who grew up with Allin in Hackney), was published by Jonathan Cape. Exhibits at the Portal Gallery, London.

ALLINGTON, Edward

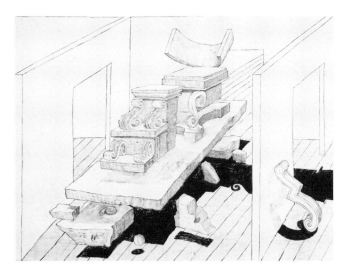

EDWARD ALLINGTON, b.1951. *'Seated in darkness'*, 1987. Ink and emulsion on paper on canvas. 72in. x 96in. Tate Gallery Collection. Photograph Edward Woodman.

ALLINGTON, Edward   b.1951

Sculptor. Born Westmorland. Studied at Lancaster School of Art 1968-71 and Central School 1971-4. 1981 first solo exhibition; then at Lisson Gallery, 1984 and 1985, Diane Brown, New York, 1986 and Galerie Monteray-Delsol, Paris, 1986. His sculpture and drawings bear witness to his great interest in Greek and Roman cultures and their recycling over subsequent centuries. Employs a variety of techniques and materials to analyse the traditional symbolic resources of Western culture. Has been represented by the Lisson Gallery since 1983.

ALLINSON, Adrian   1890-1959

Painter and sculptor. Studied at Slade, 1910-12. Worked under the guidance of Sickert* on scenes from the theatre and music hall. Contributed caricatures to the *Daily Express* and *Daily Graphic*. Through his friend, the composer Peter Warlock, he met Sir Thomas Beecham and became chief scenic designer to the Beecham Opera Company for five years. 1918 married and went to live in a small Swiss village where he painted Alpine scenery. 1925 returned to London and continued to paint, etch, carve and do wood-engravings. Exhibited at NEAC, London Group, ROI, RA and other places.

ALLINSON, Sonya M.

Painter. Born London. Studied at St. Martin's School of Art and RA Schools. Has travelled widely in order to paint. Exhibits at RA, NEAC, Royal West of England Academy and elsewhere.

ADRIAN ALLINSON, 1890-1959. *'Cotswold Blooms'*. 42¼ in. x 64in. The Fine Art Society.

MICHAEL ANDREWS, b.1928.
*'The Cathedral, The Southern
Faces Uluru (Ayers Rock)'*, 1987.
96in. x 153in. Acrylic. Anthony
d'Offay.

ALSTON, Rowland Wright   1895-1958
Painter. Studied at Slade School, at the RCA, and in Paris. Worked for many years as Curator of the Watts Gallery at Compton, Surrey. Also exhibited at the RA and in the provinces.

ALVA   1901-1973
Painter. Born Solomon Siegfried Allweiss in Berlin, Germany. 1919-25 studied music at Stern's Konservatorium, Berlin. 1928 studied painting in Paris. 1929-32 painted in France, Switzerland and Italy. 1933 settled in Paris. 1934 travelled in Palestine, Syria and Greece; first one-artist exhibition in Tel Aviv. 1938 moved to London. 1940 interned on the Isle of Man. After his move to London his subject matter turned sombre and tragic, with a concentration on Old Testament themes. 1945 first abstract painting. From late 1960s he focused increasingly on the female nude.

AMBROSE, Raymond   b.1927
Painter. Inspired by landscape and by apprehensions of the cosmic. Moved to Cornwall in 1974 and is a committee member of the Newlyn Society of Artists and a member of the Penwith Society of Artists. Solo exhibitions in Newlyn and St. Ives.

AMEY, Paul   b.1957
Painter. Studied at Oxford Polytechnic under Leonard McComb,* and then at Hornsey College of Art. Exhibition of painted cardboard reliefs held at South Hill Park Arts Centre, 1984.

ANDERSON, James Bell   1886-1938
Painter. Born Edinburgh, Scotland. Studied at Edinburgh School of Art and in Paris. Exhibited in London, Glasgow and Edinburgh. Painted portraits, landscapes and still lifes.

ANDERSON, Stanley   1884-1966
Painter and printmaker. Born Bristol, Avon. Was apprenticed for seven years as a line engraver to his father, an heraldic engraver. 1909 won a British Institution Engraving Scholarship and studied at Bristol Municipal School of Art, the RCA and Goldsmiths'

College, as well as in the National Gallery and British Museum. Fellow of the Royal Society of Painter-Etchers and Engravers. Contributed to the revival of line-engraving in the 1920s and taught at the British School in Rome, 1930-52. Specialised in townscapes and genre scenes. Was historically well informed and a good craftsman. Created CBE, 1951.

ANDERSON, Wendy
Painter. Born Elgin, Scotland. Studied at Grays School of Art, Aberdeen. First exhibited at the Ikon Gallery, Birmingham, 1984.

ANDERSON, Yvonne Ghislaine   b.1926
Painter. Born Brussels, Belgium. Moved to England during Second World War. Studied at Norwich School of Art. Worked in London as a theatrical costumier and stage designer before returning to the Norwich School of Art to teach painting and dress design for six years. Full-time painter since late 1960s. Her concern is with still life and landscape and her colour has progressively brightened. Exhibits at Royal West of England Society, with the Leicester Society of Artists and elsewhere. (Plate 18, p.86.)

ANDREW, Jim
Painter. Trained at Oldham School of Art and Manchester Regional Art College. 1960 began writing for radio. Also designs graphics for television and writes novels. Paints genre subjects from everyday life in a traditional style.

ANDREWS, Leonard Gordon   1885-1960
Painter. Born Lindfield, Sussex. Studied at Battersea Polytechnic School of Art, 1900-3, Clapham School of Art, 1903-4, Regent Street Polytechnic, 1906, Birmingham School of Art, 1908, and West Bromwich School of Art, 1909. Occupied various teaching posts and exhibited at RA and elsewhere.

ANDREWS, Michael   b.1928
Painter. Born Norwich, Norfolk. Attended classes at Norwich School of Art during his last year at school. Served in the Royal Army Ordinance Corps, 1947-9. Studied at Slade School, 1949-53. 1952 and 1954

participated in two films made by fellow Slade student, Lorenza Mazzetti. Awarded a Rome scholarship, 1953, but stayed only five months. Attracted attention in his final year at the Slade with his diploma exhibition, and was tipped by John Minton* as the most interesting artist of his generation. He has drawn ideas for his figurative paintings from literature, films and photography. At one point photographs were transferred on to the canvas to which paint was then added, the photographic image becoming semi-obscured. His interest in distortion and the use of abrupt elisions and cuts gradually gave way to photographic realism through which he still explores psychological states of mind. In 1983 a whole spate of work was inspired by a visit to Australia's Ayers Rock.

Bibl: *Michael Andrews,* Arts Council catalogue to retrospective held at Hayward Gallery, 1980.

ANDREWS, Sybil   b.1898
Painter and printmaker. Born Bury St. Edmunds, Suffolk. Studied at Heatherley's, and afterwards was associated with Claude Flight* and the Grosvenor School of Modern Art. Shared Flight's interest in the use of colour lino-cut to express an interest in dynamics and speed. 1928-37 exhibited regularly at the Redfern and Ward Galleries.

Bibl: *Sybil Andrews: Paintings and Graphic Work,* Michael Parkin Gallery, London, 1980.

ANGUS, Peggy   b.1905
Painter. Trained at RCA and won travelling scholarship to Paris, 1926. Taught at Eastbourne School of Art. 1933 moved in to the shepherd's cottage, Furlongs, near Beddingham Hill. Here she was visited by Eric Ravilious* and Percy Horton,* both artists who became associated with the Sussex Downs. After the war she took up part-time teaching in London and in a war-damaged, pre-Victorian terraced house continued to lodge a variety of talent.

ANKETELL, Judith   b.1952
Painter. Born Canada. Trained at the Sir John Cass School of Art, 1973-4 and Wimbledon School of Art, 1974-7. 1978 held one-artist exhibition at Gallery 273, Queen Mary College, London, of the sky and surrounding landscape studies made from the nineteenth floor of Hackworth Point in Bow.

ANNAN, Dorothy   b.1907
Painter. Born Brazil of British parents. Educated in France and Germany. Married the sculptor Trevor Tennant.* Exhibited frequently with the Leicester Galleries and in 1945 had her first one-artist show there.

ANNE, Sheila   b.1948
Painter. Born Ipswich, Suffolk. Studied at Ipswich and Chester Schools of Art. Held her first one-artist exhibition at the age of seventeen. Then pursued a variety of careers before returning to painting in 1976 with a ten-year retrospective at the Haste Gallery, Ipswich.

ANNESLEY, David   b.1936
Born London. 1947-56 educated in England, Australia and Southern Rhodesia. 1956-8 National Service in the RAF. 1958-62 sculpture student at St. Martin's School of Art. 1963 taught sculpture at Croydon and Central Schools of Art. 1964 taught sculpture at the Central School and St. Martin's School of Art. 1966-8 lived in America and worked with Kenneth Noland. 1966 first solo show at Waddington Galleries; another held at Flowers East, 1990. (Plate 19, p.86.)

ANNESLEY, Lady Mabel   1881-1959
Painter and engraver. Great granddaughter of Sir Francis Grant, PRA. Began to exhibit paintings at the RA from 1909. Took up wood engraving in 1920 under the supervision of Noel Rooke.* Prolific book illustrator, e.g. *Burns Songs,* for the Golden Cockerel Press.

ANREP, Boris   1883-1969
Painter and mosaicist. Born Russia. Sent to Britain as a boy to learn English. Trained in international law. Began making his name as a poet in St. Petersburg literary circles, then toured France and Italy with the artist Steletsky. Studied art in Paris where he met Henry Lamb* and Augustus John,* the second of whom gave him his first mosaic commission (the wall mosaics from Augustus John's Mallord Street, Chelsea house, now in the V & A). Selected for Russian section in 1912 Post Impressionist Exhibition. 1914 returned to Russia and entered Russian Army, and later returned to London attached to the Russian Government Committee. After the Revolution he remained either in London or Paris and became a leading mosaicist, decorating the floor of the Blake Room in the Tate Gallery, 1923, and the hallway of Ethel Sands' house, 3 The Vale, Chelsea, among many other commissions.

ANSON, Peter Frederick   b.1889
Painter. Born Portsmouth, Hampshire. Studied at Architectural Association, 1908-10, under F.L. Griggs.* Exhibited at RA, RSA, NEAC and elsewhere. Represented in the National Maritime Museum with some 200 water-colours and drawings based on British fishing ports.

ANTON, Victor   1909-1980
Sculptor and journalist. Sculptor in the mainstream of abstract modernism. He used perspex, alabaster, metal and slate and showed frequently at the Gimpel Fils Gallery. Also worked for twenty-nine years on the *Guardian-Gazette* newspapers in Chingford and Walthamstow.

APPERLEY, George Owen Wynne   1884-1960
Painter. Born Ventnor, Isle of Wight. Apart from a brief period at Herkomer's school in Bushey, he was largely self-taught. From 1905 exhibited at RA and up until the First World War regularly held solo exhibitions in London. Did much work in Spain where he also exhibited. Elected a member of the Real Academie de San Telmo and in 1945 was given the order of Alfonso X by the Spanish Government.

APPLEBEE, Leonard   b.1914
Painter. Born Fulham, London. Studied at Goldsmiths's School of Art, 1931-4, and at the RCA, 1935-8. 1940-6 served in the army. 1948 first one-person show at the Leicester Galleries. 1947 first exhibited at the RA, and did so regularly from 1956. Represented in the following collections: Arts Council, Chantrey Bequest, Tate Gallery, Aberdeen Art Gallery, National Gallery of Melbourne, Australia.

APPLEYARD, Fred   1874-1963
Painter. Born Middlesbrough, Cleveland. Studied at Scarborough School of Art, at the RCA and at the RA Schools where he won the Creswick Prize for landscape

painting. 1903 painted murals in the RA refreshment room and at Nottingham Hospital and Pickering Church. From 1900 exhibited at RA and from 1918 at RWA; he became a member of the latter society, 1926. 1910-12 worked in South Africa, and during First World War at Woolwich Arsenal. Represented in Tate Gallery collections.

ARAEEN, Rasheed   b.1935
Sculptor. Born Karachi, Pakistan. Self taught as an artist. 1962 graduated in Civil Engineering, University of Karachi. 1964 travelled to England. 1965-8 worked as an engineer with BP. 1968 gave up engineering to become a sculptor. 1969 first one person exhibition in Pakistan, at the PACC Gallery, Karachi; 1975 first one person exhibition in London at Artists for Democracy Gallery. Won an award in the 1969 John Moores Liverpool exhibition. 1978 given an Arts Council Award. 1978 founded and edited magazine *Black Phoenix* (three issues), which dealt with contemporary art from a radical Third World perspective. 1987 founded *Third Text,* a quarterly publication which aims at deepening black and Third World perspectives on contemporary visual arts. Touring retrospective exhibition of work from 1959-87 opened at Ikon Gallery, Birmingham, 1988.

Bibl: Rasheed Araeen, *Making Myself Visible*, Kala Press, London, 1984; *From Modernism to Post-Modernism: Rasheed Araeen: a retrospective, 1959-1987*, Ikon Gallery, Birmingham, 1987.

ARCHER, Frank   b.1912
Painter and printmaker. Born Walthamstow, London. Studied at Eastbourne School of Art, Brighton School of Art and RCA. 1938 awarded the Prix de Rome for engraving. Occupied various teaching posts and became Head of Fine Art at Kingston College of Art until his retirement, 1973. Senior member of the RWS and the Royal Society of Painters, Etchers and Engravers. Also exhibits at RA and in galleries in London and the provinces. Much influenced by music, medieval stained glass and Byzantine mosaics. (Plate 20, p.87.)

ARCHER, Val   b.1946
Painter. Born Northampton. Studied at Manchester, and at the Royal College of Art. Visiting lecturer at Chelsea, Goldsmiths', Sheffield and Wolverhampton Schools of Art. 1989 held solo exhibition of watercolours of fruit and flowers at Noortman Gallery, Maastricht, Netherlands. Brings to her realistic still lifes an almost surreal intensity.

ARDIZZONE, Charlotte   b.1943
Painter. Born London. Studied at St. Martin's and Byam Shaw Art Schools. One-artist exhibitions since 1970, and regular appearances at RWEA, RA and NEAC. Work in National Gallery of Australia, Dublin University and elsewhere.

ARDIZZONE, Edward   1900-1979
Painter and illustrator. Born Haiphong, Vietnam. Studied at Westminster and Central Schools of Art. 1940-6 Official War Artist. Elected ARA 1962, RA 1970. 1974 created a Royal Designer for Industry. Author and illustrator of numerous books. First one-artist exhibition in 1930 at Bloomsbury Gallery and numerous shows thereafter. Work in several major public collections, including the Tate Gallery, V & A and British Museum. His work belongs to a long tradition of British illustrators

DIANA ARMFIELD, b.1920. *'Tethered goat, Soubes'.* 15 ½ in. x 19 ¾ in. Browse & Darby. Private Collection.

and drew inspiration from Maida Vale, the raffish, but respectable area of London, where he lived and which provided the intimate scenes of London life for which Ardizzone is most famous.

Bibl: *Edward Ardizzone,* Scottish Arts Council Touring Exhibition, 1980.

ARGENIO, Antonio   b.1961
Painter. Born Bedford. Studied at the Winchester School of Art, 1982-5 and the RCA, 1986-8. Included in mixed exhibitions since 1984, and winner of a Winsor & Newton Young Artists Award, and Barclays Bank Young Painters Award. Won the Allen Lane Penguin Book Prize, 1988. Gained residency at the Delfina Studios Trust for two years from 1988.

ARIF, Saleem   b.1949
Painter. Born Hyderabad, India. Came to England at the age of seventeen. Studied sculpture at Birmingham School of Art, 1969-72, and RCA, 1972-5. On completing his training, he returned to India and also travelled widely in North Africa, Europe and the Asian sub-continent. His brightly coloured paintings reflect an interest in many cultures, as well as the influence of his own Indian and Islamic background. One-artist exhibitions in England and abroad, including 'Garden of Expectation', Winchester Gallery, 1986.

ARMFIELD, Diana   b.1920
Painter. Studied at the Slade School and Central School of Arts and Crafts. Since 1959 has taught at Byam Shaw School of Art. Paints mostly in Wales, and in France and Italy. Exhibits regularly at RA, NEAC and RWEA. Married Bernard Dunstan.* Elected ARA, 1989.

ARMFIELD, Maxwell   1881-1972
Painter, illustrator and designer. Born Ringwood, Hampshire. Studied at Birmingham School of Art and then in Paris, at a shared studio in rue de la Grande Chaumière. Travelled in Italy, looking at early Italian frescoes. 1905 returned to London. 1908 held first solo exhibition at the Carfax Gallery. 1908 married Constance Smedley, and both produced illustrations for the *Christian*

ARMITAGE, Kenneth

Science Monitor over the next few years. 1915 sailed for the USA and lived and worked there for seven years. Agreed to paint a landscape of the Grand Canyon for a railway company in exchange for two rail fares to California. With his wife in 1918, ran the stage design department at Berkeley University. Joined the Architectural League and the Tempera Society in New York. On his return to England in the 1920s concentrated on tempera portraits, flower and still life paintings. 1931 appointed ARWS and 1941 RWS. Designed his own house at Ibsley 'on the same proportion as was used in the Parthenon'. 1939 moved to an old inn at West Wycombe, Bucks., where his wife died. 1942 returned to London and concentrated on symbolic pictures and theosophical studies. Continued to exhibit with the RWS, the RA and at many dealers' galleries in London from the 1950s to '70s. 1971 Fine Art Society mounted a 90th birthday exhibition. Wrote *A Manual of Tempera Painting,* 1930, and other books.

ARMITAGE, Kenneth   b.1916

Sculptor. Born Leeds, Yorkshire. Studied at Leeds College of Art, 1934-7, and the Slade School of Art, 1937-9. 1939-46 served in the army. 1946-56 Head of Sculpture Department, Bath Academy of Art, Corsham. He destroyed all his pre-war carvings influenced by Egyptian and Cycladic sculptures, and began creating groups of figures, their shapes simplified to suggest the merging of individual particularities in a crowd. These Giacometti-influenced works were seen by the critics of the day, notably Herbert Read, to be expressive of post-war angst. 1952 first solo exhibition held at Gimpel Fils, London, the same year he was included in 'New Aspects of British Sculpture' at the Venice Biennale. 1953-5 Gregory Fellow in Sculpture at the University of Leeds. 1956 won an international prize for a war memorial for the town of Krefeld in Germany. With the move from plaster to clay as modelling material, his work developed in the late 1950s into a more monumental, hieratic style. 1958 one of three British representatives at the Venice Biennale. In the 1960s he experimented with wax, resins and aluminium, employing a style that was abstract but still had figurative connotations. 1969 made CBE. More recent shows at City Museum and Art Gallery, Stoke-on-Trent, 1980 and at Artcurial, Paris, 1985.

Bibl: *Kenneth Armitage,* Arts Council, London, 1972.

ARMOUR, George Denholm   1864-1949

Painter and illustrator. Born Waterside, Scotland. Studied at Edinburgh School of Art, and the RSA schools from 1880. Settled in London and shared a studio with Phil May. Worked as an illustrator for the following periodicals: *The Graphic, Punch,* and *Country Life.* Best known for his humorous illustrations of huntin', fishin' and shootin' scenes.

ARMOUR, Hazel   1894-1985

Sculptor. Born Edinburgh, Scotland. Educated at home before attending Edinburgh College of Art. Also studied in Paris before her marriage in 1921 to John Kennedy, after which she kept studios in Edinburgh and London. Visited South Africa twice to make studies of native heads. Commissioned to do a panel for the Scottish War Memorial in Edinburgh Castle. Exhibited in London, Edinburgh and Glasgow from 1914.

ARMOUR, Mary   b.1902

Painter. Born Blantyre, Scotland. Studied at Hamilton Academy, 1914-20, and Glasgow School of Art, 1920-5. 1937 awarded Guthrie Award at RSA. 1941 elected Associate Member of RSA. 1951-62 lecturer in still life painting at Glasgow School of Art. 1956 elected a member of Royal Scottish Society of Painters in Watercolour (RSW). 1958 elected Academician of RSA. Further awards and prizes followed. Married William Armour.*

ARMOUR, William   b.1903

Painter. Married the artist Mary Armour.* Exhibited at the RSA and was elected an associate, 1958 and a full member, 1966. For a period acted as Head of Drawing and Painting at Glasgow School of Art.

ARMSTRONG, Arthur   b.1924

Painter. Studied at Belfast College of Art, 1942-3, and also in France, Spain and England and has painted professionally since 1946. 1957 won a CEMA travelling scholarship. He has work in the Belfast Museum.

Bibl: Mike Catto, *Art in Ulster II,* Blackstaff Press, Belfast, 1977.

ARMSTRONG, Benita

Sculptor. Studied under Georg Ehrlich. Married the painter, John Armstrong.* Has exhibited many times in RA Summer Exhibitions and in other London galleries.

ARMSTRONG, Geoffrey   b.1945

Painter and sculptor. Born South Africa, the grandson of a painter. First solo exhibition at Henry Lidchi Gallery, Johannesburg; another at Drian Galleries, London, 1970.

ARMSTRONG, John   1893-1973

Painter. Born Hastings, Sussex. Educated at St. John's College, Oxford. Attended St. John's Wood Art School in an irregular fashion both before and after the First World War when he served in the Royal Field Artillery. Used tempera and held his first solo exhibition, 1928. Also achieved recognition as an interior designer and designed sets for theatre and films. Influenced by de Chirico whose work was shown in London in 1928. 1933 joined Unit One, and was an official war artist during the Second World War. He became interested in political themes and during 1950s was opposed to the proliferation of political weapons. His paintings are mostly dreamlike and surreal. 1966 elected ARA. 1975 retrospective mounted at RA in conjunction with Arts Council. Work in major public collections, including the Tate Gallery, V & A, and Arts Council.

ARMSTRONG, Shearer   b.1894

Painter. Born London. Studied at Karlsruhe and the Slade School. Exhibited at the RA, RSA, RWS, NEAC and elsewhere. Lived at St. Ives, Cornwall, for many years.

ARNATT, Ray   b.1934

Sculptor. Studied at Oxford School of Art and RCA, 1957-61. Has produced commissioned work for Lincoln College, Oxford, Weymouth Theatre, Minster Lovell Church and the Church of the Holy Family, Pontefract. Won the Sainsbury Sculpture Award, 1960.

ARNOLD, Ann   b.1936

Painter. Born Newcastle upon Tyne, Tyne and Wear. Studied at Epsom School of Art. 1961 married Graham Arnold* and has shared many exhibitions with him. Has had one-artist shows at the New Grafton Gallery, 1985, and elsewhere. 1981 illustrated *Clare's Countryside* and has designed covers for Arden Shakespeare editions. Like her husband, she was a founder-member of the Brotherhood of Ruralists. Her work reveals the extraordinary in the ordinary, with a straightforwardness of vision that she shares with the poet John Clare, whose work she admires. Represented by the Piccadilly Gallery, London.

ARNOLD, Charles Geoffrey   b.1915
Painter. Born Clayton, Yorkshire. Studied at Bradford College of Art, 1931-4, Camberwell School of Art, 1946-7, and Slade School, 1947-50. Exhibited at the RA, RWA and with the London Group. Elected ARWA, 1952.

ARNOLD, Graham   b.1932
Painter. Born Beckenham, Kent, and studied at Beckenham School of Art and RCA. Has exhibited widely, in England and abroad, with one-artist exhibitions in Brighton, Bath, Bristol, Bodmin, Chichester and London (Piccadilly Gallery). Has work in British Museum. With his wife Ann,* was a founder member of the Brotherhood of Ruralists and has been inspired by the English landscape, music and literature. Represented by the Piccadilly Gallery, London.

ARNOLD, Peter
Painter. Born Berlin, Germany. Self-taught. 1943 reached Britain as a ship's boy. Works principally in Wales. First one-artist exhibition held at the German Chamber of Industry and Commerce, London, 1975.

ARROBUS, Sydney   b.1901
Watercolour painter. Studied at Heatherley's. Exhibited at the RBA, RWS, RI, NS and SGA.

ARROWSMITH, Sue   b.1950
Painter. Born Lancashire. Studied at Nottingham School of Art, 1968-71 and the Slade, 1973-5. 1982 first solo exhibition held in London. 1985 had solo exhibition, 'Ancient Mirrors: Fragile Traces', at Serpentine Gallery, London. 1986-7 artist in residence at Wolfson College and Kettle's Yard, Cambridge.

ARTHUR, Lawrence   b.1943
Constructionist. Born Liverpool, Merseyside, where he also studied. Works with acrylic, brass and aluminium sheets and had his first one-artist exhibition at Wallasey School of Art, Wallasey, 1970. He has work in Salford City Art Gallery.

ARTHUR, Margaret   b.1930
Painter. Born Bristol, Avon. Studied at Cambridge School of Art, Chelsea School of Art and Académie Julian, Paris. First one-artist exhibition held at Phoenix Gallery, Lavenham, 1955.

ASCHERSON, Pamela   b.1923
Sculptor and illustrator. Studied at Farnham School of Art and RCA. Exhibited at RA and in the provinces. Lived for a period in France.

ASCOTT, Roy   b.1934
Sculptor. Born Bath, Avon. 1953-5 Radar Control, RAF. 1955-9 studied at King's College, Newcastle upon Tyne and held first one-artist exhibition, 'Change — Paintings and Reliefs', at Univision Gallery, Newcastle, 1961.

Moved to London and continued to exhibit in London and in galleries abroad. His work, inspired by cybernetics, deals with change and movement. He has taught at Ealing School of Art and Ipswich School of Art. Work in Arts Council Collection, Manchester City Art Gallery and elsewhere.

ASH, Bernadette   b.1934
Painter. Worked as a professional radiographer until 1973. Studied at Byam Shaw School of Painting, 1973-4, and Camberwell School of Art and Crafts, 1974-7. Has exhibited with NEAC and at RA and RWEA. Lives within the Exmoor National Park which is the subject of many of her paintings.

ASHBURN, Marian   b.1954
Painter. Studied at Edinburgh College of Art, 1972-7. Lives and works in the Orkneys. Has exhibited in mixed exhibitions at the Pier Arts Centre, Stromness, and at the RSA and the Society of Scottish Artists of which she is a member. One-artist shows at Pier Arts Centre, 1982 and 1984.

ASHBY, Derek   b.1926
Mixed media artist. Studied painting at Edinburgh College of Art and the Royal Academy Schools, London, 1948-56. Lecturer in painting at Gray's School of Art, and Robert Gordon's Institute of Technology. Makes three-dimensional constructions which explore the tonal surfaces of various metals.

ASHBY, T.H.W.   b.1927
Printmaker. Trained at Eastbourne School of Art. Has exhibited at RBA Galleries, RA and with Royal Birmingham Society of Artists.

ASHENDON, Edward James   b.1896
Watercolour painter. Born Wandsworth, London. Studied at Putney School of Art and the RCA, 1914, and 1919-22. Exhibited at the RA, RI and in the provinces.

ASHTON, Graham   b.1948
Mixed media artist. Born Birkenhead, Cheshire. Studied at Manchester College of Art, 1966-7, Coventry College of Art, 1967-70 and the University of Calgary 1970-1. 1977 held first solo exhibition. 1983-4 artist in residence at Walker Art Gallery and Bridewell Studios. Recent exhibitions at Fischer Fine Art, London, 1984, Museum of Modern Art, Oxford, 1985 and Chapter Art Gallery, Cardiff, 1985.

ASHTON, John William   1881-1963
Painter. Born York. Moved to Australia with his family and was brought up in Adelaide. Returned to England and studied painting under Julius Olsson* and Algernon Talmage,* also in Paris at the Académie Julian. Specialised in land and seascapes and exhibited at the RA and elsewhere. Elected ROI in 1913. He returned to Australia and became Director of the National Art Gallery of New South Wales and was knighted, 1960.

ASHTON, Tony   b.1948
Painter. Studied at Bath Academy of Art, Corsham, Lincoln College of Art and the West of England College of Art, Bristol, 1966-71. One-artist exhibitions at 5 Dryden Street Gallery, London and LYC Gallery, Cumbria.

ASHWORTH, John R.

CONRAD ATKINSON, b.1940. *'Wall Street Journal; Hugh McDiarmid and Buddy'*. Holly edition, 1987. 60in. x 52in. Acrylic. Ronald Feldman Fine Arts, NYC.

ASHWORTH, John R.   b.1942
Sculptor. Born London. 1955-60 lived in Canada and USA. 1968-71 studied at Manchester College of Art, and, 1971-4, at RCA. Has taught at Hornsey since 1974. One-artist exhibition at Park Square Gallery, Leeds, 1975.

ASKEW, Victor   b.1909
Painter. Born Sheffield, Yorkshire. Studied at Sheffield College of Art. 1932 came to London and painted English landscapes and London scenes. From 1944 exhibited regularly at RA and in 1948 'The Studio, St. John's Wood' was bought for the Tate Gallery. A fluent naturalist, wholly untouched by modernist art or theory.

ASPINALL, Norman   b.1929
Sculptor. Born Ashton-under-Lyne, Greater Manchester. Studied at Ashton School of Art and the Regional College of Art, Manchester, where he taught sculpture from 1961. One-artist exhibitions held at Shipley Art Gallery, Gateshead, 1957 and Crane Kalman Gallery, London,

1959. A figurative sculptor whose style in the 1950s shared characteristics with the work of Armitage* and Butler.*

ASPLIN, Syd   1902-1971
Painter. Born Coventry, West Midlands. Employed from the age of thirteen. Apprenticed as a toolmaker with Alfred Herbert's, Coventry, for whom he worked. Self-taught, he became a competent watercolourist with a wide range of techniques. Also known for his sketches of Old Coventry, done from memory, and for a series of weekly cartoons done for the *Coventry Standard*.

ASSHETON, Caroline   b.1961
Painter. Studied at Camberwell Art College and at City and Guilds, 1981-4. Travelled in Outer Mongolia and the Sahara. First solo exhibition at the Queen's Elm, Chelsea, 1986.

ATHERTON, Kevin   b.1950
Sculptor. Born Isle of Man. Attended Isle of Man College of Art, 1968-9, and Leeds Polytechnic, 1969-72. Part-time teaching at Middlesex Polytechnic, Chelsea, Maidstone and Winchester Schools of Art in the 1970s.

ATKIN, John   b.1959
Sculptor. Born Darlington, Co. Durham. Studied at Teeside College of Art, 1977-8, Leicester Polytechnic, 1978-81 and RCA, 1982-5. 1985 first solo exhibition. Exhibited at Juda Rowan, London, 1986.

ATKINS, David   b.1937
Painter and photographer. Born London. Studied at St. Martin's School of Art, 1955-9 and Royal Academy Schools, 1959-62. Has worked as a designer for Frederick Gibberd and Partners, Architects, and also as an architectural photographer. Exhibited at West Midlands Arts, 1986.

ATKINS, Ray   b.1937
Painter. Born Exeter, Devon. Studied at Bromley College of Art, 1954-6, 1958-61, and at the Slade, 1961-4. 1956-8 National Service in the Army. 1970 first solo exhibition at Piers Morris Gallery, London, followed by a second exhibition in the same year at Studio of Creative Art, Cardiff. One-man exhibitions include the Whitechapel Art Gallery, 1975. He is a prolific landscape painter, working directly from the subject. Included in the collections of the Arts Council of Great Britain, South West Arts and Somerset County Council.

ATKINS, Ron   b.1938
Painter. Born Leicestershire. Studied at Loughborough College of Art, 1954-7, and Royal Academy Schools, 1957-61. Has exhibited regularly at RA summer exhibitions and in mixed shows at Roland, Browse and Delbanco. Has work in public collections in the South West of England.

ATKINSON, Anthony   b.1929
Painter. Studied at RCA. 1950 first exhibited at RA. 1962 first solo exhibition at the Minories, Colchester. Primarily a landscape painter, working especially in the area around Buxted in Essex. Head of Colchester School of Art since 1964.

ATKINSON, Conrad   b.1940
Mixed media artist. Born Cleaton Moor, Cumbria. Studied at Carlisle College of Art, 1957-61, Liverpool College of Art, 1961-2 and Royal Academy Schools, 1962-5. 1972 first solo exhibition. Takes as his starting point the imbrication of art with politics and social reality.

Bibl: *Conrad Atkinson: 1975-80 Work About the North,* Carlisle Museum and Art Gallery, 1980.

ATKINSON, Dale   b.1962
Painter. Born Sunderland, Tyne and Wear. Studied at Sunderland Art College, 1981-2, and at Newcastle University, 1982-6. Regularly exhibits with the Anne Berthoud Gallery, London, where he has been holding solo exhibitions since 1986. Painter of bizarre images with suggestively allegorical connotations.

ATKINSON, Eric   b.1928
Painter. Born West Hartlepool, Cleveland. Studied at West Hartlepool College of Art and the Royal Academy Schools. 1956 first solo exhibition at Redfern Gallery, London, and has held many since. Head of the Department of Fine Arts at Leeds College of Art until 1969, after which he moved to Canada. Has work in many public collections, including Leeds City Art Gallery.

ATKINSON, Lawrence   1873-1931
Painter and sculptor. Born Chorlton-upon-Medlock, near Manchester. Studied singing in Berlin and Paris, then taught it in Liverpool and London. Self-taught as an artist. First exhibited in the 1913 Allied Artists Association. Joined Wyndham Lewis's Rebel Art Centre, 1914. Solo exhibition of abstract sculpture and painting held at the Eldar Gallery, London, 1921. Won Grand Prix for sculpture at Milan, 1921. Work in the Tate Gallery.

Bibl: Horace Shipp, *The New Art: A Study of the Principles of Non-Representational Art and their Application to the Work of Lawrence Atkinson,* Cecil Palmer, London, 1922.

ATKINSON, Marilyn Gore   b.1946
Painter. Born Kingston upon Hull, Humberside. Studied at Manchester College of Art, 1964-8 and RCA, 1968-71. First solo exhibition at New Art Centre, London, 1974.

ATKINSON, Terry   b.1939
Painter. Born Thurnscoe, Yorkshire. Studied at Barnsley School of Art, 1959-60, and Slade School of Art, 1960-4. Taught at Birmingham College of Art and then Coventry College of Art (now Lancaster Polytechnic) and became associated with Art and Language until 1975. Subjects that recur in his paintings are the First World War and the Somme Campaigns, and anti-nuclear politics. Has exhibited widely and taken part in many contemporary art debates.

Bibl: *Terry Atkinson: Work 1977-83,* Whitechapel Art Gallery, London, 1983; *Terry Atkinson: The Goya Series,* Gimpel Fils, London, 1987.

ATWOOD, Clare   1866-1962
Painter. Born Richmond, Surrey, daughter of an architect. Studied at the Westminster School of Art and the Slade School. First exhibited at the NEAC in 1893, became a member in 1912. First solo exhibition at the Carfax Gallery in 1912. Commissioned to paint war scenes during the First World War for the Canadian Government; four of these paintings are in the Imperial War Museum. Work in the Tate Gallery collection.

AUDSLEY, Mary   b.1919
Painter and sculptor. Studied at the Westminster School of Art, 1934-8. Began exhibiting with the London Group, at the RA and elsewhere. 1941 enlisted in the WRAF but was invalided out in 1943. The seven months she then spent in hospital were the first indication of the ill-health which was to blight her progress. Her health broke down again after her mother's death in 1947. Not until the 1970s did she re-enter an active period. Works in several media (ceramics, carving, print-making, painting and collage). Solo exhibition at Sally Hunter Fine Art, 1990.

AUERBACH, Arnold   1898-1978
Sculptor, painter and etcher. Born Liverpool. Studied at Liverpool College of Art and then in Paris. Taught at the Regent Street Polytechnic and Chelsea College of Art. Exhibited at RA and in the provinces.

Bibl: Arnold Auerbach, *Sculpture, a History in Brief,* London, 1953.

AUERBACH, Erna   1897-1975
Painter. Born Frankfurt-am-Main, Germany. Studied at Frankfurt Kunstgewerbeschule, 1917-22, in Paris, 1926,

AUERBACH, Frank

FRANK AUERBACH, b.1931. *'Head of E.O.W.V.'*, 1961. 24in. x 20in. Marlborough Fine Art. Private Collection.

GILLIAN AYRES, b.1930. *'Monte Christo'*, 1984. 84in. x 72in. Knoedler Gallery.

and Frankfurt, 1928-30. 1920-33 exhibited widely in Germany (portraits, landscapes, still lifes). From the early 1930s unable to exhibit, lecture or publish, and later prevented from painting. In England she was established as a respected artist and, after the destruction of her studio in the Blitz, as an art historian. Contributed to various journals and lectured. First one-artist show in England at Brook Street Gallery, 1938.

AUERBACH, Frank   b.1931
Painter. Born Berlin, Germany. Sent to England in 1939 and never saw his family again. Original ambition was to become an actor. Attended art classes at Hampstead Garden Suburb Institute and then the Borough Polytechnic where he responded to the teaching of David Bomberg.* Studied at St. Martin's School of Art, 1948-52 and RCA, 1952-5. 1956 first solo exhibition held at Beaux-Arts Gallery. 1978 accorded a major retrospective by the Arts Council. 1986 represented Britain at the Venice Biennale. Works slowly with a deliberately restricted range of familiar subjects, but is as obsessed with the painting's inherent vitality as he is with the 'recalcitrant, inescapable thereness of . . . everyday objects'. Represented by the Marlborough Gallery, London.

Bibl: *Frank Auerbach, Paintings and Drawings 1977-1985*, British Council, 1986.

AUMONIER, Eric
Sculptor. Member of a family firm of architectural decorators with his father William Aumonier.* 1928 one of the team of six sculptors who carved the 'Winds' on St. James's Park Underground station, he carved the 'South Wind'. Also carved the 'Empire' relief panels on the Daily Express building, London.

AUMONIER, William
Sculptor. Studied at West London School of Art. Exhibited work at the RA, 1899-1900. One of the group of artists who worked on the architectural decoration of the Victoria Law Courts, Birmingham, in the late 1880s. Father of Eric Aumonier.* Author of *Modern Architectural Sculpture*, published 1930.

AUSTIN, Frederick George   b.1902
Engraver. Younger brother of Robert Austin.* Trained at Leicester College of Art and RCA and specialised in metal work. Went to Dryads Works before the First World War and made munitions. Full-time art student after the war and in 1921 won a scholarship to RCA where he specialised in book illustration. Elected Associate of Royal Society of Painter-Etchers and Engravers and a full member, 1951, and taught at Blackheath School of Arts and Crafts.

AUSTIN, Robert   1895-1973
Etcher, engraver and watercolourist. Born Leicester. Studied at Leicester School of Art, 1909-13 and at RCA. 1915-19 served in the trenches. 1919 returned to RCA. 1921 elected Associate of the Royal Society of Painter-Etchers and Engravers. 1922-5 lived in Rome and travelled in Italy. 1926 taught engraving at RCA. 1928 elected a Fellow of the RE. 1949 elected RA. 1956 elected President of the Royal Watercolour Society. 1962 elected President of the RE.

Bibl: Campbell Dodgson, *A Catalogue of Etchings and Engravings by Robert Austin, RE 1913-1929*, London, 1930.

MICHAEL AYRTON, 1921-1975. *'Temptation of St. Anthony'*. 84in. x 62in. Tate Gallery.

AUTY, Giles   b.1934
Painter. Born East Kent. Worked in factories in the East End of London and in Yorkshire before becoming a painter. 1959 moved to West Cornwall to paint full time. His paintings depend on first-hand experience of the physical world. His distrust of theory and suspicion of contemporary trends led him to publish *The Art of Self-Deception,* 1977. 1984 he became art critic to *The Spectator.*

AYRES, Arthur James John   b.1902
Sculptor. Studied at RA Schools, also in Paris and at the British School in Rome, 1931. Exhibited at the RA, in the provinces and abroad. Elected FRBS, 1948.

AYRES, Gillian   b.1930
Painter. Born London. Studied at Camberwell School of Art, 1946-50, where she rejected ideas about painting that had originated with the Euston Road School. 1951-9 worked three days a week at the AIA Gallery, sharing the post with Henry Mundy* whom she married. 1959-66 taught at Bath Academy of Art. Continued to have a distinguished career as a teacher, resigning as Head of Painting at Winchester School of Art in 1981, in order to paint full-time. Influenced by her meeting with Roger Hilton,* she became an abstract painter in an expressionist vein. 1960-1 took part in the two 'Situation' exhibitions. 1982 elected ARA. Her one-artist shows include the Museum of Modern Art, Oxford, 1981 and the Serpentine Gallery, 1983. An exuberant, major colourist.

AYRTON, Michael   1921-1975
Painter, sculptor. Long periods of illness broke into his formal schooling. Briefly attended various art schools, including Heatherley's and St. John's Wood. 1938 visited Paris with John Minton* and admired the work of the French neo-romantics. Joined the RAF soon after war was declared, 1942 invalided out. Taught life drawing and theatre design at Camberwell. Had a diverse career as art critic, art historian, novelist, broadcaster, theatrical designer and film director, as well as painter, sculptor and etcher.

Bibl: Peter Cannon-Brookes, *Michael Ayrton: An Illustrated Commentary,* Birmingham Museum and Art Gallery, 1978.

B

BABB, Stanley Nicholson   1874-1957
Sculptor. Born Plymouth, Devon. Studied at Plymouth
Art School and the RA Schools where he won a gold medal
and a travelling scholarship. Exhibited at RA from 1898.

BACON, Francis   b.1909
Painter. Born Dublin, Ireland, the son of a racehorse
trainer. Came to London, 1925 and set up as a furniture
designer and interior decorator, spending some time in
Berlin, 1927-8. 1929 began painting in oils and received
advice from Roy de Maistre. Otherwise self-taught. In
1934 a Crucifixion by him was reproduced in Herbert
Read's *Art Now*. Lack of commercial success caused him to
abandon painting in the late 1930s. Worked in Civil
Defence during the war. 1944 returned to painting, the
year he painted *Three Studies for Figures at the Base of a
Crucifixion* and which shook visitors to the Lefevre
Gallery in the spring of 1945. Continued to gain in
reputation with a series based on Velasquez's *Pope
Innocent X* combined with a still of the screaming nanny in
Eisenstein's film, *Battleship Potemkin*. Produces images
expressive of violence and desperation. Paints portraits
mostly from photographs or memory and uses the sweep of
the brush to suggest either sudden movement or an
equivalent to the bruising of the face by the fist. Has had
numerous solo and retrospective exhibitions, including
one at the Grand Palais, Paris and elsewhere, 1972, the
Metropolitan Museum, New York, 1975, the Tate Gallery,
1985 and in Moscow, 1988. (Plate 13, p.35.)

Bibl: David Sylvester, *Interviews with Francis Bacon*, Thames &
Hudson, London, 1980; Michel Leiris, *Francis Bacon*, Thames &
Hudson, London, 1987.

BACON, Marjorie May   b.1902
Printmaker. Born Ipswich, Suffolk. Studied at RCA,
obtaining her diploma in 1927. Exhibited at the RA and
the NEAC.

BADHAM, Edward Leslie   1873-1944
Painter. Born London. Studied at Clapham School of Art,
South Kensington Government Art Schools and the Slade.
Taught at Hastings School of Art. Specialised in coastal
scenes painted at Hastings and elsewhere on the Sussex
coast.

BADMIN, S.R.   1906-1989
Watercolourist, lithographer and engraver. Born London.
Studied at Camberwell School of Art and RCA, received
his diploma in 1928. Specialised in the English country-
side and architecture, and showed at the Twenty-One
Gallery, London. 1939 he illustrated *Highways and
Byways in Essex* with F.L.M. Griggs* for Macmillan and
Co. Continued to illustrate. 1932 became an associate of
the RWS and a full member, 1939.

Bibl: Chris Beetles, *S.R. Badmin and the English Landscape*,
Collins, London, 1985.

BAGILHOLE, Robin   b.1942
Painter. Born Cornwall. Studied at Exeter and
Nottingham Schools of Art and RCA. 1975 first solo
exhibition held Thumb Gallery, London. Others include
Arnolfini Gallery, Bristol, 1977, Usher Gallery, Lincoln,
1978, Leeds Playhouse, 1979, and Thumb Gallery, 1982.
Represented in V & A and Graves Art Gallery, Sheffield.

BAILEY, Cecil   b.1907
Painter. Studied at St. Martin's School of Art, 1922. Tutor

EDWARD BAIRD, 1904-1949. *'Portrait of Walter Graham'*.
36¼ in. x 28¼ in. Dundee Art Galleries & Museums.

under David Bomberg* at the Borough Polytechnic. Solo
exhibition at the Corner Gallery, London, 1969. Founder
member of the Borough Bottega Group.

BAILEY, James   b.1922
Painter. Born London. Studied under William Chase,*
then at the Slade. Moved into theatre design after he
successfully designed sets for *Giselle* in 1946 at Covent
Garden. Solo exhibition at Redfern Gallery, London, 1963,
and at Alwin Gallery, London, in 1974.

BAILEY, Peter   b.1944
Sculptor and mixed media artist. Born Denbighshire,
Wales. Trained at Bath Academy after graduating from
University College, Aberystwyth. Taught until 1976
when he became a full-time sculptor. Represented in
Welsh Arts Council and Arts Council collections and V & A.

Bibl: *Metamorphoses: Peter Bailey*, Oriel, Cardiff, 1983.

BAILLIE, William   b.1923
Painter. Born Edinburgh, Scotland. Studied at Edinburgh
College of Art. 1963 elected member of RSW. 1968 elected
associate RSA, 1979 elected Academician. Teaches at
Edinburgh College of Art and exhibits regularly in
Scotland and London. Represented in Aberdeen Art
Gallery, RSA, Scottish Arts Council and elsewhere.

BAIN, Donald   1904-1979
Painter. Born Kilmacolm, Scotland. Encouraged by the painter W.Y. MacGregor,* he visited Paris. 1940 he moved to Glasgow and was further encouraged by J.D. Fergusson.* Whilst working in the shipyards became a founder-member of the New Art Club, Glasgow, 1940, and 1942 of the New Scottish Group. The following year he met a collector who put him on a contract to paint two pictures a week for one year. 1946-8 lived in France. 1948 designed décor for ballet, *A Midsummer Night's Dream*, for Margaret Morris. 1952 held solo exhibition in Glasgow; others followed, but ill-health curtailed his output. Interest in his work revived in the 1970s, and he held a solo exhibition at the Woodstock Gallery, London, 1978.

BAINBRIDGE, Eric   b.1955
Sculptor. Born Consett, Co. Durham. Studied at Jacob Kramer College, Leeds, 1973-4, and Newcastle Polytechnic, 1974-7. Worked in Archaeology Dept., Durham University, 1978. Studied at RCA, 1978-81. Since 1981 part-time teacher at Brighton and Falmouth Colleges of Art. Work in the Arts Council collection. First one-person exhibition at Ayton Basement, Newcastle, 1978. Represented by Galleria Salvatore Ala, Milan.

Bibl: *Eric Bainbridge: Sculpture*, Air Gallery, London, 1985.

BAINBRIDGE, John   1918-1978
Painter. Born Sydney, Australia. Studied art in Australia and came to London in 1945. Developed a fascination with the correlation between human and organic forms. His linear structures have a clinical simplicity. 1945-78 exhibited at Redfern Gallery, London, and elsewhere. Represented in V & A and in Australian public collections.

BAINES, Clare
Painter. Born New York, USA. Studied at Art Students League, New York, Regent Street Polytechnic and Byam Shaw School of Art. Has exhibited at RA in the 1960s, and at the Trafford, Marjorie Parr and Woodstock Galleries in London.

BAIRD, Edward   1904-1949
Painter. Born Montrose, Scotland. Studied at Glasgow School of Art, 1923-7, graduating with the Newberry Medal awarded to the best student of the year. Also won a travelling scholarship to Italy. Developed a passion for meticulous detail and occasionally introduced Surrealist elements into his pictures. Spent all his life at Montrose. Unable to fight during the Second World War owing to ill-health, he concentrated instead chiefly on portraiture, but kept aloof from the art world. This, and his early death, meant that he remained virtually unknown until the Scottish Arts Council organised an exhibition of his work in 1968.

Bibl: *Edward Baird,* Montrose Public Library, exhibition cat., 1981.

BAIRD, Michael   b.1929
Painter and caricaturist. Born Belfast, Northern Ireland. Studied at Belfast College of Art, 1948-52. Has exhibited at the Piccolo Gallery, Belfast, 1957, the Ritchie Hendriks Gallery, Dublin, 1960 and the Arts Council Gallery, Belfast, 1961.

BAKER, Charles Henry Collins   1880-1959
Painter and art historian. Born Ilminster, Somerset. Studied at RA Schools. Wrote art criticism for *Outlook* and the *Saturday Review.* 1914 appointed Keeper and Secretary of the National Gallery where he remained until 1932 when he joined the research staff of the Huntingdon Library in California. 1949 returned to London. Painted landscapes and exhibited with the NEAC and was Honorary Secretary of the Club, 1921-5. Published *Lely and the Stuart Portrait Painters,* 1912, *Crome,* 1921, and *Dutch Painting of the XVIIth Century,* 1926.

BAKER, Charlotte   b.1954
Sculptor and ceramicist. Born Devon. Studied at Plymouth School of Art, 1974-5, and Camberwell, 1975-8. Fellow in Ceramics at South Glamorgan Institute of Higher Education.

BAKER, Chris   b.1944
Painter. Born London. Studied at Camberwell School of Art, 1972-5 and RCA, 1975-8. 1981-2 Artist in Residence at Eton College. 1981 first solo exhibition at Eton College. He has been represented in group exhibitions and held solo exhibitions at the Paton Gallery, London, since 1983. Represented in the collections of the Metropolitan Museum of Art, New York, Arts Council of Great Britain and the Contemporary Art Society.

BAKER, Geoffrey Alan   b.1881
Painter. Born Faversham, Kent. Studied at Canterbury Art School, 1898-1902, and RCA, 1902-7. Exhibited at the RA and in the provinces. Principal of Bournemouth College of Art, 1913-47.

BALDWIN, John   b.1937
Sculptor. Born London. After serving in the RAF, he studied sculpture at Camberwell School of Arts and Crafts. Worked for fifteen years in a commercial studio producing fibreglass sculptures for architectural purposes. In his own work began making relief carvings in wood, alluding in his imagery to fables and legends, influenced to some extent by the Japanese.

BALDWIN, Mervyn   b.1934
Sculptor. Born Lincolnshire. Studied at Grimsby School of Art, 1951-3, and Leicester College of Art, 1953-5. 1960-2 won Prix de Rome (Sculpture). Has exhibited in Birmingham, London and Cardiff.

BALDWIN, Laurie   b.1942.
Painter. Born London. Studied at Ealing School of Art, 1958-63. Has exhibited in London and Liverpool (John Moores 3rd Prize). Solo exhibition held at Chenil Art Gallery, London, 1982.

BALL, Martin   b.1948
Painter. Born Leicestershire. Studied at Loughborough College of Art, Central School of Art and RCA. 1975 first one-person exhibition held at the Molton Street Gallery, London. Represented in V & A and Ashmolean Museum, Oxford.

Bibl: Artist's statement in *Artscribe,* No.5, 1977

BALL, Peter Eugene
Sculptor. Born Warwickshire. Studied at Coventry College of Art. Solo exhibitions at Marjorie Parr Gallery, London, 1970, 1972 and 1974. Has also exhibited in the Sian Gallery, Amsterdam.

BALL, Robert   b.1918
Painter and printmaker. Born Birmingham, West Midlands. Studied at Birmingham Junior School of Art, 1930-3, and Birmingham College of Art, 1933-40, and at the RCA, 1940-2. Exhibited widely. Elected ARE, 1943, ARBSA, 1943 and RBSA, 1949.

BALL, R.C.   b.1910
Painter. Born Sussex. Studied at Hastings School of Art and RCA. 1939 awarded travelling scholarship. Solo exhibitions at Ashgate Gallery, London, 1961, 1963, 1965 and 1967.

BALLOW, Yvonne
Painter. Studied at Central School of Art, Chelsea School of Art and London University. Joined a group of artists, writers, doctors and academics who lived and worked in Bloomsbury. Exhibited at RA, the Paris Salon, the London Group and the Christopher Hull Gallery.

BALMER, Barbara   b.1929
Painter. Born Birmingham, West Midlands. Studied at Coventry College of Art, West Midlands. 1951-2 summer travelling scholarship to France and Spain. Regular exhibitor at RSA, SSA, RRSW, the Glasgow Group and the Richard Demarco Gallery.

BALMER, Derek   b.1934
Painter and photographer. Born Bristol, Avon. Studied at West of England College of Art and later trained as a photographer. Solo exhibitions at the Arnolfini Gallery, Bristol, 1963, 1965 and 1968. Exhibits with London Group, RWEA, and elsewhere.

BAMBER, Anthony   b.1941
Painter. Started to paint landscapes at fifteen. Read English at Cambridge and had no formal art school training. Solo exhibition at Elvaston Gallery, London, 1974.

BAMFORD, Ian   1948-1975
Painter and sculptor. Born Rochdale, Lancashire. Studied at Rochdale College of Art, 1964-6, Coventry College of Art, 1966-9, and Liverpool College of Art, 1969-70. Included in mixed exhibitions in Rochdale, Bradford and Coventry, 1972-3. Memorial exhibition at Warwick Gallery, 1977.

BANAHAN, Christopher   b.1958
Painter. Born Nottingham. Studied at Liverpool Polytechnic, 1978-9, Trent Polytechnic, 1979-81, and at Goldsmiths' College, 1982-4. First solo exhibition at Braganza, London, 1988, followed by a second exhibition at Sue Williams, London, 1989. Included in the collections of London Borough of Camden Arts Department and the CAS.

BANBURY, William   b.1871
Sculptor. Born Leicester. Studied at Leicester College of Art, the RCA and in Paris. Exhibited at RA, RSA and in the provinces. For a time was Head of Sculpture at Aberdeen College of Art.

BAND, David   b.1959
Painter. Born Glasgow, Scotland. Studied at Glasgow School of Art, 1977-81, and RCA, 1981-3. 1983 set up Cloth studios as an amalgamation of paintings, illustrations, textile design and fashion. Has exhibited regularly since 1982, with a solo exhibition at Waterman's Arts Centre, Brentford, 1985, and Thumb Gallery, London, 1985 and 1988.

BANESS, Bridget   b.1939
Painter. Studied privately under various tutors. Drew inspiration from children with whom she worked. First solo exhibition in London, 1966; another at Woodstock Gallery, London, 1968.

BANISTER, Barbara
Painter and silversmith. Studied at RCA. Has work in silver in the collection of the Worshipful Company of Goldsmiths, Goldsmiths' Hall. Commissioned to paint a portrait of Lester Piggott winning the 1954 Derby on Never Say Die. Solo exhibition at the Rose and Crown, Fletching, Sussex, 1958.

BANKS, Brian   b.1939
Painter. Born London. Studied at St. Martin's School of Art and in private studios. Solo exhibitions in Manchester, 1967, Ansdell Gallery, London, 1968 and King's Lynn, Norfolk.

BANKS, Peter   b.1938
Painter. Born Birmingham, West Midlands. Studied sculpture and painting at Bournemouth College of Art, 1956-60. Solo exhibitions in Bournemouth, Jersey and Blandford.

BANKS, Robert   b.1911
Painter. Born Cheltenham, Gloucestershire. Studied with the Architectural Association, 1928-33. Served in the Army, awarded MC. In architectural and town planning practice until 1957. Solo exhibitions at Leicester Gallery, London, 1959, and Isaacson Gallery, New York, 1960.

BANNERMAN, Afrakuma   b.1950
Painter. Born Ghana, West Africa. Studied at Kingston Polytechnic and London University Institute. Has held several solo exhibitions in London, at the Mall Galleries and elsewhere, and at the Annexe Gallery, 1978.

BANTING, John   1902-1972
Painter. In 1921 while working as a bank clerk by day attended evening classes in art under Bernard Meninsky.* 1922 studied in Paris. 1923 clerical work in his father's book-binding factory. 1929 first exhibition at the Wertheim Gallery. Also that year did ballet designs for *Pomona* and *Prometheus* at Sadlers Wells. 1930 took a studio in Paris. 1936 contributed to the International Surrealist Exhibition in London. 1939 worked as art director in Strand Films, producing documentaries. 1941 art editor of magazine *Our Time.* 1947 lived and worked in Ireland.

Bibl: *John Banting 1902-1972: A Retrospective,* Bradbury and Birch Fine Art, London, 1983.

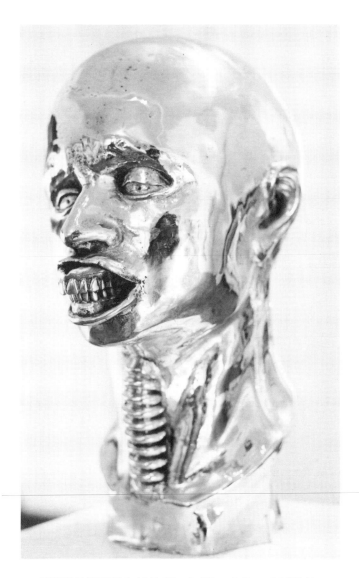

CLIVE BARKER, b.1940. *'Head of Francis Bacon'*, 1978. Brass. 37in. high. Aberdeen Art Gallery & Museums, Aberdeen City Arts Department.

BARCLAY, Stephen   b.1961
Painter. Born Ayrshire, Scotland. Studied at Glasgow School of Art, 1980-5. 1987 first solo exhibition held at Paton Gallery, London, subsequently at Raab Gallery, London. Represented in the collections of the Contemporary Art Society and the Australian National Gallery.

BARHAM, Jean   b.1924
Painter. Studied at Camberwell School of Art, 1947-51. Has held solo exhibitions at the World Trade Centre, 1973, on the *Cutty Sark*, 1979, at Greenwich Theatre, 1985, and the Woodwharf Gallery, Greenwich, 1986.

BARING, Robin   b.1931
Painter. Born London. Brought up in the country, from which he has drawn much inspiration. Decided to devote himself to painting in 1956 and studied at Central School of Art, 1956-9. Influenced by the art and ideas of Cecil Collins.* Solo exhibition at Crane Kalman Gallery, London, 1971.

BARKER, Allen   b.1937
Painter. Born Australia. Arrived in Europe, 1961. 1969 first solo exhibition held at Galerie Jungt Generation, Vienna, others include two at Lucy Milton Gallery, London, 1971 and 1973. Has work in Leicester City Art Gallery and Sheffield City Art Galleries.

BARKER, Clive   b.1940
Sculptor. Born Luton, Bedfordshire. Studied at Luton College of Technology and Art, 1957-9. Worked at Vauxhall Motors, 1960-1, and as pawnbroker in Portobello Road, 1962-4. 1964 began making objects. 1965 tutor at Maidstone School of Art. 1968 first one-person show at Robert Fraser Gallery. Has exhibited widely at home and abroad, including 'Portraits: Clive Barker', NPG, 1987. He takes a familiar image, from domestic life or art history, and transforms it by casting into chrome, giving it a chilling presence. Represented in Aberdeen Art Gallery, Arts Council, British Council, the Tate Gallery and elsewhere.

BARKER, David   b.1940
Painter. Born Scunthorpe, Humberside. Studied at Bath Academy of Art and London University. First solo exhibitions held at Interior Seven, Bath, 1966, and at Vandyck Theatre, University of Bristol, 1969.

BARKER, David Walker   b.1949
Painter. Born South Yorkshire. Studied at Sheffield College of Art and Design, 1964-8 and RCA, 1969-72. 1974 first solo exhibition held at Mappin Art Gallery, Sheffield, others include one at Bradford University, 1979 and Quinton Green Fine Art, London, 1986. Winner of many awards and fellowships. His paintings are landscape-based but explore structures that are often beneath or beyond what the eye can see.

BARKER, Kit   1916-1988
Painter. Born London. Went to USA in 1949 and lectured at Skidmore College, NY, and at California School of Fine Arts, San Francisco. Lived in Sussex after 1953. Represented in collections throughout the world, including Arts Council, CAS, and Aberdeen Art Gallery. Lived for a period in Cornwall and exhibited with other St. Ives artists. Chiefly painted landscapes often involving water or reflected light.

BARKER, Margaret   b.1907
Painter. Born London. Studied at the RCA, 1925-9 under Randolph Schwabe.* Exhibited at NEAC. Specialised in figurative paintings. Work in the Tate Gallery.

BARKLEY, Alan   b.1944
Sculptor. Born Belleville, Canada. Studied at University of Toronto, 1962-4. Assistant to sculptor Ted Bieler, 1964-6. Studied at St. Martin's School of Art, 1966-8. 1967-9 awarded Canada Council Award. Has exhibited at Stockwell Depot, 1968 and 1969, and elsewhere.

BARLOW, Bohuslav   b.1947
Painter. Born Czechoslovakia. Moved to Blackpool in 1955. Studied at Manchester and Central Schools of Art. Began exhibiting in 1973 and has had several solo exhibitions, including ones at Hartnoll and Eyre, London, 1976 and Woodlands Art Gallery, London, 1982.

BARLOW, Gillian

GILLIAN BARLOW, b.1944. *'Group portrait'*, 1978. 16½ in. x 25in. Watercolour on paper. A.C. Cooper Ltd.

BARLOW, Gillian   b.1944
Painter. Born Khartoum, Sudan. Studied at Slade School of Art, 1962-3; also studied art history at University of Sussex, 1967-72. Solo exhibitions at Hudson View Gallery, New York, 1985 and Blond Fine Art, London, 1986. 1987 visiting Professor to Baroda University, India.

BARLOW, John Noble   1861-1917
Landscape painter. Born Manchester. Studied in Paris under Le Febre and Delance. Lived much of his professional life in St. Ives, Cornwall, but painted a great deal at Lamorna, in the same tradition as Lamorna Birch.* 1906-16 exhibited at RA.

BARLOW, Nicholas   b.1940
Painter. Born London. Studied at Tunbridge Wells School of Art, Maidstone College of Art and RA Schools. Exhibits at RA and has had several solo exhibitions at the Gerdon Gallery, Wimbledon. Specialises in landscape and plant studies.

BARLOW, Phyllida   b.1944
Sculptor. Studied at Chelsea School of Art, 1960-3 and Slade School of Art, 1963-6. Solo exhibition held at Camden Arts Centre, 1971.

BARNARD, Gwen   b.1912
Painter. Studied at Chelsea School of Art, 1931-5 and Euston Road School, 1937-8. Exhibited at the Beaux Arts Gallery, London, 1947 and in various galleries since then. Published *Shapes of the River* (Gaberbocchus Press), 1955. 1976 exhibited recent paintings at Camden Art Centre.

BARNARD, Kate   b.1941
Graphic artist. Born England but educated in America, Canada and England. Studied at Bath Academy of Art and University of Reading. 1965 first one-artist exhibition at Santa Barbara Museum of Art, California. Taught at Leeds Polytechnic until 1974. Played in Mike Westwood's Brass Band.

WILHELMINA BARNS-GRAHAM, b.1912. *'Rocks, St. Mary's, Scilly Isles'*, 1953. 40½ in. x 45in. Photograph by David Roche. City Art Centre Collection, Edinburgh.

BARNARD, Thomas Henslow   b.1898
Painter. Studied at West of England College of Art in Bristol. Exhibited at RA, RWA and NEAC and was elected ARWA, 1961. Member of the Cheltenham Group of Artists.

BARNDEN, Hugh   b.1948
Painter. Born Oxfordshire. Studied at the RCA, 1968-71. Before the RCA he spent some years working with John Makepeace, designing and producing furniture. 1978 his first solo exhibition was held in Amsterdam. He has regularly exhibited at the Francis Kyle Gallery, London, since 1982.

BARNES, Archibald George   b.1887
Painter. Born Sandon. Studied at St. John's Wood School of Art and RA Schools. From 1913 exhibited at RA, and at the RP and elsewhere.

BARNES, George   b.1909
Painter and portrait sculptor. Born Boothstown, Lancashire. Studied at Huddersfield School of Art, 1925-36. Has mostly exhibited in the North of England. A work by him is in the Sir Michael Sadler Collection, University of Leeds.

BARNHAM, Denis   b.1920
Painter. Born Feltham, Middlesex. Studied at RA Schools, 1936-9. From 1937 exhibited at RA, and also at the ROI, RBA and NEAC. Employed as a war artist by the Air Ministry in 1944 and is represented in the Imperial War Museum.

BARNHAM, Nicholas   b.1939
Painter. Studied at Norwich School of Art, 1954-60. Solo exhibitions at the Thackeray Gallery, London, 1972, 1975 and 1977.

BARNS-GRAHAM, Wilhelmina   b.1912
Painter. Born St. Andrews, Scotland. Studied at Edinburgh

BARR, Ian

College of Art, 1932-7. Moved to Cornwall in 1940 where, owing to the influence of Naum Gabo, she began to paint landscapes suggestive of more than one viewpoint. 1948 visited Switzerland after which the theme of glaciers remained an important one in her work. 1949 founder-member of the Penwith Society. 1956-7 taught at Leeds School of Art. Since 1947 has held many one-artist exhibitions, including one at the Scottish Gallery, Edinburgh, 1981 and has work in the Tate Gallery, Arts Council and British Council collections, the V & A and elsewhere. (Plate 21, p.90.)

Bibl: *W. Barns-Graham. Retrospective, 1940-1989,* City of Edinburgh Museums and Art Galleries, 1989.

BARR, Ian   b.1946
Painter. Born Glasgow, Scotland. Studied at Glasgow School of Art, 1964-8, in the department of printed textiles. Solo exhibition at the Compass Gallery, Glasgow, 1973.

BARR, Richard   b.1947
Painter. Born London. Studied at Liverpool School of Art, 1969-70, Bath Academy of Art, 1970-2, and Chelsea School of Art, 1972-3. First solo exhibition held at Acme Gallery, London, 1977, another held at the Gardner Centre Gallery, University of Sussex, 1978.

BARRACLOUGH, Steve   b.1953
Painter. Born Yorkshire. Studied at Batley School of Art, 1969-71, Camberwell School of Arts and Crafts, 1971-4, and Slade School of Fine Art, 1974-6. First solo exhibitions held at the Angela Flowers Gallery, London, 1979, 1982 and 1984. Works on handmade paper, exacerbating its surface with various textural effects. Represented in V & A, New York Library and elsewhere.

BARRAND, Paul   b.1959
Painter. Born Chesterfield, Derbyshire. Studied at Sheffield Polytechnic, 1977-8, Liverpool Polytechnic, 1978-81, and Leicester Polytechnic, 1981-2. Exhibitions held include: 'Night and Day', Leicester, 1984; 'Metroland', Losaby Gallery, Leicester, 1984; Midland View 3, 1984-5.

BARRATT, Krome   b.1924
Painter. Born London. Studied at Sir John Cass College, London, 1947-51. Solo exhibitions at Drian Galleries, London, 1958, AIA Galleries, London, 1960 and 1962 and New Gallery, Belfast, 1966. His work has evolved through a number of styles, including abstract expressionism and biomorphic symbolism.

BARRETT, Christopher   b.1954
Painter. Studied at Bath Academy of Art. First solo exhibition held Bloomsbury Gallery, University of London, 1982. One of a new generation of British figurative artists.

BARRETT, Connor   1908-1987
Painter and sculptor. Born Oliver O'Connor Barrett at Eltham. Self-taught sculptor, painter, poet and composer. Has exhibited at the Royal Academy since 1933 and had one-artist exhibitions in London, Birmingham, Colchester, New York, New Orleans, Palm Beach and Potsdam.

BARRETT, Max   b.1937
Self-taught carver and sculptor. Born Penzance, Cornwall. Worked as steeplejack and steel erector. Settled back in Cornwall in 1972. Represented in galleries throughout the region. 'Gentle Wave', sited at Lands End, commissioned by the St. Ives Festival Committee, 1982.

BARRETT, Peter   b.1935
Painter. Born Bombay, India. Worked as graphic designer and illustrator. Self-taught painter. Exhibited paintings done in Greece at Drian Galleries, London, 1964.

BARRETT, Roderic   b.1920
Painter. Born Colchester, Essex. Studied at Central School of Art, 1936-40. 1947 first solo exhibition held King St. Gallery, Cambridge, others in London, Boston, Oxford and elsewhere. Recent solo exhibitions at Thackeray Gallery, London, 1976, 1977, 1978 and 1980. Represented in V & A and in the collections of the Universities of Essex and Southampton.

BARRIE, Mardi   b.1946
Painter. Born Kirkcaldy, Scotland. Studied at Edinburgh University and College of Art. First one-person exhibition at Douglas and Foulis Gallery, Edinburgh, 1963 and most recently at the Thackeray Gallery, London, 1982, 1985 and 1987. Work shown in many group exhibitions in Britain and abroad. Works in the following collections: Scottish Arts Council, Glasgow Art Gallery, Scottish National Gallery of Modern Art, Magdalen College, Oxford, University of North Wales, Laing Art Gallery, Newcastle.

BARRON, Bob   b.1945
Painter. Born Co. Durham. Studied at Sunderland College of Art, 1960-4. 1977 solo exhibition held at University Theatre, Newcastle upon Tyne. 1981 Northern Arts Award.

BARROW, John   b.1903
Painter. Born Croydon, Surrey. Chosen as one of the painters to illustrate the *Churchill Book of Golden Roses*, presented to Sir Winston and Lady Churchill in 1958 to celebrate their Golden Wedding Anniversary. Exhibited at Arthur Tooth and Sons, 1946.

BARROW, Julian   b.1939
Painter. Born Cumberland. Studied painting and drawing in Italy. Though based in London at his Tite Street studio, he travels extensively, painting landscapes, conversation pieces and paintings of country houses. Has held solo exhibitions in London, New York, Palm Beach, Jerusalem and Kuwait, including several at Hazlitt, Gooden and Fox, London.

BARRY, Simon   b.1962
Painter. Born Somerset. Studied at Marlborough College, 1975-9, and at the Ruskin School of Drawing and Fine Art, Oxford, 1980-3. 1983-4 lived in France. 1983 held first exhibition at New College, Oxford.

BARTER, Paul   b.1935
Sculptor. Born England. Studied at Bath Academy of Art. 1961 became Head of Art Department at a Surrey School. Works in welded steel and bronze as well as 'fools gold'. Solo exhibition held at John Whibley Gallery, London, 1970.

BARTHOLOMEW, Lindsay   b.1944
Painter. Born Wirral, Cheshire. Studied at the Ruskin School of Drawing, Oxford, 1961-4 where she won the

GLENYS BARTON, b.1944. *'The Rite'*, 1987. Ceramic sculpture. 17in. high, covering a base 84in. x 22in. Angela Flowers Gallery.

Ruskin prize for portraiture. 1977 first solo exhibition held at the MacRoberts Arts Centre Gallery, University of Stirling. The English countryside and its changing moods are her main sources of inspiration. Included in the collections of Trusthouse Forte, Stirling University and Robert Fleming & Co. Ltd.

BARTLETT, Charles   b.1921
Watercolourist. Studied at Eastbourne School of Art, 1937-40. Served in Royal Corps of Signals during war. Studied at RCA, 1947-50. Associate of RE. Exhibits regularly at RA, NEAC, and Royal Society of British Artists. Represented in V & A, Leeds City Art Gallery, Walker Art Gallery, Liverpool and elsewhere.

BARTLETT, Leonard   1893-1971
Painter. Born Manchester. Studied at Blackburn, Bury and Accrington Schools of Art and the RCA, 1915-21. Taught at Eastbourne Art School, 1921-5, Cambridge School of Art, 1925-9 and was Principal of Lancaster and Morecambe College of Arts and Crafts from 1929. Exhibited mostly in Lancashire.

BARTLETT, Stephen   b.1942
Painter. Born London. RCA Research Fellowship at RCA, 1965-6. 1968-80 co-founder of BIB Design Consultants.

Travels extensively in Europe, USA and Japan. Solo exhibitions at home and abroad, including one at the Montpelier Studio, London, 1983.

BARTLETT, Victoria   b.1940
Sculptor. Born England. Studied painting and sculpture at Camberwell School of Art, 1957-61, and Reading University, 1961-7. 1974 first solo exhibition held at The Egg and the Eye Gallery, Los Angeles, others include one at the Edward Totah Gallery, London, 1981. Works with cloth, acrylic and mixed media, making everyday objects and surreal conjunctions out of unexpected materials.

Bibl: *Victoria Bartlett: Sculpture,* with introduction by William Packer, Camden Arts Centre, London, 1981.

BARTON, Glenys   b.1944
Sculptor-ceramicist. Born Stoke-on-Trent, Staffordshire. Studied at RCA, 1968-71. 1973 first one-person exhibition (shared with Jacqui Poncelet) at the Waterloo Place Gallery, London. 1976 for eighteen months, worked at the Josiah Wedgwood Factory, Barlaston, Stoke-on-Trent, producing ceramic sculptures. Represented in numerous British public collections, including the V & A, the Crafts Council and the CAS.

Bibl: *Glenys Barton at Wedgwood,* Crafts Council, 1977.

BASH, Elton   b.1950
Painter. Born Birmingham, West Midlands. Studied at Birmingham College of Art, 1969-70. Travelled in France, 1972-3. Studied at Chelsea School of Art, 1973-4. 1974-7 Rome Scholar in Painting, British School in Rome. 1976 held first solo exhibition; another at Air Gallery, London, 1980.

BASKETT, Charles Henry   1872-1953
Painter and etcher. Born Colchester, Essex. Studied at Colchester and Lambeth Schools of Art. Exhibited at RA, the Paris Salon and elsewhere. Elected ARE, 1911, and RE, 1918. Principal of Chelmsford School of Science and Art until his retirement in 1932.

BASSETT
Painter. Born Cornwall. Worked in Paris with André L'Hôte, Fernand Léger and Marcel Grommaire. Returned to England after Second World War and worked in Chelsea. Has exhibited in Paris, America and London, including a solo exhibition at the Archer Gallery, London, 1972.

BATCHELOR, Bernard Phillip   b.1924
Painter. Born Teddington, Middlesex. Studied at St. Martin's School of Art under R. Kirkland Jamieson* and at the City and Guilds London Art School. Exhibited at RA, RWS, RE, NEAC and was elected ARWS, 1967.

BATE, Francis   1853-1950
Painter. Studied at RCA and the Antwerp Academy under Verlat. From 1885 exhibited at major London galleries, principally at the NEAC of which he was Honorary Secretary. Ran a small art school at the Applegate Studio, Hammersmith. One of his pupils was Roger Fry.* Published *The Naturalistic School of Painting* (1887), a pamphlet extolling impressionist values.

BATEMAN, H.M.   1887-1970
Caricaturist and illustrator. Born Sutton Forest, Australia. Studied at Westminster and New Cross Art Schools, also in the studio of Charles van Havenmaet. 1911 first solo exhibition held at Brook Street Gallery. Contributed to various magazines including *The Tatler, Illustrated Sporting and Dramatic News* and *Pearson's Weekly*. Wrote several books including *H.M. Bateman by Himself* (Collins, 1937), and was the subject of a centenary exhibition at the Festival Hall, London, 1987.

BATEMAN, James   1893-1959
Painter and engraver. Born Kendal, Cumbria. Studied sculpture at Leeds, 1910-14. Won a scholarship to RCA, but war intervened. Studied at the Slade School, 1919-21, and gave up sculpture for painting. Taught at Cheltenham and Hammersmith Schools of Art. Exhibited at the RA from 1924. Made an RA in 1942. Designed camouflage during the Second World War. Works in the collection of the Tate Gallery. Elected ARA, 1935, and RA, 1942. Painted pastoral landscapes and farmyard scenes.

BATES, Martin   b.1939
Painter. Born Derby, Derbyshire. Studied at Derby College of Art, 1959-62. Solo exhibition at Leeds Playhouse Gallery, 1975, and at Phillip Francis Gallery, Sheffield, 1982. Represented in Sheffield City Art Gallery and Derby City Art Gallery.

BATES, Roger   b.1947
Sculptor. Born Croydon, Surrey. Studied at St. Martin's School of Art, 1966-71. Began exhibiting in 1970 and in 1980 was included in 'Style in the Seventies', Artscribe travelling exhibition. Solo exhibition held at Air Gallery, London, 1982.

BATES, Trevor   b.1921
Sculptor. Pilot in RAF, 1939-45. Studied at the Slade and under Ossip Zadkine in Paris. Since 1960 Head of Sculpture Department at Hornsey College of Art. Solo exhibitions held at Waddington Galleries, 1959, the Grabowski Gallery in 1963 and 1966. Represented in National Museum of Wales, V & A and elsewhere.

BATTEN, Mark Wilfred   b.1905
Sculptor and painter. Born Kirkaldy, Scotland. Studied at Beckenham School of Art and Chelsea School of Art. Began his career as a painter and did not begin to exhibit as a sculptor until 1936. Exhibited at RA, RBS, RSA, NEAC and elsewhere. President of the Royal Society of British Sculptors, 1956-61. Published *Stone Carving by Direct Carving*, 1957, and *Direct Carving in Stone*, 1966.

BATLEY, Walter   1850-1936
Painter. Born Ipswich, Suffolk. Studied at Ipswich School of Art and the RA Schools. Joined the Ipswich Fine Art Club (later the Ipswich Art Club) of which he remained a member for sixty years. Painted landscapes at home and abroad but is best known for his Suffolk scenes in which the gentle landscape is imbued with a pronounced feeling for light.

BAWDEN, Edward   1903-1989
Painter, designer and illustrator. Born Braintree, Essex. Studied at Cambridge School of Art, 1918-22, and RCA, 1922-5, where he was influenced by his tutor Paul Nash* and established friendships with Eric Ravilious* and Douglas Percy Bliss.* First made his reputation with murals, done with Ravilious and Charles Mahoney,* for Morley College, London. Throughout the late 1920s and '30s he made a living through commercial art, also teaching one or two days a week, first at Goldsmiths' College, then at the RCA. As an illustrator he worked for the Curwen Press, the Folio Society, Chatto & Windus and Penguin Books, among others, also for *The Listener* at a time when it was renowned for the high quality of its graphic art. 1940-5 Official War Artist, first in France and then in the Middle East where he produced some of his finest watercolours. His interest in craftsmanship places him in a tradition that looks back to the Arts and Crafts Movement. Whether designing an etching, linocut or watercolour, he brought to his work an understated humour and a robust decorative generosity that is never fussy or trite. A retrospective was held at the V & A and in Canterbury, 1989.

Bibl: Douglas Percy Bliss, *Edward Bawden*, Pendomer Press, 1979.

BAWDEN, Richard   b.1936
Painter and printmaker. Born Braintree, Essex, son of Edward Bawden.* Studied at RCA. First solo exhibition held at Curwen Gallery, London, also showed at Bohus Gallery, London, 1980.

BAXTER, Douglas Gordon   b.1920
Painter. Born Kirkcaldy, Scotland. Studied at Edinburgh College of Art, 1945-50. 1948 visited Paris on a travelling

BASIL BEATTIE, b.1935. *'Legend'*, 1986. 102in. x 144in. Photograph by Leonardo Ferrante.

scholarship. Two other scholarships took him to Scandinavia, 1949 and Spain, 1950. Exhibited at RSA and elsewhere. 1961 elected SSA.

BAXTER, Glen   b.1944
Draughtsman. Born Leeds, Yorkshire. Studied at Leeds School of Art, 1960-5. Taught at V & A, 1967-74, and at Goldsmiths' College, London, 1974-86. 1974 first solo exhibition held at Gotham Book Mart Gallery, New York. Publications include *The Impending Gleam,* Thames & Hudson, 1985. An oblique satirist who employs a comic-strip style.

BAYES, Gilbert   1872-1953
Sculptor. Born London. Studied at the City and Guilds School and RA Schools, 1896-9. Exhibited at the RA from 1889, also at the Paris Salon. 1939-44 President of the RBS. 1931 carved the frieze for the Saville Theatre, London. Brother of Walter Bayes.*

Bibl: Gilbert Bayes, *Modelling for Sculpture: A Book for the Beginner,* 1930.

BAYES, Walter   1869-1956
Painter and illustrator. Born London, brother of Gilbert Bayes.* Studied evening classes at City and Guilds Technical College, 1886-1900, and then at of Westminster School of Art, 1900-2. Art critic of *Athenaeum,* 1906-16. 1911 one of founder members of Camden Town Group and the London Group, 1913. 1913 first one-person show at the Carfax Gallery. 1918-34 Head of Westminster School of Art. 1944-9 Director of Painting, Lancaster School of Arts and Crafts. Works in the collection of the Tate Gallery.

Bibl: Walter Bayes, *The Art of Decorative Painting,* 1927; Walter Bayes, *A Painter's Baggage,* 1932, both Chapman and Hall, London.

BAYNES, Keith   1887-1977
Painter. Born near Reigate, Surrey. Educated at Cambridge but owing to ill-health did not complete his degree. 1907 went to Jamaica to convalesce and returned to England 1909, having lost the sight of one eye after a haemorrhage. 1912 entered Slade. Met Sickert* and Gilman* during World War I and began to exhibit at NEAC and with the London Group from 1919. Throughout 1920s travelled widely and exhibited regularly in London. Friend of Vanessa Bell* and Duncan Grant,* and also Raoul Dufy who was a lasting influence. Moved to Rye after the death of his friend, Louis Hoare, and in 1962 moved to St. Leonards-on-Sea, Sussex. Major retrospective at the Minories, Colchester, 1969.

BEALE, Philippa   b.1946
Sculptor. Born Winchester, Hampshire. Studied at Winchester School of Art, Goldsmiths' College and University of Reading. First solo exhibition at Camden Art Centre, 1972.

BEATTIE, Basil   b.1935
Painter. Born West Hartlepool, Cleveland. Studied at West Hartlepool College of Art and RA Schools, 1958-61. Uses characters, signs, heiroglyphs, arranged in a cellular, tissue-like format. Has exhibited in many group exhibitions and held twelve one-artist exhibitions, the most recent at the Curwen Gallery, London, 1990. Admits interest in 'the multi-levels of consciousness that seem to be crammed into a fleeting moment' (*John Moores Liverpool Exhibition 15,* cat.).

BEAUCHAMP, Charles   b.1949
Painter. Born London. Studied at Chelsea School of Art, 1967, and at S.W. Hayter's Atelier 17, Paris, 1971-2. Solo exhibitions at Gimpel Fils, London, in 1974, 1976, 1980, 1983 and 1984.

BEAUCHAMP, Paul   b.1948
Sculptor. Born Barrow upon Soar, Leicestershire. Studied at Loughborough College of Art, 1967-8, Hornsey College of Art, 1968-71, and the Slade, 1971-3. 1975 awarded a Welsh Arts Council bursary. Work in the collection of the Welsh Arts Council.

BEAULAND, Frank   b.1936
Painter. Born Yorkshire. Studied at Hull College of Art, 1952-7, and Slade School of Art, 1959-61. 1962 won Boise travelling scholarship and studied in Stockholm. 1960 first exhibited at Young Contemporaries, solo exhibition at Arthur Tooth and Sons, London, 1969.

BEAUMONT, Leonard   1891-1986
Printmaker and designer. Born Sheffield, Yorkshire. Worked for *Sheffield Daily Telegraph,* 1907-15. 1912-15 attended evening classes at Sheffield School of Art with aid of studentship. 1915 joined Royal Naval Volunteer Reserve. 1919 returned to *Sheffield Daily Telegraph.* 1920s began his interest in printmaking, especially etching and lino-cuts. 1929-33 exhibited etchings at RA. 1936 moved to London and worked for United Artists Film Distributors. 1950-64 Design Consultant for Sainsbury's. Retrospective held at Mappin Art Gallery, Sheffield, 1983.

BECKER, Haidee   b.1950
Painter. Born Los Angeles, USA. Has lived in London since 1966. Studied under various artists, including Anthony Whishaw* and at the Academy in Vienna. Has exhibited at the RA and in several group shows. 1986 solo exhibition held at New Grafton Gallery. Her portrait of Uli Nimptsch* is in the NPG. Represented by the Odette Gilbert Gallery, London. Has work in the National Portrait Gallery collection.

BECKER, Harry   1865-1928
Painter. Born Colchester, Essex, the son of a German immigrant doctor. Studied at the Royal Academy Schools at Antwerp and in Paris under Carolus Duran. Lived for a period in London where he established a reputation as a lithographer. 1908 he executed murals for the new Selfridges store. Exhibited at the RA, also in Paris and Milan. 1913 moved to Wenhaston in Suffolk and brought an impressionist style to bear on his images of farm labourers.

BECKETT, Martyn   b.1918
Painter. Born North Yorkshire. Studied at Trinity College, Cambridge and served in Welsh Guards, 1939-46, winning an MC. After the war qualified as an architect. Has been a Trustee of the British Museum and Chairman of the Trustees of the Wallace Collection. His watercolours reflect his love of moorland and dale country. Exhibits at RA, Crane Kalman Gallery, London and in local Yorkshire exhibitions.

BECKETT, Sarah   b.1946
Painter. Studied at Byam Shaw School of Art, 1963-5, and Chelsea College of Art, 1977-80. 1971 first solo exhibition held at Bank of Nova Scotia, Trinidad. 1985 and 1988 exhibited Christopher Hull Gallery, London, and has work in many public collections, including the University of West Indies, Trinidad and the National Labour Museum, London.

BEDFORD, Celia   1904-1959
Painter. Studied at Chelsea Polytechnic. 1931 and 1932 solo exhibitions held at the Twenty-One Gallery, London. Exhibited regularly at NEAC, and RA and the Women's International Art Club. Represented in City Art Galleries in Birmingham, Southport and Leamington. Memorial exhibition held at Walker's Galleries, London, 1960.

BEDFORD, Richard   1883-1967
Sculptor. Born Torquay, Devon. 1903 worked as technical assistant, Department of Woodwork, V & A. Transferred to the Department of Architecture and Sculpture there, when he became Assistant Keeper in 1911. Attended sculpture evening classes at the Central School and Chelsea School of Art. 1924-38, Keeper of Architecture and Sculpture at V & A. 1938-47, ran the Circulation Department, V & A. 1947-9, Curator of Pictures for the Ministry of Works. 1936 first one-person exhibition of sculpture, Lefevre Galleries. He liked to use English marbles for his carved sculptures, and adapted animal and plant forms for his subject matter. Work in the collections of the Leicestershire Education Committee and the Royal West of England Academy.

Bibl: *The World of Richard Bedford,* The Minories, Colchester, 1968.

BEER, Clem
Painter and printmaker. Born London. Studied at Slade School of Art and then lived in Yorkshire for a number of years. 1967 first solo exhibition held at York University and another at Central London Institute, 1976. Has illustrated *The New Dragon Book of Verse,* Oxford University Press, 1977, and has work in Greenwich Libraries and elsewhere.

BEER, Richard   b.1928
Painter. Studied at the Slade School of Art, 1945-50, under Vladimar Polunin who taught stage design. Though Beer switched to painting, his sense of spectacle informed his choice of subject. He also continued to work in the theatre during the 1950s. Moved to Paris to study first at the Ecole des Beaux Arts and then at Stanley Hayter's Atelier 17 where he learn print-making. Returned to London but made regular visits to the Continent to find subjects to paint. First solo exhibition held at the Arthur Jeffress Gallery, London. Recent solo exhibitions include one at Sally Hunter Fine Art, 1990.

BEERBOHM, Max   1872-1956
Caricaturist and author. Born London. Studied at Merton College, Oxford. Published his first book of caricatures, *Caricatures of Twenty-Five Gentlemen,* 1896, having previously worked as an illustrator to *The Strand Magazine.* Many books and solo exhibitions followed and he became known as the 'incomparable Max'. 1911 helped found the National Portrait Society. Knighted in 1929. Lived for many years at Rapallo, in Italy, where he died.

BEERS, Robin   b.1943
Painter. Born London. Studied at Hammersmith College of Art, 1959-61, RCA, 1961-4, and RA Schools, 1964-7. First solo exhibition held at Galerie Tanit, Munich. Has lived and worked in Munich since 1973.

BEESLEY, Mike   b.1944
Painter. Studied at London School of Economics, 1963-7. Began painting 1965-6 and full-time since 1973. Solo exhibition at Herbert Art Gallery and Museum, Coventry, 1975.

BEESON, Jane   b.1930
Painter. Studied at Kingston School of Art, the Beaux Arts, Paris and Slade School of Fine Art, London. 1953-8 lived abroad. 1964 exhibited at the John Moores Liverpool Exhibition and in a two-person exhibition at the New Art Centre, London. The shapes in her abstract paintings are often based on microscopic slide sections of animal, plant or fungus tissue.

BEETON, Alan   1880-1942
Painter. Born London. Educated at Trinity College, Cambridge. Served as a captain in the Royal Engineers, 1914-18. Studied art in London and Paris. Exhibited at the RA from 1923, made ARA 1938. Work in the collections of the Tate Gallery and Fitzwilliam Museum, Cambridge.

BEGBIE, David   b.1956
Sculptor. Studied at Winchester and Cheltenham School of Art. Works in industrial galvanised steel mesh. 1984 and 1985 one-person exhibition held at the Brompton Gallery, London, and the Salama-Caro Gallery, London, 1988. Produced 'Crucifix' sculpture for Winchester Cathedral, Easter, 1988.

BEGGS, Guy   b.1947
Painter. Born Durban, South Africa. Came to England in 1961. Studied at Maidstone College of Art, 1963-8, RA Schools, 1968-71 and Goldsmiths' College, 1971-2. Has exhibited with the Piccadilly and Leicester Galleries in London and at the RA. A photo-realist with a liking for unexpected views. Represented in Rochdale Art Gallery.

BEHAN, Peter   b.1939
Painter. Born Dublin, Ireland. Moved to England at the age of nineteen and worked in a factory in Leicester. Moved to London and took life classes at St. Martin's School of Art. 1964 and 1966 solo exhibitions held at Roland, Browse and Delbanco, London; others include one at the Mermaid Theatre, London, 1971.

BEHRENS, Tim   b.1937
Painter. Born London. Studied at Slade School of Fine Art, 1954-8. 1960, 1962 and 1964 solo exhibitions at the Beaux Arts Gallery, London; another at Upper Street Gallery, London, 1970. Also exhibits in Italy, where he has lived since 1970.

BELCHER, George   1875-1948
Painter. Born London. Studied at Gloucester School of Art. Contributed to *Punch* as a humorous draughtsman. 1931 became ARA and 1945 elected RA, the first humorous artist for 177 years. After he retired as an illustrator he began painting still lifes and flower studies in oils.

BELL, Eileen   b.1907
Painter. Studied at St. John's Wood School and Anglo-French Art Centre, London. Member of Artists' International Association. Has exhibited in London and the provinces, most recently at the Duncalfe Galleries, Harrogate, 1988.

BELL, Graham   1910-1943
Painter. Born in the Transvaal, South Africa. Studied at Durban School of Art. 1931 came to England and remained under the influence of Duncan Grant* until he met William Coldstream* from whom he acquired a purposeful severity. 1934 exhibited with the Objective Abstractionists and shortly after this gave up painting to write art criticism for the *New Statesman,* 1934-7. 1937 returned to painting and helped found the Euston Road School. Convinced that bourgeois taste had led to decadence in art, he, like the other Euston Road teachers, promoted an unemphatic realism, mediated through the example of Cézanne. From 1938 member of the AIA. 1939 published *The Artist and His Public* with the Hogarth Press. Received support from Kenneth Clark. Killed on a training flight in the RAF. Memorial exhibition held 1946.

Bibl: Kenneth Clark, *Paintings of Graham Bell,* Lund Humphries, London, 1947.

BELL, Julian   b.1952
Painter. Grandson of Vanessa Bell* and son of Quentin Bell.* Studied at Magdalen College, Oxford, and City and Guilds London Art School. Since 1974 has worked as a self-employed artist taking on various commissions. Solo exhibitions include two at Southover Gallery, Lewes, 1982 and 1983.

BELL, Kathleen
Painter, collagist and printmaker. Studied at Slade School of Fine Art. Resident in Ireland since 1943. Member of the Women's International Art Club, London. 1966-8 President of Ulster Society of Women Artists. Has exhibited in London, Belfast, Paris and Edinburgh.

BELL, Nikki   b.1959 and
LANGLANDS, Ben   b.1955
Installation artists. Both trained at Middlesex Polytechnic and have had exhibitions at Bookworks, 1984, Interim Art, 1986, and Air Gallery, 1987, all in London.

BELL, Norman Martin   1907-1970
Painter. Born Great Meols, Cheshire. Trained at Liverpool College of Art, 1925-30, and RCA, 1931-3. Occupied various teaching posts, becoming Head of Fine Art at Liverpool College of Art, 1944. 1957-60 member of the Liverpool Academy and its President. Exhibited with the London Group and at Liverpool, Manchester and elsewhere. Represented in the Walker Art Gallery, Liverpool.

BELL, Quentin   b.1910
Painter, sculptor and potter. Son of Vanessa Bell.* Trained as an artist, studied pottery in Staffordshire and sculpture in Rome. Biographer of Virginia Woolf and author of many other books including *On Human Finery.* Has exhibited at Agnews, the Harvane Gallery, and Dan Klein in London, also at the Universities of Leeds and Newcastle upon Tyne and elsewhere. Held professorships at the Universities of Newcastle, Leeds and Sussex, before entering a vigorously productive retirement.

JOHN BELLANY, b.1942. 'Allegory'. Oil on hardboard. Left hand panel 83⅜ in. x 48in., centre, 84in. x 63in., right, 83½ in. x 48in. Scottish National Gallery of Modern Art.

BELL, Robert Anning   1863-1933

Painter and designer of mosaics, stained glass and coloured bas-reliefs. Born London. Studied at Westminster School of Art, RA Schools and in Paris. Achieved wide recognition through the RA where he exhibited regularly from 1885. Specialised in landscapes, figure subjects and religious scenes. Executed mosaics in the Houses of Parliament and Westminster Cathedral. Elected ARA, 1914 and RA, 1922.

BELL, Trevor   b.1930

Painter. Born Leeds, Yorkshire. Studied at Leeds College of Art, 1947-52. Taught at Harrogate School of Art. 1955 moved to Zennor, near St. Ives on the advice of Terry Frost.* 1958 first one-person show at Waddington Galleries. 1958-9 awarded Italian Art Scholarship. 1959 won painting prize at Paris Biennale. 1960 Gregory Fellow at Leeds University. Work in the collection of the Tate Gallery. 1989 major retrospective at New Arts Centre, London. Recent solo exhibitions include 'Expanding Themes' at the Museum of Art, Florida, 1989, and another of small paintings at Gillian Jason Gallery, London, 1990. (Plate 22, p.90.)

BELL, Vanessa   1879-1961

Painter. Born London. Attended RA Schools, 1901-4. Married the art critic Clive Bell, 1907. 1912 showed in the Second Post-Impressionist Exhibition in London. 1913-19 co-director of Roger Fry's Omega Workshops. 1915 first one-person exhibition at the Omega Workshops. 1919 joined the London Group. In the 1920s and '30s collaborated with Duncan Grant* on many interior decorative schemes, designing rugs, furnishings, murals, etc. 1932 commissioned by Allan Walton to produce designs for printed textiles. 1933-4 designed and decorated tableware for E. Brain and Co. 1940-3 painted murals for Berwick Church, Sussex. Her decorative talent is best seen at Charleston, the Sussex house where she and Duncan Grant lived.

Bibl: Frances Spalding, *Vanessa Bell,* Weidenfeld and Nicolson, London, 1983.

BELLANY, John   b.1942

Painter. Born in Port Seton, Scotland. Studied at Edinburgh College of Art, 1960-5 and RCA, 1965-8. At the age of four he was drawing the fishing boats in the village where he lived, and images of fishermen, fish, boats and the sea have continued to figure in his paintings. Attracted to Courbet's paintings whilst visiting Paris on a scholarship, 1962. Also inspired by a Max Beckman retrospective held at the Whitechapel Art Gallery, 1965. Two years later he travelled to East Germany, and visited Buchenwald concentration camp. After this his paintings became more complex, as animals became symbols for death, guilt, and sexual obsession. His style loosened and his colour became more hectic around 1973 and birds and humans sometimes merged. He suffered a serious illness in 1984 and 1988, but began drawing again whilst convalescent, producing a series of portraits which were exhibited at the Scottish National Gallery of Modern Art, 1989.

Bibl: *John Bellany: Paintings, Watercolours and Drawings 1964-86,* Scottish National Gallery of Modern Art, 1986.

BEN-DAVID, Zadok   b.1949

Sculptor. Born Yemen, moved to Israel. Studied at Bezalel Academy of Art and Design, Jerusalem, 1971-3. 1974 came to England. Studied at Reading University, 1975, St. Martin's School of Art, 1976. Taught sculpture at St. Martin's, 1977-82. Taught at Ravensbourne College of Art and Design, 1982-5. 1980 first one-person show at Air

Gallery. 1987 artist in residence, Stoke-on-Trent City Art Gallery. Represented Israel at the Venice Biennale 1988.

BENGOECHEA, Aurora   b.1948
Painter. Studied at Escuela Massana, Barcelona, 1968-9, at Chelsea School of Art, 1981-5, and at the RCA, 1986-8. First solo exhibition at Centro de Atraccion y Turismo, Palencia, Spain. 1987 her first solo exhibition in Great Britain was held at the Flaxman Gallery, London. Included in the collections of Sheffield City Art Galleries, 'Art for Schools' collection and Art Consultants, Colchester.

BENJAMIN, Anthony   b.1931
Painter, sculptor and printmaker. Born Boarhunt, Hampshire. Studied at Leger's Studio, Paris, 1951, and at Regent Street Polytechnic, 1951-4. 1958-9 French Government Award, which he used to study at Atelier 17, Paris. 1960-1 Italian Government Award. Represented Britain in the Sao Paulo Biennale. 1977 received an Arts Council Major Award. Works in the collection of the Arts Council of Great Britain, Manchester City Art Gallery, Art Gallery of New South Wales, Sydney and the British Council.

BENN, Tony   b.1956
Painter. Born Chester, Cheshire. Studied at Central School of Art, 1974-5, St. Martin's School of Art, 1975-8. 1981 first solo exhibition held at the London Elm Coop Gallery, another solo exhibition at Inkt Gallery, The Hague in 1982.

BERESFORD, Frank Ernest   1881-1967
Painter. Born Derby. Studied at Derby School of Art, 1895-1900, St. John's Wood Art School, 1900-1 and RA Schools, 1901-6. Received a British Institution scholarship for two years, and took a painting tour around the world. From 1906 exhibited at RA and abroad. During the Second World War he painted works for the RAF and the American Air Force.

BERG, Adrian   b.1929
Painter. Born London. Studied at Cambridge University and Trinity College, Dublin, at St. Martin's and Chelsea Schools of Art, 1955-61, and the RCA. Has exhibited regularly in London since 1964 as well as in Europe and North America. 1973 won a Gold Medal at the Florence Biennale. Recent solo exhibitions include 'Adrian Berg 1977-86', Serpentine Gallery, 1986. Represented by the Piccadilly Gallery, London. Specialises in park and garden scenes.

Bibl: *Adrian Berg. Paintings 1977-1986,* Arts Council, 1986

BERGMAN, Stephanie   b.1946
Painter. Born London. Studied at St. Martin's School of Art, 1963-7. 1973 first one-person show at Garage Art. Worked initially with unstretched pieces of coloured canvas, sewn together and hung on the wall. Taught at Norwich School of Art from 1967 to 1978. Works in the collection of the Arts Council and the Government Picture Collection.

BERLIN, Sven   b.1911
Sculptor. Born London of Swedish father and English mother. Studied at Beckenham School of Art, Camborne and Redruth Schools of Art. 1938 settled Cornwall. Leading member of St. Ives artists' circle and founder-

ADRIAN BERG, b.1929. *'Cambridge Gate, Regent's Park',* 1987. 14in. x 21in. Private Collection.

member of the Penwith Society of Arts. His relationship with other artists was a tempestuous one. Author of *Alfred Wallis: Primitive,* 1949, and several other books.

BERRIE, John Archibald Alexander   1887-1962
Painter. Born Manchester, Lancashire. Studied at Bootle Art School, Liverpool, London and Paris. Exhibited at the Liverpool Autumn Exhibition from 1908 and at the RA from 1924. Associate of the Royal Cambrian Academy in 1912 and member, 1923. Moved from Liverpool to London, and on to Harrogate, settling finally in Johannesburg, South Africa. Solo exhibition at Walkers Gallery, Bond Street, 1936. Represented in Walker Art Gallery, Liverpool.

BERRISFORD, Peter   b.1932
Painter. Trained at Northampton, Bournemouth and Chelsea Art Schools. Regular exhibitions at the Trafford Gallery, London and elsewhere. Represented in Hertfordshire, Leicestershire and Surrey Education Committees, and in Hull, Leicester and Northampton City Art Galleries.

BERRY, Arthur   b.1925
Painter. Born Smallbone, North Staffordshire, son of a bricklayer and a publican's daughter. Studied at Burslem School of Art and the RCA, 1943-6. An introduction to Robert Colquhoun* and Robert MacBryde* had an important influence on his life. Has taught at Manchester College of Art and North Staffordshire Polytechnic. His autobiography, *A Three and Sevenpence Halfpenny Man,* published in 1986, not only provides a vigorous account of his life but is also an invaluable witness of the changing art scene in Britain.

Bibl: *Arthur Berry Retrospective Exhibition,* Stoke-on-Trent City Museum and Art Gallery, 1984.

BERRY, June
Painter. Studied at Slade and Wimbledon Schools of Art. 1968 solo exhibitions at AIA Gallery, London, and Fringe Society, Edinburgh. Work in Kettering Art Gallery and Derby and Leicester Education Committee Collections. Paints abstracts with figurative and landscape associations.

BERRY, Paul   b.1946
Painter. Born Lowestoft, Suffolk. Studied at Leicester and Chelsea Schools of Art. Fellow in Fine Art at Cardiff College of Art. Has exhibited at home and abroad, with a solo exhibition at Greenwich Theatre Art Gallery, 1981.

BETTS, James Anthony   1896-1980
Painter. Studied at Bradford College of Art and RCA. Enjoyed a distinguished career in education, as Head of Sheffield School of Art, 1926-30. 1934-63 Professor of Fine Art, University of Reading, and Emeritus Professor at Reading from 1963 until his death. He painted regularly in Wales and the Dordogne.

BEST, Eleanor   d.1958
Painter. Born Amport, Hampshire. Studied at Slade School, 1909. Exhibited RA, RSA, NEAC and elsewhere.

BESWICK, Bobbie   b.1933
Painter. Born Bradford, Yorkshire. Studied at Bradford Regional College of Art and RCA. Represented in permanent collections in Yorkshire and has exhibited in numerous mixed and solo exhibitions in London and the North, including the Goosewell Gallery, Menston, 1972 (catalogue introduction by W.T. Oliver). Specialises in landscapes and sky paintings.

BETTANY, Peter   b.1945
Painter. Born Colwyn Bay, North Wales. Studied at Wimbledon Art School, Leicester College of Art, and California College of Arts and Crafts, Oakland. Represented in Ferens Art Gallery, Hull and University of California, Los Angeles. Solo exhibition at JPL Fine Arts, London, 1977. Represented in Arts Council Collection.

BETTS, Simon   b.1957
Painter. Born Peterborough, Cambridgeshire. Studied at Cambridge College of Arts and Technology, 1976-7, and Sheffield City Polytechnic, 1977-80. Began exhibiting in 1978 and held his first solo exhibition at Peterborough Museum and Art Gallery, 1982.

BEVAN, Oliver   b.1941
Painter. Born Peterborough, Cambridgeshire. Studied at RCA, 1960-4. Has exhibited in several mixed exhibitions and had one-artist exhibitions at the Grabowski and Angela Flowers Galleries, London, and at the Minories, Colchester, 1983.

BEVAN, Robert   1865-1925
Painter. Born Hove, Sussex. Studied at Westminster School of Art and Académie Julian, Paris. 1894 met Gauguin in Pont Aven, Brittany. 1897 married the Polish painter S. de Karlowska and visited Poland with her several times. 1905 first one-person show at the Baillie Gallery. 1911 founder member of the Camden Town Group, the London Group, 1913, and the Cumberland Market Group, 1915. Member of the NEAC, 1922. (Plate 23, p.91.)

BEVAN, Tony   b.1951
Painter. Born Bradford, Yorkshire. Studied at Bradford School of Art, 1968-71, Goldsmiths' College, 1971-4, and the Slade, 1974-6. 1976 first solo exhibition, since when he has shown in London, Cardiff, West Germany, Poland, Sydney and New York. A figurative artist, concentrating mostly on the solitary male figure in a style expressive of anxiety and alienation.
Bibl: *Tony Bevan: Paintings 1980-87*, ICA, London, 1988.

BIBBY, Judy   b.1947
Painter. Born Liverpool, Merseyside. Studied at Southport School of Art, 1962-5, Liverpool College of Art, 1965-8, and RCA, 1968-71. 1968 first solo exhibition held at Bluecoat Gallery, Liverpool, and others including one at Moira Kelly Fine Art, London, 1980, and Waterman's Art Centre, Brentford, 1986.

BICÂT, Andre   b.1909
Painter, sculptor, printer. Born of French and Anglo-Irish parents. During the 1930s worked as a theatre designer and scene painter. 1940-5 war service. 1949 first solo exhibition held at Leicester Galleries, London, and continued to exhibit regularly there until 1970. 1966-74 tutor at RCA. Represented in V & A, British Museum and many other public collections at home and abroad.

BICKERDIKE, John   1893-
Sculptor. Born Windhill, Yorkshire. Occasional student at Bradford School of Art. Joined the Army 1914-1919. 1923 one-person show held at the Twenty-One Gallery in the Adelphi.

BICKLEY, Dawn   b.1947
Collagist. Born Lancashire. Lived and studied in North Wales and accompanied her husband, Martin Bickley* to Paris, 1968. Her interest in plant life manifests itself in her collages. Exhibited at Heal's Art Gallery, 1972 and 1973.

BICKLEY, Martin   b.1947
Painter. Born Warwickshire. Lived and studied in North Wales until 1968 when he visited Paris. Makes frequent visits to France. Exhibited at Heal's Art Gallery, 1972 and 1973.

BICKNELL, John   b.1958
Painter. Born Surrey. Studied at West Surrey College of Art and Design, 1975-7, North East London Polytechnic, 1977-80, and the Slade, 1981-3. 1983 he won a Boise Scholarship to Italy. Has exhibited regularly in England and at the XXV Joan Miró Drawing Prize Competition, Barcelona, 1986.

BILLINGHURST, Alfred John   1880-1963
Painter. Born Blackheath, London. Studied at Slade School, 1899-1902, Goldsmiths' Institute, 1900, the Académie Julian in Paris, 1902, and the Ecole des Beaux Arts, 1903. Exhibited at RA, RI, RBA, the Paris Salon and elsewhere. 1921 elected RBA.

BINYON, Helen   1904-1979
Draughtsman and engraver. Taught drawing, design and wood engravings at Corsham Court, 1950-65, along with her sister Margaret. Acted at the Royal Court Theatre. In 1966 published *Puppetry Today*. Wrote a memoir of her friend, Eric Ravilious,* published 1983.

BIRCH, S.J. Lamorna   1869-1955
Painter. Born Egremont, Cheshire. Self-taught except for a period of study at the Atelier Colarossi, Paris, 1895. 1902 settled at Lamorna in Cornwall and took the name Lamorna to distinguish himself from another painter in the same area called Birch. Exhibited at the RA from 1892, becoming ARA in 1926 and RA in 1934. 1906 first one-person show at the Fine Art Society. Painted in New Zealand, 1937.

ELIZABETH BLACKADDER, b.1931. *'Pagoda Still Life'*, 1988. Watercolour/gold leaf. 33½ in. x 51in. Mercury Gallery Ltd.

BIRCH, William Henry David   1895-1968

Painter. Born Epsom, Surrey. Studied at Epsom School of Art and Goldsmiths' College School of Art, continuing his training after he had been invalided out of the war in 1915. Took up book illustration, and also worked as a part-time teacher. 1930-61 Principal of Epsom and Ewell School of Art. Inspired by Constable, he began painting landscapes around 1935. 1937 began exhibiting regularly at the RA and elsewhere. 1945 elected ROI.

BIRD, Henry Richard   b.1909

Painter and muralist. Born Northampton. Studied at Northampton School of Art and the RCA, 1930-4. Exhibited widely in London and the provinces. Member of the Art Workers' Guild and the Society of Mural Painters.

BIRLEY, Sir Oswald   1880-1952

Portrait painter. Born Auckland, New Zealand. Educated at Trinity College, Cambridge. Studied art in Dresden, Florence, and at the Académie Julian in Paris. Became an eminent society portraitist, employing a manner similar to that of John Singer Sargent* in its painterliness and confident panache.

BISHOP, Edward   b.1902

Painter and printmaker. Studied at Central School of Arts and Crafts, 1920-6. Exhibited at the RA, with the NEAC and the Leicester Galleries, Roland Browse and Delbanco and the Grosvenor Gallery. Haunted the Café Royal and became a sensitive recorder of the changing London scene. Elected RBA, 1950.

BISHOP, Henry   1868-1939

Painter. Born London. Studied at the Slade School, the Atelier Cormon, Paris, and in Brittany. Painted in Cornwall and Morocco. 1913 first one-person show at the Goupil Gallery. From 1915 exhibited at the NEAC, became a member 1929. From 1922 exhibited at the RA, made ARA 1932, and RA 1939. Work in the collection of the Tate Gallery. Specialised in landscapes and coastal scenes.

BISSIL, George   1896-1973

Painter. Born Fairford, Gloucestershire. Spent his early life at Langley Mill, near Nottingham, where his father was a miner. He worked down the mines himself for six years making this industry the subject of many of his paintings; also worked as a furniture designer and as a pavement artist. First solo exhibition at Redfern Gallery, London, 1924. Continued to show there, also at the RA and elsewhere. Work in the Tate Gallery collection.

BLACKADDER, Elizabeth   b.1931

Painter. Born Falkirk, Scotland. Studied at Edinburgh University and Edinburgh College of Art, 1949-54. 1954 awarded a Carnegie Travelling Scholarship and visited Yugoslavia, Greece and Italy. Influenced by Byzantine architecture and mosaics. 1954-5 worked in Italy. 1956 married John Houston* with whom she has since travelled widely. Her travels have fed her imagery. Flowers, cats and small objects are often arrayed vertically across the paper or canvas. Is at her most original in watercolour. Elected ARSA 1963, ARA 1971, RSA 1972 and RA 1976. Exhibits at the Mercury Gallery, London, and abroad. 1956-86 taught at the Edinburgh College of Art. Represented in the Tate Gallery and major public collections in Scotland. (Plate 24, p.91.)

Bibl: Judith Bumpus, *Elizabeth Blackadder,* Phaidon Press, Oxford, 1988.

BLACKER, Kate

BLACKER, Kate   b.1955
Sculptor. Born Hampshire. Studied at Camberwell School of Art, 1975-8, and RCA, 1978-81. 1981 included in London group exhibitions. 1982 first one-person show at Coracle Press, London and 121 Gallery Antwerp. Work in the collections of Tate Gallery, Southampton Art Gallery, Arts Council of Great Britain.

BLACKER, Thetis
Fabric artist and painter. Studied drawing privately at the same time as learning to sing. 1959 first one-person show at the Bear Lane Gallery. 1960 went to Peru on a British Council scholarship. Impressed by the textiles there, took a course at Chelsea School of Art and has since specialised in the making of batik paintings. Published *A Pilgrimage of Dreams,* 1973. Has appeared often on TV. Works in the collections of members of the Royal Family, and Churchill College, Cambridge.

BLACKETT, Vivien   b.1955
Painter. Born London. Studied at Goldsmiths' College of Art, 1974-8. 1985 first solo exhibition held at Health Centre, Brick Lane, Whitechapel. 1986 artist in residence at the National Gallery. Has work in the British Council collection.

BLAIR, Louise   b.1958
Painter. Born Kent. Studied at the Hornsey College of Art, 1976-9 and at the Chelsea School of Art, 1979-80. First solo exhibition at Cockpit Theatre, London, 1981. Has exhibited regularly at Nicola Jacobs Gallery, London in solo exhibitions since 1983. Represented in the collection of the Contemporary Art Society.

Bibl: John McEwan, *Sunday Times Supplement,* London, 8 May 1988.

BLAKE, Naomi   b.1924
Sculptor. Born Czechoslovakia. Studied at Hornsey School of Art. Lived in Milan, Rome and Jerusalem but moved to London in the 1970s. 1979 first one-person show at the Alwin Gallery, London. Public sculpture commissions for Bristol Cathedral 1980, Swansea University 1981.

BLAKE, Peter   b.1932
Painter. Born Dartford, Kent. Studied at Gravesend Technical College and School of Art, 1946-51, and entered RCA, 1950. This period of study was interrupted by National Service and he returned to the RCA, 1953-6. In his early work he excelled at creating the world of childhood in a series of works which paid detailed attention to ephemera: comics, badges, cigarette cards and packets. 1956-7 travelled in Holland, Belgium, France, Italy and Spain on a Leverhulme research award, studying popular art. In 1959 his collector's instinct found outlet in the collages and reliefs he began making, many of them itemizing kitsch items, pop stars or other aspects of popular culture. 1963 married the painter Jann Haworth* and with her became a founder member of the Brotherhood of Ruralists, 1975. 1981 elected RA. His skill as illustrator and painter has enabled him to operate as a fine artist and yet appeal to a mass audience. Retrospective held at Tate Gallery, London, 1983.

Bibl: *Peter Blake,* with essays by Michael Compton, Nicholas Usherwood and Robert Melville, Tate Gallery, 1983.

BLAKE, Vernon   1885-1930
Sculptor. 1924 one-person exhibition held at the Mansard

NORMAN BLAMEY, b.1914. *'Spring and the Student',* 1975. Oil on panel. 65in. x 55in. Private Collection.

Gallery. Director of the British School in Rome. 1925 published *Relation in Art,* and also *Way to Sketch.*

BLAKELY, Zelma   1922-78
Painter and printmaker. Studied painting, lithography and wood engraving at the Slade School. Produced many book illustrations, e.g. engravings for *The Charterhouse of Parma,* Folio Society, London, 1977.

BLAMEY, Norman   b.1914
Painter. Born London. Studied at the Regent Street Polytechnic School of Art, 1931-7. Served in the army, 1941-6. Taught at Regent Street Polytechnic until 1963 when he moved to Chelsea School of Art. Elected ROI 1952, ARA 1970 and RA 1975. Has exhibited widely in London and the provinces. Noted for his hieratic portraits and still lifes.

BLAMPIED, Edmund   1886-1966
Painter. Born Jersey, Channel Islands. Studied at the LCC Art School, Bolt Court, 1905-13. Exhibited at RA and Paris Salon. Elected ARE 1920, RE 1921 and RBA 1938. 1925 won a gold medal for lithography at the Paris International Exhibition. Lived in Jersey for many years, and during the German occupation. Specialised in landscape and figure painting, also etched, and designed stamps.

BLAND, Beatrice   1869-1951
Painter. Born Lincolnshire. Studied at Lincoln School of Art and the Slade School of Art. Exhibited NEAC, RA,

Liverpool Autumn exhibitions and elsewhere. Specialised in still life, landscape and flower paintings. Solo exhibitions at Leicester Galleries, 1922, and Arthur Tooth, 1937.

BLANK, J.N.   b.1957
Painter. Born Middlesex. Studied at Colchester School of Art, 1976-8, Chelsea School of Art, 1978-81 and Goldsmiths' College, 1982-3. 1983 solo exhibition at the Minories, Colchester. Has exhibited in a number of group shows in London, and at John Moores Exhibition, 1987.

BLISS, Douglas Percy   1900-1984
Painter and wood-engraver. Born Karachi, Pakistan. Brought up in Edinburgh and entered Edinburgh University to read Rhetoric and English Literature but also took Professor Baldwin Brown's one-year fine art course. Studied at RCA with Moore,* Ravilious* and others, including Phyllis Dodd whom he married. Close friend of Ravilious and Bawden,* and with them attended Sir Frank Short's* Saturday morning engraving classes. 1928 published his seminal work, *History of Wood Engraving* and was in the forefront of the renaissance of this medium in the 1920s and '30s. 1932-40 director of the Art Teaching course at Hornsey School of Art; also during this period published twelve illustrated books and had one-artist shows at the Lefevre and Leger Galleries. Exhibited regularly at NEAC and RA. Wrote art criticism and book reviews for various periodicals, including *The Listener* and *The Studio*. 1939-45 worked for Air Ministry and was responsible for concealment and decoy. 1946 appointed Director of the Glasgow School of Art and remained in this post until his retirement in 1965.

Bibl: *Douglas Percy Bliss: A Retrospective Exhibition,* Hatton Gallery, University of Newcastle upon Tyne, 1981.

BLISS, Rosalind   b.1937
Painter and printmaker. Born London. Daughter of Douglas Percy Bliss.* Trained as a mural painter. Worked also as a potter. Was taught engraving by her father from 1971.

BLOCH, Martin   1883-1954
Painter. Born Neisse, Silesia. 1902 studied architecture in Berlin. 1905 studied aesthetics with Heinrich Wolfflin in Munich. 1907 studied drawing with Louis Corinth in Berlin. 1923 opened Bloch-Kershbaumer School in Berlin with Anton Kerschbaumer. 1934 fled to Denmark, then to London where he opened The School of Contemporary Painting with Roy de Maistre. 1940 interned at Huyton, near Liverpool, and the Isle of Man. 1948 exhibited in Minneapolis, and Princeton, New Jersey, and in 1949 with Josef Herman at the Ben Uri Gallery. Painted many views of London in expressionist style and colour.

Bibl: *Martin Bloch: An Exhibition of Paintings and Drawings,* South London Art Gallery, 1984.

BLODGET, Michael   b.1963
Painter. Studied at Wimbledon School of Art, 1980-1, Camberwell School of Art, 1981-4, and at the RA, 1984-7. Awards include Henry Moore Scholarship, 1984; Landseer Prize, Royal Academy of Arts, 1986; residency and exhibition with *The Economist* magazine, 1986-7 and a Boise Travelling Scholarship, Slade School of Art, 1988. First solo exhibition at Alexander Roussos Gallery,

MAXWELL BLOND, b.1943. *'Woman and her reflection',* 1986. Woodcut. 11 ½ in. x 13in. Blond Fine Art Ltd.

London, 1988; in the same year he held a solo exhibition at Los Angeles Art Fair. Solo exhibitions at Anne Berthoud Gallery, London and AFR Fine Art, Washington DC, USA, 1989. Experimental painter of landscapes who works with a variety of media.

BLOIS, Flavia (Lady Burntwood)   b.1914
Painter. Born Yoxford, Suffolk. Studied at Chelsea School of Art, Euston Road School, and in Paris. Exhibited at RA, NEAC, London Group and elsewhere. Began as a portraitist, but after a period in Paris, 1939-40, she turned to landscapes.

BLOND, Maxwell   b.1943
Painter. Born Liverpool, Merseyside. Studied at Bath Academy of Fine Art and Slade School of Fine Art. Returned to Merseyside and rejected much of mainstream contemporary art. Paints landscapes, animals, flowers and figures in a symbolic style. 1969 first solo exhibition Monmouth Road, London, most recent at Blond Fine Art, Allerton Gallery, Liverpool, 1975 and 1976, and at Blond Fine Art, London, 1979.

BLOOD, Eric   b.1931
Painter. Born Wainfleet, Lincolnshire. 1946 joined the advertising department of a national holiday organisation. Served with the Royal Leicester Regiment in Korean war and was seriously injured. Returned to work in a studio specialising in commercial design. Began painting in 1965 and had solo exhibition at Woodstock Gallery, London, 1970.

BLOOMAN, Michael   b.1942
Painter. Born Essex. Studied at RCA. First visited India in 1964 and has returned many times, making a special study of the people and cities of the Rajasthan desert. Began making boldly stylised relief prints, as well as watercolours of Indian themes. Has exhibited in Jaipur, London and Oxford. Solo exhibition at Asset Gallery, London, 1975.

BLOW, Sandra b.1925
Abstract painter. Born London. Studied at St. Martin's School of Art, 1942-6, RA Schools, 1946-7, and the Accademia di Belli Arti in Rome, 1947-8. 1946 first exhibited RA. 1949-50 travelled in Spain and France. 1951 first solo exhibition Gimpel Fils, London, followed by many others at home and abroad. Elected ARA, 1971, RA, 1978. Represented in the collections of the Arts Council, Tate Gallery, V & A and many other public collections in Britain and abroad. Her abstracts employ colour, gestural brush marks and texture. For a period experimented with collages, and the combination of polythene, bamboo and paint.

BLUNDSTONE, Ferdinand Victor 1882-1951
Sculptor. Born Switzerland. Studied at South London Technical Art School and RA Schools. Won travelling Scholarship, and studied in Egypt, Greece, Italy and Paris. Exhibited at RA. Won silver medal for garden sculpture at the 1925 Paris International Exhibition. Executed a number of public memorials.

BOLTON, Sylbert b.1959
Painter. Born Jamaica, West Indies. Studied at Wolverhampton Polytechnic, 1977-80. 1980 first solo exhibition held at Wolverhampton Polytechnic, another at Wolverhampton Art Gallery, 1982.

BOLUS, Michael b.1934
Born Cape Town, South Africa. Came to England in 1957. Studied sculpture at St. Martin's School of Art, 1958-62. 1963-4 lived in Cape Town. 1964 returned to London and 1964-7 taught at St. Martin's School of Art and the Central School. 1966 first one-person exhibition at the Komblee Gallery, New York. One of the New Generation sculptors of the 1960s who worked with painted steel.

BOMBERG, David 1890-1957
Painter. Born in Birmingham, West Midlands, the son of Polish Jews, and brought up in Whitechapel. Trained at Slade School of Art. Founder member of the London Group. Associated with Wyndham Lewis* and the Vorticists but refused to sign the Vorticist manifesto. His powerful splintered compositions, as in *Mud-Bath* and *In the Hold* (both in the Tate Gallery) were exchanged in the 1920s for a more naturalistic and expressionistic approach, which records, not merely the forms of landscape, but also the artist's response to them, as well as 'the spirit in the mass'. His art continued in this vein for the next thirty years, but brought him little success. More influential was his teaching at the Borough Polytechnic where Leon Kossoff* and Frank Auerbach* were among his pupils. Retrospective exhibition held at the Tate Gallery, 1988.

Bibl: Richard Cork, *David Bomberg*, Yale University Press, 1987.

BONE, Muirhead 1876-1953
Etcher. Born Partrick, Glasgow, Scotland. Studied and qualified as an architect. Turned to art, producing his first set of Glasgow etchings in 1898, inspired by the example of Meryon and Whistler. These prints introduced him to London circles and he began exhibiting at the NEAC. 1901 moved to London, and 1902 had his first solo exhibition at the Carfax Gallery. His architectural compositions, recording London's development into a metropolis, and the publication, in 1909, of Campbell Dodgson's *catalogue raisonné* of his prints made him the most sought after printmaker after Whistler during the first quarter of this century. As his work developed, he began using dry-point alone, to produce powerful and dramatic effects. His strong draughtsmanship was also particularly suited to the lithographic medium. Appointed Official War Artist in 1916 and again in 1939. Knighted in 1937.

Bibl: *Muirhead Bone, Portrait of the Artist,* Crawford Centre for the Arts, St. Andrews, 1986 (essay by Peter Trowles).

BONE, Stephen 1904-1958
Painter and engraver. Born Chiswick, London. Studied at the Slade, 1922-4. Illustrated books written by his mother with wood engravings throughout the 1930s. 1925 awarded the Gold Medal for Wood Engraving at the International Exhibition, Paris; in the same year he toured Spain. 1926 first exhibited in England in a three-person show at the Goupil Gallery, London. 1929 travelled in Greece, Italy and the British Isles with Mary Adshead,* whom he married. 1932 Elected member of the NEAC. 1939-43 became an officer in the Camouflage Organisation in Leamington Spa; 1943-5 Official War Artist, attached to the Royal Navy. 1948-58 art critic for the *Manchester Guardian;* became a broadcaster on BBC radio in the 1950s, and contributed to the *Yorkshire Post* and the *Glasgow Herald.* His own books include *Albion: an Artist's Britain,* 1939; *The Shell Guide to the West Coast of Scotland* (illustrations by Mary Adshead); *The Silly Snail,* 1942; *The Little Boy and His House,* 1950; and *The Little Boys and their Boats,* 1953.

BOOKER, Alex b.1956
Painter and printmaker. Born Nottingham. Studied at Wimbledon College of Art, 1974-5, Exeter College of Art, 1976-9, and Chelsea School of Art, 1981-2. Since 1978 has exhibited regularly, with a solo exhibition at Atlantis Gallery, London, 1983.

BOOTH, Raymond b.1929
Artist and naturalist. Born Leeds, Yorkshire. Trained at Leeds College of Art. Began earning his living as a teacher, but after a spell in a sanatorium recovering from tuberculosis began doing botanical drawings. Is regarded as a successor to the great botanical and ornithological illustrators of the late 18th and early 19th centuries. Exhibited at the Fine Art Society, London, 1975 and 1982. Represented in British Museum, Fitzwilliam Museum, Cambridge and elsewhere.

BORDASS, Dorothy b.1905
Painter. Studied in France and Italy and travelled widely. Apart from her work as an illuminator of manuscripts, she exhibited in the 1957 Redfern Gallery exhibition, 'Tachiste, Abstract and Metavisual Painting in England Today', being one of the first to respond to American Abstract Expressionism. Solo exhibition at New Vision Centre Gallery, London, 1958. Lived at St. Ives in the 1950s and was a member of the Penwith Society and the St. Ives Society of Artists.

BOREEL, Wendela 1895-1985
Painter and etcher. Born of American and Dutch parents, she became one of the most brilliant of Sickert's pupils, especially in the field of etching. 1911 studied first at the Slade, but also attended Sickert's evening classes at the Westminster Institute, where Sickert was sufficiently impressed by her work to arrange for her to take a studio in Mornington Crescent and to be his own pupil-assistant.

WENDELA BOREEL, 1895-1985. *'In Memoriam, Berkeley Square, 1939'*. 26in. x 18in. Michael Parkin Fine Art Ltd.

She exhibited with the London Group and the NEAC. Her interest in etching dwindled after her marriage in 1924, though she continued to exhibit paintings. Exhibited at RA, NEAC and elsewhere.

BORLASE, Deidre   b.1925
Painter. Studied at RCA, 1943-6. Exhibits at RA. Married Frederick Brill,* former Principal of Chelsea Art School, and held a two-person exhibition with him, 1986.

BORNFRIEND, Jacob   1904-1976
Painter. Born Czechoslovakia. Studied at Academy of Fine Arts, Prague. Came to England in 1939 and changed his name from Bauernfriend. Spent four years working in factories before he could return to painting. An expressionist, influenced to some extent by cubism. 1950 first London solo exhibition held at Roland, Browse and Delbanco.

BOSHIER, Derek   b.1937
Painter. Born Portsmouth, Hampshire. Studied at Yeovil School of Art, 1953-7 and RCA, 1959-62, where he became one of the third wave of British Pop artists. Since 1962 has had numerous solo exhibitions, including one at Edward Totah Gallery, London, 1987. Well represented in leading public collections in Britain. Currently lives and works in Houston, Texas.

BOSWELL, James   1906-1971
Painter and illustrator. Born Westport, New Zealand. Studied at Elam School of Art, Auckland. 1925 came to London. Studied at RCA, 1925-29. Exhibited with London Group and became a Radical Socialist. 1932 joined the Communist Party and gave up painting in favour of illustration and graphic design. 1933 founder member of the Artists International Association. 1934-8 became one of the major illustrators for the *Left Review*. 1936 became art director of the Publishing Department of Asiatic Petroleum Company (now Shell), resigned 1947. 1947-50 art editor on *Lilliput*. 1951 editor of J. Sainsbury Limited house journal. 1964 designed the poster 'Let's Go With Labour' and the entire publicity campaign for the Labour Party during the General Election. Continued to exhibit, having returned to painting after the Second World War.

BOURKE, Roger   b.1945
Mixed media artist. Born Birmingham, West Midlands. Studied at Birmingham College of Art, 1963-8. 1972 first solo exhibition held at Ikon Gallery, Birmingham. His media include polyurethane expanding foam, glass reinforced polyester, liquid latex, melinex, acrylic and gauze.

BOURNE, Bob   b.1939
Painter. Born Exmouth, Devon. Studied at St. Martin's School of Art and West of England Academy. 1973 first solo exhibition held at Tooth's, London. 1973 visited Australia. Briefly experimented with near-abstraction before returning to his interest in figures in interiors. Represented in Arts Council Collection.

BOWEN, Denis   b.1921
Painter. Born Kimberley, South Africa. Studied at Huddersfield School of Art, 1938-41. Served in Royal Navy, 1941-6. Studied at RCA, 1946-50. 1953 exhibited his earliest abstract paintings with the Free Painters' Group at Three Arts Centre, London. An initiator of the Tachiste movement in the 1950s in Britain, he exhibited in the Metavisual, Tachiste and Abstract show at the Redfern Gallery, 1957. Has continued to exhibit regularly, at home and abroad, and held a retrospective at the Bede Gallery, Jarrow, 1973. Second retrospective held at Huddersfield Art Gallery, 1989. Together with John Bellany* and the Irish artist, Derek Culley, founded 'Celtic Vision', a group of contemporary Celtic artists.

BOWEN, William   b.1942
Sculptor. Born Los Angeles, USA. Studied at Pasadena City College, The Art Center School of Los Angeles, and California State College at Long Beach. 1965 moved to London. 1965-6 worked with Eduardo Paolozzi* 1967 received Tiffany Foundation Award for Sculpture. Lecturer at Coventry School of Art. Solo exhibition at Robert Fraser Gallery, London, 1969.

BOWETT, Druie   b.1924
Painter. Born Ripon, Yorkshire. Studied at Harrogate College of Art. 1957 first solo exhibition held at Midland Group Gallery, Nottingham; another at Sheffield University, 1965. Represented in Wakefield City Art Gallery. Solo exhibition at Drian Galleries, 1982. Published *Painter's Poetry* with Ryton Books, 1986.

BOWEY, Olwyn b.1936
Painter. Born Stockton, Co. Durham. Studied at West Hartlepool School of Art, and the RCA, 1955-9. From 1960 exhibited at the RA. 1960 first one-person show at the Zwemmer Gallery. Work in the collection of the Tate Gallery.

BOWLING, Frank b.1936
Painter. Born Bantica, Guyana. 1950 came to the UK. Studied at the RCA and the Slade School of Art, 1959-63. 1963-4 taught at Camberwell School of Art and at Reading University. 1966 moved to New York. 1962 first one-person show at the Grabowski Gallery. 1968 Artist in Residence, New York State Council on the Arts. 1974 returned to live in London. (Plate 25, p.94.)

Bibl: *Frank Bowling: Selected Paintings 1967-77,* Acme Gallery, London, 1977.

BOWYER, William b.1926
Painter. Trained initially at Burslem School in the Potteries, before winning a Scholarship to the RCA in the immediate post-war years. Held various teaching posts, becoming Head of Fine Art at Maidstone College of Art. Full-time painter since 1982. Well known for his portraits of cricketers in action. Exhibits at RA, RBA, RWS, NEAC and elsewhere. Represented in National Portrait Gallery and the Tate Gallery collections.

BOX, E. 1919-1988
Painter. Born London. Her married name was Eden Fleming but she adopted the pseudonym 'E. Box' when she began exhibiting. Studied at Regent Street Polytechnic, 1936-9 and married Professor Marston Fleming. Her husband's work abroad enabled her to travel widely in Europe, North America, Russia, Africa and Asia, and inspiration for some of her works was drawn from these places. Her first solo exhibition was in 1949 and fourteen others followed, one in Rome and two in New York, with retrospectives at King's Lynn, 1956 and 1979. Represented in Tate Gallery.

Bibl: *Gentle Friends: The Paintings of E. Box,* foreword by Robert Melville.

BOX, Richard b.1943
Painter. Studied at Hastings School of Art, 1960-2, and Goldsmiths' College, 1962-5. Teaches art and exhibited at Woodstock Art Gallery, 1980.

BOX, Roland b.1945
Painter. Studied in Hull and Berlin. First solo exhibition held (with another) at Ferens Art Gallery, Hull, 1958. 1980 published *Berlin Wall,* a travelling exhibition, and in 1982, *Landlord-Tenant,* a small book of selected prints, drawings and photographs. 1982 solo exhibition at Ferens Art Gallery, Hull.

BOYCE, Sonia b.1962
Painter and photographer. Born London. Studied at East Ham College of Art and Technology and Stourbridge College of Art and Technology, Birmingham. First solo exhibition, 'Conversations', held at Black Art Gallery, London, 1986; another held at the Whitechapel Art Gallery, 1988. Exhibited paintings in several major black art shows during the 1980s and has recently begun using colour photography.

BOYCOTT-BROWN, Michael b.1910
Painter. Born Hertfordshire. Studied at British Colombia College of Art, Vancouver, 1933, Académie Julian, Paris, 1933-4, Daltio-Rubbo School of Art, Sydney, 1934-7 and Westminster School of Art, 1937-8, under Mark Gertler* and Blair Hughes-Stanton.* 1938-9 assistant at Zwemmer Art Gallery. 1969 solo exhibition at Woodstock Gallery, London.

BOYD, Arthur b.1920
Painter. Born Murrumbeena, Victoria, Australia. At the age of fourteen he attended night classes at the National Gallery of Victoria School, Melbourne. 1940 conscripted into the army, discharged 1943. 1944 formed a partnership with two others to establish the Arthur Merric Boyd Pottery. 1959 moved to London. 1968 returned to Australia for some months, and since then has divided his time between his home in Suffolk and Australia. Solo exhibitions include a retrospective exhibition at the Whitechapel Art Gallery, London, 1962. Exhibits regularly with Fischer Fine Art, London, and at the Australia Gallery, Melbourne. 1978 John Read directed a BBC-ABC co-production film on Boyd, 'A Man in Two Worlds'. Is represented in several public collections, but chiefly in the Australian National Gallery, Canberra, to which he presented a large collection of pastels, sculptures, ceramics, paintings and etchings, 1975. Represented Australia at the Venice Biennale, 1988. Painter of landscapes, both impressionist and expressionist, as well as erotic or fantastic subjects, biblical or mythological scenes.

Bibl: Ursula Hoff, *The Art of Arthur Boyd,* Andre Deutsch, London, 1986.

BOYD, John b.1957
Painter. Studied at the Slade School, 1976-8 and at Newcastle University 1978-80. First solo exhibition at the Below Stairs Gallery, Newcastle, 1981.

BOYD AND EVANS
Painters. Born Fionnuala Boyd in Welwyn Garden City, Hampshire, 1944, and Leslie Evans at St. Albans, Hertfordshire, 1945. Both studied at St. Albans Art School and in Leeds, Evans also studied at Hornsey College of Art, 1967-8. Both have taught at Wolverhampton Polytechnic and began working together in 1968, using a photo-realist style. They exhibit regularly at Angela Flowers Gallery, London, and are represented in MOMA, New York, the Arts Council Collection, Manchester City Art Gallery and elsewhere. Their choice of subject matter reveals a fascination with bleak urban settings.

BOYD, Jamie b.1948
Painter. Born Melbourne, Australia. Came to England in 1959 and studied music and painting. 1968 worked at the Michael Karolyi Foundation in Vence, France, with Polish artist Kazimir Glaz. 1966 first solo exhibition at Bonython Gallery, Adelaide. Subsequent exhibitions include one at New South Wales House, London, 1980. Regularly visits Australia.

BOYD, Ronald b.1946
Painter. Studied at Duncan of Jordanstone College of Art, Dundee, 1964-9, and RCA, 1969-72. 1978 first solo exhibition held at Heatherley Gallery, London, another at Air Gallery, London, 1981.

HELEN BRADLEY, 1900-1979. *'Look, the Queen is Coming'*, 24in. x 36in. W.H. Patterson.

BOYLE, Alicia   b.1908
Painter. Born Bangkok, Thailand, of Irish parents. 1909 moved to Co. Derry, Ireland. Trained at Clapham Art Training College, 1925-9 and Byam Shaw School of Drawing and Painting, 1929-34. 1934 executed a mural for Great Ormond Street Children's Hospital. Joined AIA and held first solo exhibition in 1945 at Peter Jones Gallery, London. 1958 elected to Royal Society of British Artists. Has exhibited regularly and was given a retrospective at the Arts Council Gallery, Belfast, 1983.

BOYLE, Jimmy   b.1945
Sculptor. While serving life sentences in the Special Unit of HM Prison Barlinnie, Glasgow, Scotland, he turned to sculpture and writing. 1980 exhibited sculpture carved from the black-encrusted blocks from which the Gorbals were built, at the Pentonville Gallery, London.

BOYLE, Mark   b.1934
Sculptor. Born Glasgow, Scotland. Studied law at Glasgow University and worked as steelworker, soldier, park-keeper and head waiter while producing paintings and poetry. In 1964 he began to make reliefs of the surface of the earth, a series which continues to the present day. 1966 founded the Sensual Laboratory with his wife Joan Hills. 1978 chosen as the sole British representative at the Venice Biennale. First one-artist exhibition at Traverse Gallery, Edinburgh, 1959. Several international one-artist exhibitions have followed.

Bibl: *Journey to the Surface of the Earth*, Arts Council, 1969.

BRABY, Dorothea   1909-1987
Portrait painter and wood-engraver. Studied art in London, Florence and Paris, 1926-31. 1937-55 did book illustrations for the Golden Cockerel Press. Felt her career as an artist ended in middle age and was drawn instead into welfare work. Memorial exhibition held at Burgh House, Hampstead, 1988.

BRADAC, Jaroslav   b.1945
Painter. Born Prague, Czechoslovakia. Studied at Prague School of Art, 1959-63, and Prague Academy of Applied Arts, 1963-9. Since 1969 has lived and worked in London. 1975 first solo exhibition at Angela Flowers Gallery, London, another at Moira Kelly Gallery, London, 1980.

BRADFORD, Dorothy   b.1918
Painter. Short spells at several art colleges. 1942-5 worked in the Art Department of CEMA, London. 1950-63 art adviser to Ilkley UDC. 1971 official artist to the New Philharmonic Orchestra on US tour; also present at Leeds International Piano Competition, 1975. Concerned with relationships between figures and their activities or environment.

BRADLEY, Helen   1900-1979
Painter. Born Lees, near Oldham, Lancashire. Attended Oldham School of Art where her main interests were embroidery and jewellery. Married a textile designer and had two children. At the age of sixty-five began to paint pictures of her childhood, to show her grandchildren what life was like then. Her naïve style is both tender and precise and won praise from L.S. Lowry.* Her busy scenes admit some influence from early Persian and Moghul art.

Bibl: Helen Bradley, *And Miss Carter Wore Pink*, Jonathan Cape, London, 1971.

BRADLEY, James b.1919
Sculptor. Born Manchester. Studied and practised re-inforced concrete design. Taught art and worked for a time with Harry Thubron* and Victor Pasmore* in Leeds. His sculpture is mostly in wood and makes use of natural forms. Solo exhibition at Wells Gallery, Somerset, 1962.

BRADLEY, Martin b.1931
Painter. Born Richmond, Surrey. Self-taught. Ran away from school at age of fourteen and joined Merchant Navy. During the 1950s mixed with Soho artists and writers. Went to Spain and joined the Spanish Foreign Legion. First solo exhibition at Gimpel Fils, 1954. Has exhibited regularly since then at home and abroad. Represented in the Museum of Modern Art, New York, Chicago Art Institute and elsewhere.

Bibl: Bill Hopkins, *Martin Bradley: Fated to Paint,* GKN, Sievest, Bergstrom, Sweden, 1988.

BRADPIECE, Sarah b.1954
Sculptor. Born Surrey. Studied at West Surrey College of Art, 1970-1, Central School of Art, 1972-3, Hornsey College of Art, 1976-8 and Chelsea College of Art, 1978-9. 1980-2 Fabrication Supervisor for the film *Dark Crystal.* Included in 'The Sculpture Show' at the Hayward Gallery, 1983.

BRADSHAW, Brian b.1923
Painter. Born Bolton, Lancashire. Studied at Bolton and Manchester Schools of Art and at RCA. 1951 Rome Scholar (Prix de Rome Engraving). Exhibited at RA, Leicester Galleries, the Chenil Galleries and elsewhere. Represented in Bolton Art Gallery and Salford Art Gallery. 1960 appointed Professor of Fine Art, Rhodes University, South Africa.

BRADSHAW, Gordon b.1931
Painter. Born Liverpool, Merseyside. Studied at Liverpool College of Art. An early interest in landscape drew him first to Hertfordshire, then to the South Downs and else-where. Solo exhibition at Southampton Art Gallery, 1974.

BRAHAM, Phil b.1959
Painter. Born Glasgow, Scotland. Studied at Duncan of Jordanstone College of Art, Dundee, 1976-80, Royal Academy of Fine Art, The Hague, 1980-1. 1981-2 visiting artist to University of California, Los Angeles. 1984 first solo exhibition held at Main Fine Art, Glasgow, most recent solo show 'Fractured Landscape', at The Scottish Gallery, Edinburgh, 1988. Represented in Scottish Arts Council Collection, the Scottish National Gallery of Modern Art and elsewhere.

BRAMMER, Leonard Griffith b.1906
Printmaker and painter. Born Burslem, Staffordshire. Studied at Burslem School of Art, 1923-6 and RCA, 1926-31. Won a School of Engraving travelling scholar-ship in 1930, the same year he began exhibiting at the RA. Elected ARE, 1932 and RE 1956. Work in the Tate Gallery collection.

BRANDT, Carlos Villeneuva b.1957
Architect and painter. Born Caracas, Venezuela. 1968 moved to England. 1977-82 studied at the Architectural Association. 1983 founder member of *Narrative Architecture for Today.* 1983 first architectural exhibition, 'Discourse and Event', at the Architectural Association, London.

Exhibited in Europe, Tokyo and the United States since this date. First solo exhibition of paintings, with an installation deriving from his architectural projects, at the Albemarle Gallery, London, 1989.

Bibl: John Thackaray, *New British Design,* Thames & Hudson, London, 1987.

BRANGWYN, Frank 1867-1956
Painter. Born Bruges, Belgium. Self-taught apart from instruction given him by his architect father. Worked in the Oxford Street workshops of William Morris, 1882-4, where he was engaged in making facsimiles of Florentine tapestries. 1885 began exhibiting at RA. Travelled widely and had an international reputation. Is best known for his murals and larger easel paintings with heroic and biblical themes. 1904 elected RE and ARA. 1919 elected RA. 1941 knighted. Was honoured in his lifetime with a major retrospective in 1924 which was opened by Ramsay MacDonald, the Prime Minister.

Bibl: *Frank Brangwyn Centenary,* National Museum of Wales, 1967.

BRATBY, John b.1928
Painter. Born Wimbledon, London. Studied at Kingston Art School, 1949-50 and RCA, 1951-4. 1954 first one-person show at the Beaux Arts Gallery. 1956 included in the British Pavilion at the Venice Biennale. 1957 first prize, Junior Section, John Moores Liverpool exhibition. 1957-8 designed sets for the film *The Horse's Mouth.* 1971 retrospective held at South London Art Gallery. Known as a 'Kitchen Sink' artist in the 1950s. Turned temporarily to novel writing when the ascendancy of abstraction put his vigorous realism, indebted to Van Gogh and Soutine, out of fashion. Elected ARA 1959, and RA in 1971. Represented in Tate, Museum of Modern Art, New York, V & A and elsewhere.

BRAUND, Allin b.1915
Painter. Born Northam, Devon. Studied at Bideford School of Art, 1932-6 and Hornsey College of Art, 1936-9, where he later became a senior lecturer. The first picture he sold was bought by Dr. Bronowski. Served with the Royal Marines in Crete, Egypt and Ceylon. Exhibited at RA and elsewhere. Represented in the Museum of Modern Art, New York, the collections of the Arts Council and British Council, Leeds University, Leicester Art Gallery and elsewhere.

BRAY, Phyllis b.1911
Painter. Born London. Studied at Slade School of Art. Taught in adult eduation, East London, 1930-7. Member of the London Group from 1934. Also worked as book illustrator and lithographer. Painter in oils and water-colour of still lifes, figures and landscapes. Also designed posters and executed murals. 1932 showed with the East London Group. Represented in the Walker Art Gallery, Liverpool, and Blackpool Art Gallery.

BRAZDYS, Antanas b.1939
Sculptor. Born Lithuania. Studied at Art Institute of Chicago and RCA, 1962-4. 1965 first solo exhibition held at Hamilton Gallery, London. 1968 won First Prize Sunday Times Sculpture Competition. Represented in Arts Council collection and in Leicestershire Education Department.

JOHN BRATBY, b.1928. *'Three people at a table'*, 1955. 47 ½ in. x 47 ½ in. The British Council.

BREAKER, Charles   b.1906
Painter. Born Windermere, Lake District. Self-taught. Began to sell his work on visits to Spain, Fez, Brittany, South Africa and the Canary Islands. After the Second World War he moved to Newlyn, Cornwall, where he helped found the Newlyn Holiday Sketching Group. Moved to Penzance, painting mostly watercolours of sea and ships.

BREAKWELL, Ian   b.1943
Painter. Studied at Derby College of Art, 1961-5. 1970 first solo exhibition held at Greenwich Theatre Art Gallery. Began working with photo-texts, performance and theatre. His *Continuous Diary/ The Walking Man's Diary/ 120 Days* have been the substance of numerous solo exhibitions as well as TV programmes. 1986 published *Ian Breakwell's Diary 1964-85* (Pluto Press). 1984 represented at Venice Biennale and elsewhere.

BREAM, Antony   b.1943
Painter. Born London. Studied at the RA Schools under Peter Greenham,* 1964-7. Has exhibited widely since the early 1970s. 1981 travelled to North Yemen, where he prepared work for a book as well as for forthcoming exhibitions. 1983 exhibited in New York. Since then he has worked in Colorado, USA, Australia, France and Italy.

BRENER, Roland   b.1942
Sculptor. Born South Africa. Studied at St. Martin's School of Art, 1964-5, taught at St. Martin's, 1966-70. 1970 tutor at University of California, at Santa Barbara. One-person exhibition at the Nigel Greenwood Gallery.

BRENNAN, John   b.1949
Sculptor. Studied at Colchester School of Art, 1967-9, Bristol Polytechnic, 1969-72 and Slade, 1972-4. 1974 won Boise travelling scholarship. 1980 solo exhibition at Stanhope Gallery, London, and Lady Lodge Arts Centre, Peterborough, 1985.

BRETT, Christian.
Painter. Studied at Ruskin School in Oxford. 1970 first solo exhibition held at New Art Centre, London, and another in 1973. 1972 exhibited at Fermoy Art Gallery, King's Lynn. Lives and works in London.

BRETT, The Hon. Dorothy   1883-1987
Painter. Born London. Studied at the Slade School of Art, 1910-16. From 1914 exhibited with the NEAC. 1924 went to New Mexico in the company of D.H. Lawrence and his wife, and lived there until her death. 1950 retrospective exhibition held at the American British Gallery, New York. Work in the collection of the Tate Gallery.

Bibl: Sean Hignett, *Brett. From Bloomsbury to Mexico: A Biography,* Hodder and Stoughton, London, 1984.

Plate 18. YVONNE ANDERSON, b.1926. *'Still Life with Mug'*, c.1970. Oil on board. 18in. x 24in. Private Collection.

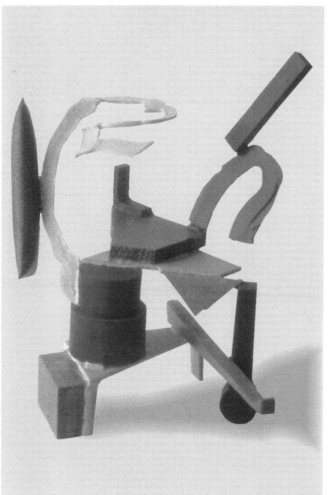

Plate 19. DAVID ANNESLEY, b.1936. *'Throne'*, 1989. Sculpture. 36in. high. Private Collection.

Plate 20. FRANK ARCHER, b.1912. *'Fountain of Youth'*, c.1949. 24in. x 22in. Private Collection.

BREWER, Paul   b.1946
Painter. Born Cardiff, Wales. Studied at Newport College of Art, 1965-9, University of Wales Institute of Science and Technology (Dept. of Applied Psychology), 1972-3, and Cardiff College of Art, 1973-4. 1974, 1975, 1976 solo exhibitions at Chapter Arts Centre, Cardiff. Represented in National Museum of Wales, Welsh Arts Council and elsewhere.

BREWS, Lee   b.1944
Painter. Born South Africa. Studied at Johannesburg Art School. 1973 settled in London. Has had numerous exhibitions, including one at Marjorie Parr Gallery, London, 1977.

BREWSTER, Martyn   b.1952
Painter. Born Oxford. Studied at Hertfordshire College of Art and Design, 1970-1, and Brighton Polytechnic, 1971-5. 1977 won Eastern Arts Award. 1986 solo exhibition, 'Paintings 1982-85', held at Warwick Arts Trust, London. Work in Arts Council Collection and elsewhere. Paints bright and colourful abstracts, suggestive of natural phenomena.

BRICKDALE, Eleanor Fortescue   1871-1945
Painter. Born Norwood, Surrey. Studied at Crystal Palace School of Art, St. John's Wood and the RA Schools. Exhibited regularly at RA and elsewhere, mostly large imaginative and historical subjects, continuing the Pre-Raphaelite tradition of close attention to detail and strong colour. Also worked as book illustrator and stained glass designer.

BRIDGWATER, Alan   b.1903
Sculptor. Studied at Birmingham College of Art, 1922-33. Exhibited at the RA, RSA, RBA, NEAC and in the provinces. Elected RSBA 1936, RBSA 1948, and ARBS 1948. Taught at Birmingham School of Art.

BRIGHT, Kate   b.1964
Painter. Born Suffolk. Studied at Ipswich School of Art, 1983-4, and Camberwell School of Arts and Crafts, 1985-8. First solo exhibition held at Galerija Arts, Ljubljana, 1989. An abstract painter on a large scale, whose touchstone is landscape. Her interest in the structure of things has led her to investigate aspects of physics and geology. Represented in 'The British Art Show', shown at the Hayward Gallery, London, 1990.

BRILL, Frederick   1920-1984
Painter. Studied at Hammersmith Art School, the Slade and the RCA whilst it was evacuated during the war to Ambleside, where he developed a passion for the North Yorkshire dales. 1946 began teaching at Chelsea Polytechnic where he became Head of Painting and eventually Principal of Chelsea School of Art. An excellent draughtsman, he also wrote lucid criticism on other artists' work, including a monograph on Matisse. He exhibited regularly at the RA and in many provincial

galleries. His work ranges from richly painted still lifes and keenly observed portraits to studies made in Venice and Rome. His landscapes of Wensleydale are particularly memorable.

BRILL, Reginald   1902-1974
Painter. Early years spent in London and Yorkshire. Studied at St. Martin's School of Art and the Slade. 1927 won the Prix de Rome for decorative painting. After two years in Rome, began teaching, first at Blackheath School of Art, then Kingston School of Art where he was Head, later Principal, 1934. Published two books, *Modern Painting,* 1946 and *Art as a Career,* 1962. 1935 planned his 'Martyrdom of Man' scheme, painting on a large scale, but also produced portraits, landscapes and still lifes. Retrospective held at Kingston Polytechnic, 1985.

BRINE, Jane   b.1940
Painter. Née Jane Pace. Studied at Bromley College of Art under Charles Mahoney* and others, and at the RA Schools under Peter Greenham* and Anthony Eyton.* Has exhibited at the RBA and the RA.

BRINE, John   b.1920
Painter. Studied at Clapham School of Art, 1935-8 and RCA where his studies were interrupted by the war. Returned in 1946, following demobilisation, and studied for three more years. 1955 appointed Master of Painting and Drawing at the RA Schools. 1961 became Head of Fine Art at Ravensbourne College of Art and Design. Has exhibited extensively, at the RA, the Royal Society of Portrait Painters, the London Group and elsewhere.

BRISCOE, Arthur   1873-1943
Painter and etcher. Born Birkenhead, Cheshire. Inspired by his experience as a child of watching great sailing ships enter Liverpool, he went to the Slade and the Académie Julian, Paris, then spent ten years etching, as a result of his friendship with James McBey.* Also for a period fell under the influence of Wilson Steer.* A superb marine painter, able to capture the essence and mood of the sea.

Bibl: *Arthur Briscoe. Edinburgh Festival Exhibition,* Bourne Fine Art, Edinburgh, 1983.

BRISCOE, Barrie   b.1936
Painter. Born Churchdown, Gloucestershire. Emigrated to Canada, subsequently studying painting and architecture at Washington State University, 1958-63. Worked as a graphic muralist and architect in North America before returning to England in 1971. Combines free-lance architecture with painting.

BRISLEY, Stuart   b.1933
Sculptor and performance artist. Born Surrey. Studied at Guildford School of Art, 1949-54, the RCA, 1956-9, the Academie der Bildendden Kunste, 1959-60, and Florida State University 1960-2. From 1980 began work on a continuing multi-media series of works entitled 'The Georgiana Collection', exploring Georgiana Street in

London where he lived. Has established an international reputation as a performance and installation artist, but since 1980 has moved closer to sculptural practice. Has been widely shown abroad, notably in the Sao Paulo Biennale, at Documenta in Kassel, and at the Serpentine Gallery, 1987.

BROADLEY, Denise   b.1913
Painter. Between 1930 and 1939 she painted in Suffolk and London, spending time also in Wales, Paris, Dieppe and Brittany. Self-taught, though spent time at the East Anglian School of Painting and Drawing run by Cedric Morris.* 1939-45 worked with the Land Army. 1945-8 taught art in a girls' school. 1949 joined the Community of the Sisters of the Church at Ham Common, but has since re-emerged and lives in Suffolk.

BROCK, Thomas   1847-1922
Sculptor. Exhibited at the RA from 1868. Elected ARA, 1883, RA, 1891, and Hon. Member of the RSA, 1910. Knighted 1911. Executed the Victoria Memorial outside Buckingham Palace, among other monuments.

BROCKBANK, Albert Ernest   1862-1958
Painter. Born Liverpool, Merseyside. Studied at Liverpool School of Art evening classes and at the Liverpool Academy while working in an office. Then studied in London and at the Académie Julian, Paris. From 1881 exhibited at the Liverpool Autumn Exhibitions and from 1886 at the RA. 1914 President of the Liverpool Academy. Represented in the Walker Art Gallery, Liverpool.

BROCKHURST, Gerald   1890-1978
Painter and etcher. Born Birmingham, West Midlands. Studied at Birmingham School of Art and RA Schools. 1915 first solo exhibition held at Chenil Gallery, London, and exhibited at RA, 1923-53. Specialised in portraiture and etching. 1933 exhibited 'Dorette' at RA. The model, Dorette Woodward, became the subject of several other paintings. 1937 elected ARA. 1938 painted Duchess of Windsor and commissioned also to paint Marlene Dietrich (unfinished). 1939 moved to New York with Dorette whom he married in 1947, after his former wife sued successfully for a divorce. (Plate 26, p.94.)

Bibl: *A Dream of Fair Women: Gerald Leslie Brockhurst RA (1890-1978): Painter and Etcher,* with introduction by Anne Goodchild, Sheffield City Art Galleries, 1986.

BROCKWAY, Michael   b.1919
Painter. Born London. Studied under Simon Bussy in France and after the war decided to take up painting professionally. Studied at Farnham and Cheltenham Art Schools and at Ruskin School of Drawing, Oxford. Exhibits at RA, NEAC and elsewhere, having several solo exhibitions in London (Walker Galleries) and elsewhere. Works in oil and tempera, but prefers watercolour for landscape painting.

BRODERICK, Laurence   b.1935
Sculptor. Born Bristol, Avon. Studied at Regent Street Polytechnic and Hammersmith College of Art. Has been carving in stone since 1953 and in 1965 began making portrait sculpture. Was for twenty-one years Director of Art at Haberdashers' Aske's School, but gave up teaching in 1981 and turned to full-time sculpture. Allows the shape of the sculpture to determine the rhythms in his work and takes his subjects from the animal world, especially the endangered species. Also sculpts nudes and ecclesiastical themes. 1979 first solo exhibition held at Belgrave Gallery, London, another at York University, 1980. Exhibits at RA, RWEA and elsewhere.

BRODZKY, Horace   1885-1969
Painter. Born Melbourne, Australia. Studied at Melbourne National Gallery art class. Moved to America and then London, arriving 1908. Attended City and Guilds Art School and joined London Group. 1915 returned to New York. 1920 edited *Rainbow* (three issues), a magazine of modern art and poetry. 1923 returned to London and continued to exhibit. 1933 published a biography of Henri Gaudier-Brzeska* and another on Jules Pascin, 1946. Continued to write, publish and broadcast. Memorial exhibition held at Fieldbourne Galleries, 1973.

Bibl: *Horace Brodzky,* Boundary Gallery, London, 1989.

BROOK, Peter   b.1927
Painter. Born Holmfirth, Yorkshire. Studied at Huddersfield and Thanet Schools of Art and at Goldsmiths' College. Member of RSBA. Works in collections of V & A, Wakefield Art Gallery, Leeds City Art Gallery, Leeds University and elsewhere. Exhibits regularly with NEAC and specialises in scenes of the urban North.

BROOKER, William   b.1918
Painter. Studied at Croydon, Chelsea and Goldsmiths' Schools of Art. 1955 first solo exhibition held, followed by a regular series of shows, including one at Agnew's, London, 1979. Represented in Tate Gallery, Oldham Art Gallery, National Gallery of Canada, National Gallery of New Zealand, Manchester City Art Gallery and elsewhere. Has taught in several art schools and in 1969 became Principal of Wimbledon School of Art.

BROSNAN, Shaun
Sculptor. Studied at Newcastle Polytechnic, from where he graduated, 1981. First solo exhibition held at Gallery Seven, Newcastle.

BROWN, Deborah   b.1929
Sculptor. Born Belfast, Northern Ireland. Studied at Belfast College of Art and at the National College of Art, Dublin, and Paris. First solo exhibition held at CEMA Gallery, Belfast, 1951; other solo exhibitions include a retrospective at Ulster Museum, Belfast, 1982, and elsewhere, and a show at the Solomon Gallery, Dublin, 1987.

Plate 21. WILHELMINA BARNS-GRAHAM, b.1912. *'Seaweed and Stone, Skull'*, 1988. Gouache on paper.
22½in. x 30½in. City Art Centre, Edinburgh.

Plate 22. TREVOR BELL, b.1930. *'Rocker with a Stop'*, 1989. Acrylic on canvas. 82in. x 112in.
Private Collection.

Plate 23. ROBERT BEVAN, 1865-1925. *'Green Devon'*, 1919. 17½in. x 21½in.
Plymouth City Museum and Art Gallery.

Plate 24. ELIZABETH BLACKADDER, b.1931. *'Still Life Nikko'*, 1987. Watercolour. 37½in. x 51in.
Mercury Gallery Ltd., London.

BROWN, Frederick

FREDERICK BROWN, 1851-1941. *'Hard Times'*. 28⅜in. x 36⅝in.
Board of Trustees of the National Museums and Galleries on Merseyside.

BROWN, Frederick   1851-1941
Painter. Born Chelmsford, Essex. Studied at South
Kensington School of Art and at the Académie Julian in
Paris. He taught at Westminster School of Art, 1877-92,
and then succeeded Legros as Slade Professor, 1892-1918.
A founder-member of the NEAC, he was also part of the
impressionist clique who showed together as 'London
Impressionists' in 1889. His famous painting, *Hard Times*
(Walker Gallery, Liverpool) starred at the NEAC's first
exhibition.

BROWN, Hugh Boycott   b.1909
Painter. Born into a family of artists. Studied at Margaret
Frobisher School, London, and elsewhere. From the 1930s
he spent long holidays in East Anglia. Became friendly
with Sir John Arnesby Brown* who encouraged him.
Entered RAF during Second World War. Specialises in
land and seascapes and exhibits regularly in England and
at the Mystic Maritime Gallery, Mystic, Connecticut,
USA. His paintings have been described as 'quiet,
unassertive and endlessly appealing'.

BROWN, James   1863-1943
Painter and musician. Born London. As a musician, was
an authority on string music and the originator of Poly-
chordia. Did not paint seriously till his middle years. In
1912 his work was noticed by the critic Frank Rutter who
introduced him to Lucien Pissarro.* They became close
friends and went painting together. Brown became
familiar with the principles of Impressionism and
developed his own interpretation of it. Never exhibited in
public and often signed his work with the pseudonym 'P.
Conway', later abandoning this for his own name. An
exhibition of his work was held at William Darby, London,
1976.

BROWN, John Arnesby   1866-1955
Painter. Born Nottingham. Studied painting privately in
Nottingham with Andrew McCallum and then at Bushey
under Sir Hubert von Herkomer, 1889-92. From 1890
exhibited at the RA; elected ARA in 1903 and RA in 1915.
1909 first one-person exhibition held at the Leicester
Galleries. 1938 knighted. Retrospective exhibition at
Norwich Castle Museum, 1935.

BROWN, Jonathan   b.1955
Sculptor. Born Winchester, Hampshire. Studied at Eastbourne College of Art, 1973-5, and Hornsey College of Art, 1975-8. Exhibited at Gardner Art Centre, Sussex University, 1981 and South Hill Park Arts Centre, Berkshire, 1982. Is interested in creating 'cathedraline structures with intention to fly'.

BROWN, Keith   b.1947
Sculptor. Born Hexham, Northumberland. Studied at Sunderland Polytechnic, 1967-71, Manchester Polytechnic, 1971-2 and the Royal College of Art, 1972-5. 1977 first one-person show at the Serpentine Gallery, London, and at Hartnell College, Salinas, California. 1977-8 artist in residence at Hartnell College, Salinas, California. 1980-2 lecturer in sculpture, Manchester Polytechnic. 1981 guest Professor, Jan Van Eyck Academie, Maastricht, Holland. Work in several collections including Northern Arts, Welsh Arts Council, South Hill Park Arts Centre, Bracknell.

BROWN, Killock   1856-1934
Sculptor. Born Glasgow, Scotland. Studied at Glasgow School of Art, the RCA and at the RA Schools. Exhibited at the RA from 1887. Taught for a time at Glasgow School of Art and executed some memorials and monuments.

BROWN, Mortimer   1874-1966
Sculptor. Born Stoke-on-Trent, Staffordshire. Studied at Hanley School of Art, c.1889-90, with Sir Alfred Gilbert, c.1890-1, at the RCA, c.1891-6 and at the RA Schools, 1896-1901. 1901-16 exhibited at the RA. 1906-27 member of the RBS. Work in the collection of the Tate Gallery.

BROWN, Neil Dallas   b.1938
Painter. Born Elgin, Scotland. Studied at Dundee College of Art, 1954-8, Hospitalfield College of Art, 1958, and Duncan of Jordanstone College of Art, Dundee, 1958-9. 1959-60 travelled on a scholarship in France, Italy and Spain. 1960-1 studied at RA Schools. 1967 visited New York on Scottish Arts Council Award. 1975 elected ARSA. 1976 elected Professional Member SSA. 1981 artist in residence, SAC Studio, Amsterdam. 1959 first solo exhibition at Duncan Institute, Cupar, regular solo shows since then, including one at Kirkcaldy Museums and Art Gallery, 1982. Represented in major Scottish collections, the Walker Art Gallery, Liverpool, and elsewhere.

BROWN, Norman   b.1942
Kinetic artist. Born London. After leaving school worked as an engineering apprentice. Began painting in his spare time. Studied at Sir John Cass College, London, 1969-70, and Hornsey College of Art, London, 1970-3. Lost interest in static images and began using elastic, string and electric motors, making web-like structures that move. Has exhibited at Reality Nouvelles, Paris, 1973, and IKI International Art Fair, Düsseldorf and at Harlow, Playhouse Gallery, 1974.

BROWN, Philip   b.1958
Sculptor. Born Leeds, Yorkshire. Studied at Jacob Kramer School of Art, Leeds, 1977-8, Manchester Polytechnic, 1978-81 and the Slade, 1981-3. 1984 won Boise travelling scholarship to Morocco. 1984-5 artist in residence, Lady Lodge Arts Centre, Peterborough. 1985 solo exhibition 'Inside Industry', at City Museum and Art Gallery, Peterborough.

BROWN, Ralph   b.1928
Sculptor. Born Leeds, Yorkshire. Studied at Leeds School of Art, 1948-51, Hammersmith School of Art, 1951-2, and the RCA, 1952-6. Awarded a scholarship to study with Ossip Zadkine in Paris, and another for study in Greece. 1957 was sponsored by Henry Moore* for a scholarship to study in Italy, and also worked in Cannes making mosaic panels for Picasso. Taught at the RCA. Work in the collections of Tate Gallery, Arts Council, Leeds City Art Gallery, CAS, the Kroller-Muller Museum, Stuyvesant Foundation, and Gallery of New South Wales, Sydney.

BROWN, Roy   b.1948
Painter and sculptor. Studied at Jacob Kramer College, Leeds, 1967-8, and Leeds Polytechnic, 1968-71. Solo exhibition at Woodstock Gallery, London, 1972.

BROWN, Sue   b.1945
Sculptor. Born Bristol, Avon. Spent childhood travelling as her father was in the Navy and lived for some years in Malta and Canada. Returned to England to train as a dancer. 1961 went to Farnham Art School. 1979 exhibited at Centre 181, Hammersmith, and Pentonville Gallery, London, 1981. Her work is concerned with the portrayal of women's place in a male-orientated society.

BROWNE, Kathleen   b.1905
Painter and printmaker. Born Christchurch, New Zealand. Studied at Canterbury School of Art, Chelsea School of Art and RCA, 1932-4. Exhibited at the RA, RSA, RBA, the Paris Salon and elsewhere. Member of the Women's International Art Club.

BROWNING, Amy Katherine   1882-1970
Painter. Born Bramingham Hall, Bedfordshire. Studied at RCA and in Paris. Exhibited at the RA, RP, ROI, NEAC, in the provinces and abroad. Won a silver medal at the Paris Salon, 1912 and a gold medal, 1922. 1912 elected ROI. Married Thomas C. Dugdale.*

BROWNSWORD, Harold   1885-1961
Sculptor. Born in the Potteries, the son of a book-keeper at Wedgwood. Studied at Hanley School of Art, then RCA, 1908-13. Headmaster of Regent Street Polytechnic, London, 1938-50. Designed and executed war memorials in Hanley, Longton, Eccleshill and Northallerton.

BRUCE, Anne   b.1927
Painter. Born Stoke Poges, Buckinghamshire. Studied theatre design, painting and drawing at the Slade School of Fine Art and Edinburgh College of Art, 1945-53. 1962 awarded a John Moores Prize. 1963 first solo exhibition at the Zwemmer Gallery, London. 1973-9 Chairwoman of the WIAC Centre. Included in the collection of the Arts Council.

BRUEN, Ru   b.1940
Mixed media artist. Born Luton, Bedfordshire. Studied at Luton College of Art, 1955-8. 1964-6 worked as a designer in London. Has exhibited in mixed exhibitions at Angela Flowers and the RA. Solo exhibition at Mappin Art Gallery, Sheffield, 1982.

BRUFORD, Marjorie (Midge)   1902-1958
Landscape and figure painter. Born Eastbourne, Sussex. Studied under Lamorna Birch* at Newlyn and in Paris. Lived at Mousehole in Cornwall and exhibited at RA, NEAC, SWA.

Plate 25. FRANK BOWLING, b.1936. *'Mirror'*, 1964-6. Acrylic on canvas. 120in. x 84in. Private Collection.

Plate 26. GERALD BROCKHURST, 1890-1978. *'Duchess of Windsor'*, 1939. 27½in. x 40in. The Al Fayed Archives.

Plate 27. STEVEN CAMPBELL, b.1953. '3 *Men of Exactly the Same Size in an Unequal Room*', 1987. 98in. x 109in. Marlborough Fine Art (London) Ltd.

Plate 28. NORMAN CLARK, b.1913. *'High Street, Sussex'*. Oil on board. 20in. x 29in. Private Collection.

BRUNDIT, Reginald G.   1883-1960
Painter. Born Liverpool, Merseyside. Studied at Bradford School of Art, the Slade School of Art and privately under John Swan. From 1922 exhibited at the RA. 1931 became ARA, and RA in 1938. Work in the collection of the Tate Gallery.

Bibl: *Reginald Brundit, R.A. 1883-1960,* Bradford Art Galleries and Museum, 1980.

BRUNELL, Geoffrey   b.1945
Maker of prints and wallhangings. Born London. Studied at Walthamstow School of Art, 1963-6, and RCA, 1966-9. 1968 won British Institute Engraving Award, 1969 Prix de Rome (Print). Has exhibited regularly since 1966 and had a solo exhibition at Oldham Art Gallery, 1986. Has work in V & A, Glasgow Art Gallery and elsewhere.

BRYANSTON, Hilary   b.1951
Painter. Born London. Studied at Newport College of Art, 1970-3. 1976 painted mural for Cardiff Community Concern. 1975 first solo exhibition at Chapter Arts Centre, Cardiff, others include one at Wolverhampton Art Gallery, 1983. An abstract artist, who uses textures and shapes that reflect the nature of the life around her.

BRYCE, Gordon   b.1943
Painter. Born Edinburgh, Scotland. Studied at Edinburgh College of Art, 1960-5. Awards include the Scottish Arts Council prize, Sir William Gillies Travelling Scholarship and the Scottish Postal Board Award, RSA. Regularly holds solo exhibitions in Britain and the USA, most recently at the Sue Rankin Gallery, London. Works in the collections of Scottish National Gallery of Modern Art; Scottish Arts Council; Aberdeen, Perth and Darlington Museums and Art Galleries; Tayside, Lothian, Grampian and Fife Regional Collections.

BRYCE, Ken   b.1956
Printmaker. Born Mancot, North Wales. Studied at Newport College of Art, and RCA. Exhibited at Ayling Porteous Gallery, Chester, 1986.

BUCHANAN, Hugh   b.1958
Watercolourist. Born Edinburgh, Scotland. Studied at Edinburgh College of Art, 1976-81. 1980 won Andrew Grant travelling scholarship to Egypt, Jordan and Syria. 1981 won Helen Rose Bequest to travel in Northern Italy and Yugoslavia. 1982 travelled and painted in Greece and South Italy, tracing the use of the sphere in architecture. 1983 worked on a series of cloud studies in Wigtownshire, Scotland. 1984 travelled and painted in Spain. Several solo exhibitions since 1980, including one at Francis Kyle Gallery, London, 1986.

BUCHANAN-CROSBIE, Anne   b.1919
Painter. Studied at Camberwell School of Art, 1950-3. Exhibited with the London Group. Was included in 'British Painting '74' at the Hayward Gallery. A solo exhibition was held at the Meridean House International, Washington, USA, 1979.

BUCKLAND-WRIGHT, John   1897-1954
Painter and printmaker. Born New Zealand, but educated in England, studying history at Oxford then architecture in London. He soon left the architectural profession for painting, but remained self-taught until he lived in Paris, 1930-9, and affiliated himself with S.W. Hayter's Atelier

17. Illustrated many books, including seventeen titles for the Golden Cockerel Press. Returned to England in 1939 and in 1940 was included among the British engravers shown at the Venice Biennale. Taught at Camberwell School of Art and then at the Slade. Published *Etching and Engraving,* 1953.

BUCKLEY, J.B.   b.1937
Painter. Born Manchester, Lancashire. Studied at Manchester School of Art and Ashton-under-Lyne School of Art. Moved into abstract art after 1963. First solo exhibition held at Woodstock Gallery, London, 1966.

BUCKLEY, Stephen   b.1944
Painter. Born Leicester, Leicestershire. Studied at Universities of Newcastle, 1962-7 and Reading, 1967-9. 1970 held first solo exhibition. 1972-4 artist in residence at King's College, Cambridge. First began weaving strips of canvas across the stretcher frame in 1969 and has continued to produce paintings that are cantilevered, bent or fragmented. Has exhibited regularly in London and New York. 1985 the Walker Art Gallery, Liverpool, together with Museum of Modern Art, Oxford, organised the retrospective 'Many Angles'. 1986 solo exhibitions in London, New York and New Haven. Has shown regularly at John Moores exhibitions.

Bibl: *Stephen Buckley: Many Angles,* by Marco Livingstone, Museum of Modern Art, Oxford, 1985.

BUDD, Rachel   b.1960
Painter. Born Norwich, Norfolk. Studied at RCA. Has won various awards, including the Jeffrey Archer prize, GLC Painting Competition. 1983 first solo exhibition at the Willow Tea Rooms, Newcastle upon Tyne. Represented in the CAS collection.

BUGG, Rod   b.1946
Sculptor. Trained at Harrow Art School, 1963-5, Newport College of Art, 1965-8 and Birmingham College of Art, 1968-9. Solo exhibitions since 1971, including one at Newcastle Polytechnic Gallery, 1986. Works with clay, often incorporating references to domestic pots in his sculpture.

BUHLER, Michael   b.1940
Painter. Born London. Studied at RCA, 1959-63. Has exhibited regularly since 1963; two solo exhibitions at the New Art Centre, London, 1966 and 1971. Represented in Arts Council Collection, University of Liverpool and elsewhere.

BUHLER, Robert   1916-1989
Painter. Studied art in Zurich, Basle and at Bolt Court School, St. Martin's School of Art and RCA, where he stayed only six weeks in 1934. Influenced by Sickert's example, he began to specialise in portraits, still lifes and landscapes. Became ARA, 1947 and RA, 1956. Tutor at the RCA, 1948-75. Commissioned portraits include: Sir John Betjeman, Sir Angus Wilson, Francis Bacon* and Arthur Koestler.

Bibl: Colin Hayes, *Robert Buhler,* Weidenfeld and Nicolson, London, 1986.

BULL, Adam   b.1965
Sculptor. Studied at Canterbury College of Art and Design, 1983-4, Cheltenham College of Art, 1984-7, and at the RA Schools, 1988. 1987 first exhibited at the Axion Centre, Cheltenham.

BULLARD, Paul   b.1918
Painter. Born London. Studied at Clapham School of Art, 1934-8 and at RCA, where his study was interrupted by war service. POW in Libya. Exhibited at RA, NEAC, and with the London Group. Became Head of Foundation Department at Camberwell School of Arts and Crafts.

BULLMORE, Edward   b.1933
Painter. Born Southland, New Zealand. Attended Canterbury College School of Art, 1951-5. 1959 studied in Florence for six months. 1960 arrived in London. Member of London Group and began exhibiting shaped paintings during the 1960s.

BURDEN, Alan   b.1938
Painter of landscapes. Born Stanmore, Middlesex. Studied and worked as a metallurgist, 1954-63. Studied at Harrow School of Art, 1962-6, and University of Newcastle upon Tyne, 1966-7. Since 1969 has exhibited regularly. 1981 solo exhibition at Colin Jellicoe Gallery, Manchester.

BURGESS, Alan   b.1936
Painter. Born West Mersea, Essex. Studied at Colchester School of Art and Manchester Regional College of Art. Solo exhibition at Playhouse Gallery, Harlow, 1973.

BURGIN, Victor   b.1941
Conceptualist. Born Sheffield, Yorkshire. Studied painting at the RCA, 1962-5. A visit to America on a Harkness Fellowship brought him into contact with the Minimalists, Robert Morris and Don Judd. On his return to England Burgin reacted against the materialist emphasis in art and began making written instructions his artwork. These did not need to be made, as on reading the instructions the person mentally made the art object in his or her own mind. Burgin went on to become a key figure within the Conceptual movement, writing abstruse articles for art journals and using photographs and text for political purposes. Regards all his activities, as writer, photographer and teacher (at the Polytechnic of Central London since 1973) as a form of political education.

Bibl: Victor Burgin, *Between*, Basil Blackwell and the ICA, 1986.

BURKE, Patrick   b.1932
Printmaker. Studied at Brighton College of Art. 1957-9 Rome Scholar (engraving). Solo exhibitions since 1962, including one at Alan Gallery, New York, 1964, and at Morley Gallery, London, 1973. 1982 Head of Painting, Brighton Polytechnic.

Bibl: *Paintings by Patrick Burke*, Brighton Polytechnic Gallery, 1987.

BURKE, Terry   b.1927
Painter. Born Bradford, Yorkshire. Studied at Bradford College of Art and Leeds College of Art. Underwent a deep religious experience in 1969 and in 1970 his first solo exhibition, at the Goosewell Gallery, Menston, reflected this. 1973 exhibited an abstract visual interpretation of the Dies Irae at the same gallery.

BURKE, Thomas   1906-1945
Painter. Born Liverpool, Merseyside. Studied at Liverpool College of Art and the RCA. Worked in Chelsea, Paris and Ireland. Was a radio officer in the Merchant Navy and a prisoner of war, 1941-5, when he designed many posters whilst imprisoned. Represented in Walker Art Gallery, Liverpool.

BURMAN, Barry   b.1943
Painter. Born Bedford, Bedfordshire. Studied at Coventry College of Art and RCA. Solo exhibitions since 1969, including one at Nicholas Treadwell Gallery, 1982. Has a liking for the strange and macabre and has recently worked mostly with black gouache and conte.

BURN, Rodney   1899-1984
Painter. Studied at Slade, 1918-22, and began painting landscapes, portraits and figure paintings. Tutor at RCA, 1929-31, and 1946, and as Senior Tutor, 1947-65. Director, School of Museum and Fine Arts, Boston, USA, 1931-4. Member of NEAC and for a period acted as Honorary Secretary. 1954 elected ARA, and RA, 1962; also a member of the Royal West of England Academy. Turned increasingly to seascapes as a source of inspiration, also making Venice and the Channel Islands aspects of his subject matter.

BURNS, Pamela   b.1938
Painter. Born London. Studied at Leicester College of Art, 1957-60, and RCA, 1960-3. 1965-7 member of Artists' International Association. 1978 included in Hayward Annual. 1980 solo exhibition at Hertfordshire College of Art and Design, St. Albans.

BURNS, Robert   1869-1941
Painter and designer. Born Edinburgh, Scotland. Initially trained as an engineer, but studied art in the evenings at Glasgow School of Art where Charles Rennie Mackintosh was a fellow student. 1889 left Scotland for London, and enrolled at Westminster School of Art. Also studied in Paris where he began to buy Japanese prints. 1892 returned to Edinburgh and began designing stained glass, silver-smithing, wrought iron work amongst other things, working for architects and exhibiting at the Scottish Guild of Handicrafts. Also executed murals, but achieved popularity with his easel paintings, influenced by the Austrian and Belgian symbolists. 1901 elected President of the Society of Scottish Artists and 1902 became associate of RSA. Quarrelled with the art establishment and turned his back on it, spending the last twenty years of his life involved with the applied arts.

Bibl: *Robert Burns 1869-1941: Artist & Designer*, Bourne Fine Art, Edinburgh, 1983.

BURNS, William   1921-1972
Painter. Born Newton Mearns, Scotland. Served in RAF, 1939-42. Studied at Glasgow School of Art, 1944-8, and Hospitalfield College of Art, Arbroath, 1947-9. 1952 elected a member of the Society of Scottish Artists. 1955 elected an associate of Royal Scottish Academy. 1958 elected member of Royal Scottish Society of Painters in Watercolour. 1970 elected a member of RSA. 1964-8 held four solo exhibitions and made regular appearances in group shows.

Bibl: *William Burns RSA, RSW, Memorial Exhibition*, Aberdeen Art Gallery, 1973.

BURNSIDE, Dudley   b.1912
Painter. Joined the RAF in 1935 and after a long and distinguished flying career retired in 1962. Thereafter he devoted much time to painting, having trained under Hayward Veal, the Australian impressionist. Represented in the Royal Air Force Museum, the British Airways Museum and the Royal Navy Collection.

Plate 29. BERNARD COHEN, b.1933. *'Of Clocks and Clouds'*, 1987-9.
Acrylic on linen. 72½in. x 72½in. Waddington Galleries Ltd., London.

Plate 30. DOROTHY COKE, 1897-1979. *'The Garden Party'*, 1929. 28in. x 36in. Private Collection.

Plate 31. PETER COKER, b.1926.
'Garden of the Villa Clos du Peyronnet,
1984. 63in. x 70in. Private Collection.

Plate 32. BERYL COOK, b.1926. *'Taxi on Curzon Street'.* Oil on board. 19in. x 24in. Portal Gallery Ltd., London.

BURR, James   b.1926
Printmaker. Studied at Bromley College of Art, 1947-9, and Slade School of Fine Art, 1949-53. 1955 spent a year etching and engraving under S.W. Hayter in Paris on a French State Scholarship. 1965 solo exhibition at Zwemmer Gallery, London. Represented in Leeds University Collection and Sunderland Art Gallery.

BURRA, Edward   1905-1976
Painter. Studied at Chelsea Polytechnic, 1921-3, and RCA, 1923-5. As a student Burra revealed a talent for popular illustration and the bizarre aspects of everyday existence. Cinema, dance and music halls and low-life bars were constant sources of inspiration. 1930 first solo exhibition at Leicester Galleries. Much of his work of the 1930s celebrated the popular culture of Harlem and Mexico, and later reflected his distress at the Spanish Civil War. Member of Unit One and exhibited in the 1936 International Surrealist Exhibition. From the late 1950s onwards he became increasingly interested in landscape and still life. Retrospective exhibition held at Hayward Gallery, London, 1985.

Bibl: Andrew Causey, *Edward Burra: Complete Catalogue,* Phaidon Press, Oxford, 1985.

BURRELL, Louie   1873-1971
Painter. Born London into a family of artists. Studied under Sir Hubert von Herkomer, 1900-3, and began to paint miniatures in order to support herself. Became a fashionable painter, painting many members of the Royal family until her health broke down and she went to Canada. From there she moved to California, finding portrait work among Los Angeles millionaires and Hollywood film stars. 1919 returned to England and suffered great poverty. Patronised by Mrs Stanley Baldwin, among others, and also went to India where she painted the Viceroy, Lord Irwin and other notables. Frequently lived on charity and died unknown. An exhibition of her work was held at the Royal West of England Academy, 1985.

BURT, Laurie   b.1925
Sculptor. Born Leeds, Yorkshire. 1939 apprenticed to firm of architectural metalworkers. 1941-6 military service in Middle East. 1946-9 worked as industrial metalworker. Studied part-time at Leeds College of Art, 1956-60. 1968 moved to London. 1971 moved to Cyprus, returning to Britain in 1979. Since 1979 has lived and worked in York. Solo exhibitions include one at Oriel Gallery, Cardiff, 1980.

BURTON, Charles   b.1929
Painter. Studied at Cardiff College of Art and RCA. From 1956 taught at Liverpool College of Art (later Polytechnic); moved to Glamorgan College of Education in 1970. First solo exhibition held at Prospect Gallery, London, 1956. Exhibits mostly in Wales and is represented in the Welsh Arts Council collection.

BURTON, Rosemary   b.1951
Painter. Studied at Slade School of Fine Art, 1972-8. Has exhibited in mixed exhibitions, including one at Barry Barker Gallery, 1979-80. Specialises in portraiture and is represented in Arts Council Collection.

EDWARD BURRA, 1905-1976. *'Toulon'*, 1927. 22¼ in. x 15½ in. The Lefevre Gallery.

BURY, Morley   b.1919
Painter. Trained at Bournemouth School of Art and Reading University. Served in army, 1940-6, and was a prisoner of war in Italy and Germany. After the war he returned to Reading University and then studied at Regent Street Polytechnic and Goldsmiths' College. Exhibitions include Looking Forward, Gallery One, Zwemmers, Heals, Camden Centre and mixed shows, e.g. Forgotten Fifties. Work in UK, Belgium, France, USA, Finland, Canada, Australia, New Zealand, Saudi Arabia and Iraq, and public collections in England. Part-time Hornsey 'O' and 'A' level art examiner.

BUSBY, George   b.1926
Painter. Born Birmingham, West Midlands. Worked for many years as a graphic designer and illustrator. 1978 left advertising world to become a full-time artist. Works mostly in watercolour and gouache, and has specialised in the industrial scene. Represented in the National Library of Wales and exhibits regularly at the Royal Birmingham Society of Artists Gallery and elsewhere.

BUSBY, John   b.1928
Painter. Born Bradford, Yorkshire. Studied at Leeds College of Art, 1948-52 and Edinburgh College of Art,

1952-4. Since 1960 has exhibited regularly and is represented in Abbot Hall Art Gallery, Kendal, Wakefield Art Gallery, and elsewhere. Solo exhibitions include one at the Goosewell Gallery, Menston, 1970.

BUSH, Harry   1883-1957
Painter. Born Brighton, Sussex. 1900 entered the Victualling Department of the Admiralty but left in 1904 to join Carlton Studios, Chelsea, where he worked under Fred Taylor, the poster and watercolour artist. Afterwards studied at Regent Street Polytechnic. 1922 began exhibiting at RA. Became known as 'Painter of the Suburbs', for he excelled in painting outer London scenes. His undramatic style has a strong feeling for atmosphere.

Bibl: *A Brush with Bush: Harry Bush R.O.I.: An English 'Plein Air' Painter,* Lowndes Lodge Gallery, London, 1985.

BUSHE, Fred   b.1931
Sculptor. Born Coatbridge, Scotland. Studied at Glasgow School of Art, 1949-53. Served in Army, 1954-8. Studied at University of Birmingham, 1966-7. 1970 became a full-time artist. 1962 first solo exhibition held at '57 Gallery, Edinburgh, others include one at Talbot Rice Art Centre, Edinburgh, 1982. Represented in Aberdeen Art Gallery and Scottish Arts Council Collection.

BUTLER, Arthur   b.1918
Painter. Born Wakefield, Yorkshire. Studied at Wakefield School of Art and RCA. Served in Royal Navy during war and lost a leg. Specialised in watercolours of architectural and landscape scenes and has exhibited widely, at RA and elsewhere. Solo exhibition at Bradford Art Galleries and Museum, 1984.

BUTLER, James   b.1931
Sculptor. Born London. Studied at Maidstone School of Art, 1948-50, St. Martin's School of Art and the Royal College of Art, 1950-2. 1953-5 National Service. Worked for a while as an architectural stone carver. Tutor in sculpture and drawing at City and Guilds of London Art School. 1972 elected RA. Executed statue of Richard III in Leicester.

BUTLER, John   b.1948
Painter. Born Whitchurch, Shropshire. Studied at Newcastle upon Tyne, 1967-8, Liverpool College of Art, 1968-71, and Birmingham College of Art, 1972-3. Founder-member of Spacex Ltd., an artists' co-operative with studios and a gallery. Solo exhibition at Winter Gardens, Malvern, 1981.

BUTLER, Paul   b.1947
Draughtsman. Born Bristol, Avon. Studied at West of England College of Art, Bristol, 1965, and Kingston-upon-Thames College of Art, 1966-9. 1976 first solo exhibition held at Parkway Focus Gallery, London; others include one at Air Gallery, London, 1980. 1985 exhibited work completed whilst artist in residence in Hounslow at Watermans Arts Centre, Brentford. Executes powerful charcoal drawings of human situations.

Bibl: *Paul Butler,* Rochdale Art Gallery, 1981.

BUTLER, Reginald   1913-1981
Sculptor. Born Buntingford, Hertfordshire. Trained as an architect, practising under the name of Cottrell Butler, 1936-50. Lecturer at the Architectural Association, 1937-9. After working as a blacksmith, 1941-5, he took up sculpture and in 1947 became assistant to Henry Moore.* 1949 first solo exhibition held at Hanover Gallery, London. 1950-3 Gregory Fellow at Leeds University. 1952 represented Britain at the Venice Biennale, the same year that he won a competition for a monument to the Unknown Political Prisoner. His original maquette (now destroyed) was enlarged into a working model, though the actual monument, intended to be over 300ft. high, was never made. His series of iron sculptures produced during the 1950s reduced the human figure to linear abstract forms. His later modelled sculpture dealt obsessively with the female figure. Retrospective exhibition held at the Tate Gallery, 1983.

Bibl: *Reg Butler,* Tate Gallery, London, 1983.

BUTLER, Vincent   b.1933
Sculptor. Born Manchester, Lancashire. Studied at Manchester School of Art and Edinburgh College of Art. Studied under Marino Marini in Milan, 1955-7. Worked in Italy until 1960, exhibiting in mixed shows. 1960-3 taught sculpture in Nigeria. 1963 returned to Edinburgh College of Art to teach. Regular contributor to Royal Scottish Academy. 1969 awarded Benno Schotz prize for portraiture. Work in Scottish Arts Council Collection and elsewhere. Solo exhibition at New Grafton Gallery, London, 1969.

BUTTERWORTH, John   b.1945
Painter. Born Lancashire. Studied at Rochdale College of Art, 1961-3, Newport College of Art, 1963-5 and Cardiff College of Art, 1965-6. 1965 won David Murray Landscape Award. Solo exhibition, 'Paper Works', using coloured paper pulp, at Southampton Art Gallery, 1983.

BYNG-LUCAS, Caroline   d.1967
Painter and sculptor. Studied in London, Paris and Rome. First exhibited at the Galerie des Jeunes Peintres, Paris, 1928. Studied sculpture with John Skeaping* in the 1930s. Solo exhibitions at the Lefevre Gallery, 1934 and the Leicester Galleries, 1939. With her sister, Frances Byng Stamper, founded the Millers Gallery, Lewes, Sussex, 1941, the first regional arts centre in the country. Set up the Millers Press to produce artists' lithographs. Retrospective exhibition at The Grange, Rottingdean, 1955.

BYRNE, James   b.1948
Painter. Born Birmingham, West Midlands. Studied at Newman's College, Birmingham. 1976-8 studied art history at Birmingham Polytechnic. 1982-3 did an MA in Fine Art at Birmingham Polytechnic. Solo exhibition at Ikon Gallery, Birmingham, 1986.

BYRNE, John   c.1940
Painter. Studied at Glasgow School of Art, 1958-61, Edinburgh College of Art, 1961-2, and Glasgow School of Art, 1962-3. 1963-4 travelled in Italy on scholarship. 1964 began work as a graphic artist with Scottish Television. 1966 went into carpet designing, also illustrated a number of Penguin book jackets, 1964-6. Began exhibiting under the name 'Patrick' and 1968 became a full-time professional painter. 1970 began making animated films. Solo exhibition at Third Eye Centre, Glasgow, 1975.

F.C.B. CADELL, 1883-1937. *'The White Room'*. 20in. x 24in. The Scottish Gallery.

CADBURY, Belinda   b.1939
Sculptor. Born Birmingham, West Midlands. Studied theatre design at Regent's Street Polytechnic, worked at Glyndebourne Opera in the property department and elsewhere. Studied life-drawing at City and Guilds London Art School. 1969-72 studied sculpture at City and Guilds. 1977 first solo exhibition held at Beehive Gallery, London. 1982 exhibited relief sculpture at Morley Gallery, London.

CADDICK, Kathleen   b.1937
Painter. Born Liverpool, Merseyside. Studied at High Wycombe Technical College, 1950-4 and High Wycombe College of Art, 1954-8. Originally worked as a freelance designer but began painting full time in the mid-1960s. Solo exhibitions at Heal's Mansard Art Gallery, 1968, 1971 and 1974. Specialises in landscape, making subtle use of shades and textures.

CADELL, Francis Campbell Boileau   1883-1937
Painter. Born Edinburgh, Scotland. On the advice of Arthur Melville,* was sent to study at the Académie Julian in Paris, 1899-1903. Remained living on the Continent for the next six years but did not begin to paint in the distinctive style associated with the Scottish Colourists until 1910. His method, with its bright colour and abbreviated drawing, well suited his aggressively good-natured, light-hearted personality. Many of his paintings are of Iona, the island he visited every summer for twenty years. Memorial exhibition held at National Gallery of Scotland, 1942.

Bibl: Tom Hewlett, *Cadell: A Scottish Colourist,* Portland Gallery, London, 1988.

CADENHEAD, William   b.1934
Painter. Born Aberdeen, Scotland. Studied at Dundee College of Art, 1951-5 and Royal Academy Schools, 1957-61. 1969 elected member of the Society of Scottish

Artists. Solo exhibitions since 1958, most recently at the Scottish Gallery, Edinburgh, 1983. Works in Scottish Arts Council, Steel Company of Wales and with HM Queen Elizabeth the Queen Mother.

CAIN, Gordon   b.1947
Sculptor. Studied at Rochdale College of Art, 1964-6, and St. Martin's School of Art, 1966-9. 1979 solo exhibition at Cartwright Hall, Bradford. Works in mixed media, with cement, felt, sheet acrylic, paper, string, wood, steel, nylon cord, chalk and stone.

CAINE, Osmund   b.1914
Painter. Born Manchester, Lancashire. Studied at Birmingham College of Art and in Italy, as well as music at the Guildhall School of Music. Has exhibited at RA since 1946 as well as elsewhere in London and the provinces. Has executed many commissions for stained glass, mosaic, illustration and display. Interested in the Arthurian legend and other mysteries.

CAINS, Gerald A.   b.1932
Painter. Studied at Southern College of Art, Portsmouth. Exhibits at Royal West of England Academy and elsewhere.

CAIRNS, Cecilia   b.1944
Painter. Born Melbourne, Australia. Studied at Melbourne and La Trobe Universities. While in Australia won several awards for painting and exhibited in Melbourne and Canberra. 1976 came to London and held first solo exhibition at the Bookshop Gallery, Hampstead, 1979. Also exhibited at New South Wales House, 1979.

CAIRNS, Joyce   b.1947
Painter. Studied at Gray's School of Art, 1966-71, and RCA, 1971-4. Lives and works in Aberdeen. 1980 first solo exhibition held at Compass Gallery, Glasgow, and most recent at Third Eye Centre, Glasgow, 1987. A figurative artist, whose complex narrative paintings employ both flat and illusionistic space and make frequent allusions, through the use of naval imagery, to the threat of war. Work in Aberdeen Art Gallery, Scottish Arts Council and Aberdeen University. (Plate 17, p.43.)

CALDECOTT, Jon   b.1924
Painter. Self-taught. A hotelier by profession, he commenced sketching and painting during his army service in the war. Later he took up oil painting and exhibited at Woodstock Gallery, London, 1963.

CALDERON, William Frank   1865-1943
Painter. Studied at Slade School of Art under Legros. From 1881 exhibited at RA. 1894-1916 founder and Principal of the School of Animal Painting, Kensington.

CALLAM, Edward
Painter. Born Buckinghamshire. Studied art first under F.F. May and then with a group of artists from Goldsmiths' College. 1950 elected member of the Society of Industrial Artists. 1955 elected member of Royal Institute of Oil Painters. 1959 awarded life fellowship to International Institute of Arts and Letters. Has exhibited regularly, with a solo exhibition at Luton Museum and Art Gallery, 1969.

CALLAND, Ruth   b.1963
Painter. Born Scunthorpe, Humberside. Studied at Lanchester Polytechnic, Coventry, 1982-7 and at Chelsea School of Art, 1986-7. 1987 awarded the Boise Travelling Scholarship, and 1987-8 a Painting Fellowship at Cheltenham College of Art. Represented in 'New Contemporaries' at the ICA, London, 1986, followed by an exhibition at the Paton Gallery, London, 1987 with Stephen Barclay* and Paul Storey.*

CALLENDER, Robert   b.1932
Sculptor. Born Mottingham, Kent. Studied at South Shields Art School, 1948-9, Edinburgh University, 1951-4, and Edinburgh College of Art, 1954-9. Has received several awards, including a Scottish Arts Council Major Award. 1963 first solo exhibition held, and at Mercury Gallery, London, in 1986 he exhibited work concerned with man's involvement with sea, tides, weather, crafts and craftsmanship. President of SSA, 1969-73.

CALLON, Colin J.   b.1932
Painter. Born St. Helens, Lancashire. Self-taught. Has exhibited throughout the north west of England, his first solo show held in 1977 at the Memorial Art Gallery, Swinton. Painter of landscapes, portraits and animals.

CALOW, Jane   b.1953
Painter. Born Tynemouth, Tyne and Wear. Studied at Stourbridge College of Art, Worcestershire, 1971-4. 1977 firt solo exhibition held at Hereford City Art Gallery, most recent at William Morris Gallery, London, 1984. Has concentrated on agricultural workers and on unemployment.

CAMERON, Sir David Young   1865-1945
Painter. Born Glasgow, Scotland. Trained at evening classes at the Glasgow School of Art and then entered the Royal Institution, Edinburgh, 1885. 1892 and 1893 he exhibited at the NEAC and became one of Britain's most prolific etchers and possibly its most famous. His paintings of Scottish landscapes use boldly simplified shapes and strong colour. Elected RE, 1895, RSA, 1918 and RA, 1920. Knighted 1924 and in 1933 appointed King's Painter and Limner in Scotland. Trustee of the Tate Gallery and an eloquent speaker.

Bibl: *Sir D.Y. Cameron: Centenary Exhibition*, Arts Council of Great Britain, 1965.

CAMERON, Eric   b.1936
Painter. Studied art at King's College, Newcastle, 1953-7 and History of Art at the Courtauld Institute, London, 1957-9. 1967 exhibited 'Process Paintings' at Queen Square Gallery, Leeds.

CAMERON, Gordon Stewart   b.1916
Painter. Born Aberdeen, Scotland. Studied at Gray's School of Art, Aberdeen, 1935-40. Represented in several public Scottish collections and elected RSA, 1971.

CAMM, Beatrice
Painter. Born London. Studied at Penzance School of Art, and Regional College of Art, Hull. 1951-60 travelled extensively, after which she studied at Hornsey College of Art. Solo exhibitions at Woodstock Gallery, London, 1968 and 1969.

CAMP, Jeffrey

JEFFERY CAMP, b.1923. 'Serenissima', 1986. 117in. x 78in. Nigel Greenwood Gallery, London.

CAMP, Jeffrey   b.1923
Painter. Born Oulton Broad, Suffolk. Studied at Lowestoft School of Art, Ipswich School of Art and Edinburgh College of Art, 1941-4. 1955 painted altarpiece for St. Alban's Church, Norwich. 1961 became member of the London Group. 1963 married Laetitia Yhap.* Since 1947 numerous solo exhibitions held at Beaux Art Gallery, London and elsewhere. Often shapes his canvas according to the demands of his figurative subjects.

Bibl: Jeffrey Camp, *Draw: How to Master the Art*, André Deutsch, 1981, reprinted 1988; *Jeffrey Camp: Paintings 1949-1988*, Royal Albert Memorial Museum, Exeter, 1988.

CAMPBELL-GRAY, Iona   b.1962
Painter. Born London. Studied at St. Martin's School of Art, 1981-2, Winchester School of Art, 1982-5 and Chelsea School of Art, 1985-6. Abstract artist, who employs musical connotations.

CAMP, Sokari Douglas   b.1958
Sculptor. Born Nigeria. Studied at California College of Arts and Crafts, Central School of Art and RCA. 1982 first solo exhibition held at Africa Centre, London, and, most recently, at the Dorman Museum, Middlesborough, 1987. Her work draws upon the culture of the Kalahari people, but fuses African and Western experience, using a variety of materials with great ingenuity and wit to create images concerned with belief and ritual.

Bibl: *Alali — Festival Time: Sokari Douglas Camp*, introduction by Stephanie Brown, Dorman Museum, Middlesborough, 1987.

CAMPBELL, Alex   b.1932
Painter. Born Edinburgh, Scotland. Studied at Edinburgh College of Art and Edinburgh University, 1951-7. Solo exhibitions since 1966. Exhibited at Mercury Gallery, Edinburgh, 1983. Work in Scottish Arts Council and other public and private collections.

CAMPBELL, Christopher   b.1908
Painter. Born Clontarf, Ireland. Studied at National College of Art, Dublin and first exhibited at RHA in 1929, and continued until 1945. 1947 became an art teacher at Kilkenny Technical Schools for four years. Also worked for a period in the Harry Clarke Stained Glass Studios.

CAMPBELL, Clifton
Painter. Born Jamaica, West Indies. Studied at St. Martin's School of Art, and became a designer, for theatre and television, working for the Royal Opera House, Covent Garden, and the National Theatre Old Vic. 1967 held solo exhibition at University of Birmingham and at Woodstock Gallery, London, 1968.

CAMPBELL, George   b.1917
Painter. Born Arklow, Ireland and educated in Belfast and Dublin. Is descended from a family of artists and has held exhibitions in Dublin, Belfast, New York, Boston, London, Gibraltar and Cape Town. Work in many public collections, including Dublin Municipal Gallery of Modern Art and Leicestershire Educational Committee.

CAMPBELL, Henry
Painter. Studied at Alexandria College of Art. Served in RAF before and during the war and studied cubists and surrealists while a prisoner of war. Continued painting for two years after the war in a French Trappist monastery. Returned to England to study at St. Mary's College, Twickenham, and to teach. Solo exhibitions at Woodstock Gallery, London, 1966 and 1967.

CAMPBELL, Peter   b.1931
Painter. Born London. Studied graphic design at the London School of Printing and Graphic Arts and painting and drawing as a part-time student at Goldsmiths' College. 1965 began working as a full-time artist and has exhibited regularly in group and solo exhibitions, including a solo show at Christchurch Mansion, Ipswich, 1986.

CAMPBELL, Scott   b.1924
Relief artist. Studied at King's College, University of Durham, 1948-53. Worked for the North-East Regional Office of the Arts Council, 1953-5, moving to the Department of Fine Art, King's College, Newcastle upon Tyne. Exhibited 'Reliefs and constructions' at Drian Gallery, London, 1960.

CAMPBELL, Steven   b.1953
Painter. Born Glasgow, Scotland. 1970-7 worked as steel works maintenance engineer. Studied at Glasgow School

of Art, 1978-82 and won various awards and medals. Since 1983 solo exhibitions held in New York, Glasgow, Chicago, London, Munich and elsewhere. Paints large narrative pictures in which tweed-clad figures, partly inspired by P.G. Wodehouse's stories, perform strange rituals in a surreal world. (Plate 27, p.95.)

Bibl: *Steven Campbell: Recent Paintings,* Marlborough Fine Art, 1987.

CAMPION, Oliver   b.1928
Painter. Studied at Central School of Art and the Slade. 1968 and 1971 solo exhibitions at the Mayor Gallery, London, and at the New Grafton Gallery, 1975, 1981 and 1987. Work has been purchased by Leicester Education Committee, *Financial Times,* University College, London and Magdalen College, Oxford. A bold colourist and francophile.

CAMPION, Sidney   b.1891
Sculptor and painter. Born Leicester. Worked as a journalist, studying law in his spare time, and was called to the Bar in 1930. 1940 became Chief Press and Broadcast Officer at GPO Headquarters where he remained until his retirement in 1957. Attended various evening and part-time art courses, producing painting and sculpture in his spare time. Solo exhibition at Tower Gallery, Christchurch, Greyfriars, 1964.

CAMRASS, David   b.1939
Sculptor. Born London. Lived in Israel and served in Israeli Army, 1957-9. 1962 moved to Glasgow to work with Benno Schotz.* Exhibited with RSA and at Royal Glasgow Institute of Fine Arts.

CANNEY, Michael   b.1923
Constructivist. Born Falmouth, Cornwall. Studied at Redruth and Penzance Schools of Art and at the St. Ives School of Painting. 1942-7 served as a draughtsman in Royal Engineers. 1947-51 studied at Goldsmiths' School of Art. 1950-2 incapacitated with tuberculosis and convalesced in Cornwall. Influenced, variously, by Christopher Wood,* Peter Lanyon,* abstract expressionists and the constructivist tradition. Exhibits widely.

Bibl: *Michael Canney: Recent Works,* Newlyn Orion Gallery, 1983.

CANT, James   1911-1982
Painter. Born Melbourne, Australia. Studied at art schools in Sydney, in Paris and London at Central School of Arts and Crafts. 1935 began exhibiting at Mayor Gallery and was invited to become a member of the British Surrealist Group. Member of AIA. Returned to Australia at outbreak of Second World War, and remained there, painting, lecturing and making murals until his death.

Bibl: *James Cant 1911-1982: Retrospective,* Ron Radford, 1984.

CANZIANI, Estella Louisa Michaela   1887-1964
Painter. Born London. Studied at Cape and Nichol School in South Kensington and at Royal Academy Schools. Exhibited at RA and elsewhere. Member of the Society of Mural Decorators and Painters in Tempera. Wrote and illustrated *Costumes, Traditions and Songs of Savoy,* 1911, *Piedmont,* 1913 and *Roundabout Three Palace Green,* 1939.

HILDA CARLINE, 1889-1950. *'Self Portrait',* 1923. 24½ in. x 22¾ in. The Tate Gallery.

CARDER, Malcolm   b.1936
Constructivist sculptor. Studied at Kingston College of Art, 1955-9. 1967 commissioned to exhibit in British Pavilion Expo '67, Montreal. 1968 first solo exhibition held at Axiom Gallery, London. Work in Arts Council Collection, Tate Gallery and elsewhere.

CAREW, Keggie   b.1957
Painter. Born Gibraltar. Self-taught. Spent two years travelling in North, Central and South America where she studied Mayan, Incan and indigenous art forms. Returned to London and worked in publishing, also wrote and illustrated children's stories for television. 1981 began to paint full-time. Solo exhibitions at Cibeal Cincise, Co. Kerry, 1984, and Gessnerallee, Zurich, 1985.

CARLINE, George   1855-1920
Painter. Born Lincoln. Studied at Heatherley's in London, also in Antwerp and Paris. From 1886 exhibited at the RA and elsewhere. 1896 solo exhibition at Dowdeswell Galleries, London. Illustrated Andrew Lang's *Oxford,* published 1915. Father of Hilda,* Richard,* and Sydney Carline.*

CARLINE, Hilda   1889-1950
Painter. Born London. Studied in Paris and at the Slade. Both her brothers, Sydney* and Richard* Carline, were accomplished artists and through them she met Stanley Spencer,* whom she married in 1925. Despite her definite

SYDNEY CARLINE, 1888-1929. *'The destruction of an Austrian machine in the Gorge of the Brenta Valley, Italy'*, 1918. 30in. x 36in.
Imperial War Museum.

opinions about art, her painting was to some extent
influenced by Spencer's, from whom she was eventually
divorced. Represented in the Tate Gallery and Hove
Museum of Art.

CARLINE, Nancy   b.1909
Painter. Born London (née Higgins). Studied at Slade,
under Professor Tonks* and Allan Gwynne-Jones.*
1933-5 worked at Sadlers Wells Ballet, afterwards
attending Vladimir Polunin's class for stage design.
Towards the end of the 1930s resumed painting and briefly
attended the Euston Road School. Married Richard
Carline* and lived in Hampstead until 1982 when she
moved to Oxford where she now lives. Has exhibited
frequently with the London Group, the Artists International Association, the NEAC, and the RA.

Bibl: *Nancy Carline,* introduction by Richard Morphet, Camden
Arts Centre, London, 1985.

CARLINE, Richard   1896-1980
Painter. Son of the painter George Carline;* his brother
Sydney* and his sister Hilda* were also painters. Studied
at Percyval Tudor-Hart's Académie de Peinture, Paris

and London, 1913. 1916 joined Middlesex Regiment, then
the Royal Flying Corps in 1917, painting camouflage on to
aeroplanes. 1918 Official War Artist, posted to Middle
East in January 1919 and executed aerial views of the war
zones. First exhibition, shared with his brother Sydney at
the Goupil Gallery, 1920, showed paintings and drawings
of the Middle East. 1920 elected to the London Group.
1921-4 studied part-time at the Slade School under
Tonks.* 1924-9 taught intermittently at the Ruskin
School, Oxford. 1931 first one-person show at the Goupil
Gallery. 1935 he wrote the main text in *Arts of West Africa,*
edited by Michael Sadler, and organised an exhibition of
Negro Art for the Adams Gallery. 1937-8 on behalf of the
AIA spent nearly a year in USA and Mexico, investigating
art projects. 1938 founder member of the Artists' Refugee
Committee, Hampstead. 1938-43 designed camouflage for
factories and aeroplanes under the aegis of the Air
Ministry. 1944 helped found the Hampstead Artists'
Council. 1946-7 First Art Counsellor of UNESCO. 1951-3
Chairman of the AIA. 1956 elected Vice Chairman of the
UK National Committee of the International Association
of Artists. 1957 and 1963 selected and accompanied two
exhibitions of British Art for China as part of Britain-

China Friendship Association. 1968 published *Draw they Must*, a history of art teaching and examining. 1978 published *Stanley Spencer at War*. Represented in the Tate Gallery and the Imperial War Museum.

CARLINE, Sydney   1888-1929
Painter. Born London. Studied at Slade School of Art, and in Paris, 1912-13. 1914 painted in Westmorland. Joined the army and trained as a dispatch rider before becoming a pilot in the Royal Flying Corps, 1916. 1918 became a war artist and tried to represent war as seen from the air, completing seven large oils on this subject. 1922 appointed Ruskin Master of Drawing at Oxford. Exhibited with the School of Art London Group, became a member, 1924. Died of pneumonia after a visit to John Nash* on a frosty evening.

CARLISLE, Fionna   b.1954
Painter. Born Wick, Scotland. Studied at Edinburgh College of Art, 1972-6. 1982 awarded Scottish Arts Council Bursary. Solo exhibitions at 369 Gallery, Edinburgh, in 1978, 1979, 1980, 1981, 1982, 1986. Known primarily for her paintings of women, but has also painted jugglers, sailors and fishermen. Has lived in Crete since 1984.

CARLO, Michael   b.1945
Printmaker. Born Suffolk. Studied at Colchester School of Art and RCA. Has exhibited widely, including solo exhibitions at the Portland Gallery, Manchester, the Pottergate Gallery, Norwich, and Amalgam, London, 1974. Chiefly concerned with interpretations of the Suffolk landscape, his work is in the collections of London Transport, the Bank of America, British Home Stores and elsewhere.

CARLSON, Ronald   b.1936
Painter. Born Newport, South Wales. Studied at Newport College of Art, 1952-6, and at the RCA, 1956-9, where he won a two year travelling scholarship. Held solo exhibitions in the early 1960s at the Howard Roberts Gallery, Cardiff, and at Keele University. Since then he has exhibited in numerous group shows and is represented in the Welsh Arts Council collection.

CARNEGIE, Andrew   b.1950
Painter. Born London. Studied at Byam Shaw School of Painting and Drawing, 1968-71, and Royal Academy Schools, 1971-4. 1970 began exhibiting and has won various awards and prizes. Solo exhibitions at The Gallery at Upstream, London, 1977.

CARO, Anthony   b.1924
Sculptor. Born London. Studied engineering at Christ's College, Cambridge, before turning to sculpture. Trained at Regent Street Polytechnic, 1946-7 and Royal Academy Schools, 1947-50. 1951 assistant to Henry Moore.* 1952 began teaching sculpture at St. Martin's School of Art. 1956 first solo exhibition held at Gallerie der Naviglio, Milan. 1959 met Clement Greenberg and visited USA, and the following year made his first abstract steel sculpture. 1963 taught at Birmingham College, Vermont, and again in 1965. Also taught at St. Martin's School of Art and since the '60s has been a leading figure in British sculpture, with an international reputation and numerous exhibitions at home and abroad. 1969 awarded CBE; knighted 1987.

Bibl: Diane Waldman, *Anthony Caro*, Phaidon, Oxford, 1982.

ANTHONY CARO, b.1924. *'Descent from the Cross (after Rembrandt)'*, 1988-9. Steel rusted and waxed. 90in. x 72in. x 69in. Annely Juda Fine Art.

CARPANINI, David   b.1946
Painter and etcher. Studied at Gloucestershire College of Art, RCA and University of Reading. Exhibits at RA, Royal West of England Academy, the RBA and elsewhere. His subject matter is the industrial scene of South Wales, a landscape composed of bleak hills, terraced houses and groups of figures.

CARPANINI, Jane   b.1949
Painter. Born Bedfordshire. Studied at Luton College of Technology, Brighton Polytechnic and University of Reading. Exhibits at RA, Royal West of England and the RBA. Has work in National Library of Wales, Aberystwyth. Elected member of the RBA and associate of RWS.

CARPENTER, John   b.1921
Painter. Born Falmouth, Cornwall. Studied at Falmouth School of Art. His training was interrupted by the war, after which he tried to find expression as an actor, but eventually returned to painting, studying at Dartington Hall Art Centre and the Bath Academy of Art. Exhibits at Royal West of England Academy, the Royal Institute Galleries and with the St. Ives Group.

JOANNA CARRINGTON, b.1931. *'Interior with books'*, 1988. Oil on board. 28in. x 28in. Sue Rankin Gallery.

CARPREAU, Henri   b.1923
Painter. Born in Java of Dutch and French extraction. Educated in The Hague and trained as a teacher of English. Studied at Bournemouth College of Art. During the Second World War he was interned as a hostage and did drawings of camp life. 1951 he came to England and trained as an art teacher at Bournemouth College of Art. Since 1968 has been a full-time artist, abandoning his romantic style in 1970 for a more analytical approach. Solo exhibition at Drian Galleries, 1981.

CARR, David   1915-1968
Painter. Born Petersham, Surrey. Studied at Byam Shaw School of Art and at Benton End Art School under Cedric Morris* and Lett Haines.* In the 1950s he established a friendship with the painters Robert Colquhoun* and Robert MacBryde.* Became fascinated by the relationship between men and machinery. In 1967 a visit to America made a great impression and the drawings he made on his return home were posthumously exhibited by Berth and Schaeffer in New York, 1969. Founder-member of Norfolk Contemporary Art Society.

Bibl: Bryan Robertson and Ronald Alley, *David Carr: The Discovery of an Artist,* Quartet Books, London, 1987.

CARR, David   b.1944
Painter. Born Middlesborough, Cleveland. Studied at Slade School of Fine Art, 1962-6. Exhibited at RA and London Group. 1972 first solo exhibition held at Stanhope

Institute Gallery. Works in the possession of the Greater London Council and elsewhere. Teaches at the Camden Arts Centre.

CARR, Henry   1894-1970
Painter. Born Leeds, Yorkshire. Studied at Leeds College of Art and RCA. Served in the Royal Field Artillery during the First World War and during the Second World War was a war artist in North Africa and Italy. Later taught at Beckenham Art School for seventeen years, becoming Head of the School. Exhibited at RA and in many London and provincial galleries. 1956 won a Gold Medal in the Paris Salon. Commissioned to paint many portraits and wrote books on portrait painting and drawing.

CARR, Tom   b.1909
Painter. Born Belfast, Northern Ireland. Studied at Slade School of Fine Art. 1935 exhibited with the Objective Abstractionists at the Zwemmer Gallery. 1937 shared an exhibition at the Storran Gallery with Victor Pasmore* and Claude Rogers.* 1940 first solo exhibition held at Wildenstein Galley; regular shows followed, at the Leicester Galleries, Redfern and elsewhere. Widely regarded as the most distinguished living Irish water-colour painter. Work in Tate Gallery, Whitworth Art Gallery, with HM the Queen Mother and other leading public and private collections.

Bibl: *Tom Carr: Retrospective,* Ulster Museum, Belfast, 1983.

CARRICK, Alexander   1882-1966
Sculptor. Born Musselburgh, Scotland. Trained as a stonecarver in the studio of Birnie Rhind in Edinburgh. Studied at Edinburgh College of Art and RCA. Began teaching at Edinburgh College of Art, 1914, and returned there after military service, 1916-18. Worked closely with architects, and in the 1920s executed several war memorials. Continued to execute major commissions, and as head of sculpture at Edinburgh College of Art, 1928-c.1942, inspired a generation of Scottish sculptors. Exhibited at the RSA, GI and RA.

CARRINGTON, Donald P.   b.1907
Painter. Born Durwood, near Wakefield, Yorkshire. Studied at Wakefield School of Art, 1924-6, and RCA, 1926-30. Exhibited at RA and widely in the provinces. From 1936 was Head of the School of Drawing and Painting at Leicester College of Art.

CARRINGTON, Dora   1893-1932
Painter. Trained at the Slade School of Art where she met John Nash,* who aroused her interest in wood engraving, and Mark Gertler,* whose powerful, almost symbolic portraits, influenced her own. Rejected Gertler as a lover in preference for the companionship of the homosexual essayist and biographer, Lytton Strachey, with whom she set up home, first at Tidmarsh Mill near Pangbourne, then at Ham Spray House in the village of Ham in Wiltshire. 1921 married Ralph Partridge, living with him and Strachey in a ménage à trois. Turned more to decorative work, emulating the example of Vanessa Bell* and Duncan Grant,* but adopted a more naïve style. Took her own life after Strachey's death.

Bibl: Noel Carrington, *Carrington: Paintings, Drawings and Decorations,* Polytechnic Press, Oxford, 1979.

CARRINGTON, Joanna   b.1931
Painter. Born Hampstead, London. At sixteen attended Cedric Morris's* school in Essex, afterwards studying in Fernand Léger's studio in Paris. Returned to England and studied at Central School of Arts and Crafts. Exhibits with the London Group and elsewhere. 1962 first solo exhibition held at The Establishment Gallery in Greek Street. Divides her time between Brittany and Hove, and exhibited at Sue Rankin Gallery, London, 1988.

CARRUTHERS, Derek   b.1935
Painter. Born Penrith, Cumbria. Studied art at King's College, Newcastle, and identified with Pasmore's* 'constructivist' teaching. Gradually became dissatisfied with the severe formality associated with the constructivists, and moved towards a more sensuous approach. 1983 visited India and was impressed by the Ajanta carvings. Has work in several public collections, including Bradford City Art Gallery and Abbot Hall Gallery, Kendal.

CARRUTHERS, Robert   b.1925
Sculptor. Studied at Cheltenham College of Art and RCA. 1953-4 awarded Royal College Major Travelling Scholarship and subsequently taught at RCA. 1958 awarded French Scholarship. 1970 solo exhibition at Museum of Modern Art, Oxford.

CARSON, Robert Taylor   b.1919
Painter. Born Belfast, Northern Ireland. Studied at Belfast College of Art, 1936-41. During the last years of the war he was seconded by the US Air Force as an unofficial war artist in Northern Ireland. Has shown extensively, at the RHA, RA and the Royal Ulster Academy. Represented in numerous public and private collections, including that of the King of Denmark.

CARSWELL, John   b.1931
Painter and constructivist. Born London. Studied at Wimbledon School of Art, 1948-50 and RCA, 1950-2. 1950 settled in the Near East and became an assistant professor at the American University of Beirut. Has exhibited with the Young Contemporaries, 1950-2, and the London Group. 1962 solo exhibition at Hanover Gallery, London.

CARTER, B.A.R.   b.1909
Painter. Born Kenilworth, Warwickshire. Initially studied modern languages at the Universities of Grenoble, Innsbruck and Cambridge, prior to taking up art. Studied at Central School of Arts and Crafts, 1932-4, and the Euston Road School, 1938-9. From 1948 exhibited at the London Group. 1945-8 taught at Camberwell School of Art, and later, at the Slade.

CARTER, Bernard   b.1920
Painter. Served in RAF during the war and studied painting at Goldsmiths' College of Art. After several years of art lecturing joined the staff of the National Maritime Museum, and became head of the picture department, 1970. Paints tranquil scenes in a semi-naïve style and exhibits regularly at Portal Gallery, London.

CARTER, Frederick   1885-1967
Painter-etcher. Born Bradford, Yorkshire. Studied in Paris, Antwerp and London, as well as etching under Frank Short.* Exhibited at RA and elsewhere and elected ARE, 1910. His artistic life before and after the First World War centred around the Fitzroy Street area of London, and the Dieppe restaurant in Dean Street. He became a mystic symbolist artist, involved with Aleister Crowley and worked on illustrations for D.H. Lawrence's *Apocalypse.*

CARTER, Howard   b.1938
Painter. Born Romford, Essex. Studied at South-East Essex School of Art, 1956-60, and RCA, 1960-3. Winner of various awards and scholarships and specialises in architectural paintings and drawings. Solo exhibition at Gadsby Gallery, London, 1974.

CARTER, John   b.1942
Constructionist. Born Middlesex. Studied at Twickenham School of Art, 1958-9, Kingston School of Art, 1959-63. During 1963-4 lived in Italy on a scholarship. 1966 worked as an assistant to Bryan Kneale* and in 1966-7 travelled in USA for three months on another scholarship. 1968 first solo exhibition held at Redfern Gallery, London, and recently has held solo exhibitions at Nicola Jacobs, London, 1980 and 1983. Has work in several public collections including the Arts Council and Oldham Art Gallery.

Bibl: *John Carter: paintings, drawings and structures 1965-83,* Warwick Arts Trust cat. 1983.

CARTER, Kenneth   b.1928
Sculptor. Born Yorkshire. Studied at Hull and Leicester Colleges of Art. Since the early 1960s has exhibited regularly in Britain, with solo exhibitions at the Ferens

CARTER, Stephen

TONY CARTER, b.1943. *'Miracle at Cana — on the turning of water into wine'* (detail), 1983-5. Mixed media.
Private Collection.

Art Gallery, Hull, Keele and Exeter Universities. In 1974 he completed a series of fifteen reliefs for Exeter Cathedral.

CARTER, Stephen   b.1949
Painter. Born Kingston upon Thames, Surrey. Studied at Canterbury College of Art, 1967-8, and Birmingham Polytechnic, 1968-72. Since 1970 has exhibited in various mixed shows and had a solo exhibition at Hetley Fine Art, London, 1982.

CARTER, Tony   b.1943
Conceptual sculptor. Born in the West Riding of Yorkshire. Studied at University of Newcastle upon Tyne, 1962-6, and University of Reading, 1966-8. 1975 held his first solo exhibition at Garage Ltd., London, and in 1983 had a solo exhibition at the Serpentine Gallery, London. Has work in Arts Council Collection and CAS.

Bibl: *Tony Carter: Images of subject/object duality 1968-82,* Arts Council, 1983.

CARTER, William   1863-1939
Painter of portraits, animals and still lifes. Born Swaffham, Norfolk, the son of Samuel John Carter, painter, and brother of Howard Carter, the Egyptologist who discovered the tomb of Tutankhamun. Studied at the RA Schools and then exhibited regularly at the RA from 1883. 1889-1908 showed at the Paris Salon. 1915 made RP. Work in the Tate Gallery collection.

CARTMEL, Hilary   b.1958
Sculptor. Born Wendover, Buckinghamshire. Trained at Exeter College of Art and Design, 1976-7 and Trent Polytechnic, 1977-80. 1982 artist in residence at Carlton Hayes Hospital, Leicestershire. 1982 first solo exhibition at Air Gallery. Her work, initially made out of rough-hewn sections of wood, crudely aligned, produced imagery of shells, hermit crabs and the figure, which explored a view of femininity contrary to received opinion.

CARTWRIGHT, Lucette
Sculptor. Born London, of French parents. Studied at Regent Street Polytechnic under Harold Brownsword.* Winner of a British Institute Scholarship and the Feodora Gleichen award. Influenced by Florentine art, her figurative sculpture is mostly life-size and concerned with dramatic action. Work by her was exhibited in Holland Park, London, 1970, and at the John Whibley Gallery, Cork Street, 1973.

CARTWRIGHT, Reg   b.1938
Painter. Born Leicester. Originally wanted to be a musician and served in the army as a bandsman. 1969 started painting in oils and in a naïve style, reminiscent of Henri Rousseau, captures the English countryside and village life. Since 1970 a regular exhibitor at the Portal Gallery, London.

CARVALHO, Bryan   b.1942
Painter. Studied at Chelsea School of Art, 1959-61, and Hornsey, 1967-70. 1969 first exhibited at the AIA Gallery and in 1970 was artist in residence at the University of Sussex. 1970 exhibited at Gardner Centre Gallery, University of Sussex.

CASSELDINE, Nigel   b.1947
Painter. Born London. Studied part-time at John Cass and Camberwell Schools of Art, 1967-72, while he worked as a studio assistant to F.V. Magrath. 1972 formed the Romeny Studio Workshop. 1985 elected Associate of the Royal West of England Academy. 1988 awarded the Brandler Painting Prize.

CASSON, Sir Hugh   b.1910
Architect and illustrator. Trained as an architect and has been in private practice since 1937. Likes the medium of watercolour. Has illustrated numerous books, including *The Old Man of Lochnagar,* with text by the Prince of Wales. President of the Royal Academy of Arts, 1976-84.

CASTLE, James   b.1946
Sculptor. Born Aberdeen, Scotland. Studied at Ealing School of Art, 1967-8 and Winchester School of Art, 1968-71. During 1971 travelled in Turkey, Greece and Italy on a scholarship. 1971-3 assistant to Brian Kneale.* First solo exhibition at Artspace Galleries, Aberdeen, and since then at Crawford Centre, St. Andrew's University, 1984 and Open Eye Gallery, Edinburgh, 1985. Has moved from abstract work to carved laminated wood sculpture with humorous, figurative content.

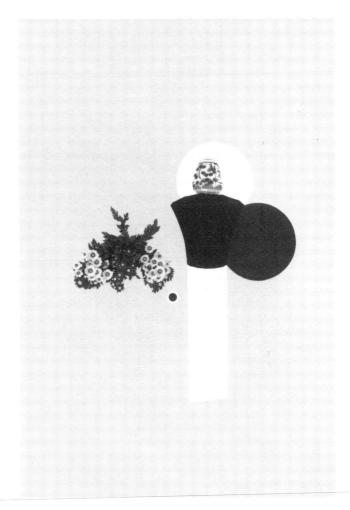

HILARY CARTMEL, b.1958. *'Katherine (in languid pose)'*, 1987. Steel. 36in. high. Private Collection.

PATRICK CAULFIELD, b.1936. *'Reception'*, 1988. 120in. x 81in. Acrylic on canvas. The artist, courtesy Waddington Galleries.

CASTLE, Philip   b.1929
Naïve painter. Self-taught. Began painting whilst studying physics at Dublin University. Became a full-time painter, spending much time in the Mediterranean, painting hill villages, ports and fortified towns. Regular exhibitor at the Portal Gallery, London.

CATLING, Brian   b.1948
Sculptor. Born London. Studied at NE London Polytechnic, 1968-71 and under Bernard Meadows* at RCA, 1971-4. 1977 first solo exhibition held at Air Gallery, also at South Hill Park Gallery, 1984. His sculpture is directed by a metaphysical approach to physical materials and by a fascination with enigmatic presence and emotive associations.

Bibl: *Brian Catling,* Norwich School of Art, 1984.

CATLING, Darrel
Painter. Born London. Works as a film director, painter and writer. Mixes oils with papier collé, painting in two styles, figurative and neo-abstract. 1966 exhibited at the John Whibley Gallery, and also in a solo exhibition, 1967.

CATTRELL, Louise   b.1957
Painter. Studied at Dundee College of Art, 1975-80, and at RCA, 1980-3. 1980 awarded the Duncan of Drumfork Scholarship and the Farquhar Reid Scholarship, and the John Minton Award from the RCA, 1983. First solo exhibition at the Peterborough City Art Gallery, 1985.

CAUGHLIN, Ian   b.1948
Painter. Born Lancaster, Lancashire. Studied at St. Martin's School of Art, 1966-71. Lived and worked in Italy, 1973-5. 1979 first solo exhibition at House Gallery, London. 1981 first artist in the Riverside Studios placement. 1981 won Elephant Trust award. Work in Arts Council and Government Art Collections. Has also done paintings for hospitals.

CAULFIELD, Patrick   b.1936
Painter. Born London. Studied at Chelsea School of Art, 1956-60, and RCA, 1960-3 where he became one of the third generation of Pop artists. Began working with a deliberately anonymous style, using an even, uninflected black outline and flat colour, to bring out the irony in his

CAUSER, William Sydney

presentation of cliché subjects. Taught at Chelsea School of Art, 1963-71. Also makes prints and won the *Prix des Jeunes Artistes* for graphics at the 4th Biennale des Jeunes in Paris, 1965. A retrospective was held in Liverpool and at the Tate Gallery, 1981.

Bibl: *Patrick Caulfield. Painting 1963-81,* London, Tate Gallery/Liverpool, Walker Art Gallery, 1981.

CAUSER, William Sydney 1876-1958
Painter. Born Wolverhampton, West Midlands. Studied at Wolverhampton School of Art, also in London and Italy. Exhibited at RA, RSA, NEAC and elsewhere. Held solo exhibitions at the Leger Gallery and the Fine Art Society, both in London. Painted in Spain immediately prior to the Spanish Civil War and was forced to leave the country in haste. Represented in several public collections.

CAWTHRA, Hermon b.1886
Sculptor. Trained at Salts Art School, Shipley, Yorkshire, 1904, and Leeds School of Art, 1907-9, RCA, 1909-11 and RA Schools, 1912-16. Principal works include: Burns Statue, Dumfries; figures at Leeds Civic Hall; Manchester Town Hall extension and bust of King George V, Mombasa. Head of the Sculpture School at Bournemouth Municipal College. 1937 elected FRBS.

CEBERTOWICZ, Janina b.1953
Painter. Studied at Manchester Polytechnic, 1971-2, Bath Academy of Art, 1972-5, and Manchester Polytechnic, 1977-8. 1983 first solo exhibition at Bede Gallery, Jarrow. Paints Greece, Rossendale, and her family.

CECIL, Rose b.1956
Painter. Studied at Byam Shaw School of Art and City and Guilds of London Art School. Travelled widely then worked for Afghan Aid for two years. 1984 exhibited at Fermor Antiques, London, and in 1985 visited Rotherhithe and began making a record of Docklands 'pre-dinky, pre-yuppy'; these paintings were exhibited at Michael Parkin Gallery, London, 1988.

CHADWICK, Helen b.1953
Sculptor and mixed media artist. Studied at Brighton Polytechnic and Chelsea School of Art, 1973-7. Lives and works in East End of London. Most recent exhibitions include: 'Of Mutability', ICA, 1986; 'Staging The Self', NPG, 1986; 'The Mirror and the Lamp', Fruitmarket Gallery, Edinburgh, 1986; 'Allegory of Misrule', Kunstverean Freeburg, South Germany and elsewhere, 1987. 1987 short-listed for the Turner Prize. Uses the photocopying machine, the computer and the microscope to generate works about sensuality, desire and fleshly decay.

Bibl: 'Allegory of Misrule', Birmingham City Museum of Art Gallery, 1987; Helen Chadwick, *Enfleshings,* with an essay by Marina Warner, Secker & Warburg, London, 1989.

CHADWICK, Lynn b.1914
Sculptor. Born London. Trained and worked as an architectural draughtsman. In the 1940s started to make metal mobiles. 1951 commissioned to make three works for the Festival of Britain exhibition on the South Bank. 1953 awarded a national prize in the Unknown Political Prisoner Sculpture competition; 1956 awarded the International Sculpture Prize at the Venice Biennale. 1959 won First Prize at the Concorso Internazionale del Bronzetto in Padua. March 1986 exhibition held at the Marlborough

HELEN CHADWICK, b.1953. *'Ego geometria sum',* 1983-4. Installation at Riverside Studios, London.

Gallery, New York. Represented in most major collections worldwide.

CHADWICK, Oliver b.1942
Painter. Entered a commercial art studio on leaving school but abandoned it to become a salesman of antique silver. His paintings contain references to his interest in anthropology and primitive religion. Solo exhibitions at Woodstock Gallery, London, 1964 and 1965.

CHAIMOWICZ, Marc Camille b.1945
Mixed media artist. Born Paris and moved to England as a child. Studied at Ealing, Camberwell and Slade Schools of Art. 1972 first solo exhibition held at Gallery House, and has exhibited or presented performances at galleries in London and abroad regularly since. 1976-8 wrote a column on performance for *Studio International.* Represented by Nigel Greenwood. Performances of 'Doubts' and 'Partial Eclipse' given since 1979 in America and Europe.

CHATLOW, Michael b.1944
Painter. Born Herefordshire. 1961 worked as an illustrator. Studied at Hammersmith College of Art, 1967, and Central School of Art, 1967-70. 1971-3 Commonwealth Painting Scholarship in India. 1973 first solo exhibition held in Baroda, India, and his most recent at Christopher Hull Gallery, London, 1984.

CHALK, Martyn b.1945
Relief artist. Born Trowbridge, Wiltshire. Studied at Portsmouth College of Art. 1972 held first solo exhibition, and at Juda Rowan Gallery, London, 1984 and 1987. Has also made eight reconstructions of Tatlin reliefs, which have been widely exhibited.

LYNN CHADWICK, b.1914. *'Couple on seat'*. Bronze, edition of 6. Male: 89in. x 93¾in. x 44in. Female: 96in. x 78¾in. x 55in. Marlborough Fine Art (London) Ltd.

CHALKER, Jack Bridger   b.1918
Painter. Studied at Goldsmiths' College, 1936-9 and RCA where his studies were interrupted by war. 1939-45 saw war service with the Royal Field Artillery, then was attached to the Australian Army as a war artist. 1949 became Director of Art at Cheltenham Ladies' College. 1958 appointed principal of the West of England College of Art; later became lecturer in art and design at Bristol University. Exhibited at the RBA, with the Royal Society of Portrait Painters, the NEAC and elsewhere.

CHALKLEY, Brian   b.1948
Painter. Studied at Chelsea School of Art, 1970-3 and the Slade, 1973-5. Following his six month placement as Artist in Industry with the British Steel Corporation, Teesside, 1983-4, he had a number of solo shows in the north east and at Howard Gardens Gallery, Cardiff, 1985. Solo exhibition at Creaser Gallery, London, 1990.

CHALLENGER, Michael   b.1942
Painter, sculptor and printmaker. Studied at Goldsmiths' College of Art, 1960-4, and Slade School of Art, 1964-6. Has

exhibited widely, at home and abroad, including a solo exhibition at London Arts Gallery, 1972. Work in many public art collections, including Bradford City Art Gallery and Boston Museum of Fine Arts.

CHAMBERLAIN, Brenda   1912-1971
Painter, poet and writer. Born Bangor, Wales. Studied at RA Schools, 1931-6. 1936-45 lived near Bethesda, Snowdonia and with her husband, John Petts, and Alan Lewis, published the *Caseg Broadsheets,* poems and engravings. 1946-62 lived and worked on Bardsey Island, Gwynedd. Awarded two gold medals at the Royal National Eisteddfod, in 1951 and 1953, and was given two touring exhibitions by Welsh Arts Council. In London exhibited at Gimpel Fils, 1950-5, and at the Zwemmer Gallery in 1962. 1962-7 lived on the Aegean island of Hydra. Worked with the dancer, Robertos Saragas, and the musician, Halim el Dabh. (Her visual imagery is discussed by Maurice Cooke in the *Anglo-Welsh Review,* Vol.20, No.46, Spring 1972.)

Bibl: *Brenda Chamberlain,* Mostyn Art Gallery, Llandudno, 1988.

CHAMBERLAIN, Christopher

CHAMBERLAIN, Christopher   b.1918
Painter. Born Worthing, Sussex. Studied at Clapham School of Art, 1934-8, the RCA, 1938-9 and 1946-8. From 1951 exhibited at the RA. 1953 first solo exhibition at the Trafford Gallery. Taught painting at Camberwell School of Art and Bromley College of Art. Likes to paint the area that is familiar to him. Work in the Tate Gallery collection.

CHAMBERLAIN, Maurice   b.1934
Painter. Born Doncaster, Yorkshire. Studied at Doncaster College of Art, 1949-51 and RCA, 1955-8. 1964 had first solo exhibition and most recently at the Manor House Art Gallery, Ilkley, 1986. Work in various public collections in Yorkshire, including Cartwright Hall, Bradford.

CHAMBERLAIN, Trevor   b.1933
Painter. Born Hertford, Hertfordshire. Self-taught. Before taking up painting professionally in 1964 he worked as an architectural assistant in the Royal Engineers. 1976 won Lord Mayor of London's Art Award. President of Chelsea Art Society and member of Royal Institute of Oil Painters, Royal Society of Marine Artists and National Society of Painters, Sculptors and Printmakers. Exhibits at RA and elsewhere.

CHAMBERLAIN, Walter   b.1936
Painter and printmaker. Born Bolton, Lancashire. Studied at Bolton College of Art, 1949-56 and RCA, 1958-61. 1964 exhibited at Ferens Art Gallery, Hull, with two others and regularly since then in galleries in the north, including a solo exhibition at Ferens, 1984.

CHAMBERS, Stephen   b.1960
Painter. Born London. Studied at Winchester School of Art, 1978-9, St. Martin's School of Art, 1979-82 and Chelsea School of Art, 1982-3. 1983-4 awarded Rome Scholarship. 1985 Artist-in-Residence at Portsmouth Polytechnic. 1985-7 Painting Fellow at Winchester School of Art. 1987 first solo show, 'Strange Smoke' at the Winchester Gallery; recent one at Flowers East Gallery, 1989. Work in the Arts Council collection.

CHAMPION, Andrew   b.1966
Mixed media artist. Studied at Epsom School of Art, 1983-5 and at Camberwell. Exhibited at John Moores, 1987.

CHANDA, Alec   b.1962
Painter. Studied at Richmond College, Twickenham, 1978-9, and at Camberwell School of Arts and Crafts, 1979-83. 1983-5 travelled to Indonesia, Australia and India. Since 1985 she has regularly painted in Italy. 1985 first exhibited in the Whitechapel Open, London.

CHANDLER, Eileen   b.1904
Painter. Born London. Studied at Hornsey and RA Schools. 1930 married Roland M. Chandler, illustrator to the *Strand Magazine*. After 1946 spent many years painting abroad, painting landscapes and portraits, including one of Queen Sylvia of Sweden. Solo exhibition at Guy Morrison, London, 1988.

CHANTREY, Melvyn   b.1945
Painter. Born Hyde, Cheshire. Studied at Manchester College of Art and Design. Lives and works in Manchester. Solo exhibitions at Bluecoat Gallery, Liverpool, in 1976 and 1978 and at Bletchley Leisure Centre, Milton Keynes,

1980. Work by him belongs to Manchester and Liverpool Universities.

CHAPLIN, Bob   b.1947
Printmaker and photographer. Solo exhibitions since 1970 (University of East Anglia), including one at Riverside Studios, Hammersmith, 1979. Prizewinner at the 4th and 5th British International Print Biennales, 1974 and 1976. Work in the Arts Council, British Council and Tate Gallery collections.

CHAPLIN, Stephen   b.1934
Painter. Born London. Studied at Slade and Courtauld Institute, 1952-8. Since 1966 Lecturer in History of Art at Leeds University. Solo exhibitions at University Gallery, Leeds, 1970, Hatton Gallery, Newcastle, 1972, and also at Park Square Gallery, Leeds, 1972.

CHAPMAN, Anthea
Painter. Born Sussex. Studied at Brighton College of Art. 1962 first solo exhibition at The Comedy Gallery, London. Also exhibits at RA and in schools. Works in the Nuffield Scheme for Pictures in Hospitals and Stoke-on-Trent Art Gallery.

CHAPMAN, Bobbie   b.1947
Printmaker. Born Northamptonshire. Studied at Northampton School of Art, 1963-5, Ravensbourne College of Art and Design, 1965-8 and RCA, 1968-71. Has been filmed in his workshop for an Anglia Television documentary, *Arts for everyone*. 1972 first solo exhibition at Nottingham Adult Education Centre. Has work in North London Polytechnic and Scunthorpe Museum and Art Gallery.

CHAPMAN, George   b.1908
Painter. Born London. Studied at Gravesend, Slade and RCA. Abandoned various realist and abstract styles, when he discovered the mining valleys of South Wales which transformed his vision and his purpose. In 1960-1 a BBC *Monitor* film was made about him and his work. 1956 first solo exhibition at Piccadilly Gallery, London. Work in many public collections, including V & A and Whitworth Art Gallery, Manchester.

CHAPMAN, Max   b.1911
Painter. Born Dulwich, London. Studied at Byam Shaw Art School, 1927-30. 1931 won travelling scholarship to Italy. 1939 first solo exhibition at Storran Gallery, London, then at Leger Gallery, Molton Gallery and elsewhere. Also writes art criticism, for *Arts Review* and other publications.

CHAPMAN, Richard   b.1951
Draughtsman. Born Epping, Essex. Trained as a graphic designer, 1967-70. Studied at Lanchester Polytechnic, 1971-5 and the City University, 1976-7. 1975 first exhibited in a group exhibition at the Serpentine. 1981 solo exhibition at The Hexagon, Reading.

CHAPMAN, Robert   b.1933
Painter. Primarily self-taught, though has studied tempera and fresco under Annigoni. Since 1970 has exhibited in London (Foyles Gallery) and elsewhere. 1972 first solo London exhibition held at Woodstock Gallery. On 14 October 1975 he delivered the manifesto, 'The

Indictment of "Abstract" Influence in Art this Century and its effect upon the People' at University College of Swansea.

CHARALAMBOU, Sotikaris   b.1947
Painter. Born England. Studied at St. Martin's School of Art, 1971-5. Included in 'Critic's Space 4' at Air Gallery, London, 1987.

CHARLTON, Alan   b.1948
Painter. Born Sheffield, Yorkshire. Since 1979 solo exhibitions in Dusseldorf, Amsterdam, Eindhoven, London, Paris, Edinburgh, Zurich and Brussels. Included in several major mixed shows including 'The New Spirit in Painting' at RA, London, 1981 and 'Documenta 7', Kassel, 1982. Has specialised in abstracts painted in differing shades of grey.

CHARLTON, Evan   1904-1984
Painter. Born London. Studied at University College, London, 1923-7, and at Slade, 1930-3. 1935-8 taught at West of England College of Art. 1938-45 Head of Cardiff School of Art. 1939-44 war artist. 1945-66 HM Inspector (Art) for Wales. After retirement he continued as a full-time painter, exhibiting widely at RWEA, NEAC and elsewhere. Represented in the National Museum of Wales and Welsh Arts Council.

CHARLTON, Felicity   b.1913
Painter. Born Bristol, Avon. Studied at West of England College of Art, 1932-7. Exhibits with RWEA, the South of Wales Group, the Royal National Eisteddfod of Wales and with Welsh Arts Council. Examples of her work are in the National Museum of Wales and Welsh Arts Council.

CHARLTON, George   b.1899
Landscape painter and illustrator. Born London. Studied at the Slade School from 1914 and joined the staff there in 1919. From 1916 exhibited at the NEAC, 1926 became member and 1958 Treasurer. 1924 first solo exhibition at the Redfern Gallery. From 1931 Examiner in Art for the University of London school examinations. 1949-59 taught at Willesden School of Art. Works in the Tate Gallery collection.

CHARLTON, Mervyn   b.1945
Painter. Born Woodford, Essex. Studied at Loughton College of Further Education, 1972-4 and Nottingham Art College, 1974-7. 1981 and 1982 solo exhibitions at Moira Kelly, London. Has work in Leicestershire Schools Collection and South Eastern Arts Collection.

CHARNLEY, Clare   b.1949
Painter. Born Leeds, Yorkshire. Studied at Leeds College of Art, 1968-71. 1976 first solo show at Leeds Playhouse, also at Air Gallery, London, 1980.

CHAROUX, Siegfried   1896-
Sculptor. Born Vienna, Austria, of French origin. Studied at the Vienna School of Arts and Crafts, and the Vienna Academy. Worked as a political cartoonist until 1933. Made monuments in Vienna during this time, to Lessing, Blum and Matteotti. 1935 came to England, and was naturalised, 1946. 1948 carved stone figures for the new School of Anatomy and Engineering Laboratory at Cambridge. Made memorial to Amy Johnson for her home town of Hull. 1949 ARA, 1956 RA. 1958 solo exhibition of

MICHAEL CHASE, b.1915. 'Orvieto Olive'. Watercolour. 20in. x 16in. Private Collection.

watercolours at the Piccadilly Gallery. Has bronze figures sited on the South Bank, London. Work in the Tate Gallery collection.

CHASE, Michael   b.1915
Painter. Son of the painter, William A. Chase.* Saw war service in the Royal Armoured Corps. After a couple of false starts, he began to run the Kensington Art Gallery, and also to paint in watercolour. Continued to exhibit spasmodically in the 1950s, though his painting was curtailed by running the Zwemmer Gallery, London, 1954-65. Moved to East Anglia, and in 1966 became director of the Minories, Colchester. Married Valerie Thornton* that same year. Has been painting full-time since 1974. Recent solo exhibitions include one at the Stonegate Gallery, York, 1987.

CHASE, William Arthur   1878-1944
Painter. Born Bristol, Avon. Studied at City and Guilds School of Art, London, and at the Regent Street Polytechnic. Exhibited at the RA and other leading venues. Painted in England, Northern Italy, and South America. Father of Michael Chase.*

CHATTAWAY, William   b.1927
Sculptor. Born Coventry, West Midlands. Studied at Coventry Art School, 1943-5, and Slade School of Art,

CHATWIN, Michael

1945-8. 1950 settled in Paris. 1963 first solo exhibition at Galerie Jeanne Castel, Paris.

Bibl: *William Chattaway: Drawings and Sculpture,* Herbert Art Gallery and Museum, Coventry, exh. cat., 1969.

CHATWIN, Michael   b.1943

Painter, printmaker and constructionist. Studied at Oxford School of Art. Taught 1968-78, but since then has been a full-time painter in Newlyn, Cornwall. 1988 solo exhibition at Newlyn Art Gallery.

CHEESE, Bernard   b.1925

Printmaker. Studied at Beckenham School of Art and RCA. Has work in V & A, Leeds Art Gallery, Boston Museum of Fine Art, Library of Congress, Washington and elsewhere.

CHEESE, Chlöe   b.1952

Painter and illustrator. Born London. Studied at Cambridge School of Art, 1970-3, and RCA, 1973-6. 1974 worked in Paris studio. 1979 first solo exhibition at Curwen Gallery, London, and since then has exhibited frequently in London (Thumb Gallery) and abroad. Has work in Arts Council and British Council Collections. As an illustrator has worked for many clients in London, Holland and Japan.

CHEESEMAN, Harold   b.1915

Painter. Born Rye, Sussex. Studied at Hastings School of Art, 1932-5, and RCA, 1935-8. 1946-78 taught at Farnham School of Art. 1964 elected Associate of the RWS. 1970 Fellow of Royal Society of Arts. 1974 elected Fellow of RWS. Many solo exhibitions since 1954. A retrospective was held at West Surrey College of Art and Design, 1970.

CHELL, Edward   b.1958

Painter and sculptor. Born Huddersfield, Yorkshire. Studied at Newcastle upon Tyne University, 1977-81. Placements include Grizedale Forest, Cumbria, 1985, artist in residence, Springfield Comprehensive School, Jarrow, 1986, and Shepherd's Offshore Industries, 1986. Has work with Northern Arts Association and Grizedale Forest Society.

CHENG-WU, Fei   b.1914

Painter. Born China. Studied art in Nanking. Came to London, 1946 and studied at Slade, 1947-50. Has exhibited at RA, RWEA, NEAC, London Group and had three solo shows at the Leicester Galleries, the last in 1963. He has work in various public collections, including Sheffield City Art Galleries and Derby Museum and Art Gallery. Published *British Drawing in the Chinese Manner,* Studio Publications, 1957.

CHENTOFF, Polia   1896-1933

Painter and sculptor. Born Vitebsk, Russia. Moved with her mother to Paris and exhibited at the Salon. Illustrated several books of children's stories which were published in Berlin. Late 1920s moved to London and in 1932 married the painter Edmond Kapp.* June 1930 solo exhibition of paintings at the Paul Guillaume and Brandon Davis Gallery, and of engravings, woodcuts and illustrations at the Bloomsbury Gallery. Died of a cerebral tumour.

CHESHER, A.W.   1895-1972

Naïve painter and farmer. Self-taught. Began painting in order to record the various types of steam traction engines which were used in agriculture. His pictures aim to convey a pageant of rural antique Britain. Exhibits at Portal Gallery, London.

CHESTERFIELD, Diane   b.1943

Painter. Born Portsmouth, Hampshire. Studied painting and music at Bath Academy of Art, Corsham. 1978 held solo exhibition at Dryden Street Gallery, London.

CHESTERMAN, Jack   b.1938

Painter. Born Lahore, India. Served in the Household Cavalry 1953-4, worked as farm labourer, 1957-9. Studied at Leeds College of Art, 1960-1 and RCA, 1962-4. Solo exhibition at the Manor House, Ilkley, 1978.

CHESTERMAN, William

Painter. Born Chantilly, near Paris, of English and French parentage. Studied at Ecole des Beaux Arts and studied history of art at the Louvre. Met many influential painters of the day, including Raoul Dufy who became a close friend. Lives and works in Hampshire. Exhibited at Salisbury Library, 1984.

CHESTON, Charles   1882-1960

Painter. Studied at Slade 1899-1902. Member of NEAC and RWS. Devoted companion to his invalid artist wife, Evelyn Cheston,* in their various homes mostly in Dorset and the West Country. His work is close in style to hers, though considered less good. Elected ARE, 1927 and RWS, 1933. Work in the Tate Gallery collection.

CHESTON, Evelyn   1875-1929

Watercolourist. Born Evelyn Davy in Sheffield, Yorkshire. Studied at Slade where she shared a painting prize with Augustus John. Fell ill with Bright's disease which left her severely invalided and only able to paint for short periods, but went on painting, often in the company of her husband, Charles Cheston,* whom she married in 1904. Painted out of doors, with a vivacity and spontaneity inspired by the example of Constable. Memorial exhibition held at Mappin Art Gallery, Sheffield, 1931.

Bibl: Charles Cheston, *Evelyn Cheston,* Faber, London, 1931.

CHEVALLIER, Annette   b.1944

Painter. Born West Sussex. Studied at West Sussex College of Art and at Chelsea College of Art. 1976 organised an etching workshop at Brixton Arts Centre. Moved to Tynemouth and exhibited in both solo and group exhibitions in the North. 1980 exhibited abstract paintings with overtones of landscape at the Camden Arts Centre, and in 1985-6, making increased use of rich colour, she had a solo exhibition at the City of Edinburgh Art Centre.

CHEVSKA, Maria   b.1948

Printmaker and painter. Studied at Byam Shaw School of Art, 1968-72. 1977 held first solo exhibition at the Women's Art Alliance; other solo exhibitions include one at the Air Gallery, 1982. Uses words, photographs and the drawn mark to question received notions of femininity. 1985 she had a solo exhibition at Nottingham's Midland Group, entitled 'Of Pyramids and Sailing Shoes'. Represented by Anderson O'Day, London.

CHEYNE, Ian   1895-1955

Painter and printmaker. Born Broughty Ferry, Scotland. Studied at Glasgow School of Art under Maurice Greiffenhagen.* Exhibited at the SSA, RSA, GI and at the

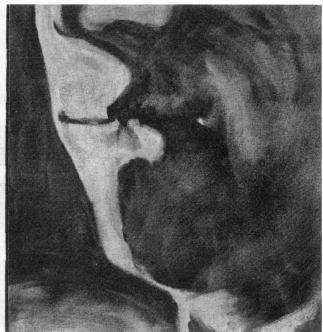

MARIA CHEVSKA, b.1948. 'Clench (ii)', 1990. 16 ½ in. x 32in. Anderson O'Day Gallery.

Redfern and Cooling Galleries in London. Originally a painter, he grew increasingly interested in colour woodcuts to which he brought an Art Deco style and a grasp of design partly inspired by Japanese prints.

CHILD, St. John   b.1936
Painter. Born London, the grandson of W. Fishley Holland, the well-known potter. Studied at RCA and has taught pottery and painting in London and Brighton. Has exhibited regularly at Redfern, Mayor, Woodstock Galleries and elsewhere and has a collection of ten large paintings on permanent loan to the University of Sussex.

CHILTON, Michael   b.1934
Painter. Born Leeds, Yorkshire. Studied at Slade, 1952-6. 1956 went on a travel scholarship to Spain, and 1959 on an Abbey Minor Travel Scholarship to Western Europe. 1975 first solo exhibition held at Suzanne Fischer Gallery, Baden-Baden and at Ferens Gallery, Hull. Has work in Leeds City Art Gallery and elsewhere. His subject matter is the 'natural landscape, in actuality and memory'.

Bibl: *Michael Chilton: Paintings and pastel drawings 1972-76,* Whitechapel Art Gallery, 1976.

CHORLTON, Graham   b.1953
Painter. Born Leicester. Studied at Leeds University, 1972-6 and Birmingham Polytechnic, 1977-8. Solo exhibitions include one at Wolverhampton Art Gallery, 1983. Paints city locations and interiors.

CHOWDHURY, Paul Gopal   b.1949
Painter. Studied at Camberwell School of Art and Slade. 1975-7 Gregory Fellow at Leeds University. 1981 solo exhibitions at Newcastle upon Tyne Polytechnic, at the Metropole Arts Centre, Folkestone, and Ian Birkstead Gallery, London. Selected the figurative section of the Hayward Annual Exhibition, 1979.

CHOWNE, Gerard   1875-1917
Painter. Born India. Studied at Slade School of Art, 1893-9, also studied in Paris and Rome. From 1903 exhibited at the NEAC and 1911 had his first solo show at the Carfax Gallery, London. Served with the Salonika Force and died of wounds in Macedonia. Work in Bradford City Art Galleries and the Tate Gallery.

CHRISTIAN, Yolanda   b.1957
Painter and printmaker. Born Liverpool, Merseyside. Studied at Liverpool Polytechnic, 1976, Wolverhampton Polytechnic, 1977-80, Ecole des Beaux Arts, Marseilles, 1979 and Slade, 1980-2. 1983 organised an exhibition 'Private Lives' at Swiss Cottage Library. Solo exhibitions include 'People and Places', at Woodlands Art Gallery, London, 1983.

CHRISTIE, Ann   b.1939
Painter. Studied at Edinburgh College of Art, 1957-61. 1963 held her first solo exhibition at the University of Hull and another at the City Hotel Restaurant, New Elvet, Durham, 1964.

CHRISTIE, James Elder   1847-1914
Painter. Born Fife, Scotland. Studied at Paisley School of Art, Royal Academy Schools and Académie Julian in Paris. Closely associated with H.H. La Thangue* and T. Stirling. Was partly responsible for founding the Chelsea Art Club. His paintings of children delighted Walter Sickert.*

CHRISTIE, Tessa   b.1941
Painter. Daughter of a Naval Officer and has travelled extensively. Studied at Farnham School of Art and Slade. Has made many drawings in the National History Museum and of underwater life in the National Institute of Oceanography. Solo exhibitions at Sussex University, 1968 and Drian Galleries, London, 1969.

KATHERINE CHURCH, b.1910. *'Fawley Bottom'*, 1937. Watercolour. 30in. x 36¼ in. Sally Hunter Fine Art.

CHRISTOFIDES, Andrew b.1946
Painter. Born Cyprus. Studied at University of New South Wales, Australia and worked as an economist within the Treasury Department, Australia, 1971-3. Studied at Byam Shaw School of Art, 1974-5, and Chelsea School of Art, 1975-8. 1978-9 won Abbey Major Scholarship and lived and worked in Rome, travelling extensively in Italy. 1979-80 Picker Fellowship at Kingston Polytechnic. 1980 solo exhibition at House Gallery, London.

CHRISTOPHERSON, John b.1921
Painter. Born Blackheath, London. Permanent civil servant at the Geological Museum until 1959. Resigned to devote himself to full-time painting and has held regular solo exhibitions since 1961. At the start of his career was encouraged by Jean Dubuffet whose technique and experiments with texture inspired him. Has work in Arts Council Collection, Sheffield City Art Galleries, Pembrokeshire County Museum and several distinguished private collections. His pictures, deliberately drawn and heavily textured, are often painted on a dark ground. Also produced collages, frottages and mixed-media drawings. Feels that collage expresses the forlorn poetry of the disregarded through transformation of disparate materials. 1972-3 held retrospective at Woodlands Art Gallery, London. 1983 solo exhibition at Sandford Gallery, Covent Garden.

CHRONIN, Ann b.1950
Sculptor. Studied at Limerick School of Art and Design, 1979-83, and at Birmingham Polytechnic, 1983-4. First exhibited at the Ikon Gallery, Birmingham, 1984.

CHURCH, Katherine b.1910
Painter. Born London. Studied at Brighton School of Art, the RA Schools, 1930-3, and at the Slade School, 1933-4. A friend of John Piper* and Ivon Hitchens.* Married the writer Anthony West. First exhibited at the Wertheim Gallery, 1933, and showed at the Lefevre Gallery, London, in the 1930s and '40s. Invited to contribute to the 'Figures in their Setting' exhibition at the Tate Gallery, 1953. Showed regularly with the London Group, also at the Hamilton Gallery, London, in the 1970s. Another solo exhibition held at Sally Hunter and Patrick Seale Gallery, London, 1984.

CHURCHILL, John Spencer b.1909
Painter and stockbroker. Nephew of Sir Winston Churchill.* First painted professionally in 1932, studying in Rome, Munich, Madrid and London under Sir William Nicholson* and Bernard Meninsky.* First came to public attention in 1936, during the Spanish Civil War, when his sketches from Malaga were published in *The Illustrated London News.* Executed a relief freize depicting the battle

of Blenheim for the 'Marlborough Pavilion' at Chartwell, at Lady Churchill's request. Has continued to paint many murals.

CHURCHILL, Sir Winston   1874-1965
Painter, soldier, politician, statesman and historian. Born at Blenheim Palace, Oxfordshire. 1900 entered Houses of Parliament as member for Oldham. 1906 Under Secretary of State for the Colonies, 1910 Home Secretary, 1911 First Lord of the Admiralty. 1915 began to paint, self-taught. 1917 Minister of Munitions, 1919 Secretary of State for War and Air. 1921 began to paint for the first time in the Middle East, later stayed regularly in Morocco, where he worked with the painter Sir John Lavery.* 1922 bought Chartwell, Kent, and began his long series of paintings in the South of France. 1924 Chancellor of the Exchequer. 1930 started to paint his 'Bottlescapes', his own form of still life. 1932 'Painting as a Pastime' published in an anthology of his *Thoughts and Adventures*. 1940-5 Prime Minister. 1947 exhibited at the RA summer exhibition for the first time with two works, under the name of David Winter, one of which is now in the collection of the Tate Gallery. 1948 elected as the first Honorary Royal Academician Extraordinary. 1950 decided that a catalogue of his pictures should be prepared, which was completed by 1967. 1951-5 Prime Minister for the second time. 1958 world tour of his paintings, to USA, Canada, Australia and New Zealand. 1959 exhibition at the RA. 1965 exhibition in the Churchill Pavilion at the New York World Fair.

Bibl: *Sir Winston Churchill, 1874-1965* (Centenary exhibition), Somerset House, London, 1974.

CINA, Colin   b.1943
Painter. Born Glasgow, Scotland. Studied at Glasgow School of Art, 1961-3 and Central School of Art and Design, 1963-6. 1966 won a Peter Stuyvesant Foundation Travel Bursary and visited USA. 1967, 1969 and 1973 solo exhibitions at Arnolfini Gallery, Bristol, and since then has exhibited regularly at Angela Flowers Gallery, London, and elsewhere. Works with accepted illusion systems to create abstract canvases that explore structure, surface, space and colour. Has work in Arts Council Collection, V & A, Bristol City Art Gallery and elsewhere.

Bibl: *Colin Cina: Paintings and Drawings 1966-75*, Third Eye Centre, Glasgow, 1975.

CLAIRMONTE, Christopher   b.1932
Painter. Studied at Wimbledon School of Art and RCA. Has exhibited widely in the UK and abroad. Solo exhibition at the Patrick Searle Gallery, London, 1981.

CLAPCOTT, Helen   b.1952
Painter. Born Blackpool, Lancashire. Studied at Liverpool School of Art and RCA. Won David Murray travelling scholarship and went to Morocco, also the Elizabeth Greenshields Foundation Scholarship. Since 1976 has exhibited at RA, and has had solo exhibitions at New Ashgate Gallery, Farnham, 1983, Salford City Art Galleries, 1984, Stockport War Memorial Gallery, 1984, and the Ginnel Gallery, Manchester, 1984.

CLAPHAM, Peter   b.1924
Painter and sculptor. Born London. Studied at Architectural Association, 1947-52. 1971 first solo exhibition held at Battelle Gallery, Geneva. Has work in St. Mary's College, Durham University, Arts Council collection and elsewhere.

Bibl: *Peter Clapham: space light structures at Kenwood*, Greater London Council, 1971.

CLARE, Stephen   b.1958
Painter. Born Walsall, Staffordshire. Studied at Walsall School of Art, 1975-6 and Sir John Cass College of Art, London, 1977-80. Has exhibited in various London galleries, including Adam, 1985, and Jablonski, 1986.

CLARK, Anthony   b.1942
Painter. Born Sunderland, Tyne and Wear. Studied at Sunderland College of Art, 1959-63 and RCA, 1963-6. 1966 winner of the Sir James Knott Scholarship and studied in Paris. Solo exhibitions at RCA, 1966, Sunderland Art Gallery, 1969, the University of Surrey, 1970, ICI Gallery, Billingham, 1970, and DLI Museum and Arts Centre, Durham, 1971.

CLARK, Jean Manson   b.1902
Painter. Born Sidcup, Kent. Studied at Sidcup School of Art and RA Schools and at the Académie Julian, Paris. Married artist John Cosmo Clark.* Exhibited at NEAC and elsewhere. 1972 elected member of RWS. Paints landscapes, townscapes and flower paintings but has also specialised in murals.

CLARK, John   b.1943
Painter. Born Yorkshire. Studied at Hull College of Art 1961-6 and Indiana University, USA, 1966-8. 1972 and 1975 solo exhibitions at Park Square Gallery, Leeds. Has work in Arts Council of Northern Ireland collection and at Indiana University.

CLARK, John Cosmo   1897-1967
Painter. Studied at St. Mark's School, Chelsea and Goldsmiths' College. Served in First World War and awarded the MC. Studied at RA Schools, 1918-21. 1921 onwards taught life painting at Camberwell School of Arts and Crafts. 1938 appointed Head of Hackney School of Art. Exhibited at RA and NEAC. 1958 elected RA. Painted chiefly street scenes, open air markets, cafes, boat houses, boxing booths and figurative scenes.

CLARK, Judy   b.1949
Mixed media artist. Born Portsmouth, Hampshire. Studied at Portsmouth College of Art, 1969-71, and Slade School of Fine Art, 1971-3. Exhibited at Angela Flowers, London, 1972, and had a solo exhibition at Garage Art Ltd., London, 1973, in which she presented rubbings of male and female skin. Interested in forensic techniques, especially fingerprinting. Works in the Tate Gallery and Arts Council collections.

Bibl: Caroline Tisdall, 'Bodyworks', *The Guardian*, 14.12.1973.

CLARK, Michael   1918-1990
Sculptor. Born Cheltenham, the son and grandson of sculptors. Studied at City of London Art School and then served with the Cameronians in the North African and Italian campaigns. Associate member of the RSBS in 1947 and served as its President from 1971 to 1976. His work can be found in many British churches and cathedrals, e.g. Christ over the West Door of Westminster Abbey and Our Lady of the Assumption at Aylesford, Kent.

CLARK, Norman   b.1913
Painter. Born Ilford, Essex. Studied at Central School of Art and Crafts, 1929, and the RA Schools, 1930-5, where he won many prizes including the Landseer Prize for mural decoration. Leverhulme Scholar, 1935. Exhibits at the RA, ROI and in the provinces and is a member of the RWS. Taught for some years at Brighton Art School where he was a friend and associate of Dorothy Coke.* Member of the Society of Sussex Painters. Represented in the Harris Museum, Preston, and the Imperial War Museum. (Plate 28, p.95.)

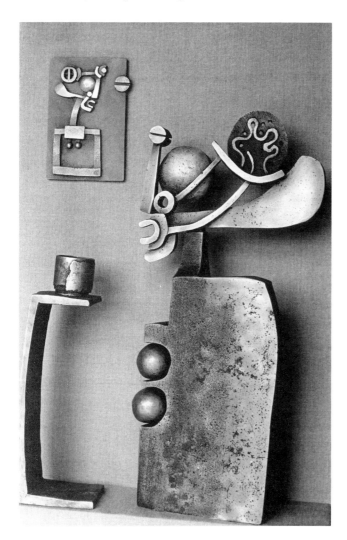

GEOFFREY CLARKE, b.1924. *'Perception I'*, 1987-8.
Cast aluminium. 40in. x 28in. x 9in. Private Collection.

CLARK, Philip Lindsey   b.1889
Sculptor. Born London. Studied at Cheltenham School of Art, 1905-10, at City and Guilds School, Kennington, 1910-14, and RA Schools, 1919-21. From 1920 exhibited at the RA, and from 1921 at the Paris Salon. Has executed war memorials as well as religious commissions.

CLARK, Robert   b.1951
Painter. Born Lancashire. Studied at Leeds College of Art, 1971-4. Solo exhibitions at Leeds Polytechnic, 1975 and elsewhere, including Abbot Hall Gallery, Kendal, 1981.

CLARKE, Brian   b.1953
Painter and stained glass designer. Born Oldham, Lancashire. Studied at art colleges in Oldham, Burnley and Bideford, 1965-72. 1973 set up his own studio in Preston, working both as painter and stained glass designer. 1974 awarded Winston Churchill Memorial Fellowship to study contemporary stained glass in Western Europe. Began to paint for specific architectural settings. 1979 he was the subject of a BBC TV *Omnibus* documentary. Solo exhibition at Mayor Gallery, London, 1990. Has completed architectural projects in Europe, America and the Far East.

CLARKE, Denis   b.1952
Painter. Born Sydney, Australia. Studied at Sydney and awarded a New South Wales Travelling Art Scholarship. Moved to London to do a postgraduate course at St. Martin's School of Art, studying also part-time at the Byam Shaw School of Art, Morley College and Chelsea School of Art. 1975 first solo exhibition held in Sydney; most recent solo exhibition held at New South Wales House, London, 1983.

CLARKE, Geoffrey   b.1924
Sculptor. Born Darley Dale, Derbyshire. Studied at the RCA, 1948-52. 1953-62 commissioned to make the High Altar Cross, candlesticks, the Flying Cross and the Crown of Thorns in Coventry Cathedral. Further commissions include: an iron sculpture for the Time Life Building, London; relief sculptures for the liners *Canberra* and *Oriana*; a bronze sculpture for the Thorn Electric Building, London. Has also made sculpture for the Universities of Oxford, Cambridge, Exeter, Liverpool, Manchester and Loughborough. Work in the Tate Gallery, Arts Council, and British Council collections.

CLARKE, Jeff   b.1935
Painter. Studied at Brighton College of Art. 1955-7 won a British Institution Fund Scholarship, and 1956-8 Rome Scholar. Since 1958 has exhibited at regular intervals and has work in Jesus College, Oxford, and elsewhere.

CLARKE, Pat   b.1940
Painter. Studied at Reigate Art School. Has had ten solo exhibitions in London and the provinces, is a member of the National Society of Painters, Sculptors and Printmakers and the Association of Artists and Designers in Wales. Solo exhibition at Aberystwyth Art Centre, 1983.

CLARKE, Peter   b.1951
Painter. Born Burnley, Lancashire. Studied at Burnley Municipal College, 1967-9, Bristol Polytechnic, 1969-72 and Chelsea College of Art, 1977-8. Is a member of Liverpool Artists Workshop. 1981 first solo exhibition at Bluecoat Gallery, Liverpool. 1978 moved to Liverpool, and Merseyside became the subject of his work. He explores its ravaged condition and its social and political tensions.

Bibl: *Peter Clarke: Constructed Views,* Rochdale Art Gallery, 1984.

CLARKE-HALL, Edna   1879-1979
Painter and illustrator. Born Shipbourne, Kent. Trained as an artist on the encouragement of the barrister William Clarke-Bell whom she married in 1898. Won many prizes at the Slade where she was a pupil of Professor Tonks.* Lived at Thames Ditton and exhibited with NEAC. Took lessons in oil painting from Gwen John* but soon abandoned this medium for watercolour. Became obsessed with the novel, *Wuthering Heights,* and produced hundreds of related drawings, 1900-10, returning to this tale in a series of etchings in the 1920s. A brilliant draughtswoman, she made the world around her the subject of her art. Even at its most economical, her line is never facile, but is animated by the nervous tension which periodically caused her mental stress. Is represented in Tate Gallery, V & A, British Museum and elsewhere.

CLARKSON, Jack   1906-1986
Sculptor. Born Silsden, Yorkshire. Studied at Keighley School of Art and RCA, 1927-30. For many years he was Head of Sculpture and Pottery at Sheffield College of Art, and afterwards became Principal of Newcastle under Lyme Art School, a position he held until his retirement in

1968. Exhibited widely, at the RA, RSA and elsewhere. Represented in the collections of Hanley Art Gallery and Newcastle under Lyme Art Gallery.

CLARKSON, Pamela b.1946
Painter. Born Lancashire. Studied at Manchester College of Art, 1963-4, Central School of Art and Design, 1964-7 and RCA, 1967-70. 1973-4 visited Chile, and has exhibited regularly at home and abroad.

Bibl: *Pamela Clarkson: Paintings and Prints* (with an essay by Patrick Heron), Penwith Galleries, 1978.

CLATWORTHY, Robert b.1928
Sculptor. Born Bridgwater, Somerset. Studied at West of England College of Art, Bristol, 1944-6, Chelsea School of Art, 1949-51, and Slade, 1951-4. Solo exhibitions at Hanover Gallery, London, 1955 and 1956, Waddington Galleries, 1965, Basil Jacobs, London, 1972. 1968 elected ARA and 1973, RA. Diploma Galleries, RA, 1977 and Quinton Green, London, 1986. Represented in Tate Gallery, V & A and elsewhere.

CLAUSEN, George 1852-1944
Painter. Born London, the son of a painter of Danish descent. Studied at South Kensington School of Art and at the Académie Julian in Paris. Influenced by the French artist, Bastien-Lepage, he did much to promote his work in England. Elected ARWS, 1877, ARA, 1895, RWS, 1898. Professor of Painting at the RA Schools, 1904-6, later became Director of the Schools. A founder member of the NEAC, he changed his allegiance to the Royal Academy and was elected RA, 1908. Knighted 1927.

Bibl: *Sir George Clausen, RA, 1852-1944,* with introduction by Kenneth McConkey, Tyne & Wear and Bradford Museums, 1980.

CLEAVER, James b.1911
Painter. Studied at Camberwell School of Arts and Crafts, 1930 and then RCA. 1939 worked on camouflage of factories and civilian installations, then joined the Army. After a varied career he returned to his early interests in landscape and marine painting and studied under R.V. Pitchforth.* Exhibited at RA.

CLEGG, J. David b.1933
Painter. Born Manchester. Studied at Slade. Primarily a landscape painter. Exhibits in mixed exhibitions, with solo exhibitions at the Tib Lane Gallery, Manchester and Hamwic Gallery, Southampton.

CLIFFORD, Henry Charles 1861-1947
Painter. Born Greenwich, London. Studied painting in Paris under Bouguereau, Constant and Tony Fleury. Exhibited at the RA and other major exhibition venues. Specialised in landscapes and town scenes. 1912 elected RBA.

CLIFFORD, Therasa b.1961
Sculptor. Born Cork, Ireland. Studied at Limerick School of Art, 1979-83, and Birmingham Polytechnic, 1983-4. First exhibited at EVA, Limerick, 1982.

CLINCH, John b.1934
Sculptor. Born Folkestone, Kent. Attended Kingston School of Art, 1951-5. National Service, 1955-7. Attended Sculpture School, RCA, 1957-61. 1960 onwards included in group exhibitions. 1979 received Arts Council Major Award.

CLOUGH, Prunella b.1919
Painter. Born London. Studied at Chelsea School of Art, 1938-9. 1940-5 worked at various clerical and draughts-man's jobs. 1946-9 lived in London but made visits to East Anglia. 1950-60 developed an interest in urban, industrial subjects, some derived from visits to the Midlands. During the immediate post-war years worked in a neo-romantic style that soon gave way to a concern with the urban environment and the activities of workmen. Many of her subjects during the late 1950s were based on factories, even when she moved away from the figurative and into abstraction. The urban wasteland remains her starting point. The various sensations it provides are then distilled into metaphysical abstracts in which the energy of our everyday environment is clarified. 1947 first solo exhibition held at Leger Gallery; others include Leicester Galleries, 1953, a retrospective at the Whitechapel Art Gallery, 1960, Serpentine Gallery, 1976 and Warwick Arts Trust, 1982.

Bibl: Malcolm Yorke, *The Spirit of the Place: Nine Neo-Romantic Artists and their Times,* Constable, London, 1988.

CLOUGH, Thomas Collingwood b.1903
Painter. Born Glen Conway, Wales. Studied at the Slade School, 1925-7, and the RCA, 1928-30. Exhibited at the RA, and with the NEAC and the London Group. Painted in North Wales, Brittany and British Colombia. Taught at the Sir John Cass School of Art.

CLUETT, Shelagh b.1947
Sculptor. Born Dorset. Studied at St. Martin's School of Art, 1966-7, Hammersmith College of Art, 1967-8, Hornsey College of Art, 1968-71, and Chelsea School of Art, 1971-2. 1979 won a Greater London Arts Association Major Award. Since 1972 has exhibited regularly and been associated with the Nicola Jacobs Gallery, London. Her work, contrary to traditional expectations of sculpture, transcends material presence with its melodic linearity and grace.

CLUTE, Judith b.1942
Painter. Born Edmonton, Canada. Moved to England in 1969. Has exhibited regularly since 1961. Held a solo exhibition at Triad Regional Arts Centre, Bishop's Stortford, 1974. Juxtaposes images drawn from diverse sources and media, to create ambiguity and tension.

CLUTTON-BROCK, Alan 1904-1976
Painter. Son of the art critic, Arthur Clutton-Brock. Studied at Westminster Art School, took up journalism, and became art critic to *The Times.* Wrote several books on art, including a short life of William Blake and continued to paint for pleasure, mostly landscapes.

CLYDE, Maggie b.1952
Printmaker. Born Glasgow, Scotland. Trained at Edinburgh College of Art, 1970-5 and RCA, 1976-9. Has won several prizes and awards and held her first solo exhibition, 1976. Has work in Scottish Arts Council and Arts Council collections and in Sheffield City Art Galleries.

COATES, George
Painter. Born Australia, the son of a lithographer. Studied at the North Melbourne School of Art and the National Gallery Drawing School, Melbourne. Apprenticed to a glass stainer, 1884. Set up painting classes in his own studio, 1895-6. Came to England, 1897. Studied at the Académie Julian, 1898-1900. 1910 visited Italy. 1913 first solo exhibition in Melbourne, followed by others in Melbourne and Sydney, 1921. 1915-19 served in the RAMC. From 1902 exhibited at the RA. 1928 founder

COATES, Tom

member of the London Portrait Society. 1931 memorial exhibition at the New Burlington Galleries. Work in the Tate Gallery collection.

COATES, Tom   b.1941

Painter. Born Birmingham, West Midlands. Studied at Bournville College of Art, 1955-9, at Birmingham College of Art, 1959-61, and at the RA Schools, 1961-4. Regular exhibitor at RA, RSBA, RSW and the Royal Society of Portrait Painters. Awards include the De Lazlo medal, the Critics' Prize, 1987, first prize for the Sunday Times Watercolour Exhibition, 1988, and third prize, 1989. Member of the RSPW, the RSPP and the NEAC. 1988 elected President of RSBA. His work upholds the best traditions of the NEAC with vigorous execution and tonal balance.

COBB, John   b.1946

Sculptor. Studied at Great Yarmouth College of Art, 1966, Coventry College of Art, 1967-70 and RCA 1970-3. 1972 won RCA Minor Travel Award. Has won several awards and has exhibited regularly since 1973 when he was represented at the 8th Paris Biennale. Teaches at Central School of Art. Represented by Anne Berthoud Gallery, London. Works chiefly with wood.

Bibl: *John Cobb: Sculpture 1976-1988*, Norwich School of Art, 1988.

COCHRANE, Stephen

Mixed media artist. Studied at Hornsey College of Art and RCA. 1976 first solo exhibition held at Gordon Maynard Gallery, London; since then has worked on various projects and exhibitions with the musician, Lol Coxhill, in England and in Europe. Exhibited at Air Gallery, London, 1982.

COCKER, Douglas   b.1945

Sculptor. Born Perthshire, Scotland. Attended Duncan of Jordanstone College of Art, Dundee, 1963-8. Taught at Northampton College of Art, 1972, and at George College, Ontario, Canada, 1977. 1969 first one-person show at the New 57 Gallery, Edinburgh. 1977 Arts Council of Great Britain Major Award, 1979 East Midlands Arts Major Award. 1984 elected Associate of RSA. 1985 elected chairman of the Federation of Scottish Sculptors. Since 1981 lecturer in sculpture, Gray's School of Art, Aberdeen. Represented in public collections, e.g. Arts Council of Great Britain, Scottish Arts Council, Glasgow Art Gallery and Museum.

Bibl: *Doug Cocker, Sculpture and Related Works 1976-86*, Third Eye Centre, Glasgow, 1986.

COCKRAM, George   1861-1950

Watercolourist. Born Birkenhead, Cheshire. Studied at Liverpool School of Art, 1884 and in Paris, 1889. Decided to devote himself entirely to landscape views in watercolour. Lived and worked in North Wales. 1885-1924 exhibited at the RA. From 1891 member of the Royal Cambrian Academy, the RA from 1913 and the Manchester Academy from 1922. Work in the Tate Gallery collection, bought by the Chantrey Bequest.

COCKRILL, Maurice   b.1936

Painter. Born Hartlepool, Cleveland. Studied at Wrexham Art School and University of Reading, 1960-4. 1969-80 taught at Liverpool Polytechnic. Solo exhibitions include the Serpentine Gallery, 1971, Bluecoat Gallery, Liverpool, 1982, Edward Totah Gallery, London, 1984 and 1985-6, as well as many others. Has work in Arts Council collection, University of Liverpool, Walker Art Gallery, Liverpool and elsewhere. An expressionist painter, with frequent references to Old Masters.

CODRINGTON, Isabel

Painter. Studied at RA Schools. Exhibited at RA, Paris Salon and Goupil Gallery, London. Represented in Imperial War Museum. Solo exhibition of etchings at Colnaghi's, London, 1933.

COE, Sue   b.1951

Mixed media artist. Studied at Chelsea School of Art, 1968-71 and RCA, 1971-4. 1974 moved to New York. 1979 solo exhibition at the Thumb Gallery, London, and Moira Kelly Fine Art, London, 1982. Her drawings are satirical and feminist.

COHEN, Alfred   b.1920

Painter. Born Chicago, USA. Studied at Art Institute in Chicago, 1945-9. 1949 awarded a foreign travel fellowship and travelled and worked in Europe. 1960 settled in England. 1963 moved to Kent. Many solo exhibitions since 1958, including 'Aspects of The Thames' at Kaplan Gallery, London, 1961.

COHEN, Bernard   b.1933

Painter. Born London. Studied art at South-West Essex Technical College and School of Art, 1949-50, St. Martin's, 1950-1 and Slade, 1951-4. 1954 awarded French Government Scholarship and spent one year travelling in France, followed by two years living mostly in Paris. 1958 first solo exhibition at Gimpel Fils, London. 1960 participated in Situation exhibition, and in the New London Situation, 1961. 1966 represented at Venice Biennale. 1969-70 spent a year lecturing and travelling in America. 1972 given Arts Council retrospective at Hayward Gallery and elsewhere. 1980-7 Head of Painting, Wimbledon School of Art. 1988 appointed Professor and Director of Slade School. Represented by Waddington Galleries, London. (Plate 29, p.98.)

COHEN, Gerda   b.1925

Painter. Born Vienna, Austria. Came to England in 1939. Studied at Cardiff School of Art. In 1960 began to use her paintings as a means of expression for past experiences and for emotional reactions to the world today.

COHEN, Harold   b.1928

Painter. Born London. After serving in RAF studied at Slade School of Art, 1948-52. 1952 spent six months in Italy on an Abbey Minor Travelling Scholarship. After two years teaching at Camberwell School of Art, opened small furniture workshop, 1955. 1951 first solo exhibition held in Oxford, followed by three London shows with Gimpel Fils. Has continued also to design furniture and textiles. Work in Arts Council Collection and Tate Gallery.

COHEN, Nathan   b.1962

Constructivist. Born London. Studied at Slade School of Art, 1980-4 and Chelsea School of Art, 1985-6. Since 1985 has exhibited regularly. In 1986 an exhibition of spare, painted aluminium reliefs was shown at Annely Juda Fine Art, London.

WILLIAM COLDSTREAM, 1908-1987. *'On the Map'*, 1937. 20in. x 20in. Tate Gallery.

COKE, Dorothy   1897-1979
Painter. Born Southend-on-Sea, Essex. Studied at Slade School of Fine Art, 1914-18. 1920 elected member of NEAC. 1935 elected ARWS. 1940 commissioned by the War Artists Advisory Committee to draw the various branches of the Women's Services: the WAAF, ATS and Nursing Services. 1943 elected RWS. 1945-67 taught at Brighton College of Art. (Plate 30, p.98.)

COKER, Peter   b.1926
Painter. Born London. Studied at St. Martin's School of Art, 1942 (evening classes). 1943-6 served with Fleet Air Arm. 1947-50 studied at St. Martin's, and 1950-4, RCA. 1956 first solo exhibition at the Zwemmer Gallery, London, and was included in John Berger's 'Looking Forward' exhibition at South London Art Gallery. 1962 moved to East Anglia. 1965 elected ARA. Has exhibited regularly and in 1972 was given a retrospective at The Minories, Colchester. Retrospective exhibition held at Chelmsford and Essex Museum, 1978. Works often with thick paint and the palette knife in figurative and landscape paintings which, in the 1950s, associated him with the 'Kitchen Sink' School. (Plate 31, p.99.)

COLDSTREAM, William   1908-1987
Painter. Born Northumberland. Educated privately and studied at Slade under Professor Tonks,* 1926-9. 1931 joined the LAA and 1933 became a member of the LG. The following year he abandoned art and began working for the GPO Film Unit with John Grierson on documentary films. 1937 returned to painting in a realist style, convinced that art should be directed to a wider public than modernist styles had reached. Founded, with Claude Rogers* and Victor Pasmore,* the Euston Road School, which emphasised observation and objective appraisal of the subject. 1940 joined the Royal Artillery, but later transferred to the Royal Engineers. 1943 appointed official war artist. After demobilisation, taught at Camberwell until 1949 when appointed Slade Professor, filling this post until 1975. 1958-71 chaired the national advisory committee for art education and was an able administrator. As a painter, his purposeful severity and emphasis on measured observation influenced many, including Euan Uglow.* Knighted 1956.

COLE, Elsie Vera   1885-1968
Painter. Born Braintree, Essex. Studied at Norwich and Chelmsford Schools of Art. Exhibited at the RI, RWA, SWA and with the Norwich Art Circle. Taught at Norwich School of Art, 1919-41. Published *A Sketch book of Norwich,* 1920.

COLE, Henry George   1875-1957
Painter and engraver. Born Plymouth, Devon. Studied at Plymouth School of Art. Exhibited widely at the RA and other leading artistic institutions. 1948 had a solo exhibition at Plymouth Art Gallery and in 1956 at St. George's Gallery, Cork Street.

COLE, John Vicat   b.1903
Painter. Born London, son of Rex Vicat Cole.* Specialised in landscape and stained glass designs. Exhibited at the RA, the Paris Salon, ROI, RBA, NEAC and in the provinces. Won a silver medal at the Paris Salon, 1952 and a gold medal, 1954. Elected ARBA, 1929, RBA, 1930, ROI, 1932, and a member of the NEAC, 1965.

COLE, Leslie   b.1910
Painter. Born Swindon, Wiltshire. Studied at Swindon Art School and RCA, 1934-7, receiving his diploma in mural decoration, fabric painting and lithography. 1937 began teaching at Hull College of Art. 1940 requested work as a war artist and was at first turned down, but persisted and was given work. 1942 he was sent to Malta as an offical war artist, and in 1944 was sent to France, then Greece, Germany and the Far East, becoming one of Britain's most productive war artists. 1944 entered the Royal Marine Commandos. After the war he moved to London and taught at Central School, and Brighton College of Art. Nothing, however, after 1946 matched the intensity of his wartime experience. Included in exhibition, 'To the Front Line', Imperial War Museum, 1985.

Bibl: *To the Front Line: Leslie Cole: Paintings of the Second World War,* Imperial War Museum, 1986.

COLE, Rex Vicat   1870-1940
Painter. Born London. Son of landscape painter George Vicat Cole. Attended St. John's Wood Art School. Exhibited at RA, the Paris Salon and elsewhere. With Byam Shaw he formed the Byam Shaw and Vicat Cole School of Art, 1910. He published several books including *The Art and Life of Byam Shaw*, 1933.

COLE, Yvonne   b.1953
Printmaker. Born Surrey. Studied at Kingston College of Art. 1980 first solo exhibition held at Thumb Gallery; since then has exhibited frequently in London and elsewhere, continuing her association with the Thumb Gallery.

COLEMAN, John   b.1956
Painter. Born Haslemere, Surrey. Studied at West Surrey School of Art and Camberwell School of Art. Exhibited with the group Work From Common Knowledge, 1982-5. Also writes reviews and art criticism. Responsible for the film 'Sea Passages' shown on Channel 4 in the summer of 1988.

COLES, Susan   b.1952
Printmaker. Born Darlington, Co. Durham. Studied at Cardiff College of Art, 1970-4. 1974 first solo exhibition at Darlington Art Gallery, and was given a Production Award from Northern Arts.

COLLET, Ruth   b.1909
Painter. Studied at Slade School of Art, and later with Marian Kratochwil* and Kathleen Brown. Studied etching with S. William Hayter.* Has exhibited at RA, NEAC and elsewhere, and had a solo exhibition at the Annexe Gallery, London, 1982. Represented in the collection of the Ben Uri Gallery, London.

COLLIER, The Hon. John   1850-1934
Painter of portraits and subject pictures. Born London. Studied art at the Slade School, in Paris and in Munich; encouraged by the painters Alma-Tadema and Millais. From 1874-1934 exhibited at the RA. 1882 published *The Primer of Art*, 1886 *A Manual of Oil Painting,* and 1905 *The Art of Portrait Painting*. 1915 first solo exhibition, of landscapes, held at the Leicester Galleries. 1921 retrospective exhibition held at Sunderland Art Gallery. 1921 OBE. Work in the Tate Gallery.

COLLIN, C.F.   1890-1937
Painter. Born Sunderland, Tyne and Wear. Studied at RCA and was influenced by the Second Post-Impressionist Exhibition in 1912-13. On a travelling scholarship, he saw the mosaics at Ravenna and afterwards sought in his own paintings to equal their brilliance and permanency. 1930-6 used egg tempera and powder colour. 1923 moved to South of France and 1937 to California. A little known modernist with a strong sense of design.

COLLINGBOURNE, Stephen   b.1943
Sculptor. Studied at Darlington College of Art, 1960-1, and Bath Academy, Corsham, 1961-4. Works in steel. Describes his sculptures as drawings in space. Tries also to give preformed objects a new identity. 1968 first solo exhibition held at Dartington Hall, Devon, followed by regular shows, including a solo exhibition at the MacRobert Arts Centre Gallery, University of Stirling, 1979.

COLLINGS, David   b.1949
Painter. Born London. Moved to Cornwall in 1963 and has worked as a professional artist since 1974. Has exhibited widely all over Britain as well as at the Newlyn Orion Galleries in Cornwall; he also teaches handicapped children at Nancealverne Special School in Penzance.

COLLINS, Cecil   1908-1989
Painter. Studied at Plymouth School of Art, 1923-7, and RCA, 1927-31. His earliest work was essentially naturalistic, but during the 1930s he fell under the influence of Klee, Picasso and (briefly) European surrealism. A meeting with Mark Tobey, the American abstract expressionist, in 1938 encouraged an interest in the art and philosophy of the Far East. 1940 first began his series of images on the same theme as his book, *The Vision of the Fool,* published 1947. Often labelled a neo-romantic, Collins has consistently been concerned with (in his own words) 'art as a metaphysical experience... with exploring the mystery of consciousness'. Much of his imagery deals with visionary experience and the notion of a spiritual quest. Retrospectives include Whitechapel Art Gallery, London, 1959, and Tate Gallery, 1989. An Arts Council film about his work, *The Eye of the Heart,* was made in 1978.

Bibl: *Cecil Collins,* with essay by Judith Collins, Tate Gallery, 1989.

COLLINS, Elizabeth   b.1905
Painter and sculptor. Studied sculpture at Leeds School of Art and at the RCA in the 1920s. While still a student she married Cecil Collins,* a fellow student. Her most productive period was during 1937-45 when staying at Dartington Hall, the home of Leonard and Dorothy Elmhirst. Her work has affinities with folk art and child art. Her paintings juxtapose fantastical images with references to the actual world. Retrospective exhibition at the Albermarle Gallery, London, 1989.

CECIL COLLINS, 1908-1989. *'The Shepherd Fool',* 1945. Ink and watercolour. 15in. x 22½in. Private Collection. Photograph by Clive Hicks.

COLLINS, Frank   b.1938
Painter. Born London. Studied at Camberwell School of Art, 1954-8. 1958 received a French Government Scholarship and studied etching with S.W. Hayter in Paris. Studied at RCA, 1960-3. Has travelled round the world and taught in various London art schools. Solo exhibitions include one at the Whitechapel Art Gallery, London, 1974.

COLLINS, George Edward   1880-1968
Painter and etcher. Born Dorking, Surrey. Studied at Epsom and Lambeth Schools of Art. Exhibited at the RA, RI, RBA and in the provinces. Elected RBA, 1905, and a member of the Royal Cambrian Academy, 1941. Illustrated a number of books on natural history.

COLLINS, Hannah   b.1956
Painter and photographer. Born London. Studied at Slade, 1974-8. 1976 worked in Belfast. 1977 began exhibiting in London and elsewhere. Exhibited 'The Large Book and Other Drawings 1980-81' at the Ikon Gallery, Birmingham, 1981.

COLLINS, Niamh   b.1956
Painter. Born Dublin, Ireland. Studied at Somerset College of Art, 1973-4, Portsmouth Polytechnic, 1974-7, and at the RCA, 1978-81. 1983 first solo exhibition at

Centre 181, Hammersmith, London. Represented by Anderson O'Day, London.

COLLIS, Maurice   1889-1973
Painter and critic. Studied history at Oxford and in 1911 entered the Indian Civil Service. Served in Burma for twenty-three years, retiring in 1936. Began to write, became an authority on Oriental subjects, and wrote a biography of Stanley Spencer and another on Nancy, Lady Astor; also wrote art criticism for the *Observer* and *Time and Tide.* 1956 began painting, and at the age of seventy-one, exhibited his work at the Kaplan Gallery, London, 1959-60. Published an autobiography, *The Journey Up: Reminiscences,* 1970.

COLLISTER, Alfred James   1869-1964
Painter. Born Isle of Man. Studied at Douglas School of Art. 1899 began exhibiting at the Royal Society of British Artists and by 1900 had been elected a full member. From then on exhibited three or four watercolours annually. Taught at various art schools and had many distinguished pupils, including R.O. Dunlop.*

COLQUHOUN, Ithell   1906-1988
Painter and writer. Born Shillong, Assam, India. Studied at Slade School of Fine Art. 1930-40 lived in London and Paris and was involved with Surrealism. 1940-50 painted

COLQUHOUN, Robert

with automatic processes, wrote surrealist poetry and regularly visited Cornwall. 1950-60 wrote topographical books and a novel, exhibited widely on the Continent and moved to Cornwall. 1960-70 developed Merz Collages (the term 'Merz' refers to the use of found objects and papers in these collages, a technique evolved originally by the Dadaist, Kurt Schwitters) and landscapes that evolve not from reality but from the realm of fantasy and the imagination. Continued to write surrealist novels and poetry. From 1970 onwards began to research into the occult and alchemy. Held a retrospective at the Newlyn Orion Gallery, 1976.

COLQUHOUN, Robert   1914-1962
Painter. Born Kilmarnock, Scotland. Studied at Glasgow School of Art, 1933-8, where he met, and from then on was associated with, Robert MacBryde.* 1938 travelled Europe on a scholarship. 1939 painted for a year at Ayrshire, then entered the Royal Army Medical Corps. 1941 invalided out of army and moved to London, receiving initial support from Peter Watson, the arts patron and collector. Joined Civil Defence Corps as an ambulance driver and from then until 1944 painted mostly at night owing to day shifts on Civil Defence work. 1942 his first group of pictures was exhibited in London, in Lefevre Gallery's 'Six Scottish Painters'. Early influences of Gauguin and Wyndham Lewis were still visible. 1943 Jankel Adler* arrived from Glasgow and settled into studio in the same building as Colquhoun, MacBryde and John Minton.* 1943 first solo exhibition at Lefevre Gallery; 1944 his second solo exhibition at the Lefevre Gallery included paintings of Hebridean women, card players and grieving women. 1945 held a third solo exhibition of women with leaping cats. 1945 began experimenting with monotypes. 1947 fourth solo show at Lefevre. 1947 met Frances Byng Stamper, of Miller's Press, who became a friend and patron. Colquhoun spent nearly two years in Lewes where he was provided with a studio. 1948 executed designs for Scottish ballet, *Donald of the Burthens*. 1949 visited Italy. 1950 moved to Tilty Mill, in Essex, home of the poet George Barker and his wife Elizabeth Smart. 1953 did designs for *King Lear* at Stratford. 1958 retrospective held at the Whitechapel Art Gallery, London.

Bibl: *Robert Colquhoun,* City of Edinburgh Museum and Art Gallery, 1981.

CONDER, Charles   1868-1909
Painter. Born London, a descendant of Roubiliac, the sculptor. Taken to India as a child and sent home 1873. At the age of seventeen went to New South Wales to join his uncle and then began painting. 1890 returned to Europe and studied in Paris at Académie Julian and the Louvre. Joined NEAC and exhibited regularly there and at the Carfax Gallery until his untimely death.

Bibl: John Rothenstein, *The Life & Death of Conder,* London, 1938.

CONN, Roy   b.1931
Painter. Born London. Trained as a structural engineer and is self-taught. 1958 moved to St. Ives and became a member of the Penwith Society of Arts. Solo exhibitions at Rowan Gallery, London, 1966, and Arnolfini Gallery, Bristol, 1969. A hard-edge abstract artist.

CONNARD, Philip   1876-1958
Painter. Born Southport, Lancashire. Won a scholarship to RCA in 1896 and a British Institute travelling scholarship, 1898. Did illustration work for the Bodley Head and secured a teaching post at Lambeth School of Art. Became

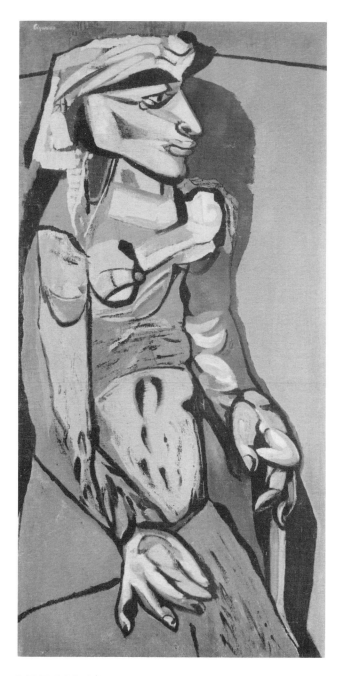

ROBERT COLQUHOUN, 1914-1962. '*Woman in Green*', 1949. 39¾in. x 20¼in. Aberdeen Art Gallery & Museums, Aberdeen City Arts Department.

a member of the NEAC and refused to acknowledge modernist developments. Often accompanied P.W. Steer* on painting holidays. 1914 joined the army and was invalided out in 1916 after the Battle of the Somme. Exhibited at RA, elected ARA 1918, then RA 1925. His work falls into four categories: decorative; stylised landscapes; portraits and interiors; realistic landscapes and seascapes; and watercolours capturing evanescent effects of light and atmosphere. 1945-49 served as Keeper of the RA and was appointed CVO in 1950.

CONROY, Stephen   b.1964
Painter. Born Helensburgh, Scotland. Studied at Glasgow School of Art, 1982-7. In 1986, before commencing his post-

CHARLES CONDER, 1868-1909. *'Silver Sands'*, c.1906. 25in. x 30in. Cartwright Hall, Bradford.

STEPHEN CONROY, b.1964. *'Further and Better Particulars'*, 1989. 54⅛in. x 72in.
Marlborough Fine Art (London) Ltd.

CONSTABLE, Martin

graduate year, was invited by Dumbarton District Council to hold a solo exhibition. Unlike most of his contemporaries who prefer loose brushwork and strident colour, Conroy meticulously plans his compositions, using chiaroscuro and a shallow pictorial space. Most of his pictures evoke an Edwardian world in which the interaction between the figures remains enigmatic. Memories of Degas, Seurat, Sickert* and Cowie* permeate his pictures.

Bibl: *Stephen Conroy: Living the Life,* Marlborough Fine Art, London, 1989.

CONSTABLE, Martin   b.1961
Painter. Born Toronto, Canada. Studied at Richmond upon Thames Polytechnic, 1978-9, St. Martin's School of Art, 1979-80, Coleg Elidyr Camphill, South Wales, 1980-1, and Camberwell, 1983-6. Has exhibited in various group shows, including John Moores, 1987.

CONSTANCE, Diana   b.1934
Painter. Born New York City, USA. Studied at Art Students League, New York, and University of New Mexico. 1961-6 lived in Rome and took up photography. 1966 moved to England. Since 1960 has had seven solo exhibitions and in 1988, at the People's Gallery, Kentish Town, exhibited a series of drawings entitled 'Aids (and nobody wants to know)'.

CONVEY, Frances   b.1956
Painter. Born Paisley, Scotland. Worked as a mechanical engineer before studying at Edinburgh College of Art, 1979. 1983 awarded the Carnegie Travelling Scholarship and two other prizes. Solo exhibitions at Edinburgh University Festival Club, 1984, and Mercury Gallery, Edinburgh, 1985.

COOK, Barrie   b.1929
Painter. Born Birmingham, West Midlands. Studied at Birmingham College of Art. Taught in secondary schools and at Coventry College of Art and Stourbridge College of Art. 1975 made Senior Fellow in Fine Art at Cardiff College of Art and in 1977, Gregynog Fellow, University of Wales. 1967 first solo exhibition held at Birmingham and Midland Institute; others include shows at the Whitechapel Art Gallery, 1974, and Oriel, Cardiff, 1977.

COOK, Beryl   b.1926
Painter. Born Beryl Lansley in Egham, Surrey. On leaving school she worked in an insurance office. 1943 her family moved to London and she briefly worked on stage before becoming a model for a number of dress firms. This developed her lifelong fascination with the way people dress and look. 1946 she left London, moving with her mother and one sister to a house and tea-garden at Hampton. There she married John Cook. 1956 moved with her husband to Stoke-by-Nayland in Essex where they managed a pub. They next moved to Rhodesia, where she did a variety of jobs, also deciding to become a painter. She continued with this aim after their return to England, at first painting only in the winter, and running a boarding home for Plymouth holidaymakers in the summer, a job that enabled her to observe a variety of human manners at close quarters. Has since become one of England's most popular living artists. Her second book of painting, *Private View* (1980) became a best seller. Her subject matter continues to reflect the immediate circumstances of her life, the pubs she frequents, and the human life she sees

RICHARD COOK, b.1947. *'Portrait of Saskia',* 1989. Charcoal on paper. 28in. x 19in. Odette Gilbert Gallery.

around her. Always a scene is portrayed with humour and understanding. (Plate 32, p.99.)

COOK, Christopher   b.1959
Painter and etcher. Born Yorkshire. Studied at Exeter College of Art, 1978-81 and RCA, 1983-6. 1983 drawings and poems published in *New Nerves,* and 1984 *The Choosing* 1984 executed mural project for V & A, also Royal Overseas League prizewinner. 1985 given John Minton travel award. 1986 won Italian Government Scholarship to Bologna. First solo exhibition held in the Library Gallery, Exeter University, 1982. Shows with Benjamin Rhodes, New Burlington Place, London.

COOK, David   b.1957
Painter. Born Dunfermline, Scotland. Began work as a bricklayer before entering Duncan of Jordanstone College of Art, 1979. First solo exhibition held at 369 Gallery, Edinburgh. 1985 given the Guthrie Award by the RSA.

COOK, Ebenezer Wake   1843-1926
Painter. Born Malden, Surrey. Specialised in landscape and exhibited at the RA from 1875 onwards. Worked on the Continent, particularly in Switzerland and Italy. Became well known for his innovative views on art education and gave lessons to Vanessa Bell.*

COOK, Richard   b.1947
Painter. Born Cheltenham, Gloucestershire. Studied at
St. Martin's School of Art, 1966-70, and RCA, 1970-3. 1985
moved from London to Cornwall. 1981 solo exhibitions at
House, London, and at Odette Gilbert Gallery, London,
1989. Represented in Arts Council collection and British
Museum.

COOKE, Jean   b.1927
Painter and sculptor. Born London. Studied at the Central
School of Arts and Crafts, Goldsmiths' College,
Camberwell School of Art, City and Guilds School and at
the RCA under Carel Weight* and Ruskin Spear.*
Married the painter John Bratby* in 1953. Exhibits at the
RA, RBA and with the London Group.

COOKSEY, May Louise Greville   1878-1943
Painter. Born Birmingham, West Midlands. Studied at
Leamington and Liverpool Schools of Art, and won silver
and bronze medals at South Kensington School of Art.
Received a travelling scholarship and visited Italy.
Exhibited at RA and elsewhere. Taught at South
Kensington School. Later lived at Freshfield in Lanca-
shire. Ecclesiastical artist, landscape and figure painter
and etcher.

COOPER, Alfred Egerton   1883-1974
Painter. Born Tettenhall, West Midlands. Studied at
Bilston School of Art and the RCA, received his diploma in
1911. Specialised in portraits, figure subjects and landscapes. Exhibited at the RA, RBA, the Paris Salon and
elsewhere. Served in the Artists' Rifles, 1914-18 during
which time the sight in one eye was impaired by chlorine
gas. Painted a portrait of George VI in 1940. His portrait of
Winston Churchill, painted in 1943, was widely reproduced.

COOPER, Austin   b.1890
Maker of abstract collages. Born Manitoba, Canada.
Settled in Cardiff, 1896. Studied at Cardiff College of Art,
Allan Frazer College of Art, Arbroath, 1905-9, then
evening classes at City and Guilds School, London. Served
in Flanders during the First World War, then returned to
Canada. Finally settled in London, 1922. Worked as a
poster designer until 1943 when he began to paint and
make collages. First solo exhibition at London Gallery,
1948; many further shows with Gimpel Fils Gallery,
London. Work in the Tate Gallery and Canadian collections.

COOPER, David   b.1952
Painter. Born Rotherhithe, London. Worked as a Mason
Pavior for London Borough of Southwark, 1968-78.
Studied at Goldsmiths' College of Art, 1978-82. 1982 first
exhibited in 'New Contemporaries' Stowells Annual
Award. His paintings combine real environments with
imaginative events. Included in the collections of
Leicestershire Education Authority.

COOPER, Eileen   b.1953
Painter. Born Glossop, Derbyshire. Studied at Goldsmiths'
College, 1971-4 and RCA, 1974-7. Regular solo exhibitions
since 1979, including Blond Fine Art, London, 1985 and
Castlefield Gallery, Manchester, 1986. Widely acclaimed
for her figurative paintings exploring female experience.
Represented by the Benjamin Rhodes Gallery, London.

JEAN COOKE, b.1927. *'Self portrait'*, c.1959. Tate Gallery.

EILEEN COOPER, b.1953. *'Scarecrow'*, 1987. 66in. x 60in.
Benjamin Rhodes Gallery.

COPAS, Ronnie   b.1932
Painter. Born London. Moved to Cornwall where he worked as a ferryman to St. Michael's Mount. Self taught. Works in egg tempera on wood panel coated with gesso. His scenes are often distorted, as if seen through a fish-eye lens, and are based on Cornish or Spanish life.

COPE, Arthur   1857-1940
Painter. Son of the artist Charles West Cope. Studied at Carey's and the RA Schools. Specialised in portraiture and landscape. Exhibited regularly at the RA from 1876 and ran an art school at South Kensington, where his pupils included Nina Hamnett* and Vanessa Bell.* Painted portraits of Edward VII, George V, Lord Kitchener and other important figures of his day. Knighted in 1917.

COPEMAN, Constance Gertrude   1864-1953
Painter. Born Liverpool, Merseyside. Studied at Liverpool School of Art. 1885-1938 exhibited at Liverpool Autumn exhibitions and from 1894 at RA. Her etchings and sketching albums are in Liverpool City Libraries. Specialised in landscape and portraiture. 1897 elected ARE.

COPLEY, John   1875-1950
Painter and printmaker. Born Manchester. Studied at Manchester School of Art, in the studio of Watson Nicol and Arthur Cope* and at the RA Schools, then spent ten years in Italy. Exhibited at the RA, RSA, RBA and with the NEAC. Took up lithography in 1907 and was Hon. Secretary of the Senefelder Club, 1910-16. Won the major award at the First International Exhibition of Lithographs at the Chicago Art Institute, 1930. Elected RBA, 1933. Retrospective exhibition at Agnews, 1990.

COPNALL, Edward Bainbridge   1903-1973
Sculptor and painter. Born Capetown, South Africa. Studied at Goldsmiths' College, London, and RA Schools. 1929 turned to sculpture. 1945-53 Head of Sir John Cass College. Commissions include figures on the RIBA building, Portland Place, 1931-4, St. Columba's, Pont Street and 72 carvings for the *Queen Mary* and *Queen Elizabeth.* 1946 awarded MBE. 1961-6 President of Royal Society of British Sculptors. Father of John Copnall.*

COPNALL, Frank   1870-1949
Painter. Born Ryde, Isle of Man. Began a business career in Liverpool around 1885 and painted in his spare time. Took up portrait painting as a career in 1897, as the result of a commission. Exhibited at the Liverpool Autumn Exhibition from 1894 and at the RA from 1902, and at various London and provincial societies. Member of the Liverpool Academy and the Liver Sketching Club. Represented in the Walker Art Gallery, Liverpool.

COPNALL, John   b.1928
Painter. Born Sussex, son of Edward Copnall.* Studied at AA School of Architecture, 1945-6 and at the RA Schools, 1949-54. 1955 moved to Spain, returning to England to live, 1968. 1970 awarded Edwin Abbey Scholarship. 1955 first solo exhibition at the Piccadilly Gallery, London. When Copnall left the RA he was committed to figurative painting. He later turned to abstraction whilst living in Spain. His recent work is often based on the pentangle which is built up out of disjointed strokes of vibrant colours. Included in the collections of Aberdeen Art Gallery and Museum, Arts Council of Great Britain,

Bristol and York Universities, Ateneum Museum, Helsinki and the Sara Hilded Foundation Museum, Tampere, Finland.

COPNALL, Teresa Norah   1882-1972
Painter. Born Teresa Norah Burchart at Haughton-le-Skern, near Darlington, Co. Durham. Trained at Brussels, the Slade and Herkomer's School. Married the Liverpool portrait painter, Frank Copnall.* Lived at Hoylake. Exhibited at Liverpool Autumn Exhibitions, RA and Paris Salon. Specialised in portaits and flowers.

COSGROVE, James   b.1939
Printmaker, painter and sculptor. Born Glasgow, Scotland. 1955 joined the Army as a cartographic draughtsman, then worked ten years as a telecommunications officer for a telephone exchange before studying at Glasgow School of Art, 1967-71. Joined staff at Glasgow School of Art on graduating. 1980 solo exhibition at Glasgow Print Studio; 1986, solo exhibition at Corners Gallery, Glasgow.

COSMAN, Milein   b.1922
Painter. Born Dusseldorf, Germany. Came to England in 1939 and trained at Slade, 1939-42. Member of the FDKB (The German League of Culture, founded in Hampstead in 1939 with Kokoschka officially as its head). Close friend of John Heartfield, the German collagist. 1942 joined Artists' International Association. Subjects during the war years included portraits of members of FDKB and other eminent artists and intellectuals, and sketches of everyday life. For ITV she has organised and presented school programmes on drawing.

COTTON, Alan   b.1936
Painter. Born Redditch, Worcestershire. Studied at Redditch School of Art, Ruskin Hall, Bourneville School of Art and at Birmingham College of Art. Began painting full-time, 1982. Exhibited numerous times in Great Britain; has also exhibited at the Canada Arts Gallery, Victoria, where he gave a number of lectures. In February 1987 he visited Florida, USA on a lecture tour. Writes for art magazines and the Open University, and has written a book on child art *Learning and Teaching through Arts and Crafts.* He has been featured in a number of TV films about his work as a painter. Produces landscapes, often in oils, applying the paint with a palette knife, thereby conveying the scene through geometric shapes of colour.

COUCH, Christopher   b.1946
Painter. Born Warwickshire. Studied at Leamington School of Art, 1962-3, and the Slade School, 1963. 1981 first one-person show at House Gallery. 1982 first artist in residence at Birmingham City Art Gallery.

COULTER, Michael   b.1937
Painter. Born Shropshire. Studied at Hereford, Stafford and Leeds Colleges of Art. 1983 first exhibited at the RSW and the RA Summer Exhibitions. Has lived in Suffolk since 1966 and paints locally around the River Orwell and River Stour. 1989 solo exhibition at the John Russell Gallery, Ipswich.

COUNSELL, Melanie   b.1964
Installation artist. Born Cardiff, Wales, Studied at South Glamorgan Institute of Higher Education, 1982-6, and Slade School of Fine Art, 1986-8. First solo exhibition held

at Matt's Gallery, London, 1989. Most of her work is 'site-specific' and has dealt with aspects of grief, melancholy, human tragedy or loss. Represented in 'The British Art Show' at the Hayward Gallery, London, 1990.

COUNSELL, Nicola   b.1963
Painter. Born Kidderminster, Worcestershire. Studied at Birmingham College of Art, 1982-5 and at Cyprus College of Art Summer School, 1987. First solo exhibition at the Solomon Gallery in 1986, followed by another exhibition there in 1987. Prizewinner, Royal Society of Oil Painters Exhibition, 1987.

COUTINHO, Graca   b.1949
Painter. Born Lisbon, Portugal. Studied at School of Fine Art, Lisbon, 1967-71. Moved to London, 1971 and studied at St. Martin's School of Art, 1974-7. Since 1975 has held several solo exhibitions in Lisbon, Oporto and London and has been represented in group shows throughout Europe and South America, including the Sao Paolo and Paris Biennales. Included in 'Critic's Space 4' at Air Gallery in London, 1987. Solo exhibition at Todd Gallery, London, 1989.

COVENTRY, Frederick Halford   b.1905
Mural painter. Educated in New Zealand. Studied at the Julian Ashton School in Sydney, 1926-8, and at the Grosvenor School of Art, 1929. Exhibited at the RA and abroad. Member of the Art Workers Guild, 1945, and elected to the Society of Mural Painters, 1947.

COWIE, James   1886-1956
Painter. Born on a farm in Aberdeenshire, Scotland. Studied English Literature at Aberdeen University, but was increasingly attracted to the visual arts. Studied at Glasgow School of Art, 1912-14. Conscientious objector 1916-18, and worked for Pioneer Corps. Taught at Bellshill Academy, near Glasgow. Held first solo exhibition at the McLellan Galleries, Glasgow, 1935. That same year, appointed Head of Painting at Gray's School of Art, Aberdeen. 1937 became warden of the Patrick Allen Fraser School of Art, Arbroath. His study of the Old Masters coupled with his meticulous draughtsmanship, had given his work a striking formality in the 1920s and 1930s. In the 1940s he became interested in Surrealism and began to experiment with perspective and other pictorial devices.

Bibl: Cordelia Oliver, *James Cowie,* Edinburgh, 1980.

COWPER, Frank Cadogan   1877-1958
Painter. Born Wicker, Northamptonshire. Studied at St. John's Wood Art School, 1896 and RA Schools, 1897-1902, and spent six months in the studio of Edwin A. Abbey.* Exhibited at the RA from 1899, specialising in historical subjects, portraits and landscapes. Elected ARWS, 1904, ARA, 1907, RWS, 1911 and RA, 1934. Work in the Tate Gallery collection.

COX, E. Albert   1876-1955
Mural painter and illustrator. Born Islington, London. Studied at Whitechapel People's Palace and at Bolt Court. Worked first as a designer for a manufacturing chemist and later assisted Sir Frank Brangwyn.* Exhibited at most of the leading art venues. Elected RBA, 1915, RI, 1921 and ROI, 1923.

RAYMOND COXON, b.1896. *'Edge of the Forest'.* 12in. x 26in. Private Collection.

COXON, Raymond   b.1896
Painter and muralist. Born Hanley, Stoke-on-Trent, Staffordshire. Served with the Cavalry in Palestine in the First World War. Studied at Leeds College of Art, 1919-21 and RCA, 1921-5. 1926 married Edna Ginesi.* 1927 formed, with Henry Moore,* Leon Underwood* and others, the short-lived British Independent Society. 1928 first one-artist exhibition with the London Artists' Association at the Cooling Galleries. Member of the London Group and the Chiswick Group. 1940-5 Official War Artist.

Bibl: *Raymond Coxon: Retrospective Exhibition,* Stoke-on-Trent Museum and Art Gallery cat., 1987.

CRABTREE, Jack   b.1938
Painter. Born Rochdale, Lancashire. Studied at Rochdale College of Art, St. Martin's School of Art and RA Schools. 1975 first solo exhibition. Has specialised in paintings of miners.

CRADDOCK, Kenneth Julius Holt   1910-1989
Painter. Born Bolton, Lancashire. Studied at Bolton School of Art and Manchester School of Art, graduating 1939. Wartime service spent as a draughtsman with de Havillands at Trafford Park, Manchester. Began teaching at Manchester School of Art in 1946, moving to Hereford School (later College) of Art as its Principal in 1951. Retired 1970. Exhibited with the Manchester Academy of Fine Arts, also at the RA. Also worked as an illustrator, for the *Manchester Evening News,* among others.

CRAGG, Tony   b.1949
Sculptor. Born Liverpool, Merseyside. Trained at Gloucestershire College of Art, 1969-70, Wimbledon School of Art, 1970-3 and RCA, 1973-7. 1977 moved to live and work in Wuppertal, West Germany. From 1977 taught at Dusseldorf Academy for a few years. Has vast studio at Wuppertal which had formerly been a textile factory. 1970 first solo exhibition at Lisson Gallery, London. 1988 awarded the Turner Prize, and represented in Britain at the Venice Biennale. Work in Tate Gallery, Arts Council and British Council collections.

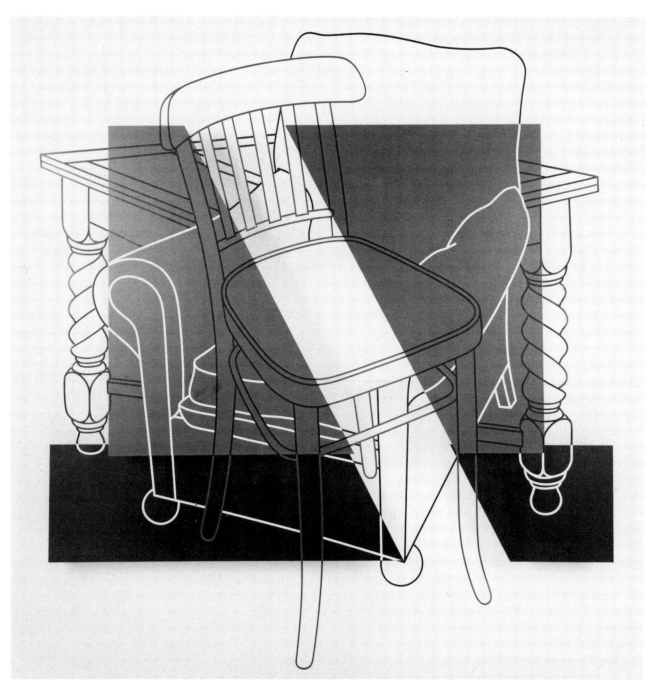

MICHAEL CRAIG-MARTIN, b.1941. *'Domestic Life',* 1985. Oil on aluminium with painted steel. 85in. x 81in. x 7in.
The artist, courtesy Waddington Galleries.

CRAIG, Edward Gordon   1872-1966
Theatrical designer and wood engraver. Self-taught.
Produced over 500 engravings and exhibited widely in
Europe. Was an influential figure within the theatre
world and author of *The Art of the Theatre,* 1905, and
Towards a New Theatre, 1913, among other works.

CRAIG-MARTIN, Michael   b.1941
Mixed media artist. Born Dublin, Ireland. Resident in
USA, 1946-66. Studied at Yale University, 1961-6. Since
1966 resident in Great Britain. 1969 first solo exhibition
held at Rowan Gallery; since then frequent solo shows in
England and abroad. 1970-2 artist in residence, King's

College, Cambridge. Since 1973 has taught at Goldsmiths'
College, London. 1981-2 spent a year in USA.

Bibl: *Michael Craig-Martin,* Waddington Galleries, 1988.

CRAMPTON, Sean   b.1918
Sculptor and engraver. Born Manchester. Studied at the
Victoria Junior School of Art, Birmingham, 1930-3, and at
the Birmingham School of Art and in Paris. Exhibited at
the RA and elsewhere. Became ARBS, 1953, FRBS, 1965
and PRBS, 1966.

CRAWFORD, Hugh Adam   1898-1982
Painter. Born Busby, Scotland. Studied at Glasgow School

JOHN CRAXTON, b.1922. *'Four Figures in a Mountain Landscape'*, 1950-1. 63in. x 84in. Collection Bristol City Art Gallery.

of Art, 1919-23 and part-time at Central School of Arts and Crafts and St. Martin's School of Art, 1924-5. Joined staff of Glasgow School of Art, 1925 and taught Colquhoun,* MacBryde,* Eardley* and others. Head of Gray's School of Art, Aberdeen, 1948-54, and Principal of Duncan of Jordanstone College of Art, Dundee, 1954-64. Specialised in portraits and painted murals, including some for John Brown's shipyard and Scottish Brewers, Glasgow.

CRAWHALL, Joseph   1861-1913
Painter. Born Morpeth, Northumberland. Was first taught by his father and then at Aimé Morot's atelier in Paris. Was associated with the 'Glasgow Boys' and specialised in paintings of animals and landscape. Member of the RWS, 1887-93 and the NEAC, 1909-13.

CRAXTON, John   b.1922
Painter. Born London. 1936 visited Paris and saw Picasso's *Guernica* and Miro's *The Reaper*. 1939 lived in Paris and studied life drawing at La Grande Chaumière. Studied at Westminster Art School and Central School of Art under P.F. Millard* and Eric Schilsky.* 1941 studied drawing at Goldsmiths' College under Clive Gardiner* and shared premises with Lucian Freud.* 1943 made the

first of many visits to Pembrokeshire with Graham Sutherland.* 1944 first solo exhibition at Leicester Galleries, London. 1948 visited Crete for the first time. Travelled widely over next few years, for periods lived abroad but kept a studio in London. Retrospective held at Whitechapel Art Gallery, 1967. Represented by Christopher Hull Gallery, London.

Bibl: Malcolm Yorke, *The Spirit of the Place: Nine Neo-Romantic Artists and their Times,* Constable, 1988.

CREBER, Frank   b.1959
Painter. Studied at the University of Newcastle upon Tyne, 1977-81, and at Chelsea School of Art, 1986-7. Awards include Herbert Read Fellowship, Chelsea School of Art, 1986; Picker Fellowship, Kingston Polytechnic and joint Winner, Barclays Bank Young Painters Award, 1987. First solo exhibition at Sue Williams, London, 1989.

CREE, Janet   b.1910
Portrait painter. Born London. Studied at the Byam Shaw School, 1928-33. Married the barrister John Platt-Mills, 1936. Exhibited at the RA from 1933-7. Executed portraits in tempera in a quattrocento style. Work in the Tate Gallery collection, bought by Chantrey purchase.

CREFFIELD, Dennis

DENNIS CREFFIELD, b.1931. *'Bristol Cathedral'*. Drawing. The South Bank Centre.

CREFFIELD, Dennis   b.1931
Painter. Born London. Studied at Borough Polytechnic under David Bomberg* and at Slade School of Art. 1964 became Gregory Fellow in Painting, University of Leeds. Since 1962 member of the London Group. 1966 first solo exhibition held at Leeds City Art Gallery. 1987 'Drawings by Dennis Creffield: English Cathedrals' was toured by the South Bank Centre.

CRIBB, Herbert Joseph   1892-1967
Stonecarver. Apprenticed to Eric Gill* in London, 1906. Sent by Gill to cut the inscription on Epstein's monument to Oscar Wilde at Père Lachaise cemetery in Paris. Moved to Ditchling with Gill and after war service returned to open his own workshop there. At the foundation of the Guild of St. Joseph and St. Dominic he moved into the Guild's Workshop, taking over from Gill in 1924. 1960 he carved a memorial plaque for Gill's birthplace, 32 Hamilton Road, Brighton.

CROOK, P.J.   b.1945
Painter. Born Pamela Jane Hagland in Cheltenham, Gloucestershire. Studied at Gloucestershire College of Art, specialising in textiles and printmaking. 1965 moved to London and worked as a freelance textile designer, also developed a business in decorated wooden objects for fashionable shops and boutiques. Moved to Weston-super-Mare and, in 1977, began exhibiting at the Portal Gallery, London. Exhibits regularly at the RWEA and the Portal

TOM CROSS, b.1931. *'Cape Cornwall'*, 1988. Mixed media. 30in. x 30in. Private Collection.

Gallery. Often uses mirrors and strong light sources to help transport the viewer into another, strange world.

CROSBIE, William   b.1915
Painter. Born Hankow, China, where his father, a Scot, was employed as a marine engineer. Returned with his family to Glasgow, 1926. Trained as an accountant and worked as a salesman. Studied at Glasgow School of Art, 1932-5. Awarded travelling scholarship and studied in Paris under Ferdinand Léger, also took drawing lessons from Aristide Maillol. Influenced by the French Surrealists. During the 1940s and '50s became well known as a muralist, producing large scale work for the 1938 Glasgow Empire Exhibition and elsewhere. Held many solo exhibitions in Glasgow and Edinburgh and had a retrospective at the Scottish Gallery, Edinburgh, 1980.

CROSBY, Clement   b.1958
Painter. Trained at Portsmouth College of Art, 1978-9, and Trent Polytechnic, 1979-82. 1988 mounted his first solo exhibition in his flat (provisionally entitled 'Vanguard Gallery').

CROSS, Dorothy   b.1956
Sculptor. Born Ireland. Studied at the Cork School of Art, 1973-4, and Leicester School of Art, 1974-7; further study at the San Francisco Art Institute, 1978-82. 1980 first solo show at the Triskett Art Centre, Cork; most recent at the Douglas Hyde Gallery, Dublin, 1988. Explores social issues and male and female relationships in her sculpture.

CROSS, Tom   b.1931
Painter. Born Manchester. Studied at Manchester Regional College of Art and at the Slade, 1953-6. 1956-8 travelled and painted in Italy and France on Italian and French Government scholarships. 1963 began to teach painting at Reading University. 1976-87 Principal of Falmouth School of Art, Cornwall. 1984 published *Painting the Warmth of the Sun,* a book about St. Ives' artists.

GRAHAM CROWLEY, b.1950. 'The Chain Store', 1987. 80in. x 100in. Edward Totah Gallery.

CROWLEY, Graham   b.1950
Painter. Born Romford, Essex. Studied at St. Martin's School of Art, 1968-72 and RCA, 1972-5. 1976 and 1978 received Arts Council awards and 1982-3 was artist in residence at St. Edmund Hall, Oxford. Has held solo exhibitions in London and New York and is currently Senior Fellow at South Glamorgan Institute of Higher Education.

CROWTHER, Michael   b.1946
Painter. Born Co. Durham. Studied at Leeds College of Art. 1970 joined Cardiff College of Art as lecturer and 1977 won a Welsh Arts Council bursary. 1978 first solo exhibition at Open Studio, Cardiff. Included in the Arts Council's 'British Art Show', 1980.

CROZIER, William   1897-1930
Painter. Born Edinburgh, Scotland. Entered Edinburgh College of Art in 1915. Won the Carnegie Travelling Scholarship and studied in Paris under André Lhote. Exhibited at RSA from 1920 and the SSA from 1922. Elected ARSA, 1930. Best known for his landscapes of France and Italy and especially for his carefully constructed views of Edinburgh. Had an influence on William MacTaggart* with whom he shared a studio. A haemophiliac, he died at the age of thirty-three.

Bibl: *Royal Scottish Academy Annual Report*, Edinburgh, 1930.

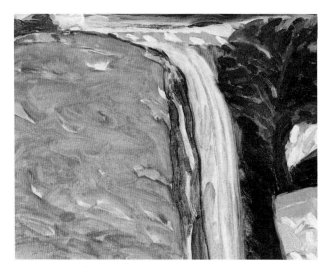

WILLIAM CROZIER, b.1930. 'McCarthy's Lane', 1988. 16in. x 20in. Private Collection.

CROZIER, William   b.1930
Painter. Born Yoker, Scotland. Studied at Glasgow School of Art, 1949-53. Worked for two yers as a theatre director. Since 1955 has lived in Paris, Dublin, Malaga and London.

CRUMPLIN, Colin

Has taught at Bath Academy of Art, Corsham, Central School of Arts and Crafts, and Winchester School of Art where he was Head of Fine Art until 1987. Retired to devote himself to full-time painting. In the late 1950s developed a powerful abstract idiom loosely based on the study of landscape motifs. 1957-70 held eight solo exhibitions at the Drian Galleries, London. Also exhibited elsewhere and in the 1980s returned to more recognisable depictions of landscape, often employing strong colour.

Bibl: *William Crozier, Paintings,* The Scottish Gallery, Edinburgh, 1985.

CRUMPLIN, Colin   b.1946

Painter. Studied at Leicester College of Art, 1964-5, Chelsea School of Art, 1965-8 and Slade, 1968-70. Solo exhibitions held at Salisbury Festival 1985 and Axiom Gallery, Cheltenham, 1986.

CUBITT, James   b.1914

Sculptor. Studied at Ruskin School of Art, Oxford and the Architectural Association School, London. 1940-5 war service as a Major in the Royal Engineers. 1946-8 taught at Department of Architecture, Kingston School of Art, and in 1948 began a private architectural practice. 1957 started sculpture at St. Martin's School of Art, London. First one-person show at John Whibley Gallery, London, 1962.

CUDDIHY, Micky   b.1952

Painter. Born New York, USA. Moved to England in 1962. Studied at Edinburgh College of Art, 1969-71, Central School of Art, 1971-4 and at Chelsea School of Art, 1974-5. 1976 won the Arts Council Visual Arts Award. 1980 first solo exhibition at 'The Gallery', ACME Studios, London. Has exhibited regularly with the London Group since 1975.

CUDWORTH, Jack   b.1930

Painter. Born Leeds, Yorkshire. Studied at Leeds College of Art. 1954-75 lived in Dublin, then moved back to England. Exhibited regularly at the Royal Hibernian Academy, and the RA summer exhibition. (In the evenings, he takes on his other profession as clarinettist 'Phil Butler', well known in jazz circles.) 1977 first one-person show in London at Belgrave Gallery. Work in public collections including Arts Council of Ireland, the Arts Council of Northern Ireland, the Haverty Trust.

CUDWORTH, Nick   b.1947

Painter and graphic artist. Born Derby. Studied at Derby College of Art, 1964-6, Chelsea School of Art, 1966-9. Awarded Leverhulme Scholarship, which he spent in the USA. 1970-1 spent a year as a rock musician. 1969 first one-person show at Newcastle University. 1971-3 ward orderly in geriatric hospital and lecturer in graphic design at Derby College of Art and Trent Polytechnic, Nottingham. 1973-8 postman, musician, lecturer in drawing at Winchester School of Art. Full-time artist since 1979. Solo exhibition at Nicholas Treadwell Gallery, London, 1981.

Bibl: *Satie's Faction* (a folder of eight prints). The Cephalophones Postcard Edition, published with South West Arts, 1975.

CULBERT, Bill   b.1935

Painter and sculptor. Born New Zealand. Studied at Canterbury College School of Art, New Zealand, 1953-6, and at RCA, 1957-60. 1960-1 taught painting at Hornsey College of Art. 1961 first one-person show at the Commonwealth Institute Art Gallery, London. 1962 appointed Fellow in Fine Art, Nottingham University. 1964 awarded first prize, Open Painting competition, Arts Council of Northern Ireland. 1970 designed stage set/light sculpture for *Lament of the Waves,* for the Royal Ballet, Covent Garden. 1981 won Greater London Arts Association Award to Artists. 1982 Arts Council of Great Britain Holographic Bursary. 1985 artist in residence, Museum of Holography, New York.

Bibl: *Bill Culbert: Selected Works 1968-86,* ICA, London, 1986.

CULLEARN, David   b.1941

Painter. Born Bradford, Yorkshire. Worked as a carpenter and joiner and then studied at Leeds School of Architecture until 1964. Partner in architectural practice with offices in Manchester and Ascot. Regular walking and painting tours throughout Britain each year are taken in the Outer Isles or the West Coast of Scotland. 1975 walked the complete length of the Outer Hebrides. 1980 first one-person show at Phillips and Sons Gallery, Marlow, Bucks.

CULLEN, Patrick   b.1949

Painter. Born Addlestone, Surrey. Studied at St. Martin's School of Art, 1972-3, and Camberwell School of Art, 1973-6. Work included in RA summer exhibitions. 1978 first one-person show at Ogle Gallery, Eastbourne. Work in the collection of Sheffield City Art Galleries.

CULLERNE-BROWN, Matthew   b.1956

Painter. Born London. Studied at Camberwell School of Arts and Crafts, 1975-9, and at Slade School of Fine Art, 1979-81. Included in mixed exhibitions, e.g. Northern Young Contemporaries and New Contemporaries from 1979. 1984 first one-person show at Air Gallery. From 1984 visiting lecturer at Birmingham Polytechnic and St. Martin's School of Art.

CULLIMORE, Michael   b.1936

Painter. Born Bradford on Avon, Wiltshire. Studied at Swindon School of Art and Goldsmiths' College of Art. Worked as a labourer in an East End foundry casting ships' propellers. 1962-83 lived in North Wales, then returned to Wiltshire. 1968 one-person exhibition at Bangor Art Gallery. 1962-82 Deputy Curator, then Curator of Oriel Gallery, Bangor. Work in public collections including Welsh Arts Council, Contemporary Arts Society for Wales, Ceolfrith Gallery Collection, Sunderland. Retrospective touring exhibition organised by Aberystwyth Arts Centre, 1983.

Bibl: Michael Cullimore: *'I am awake in the Universe:' Paintings and Watercolours 1968-82,* Aberystwyth Arts Centre, 1983.

CULLINAN, Charlotte   b.1959

Painter. Studied at Canterbury College of Art, 1977-8. Ravensbourne College of Art, 1978-81 and the RCA, 1982-4. Included in mixed exhibitions since 1984. First one-person show at Roger Francis Gallery, London, 1985.

CUMING, Fred   b.1930

Painter. Born London. Trained at Sidcup School of Art, 1945-9. 1949-51 National Service. Studied at RCA, 1951-5. Awarded Abbey travel scholarship and visited Italy. Elected ARA, 1964 and RA, 1974. 1986 won Sir Brinsley Ford Award, NEAC. Regular exhibitor at RA.

CUMISKEY, Mike   b.1940
Sculptor. Born Stockton on Tees, Cleveland. Studied at Middlesborough College of Art, 1956-60. Taught in London and Teesside, 1960-5. From 1966 has worked as artist/designer for Skelmersdale Development Corporation, in Skelmersdale New Town. 1961 first one-person show at Studio Club Gallery, London; also in 1961 won second prize in National Coal Board 'Trophy Design' competition.

CUMMING, Diana   b.1929
Painter. Born Hereford. Studied at the Slade School of Art, 1950-4. 1954 won travelling scholarship in Paris. 1954-6 British School at Rome scholarship. From 1955 work included in mixed exhibitions. 1964 first one-person show at the Beaux Arts Gallery. 1987 retrospective exhibition at the Serpentine Gallery, London. Work in the collection of the CAS, Arts Council, Hereford Art Gallery, Walker Art Gallery, Liverpool.

CUMMING, James   b.1922
Painter. Born Dumfermline, Scotland. Studied at Edinburgh College of Art, 1939-41, then served with the RAF, 1941-6. 1946 resumed studies at Edinburgh College of Art, awarded postgraduate and travelling scholarships. 1950-82 Tutor in Painting, Edinburgh College of Art. 1951 RSA award. 1955 first one-person show at Gallery One, London. 1958-68 contributed as broadcaster to BBC radio and TV programmes on art. 1964 awarded International Scholarship in the Humanities, Harvard University, USA. 1970 elected RSA. In 1973 became Treasurer of the RSA and between 1978 and 1980 acted as its Secretary. Works in numerous public collections, including Aberdeen, Eastbourne, Edinburgh, Glasgow, Kirkcaldy, Paisley, Perth Art Galleries.

CUMMINS, Gus   b.1943
Painter. Studied at Sutton and Wimbledon Schools of Art. 1967 he was president of the Young Contemporaries Group. Regular group exhibitions since 1981. Lives and works in Hastings. Represented in the Contemporary Art Society's collection.

CUNDALL, Charles RA, RWS   1890-1971
Painter. Born Stretford, Lancashire. Studied at Manchester School of Art. Scholarship to RCA, 1912. 1914 war service in First World War. After being wounded in the right arm in 1916 he learnt to paint with his left hand and returned to RCA from where he transferred to the Slade. Painted at Colarossi's atelier in 1920. Joined NEAC. During the 1920s and 1930s he travelled extensively in Europe. Official War Artist to the Royal Navy and Air Force, 1939-45. Elected RA 1944. After the war he continued to paint and travel widely. Works represented in the Tate Gallery (Chantrey Bequest) and the Imperial War Museum among other public collections.

CUNDELL, Nora L.M.   1889-1948
Painter and writer. Born London, the granddaughter of the artist Henry Cundell. Studied at Blackheath Art School, the Westminster Technical Institute under Sickert, and at the Slade School, 1911-14 and in 1919. Exhibited at the RA, NEAC and the Paris Salon. 1925 first solo exhibition at the Redfern Gallery. 1930 founder member of the National Society. Wrote and illustrated *Unsentimental Journey,* published 1940. 1949 memorial exhibition held at the RBA Galleries. Work in the Tate Gallery.

CUNNINGHAM, John   b.1926
Painter. Born Lanarkshire, Scotland. Studied at Glasgow School of Art and taught painting there, 1967-85. Regular exhibitor at the RSA. Has work in many Scottish public collections, including the Hunterian Art Gallery and Strathclyde University.

CUNNINGHAM, Vera   1897-1955
Painter. Studied at Central School of Art. 1922 began exhibiting with the London Group and became a member, 1927. 1929 first solo exhibition held at Bloomsbury Gallery. Through her teacher Bernard Meninsky* she was introduced to Matthew Smith* and became his favourite model. Her most assured painting was produced during the Second World War, in between her duties as a London air raid warden. In these paintings, gargantuan figures and grotesque nudes seem to caricature the nudes of Matthew Smith, suggesting an alarming tension between her role as artist and as model.

CURRIE, John   c.1884-1914
Painter. Born Chesterton, Newcastle under Lyme. Studied at Newcastle and Hanley Schools of Art and won two scholarships. Worked as a ceramic artist until he became Master of Life Painting at Bristol. 1910 studied part-time at the Slade School, making friends with Mark Gertler.* Left his wife in 1911 after only four years of marriage. Worked briefly in Cornwall. Set up home with Miss Dolly Henry in Hampstead until, in a fit of jealousy, he shot himself and her, and died the following day. Work in many public collections, e.g. Stoke-on-Trent Art Gallery.

CURRIE, Ken   b.1960
Painter and printmaker. Born North Shields, Tyne and Wear. Studied Social Science at Paisley College, 1977-8 and painting at Glasgow School of Art, 1978-83, which included a postgraduate year. 1982 first solo exhibition, 'Art and Social Commitment', at Glasgow Arts Centre. Commissioned to paint murals for Glasgow's People's Palace with scenes based on Scottish labour history. Solo exhibition at Third Eye Centre, Glasgow, 1988.

CURSITER, Stanley   1887-1976
Painter. Born Kirkwall, Orkney. Was apprenticed as a chromolithographic designer before he entered Edinburgh College of Art. Responded to Post-Impressionist and Futurism, applying a fragmented modernist style to Scottish scenes. Became Keeper at the Scottish National Portrait Gallery and the Director of the National Gallery of Scotland, 1930-48. 1948 appointed King's Painter and Limner in Scotland and retired from the National Gallery of Scotland to his native Orkney, to paint landscapes and record Orcadian life in articles.

Bibl: *Stanley Cursiter Centenary Exhibition,* Pier Arts Centre, Orkney, 1987.

CUTHBERT, Rosalind   b.1951
Painter. Born Weston-super-Mare, Somerset. Studied at Somerset College of Art, 1969-71, Central School of Art, 1971-4, and the RCA, 1974-7. First solo exhibition held at the RCA, 1976; another at the Crest Gallery, 1980. Represented in the collection of the National Portrait Gallery.

ALFRED DANIELS, b.1926. *'Village Fete'*, 1986. 40in. x 30in. Private Collection.

DACHINGER, Hugo   b.1908
Painter and collagist. Born Gmuden, Upper Austria.
Studied art in Leipzig, 1929-32. Returned to Austria to
promote a new idea for a lettering system which he also
took to Poland, while continuing to paint and draw. 1938
emigrated to England, via Denmark. 1940 interned. On
his release impositions on his business obliged him to
concentrate on his painting. 1941 first one-artist
exhibition 'Art Behind Barbed Wire' held at Redfern
Gallery; further exhibitions followed.

DACHINGER, Meta   1916-1983
Painter. Born Nuremberg, Germany. Studied under the
painter Hublitz. After Hitler came to power, she went to
Italy and continued her studies in Turin, producing
mainly still lifes and portraits. 1939 emigrated to
England, living for a period in North Wales before
returning to London. 1943 married the painter Hugo
Dachinger.* After the birth of her children she produced
mainly watercolours.

DAGNALL, Thompson William   b.1956
Sculptor. Born Liverpool. Studied at Liverpool Polytechnic,
1974-5, Brighton Polytechnic, 1975-8, Chelsea College of
Art, 1978-9. First solo exhibition at Festival Hall, 1984.

DAINTREY, Adrian   1902-1988
Painter. Studied at Slade School. Received encouragement
from Augustus John* and Matthew Smith.* Lived in
Paris for some years, making regular return visits to
London. Much travelled artist, whose best work is his
drawings in pen and wash of people and places. 1953-61
was art critic for *Punch.* 1964 published his autobiography,
I Must Say, which conveys his urbane, perceptive and
amusing character.

DALBY, Claire   b.1944
Botanical illustrator. Born St. Andrews, Scotland.
Studied at City and Guilds, London Art School, 1964-7.
1966 first exhibited at RA. 1973 elected Associate of RWS,
and full member, 1977. 1978 elected Associate of the RE.

DALEY, Anthony   b.1960
Painter. Born Jamaica. Studied at Leeds College of Art, 1978-9, Wimbledon College of Art, 1979-82, and Chelsea School of Art, 1982-3. Solo exhibition at Angela Flowers Gallery London, 1986 and 1988. Considers himself to be a still life and history painter.

DALLEY, Terence   b.1935
Draughtsman. Born Kenya. Studied at St. Martin's School of Art, 1954-7, and RCA, 1957-60. Visited Ulm, Germany, on an exchange scholarship and on his return to London worked for a printing house, in advertising and as a designer-illustrator. 1971 solo exhibition, 'The Silent Docks and London Streets', at Upper Grosvenor Galleries, London.

DALTON, Lisa   b.1954
Painter. Born London. Studied at Chelsea School of Art, 1974-8. 1979 first solo exhibition held at Robin Gibson Gallery, Sydney, Australia. Specialises in still lifes, landscapes and portraits.

DALWOOD, Dexter   b.1960
Painter. Born Bristol. Studied at St. Martin's School of Art, London, 1981-5. Awarded Commonwealth Scholarship to Baroda Univeristy Faculty of Fine Arts, Gugurat, India, 1985-6. 1986 first solo exhibition at the Paton Gallery. Represented in group exhibitions since 1983 when his work was included in 'New Contemporaries', at ICA, London. Represented in collections of the Arts Council of Great Britain and the British Council.

DALWOOD, Hubert   1924-1976
Sculptor. Born Bristol, Avon. Apprenticed to the British Aero Company as an engineer, and then served as an engineer in the Royal Navy, 1944-6. Studied at Bath Academy of Art, 1946-9, under Kenneth Armitage.* 1955-9 Gregory Fellow at Leeds University. 1962 awarded first prize for sculpture at the Venice Biennale. 1966-73 Head of the Sculpture Department at Hornsey College of Art, 1974-6 Head of Sculpture at the Central School of Art. Commissioned to make sculpture for the Universities of Oxford, Liverpool and Leeds. Retrospective exhibition at the Hayward Gallery, London, 1979.

DALY, Jehan   b.1918
Painter. Born Llanelly, Wales. Studied at Kidderminster Art School and the RCA where he made friends with John Ward.* Has exhibited at the RA and with the NEAC but has consistently avoided artistic fashions or unwanted limelight.

DANIELS, Alfred   b.1926
Painter. Born London. Trained at Woolwich Art School and RCA. Tutor in drawing at RCA and Hornsey College of Art. His paintings are mostly of places he knows well and which are under threat from developers. This concern to document is allied to a highly personal vision. Solo exhibitions at the John Whibley Gallery, London, 1968 and 1971. Elected member of RSW, 1972, and member of RBA, 1982.

DANIELS, Harvey   b.1936
Painter and printmaker. Born London. Studied at Willesden School of Art, 1951-6, Slade, 1956-8 and Brighton College of Art, 1958-9. 1963 first solo exhibition held at FAR Gallery, New York. Has work in many private collections in England and America, including Museum of Modern Art, New York.

DANNATT, George   b.1915
Painter. Born Blackheath, London. Worked as a chartered surveyor by day and a music critic for the *News Chronicle* by night until 1956, when he began painting seriously. 1970 first exhibited at the Penwith Galleries, St. Ives, and 1973 at the Newlyn Art Gallery. 1974 elected member of the Newlyn Society of Artists. 1980 first solo exhibition held at Galerie Schreiner, Basle, Switzerland; others include an exhibition at Michael Parkin Gallery, London, 1988. An abstract artist, who takes his starting point from the St. Ives School.

DARACH, Peter   b.1940
Painter. Born Derbyshire. Studied at Derby College of Art, 1959-61 and RCA, 1962-5. Exhibited in mixed exhibitions in the 1960s. 1983 solo exhibition at Artspace, Aberdeen, which toured to Newcastle and Glasgow.

DARWIN, Robin   1910-1974
Painter. Studied at Cambridge University and Slade, 1929. 1939-44 employed by the Ministry of Home Security. While working for the Council of Industrial Design, 1945-6, he produced a report, 'The Training of the Industrial Designer', proposing curriculum changes at the RCA, which led to his appointment as Principal in 1948, a post he held until 1971, overseeing a famous period in the RCA's history, now rightly known as 'the Darwin era'. In his spare time he continued to execute sensitive, close-toned landscapes, figure subjects and still lifes. Knighted in 1964.

Bibl: Christopher Frayling, *The Royal College of Art,* Barrie and Jenkins, London, 1987.

DAVENPORT, Ian   b.1966
Painter. Born Sidcup, Kent. Studied at Northwich College of Art and Design, 1984-5, and Goldsmiths' College, 1985-8. Represented by Waddington Galleries, London. Works with household and industrial paints and often uses repetition (in his words 'a kind of exuberant methodicalism') in abstracts that make much play upon the fluidity of paint. Represented in 'The British Art Show', at Hayward Gallery, London, 1990.

DAVEY, Grenville   b.1961
Sculptor. Born Launceston, Cornwall. Studied at Exeter College of Art and Design, and Goldsmiths' College, 1981-5. Solo exhibitions at the Lisson Gallery, London, 1987 and 1989. Represented in 'The British Art Show' at the Hayward Gallery, London, 1990.

DAVIE, Alan   b.1920
Painter. Born Grangemouth, Scotland, the son of a painter and etcher. Studied at Edinburgh College of Art, 1937-41. Made silver jewellery as well as paintings and became involved in jazz. Served with the Royal Artillery during Second World War. 1947 worked briefly as a full-time jazz pianist. 1948 made extensive travels through Europe, seeing among other things paintings by Jackson Pollock in Peggy Guggenheim's collection in Venice. Their influence was added to his interests in Klee, Picasso and African art. 1950 first solo exhibition at Gimpel Fils, London. 1955 became interested in Zen Buddhism and oriental mysticism. 1956 visited New York, meeting leading Abstract Expressionists and seeing primitive art

DAVIES, Anthony

in the American Natural History Museum. 1956-9 Gregory Fellow in Painting at University of Leeds. 1960 took up gliding which exercised a certain influence on his art. His abstract, eclectic paintings are crammed with allusions to magic, eroticism, religion and sacrifice. Recently his work has become formally more coherent, with symbols often now derived from Indian manuscripts.

Bibl: *Alan Davie,* City of Aberdeen Art Gallery and Museum catalogue, 1977.

DAVIES, Anthony   b.1947
Printmaker. Born Hampshire. Studied at Winchester School of Art, 1966-70, RCA, 1970-3, and was Prix de Rome Scholar, British School in Rome, 1973-5. 1975 first solo exhibition held at Winchester School of Art Gallery; others include Octagon Gallery, Belfast, 1982 and the Hendriks Gallery, Dublin, 1987. Represented in Ferens Art Gallery, Hull, Bolton Museum and Art Gallery and elsewhere.

Bibl: *No Surrender '86: Prints by Anthony Davies,* 'On-the-Wall', Belfast, 1987.

DAVIES, Audrey   b.1935
Painter. Obtained Art Teachers Diploma in Cardiff, 1957. Her chief interest is the Herefordshire landscape and the seasonal variations. Has exibited in the Hereford City Art Gallery and held a solo show at Compendium Galleries, Birmingham, 1970.

DAVIES, Gareth   b.1956
Painter. Born Ferryside, Dyfed, Wales. Studied at Dyfed College of Art, 1977-8, and Epsom School of Art, 1978-81. Included in group exhibitions since 1981. First solo exhibition, 'Enter the Dragon', at Carmarthen Library Gallery, 1987. Most recent, entitled 'Flag Days', at the Glynn Vivian Art Gallery, Swansea, 1989. Interested in depicting the human being's 'display of identity'.

DAVIES, Gerald   b.1957
Painter. Born South Wales. Studied at Wolverhampton Polytechnic, 1976-80 and RCA, 1981-4. 1984 awarded John Minton Prize. 1985 first solo exhibition at Roger Francis Gallery, London. Works chiefly with charcoal or graphite in pictures that deal with the human predicament.

DAVIES, Gordon   b.1926
Painter. Served in army during Second World War. Studied at Camberwell College and RCA. Works as a craftsman, designs fabrics and wallpaper, among other things, but also paints landscapes and architectural subjects. Exhibits at RA and has solo exhibitions at King Street Galleries, London.

DAVIES, Hugh   b.1946
Painter. Born Germany but educated in England. Studied at Brighton College of Art, 1964-8, and Chelsea School of Art, 1968-9, where he now teaches. Began exhibiting in 1969, holding his first solo exhibition at the Woburn Gallery, Woburn Abbey, 1973; others held at the Redfern Gallery, London, 1984 and 1985, and at the Cartwright Hall, Bradford, 1986. Represented in the University of Sussex collection.

DAVIES, Ivor   b.1935
Painter. Studied at Cardiff College of Art, 1952-6 and Swansea College of Art, 1956-7. 1957-9 taught art in a London school and visited many exhibitions. After 1959

travelled and worked abroad until 1963 when he joined the Fine Art Department, Edinburgh University. Experimented with kinetic art and participated in the International Destruction in Art Symposium in London, 1966. Solo exhibition at Oriel Gallery, Cardiff, 1974; others include one at Newport Museum and Art Gallery, 1987.

DAVIES, John   b.1946
Mixed media artist. Born Cheshire. Studied at Manchester College of Art and Hull College of Art, 1963-7, and Slade, 1967-9. Sculpture fellowship at Gloucestershire College of Art, 1969-70. Sainsbury Award, 1970-1. Numerous solo exhibitions since 1972, including two at Whitechapel Art Gallery, London, 1972 and 1975, and Marlborough Fine Art, 1980 and 1984. His figurative art focuses on the human figure and head. 'All I hope', the artist has written, 'is that there is something of the human circus — life's circus here.' (Plate 33, p.166.)

Bibl: *John Davies: Recent Sculpture and Drawings,* Marlborough Fine Art, London, 1984.

DAVIES, B. Kevill   b.1954
Painter. Born Dorset. Studied at Bournemouth and Poole College of Art and Design, 1973-7. Recent group exhibitions include John Moores, 1987, the RA Summer exhibitions and Contemporary Art Society Market.

DAVIES, Kate   b.1960
Sculptor. Studied at Hertfordshire College of Art and Design, 1978-9, Falmouth School of Art, 1979-80 and at the Slade School of Art, 1983-6. First exhibited in the 1986 Biennale of European Art in Toulouse, followed by a two person show at the Phoenix Gallery, Kingston, 1987.

DAVIES, Marissa   b.1962
Painter. Studied at the National College of Art and Design, Dublin, 1979-80, also at Somerset College of Art and Technology, Gloucester College of Art and Design and the RCA, 1986-8. Commissioned to execute a mural for the Guildhall School of Music and Drama, 1988. First solo exhibition at the Albermarle Gallery, London, 1989; another at the Anna Mei Chadwick Gallery, London, 1990.

DAVIES, Philip   b.1953
Painter. Born Pudsey, West Yorkshire. Studied at Loughborough College of Art, 1972-5, and RCA, 1978-81. First solo exhibition at the Polytechnic Gallery, North Staffordshire. Held exhibition of recent paintings at Christopher Hull Gallery, 1988.

DAVIES, Richard   b.1944
Printmaker. Born Isle of Wight. Studied at Portsmouth College of Art and afterwards travelled extensively in Europe on travel scholarships. Studied at RCA, spending part of his time in Paris at the Cité International des Arts and in the studio of M. Jean Jacque de Broutelle. Numerous exhibitions, including one at the Redfern Gallery, London, 1983.

DAVIS, Iiona Julia   b.1945
Painter. Born England. Studied modern history at St. Catherine's College, Oxford. A member of the Free Painters Group and the Artists International Association in the 1960s. First solo exhibition held at Woodstock Gallery, London, 1960.

DAVIS, Lady Mary   1866-1941
Painter and designer of fans. Born London, née Mary Halford. Studied at Ridley Art School. Married Edmund Davis in 1889. (He was knighted in 1927 and died in 1939 when his collection from Chilham Castle, including Whistler's 'At the Piano' was sold.) Charles Conder* was a friend of the Davises and influenced Lady Davis's decorative style. Exhibited at the RA from 1896 and the Paris Salon from 1898, and elsewhere. Has work in the Tate Gallery collection.

DAVIS, Robin   b.1928
Painter. Studied modern history at St. Catherine's College, Oxford. A member of the Free Painters Group and the Artists International Association in the 1960s. First solo exhibition held at Woodstock Gallery, London, 1960.

DAVISON, Francis   1919-1984
Painter and collagist. Worked intermittently as teacher whilst writing poetry. Began drawing and painting in mid-1940s, making his first collage in 1952. Married Margaret Mellis* and lived in Suffolk. Abandoned paint for collage, and developed an almost painterly expressiveness in his handling of torn paper. Scarcely exhibited in his lifetime, but was given an exhibition at the Hayward Gallery, 1986. (Plate 34, p.167.)

DAWBURN, Joseph Yelverton   1856-1943
Painter. Born Liverpool, Lancashire. Read mathematics at Queen's College, Cambridge, 1874-7, then law and was called to the bar 1881 but practised little as he did not enjoy this profession. Studied under the Liverpool artist John Finnie at the Liverpool Institute School of Art and went on sketching tours on the Continent with his brother. From 1887 exhibited at the Liverpool Autumn Exhibitions and from 1897 at the RA. 1908-12 President of the Liverpool Academy. Member of the Liver Sketching Club. Represented in the Walker Art Gallery, Liverpool.

DAWNAY, Denis   1921-1983
Painter. Studied at Euston Road School. Began exhibiting at RA in late 1930s, but was unable to sustain a full career as an artist, owing to diabetes and, from 1945, tuberculosis. Friend of King George VI and other members of the Royal Family. In the 1950s and '60s gave painting instruction to HRH Prince Philip, Duke of Edinburgh. Executed meticulously detailed watercolours, in a style very different from that associated with the Euston Road School.

DAWSON, Montagu J.   1894-1973
Marine painter. Born Chiswick, London, son of a sea captain, and grandson of Henry Dawson, a landscape painter. Studied painting under C. Napier Hemy. Entered a commercial studio, specialising in the illustration of nautical subjects. Served at sea during the First World War. Following his discharge from the Navy he took up painting full-time. Exhibited at the RA, 1917-36. Represented in many public collections.

DAWSON, Eric   b.1918
Painter and illustrator. Encouraged by his art master, Rupert Shepherd, he gained a scholarship to West Ham Art School. Served in army during war. Taken up by Edward Ardizzone* after his illustration work appeared in *Parade* and other service magazines. After demobilisation in 1946 he became a commercial artist, also continued to paint and draw for himself. First solo exhibition in London held at Sally Hunter Fine Art, 1987.

DAY, Bryan   b.1934
Painter. Educated at Doncaster and moved to Cumberland in 1959. Exhibits at RSA and RSW. Solo exhibitions at The Border Gallery, Carlisle, 1969, at Maryport, 1972 and at Norham House, Cockermouth, 1973. An expressionist artist, with a preference for colours and shares some stylistic affinities with another Cumbrian artist, Sheila Fell.*

DAY, Melvyn   b.1923
Painter. Born Hamilton, New Zealand. Studied at Elam School of Art, Auckland, 1935-40. Studied history of art at Courtauld Institute of Art, after coming to England. Solo exhibition at Commonwealth Institute Art Gallery, 1966.

DEACON, Peter   b.1945
Painter. Born England. Studied at Portsmouth College of Fine Art, 1963-7 and Slade School of Art, 1968-70. 1970-2 lived and worked in Rome on Abbey Major Scholarship. 1973 appointed Fellow in Fine Art, University of Nottingham. 1972 first solo exhibition held at Zella Gallery, London; also held three exhibitions at Nottingham University Art Gallery, 1973, 1974 and 1975.

DEACON, Richard   b.1949
Sculptor. Born Bangor, Wales. Studied at Somerset College of Art, 1968-9, St. Martin's School of Art, 1969-72, the RCA, 1974-7, and Chelsea School of Art, 1977-8. Ceased making objects in 1978-9 and spent a year in the USA, making pots and drawing. Recent solo exhibitions at the Orchard Gallery, Londonderry, Riverside Studios, London, the Fruitmarket Gallery, Edinburgh and Le Nouveau Musée, Lyon. 1984 shortlisted for the Turner Prize; awarded the Turner Prize, 1987. His sculpture uses a simple armature to convey allusions to lyrical and poetic ideas often drawn from literature.

DEAN, Catherine   1905-1983
Painter. Born Liverpool, Merseyside. Won scholarship to Liverpool School of Art, 1921 and another to RCA, 1926-9. Taught art in schools and colleges and in 1931 married the painter, Albert Houthuesen.* 1940 Tate Gallery acquired her *Sheep's Skull and Ferns*. First solo exhibition held at Mercury Gallery, London, 1982.

DEAN, Diana   b.1942
Sculptor. Studied at Bath Academy of Art, Corsham, 1961-4. Exhibited in AIA 'Sculpture '64' exhibition and was awarded the Sculpture Prize.

DEAN, Elizabeth   b.1929
Sculptor. Born Birmingham, West Midlands. Trained as a radiographer and did not turn to sculpture until she was over thirty. Studied briefly at Northampton School of Art and Khartoum School of Fine Art in the Sudan. 1966-7 lived and worked as a portrait sculptor in Uganda and studied welding under George Kakooza, at Makers University, Kampala. 1968-70 studied further in Singapore, after which she returned to live in Northampton. Solo exhibition at Central Art Gallery, Northampton, 1973.

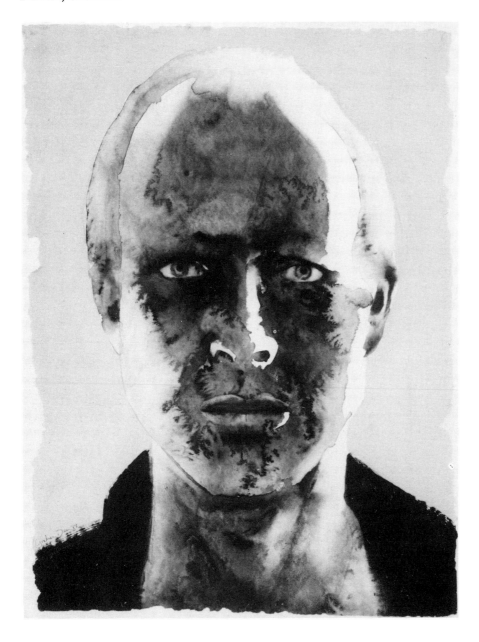

GRAHAM DEAN, b.1951.
'Self-portrait'. Watercolour and
acrylic on paper. 22¾in. x 17in.
Austin/Desmond Fine Art.

DEAN, Graham   b.1951
Painter. Born Birkenhead, Cheshire. Studied at Laird
School of Art, Birkenhead, 1968-70 and Bristol Polytechnic,
1970-3. 1973-4 worked for a publisher for nine months,
and since then has been a full-time painter. 1973 first solo
exhibition at Bristol Arts Centre, and has had solo
exhibitions at Nicholas Treadwell Gallery, London and
elsewhere. Paints assertive watercolours in vivid colours.

Bibl: *Graham Dean: Paintings, drawings, photographs and films*,
South Hill Park Arts Centre, 1981.

DEAN, Margaret
Painter. Trained at Liverpool College of Art, 1955-61.
1962 first solo exhibition held at Blackstone Gallery,
Leeds; others include one at University of Keele, 1966.
Interested in the alternating current between the real and
the absurd. Many of her paintings derive from the 'Alice in
Wonderland' theme.

DEBENHAM, Alison   1903-1967
Painter. Studied at Slade School, 1923-6. 1928 lived in
Paris. 1929 moved to South of France and worked with
Simon Bussy, the French painter and pastellist. 1932
began exhibiting in London and Paris with first solo show
at the Galerie Vignon, Paris, 1932. Memorial exhibition
held at Richmond Hill Gallery, 1968.

Bibl: *Alison Debenham* (with introduction by Claude Rogers),
Belgrave Gallery, London, 1976.

DE CORDOVA, Denise   b.1957
Sculptor. Born Birkenhead, Cheshire. Studied at Laird
School of Art, Birkenhead, 1975-6, Brighton Polytechnic,
1977-80, and RCA, 1980-3. 1981 given an RCA travelling
scholarship, spent at Carrara in Italy. 1983-4 sculpture
scholarship, British School at Rome. 1985 first one-person
show at the Camberwell School of Art Gallery. 1987
sculpture residency at the Europaischer Skulptusenpark,
Willebadessen, West Germany, and artist in residence at
Seven Kings School, Ilford.

DEE, John   b.1938
Sculptor. Born Northampton. Studied at Reading University and Slade, 1956-62. Began teaching at Sunderland Polytechnic, 1964. 1978 moved to Cumbria. 1965 first solo exhibition held at Arnolfini Gallery, Bristol; others include one at the Bede Gallery, Jarrow, 1985. Represented in Portsmouth City Art Gallery, the Arts Council Collection and elsewhere.

DE FRANCIA, Peter   b.1921
Painter and draughtsman. Born France. Educated in Paris and Academy of Brussels. After army service studied painting at Slade. 1949-51 worked in Canada and USA. 1951-3 in charge of planning and production of BBC television art programmes. Taught at Morley College, St. Martin's School of Art, Goldsmiths' and RCA. One-artist exhibitions in Milan, London, Amsterdam, Prague and New York. 1973-86 Professor of Painting at RCA. Influenced by Picasso and George Grosz, his tersely expressive paintings and drawings are often motivated by political concerns.

Bibl: *Peter De Francia: Painter and Professor*, Camden Arts Centre, 1987.

DE GLEHN, Wilfred Gabriel   1870-1951
Painter and stained glass designer. Born London. Studied at RCA and at the Ecole des Beaux Arts, Paris. First solo exhibition at the Carfax Gallery, 1908. Exhibited with the NEAC; became a member in 1900. Elected ARA, 1923 and RA, 1932. Travelled widely and exhibited internationally. A fluent portrait painter and landscapist, in a style indebted to the example of John Singer Sargent.*

DE GREY, Roger   b.1918
Painter. Born Penn, Buckinghamshire, a nephew of Spencer Gore.* Studied at Chelsea School of Art, 1936-9. Served in army during war and was awarded the United States Bronze Star. 1946-7 returned to Chelsea School of Art. 1953 joined staff of the Painting School at RCA. Became Principal of City and Guilds, London Art School. 1962 elected ARA, RA 1969, 1984 President of RA. Exhibited first with the London Group and then the RA, also with the Leicester Galleries, at Agnew's and elsewhere. Has work in Tate Gallery, Arts Council and many other public collections. 1979 won the Wollaston Award for the most distinguished work in the RA Summer Exhibition.

DELLOW, Jeff   b.1949
Painter. Studied at St. Martin's School of Art, Maidstone College of Art and the Slade School of Art. 1974-5 was awarded a Cheltenham Fellowship. 1987 first solo exhibition at the Castlefield Gallery, Manchester. Included in the collections of the Arts Council of Great Britain and the Roehampton Institute. Abstract painter, inspired by experience of place, narrative and the 'presence' suggested by colour and shape. Recent solo exhibitions include one at the Todd Gallery, London, 1989.

DEMARCO, Richard   b.1930
Painter. Born Edinburgh, Scotland, of Italian extraction. Studied at Edinburgh College of Art, 1949-53, and for the last two years specialised in mural paintings under Leonard Rosoman* and graphic design under John Kingsley Cook. Has executed murals, designed record sleeves and wallpapers and done illustration work. Also exhibited at RSA, SSA and RSW. Solo exhibitions include

'Edinburgh in watercolour', at Douglas and Foulis Art Gallery, Edinburgh, 1962. Eventually moved into art administration, opened his own gallery in Edinburgh and became one of Scotland's most energetic entrepreneurs.

DE MONCHAUX, Cathy   b.1960
Sculptor. Born London. Studied at Camberwell School of Art, 1980-3, and Goldsmiths' College, 1985-7. First solo exhibition held at Winchester Gallery, 1985; others include one at Laure Genillard Gallery, London, 1990. Represented in 'The British Art Show' at the Hayward Gallery, London, 1990.

DENAHY, John   b.1922
Painter. Started painting and drawing during service with the Royal Navy in the Second World War. Later studied at Eltham Art Centre where he taught for 22 years. Exhibits at RA, RWEA, NEAC and elsewhere.

DENBY, Philippa   b.1938
Sculptor and painter. Trained at Central School of Art. Paints landscapes and flowers. Also sculpts figures in wax which are then cast in bronze. Solo exhibitions include one at the Guild Gallery, London, 1986.

DENISON, David   b.1939
Painter. Self-taught. Began painting when he joined the Prison Service in 1963 after serving three years in RAF. Has worked in various prisons and since 1975 was tutor at Prison Officer's Training School, Wakefield. 1970 first solo exhibition held at the Manor House, Ilkley; others include an exhibition at Wakefield Art Gallery, 1974 and one at Cartwright Hall, Bradford, 1980.

DENNIS, Jeffrey   b.1958
Painter. Born Colchester, Essex. First solo exhibition held at 5 Dryden Street Gallery, London, 1979. Now represented by Salvatore Ala Gallery, New York, where he has showed in 1985, 1986, 1987 and 1988. In his paintings small images occur in an overall field like motifs in a wallpaper. 'The characters in my paintings', Dennis writes, 'are colonists in this difficult terrain. They bring all sorts of awkward luggage and allegiances from their previous homes, and stake out new territory.' Represented in 'The British Art Show' at the Hayward Gallery, London, 1990.

Bibl: *Jeffrey Dennis: Recent Paintings* (with introduction by Stuart Morgan), Whitechapel Art Gallery, 1986.

DENNISON, Christabel   1884-1925
Painter. Born Watford, Hertfordshire. Studied under Sir Hubert von Herkomer at Bushey, 1903. 1905 visited Paris. Began exhibiting in London and in 1910 served on the hanging committee of the Allied Artists' Association with Jacob Epstein* and Charles Ginner.* Served as a nurse during the First World War. After the war she led a precarious existence, but continued to paint, draw and model. Under-nourished, she had little reserve when illness struck. She caught measles, followed by pneumonia and died after ten days.

Bibl: *Christabel Dennison* (with an introduction by Charles Ginner), Whitechapel Art Gallery, 1928.

DENNY, Robyn   b.1930
Painter. Born Abinger, Surrey. Studied at St. Martin's School of Art, 1951-4 and at RCA, 1954-7. Taught painting at Hammersmith College of Art, 1957-9 and Bath Academy of Art, 1959-65, also at the Slade. 1957 first one-

artist exhibition at Gallery One, London. 1973 retrospective exhibition at Tate Gallery. One of the first artists in England to respond to American abstract expressionism and to establish an abstract style free of natural associations. At one point, in order to emphasise the objectivity of his paintings, he exhibited them resting on the floor, on the spectator's own ground. His abstract paintings have become increasingly refined.

Bibl: *Robyn Denny* (with introduction by Robert Kudielka), Tate Gallery, 1973.

DENTON, Kenneth   b.1932
Painter. Spent most of his early life in Kent. Won a scholarship to Rochester School of Art. Worked as interior designer and painted inn signs for major brewing companies. 1967 turned to full-time painting. 1976 elected member of the Royal Society of Marine Artists. His work in this field has been reproduced by the Medici Society and Foyle's. Solo exhibitions include two at Folkington Manor, Polegate, Sussex, 1982 and 1985.

DERHAM, Brigid   b.1943
Painter. Born London. Studied at Slade School of Fine Art, 1961-6. 1962 won Walter Neurath Prize for drawing and painting. 1965 awarded Italian Government Scholarship for study in Italy; 1965 the Ian Stevenson Travelling Scholarship; 1966 the Boise Travelling Scholarship. 1971 first solo exhibition held at New Art Centre, London.

DE ROSE, Gerard   1918-1987
Painter. Born Accrington, Lancashire. Studied at his local art school where he gained a scholarship to the RCA, receiving his diploma in 1949. Specialised in industrial landscapes and portraits. Exhibited at RA, and elsewhere. Left instructions that he was to be buried with a telephone, alcoholic refreshment and a box of cigars.

DE SAUSMAREZ, Maurice   1915-1969
Painter. Studied at the RCA, 1936-9. Exhibited at the RA, RBA and with the NEAC and the London Group. Elected RBA, 1952 and ARA, 1964. From 1950 was Head of Fine Art at the University of Leeds.

DESOUTTER, Roger   b.1923
Painter. Trained as an engineer and worked on the design of jet engines until 1945, sketching in his spare time. 1947 joined family engineering business of which he is now Chairman. 1962 acquired a boat and became a keen amateur yachtsman. Since 1974 has exhibited regularly with the Royal Society of Marine Artists. Many of his paintings have been reproduced as greeting cards and fine art prints.

DETMOLD, Charles Maurice   1883-1908
Painter, etcher, illustrator. *See under* Edward Julius Detmold.

DETMOLD, Edward Julius   1883-1957
Painter, etcher and illustrator. Born Putney, twin brother of Charles Maurice Detmold.* Exhibited with his brother for the first time at the RA at the age of thirteen. Advised by Burne-Jones to avoid traditional art training. With Charles Maurice Detmold bought a printing press and produced many prints and book illustrations. Praised by M.H. Spielmann in the *Magazine of Art* in 1900 and in the same year both brothers held a large exhibition at the Fine Art Society, London. From then on they enjoyed notable success, especially with their drawings and prints of plants and animals inspired partly by Dürer. Their partnership ended tragically in 1908 when Charles Maurice committed suicide by inhaling chloroform, in a fit of remorse after chloroforming the family cats on the instructions of his uncle. Edward Julius continued working, but his art began to be criticised and his output declined. However, during the 1920s he entered upon another richly creative phase, although he relied more on fantasy than observation. Took his own life, after a period of growing despair.

Bibl: Nicholas Alfrey and Richard Verdi, *Charles Maurice and Edward Julius Detmold: A Centenary Exhibition,* Heslington Hall, University of York and elsewhere, 1983.

DEVANE, John   b.1954
Painter. Born Blackpool, Lancashire. Studied at Liverpool College of Art, 1972-5 and at RCA, London, 1977-80. Represented in group exhibitions since 1974. Since 1983 has shown at the Paton Gallery, London. In 1978 he was commissioned by the Imperial War Museum to give an artistic record of military life in Cyprus. Work in the Unilever collection.

DEVAS, Anthony   1911-1958
Painter. Born Bromley, Kent. Studied at Slade School of Fine Art, 1927-30. Associated with members of the Euston Road School. Remained an unashamedly reactionary painter, specialising in portraits and painting with freshness and charm. Elected ARA, 1953. 1957 painted the Queen for the Honourable Artillery Company. A memorial exhibition of his work was held at Agnew's, 1959.

DEVEREUX, Richard   b.1956
Sculptor. Born Lincoln. Studied at Portsmouth College of Art, 1974-7. First solo exhibition held at Axis Gallery, Brighton, 1979.

Bibl: *Assembled Rites: Works by Richard Devereux,* Artsite Gallery, Bath, 1987.

DEWHURST, Harry
Wood engraver. Born Ramsbottom, Lancashire. Spent most of his working life in London as a school master. Began wood engraving in the 1950s and concentrated more fully on this work after he retired to Suffolk. Solo exhibition held at Gainsborough's House, Sudbury, 1982.

DEWHURST, Wynford   1864-c.1941
Painter. Born Manchester. Studied at the Ecole des Beaux Arts, Paris, and the Académie Julian. Continued to make return visits to France to paint in the valley of the Seine. A follower of Monet, he published *Impressionist Paintings: Its Genesis and Development,* 1904.

DHANJAL, Avtarjeet   b.1939
Sculptor. Born Punjab, India. Worked as a carpenter and signwriter before entering art school at Chandigarh. Much travelled. Studied at St. Martin's School of Art. One-artist shows in California and Cleveland, USA; another at Gallery 27, Tonbridge, Kent, 1976. Works mainly in aluminium, using shapes derived from nature. Represented in Chandigarh Museum, the National Lalit Kala Akademi in India and the National Collection of Kenya.

DIBBLE, Cornelia
Painter. Born Gouroch, Scotland. Descended from two generations of painters. Studied at Bromley College of Art and RA Schools. By 1977 had held four solo exhibitions at the Portal Gallery, London.

DICK, Alan
Painter. Born Aberdeen, Scotland. Studied at Gray's School of Art, Aberdeen and Chelsea School of Art. 1982 first solo exhibition held in London. 1984 exhibited paintings of 'Pop Stars' at the Cadogan Gallery, London.

DICK, Sir William Reid   1879-1961
Sculptor. Born Glasgow, Scotland. Trained at Glasgow School of Art up to 1907 and then at City and Guilds School of Art, Lambeth. Exhibited regularly at RA from 1908, and made ARA, 1921, and RA, 1928. Received many official commissions. 1935 knighted. 1935-8 President of the Royal Society of British Sculptors. 1938-52 sculptor to King George VI, and Queen's Sculptor in Ordinary for Scotland from 1952 until his death. Commissions include the Kitchener Memorial Chapel in St. Paul's Cathedral and the Tombs of King George V and Queen Mary, St. George's Chapel, Windsor.

DICKINS, Lynne   b.1948
Painter. Studied at St. Martin's School of Art, 1967-8, and Wimbledon School of Art, 1968-72. 1979 moved to Wales and held a solo exhibition at Chapter Gallery, Cardiff, 1980. Her art is not representational, although landscape remains its source.

DICKER, Kate   b.1953
Painter. Born Southsea, Hampshire. After seven years as a secretary in farming and estate management studied at West Sussex College of Design, 1979-80, and Camberwell School of Art, 1980-3. 1982 began exhibiting and in 1985 held 'An Exhibition of Watercolours and Drawing: Many London Locations' at Leighton House, London.

DICKINSON, Timothy   b.1941
Painter. Born Huddersfield, Yorkshire. Studied at Birmingham College of Art, 1957-62. Taught at Sutton Coldfield School of Art, 1962-9 and then at Chesterfield College of Art. 1969 first solo exhibition held at Compendium Gallery, Birmingham; others include two at the Piccadilly Gallery, London, 1980 and 1981.

DICKSEE, Frank   1853-1928
Painter. Born London. Studied at the RA Schools, from 1871. Initially worked as an illustrator. From 1876 exhibited regularly at the RA, becoming well known as a painter of romantic, historical and literary subjects and portraits. Elected ARA, 1881, RA, 1891, and PRA 1924-8. Knighted 1925, KCVO, 1927. He was a strong opponent of modern art.

DICKSON, Jennifer   b.1936
Painter and printmaker. Born Piete Retief, South Africa. Came to England 1954. Studied at Goldsmiths' College, 1954-9, and worked, periodically, in S.W. Hayter's Atelier 17, Paris, 1960 and 1961. Travelled widely in Europe, Africa and USA and exhibited widely in group exhibitions. 1962 solo exhibition at New Vision Centre Gallery, London; others at the Zwemmer Gallery, London, 1965, and University of Sussex Arts Centre, 1967. Represented in Victoria and Albert Museum, National Gallery of Canada and the Hermitage, Leningrad.

DICKSON, Rodney   b.1956
Painter. Born Bangor, Northern Ireland. Studied at Liverpool Polytechnic, 1979-83 and held solo exhibitions at Bluecoat Gallery, Liverpool and at Murdoch Lothian, 1983-4. After moving to Devon had further solo shows in Exeter. Has also exhibited in London and Amsterdam. Solo exhibition at the Arts Council Gallery, Belfast, 1987.

DIGGLE, Philip   b.1956
Painter. Born Manchester. 1979 started painting on stage at the Kim Philby Club, Manchester, together with the poet John Cooper Clarke. 1985 exhibited abstract gestural paintings, close in spirit to Alan Davie,* at Angela Flowers Gallery, London. Also makes videos. 1985 exhibited 'The Macbeth Suite of Paintings' at Warwick Arts Trust, London.

DILWORTH, Norman   b.1933
Sculptor. Born Wigan, Lancashire. Studied at Slade School of Fine Art. First exhibited at Young Contemporaries, London, 1953-5. Awarded French Government Scholarship and studied in Paris, 1956-7. In the 1960s took 'the properties and dimensions of the elements' as the starting point for his sculptures. First solo exhibition at Redmark Gallery, 1968, more recent at Galerie Lydia Megert, Bern, 1981.

Bibl: *Norman Dilworth: Sculpture and Reliefs 1972-80,* South East London Gallery, 1981.

DIMITRIJEVIC, Braco   b.1948
Artist. Born Sarajevo, Yugoslavia. Lives and works in London. First one man show at the age of ten. Attended Academy of Fine Arts Zagreb, 1968-71 and St. Martin's School of Art, 1971-3. 1976-7 held a DAAD fellowship in Berlin. 1979 awarded Prix Jean Dominique Ingres from Académie de Muséologie Evocatoise France. Works mostly with found objects and chance events to create installations that tease the imagination. First mature one-man exhibition at RU Djuso Djakovic, Sarajevo; others include two at the Tate Gallery, 1982 and 1985.

DINGWALL, Kenneth   b.1938
Painter and constructivist. Born Devonside, Scotland. Studied at Edinburgh College of Art, 1955-60, and Athens Art School, 1961-2. 1972 received a Scottish Arts Council Award. 1973-4 visiting professor at Minneapolis College of Art, USA. Lectures at Edinburgh College of Art. Solo exhibitions at The Gallery, Hydra, Greece, 1962, the Scottish Gallery, Edinburgh, 1969, Stevens Gallery, Minneapolis, 1974, Graeme Murray Gallery, Edinburgh, 1977 and House, 62 Regents Park Road, London, 1977. Has moved from abstract colour-field paintings to small minimalist wooden constructions.

DINKEL, Ernest   b.1894
Painter and designer. Born Huddersfield, Yorkshire. Served in France, 1916-19. Studied at Huddersfield School of Art and the RCA, 1921-5. Won a travelling scholarship which took him to Italy. From 1927 exhibited at the NEAC and the RA. 1925-40 taught painting at the RCA; 1940-7 Head of Stourbridge School of Art; 1947-59 Head of the Design School, Edinburgh College of Art. Work in the collection of the Tate Gallery.

DINKEL KEET, Emmy G.M.   b.1908
Painter. Studied at Southend College of Art, 1927-30 and RCA, 1930-3. Also studied peasant art and design in Hungary. Exhibits at RA, RWA, RSA and elsewhere. Married to Ernest Dinkel.*

JESSICA DISMORR, 1885-1939.
'Hampstead', 1924. Watercolour.
Private Collection.

DINKEL, Michael   1905-1983
Painter. Born Huddersfield, Yorkshire. Studied at
Huddersfield School of Art and the RCA where in 1926 he
won a travelling scholarship. Painted in tempera and oils
in a style influenced by Italian quattrocento painting.
Also worked in many fields of decorative design from
stained glass to inn signs. Executed poster designs for
London Transport. 1940, became Principal of Stourbridge
School of Art where he developed his enthusiasm for glass
designs and engraving. 1947-59 Head of Design,
Edinburgh College of Art, from whence he retired to the
Cotswolds. Represented in the collections of the Tate
Gallery, Laing Art Gallery, Newcastle upon Tyne and
Dudley Art Gallery.

DISHER, Eve   b.1894
Painter. Born North London. Trained at Hornsey College
of Art. At age of twenty-four ran away from home to marry
Maurice Willson Disher, author and theatre critic of the
Evening Standard. Took part in the artistic ferment of the
1920s and 1930s, having associations with Duncan
Grant* and later with the documentary film-maker John
Grierson. During these years shared a studio with Vera
Cunningham* and was profoundly influenced by her
work. Travelled widely. Solo exhibitions at Foyles Art
Gallery, 1987. (Plate 35, p.167.)

DISMORR, Jessica   1885-1939
Painter. Born Gravesend, Kent. Studied under Metzinger,

Segonzac and Blanche at Atelier La Palette, Paris, 1910-13. 1913 met Wyndham Lewis* and became associated with the Vorticists, signing the Vorticist Manifesto in 1914 and exhibiting with them, 1915. 1920 exhibited with Lewis's Group X. 1925 first solo exhibition held at Mayor Gallery, London. 1926 elected to London Group and 7 & 5 Society. During 1930s exhibited with the Association Abstraction-Creation. Favoured close light tones and, in her figurative work, near geometric stylisation of form.

Bibl: Richard Cork, *Vorticism and Abstract Art in the First Machine Age,* Gordon Fraser, London, 1976.

DIXON, Charles   1872-1934
Painter. Son of the artist, Alfred Dixon. Began exhibiting at RA at age of sixteen. 1900 made member of RI. Became a well known marine artist. His chief recreation was yachting and he was a founder member of the Yacht Club at Itchenor, Sussex, where he lived.

DIXON, Harry   1861-1942
Sculptor, painter and printmaker. Born Watford, Hertfordshire. Studied at Heatherley's School, c.1880 and at the Académie Julian, Paris, from c.1883-7. 1885-1928 exhibited at the RA, mostly figures of wild animals. 1892 made the lions which guard the entrance to the Imperial Institute, London. 1904 member of the RBS. Illustrated a number of books on animals and *Human Anatomy for Art Students,* by Sir Alfred Fripp. Work in the Tate Gallery collection.

DOBBIN, Stanley   b.1929
Printmaker. Born Birmingham, West Midlands. Studied at Birmingham College of Art, 1947-52. Began exhibiting woodcuts in 1959, having become interested in this medium after seeing work by the German Expressionists. Solo exhibitions include one at Hanover Galleries, Liverpool, 1986.

DOBSON, Frank   1886-1963
Sculptor. Born London, son of a commercial artist. Studied at Leyton School of Art, 1900-2 and served as apprentice studio boy to Sir William Reynolds-Stephens, 1902-4. 1904-6 painted in Cornwall. 1906-10 won a scholarship and studied at Hospitalfield Art Institute, Arbroath, Scotland. 1910-12 further study at City and Guilds School, Kensington. 1913-14 shared a studio in Cornwall with Cedric Morris* and held first solo exhibition at Chenil Galleries, Chelsea, 1911. 1914-18 served in the Artists' Rifles. Participated in Wyndham Lewis's* short-lived Group X, 1920. 1924 elected President of the London Group and represented Britain at Venice Biennale, 1924 and again in 1932. 1946 appointed Professor of Sculpture at RCA. 1947 awarded CBE. 1953 elected RA. Held numerous solo exhibitions and was given a memorial show by the Arts Council in London, 1966.

Bibl: Robert Hopper, *True and Pure Sculpture: Frank Dobson, 1886-1963,* Kettles Yard, Cambridge, 1981.

DOBSON, Mary
Painter and illustrator. Trained at Bournemouth Art School and Chelsea Polytechnic. Worked as a free-lance illustrator, 1936-9. Served in WRNS, 1939-47. 1953 held first solo exhibition. Member of the Council of SWA. Executed a stained glass window for the Fisherman's Church, Hastings, and specialised in stained glass and mosaic panels.

ALAN DODD, b.1942. *'Assumption',* 1974-5. 36in. x 29in. Private Collection.

DOCHERTY, Michael   b.1947
Painter and sculptor. Born Alloa, Scotland. Studied at Edinburgh College of Art, 1964-9. Awarded Andrew Grant Travelling Scholarship to France and Spain. 1970 first solo exhibition at the Demarco Gallery, Edinburgh International Festival, followed in the same year by a second solo exhibition at the Demarco Gallery and one at the Manchester City Art Gallery and Museum. Works extensively with found objects which he then paints. Represented in several major Scottish collections.

Bibl: *Michael Docherty,* 35min. colour, STV, 1970.

DOCKLEY, Peter
Sculptor. Studied at Hornsey College of Art and since then has been involved with the environmental theatre pieces and events in public places. 'Street Altar' and 'Stream' held at Arnolfini Gallery, Bristol, 1973.

DODD, Alan   b.1942
Painter. Born Kennington, Kent. Studied at Maidstone College of Art, 1958-63 and RA Schools, 1963-6. 1965 and 1966 won various scholarships. 1969 first solo exhibition held at New Grafton Gallery; others held 1970 and 1972 at same gallery. 1977 began exhibiting with the London Group. Much of his current work has taken the form of mural painting.

DODD, Francis

DODD, Francis   1874-1949
Painter and printmaker. Born Holyhead, Wales. Trained at Glasgow School of Art and in Paris and Italy. On his return to England he established a studio in Manchester, encouraged the young Henry Lamb* and quickly attained a reputation through the NEAC. 1923-49 exhibited at RA, 1927 elected ARA, and 1935 RA. Painted suburban scenes and excelled at portraiture. His greatest achievement is *Interrogation* in the Imperial War Museum.

DODGSON, Catherine   1883-1954
Painter. Studied at Ruskin School, Oxford, RA Schools and, briefly, at the Slade. 1913 married Campbell Dodgson, Keeper of Prints and Drawings in the British Museum. Subjugated her own artistic interest to social and other duties. 1923 exhibited an oil painting for the first time at the RA. Not until the 1930s did she cultivate her artistic inclinations. 1936 and 1939 she had two exhibitions at Colnaghi's and 1933-45 exhibited a dozen portrait drawings at the RA. Her husband's illness and death in 1948 depleted her energies; she had only just begun to resume her former interests when she died after an operation.

DODGSON, John   1890-1969
Painter. Studied at Slade School of Fine Art, 1913-15. Served with the RASC, 1916-18. 1919 briefly assistant director at National Gallery. 1928 first solo exhibition at Claridge Gallery, London. Associated with the Euston Road School and showed with London Artists' Association, 1932-4. 1947 elected member of London Group, and 1950-2 President. 1939-45 served again with the RASC. Taught at Camberwell and Chelsea Schools of Art. 1959 solo exhibition at Beaux Arts Gallery, London. 1964 his studio in Suffolk burnt to the ground. His paintings began with observation but underwent formal adjustment owing to his love of fantasy.

Bibl: *John Dodgson 1890-1969,* South London Art Gallery, 1971.

DODS-WITHERS, Isobelle Anne   1876-1939
Painter. Born Congalton Mains, Scotland. Studied at Edinburgh College of Art. Exhibited widely, at Royal Institute of Oil Painters, the Pastel Society and the Women's International Art Club, and abroad. Specialised in townscapes, mostly in Southern Europe.

DOLBY, James Taylor   1909-1975
Wood-engraver. Studied at Keighley School of Art, 1925-9, and RCA, 1929-33, under Robert Austin,* Malcolm Osborne and Edward Johnston. After the war, until he retired, he was head of Blackburn School of Art.

DONAGH, Rita   b.1939
Painter. Born Wednesbury, Staffordshire. Began taking evening classes in life drawing at Bilston College of Further Education, 1954-6. Studied at University of Durham, Newcastle upon Tyne, 1959-62. Married Richard Hamilton.* Has occupied various teaching positions at Newcastle, Reading, the Slade School of Fine Art and Goldsmiths' College. In 1978 was one of the selectors of the Hayward Annual. Trustee of the Tate Gallery, 1977-84. Recent solo exhibitions include one at the Nigel Greenwood Gallery, London, 1984.

Bibl: *Rita Donagh. Paintings and Drawings,* Whitworth Art Gallery and Arts Council, 1977; *A Cellular Maze* (with Richard Hamilton), ICA, London, 1984.

MICKY DONNELLY, b.1952. *'Shillelagh Dreaming — Holy Cow',* 1989. 74in. x 54in. Private Collection.

DONALDSON, Antony   b.1939
Painter. Born Godalming, Surrey. Studied at the Regent Street Polytechnic, 1957-8 and the Slade School of Art, 1958-63. From 1958 included in mixed exhibitions, e.g. Young Contemporaries. 1962 first solo exhibition at the Rowan Gallery. 1962 joined the teaching staff at Chelsea College of Art. 1963 won Second Prize in the John Moores exhibition. 1976 solo exhibition at Felicity Samuel Gallery. Painter of popular imagery derived mainly from advertising imagery. Work in the Tate Gallery collection.

DONNELLY, Micky   b.1952
Painter and sculptor. Born Belfast, Northern Ireland. Studied at the Art and Design Centre, Belfast, 1971-3 and 1976-9. Attended British School in Rome, 1985-6. 1987 first solo exhibition at the Art and Research Exchange, Belfast. Has work in the British Council collection and elsewhere. Represented by Anderson O'Day, London.

DONOVAN, Phoebe   b.1902
Painter. Born Wexford, Ireland. Studied at Dublin School of Art and the Royal Hibernian Academy Schools, also, during the 1930s, at Regent Street Polytechnic. Specialised in animal portraits. Exhibits at the Royal Hibernian Academy, the RWS and elsewhere.

148

DOOLEY, Arthur b.1929
Sculptor. Born Dingle, Liverpool. Left school at fourteen and spent nine years with the Irish Guards. Became a Catholic convert and did various jobs on leaving the army, including sweeping out St. Martin's School of Art. 1961 first solo exhibition held in Liverpool. 1964 executed the Fourteen Stations of the Cross for St. Mary's Church, Leyland. Solo exhibitions include one at Upper Street Gallery, London, 1971.

DORF, Barbara b.1933
Painter. Studied at Slade and University College, London. Exhibits RA, NEAC and in galleries in London, Paris and Belgrade. Represented in British Museum, Lady Margaret Hall, Oxford and elsewhere. Solo exhibitions include one at Michael Parkin Gallery, London, 1978.

DORRIAN, Patrick b.1953
Painter. Born Glasgow, Scotland. Studied at Glasgow School of Art and Hospitalfield, Arbroath. Began exhibiting in 1977 and shows regularly at the RSA and RSW. Solo exhibitions include one at Smith Art Gallery and Museum, Stirling, 1985. His central theme is the human figure. Paints large expressionist oils, often pessimistic in mood.

DOUBLEDAY, John b.1947
Sculptor. Born Langford, Essex. After leaving school drew for several months in the Musée Bourdelle, Paris, where he was especially influenced by the sculptors Despaiu and Maillol. Studied at Carlisle Art School and Goldsmiths' College of Art. Since 1967 has exhibited regularly in Britain, Holland and Germany. Began an association with the Alwin Gallery, London, 1972. Solo exhibition at Wolverhampton Art Gallery, 1975. Represented in British Museum, V & A, National Museum of Wales and elsewhere.

DOUGLAS, Sheila b.1924
Painter. Born Todmorden, Yorkshire. Studied at Leeds School of Art and at the Slade. Exhibited at Liverpool Academy, Leicester Galleries and Redfern Galleries.

DOUGLAS, Sholto Johnstone 1871-1958
Painter. Studied at Académie Julian, Paris, in Antwerp and at Slade School of Fine Art. By the 1890s was launched on his successful career as society portraitist. Was compared with John Singer Sargent.* Moved to London and was commissioned to paint the 'dazzle' ships during the First World War; fifty-two of these paintings are in the Imperial War Museum. 1926 moved to South of France, to sketch the Provençal countryside. 1939 returned to Britain and continued painting until his death.

DOUTHWAITE, Patricia b.1939
Painter. Born Glasgow, Scotland. Studied dance with Margaret Morris whose husband J.D. Fergusson* encouraged her to paint. Self-taught. 1958 went to live in Suffolk with a group of painters, including Robert Colquhoun,* Robert MacBryde* and William Crozier.* 1959-88 travelled widely. 1975 created a multi-media performance work, *Inanna.* Solo exhibitions include a retrospective at Third Eye Centre, Glasgow, 1988. Represented in Aberdeen Art Gallery, Ferens Art Gallery, Hull, and elsewhere.

DOWER, Natalie b.1931
Painter and constructivist. Born London. Studied at St. Martin's, 1948-9, Camberwell, 1949-51 and Slade, 1951-4. Makes painted wood constructions and works on paper. Exhibitions at Riverside Studios 1981, Hayward Annual 1982, Air Gallery 1983, Curwen Gallery 1987. Has lived in Morocco and Portugal. Worked figuratively until 1968 when she became interested in logical systems.

DOWKER, Ann
Painter and etcher. Born Sheffield, Yorkshire. Studied at Bath Academy of Art, Corsham, and later attended evening classes at St. Martin's School of Art, London. 1978 began studying etching at the Camden Institute, followed by lithography in 1981 at the Central School of Art, London. 1981 first exhibited at the House Gallery, London. Her themes are drawn from the Italian masters and everyday events. Included in the collections of the Government Art Collection and the Australian Embassy. Often bases her images on passages within Old Master paintings.

DOWLING, Jane b.1925
Painter. Studied at St. Anne's, University of Oxford, 1943-6, Slade School of Art, 1943-6, Ruskin School of Art, 1946-9, Byam Shaw School of Art, 1951-61 and Central School of Art, 1961-3. 1964 married Peter Greenham.* Solo exhibitions at New Grafton Gallery, London, 1974, 1978 and 1982. Also exhibits at RA and NEAC.

DOWLING, Terry b.1946
Graphic artist. Born Wrexham, North Wales. Studied graphic design at Manchester College of Art and Design, 1964-9, and illustration and ceramics at RCA, 1969-72. 1972 awarded travelling scholarship to Europe. 1976 solo exhibition at Bluecoat Gallery, Liverpool.

DOWNING, Peter b.1929
Painter. Born Leeds, Yorkshire. Trained at Leeds College of Art and RCA. 1960 and 1961 three solo exhibitions in Coventry and two at Bear Lane Gallery, Oxford; others include one at Park Square Gallery, Leeds, 1971.

DOWNS, George 1901-1983
Painter. Born Macclesfield, Cheshire. Self-taught; began painting by chance at the age of thirty-five. Befriended by the painter Julian Trevelyan,* Downs joined the AIA. Contributed to *The Daily Worker* newspaper. Painted murals in restaurants. 1939 first exhibited with the AIA. Retrospective exhibition at the Drian Gallery, 1978 and at Buxton Museum and Art Gallery, 1988.

DOWNS, Michael b.1953
Painter. Born Skipton, Yorkshire. Studied at Bath Academy of Art, 1972-6. Worked as a full-time mural painter, 1976-7. 1982 had an influential meeting with Frank Stella, the hard-edge abstract painter. 1984 solo exhibition at Sunderland Arts Centre.

DOYLE, John b.1928
Painter. Began his career in industry. Self-taught. Has exhibited twice in Canterbury Cathedral and in 1977 painted a picture for Archbishop Coggan to present to the Pope. 1981 and 1985 exhibited at Spink and Son, London. Painter of famous places in an untroubling style. Member of RWCS and exhibits regularly at RA.

PAMELA DREW, b.1910. *'RAAF Sunderland Flying Boat'*, 1942. Oil on board. 24in. x 18in. G.T. Cochrane.

DOYLE, Michael   b.1899
Sculptor. Born North Shields, Tyne and Wear. Began work as a miner and was president of Lambton Miners' Lodge for thirty-two years, receiving the unique distinction of having his portrait put on the Lodge banner, alongside that of Hugh Gaitskell. A lifelong interest in religious sculpture prompted him, at the age of forty-four, to take up woodcarving and since then has had exhibitions in Durham and Sunderland and received several commissions.

DRAPER, Kenneth   b.1944
Sculptor. Born Killamarsh, Yorkshire. Studied at Chesterfield and Kingston School of Art, from where he graduated, 1964, and at the RCA, 1965-8. He has travelled widely, visiting America, East Africa and Asia. His work has been particularly influenced by his travels in India and Pakistan and the Menorcan landscape. 1969 first solo exhibition at the Redfern Gallery. 1977 won a major Arts Council Award; in the same year he was elected to the Faculty of the British School in Rome. Included in the collections of the Arts Council of Great Britain; CAS; Fitzwilliam Museum and Art Gallery, Cambridge; National Museum of Wales, Cardiff; Courtauld Institute, London; Cartwright Museum and Art Gallery, Bradford;

Leicestershire Education Authorities; Mappin Art Gallery, Sheffield; Minories, Colchester; Welsh Arts Council. Elected ARA, 1990.

DRAPER, Paul   b.1947
Graphic artist. Educated in Cambridge and London, gained a Diploma in Interior Design. A Freeman of the Painter Stainers' Company and a Fellow of the Royal Society of Arts. 1976 exhibited 'Drawings of eighteenth-century buildings in East London' at the Geffrye Museum.

DRESSLER, Conrad   1856-1940
Sculptor and potter. Born London, of German descent. Studied at RCA and in France. 1886 stayed with Ruskin at Coniston. 1891-1918 member of the Art Workers' Guild. Set up a foundry in Chelsea and carried out *cire-perdue* casting. Also met William de Morgan who furthered his interest in pottery. 1893-5, worked as a potter in Birkenhead with Harold Rathbone, then set up his own kiln with R.W. Hudson in Buckinghamshire and made tiles. He was the inventor of the tunnel kiln. 1883-1907 exhibited at the RA. 1905-20, FRBS, then went to live in Paris and America. Two portrait busts of Ruskin exist, one in the Tate Gallery and the other at the Ruskin Memorial

Hall, Bournville. Dressler said of Ruskin 'His art teaching was lost upon me, but his spiritual teaching still illuminates my life'.

DREVER, Timothy   b.1935
Constructivist. Studied mathematics at Cambridge and taught for three years in Istanbul. 1962 started painting full-time and 1964 returned to London after living for two years in Vienna. Solo exhibitions include one at Lisson Gallery, London, 1968.

DREW, Pamela   1910-1989
Painter. Born Burnley, Lancashire. Studied under Dorothy Baker at Christchurch, Hampshire, with Iain McNab* at Grosvenor School of Modern Art, and with Roger Chastel in Paris. Air Ministry Accredited War Artist. Represented in the Imperial War Museum, National Maritime Museum, RAF Museum, Hendon and elsewhere. Recent solo exhibitions include one at the Abbot Hall Art Gallery, Kendal, 1982.

DREW, Sannie
Painter. Born in Mussooree, India. Educated in England where she was taught painting by Mary Hogarth.* 1923 returned to India and married. 1929-34 lived in England and studied at Chelsea Polytechnic. Later studied at Edinburgh College of Art. Solo exhibitions since 1952, including one at Bear Lane Gallery, Oxford, 1971. Member of the Artists International Association, and the Women's International Art Club.

DRING, James   1905-1985
Painter. Studied at RCA. Taught at St. Martin's School of Art, 1943-72. Exhibited at RA, ROI, RBA and other places. Represented in V & A, Southampton Art Gallery and elsewhere. Painted landscapes in a vaguely impressionist manner.

DRING, William   1904-1990
Painter. Studied at the Slade School of Fine Art in the 1920s. Official War Artist in Second World War; many of his drawings were executed in pastel, a medium in which he specialised. 1944 became ARA, and 1955 RA. A skilled technician, in oil, watercolour and pastel, he is best known for his portraits, family groups and landscapes. His drawing is always tight and precise and the forms carefully modelled. 1990 solo exhibition held at Agnew's, London.

DRUMMOND, Malcolm   1880-1945
Painter and printmaker. Born Boyne Hill, Berkshire. Studied at Christ Church, Oxford, 1899-1903, Slade School of Art, 1903-7, and Westminster School of Art, 1908, under Walter Sickert.* A member of Sickert's Fitzroy Street Group, he afterwards joined the Camden Town Group and the London Group. Did little painting during First World War, but for two years after the war was very productive, painting scenes from the Hammersmith Palais de Danse and in the Law Courts. 1922 executed 'The Sacred Heart' altarpiece for St. Peter's Church, Edinburgh. 1926 executed 'Stations of the Cross' for the Church of the Holy Name, Birkenhead. 1937 lost the sight of one eye and in 1942 became totally blind. 1963-4 Arts Council retrospective held. (Plate 3, p.15.)

MALCOLM DRUMMOND, 1880-1945. 'Hammersmith Bridge', 1912-13. 28in. x 18in. Huddersfield Art Gallery.

DRURY, Alfred   1856-1944
Sculptor. Born London. Studied at Oxford School of Art and at the RCA under Dalou, whom he followed to Paris and worked with, 1881-5. Returned to London and worked as an assistant to the sculptor Edgar Boehm. From 1885 exhibited at the RA. 1913 became an RA. 1905 executed sculpture for the War Office, 1908 the facade of the V & A Museum, and many war memorials throughout the country. 1932 received the RBS silver medal for his sculpture of Sir Joshua Reynolds in the courtyard of Burlington House, Piccadilly. Work in the collection of the Tate Gallery.

DRURY, Paul   1903-1987
Printmaker. Son of Alfred Drury,* distinguished sculptor and RA. Studied at Goldsmiths' School of Art , 1920-6. 1924 won an Open Scholarship in engraving from the British Institute. Influenced by Dürer, Rembrandt and F.L.M. Griggs.* 1926-31 worked as an assistant to his father. Executed portraiture as well as pastoral views of the English countryside, partly inspired by the 1920s

revival of interest in Samuel Palmer. Following the effect of the slump on the print market, he returned to Goldsmiths' as teacher and eventually became Principal. Also President of the RE, sustaining an interest in print-making in the years when its popularity waned.

Bibl: *Paul Drury: Artist and Printmaker.* Goldsmiths' College Gallery, 1984.

DUBERY, Fred   b.1926
Painter. Studied at Croydon School of Art, 1949-50 and RCA, 1950-3. Has taught at the RA Schools since 1964 and in 1984 was appointed Professor of Perspective at the RA. Solo exhibitions at the Trafford Gallery, London, 1957 and 1963, and at the New Grafton Gallery, London, 1974 and 1989. Mostly paints the Suffolk landscape as well as interiors and still lifes, but his traditional subjects are always painted from an unexpected angle and have a mysterious poetic quality.

DUBSKY, Mario   1939-1985
Painter. Born London. Studied at Slade School of Fine Art, 1956-61. 1963-5 won Abbey Major Rome Scholarship to British School at Rome. 1969-71 Harkness Fellowship in painting, New York. 1982 artist in residence, at the British School in Rome. Influenced by Picasso in the 1950s and haunted by memories and images of war, he fashioned a figurative art that had moved into abstraction by the mid-1960s, but returned to figuration with urgent moral and sexual themes. First exhibition held at Grosvenor Gallery, London, 1969. Last solo exhibition at South London Art Gallery, 1984.

Bibl: *Mario Dubsky: Paintings and Drawings 1973-84,* South London Art Gallery, 1984.

DUCKWORTH, Ruth   b.1919
Sculptor and potter. Born Hamburg, Germany. 1936 came to England and studied at Liverpool School of Art. Until 1956 did free-lance sculpting and earned her living carving tombstones. Studied pottery at Central School of Arts and Crafts and at Hammersmith School of Art. First solo exhibition of her sculpture at Apollinaire Galleries, London, 1951.

DUERDOTH, Philip Robert   b.1962
Painter. Studied at Chelsea School of Art and Ravensbourne College of Art. Solo exhibitions at Odette Gilbert Gallery, London 1987, 1989 and 1990.

DUFF, Leo   b.1954
Painter. Born Belfast, Northern Ireland. Studied at Brighton College of Art, 1972-6 and RCA, 1976-9. 1979 first solo exhibition held at Tom Caldwell Gallery, Belfast; others include one at Thumb Gallery, London, 1984. Also participates in the annual Association of Illustrators exhibition.

DUFFY, E.A.J.   b.1916
Painter. Born Croydon, Surrey. Much of his professional work has been concerned with insect and plant life in the tropics, particularly in relation to forestry. The influence of this is apparent in his work. Solo exhibition at Woodstock Gallery, London, 1971.

DUFFY, Terry   b.1948
Painter. Born Liverpool, Merseyside. His art is rooted in the urban environment. 1984 did a series of paintings on the Toxteth riots, which formed part of an exhibition at the Harris Museum and Art Gallery. Has also made the nuclear holocaust one of his themes.

DUGDALE, Thomas   1880-1952
Painter and textile designer. Born Blackburn, Lanca-shire. Studied at Manchester School of Art, the RCA, the City and Guilds School, Kennington, the Académie Julian and the Atelier Colarossi in Paris. Exhibited at the RA, mostly portraits, 1901-52. Served in Egypt, Gallipoli and Palestine during the First World War. 1919 solo exhibition at the Leicester Galleries of paintings of Palestine. 1916 married the painter Amy K. Browning.* 1936 made ARA and 1943, RA. Work in the Tate Gallery collection.

DUGUID, John   1906-1961
Painter. Studied at the Bauhaus, Germany, 1931-2. Lived and worked in Chile, 1934-8. Exhibited at the RA, London Group and elsewhere. 1960 solo exhibition at the Grabowsky Gallery, London. 1962 retrospective held at Canning House, 2 Belgrave Square, London.

DUKE, Lucy   b.1955
Painter. Studied at Camberwell School of Art, 1975-8. 1985 first solo exhibition held at Clarendon Gallery, London. 1988 exhibited recent pastels and watercolours at Christopher Hull Gallery, London.

DULAC, Edmund   1882-1953
Illustrator. Born Toulouse, France. Studied at Ecole des Beaux Arts, Toulouse. 1904 settled in London, and soon had regular work as an illustrator, for *The Pall Mall Gazette* and other publications. The 1907 commission to illustrate *Stories from the Arabian Nights,* retold by Laurence Houseman, which came from Hodder and Stoughton, made his reputation and allowed him to develop his love of the exotic. 1909 his orientalism again found expression in his illustrations to *The Rubáiyát of Omar Khayám.* Went on to enjoy an extremely active career, designing stamps, books and gravestones.

Bibl: *Edmund Dulac: Illustrator and Designer 1882-1953,* Sheffield City Art Galleries, 1983.

DUNBAR, Evelyn   1906-1960
Painter. Studied at Rochester School of Art and Chelsea, also at RCA, 1929-33. 1933-6 painted murals at Brockley School, Kent and was a member of the Society of Mural Painters. One of the first women to be made an official war artist and who concentrated particularly on the activity of the Land Army and the Land Girls. 1958-60 she was commissioned to do a mural at Bletchley Training College, Buckinghamshire.

DUNCALF, Stephen   b.1951
Object maker and painter. Born Widnes, Lancashire. Studied at Trent Polytechnic, 1970-3, and RCA, 1974-7. Began making objects as a reaction to the traditions and constraints of a two-dimensional surface. The first painting, *per se,* did not occur until 1972. Thereafter paintings and objects played off each other. Three solo exhibitions at the Coracle Press Gallery, London. 1986 he showed seven large paintings at the Victoria Miro Gallery, London, and had a solo exhibition at South London Art Gallery.

EVELYN DUNBAR, 1906-1960. *'Land Army girls going to bed'*. 20in. x 30in. Imperial War Museum.

DUNCAN, Jean
Painter. Born Edinburgh, Scotland. Studied at Edinburgh College of Art, 1951-5, Moray House College of Education, 1955-6 and Ulster Polytechnic, 1960-1. 1967 began exhibiting and held a solo exhibition, 'Sense and Symbols', at Octagon Gallery, Belfast, 1986.

DUNCAN, John   1866-1945
Painter and symbolist. Born Dundee, Scotland. Studied at Dundee School of Art and at the school of Verlat in Antwerp and in Dusseldorf. A member of the Dundee Graphic Arts Association. With Patrick Geddes he executed twelve paintings for the University Hall Common Room of Ramsay Lodge, Edinburgh. Painted on Barra and Iona and eventually abandoned his dream-like Celtic style. Believed unrequited love more conducive to creativity than physical satisfaction. Turned to designing stained glass whilst as a painter excelled at myth and legend.

Bibl: *John Duncan 1866-1945*, City of Edinburgh Art Centre, 1986.

DUNCAN, Joseph   b.1920
Painter. Born of Irish parents. Studied at Slade School and at the Sorbonne, Paris. Has lived and worked in Paris, Sardinia and Rome. 1952 first solo exhibition at Galerie Hervieu, Nice; others include one at the ICA, London, 1955. Since then has exhibited regularly in Paris, and

elsewhere, and is represented in numerous public collections.

DUNKLEY, Sue   b.1942
Painter. Born Leicester. Studied at Bath Academy of Art, 1959-61, Chelsea School of Art, 1961-3 and Slade School of Fine Art, 1963-5. 1963 visited Australia and taught at the art school in Sydney. 1965 won a Boise travelling scholarship and visited Italy. Solo exhibitions at Polytechnic of Central London, 1973, at Thumb Gallery, London, 1979, 1980 and 1982, and Curwen Gallery, London, 1986.

DUNLOP, R.O.   1894-1973
Painter. Born Dublin, Ireland. Studied part-time at Manchester and Wimbledon Schools of Art and in Paris. 1923 founded the Emotionist Group of artists and writers. Elected ARA and RA. An *alla prima* painter of traditional subjects.

DUNLUCE, Alexander   b.1935
Painter and conservationist. Born London. Studied at Ruskin School of Art, 1954-7. 1964 appointed restorer at the Tate Gallery and remained there until 1969 when he joined the Ulster Museum. 1971 he returned to the Tate Gallery and became Keeper of Conservation. Solo exhibitions at Bath Festival Gallery, 1975, and at Crane Arts, London, 1975, 1977 and 1983.

BERNARD DUNSTAN, b.1920. *'Auberge des Belles choses'*, 1985. 14in. x 12in. Private Collection.

DUNLUCE, Sarah   b.1941
Painter. Born Sarah Harmsworth. Was taught drawing by Mrs Cox, a pupil of Sickert. Studied at Byam Shaw School of Art, 1960-2. 1961 exhibited at Leicester Galleries. 1963 married Viscount Dunluce,* painter and picture restorer. 1970 solo exhibition at Crane Kalman Gallery, London.

DUNN, Alfred   b.1937
Sculptor. Born Wombwell, Yorkshire. Studied at Barnsley and Leeds Schools of Art and RCA. Exhibited at Redfern Gallery, London, 1965, 1966, 1969, 1971, 1975 and 1978. Works with a variety of materials and is also a professional printmaker.

DUNN, Anne   b.1929
Painter and collagist. Born London. Studied at Chelsea Polytechnic, 1947-9 and Académie Julian, Paris, 1952. Since then has lived and worked in France, the USA and Canada. Regular solo exhibitions since 1957 at Leicester Galleries, London, Fishback Gallery, New York. Represented in Arts Council collection and elsewhere. Married first Michael Wishart, then Rodrigo Moynihan.*

DUNSTAN, Bernard   b.1920
Painter. Born Middlesex. Studied at Byam Shaw School of Art and Slade School of Art, 1939-41. Taught at West of England School of Art, Bristol, 1946-9 and subsequently at a number of art schools until the 1970s. 1946 elected a member of NEAC, 1949 a member of the RWEA, 1979-83 President, 1959 elected ARA and RA 1968. 1952-70 he exhibited biennially at Roland, Browse and Delbanco. He has published six books on painting methods and is

represented in numerous public collections. His painting continues the 'intimiste' style of Bonnard and Vuillard with remarkable freshness.

DUNSTONE, Brian   b.1943
Sculptor. Born Prestwick, Scotland. Studied at Northampton School of Art, 1960-2, Hammersmith College of Art, 1962-5, and RCA, 1965-8. 1968-70 won Prix de Rome. 1974-6 Calouste Gulbenkian Fellowship, artist in residence, Hertfordshire. 1976 solo exhibition at House, 62 Regents Park Road, London.

DURDEY, Edward   b.1954
Painter. Born Stoke-on-Trent, Staffordshire. Lived in Hong Kong, 1961-71. Worked as telephone engineer, 1971-4. Studied at Wimbledon College of Art, 1975-8, and RCA, 1979-82. 1983-4 travelled in India, China, South East Asia, Australia and America. Since 1976 has exhibited in group shows. Represented by the Benjamin Rhodes Gallery, London.

DURHAM, Terry   b.1936
Painter. Born East Ardsley, Yorkshire. Studied at Batley and Leeds Colleges of Art, but mainly self-taught. 1963 began exhibiting at New Vision Centre, London. Solo exhibitions at Queen Square Gallery, Leeds, 1965, and Nicholas Treadwell Gallery, London, 1969.

DURRANT, Jennifer   b.1942
Painter. Born Brighton, Sussex. Studied at Brighton College of Art, 1959-63 and Slade, 1963-6. 1975 first solo exhibition held at University of Surrey, Guildford. 1979-80 was artist in residence at Somerville College, Oxford. Recent solo exhibitions include Nicola Jacobs Gallery, 1985, and Serpentine, 1987. The many influences on her abstracts include Mark Rothko, Arthur Dove, Ken Kiff,* and psychotherapy.

Bibl: *Jennifer Durrant. Paintings,* Serpentine Gallery, 1987.

DURRANT, Roy Turner   b.1925
Painter. Born Lavenham, Suffolk. Studied at Camberwell School of Art, 1948-52. Member of Artists International Association and Cambridge Society of Painters. 1960 Published *A Rag Book of Love* (poems), with the Scorpion Press. Represented in Southampton Art Galleries, Kettles Yard, Cambridge and elsewhere. Solo exhibitions include four with the Loggia Gallery, London.

DURST, Alan   1883-1970
Born Alverstoke, Hampshire. Served in the Royal Marines 1902-13 and in the First World War. Studied at the Central School of Art, 1913 and 1920. 1919-20 Curator of the G.F. Watts Museum, Compton. 1920 started to practise as a sculptor. 1925-40 and again in 1945-48 taught wood carving at the RCA. 1930 first one-person exhibition at the Leicester Galleries. 1931 carved figures on the front of the Royal Academy of Dramatic Art, London, and works for many churches, including figures on the west front of Peterborough Cathedral.

Bibl: Alan Durst, *Woodcarving,* Studio Publications, London, 1938.

DURWARD, Graham   b.1956
Painter. Born Aberdeen, Scotland. Solo exhibitions at the 369 Gallery, Edinburgh, 1979, 1981 and 1983 and the Frejus/Ordorer Gallery, New York, 1984.

JOAN EARDLEY, 1921-1963. *'Breaking Wave'*, 1960. 48in. x 55in.
Kirkcaldy Museum and Art Gallery, Kirkcaldy, Fife.

EACHUS, Paul   b.1944
Painter. Born Waterloo, Lancashire. Studied at Liverpool
College of Art and the RCA. Included in mixed exhibitions
from 1970, beginning with the Young Contemporaries.
1974 given Arts Council working grant and 1979 a British
Council grant to work abroad. One-person exhibition at
the University of Bradford Art Gallery, 1983.

EADIE, Ian   1913-1973
Painter. Born Dundee, Scotland. Studied at Dundee
College of Art, 1931-5. 1936-7 awarded travelling
scholarship to France and Italy, attended the Ecole des
Beaux Arts, Paris. Designed and painted murals for the
1938 Empire Exhibition. 1938 began to exhibit at the
RSA. 1939 worked in London and studied under Mark
Gertler* at Westminster School of Art. 1939-40 taught at
Dundee College of Art. 1940-6 war service with the Gordon
Highlanders in North Africa and Europe. 1944 had a one-
person travelling exhibition through Scotland of war
drawings and paintings; eighteen pictures acquired by the
Imperial War Museum. In the 1950s and '60s was
commissioned to produce murals for public and
commercial buildings throughout Scotland.

EADIE, Robert   1877-1954
Painter and printmaker. Born Glasgow, Scotland. Studied
art in Munich and Paris. Showed in mixed exhibitions at
the Paris Salon and in Edinburgh, Glasgow and London.
1916 elected RSW. Work in the collection of Glasgow Art
Gallery.

EAGLETON, Aileen   b.1902
Painter and wood engraver. Born Bexley, Kent. Studied
art under Louis Thomson in London. Exhibited work at
the RA, RI, ROI and the Paris Salon.

EAGLETON, Godfrey Paul   b.1935
Painter. Born London. Studied at Camberwell School of
Art, 1951-5 and the Slade School, 1957-9. 1955-7 period of
National Service spent in Cyprus. 1964 first one-person
exhibition at the Opus Gallery, London.

EARDLEY, Joan   1921-1963
Painter. Born Warnham, Sussex. Her father died when
she was seven, two years after the family had moved to
London. In 1939 the family moved to Glasgow. 1940-3 she
studied at the Glasgow School of Art, and was encouraged
by Hugh Adam Crawford.* Because of the war she could
not take up the post-diploma Scholarship awarded in 1943
so for two years worked as a joiner's labourer. From 1943
for several years she visited Arran and in particular
Corrie. In the summer of 1946 she studied at the Patrick
Allan-Frazer School of Art, Hospitalfield, near Arbroath,
then directed by James Cowie.* 1948 became a
professional member of the Society of Scottish Artists, also
in that year returned to Glasgow School of Art to take up a
post-diploma Scholarship which enabled her to travel for
eight months. Visited Paris, Florence, Assisi, Sienna,
Rome and in particular Venice. On her return taught at
the Glasgow School of Art two evenings a week. Her first
studio was in Cochrane Street, near the City Chambers,

but she later moved to an old photographer's studio at 204 St. James's Road in the Townhead area of Glasgow. Claimed there was no social or political impetus behind her painting of these streets. Around 1950 her interest in Catterline began, where she painted its fields and coastline all year round. 1955 elected an Associate of RSA and eight years later was made an academician. 1963 an honorary membership of the Glasgow Society of Lady Artists' Club was bestowed. Died of cancer.

Bibl: *Joan Eardley: Memorial Exhibition,* 1964 Glasgow Art Gallery and Museum; Cordelia Oliver, *Joan Eardley, RSA,* Mainstream Publishing, Edinburgh, 1988.

EARLE, Maud   d.1943
Painter of animals. Born London, daughter of the animal painter George Earl, and was taught by him. From 1884 exhibited at the RA and at the Paris Salon. Painted Queen Victoria's and King Edward VII's dogs. Many one-person shows.

EARLY, Tom
Painter. Studied medicine. Started painting in 1946 encouraged by Ben Nicholson.* 1946-52 painted in St. Ives. 1950 elected exhibiting member of Penwith Society of Arts. 1953 returned to medicine. 1958 began painting again and has exhibited at the Midland Group Gallery, Nottingham and elsewhere. 1961 founder member of the Derby Group of Artists.

EARNSHAW, Anthony   b.1924
Painter and maker of assemblages. Born Ilkley, Yorkshire. Earned his living as a crane driver. Self-taught. Started to paint in the mid-1940s. Produced four publications: *Museum,* 1968; *Wintersol,* 1971; *25 Poses,* 1973; and *Secret Alphabets 1-8,* 1985. 1971-2 drew a comic strip 'Wokker' in collaboration with Eric Thacker, for the *Times Educational Supplement.* 1987 retrospective exhibition of work (1945-87) held at Leeds City Art Gallery.

EARTHROWL, Eliab George   1878-1948
Painter and etcher. Born London. Studied at Goldsmiths' College. Exhibited at the RA. 1924 elected ARA. Member of the Print Makers' Society of California.

EASBY, Steve   b.1958
Painter. Born Derby. Studied painting in Liverpool. Depicts with minute detail formal gardens, parks, hot air balloons, and children's games, all slightly surreal. Adds depth to his pictures by adding a frame of leaves, made out of layers of tissue paper, varnished and painted. Exhibits at the Portal Gallery, London.

EASSON, Richard   b.1948
Painter. Born Oakley, Scotland. Studied at Edinburgh College of Art, 1965-71. Has exhibited in group shows and held solo show at New 57 Gallery, Edinburgh, 1972.

EAST, Alfred   1849-1913
Painter. Born Kettering, Northamptonshire. Began work in his brother's shoe factory. Sent to Glasgow on business, attended evening classes at the Government Art School. 1880 studied in Paris at the Ecole des Beaux Arts and the Académie Julian. Influenced by the Barbizon painters. Settled in London, 1884. Exhibited at RA from 1883, every year until his death. Elected ARA, 1899, RA, 1913. Knighted, 1910. Vivid landscapist, working with broad masses on a large scale.

EASTON, John   b.1929
Painter. Born London. Trained as an architect and town planner and worked in England, Europe, the Middle East and Australia. Studied painting and sculpture part-time at St. Martin's School of Art and East Sydney College. One-artist show at Compendium 2, 137 Fulham Road, 1969.

EASTWOOD, Walter   1867-1943
Painter. Born Lancashire. Studied at Heywood School of Art. Included in mixed exhibitions at provincial galleries in the north of England. First President of the Lytham St. Anne's Art Society.

EASYDORCHIK, Edwin   b.1949
Painter. Born Northumberland. Studied at Central School of Art, 1968-71. 1971 travelling scholarship taken in Italy. 1973-5 postgraduate painter, University of Newcastle upon Tyne. 1975 first one-person show at Sunderland Arts Centre. 1979 given Arts Council Purchase Award. Since 1982 Lecturer in Painting at the University of Newcastle upon Tyne. Work in the collections of the Arts Council and the British Council.

EAVES, John   b.1929
Painter and collage maker. Born Bristol, Avon. Studied at Bath Academy of Art. One-artist exhibitions held at Beaux Art Gallery, 1953, Forum Galleries, Bristol, 1963, Arnolfini, Bristol, 1966 and elsewhere.

ECCLESTON, Harry   b.1923
Painter and printmaker. Born Bilston, Staffordshire. Studied at Birmingham College of Art, 1939-42 and at the RCA, 1947-51. Included in mixed exhibitions at the RA, RE, NEAC and RWS. 1949 elected ARE, RE, 1961 and ARWS, 1964.

EDEN, William Denis   1878-1949
Painter. Born Liverpool, Merseyside, the son of William Eden, a painter in watercolour. Studied at the St. John's Wood Art School, London, from 1894, and RA Schools from 1897. Exhibited at the RA from 1899, principally genre and history pictures.

EDGCUMBE, Ursula   1900-1985
Painter and sculptor. Born Sandy, Bedfordshire, daughter of Sir Robert Edgcumbe. Studied art at Slade School, 1916-21. After the Slade worked as an architectural carver. Joined the National Society of Painters, Sculptors, Engravers and Potters at its foundation in 1929 and regularly exhibited with them. 1936 first one-person show of sculpture at Leger Galleries. 1940 abandoned sculpture for painting.

EDKINS, John   1931-1966
Painter. Born Bromley, Kent. Studied at Ealing School of Art, 1945-50 and at RCA, 1954-7. Went to Greece on a travelling scholarship, and subsequently taught at Bideford School of Art. 1961 settled in Liverpool, and taught at Liverpool College of Art. Exhibited with the Liverpool Academy and elsewhere. 1965 won a £100 prize in the John Moores Exhibition.

EDMOND, Mary   b.1929
Painter. Born Gallimuir, Scotland. Studied at Edinburgh College of Art, 1948-54, where the Principal, Robert Lyon, thought he detected the influence of Gwen John* on her

work, in both style and subject matter. Later published (under her married name, Mary Taubman) a book on this artist. 1988 held a solo exhibition at the Fine Art Society, Edinburgh. Also exhibits occasionally at the RSA and the Royal West of England Academy.

EDMONDS, Edith   **fl.c.1920-1955**
Painter. Studied at Liverpool School of Art, 1921-2 and at the Atelier Delbos, Paris, 1923-4. Exhibited in mixed shows at the Paris Salon, the RA and the RBA.

EDMONDSON, Simon   **b.1955**
Painter. Born London. Studied at City and Guild Schools of Art, 1973-4, Kingston Polytechnic, 1974-7, and Chelsea School of Art, 1977-8 and Syracuse University, New York, 1978-80. 1979 first solo exhibition held at Fairbanks Gallery, Syracuse. Solo shows also at Nicola Jacobs Gallery, London, 1982, 1986 and 1987.

EDWARDES, May   **c.1910-1960**
Painter of miniatures. Studied at the Cope and Nichol School of Art, and the RA Schools, 1907-12. Exhibited at the RA, the RI and the Paris Salon.

EDWARDS, Cyril   **c.1902**
Painter. Studied at Regent Street Polytechnic School of Art. Included in mixed exhibitions at the RA, the ROI and the Paris Salon. 1935 elected RBA and 1936 RI. Work in the collection of the Laing Art Gallery, Newcastle upon Tyne.

EDWARDS, Geoff   **b.1942**
Painter. Born London. First one-person show at the Arts Laboratory, London, 1968. Member of the Penwith Society of Arts in Cornwall.

EDWARDS, Helen   **1882-**
Painter. Born Eastbourne, Sussex (née Sutton). Studied art in St. Ives, Cornwall under Algernon Talmage,* 1906-8, and in Reading, Berks., with H. Dawson Barkas, 1909. Exhibited at the RBA and the Portrait Society. 1933 elected RWS.

EDWARDS, Jeffery   **b.1945**
Painter and printmaker. Born London. Studied at Leeds College of Art, 1964-7, RCA, 1967-70. 1970 won KMP Printmaking Prize. 1972 first one-person show at the Serpentine Gallery. Work in the collection of Tate Gallery, V & A, British Council, Arts Council, Brooklyn Museum, New York.

EDWARDS, John   **b.1938**
Painter. Born London. Studied at Hornsey College of Art, 1954-6 and 1958-60. Awarded British Council Scholarship to Belgium, 1963-4. Taught at St. Martin's School of Art, Chelsea School of Art and Brighton School of Art, 1964-73. 1967 first one-person show at Rowan Gallery, London. 1976 artist in residence, University of Syracuse, New York. Work in public collections, Arts Council, Department of the Environment, Gulbenkian Foundation, Leicestershire Education Authority, Towner Art Gallery, Eastbourne. Since 1980 Head of Painting at St. Martin's School of Art.

EDWARDS, John Colin   **b.1940**
Painter. Born Kidderminster, Worcestershire. Began as an apprentice carpet designer. Met Annigoni and studied with him in Florence. Back in London, studied at the RA Schools. First one-person show at the Federation of British Artists Galleries, London.

JOHN D. EDWARDS, b.1952. *'French Balcony',* 1987. 48in. x 48in. Private Collection.

EDWARDS, John D.   **b.1952**
Painter. Born North London. Studied at Central School of Art. Taught by John Hoyland* and Patrick Heron.* 1973 first President of the New Contemporaries. Travelled extensively in Europe and the West Coast of America 1975-9. Worked as Barry Flanagan's* assistant on major pieces including the Weather Vane for the Tate Gallery from 1983. 1985 first solo exhibition at Odette Gilbert Gallery, followed by others in 1987 and 1989.

EDWARDS, Lionel   **1878-1966**
Painter of horses. Born Bristol, Avon. Attended Frank Calderon's school of painting in Baker Street, London. Youngest member of the London Sketch Club. 1914-18 served in Army Remount Service. Contributed articles and pictures to *Country Life* and provided illustrations for numerous books on horses, e.g. *The Aga Khan's Horses,* 1938. 1927 elected RI. 1959 commissioned to paint the annual inspection of the Household Cavalry Mounted Regiment. His style of sky painting is immortalised in a poem by John Betjeman.

Bibl: Lionel Edwards, *Reminiscences of a Sporting Artist,* 1948.

EDWARDS, Peter D.   **b.1959**
Portrait painter. Born Chirk, North Wales. Attended Shrewsbury School of Art, 1974-5 and Gloucester College of Art and Design, 1975-8. From 1980 sent work to RA summer exhibitions. 1985 received special commendation for John Mayer Portrait Award, National Portrait Gallery. 1986 his painting, 'Liverpool Poets', was purchased by the NPG. 1986 first one-person show at Oriel 31 Gallery, Welshpool.

EGGINTON, Frank   b.1908
Painter of Irish landscapes. Son of the painter Wycliffe Egginton.* Lived in Donegal, Ireland. ARCA Exhibitions at Fine Art Society Gallery, March 1937 and February, 1939.

EGGINTON, Wycliffe   1875-1951
Painter of Scottish landscapes. Born Birmingham, West Midlands. Educated in Birmingham. 1913 elected RI. Exhibited at the RA, RI and the Paris Salon. Exhibitions at Fine Art Society Gallery, November 1936 and November 1938.

EGON, Nicholas
Painter, mainly of portraits of women. Began by painting abstract pictures but changed to figure painting in the late 1940s. 1950 produced works for an exhibition entitled 'Tribute to Greece', shown at Parsons and Sons Limited, 70 Grosvenor Street, London. 1952 published *Some Beautiful Women*.

EHRLICH, Georg   1897-1966
Sculptor and printmaker. Born Vienna, Austria. Studied at the Vienna Kunstgewerbeschule, 1912-15. Served in Austrian Army during First World War. 1920 exhibition of prints held at Hans Goltz Gallery, Munich, thereafter exhibited regularly. 1926 began to sculpt. 1919-21 lived in Munich, 1921-3 Berlin, 1923-37 Vienna. 1937 awarded Gold Medal at the World Exhibition, Paris. 1937 came to London as a refugee and took British nationality. 1961 awarded Sculpture Prize of City of Vienna. 1962 elected ARA. Work in the collection of the Tate Gallery.

EINZIG, Susan   b.1922
Painter and illustrator. Born Berlin, Germany. Educated at Breuer School of Design, Berlin, 1937-8 and, after emigrating to England, at Central School of Arts and Crafts, 1939-42. 1942-5 did war work in industry. 1945 exhibited with London Group. 1946 won National Book League Award for Best Illustrated Children's Book. Since 1945 has worked as free-lance illustrator and painter, until recently preferring intimate media to working in oils. Taught at Camberwell and Chelsea Schools of Art.

EISENMAYER, Ernst   b.1920
Painter and sculptor. Born Vienna, Austria. 1939 arrested and sent to Dachau Concentration Camp. Released due to intervention of Professor J.L. Brierley, Fellow of All Souls, Oxford and came to London, 1939. Became a jewellery designer and sent paintings to mixed exhibitions, e.g. The London Group, the AIA, and the RA summer exhibitions. 1961 first one-person show at the John Whibley Gallery, London. 1964 first one-person show of sculpture at the Mercury Gallery, London.

ELAND, John   1872-1933
Painter of portraits, printmaker and sculptor. From 1893 studied at the RA Schools and then in Paris. From 1894 exhibited at the RA. Member of the Senefelder Club. Died in New York.

ELDERFIELD, John   b.1943
Painter and art historian. Born Yorkshire. Studied at University of Manchester, School of Architecture, 1961-2, University of Leeds, Fine Art Department, 1962-6. Taught at Winchester School of Art, 1966-70. 1970 awarded Harkness Fellowship to study in USA. 1972

visiting Professor, Department of Fine Art, University of Guelph, Canada. 1973 Lecturer in History of Art, Department of Fine Art, University of Leeds. Curator of MOMA, New York. 1974 first one-person show at Park Square Gallery, Leeds.

ELDRIDGE, Harold Percy   b.1923
Painter and muralist. Born London. Studied at Camberwell School of Arts and Crafts, 1938-42, and at the RCA, 1947-50. Included in mixed exhibitions at the RA, RBA and the London Group.

ELDRIDGE, Mildred   b.1909
Painter and book illustrator. Born London. Studied at Wimbledon School of Art, at the RCA and at the British School in Rome. Included in mixed exhibitions at the RA, RSA and RWS. Work in public collections. Recorded Wales for Pilgrim Trust, 1944-6.

ELKAN, Benno   1877-1960
Sculptor. Born Dortmund, Germany. Studied painting at Munich and Karlsruhe. Self-taught in sculpture. 1933 settled in London. Sent work to RA summer exhibitions.

ELLIS, Lionel   b.1903
Painter. Born Plymouth, Devon. Studied at Plymouth School of Art, 1917-22 and the RCA, 1922-5. 1925 visited Florence and Rome on RCA Travelling Scholarship. 1930, *Herrick, Theocritos, Catullus* with fifty of his wood engravings, published by the Franfrolico Press. Also in 1930 founder member of the National Society of Painters and Sculptors. 1934 first one-person exhibition at the Redfern Gallery, London. 1937-68 taught painting and sculpture at Wimbledon School of Art. 1950 founder member of the Society of Animal Painters (he loved to paint horses). 1973 retrospective exhibition at Plymouth Art Gallery.

ELLIS, Noel   b.1917
Painter. Born Plymouth, Devon. Studied at Plymouth School of Art and at the RCA until 1948. Included in mixed exhibitions at the RA, RBA, NEAC and with the London Group.

ELLIS, Peter   b.1950
Sculptor and performance artist. Born Prestbury, Cheshire. Attended Manchester College of Art, 1969-70, Wolverhampton College of Art, 1970-3, Chelsea School of Art, 1973-4. Junior Fellow in Fine Art at Cardiff College of Art, 1974-5. Included in mixed exhibitions since 1974, including a piece in the International Performance Festival in Birmingham that year. 1975 published his own book work *MSS*. 1977 first one-person show at Chapter Gallery, Cardiff.

ELLWOOD, George   1875-1955
Decorative artist and designer. Born London. Studied in London, Paris, Vienna, Berlin and Dresden. Showed in mixed exhibitions at the RA, RI and the Paris Salon. Publications include *Studies of the Human Figure*, 1918, *The Art of Pen Drawing*, 1927, and other books.

ELWELL, Frederick   1870-1958
Painter. Born Beverley, Yorkshire. Studied at Lincoln School of Art, the Academy Schools in Antwerp and the Académie Julian, Paris. Exhibited at the Paris Salon from 1894 and at the RA from 1895. 1914 married Mary Bishop

JOHN ELWYN, b.1916. *'Whitewashed walls'*, 1961. 30in. x 40in. Private Collection

(1874-1952), a painter of landscapes. 1931 elected ARA, and 1938 RA.

ELWES, Simon   b.1902
Painter of portraits. Born near Rugby, Staffordshire. Studied at the Slade School, 1918-21, and then in Paris until 1926. From 1927 exhibited at the RA. 1956 elected ARA, and 1967 RA. Official war artist in India and South East Asia during the Second World War.

ELWYN, John   b.1916
Painter. Studied at Carmarthen Art School, 1935-8, West of England College of Art, Bristol, 1937-8, and RCA, 1938-40. Taught at Portsmouth College of Art, 1948-53, and Winchester School of Art, 1953-77. Solo exhibitions include two at the Leicester Galleries, London, 1965 and 1968, and another at Howard Roberts Gallery, Cardiff, 1965. Represented in National Museum of Wales, Cardiff, the Glynn Vivian Gallery, Swansea, and elsewhere. Honorary member of the Royal Cambrian Academy.

EMANUEL, Frank   1865-1948
Painter and printmaker. Born London. Studied art at the Slade School, where he won the first medal for life drawing, and at the Académie Julian in Paris. 1896 first exhibited at the RA, and the Paris Salon. Travelled extensively in Europe, South Africa and Ceylon. 1918-30 taught etching at Central School of Arts and Crafts. Wrote letters to *The Listener* and elsewhere in the 1930s denouncing modern art.

EMERSON, Robert   1878-1944
Sculptor. Born Rothley, Leicestershire. Studied at Leicester College of Art, and in London and Paris. 1913 elected FRBS. Taught at Wolverhampton School of Art.

EMERY, Janette   b.1964
Sculptor. Studied at Cambridge College of Arts and Technology, 1982-3, Chelsea School of Art, 1983-6, and at the RA Schools, 1986-9. Awards include the Italian Institute of Culture Travelling Scholarship, 1985, and RA

RICHARD EURICH, b.1903. 'Men of Straw', 1957. Oil on board. 20in. x 40in. Nottingham Castle Museum and Art Gallery.

Gold Medal, 1988. 1984 first exhibited in Elsom Pack and Roberts Architectural Competition. This was followed by her inclusion in an RIBA touring exhibition in America, 1985.

ENGELBACH, Florence   1872-1951
Painter. Born Spain of English parents. Studied art at the Westminster School of Art, the Slade School and in Paris. 1901 began exhibiting at the RA. 1902 married and stopped painting until 1931, then resumed and worked mostly on flower paintings. Exhibited at the Beaux Arts, Tooth's and Leicester Galleries in London. Specialised in flowers, portraits, still lifes and landscapes.

ENGLISH, Grace   1891-1956
Painter. Born London. Studied in Paris and Germany. Whilst staying at Karlsruhe she met I.A.R. Wylie and did illustrations for her book on the Black Forest. Around 1912 returned to England and entered the Slade School of Art. 1914-18 did munitions work and machine drawing. After the First World War she studied etching at South Kensington under Sir Frank Short.* Specialised in portraits, pictures of ballet dancers and flower pieces. Exhibited regularly at the RA and with the NEAC. During the last six years of her life ill-health affected the size of her work but not its quality. Represented in Leeds City Art Gallery and the Imperial War Museum.

ENGLISH, Stanley   b.1908
Sculptor. Born Romford, Essex. Studied at Lambeth School of Art and the RA Schools. Included in mixed exhibitions, e.g. RA summer exhibitions. 1946 teacher of ceramics, Liverpool College of Art.

EPSTEIN, Jacob   1880-1959
Sculptor. Born New York of Russian and Polish parents. Studied at the Art Students League, New York and at night school, 1896-9. Left America for Paris. Studied at Ecole des Beaux Arts and the Académie Julian, Paris,

1902-4. 1905 settled in London, 1907 became a British citizen. Worked for a while in Paris, c.1911-2 and befriended Picasso, Modigliani and Brancusi. 1907-8 his first major commission was eighteen figures for the BMA headquarters in the Strand. 1913 founder member of the London Group, and first one-person show at the Twenty-One Gallery. Other public commissions include: 1924 'Rima', a memorial to the writer, W.H. Hudson, for Hyde Park; 1928-9 Night and Day on London Underground Transport Building, St. James's; 1952 Madonna and Child, Cavendish Square; 1953-4 Christ in Majesty, Llandaff Cathedral; 1957-8 St. Michael and Lucifer, Coventry Cathedral. 1954 knighted.

Bibl: *The Sculptor Speaks,* Heinemann, London, 1931; *Let there Be Sculpture,* Michael Joseph, London, 1940, revised as *An Autobiography,* 1955; E. Silber, *Jacob Epstein: Catalogue Raisonné of his sculpture,* Phaidon, Oxford, 1987.

ERNEST, John   b.1922
Sculptor. Born Philadelphia, USA, the son of Russian Jewish *émigrés.* Studied at the Philadelphia Museum School of Industrial Art in 1940, and at St. Martin's School of Art, London, 1952.6. Served with US Merchant Marines, 1942-4. Lived in Sweden, 1946-9, France, 1949-51 and then settled in England. Started making constructions, 1954 and worked exclusively in that category since 1956. His works display his interest in mathematical structures. Work in the collection of the Tate Gallery and Arts Council.

ERTZ, Edward   1862-1954
Painter and printmaker. Born Chicago, USA. Worked in Chicago and New Orleans as an engraver and illustrator. 1885 went to New York and produced illustrations for *The Century Magazine.* 1888 went to Paris and began to exhibit at the Paris Salon from 1889. 1892-9 Professor of Drawing and Painting at Académie Délécluse, Paris.

Moved to England. Exhibited at the RA and the RBA. 1902 elected RBA.

ETCHELLS, Frederick   1886-1973
Painter. Studied at RCA, c.1908-11, after which he rented a studio in Paris. Came under the influence of French Post-Impressionism and was represented in Roger Fry's* Second Post-Impressionist Exhibition, 1912-13. For a period was associated with Fry and his circle and was employed at the Omega Workshops. Left this for Wyndham Lewis's Rebel Art Centre, and joined the Vorticist camp, contributing illustrations to *Blast*. Founder member of the London Group. Took up architecture in mid-1920s and translated Le Corbusier's *Towards a New Architecture*.

ETCHELLS, Jessie   1892-1933
Painter and designer. Born Newcastle-upon-Tyne, the younger sister of the painter Frederick Etchells.* Self-taught as an artist but guided by her brother. Roger Fry* included her work in his Second Post-Impressionist exhibition at the Grafton Galleries, London, 1912. Joined Fry's Omega Workshops in the summer of 1913, left it in the autumn, after the secession of her brother. Left Britain, 1914, for Canada, with her future husband, David Leacock. Remained there the rest of her life, which after marriage had less room for painting. Works in the collection of Rochdale Art Gallery and Charleston Farmhouse, Lewes, Sussex.

EURICH, Richard   b.1903
Painter. Born Bradford, Yorkshire, the son of a bacteriologist. Studied at Bradford School of Art and at the Slade. 1929 befriended by Sir Edward Marsh who helped obtain his first one-artist show at the Goupil Gallery. Subsequent exhibitions held at the Redfern Gallery. Much influenced by Christopher Wood.* Served in Royal Navy as a war artist, concentrating on the theme of survival at sea. From 1949 taught at Camberwell. His landscapes are often both intricately detailed and panoramic in scope, and his narrative pictures rich in incident. Represented by the Fine Art Society. Elected ARA, 1942, and RA, 1953.

Bibl: *Richard Eurich, RA: A Retrospective Exhibition*, Bradford Art Galleries and Museums, 1980.

EVANS, David   1929-1988
Painter. Born London. Studied at Central School of Art and Crafts under Keith Vaughan.* As a young man he produced photomontages and designed a mural for a Knightsbridge soup kitchen. Moved to East Anglia, became a watercolourist and worked in a tiny studio overlooking his vegetable garden. The somewhat predatory nature of his garden scenes suggests the influence of Edward Burra.* He never lived off the proceeds of his sales but did part-time jobs, working for a period as a porter in a psychiatric unit and recreating his experience of this in hallucinatory images testifying to the patients' distress.

EVANS, Garth   b.1934
Sculptor. Born Cheadle, Cheshire. Studied at Manchester College of Art and the Slade School, 1955-60. 1962 first one-person exhibition at the Rowan Gallery. 1972 commissioned to make a sculpture for the Peter Stuyvesant Sculpture Project in Cardiff. Since early 1980s has lived and worked in USA. Represented in the following collections: Tate Gallery, Arts Council, V & A, Metropolitan Museum of Art, New York.

EVANS, Merlyn   1910-1973
Painter. Born Cardiff, Wales. Studied at Glasgow School of Art and the RCA. 1931-3 studied in Paris, Berlin, Italy

NICHOLAS EVANS, b.1907. *'A great step forward. (The first Davy lamp.)'*, 1982. 48in. x 48in. Private Collection.

and Copenhagen. 1932 awarded Royal Exhibition from the RCA. From 1931 included in mixed exhibitions. 1934-6 contacts with Mondrian, Kandinsky, Moholy-Nagy and other artists in Paris confirmed Evan's commitment to abstraction, manifest in his student work. 1936 took part in International Surrealist Exhibition, London. His paintings, which often link mechanical and natural forms, are essentially Celtic and romantic in spirit. 1938-42 lived in Durban, South Africa. Served in South African Army, then the British Army, during the war. 1939 first one-person show at City Art Gallery, Durban. 1954 mural painting entitled 'Metropolitan Crowd'. 1961 designed mural for Southampton General Hospital, and awarded prize in 4th International Exhibition of Graphic Art, Ljubljana, Yugoslavia. 1965 Tutor in painting at RCA. 1966 awarded Gold Medal, National Eisteddfod of Wales. Retrospectives at Whitechapel Art Gallery, 1956, and Welsh Arts Council exhibition, 1974.

Bibl: *The Political Paintings of Merlyn Evans, 1930-50*, Tate Gallery cat., 1985.

EVANS, Nicholas   b.1907
Painter. Born Aberdare, South Wales, where he still lives and works. Employed as an engineman with British Rail. Began to paint when he took early retirement. Self-taught. 1972-7 exhibited annually in the Royal National Eisteddfod of Wales, and was awarded first prize, 1975. 1978 Bursary from the Welsh Arts Council. 1978 first one-person exhibitions at Browse and Darby, London and at Oriel, Cardiff. Work purchased by the CAS and the Welsh Arts Council.

EVANS, Ray   b.1920
Painter and illustrator. Studied at Manchester College of Art, 1946-8, and at Heatherleys School under Iain Macnab.* His publications include *Travelling with a Sketchbook*, 1980, and *Learn to Paint Buildings*, 1987. Has also produced calendars, prints and paintings for Art for

ANTHONY EYTON, b.1923.
'Spitalfields through a window'.
57in. x 47in.
Browse & Darby Gallery.

Offices, British Rail, British Petroleum, Whitbread, Abbey National and others. Represented in the National Library of Wales and elsewhere. (Plate 36, p.170.)

EVES, Reginald G.   1876-1941
Painter of portraits and topographical subjects. Born London. Studied at the Slade School, 1891-5. Lived and worked in Yorkshire, 1895-1900, then settled in London and as a portrait painter. Copied at the National Gallery and was encouraged by Sargent. From 1901 exhibited at the RA. ARA, 1933, RA 1939. 1935 first solo exhibition at Knoedlers, 1940-1 Official War Artist. Painted portraits of many celebrities, e.g. Thomas Hardy and Max Beerbohm, both of which are in the Tate Gallery collection. 1947 memorial exhibition held at the RBA Galleries.

Bibl: Adrian Bury, *The Art of Reginald G. Eves,* RA publications, London, 1940.

EWART, David Shanks   1901-1965
Painter. Born Glasgow, Scotland. Spent a year in business before studying at Glasgow School of Art; graduated 1924. Studied in France and Italy on a travelling scholarship. Exhibited regularly at the RSA, the Royal Glasgow Institute of the Fine Arts, and occasionally at the RA. 1934 elected ARSA. Lived all his life in Glasgow, but from 1946 onwards spent several months each year in America painting portraits of industrialists and their wives.

EYTON, Anthony   b.1923
Painter. Born Middlesex. Son of the painter Phyllis Eyton who died in a hunting accident at the age of twenty-nine. Like his mother, Eyton's chief concern is with light and nature. Whilst at Canford School in Dorset he received lessons from the visiting teacher, William Coldsteam.* Spent one term at Reading University before serving in the Army, 1942-7. Studied at Camberwell School of Art, 1947-51. Awarded an Abbey Major Scholarship and spent 1951-3 in Italy. 1954 began exhibiting at RA. Specialises in crowd scenes, on beaches, in streets, railways, factories and elsewhere, but also paints from nature in his garden at Brixton. 1969-71 lived in Canada and owing to his experience of American Abstract Expressionism adopted a more fluid approach; his paintings remain representational but the marks, shapes and colours execute an independent, abstract dance. 1976 elected ARA and 1985, RA. Has taught at Camberwell and the RA Schools and travels widely. Recent solo exhibitions include one at Browse and Darby, London, 1990. Work in Arts Council collection, Tate Gallery, Imperial War Museum, Guildhall Art Gallery and elsewhere.

JAMES FAIRGRIEVE, b.1944.
'*Dark Sky*'. 48in. x 48in. Acrylic.
Private Collection.

FAIRCLOUGH, Michael   b.1940
Painter and printmaker. Born Blackburn, Lancashire. Studied at Kingston School of Art, 1957-61, the British School in Rome, 1964-7, and Atelier 17, Paris, 1967. Solo exhibitions include one at the Bohun Gallery, Henley on Thames, 1981. Represented in the V & A Museum, Ashmolean Museum, Oxford, New York Public Library and elsewhere. Commissions include a mural for Farnham Post Office, 1970 and a National Trust special commemorative issue of five stamps, 1981.

FAIRCLOUGH, Wilfred   b.1907
Painter and printmaker. Studied at RCA, 1931-4, and the British School in Rome, 1934-7. Has exhibited internationally, also at the RA, RE and RSA. Elected ARWS, 1961, and RWS, 1967. 1962-72 Principal of Kingston College of Art.

FAIRGRIEVE, James H.   b.1944
Painter. Born Prestonpans, Scotland. Studied at Edinburgh College of Art, 1962-8. 1968 received David Murray Landscape Award (Royal Academy). 1969 first solo exhibition held at New 57 Gallery, Edinburgh; others include one at the Mercury Gallery, London, 1980. 1969 elected a Professional Member of the Society of Scottish Painters; 1975 Associate of the Scottish Academy and Member of the Royal Scottish Society of Watercolourists; 1978 President of the Society of Scottish Painters. Represented in Scottish Arts Council Collection.

FAIRHURST, Jack Leslie   b.1905
Painter. Born London. Studied at Camberwell School of Art and the RCA, 1937-43. Was Hon. Secretary of the London District National Society of Art Education. Exhibited in mixed exhibitions in London and the provinces. 1941-57 Head of Richmond School of Art.

FAIRLEY, George   b.1920
Painter. Born Dunfermline, Scotland. Studied at Edinburgh College of Art. War service in RAF. 1950 held first solo exhibition at Gimpel Fils, London, and another in 1953.

FALCONBRIDGE, Brian   b.1950
Sculptor. Born Norfolk. Studied at Canterbury College of Art, 1968-9, Goldsmiths' College, 1970-3 and Slade School of Fine Art, 1973-5. Has taught in a variety of art schools and held a solo exhibition at House, 62 Regents Road, London, 1977.

FANTONI, Barry   b.1940
Painter and cartoonist. Born Stepney, London, of Italian and Jewish parents. Studied at Camberwell School of Art. 1963 first solo exhibition held at Woodstock Gallery, London. Also plays the tenor sax and executes cartoons for *The Times*.

FARGHER, Tim   b.1952
Painter. Born Lincolnshire, but spent the first eight years of his life living in Europe. Studied at St. Martin's School

FARLEIGH, John

of Art, and after a period of travel and work in other fields, graduated in 1979. Since then has exhibited regularly in London and Suffolk where he lives on the coast. His work centres on landscape, portraiture and allegorical figure paintings. Solo exhibitions include one at Long and Ryle Art International, London, 1990.

FARLEIGH, John   1900-1965
Painter and engraver. Originally intended to be a stained glass artist and was apprenticed to a commercial art studio. 1918 entered army and after demobilisation trained at Central School of Art. During the Second World War found himself unemployed, 'starving gracefully and with moderate tact'. 1947 a founder member of the Crafts Centre in London. 1940 his autobiography, *Graven Image,* published, and in 1942 the essay, 'The Future of Wood Engraving'. 1986 an exhibition of his wood-engravings was held at the Ashmolean Museum, Oxford.

FARMER, Bernard   b.1919
Painter. Born London. Studied at Chelsea Polytechnic School of Art. 1956 first solo exhibition held at AIA Gallery, London; others include one at Circle Gallery, London, 1970. Represented in Arts Council Collection.

FARMER, Peter   b.1936
Painter. Born Luton, Bedfordshire. Studied at Central School of Art. Illustrated H.E. Bates's *The Day of the Tortoise* and has decorated harpsichords for Morley and Sons. 1961 first solo exhibition held at Redfern Gallery, London; others include solo shows at Mercury Gallery, London, 1964, 1965, 1970 and 1973, and at the Casson Gallery, London, 1974, 1975 and 1977. Specialises in designs for ballet and theatre.

FARNHAM, John   b.1942
Sculptor. At age of sixteen he joined his father's business helping on construction work for Henry Moore.* 1965 started working as assistant to Moore and since 1969 has been engaged on his own work. 1973 executed work for Gawthorpe Festival in Burnley. 1976 solo exhibition at New Art Centre, London; another at Leeds City Art Gallery, 1984.

FARQUHARSON, Joseph   1846-1935
Painter. Born Edinburgh, Scotland. Studied at the RSA Life School, Edinburgh. Exhibited at the RA from 1873. Elected ARA, 1900, RA, 1915. Visited Egypt, 1885. Specialised in portraits and landscapes and is especially famous for his snow scenes.

FARRELL, Anthony   b.1945
Painter. Born Epsom, Surrey. Studied at Camberwell School of Art, 1963-5 and at the RA Schools, 1965-8. 1972 first solo exhibition at Brunel University. Draws his themes from Southend, depicting people at leisure by the sea. Included in the collections of the Arts Council and Epping Forest Museum.

FARRELL, Michael   b.1940
Painter. Born Kells, Ireland. Studied at St. Martin's School of Art, and London and Colchester College of Art, 1957-61. 1966 spent a year in New York on the Macauley Fellowship. 1971 moved to Paris. Solo exhibitions include one at New Art Centre, London, 1977 and another at the Douglas Hyde Gallery, Trinity College, Dublin, 1979. Represented in Manchester City Art Gallery, Trinity College of Dublin and elsewhere.

FARRER, Julia   b.1950
Painter. Studied at Slade School and on a Harkness Scholarship, in USA, 1974-6. Her abstract paintings distil the rhythms and rhymes inherent in nature. They achieve clarity and stillness through a deliberate suppression of personal expression.

FARTHING, Stephen   b.1950
Painter. Born Leeds, Yorkshire. Studied at St. Martin's School of Art, 1969-73 and RCA, 1973-6. Appeared regularly at John Moores exhibitions in the 1980s. Solo exhibitions at Edward Totah Gallery, London, 1984 and 1986. Since 1985 has been Head of Painting at West Surrey College of Art and Design.

FAULKNER, Amanda   b.1953
Painter. Born Dorset. Spent two years in South America making, with another, a film of the Canai Indians of Equador. Also worked there as an illustrator of books on the mythology of an Amazonian group. Studied at Bournemouth College of Art, 1978-9, Ravensbourne College of Art, 1979-82 and RCA, 1982-3. 1983 first solo exhibition held at Woodlands Art Gallery, Blackheath, and since then has exhibited regularly at Angela Flowers Gallery, London. A figurative artist who uses specifically female experience as her subject matter. Represented in Arts Council and Unilever collections.

FAULKNER, Patricia   b.1946
Painter. Studied at West Sussex College of Art, 1962-4, Kingston College of Art, 1964-7 and RCA, 1967-70. Awarded the silver medal at the RCA. Exhibits at RA and at Mercury and Piccadilly Galleries, London. A fantasist, who uses classical and literary sources.

FAULKNER, Trevor   b.1929
Sculptor. Born Sheffield, Yorkshire. Studied at Sheffield School of Art, 1946-50 and the RCA, 1952-5. Works in ferrous and non-ferrous metals. Principal Lecturer at Sheffield City Polytechnic. Published *Manual of Direct Metal Sculpture,* 1978. Work in the Ulster Museum.

FAUSSET, Shelley   b.1920
Sculptor. Born Berkshire. On leaving school became a pupil of Eric Gill* and a student apprentice to J.M. Dent and Sons. Founded the Linden Press. Worked as farm worker during Second World War and also served in the Friends Ambulance Unit on the Continent. 1946 became resident assistant to Henry Moore.* Studied at Chelsea School of Art and Slade, 1948-54. Taught at Cambridgeshire College of Art and Technology, and moved to Central School of Art and Design to become Head of Foundation Studies. 1958 first solo exhibition held at Heffers, Cambridge; others include two at Mercury Gallery, London, 1973 and 1977.

FAWCETT, Raymond   b.1934
Painter. Born Yorkshire. Studied at Beckenham School of Art and RCA. Much travelled and taught at Hammersmith College of Art. Solo exhibition of abstract paintings held at Drian Galleries, 1960.

STEPHEN FARTHING, b.1950. *'Summer House'*, 1987. 81in. x 68in. Edward Totah Gallery.

FAWCETT, Rosemary   b.1947
Painter. Born Yorkshire, but spent her childhood in the Scottish border country. Trained as a textile designer and painter. Describes her paintings as 'Romantic Realism' and is much influenced by 14th and 15th century Northern artists. Her work is characterised by fine detail and a dream-like exaggeration.

FAWSETT, Evelyn
Painter. Wanted to be an artist at the age of four, but this idea was not approved and she went to a horticultural college and worked on the land until the end of the First World War. Joined a firm of landscape gardeners and married the artist, Cecil Heathfield.* Held her first solo exhibition in her seventies at Woodstock Gallery, London, 1966.

FEATHER, Yan Kel   b.1920
Painter. Of Austro-Russian parentage. Spent childhood in Liverpool. 1942 first exhibited at Hereford Art Gallery. 1960-70 member of the Liverpool Academy. 1981 solo exhibition at Salt House Gallery, St. Ives, with introduction to catalogue by Rose Hilton.*

FEATHERSTON, Bill   b.1927
Sculptor. Born Canada. Resident in England since 1961. Abstract carvings influenced by Barbara Hepworth* and Henry Moore.* Has exhibited at the New Vision, the Rawinski and the Grabowski Galleries, London.

FECHENBACH, Hermann   b.1897
Painter and engraver. Born in Württemburg, Germany. Injured during First World War. 1918 trained at Stuttgart Handicraft School for invalids. Also attended academies in Stuttgart and Munich. 1923 went to Florence, followed by periods in Pisa, Venice, Vienna and Amsterdam. 1924 returned to Stuttgart, painting in style of 'Die Neue Sachlichkelt'. 1933 the Nazis removed his name from the official state register, forbidding him to exhibit. 1938 Nazi persecution caused him to flee to Palestine and thence to England. 1940 interned as a suspect alien; whilst interned produced 'Refugee Impressions', a series of linocuts. Released 1941. Has exhibited in England since 1951, working in isolation.

FEDARB, Daphne   b.1912
Painter. Born London (née Brock). Studied at Beckenham

Plate 33. JOHN DAVIES, b.1946. *'Lined Head'*, 1985-8. Resin, fibreglass, stone dust and acrylic. Height 64½in. Marlborough Fine Art (London) Ltd.

Plate 34. FRANCIS DAVISON, 1919-1984. *'Bright Colours bound with Black'*, c.1978-82. Collage. Private Collection.

Plate 35. EVE DISHER, b.1894. *'Portrait of Mrs. Mary St. John Hutchinson'*, 1930. Gouache on board. 16½ in. x 13½ in. Sandra Lummis Fine Art, London.

FEDARB, Ernest

School of Art, 1928-30 and Slade, 1931-4. Married Ernest Fedarb* and with him exhibited at the Fine Art Society, 1935. Studied under Mark Gertler* and Bernard Meninsky* at Westminster School of Art, 1936-9. 1948 became member of RBA. Exhibited RA, NEAC and elsewhere. 1982 awarded the De Lazlo Medal, RBA.

FEDARB, Ernest   b.1905
Painter. Born Canterbury, Kent. Studied at Sidney Cooper School of Art (Canterbury) and Beckenham School of Art. 1934 elected member of National Society of Painters, Sculptors, Engravers and Potters. 1935 held joint exhibition with his wife, Daphne,* at the Fine Art Society, in the same year he joined the staff of Westminster School of Art. Other teaching posts included one at Hammersmith School of Art, 1944, and was an HMI for Art, 1947. 1985 elected President of the National Society of Painters, Sculptors and Printmakers.

FEDDEN, Mary   b.1915
Painter. Born Bristol, Avon. Studied at Slade School of Art, 1932-6. 1956 became a member of the London Group and Chairperson of the Women's International Art Club until 1959. Tutor of painting at RCA, 1958-64. Married Julian Trevelyan* and has held numerous solo exhibitions since 1953. Has also executed several mural commissions including one for the Charing Cross Hospital in 1980 with Julian Trevelyan. Her most recent exhibitions have been at the New Grafton Gallery, London. Represented in Royal West of England Academy, Sheffield City Art Gallery, Ferens Art Gallery, Hull and elsewhere. (Plate 37, p.171.)

FEDDEN, Romilly   1875-1939
Painter. Born Henbury, Gloucestershire. Studied under Herkomer at Bushey, at the Académie Julian, Paris, and in Spain. Exhibited at the RA and other leading London galleries, as well as abroad. Published *Modern Water Colour,* 1918, and *Golden Days from the Fishing Log of a Painter in Brittany,* 1919. Lived mostly in France, by the Seine, and painted extensively on the Continent.

FEI, Cheng-Wu   b.1914
Painter. Born China. Studied at National Central University, China, 1930-4, and the Slade School, 1947-50. Has exhibited at RA, RI, RWA, RWS, NEAC and held several solo exhibitions at the Leicester Galleries. Has promoted in England brush drawing in the Chinese manner.

FEIBUSCH, Hans   b.1898
Painter, muralist and sculptor. Born Frankfurt, Germany. After serving in First World War went to Munich to study medicine. Left medical school to study painting under Carl Hoefer in Berlin. Won Rome prize and went to Italy and then studied for two years in Paris under André Lhote. 1933 returned to Frankfurt and won Prussian state prize for painting and, at the same time, aroused Nazi antagonism. The same year he emigrated to England where he began to exhibit at the Lefevre Gallery but concentrated on murals. In the early 1970s failing eyesight oliged him to abandon painting for sculpture.

FEIGL, Fred   1884-1965
Painter. Born Prague, Czechoslovakia. Studied at Prague Academy of Art, 1904-5, but was expelled for 'revolutionary artistic activity'. Founder member of 'Osma' group, being

CHENG-WU FEI, b.1914. *'Cat',* 1977/8. Watercolour. Approx. 26in. x 20in. Private Collection.

anti-traditionalist and an admirer of Van Gogh, Gauguin and Münch. 1905-7 studied in Antwerp and Paris. 1907 returned to Prague. 1910 went to Hamburg. 1912 first one-artist show in Berlin. 1917 co-founder of 'Freie Bewegung', Vienna. After the German occupation of Czechoslovakia in 1938 he was arrested trying to emigrate and sent to a concentration camp in Westphalia. 1939 was aided by Artists' Refugee Committee and Czech Refugee Trust Fund and arrived in England. Later exchanged revolutionary work for mostly landscapes.

FEILER, Paul   b.1918
Painter. Born Frankfurt, Germany. Came to England in 1933. Studied at Slade School of Art, 1933-9. 1939 was interned in Canada, but returned to England in 1941 and became art master at Eastbourne until 1946. 1946 joined the staff at West of England College of Art, where he taught until 1975. 1953 first one-person show at the Redfern Gallery, London. 1954 bought a disused chapel in Cornwall, which has been his home ever since. Work in public collections, including Arts Council, CAS, Aberdeen Art Gallery, Bath Art Gallery, Birmingham City Art

Gallery, Glasgow, Doncaster, Leeds, Manchester, Newcastle, Norwich, Plymouth, Sheffield, Wakefield, and the Tate Gallery.

FEILD, Maurice   1905-1988
Painter. Studied at Slade School, 1924-8. Became art teacher at the Downs School, Colwall, 1928, and in 1937 organised an exhibition of his pupils' work at the Redfern Gallery, London. Worked during holiday periods at the Euston Road School, and exhibited with the London Group. 1948 held solo exhibition at the City Art Gallery, Worcester. Moved to the Slade School as a member of staff, and in 1950 to St. Albans School of Art.

FELCEY, Trevor   b.1945
Painter. Born Ferring, Sussex. Studied at Camberwell School of Art, 1963-6 and at the RCA, 1966-9. He was awarded the David Murray and Andrew Lloyd Scholarships. First solo exhibition at Brunel University, 1976. Primarily a landscape artist.

FELL, Michael   b.1939
Painter and graphic artist. Studied at St. Martin's School of Art and at City and Guilds School, Kennington. Awarded a travelling scholarship to Italy. Has exhibited in London and Suffolk and had a one-artist show at the Jordan Gallery, Camden Lock, London, 1974.

FELL, Sheila   1931-1979
Painter. Born Aspatria, Cumberland. Studied at Carlisle School of Art and St. Martin's School of Art. 1957 won second prize in John Moores Liverpool Exhibition. 1958 awarded a Boise Scholarship and travelled to Italy, Greece and France. 1969 elected ARA. Taught at Chelsea School of Art and lived in London but made regular trips to the North. Exhibited at Beaux Arts Gallery. 1974 elected RA. Regarded by Lowry* as the finest English landscape painter of this century. Work in the Tate Gallery, Arts Council collection and elsewhere.

Bibl: *Sheila Fell,* with essay by Helen Lessore, South Bank touring exhibition held RA and elsewhere, 1990.

FENNELL, Hazel   b.1936
Painter. Born Penzance, Cornwall. Studied at Bournemouth College of Art, 1953-9 and Central School of Art and Crafts, 1960, where she specialised in lithography. 1964 joined AIA. Has exhibited regularly since 1959, including paintings of aircraft and racing cars at the ICA, London, 1972.

FENNER, Rachel   b.1939
Sculptor. Born Scarborough, Yorkshire. Studied at Wimbledon School of Art, 1958-62, and RCA, 1962-6. 1979 appointed 'City Sculptor' to Portsmouth. 1976 first solo exhibition held at House, London, and 1979 was given a Southern Arts Touring Exhibition. Her work reflects an interest in socio-environmental problems.

FENWICK, Catherine   b.1955
Sculptor. Born London. Studied at Gloucestershire College of Art and Design, 1973-7. 1978 first solo exhibition held at Jordan Gallery, and another at the Ikon Gallery, Birmingham, 1980. Her sculptures are less than a foot tall, yet dense in allusion, often referring to decay, violence or distress.

J.D. FERGUSSON, 1874-1961. *'A Lowland Church',* 1916. 20in. x 22in. Dundee Art Galleries and Museums.

FERGUSON, Ken   b.1937
Painter. Born Northumberland. 1952-8 trained as an apprentice painter and decorator. 1958-69 was a professional soldier. 1970 began to paint and became associated with the Ashington Group. 1981 solo exhibition, 'A Trip to Appleby Horse Fair', held at Printmakers Workshop Gallery, Edinburgh.

FERGUSSON, J.D.   1874-1961
Painter. Born Leith, Scotland. Abandoned medical studies to devote himself to painting. Encouraged by the example of Whistler and the Glasgow Boys made regular visits to Paris from the mid-1890s, where he studied the Impressionists and frequented the Académie Colarossi. 1905 first solo exhibition held at Baillie Galleries, London. 1907 settled in Paris and adopted a Fauve style. 1908 began to sculpt carving directly in wood and stone, in a Cubist manner. Became art editor of the magazine *Rhythm,* 1911 and in his own work sought to emulate the vitality and sensuousness he experienced in contemporary music and dance. 1913 included in the 'Post Impressionist and Futurist Exhibition' at the Doré Galleries, London, the same year that he met the dancer Margaret Morris, whom he married. Became associated with Cadell, Hunter and Peploe as a Scottish Colourist. During the 1930s was president of the Groupe des Artistes Anglo-Americans in Paris. 1939 moved to Glasgow, and was a founder member of the New Art Club in 1940 from which emerged the New Scottish Group in 1942.
Bibl: *Colour, Rhythm, and Dance. Paintings and Drawings by J.D. Fergusson and his circle in Paris,* Scottish Arts Council cat., 1985.

FERNEE, Kenneth   b.1926
Painter. Born London. Head of Art Department in a Devon Comprehensive School. Paints landscapes and seascapes in the South West and in Wales. Solo exhibition at John Whibley Gallery, London, 1971.

Plate 36. RAY EVANS, b.1920. *'Place D'Jemmaa El FNA, Marrakech'*, 1990. Watercolour. 10½ in. x 10½ in. Private Collection.

Plate 37. MARY FEDDEN, b.1915. *'Playing Cards'*, 1989. 24in. x 20in.
Private Collection.

Plate 38. STANHOPE FORBES, 1857-1947. *'A Fish Sale on a Cornish Beach'*, 1885. 48⅝in. x 61¼in.
Plymouth City Museum and Art Gallery.

FERRABY, Paul

DAVID FERRY, b.1957.
'Continuous and Universal',
c.1981. Etching and aquatint.
Collection of University College.

FERRABY, Paul   b.1951
Painter. Born into an Army family and travelled abroad extensively as a child. Influenced, as a boy, by Chinese painting in Singapore. Studied at West Surrey College of Art. Solo exhibition at Century Galleries, Henley-on-Thames, 1989.

FERRIS, Sydney   b.1902
Painter. Studied at Camberwell School of Art and Crafts and Goldsmiths' College where he studied etching and engraving under Stanley Anderson.* Having earlier obtained a technical training, he worked as a structural engineer but exhibited regularly at the RA, RBA, NEAC,

RWS and elsewhere. Represented in the Imperial War Museum.

FERRY, David   b.1957
Painter. Studied at Blackpool College of Higher and Further Education, 1974-6, Camberwell School of Arts and Crafts, 1976-9, Slade, 1979-81, and Camberwell (extended studies in printmaking), 1981-2. 1982 held his first solo exhibition at the Grundy Art Gallery, Blackpool, and his most recent at the Herbert Read Gallery, Canterbury College of Art, 1987. His fascination with structure has created in his 'Star Chamber' series, awesome, inexplicable instruments of fear and destruction.

FESENMAIR, Helene   b.1937
Sculptor. Born New Ulm, Minnesota, USA. Studied at Smith College, Massachusetts, 1955-9, and Yale University, 1959-61. 1961-8 worked and exhibited in New York, studying at New York Studio School and travelling to archeological sites in Greece, Peru and the Yucatan. 1969-70 worked in Venezuela before moving to London in 1970. Solo exhibitions include two at New Art Centre, London, 1974 and 1975.

FEW, Elsie   1909-1980
Painter and collagist. Born Jamaica, West Indies. Studied at Slade, 1929-31, and abroad, visiting Paris, Vienna, the Balkans, Greece and Italy. 1936 held her first solo exhibition in Jamaica. 1937 married Claude Rogers* and 1937-9 worked occasionally at the Euston Road School. 1943 elected member of the London Group. 1945-8 was an art editor at Chatto and Windus, 1946-69 headed the art department at Gipsy Hill College. As a collagist she came to believe that the tearing of paper is important, visually and for its textural effect. Her later collages are freer than the earlier ones. Memorial exhibition held at Bury St. Edmunds Art Gallery, 1981. Represented in the V & A, Royal West of England Academy, New York Public Library and elsewhere.

FIELD, Norman   b.1917
Sculptor. Born Croydon, Surrey. Educated at Royal Military College, Sandhurst. 1970 first solo exhibition held at John Whibley Gallery, London. 1969 his sculpture of Rugby Players was selected for the 2nd Biennale exhibition of Sport and the Fine Arts at Madrid. Sculpts birds, figures and plant life.

FIELDING, Brian   1933-1987
Painter. Born Sheffield, Yorkshire. Studied at Sheffield College of Art, 1950-4 and RCA, 1954-7. 1958 won Abbey Minor Travelling Scholarship to Italy and France. 1958 first solo exhibition at Hibbert Gallery, Sheffield; others include one at Morley Gallery, London, 1984. An abstract gestural artist.

Bibl: *Brian Fielding. New Paintings and Paintings 1960-1983*, Mappin Art Gallery, Sheffield, and elsewhere, 1986.

FIELDS, Duggie   b.1945
Painter. Born Salisbury, Wiltshire. Studied architecture briefly at Regent Street Polytechnic before going to Chelsea School of Art in 1964. As a student his work moved through minimalism, conceptionism, constructivism to a more hard-edge post-Pop figuration. First solo exhibition held at Hamet Gallery, London. In the 1980s his work was seen to include elements of post-modernism. 1983 an exhibition of his was sponsored by the Shiseldo Corporation in Tokyo and his work featured simultaneously on television, in magazines and billboard and subway advertising throughout the country.

Bibl: *Duggie Fields. Paintings 1982-87*, Albemarle Gallery, 1987.

FILDES, Luke   1843-1927
Painter. Born Liverpool. Studied at Chester School of Art and the RCA. Began work as an illustrator, for *The Graphic* and other magazines. Began exhibiting at the RA, 1872. With Herkomer, he became associated with the social realism of the 1870s but once he achieved success he changed to portraiture in order to maintain the life style he enjoyed. One of his most famous paintings is *The Sick*

BRIAN FIELDING, 1933-1987; *'Drift'*, 1977. Acrylic. 80in. x 69in. The Trustees of the Brian Fielding Estate.

Child (Tate Gallery). Elected ARA, 1879, and RA, 1887. Painted State portraits of King Edward VII, 1902, and King George V, 1912. Knighted, 1906, and KCVO, 1918.

FINESTONE, Laurie Ann   b.1949
Draughtswoman. Born New York City. Studied music and visited museums. Studied etching in Santa Reparate Graphic Studio in Florence. Moved to Bath and worked for seven years with the Bristol Printmaking Co-operative. Moved to Penzance. Solo exhibition at Newlyn Art Gallery, Penzance, 1983.

FINK, Peter   b.1948
Sculptor. Born London. 1969 graduated as an engineer at University of Prague. Studied sculpture at St. Martin's School of Art, 1969-72. 1978 graduated in philosophy, University of London. Has shown in group exhibitions since 1973 and had a solo exhibition at Hull City Museum, 1984. Commissions include 'Sculpture for Jerusalem', 1986.

FINLAY, Ian Hamilton   b.1925
Sculptor. Born Nassau, Bahamas. Spent a brief period at Glasgow School of Art followed by Service in Germany. Took a variety of agricultural labouring jobs and in 1958 began publishing short stories, poetry and plays. 1961 founded the Wild Hawthorn Press and the magazine, *Poor. Old. Tired. Horse* and the broadsheet, *Fishsheet*. First became known as a concrete poet. 1963 made his first free-standing poems. Exhibited in all major concrete poetry exhibitions. Created a garden to house his work at

Plate 39. ANTHONY FRY, b.1927. *'At the Edge of the Desert'*. 60in. x 72in. Private Collection.

Plate 40. ROGER FRY, 1866-1934. *'Edith Sitwell'*, 1918. 24in. x 18in. Sheffield City Art Galleries.

Plate 41. MARGARET GERE, 1878-1965. *'There is no Friend like a Sister'*. Watercolour. 8½in. x 10in. Private Collection.

Plate 42. TIMOTHY GIBBS, b.1923. *'Garden'*. 26in. x 32in. Clarendon Gallery.

175

FINN, Elizabeth

Stonypath, Lanarkshire, also as a living homage to classical tradition. Believes that 'The more man is in control of his environment, the more he has to create a world of orderliness for himself to live in. Art can create an order and clarity not attained to in life by most people.' Much of his work aspires to a styleless quality and is executed by various collaborators.

Bibl: Yves Abrioux, *Ian Hamilton Finlay: A Visual Primer*, Reaktion Books, Edinburgh, 1985.

FINN, Elizabeth   b.1933
Painter. Born Liverpool. Studied at Manchester Academy of Fine Art. First solo exhibition at Capital Art Centre, Great Falls, United States. She has exhibited widely in group exhibitions in the United Kingdom and the United States. Represented in Salford Art Gallery and Stockport Art Gallery.

FINNEMORE, Joseph   1860-1939
Painter, etcher and illustrator. Born Birmingham, West Midlands. Studied at Birmingham School of Art and at the Antwerp Academy under Verlat. Returned to England in 1881 and exhibited at major art venues. After further travels in Malta, Greece, Turkey and Russia he settled in London and worked as an illustrator for *The Graphic, The Sphere* and other magazines. Elected RBA 1890, RI 1898, and RSBA 1901.

FIRMSTONE, David   b.1943
Painter. Born Middlesbrough, Cleveland. Studied at Middlesbrough College of Art, 1958-63. Began exhibiting in 1963 and in 1965 held a solo exhibition at Silver Coin Art Gallery, Harrogate.

FISHER, John   b.1938
Painter, sculptor, printmaker. Born Coventry, Warwickshire. Trained at Camberwell School of Art. Practised in several media until late 1970s since when he has worked mostly in oils. 1980 visited Isle of Mull where he developed a lasting fascination for mountains and hills. Since 1986 has been represented by the Francis Kyle Gallery and held his first solo show there, 1988.

FISHER, Mark   1841-1923
Painter. Born Boston, USA. Studied at Gleyre's Atelier in Paris in 1893, at the same time as Sisley. Returned to America before settling in England in 1872. A foremost English impressionist, exhibiting at NEAC, RA, and elsewhere. Elected ARA, 1911 and RA, 1919. Father of Margaret Fisher Prout.*

FISHER, Myrta   b.1917
Painter. Born Wimbledon, London. Studied at Huddersfield Art School, Slade and Central School of Arts and Crafts. Solo exhibition at Ansdell Gallery, London, 1971.

FISHER, Roger   b.1919
Painter. Born Dover, Kent. Spent thirty-seven years in the Royal Navy. Member of the Wapping Group of Artists and Armed Forces Art Society. Specialises in marine paintings.

FISHER, Rowland   1885-1969
Painter. Born Gorleston, Norfolk, the son and grandson of master mariners. Was apprenticed to a timber firm in Southtown where he remained for fifty years, retiring as sawmill manager in 1950. Co-founder of the Great Yarmouth and District Society of Artists, following Arnesby Brown* as its President. His paintings of ships, docks and quays chart the fortunes of the Yarmouth fleet as it changed from sail to diesel. Holidays in Cornwall led to his election as member of the St. Ives Society of Artists; he also became a member of the Royal Society of Marine Artists.

Bibl: *Rowland Fisher, RSMA, ROI, A Centenary Exhibition*, Great Yarmouth Museum's Exhibition Galleries, 1985.

FISHER, Samuel Melton   1860-1939
Painter. Born London. Studied at Lambeth School of Art and the RA Schools, 1876-81, winning a gold medal and a travelling scholarship. Later studied in Paris under Bonnaffe, and subsequently lived for ten years in Italy painting Venetian subjects. From 1878 exhibited at RA and also internationally. 1917 elected ARA and 1924 RA. Probably for financial reasons he devoted himself to portraiture during the last part of his career.

FISHER, Sandra   b.1947
Painter. Born New York City, USA. Studied at Chouinard Art School, California Institute of the Arts, Los Angeles. Moved to London, 1971. Guest lecturer at various art schools. 1983 married R.B. Kitaj.* 1982 first solo exhibition held at Coracle Press Gallery, London; others include one at the Odette Gilbert Gallery, London, 1989. Has illustrated Thomas Meyer's translations of *Sappho* (1982) and his poems, *Sonnets and Tableaux* (1987).

FISHWICK, Clifford   b.1923
Painter. Born Accrington, Lancashire. Studied at Liverpool College of Art. 1957 first solo exhibition held St. George's Gallery, London; others include one at the Royal Albert Memorial Museum, Exeter, 1960. 1958-70 Principal of Exeter College of Art. Recent solo exhibitions include one at Austin/Desmond Fine Art, London, 1989.

FITTON, James   1889-1982
Painter and cartoonist. Born Oldham, Lancashire. Apprenticed to a fabric designer and attended evening classes at Manchester School of Art. Met L.S. Lowry.* 1920 moved to London. Attended evening classes at Central School of Arts and Crafts under A.S. Hartrick.* Also visited Russia. 1929 first exhibited at RA. 1932-52 member of London Group. 1933 first solo exhibition at Arthur Tooth and Sons. Worked for *Left Review* and did posters for the Ministry of Food and London Underground. 1944 elected ARA, and 1954 RA. 1968-75 trustee of British Museum. 1970-82 Honorary Surveyor of Dulwich College Picture Gallery.

Bibl: *James Fitton RA. 1899-1982*, Oldham Art Gallery, 1983.

FITZJOHN, David   b.1963
Painter. Born Wembley, Middlesex. Studied at High Wycombe College of Higher Education, 1981-2, and Canterbury College of Art, 1983-6. 1982-6 took part in group shows in Aylesbury and Canterbury.

FITZPANE, Mary   b.1928
Painter. Born Catterick, Yorkshire. Studied at Leeds College of Art during the war years, afterwards at Central School of Art and Crafts and the RCA. Has exhibited widely. Also does book illustration and china decoration.

SANDRA FISHER, b.1947. *'The Lovers'*. 20in. x 25in. Private Collection.

FLANAGAN, Barry   b.1941
Sculptor. Born Prestatyn, North Wales. Studied at Birmingham College of Art and Crafts, 1958. 1960 moved to London, worked on sets for Pinewood Studios and attended Anthony Caro's* Friday evening classes. 1961 spent three months at Flintshire Technical College. 1964-6 studied at St. Martin's School of Art. 1966 first solo exhibition at Rowan Gallery, London. Numerous solo exhibitions at home and abroad including a retrospective at the van Abbemuseum, Eindhoven, 1977 (also shown at Arnolfini, Bristol, and Serpentine, London). Has moved from using hessian, cloth and sand through a return to carving, modelling and bronze casting. (Plate 16, p.42.)

FLANAGAN, T.P.   b.1929
Painter. Born Enniskillen, Northern Ireland. Studied at Belfast College of Art. Exhibits in Dublin and London (RA), and is represented in the Herbert Art Gallery, Coventry, the Ulster Museum and the Arts Council of Northern Ireland Collection.

FLANDERS, Dennis   b.1915
Painter and etcher. Studied at Regent Street Polytechnic, St. Martin's School of Art and Central School of Arts and Crafts. Exhibited at RA and other leading London galleries and in the provinces. First solo exhibition held at Colnaghi's, London, 1947. Represented in several public collections and elected ARWS and RBA, 1970.

FLATTELY, Alistair   b.1922
Painter. Born Inverness, Scotland. Studied at Glasgow University and Edinburgh College of Art. Has exhibited widely, at the RSA, SSA, RA and RWA, among other places. Became Head of Grays School of Art, Aberdeen. Represented in public collections in Aberdeen, Glasgow, Dundee and Cheltenham.

FLATTER, Joseph Otto   b.1894
Painter. Born Vienna, Austria. Studied at Vienna Academy of Fine Arts, but his career was interrupted by service in Austrian Army. Made his name as portrait

Plate 43. HAROLD GILMAN, 1876-1919. *'The Tea Cup'*.
Ivor Braka Ltd., London.

Plate 44. MERVYN GOODE, b.1946. *'Winter Light through the Ivy, Treyford, W. Sussex'*. 36in. x 48in. Private Collection.

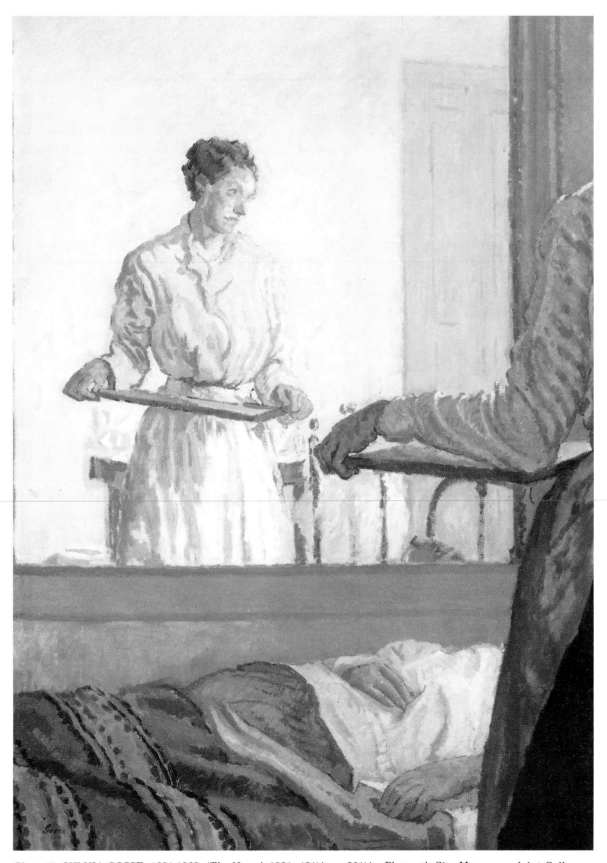

Plate 45. SYLVIA GOSSE, 1881-1965. *'The Nurse'*, 1931. 42½ in. x 30¼ in. Plymouth City Museum and Art Gallery.

FLEETWOOD-WALKER, Bernard

painter. 1935 settled in England. Interned for three months at start of 1939-45 war but was released to produce propaganda cartoons for Ministry of Information. Work also used by Refugee governments and American press. Commissioned by Ministry of Information to draw Nazi defendants at Nuremberg trials. After the war worked as satirical artist and collected and restored Old Masters. 1976 began a series of tempera paintings based on history, literature and personal experience.

FLEETWOOD-WALKER, Bernard 1893-1963

Painter. Born Birmingham, West Midlands. Trained at Birmingham School of Art and Crafts, also in London and Paris. Served with Artists' Rifles during First World War and was wounded and gassed. A prodigious worker, who spent all his life in Birmingham and excelled at portraiture, especially pictures of children. 1946 elected ARA, and 1956 RA; also a member of Royal Watercolour Society. 1966 a memorial exhibition was held by the Royal Birmingham Society of Artists.

FLEISHMANN, Arthur 1896-1990

Sculptor. Born Bratislava, Czechoslavakia, but lived most of his life in London. Studied medicine in Budapest and Prague and qualified as a doctor of medicine but his interests turned to art and he was awarded a scholarship to the Master School of Sculpture in Vienna. Taught at the Women's Art Academy, Vienna, then moved to Sydney in Australia for ten years, finally settling in London in 1948, in the St. John's Wood studio that had once belonged to the Victorian sculptor, Sir George Frampton.* Pioneered the use of perspex in sculpture, but also specialised in portrait busts, and was the only artist to have sculpted four popes from life. His devotion to the Catholic faith was central to his work and he executed many commissions for churches in England and on the Continent. Commissions include a Silver Jubilee Memorial for the Queen at St. Katherine's by the Tower, London, 1977.

FLEMING, Ian b.1906

Painter and printmaker. Born Glasgow, Scotland. Studied at Glasgow School of Art, 1924-9, and was appointed to the staff, 1931. 1940-6 war service, after which he returned to Glasgow School of Art. 1946 elected member of RSW, and 1947 of Royal Scottish Academy. 1956 elected Academician RSA. 1954-72 Head of Gray's School of Art, Aberdeen. Moved from a very factual use of line engraving to a more atmospheric use of drypoint. In the 1970s he began the print series *Creation* and *Comment* which introduced texts into semi-abstract compositions reflecting the human dilemma. Elected Chairman of Peacock Printmakers, 1974.

FLIGHT, Claude 1881-1955

Painter and printmaker. Born London. After a mixed start, in engineering, then as a librarian, farmer and beekeeper, Flight started studying art in 1912, aged thirty-one, at Heatherley's. C.R.W. Nevinson,* a former student, introduced Flight to Marinetti and Severini. Flight's own futurism took the form of linocuts. 1919 he became a founder member of the 7 and 5 Society, 1923 a member of the RBA, and 1928 of the Grubb Club. 1925-30 with Iain McNab* he ran the Grosvenor School of Modern Art. Flight founded a school of colour linocuts, and in his own work sustained the futurist interest in the representation of speed and movement.

Bibl: Michael Parkin, *Claude Flight and his circle,* Fine Art Ltd., 1975.

FLINT, Robert Purves 1883-1947

Painter and etcher. Born Edinburgh, Scotland, younger brother of William Russell Flint.* Educated at Daniel Stewart's College, Edinburgh. 1926 held solo exhibition at the Leicester Galleries, London. Worked much abroad, especially in France. Elected RSW, 1918, ARWS, 1932 and RWS, 1937.

FLINT, Sir William Russell 1880-1969

Painter. Born Edinburgh, Scotland. Apprenticed as a lithographic artist and designer with a firm of printers, also attended evening classes at the Royal Institution School of Art. 1900 came to London and was employed as a medical illustrator. 1903 appointed to staff of *The Illustrated London News* and attended evening classes at Heatherley's Art School. Did colour illustration work for the Medici Society and began exhibiting regularly at the RA. Elected ARA, 1924, and RA, 1933. 1936-56 President of the Royal Society of Painters in Watercolours. Painted landscapes, seascapes and 'feminine grace'. Also won acclaim for his gypsies, flamenco dancers and languorous nudes.

Bibl: Sir William Russell Flint, *Minxes Admonished; or Beauty Reproved,* Golden Cockerel Press, 1955.

FLORENCE, Mary Sargent 1857-1954

Painter. Born London. Studied at Slade School of Art under Legros and in Paris under Merson. 1888 she married Henry Smyth Florence, an American musician. Exhibited at RA and NEAC, becoming a member of the NEAC, 1911. Represented in the Tate Gallery collection.

FLOYD, Christina b.1949

Painter. Born London. Studied at Central School of Art, 1968-9, Hornsey College of Art, 1969-72 and RCA, 1972-5. 1977 first solo exhibition held at University of Pittsburgh Gallery; other solo shows include one at South London Art Gallery, 1985. Represented in Leicester Education Authority Collection.

FLOYD, Roderick b.1904

Painter. Born Paris of Anglo-French parentage. Studied at Chelsea Polytechnic and elsewhere. Solo exhibitions held in London include one at Woodstock Gallery, London. Blends representational and abstract worlds into evocative harmonies.

FOLKES, Peter L. b.1923

Painter. Born Beaminster, Dorset. Studied at West of England College of Art before and after military service, 1942-7. 1952 elected associate of Royal West of England Academy, and 1959 an academician. 1969 elected member of RI. 1977 solo exhibition at Gainsborough House, Sudbury, Suffolk.

FOLLETTE, Patricia b.1929

Painter. Born Birmingham, West Midlands. Studied at Birmingham College of Art 1951-5. Solo exhibition at Compendium Gallery, Birmingham, 1967, another at Griffen-Garnett Galleries, Shrewsbury, 1968.

FOOT, Victorine b.1920

Painter. Born Knowles Bank, Kent. Studied at Central School of Art and Chelsea School of Art, 1941-5. Executed camouflage work for the Navy during the Second World War. 1946 married the sculptor Eric Shilsky. 1949 gained her diploma from Edinburgh College of Art. 1949 first solo

CLAUDE FLIGHT, 1881-1955. *'Speed'*, c.1926. 8¼ in. x 11in. Linocut. Michael Parkin Fine Art Ltd.

VICTORINE FOOT, b.1920. *'A kite in Venice'*. 25in. x 30in. Private Collection.

FORBES, Ronald

exhibition at the Institute Français, Edinburgh. 1950-1 taught at Edinburgh College of Art, and 1961-79 at Oxenford Castle School. Exhibited with the NEAC, London Group, RA, RSA and the Society of Scottish Artists among others. Work in the collection of the War Artists Advisory Commission.

FORBES, Ronald   b.1947
Painter and film maker. Born Perthshire, Scotland. Studied at Edinburgh College of Art, 1964-9. 1971 founder chairman of the Glasgow League of Artists. Member of Society of Scottish Artists. Moved to Cork, Eire, to teach at Crawford School of Art. Exhibited 'Recent TV Series Paintings' at Drian Galleries, London, 1975. Represented in Scottish Arts Council collection and elsewhere.

FORBES, Stanhope Alexander   1857-1947
Painter. Born Dublin, Ireland. Studied at Lambeth School of Art and Royal Academy Schools, 1874-8. 1880 he enrolled at Bonnat's Atelier in Paris. In the early 1880s worked during the summers in Brittany with Henry La Thangue* under the influence of Bastien-Lepage. 1884 settled in Newlyn and in 1885 sent *A Fish Sale on a Cornish Beach* to the RA Summer Exhibition; it earned him much acclaim and effectively made him the leader of the Newlyn School. 1886 a founder-member of the NEAC but was suspicious of the Whistler influence within it. Elected ARA, 1892 and RA, 1910. With his wife, Elizabeth, opened the Newlyn School of Art and while other of their contemporaries moved on, he and his wife remained in Newlyn to influence a younger generation that included Laura Knight.* (Plate 38, p.171.)

Bibl: *Painting in Newlyn,* Barbican Art Gallery, 1985.

FORBES, Vivian   1891-1937
Painter. First solo exhibition held in Chicago in 1921, followed by five in London 1924-36. Represented in Tate Gallery, London Museum, Chicago Art Institute and elsewhere. Memorial exhibition held at Redfern Gallery, London, 1938.

FORD, Anita   b.1948
Printmaker and collagist. Trained at Coventry and Loughborough Colleges of Art. 1971 won an Italian State Scholarship and studied in Venice for a year. First solo exhibition held at Camden Institute, London, 1974. 1979 visited Israel and contributed to the 'Israel Observed' project. Solo exhibition at Graffiti, London, 1983, of collages and monoprints.

FORD, George Henry   b.1912
Sculptor. Studied at Hornsey School of Art under Harold Youngman.* Exhibited at the RA, RSA and in the provinces. Elected ARBS, 1944, and FRBS, 1955.

FORD, Jane   b.1944
Painter. Born Sutton Coldfield, West Midlands. Lived in USA in 1963. Studied at Falmouth College of Art, 1964-5 and at the Slade, 1965-8. 1968 awarded the Boise Travelling Scholarship and the Milner Kite Travelling Bursary. Since 1981 she has made long visits to Cyprus, occasionally working with archaeologists. First solo exhibition at King Street Gallery, Bristol, 1985.

FORD, Laura   b.1961
Sculptor. Studied at the Bath Academy of Art, 1978-82 and at the Chelsea School of Art, 1985. 1987 first solo exhibition

at Nicola Jacobs Gallery, London. Included in the collections of the Arts Council, Contemporary Arts Society, Unilever, Penguin Books, and the Government Art Collection.

FORD, Peter   b.1937
Printmaker. Born Hereford. Studied at Hereford College of Art, 1955-6, St. Mary's College, Twickenham, 1957-60, Brighton College of Art, 1960-1 and Institute of Education, London University, 1966-7. Regular solo exhibitions since 1979. Also exhibits at the RA, Printmakers Council exhibitions, and RWA.

FOREMAN, Margaret   b.1951
Painter. Born Malaya. Moved to Guernsey in 1967. Studied at Goldsmiths' College, 1969-73, and RA Schools, 1973-6. While at RA Schools she won several prizes. Since 1971 has exhibited at RA and had a solo exhibition at the Belgrave Gallery, London, 1977.

FOREMAN, William   b.1939
Painter. Born London. Entered RAF, but encouraged by Angus McNab,* abandoned it for painting. 1961 first exhibited in Gibraltar. 1963 became a member of the Cambridge Drawing Society. Since 1974 has had regular solo exhibitions, most at the Richmond Gallery, London.

FORGE, Andrew   b.1923
Painter and writer on art. Born Hastingleigh, Kent. Studied at Camberwell School of Art, 1947-9. Exhibited with the London Group, became a member 1961 and President, 1965-71. Tate Trustee, 1964-71.

FORREST, Norman John   b.1898
Sculptor. Born Edinburgh, Scotland. Studied at Edinburgh College of Art and under the sculptor, Thomas Good. Exhibited at RSA, SSA, GI and elsewhere. Elected ARSA, 1943.

FORRESTER, Robin   b.1937
Painter. Born near Linlithgow, Scotland. Studied in London, Milan and Edinburgh. Has worked extensively on the Island of Mull which is the scene of many of his landscape paintings. First solo exhibition held at Traverse Restaurant Gallery, Edinburgh, 1965.

FORSTER, Andrew
Sculptor. Born Halifax, Nova Scotia. Moved to England at the age of seventeen. Studied at Guildhall School of Art, London and St. Martin's School of Art. 1963 moved to York to work as assistant at archaeological digs. 1966 moved to Amsterdam and began doing walking pieces in its streets. Involved in the conceptual movement in late '60s and early '70s. Exhibited in 'When Attitudes Become Form' in 1969. Uses quotations, installation work and film. 1981 he began an extensive series of steel pieces.

FORSTER, Noel   b.1932
Painter. Born Steaton Delaval, Northumberland. Studied at University of Newcastle upon Tyne, 1953 and 1955-7. 1964 held first solo exhibition. 1975-6 artist in residence at Baillol College, Oxford. 1978 won first prize at John Moores exhibition. 1984 solo exhibition at Air Gallery, London. Since 1984 principal lecturer in painting at Camberwell School of Art. Abstract artist, much of his work has used crossed ribbons of colour. Represented by the Anne Berthoud Gallery.

FORSYTH, Karen   b.1953
Painter. Born Aberdeen, Scotland. Studied at Oxford University. 1979 awarded a D. Phil. on Richard Strauss and Hofmannsthal. 1987 first represented in 'Four New British Artists' at The Raab Gallery, London, followed by another exhibition at the same gallery later in the year.

FORTESCUE-BRICKDALE, Eleanor   1872-1945
Painter. Born Upper Norwood, Surrey. Studied at Crystal Palace School of Art and RA Schools. 1899-1932 exhibited at RA. Labelled a 'Pre-Raphaelite revivalist'. A friend and contemporary of Byam Shaw,* she taught at his school, founded in 1911. Executed many illustrations for books and remained wholly untroubled by any modernist influence. Painted imaginative and historical subjects. Also designed stained glass.

Bibl: *Centenary Exhibition of Works by Eleanor Fortescue-Brickdale, 1872-1945,* Ashmolean Museum, Oxford, 1972.

FOSSICK, Michael   b.1947
Painter. Born Sheffield, Yorkshire. Studied at Harrogate School of Art, Bradford College of Art and Slade School of Fine Art. 1971 awarded Boise travelling scholarship and went to America. 1982 first solo exhibition 'Images from a Secret Place', held at Wakefield Art Gallery.

FOSTER, Colin
Sculptor. Studied at Leicester Polytechnic, 1972-3, Trent Polytechnic, 1973-6 and Manchester Polytechnic, 1976-7. 1978-9 sculpture fellow to the Artescape Trust, Lincolnshire and Humberside Arts Award. 1976 began exhibiting and in 1983 had a solo exhibition at Festival Gallery, Bath. Commissions include sculpture for William Watts Steel, Nottingham, 1975.

FOSTER, Frank   b.1920
Painter and stained glass artist. Born Swansea, South Wales. Studied at Swansea College of Art, 1947-9. Practised as a stained glass artist, carrying out commissions in many countries until 1969, when he began painting full time. Solo exhibition at Woodstock Gallery, London, 1973.

FOSTER, John   b.1951
Sculptor. Born London. Studied at Epsom School of Art, 1969-73. 1974 won Sainsbury Sculpture Award. 1971-5 worked at Stockwell Depot, London. 1975 moved to Gresham Farm, Norfolk. Began exhibiting in 1973 and, among other shows, was included in Serpentine Gallery Summer Show II, 1979.

FOSTER, Mary Melville   1890-1968
Painter. Born Yorkshire. Her family moved to New Zealand when she was one year old. Returned aged fifteen, studied in Paris and participated in the modern movement. Exhibited at London Group and NEAC, later at the RA. Two solo exhibitions, at Wertheim Gallery, London 1932, and French Gallery, London, 1934. At the age of seventy-five she held a retrospective at Stroud, Gloucestershire.

FOSTER, Richard   b.1945
Painter. Grew up in Norfolk. Studied painting in Florence with Signorina Simi and in London at the City and Guilds. Regular exhibitor at the Royal Society of Portrait Painters and at RA. 1972 received one of the Lord Mayor's Awards for his London views. 1972 solo exhibition at Jocelyn Fielding Fine Art, London.

FOSTER, Stephen John   1953-1978
Sculptor. Born Epping, Essex. Studied at Colchester Polytechnic, 1972, Bristol Polytechnic, 1973, but suffered a breakdown after the first term. Spent a year at home, painting and sculpting and was confirmed C. of E. 1975 returned to Bristol until 1977. 1978 began a postgraduate course at Slade but suffered a final breakdown in first term. 1980 memorial exhibition held by Harlow Art Trust.

FOSTER, Tim   b.1951
Painter. Born Hornchurch, Essex. Studied at University of Reading. Began exhibiting in 1969 and in 1982 was represented in the Hayward Annual. 1979 began lecturing in art history. Also makes films and publishes.

FOSTER, Vivienne   b.1936
Painter. Born West Riding of Yorkshire. Studied at St. Martin's School of Art and began exhibiting in mixed shows, 1961. 1966 first solo exhibition held at Woodstock Gallery, London.

FOTHERBY, Lesley   b.1946
Painter. Born London. Studied at Bath Academy of Art, Ravensbourne College of Art and Leicester Polytechnic. Inspired by the Yorkshire Dales. Exhibits regularly at Royal Horticultural Society. Solo exhibition at Chris Beetles Ltd., London, 1985.

FOUNTAIN, Cherryl   b.1950
Painter. Studied at Reading University and RA Schools, 1974-7. 1983 solo exhibition at Royal Museum, Canterbury. Since 1975 regular exhibitor at RA. Winner of many prizes and awards. Recent solo exhibitions include one at the New Grafton Gallery, London, 1986.

FOX, Christine   b.1922
Sculptor. Born Bridlington, Yorkshire. Studied at Bath Academy of Art. Much influenced by periods in Asia and Africa. 1976 did a three-month apprenticeship with a traditional Ashanti goldweight caster in Ghana. 1976 solo exhibition at Marjorie Parr Gallery, London.

FOX, Mary
Painter. Born Atherstone, Warwickshire. Studied at Leicester School of Art and Central School of Art. Solo exhibitions at John Whibley Gallery, London, 1960, 1967 and 1969, another at Sue Rankin Gallery, London, 1986. Represented in Arts Council Collection, V & A, and elsewhere.

FOX-PITT, Douglas   1864-1922
Painter. Born London. Studied at the Bartlett School of Architecture, 1881-2 and 1889-90, also at the Slade School. From 1907 exhibited at the RBA, and was a founder-member of the London Group. Painted mostly in watercolour. A friend of Walter Sickert,* and painted with him in Dieppe. Travelled widely and illustrated Count Sternberg's *Barbarians of Morocco.*

FRADAN, Cyril   b.1928
Painter. Born Johannesburg, South Africa. Studied at Witwatersrand University. Studied at Académie Julian, Paris, 1952-3. 1960 settled permanently in London. 1961 first solo exhibition held at Woodstock Gallery, London; others include one at Tib Lane Gallery, Manchester, 1969.

FRAMPTON, George

FRAMPTON, George   1860-1928

Sculptor. Born London. Studied at Lambeth School of Art under W.S. Frith and at the RA Schools, 1881-7, where he won a gold medal and a travelling scholarship. From 1884 exhibited at RA. 1894 elected ARA, and 1902, RA. 1911-12 President of the RBS. 1908, knighted. Produced mostly portrait and figure subjects, frequently enriching his art through a combination of materials, such as bronze, ivory and semi-precious stones. He is best known for his portrait of Peter Pan in Kensington Gardens, and the lions at the North Entrance to the British Museum.

FRAMPTON, Meredith 1894-1982

Painter. Born London, son of the sculptor Sir George Frampton.* Studied at the RA Schools from 1913 and exhibited at RA from 1920. Elected ARA, 1934 and RA, 1942. Elected a member of the Art Workers Guild in 1925 and like other members of their guild placed much emphasis on sound technique. He specialised in portraits which he prepared with great care, bringing an exceptional lucidity to his portrayal of appearances. Though he painted with meticulous realism, his portraits are also designed to bring out the abstract beauty inherent in objects. The extreme stillness found in his pictures gives them an enigmatic effect. Though he showed thirty-two paintings at the RA between 1920 and 1945, he suffered neglect after that date, in part because for the last thirty-seven years of his life he did no painting at all owing to failing eyesight. Not until 1982, when the Tate Gallery mounted a retrospective, did he regain the attention he deserves.

Bibl: *Meredith Frampton,* with introduction by Richard Morphet, Tate Gallery, 1982.

FRANCIS, Michael   b.1922

Painter. Served as a fighter pilot in the RAF during the Second World War. After demobilisation he won a scholarship to the Slade School of Fine Art, 1946-50. During the 1950s exhibited annually at the Royal Society of Portrait Painters and the RBA. Continued to exhibit in the 1960s in London and the provinces. Represented in the collections of Bournemouth Art Gallery, and the Leicester Education Authority.

FRANCIS, Mike   b.1938

Painter. Born Tooting, South London. Self-taught. 1964 first solo exhibition held at Furneaux Gallery, London. Regularly exhibits, especially at Nicholas Treadwell Gallery, London.

FRANKEL, Gerhart   1901-1965

Painter. Born Vienna, Austria. Largely self-taught artist, exhibiting frequently until 1930. 1938 fled to London with his family. 1950 exhibited at Venice Biennale. 1961 received honorary professorship from Austrian Government. Early 1960s produced a cycle of paintings inspired by reports of concentration camps.

FRANKLAND, Trevor   b.1931

Painter. Born Middlesbrough, Cleveland. Apprenticed as a shipyard draughtsman. Studied at Birkenhead School of Art and RA Schools. 1970 held first solo exhibition at Billingham Art Gallery, and 1977 took part in a three-man show at Battersea Arts Centre. Represented in Middlesbrough Art Gallery and Shipley Art Gallery, Gateshead.

FRANKLIN, Ben   b.1918

Sculptor. Born Petworth, Sussex. Worked as a lithographic artist, 1933-9. Studied part-time at Croydon School of Art, 1936-9. 1939-46 war service, the Devonshire Regiment. Resumed studies at Croydon School of Art and resolved to become a sculptor. 1947-50 studied at Goldsmiths' College. Has exhibited regularly since 1950, executing many commissions, including one for Winstanley Secondary School, Braunston, Leicestershire, 1960-1. Most recent exhibition at the James Hockey Gallery, Farnham, 1988.

FRANKLIN, Ruth   b.1948

Sculptor. Born London. Studied at Hornsey College of Art, 1965-6. 1966-70 worked as a designer and art director in advertising agencies. 1971 travelled to Israel, Iran and Afghanistan. 1972 studied ceramics at Croydon College of Art, transferring to Harrow College of Art, 1973-5. 1975 moved into the Barbican Arts Group. 1977 travelled in West Africa for nine months. 1985 solo exhibition at Ceolfrith Gallery, Sunderland Arts Centre. Uses a mixture of materials and has an interest in archetypal primitive forms.

FRANKLYN, Lesley   b.1938

Painter. Born Singapore. Studied at Chelsea School of Art and whilst living in a barge on the Thames painted several abstract pictures of the river. Has exhibited at Mermaid Theatre, Woodstock Gallery, London and at Thorndike Theatre, Leatherhead.

FRASER, Alexander   b.1940

Painter. Born Aberdeen, Scotland. Studied at Gray's School of Art, Aberdeen, 1958-62. 1964 won a travelling scholarship to France and Italy. 1971 elected associate of RSA, 1978, elected member. Winner of various awards. 1964 first solo exhibition held at 57 Gallery, Edinburgh; others include another at this same gallery, 1984. Represented in Aberdeen Art Gallery, Dundee Art Gallery, Hunterian Museum, Glasgow, and elsewhere.

FRASER, Claud Lovat   1890-1921

Painter and designer. Born London. Originally studied law, but in 1911 abandoned this and entered Westminster School of Art under Walter Sickert.* Left after one year and abandoned oils, thereafter working mostly with watercolour and pen and ink. 1913 held his first solo exhibition in his own studio. He issued, with two friends, modern versions of the old street ballad sheets and chapbooks. 1915 joined army and served in France and Flanders. Gassed and shell-shocked, he returned home and eventually entered War Office to work on visual propaganda. 1917 began designing for the theatre. Also began designing textiles for the firm of William Foxton. Taken suddenly ill with a duodenal complaint, he died soon after an operation.

Bibl: *Claude Lovat Fraser,* V & A exhibition cat., 1969, with essay by the artist's widow, Grace Lovat Fraser.

FRASER, Cynthia

Painter. Educated in France and Jersey. After six years in the ATS and the birth of a son, she studied at Edinburgh College of Art, 1949-53. Has exhibited in the Paris Salon, RA, and RSA. 1968-9 was President of the Scottish Society for Women Artists. Represented in the collections of HM The Queen, the Scottish Arts Council, Huddersfield Art Gallery and elsewhere.

FRASER, Donald Hamilton   b.1929
Painter. Born London. Served in RAF, 1947-9. Studied at St. Martin's School of Art, 1949-53. 1953-4 awarded French Government Scholarship. 1953 first solo exhibition at Gimpel Fils, London. Subsequent exhibitions at Gimpel Fils, Galeries Craven, Paris (1956) and elsewhere. Represented in Arts Council Collection, National Gallery of Victoria, Melbourne, Wadsworth Athenaeum, Hartford, Connecticut, and elsewhere. Fraser combines the Scottish colourist tradition of strong colour with a near abstract approach to landscape.

FRASER, Eric   1902-1983
Painter and illustrator. Born London. Attended evening classes at Westminster Institute under Walter Sickert,* and later studied at Goldsmiths' School of Art. 1926 received his first commission from the *Radio Times* and continued to work for this publication until his death. He also did designs for the Folio Society and for *Vogue,* for murals or for postage stamps; all displayed that disciplined vitality that is the keynote to his style. Taught at Camberwell School of Art, 1928-40.

FRASER, Ian   b.1933
Painter. Born Newcastle upon Tyne, Tyne and Wear. Studied at Leeds College of Art, 1949-53, and RCA, 1955-8. Has taught lithography and etching at Hammersmith College of Art and Ealing School of Art. Represented in V & A, Metropolitan Museum of Art, New York, and elsewhere.

FRASER, Simon   b.1950
Painter and printmaker. Born Inverness, Scotland. Studied at Ruskin School of Drawing and Painting, Oxford, 1968-70, Gray's School of Art, Aberdeen, 1971-3. 1973 Official Artist on Arctic Lapland Expedition. Has worked with the poet George Mackay Brown and others on a sequence in celebration of St. Magnus, patron saint of Orkney. 1973 first solo exhibition at Plymouth Hoe Theatre, and most recent at 369 Gallery, Edinburgh, 1988.

FRAUGHAN, Charles   b.1929
Sculptor. Born Liverpool, Merseyside. Employed as a millwright and became fascinated by welding. 1969 held first solo exhibition at Gateway Theatre, Chester, followed by a two year fellowship with British Steel Corporation. Teaches welding to secondary school-children and has continued to hold solo exhibitions in the North, also executing large commissions for public sites, including the Anglican Cathedrals at Manchester and Liverpool.

FRAZER, William Miller   1864-1961
Painter. Born Scone, Scotland. Studied at RSA Schools. Exhibited mainly in Scotland, also in London and abroad. Elected SSA, 1908, ARSA, 1909 and RSA, 1924. Elected President of the Scottish Arts Club, 1926.

FREEDMAN, Barnett   1901-1958
Painter. Worked as a signwriter, stonemason's and architect's assistant, attending evening classes at St. Martin's School of Art, 1916-22. 1922-5 went on an LCC scholarship to RCA. 1930-40 instructor in still life at RCA. 1940-6 official war artist. 1946 awarded CBE. An ambitious figurative artist, but best known for his revival of colour lithography and for his book illustrations. Also designed for the George V Jubilee postage stamp and posters for Shell-Mex and London Transport. Visiting instructor at RCA from 1928, also at the Ruskin School, Oxford.

Bibl: *Barnett Freedman*, Arts Council Memorial Exhibition cat., 1958.

FREEDMAN, Beatrice Claudia   b.1904
Painter and illustrator. Born Formby, Liverpool, née Guercio. Studied at Liverpool School of Art and at the RCA. Married Barnett Freedman.* Exhibited at the RA.

FREEDMAN, Harriet   b.1949
Sculptor. Born London. Studied at St. Martin's School of Art and Ealing School of Art. Began making soft sculptures while at art school. 1972 solo exhibition at Buckingham Gallery, London. Her work imitates real objects but is stuffed and sewn. Sometimes she conceals real objects alongside invented ones.

FREEMAN, Barbara   b.1937
Painter. Born London. Studied at St. Martin's, Camberwell and Hammersmith Schools of Art. Winner of various awards and began exhibiting in 1964. Recent solo exhibitions include two at the Fenderesky Gallery, Belfast, 1984 and 1986 and 'Two Cities: Rome — New York' at Art Space Gallery, London, and elsewhere, 1987-8.

FREEMAN, John   b.1958
Painter. Born London. Studied at Bath Academy of Art, 1976-7, Chelsea School of Art, 1977-80 and worked with Westminster City Council, 1980-4. 1986 artist in residence, Royal Surrey County Hospital. 1988 first solo exhibition in London held at Camden Art Centre. Paints portraits with the picture space fragmented, each fragment containing an image of importance to the sitter.

FREEMAN, Michael   b.1936
Painter. Born Swansea, South Wales, 1955-9. Trained as an art teacher at Swansea College of Art, 1959-61 taught art in London, afterwards becoming a librarian until 1970 when he returned to teaching. 1968 first solo exhibition at Galerie Hessler, Munich. Others include 'Michael Freeman: Paintings and Drawings 1964-1984' at Glynn Vivian Art Gallery and Museum, 1985.

FREEMAN, Ralph   b.1945
Painter. Born London. Studied at St. Martin's School of Art and Harrow School of Art, 1961-5. 1964-6 studied jazz and worked as a painter. 1968-80 worked as artist and designer in London, Hamburg and Frankfurt. 1982 became member of Hampstead Artists Council. 1984 first solo exhibition held at Royal Free Gallery, London; others include one at Louise Hallett Gallery, London, 1988.

FREER, Mavis   b.1927
Painter. Born Chesterfield, Derbyshire. Studied at Chesterfield School of Art and Goldsmiths' College of Art, 1943-9. 1976 first solo exhibition held in Canterbury, and another at Woodlands Art Gallery, London, 1977.

FREETH, H. Andrew   b.1912
Painter and etcher. Born Birmingham, West Midlands. Studied at Birmingham College of Art and the British School at Rome, 1936-9. From 1936 exhibited at the RA, also at the RWS, RE, RBA and elsewhere and held several solo exhibitions. Elected ARE, 1938, RE, 1946, ARWS,

FREETH, Peter

1948, RP, 1949, RWS and ARA, 1955 and RA, 1965. 1943 went to the Middle East as an official war artist to the RAF.

FREETH, Peter b.1938

Printmaker. Born Birmingham, West Midlands. Studied at Slade School, 1956-60, where he was taught etching by Anthony Gross.* 1960 awarded Prix de Rome (engraving) and spent next three years in Italy. Has taught at RA Schools and Camden Institute. His work has been seen in mixed exhibitions at the Redfern Gallery, Anne Berthoud Gallery, Agnews, Air Gallery and elsewhere. Represented in V & A, British Museum and Arts Council Collection. Elected ARA, 1990.

FREEMANTLE, Chloë b.1950

Painter. Born London. Studied at Byam Shaw School of Art. Has lived and worked abroad much of the time, travelling to China, Japan and Hong Kong, in 1982 and held an exhibition of work based on these travels at Christopher Hull Gallery, London, 1983.

FRENCH, Annie 1872-1965

Painter and illustrator. Born Glasgow, Scotland. Studied at Glasgow School of Art. Executed book illustrations, greeting cards, and pen and watercolour compositions on vellum in a similar style to her near contemporary, Jessie M. King.* 1909 took over King's post at the Glasgow School of Art Department of Design. 1914 married the artist George Wooliscroft Rhead (1854-1920) and settled in London.

FRENCH, Brian

Painter. Born London. Studied at Goldsmiths' College and RCA. 1960 began exhibiting at the Grabowski Gallery, London; other solo exhibitions include one at Compendium Gallery, London, 1968.

FRENCH, Dick b.1946

Painter. Born South Shields, Tyne and Wear. Studied at Sheffield College of Art, 1962-7 and RCA, 1967-70. Recent exhibitions have included South Hill Park, 1985, City Arts Gallery, 1986 and John Moores exhibitions, 1976 and 1987. Represented in Wolverhampton and Sheffield City Art Galleries.

FRENCH, Gerald b.1927

Painter. Mainly self-taught, but studied part-time at Regional College of Art, Bradford. Has exhibited in Yorkshire and RA and is represented in the Abbot Hall Gallery, Kendal. Solo exhibition at the Lane Gallery, Bradford, 1963.

FRERE-SMITH, Matthew b.1923

Sculptor. Studied at RCA. Works with a variety of materials and has executed numerous architectural commissions. Held his first solo exhibition at the King's Lynn Festival, Norfolk, 1962.

FREUD, Lucian b.1922

Painter. Born Berlin, Germany, son of Ernst Freud, the architect, and grandson of Sigmund Freud. Came to England in 1932. Studied at Central School of Art and Goldsmiths' College and, briefly, under Cedric Morris* and Lett Haines* in Suffolk. 1942 invalided out of Merchant Navy. 1944 first exhibited at Lefevre Gallery, London. His combination of meticulous accuracy and disquieting intensity earned him the soubriquet, 'The Ingres of Existentialism', from Herbert Read. After he exchanged the use of sable brushes for hog's hair, he began to paint more broadly, the modelling of flesh emphasising still further the physicality of his subject matter. The bulk of his work is portraiture. A retrospective exhibition of his work was held at the Hayward Gallery, London, in 1974 and again in 1988. Unquestionably the greatest realist of his day.

Bibl: Lawrence Gowing, *Lucian Freud*, Thames and Hudson, London, 1982.

FRIEDMAN, Bernard b.1940

Painter. Born London. Studied at Seaford College, 1953-7. Held first solo exhibition at Drian Galleries, London, 1963.

FRINK, Elizabeth b.1930

Sculptor. Born Thurlow, Suffolk. Studied at Guildford School of Art and Chelsea School of Art. First captured attention in 1951 at an exhibition at the Beaux Arts Gallery, London. Since then has exhibited regularly and was for twenty-seven years associated with Waddington's, London. Her main subjects are man, dog and horse. The appeal of her work lies in its directness, the excision of all artiness in a frank statement of feeling. Often the anatomy is exaggerated or incorrect; the life-likeness grows more out of her interest in the spirit of the subject: the urgency animating *Running Man*, the alertness in *Barking Dog*. During the Algerian war she began making heads, blinded by goggles and which have a threatening facelessness. Public commissions include *Wild Boar* for Harlow New Town, *Blind Beggar and Dog* for Bethnal Green, a lectern for Coventry Cathedral, *Shepherd* for Paternoster Square beside St. Paul's Cathedral and a *Walking Madonna* for Salisbury Cathedral. Has exhibited widely at home and abroad. 1982 created DBE. Now lives and works in Dorset where her garden has become an arena for her work. 1985 retrospective at RA. Represented in the Tate Gallery and public collections world-wide.

Bibl: Edwin Mullens, *The Art of Elisabeth Frink*, Lund Humphries, London, 1972; *Elisabeth Frink: Sculpture:Catalogue Raisonné*, introduction by Bryan Robertson, Harpvale Books, Salisbury, 1984.

FRIPP, Paul 1890-1945

Painter. Born Mansfield, Nottinghamshire, into a family of artists. Studied at Bristol and Leicester Schools of Art. Won scholarship to RCA. 1914 entered army. 1919 resumed studies. Became director of art at Cheltenham Ladies' College. 1931 moved to Devon, to become Principal of Bideford School of Art. Further teaching appointments followed. Also a keen amateur photographer. Exhibited RA, NEAC and elsewhere but rarely had a solo exhibition. He is said to have made a major contribution to Cheltenham cultural life in the 1920s.

FRITH, Jack, RSW

Painter. Born Edinburgh, Scotland. Studied at the Edinburgh College of Art, graduating in 1939. War service, 1940-6. 1959 first solo exhibition at the Scottish Gallery. Since the 1950s he has exhibited regularly at the Royal Scottish Academy and the Royal Scottish Society of

PAUL FRIPP, 1890-1945. *'A Cotswold Farm'*, 1928. Watercolour. 11¼ in. x 14¾ in. Cheltenham Art Gallery and Museum.

Painters in Watercolours. 1961 elected to RSW. Author of *Scottish Watercolour Painting* (Ramsey Head, 1979). Represented in collections such as the Aberdeen Art Gallery, the Scottish Arts Council and in the collection of the University of Dundee.

FROOD, Hester   1882-1971
Painter and etcher. Born New Zealand. Educated in England and studied art at Exeter and in Paris. Exhibited at RA, NEAC, and IS. Elected ARE, 1920. Held solo exhibitions of her architectural subjects at Colnaghi's, London, in 1925, 1943, 1946 and 1949.

FROST, Anthony   b.1951
Painter. Born Redruth, Cornwall, son of Terry Frost.* Studied at North Oxfordshire Technical College and School of Art, 1967-70 and Cardiff College of Art, 1970-3. 1979 held first solo exhibition at Newlyn Art Gallery; others include two more at Newlyn Art Gallery, 1983 and 1986. Abstract painter, who frequently makes use of the diamond shape and strong colour.

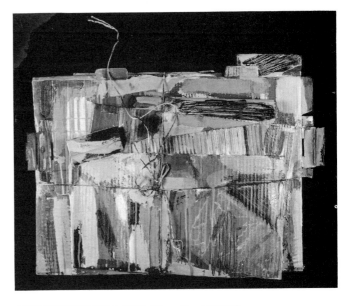

ANTHONY FROST, b.1951. *'Wrap it up'*, 1987-8.
Acrylic on cardboard, string and wood. Private Collection.

FROST, Terry

TERRY FROST, b.1915. *'Movement: Green, Black and White'*, 1951-2. 44in. x 34in. Scottish National Gallery of Modern Art.

FROST, Terry   b.1915
Painter. Born Leamington Spa, Warwickshire. 1939 entered army. 1941 captured and spent rest of war in concentration camps, meeting Adrian Heath* who encouraged him to paint. 1945 began attending evening classes at Birmingham Art College. 1946 moved to Cornwall and attended St. Ives School of Painting. 1947 held first solo exhibition at G.R. Downing's bookshop in St. Ives, and that autumn began studying at Camberwell School of Art. 1949 painted his first abstract picture. 1947-50 exhibited with the St. Ives Society of Artists. 1950 settled in St. Ives and in 1951 worked for a period as assistant to Barbara Hepworth.* 1951 met Roger Hilton* and began using construction and collage. 1952 held his first solo exhibition in London, at the Leicester Galleries. 1954-6 Gregory Fellow at Leeds University. Taught at Leeds School of Art, Coventry Art College and Reading University.

Bibl: *Terry Frost: Paintings, drawings and collages,* Arts Council cat., 1976-7.·

FROUD, Jonathan   b.1958
Sculptor. Born Hengistbury Head, Dorset. Studied at Bournemouth and Poole College of Art, 1975-6, Brighton Polytechnic, 1976-9 and RCA, 1979-82. Winner of various awards. 1982-3 worked in South Africa. 1984-5 Fourth Merseyside artist in residence at Bridewell Studios and Walker Art Gallery, Liverpool.

Bibl: *Jonathan Froud: Made up about it,* Walker Art Gallery, Liverpool, 1985.

FROY, Martin   b.1926
Painter. Born London. Studied at Slade School of Fine Art, met William Coldstream* and others, 1949-51. 1951-4 Gregory Fellow in Painting, University of Leeds. 1963 won Leverhulme Research Award for six months study in Italy. 1952 first solo exhibition held at Hanover Gallery, London. Professor of Fine Art, Reading University. Represented in Tate Gallery and elsewhere.

Bibl: *Martin Froy: Paintings, constructions, drawings, 1968-82,* Serpentine Gallery, London, cat. (Arts Council), 1983.

FRY, Anthony   b.1927
Painter. Born Theydon Bois, Essex. Studied at Edinburgh College of Art and Camberwell School of Art. 1950-2 won the Rome Prize. Has taught at Bath Academy and Camberwell. 1955 first solo exhibition held at St. George's Gallery, London. Represented in Tate Gallery, Arts Council Collection, Royal West of England Gallery and elsewhere. (Plate 39, p.174.)

FRY, Lewis George   1860-1933
Painter. Born Clifton, Bristol, Avon. Educated at New College, Oxford. Studied art in London under Francis Bate* and at the Slade. Member of the Art Workers' Guild.

FRY, Roger   1866-1934
Painter and critic. Born London. Read natural sciences at Cambridge, after which he studied painting under Francis Bate* in London and at the Académie Julian in Paris. Became a specialist in Italian Renaissance art, founded *Burlington Magazine* and acted as European Adviser to Metropolitan Museum of Art in New York, until a disagreement with the Chairman of its trustees terminated his appointment. Organised two post-impressionist exhibitions in London, in 1910 and 1912, awakening a London audience to modern art. From then became an influential figure among the avant-garde. Continued to paint, moved through a variety of styles, also published some of his many articles in book form as *Vision and Design* (1920) and *Transformations* (1926). Also wrote an influential monograph on Cézanne (1927). His reputation as critic and lecturer exceeded his reputation as painter. (Plate 40, p.174.)

Bibl: Frances Spalding, *Roger Fry: Art and Life,* Granada, London, 1980.

FRY, Simon   b.1944
Painter. Studied at Bournville School of Art, 1960-2 and Birmingham School of Art, 1962-6. Solo exhibition at Compendium Galleries, London, 1970.

FRYER, Malcolm   b.1937
Painter. Born Manchester. Studied at Lancaster College of Art. Lectured at Blackpool School of Art and acted as Curator of the Haworth Art Gallery, Accrington. Exhibits in group and solo exhibitions and concentrates on

ROGER FRY, 1866-1934. *'Boats in a Harbour'*, 1915. 28⅛in. x 35⅝in. Wakefield Art Gallery and Museums.

landscape painting, the Lancashire countryside and the Haworth Moors. Solo exhibition at University of Hull, 1969.

FULLARD, George   1923-1974
Sculptor. Born Sheffield, Yorkshire. Studied at Sheffield College of Art, 1938-42. 1942-44 served in the army and was severely wounded in Battle of Cassino. 1944-5 convalesced. 1945-7 studied at RCA. 1947 won travelling scholarship to visit Rodin Museum, Paris. 1974 retrospective exhibition at the Serpentine Gallery. Represented in the collection of the Tate Gallery, Arts Council, CAS, and the National Gallery of South Australia. Haunted by his wartime experience, Fullard in his work marries memories of it with observation of children's games, his work often creating an amalgam of the playful and terrifying. Three of his sculptures inhabit public places in Sheffield's city centre.

Bibl: *George Fullard 1923-1973*, Arts Council cat., 1974.

FULLER, Leonard John   1891-1973
Painter. Studied at Clapham School of Art and at the RA Schools. Won a British Institution Scholarship in painting, 1913. From 1919 exhibited at RA, also at the RP, ROI, RSA and elsewhere. 1927 won a silver medal at the Paris Salon. 1922-3 taught painting at St. John's Wood Art School, and from 1938 was Principal of the St. Ives School of Painting. Lived in St. Ives for many years where he became Chairman of the St. Ives Society of Artists, 1942-6; member of the Penwith Society of Arts and of Newlyn Society of Artists.

FULLER, Martin   b.1943
Painter. Born Leamington Spa, Warwickshire. Studied at Mid-Warwickshire School of Art, 1960-2, and Hornsey College of Art, 1962-4. 1968 first solo exhibition held at Arnolfini Gallery, Bristol; others include those at the Thumb Gallery, London, 1976 and 1979. Represented in Bristol City Art Gallery. Solo exhibition at Austin/ Desmond Fine Art, London, 1990.

VIOLET FULLER, b.1920. *'Snow in Essex'*. 28in. x 34in. Private Collection.

FULLER, Violet   b.1920
Painter. Born London. Studied at Hornsey College of Art, 1937-40 and Stroud School of Art, 1942-4. Fellow of Society of Free Painters and Sculptors. Solo exhibitions at Woodstock Gallery, London, 1958, 1961, 1963 and 1967. Also exhibits at RA, RI, RBA, NEAC and WIAC.

FULTON, Hamish   b.1946
Sculptor. Born London. Studied at St. Martin's School of Art and RCA. Since 1969 has exhibited at home and abroad. 1979 his 'Selected Walks' shown at the Whitechapel Art Gallery. A sculptor whose use of photography to create exhibitions out of his experience in landscape has often linked his name with that of Richard Long.*

FURNIVAL, John   b.1933
Painter. Studied at Wimbledon College of Art. Joined Royal Fusiliers, then returned to study at RCA. Has taught at Gloucestershire College of Art and Gloucestershire City College where he met Dom Sylvester Houedard and became interested in printing. 1964 started Openings Press. 1972 solo exhibition at Arnolfini Gallery, Bristol. Also exhibits in international shows of visual and concrete poetry.

FURSE, Paul   b.1904
Painter. Son of the artist Charles Furse. Entered Navy in 1916 and painted in his spare time. After retiring as a Rear Admiral in 1959 he devoted his time to botanical painting, working at Kew and the British Museum. Solo exhibition at the Tryon Gallery, London, 1956.

FUSSELL, Michael   1927-1974
Painter. Born Southampton, Hampshire. Studied at St. Martin's School of Art, 1946-50 and at RCA, 1950-3. 1956 held his first solo exhibition at the Beaux Arts Gallery, London. Moved from using sombre tonalities to lighter tones in the 1960s. Experimented with Kleenex soaked in white paint and laid on the canvas in such a way that the folds create ridges and declivities. These won him considerable acclaim but he abandoned them within a year. Became head of the painting department at Wimbledon School of Art, and continued to produce abstract paintings. Influenced by Gurdjieff.

Bibl: *Michael Fussell: A retrospective exhibition of paintings and drawings,* published by House, 62 Regents Park Road, 1976.

FYE, Deryk   b.1947
Painter. Born Whitehaven, Cumbria. Studied at Carlisle College of Art and Design, 1964-6, Leicester Polytechnic, 1966-9 and Slade School of Fine Art, 1969-71. 1981 first solo exhibition held at Warrington Art Gallery; others include one at Oriel Gallery, North Wales, 1981. Represented in Leicester City Art Gallery and elsewhere.

GABAIN, Ethel   1883-1950

Painter. Born Le Havre, France. Studied at Slade, Central School of Arts and Crafts and in Paris. 1913 married the artist John Copley.* Became well known as a lithographer, and in her oil painting specialised in portraits, especially actresses in character roles. Her portrait of Flora Robson (Manchester Art Gallery) won the De Laszlo silver medal, 1933. Exhibited at RA and elsewhere. Works in Walker Art Gallery, Liverpool, and Tate Gallery.

GAGE, Edward   b.1925

Painter. Born Gullane, Scotland. Studied at Edinburgh College of Art, 1941-2 and 1947-50. 1952 began designing for the stage and doing illustration work for *Radio Times* and elsewhere. 1960-4 President of the Society of Scottish Artists. 1964 first solo exhibition at The Scottish Gallery. Represented in several leading Scottish public art collections. 1978 published *The Eye in the Wind: Scottish Painting since 1945.*

GAISFORD, Paul   b.1941

Painter. Born Dorking, Surrey. Studied at Camberwell School of Art, 1956-61, Slade School of Fine Art, 1961-4, and at Berlin Academy, 1964. Winner of various prizes and has exhibited at the Ibis and Langton Galleries in London.

GALLINER, Edith   b.1914

Painter and collagist. Born London of a German-Jewish family who returned to Hamburg in 1914. Attended Karl-Marx in Berlin. 1933 emigrated to England. Attended art school in London, followed by silversmith training in

ETHEL GABAIN, 1883-1950. *'Diana Wyndham in "Silent Knight"'*, 1938. 40in. x 30in. Merseyside County Art Galleries.

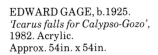

EDWARD GAGE, b.1925.
'Icarus falls for Calypso-Gozo',
1982. Acrylic.
Approx. 54in. x 54in.

GALVIN-HARRISON, Christopher

Paris. 1938-9 acted as travel companion to Jewish children from Berlin to London. After a period teaching painting and drawing, she worked freelance in London and in Berlin, 1961-6.

GALVIN-HARRISON, Christopher   b.1956
Painter. Born Birmingham, West Midlands. Studied at Amersham College, 1977-8 and Camberwell School of Arts and Crafts, 1979-82. 1981 first solo exhibition held at Henrik Kampmann Galleri, Copenhagen; others include one at the Herbert Art Gallery, Coventry, 1985. 1982 won Thames and Hudson Drawing Award.

GAMMON, Reg   b.1894
Painter. His professional career began in 1918, following war service, and he contributed illustrations to *Punch* and elsewhere. Wrote and illustrated a country feature for *Cyclists Touring Club Gazette* from 1924 for some sixty years. Joined the *News Chronicle* in 1930 and ran his own feature 'The Week in the Country'. Exhibited at RA, RI and NEAC. 1966 elected RWA and ROI. 1985 a retrospective was held at the Royal West of England Academy.

GANLEY, Helen   b.1940
Painter. Studied at Slade School of Fine Art, 1958-62, and taught at Ruskin School of Drawing in Oxford, 1965-74. Has exhibited in various mixed shows in and around Oxford and held her first solo exhibition at Chapel Gallery, Bladon, 1973; another was held at the Mercury Gallery, London, 1976.

GARAWAY, Michael
Painter. Studied at Preston Polytechnic, 1976-7, Manchester Polytechnic, 1977-80 and Rochdale College of Art, 1986-7. 1987 became a graphic artist with Impact Environmental Services, Old Trafford, Manchester. 1981 began exhibiting and in 1988 held solo exhibition, 'Urban Vision' at the Atkinson Art Gallery, Southport. His concern is with the urban and industrial landscape and with the potential of microcomputers and basic graphics software as tools for drawing.

GARBE, Louis Richard   1876-1957
Sculptor. Born London. Studied at Central School of Arts and Crafts and RA Schools. From 1908 exhibited at RA. Elected FRBS, 1920, ARA, 1929 and RA, 1936. 1901-29 taught sculpture at Central School, and 1929-46 was Professor of Sculpture at RCA. Represented in several public collections. Specialised in figure and animal subjects.

GARDEN, William Fraser   1856-1921
Painter. Little is known about this artist. He was the fourth of five sons of Dr. Robert Winchester Fraser, of Hemingford Grey Manor House. In order to distinguish himself from two of his brothers, who also painted, he reversed his last two names. Lived at Hemingford Abbotts until 1898 and later at Holywell, both in Cambridgeshire.

GARDINER, Brian   b.1932
Glass etcher. Born Bristol, Avon. Apprenticed to a signwriting firm, 1950-3. Studied graphic design (part-time), at West of England College of Art, Bristol, 1951-2. 1953-6 in RAF, Middle East, 1956-7 glass etching trainee, Bristol. 1957-60 studied fine art at Newport College of Art, Gwent. 1959 began exhibiting. 1960-3 studied at RCA. 1960-82 received numerous private and commercial commissions, including work for S.A. Brain and Co. Ltd., Cardiff. 1982 solo exhibition held at The Gallery, South Glamorgan Institute of Higher Education.

GARDINER, Clive   1891-1960
Painter. Born Blackburn, Lancashire. Studied at Slade School of Art, 1909-12, and RA Schools, 1913-14. Served in Ministry of Munitions during the First World War. Influenced by Puvis de Chavannes, began to exhibit in 1920s at NEAC and RA. After a period as a part-time teacher became Headmaster of Goldsmiths' College School of Art in 1929, a post he filled until 1952 when his status was raised to Principal; he retired in 1957. His early work as a poster designer influenced some of his students, including Graham Sutherland.* Admired Cézanne, Derain, Picasso and Braque, imitating aspects of their work in his painting. Also executed several murals, including some for London University's Students Union with Betty Swanwick.*

Bibl: *Clive Gardiner 1891-1960,* South London Art Gallery, 1967.

GARDINER, Gerald   b.1902
Painter. Born London. Studied at Beckenham School of Art, 1919-23 and RCA, 1923-7. Exhibited at RA, RSA, NEAC and in the provinces. Elected ARWA, 1949, and RWA, 1954.

GARDINER, Jeremy   b.1957
Painter. Born Munster, Germany. Studied at Newcastle University, Fine Art Department, 1975-9, and RCA, 1980-3. 1980 first solo exhibition held at Parnham House, Beaminster, Dorset; others include one at Gallery 39, London, 1984. Began using a computer as a tool for his painting whilst at RCA.

GARDNER, Diana
Painter. Studied at Regent Street Polytechnic and Westminster School of Art. Joined Society of Wood-Engravers. Has engraved book illustrations, designed book jackets, written a novel and short stories. After twelve years in publishing she began to concentrate on watercolour and pen and ink. 1970 first solo exhibition held at Waterhouse Gallery, London. In addition to solo shows, exhibits regularly at the RBA, the RI and with the Royal Society of Wood-Engravers.

GARDNER, Ian   b.1944
Painter. Born Lancaster, Lancashire. Studied at Lancaster School of Art, 1961-5 and Nottingham School of Art, 1965-6. 1973 held first solo exhibition at Thumb Gallery, London. Has held a series of teaching posts at art colleges, but since 1979 has painted full-time. Also a founder of the New Arcadians, a fluctuating group of artists committed to landscape painting and the reinterpretation of traditional styles. Gardner's own paintings reflect a debt to Girtin and are often of sites painted by either Girtin or Turner.

WILLIAM GARFIT, b.1944. '*Where salmon leap*'. 24in. x 36in. Private Collection.

GARFIT, William   b.1944
Painter. Born Cambridgeshire. Studied at Cambridge School of Art, Byam Shaw School, and RA Schools. Landscape painter, in sturdily traditional style, specialising in East Anglia where he lives. Since 1965 has exhibited frequently at RA, RSBA, NEAC, and Royal Society of Portrait Painters. Also does illustrations for *The Shooting Times*.

GARLAND, Margaret   1900-1977
Painter. Born Oxford. Studied at RCA 1924-7. During most of the 1930s exhibited at Bath Academy of Art. During the war taught for a time at Bath Technical College. 1947 joined Bath Academy of Art under Clifford Ellis, through whom at an earlier date she had met Walter Sickert.* Influenced in part by David Bomberg* and Frances Hodgkins,* she remained shut within a circle of artists at Bath and her reputation has not extended much beyond that city.

GARNETT, Angelica   b.1918
Painter. Born Sussex, daughter of Vanessa Bell* and Duncan Grant.* Studied for four months in Paris in 1935.

1936 studied drama under Michael Saint-Denis and George Devine. 1938 studied painting at Euston Road School. 1942 married David Garnett, novelist and editor, and continued to paint. 1967-8 worked with George Bergen in New York. Has exhibited in solo and group exhibitions, in London, Sussex and Dallas. Also has a reputation as a designer of book jackets and textiles, and for executing painted decorations in the various houses in which she has lived.

GARRARD, Charles   b.1952
Sculptor and filmmaker. Born London. Studied at Cardiff and Chelsea Schools of Art. Exhibited at the Ikon Gallery, 1987.

GARRARD, Peter John   b.1929
Painter. Studied at Byam Shaw School of Painting and Drawing. Began exhibiting with NEAC and became a member of the Royal Society of Portrait Painters and Vice-President of the RSBA. At one time editor of *The Artist* and author of *Learn to Paint in Oils* (Collins, 1980). 1978 awarded the De Laszlo Medal by the RBA. Exhibits regularly at RA, RBA, NEAC and elsewhere.

ROSE GARRARD, b.1946. Talisman: *'The sea shell from her childhood'*, 1988. Acrylic and wash on paper. 48in. x 31 ½ in. Louise Hallett Gallery.

GARRARD, Rose   b.1946
Mixed media artist. Studied at Birmingham College of Art and Chelsea School of Art. Went on a scholarship to the Ecole des Beaux Arts in Paris and won the Prix d'Honneur for her sculpture. Her work encompasses painting, sculpture, performance and installation. Has exhibited at major galleries and museums at home and abroad and is represented in the Tate Gallery. The subject of her work is often her quest for the reclamation of the past, both as woman and artist. 1988 solo exhibition at Louise Hallett Gallery, London.

Bibl: *Rose Garrard: between ourselves*, Ikon Gallery, Birmingham, 1984.

GARRETT, Albert Charles   b.1915
Painter. Born Kingsclere, Hampshire. Studied at Camberwell School of Art, 1947-9, Anglo-French Art Centre, 1949-50 and Slade School, 1950-1. Exhibited at principal London galleries and is represented in several public art collections.

GARSIDE, Oswald   1879-1942
Painter. Born Southport, Lancashire. Exhibited at RA from 1902, also at the Paris Salon and elsewhere. Went to Paris on a Lancashire County Council Scholarship to study at the Académie Julian for three years, afterwards spending time in Italy. Elected RI, 1916, R.Cam.A., 1924 and RBI, 1925. Member of the Liverpool Academy of Arts, Manchester Academy of Fine Arts and President of the Midland Sketching Club. Specialised in watercolour.

GARSON, George   b.1930
Painter. Born Edinburgh, Scotland. Studied at Edinburgh College of Art, graduating with a post-diploma scholarship in stained glass and glass design. Has held several solo exhibitions of paintings, including one at the University of Hull, 1970. Has executed several public commissions, for St. Andrews University, Glasgow University and elsewhere.

GARSTIN, Alethea   b.1894
Painter. Born Penzance, Cornwall, daughter and pupil of the leading Newlyn impressionist Norman Garstin.* She remained based in Penzance until 1960, when she moved to Zennor, where she still lives. Before and after the First World War she painted frequently in northern France, particularly Brittany. Rome, Morocco, Kenya, the Carribean, Ireland and London have all provided her with

NORMAN GARSTIN, 1847-1926.
'Le Promenade de l'Après Midi'.
32in. x 39½in.
David Messum Fine Paintings, London.

subjects. Represented in Bristol City Art Gallery, Plymouth City Art Gallery and elsewhere.

Bibl: *Norman and Alethea Garstin,* Penwith Gallery, St. Ives, 1978.

GARSTIN, Norman   1847-1926

Painter. Born Ireland. Brought up by his grandparents after his father committed suicide and his mother developed a severe form of muscular paralysis. After several false starts he decided to take up art as a profession and studied at Verlat's Academy in Antwerp, and under Carolus-Duran in Paris. Travelled in Italy and to Morocco before settling in Newlyn in 1886 where he became part of the Newlyn School, later moving to Penzance. More than others in this school, he displayed a preference for scenes from modern life. Also excelled at painting a cool, silvery tonality, created by rain on the streets or light on wet sand. To subsidise his painting he wrote articles for art journals and also taught. His interest in asymmetrical balance grew out of his love for Japanese art and his admiration for the work of Whistler. He also admired Manet and despised anecdotal content. During the latter part of his career turned to sentimental costume painting, presumably due to financial pressures.

Bibl: *Norman and Alethea Garstin,* Penwith Gallery, St. Ives, 1978.

GARWOOD, Tirzah   1908-1951

Painter and wood-engraver. Born Gillingham, Kent. Studied at Eastbourne School of Art, 1925-8, where she

TIRZAH GARWOOD, 1908-1951. *'The Train Journey',* c.1929.
Wood engraving. Private Collection.

GASCOIGNE, George Edward

HENRI GAUDIER BRZESKA, 1891-1915. *'Seated Nude'*.
Chalk. 15in. x 10in. Mercury Gallery Ltd.

was taught wood engraving by Eric Ravilious* whom she later married. 1928 commissioned by BBC to illustrate *The Pilgrim's Progress*. 1929 studied at Central School of Art. 1931 did work for Golden Cockerel Press. 1933 with Ravilious executed a mural for Midland Railway Hotel, Morecambe. After the death of Ravilious in 1942 she began oil painting and making collages. 1952 memorial exhibition of her work held at Towner Art Gallery, Eastbourne; another retrospective held at same gallery, 1987.

GASCOIGNE, George Edward   1896-1971
Painter. Born London. On leaving school was apprenticed to a firm of lithographers. 1916 was imprisoned as a conscientious objector and not released until spring of 1919. Tried to establish himself as a freelance commercial artist whilst studying part-time at Hammersmith School of Art. 1934 obtained work in Carlisle. Apart from commercial work he painted landscapes and portraits, and remained a pacifist all his life. 1972 a commemorative exhibition of his work was held at Carlisle City Art Gallery.

GASKELL, George Percival   1868-1934
Painter. Born Shipley, Yorkshire. Educated at Cambridge. Studied art at RCA, in Paris and Italy. Exhibited at RA,

RE, RI, RBA and at the Paris Salon. Elected RBA, 1896, ARE, 1908, RE, 1911. Member of the Art Workers' Guild and for over thirty years was Headmaster of the Regent Street Polytechnic School of Art.

GATES, Eleanor   b.1957
Painter. Born Sheffield, Yorkshire. Studied at Newcastle upon Tyne Polytechnic, 1977-8, Sheffield City Polytechnic, 1978-80 and Chelsea School of Art, 1981-2. 1980-1 Fellowship held at Sunderland Polytechnic. 1983 artist in residence in West Germany, during which she worked at Worpswede. 1981 first solo exhibition held at Dryden St. Gallery, London; others include one at Cooper Gallery, Barnsley, 1986.

GATHERCOLE, Roy   b.1945
Painter. Studied at Ravensbourne College of Art, 1962-6, and at Leeds, 1966-7. 1967-8 Fellow in Painting at Carlisle College of Art. 1968 solo exhibition at Carlisle City Art Gallery. Teaches at Carlisle College of Art.

GAUDIER-BRZESKA, Henri   1891-1915
Sculptor. Born St. Jean-de-Braye, near Orleans, France. Visited London for two months in 1906 on a travelling scholarship and returned 1907 on a second scholarship to spend two years in Bristol and Cardiff studying English business methods. 1909 another bursary sent him to Nuremberg and Munich. His interest in art and in drawing had been growing all the while and in 1911 he left France for London with Sophie Brzeska, a Polish woman twenty years his senior whom he had met in a library and whose name he adopted. By 1912 he had made contact with several names in artistic and literary London. He had met Jacob Epstein* and begun carving, but it was not until 1913 that he gave up his job as a clerk with a shipping broker in order to devote himself wholly to art. His association with Vorticism, and in particular the ideas of T.E. Hulme, developed his respect for the machine and its principles into his work, but his innate feeling for animals and for the human form suggests that this influence was not wholly assimilated. He was killed in action in 1915 and a memorial exhibition was held at the Leicester Galleries, London, three years later.

Bibl: Roger Cole, *Burning to Speak. The Life and Art of Henri Gaudier-Brzeska*, Phaidon, Oxford, 1978; *Henri Gaudier-Brzeska, Sculptor 1891-1915*, Cambridge, Kettle's Yard Gallery, 1983.

GAULD, David   1866-1936
Painter. Born Glasgow, Scotland, and studied in Glasgow. Apprenticed to a Glasgow lithographer, working also as an illustrator for the *Glasgow Weekly Citizen*. Designed stained glass for several years and afterwards devoted himself entirely to painting. 1896 visited the artists' colony Grez-sur-Loing, in France. Elected RSA, 1924. Specialised in landscape and cattle pictures.

GAULT, Annabel   b.1952
Painter. Studied at West Surrey College of Art, 1973-7, and RA Schools, 1977-80. 1977 began exhibiting and held her first solo exhibition at the Oxford Gallery, 1981. Represented in the Arts Council Collection.

GAULT, George   b.1916
Painter. Born Belfast, Northern Ireland. 1934-7 served in the Royal Artillery. 1939 recalled to serve in the Second

WILLIAM GAUNT, 1900-1980. *'Diplomatic Occasion at the Hotel Grande Bretagne, Athens 1930'.* Pen and ink with watercolour. 9¾ in. x 14¾ in. Michael Parkin Fine Art Ltd.

World War. After the war studied at Camberwell School of Art and Crafts. Has exhibited at London Group, RA, Paris Salon, Royal Society of Portrait Painters, Roland, Browse and Delbanco, Blackheath Gallery and Woodlands Art Gallery, London.

GAULT, Kate   b.1954
Painter. Born Midhurst, Sussex. Studied art in Florence in 1970 and then at Byam Shaw School, London. Was diverted for a period into contemporary dance, worked with Eric Hawkins in New York, 1977, and continued to paint in her spare time. 1982 returned to London (after working as a dancer and choreographer in Holland and Ethiopia) to become a full-time painter. Moved to Ariège, France, 1984. Solo exhibition at Christopher Hull Gallery, London, 1985.

GAUNT, William   1900-1980
Painter and author. Born Hull, Yorkshire, son of a designer and chromolithographer. 1918 served in a 'Young Soldiers' battalion. 1919-22 studied History at Oxford. Studied part-time at Ruskin School of Art, Oxford and figure drawing at Westminster School of Art under Bernard Meninsky.* First solo exhibition held at Redfern Gallery, London, 1930. Edited the Special Number of *The*

Studio magazine in 1920s and published *London Promenade,* 1930, drawings of London life. Better known are his books, *The Pre-Raphaelite Tragedy,* 1941, and *The Aesthetic Adventure,* 1946, among many others. From 1957 Special Correspondent to *The Times* on art subjects; also editor of numerous illustrated works, mainly on the Fine Arts. 1975 a retrospective exhibition of his work was held at Michael Parkin Gallery, London.

GAVIN, Charles   b.1944
Painter. Born Edinburgh, Scotland. 1968 moved to Paris to undertake independent art studies. 1970 accepted into L'Ecole des Beaux Arts. 1972 returned to Edinburgh. 1973 moved to London. 1975-6 lived and worked in Spain. 1979 moved to the south west. 1972 held first solo exhibitions; others include one at Plymouth Arts Centre, 1984. 1985 artist in residence, Barne Beaton Secondary School, Plymouth.

Bibl: *Charles Gavin: Recent Work,* City of Edinburgh Art Centre, 1986.

GAY, Bernard   b.1921
Painter. Studied at Willesden School of Art. Has exhibited at Gimpel Fils, Roland Browse and Delbanco, Redfern, Leicester Galleries, Wildenstein's, Piccadilly Gallery,

GEAR, William

WILLIAM GEAR, b.1915. *'Landscape Image No.1'*, 1961. 72in. x 48in. City of Birmingham Museum and Art Gallery.

London, and at Austen Hayes, New York. 1965 exhibited small abstract pictures at the ICA, London. Became Head of the School of Interior Design at the London College of Furniture.

GEAR, William   b.1915

Painter. Born Fife, Scotland. Studied at Edinburgh College of Art, 1932-9. Worked in Paris, 1947-50, but spent the summer of 1948 painting at St. Ives. Was one of the first in Britain after the Second World War to move into pure abstraction, his style, owing much to French *tachisme,* depending on strong colour softly brushed into the spaces created by a lattice-like armature. Won a prize in the '60 paintings for '51' exhibition, timed to coincide with the Festival of Britain. 1964-75 Curator of the Towner Art Gallery, Eastbourne, and 1964-75 head of the Fine Art Department at Birmingham College of Art. Has received numerous prizes and awards and was elected fellow of the Royal Society of Arts, 1970. Has held many one-artist exhibitions in Britain and abroad. Work in Tate Gallery and other public collections.

GEARY, Kevin   b.1952

Painter. Born Lincoln, into a family containing three generations of marine artists. First solo exhibition opened by the Rt. Hon. Harold Wilson who also lent his portrait. Member of the Contemporary Portrait Society. His sitters have included Lord Goodman, Mrs Golda Meir, Vladimir Ashkenazy and others.

GEARY, Mike   b.1932

Painter. Born Twickenham, Middlesex. Studied at Worthing Technical College and College of Art, 1949-51. 1986 exhibited at the National Theatre, London, paintings based on his experience of running the New York City marathon October, 1984 and the London marathon April, 1985.

GEDDES, Fionna   b.1949

Painter, collagist and weaver. Born Glasgow, Scotland. Studied at Newcastle College of Art, 1968-9 and Edinburgh College of Art, 1973-4. 1974 awarded travelling scholarship to Morocco and South Spain. 1976 elected professional member SSA. 1976 secretary and founder member of STAG. 1975 held first solo exhibition at the Stirling Gallery, Stirling. Her interest in textural sensations led to an interest in weaving, knotting and binding, and she has been included in tapestry shows though still regards herself primarily as a painter.

GEDDES, Margaret   b.1914

Painter and abstract artist. Born Surrey. Studied at Westminster School of Art and began exhibiting while still a student. Apart from the war years, when she worked as draughtsman in the Fire Staff Department of the Home Office, she has exhibited regularly at group shows in London (Redfern, Leicester Galleries) and the provinces, with the London Group and the Women's International Art Club, of which she was chairperson, 1951-5. Represented in Leicestershire Education Authority Collection and elsewhere.

GENTLE, Nicola   b.1951

Painter. Born London. Studied at Winchester School of Art, since when the garden has been a recurrent theme in her paintings. This preoccupation, combined with the influence of Vanessa Bell's* and Duncan Grant's* decorative work, were displayed in her paintings of Sissinghurst and Charleston, exhibited at the Bloomsbury Workshop, London, 1989.

GENTLEMAN, David   b.1930

Illustrator and designer. Born London. Studied at RCA and stayed on to teach for two years. Since then has undertaken a wide range of work as illustrator and designer, including wall decorations for London Underground's Embankment tube station. Other major commissions include work for Shell, the British Steel Corporation, Penguin Books, many other English publishers and Limited Editions Club in New York.

GEORGE, Adrian   b.1944

Painter. Born Cirencester, Gloucestershire. Studied at RCA. Since 1978 has been represented by the Francis Kyle Gallery, London, holding regular solo exhibitions. 1983 exhibited oil paintings at the Museo Municipal, Madrid, and 1984 held his first solo exhibition in New York. Represented in V & A and National Portrait Gallery, London.

DAVID GENTLEMAN, b.1930. *'Park Lane'*, 1984. Pen and wash watercolour. From *David Gentleman's London*.

PATRICK GEORGE, b.1923. *'Two Ash Trees — Hickbush'*. 40in. x 42in. Private Collection.

MARK GERTLER, 1891-1939. *'The Fruit Sorters'*, 1914. 30in. x 25in. Leicestershire Museums, Arts and Records Service.

GEORGE, Patrick   b.1923

Painter. Born Manchester. Studied at Edinburgh College of Art and Camberwell School of Art where he was influenced by the continuation of the Euston Road School method as taught by William Coldstream.* 1949 joined staff of Slade School of Art. Solo exhibitions include one at Gainsborough's House, Sudbury, 1975, and a retrospective at the Serpentine Gallery, London, 1980 (catalogue introduction by Lawrence Gowing*). Confines himself to traditional subjects, painted with meticulous attention to the delicate relationship between the reality of the image and the reality of nature.

GERE, Charles   1869-1957

Painter. Born Gloucester. Studied at Birmingham Municipal School of Art. 1895 first visited Italy, making return visits in 1898 and 1900. Settled in Painswick, with his sister, Margaret Gere,* taking annual sketching holidays abroad. Often painted in tempera, his favourite medium, His landscapes are gentle and subdued, precise and lyrical. Within the limitations of his art produced work of poetic intensity. Also worked as an illustrator with William Morris for the Kelmscott Press and later for the Ashendene Press. Exhibited at RA from 1890. Member of NEAC, 1911, RWS, 1926, ARA, 1934 and RA, 1939. A memorial exhibition of his work was held in Gloucester, 1963.

GERE, Margaret   1878-1965

Painter. Born Leamington Spa, Warwickshire. Studied at Birmingham Municipal School of Art. 1900 visited Italy. 1905 entered Slade School of Art and whilst there became a friend of Ethel Walker* and Virginia Woolf. Settled in Painswick with her brother Charles Gere,* accompanying him on his annual sketching trips abroad. 1900-17 exhibited at Royal Birmingham Society of Artists and also at the NEAC and the Cheltenham Group of Artists. (Plate 41, p.175.)

Bibl: Gaynor Andrews and George Breeze, *Margaret Gere 1878-1965,* Cheltenham Art Gallery and Museums, 1984.

GERRARD, Charles Robert   1892-1964

Painter. Born in Antwerp of English parentage. Studied at Lancaster School of Art, 1907-14, and RCA, 1917-22. Exhibited at RA, NEAC and extensively abroad. Held solo exhibitions in London in 1924, 1927, 1931 and 1933. Worked much abroad, especially in India where he was the director of the Sir Jamsetji Jeejeebhoy School of Art, Bombay. Published a set of pictorial charts illustrating Hindu and Muslim painting, architecture and scripture.

GERTLER, Mark   1891-1939

Painter. Born Spitalfields, London, the son of Polish refugees. In Gertler's childhood his family, in desperate poverty, moved to Austria, then America, before settling back in London in 1896. Studied at Regent Street Polytechnic, 1906, but the following year, at his father's insistence, apprenticed himself to a stained glass works. 1908 entered the Slade, with financial assistance from the Jewish Education Aid Society and in 1910 won the Slade prize for portrait painting. 1912 left Slade, having already made friends with the patron, Edward Marsh, and the artist, Dora Carrington,* who brought him into connection with the Bloomsbury set and with Lady Ottoline Morrell. 1916 painted his most famous picture, *Merry-Go-Round* (Tate Gallery). 1921 first solo exhibition held at Goupil Gallery. Periods spent in sanatoria in early

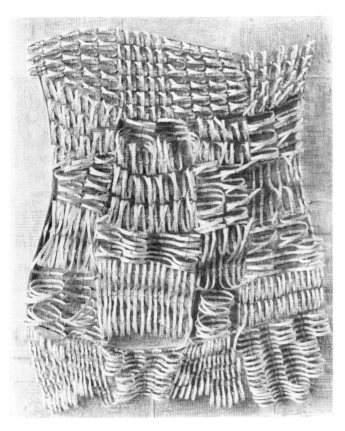

ARTHUR GIARDELLI, b.1911. *'The Vessel'*. Printed paper, pencilled and set into a carved out wooden ground. 28¾in. x 23¼in. Private Collection.

ROBERT GIBBINGS, 1889-1958. *'Melliha, Malta'*, 1919. Wood engraving. Approx. 7½in. diameter. Garton & Co.

1920s owing to tuberculosis. Continued to paint and exhibit despite ill-health, unhappiness and hardship, but finally committed suicide.

Bibl: John Woodeson, *Mark Gertler: Biography of a Painter, 1891-1939,* Sidgwick and Jackson, London, 1972.

GIARDELLI, Arthur   b.1911
Painter and collagist. Born London. Took a degree at Oxford and studied at Ruskin School of Art. Taught in a school in Merthyr Tydfil which was visited by Cedric Morris* who came to teach the unemployed, and also helped Giardelli who afterwards went to Morris's art school in Suffolk. Began incorporating real materials into his work, especially those found on the sea's edge. Joined staff of University College of Wales, Aberystwyth. Since 1960 has exhibited regularly in group and solo exhibitions and is represented in the National Museum of Wales, Keble College, Oxford, Arts Council Collection and elsewhere.

Bibl: Meic Stephens (ed.), *Artists in Wales,* Gwasg Gomer, 1971.

GIBB, Phelan   1870-1948
Painter. Born Alnwick, Northumberland. Studied at Glasgow School of Art. Exhibited at the RSA, RSW, GI and abroad. Lived at Milngavie and later at Killin, Perthshire. Friend of Matisse, Braque and Gertrude Stein in pre-1914 Paris where he held a solo exhibition at Bernheim-Jeune, 1913.

GIBBINGS, Robert   1889-1958
Wood-engraver. Studied at Slade, 1911-13, and on his spare days and evenings with Noel Rooke* who had started classes in wood engraving and book design at the Central

Schools. Served in the Gallipoli campaign and at Salonica during the First World War and was invalided out to Malta; there produced wood engravings using powerfully massed areas of black and white, leaving the spectator to complete the shapes of the buildings in those places where the paper was left blank. 1920 founder-member of the Society of Wood-Engravers. Turned to book illustration and eventually bought up the Golden Cockerel Press, one of the foremost private printing presses in England. 1933 was forced to sell up but continued as a free-lance book illustrator. Also lectured in book design at Reading University.

Bibl: *Aspects of the Work of Robert Gibbings,* University of Reading, 1975.

GIBBONS, John   b.1949
Sculptor. Born Ireland. Studied in Ireland, 1969-72, and at St. Martin's School of Art, 1972-5. Solo exhibitions include one at Nicola Jacobs Gallery, London, 1981, and the Serpentine Gallery, London, 1986. Works in steel, using prefabricated materials. Work in the collections of the Tate Gallery and the Arts Council.

GIBBS, Evelyn   b.1905
Painter. Studied at Liverpool School of Art and RCA. 1929 won the Rome Scholarship for Engraving. Taught at Goldsmiths' College and moved with it when it was evacuated to Nottingham during the war. 1929 elected ARE. 1943 founded Midland Group of Artists. Represented in Nottingham Art Gallery and British Museum. Exhibits regularly at RA. Has also shown at Leicester Galleries, London.

GIBBS, Jonathan   b.1953
Painter and collagist. Studied at Lowestoft College of Further Education, 1971-2, Central School of Art and Design, 1972-6 and Slade, 1976-8. 1978-9 awarded Cheltenham Painting Fellowship. 1979 won Boise Travelling Scholarship to Italy. 1980 solo exhibition of drawings and collages held at Ikon Gallery, Birmingham.

GIBBS, Timothy   b.1923
Painter. Born Epping, Essex. Studied at Trinity College, Oxford, then at Ruskin School of Art, 1947-8. 1955 held first solo exhibition at Piccadilly Gallery and subsequently at the Leicester Galleries, 1962. Has exhibited at RA and with London Group. Represented in Kensington Borough Council collection. (Plate 42, p.175.)

GIBILARO, Jason   b.1962
Painter. Studied at St. Martin's School of Art, 1980-1, and at Brighton Polytechnic School of Art and Design, 1981-4. 1984 first exhibited in 'Stowells Trophy', at RA. 1986 awarded the Laing Calendar and Royal Overseas League Travel Prize.

GIBSON, James   b.1948
Painter. Born Glasgow, Scotland. Studied history of art at Edinburgh University. Taught English for a number of years. No formal art teaching but began painting in 1977. 1985 first solo exhibition held at Compass Gallery, Glasgow.

GIBSON, Jean   b.1935
Sculptor, Born Stoke-on-Trent, Staffordshire. Studied at Wimbledon School of Art and RCA. Won travelling scholarship to Italy. 1965 first solo exhibition held Leicester Galleries, London; another 1969. Abstract sculptor who works with resin, fibreglass and perspex. Commissions include two panels for the P & O liner, *Oriana*. Married Anthony Whishaw.* Exhibited at Nicola Jacobs Gallery, London, 1981.

GIBSON, Leslie Donovan   1910-1969
Painter and printmaker. Educated at Durham University. 1928-30 travelled and painted in Finland, Germany, Belgium, France and Spain. Studied at RCA, 1930-3. Continued travelling, at intervals, in between teaching art. 1939-40 war service. Invalided out of army, lived first in London then Wiltshire. A versatile artist, who produced traditional subjects in a variety of media.

GIBSON, Lloyd   b.1945
Sculptor. Studied at Newcastle University 1964-8. Winner of many awards. 1971 began exhibiting. Solo exhibitions include one at the Mappin Art Gallery, Sheffield, 1978, and another at the Lewis Johnstone Gallery, London, 1981. Works with mixed media, creating wall pieces and installations that have a capacity to disturb.

GIBSON, William Alfred   1866-1931
Painter. Born Glasgow, Scotland, and studied in Glasgow. Exhibited at RA, RSA, GI and abroad. Served in the Boer War with the 6th Battalion Scottish Imperial Yeomanry. Worked as a landscapist in Scotland, England, Holland and France. Member of the Glasgow Art Club and represented in several public Scottish art collections.

GILBERT and GEORGE
Born (respectively) 1943, in the Dolomites of Ladino stock, and 1942 in Devon. Gilbert studied at Wolkenstein School of Art in South Tyrol, Italy, the Hallein School of Art, Austria, and the Academy of Art, Munich. George studied at Dartington Adult Education Centre and Dartington Hall College of Art, Devon, and at the Oxford School of Art. They met in 1967 when both were studying sculpture at St. Martin's School of Art, and began collaborating a year later. Deciding to abandon the making of sculpture, they donned the 'responsibility suits of our art' and became 'living sculptures'. Thereafter everything they did became 'art'. 1971 they began also making photo-pieces which soon became the main focus of their work, and in 1977 they gave up living sculpture presentations, although their house and life style still remains part of their ongoing work of art. 1984-5 major exhibition toured America and another, which began in Bordeaux in 1986, ended at the Hayward Gallery, 1987.

Bibl: *Gilbert and George: The Complete Sculptures 1971-85,* Thames & Hudson, London, 1986.

GILBERT, Alfred   1854-1934
Sculptor and designer. Born London. Studied at Heatherley's School from 1872, under Boehm at the RA Schools, at the Ecole des Beaux Arts, Paris, 1875-8, and in Rome, 1878-84. Exhibited at the RA from 1882. Elected ARA, 1887, RA, 1892, resigned 1909. His highly detailed work displays a love of linear arabesques, made possible by the revival of the lost-wax method of bronze casting. Also sometimes added to his work semi-precious gems, ivory, tin or mother-of-pearl, combining skilled craftsmanship with a flair for capturing dramatic poses. His best known works include Eros at Piccadilly Circus, the Duke of Clarence Tomb at Windsor and the Queen Alexandra Memorial at Marlborough Gate. Lived in Belgium and Italy for some years, returning to England, 1926. Re-elected RA, 1932, the year in which he was also knighted. (For illustration see p.16.)

GILBERT, Donald   1900-1961
Sculptor. Born Burcot, Worcestershire, son of the sculptor, Walter Gilbert. Studied under his father and with Sir Alfred Gilbert,* also at Birmingham Central School of Art, the RCA and RA Schools. Exhibited at RA, RWA, RHA, GI, Paris Salon and in the provinces.

GILBERT, Richard   b.1957
Painter. Born Plymouth, Devon. Studied at Falmouth School of Art, 1977-8, Wimbledon School of Art, 1978-80, Chelsea School of Art, 1983-4 and British School in Rome, 1984-5. 1988 held first solo exhibition at Raab Gallery, London. Figurative artist, working in pastel and oils, with vibrant colours and textures.

GILCHRIST, Philip Thomson   1865-1956
Painter. Born Stanwix, near Carlisle, Cumbria. Spent some years as a partner in the calico printing business and then studied art under Tom Mostyn. Exhibited at RA from 1900, also at the RSA, RBA and in the provinces. Elected RBA, 1906 and was also a member of the Liverpool and Manchester Academies of Art. Represented in public collections in the North West. Specialised in landscape and marine subjects.

GILES, Graham   b.1942
Painter. Born London. Studied at Regent Street Polytechnic, 1960-4. Has held several exhibitions since 1971, most recently at Cadogan Contemporary, 1986 and 1988.

GILES, Maggi   b.1938
Ceramics artist. Born Cornwall. Studied at Bromley School of Art in Kent. 1956-60 worked as a commercial artist for the D.H. Evans department store. For a period worked in Holland in the Royal Delft Blue Porcelain Factory and 1970 held her first solo exhibition in the Stedelijk Museum, Amsterdam. Set up her own studio in Amsterdam and began making large ceramic reliefs for public buildings. Solo exhibition at Southampton Art Gallery, 1978.

GILES, Tony   b.1925
Painter. Born Taunton, Somerset. 1941-5 apprenticed to the Admiralty Hydrographic Department in Cartographic Drawing. Has worked for the Admiralty and local government; retired in 1981. Member of the Penwith Society of Arts. First solo exhibition held at Penwith Gallery, 1962. Others include one at Park Gallery, Cheltenham, 1988. Exhibits at RA and represented in Stoke-on-Trent Museum and Art Gallery and elsewhere.

GILHESPY, Tom   b.1944
Sculptor. Born Ferry Hill, Co. Durham. Studied at Leicester College of Art, 1962-6. 1966-7 won Italian Government Scholarship. Has taught at Newport College of Art and in 1981 became head of Sculpture Department at Birmingham Polytechnic. 1981 held a solo exhibition at Chapter, Cardiff. Represented in the Welsh Arts Council Collection.

GILI, Katherine   b.1948
Sculptor. Born Oxford. Studied at Bath Academy of Art, 1966-70, and at St. Martin's School of Art, 1971-3. 1977 first solo exhibition at the Serpentine Gallery, London. Working with steel she produces abstract and experimental pieces. Her more recent work, while not representational, seeks to express the movements of the human form. Included in the collections of the City of Lugano Collection, Switzerland; Arts Council of Great Britain; Cartwright Hall Museum, Bradford.

GILL, Colin Unwin   1892-1940
Painter. Born Bexley Heath, Kent. Studied at Slade School and was awarded the Rome Scholarship in Decorative Painting, 1913. Served in France 1915-8, and was official war artist, 1918-9. Exhibited with the NEAC from 1914, became a member in 1926; also showed at the RA from 1924. Taught painting at the RCA, 1922-5. 1939 went to Johannesburg, South Africa, to paint decorations in the Magistrates Court and died there before completing the scheme.

GILL, Eric   1882-1940
Sculptor and engraver. Born Brighton, Sussex, the son of a congregationalist minister. He became articled to W.H. Caroe, architect to the Ecclesiastical Commissioners in London in 1900. Attended evening classes at Central School of Arts and Crafts and studied letter design under Edward Johnston; he also began to carve in stone. By 1904 was making a living from letter engraving. 1910 began making figure sculpture and held his first solo exhibition at the Chenil Gallery, London, 1911. He set up an artistic

ERIC GILL, 1882-1940. *'Sonnets and Verses'*. Garton & Co.

community in Ditchling and was converted to Roman Catholicism, 1913. 1924 moved to Capel-y-ffin in Wales and over the next four years produced much of his best engraved work, mainly for Gibbing's* Golden Cockerel Press. 1928 moved again to High Wycombe, Buckinghamshire. Though a controversial figure in that his sexual improprieties remained in conflict with his Catholic faith, Gill is nowadays regarded as one of the greatest craftsmen of this century, a typographer and lettercutter of skill and a masterly wood-engraver.

Bibl: Malcolm Yorke, *Eric Gill: Man of Flesh and Spirit*, Constable, London, 1981; Fiona MacCarthy, *Eric Gill*, Faber and Faber, London, 1989.

GILL, Macdonald   1884-1947
Architect, mural painter and cartographer. Born Brighton, Sussex, brother of Eric Gill.* Studied at Chichester School of Art and the Central School of Arts and Crafts. 1901-3 articled to an architect, afterwards became an assistant to Sir Charles Nicholson. Elected FRIBA, 1931. As a mural painter worked with Roger Fry* and others on decorations for the Borough Polytechnic. Also painted murals for Lincoln Cathedral, the House of Commons and Lindisfarne and Howth Castles.

WILLIAM GILLIES, 1898-1973. *'Double Still Life'*, 1954. 23 ½ in. x 51 ¼ in. Scottish National Gallery of Modern Art.

GILL, Madge   1882-1961
Painter and fantasist. Born London. Little is known about this artist except that she seems to have spent all her life in East London. In May 1937 the magazine *Prediction* published her own account of her automatic writings and drawings. In her drawings she endlessly tried to create some kind of heavenly city, producing elements that prefigure Bridget Riley* and Vasarely. On 18 July 1942 *Psychic News* published an interview with the artist. She exhibited in the 1930s in the East End Academy and the Whitechapel Art Gallery and in 1942 contributed to an exhibition 'Artists Aid Russia' at Hertford House. An exhibition of her work was shown at the Leeds Playhouse, 1976 and at the Grosvenor Gallery in London.

GILLESPIE, Michael   b.1929
Sculptor. Studied at Hammersmith College of Art and then taught himself bronze casting, from which he made a living and learnt a lot through casting for others, including Jacob Epstein.* Has had several solo exhibitions, including one at the Gilbert Parr Gallery, London, 1977. Also exhibits at RA and elsewhere. Most of his work is abstract and he takes his standards more from musical than visual experience.

GILLESPIE, Rowan   b.1953
Sculptor. Born Dublin, Ireland. Studied at York School of Art, Kingston College of Art, London and Statens Kunst Skole, Oslo. Since 1975 has exhibited widely in Norway and held his first solo exhibition in Ireland in Lad Lane, 1976. 1979 was commissioned by the Bank of Ireland to design and cast the GAA 'All-Stars Trophies'.

GILLICK, Ernest George   1874-1951
Sculptor. Born Bradford, Yorkshire. Studied at RCA and won a travelling scholarship. Exhibited at RA and was elected ARA, 1935. 1938 was elected FRBS; 1935 Master of the Art Workers' Guild. Married the sculptor Mary Tutin (Mary Gillick*).

GILLICK, Mary   d.1965
Sculptor and medallist. Née Tutin. Studied at RCA and in 1905 married Ernest George Gillick.* Exhibited at RA and other leading galleries. Also painted in her spare time.

GILLIE, Ann   b.1906
Painter and collagist. Born Newcastle upon Tyne, Tyne and Wear. Studied at Newcastle University, Fine Art Department, 1923-8. 1928-33 worked as a designer at Heal's in London and also for the stage. 1934 settled in Tyneside. Has exhibited at RA, RSA, the Molton Gallery, London, and with the Artists International Association. Represented in the Laing Art Gallery, Newcastle upon Tyne, Shipley Art Gallery, Gateshead and elsewhere. Has been called one of the North East's most significant but least publicised artists.

GILLIES, William   1898-1973
Painter. Born Haddington, Scotland. Studied for two terms at Edinburgh College of Art, 1916. 1917 called up for war service. 1919 resumed studies at Edinburgh College of Art. 1924 awarded travelling scholarship and studied in Paris under André L'Hôte. 1932 invited to become a member of the Society of Eight. 1946 became head of School of Painting, Edinburgh College of Art. 1947 elected Academician of RSA. 1950 elected member of RSW. 1957 awarded CBE. 1960 became Principal of Edinburgh College of Art. 1963 elected President of RSW. 1964 elected ARA and in 1971 elected RA. One of Scotland's leading painters, famous for his rendering of landscape. Knighted in 1970. Much of his output was bought by Dr. R.A. Lillie who bequeathed some 300 pictures to the National Gallery of Scotland, most of which are now in the Scottish National Gallery of Modern Art, Edinburgh.

Bibl: T. Elder Dickson, *W.G. Gillies,* University Press, Edinburgh, 1974; *William Gillies and the Scottish Landscape,* Scottish Arts Council, 1980.

HAROLD GILMAN, 1876-1919.
'Tea in the Bed-Sitter', 1916-17.
33in. x 37in. Huddersfield Art Gallery.

GILLINGHAM, Tim   b.1958

Painter. Studied at Southend-on-Sea College of Art and Design, 1977-8, and Newcastle upon Tyne Polytechnic 1978-82. Whilst working in the theatre and with community ventures, he has progressed as a painter through abstaction to figuration. His paintings reflect the noise and rush of contemporary urban life. 1985 held a solo exhibition at Kingsgate Gallery, London.

GILLMAN, Tricia   b.1951

Painter. Studied at University of Leeds and University of Newcastle, 1970-7. 1975 first solo exhibition held at Parkinson Gallery, Leeds; others include one at the Arnolfini Gallery, Bristol, 1985 and the Benjamin Rhodes Gallery, London. Her brightly coloured paintings are abstract with figurative connotations.

GILMAN, Harold   1876-1919

Painter. Born Rode, Somerset. Educated at Brasenose College, Oxford, for one year. Studied at Hastings Art School, 1896, and transferred from there to the Slade, 1897. 1904 visited Madrid and spent a year copying the works of Velasquez and Goya. 1905 visited America. 1906 joined Walter Sickert's* Fitzroy Street Group, and in 1911 helped found the Camden Town Group. 1912 visited Sweden and Norway. 1914 termed himself a Neo-Realist, with Charles Ginner.* 1918 commissioned by the Canadian Government to paint Halifax Harbour for the War Memorial at Ottawa. A leading English Post-Impressionist, his mostly lodging-house interiors display strong colours inspired by Van Gogh and Gauguin. Died in the severe flu epidemic that swept Britain, 1918-9. (Plate 43, p.178.)

Bibl: *Harold Gilman,* with essays by Andrew Causey and Richard Thompson, Arts Council cat., 1981

EDNA GINESI, b.1902. *'Thameside'.* 40in. x 50in. Private Collection.

GINESI, Edna   b.1902

Painter, interior decorator and ballet designer. Born Leeds, Yorkshire, of Italian descent. Studied at Leeds College of Art and RCA, 1920-4 where she became a close friend of Henry Moore.* 1924 awarded West Riding Travelling Scholarship and visited Holland, Belgium, France and Italy. 1932 first one-artist exhibition at Zwemmer Gallery. 1931-2 designed decor for the Camargo Ballet. Travelled widely in Europe and North America and was in Spain during the Civil War, 1936. 1956 retrospective exhibition held at Bradford.

CHARLES GINNER, 1878-1952. *'Cottages: Brook Green, Isle of Wight',* 1929. 21in. x 28in. Leicestershire Museums, Arts and Records Service.

GINGELL, John   b.1935

Installation artist. Born Kent. Trained at Goldsmiths' College. Moved to Cardiff, 1966, eventually became Principal Lecturer in the South Glamorgan Institute of Higher Education. During the 1970s made and exhibited environmental work. 1978 he exhibited 'Fragile Stones Make Art' at the National Museum of Wales, and then embarked on a major land sculpture commissioned by Gwent Education Authority. Exhibited an installation called 'Gardens of Pleasure' at Oriel, Cardiff, 1983.

GINNER, Charles   1878-1952

Painter. Born Cannes, France. Studied at College Stanislas in Cannes. Worked in an architect's office in Paris 1899-1904, finally overcame parental disapproval, and studied art at the Academie Vitti and the Ecole des Beaux Arts. Inspired especially by Van Gogh, his strong colours won him much disapproval. 1909 he visited Buenos Aires and held his first exhibition there; by the end of that year he had settled in London. Joined the Fitzroy Street Group and, in 1911, the Camden Town Group, becoming one of the prominent figures within the latter. He also joined the London Group, 1913 and the Cumberland Market Group, 1914. In April, 1914 he and

Harold Gilman* held a joint exhibition at the Goupil Gallery, calling themselves 'Neo-Realists'. Ginner's style from then on changed little and is characterised by small, brick-like touches of thick paint which steadily fill every part of the picture. The same deliberate, almost mechanical approach is applied to street scenes and to landscapes, his work having dignity and calm. Joined NEAC, 1920 and was elected ARA, 1942. Served as an Official War Artist during the First World War.

Bibl: *Charles Ginner: Paintings and Drawings,* Arts Council cat., 1953; *Charles Ginner,* Fine Art Society, London, 1985.

GLASGOW, Edwin   1874-1955

Painter. Born Liverpool, Merseyside. Educated at Wadham College, Oxford. Exhibited at RA, RI, Paris Salon and the provinces. Keeper and Secretary at the National Gallery, London, 1933-5. Published *The Painter's Eye,* 1936.

GINSBERG, Michael   b.1943

Painter. Born London. Studied at Central and Chelsea Schools of Art, 1965-9. 1976 won Greater London Arts Association Visual Arts Award and 1978 the Mark Rothko Memorial Award. 1981-2 painted centenary murals for St.

Charles Hospital, London. 1969 first solo exhibition held at Lisson Gallery, London; others include Acme Gallery, London, 1983, and Benjamin Rhodes Gallery, London, 1986 and 1989-90. Abstract painter, often using an irregular format. Represented in the National Museum of Wales, York City Art Gallery and elsewhere.

GIRLING, Sheila
Painter. Born Birmingham, West Midlands. Studied at the RA. 1978 first solo exhibition at Edmonton Art Gallery, Edmonton, followed by a second solo exhibition in the same year at Alberta Art Gallery, Calgary, Canada. She has exhibited widely in Great Britain and the United States. Included in the collections of Everson Museum, Syracuse, USA, FUBA Collection, Johannesburg, South Africa, Warwick Arts Trust and Triangle Arts Trust. Married to the sculptor, Anthony Caro.* Solo exhibition held at Francis Graham Dixon Gallery, London, 1985.

GLADWELL, Rodney   b.1928
Painter. Born Didcot, Berkshire. Studied at Académie Colarossi, Paris. First solo exhibition held at Sussex University, 1962-3. Also showed at Molton Gallery, London, and Lefevre Gallery, London. His paintings hover between abstraction and figuration and play on this ambiguity.

GLASS, William Mervyn   1885-1965
Painter. Studied at Aberdeen School of Art, at the RSA Life School in Edinburgh, and in Paris and Italy. Exhibited at the RA, RSA, GI and elsewhere. Elected ARSA, 1934, and 1930-3 was President of the SSA. Specialised in landscapes and coastal scenes.

GLUCK, Felix   1923-1981
Artist and publisher. Born Bavaria, Germany. Studied at Free Academy of Art, Budapest, 1941-4. Imprisoned in Mauthausen concentration camp, 1944-5. 1948 came to England and studied at King's College, University of Durham. 1950 returned to Hungary and worked as art editor for the Hungarian State Publishing House. 1956 fled to England and became art editor at Rathbone Books. Solo exhibition at Woodstock Gallery, London, 1962. Lectured at Hornsey College of Art, 1966-9, and Chelsea College of Art, 1969-71. Retrospective held at Orleans House Gallery, Richmond, 1986.

GLUCK   1895-1976
Painter. Born Hannah Gluckstein, into the family that founded the J. Lyons & Co. catering empire. She did not want her wealth or her patronymic to be known and adopted for her name the harsh monosyllable 'Gluck'. Studied briefly at St. John's Wood Art School, afterwards visited Lamorna at the invitation of Alfred Munnings.* Returned to London to live in Hampstead but retained a small cottage and studio in Borah, Cornwall. Scorned art school teaching and resolved early on to show her work only in solo exhibitions, of which she held five, the last at the Fine Art Society in London, 1973, after a gap of thirty years. Also designed her own frames which were stepped up towards the centre, so that when painted the same colour as the wall they die away into it. The fastidiousness found in her person (she always dressed in male attire, had her hair cut at a gentlemen's hairdressers in Bond Street and turned androgyny into high fashion) is also found in her art. Friendship with Constance Spry furthered her

GLUCK, 1895-1976. 'Bettina', 1917. 15½ in. x 19½ in.
The Fine Art Society, London.

interest in flower painting. She is also renowned as a penetrating, if sometimes unflattering, portraitist.

Bibl: Diana Souhami, *Gluck, her biography*, Pandora, London, 1988.

GOBLE, Anthony   b.1943
Painter. Born Newtown, Mid Wales. Studied at Wrexham School of Art and Coleg Harlech. Has practised as a painter since 1965, and subsidised himself with occasional prosaic jobs. Also writes poetry and held his first solo exhibition, 1974, at University College of North Wales, Bangor. Has received many awards and grants and is represented in the Welsh Arts Council Collection and elsewhere. His paintings of heads come close at times to those of Frank Auerbach.*

GODFREY, Angela   b.1939
Sculptor. Studied at King's College, Newcastle upon Tyne. Works in stone, wood, metal and with modelling materials. Executed a commission for a frontal to the High Altar in a Catholic Church in St. Albans. Solo exhibition at Elisabeth Gallery, Coventry, 1964.

GODWIN, Keith   b.1916
Sculptor. Born Warsop, Nottinghamshire. Studied at Mansfield Art School, 1934-5, Nottingham College of Art, 1935-6, Leicester College of Art, 1936-9 and RCA, 1939, 1946-8. Exhibited at RA, RBA, with the London Group and in the provinces. Elected RBA, 1950.

GOGIN, Charles   1845-1931
Painter. Born London, the son of a Frenchman from Orleans. Educated in France and Germany and after a period in a stockbroker's office, turned to painting. Studied at RA Schools and in Paris. First exhibited at the RA in 1876, and with the NEAC, 1886, though was not a founder member.

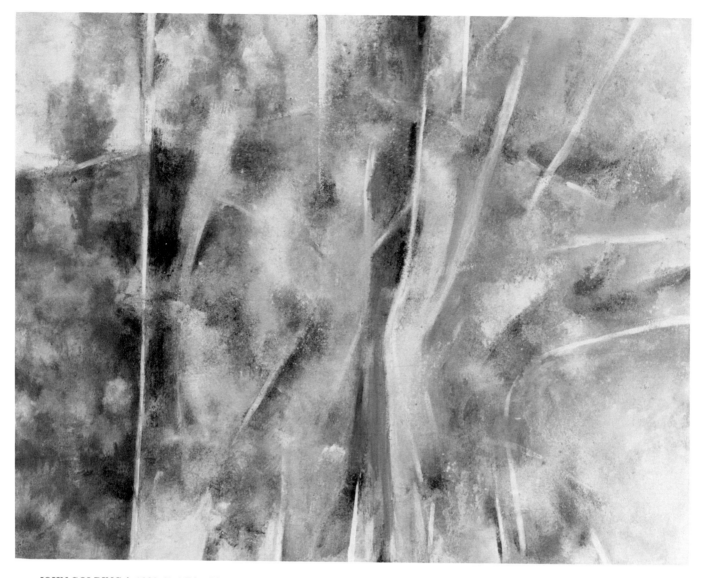

JOHN GOLDING, b.1929. '1.4 (Blue Mounting)', 1985. Mixed media on cotton duck. 52in. x 66in. Mayor Rowan Gallery.

GOLDBERG, Simon
Painter. Born London. Studied at St. Martin's School of Art and then RCA. Taught printmaking at Hull College of Art. Founder member in the early 1960s of the Avenue Group. Represented in V & A, Leeds City Art Gallery and Ferens Art Gallery, Hull.

GOLDEN, Grace   b.1904
Painter. Born East London. Studied at Chelsea School of Art, 1920-3, and the RCA, 1923-6. A small legacy in 1934 enabled her to interrupt a career in illustration for painting. Exhibited at RA, 1936-40, also at the Fine Art Society and the Leicester Galleries. 1951 she published *Old Bankside,* which combined her interest in history, especially that of the theatre, with her love of the river.

GOLDING, John   b.1929
Painter and art historian. Born Hastings, Sussex, of Anglo-Mexican parents and spent much of his early life in Mexico. Studied at University of Toronto and worked professionally as a stage designer. Subsequently he came to London to study art history at the Courtauld Institute of Art, London University, where he obtained a PhD, 1957. His doctoral thesis was published under the title *Cubism: 1907-14* but even while at the Courtauld he had decided to turn from art history to painting. Has exhibited regularly in London, at Mayor Rowan Gallery, and abroad.

GOLDSMITH, William   b.1931
Painter. Born Lincolnshire. Studied for two years at Bristol School of Art and for three years at RCA, afterwards travelled to Italy, France and Germany. Exhibited at the RBA Galleries, 1953 and at the Beaux Arts Gallery, London, 1954. A representational painter, whose realism is merged with a semi-cubist style.

GOLDSWORTH, Andy   b.1956
Photographer and sculptor. Studied at Bradford Art College, 1974-5, and Preston Polytechnic, 1975-8. Held first solo exhibition at LYC Museum and Art Gallery, Banks, Cumbria, 1980. Working with sticks, snow or leaves, he creates delicate outdoor sculpture that is

impermanent but shown in galleries in the form of photographs. A more diverse artist than Richard Long* but not so well known.

Bibl: *Andy Goldsmith: Mountain & Coast, Autumn into Winter, Japan, 1987,* Gallery Takagi, Nagoya, 1988.

GOODCHILD, Max   b.1952
Painter. Born Dorset. Studied at Bristol Polytechnic 1978-81. First solo exhibition at Bath University, 1982.

GOODE, Mervyn   b.1948
Painter. Born Peterborough, Cambridgeshire. Studied landscape architecture at Gloucestershire College of Art, 1967-69, and is self-taught as a painter. First solo exhibition held at Highton Gallery, London, 1970. Since then has held many solo exhibitions in London and the Home Counties and shows sporadically at the ROI. Moved to East Hampshire, near the village of Selbourne, in order to immerse himself in the landscape he loves to paint. Is also associated as a landscape painter with West Sussex. Many of his paintings have been reproduced by the Medici Society as greetings cards. (Plate 44, p.178.)

GOODEN, Stephen   1892-1955
Printmaker and illustrator. Born Rugby, Warwickshire. Studied at Slade School and began engraving in 1923. Served in France, 1915-8. Elected ARA, 1937, and RA, 1946. Created CBE, 1942. Illustrated a number of books and is represented in several public collections.

GOODFELLOW, Reginald   1894-1985
Painter. Apprenticed to a structural engineer on leaving school and served with the Royal Engineers in Mesopotamia during the First World War. Employed as engineer by Ministry of Works and did not begin formal art training until 1927 when he enrolled for classes at Westminster School of Art under Walter Bayes.* His engineering career continued until 1959 alongside his painting. His work was shown at the Parkin Gallery, London, the year after his death along with that of Walter Bayes, in a show entitled 'Pupil and Master'. Woodcuts by Goodfellow are in the British Museum.

GOODMAN, Victoria
Painter. Studied under John Skeaping* in France. 1979 came to England to study at the RA. Since 1982 has been earning her living as an artist, developing an interest in collage and landscape. Winner of the Winsor and Newton 'Young Artist of the Year' Award, 1984.

GOODWIN, Arthur   b.1922
Painter. Born Lancashire. Studied in Liverpool. Taught drawing and painting at Hull College of Art. Did research into Art Education and became Head of Fine Art, Exeter College of Art. His interests also extend to history of art, poetry, philosophy and history. First solo exhibition held at Hull University, 1960. Has worked on mural commissions executed in mosaics. Represented in Ferens Art Gallery, Hull.

GOPAL-CHOWDHURY, Paul   b.1949
Painter. Studied at Camberwell School of Art, 1967-8, and Slade School of Fine Art, 1968-73. Has taught at Chelsea School of Art, Leeds University and the Byam Shaw School of Art. 1973 awarded Boise travelling scholarship and French Government scholarship (taken 1974). 1975-7 Gregory Fellow, Leeds University. 1983-4 Artist in

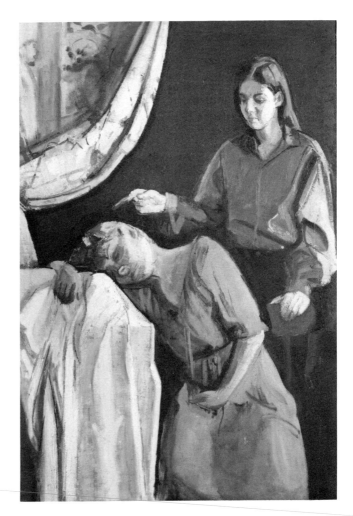

PAUL GOPAL-CHOWDHURY, b.1949. *'Joey and Adrianna I',* 1986. 59¾in. x 41¾in. Benjamin Rhodes Gallery.

Residence at Gonville and Caius College and Kettle's Yard Gallery, Cambridge. First solo exhibition held at Newcastle upon Tyne Polytechnic Art Gallery, 1980. Has exhibited since then with the Ian Birksted Gallery, and Benjamin Rhodes Gallery, both in London.

GORDINE, Dora   b.1906
Sculptor. Born St. Petersburg, Russia. Studied in Paris and was encouraged by Maillol. Exhibited at the RA from 1928. First one man exhibition at the Leicester Galleries, 1928. 1929-35 made figures for Singapore Town Hall. 1936 moved from Paris to London. Designed her own house and studio in Richmond. Elected ARBS 1938 and FRBS in 1949. 1948 spent a year in America working in Hollywood. 1959 revisited America. Represented in the Tate Gallery.

GORDON, Esmé   b.1910
Painter. Born Edinburgh, Scotland. Studied architecture at Edinburgh College of Art, 1927-34. 1931 began exhibiting with the RSA. 1937 set up in practice as an architect. 1942-5 served with Royal Engineers in Europe. 1955-7 President of Edinburgh Architectural Association. 1957 elected an associate of the RSA and 1967 elected academician. 1972-7 Hon. Secretary of the RSA. Specialises in watercolours of architectural subjects.

GORDON, Hilda May

GORDON, Hilda May 1874-1972
Painter. Studied under Herkomer and Brangwyn* at the Bushey School of Art. Set off in 1922 to paint her way around the world, returned 1928. She experienced many hazardous moments, and lived in native huts, houseboats, tents and palaces. At Bali she sketched a volcano in the act of eruption.

Bibl: Patrick Conner, *Hilda May Gordon: A Colourist Abroad,* Martyn Gregory Gallery, London, 1987.

GORDON, Mel b.1943
Painter. Born Bradford, Yorkshire. Studied at Bradford College of Art, 1961 and Birmingham Polytechnic, 1964, also that year won the Max Beckmann Scholarship to New York. Began exhibiting 1965 and has exhibited regularly ever since. Represented in Arts Council Collection, Birmingham City Art Gallery, V & A and elsewhere.

GORE, Frederick b.1913
Painter. Studied painting at the Ruskin School while reading classics at Oxford. Later studied at Westminster Art School and Slade, and on leaving had his first solo exhibition at the Redfern Gallery, London. 1940-6 served in the army. 1949-62 had five solo exhibitions at the Redfern Gallery, two at the Mayor Gallery and in 1963 one at the Juster Gallery, New York. Elected ARA 1964 and RA 1973. Has also published books on art and contributed many essays to catalogues. Represented in Southampton Art Gallery, Plymouth Art Gallery, Reading Art Gallery and elsewhere.

GORE, Spencer 1878-1914
Painter. Born Epsom, Surrey. Studied at Slade School of Art, 1896-9, and became friendly with Harold Gilman.* Visited Spain in 1902 with Wyndham Lewis,* and in 1904 visited Walter Sickert* in Dieppe. He returned to Dieppe during the summers of 1905 and 1906, having become a friend and colleague of Sickert, a member of his Fitzroy Street Group and shared his fondness for music halls. Like Gilman and Charles Ginner,* Gore became a central figure within the Camden Town Group in 1911. Inspired by Gauguin, he began applying strong colour to the landscapes he painted at Letchworth and elsewhere. In March 1914 he got wet while painting, contracted pneumonia and died.

Bibl: *Spencer Frederick Gore 1878-1914,* Anthony d'Offay Gallery cats., 1974 and 1983

GORMAN, Michael b.1938
Painter. Born Wolverhampton, West Midlands. Studied fine art at the University of Newcastle, 1965-9. Teaches at Exeter College of Art. First solo exhibition at the Serpentine Gallery, 1972. Winner of the Westward Television Open Competition, 1971. Solo exhibitions include two at the Nicholas Treadwell Gallery, London, 1972 and 1974.

GORMAN, Richard b.1946
Painter. Born Dublin, Ireland. Graduated from Dun Laoghaire School of Art and Design, Ireland, 1980. First solo exhibition at the Project Gallery, Dublin, 1983. Regularly exhibits in Europe. Contributed to Ireland & Cuba Printers Exchange, 1986, followed by a solo exhibition in Tokyo, 1989. Exhibits with the Benjamin Rhodes Gallery, London. Solo exhibition with the Kirlin Gallery, Dublin, 1990. Included in the collections of the Arts Council of Ireland and Allies Irish Banks.

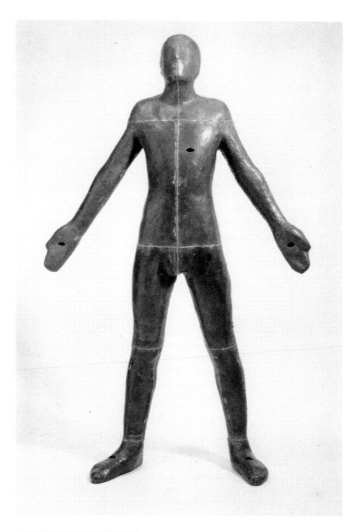

ANTHONY GORMLEY, b.1950. *'Untitled (for Francis)',* 1985. 74¼ in. x 47in. x 13⅜in. Metal and acrylic. Tate Gallery.

GORMLEY, Antony b.1950
Sculptor. Born London. Studied at Trinity College, Cambridge, 1968-70, Central School of Art and Design, 1973-4, Goldsmiths' College, 1975-7 and Slade, 1977-9. First solo exhibition held at Serpentine Gallery, London, 1981; another at the Whitechapel Art Gallery in the same year. Others include one at Salvatore Ala, New York, and Riverside Studios, London, both 1984. Gormley's sculptures are often figurative, made of lead and based on casts of his own figure.

GORTON, Lesley Ann b.1939
Painter. Born Brighton, Sussex. Studied at Brighton College of Art and Crafts. 1958 won a travelling scholarship to Holland, 1961 visited Nigeria. Became an art teacher but continued to paint and joined the Society of Sussex Painters. Represented in Worthing Municipal Gallery.

GOSSE, Sylvia 1881-1965
Painter and etcher. The daughter of Sir Edmund Gosse, the prominent essayist and critic and also Librarian to the House of Lords, she was brought up among her father's

formidable circle of friends which included Thomas Hardy, Henry James, Swinburne and Browning. Became interested in painting as a child at Dinon, and on her return from France studied at the St. John's Wood School of Art; followed by three years at the RA Schools. Was only allowed to become a professional artist through the prompting of Sickert,* who by 1909 was a family friend; her style owes much to his example. Member of NEAC and London Group. Has work in many public collections, including Sheffield City Art Galleries and Walker Art Gallery, Liverpool. (Plate 45, p.179.)

GOTCH, Thomas Cooper   1854-1931
Painter. Born Kettering, Northamptonshire. Studied at Heatherley's and the Slade, and with Jean-Paul Laurens in Paris, 1880-3. He visited Newlyn, Cornwall, in 1881 where he married the painter, Caroline Yates, and they settled there in 1887. A founder member of the NEAC, he was influenced by Bastien-Lepage and favoured narrative subjects. President of the Royal British Colonial Society of Artists, 1913-28.

GOTLIB, Henryk   1890-1966
Painter. Born Cracow, Poland. Studied in Cracow, Munich and Paris. First solo exhibition held in Warsaw, 1918. In Cracow he became leader of the Polish avant-garde 'Formist' movement. 1938 married an Englishwoman and in 1939 found himself in England, an enforced exile. Exhibited in London but his popularity gradually declined and he became an isolated and lonely figure. A retrospective of his work was held at the Boundary Gallery, London, 1988. Represented in the Tate Gallery, Scottish National Gallery of Modern Art and elsewhere.

GOUGH, Paul   b.1958
Painter. Studied at Wolverhampton Polytechnic, 1976-9, and RCA, 1980-5, also at the Ecole des Beaux Arts, Metz, 1979 and Gray's School of Art, Aberdeen, 1982. Began exhibiting in 1979 and held his first solo exhibition in 1987 at the Derby Hall Art Gallery, Bury. Another was held at Waterman's, Brentford, 1988. Uses images from past warfare to explore present world tensions.

GOUK, Alan   b.1939
Painter. Born Belfast, Northern Ireland. Studied architecture part-time at Glasgow School of Art, 1957-9, and at Regent Street Polytechnic, 1959-60, and psychology and philosophy at Edinburgh University, 1961-4. 1964-7 worked as Fine Arts Exhibition Officer for British Council and travelled with exhibitions throughout Europe. 1967 became a lecturer at St. Martin's School of Art. 1969 and 1983 visited Morocco, and the USA in 1972 and 1981. 1967 first exhibited at John Moores Liverpool Exhibition at the Walker Art Gallery, Liverpool, where he was a prizewinner. 1986 first solo exhibition in London at Gallery One. Included in the collections of the Arts Council of Great Britain, Scottish Arts Council and the Calouste Gulbenkian Foundation. Gouk's central concern is the physical quality of paint and the way in which brushstrokes abut or blend into one. In the 1970s he abandoned acrylics for oils, using increasingly thick creamy paint. He has written extensively for contemporary art journals and is currently Head of Advanced Painting and Sculpture at St. Martin's School of Art.

GOVIER, Gordon   b.1946
Sculptor. Born Weston-super-Mare, Somerset. Studied at

HENRYK GOTLIB, 1890-1966. *'Nude by Garden Door'*, 1942. 30in. x 25in. Scottish National Gallery of Modern Art.

Hereford School of Art, 1962-4 and Wolverhampton College of Art, 1964-7. Has taught at Hereford College of Art. Began exhibiting in 1969, having his first solo show the following year at Nicholas Treadwell Gallery, London, where he has continued to exhibit.

GOWING, Lawrence   b.1918
Painter and art historian. Born Stamford Hill, London. Introduced to painting by a teacher at his school and given a letter of introduction to William Coldstream.* Joined Euston Road School and followed Coldstream's example producing works of great subtlety, lyricism and restraint. Enjoyed friendship with Adrian Stokes* and marriage to Julia Strachey, whom he painted. Taught at Camberwell School of Art, 1944-7 and from 1948 for ten years was Professor of Fine Art at King's College, University of Durham. 1959 became Principal of Chelsea School of Art and 1965-7 worked as Keeper of British Art and Deputy Director of the Tate Gallery, before taking up the Professorship at Leeds University, from whence he moved in 1975 to become Slade Professor of Fine Art at the University of London. His distinguished career as a teacher was paralleled by his publications which include books on Vermeer, Matisse and Lucian Freud, among other subjects. The penetrating subtlety of thought, found in his writings, has also made him a questing artist, his interests persistently developing, until he begun to use his own body as a kind of template in front of the picture surface, the pose adopted reminiscent of Vitruvian man. A

RIGBY GRAHAM, b.1931.
'Brighton Beach', 1979.
Watercolour. 10in. x 13¾in.
Private Collection.

retrospective of his work was held at the Serpentine Gallery, London, 1983, in which year he was also knighted.

Bibl: *Lawrence Gowing,* Arts Council cat., 1983.

GRAHAM, Brian   b.1945
Painter. Born Poole, Dorset. Studied at Bournemouth College of Art. Works as an art director with an advertising agency and has paintings in many private collections, including those owned by Lord Weymouth and Eton College.

GRAHAM, David   b.1926
Painter. Studied at Hammersmith School of Art, St. Martin's School of Art and RCA. Held first solo exhibition at the Guildhall Art Gallery, London, 1976. Others include an exhibition of recent work and 100 paintings of Israel at the Herbert Art Gallery, Coventry, 1987. Regular exhibitor at RA, Paris Salon and elsewhere and a member of the Royal Society of Portrait Painters. Represented in London Museum, Barbican and elsewhere.

GRAHAM, George   1882-1949
Painter. Born Leeds, Yorkshire. Studied for two years to become an architect, taking drawing lessons in the evenings at Leeds School of Art. Then studied at the London School of Art under Frank Brangwyn* and others. Developed a fascination with the Yorkshire Dales, where he lived during a large part of his life. A prolific exhibitor at both London and provincial exhibitions, he became a member of ROI, RI, RSW and RBA. Became President of the Society of Yorkshire Artists and secretary of the Society of Sussex Painters.

GRAHAM, Henry   b.1930
Painter. Trained at Liverpool College of Art. Elected to Liverpool Academy of Fine Art. Landscape is the subject that has primary importance in his life, together with a highly personal reaction to the insignia of modern life. In London he has exhibited at the Archer Gallery, the New Art Centre and the Portal Gallery.

GRAHAM, Rigby   b.1931
Painter and bibliophile. Born Stretford, Manchester. Studied at Leicester College of Art, 1947-54. First solo exhibition held at Gadsby Gallery, Leicester, 1963. He exhibited again in the same gallery, 1966, 1969, 1971 and 1974. His interest in the romantic landscape tradition, particularly in Graham Sutherland,* Paul Nash* and John Piper,* as well as John Minton,* has fed his work.

Bibl: *Rigby Graham,* Wymondham Art Gallery, Leicestershire, 1979.

GRAINGER, Esther
Painter. Studied at Cardiff School of Art. Taught art, and became a lecturer at Cardiff College of Education. First solo exhibition held at Newport Museum and Art Gallery, 1950. Others include one at Oriel, Cardiff, 1976. Represented in the Welsh Arts Council Collection.

GRAINGER, James   b.1956
Painter. His paintings are often humorous, playing on the sense of 'typical' British life. Illustrated *Vicarage Allsorts.* Exhibits with the Portal Gallery, London, where he first showed his work, 1977.

GRAINGER, Rowan   b.1936
Painter. Born Epsom, Surrey. On leaving school he spent two terms at Brighton College of Art before being called up for National Service in the Army where he trained as a tactical sketcher and attended evening classes at Farnham School of Art. Trained as an actor before returning to his original intention of becoming an artist and studied for a short time at the Bath Academy of Art. First solo exhibition held at Alwin Gallery, London, 1970. Also exhibits at RA, London Group and elsewhere.

KEITH GRANT, b.1930. *'Icebergs in Disko Bay, Ilulissat'*, 1990. 43in. x 60in. Private Collection.

GRANGER, Michael   b.1924
Painter. At first an apprenticed engineer at Rolls-Royce, Derby. 1942 he entered the Fleet Air Arm to serve as a pilot. 1946 began training as a painter at Derby College of Art and after four years, went to the University of London Institute of Education for one year. Became Head of the Art Department at the Herbert Strutt School, Belper. Exhibited regularly with the Midland Group of Artists.

GRANGER-TAYLOR, Nicolas   b.1963
Painter. Born London. Studied at Kingston Polytechnic, Bristol Polytechnic and RA Schools. First solo exhibition held at Cadogan Contemporary Art, London, 1988.

GRANT, Alistair   b.1925
Painter. Born London. Studied at Birmingham College of Art and RCA. Solo exhibitions at the Zwemmer Gallery, London, 1955-7. Also exhibits regularly at RA, London Group, RBA and elsewhere. Represented in V & A, Boston Library and elsewhere.

GRANT, Duncan   1885-1975
Painter. Born Rothiemurchus, Scotland, but spent his early childhood in India where his father's regiment was based. Studied at Westminster School of Art, whilst living in the home of his cousins, the Stracheys, and for a year, in 1907, under Jacques-Emile Blanche at La Palette, in Paris. Exposed to the French Post-Impressionists at Roger Fry's* two exhibitions of 1910 and 1912, he entered his most inventive period, in part indebted to his simultaneous admiration for Byzantine mosaics. 1913 became a director of Roger Fry's Omega Workshops and for the rest of his career frequently involved himself with decorative commissions. A pacifist during the First World War, he began his association with the house, Charleston, in

Sussex, while working as a farm labourer. A lifelong companion of Vanessa Bell,* he exhibited regularly, at the London Group, with the London Artists' Association and elsewhere. His decorative work includes murals for a chapel in Lincoln Cathedral and for Berwick Church, Sussex. A retrospective was held at the Tate Gallery, 1959. (Plate 7, p.23.)

Bibl: Richard Shone, *Bloomsbury Portraits*, Phaidon, 1976.

GRANT, Fiona M.   b.1948
Painter. Born Edinburgh, Scotland. Studied at Duncan of Jordanstone College of Art, Dundee. Has exhibited in the Scottish Young Contemporaries and held her first solo exhibition at New 57 Gallery, Edinburgh, 1972.

GRANT, James Ardern   1885-1973
Painter and printmaker. Born Liverpool, Merseyside. Studied at Liverpool School of Art where he subsequently taught, and at the Académie Julian, Paris. Exhibited at Liverpool Autumn Exhibitions, 1908-21. Member of the Sandon Studios Society, c.1912. Moved permanently to London after his marriage in 1913. Member of RP, RE and Vice-Principal of the LCC Central School of Arts and Crafts.

GRANT, Keith   b.1930
Painter. Born Liverpool, Merseyside. Studied at RCA. Since 1959 has held numerous exhibitions in England, Iceland, Italy and Norway. Major public commissions have included mosaic murals for Newcastle upon Tyne subway which were inaugurated by Her Majesty the Queen in 1981. The 1960s saw the beginning of his absorption with the far North, with the lands and seas beyond the Arctic Circle. Exhibits with the Francis Kyle Gallery, London.

GRANT, Ian Macdonald

DERRICK GREAVES, b.1927. *'Portrait of the artist's mother'*, 1978. Collage drawing on paper on canvas. 32in. x 66in. Sheffield City Art Galleries.

GRANT, Ian Macdonald   b.1904
Painter. Studied at Glasgow School of Art, 1922-6, in Paris, 1927, and at RCA, 1927-30. Exhibited at RA, RSA, RBA, with the NEAC and in the provinces. Specialised in portraiture and landscape.

GRAY, Douglas Stanning   1890-1959
Painter. Born London. Studied at art schools in Clapham and Croydon and then at RA Schools, where he came under the influence of John Singer Sargent.* Ignored all the modernist developments after Impressionism. Served in the Army during the First World War and was twice wounded. 1920 began exhibiting at the RA. Specialised in portraits and outdoor scenes. 1928 became a founder member of the London Portrait Society. 1933 elected a member of the Royal Society of Portrait Painters. A highly skilled artist, he remained one of the most distinguished of Sargent's followers.

GRAY, John   b.1942
Painter. Born Greenock, Scotland. Studied at Sutton and

Cheam School of Art, 1963-5, Guildford School of Art, 1965-7 and Hull College of Art, 1971-4. Solo exhibition held at Ferens Art Gallery, Hull, 1975.

GRAY, Joseph   1890-1963
Painter. Born South Shields, Tyne and Wear. Worked as an illustrator for the *Dundee Courier*. 1914 joined the 4th/5th Black Watch. Invalided out and afterwards worked for *The Graphic,* contributing war drawings. 1939-44 attached to the camouflage section of the Royal Engineers and Signals Board. A landscape artist who is represented in the British Museum, the V & A, the Imperial War Museum and elsewhere.

GRAY, Ken   b.1943
Electronic sculptor. Born London. 1961 started civil engineering. 1966 worked on marine survey and began to draw and paint. 1968 gave up civil engineering to study art, entered Brighton College of Art, 1969. 1970 began to use electronic components by incorporating them into paintings. 1972 held his first exhibition of electro-sculpture. Represented in Baroness Thyssen collection, Lausanne, Aberdeen Art Gallery and elsewhere.

GRAY, Reginald   b.1932
Painter. Born Dublin, Ireland. Studied at National College of Art, Dublin, and spent some time with Cecil ffrench-Salkeld studying Old Master techniques. 1956-8 worked in theatre design. 1958 moved to London. Represented in the City of York Art Gallery and elsewhere.

GRAY, Ronald   1868-1951
Painter. Born Chelsea, London. Studied at Westminster School of Art and at the Académie Julian in Paris. Visited America in 1908, 1909 and 1910. Exhibited with the NEAC; became a member 1923. Elected ARWS, 1934, and RWS, 1942. Influenced by P. Wilson Steer.*

GREAVES, Derrick   b.1927
Painter. Born Sheffield, Yorkshire. 1943-8 apprenticed as a sign-writer. 1948-52 studied at RCA. 1952-4 won Abbey Major Scholarship to study in Italy. 1953 held first solo exhibition at Beaux Arts Gallery, London, and another, 1955. Became known as one of the Beaux Arts Quartet, better known as the Kitchen Sink School, but he later exchanged the gritty realism of his early style for a more distilled form of image-making, closer in style to that of Patrick Caulfield* than any realist. His paintings are concise, subtle and often witty. His work is represented in many public collections at home and abroad.

Bibl: *Forty from Ten. Forty Pictures by Derrick Greaves, from the decade 1976-86,* Loughborough College of Art, 1986.

GREAVES, Walter   1846-1930
Painter. Born London, the son of a boatbuilder and waterman. Trained with his brother Henry as a shipwright. Met Whistler* in the early 1860s, and began helping him in his studio. In turn Whistler taught Walter and Henry to paint, and to move away from mimetic accuracy. A break in Greaves' friendship with Whistler did not prevent him continuing to revere his master, whose style and dress he continued to imitate. He haunted the streets of Chelsea trying to sell his work for a few shillings.

Bibl: *Walter Greaves and the Goupil Gallery,* Michael Parkin Fine Art Ltd., 1984.

ANTHONY GREEN, b.1939. *'Paradise'*, 1988. 82in. x 86½ in. Mayor Rowan Gallery.

GREBBY, Anne   b.1944
Painter. Born Lincoln. Studied at Birmingham and Hornsey College of Art and then at the British School in Rome. Has exhibited at the Paton Gallery, London, and elsewhere. Lives in Sheffield and currently Head of Painting and Printmaking at Sheffield City Polytechnic.

GREEN, Alan   b.1932
Painter. Born London. Studied at Beckenham School of Art, 1949-53. National Service, Korea and Japan, 1953-5. Studied at RCA, 1955-8. 1958-9 won RCA Major Travelling Scholarship to France and Italy. First solo exhibition held at AIA Gallery, London, 1963. Has exhibited regularly since then, at home and abroad, in solo and group exhibitions. Represented in Arts Council Collection and elsewhere. In the 1960s worked through collage, relief and assemblage to grid paintings, reaching, finally, flat, single colour abstracts. This process remains a part of his content; also displays a predilection for greys and blacks.

Bibl: *Alan Green: Recent Paintings and Drawings,* Juda Rowan Gallery, 1985.

GREEN, Alfred Rozelaar   b.1917
Painter. Born London, of Anglo-Dutch parentage. Studied at Central School in London and then Académie Julian and Gromaire's atelier in Paris. Founder of the Anglo-French Art Centre in London, 1946-51.

GREEN, Anthony   b.1939
Painter. Born London. 1947 first visit to France. Studied at Slade School of Fine Art, 1956-60. 1960-1 won French Government Scholarship to Paris. 1961 married Mary Cozens-Walker who has continued to appear in many of his paintings. 1964 elected member of the London Group. 1966 began exhibiting at RA. 1967-9 Harkness Fellowship to RA. 1971 elected ARA and 1977 RA. A figurative artist who uses shaped canvases and a fluctuating viewpoint which leaves the impression that we are floating over his richly detailed, bizarre scenes and looking at them from all angles.

GREEN, Barry   b.1940
Painter. Born Melbourne, Australia. 1957-61 studied art history, graphics and communication at the Royal

GREEN, John

PETER GREENHAM, b.1909. *'Sheridan Russell (or Portrait of an Old Man)'*. Private Collection.

Melbourne College of Art. 1961-70 worked in various design studios. 1970-1 travelled extensively in Europe and Asia and 1971 settled in Britain. Exhibits at RA and Piccadilly Gallery, London.

GREEN, John   b.1932
Sculptor. Born Suffolk. Apprenticed to a stonemason, 1946-51. Studied at Ipswich School of Art, 1951-4, and RCA, 1954-7. Has executed various commissions for public buildings and had a solo exhibition at the John Whibley Gallery, London, 1970.

GREEN, Margaret
Painter. Born West Hartlepool, Co. Durham. Studied at West Hartlepool School of Art and RCA, 1944-7. Exhibits at RA, NEAC, London Group and elsewhere. Represented in public art galleries in Carlisle, Coventry, Leeds and Nottingham. Solo exhibition at New Grafton Gallery, London, 1972.

GREEN, Paul   b.1951
Sculptor. Born Pontypridd, Wales. Studied at Maidstone College of Art, 1969, Cardiff College of Art, 1971-4, and Slade, 1974. Moved into making environmental sculpture and back to the producing of small sculpture. Solo exhibition at Oriel, Cardiff, 1975.

GREEN, Roland   1896-1972
Painter, etcher and illustrator. Born Rainham, Kent. Studied at Rochester School of Art and at Regent Street Polytechnic. Held many solo exhibitions, notably at Ackermann Galleries in Bond Street. Spent much time studying bird life and their flight patterns. Lived rather like a hermit, alone at Hickling Broad, Norfolk. Wrote and illustrated *How to Draw Birds* and *Wing Tips;* also illustrated books by other authors.

GREENBURY, Judith   b.1924
Painter. Born Bristol, Avon. Studied at West of England College of Art and Slade School of Fine Art. Elected ARWA 1970 and RWA 1979. Held her first solo exhibition at Postgraduate School, Oxford, 1966, and another at Forest Gate Gallery, London, 1981.

GREENGRASS, Sarah   b.1951
Painter. Trained at University of Newcastle upon Tyne and Chelsea School of Art. First solo exhibition 'The Child Within' held at Ikon Gallery, Birmingham, 1987. Began as an abstract artist but moved into figuration, using bold colour.

GREENHAM, Peter   b.1909
Painter. Studied at Byam Shaw School of Art and afterwards became a schoolmaster. Elected ARA 1951 and RA 1960 and became Keeper of the RA Schools. He was also for two years art critic of *The Scotsman*. Especially renowned for his portraits, he has painted Michael Ramsay, the former Archbishop of Canterbury and Dr. F.R. Lewis, among others. His paintings, which are quiet and restrained, are greatly admired by discriminating collectors.

Bibl: *Peter Greenham. Paintings and Drawings with Paintings by Jane Dowling,* Royal Academy, 1985.

GREENHAM, Robert   1906-1976
Painter. Born Streatham, London. Studied at Byam Shaw Art School and RA Schools. Elected ROI and RBA, 1931. In his early pictures he employed tempestuous handling; his later work had a calmer surface and more deliberate design. He specialised in paintings of the English seaside, executed with vigour and delight. An exhibition of his beach scenes was held at the Maclean Gallery, London, 1981.

GREENHILL, Mina
Painter. Born London. Studied painting and etching in Italy, 1921-2, and at Chelsea Art School, 1922-7, where she studied etching under Graham Sutherland.* Has exhibited at the RA, with the London Portrait Society and elsewhere. Had a solo exhibition at the Woodstock Gallery, London, 1966.

GREENWOOD, John Frederic   1885-1954
Painter and printmaker. Born Rochdale, Lancashire. Studied at Shipley and Bradford Art Schools, 1904-8, and at the RCA, 1908-11. Taught at various schools and colleges of art in Yorkshire. Elected ARE, 1922, RE, 1939 and RBA, 1940. Lived in Ilkley, Yorkshire and exhibited extensively abroad. Best known for his watercolours.

GREENWOOD, Robin   b.1950
Sculptor. Born Manchester. Studied at Wimbledon School of Art, 1968-71, and St. Martin's School of Art, 1971-2. 1978 won an Arts Council Major Award. 1976 first solo exhibition at P.M.J. Self Gallery, London. His work in the 1980s contributed to the re-evaluating of the human figure as a source for sculpture. His concern with three-dimensionality leads him to explore, in abstract terms, physical movement.

GREETHAM, Geoffrey   b.1934
Sculptor. Born Keighley, Yorkshire. Studied at Keighley School of Art and Camberwell School of Art. 1962-5 assistant to Henry Moore.* 1965-7 Sculpture Fellowship at Coventry College of Art. Solo exhibition at Drian Galleries, London, 1969.

GREG, Barbara   b.1900
Wood-engraver. Studied at the Slade, 1919-23, Central School of Art, 1921-3, and Westminster School of Art, 1926-7. Married the artist Norman Janes* and with him produced a number of wood engravings based on musical subjects for pianola rolls. Her wood engravings reflect an admiration for Thomas Bewick. Also produced book illustrations, watercolours and coloured lino cuts. Exhibited at principal London galleries from 1926. Elected ARE, 1940, and RE, 1946.

GREGSON, Stephen   b.1955
Painter. Studied at Croydon College of Art. Awarded the David Murray Scholarship by RA, 1976. First solo exhibition held at Hamster Gallery, Preston, 1979. Others include one at the Christopher Hull Gallery, London, 1983.

GREIFFENHAGEN, Maurice   1862-1931
Painter and illustrator. Born London. Studied at RA Schools where he won several prizes. First became well known as a magazine and book illustrator during the 1890s, working mainly in black and white. Later became a noted illustrator of H. Rider Haggard. Around 1900 portraiture took over from illustration. 1906-29 was head of the Life Department at Glasgow School of Art. 1886 member of the NEAC; 1916 elected ARA, and 1922 RA.

GRESTY, Hugh   1899-1958
Painter. Born Nelson, Lancashire. Studied at Goldsmiths' College. Specialised in architectural subjects and exhibited at the RA, RBA, RI and in the provinces. Elected RBA, 1927, RI, 1935.

GRIEVE, Peter   b.1936
Sculptor. Born London. Studied at Bromley College of Art, 1954-7 and RA, 1957-61. 1961-4 taught in Greece. First solo exhibition held at Richard Demarco Gallery, Edinburgh, 1972.

GRIEVE, Walter Graham   d.1937
Painter. Studied at the RSA Life School in Edinburgh and at the School of Board of Manufacturers. Exhibited chiefly in Scotland, also in Liverpool, London and on the Continent. Elected RSA, 1929.

GRIFFIN, Rachel   b.1962
Painter. Studied at St. Alban's College of Art and completed a course in Textile Design. Has had a one-artist exhibition at the Barbican Centre, London.

GRIFFIN-BERNSTORFF, Ann
Painter. Born Limerick, Ireland. Studied at the National College of Art, Ireland, and in Paris. Influenced by early Italian and North American portraits. Her figures are depicted with a gentle humour, and are often dreamy and nostalgic. Exhibits with the Portal Gallery, London. She held her first solo exhibition with the Portal Gallery, 1989, and has also exhibited in Ireland and Chicago.

FREDERICK LANDSEER GRIGGS, 1876-1938. 'The Almonry', 1925. Etching. 55½ in. x 23½ in. Garton & Co.

GRIFFITHS, Mike
Painter. Born London. Studied at Brighton Polytechnic. 1976 began exhibiting; 1979 held first solo exhibition at The Gallery, Brighton Polytechnic.

GRIGGS, Frederick Landseer   1876-1938
Printmaker. Born Hitchin, Hertfordshire. First became interested in etching in 1896. At first made perspective drawings for local architects, and in 1900 began to make drawings for Macmillan's *Highways and Byways* guide books, illustrating thirteen in all. 1903 moved to Chipping

GRIMM, Stanley

Camden in Gloucestershire. 1912 began to etch seriously, and in 1921 Colnaghi's became his publishers. Produced fifty-seven prints in all and was successful until the 1930s and the Depression years. His often fantastic inventions are characterised by formal severity. He also designed lettering, typefaces and book covers, and painted in watercolour. Before turning to art he had trained as an architect and executed small architectural commissions. The Wall Street crash in 1929 affected the print market, and he died in relative poverty. His work reflects a profound feeling for architecture, and an admiration for Samuel Palmer. 1922 elected ARA, and 1931 RA; was also a member of the Council of the Society for the Protection of Ancient Buildings.

GRIMM, Stanley 1891-1966
Painter. Born London. His father was of Baltic origin and his mother died shortly after his birth, as a result he was brought up by his father's family in Riga, Latvia. Tradition has it that his family was connected with the Brothers Grimm. 1911 went to Munich to study art. 1918 he returned to Russia and was soon painting posters and decorations for the first anniversary of the October Revolution. Settled finally in London, in Chelsea, and exhibited extensively at many London galleries, including the Redfern, the Beaux Arts and Wertheim.

GRIMSHAW, Reginald b.1910
Painter. Born Farsley, Yorkshire. Studied at Pudsey School of Art, 1927-30, Leeds College of Art, 1930-1, and at the RCA, 1931-4. Exhibited at the RA, RBA and elsewhere. Became Head of Oxford School of Art.

GRIMWOOD, Brian b.1948
Illustrator. Born Beckenham, Kent. Studied graphics at Bromley Technical High School, 1961-4. Solo exhibitions at Thumb Gallery, London, 1978 and 1980. Specialises in comic drawings of animals which reflect human behaviour.

GRINLING, Anthony Gibbons 1896-1982
Sculptor. Born Stanmore, Middlesex. Educated at Harrow, where he won the art prize. After the First World War he went to Taormina, Sicily, to recuperate from the effects of gas, and studied carving and modelling with Lipari, 1919-20. On returning to England, he was obliged to work in the family firm, but continued to make sculpture, often working closely with the architect Serge Chermayeff. Commissions include garden statues for Queen Mary's Doll's House, 1924, a bas-relief for the Cambridge Theatre, 1930, and a room of tubular steel sculpture and furniture for Whiteley's, 1934. First solo exhibition at Tooth's, London, 1934. Exhibited at RA from 1946.

GROOM, Jon b.1953
Painter. Born Powys, Wales. Studied at Cardiff College of Art, 1971-2 and 1974-6, Sheffield Polytechnic, 1972-3, and Chelsea School of Art 1976-7. 1978 first solo exhibition at Riverside Studios, also at Rochdale Art Gallery, 1983, Ruth Siegal Gallery, New York 1985. Fellow in Painting at Gloucester College of Art and Design since 1977. Recent solo exhibitions include those at Nicola Jacobs Gallery, London, 1983, 1986 and 1988.

GROSS, Anthony 1905-1984
Painter and etcher. Born Dulwich, London, of Anglo-Hungarian parentage. Began etching in 1921 and

throughout that decade travelled extensively in Europe. Became an Official War Artist during the Second World War and held a solo exhibition at the National Gallery, London. Regular exhibitor in galleries at home and abroad. His style is characterised by wit and invention, for tone and texture are created by variegated marks rather than by cross-hatching. In 1955 he bought a house in France, in the Lot department, and went there regularly to paint. 1968 held a retrospective exhibition at V & A. 1971 he was the subject of a BBC film, *A Printmaker's Workshop,* by John Read.

GUEVARA, Alvaro 1894-1951
Painter. Born Chile. Arrived in England in 1910 and attended Bradford Technical College, evening classes at Bradford School of Art and then won scholarships to the Slade, where he studied, 1912-15, during one of its most brilliant periods. 1916 exhibited at Roger Fry's* Omega Workshops and became a close friend of Edith Sitwell around this time. 1926 was elected a member of the NEAC. 1930 moved to France, after marrying the Irish painter Meraud Guinness (see Meraud Guevara*) in 1929, and remained there until the German invasion. Arrested in 1941 and returned to Chile. Fascinated by boxers, swimming pools and characterful women.

Bibl: Diana Holman-Hunt, *Latin among Lions: a Biography of Alvaro Guevara,* London, 1975.

GUEVARA, Meraud b.1904
Painter. Born Meraud Guinness. Married the Chilean painter Alvaro Guevara* in 1929 in London, and went to live with him in France. Her parents were not delighted by the marriage of their society daughter to a Bohemian painter who was also a boxer. Painted strong simple compositions of still lifes and portraits, often with animals. Lived and worked in Paris and Provence during the 1930s to 1950s. Solo exhibition at the Ohan Gallery, 1959, when she showed some abstract paintings on a plaster base. Works in the Tate Gallery, along with a portrait of her by Alvaro Guevara, painted 1930.

GUINSBERG, Ilona
Painter. Born Johannesburg, South Africa. Studied at Witswatersrand, Johannesburg. 1973 emigrated to England. 1976-8 worked for the Arts Council, while running her own Contemporary Graphics company. 1978-85 she worked as Research Assistant to Sir Lawrence Gowing* at the Slade. 1983-6 she founded and ran the Friends of the Slade, UCL. 1982 won the Richard Ford Award to study paintings in Spain. 1979 first exhibited at Ben Uri Gallery, London. Commissioned to illustrate *African Folk Tales* in 1989.

GUNN, Herbert James 1893-1964
Painter. Born Glasgow, Scotland. Studied at Glasgow School of Art, Edinburgh College of Art and at the Académie Julian in Paris under J.P. Laurens. Exhibited at RA, RSA, Paris Salon and elsewhere. Elected ARA, 1953, and RA, 1961. 1953-4 painted the State Portrait of HM the Queen. Knighted.

GUTHRIE, James 1859-1930
Painter. Born Greenock, Scotland. Painted with Walton and Crawhall* in 1879 and studied with John Pettie in London. His conversion to French painting came from the French art he saw in London and a trip to Paris in 1882. Guthrie's adventurous use of pastel was admired by the

London impressionists. Worked for a period at the artists' colony at Cockburnspath, afterwards living in Glasgow, then London and finally Edinburgh. Elected ARSA, 1888, RSA, 1892 and PRSA, 1902-19. Knighted in 1903.

GUTHRIE, James Joshua   1874-1952

Painter and illustrator. Born Glasgow, Scotland. Studied at Heatherley's School of Art and with the British Museum Students' Group while working in the family firm in London. An artist of diverse talents, he produced paintings, illustrations, book and bookplate designs, etchings and wood engravings. He played a significant role in the revival of the latter, and in the development of private presses. His characteristic graphic style has been described by John Russell Taylor as 'a sort of folk-weave art nouveau'. Exhibited at the Arts and Crafts Society, the IS and at the Barcelona International Exhibition.

GUTHRIE, Kathleen   b.1905

Painter. Born Feltham, Middlesex, née Maltby. Studied at Slade School, 1921-3, and RA Schools, 1923-6. Exhibited at RA and with the London Group and held several solo exhibitions. Married Robin Guthrie* in 1927 and, after a divorce, remarried in 1941. Signed her early work 'K. Maltby', using 'Kathleen Guthrie' from 1927 onwards.

GUTHRIE, Robin   1902-71

Painter. Born Hastings, Sussex, son of James Guthrie.* Studied at Slade School, 1918-22. Began exhibiting at NEAC, 1923; became a member, 1928. From 1931 exhibited at RA. 1931-3 Director of the Boston Museum School of Fine Arts, USA. 1951-4 taught at St. Martin's School of Art and RCA.

GUY, Alexander   b.1962

Painter. Born St. Andrews, Scotland. Studied at Duncan of Jordanstone College of Art, Dundee, 1980-4 and RCA, 1985-7. 1986 first solo exhibition at Seagate Gallery, Dundee, followed in 1987 by a solo exhibition in Aberdeen. Since 1983 represented in group exhibitions in Scotland and England. 1984-5 awarded first prize in 'Scottish Young Contemporaries'. Represented in the Scottish Arts Council Collection, Peoples Palace, Glasgow and in the collections of Dundee College of Art and Cambridge University.

GWYNNE-JONES, Allan   1892-1982

Painter. Born Richmond, Surrey. Initially qualified as a solicitor, but also began to paint in watercolour in 1912. Served in the Welsh Guards during the First World War. Wounded twice and awarded DSO, 1916. Afterwards studied at the Slade, 1919-22. Joined the RCA, 1923 and became Professor of Painting. During the 1920s he produced a number of etchings of rural subjects but is best known for his portraits and still lifes painted in an undemonstrative style but which achieved great intensity. 1930 moved to Slade School where he taught until 1958.

ARTHUR HACKNEY, b.1925.
'Winter orchard with stone wall'.
Gouache. 30in. x 24in.
Private Collection.

HACKER, Arthur   1858-1919
Painter. Born London. Studied at the RA Schools, 1876-81, and at Bonnat's in Paris, 1880-1. A founder member of the NEAC he, like others, was influenced by Bastien-Lepage, but later abandoned his naturalistic style for historical, mythological and symbolist themes. Exhibited at the RA from 1878. Elected ARA, 1894, and RA, 1910.

HACKER, John   b.1936
Painter. Born London. Studied at Kingston School of Art, 1958-61, and RCA, 1961-4. 1965 spent a year in Egypt, working on drawings of a temple in Luxor for the Oriental Institute, Chicago University. Various teaching jobs followed. Solo exhibitions include one at Achim Moeller Limited, London, 1975.

HACKNEY, Alfred   b.1926
Painter and printmaker. Born Stainforth, Yorkshire. Brother of Arthur Hackney.* Studied at Burslem School of Art, at Edinburgh College of Art and, with the help of a travelling scholarship, in France and Italy. Exhibited at principal exhibition venues in London and Scotland. Elected ARE, 1951.

HACKNEY, Arthur   b.1925
Painter. Born Stainforth, Yorkshire. Brother of Alfred Hackney.* Studied at Burslem School of Art and RCA. 1949 awarded a travelling scholarship and studied for a year in France and Italy. 1942-6 served in Royal Navy. 1951 began teaching at Farnham School of Art. Exhibited regularly in London and abroad. Elected ARE, 1948, ARWS, 1950, RWS, 1957 and RE, 1960. Represented in the V & A, Nottingham Art Gallery and elsewhere.

HADDELSEY, Vincent   b.1934
Illustrator. Born Grimsby, Lincolnshire. In 1952 left for Canada and spent many years in British Columbia.

Developed an enduring passion for horses. Solo exhibition held at Usher Gallery, Lincoln, 1985.

Bibl: *Haddelsey's Horses*, St. Martin's Press, NY, Jonathan Cape, London, 1978; *The Horse — Our Heritage*, Niggli, 1969.

HADDOCK, Aldridge   b.1931
Painter. Born Co. Durham. Began his career as a fighter pilot in RAF and saw active service in France and Germany. At the age of twenty-six took up medicine and practised in Grimsby. Was self-taught as a painter. Held several solo exhibitions, in the Midlands, London and New York. Represented in Preston Art Gallery, Wakefield City Art Gallery, Sheffield City Art Galleries and elsewhere.

HADFIELD, Tim   b.1953
Painter. Born Lincoln. Studied at Ravensbourne College of Art, 1971-2, Hornsey College of Art, 1972-5, Chelsea School of Art, 1975-6, and Royal Academy of Fine Arts, The Hague, 1976-7. 1977 first solo exhibition held at Royal Academy of Fine Arts, The Hague. 1988 most recent solo show held at New Art Centre, London, in which the signal feature was the illusionistic representation of raw materials.

HAGEDORN, Karl   b.1889
Painter. Born Berlin, Germany. Moved to England, 1905 and adopted British nationality, 1914, served in the British army during the First World War. Studied at Manchester, Slade School and in Paris. Exhibited at the RA, RBA and with the NEAC. 1925 received the Grand Prix at the International Exhibition of Decorative Art, Paris. 1935 elected RBA.

HAGGAR, Reginald George   b.1905
Painter. Studied at Ipswich Art School, 1920-6, and at the RCA, 1926-9. Exhibited at the RA, RSA, RWA and elsewhere. 1945 became President of the Society of Staffordshire artists. 1952 elected RI.

CHRISTOPHER HALL, b.1930.
'Kwai's Shop, Bootle', 1976.
13in. x 15in.
Private Collection.

HAGGER, Brian   b.1935
Painter. Born Bury St. Edmunds, Suffolk. Studied at Ipswich School of Art, 1952-6, and RCA, 1958-61. Worked for a period as studio assistant to William Scott.* Had four solo exhibitions at the Bramante Gallery, London, and then moved to the Thackeray Gallery, London. Specialises in urban landscapes.

HAIG, The Earl George Alexander Eugene Douglas   b.1918
Painter. Born Kingston Hill, Surrey. Educated at Christ Church, Oxford. 1939-42 served MEF with Royal Scots Greys. 1942-5 prisoner-of-war in Italy and Germany. 1945-7 studied at Camberwell School of Art. Has sat on numerous committees and held dozens of solo exhibitions, at the Scottish Gallery, Edinburgh, 1945-88.

HAILE, Sam   1909-1946
Painter. Attended evening classes at Clapham School of Art, and then won a scholarship to the RCA, 1931-5. Trained first as a painter, then under Staite Murray in the Pottery School. He first achieved fame as a potter, using shapes closely related to the organic forms in his paintings. The latter, though indebted to surrealist theory and practice, remained a more private activity. Experimented with automatist drawing and communicated his preoccupation with sexuality, suffering, violence and the threat of Fascism. Killed in a car accident

Bibl: *Sam Haile*, Birch and Conran, London, 1987.

HAILSTONE, Bernard   1910-1987
Painter. Studied at Goldsmiths' School of Art and the RA Schools. At outbreak of Second World War he joined the Auxiliary Fire Service and did portraits of his comrades as well as scenes of the Blitz. 1941 made an official war artist and was attached to the Ministry of Transport. 1944 went to South-East Asia to paint Lord Mountbatten and key members of his staff. He became President of the Royal Society of Portrait Painters.

HALE, Kathleen   b.1898
Painter and lithographer. Born Broughton, Scotland. Studied at Manchester School of Art, Reading University, 1915-17, Central School of Arts and Crafts, 1928-30 and at the East Anglian School of Painting and Drawing under Cedric Morris,* 1938. Exhibited with the NEAC, the London Group and elsewhere. Wrote and illustrated many children's books, including *The Marmalade Cat*.

HALL, Adrian   b.1943
Painter. Born Cornwall. Studied at Plymouth College of Art, 1959-63, RCA, 1964-7, and Yale University, 1967-9. 1971-3 artist in residence, University of Auckland, New Zealand. 1967 first solo exhibition held; others include one at the Felicity Samuel Gallery, London, and another at Project Gallery, Dublin, 1978.

HALL, Christopher   b.1930
Painter. Studied at Slade School of Art. First solo exhibition held at Arthur Jeffress Gallery, London, 1958. Others include six at the New Grafton Gallery, London. Often paints the back streets of towns such as Reading, Bristol and Maryport. Represented in the London Museum, the National Library of Wales and elsewhere.

NIGEL HALL, b.1943. *'Turkish Leaf'*, 1988. Cast bronze (unique). 75 ½ in. x 43in. x 34in. Annely Juda Fine Art.

HALL, Clifford   1904-1973
Painter. Born London. Studied at Richmond Art School and Putney Art School, 1922-5, and RA Schools, 1926-7. 1928-9 lived in Paris and studied under André L'Hôte. 1935 held first solo exhibition at Beaux Art Gallery. Worked with a stretcher party during the Second World War. Exhibited regularly at Roland, Browse and Delbanco, the Anthony d'Offay Gallery and elsewhere. Represented in Bradford City Art Gallery, V & A, London Museum, Imperial War Museum and elsewhere.

HALL, Fergus   b.1947
Painter. Born Paisley, Scotland. Studied at Glasgow School of Art. His father's work as a scenic artist enabled him to become familiar with the colourful atmosphere of the theatre from an early age. His paintings highlight a fascination with the bizarre and curious, displayed in a fantasy world. Regularly exhibits with the Portal Gallery, London.

HALL, Frederick   1860-1948
Painter. Born Shillington, Yorkshire. Studied at Lincoln School of Art, 1879-81, and Antwerp Academy of Fine Arts under Charles Verlat, 1882-3. Returned to London and exhibited at the RSBA, the Grosvenor Gallery, the New Gallery and the NEAC, from which he resigned, 1890. He exhibited regularly at the RA. 1884-97 lived in Newlyn, Penzance, then moved to various places but in 1911 settled near Newbury, Berkshire, where he remained for the rest of his life. 1921-32 commissioned by the commerical printers, Thomas Forman and Sons, Nottingham, to paint country scenes for reproduction.

HALL, Nigel   b.1943
Sculptor. Born Bristol, Avon. Studied at West of England College of Art, Bristol, 1960-4 and RCA, 1964-7. 1967-9 Harkness Fellowship. 1967 first solo exhibition held at Galerie Givaudan, Paris. Numerous solo exhibitions followed, including one at Annely Juda Fine Art, London, 1987. Works in metal using abstract forms.

HALL, Oliver   1869-1957
Painter and printmaker. Born Tulse Hill, London. As a boy he copied magazine illustrations, some of which gained him entry to the RCA where he studied, 1887-90. Later attended evening classes at Lambeth and Westminster Schools of Art. Much influenced by the Liverpool painter, Daniel Alexander Williamson, and spent some months working with him at Williamson's home in Broughton in Furness, Cumbria. Travelled England in search of subjects to paint, journeying also to Spain, Italy and France. From 1890 exhibited at RA, and 1895 elected RE (re-elected 1926), also ARA, 1920 and RA, 1927. 1898 held his first solo exhibition at the Dowdeswell Gallery, London. Father of Claude Muncaster.*

HALL, Patrick   b.1906
Painter. Born York. Specialises in watercolours of landscapes and town scenes. Exhibited at the RA, with the NEAC, in the provinces and with the Marjorie Parr Gallery, and Montpelier Gallery, London. Has painted many Suffolk views. (Plate 46, p.246.)

HALL, Patrick   b.1935
Painter. Born Tipperary, Ireland. Studied at Chelsea School of Art, 1958-9, and Central School of Art, 1959-60. 1980 first solo exhibition held at Lincoln Gallery, Dublin; others include one at the Hendriks Gallery, Dublin, 1987. Has based a group of work on 'The Flaying of Marsyas', taking a view of love and cruelty influenced in part by the severe years he spent in Spain. Appointed member of Aosdana by the Irish State in 1982 for his 'outstanding contribution to the arts in Ireland'. Represented in the collections of the Irish Arts Council, Hugh Lane Municipal Gallery of Modern Art, Dublin and in the National Institute of Higher Education, Limerick.

Bibl: Andrew Brighton, *Heart and Other Recent Paintings by Patrick Hall,* Aidan Dunne, London; *Life Lines: the Paintings of Patrick Hall,* Pentonville Gallery, London, 1987.

HALL, Sharon   b.1954
Painter. Born Darlington, Co. Durham. Studied at Coventry Polytechnic, 1976-9, and at the Slade, 1979-81. Awards include the Jeremy Cubitt Prize, the Sir James Knott Scholarship and a French government scholarship, 1981. 1984 she won two GLA awards; 1983 first solo exhibition at the Lanchester Gallery, Coventry followed by a second solo exhibition at the Angela Flowers Gallery, London, 1988.

HALLÉ, William   b.1912
Painter. Born Richmond. His mother was a direct

descendant of Sir Peter Lely, court painter to Charles II. A book of reproductions in a public library confirmed his desire to become a painter. Working visits to South Africa. First solo exhibition at the Alder Gallery, Johannesburg. Three at Wildenstein's, London and four at the O'Hana Gallery, London, the last in 1962.

HALPERN, Henia
Painter and sculptor. Born Poland and educated in Vienna. A teacher by profession, she began to paint and sculpt in 1952, remaining, by temperament and conviction, a primitive artist. Exhibits with the Women's International Art Club.

HALSEY, Mark   b.1961
Painter. Born Hull, Yorkshire. Studied at Hull College of Higher Education, 1980-7. 1983 began exhibiting and held a solo exhibition at Posterngate Gallery, Hull, 1985. His images often concern a central solitary figure.

HALT, Christine   b.1954
Constructivist. Born London. Studied at Ravensbourne College of Art and Slade School, 1975-80. 1987 GLA artist in school residency. 1986 first solo exhibition held at Exhibiting Space, London; another held at Annely Juda Fine Art, London, 1988.

HAMANN, Paul   1891-1973
Portaitist. Born Hamburg, Germany. Studied at the Arts and Crafts School in Hamburg and with Rodin in Paris. 1914-18 served in the First World War. Married the painter Hilde Guttman. 1926-33 worked in the artists' colonies of Worpswede and Breitenbachplatz, and was a member of the 'Hamburg Sezession'. 1919-33 President of the Kunstlerfest, Hamburg. Late 1920s began producing 'life masks' of personalities in British and European cultural life. 1933 emigrated to Paris. 1936 moved to London. Established a private art school with his wife. 1938 founder member of FDKB (Free German League of Culture). 1940 interned in Isle of Man. Member of the Hampstead Artists Council.

HAMBLING, Maggi   b.1945
Painter. Born Suffolk. Studied with Arthur Lett-Haines* and Cedric Morris* at the East Anglia School of Painting and Drawing, 1960-2, Camberwell, 1962-7, and Slade, 1967-9. 1969 won Boise Travel Award to New York. 1987 first solo exhibition held. 1980-1 was the first artist in residence at the National Gallery, London. Has exhibited widely and was given a solo exhibition at Serpentine Gallery, 1987. A figurative artist who uses expressionist colour and handling, she has also made a reputation with her portraits of Max Wall, Dorothy Hodgkin, A.J.P. Taylor and others. (Plate 47, p.246.)

Bibl: *Maggi Hambling: Paintings, Drawings and Watercolours*, Serpentine Gallery, London, 1987.

HAMER, Christopher   b.1953
Painter. Born Lancashire. Studied at Rochdale College of Art, 1970-2, Maidstone College of Art, 1972-5, and University of Reading, 1975-7. 1977-8 Gloucestershire College of Art Painting Fellowship. Establishes a dialogue between the squares, triangles and rectangles he uses and the structural shape of the stretcher.

HAMILTON, James Whitelaw   1860-1932
Painter. Born Glasgow, Scotland. Studied in Glasgow and in Paris, in the studios of Dagnan-Bouveret and Aime Morot. Mostly exhibited in Scotland, but showed also in London and abroad. 1897 won Gold Medal at the Munich International Exhibition. Elected ARSA, 1911, and RSA, 1922. Mostly found his landscape settings around his home at Helensburgh in Dumbartonshire, also on the east coast of Scotland. Became Governor of the Glasgow School of Art.

HAMILTON, Patrick   b.1923
Painter. Born Kent. Educated at Wellington College and Cambridge. 1939-45 active service in Royal Navy. After the war joined British Petroleum and later went into publishing. Began drawing seriously at the age of forty-five. Moved to Florence and studied under Signorina Simi, to whom he dedicated a published book of his drawings. Exhibits at the King Street Galleries, St. James's, London.

HAMILTON, Richard   b.1922
Painter and printmaker. Born London. Left school at fourteen and worked in advertising, attending evening classes at St. Martin's School of Art and Westminster Technical College. Studied at RA Schools, 1938-40, leaving to do war service as an engineering draughtsman. Returned to RA Schools 1946 and was expelled. Studied at Slade School of Art, 1948-51. 1953 began teaching at the University of Newcastle. 1952 a founder member of the Independent Group at the ICA, his contribution to 'This is Tomorrow' exhibition at the Whitechapel Art Gallery in 1956 heralded the Pop Art movement. Since then his work, both in content and method, has investigated modern processes, culture and styling. Has reconstructed Duchamp's *Large Glass* and, on occasion, collaborated with Dieter Roth. He published *Collected Works 1953-1982* in 1982, and in 1983 collaborated with Rita Donagh* on an exhibition based on the Maze Prison at the Orchard Gallery, Londonderry.

Bibl: *Richard Hamilton*, with essay and cat. by Richard Morphet, Tate Gallery, 1970.

HAMMERSCHLAG, Alice Berger   1917-1969
Painter. Born Vienna, Austria. Studied at Vienna Academy of Arts and the Kunstgewerbeschule. Moved to Belfast, Northern Ireland. Member of the Women's International Art Club and the Free Painters and Sculptors, London. Her early canvases were reminiscent of the work of the German artist, Feininger, with their use of facets. As her interest in abstract art developed, she used light structures and sound rhythms as the subject of her art. 1959 first solo exhibition at the New Vision Centre Gallery, London. Others include shows at the Dawson Gallery, Dublin, 1965 and 1968. A retrospective was held at the Arts Council Gallery, Belfast, 1970.

HAMMOND, Geoffrey   b.1938
Painter. Born Kent. Studied at Goldsmiths' College and became Head of a Remedial Department at a large primary school. Exhibited at the Furneaux Gallery, Wimbledon, and the Gallery Vincitore, Brighton, and held his first solo show at the Woodstock Gallery, London, 1968.

HAMNETT, Nina   1890-1956
Painter. Born Tenby, Wales. Studied at several art schools in Dublin, the Pelham School in South Kensington and the London School of Art, while her family moved around due to her father's military career. Set up by herself in a studio in Grafton Street, 1911. Joined Roger Fry's* Omega

LIAM HANLEY, b.1933.
'Top Road, Reed Joint', 1988.
12in. x 16½in.
Private Collection.

Workshop, 1913 and under its aegis painted murals for a London flat, 1916. Taught drawing part-time at the Westminster Technical Institute in 1919 on the recommendation of Walter Sickert.* Moved to Paris in 1919 and acted as unofficial artistic ambassador between London and Paris until the 1930s. Painted penetrating portraits of the artistically famous, e.g. Sickert, Edith Sitwell, Poulenc, W.H. Davies, Anthony Powell, Lytton Strachey and Roger Fry. Illustrated Osbert Sitwell's book, *The People's Album of London Statues* in 1928. Wrote two volumes of autobiography, *Laughing Torso*, published 1932, and *Is She a Lady?*, published 1955. Exhibited in mixed exhibitions from 1913 until the 1940s, when her gift for anecdote, fuelled by drink, took over from her painting. Crucial member of the social life of Soho in the 1940s and 1950s. Solo exhibition of watercolours at the Independent Gallery, 1921.

Bibl: Denise Hooker, *Nina Hamnett: Queen of Bloomsbury*, Constable, London, 1986; Teresa Grimes, Judith Collins, Oriana Baddeley, *Five Women Painters*, A Channel 4 Book, 1989.

HAMPER, Nicholas   b.1956
Painter. Born Chatham, Kent. Studied at Slade School of Art, 1975-9 and RCA, 1980-2. 1983-4 travelled in Australia. 1984 first solo exhibition at Rex Irwin Gallery, Sydney; another held at Fischer Fine Art, London, 1985.

HANLEY, Liam   b.1933
Painter. Born London, son of novelist James Hanley. Studied briefly at Central School of Art but is largely self-taught. Held first solo exhibition in 1962 at the Royal Society of Arts. Others include regular shows at the Thackeray Gallery in London, the Phoenix Gallery in London, Kingston and Lavenham, and at Abbot Hall, Kendal. His landscapes have a clarity and precision that is distinctive.

HARCOURT, George   1868-1947
Painter. Born Dumbartonshire, Scotland. Exhibited at leading exhibition venues in London from 1893, also at the Paris Salon where he won a gold medal, 1923. Elected ARA, 1919, RA, 1926.

HARDAKER, Charles   b.1934
Painter. Born Oxford. Studied at Birmingham College of Arts and Crafts and at RCA, becoming an Associate. Primarily a landscape and still life painter, but also does commissioned portraits. Exhibits at RA, the Royal Society of Portrait Painters and NEAC. Represented in Tate Gallery and elsewhere.

HARDIE, Gwen   b.1962
Painter and sculptor. Born Fife, Scotland. Trained at Edinburgh College of Art, 1979-84, and in West Berlin on a DAAD annual art scholarship, 1984-5. Soon after arriving in Berlin she was advised by Georg Baselitz to abandon her studied and precise depictions of the human figure for more liberated, dynamic means of representation. She subsequently produced a series of works based on elements of her own body, applying paint, not with a brush, but a sponge in order to hinder any tendency to bravura technique. 1984 held first solo exhibition at Main Fine Art, Glasgow. Solo exhibition at Fischer Fine Art, 1990. Has work in Metropolitan Museum, New York, British Council Collection and other public collections.

Bibl: *Gwen Hardie. Paintings and Drawings*, The Fruitmarket Gallery, Edinburgh, 1987.

HARDIE, James   b.1938
Painter. Born Motherwell, Scotland. Studied at Glasgow School of Art, 1955-9. 1968-80 lectured at Aberdeen College of Education. 1970 started flying. Since 1980 lecturer at Glasgow School of Art. 1961 first solo exhibition held at Blythswood Gallery, Glasgow; others include one at the Compass Gallery, Glasgow, 1988.

GWEN HARDIE, b.1962. *'Coupling'*, 1988.
Acrylic. 78¾in. x 78¾in.
Fischer Fine Art Ltd.

JAMES HARDIE, b.1938. *'Brooklyn
Bridge Study — Fear of Flying'*.
Compass Gallery, Glasgow.

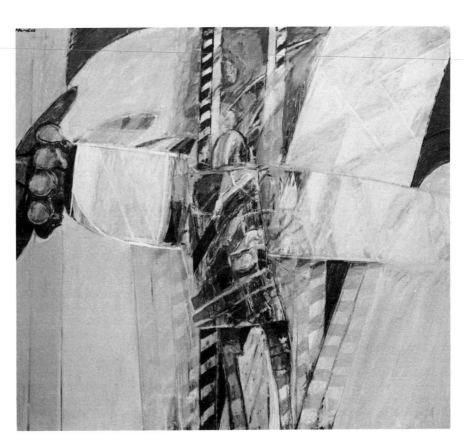

HARDIE, Martin   1875-1952
Painter and curator. Born London, nephew of Charles Martin Hardie, the Scottish painter, and also of John Pettie, RA, in whose studio he spent many hours of his youth. Educated at Cambridge, after which he joined the staff of the V & A. His own watercolours have, according to James Laver, 'a curious tranquillity, an inward peace'. He rarely drew figures, concentrating on the landscapes he found when travelling abroad. Had an informed grasp of technique and became a master of evanescent effects. Wrote many books including *Water-colour Painting in Britain.* Created CBE, 1935.

HARDING, David   b.1944
Painter. Born Bath, Avon. Studied at High Wycombe School of Art, 1961-5 and Slade, 1965-7. Has exhibited widely in group shows and has taught at Bath College of Higher Education since 1972.

HARDING, Robert   b.1957
Painter. Born London. Studied at Salisbury School of Art, 1973-6 and Camberwell, 1976-9. Has exhibited in various group exhibitions in London since 1984, and at John Moores, 1982 and 1987.

HARDY-HENRION, Daphne
Sculptor. Studied in Holland and at RA Schools, where she won a Gold Medal. 1946 solo exhibition at Beaux Arts Gallery, London. Exhibited at RA and with Women's International Art Club. Produced a nine-foot-high statue for 1951 South Bank Exhibition and a 'Tobias and the Angel' for a St. Albans Primary School. Another solo exhibition held at AIA Gallery, London, 1957.

HARLING, Simon   b.1950
Painter. Studied graphic design at London College of Printing. After working three years as a designer and illustrator in a publishing house, he decided to become a full-time landscape painter. Exhibits at Portal Gallery, London.

HARMAN, Gill   b.1928
Painter. Studied at King's College, Newcastle. Has taught part-time in H.M. Prison, Durham, for the Durham University Extra-Mural Board. Has exhibited in London and the provinces. Solo exhibitions include one at the University of Hull, 1967.

HARMAN, Rod   b.1942
Painter. Studied at Brighton College of Art and RCA. Teaches at Hastings College of Further Education. 1979 solo exhibition at Woodlands Art Gallery, London, of work based on burial and requiem themes.

HARMAR, Fairlie (Viscountess Haberton)   d.1945
Painter. Born Weymouth, Dorset. Entered the Slade School, 1894. Became a member of NEAC, 1917. Exhibited at the Lefevre Gallery, London. 1933 married the 7th Viscount Haberton. Represented in Tate Gallery and elsewhere.

HARPLEY, Sydney   b.1927
Sculptor. Studied at Hammersmith School of Art, 1950-3 and RCA, 1953-6. Elected RA. His portrait bust commissions include the Rt. Hon. Edward Heath and H.S.H. Prince Albert of Monaco. Exhibits at RA, RSA and elsewhere.

HARRIGAN, Claire   b.1964
Painter. Born Kilmarnock, Scotland. Studied at Glasgow School of Art, 1982-6. 1988 first solo exhibition at the Macaulay Gallery, Stenton.

HARRIS, Alfred   b.1930
Painter and collagist. Born London. Studied at Willesden School of Art, 1947-9 and RCA, 1950-2. Has exhibited at the Beaux Arts, Ben Uri, Grosvenor, New Art Centre and Prospect Galleries in London and was awarded the Amy Drucker Prize, 1955.

Bibl: *Alfred Harris: ten years in retrospect,* Bedford Way Gallery, University of London Institute of Education, 1979, with preface by Pierre Rouve.

HARRIS, Anthony   b.1931
Painter. Studied at Reading University part-time, 1946-8, and full-time, 1948-53. Studied art history at Courtauld Institute of Art, 1954-5. Became Principal of St. Albans School of Art, 1967-75, and Vice-Principal of Chelsea School of Art, 1975-86. 1982 elected Master of the John Ruskin Guild of St. George. 1986 appointed head of Camberwell School of Art and Crafts and Assistant Rector of the London Institute. Has exhibited widely, in London, the provinces and in Italy.

HARRIS, Charles
Painter. Studied at Epsom College of Art and Design, 1970-1, Hammersmith College of Art, 1971-4 and RA Schools, 1977-83. Winner of various prizes including the David Murray Scholarship in Landscape Painting. Exhibits at RA and with most professional exhibiting societies.

HARRIS, Edwin   1891-1961
Painter. Born Sussex and lived in the country almost all his life. A landscape artist in tempera and watercolour who is especially associated with West Sussex. Exhibited at RA, RI, RSBA and elsewhere. His work has been reproduced by the Medici Society, Raphael Tuck and Eyre and Spottiswoode. Represented in Hove, Newport and Worthing Art Galleries. Also a first-class cricketer who played for his home town of Littlehampton and for his county.

HARRIS, Geoffrey   b.1928
Sculptor. Studied at Leeds College of Art, 1948-51. 1951 awarded travelling scholarship to Rome. Studied at RCA, 1951-4. 1954 assistant to Leon Underwood.* 1955 assistant to William Bloye, FRBS. 1957-60 assistant to Henry Moore.* Has exhibited regularly since 1959 in mixed exhibitions. Included in the 'Artists in Focus' exhibition, AIA Gallery, London, 1983.

HARRIS, Jeffrey   b.1932
Painter. Born Leeds, Yorkshire. Studied at Leeds College of Art. 1953 won travelling scholarship to Paris. 1956-64 worked and lived in St. Ives, Cornwall. Has exhibited in St. Ives and at the Rowan Gallery and New Arts Centre in London.

HARRIS, Jon   b.1943
Painter. Born Stoke-on-Trent, Staffordshire. Began a degree in architecture at Cambridge but did not complete it. Began painting and held his first solo exhibition at Trinity Hall, Cambridge, 1964. Exhibits mostly in East Anglia.

GEOFFREY HARRIS, b.1928. *Double figure*, 1968. Stone. 44in. Private Collection.

HARRIS, Lyndon Goodwin   b.1928
Painter, etcher and stained glass artist. Born Halesowen, Worcestershire. Studied at Birmingham College of Art, Central School of Arts and Crafts and Slade School, 1946-50. Began exhibiting at the RA at the age of thirteen. Won a gold medal at the Paris Salon, 1956. Elected RWA, 1947, RSW, 1952 and RI, 1958.

HARRIS, Mark   b.1954
Painter. Born Singapore. Studied at Edinburgh College of Art, 1977-8, RCA, 1979-82, Brera Academia di Belle Arti, Milan, 1982-3. 1985 visiting artist, School of the Art Institute of Chicago. 1984 first solo exhibition held at Studio Carolo Grossetti, Milan; others include one at Juda Rowan Gallery, London, 1986. Winner of several scholarships and awards, including the Fulbright Scholarship, 1986. Abstract artist who uses swirling movement and high-pitched colour.

HARRIS, Robin   b.1949
Painter. Born London. Studied at Hammersmith College of Art, 1967-8, Liverpool College of Art, 1968-71 and RCA, 1971-4. 1972 visited USA and Canada. 1974 visited Middle East, Central and Eastern Europe. 1975 solo exhibition at Park Square Gallery, Leeds. Exhibited '30 Images Concerning the Universal Declaration of Human Rights' at the Herbert Art Gallery and Museum, Coventry, 1987.

HARRIS, Rohan   b.1963
Painter. Born Amersham, Buckinghamshire. Studied at Chelsea School of Art, 1981-5. First one-person show at Knoedler Gallery, London, 1988.

HARRIS, Tomás   1908-1964
Painter. Born London of an English father and Spanish mother. His father created the Spanish Art Gallery in London. Studied at Slade and British Academy in Rome. 1943 first solo exhibition held at Reid and Lefevre. After the war he divided his time between England and Spain, and held a solo exhibition at the Museum of Modern Art in Madrid, 1947.

HARRISON, Andrew   b.1947
Painter. Born Birkenhead, Cheshire. Studied at Wallasey Art School, and Winchester Art School, 1966-70. Worked in various kinds of employment, exhibiting in and around Merseyside, having a solo exhibition at the Atkinson Art Gallery, Southport, 1978.

HARRISON, Anthony   b.1931
Painter and printmaker. Born Truro, Cornwall. Studied architecture at the Northern Polytechnic in London from 1949. 1951 studied painting at Chelsea School of Art on an LCC Scholarship and in 1952 continued his studies under Keith Vaughan* and Merlyn Evans* at Central School of Arts and Crafts. 1955 began exhibiting his prints regularly at the St. George's Gallery.

HARRISON, Claude   b.1922
Painter. Born Leyland, Lancashire. Studied at Preston College of Art, 1939-41, Liverpool College of Art, 1941-2, and RCA, 1947-50. Exhibits regularly at RA and has held solo exhibitions in London, Italy and USA. Lives and works in Cumbria. Published *The Portrait Painters' Handbook* (1968) and *The Book of Tobit* (1969).

HARRISON, Claude
Painter. Chiefly a painter of portraits, conversation pieces and imaginative figure compositions that draw on the *commedia dell'Arte*. A sense of timelessness informs his works in which figures are set in barren, surreal landscapes. First solo exhibition with the Portal Gallery, 1987. He has also exhibited in the USA and Italy.

CLAUDE HARRISON, b.1922. *'Hat Trick'*, 1973. 30in. x 25in. Private Collection.

HARRISON, Lillian   1899-1965

Painter. Born Wakefield, Yorkshire. Studied English at Somerville College, Oxford. At first taught English, then art, after moving to Hull. Member of the National Society of Painters and FRSA. Exhibited in Hull and London and held her first solo exhibition in the University of Hull's senior common-room, 1966.

HARRISON, Liz   b.1947

Painter and collagist. Born Coventry, Warwickshire. Studied at Stoke-on-Trent College of Art, Cardiff College of Art and Manchester College of Art and Design, 1963-8. Also studied at Slade School, 1968-70. Solo exhibitions include '24 days in the life of a papaver: a environment', held at Whitechapel Art Gallery, 1976.

HARRISON, Margaret   b.1940

Mixed-media artist. Studied at Carlisle College of Art, RA Schools and Academy of Art, Perugia. 1971 held her first solo exhibition. Her work reflects feminist and political interests. Represented in Arts Council Collection and elsewhere.

Bibl: Audio Arts Publication, taped conversation with Lucy Lippard, 1979.

HARRISON, Michael   b.1945

Printmaker. Born Leicester. Studied at Leicester College of Art and Central School of Art and Design. 1970 first solo exhibition held at Winchester School of Art; others include one at Graffiti, London, 1978. Represented in several public collections in Britain.

HART, John   b.1921

Painter. Born Manchester, Lancashire. Studied at Liverpool College of Art, 1946-51. 1953 first solo exhibition held at Beaux Arts Gallery, London. 1958 worked in Cassis and

Paris. 1960s held regular exhibitions at the Molton Gallery, London.

Bibl: *Hart's Camden Exhibition*, Camden Arts Centre, 1975.

HARTLEY, Elizabeth Jane   b.1952
Painter. Born Sheffield, Yorkshire. Studied at Birmingham Polytechnic, 1970-4, and Goldsmiths' College, 1975-6. 1972 began exhibiting at the Northern Young Contemporaries, Manchester, and has continued to exhibit, mostly in the Midlands.

HARTRICK, A.S. (Archibald Standish)   1864-1950
Painter and printmaker. Born India. Studied at Edinburgh University and Slade School of Art and at the Académie Julian and Atelier Cormon in Paris. Spent summer of 1886 with Gauguin at Pont-Aven. 1890 moved to London and joined staff of *The Daily Graphic,* moving on in 1893 to *The Pall Mall Magazine.* 1893 became member of NEAC and 1906 of the International Society of Sculptors, Painters and Gravers. 1920 became a member of the RWS. Published *Lithography as a Fine Art,* 1932. Wrote and illustrated books, including *A Painter's Pilgrimage through Fifty Years,* 1932. Taught at Camberwell and Central Schools of Art and was awarded an OBE. The Arts Council mounted a memorial exhibition, 1951. Represented in the V & A and the Tate Gallery.

HARTWELL, Charles Leonard   1873-1951
Sculptor. Born Blackheath, London. Studied at the City and Guilds School, Kennington, where he won a silver medal for sculpture, and at the RA Schools from 1896, winning silver and bronze medals. Also received private tuition from Onslow Ford and Hamo Thorneycroft.* Exhibited at the RA from 1900. Elected ARA, 1915, and RA, 1924. Specialised in figure subjects and portraiture.

HARTWELL, Richard   b.1946
Printmaker. Born Cambridge. Studied at Hornsey College of Art and Central School of Art. 1970 first solo exhibition held at Camila Speth, Berlin. His work has dealt with, among other things, the use of graphic symbols in communication.

HARVEY, Daniel   b.1959
Sculptor. Born Dorking, Surrey. Studied at Cardiff College of Art, 1977-8 and RCA, 1983-6. 1987 held first solo exhibition at Birch and Conran, London.

HARVEY, Dorothea S.   b.1928
Painter. Born Yorkshire. Her paintings attempt to translate music into art forms. Works mainly in pastel, ink and tempera and exhibits in group shows in Britain and abroad.

HARVEY, Harold   1874-1941
Painter. Studied under Norman Garstin* and afterwards in Paris at the Académie Julian. Exhibited at the RA from 1898, also in the provinces and abroad. Held solo exhibitions at the Leicester Galleries in 1918, 1920 and 1926. Represented in several public collections. (Plate 48, p.247.)

HARVEY, John Wynn   1923-1989
Sculptor. Studied, after the war, at the Central School of Art. In the 1960s he turned away from the visual arts to literature, writing *Within Without, Beside the Sea* and *The Diaries of Oliver Harvey,* his father having been Anthony Eden's private secretary. Moved to Wales, where he concentrated again on painting and sculpture. Had solo shows in London and Shrewsbury.

HARVEY, William   b.1957
Painter. Born Hampshire. Studied at Yeovil College of Art, 1977-9, Gwent College of Higher Education, 1980-3, and Birmingham Polytechnic, 1983-4. Exhibited two or three times a year throughout the 1980s, and 1986 had a solo exhibition at Worcester City Art Gallery, Winchester Gallery and Spitalfields Workspace. 1986-7 Fellow in Painting at South Glamorgan Institute of Higher Education, Cardiff. Has executed murals for West Midlands County Council and the Chinese Quarter, Birmingham. Solo exhibition at Sue Williams, London, 1988. Included in the collection of the Arts Council.

HARWOOD, Lucy   1893-1972
Painter. Born Belstead Park, Ipswich, Suffolk. An early aspiration to play the piano was destroyed by an operation which left her partially paralysed on her right side. Turned to painting (with her left hand) and attended Slade School of Art, before the First World War. 1937 began attending Cedric Morris's* East Anglian School of Painting and Drawing, with which she became closely associated. A commemorative exhibition of her work was held at The Minories in Colchester, 1975.

HASELDEN, Ron   b.1944
Sculptor and film maker. Born Gravesend, Kent. Studied at Gravesend School of Art. Lectures at University of Reading. Has moved through sculpture, then photography into film and installation, exhibiting regularly since 1975.

HASSALL, Joan   b.1906
Painter and wood engraver. Daughter of John Hassall.* Studied at RA Schools and the LCC School of Photo-engraving and Lithography. Exhibited at the RA, RSA, SWA and with the NEAC. Elected ARE, 1938, and RE, 1948.

HASSALL, John   1868-1948
Painter. Born Walmer, Kent. Studied under Prof. P. van Havermaet at the Antwerp Academy. Began exhibiting at the RA, 1894. Interested by a circular letter sent to promising young artists, John Hassall began producing posters for Messrs. David Allen and Sons. Painted a very large watercolour every year for the RI Exhibition and attended the London Sketch Club every week. Outside of art his great interest was prehistoric flint implements and his collection is now housed in the Museum of Ethnography, Cambridge.

HASTE, David   b.1938
Painter. Studied at Ipswich and St. Martin's Schools of Art, 1964-8 and RCA, 1968-71. 1967 began exhibiting in mixed shows and had his first solo show at the Thumb Gallery, London, 1978.

HASTED, Michael

HASTED, Michael b.1946
Painter. Began work as an actor and then a photographer before turning to painting in 1973. Adopted a surrealist style, using the heightened mimetic realism of Dali. 1974 first solo exhibition at Galerie Baumeister, Berlin; another held at the London Arts Gallery, 1975.

Bibl: *Novum Gebrauchsgraphik,* November 1973.

HASTINGS, George b.1960
Painter. Born Gateshead, Co. Durham. Studied art history and printmaking at University College of Wales, Aberystwyth, after obtaining a BA in Fine Art. Lectures in art history but continues to paint. 1981 his first solo exhibition was held at the Aberystwyth Arts Centre and his most recent at the Grosvenor Gallery, London, 1987. His paintings, both landscapes and abstracts, exhibit a debt to the neo-romantic painters of the 1940s.

HASTINGS, John (15th Earl of Huntingdon) b.1907
Painter. Studied under Professor Tonks* at the Slade School and later spent two years in the South Pacific. 1931 held his first solo exhibition in San Francisco. Met Diego Rivera and became his pupil and assistant, helping him with the murals for the San Francisco Stock Exchange Lunch Club and others. Hastings, himself, painted murals for the Hall of Science in the World's Fair, Chicago, 1933. Exhibited at the Lefevre and Wertheim Galleries in London. Also continued to execute murals. Married the writer Margaret Lane.

HATOUM, Mona b.1952
Sculptor. Born Beirut, Lebanon. Studied at Byam Shaw School of Art, 1977-9, and Slade School of Art, 1979-81. Since graduating has occupied several artist-in-residences. 1989-92 Senior Research Fellow in Fine Art, South Glamorgan Institute of Higher Education, Cardiff. Her work is 'minimal' but reverberates with meanings often relating to the theme of division, psychic and physical. Violence and danger are not just implied but were actually present in the work she exhibited at 'The British Art Show' at the Hayward Gallery, 1990, and which consisted of an iron frame and six electric elements.

HATTON, Brian 1887-1916
Painter. A child prodigy who was admired by G.F. Watts. Studied at George Harcourt's Abroath painting school, under Lanteri at South Kensington and for a few months at the Académie Julian in Paris. Exhibited at RA, Royal Society of Portrait Painters and elsewhere, before he enlisted in the Worcestershire Yeomanry and was killed in action.

HATWELL, Elizabeth b.1937
Painter. Born Brighton, Sussex. Studied at Chelsea School of Art, 1962-6. Teaches at Edinburgh College of Art. 1976 first solo exhibition held at Stirling Gallery; another at the Scottish Gallery, Edinburgh, 1979. Represented in Scottish Arts Council Collection.

HAUGHTON, David b.1924
Painter. Born London. Studied at Slade School of Art. 1947 moved to St. Just, Penwith and later was a founder member of Penwith Society of Artists. His fascination with the town of St. Just and its surrounding landscape gradually developed into an obsession with abstract surfaces. His work has a religious intensity and a marked dependence on line. Represented in Arts Council Collection, V & A and Metropolitan Museum of Art, New York.

Bibl: *David Haughton: Paintings, drawings and prints, 1948-1979,* Newlyn Art Gallery, 1979.

HAVERS, Mandy b.1953
Sculptor. Born Portsmouth, Hampshire. Studied at Portsmouth College of Art and Design, 1971-2, Lanchester Polytechnic, 1972-5, and Slade School, 1976-8. With others formed the Canal Basin Trust to preserve and develop warehouse studios. 1979 included in Peter Moore's Liverpool Project 5. Solo exhibitions include 'Figures in Leather' at Oriel 31, Welshpool, Powys, 1986.

HAVINDEN, Ashley 1903-1973
Painter and designer. Born Rochester, Kent. 1920-2 trained in lithographic and photogravure printing. 1922 joined the London advertising agency, W.S. Crawford Ltd., also taking evening classes in design and drawing at Central School of Arts and Crafts. 1933 for a few months learnt carving and drawing under Henry Moore.* Designed rugs, fabrics and the catalogue for MARS Group Exhibition, 1938. Created OBE.

HAWKEN, Anthony b.1948
Sculptor. Studied at Medway College of Art, 1968 and RA Schools, 1968-71. Won a Landseer Scholarship and Bronze Medal. 1972 worked as assistant to Leon Underwood.* 1977 elected to Royal Society of British Sculptors. Solo exhibitions include one at Woodlands Art Gallery, 1987.

HAWKER, Derrick b.1936
Painter and abstract artist. Born Seaton, Devonshire. Studied at Newton Abbot College of Art and Cardiff. Has taught at Shrewsbury School of Art. Solo exhibition at Woodstock Gallery, London, 1964.

HAWKER, Susan b.1949
Painter. Born Surrey. Studied at Sutton School of Art, 1965-6, Epsom School of Art, 1968-71 and RCA, 1971-4. Awarded a John Minton Scholarship and two John Murray awards. 1975 elected an associate member of the RWS. Represented in Carlisle City Art Gallery. First solo exhibition held at Thackeray Gallery, London, 1976.

HAWKES, Julian b.1944
Sculptor. Born Gloucestershire. Studied at West of England School of Art, Bristol, 1963-6 and Slade School of Art, 1967-9. 1969-75 worked as assistant to Phillip King.* 1975 held first solo exhibition at Woburn Arts Centre, Woburn Abbey; others include one at the Juda Rowan Gallery, London, 1983. Represented in Arts Council Collection.

HAWKINS, Dennis b.1925
Printmaker. Studied at Ruskin School, 1947-9, and Slade School of Art, 1949-52. 1958 first solo exhibition held at New Vision Centre, London; others include two at the Zwemmer Gallery, London, 1962 and 1964. Represented in the Arts Council Collection, the V & A, Seattle Museum of Modern Art and City Art Galleries in Birmingham, Exeter, Norwich, Liverpool, Portsmouth and Eastbourne.

HAWKINS, Peter
Sculptor. Born London. Studied at Kingston School of Art, Chelsea School of Art and RCA, 1949-59. 1959-61 travelled in Brazil, Bolivia and Peru. 1958 began

exhibiting; solo exhibition at the Grabowski Gallery, London, 1962.

HAWLEY, Helen   b.1937
Painter and printmaker. Born Saskatchewan, Canada. Studied at University of Saskatchewan and then history of art at the University of Paris. 1962 moved to England and studied printmaking at Morley College and Chelsea School of Art. Combines her work as an artist with a part-time job in a London music library. Solo exhibitions at Gallery 273, Queen Mary College, London, 1980.

HAWORTH, Jann   b.1942
Sculptor. Born Hollywood, USA. Studied at University College, Los Angeles, 1959-61 and Slade School of Art, 1962-3. Married the artist, Peter Blake.* 1966 first solo exhibition held at Robert Fraser Gallery, London; others include one at the Arnolfini Gallery, Bristol, 1972. Using fabrics, she makes three-dimensional figurative sculptures that evoke a sense of drama and magic.

HAYES, Colin   b.1919
Painter. Born London. Educated at Christ Church, Oxford and served in the Royal Engineers in the Middle East, 1940-5. Studied at the Ruskin School of Drawing, 1946-7. Taught at the RCA, 1949-84. Has exhibited at various London galleries including Agnew's and the New Grafton. Has written several books on artists including Renoir (1961), Stanley Spencer (1963) and Rembrandt (1969). Represented in collections belonging to the Arts Council, British Council, Carlisle Art Gallery and others.

HAYMAN, Patrick   1915-1988
Painter. Born London. 1936-47 lived in New Zealand. 1938 started painting in Dunedin. 1947 returned to England and 1950-3 lived in Cornwall, mainly St. Ives. 1958-63 founder-editor of *The Painter and Sculptor* magazine. First solo exhibition held at Robin Nance, The Wharf, St. Ives. Numerous solo exhibitions since then, including one at the Whitechapel Art Gallery, London, 1963. A figurative artist who used themes from the subconscious, myths and dreams. Represented in the Tate Gallery, Arts Council Collection, National Gallery of Modern Art, Edinburgh, the National Art Gallery of New Zealand, Wellington, and elsewhere.

HAYTER, Stanley William   1901-1989
Painter and printmaker. Born London, the son and great-nephew of artists. Studied in his father William Harry Hayter's studio and at the Académie Julian, Paris. 1927 founded the Atelier 17 in Paris which became a highly influential printing school. For a period it transferred to New York but was reopened in Paris in 1950, the New York branch closing in 1955. First solo exhibition held at Claridge Gallery, London, 1928. Association with the Surrealists encouraged an interest in automatic writing. Represented in many public collections.

HAYWARD, Alfred   1875-1971
Painter. Born London. Studied at RCA, 1891-4, and at Slade School, 1895-7. Exhibited at RA, the Paris Salon, with the NEAC and elsewhere. Elected member of the NEAC, 1910. Made frequent visits to Italy and held an exhibition of Venetian subjects at the Leicester Galleries, London, 1924. Offical war artist, 1918-19. Represented in several public collections.

MARY HEADLAM, 1874-1959. '*A Corner of the Apothecary's Garden*'. Pencil and watercolour. 8¾ in. x 9½ in. Sheffield City Art Galleries.

HEAD, Tim   b.1946
Painter, photographer, sculptor and mixed-media artist. Born London. Studied fine art at University of Newcastle upon Tyne, 1965-9, and sculpture at St. Martin's School of Art, 1969-70. 1968 worked for the sculptor Claes Oldenburg in New York. 1971-9 lecturer at Goldsmiths' College. 1972 first one-person show at MOMA, Oxford. 1972 first made installations using mirrors and projections, creating odd illusory spaces. Published an artist's book *Reconstruction,* a sequence of photographs, 1973. 1975 Gulbenkian Foundation Award. 1977-8 Fellowship at Clare Hall, Cambridge. 1987 won first prize for painting at John Moores Liverpool exhibition. Now interested in the imagery of food. Represented in numerous public collections. (Plate 49, p.247.)

HEADLAM, Mary   1874-1959
Painter and etcher. Born Norfolk, daughter of Admiral Sir John Corbett, an amateur watercolourist. Studied at Slade School, 1892-c.1896. In 1898 began to submit work for NEAC exhibitions. 1909 married Horace Headlam; on his death in the 1930s took a cruise to the West Indies, which inspired exotic watercolours. During the Second World War she moved to Devon, but returned to London, 1954-9. Produced illustrations for *The Magic City* by Netta Syrett, 1903, and *Kilmeny* by James Hogg, 1905. Possibly studied etching under Graham Sutherland* in the 1920s.

HEADLEY-NEAVE, Alice
Painter. Born Hastings, Sussex. Studied at the Slade and RA Schools where she won the Landseer Scholarship. Primarily a portrait painter. Exhibited widely in mixed exhibitions, e.g. RA, Paris Salon, Royal Society of Portrait Painters and NEAC. Member of the Industrial Painters Group. Held five solo exhibitions, including one at the Robert Peck Art Gallery, Rye, 1963.

HEALE, David   b.1954
Painter. Lives in Welwyn Garden City, Herts. Studied at St. Albans School of Art, 1972-3, Bath Academy of Art, 1973-6 and Brighton Polytechnic, 1976-7. Included in

HEALE, Jonathan

mixed exhibitions at the Morley Gallery, Digswell House. Solo exhibition which toured in 1982, was shown at Stevenage Leisure Centre, Peterborough City Museum and Bury St. Edmunds Art Gallery. Solo exhibition 'Paintings and Constructions', held at Swiss Cottage Library, London, 1988. Paints on wood and makes shaped works.

HEALE, Jonathan   b.1949
Painter and printmaker. Born Liverpool, Merseyside. Studied at Southampton College of Art, 1966-7, Chelsea School of Art, 1967-70 and RCA, 1970-1. 1971-5 lived and worked in Los Angeles and London. 1975 moved to a farmhouse in Montgomery, Wales and set up his printing press there. 1978 published his book of woodcuts *Art Alphabet,* a 20th century version of William Nicholson's famous alphabet of 1898. 1978 first one-person show 'The Sky at Night', at Leighton House, London. Work in the collections of Birmingham City Art Gallery and the Welsh Arts Council.

HEALEY, John   b.1894
Maker of sculptures in light and luminous pictures. Born London. Studied at University of London. Early years taken up managing a family textile business. At retirement he began researches into the field of light. First solo exhibition of his luminous shows in Holland 1966, Brighton 1967 and New York, 1967. 1966 awarded Richardson Medal as Inventor of the Year and 1967 received two gold medals at Brussels International Invention Exhibition.

HEARD, Andrew   b.1958
Painter. Studied history and history of art at the University of London. Exhibited in solo exhibitions at Jean Bernier in Athens, with 'Art and Project' in Amsterdam, and with the Friedman-Guinness Gallery, Heidelberg. First solo exhibition in Great Britain at Salama-Caro Gallery, London, 1988.

HEARD, Peter   b.1939
Naïve painter. Untrained. By profession a civil engineer and bridge builder. Started to paint in 1970. Paints the British at work and play. One-person shows at the Portal Gallery, 1978 and 1980.

HEATH, Adrian   b.1920
Painter. Born Matmyo, Burma. Came to England in 1925. Studied at Newlyn, Cornwall, under Stanhope Forbes* in 1938, then at the Slade School in Oxford in 1939. 1940 joined the RAF. 1941-5 he was a prisoner of war in Germany where he met Terry Frost.* 1945-7 returned to Slade. 1947 lived in France. 1948 returned to England. Had an exhibition at the Musée de Carcassonne, France; 1949 first exhibited with the London Group. Stayed in St. Ives in 1951 and was instrumental in linking the St. Ives-based abstractionists with the constructivists, through weekend exhibitions held in his studio. 1951 helped to organise the first post-war Abstract Art exhibition at the AIA Gallery. 1953 his first one-artist exhibition was held at the Redfern Gallery. 1953 published *Abstract Art: Its Origin and Meaning.* 1954-64 Chairman of the AIA. From 1955 he taught at Bath Academy of Art. 1969 artist in residence at Sussex University. Lives and works in London. Has work in numerous public collections. (Plate 50, p.247.)

HEATHFIELD, Cecil
Painter. Born London. Studied at Croydon School of Art and at the Bolt Court School, Fleet Street, under Walter Bayes.* Ran his own studio in London for twenty years, concentrating on commercial design. In 1950s became Art Adviser to the East Sussex Education Committee. Chairman of the Brighton Arts Club, President of the Lewes Art Club, exhibitor with the RBA and at the Sussex Galleries. Work in the collections of Hove and Brighton Art Galleries.

HEATON, Doreen   b.1930
Painter. Studied at Bath Academy of Art 1949-53, travelled in France, Italy and Spain. (Married a Pole and became Mrs Potworowska.) 1961 first solo exhibition at the MDM Gallery, Warsaw, with another in Poznan, 1962. Shows at the Drian Galleries, London.

HEBBORN, Eric   b.1934
Sculptor. Born London. Studied at RA schools from 1949. Began to exhibit in mixed shows, e.g. Young Contemporaries. 1959-61 resumed sculpture studies in Italy and won the Prix de Rome. 1976 one-person show at Villa Gregoriana Tivoli, and at the Alwin Gallery, London, 1978.

HEBDEN, Rosemary   b.1924
Painter and printmaker. Untrained. Head of Art and Crafts Department, Nottingham College of Education in the 1960s. One-person shows at the Marjorie Parr Gallery, Woodstock Gallery and the Galerie Contemporaine, Geneva.

HEDGES, Janet   b.1955
Sculptor. Born Oxfordshire. Studied at Banbury School of Art, 1973-4, and Sunderland Polytechnic, 1974-7. 1979 first solo exhibition at Bampton Arts Centre, Oxfordshire. Makes sculpture which utilises natural materials and the passage of time, so that something new is made by accumulation.

HEESON, Crispin   b.1950
Painter. Born Oundle, Leicestershire. Studied at Norwich School of Art 1970-1 and Byam Shaw School of Art. Included in mixed exhibitions from 1966. 1984 solo exhibition at the City Museum and Art Gallery, Peterborough. In 1982 commissioned to paint a mural in Girdlers Road, Hammersmith, London.

HEMMING, Adrian   b.1945
Painter. Born Leicester. Studied at Lincoln College of Art 1969-70, Brighton Polytechnic 1970-5. 1979 founder member of the Tichbourne Studios, Brighton. 1980 first solo exhibition at Brighton Polytechnic Gallery. Included in group exhibitions from 1977. 1976 won several Arts Council and South East Arts awards. Visiting Lecturer at Brighton Polytechnic from 1982. Currently interested in painting saints and sinners.

HEMPTON, Paul   b.1946
Painter. Born Wakefield, Yorkshire. Studied at Goldsmiths' College of Art, 1964-8 and RCA, 1968-71. 1971-3 appointed Fellow in Fine Art, Nottingham University. 1972 first solo exhibition at Nottingham University Art Gallery. 1980 represented Great Britain at 11th Biennale de Paris; 1981 at Biennale de Art, Medellin, South America; 1985 at 4th Biennale of European Graphic Art, Germany. Works in the collections of the Arts Council and V & A.

PAUL HEMPTON, b.1946.
'Ravine Traces', 1987.
66in. x 54in. Private Collection.

HEMSOLL, Eileen Mary   b.1924
Painter. Studied at Birmingham College of Art, 1941-6.
Exhibited at RA, RSBA, RWEA and elsewhere. Paints in
enamel on earthenware, also with oil, oil pastel and
watercolour. Elected to the Royal Birmingham Society of
Artists, 1978.

HEMSWORTH, Gerard   b.1945
Painter. Born London. Studied at St. Martin's School of
Art 1963-7. 1970 first solo exhibition at Nigel Greenwood
Gallery. Recent major exhibition at the ICA. Uses
figurative imagery to produce paintings which examine
reality and meaning by the use of odd juxtapositions.
Teaches at Goldsmiths' College, London.

HENDERSON, E. Hope
Painter. Studied at Edinburgh College of Art, and took a
postgraduate year there. Included in mixed exhibitions
such as the RA, the SSA. First one-person exhibition at the

Harbour Cottage Art Gallery, Kirkcudbright. Solo
exhibition at the Woodstock Gallery, 1969.

HENDERSON, Elsie (Baroness de Coudenhove)
1880-1967
Painter and sculptor. Born Eastbourne, Sussex. Studied at
the South Kensington Schools and at the Slade and then
travelled abroad. 1908-9 and 1912 she spent time in Paris,
working in several ateliers. 1916 enrolled at Chelsea
Polytechnic to learn lithography. 1924 showed with Paul
Nash* and Frederick Whiting at the Leicester Galleries.
Became a close friend of the painter Orovida Pissarro.*
1928 married Henri Baron de Coudenhove, French Consul
in Guernsey. Lived in Sussex during the latter part of her
life, painting watercolours, but is best known for her
outstanding animal drawings of the 1920s. Commissioned
by London Transport to design a poster advertising London
Zoo for the Underground. First solo exhibition in 1985,
followed by a second one, at Sally Hunter Fine Art, London,
1990. Has work in the Fitzwilliam Museum, Cambridge,
the Tate Gallery, the British Museum and elsewhere.

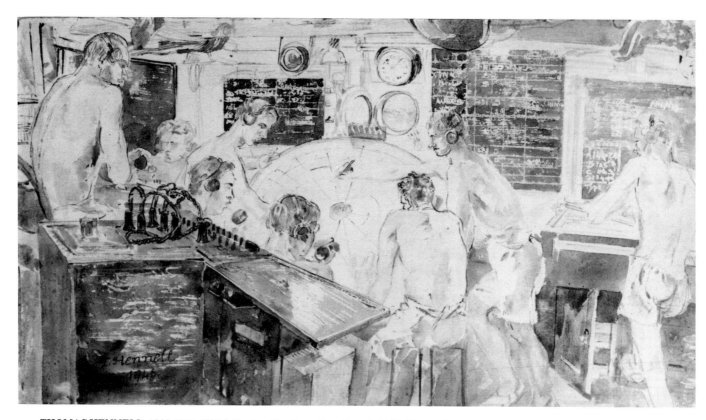

THOMAS HENNELL, 1903-1945. *'HMS Hunter. The Operations Room'*, 1945. Watercolour. 13⅜in. x 25⅛in. Imperial War Museum.

HENDERSON, Ewen b.1934
Painter, sculptor and potter. Born Staffordshire. Spent
seven years working for a timber factory in Cardiff.
Studied at Goldsmiths' College of Art and then ceramics at
Camberwell School of Art until 1968. Has taught at
Goldsmiths' College and Camberwell. 1974 first solo
exhibition at Marjorie Parr Gallery, London. Work in the
collections of the Kyoto Museum of Modern Art, Japan, the
V & A, Ulster Museum, Belfast, Glasgow City Art Gallery,
and Boymans van Beuningen Museum, Rotterdam.

HENDERSON, John b.1943
Painter. Born Torquay, Devon. Studied at Falmouth
School of Art until 1964 and then taught there 1965.
1966-8 awarded Dutch Government Scholarship. 1975
moved to live and work in Cornwall. 1973 first solo
exhibition at the DM Gallery, London. Work in the
collection of South West Arts and the National
Westminster Bank.

HENDERSON, Kevin b.1963
Sculptor. Born Singapore. Studied at Gray's School of Art,
Aberdeen, 1981-6, and Oregon State University, 1982-3.
First solo exhibition held at Eden Court Theatre,
Inverness, 1987. Represented in 'The British Art Show'
held at the Hayward Gallery, 1990. Works with discarded
materials and recurring motifs. Prefers simple
organisation to elaborate composition.

HENDERSON, Madeleine b.1938
Painter and sculptor. Born London of Italian and
Australian parents. Studied sculpture at the Academies of
Fine Arts in Florence and Rome. 1960-72 lived and worked

in Australia, Copenhagen and Oslo. 1972 moved to live
and work in London. Solo exhibition of sculpture at the
DM Gallery, London, 1972.

HENDERSON, William b.1941
Painter. Born Ringmer, Sussex. Studied at Brighton
College of Art, 1959-63, and the Slade School, 1963-5.
From 1965 included in mixed exhibitions. 1975 first solo
exhibition, Summer Show 3, at Serpentine Gallery; 1983
mid-term retrospective exhibition at Arnolfini Gallery.
1983 prizewinner, Tolly Cobbold Eastern Arts 4th Annual
Exhibition. 1980s taught at St. Martin's School of Art.
Work in the collections of the Arts Council, V & A, Tate
Gallery, CAS, Bradford Art Galleries and Museums.

HENNELL, Thomas 1903-1945
Painter. Born at Ridley Rectory, Kent. Studied at the
London Polytechnic School of Art, 1921-6. 1928-32 taught
art at Bruton School, Somerset and Kingswood School,
Bath. At that time began to make drawings of country
crafts and farm implements. 1934 published his first book,
Change in the Farm, with his own illustrations. During
the mid-1930s he suffered a breakdown and was confined
to Claybury Mental Hospital, later recounting his
experience there in *The Witnesses*, published 1938. 1936
first book of poetry published by the OUP. 1938 elected
Associate of RWS. 1940 commissioned by the Pilgrim
Trust to make drawings for the Recording Britain scheme.
1941-2 commissioned by the Ministry of Information to
record aspects of toolmaking and landwork in wartime.
1943 spent three months in Iceland as an Official War
Artist. 1944 his watercolours of Iceland exhibited in the
National Gallery. 1944-5 sent to France as a War Artist

attached to the Royal Navy, then flew to India attached to the RAF. Captured by terrorists in Java and reported missing.

Bibl: Michael Macleod, *Thomas Hennell: Countryman, Artist and Writer,* Cambridge University Press, 1988.

HENNESSEY, Kevin   b.1920

Painter. Born London. Studied at Kingston School of Art, then six years war service in the Queen's Royal Regiment and the Intelligence Corps. Art studies continued at Chelsea School of Art after the war. Showed work in mixed exhibitions including the RA, Royal Society of Portrait Painters and NEAC. Had five one-person shows. From 1949 taught at Folkestone School of Art.

HENRI, Adrian   b.1932

Poet and painter. Born Birkenhead, Cheshire. 1938 his family moved to Rhyl, North Wales. Studied fine art at King's College, University of Durham, 1951-5. 1957 scenic artist at the Liverpool Playhouse. 1958 first included in a mixed exhibition. 1962 first event/happening entitled 'City' in Liverpool, in collaboration with Roger McGough. 1963-7 further events in Liverpool. 1967 published *The Mersey Sound,* a collection of poems. 1968 first solo exhibition at the ICA Gallery. 1969 *The Liverpool Scene* series produced for Granada Television. 1971 *Autobiography* published by Jonathan Cape. 1972 elected President, Liverpool Academy of Arts. 1974 *Environments and Happenings* published by Thames and Hudson. From 1978 visiting Lecturer in Film and Art History at Liverpool Polytechnic. 1980 mural commissioned for the Royal Liverpool Hospital, and another 1983. 1982 published *Eric the Punk Cat,* a children's book. 1985 writer in residence, Runcorn Secondary Schools.

HENRIQUES, Rose L.

Self-taught painter. Married Sir Basil Henriques, a magistrate in East London. Occupied mostly with social work in the East End. Executed a large series of paintings and drawings of the East End during the Blitz, now in the collection of the London Museum. 1961 solo exhibition of scenes of Stepney held at the Whitechapel Gallery.

HENRY, David Reid   b.1919

Painter and illustrator of bird subjects. Born Ceylon. His father, George Henry, was a well-known illustrator of ornithological works. Studied in the studio of George Lodge, the bird painter, during his spare time while at Sandhurst. His army service took him to North Africa with a tank regiment. Since the war has lived and worked in Africa for a considerable period of time. 1969 first solo exhibition of paintings of birds held at the Sladmore Gallery.

HENRY, George   1858-1943

Painter. Born Irvine, Scotland. Studied at Glasgow School of Art and afterwards in W.Y. MacGregor's studio. In 1881 he painted in the Trossacks and at Brig O'Tusk with Crawhall,* Walton* and Guthrie* and was one of the first 'Glasgow Boys' to join the NEAC in 1887. In 1885 he met E.A. Hornel* and shared a studio with him at Kirkcudbright. They both subscribed to the Celtic revival and in 1889 together painted *The Druids.* Both visited Japan 1893-4 and were inspired by Japanese prints. Henry was also influenced by Whistler and Bastien-Lepage. Elected RSA, 1902, and RA, 1920. Worked

DAVID HEPHER, b.1935. *'No.22',* 1972. 76½ in. x 96in. Flowers East.

principally in Glasgow, but moved to London in 1901 where he became a successful portrait painter. Represented in Glasgow City Museum and Art Gallery, the Walker Art Gallery, Liverpool and elsewhere.

HENRY, Paul   1876-1958

Painter. Born Belfast, Northern Ireland. Apprentice designer at the Broadway Damask company in Belfast for a year, then entered Belfast School of Art. 1900 left Belfast to study art in Paris, first at the Académie Julian and then at Whistler's studio. From Paris lived first in London until c.1909, then near Guildford until his return to Ireland, 1912. 1920 moved to Dublin with his wife, the painter Grace Henry, and founded the Dublin Painters, a group of ten artists. During this period he designed posters and produced paintings for posters for the railways; a painting entitled 'Connemara Landscape' had larger sales than any other London, Midland and Scottish Railways poster. 1929 elected member of the Royal Hibernian Academy. Regular exhibitor at the RA. Lost his sight in 1945 and remained virtually blind for the rest of his life. Commemorative exhibition at Trinity College, Dublin, 1973.

HEPHER, David   b.1935

Painter. Born Surrey. Studied at Camberwell School of Art and the Slade School, 1955-61. From 1960 included in mixed exhibitions. 1971 first solo exhibition at the Serpentine Gallery. 1974 awarded first prize for painting at the Tokyo Biennale. 1974 retrospective exhibition at the Mappin Art Gallery, Sheffield. Paints realistic works on the subject of urban domestic architecture.

HEPPLE, Norman   b.1908

Portrait painter. Born London. Son of the painter Robert Hepple, and nephew of Wilson Hepple, the Northumberland animal painter. Studied at Goldsmiths' College of Art, and the RA Schools. During the Second World War, became Official War Artist to the National Fire Service. His war paintings are in the Imperial War Museum. 1948 elected member of the RP and president 1979-83. 1954 elected ARA and RA in 1961. Painted many royal portraits, including H.M. The Queen, The Queen Mother, Prince Philip and Prince Charles. Paints landscapes, horses and flowers for relaxation. Solo exhibition at Spink Gallery, 1987.

HEPWORTH, Barbara   1903-1975

Sculptor. Born Wakefield, Yorkshire. Studied at Leeds College of Art and RCA. 1924 lived in Italy on a scholarship, studied the Italian technique of marble-carving and married the sculptor, John Skeaping.* Returned to London, and in 1928 moved to Parkhill Road Studios, Hampstead, where her neighbours were Henry Moore* and Ben Nicholson.* (Her marriage to Skeaping was dissolved in 1933.) In 1932 and 1933 she and Nicholson visited the Paris studios of leading French artists. 1933 she joined Abstraction-Création, an international Paris-based exhibiting society. Moved into an abstract phase and, like Moore, introduced the use of a hole into carved sculpture. With Nicholson and others, was for a period at the forefront of the modern movement in England. When war broke out, she moved with Nicholson and their triplet children to Cornwall, and did not sculpt again until 1943. From then on the Cornish sea and landscape was held in dialogue with her art. She also began employing strings to explore the tension or space within a sculpture. From 1951 lived permanently at Trewyn Studios, St. Ives after the dissolution of her marriage. Received many commissions from home and abroad and held retrospectives at the Whitechapel Art Gallery (in 1952 and 1962) and at the Tate (1968). Created DBE in 1965. After her tragic death in a fire her studio was opened as a public museum.

Bibl: *Barbara Hepworth*, Tate Gallery, 1968; Barbara Hepworth, *A Pictorial Autobiography*, Adams & Mackay, London, 1970.

HERMAN, Josef   b.1911

Painter. Born Warsaw, Poland. Studied at Warsaw School of Art for eighteen months from 1930, and then worked as a freelance graphic artist. 1932 held his first solo exhibition at a Warsaw dealer's gallery, Koterba, showing watercolours of scenes of the life of working people. 1935-6 founded, with the Polish painter, Zigmunt Bobowsky, a group of artists called The Phrygian Cap, who drew their subjects from working people. 1938-9 moved to Brussels, and after the German invasion of Belgium in 1940, travelled to France and Britain, settling in Glasgow for four years. There he renewed his friendship with the painter Jankel Adler* whom he had known since 1936. 1943 moved to London and then to the mining village of Ystradgynlais in South Wales. 1944 set up a studio there in the PenyBont Inn; lived in the village for eleven years. 1948 became a naturalised British subject. 1946 the London gallery Roland, Browse and Delbanco held the first of over twelve exhibitions of his work. Commissioned by the Festival of Britain organisers to paint a large painting of Miners for the Pavilion of Minerals, on the South Bank. 1952 became a member of the London Group. 1955 first retrospective exhibition, shared with L.S. Lowry,* at Wakefield Art Gallery, followed by another retrospective in 1956 at the Whitechapel Art Gallery. 1962 awarded a gold medal by the Royal National Eisteddfod of Wales. 1975 third retrospective exhibition at Glasgow City Art Gallery. 1975 published an autobiography *Related Twilights: Notes from an Artist's Diary — Places and Artists*. Great collector of African sculpture. (Plate 51, p.250.)

HERMES, Gertrude   1901-1983

Painter, sculptor and printmaker. Born Bromley, Kent. Studied painting at the Beckenham School of Art, 1919-20. Spent a year in Germany. 1921-5 studied at Leon Underwood's* School of Painting and Sculpture. Began wood engraving in 1922 and sculpture in 1924. 1926 married the painter and printmaker Blair Hughes-Stanton* (marriage dissolved in 1932). Collaborated with her husband on the wood engravings for the Cresset Press volume of *The Pilgrim's Progress,* published in 1926. Other wood engravings for illustrated books include blocks for *A Floriledge,* published 1929. 1932 designed a mosaic floor and carved centre stone of a fountain for Shakespeare Memorial Theatre, Stratford. 1935 elected member of the London Group. 1937 designed a 30ft. sculptured glass window for the British Pavilion at the International Exhibition of Arts and Industry in Paris. 1939 selected as one of seven engravers to represent Britain at the Venice Biennale. Taught at Camberwell School of Art, Westminster School of Art and St. Martin's School of Art. 1940-5 went to Canada with her children; worked as a technical draughtsman in offices of aircraft and shipbuilding factories. 1945 returned to London. Teaching commitments from then until the 1960s at Camberwell School, St. Martin's, Central School, Royal Academy Schools. 1951 elected a Fellow of the RE. 1963 exhibited a wide range of her diverse work, for the first time, at the Metropole Art Centre, Folkestone. Retrospective exhibition at the Whitechapel Art Gallery, 1967. Work in the collection of the Tate Gallery.

HERON, Hilary   b.1923

Sculptor. Born Dublin, Ireland. Works in brass and natural boulders. 1948 awarded the Mainie Jellet Travelling Scholarship. Included in numerous Irish group exhibitions since that date. 1956 represented Ireland at the Venice Biennale. 1964 solo exhibition at Waddington Galleries, London.

HERON, Patrick   b.1920

Painter and art critic. Born Leeds, Yorkshire. Lived in West Cornwall, 1925-9. Studied part-time at the Slade School, 1937-9. 1940-4 worked as an agricultural labourer. 1944-5 worked as an assistant at the Bernard Leach pottery, St. Ives. 1945-7 art critic of *New English Weekly*. 1947-50 art critic for the *New Statesman* and *Nation*. 1947 first solo exhibition at Downing's Bookshop, St. Ives. 1953-6 taught at Central School. 1955 published *The Changing Forms of Art*. 1955-8 London correspondent of American magazine *Art Digest*. 1956 moved to Eagle's Nest, Zennor, near St. Ives. 1959 awarded Grand Prize, Second John Moores exhibition, Liverpool. 1965 awarded Silver Medal at VIII Bienal de Sao Paolo. 1973 delivered Power Lecture in Contemporary Art — 'The Shape of Colour' — in several Australian cities. Created CBE 1977. 1978 delivered E. William Doty Lectures in Fine Arts at University of Texas at Austin. 1980-7 Trustee of the Tate Gallery.

Bibl: *Patrick Heron,* edited by Vivien Knight, Lund Humphries, London, 1988.

HERON, Susanna   b.1949

Jeweller and sculptor. Daughter of the painter Patrick Heron.* Born Cornwall. Studied at Falmouth School of Art, 1967-8 and the Central School, 1968-71, where she specialised in jewellery. Exhibited her work widely during the 1970s. 1978-9 spent a year in the USA on a British

Council Bicentennial Arts Fellowship. First solo exhibition 'Bodywork', organised by the Crafts Council. 1981 began to make a distinction in her work between pieces which could be worn and pieces which had an autonomous nature. From 1981 part-time teacher at Middlesex Polytechnic. Solo exhibition of sculpture at the Whitechapel Gallery, 1985.

HERSCH, Eugen   1887-1967
Painter. Born Berlin, Germany. Studied at the Imperial Academy of Arts, Berlin and in Rome, and was a recipient of the Prix de Rome, 1910. Official War Artist in the First World War. Painted portraits of many leading European personalities. 1940 interned at Huyton, near Liverpool. Painted portraits, still lifes, landscapes and figure subjects. Also known for mural paintings, notably 'Triptych in Blue' at Wandsworth Town Hall. Had several one-person shows and was a regular exhibitor at the RA.

HESELTINE, John
Painter. Studied at the South East Essex College of Art, graduating in 1942. Served for four years in the Royal Navy Coastal Forces and exhibited in two War Artists' exhibitions. Included in mixed exhibitions at the V & A, the Royal Society of Portrait Painters and the Royal Watercolour Society. 1969 he was commissioned by the International Publishing Corporation to paint the Investiture of HRH The Prince of Wales, and for the same organisation he painted a portrait of Princess Anne. Commissioned work included a portrayal of *HMS Hermes* in action during the Falklands campaign, for the Royal Navy.

HETHERINGTON, Guy   b.1948
Painter. Born Penrith, Cumbria. Studied at Kingston School of Art, 1968-72. Visiting tutor to Chelsea School of Art, 1972-6. From 1973 included in mixed exhibitions. First solo exhibition at House Gallery, 1976.

HEWINSON, Morgan   b.1913
Painter. Born Monmouthshire, Wales. Studied at Newport College of Art and there won a scholarship to the RCA where he stayed until 1937. 1948 appointed to the staff of Manchester College of Art and by his retirement in the late 1970s was Senior Lecturer at Manchester Polytechnic's Faculty of Art and Design. Member of the Manchester Academy of Fine Arts. Represented in public art galleries at Bolton, Swansea, Stockport, Newport, Huddersfield, Sheffield and elsewhere.

HEWITT, Geoffrey   b.1930
Painter. Born Horden, Co. Durham. Graduated from the RCA, 1953, where his tutors were John Minton,* Ruskin Spear* and Carel Weight.* Taught at Sunderland College of Art, 1953-5, then taught at the College of Arts, Birmingham. Included in mixed exhibitions, e.g. the RA, the RSA, the London Group, and the RBA. First solo exhibition at the Shipley Art Gallery, Gateshead, 1956.

HEWKIN, Andrew   b.1949
Painter. Born Sutton Coldfield, Warwickshire. Studied glass and ceramics at Stourbridge College of Art, 1966-7, sculpture and painting at West of England College of Art, 1967-70, and painting at the RCA, 1970-3. 1972 won a

John Minton travelling scholarship and visited Greece, Turkey and Cyprus. 1974 first solo exhibition at Trafford Gallery. 1974-5 travelled extensively in Kenya, Tanzania, Malawi, Zambia and the West Indies. Exhibited occasionally at the RA.

HEWLETT, Francis   b.1930
Painter. Born Bristol, Avon. Studied at Bristol School of Art, 1948-52. Awarded a French Government Scholarship, 1952-3 and lived and worked in Paris. Studied at Slade School of Art, 1953-5, travelled in Italy, 1955. From 1957 taught at Falmouth School of Art, Cornwall and became head of painting. 1964 first solo exhibition at the New Art Centre. Work in the collections of Plymouth City Museum and Art Gallery and King's College, Newcastle. Works in a variety of media in a figurative style. He also worked as a sculptor using polychrome ceramic.

HEWLINGS, Charles   b.1948
Sculptor. Studied at Fine Art Department, Newcastle University, 1967-71, and St. Martin's School of Art, 1971-3. From 1973 sent work to group exhibitions; first solo exhibition at the Acme Gallery, 1976. Works in wood, steel, stone, slate, rope, etc.

HEWSON, Ann   b.1933
Sculptor. Born London. Studied briefly at South West Essex Technical College. Later attended evening classes at Regent Street Polytechnic where one of her teachers was Clifford Hall, whom she married in 1956. Shared an exhibition with Nigel Lambourne at the Belgrave Gallery, 1976.

HEY, Cicely   b.1896
Painter. Born Faringdon, Berkshire. Studied at Central School of Arts and Crafts and under Walter Sickert* who also painted her. Married the art critic Robert Tatlock. Exhibited with the NEAC, the London Group and elsewhere.

HEYWOOD, Sally   b.1964
Painter. Born Liverpool, Merseyside. Studied at RA Schools, 1984-7 and as a Painting Fellow at Gloucester College of Art and Design, 1987-8. 1987 first solo exhibition at Midland Bank Headquarters, London. Represented in group exhibitions since 1987 when she was exhibited at the Warburg Institute, London and at the Galérie Cafe, Saalech, Austria. Included in the collection of the Metropolitan Museum of Art, New York.

HIBBERD, Steven   b.1961
Painter. Born Dronfield, Derbyshire. Studied at Chesterfield College of Art, 1979-80, Cardiff College of Art, 1980-3 and at Birmingham Polytechnic, 1983-4. 1982 first exhibited at Stowells Trophy, followed by Whitworth Young Contemporaries, at Whitworth Art Gallery, Manchester, 1983.

HICKS, Jerry   b.1927
Painter. Studied at Slade School, at Oxford, 1944-5, and at the Slade in London, 1948-50. Has exhibited at the RA, RWA, RBA and elsewhere. Head of Art at Cotham Grammar School, 1951-81. Specialises in portraits.

NICOLA HICKS, b.1960. *'Shudder in the Citadel'*, 1988. Painted plaster and straw. 69½ in. x 77in. x 37½ in. Flowers East.

HICKS, Nicola   b.1960
Sculptor. Born London. Studied drawing and sculpture at Chelsea School of Art and the RCA. 1985-6 first solo exhibition at the Angela Flowers Gallery, London. 1986 artist in residence at Brentwood High School, Essex. 1986-7 commissioned to sculpt a monument in Battersea Park. Included in the collections of Drumcroon Education Centre, Wigan, Ipswich County Council, Contemporary Arts Society and Brentford High School, Essex. Specialises in animal sculpture.

HILDER, Rowland   b.1905
Painter. Born Great Neck, Long Island, USA. In 1915 travelled to England on the *Lusitania*. His family settled at New Cross, South London. 1921 entered Goldsmith's School of Art where he studied etching and drawing. Influenced by Muirhead Bone* and Frank Brangwyn* who was recommended to him by Graham Sutherland.* 1924 won a travelling scholarship and visited the Low Countries. 1925 began to illustrate books and in this way got to know John Masefield. Also did illustrations for Jack Beddington at Shell Mex. Became well known for his paintings and drawings of the Kentish landscape. Did camouflage work during the war and illustrated the *Army Manual on Camouflage*. Set up the successful Heron Press. Also worked with his wife, Edith, and Geoffrey Grigson, on the *Shell Guide to Flowers of the Countryside*. 1958 painted the *Shell Guide to Kent,* the first of the country guide pictures. His paintings of Kent look back to a pre-industrial age and have done much to sustain the myth of rural England.

HILL, Adrian Keith Graham   b.1895

Painter. Born Charlton, Kent. Studied at St. John's Wood Art School, 1912-14, and at RCA, 1919-20. Exhibited at RA, RBA, RI and with the NEAC and the London Group. Elected RBA 1926, ROI, 1929, SGA, 1931, and PROI, 1968. Represented in several public collections.

HILL, Derek   b.1916

Painter and stage designer. Born Southampton, Hampshire. Studied in Munich, Vienna and Paris, and stage design in Russia, China and Japan. Worked initially as a stage designer but from 1938 onwards turned increasingly to painting, holding his first solo exhibition at the Nicholson Gallery, London, 1943. Director of Art, British School at Rome, 1953-5 and 1957-9. Brings to his portraits a freshness and immediacy. Lives and works in Ireland.

Bibl: Greg Gowrie, *Derek Hill: An Appreciation*, Quartet Books, London, 1987.

HILLIER, Tristram   1905-1983

Painter. Born Peking, China. Studied at Slade, 1926-7, and under Andre Lhôte at the Atelier Colarossi, Paris. 1930-2 lived in Gascony. 1931 first one-artist exhibition at Alex Reid and Lefevre. 1933 settled in London. 1934 participated in Unit One. 1935-6 lived and worked mostly in Spain. 1937-40 lived and worked in France, and left after the German invasion. After the war he settled in Somerset and became a Roman Catholic. Exhibited regularly at Arthur Tooth's, London, and at RA. His work is characterised by a disquieting stillness and meticulous technique. (Plate 52, p.250.)

Bibl: *A Timeless Journey. Tristram Hillier R.A.*, cat. to retrospective held at Cartwright Hall, Bradford, 1983.

HILTON, Roger   1911-1975

Painter. Born Northwood, Middlesex. Studied at the Slade, 1929-31 and 1935-6, also under Bissière at the Académie Ranson, Paris. 1936 held his first solo exhibition at the Bloomsbury Gallery, London. Joined the army in 1939, serving in the Commandos. Captured 1942 and remained a POW until 1945. Turned to abstract art around 1950, encouraged by friendship with a member of the Cobra Group. Travelled to Paris and Amsterdam to study the work of Mondrian and himself began producing very austere abstracts, using only black, white, and small segments of earth colours. Taught at Central School of Art and Design, 1954-6, during which time he began making visits to Cornwall, staying first with Patrick Heron,* then renting a studio for summer use at Newlyn. Finally moved permanently to Cornwall in 1965 and became part of the St. Ives group. Landscape connotations began to infiltrate his abstracts, and figurative ingredients returned, but his style remained vigorously abrasive, like his personality. Humour entered his late work when, confined to bed during the last two-and-a-half years of his life, he found emotional release through the painting of gouaches in which hectic colours and childlike drawing combined with his aesthetic cunning and immense zest for life.

Bibl: *Roger Hilton, Paintings and Drawings 1931-1973*, London, Arts Council, 1974; *Roger Hilton's Night Letters*, with an introduction by Michael Canney, Newlyn Orion Galleries, Newlyn, 1980.

HILTON, Rose   b.1931

Painter. Grew up in Kent. After initial training at Beckenham Art School went on to study at the RCA, 1954-7. Went to Rome on an Abbey Scholarship. 1959 met

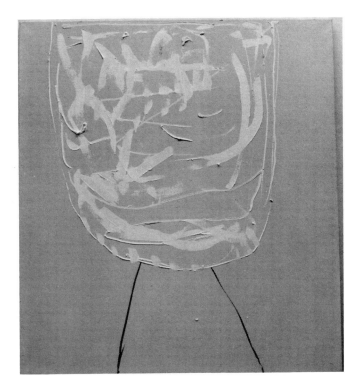

ROGER HILTON, 1911-1975. *'Oct. '60'*, 1960. 52in. x 55in. Waddington Galleries.

Roger Hilton* and with him moved to Botallack, a small mining hamlet on the tip of Cornwall. Here she brought up her children and supported her husband in his work, painting little except through her teaching in an adult education programme. 1975 she began painting again consistently after her husband's death and also took drawing lessons from Cecil Collins.* Solo exhibitions in Newlyn, Plymouth and London, including a major show at the Newlyn Art Gallery, 1987, and another at Michael Parkin Gallery, London, 1988.

HILTON, Matthew   b.1948

Photographer/printmaker. Born London. Studied photography and film making at Bournemouth Art College. 1981 first exhibition of photographs held at Holdsworth Gallery, Hebden Bridge, Yorkshire, followed by an exhibition of his lino prints at the same Gallery, 1982. 1983 awarded North West Arts Printmaking Bursary, Manchester Print Workshop.

HINCHCLIFF, Woodbine K.   fl.1890-1930

Painter. Son of the engraver John James Hinchcliff, under whom he studied. First exhibited at RA, 1895. 1897 moved to North Devon, but continued to exhibit in London. 1901 returned to London, working from the Rossetti Studios, Chelsea. 1904 was commissioned by J.M. Dent, the publisher, to illustrate the book, *Paris and its Story* by T. Okey, published in 1906. A skilled naturalist, who worked in a sensitive, semi-impressionist style. Moved to Australia and became an exhibiting member of the Royal Art Society of New South Wales.

HINCHCLIFFE, Richard George   1868-1942

Portrait painter. Born Manchester. Studied at Liverpool School of Art, the Slade School and Académie Julian, Paris, and at the Royal Academy, Munich where he

HINES, Naomi

gained a gold medal, 1900. Exhibited at the Liverpool Autumn Exhibition from 1901 and the RA from 1907. A President of the Liverpool Academy, Royal Cambrian Academy and the Liver Sketching Club.

HINES, Naomi b.1965
Painter. Studied at West Surrey College of Art and Design, 1984-7. 1987 first represented in a group exhibition at the Young Unknowns Gallery, London. 1988 she was exhibited in a group show at the Square Gallery, London. Also involved in set design and scenery painting for fringe theatre.

HIRST, Barry b.1934
Painter. Born Padstow, Cornwall. Studied at Camberwell School of Art, 1950-2 and 1954-6, and at the Slade, 1956-8. Has taught at various art schools and in 1971 was made Head of Fine Art at Sunderland Polytechnic. 1965 first solo exhibition held at Hanover Gallery, London. Others include one at the Mercury Gallery, London, 1986, and the Mercury Gallery, Edinburgh, 1987. Has illustrated several private press books of poetry.

HIRST, Derek b.1930
Painter. Born Doncaster, Yorkshire. Attended Doncaster School of Art, 1948, and RCA, 1948-51. 1953 first visited Catalonia in Spain, visits which continued annually until 1973. 1961 lived and worked in Andalusia, Southern Spain. 1966 first Artist-in-Residence at the University of Sussex. 1961 first one-person show at Drian Gallery, London. Others include one at Pallant House, Chichester, 1987. Represented by Angela Flowers Gallery, London.

HITCHCOCK, Harold b.1914
Painter. Born London. His mother was a descendant of George Stubbs. After a visit to the National Gallery he developed a lifelong love for the work of Claude Lorraine. Largely self-taught, he paints entirely from imagination mystical landscapes influenced by the Arthurian legends, Samuel Palmer, the Pre-Raphaelites and Claude. 1984 an exhibition of his work was held at the Christopher Wood Gallery, London.

HITCHEN, Stephen b.1953
Sculptor. Born Liverpool, Merseyside. Studied at St. Helen's College of Art, 1971-2, Liverpool Polytechnic, 1972-6 and Manchester Polytechnic, 1976-7. 1978 solo exhibition at Atkinson Art Gallery, Southport.

HITCHENS, Ivon 1893-1979
Painter. Born London. 1909-11 he travelled in New Zealand after a severe illness. 1911 attended St. John's Wood School of Art, moving that same year to the RA Schools where he studied 1911-12, 1914-16 and 1918-19. Founder-member of the 7 & 5 Society. 1925 first solo exhibition at Mayor Gallery. 1929 member of London Artists' Association. 1931 member of London Group. During the 1930s came under the influence of Braque. Contributed to the exhibition, 'Objective Abstractions', held in 1934 and for a period experimented with abstraction. 1936 began using the double-square horizontal format for abstracted landscapes in which the sweep of a broad full brush can connote seasonal moods, a stretch of sky or water or the movement of wind. 1940 moved to Sussex after the bombing of his London home, acquiring six acres of land at Lavingham Common, near Petworth, where he lived for the rest of his life. 1945 first retrospective held at Temple Newsam House, Leeds. Another held at RA, 1979. A major landscape artist, employing a non-factual style which allowed him to plan his pictures, like music, in movements, thereby appealing, as he said, with a 'clear tune' to the spectator's 'aesthetic ear'. (Plate 53, p.251.)

DAVID HOCKNEY, b.1937. *'Japanese Painting'*, 1981. Acrylic. 60in. x 60in. Tradhart Ltd.

Bibl: Alan Bowness, *Ivon Hitchens,* London: Lund Humphries, 1973; *Ivon Hitchens: Forty-Five Paintings,* Serpentine Gallery, London, 1989.

HITCHENS, John b.1940
Painter. Born Sussex. Son of Ivon Hitchens* to whose art his own is related, in its concern with landscape, the sweep of the brushmarks and the preference for horizontal formats. 1964 first solo exhibition held at Marjorie Parr Gallery, London; others include one at Montpelier Studio, London, 1986.

HITCHINS, Ron b.1926
Relief-maker. Born London. First became well-known for his Spanish dancing, and appeared on films, on stage and television. Began working with ceramics, before exchanging this for resin bonded fibreglass, for door-size relief panels. 1966 first solo exhibition held at John Whibley Gallery, London.

HITCHMOUGH, Colin b.1943
Sculptor. Born Widnes, Lancashire. Studied at Liverpool College of Art, 1963-7 and Birmingham College of Art, 1967-8. Solo exhibitions at the Bluecoat Gallery, Liverpool, 1967, 1968 and 1970, and at the Ikon Gallery, Birmingham, 1971 and 1974. Represented in the Museum of Modern Art, Oxford.

HOARE, Jeff
Painter. Studied at Chelsea School of Art and Swansea University. Taught art in London schools and designed sets for Brecht's *Caucasian Chalk Circle.* Numerous solo exhibitions at Piccadilly Gallery, Marjorie Parr Gallery, London, and elsewhere.

HOCKNEY, David b.1937
Painter and printmaker. Born Bradford, Yorkshire. Studied at Bradford School of Art, 1953-7. As a conscientious objector, he did his National Service as a hospital orderly. During this period he read Proust and

FRANCES HODGKINS,
1869-1947. *'Wings over Water'*.
27in. x 38in.
Leeds City Art Galleries.

was inspired by an Alan Davie* exhibition at Wakefield. Studied at the RCA, 1959-62, where he was encouraged by his fellow student, R.B. Kitaj,* to move away from abstraction. From then on his personal interests, including his homosexuality, became the subject of his art. Impressed by the 1960 Picasso exhibition at the Tate Gallery, he titled his own contribution to the 1962 Young Contemporaries show 'Demonstrations of Versatility', announcing his decision to be unbounded, like Picasso, by any single style. After a visit to Egypt in 1963 and on the proceeds of his successful series of etchings, *A Rake's Progress,* he moved to Los Angeles. There he exchanged oils for acrylic paint which encouraged his preoccupation with flatness and clearer definition. His use of photographs for source material further encouraged a more realist style. 1966 he produced *Illustrations for Fourteen Poems from C.P. Cavafy,* a series of etchings which led on to his illustrations for six of the fairy tales by the Brothers Grimm, published 1970. Since then he has continued to work in a variety of media, producing photo-portraits, designs for theatre and opera, Fax art, as well as etchings, lithographs and paintings. A brilliant draughts-man, some of his best work has been produced with pen and ink. Since the mid-1970s his paintings have also begun to explore notions of artifice and style in a freshly inventive manner. His first major retrospective was held at the Whitechapel Art Gallery, 1970. Since then he has exhibited world wide, as an artist of international stature.

Bibl: *David Hockney by David Hockney,* Thames & Hudson, London, 1976; Marco Livingstone, *David Hockney,* Thames & Hudson, London, 1980; *David Hockney: A Retrospective,* Los Angeles County Museum of Art, 1988.

HODGES, Paul   b.1950
Painter. Born Cardiff, Wales. Studied at Bath Academy of Art, 1972-3, and Sheffield College of Art, 1973-6. 1979 first solo exhibition held at University Gallery, Sheffield, and another at the Compass Gallery, Glasgow, 1980.

HODGKIN, C. Eliot   1905-1987
Painter. Born Purley, Berkshire. Studied at the Byam Shaw School of Art and the RA Schools. Held first solo exhibition at the Picture Hire Gallery, London, 1936; also

exhibited at the RA. During the Second World War served as an air-raid warden and painted many pictures of the Home Front. Author of *55 Views of London* (1948) and *A Pictorial Gospel* (1949).

Bibl: *Eliot Hodgkin: Painter and Collector,* introduction by Sir Brinsley Ford, Hazlitt, Gooden & Fox, London, 1990.

HODGKIN, Howard   b.1932
Painter. Born London. Soon after the outbreak of war was evacuated to America, and returned 1943. Studied at Camberwell School of Art, 1949-50, and the Bath Academy of Art at Corsham, 1950-4. Taught for some years at Charterhouse School, then the Bath Academy of Art, and finally at Chelsea School of Art. Artist-in-residence at Brasenose College, Oxford, 1976-7 and made CBE, 1977. The starting point for many of his paintings has been the memory of an encounter with people or a place. In his recreation of the emotional reality of the occasion, Hodgkin deliberately avoids the illustrational and for many years worked with shapes — the disc, stripe or loop — that are impersonal. Working mostly on wood, he constantly alters the image by radical additions, allowing traces of the earlier state to show through. In this way he achieves a rich density of colour with spatial complexity. Has also produced etchings, aquatints and lithographs in a painterly fashion. His prints, *Indian Leaves,* made on wet, hand-made paper in Ahmedabad, were shown at the Tate Gallery, 1982. Their colours owed much to Mughal miniatures which Hodgkin collects. His exhibition 'Forty Paintings 1973-84' was shown at the Venice Biennale, 1984 and afterwards travelled to America and Germany before returning to London to inaugurate the reopening of the Whitechapel Art Gallery. 1985 won the Turner Prize. 1986 won first prize in the Bradford Print Biennale with *David's Pool.* (Plate 54, p.251.)

Bibl: *Howard Hodgkin: Forty Paintings 1973-84,* Whitechapel Art Gallery, London, 1984.

HODGKINS, Frances   1869-1947
Painter. Born New Zealand. Came to London in 1900, having earned the money to do so from piano lessons, selling watercolours and black and white illustrations for

EILEEN HOGAN, b.1946.
'Tooting Common', 1988.
48in. x 48in. Private Collection.

newspapers. Travelled in Europe, painting watercolours influenced by Arthur Melville.* Spent ten years in Paris, taking a watercolour class of her own at Colarossi's. Returned to England shortly before the First World War and received encouragement from Cedric Morris.* 1923-6 lived in Manchester. Exhibited with the London Group and 7 & 5 Society. An association with the St. George's Gallery and then the Lefevre Gallery, London, brought her fame in her sixties. She favoured still lifes placed in front of landscape and often worked in the Constable country in East Anglia.

HODGSON, Carole   b.1940
Sculptor and collagist. Born London. Studied at the Slade School of Art. Lecturer at Reading University, the University of Wisconsin, USA, Norwich School of Art and the Institute of Education, London University. 1973 first one-person show at the Angela Flowers Gallery, London. 1987 bronze sculpture commissioned by British Aerospace sited at the Fairfield Development, Kingston upon Thames. Represented in Arts Council Collection and elsewhere.

HODGSON, Clive   b.1953
Painter. Born Nottingham. Studied at St. Martin's School of Art, 1971-2, and at the Slade School of Art, 1972-7. Awards include a Boise Scholarship from the Slade School of Art and Sotheby's Prize for the Most Outstanding Painting, Whitechapel Open Exhibition, Whitechapel Art Gallery, 1988. First exhibited at Browse and Darby, 1977.

Solo exhibition at the Anne Berthoud Gallery, London, 1988. Painter of oblique figurative allegories. Included in the collections of Arts Council of Great Britain, University College, London and Leicestershire Schools Collection.

HODGSON, Trevor   b.1931
Painter. Born Yorkshire. Studied at Lancaster College of Art and London University. Solo exhibitions in London and America, also one at University of Hull, 1969.

HOFFNUNG, Gerard   1925-1959
Draughtsman. Born Berlin, Germany. Came to England in 1939. Studied at Hornsey School of Art, but was failed for not taking the life classes seriously. Became a humorous illustrator, having an especial fondness for musicians and their instruments; he originated a series of humorous concerts at the Royal Festival Hall, London. He also taught art, played the oboe, visited prisons, wrote books and spoke at the Oxford and Cambridge Unions.

HOGAN, Eileen   b.1946
Painter. Born London. Studied at Camberwell School of Art, 1964-7, the RA Schools, 1967-70, and RCA, 1971-4. 1972 first solo exhibition held at New Grafton Gallery, London; others followed, in Cambridge and elsewhere. 1978 established the Burnt Wood Press, and joined the staff at Camberwell School of Arts and Crafts. 1980 held a solo exhibition at FIN, London. 1983-6 established the Camberwell Press. 1986 elected ARWS, and was commissioned to paint HM the Queen presenting colours

PAUL HOGARTH, b.1917. *The Djurgarden with Nordiska Museet and Tivoli Tower from Strandvagen*, 1986. Watercolour. From *Graham Greene Country*, 1986.

to the Portsmouth Fleet. A romantic figurative painter, with a liking for geometric grids underlying her compositions.

HOGARTH, Paul   b.1917
Topographical artist. Born Kendal, Westmorland. Studied at Manchester College of Art, 1933-6 and St. Martin's School of Art, 1936-7. After the war he resumed his career as an illustrator and graphic designer and travelled widely. Published *Looking at China*, 1955, *People Like Us*, 1958, *Brendan Behan's Ireland*, 1962, and *Brendan Behan's New York*, 1964. 1965 he collaborated with Robert Graves on *Majorca Observed*. 1966 with Malcolm Muggeridge he produced *London à la mode*. Also contributed to numerous magazines and journals and taught at the RCA. An exhibition in honour of his 60th birthday was held at the Fitzwilliam Museum, Cambridge, 1977.

HOGBEN, Philip   b.1945
Painter. Studied at Derby College of Art, 1961-5, and Winchester School of Art, 1965-6. Since 1977 has exhibited regularly with the Newlyn Group at the RWEA and elsewhere. Exhibits mostly in the West Country and in Germany.

HOLDEN, Cliff   b.1919
Painter. Born Manchester. Studied painting and sculpture, worked for a period with David Bomberg* and became a founder member of the Borough Group, 1946-51, and its first President. Has exhibited in numerous group and solo exhibitions, and was represented in the 1957 Redfern Gallery show, 'British Abstract, Tachiste and Metavisual Painters'. Solo shows include one at the Drian Galleries, 1962.

HOLDEN, Denis
Painter. Studied at St. Martin's and Central School of Art and the Bath Academy of Art. 1953-60 lithographic artist with Shell-Mex and B.P. Limited. Member of the Islington Art Circle and Finsbury Art Group. 1964 solo exhibition at Woodstock Gallery, London.

HOLDEN, (Mrs) Lily B.
Painter. Trained as a pharmacist in Liverpool and then apprenticed with Boots the Chemist until her marriage. In the early 1950s attended part-time classes at Wallasey School of Art. Member of Deeside Art Group.

HOLDERNESS, Grizelda   b.1953
Pastellist. Born Salisbury, Zimbabwe. Came to England

HOLDERNESS, Helen

EDGAR HOLLOWAY, b.1914. *'Self portrait'*, 1932. Etching. 61½ in. x 88½ in.

in 1972. Studied at Bristol School of Art, 1972-3 and Central School of Art and Design, 1973-6. 1982, 1983 and 1985 had solo exhibitions at the Thumb Gallery, London. Has also designed many book covers and in 1983 won the Pan Young Illustrator of the Year Award.

HOLDERNESS, Helen
Painter. Studied at Slade School of Art under Professor Tonks,* 1924-6, and Central School of Arts and Crafts, 1935-9. Solo exhibitions at Kensington Art Gallery, Goupil Gallery, Small Gallery, FBA, 1964, and Woodstock Gallery, London, 1968. Member of South London Group.

HOLLAND, Derek   b.1927
Painter. Born Chesterfield, Derbyshire. Studied at Chesterfield College of Arts and Central School of Arts and Crafts. Taught at Central School, afterwards became Head of Art at Plymouth College. Exhibited in mixed exhibitions throughout 1950s and 1960s, having a solo exhibition at the Sheviock Gallery in East Cornwall, 1968.

HOLLAND, Harry   b.1941
Painter. Born Glasgow, Scotland. Studied at St. Martin's School of Art, 1965-9. His paintings show figures engaged in everyday actions in such a way that the scene becomes disturbing and near hallucinatory. Light is an important ingredient, distilling a monumentality that recalls Edward Hopper and Balthus. 1975 first solo exhibition held at Oriel, Cardiff, and 1979 at the Nicholas Treadwell Gallery. Others include one at the Andrew Knight Gallery, Los Angeles, 1987. Represented in Tate Gallery, Metropolitan Museum of Art, New York and elsewhere.

HOLLAND, James   b.1948
Painter. Born Ashington, Northumberland. Studied at Newastle upon Tyne University, 1966-71, and Courtauld Institute, University of London, 1971-2. 1976 solo exhibition at Dudley Art Gallery.

HOLLINGSWORTH, Ruth   fl.1906-1934
Painter. Studied at the Slade and London School of Art. Exhibited NEAC, RA, Society of Women Artists and elsewhere. Specialised in landscape, still lifes and flowers.

HOLLINGWORTH, Mick   b.1945
Painter. Studied at Colchester School of Art, 1964-5, and Nottingham College of Art, 1965-8. Figurative artist. 1980 solo exhibition at Gainsborough's House, Sudbury, Suffolk.

HOLLWEG, Alexander   b.1936
Sculptor. Born London. Solo exhibitions held at Whitechapel Art Gallery, London, 1970, and Felicity Samuel Gallery, London, 1972.

HOLLOWAY, Edgar   b.1914
Painter and etcher. Born Doncaster, Yorkshire. Intended going to art school but was already selling his work through his father's framing shop at the age of fourteen and felt little need for instruction. Learnt his skill at etching from books, especially Ernest Lumsden's *The Art of Etching*. 1931 first solo exhibition held. Moved to London, attended life classes at the Slade, met Alec Buckels and through him, Herbert Read, Stephen Spender and T.S. Eliot, whose portraits Holloway drew and etched. Visited Eric Gill* at Capel y ffin and married his favourite model, Daisy Monica Hawkins. Exhibited at RA.

Bibl: *Edgar Holloway,* The Robin Garton Gallery, London, 1979.

HOLMES, Charles   1868-1936
Painter and etcher. Born Preston, Lancashire. Educated at Brasenose College, Oxford. Two years later he produced the first of his industrial scenes and the same year entered a publishing business in London. Came under the influence of Charles Ricketts* and took up etching, executing some 85 plates between 1892 and 1897. 1900 began to exhibit with the NEAC, became a member, 1904. 1903-9 editor of the *Burlington Magazine,* 1904-10 Slade Professor at Oxford, 1909-16 Director of the National Portrait Gallery, and 1916-28 of the National Gallery. 1909 first solo exhibition held at Carfax Gallery, London. Knighted 1921, KCVO, 1928, ARWS, 1924 and RWS, 1928. Also wrote many books on art.

HOLT, Eric   b.1944
Painter. Born Sutton, Surrey. Studied at Epsom School of Art 1959-62. Undertook various forms of employment, producing also two paintings a year, 1962-72. 1972 held his first solo exhibition at Maltzahn Gallery, London, and has since then exhibited regularly, at the RA and elsewhere. His figurative scenes owe something to Stanley Spencer* in their use of distortion.

HOLT, Gila
Painter. Born London. Studied at Hammersmith School of Art. Her paintings have benefited from her study of other arts, notably dancing and music. After many years as a professional musician and singer she returned to painting full time and has had several exhibitions in London and Israel, including one at Heal's, London, 1966.

HOLT, Jeremy   1931-1965
Painter. Studied at Camberwell and Chelsea Schools of Art. Established a considerable reputation as a portrait painter in England, America and Canada, though his preferred subject was landscape. Solo exhibition held at New Grafton Gallery, 1977.

HOLT, Lilian   1898-1983
Painter. Attended classes in the 1940s at the Borough Polytechnic at David Bomberg's* suggestion. Married Bomberg, channelling much of her energy into nurturing his career. 1971 held solo exhibitions at the Woodstock Gallery, London, and 1980 had a retrospective at the Ben Uri Art Gallery, London, with catalogue introduction by Richard Cork.

HOLTAM, Brenda   b.1960
Painter. Studied at Gloucester College of Art and Design, Falmouth School of Art and RA Schools. First began exhibiting at the RA, 1985. Has shown also at the Newlyn Orion Gallery, 1981, and at the RWS.

HOLZHANDLER, Dora   b.1928
Painter. Born in Paris of Russian parents. Came to England at the age of six and in 1943 attended St. Martin's School of Art. Returned to Paris in 1946 for a short period of further study. 1958 first exhibited at the Beaux Arts Gallery, London. Other solo shows include one at the Langton Gallery, London, 1978.

HONE, Evie   1894-1955
Painter and stained-glass designer. Born Dublin, Ireland. Went to London after the First World War and studied at Westminster School of Art and Central School of Art. In 1920 went to Paris with her lifelong friend Mainie Jellett* and worked in the studio of André L'Hôte. In 1921 he persuaded the French Cubist Albert Gleizes to accept them as his first pupils and worked with him each year until 1931. Elected to the 'Abstraction-Création' exhibiting group. Exhibited regularly in Dublin and became a founder-member of the Irish Exhibition of Living Art. Produced her first piece of stained glass in 1933, carrying out some 48 commissions in all.

HOOD, Harvey   b.1946
Sculptor. Born Staffordshire. Studied at Birmingham College of Art, and RCA, 1969-72. In 1973 began living in the Forest of Dean. 1979 solo exhibition at Oriel, Cardiff. Works in wood, with a respect for traditional craft skills.

HOOPER, George   b.1910
Painter. Born India. Arrived in England, 1922. On leaving school he entered employment in a bank for two years then studied at the Slade School of Fine Art and then RA Schools, 1931-5. Spent two years in Italy on a Rome Scholarship, returned to England and during the war joined the ARP. Made watercolours of buildings and sites of national importance for the Pilgrim Trust's *Recording Britain* project. After the war he taught part-time and kept

himself apart from other artists, except for Duncan Grant* whose old-fashioned courtesy and charm he enjoyed. Represented in the V & A and British Museum.

HOPE, Laurence   b.1928
Painter. Born Sydney, Australia. Studied at East Sydney Art College, 1943-6. 1949 held first solo exhibition in Brisbane. 1963 came to London and during the next six years travelled widely in Europe and North Africa. 1968 held his first solo exhibition at the Clytie Jessop Gallery, London; another held at the Commonwealth Art Gallery, London, 1972.

HOPE, Polly   b.1933
Fabric sculptor. Born Colchester, Essex. Originally trained as a dancer and joined the Festival Ballet. Left ballet because of her excessive height and enrolled at Heatherley's School of Art, afterwards studying at Chelsea Polytechnic, 1950-2. 1973 made her first fabric sculptures. Divides each year between London and Greece. Her work includes a commissioned portrait of Sir Roy Strong.

Bibl: *Polly Hope: soft art and drawings 1971-82,* Warwick Arts Trust, 1982.

HOPKIN, Elizabeth   b.1920
Naïve painter. A housewife who began painting scenes of her childhood in the Upper Swansea Valley to portray life in a mining community as it was in the 1920s. Self-taught. Solo exhibition at Portal Gallery, London, 1976. Also exhibits in Los Angelés.

HOPKINS, Clyde   b.1946
Painter. Born Bexhill, Sussex. Studied at Reading University, 1965-9. Has taught at various art schools and exhibited in many solo and group shows. 1980 was awarded a Mark Rothko Fellowship and travelled to North America, making another visit in 1984. Solo exhibition held at Serpentine Gallery, 1986, and elsewhere.

Bibl: *Clyde Hopkins: Paintings,* Arts Council cat., 1985-6.

HOPKINS, Phill   b.1961
Sculptor. Born Bristol, Avon. Studied at Goldsmiths' College, University of London, 1982-5. 1987 artist-in-residence at Alhambra Theatre, Bradford. 1984 first solo exhibition held at Hartcliffe Arts Festival, Hartcliffe, Bristol; another at St. Paul's Gallery, Leeds, 1988.

HOPKINSON, John   b.1941
Painter. Born Cleethorpes, Humberside. Studied at Grimsby School of Art, but left without a diploma and begun labouring in a Scunthorpe steel works. In 1978 Fox Fine Arts, London, enabled him to paint full-time, and gave him his first solo exhibition in that year.

HORNEL, Edward Atkinson   1864-1933
Painter. Born Bacchus Marsh, Victoria, Australia. Spent his early life in Scotland. Studied at the Trustees Academy, Edinburgh, 1881-3, and in Antwerp under Verlat in 1887. Around 1890 began exhibiting in Glasgow and became a prominent member of the Glasgow School. 1893-4 visited Japan and Ceylon, and Australia, 1907. Influenced by Oriental art, Monticelli and Matthew Maris. Painted mainly children and flowers in a rich mosaic of colour.

Bibl: *Edward Atkinson Hornel 1864-1933,* Fine Art Society, Glasgow, 1982.

Plate 46. PATRICK HALL, b.1906. *'Business Canale Grande, Venice'*. 16in. x 14½in. Private Collection.

Plate 47. MAGGI HAMBLING, b.1945. *'Sunrise 1989'*. 84in. x 36in. Private Collection.

Plate 48. HAROLD HARVEY, 1874-1941. *'Sport on the Shore — A Crab Race'*. 12in. x 16in.
Plymouth City Museum and Art Gallery.

Plate 49. TIM HEAD, b.1946. *'Flesh & Blood II'*, 1988. Acrylic
on canvas. 60in. x 48in. Nicola Jacobs Gallery, London.

Plate 50. ADRIAN HEATH, b.1920. *'Sogne No. 2'*, 1986.
50in. x 36in. Private Collection.

HORNER, Jocelyn

JOCELYN HORNER, 1902-1973. 'The Annunciation', c.1949. Plaster. 20½ in. high. Leeds City Art Galleries.

HORNER, Jocelyn   1902-1973
Sculptor. Born Halifax, Yorkshire. Studied at Leeds School of Art in 1920, where her fellow pupils were Barbara Hepworth* and Henry Moore.* Produced little during the 1930s and during the Second World War was occupied aiding the disabled. After 1945 she returned to Leeds School of Art as a student, and subsequently became a teacher of art. The 1950s saw renewed productivity. Admired Jacob Epstein* and sought linear elegance in her own work. During the 1960s she executed many portrait commissions.

Bibl: *Jocelyn Horner, Sculptor, 1902-1973*, Temple Newsam, Leeds, 1974.

HOROVITZ, Michael   b.1935
Painter, performance poet, songwriter-singer, literary journalist. Born Frankfurt, Germany. Studied English at Brasenose College, Oxford, 1954-9, during which time he published *The Blake Renaissance*. Visited Paris regularly

between 1954 and 1959 which led to new visual art activity. 1959 started *New Departures* with Anna Lovell, Cornelius Cardew and John McGrath, and *Live New Departures* arts circuses, which were platforms for intermedia experimentations. 1966-71 he began his *Carnival*. 1971-81 he made extended tours of Canada and the United States; 1981 launched *Poetry Olympics* from Westminster Abbey. His visual work is influenced by the Nicholas de Staël memorial show, London, 1956, the exhibition of new American painting, London, 1958, and by Alan Davie.* The breadth of his interest is reflected in the diversity of visual images he produces in paintings, collages and picture-poems. They are created out of an eclectic range of images in which the paint, form and colour are handled loosely, highlighting his pleasure in the materials for their own sake.

HORROCKS, Nancy
Painter. Studied at Chelsea Art School and the Slade. Has worked in St. Ives and London and exhibited in the AIA, New Vision and other galleries.

HORSFIELD, Nicholas   b.1917
Painter. Studied at RCA, 1935-8. 1948-56 worked as Arts Council Regional Officer, Visual Arts, Manchester. 1954 became member of Liverpool Academy of Art. 1963 first solo exhibition held at Bluecoat Gallery, Liverpool; others include one held at the Chateau-Musée, Dieppe and Camden Arts Centre, 1984. An expressionist element in his work liberated him from slavish imitation of appearances and his landscapes can come close to pure abstraction.

HORSFIELD, Susan   b.1928
Painter. Born India. Travelled extensively in Africa where for some time she worked for an interior decorator in Nairobi and taught in a government school. Trained at the Regent Street Polytechnic under P.F. Millard.* 1959 first solo exhibition at Walker Galleries, London. Exhibited with the London Group, the RSBA and Women's International Art Club.

HORTON, James V.   b.1948
Painter. Studied at Sir John Cass School of Art, 1964-6, City and Guilds School of Art, 1966-70, and RCA, 1971-4. First solo exhibition held at Hay Galleries, Hay-on-Wye, 1974. Others followed, in Belfast, Dublin, Cambridge, and Stockholm. Has also exhibited in various group shows. Regular contributor to *The Artist* since 1977 and published *Learn to Draw the Figure*, 1984.

HORTON, Percy   1897-1970
Painter. Studied at Brighton School of Art, 1912-16. An absolute conscientious objector, he served two years hard labour in Carlton Prison, Edinburgh, 1916-18. Studied at Central School of Art and Design, 1918-20, and RCA, 1922-5. 1930-49 taught at RCA and afterwards at Ruskin School, Oxford. As a member of the Artists International Association in the 1930s he believed artists should be socially committed and adopted a restrained, conservative style (partly inspired by Cézanne) with which to portray people.

Bibl: Janet Barnes, *Percy Horton: Artist and Absolvetist,* Sheffield City Art Galleries, 1982.

HOSIE, David   b.1962
Painter. Born Glasgow, Scotland. Studied at Edinburgh

PERCY HORTON, 1897-1970. *'The Unemployed Man'*, 1936.
Oil on plywood. 17 ½ in. x 14in. Sheffield City Art Galleries.

SHIRAZEH HOUSHIARY, b.1955. *'Sacred Threshold'*, 1986.
Zinc and copper. 79 ½ in. x 30in. x 30in. Lisson Gallery, London.

College of Art 1980-6. Since 1986 part-time lecturer in painting at Edinburgh College of Art. From 1985 included in mixed exhibitions in Edinburgh and Glasgow. 1987 first one-person show at Raab Gallery, London and Berlin. Work in the collection of the Royal Scottish Academy and the City Art Centre, Edinburgh.

HOSKIN, John   b.1921
Sculptor and painter. Born Cheltenham, Gloucestershire. Trained and worked as an architectural draughtsman. 1951 started to paint and sculpt, and is self-taught. 1956 one-person show at the Aldeburgh Festival, and at the Serpentine Gallery, 1975. 1957-67 Head of the Sculpture School at Bath Academy of Art and Head of Painting at Winchester School of Art, 1978. Commissioned to make a reredos for St. Stephens Church, Southmead, Bristol, and one for Nuffield College Chapel, Oxford.

HOSKING, Knighton   b.1944
Painter. Born Sidmouth, Devon. Studied at Central School of Art and Design, 1963-6. 1966 won Peter Stuyvesant Foundation Bursary for travel in USA. 1970 first solo exhibition held at Wolverhampton Polytechnic; others include one at the Serpentine Gallery, London, 1974, and another at the Ikon Gallery, Birmingham, 1980.

HOSKINS, Ned   b.1939
Painter. Born Croydon, Surrey. Studied at Harrogate School of Art, 1955-60, and RCA, 1961-4. 1973-4 Fellow in Fine Art, University of Southampton. Solo exhibitions include one at Brighton Museum and Art Gallery, 1986,

entitled 'Sussex Revisited'. Indebted in his understanding of landscape to an unorthodox art class on the Yorkshire Moors given by Terry Frost.*

HOUSHIARY, Shirazeh   b.1955
Sculptor. Born Shiraz, Persia. Has lived in London since 1963. Studied at Chelsea School of Art, 1976-9 and was Junior Fellow at Cardiff College of Art, 1979-80. Included in mixed exhibitions since the Venice Biennale, 1982. 1980 one-person show at the Chapter Arts Centre, Cardiff; another held at Lisson Gallery, 1984. 1987 first major museum exhibition at the Centre d'Art Contemporain, Geneva. Work in the collections of the Tate Gallery and Southampton Art Gallery.

Bibl: *Shirazeh Houshiary,* with introduction by Lynne Cooke, Lisson Gallery, London, 1984.

Plate 51. JOSEF HERMAN, b.1911. *'Suffolk Landscape'*, 1974. 28in. x 36in.
Private Collection.

Plate 52. TRISTRAM HILLIER, 1905-1983. *'The Slipway at Peniche'*, 1948. 25¼in. x 37½in.
Aberdeen City Arts Department, Art Gallery and Museums.

Plate 53. IVON HITCHENS, 1893-1979. *'Folded Stream'*, 1947. 20in. x 40½in. Bernard Jacobson Gallery, London.

Plate 54. HOWARD HODGKIN, b.1932. *'Bedroom in Carennac'*, 1971-2. Oil on panel. 42½in. x 46⅝in. Waddington Galleries Ltd., London.

ALBERT HOUTHUESEN,
1903-1979. 'Crown of Thorns',
1939-40. 36in. x 48in.
Tate Gallery.

HOUSTON, Ian   b.1934
Painter. Born Gravesend, Kent. Since 1964 has lived in Norfolk. Widely acclaimed as one of Britain's leading marine artists. Honorary member of the East Anglian Group of Marine Artists and a Gold Medallist (1984) of the National Society of French Artists. 1984 held an exhibition, 'Our Maritime Heritage: Coastline Landscapes' at Falmouth Art Gallery.

HOUSTON, John   b.1930
Painter. Born Buckhaven, Scotland. Studied at Edinburgh College of Art and afterwards went to Italy on a travelling scholarship. Influenced by William Gillies* and, later, by American Abstract Expressionism. First visited America in 1969 and after his return returned to landscape painting with a new access of energy, never again painting in a wholly abstract manner, though continuing to use strong colour. Elected associate of the RSA, 1964 and academician in 1972. Member of the RSW and the Society of Scottish Artists. Married to Elizabeth Blackadder.* Teaches at Edinburgh College of Arts. (Plate 55, p.254.)

Bibl: *Works on Paper 1962-1987. John Houston,* Talbot Rice Gallery, Edinburgh, 1987.

HOUSTON, Sally   b.1954
Sculptor. Born Belfast, Northern Ireland. Studied at Edinburgh College of Art. 1976 began exhibiting in group shows, and held her first solo exhibition at the Octagon Gallery, Belfast, 1982.

HOUTHUESEN, Albert   1903-1979
Painter. Born Amsterdam, Holland. Taught by his father, also a painter. Moved to London 1911. Attracted notice of Sir William Rothenstein,* later winning a scholarship to RCA, 1923. Exhibited at Fine Arts Society, Colnaghi, Mercury and Waddington Galleries. Despite constant ill health, he was a prolific and wide-ranging painter of audacious and powerful vision, symbolically expressed in vibrant colour, notably in tumultuous sea-scapes with menacing rocks: also a series of tragic clowns. In 1977 he was the subject of a BBC TV Omnibus programme: *Walk to the Moon.* Represented in Tate Gallery, Leeds City Art Gallery and elsewhere. Married the painter Catherine Dean.*

HOWARD, Anita   b.1926
Painter. Born London. 1945-8 served in WRAC in Singapore and Hong Kong. Studied at Provincetown, Massachusetts, USA, 1950-2, at Regent Street Polytechnic and the Central School, 1954-7. 1976 first solo exhibition held at Camden Arts Centre; another at Royal Free Hospital, Hampstead, 1978.

HOWARD, Charles   1899-1978
Painter. Born Montclair, New Jersey, USA. Studied at University of California. 1922 took up painting and for two years travelled in France and Italy. 1926 first solo exhibition at Whitney Studio Club, New York. 1933-40 lived in London. 1936 associated with the Surrealists and exhibited in the International Surrealist Exhibition. 1946 returned to England and in 1963 became a British citizen.

HOWARD, Ian   b.1952
Painter. Born Aberdeen, Scotland. Studied at Edinburgh University, and Edinburgh College of Art, 1970-5. 1976 won a travelling scholarship to Italy. 1983 elected associate of the RSA. Has exhibited regularly since 1973 and in 1985 held a solo exhibition at the Compass Gallery, Glasgow. Like Graham Crowley* and Stephen Farthing,* Howard imbues inanimate objects with human qualities. 1986 appointed Head of Painting at Duncan of Jordanstone College of Art, Dundee.

Bibl: *Ian Howard: Paintings, Prints and Related Works,* Third Eye Centre, Glasgow, 1987.

KEN HOWARD, b.1932. *'In the Studio'*. New Grafton Gallery.

HOWARD, John   b.1902
Painter. Born London. Studied at Slade School of Art and won second prize in the summer competition of 1921. Influenced by Sickert* through the teaching of John Wheatley* who taught him to look at the space behind the model and to paint in 'blobs'. Exhibited with the London Group, the NEAC and at the Goupil Gallery. Spent periods abroad during the 1920s. Solo exhibitions include one at Cadogan Contemporary Art, London, 1988.

HOWARD, Ken   b.1932
Painter. Studied at Hornsey College of Art, 1949-53 and RCA, 1955-8. 1958-9 won British Council Scholarship to Florence. Member of NEAC. 1981 elected RWA, and 1983 ARA. 1955 first solo exhibition held at Plymouth Art Centre; others include seven at the New Grafton Gallery, London, 1971-86. Elected RA, 1989

HOWARD, Patricia D.
Painter. Born Surrey, the granddaughter of the artist, Frank Holl. In 1948 she had two solo exhibitions at Salford and Manchester, which included industrial scenes. 1951 moved to Eastbourne and specialised in lithography and linocuts. Studied at Eastbourne School of Art. Exhibits at RA. Fellow of the RSA. Represented in Brighton and Eastbourne art galleries.

HOWARD-JONES, Ray   b.1903
Painter. Born in Berkshire of Welsh parents. Studied at Slade School in the early 1920s. During the war he became an accredited painter with the Royal Navy, the Army and the RAF, working on coastal defence. Also undertook several commissions from the War Artists Advisory Committee. 1949 chose to live and paint for nine years on the uninhabited island of Skomer. 1958 designed a 40ft.

Plate 55. JOHN HOUSTON, b.1930.
'Stormy Sunrise', 1989. 40in. x 40in.
Mercury Gallery, London.

Plate 56. PETER HOWSON, b.1958. *'Death of Innocence',*
1989. 120in. x 96in. Flowers East, London.

Plate 57. JOHN HUBBARD, b.1931. *'Double Courtyard'*, 1989.
60¼in. x 35in. Fischer Fine Art Ltd., London.

Plate 58. ROBERT HURDLE, b.1918.
'Canal, Maida Vale', c.1948.
19in. x 23in. Private Collection.

HOWE, Beatrice

mosaic for Thompson House in Cardiff. Solo exhibition at the Leicester Galleries, London, 1961, at which she showed abstract paintings as well as landscapes and seascapes; another was held at the same gallery, 1964. Represented in the National Museum of Wales, Imperial War Museum, Glynn Vivian Museum, Swansea and elsewhere.

HOWE, Beatrice   1867-1932
Painter. Born Bideford, Devon. Studied at the Herkomer School at Bushey and in Paris at the Académie Delacluse. Influenced by Bonnard and Vuillard. Exhibited regularly at the Salon from 1902 onwards, also at the Royal Glasgow Institute of Fine Arts. Represented in Tate Gallery and elsewhere. Was fascinated by the mother and child subject and by gently luminous colour.

HOWE, Robert   b.1945
Painter. Born Leeds, Yorkshire. Studied at Doncaster School of Art but left after one year as he felt the teaching was too academic. Continued painting whilst doing odd jobs, exhibiting on Green Park railings in London. 1967 solo exhibition held at ICA; another at Portal Gallery, London, 1979.

HOWELL, Joan
Painter. Studied at Chelsea School of Art, 1953-8, followed by two years study at LCC Teachers' Training Centre. Studied Graphic Design, Illustration and Printing at St. Martin's School of Art, 1962-4. First solo exhibition held at Woodstock Gallery, London, 1968.

HOWIE, James   b.1931
Painter. Born Dundee, Scotland. Studied at Dundee College of Art, 1949-54. 1955 visited Paris. 1955-7 National Service, and also studied pottery at Liverpool College of Art during this period. 1959 moved to London. 1960 featured in a 'Monitor' film with Anthony Whishaw* and Sonia Lawson.* 1960 first solo exhibition held at New Art Centre, London; another at Richard Demarco Gallery, Edinburgh, 1969.

HOWKINS, Colin
Painter. Born Birmingham, West Midlands. Studied at Birmingham College of Art and Design. 1986 solo exhibition at City Museum and Art Gallery, Worcester. Abstract artist inspired by the landscape of West Wales.

HOWLIN, John   b.1941
Painter. Studied at Hammersmith School of Art, 1957-9. 1963 first solo exhibition held at Chester Beatty; others include Kasmin Gallery, London, 1965, and Arnolfini Gallery, Bristol, 1968.

HOWSON, Peter   b.1958
Painter. Born London. Moved to Scotland in 1962. Studied at Glasgow School of Art, 1975-7, and 1979-81. In between he took on various jobs, including joining the Scottish Infantry. 1985 Artist-in-Residence, St. Andrew's University. 1983 first solo exhibition, 'Wall Murals', held at Feltham Community Association, London; 1987 and 1989 at Angela Flowers Gallery. His work chronicles Glasgow's working-class male population, an overtly masculine world of footballers, pub-goers, boxers and body-builders. This vividly Glaswegian imagery gains in urgency through Howson's theatrical use of dark settings and artificial light. Represented in Scottish Arts Council Collection,

People's Palace, Glasgow, and elsewhere. (Plate 56, p.254.)

Bibl: Waldemar Januszczak, *Peter Howson,* Angela Flowers Gallery, London, 1987.

HOYLAND, Francis   b.1930
Painter. Born Birmingham, West Midlands. Studied at Camberwell School of Arts and Slade School of Art. Exhibited at the Galerie de Seinem, 1958, at the Beaux Arts Gallery, London, 1960, and at South London Art Gallery, 1969.

HOYLAND, John   b.1934
Painter. Born Sheffield, Yorkshire. Studied at Sheffield College of Art, 1956-60, and RA Schools, 1960. Has taught in various schools and been Artist-in-Residence in the Studio School, New York and at Melbourne University, Australia. First came to prominence at the Situation exhibitions in 1960 and 1961 and has since continued to develop an abstract language of art that is primarily dependent on colour applied with bravura vitality. Has also produced a steady flow of silk screens, etchings and lithographs, but is perhaps most noted as a printmaker for his monotypes. 1979 retrospective held at Serpentine Gallery, London. Elected ARA, 1983. Represented by Waddington Fine Art. (Plate 14, p.38.)

Bibl: *John Hoyland: Paintings 1967-1979,* Arts Council, London, 1979; Mel Gooding, *John Hoyland,* Lund Humphries, London, 1990.

HOYLAND, Philippa   b.1924
Painter. Studied at Central School of Arts and Crafts. Works shown at 'Young Contemporaries' and in John Berger's 'Looking Forward' exhibition, at the South London Gallery, RWEA, the LG, and RA. Married to Francis Hoyland.* 1982 solo exhibition at the Annexe Gallery, London.

HOYTON, Edward Bouverie   b.1900-1988
Etcher. A student at Goldsmiths' College in the 1920s, Hoyton learnt etching from F.L. Griggs* and became a Rome Scholar in Engraving, 1926. A contemporary of Graham Sutherland,* he too admired Palmer. Principal of Penzance School of Art, 1941-66. Represented in several public collections.

HUBBARD, Eric Hesketh   1892-1957
Painter and etcher. Born London. Studied at Heatherley's, Croydon School of Art and Chelsea Polytechnic. Exhibited at the RA, the Paris Salon, the RBA, ROI, IS, in the provinces and abroad. Elected ARWA, 1916, ROI, 1921, and RBA, 1923. Published a number of books on the making of art and specialised in landscape and architectural scenes.

HUBBARD, John   b.1931
Painter. Born Ridgefield, Connecticut, USA. Studied at Harvard University. Served in US Army, based in Japan, 1953-6. Studied at Art Students' League, New York, 1956-8, and at Provincetown, Massachusetts, with Hans Hoffman. 1958-60 lived in Rome. 1960 moved to England and has lived in Dorset since 1961. 1988 resident artist at the Poet's House, New Harmony, Indiana, USA. 1961-75 held nine solo exhibitions at New Art Centre, London; others include one at Fischer Fine Art, London, 1988. (Plate 57, p.255.)

HUBBUCK, Rodney   b.1940
Painter. Born Hampshire. Studied at Portsmouth College

EDWARD BOUVERIE HOYTON, 1900-1988. *'Bagworthy Farm'*, c.early 1930s. 11 ¼ in. x 7 ¾ in. Etching. Private Collection.

of Art, Corsham and Brighton. 1967 first solo exhibition held at All Hallows, London Wall; others include a retrospective at Portsmouth Museum and City Art Gallery, 1979.

HUBY, Peter   b.1946
Etcher. Born Hull, Yorkshire. Worked in various jobs until 1973 when he began etching, building his own press with help from a shipyard fitter. Took his subject matter from that of a city decaying and half empty, obscurely menaced by war. 1978 solo exhibition at York City Art Gallery.

HUDSON, Juley   b.1963
Sculptor. Born Carshalton, Surrey. Studied at Reigate School of Art, 1981-3, and Chelsea School of Art, 1983-6. 1986 awarded the Morland Lewis Award. 1986 first exhibited at the Royal Festival Hall, London.

HUDSON, Tom   b.1922
Sculptor. Born Durham. Studied painting at Sunderland College of Art, then art history at the Courtauld Institute, London. Began teaching art, lecturing in Basic Design at Leeds College of Art, 1956-60, at Leicester College of Art, 1960-64, afterwards moving to Cardiff College of Art. 1965-6 visiting artist at Sheffield University. Has exhibited regularly since 1964. Abstract artist who works with synthetic materials.

HUGGINS, Dawn   b.1937
Sculptor. Born Bristol, Avon. Studied at West of England College of Art, 1954-60. 1963 solo exhibition held at Wells Gallery, Somerset.

HUGGINS, John   b.1938
Sculptor. Born Wiltshire. Studied at West of England College of Art. Held numerous solo and group exhibitions in the West Country before having his first solo London exhibition at the Alwyn Gallery, 1978. Member of the Royal Society of British Sculptors, and the Royal West of England Academy.

HUGHES, Eleanor Mary   1882-1959
Painter. Born Christchurch, New Zealand. Studied in London and in Newlyn where she met and married the painter, Robert Hughes.* Settled in Lamorna and painted the Devon and Cornish countryside. 1911 began exhibiting at RA and later at the RI. 1933 elected member of RI.

HUGHES, Frances   b.1905
Painter. Born Hatherop, Gloucestershire. Studied at Chelsea Polytechnic, Central School of Arts and Crafts and Westminster School of Art. Settled in North Wales after the war and painted landscapes, at home and abroad. Solo exhibitions include one at the Woodstock Gallery, London, 1969.

Plate 59. GWYTHER IRWIN, b.1931. *'July 1989'*. Watercolour. 48in. x 60in. Private Collection.

Plate 60. BILL JACKLIN, b.1943. *'Washington Square at Night'*. 78in. x 78in. Marlborough Fine Art (London) Ltd.

Plate 61. LUCY JONES, b.1955. *'Yellow Bridge'*, 1989. 68in. x 82¾in. Flowers East, London.

HUGHES, Ian   b.1958
Painter. Born Glasgow, Scotland. Studied at Duncan of Jordanstone College of Art, Dundee, 1976-8. 1980 part-time work in Kelvingrove Museum and Art Gallery, Glasgow. 1981-2 worked part-time with the mentally ill, initially in the Art Therapy Department, Stobhill Hospital, Glasgow, and then at the Royal Edinburgh Psychiatric Hospital. 1985 first one-person exhibition at 369 Gallery, Edinburgh. 1985 won 'Young Artists' Bursary from Scottish Arts Council. 1986 won second prize in Inverclyde Bienniale. At the 369 Gallery, in 1987, exhibited paintings based on photographs of Kafka. 1988-9 Artist-in-Residence at the Scottish National Gallery of Modern Art, followed in February 1989 by an exhibition of works produced during his residency. His work combined painting and photography, religious imagery and references to the Old Masters with images from medical text books and of the mentally ill.

Bibl: *Ian Hughes: Works 1988,* Scottish National Gallery of Modern Art, 1989.

HUGHES, Kenneth   b.1927
Sculptor. Studied at Liverpool College of Art, 1949-51 and Slade School of Fine Art, 1951-5. 1959 won an Italian Government Scholarship. 1960-5 taught at Birmingham College of Art, and Bath Academy of Art. 1969 solo exhibition at the Ikon Gallery, Birmingham.

HUGHES, Malcolm   b.1920
Constructivist. Born Manchester. Studied at Regional College of Art, Manchester, and RCA. Taught at Bath Academy of Art and Chelsea School of Art. 1982 Honorary Research Fellow at University College, London and Emeritus Reader in Fine Art. 1965 first solo exhibition held at ICA, London; others include one at the Juda Rowan Gallery, London, 1983, and Annely Juda Gallery, 1989.

HUGHES, Margaret   b.1930
Painter. Studied at Wimbledon School of Art, the Slade, and London University. From 1954 exhibited portraits and landscapes at Liverpool Academy and has work in Walker Art Gallery, Liverpool.

HUGHES, Nigel   b.1940
Painter. Studied at RA Schools and has since been a full-time painter, travelling widely and exhibiting regularly. Commissions include works owned by HRH the Prince of Wales, the Grenadier Guards, the National Trust and the Tower of London.

HUGHES, Patrick   b.1939
Painter and printmaker. Born Birmingham, West Midlands. Trained as a teacher at Leeds Training College. First solo exhibition held in London, 1961. Since then has exhibited regularly at the Angela Flowers Gallery, London, throughout the United Kingdom, in America and Canada. His work is often associated with the image of the rainbow in many guises and surreal situations, either wrapped as a present, piled into a dustbin or hung over the line to dry. Publications include (with George Brecht) *Vicious Circles and Infinity, a panoply of paradoxes* (1976) and (with Paul Hammond) *Upon the Pun* (1978). Member of the Penwith Society of Arts. Represented in the V & A, Tate Gallery, Arts Council collection and elsewhere.

HUGHES-STANTON, Blair   b.1902
Painter and wood-engraver. Studied at Byam Shaw School, RA Schools and under Leon Underwood.* Member of the London Group and the Society of Wood-Engravers. Produced a number of books for the Gregynog Press, 1930-3, and also did illustrations for the Golden Cockerel and Cresset Presses. Won an International Prize for Engraving at the Venice Biennale, 1938. Married the sculptor, Gertrude Hermes.* Represented in the British Museum, the V & A and many other galleries throughout Britain.

HUGHES-STANTON, Herbert Edwin Pelham 1870-1937
Painter. Born London. Father of Blair Hughes-Stanton.* Self-taught, apart from help received from his father, also a painter. Exhibited at principal London galleries. Elected ARA, 1913, and RA, 1919, also ARWS, 1909, RWS, 1915, and PRWS in 1920. Knighted 1923. Worked much in France. A prolific artist, who consistently produced three watercolours a day.

HUGO, David   b.1958
Sculptor. Born Nottingham. Studied at Wolverhampton Polytechnic, 1977-80, and RCA, 1981-4. 1985 first solo exhibition at Lanchester Gallery, Coventry. Since 1978 represented in group shows. 1988 awarded Residency at Delfina Studios Trust for two years.

HULBERT, Thelma   b.1913
Painter. Born Bath, Avon. Studied at Bath School of Art, 1927-33, and at the Euston Road School during the late 1930s. 1950 first solo exhibition held at Heffers, Cambridge; another at the Whitechapel Art Gallery, London, 1962; others include two at the Christopher Hull Gallery, London, 1981 and 1984.

HULL, James   1921-1990
Painter. Born London. Self-taught. Began work as a toy-maker and scenery designer. First caught attention in 1948 with his pen and ink drawings of figures in ruined landscapes. Encouraged by the critic, Herbert Read, he held his first solo exhibition at Brook Street Gallery, London, 1949. 1951 designed and painted a mural, *The Story of Coal,* for the Festival of Britain's Dome of Discovery. Included in the 'British Abstract Art' exhibition held at Gimpel Fils, London, 1951. 1952 visited Paris. 1953 began to exhibit in New York at the Passedoit Gallery. Continued to exhibit abstracts in London and took part in the 'This is Tomorrow' exhibition at the Whitechapel Art Gallery, 1956. Towards the end of the 1950s his pre-war interest in architecture revived and he won a competition to design the interior of the *Daily Mail* building. For the next decade he was employed by the IPC conglomerate as a design consultant. 1971 moved to Ibiza with his wife; soon after they arrived his younger daughter died. He then cut himself off from family and friends and travelled in America and Africa. 1980 returned to London, impoverished and in ill health. Began to paint again and in 1989 showed with others at Adrienne Resnick's North London Gallery.

HUME, Gary   b.1962
Painter. Born Kent. Studied at Liverpool Polytechnic, 1985-6, and Goldsmiths' College, 1986-8. First solo exhibition held at Karsten Schubert Ltd., London, 1989. A neo-minimalist. Represented in 'The British Art Show' at the Hayward Gallery, 1990.

HUMPHREYS, David   b.1937
Painter. Born Clapham, London. Studied Fine Art at

LESLIE HUNTER, 1879-1931.
'Reflections, Balloch', 1929-30.
25in. x 27⅞in.
Scottish National Gallery of
Modern Art.

Durham University, 1958-62. 1960 held first solo exhibition at Richmond Hill Gallery, Surrey. 1981 exhibited 'The Constructivist Works, 1960-1970' at the Richmond Studios. Represented in Arts Council Collections, Leicester University and elsewhere.

HUNT, Cecil Arthur   1873-1965
Painter. Born Torquay, Devon. Educated at Trinity College, Cambridge. Elected RBA, 1914 but did not become a full-time painter until his election as ARWS in 1919, at which time he ceased to practise at the bar. Elected RWS, 1925, and VP, RWS, 1930-3. Specialised in landscape and travelled widely in Britain and on the Continent in search of subjects.

HUNT, Georgina
Painter. Studied at Slade School of Fine Art. 1967 first solo exhibition held at Drian Gallery, London; others include four at Space Studios, London, 1974-8. 1982 solo exhibition at Camden Arts Centre. Abstract artist, who uses a spray-gun instead of brushes.

HUNT, Robert   b.1929
Painter and illustrator. Studied at Camberwell School of Arts and Crafts, 1943 and 1945-8. Lectured on illustration 1959-65. 1966-72 Picture Director for the British Printing Corporation. Since 1982 has been House Illustrator for *The Economist* and photography and art consultant to Orbis Publishing.

HUNTER, Alexis   b.1948
Painter. Born Parnell, Auckland, New Zealand. Assistant preparator of Auckland Institute and Museum, 1965-71. Studied at Elam School of Fine Arts, University of Auckland, 1966-9. 1969 won a Travel Award, University of Otago, Dunedin. 1971 worked on a series concerned with

popular visual culture in New Zealand. 1972 moved to London. 1972-5 member of Women's Workshop of the Artists' Union. 1973 began working with collage, tinted photographs and began photographing tattoos. She also made a film, *Anatomy of a Friendship*, in the same year. 1976-7 member of Women's Art Alliance which led her to curate exhibitions with the Alliance Gallery Collective. 1977 began lecturing on feminist issues in art. 1976-81 she made many photo-narratives exhibited in public institutions and spaces, which dealt with the social conditioning of women. She returned to painting in 1981 and began exploring mythologies in a series titled *Male Myth*. In 1983 as printmaker in residence at Lowik House, Cumbria, she was able to explore animal imagery. 1985 visited Tahiti, and later travelled in Europe and Tangiers. 1971 first solo exhibition at Mollers Gallery, Auckland; 1973 first solo exhibition in Great Britain at the Architectural Association, London. She has had a long standing interest in theories of creativity, investigating the role of the unconscious, and focusing on female creativity and the idea of the muse; also offers a radical questioning of traditional representation of female sexuality. Included in the collections of Auckland City Art Gallery; Arts Council of GB; Camden Council; CAS; GLA; Imperial War Museum; Northern Arts, Newcastle upon Tyne; Scottish National Gallery of Modern Art; Zurich Museum; University of Houston, Texas, USA.

Bibl: *Alexis Hunter: Fears/Dreams/Desires: A Survey Exhibition 1976-1988*, Auckland City Art Gallery, 1988.

HUNTER, Leslie   1879-1931
Painter. Born Rothesay, Isle of Bute, Scotland. His family emigrated to California in 1892 leaving Hunter there, on their return to Scotland in 1899. He found employment as an illustrator and worked his passage to Paris, 1904.

HUNTER, Margaret

DEREK HYATT, b.1931. *'Tracks and Signs (Langtar Moor)'*, 1970. 16in. x 12in. Private Collection.

Returned to San Francisco, 1906, and his first solo exhibition there was destroyed in the 1906 earthquake. Returned then to Glasgow and continued his self education as an artist. First solo exhibition in Glasgow, at Alex Reid's gallery, 1913. Showed in mixed exhibitions with Peploe,* Cadell* and Fergusson* in the 1920s. First solo show in London at Reid and Lefevre, 1928. The French Government purchased a painting of Loch Lomond in 1931. He became a well known figure in Glasgow art circles, occupying a number of studios, arguing with himself and following an erratic life style. He had little regard for money, was unconscious of disorder and was frequently hard up. Worked on his uncle's farm throughout the greater part of the First World War. Associated with the Scottish Colourists. Lived in France from 1927, moving from place to place, until a breakdown compelled his removal to a hospital at Nice.

Bibl: Roger Billcliffe, *The Scottish Colourists*, John Murray, London, 1989.

HUNTER, Margaret b.1948
Painter. Born Irvine, Scotland. Studied at Glasgow School of Art, 1981-5, and under Georg Baselitz at the Hochschule der Kilnste, Berlin, 1985-6. Since then has divided her time between Berlin and Scotland. Solo shows in Berlin and Ayr, Scotland, 1986, and in 1988 at the 369 Gallery, Edinburgh and the Vanessa Devereux Gallery, London. Interested in the female figure rendered in an expressive manner. Works in the collection of the Scottish National Gallery of Modern Art, Edinburgh.

HUNTER, Robert b.1920
Painter. Born Liverpool, Merseyside. 1938, joined the Territorials; saw war service in Norway, Egypt, Syria, Palestine, France, Germany and Italy, where he was awarded the MC at Anzio. Trained at Liverpool College of Art, 1946-50. 1952 moved to Wales and taught for over thirty years at Trinity College, Carmarthen. Founder-member of the Welsh '56' Group which was responsible for the development and encouragement of abstract painting and sculpture in Wales. Has exhibited regularly in Wales and London. Represented in Welsh Arts Council Collection, the National Museum of Wales and elsewhere.

HUNTING, Leonard b.1951
Painter. Born Leicester. Studied at Leicester College of Art. Visited France in 1951, studying in the atelier of Maurice Brianchon at the Ecole des Beaux Arts in Paris. Has held exhibitions in Paris, London, New Mexico and San Francisco, as well as at the Gadsby Gallery, Leicester, 1967.

HURDLE, Robert b.1918
Painter. Born London. Studied at Richmond School of Art, 1935-7, and at Camberwell School of Art, 1947-9. Occupied teaching posts at the West of England College of Art, Bristol Polytechnic and Bristol University. Exhibits at the RWA and mostly in the West Country. (Plate 58, p.255.)

HURREN, Eric b.1922
Painter. Served in the Infantry, 1943-7. Studied at Canterbury College of Art, and at Isrlohn and Cottingen in Germany. Has exhibited at the RA, with the NEAC and elsewhere.

HURRY, Leslie 1909-1978
Painter and theatre designer. Studied at St. John's Wood Art School and RA Schools. From 1930 onwards he travelled extensively in Britain and Ireland living on the results of commissions given by the owners of large estates. 1941 began to exhibit at the Redfern Gallery, after which he was commissioned by Robert Helpmann to design sets for his ballet, *Hamlet*. This began Hurry's successful career as a theatre designer, working with many companies in England and Canada. Represented in the V & A, Brighton Art Gallery and elsewhere.

HURST, Steve b.1932
Sculptor. Born Cairo, Egypt. Moved to England, 1939.

TIMOTHY HYMAN, b.1946. *'Passage through Austria'*, 1982. 23 ¾ in. x 40in. Blond Fine Art Limited.

Studied at Ruskin School of Drawing, Oxford, before doing army service in Malaya, 1953-8. Studied at Goldsmiths' College, 1959. 1967-8 worked in USA as a welder. 1979-82 held various teaching positions, including Head of Sculpture, Art and Design Centre, Belfast. 1985 solo exhibition at the Arts Council Gallery, Belfast.

HUSSAIN, Kabir   b.1960
Sculptor and installation artist. Born Nara, Pakistan. Studied at the Jacob Kramer College, Leeds, 1979-80, South Glamorgan Institute of Higher Education, 1980-3, and at Chelsea School of Art, 1983-4. Began exhibiting in 1984 and held two solo exhibitions in Wales, 1988. Represented in 'The British Art Show' at the Hayward Gallery, 1990.

HUTCHINSON, Louise
Sculptor. Born Mayenne, France. Educated in Freiburg, Geneva and London. Before she became a sculptor was well known as a photographer (Liz Osborne). 1945 began working in East Bergholt, Suffolk. Self-taught. 1953 was selected as one of the artists in the British section of the Unknown Political Prisoner Competition. 1953 and 1956 held two solo exhibitions at the Beaux Arts Gallery, London.

HUTCHINSON, Suzanne   b.1957
Painter. Born Lincolnshire. Studied at Bath Academy of Art, 1975-6, Brighton Polytechnic, 1976-9 and Chelsea School of Art, 1979-80. 1982 first solo exhibition held at Brighton Polytechnic; another at Nicola Jacobs, London, 1983. 1981 designed and painted backdrop for the 'David

Glass Mime' production of *Petruschka*. German-expressionist influenced figurative artist.

HUTCHINSON, William Oliphant   1889-1970
Painter. Born Kirkcaldy, Scotland. Studied at Edinburgh College of Art, 1909-12, and in Paris. Exhibited at the RA, RSA, Paris Salon, GI, IS and with the NEAC. Became Director of Glasgow School of Art, 1933-43. Elected ARSA, 1937, RSA, 1943, and PRSA, 1950. Knighted 1953.

HUTLER, David   b.1935
Painter. Studied at St. Martin's School of Art and Hornsey School of Art. Paints Mediterranean landscapes, partly inspired by Claude Lorraine. 1969 and 1972 held two solo exhibitions at the John Whibley Gallery, London.

HUTTER, David   1930-1990
Born London. Studied graphic art at St. Martin's and Hornsey Schools of Art, then worked as a commercial artist, in film animation and provided a strip for a gardening magazine. Through part-time teaching committments he gave talks on art history in Brixton and Wandsworth Prisons. Liked to paint landscapes, flowers and the nude male in the medium of watercolour. Solo exhibitions at the Ebury Gallery, 1982 and St. Jude's Gallery, Kensington, 1988.

HUWS, Bethan   b.1961
Sculptor. Born Bangor, Wales. Studied at Middlesex Polytechnic, 1981-5, and RCA, 1986-8. Works with natural materials on an extremely small scale. Solo exhibitions include one at the Anthony Reynolds Gallery,

HUXLEY, Paul

London, 1988. Represented in 'The British Art Show' held at the Hayward Gallery, 1990.

HUXLEY, Paul   b.1938
Painter. Born London. Studied at Harrow School of Art, 1953-6, and RA Schools, 1956-60. 1965-7 lived in New York City. 1974 Visiting Professor at Cooper Union, New York. 1975-82 trustee of the Tate Gallery. 1976 appointed Visiting Tutor at RCA. 1986 appointed Professor of Painting at RCA. 1987 elected ARA. 1963 first solo exhibition held at the Rowan Gallery and has exhibited since then regularly at the same gallery (now Mayor Rowan). An abstract artist, who uses geometric shapes on a large scale and with authority.

Bibl: *Paul Huxley's Recent Paintings,* Mayor Rowan Gallery, London, 1989.

HYATT, Derek   b.1931
Painter. Born Ilkley, Yorkshire. Studied at Leeds College of Art, Norwich School of Art and RCA. Solo exhibitions include four at New Art Centre, London, 1960-6. 1958-60 awarded J. Andrew Lloyd Scholarship for landscape painting. Other solo exhibitions include one at Waddington and Tooth Gallery, London, 1977, and at Austin Desmond Fine Art, London, 1989. Represented in Bradford Museums and Art Galleries and elsewhere.

HYMAN, Timothy   b.1946
Painter. Born London. Studied at Slade School of Fine Art, 1963-7. 1968 travelled in USA. On his return painted and taught and in 1977 began writing art criticism for the *London Magazine.* 1981 first solo exhibition held at Blond Fine Art. Spokesman for the revival of a British figurative art, selecting the 'Narrative Paintings' exhibition held at the Arnolfini, Bristol, and elsewhere, 1979-80.

HYNES, Gladys   1888-1958
Painter and sculptor. Born India, and moved to London at the age of three. Studied at the London School of Art under Frank Brangwyn.* 1906-7 her family moved to Penzance, where she studied under Stanhope* and Elizabeth Forbes* at their School of Painting at Newlyn. She left Cornwall in 1919 and spent the rest of her life in Hampstead, London. Much influenced by Italian Renaissance art in her figurative painting and by Jacob Epstein* in the *Mother and Child* that she executed for St. Dominic's Priory, Southampton Row. Illustrated Ezra Pound's *Cantos* and exhibited at RA, LG, IS and Paris Salon.

GLADYS HYNES, 1888-1958. *'Private View',* 1937. 48in. x 36in. Michael Parkyn Fine Art Ltd.

I

IBBERSON, Vincent
Painter. Born Bolton on Dearne, Yorkshire. Lived in Brazil, 1950-60. Gained a Ph.D. in Chemical Engineering from London University. Self-taught. 1956 first solo exhibition held in Rio de Janeiro, and first in London, 1963, at the Woodstock Gallery. Interested in colour theories.

ICKE, Gillian
Painter. Born London. Gained a Froebel teaching diploma from Bedford College of Education. Taught art in schools in the UK and Singpore. 1966 studied under the painter Kenneth Webb, Director of the Irish School of Landscape Painting. Shown in mixed exhibitions, e.g. the NS, ROI, RI, SWA. 1975 first solo exhibition at Haverfordwest County Library.

ILLSLEY, Bryan   b.1937
Painter and sculptor. Born Surbiton, Surrey. Studied to be an apprentice stone carver. Took classes at art school to defer National Service. Lived at St. Ives but moved to London in 1986. 1988 one man show at Contemporary Applied Arts.

IMMS, David   b.1945
Painter and printmaker. Studied at Derby College of Art and the Central School of Art. Won purchase Award, 6th British Drawing Biennale, Cleveland. 1974 first solo exhibition at MacRobert Arts Centre, Stirling University. Takes his subject matter from the cycles of nature and the prehistoric cultures of the West Country. Represented in the collections of the V & A, Bolton, Derby, Sheffield, Portsmouth and Kéttering Art Galleries.

INGHAM, Bryan   b.1936
Painter. Born Preston, Lancashire. Studied at St. Martin's School of Art, under Anthony Caro* and others, and at the RCA, also studied at the British Academy in Rome. Lives in Cornwall, but also has a studio at Workswede in Germany. In his paintings representational details are worked into an abstract composition in which there is often much play upon overlap. Rauschenberg and Scwitters have influenced his art, as has Ben Nicholson,* chiefly because of a shared geography and subject matter.

INGLIS, Judy   b.1952
Painter. Born Cornwall. Studied at Exeter College of Art and Design, 1971-2, Sheffield City Polytechnic, 1980-3, and at the RCA, 1984-7. Awarded a Fellowship in painting at Gloucester College, 1987-8. Other awards include the Bursten Award, RCA, 1987. First solo exhibition at the Mappin Art Gallery, Sheffield, 1984. Exhibited with Sue Williams, London, 1988 and 1990. Included in the collections of Sheffield City Art Galleries.

INLANDER, Henry   b.1925
Painter. Born Vienna, Austria. Educated in Vienna, Trieste and London. Arrived in England, 1938, became British citizen, 1947. Studied at the Slade School, winning the Rome Scholarship, 1952. From 1954 included in mixed exhibitions. 1955 first solo exhibition at the Leicester Galleries and won the Daily Express Young Artist Prize in the same year. 1955-6 Art Adviser to the British School in Rome. 1957 visiting lecturer, Camberwell School of Art. 1960-2 won Harkness Fellowship to the USA. 1961 one man exhibition at the Peridot Gallery, New York. 1969 visiting artist, Department of Fine Art, University of

JAMES DICKSON INNES, 1887-1914. *'Bala Lake'*, 1911. Oil on panel. 12⅞ in. x 16⅛ in. Manchester City Art Galleries.

Calgary. Works in the collection of the Tate Gallery, Arts Council, the CAS, the DoE, and in Canada and Australia.

INNES, Callum   b.1962
Painter. Born Edinburgh, Scotland. Studied at Gray's School of Art, Aberdeen, 1980-4, and at Edinburgh College of Art, 1984-5. First solo exhibition held at Artspace Gallery, Aberdeen, 1986; another at the 369 Gallery, Edinburgh, 1988. Represented in 'The British Art Show' held at the Hayward Gallery, 1990.

INNES, Charles   b.1946
Painter. Showed a series of 'Medieval illustrations' at the Woodstock Gallery, 1972, and a series of urban landscapes of Nottingham and Bristol at the same gallery, 1974.

INNES, George   1913-1970
Sculptor. Born Glasgow, Scotland. Studied at Glasgow School of Art. In 1938 he showed four stone carvings at the Glasgow Empire Exhibition. Served in the army during the Second World War when his hands were badly burnt, which curtailed his carving. In the late 1940s and '50s he reduced his figures to geometrical facets. Work in the collection of Kirkcaldy Museum and Art Gallery.

INNES, James Dickson   1887-1914
Painter. Born Llanelli, Wales. Studied at Carmarthen Art School, 1904-5 and at the Slade School, 1906-8. 1906 met Derwent Lees,* a fellow student at the Slade and formed a close working relationship. 1908 taught painting at the Slade School and first became friendly with the painter Augustus John.* Tuberculosis diagnosed; 1908-13 travelled and painted in France, Spain, Ireland, England, North and South Wales. His illness increased and he visited Morocco and Teneriffe in 1913 in attempt to recuperate. He died in a nursing home in Kent but is buried in Devon.

INNES, William Henry   b.1905
Painter. Served in the RAF during the war and first exhibited in a collection of paintings by wartime

DAVID INSHAW, b.1943. *'Wiltshire Landscape'*, 1988. 51in. x 60in. Waddington Galleries.

servicemen. Specialises in land and seascapes. Has exhibited at the RA, the Royal Society of Marine Artists, the ROI, NEAC and elsewhere.

INSHAW, David   b.1943

Painter and printmaker. Born Staffordshire. Studied at Beckenham School of Art, 1959-63, and the RA Schools, 1963-6. 1964 won a French Government Scholarship to study in Paris. 1969 first solo exhibition at the Arnolfini Gallery, Bristol. 1971 moved to Devizes. 1973 first meeting with the painter Peter Blake.* 1975 first meeting of the Brotherhood of Ruralists at Wellow, Somerset. Those present were Inshaw, Blake, Jann Haworth,* Graham* and Ann Arnold,* Graham* and Annie Ovenden.* 1975 appointed Fellow in Creative Art at Trinity College, Cambridge. 1977 returned to Devizes. 1981-2, worked on TV film, *Between Dreaming and Waking*. 1983 left the Ruralists. 1984 solo exhibition held at Waddington Galleries.

IRELAND, Patrick   b.1934

Painter and sculptor. Born Brian O'Doherty at Ballaghaderrin, Ireland. 1939 briefly kidnapped by gypsies. 1956 met Jack Butler Yeats* who recommended him for a scholarship to the USA. 1957 travelled to Harvard on a Nuffield Grant from Cambridge, to study the psychology of perception. 1961-4 moved to New York to work as art critic for the *New York Times*. 1965 began his Five Senses Series. 1966 invited Marcel Duchamp for dinner. 1967 made first Ogham drawings and sculptures, and published *Object and Idea*. 1968 began a life-long photographic self-portrait. 1972 returned to Dublin and changed his name to Patrick Ireland in response to Bloody Sunday in Derry. 1973 began his 'Rope' drawings series in New York. 1975 began to superimpose multiple systems in drawings. 1978 exhibited a painted room, 'Camera', at Visual Arts Museum, New York. Since then has created installations and produces performances. 1986 major exhibition of Drawings 1965-85, at the National Museum

ALBERT IRVIN, b.1922. 'Merlin', 1987. Acrylic. 60in. x 72in. Gimpel Fils Gallery.

of American Art, Smithsonian Institution, Washington DC, USA.

IRONSIDE, Robin   1912-1965
Painter and art critic. Born London. Studied art history at the Courtauld Institute. Assistant Keeper at the Tate Gallery, 1937-46. 1947 first solo exhibition at the Redfern Gallery; 1948 designed Strauss's *Der Rosenkavalier* for Covent Garden and collaborated with his brother Christopher on other opera and ballet designs. He published a book on P. Wilson Steer, 1944 (Phaidon). 1952, 1954, 1957 and 1964 exhibited with the Durlacher Bros. Gallery in New York. 1966 retrospective exhibition at the New Arts Centre.

IRVIN, Albert   b.1922
Painter. Born London. Studied at Northampton School of Art, 1940-1, and Goldsmiths' College, 1946-50. Taught at Goldsmiths', 1962-83. Recent solo exhibitions include Third Eye Centre, Glasgow, 1983, Ikon Gallery, Birmingham, 1984, Gimpel Fils, London, 1986. 1986 he won the Giles Bequest Prize at the Bradford International Print Biennale. Abstract artist, who works with loaded, gestural brushstrokes.

IRWIN, Gwyther   b.1931
Painter, sculptor and maker of collages. Born North Cornwall. Studied art at Bryanston School where he was taught by the painter Roger Hilton.* Studied at the Central School, 1951-4. 1957 first solo exhibition at Gallery One. 1964 he was one of the artists chosen to represent Great Britain at the Venice Biennale. 1965-8 made a relief in Portland stone for BP House, Moorfields, London. 1969-84 Head of Fine Art, Brighton Polytechnic. 1978 won Greater London Arts Award. 1987 retrospective exhibition at Gimpel Fils Gallery. (Plate 59, p.258.)

JACKLIN, Bill   b.1943
Painter and printmaker. Born London. Studied graphics at
Walthamstow School of Art, 1960-1, afterwards worked for a
year as a graphic designer. Studied painting at Walthamstow School of Art, 1962-4, and RCA, 1964-7. Has taught at
various British art schools and colleges, 1967-75. First solo
exhibition held at Nigel Greenwood's, London, 1970. 1985
moved to New York where he now lives and works. Recent
solo exhibitions include one at the Marlborough Gallery,
London, 1988. Likes to record the sociological behaviour of
the modern metropolis, continuing a tradition begun by
the Impressionists. Represented in many public collections
in America and Britain. (Plate 60, p.259.)

Bibl: *Bill Jacklin, Urban Portraits*, introduction by Robert
Rosenblum, Marlborough Gallery, London, 1988.

JACKSON, Francis Earnest   1872-1945
Painter. Born Huddersfield, Yorkshire. Studied at the
Académie Julian and the Ecole des Beaux Arts in Paris.
Taught at Central School of Arts and Crafts, 1902-21, the
RA Schools, 1921-39 and acted as Principal of the Byam
Shaw School, 1926-40. Also produced lithographs and
posters and was a member of the Senefelder Club. Elected
ARA, 1944.

JACKSON, Vanessa   b.1953
Painter. Studied at St. Martin's School of Art, 1971-5, and
the RCA, 1975-8. Abstract painter who works on a large
scale. The shapes and spaces in her pictures relate to a
sense of human proportion, stretch and balance. Has held
solo exhibitions at the National Theatre, 1978, AIR
Gallery, 1981, and Vortex Gallery, 1984 (both London) at
Gotham Book Mart Gallery, New York, 1986, and
Winchester Gallery, 1990. Has occupied various teaching
positions and is currently Head of Painting at Winchester
School of Art.

JACOMB-HOOD, George Percy   1857-1929
Painter, etcher and illustrator. Born Redhill, Surrey.
Studied at Slade School and in Paris. Exhibited at RA from
1878, also at the Grosvenor Gallery. Elected RE, 1881, and
a member of the NEAC, 1886. Did illustrations for *The
Graphic* and *The Illustrated London News*. As a painter
specialised in portraits and genre subjects.

JAGGER, Charles Sargeant   1885-1934
Sculptor. Born Kilnhurst, near Sheffield, Yorkshire.
Apprenticed as a metal engraver to Mappin & Webb at the
age of fourteen. He learnt engraving, inlaying and relief,
skills that laid the basis for his development as a sculptor
of bas-relief. 1907 won scholarship to RCA, where he
studied, 1908-11, under Edward Lantéri. 1914 won a Prix
de Rome scholarship, but owing to the outbreak of war he
never took it up. Enlisted in the Artists' Rifles and served
at Gallipoli and on the Western Front. Wounded three
times and twice gassed. Received commissions from the
British War Memorials Commission. His largest and most
important commission was the Royal Artillery Memorial
at Hyde Park Corner, 1921-5. Continued to enjoy
commissions from private patrons and from ecclesiastical
bodies. His *Christ the King* was produced for Liverpool's
Roman Catholic Cathedral. Died young from a heart
attack caused by war wounds and overwork.

Bibl: *Charles Sargeant Jagger: War and Peace Sculpture,* Imperial
War Museum, London, 1985.

TESS JARAY, b.1937. *'Six Red Steps'*, 1987. 77in. x 47in.
Private Collection.

JAMES, Francis Edward   1849-1920
Painter. Began exhibiting in 1884, mainly at the RBA and
RWS. Elected ARWS, 1908, and RWS, 1916. Painted
mostly landscape and architectural subjects in watercolour.

JAMIESON, Robert Kirkland   1881-1950
Painter. Born Larnark, Scotland. Studied at Glasgow
Training College for Teachers and in Paris. Exhibited at
the RA, RBA, with the NEAC and the London Group.
Elected RBA, 1923. Headmaster of Westminster School of
Art, 1933-9 and Principal of St. Martin's School of Art,
1945-7. Specialised in landscape.

JANES, Alfred   b.1911
Painter. Born Swansea, Wales. Studied at Swansea School
of Art and the RA Schools. 1936-40 taught at School of Art.
1940-6 military service with Pioneer Corps in North
Africa. After the war he continued teaching art, and
exhibited regularly, in Swansea, London and elsewhere.

JANES, Norman   1892-1980
Painter and illustrator. Born Egham, Surrey. Studied at Regent Street Polytechnic, 1909-14, whilst working freelance as an advertising designer. After army service studied at Slade School of Fine Art, 1919-22, and at the RCA, 1923-4, also taking evening classes in etching at the Central School of Art. Elected ARE, 1922, RE, 1938. Solo exhibitions at the Beaux Arts Gallery, London, 1932 and 1945. Lectured in etching and wood-engraving at Hornsey School of Art, 1928-60, and at the Slade, 1936-50. Worked mostly in watercolour and prints, less often in oils. Executed many designs for the Oxford University Press.

JAPP, Darsie   1883-1973
Painter. Born Liverpool, Merseyside. Studied at evening classes at Lambeth School of Art under Philip Connard* and at the Slade School, 1908-9. Exhibited with the NEAC, and became a member in 1919. Left England in 1926 and for the next 27 years lived in France and Spain; returning in 1953. Some years later he left England again for Portugal. Specialised in landscape and figure subjects.

JARAY, Tess   b.1937
Painter and printmaker. Born London. Studied at St. Martin's School of Art, 1954-7, and Slade School, 1957-60. Awarded a travelling scholarship, 1960 and a French Government scholarship, 1961. Since 1959 included in mixed exhibitions. 1963 first solo exhibition at Grabowski Gallery. 1964-8 taught at Hornsey College of Art. Commissioned to paint a mural for British Pavilion, Expo '67, Montreal. 1980 visited Australia. 1984 taught at the Slade School. 1984 solo exhibition of recent paintings at the Whitworth Art Gallery, Manchester University and a retrospective exhibition of graphic work at the Ashmolean Museum, Oxford.

JARDINE, George   b.1920
Painter. Born Wallasey, Cheshire. Studied at Wallasey School of Art until 1936, then the RCA. Started to make collages in 1936 and continued so until c.1950. These helped release his imagination, 'unhindered by rationality'. Interested in Indian and Persian art and miniatures, which influenced his detailed and imaginative compositions. Work in the collection of the Arts Council. Dame Janet Baker chose Jardine's work for an Arts Council touring exhibition, 1987. Solo exhibition at the Williamson Art Gallery, Birkenhead, 1981.

JARMAN, Derek   b.1942
Painter and film maker. Studied art history at King's College, 1960-2 and painting at the Slade School, 1963-7. Won a Peter Stuyvesant award for painting, 1967. 1967 included in mixed exhibitions, beginning with the Young Contemporaries. 1968 first solo exhibition at the Lisson Gallery. 1967 began designing for the ballet, opera, theatre and films. 1975 made his first film *Sebastiane*; has since made *The Life of Caravaggio* and *War Requiem*. 1987 nominated for the Turner Prize.

JARVIS, Roland   b.1926
Painter and printmaker. Born France and lived there until the age of twelve. Studied engineering at university in England, then studied painting at the Guildford and Chelsea Schools of Art and in Paris. Teaches printmaking at Camberwell School of Art. Included in mixed exhibitions in Britain and abroad. Solo exhibition at South London Art Gallery, 1974.

GEORGE JARDINE, b.1920. *'Hen People Flying Kites'*. Oil and printed musical score. 21¾in. x 15½in. Williamson Art Gallery and Museum, Birkenhead.

JEANS, Francis
Painter. Born London. Studied at Wimbledon School of Art, 1967-70 and also at Bournemouth and Hornsey College of Art. Likes to paint townscapes, still lifes and landscapes. Solo exhibition at Brunswick Gallery, 1978.

JEFFERSON, Alan   b.1918
Painter. Born London. Studied at Wimbledon School of Art and the RCA, 1937-9 and after war service, 1946-7. In the '60s taught at Portsmouth College of Art. Since 1953 included in group exhibitions. 1965 first solo exhibition at Bear Lane Gallery, Oxford.

JEFFREYS, Marcel   1872-1924
Painter. Born Milan, Italy. Self-taught. Travelled to Brussels, Paris and London. Painted the theatres and music halls of London during the First World War. Liked to paint water and harbours, and flowers. Died young after a long illness. Exhibition at Kaplan Gallery, 1964.

JEFFRIES, Neil   b.1959
Sculptor. Born Bristol, Avon. Studied at St. Martin's School of Art and the Slade, graduated in 1984, then spent a year at Kingston Polytechnic on a Picker Fellowship. Since 1985 included in group shows. 1986 solo exhibition of reliefs at Arnolfini Gallery, Bristol. Work in the collections of the Arts Council and the British Council.

JEGEDE, Emmanuel   b.1943
Sculptor. Born Nigeria. Studied sculpture in Nigeria, 1960-3. Studied painting and decorating at Willesden College of Technology, London, 1963-6, and bronze casting at Hammersmith College of Art, 1966-9. 1968 first solo exhibition at Woodstock Gallery. Writes poetry and teaches drumming and batik painting. 1973 held exhibitions of sculpture and prints at the Commonwealth Institute and the Woodstock Gallery.

JELLETT, Mainie   1877-1944
Painter. Born Dublin, Ireland. Studied art privately, c.1912-14, then at the Dublin School of Art, 1914-16. Left for London and studied under Sickert* at the Westminster Technical Institute, 1917-19. 1921-30 went to Paris to study under the painter André L'Hôte. 1924 first joint exhibition held with Evie Hone* in Dublin. 1925 began to exhibit at the Paris Salon des Independants. 1926 published article entitled 'Cubism'. 1937 commissioned by the Irish Government to decorate the Irish Pavilion at the Glasgow Fair. 1926-41 showed her work in Dublin. 1943 chairman of committee formed to establish Irish Exhibition of Living Art. 1944 memorial exhibition of work in Dublin Painters Gallery. 1974 retrospective exhibition at the Neptune Gallery, Dublin. Work in Tate Gallery collection.

JELLICOE, Colin   b.1942
Painter and printmaker. Born Manchester. Studied at Manchester College of Art from 1959. 1963 opened an art gallery in Rusholme, Manchester. From 1964 included in mixed shows. Solo exhibition at Stockport Art Gallery in 1967.

JENKINS, Derek   b.1937
Painter and printmaker. Born Cardiff, Wales. Trained in fabric design and calligraphy at the West of England College of Art, 1954-8. Taught in schools in London and Bristol and from 1972 has been Head of the Art Department at Falmouth School of Art. Started to paint in 1975, having concentrated up till then on pottery. Inspired chiefly by the coastline and maritime activity of Cornwall. Member of the Newlyn Society of Artists. Exhibition of paintings and prints at Falmouth Art Gallery, 1983.

JENKINS, Robert   b.1945
Painter. Born Manchester. Studied at Manchester College of Art, 1963-5. Went to Paris, 1966. First exhibited at Detra Gallery, Manchester, 1970. 1971 began working voluntarily with deprived children. 1972 worked full-time as a social worker. 1979 taught painting part-time at Moston College. 1981 first solo exhibition at Ginnel Gallery, Prestwich, Cheshire, then visited Egypt. Further exhibition at Ginnel Gallery, Manchester, 1983.

JENKINSON, Edith   1893-1975
Painter. Born London. Studied at the Byam Shaw School of Art, where she befriended Winifred Nicholson.* Painted mostly light and airy flower pieces. Exhibited with the 7 & 5 Society as a guest member. Stopped painting when she married Lt. Colonel Justin Hooper, and undertook much travel.

JENNINGS, Chris   b.1949
Photographer and printmaker. Born Oxford. Studied at Wimbledon School of Art and Hornsey College of Art,

1967-70. From 1969 included in mixed exhibitions. Since 1975 has been photographing and drawing the standing stones of the British Isles. 1978 won British Council travel award. 1980 exhibition at Elise Meyer Gallery, New York.

JENNINGS, Humphrey   1907-1950
Painter. Born East Anglia. Studied literature at Cambridge where he became interested in the theatre. From 1934 has lived in London and worked on films. Directed films for Crown Film Unit during the war. Kept his painting secret until he showed paintings and collages at the Surrealist exhibition, 1936 and in a solo show, 1938, at the London Gallery. Died in Greece while working on a film. Memorial exhibition of paintings held at the ICA, 1957.

JOHN, Augustus   1878-1961
Painter. Born Tenby, Wales. Attended the Slade School, 1894-8. Visited Paris 1898 and returned there every year. In 1899 first exhibited with the NEAC. 1901 married Ida Nettleship. 1901-2 taught art in Liverpool. 1903 met Dorelia McNeil who joined John and Ida in a ménage-à-trois, until the death of Ida in 1907. 1903 first exhibition, shared with his sister, Gwen,* held at the Carfax Gallery. 1901-4 Professor of Painting at Liverpool University. 1911-14 worked with Innes* and Lees* in Wales. 1921 elected ARA, 1928 RA, 1938 resigned, 1940 re-elected. 1940-61 member of London Group. 1942 awarded OM. 1940 retrospective held at Temple Newsam, Leeds. 1949 another at Scott and Fowles, New York, the RA, 1954 and the Graves Art Gallery, Sheffield, 1956. Wrote *Chiaroscuro, Fragments of an Autobiography* in 1952. One of the most prominent artistic personalities of his day, famous for his bohemianism, womanising and fascination with the gypsies; also renowned as a brilliant draughtsman. His portraits achieve striking likenesses and are frequently painted with great bravura, but he is nowadays less highly regarded than his sister.

Bibl: Michael Holroyd, *Augustus John*, Heinemann, London, Vol.I, 1974, Vol.II, 1975.

JOHN, Gwen   1876-1939
Painter. Born Haverfordwest, Wales, elder sister of Augustus John.* Studied at the Slade School, 1894-7 and at Whistler's School in Paris. From 1898 lived and worked in Paris. From 1900 exhibited with the NEAC in London. 1903 showed with Augustus John at the Carfax Gallery. 1926 first and only solo exhibition at the New Chenil Galleries. A friend of Rodin, she posed for his Monument to Whistler. Influenced by Whistler's love of subtle tonalities, she restricted her palette to mauve, pink, blue and grey colour harmonies. Though she appears to have left England to escape her brother's dominating presence, in Paris she fell heavily in love with Rodin and in 1914 moved to Meudon in order to be near his house. Her passion for Rodin reduced her output as an artist for several years. She emerged from it confirmed in her desire to paint. 1913 was received into the Roman Catholic Church and enjoyed friendship with the Catholic writer on art, Jacques Maritain. Her subject matter, consisting mostly of portraits of women and interiors, is reduced to its essence. She became a recluse and died in the street in Dieppe. The 1946 memorial exhibition at the Matthiesen Gallery established her reputation, which still continues to grow. 1952 memorial exhibition at the Tate Gallery

(shared with Frances Hodgkins* and Ethel Walker*). 1985 major retrospective at the Barbican Art Gallery, London. (Plate 4, p.18.)

Bibl: Susan Chitty, *Gwen John*, Hodder & Stoughton, London, 1981; Cecily Langdale, *Gwen John: A Catalogue Raisonné of the Paintings and a Selection of the Drawings*, Yale University Press, 1986.

JOHN, Vivien   b.1915
Painter. Daughter of Augustus John,* youngest of nine children. Born Alderney Manor, Dorset. Studied at the Slade School and at the Euston Road School. Served as Red Cross Nurse during the Second World War. Married a doctor after the war and went with him to Moscow for a year in 1947. 1950s first solo exhibition at Walker's Gallery, another at Liverpool University, 1967. 1960 took further lessons in art at the Regent Street Polytechnic. 1960s lived in Malaysia with her husband. 1971 solo exhibition at Upper Grosvenor Galleries.

JOHNSON, Ben   b.1946
Painter and printmaker. Studied at the RCA. Solo exhibition at Wickesham Gallery, New York, 1969. Work in the collections of the Tate Gallery, the British Council, the CAS, and Glasgow City Art Gallery, among others. Paints in a super-realist style, choosing architectural features as subject material.

JOHNSON, Colin T.   b.1942
Painter. Born Blackpool, Lancashire. Studied at Salford School of Art and Manchester College of Art, 1957-60. Painted at St. Ives, Cornwall each summer. 1968 received a commission from Granada Television. From 1970-3 he concentrated on painting urban scenes. 1975 painted a mural for BBC Television, North West. 1980 artist in residence, Manchester International Music Festival. 1984 artist in residence, City of London Festival. 1986 artist in residence, Wigan International Jazz Festival. 1986 exhibition at the Art Gallery, Scarborough.

JOHNSON, Jane   b.1951
Book illustrator. Born London. After university she entered the publishing world, designing children's books for Jonathan Cape. Worked on her own illustrations in the evenings, leading to her first book *Sybil and the Blue Rabbit* (1980), which won prizes. Also published greeting cards and magazine illustrations. 1986 solo exhibition of artwork at Chris Beetles Gallery, London.

JOHNSON, Michael   b.1937
Painter. Studied at Bath Academy of Art, 1954-8. Showed at the Drian and Grosvenor Galleries, London, 1960s. Taught at Bath Academy, 1961-70. Now teaches at Chelsea School of Art and Kingston Polytechnic. 1982 exhibition of recent paintings at The Bridge Street Gallery, Bath.

JOHNSTON, Alan   b.1945
Painter. Born Scotland. Studied at Edinburgh College of Art, 1967-70, and the RCA, 1970-2, then spent time in Germany, working near Dusseldorf, where he developed his personal style of minimalist pencil drawings. First solo exhibition at Konrad Fischer Gallery, Dusseldorf, 1972. Another show of drawings, some done directly on to the gallery walls, at Von der Heydt Museum, Wuppertal, 1974. Numerous one man shows at the Graeme Murray

Gallery in Edinburgh. Recently he has worked on large canvases and has made sculpture.

Bibl: *Alan Johnston 1978-88*, Pier Arts Centre, Stromness, Orkney, 1988.

JOHNSTONE, William   1897-1981
Painter. Born Denholm, Scotland. Worked on his parents' farm. Joined labour camps in 1918, employed as a farmer. 1919-23, studied at Edinburgh College of Art, and then taught evening classes there, 1923-5. 1925 he went to Paris to study at the Grande Chaumière, the Académie Colarossi and with André L'Hôte. Returned to Selkirk in 1927, then to California with his wife in 1928, back to Scotland in 1929, and to London in 1931. Teaching posts in the 1930s include the Regent Street Polytechnic, Hackney School of Art and the Royal College of Needlework. First solo show at Wertheim Gallery, London, 1935; another in the same year at Aitken and Dott, Edinburgh. After the Second World War, he established Camberwell School of Arts and Crafts as a leading art school, attracting some of the most talented artists of the day on to its staff. Moved to Central School of Arts and Crafts, 1947 and attempted the same but with less noticeable success. As a painter, he moved into abstraction often working on a large scale.

JOICEY, Richard
Marine painter. Born London, the son of Violet Loraine, the actress. Studied at the Sir John Cass College of Art. Served with the Royal Navy and was awarded the George Medal, 1956, for saving lives in a shipyard fire. Since 1968 has worked as a full-time artist and exhibits regularly with Royal Society of Marine Artists and the RI. President of the Chichester Art Society. 1980 exhibition of marine watercolours at Clarges Gallery.

JONAS, Harry   1893-1990
Painter. Born London. Studied at St. John's Wood School of Art, then began painting seriously in a studio in Chelsea. Moved to another studio in Brook Green which he shared with the painter John Armstrong.* Travelled extensively, especially during the 1920s and befriended Utrillo, Modigliani and Picasso in Paris. Became a society portraitist, painting Lord Beaverbrook, Iris Mountbatten and Elsa Lanchester among others. Included in mixed exhibitions at the RA, the Grosvenor and Leicester Galleries. Held solo exhibitions at the Grosvenor Gallery and the Mattheisen Gallery. Founded a little group of younger artists, 'The Guild of St. Luke' which included Joseph Sickert, son of Walter* and Francis West.* Work by Jonas is in the collections of the Beaverbrook Gallery, Montreal, Manchester City Art Gallery and the National Portrait Gallery.

JONAS, Johnny   b.1948
Painter. Studied at Charterhouse. Joined Lloyds in 1966, to finance himself as an artist. Won a place at the Fine Arts Academy, Florence, 1972. He continued his studies at the Academy in Perugia, and received tutorship from Bob Maione, 1974. 1975 returned to England and began to concentrate on portraiture and landscape painting. 1979 moved to Grimaldi, France, and commenced a series of paintings depicting everyday life in the streets and cafes, and the night life of the Riviera. 1980 first solo exhibition at the Mall Gallery, London. On returning to England, 1984, he began a series of paintings depicting sporting scenes, including Royal Ascot, cricket and bowls.

JONES, Adrian   1845-1938

Painter and sculptor. Born Ludlow, Shropshire. Studied at the Royal Veterinary College, then joined the army, serving with the Royal Horse Artillery, the 3rd Hussars. 1879 painted two studies of racehorses. 1881 joined the 7th Hussars in the Boer War, and befriended the sculptor Charles Birch. 1884 with Birch's encouragement exhibited bronze statuette of a hunter at the RA and joined the 2nd Life Guards with whom he stayed until the end of his military career. 1886-1921 exhibited paintings and bronzes of horses at the RA. 1891 exhibited at the RA 'Triumph' a quadriga, which sowed the seed for the massive bronze group, the 'Quadriga of Peace'. Moved to bigger studio in Chelsea to work on a large scale. 1900 received five Royal commissions for paintings and bronzes of their horses. 1903 his Royal Marines Memorial unveiled by the Prince of Wales. 1907 monument to the Duke of Cambridge unveiled by Edward VII. Received MVO, and began work on the Quadriga of Peace. 1912 Quadriga of Peace erected on arch at Hyde Park Corner. 1923 awarded the Royal Society of British Sculptors Gold Medal, the highest distinction for a sculptor. 1924 Cavalry War Memorial unveiled by the Prince of Wales. 1933 published *Memoirs of a Soldier Artist*. 1934 made an Honorary Associate of the Royal College of Veterinary Surgeons.

JONES, Barbara   d.1978

Painter, designer, illustrator and author. Born Croydon, Surrey. Studied at RCA. Her remarkable breadth of interest made her a pioneer in the field of popular culture, as her book, *The Unsophisticated Arts* (1951), demonstrates. She painted landscapes, wrote books on design history, grottoes and death, designed murals and mosaics, organised an exhibition of British Popular and Traditional Art for the Whitechapel Gallery and was, both in her art and person, an original talent who never achieved the recognition she deserved.

JONES, Ben   b.1947

Sculptor. Born Builth Wells, Wales. Studied at Thames Polytechnic, 1966-9, with a trip to Mexico, and then St. Martin's School of Art, 1969-71. 1971 set up a studio in Euston Road, London and began writing about art. From 1969 included in mixed exhibitions. 1976 founding editor of *Artscribe* magazine. 1976-9 visiting lecturer in sculpture at various art colleges. 1979 began to paint. 1981 moved from London to rural Wales. 1984 elected to Welsh Sculpture Trust executive, and founded the Powys Sculpture Trail. 1985 solo exhibition at Oriel Gallery, Cardiff.

JONES, Bryn   b.1927

Painter. Born East London of Welsh parents. Educated at Cambridge and then in the Arts Faculties of Cairo and Hong Kong Universities. In 1955 began to paint and was included in mixed exhibitions in London galleries. Solo exhibitions at the Drian Galleries, 1962 and 1963.

JONES, Christopher   b.1958

Painter. Born High Cross, Bedfordshire. Studied at Newcastle upon Tyne University, 1977-81. Moved to Cumbria so that he could paint in the Lake District, 1981-2. Studied at Chelsea School of Art, 1982-3. 1983-4 Fellow in Fine Art at Gloucester College of Art and Technology. 1984 two month visit to Spain on a Boise travelling scholarship. From 1981 included in mixed exhibitions; 1985 solo exhibition at Nottingham University Art Gallery.

JONES, Colin   b.1934

Sculptor. Studied at Goldsmiths' College of Art under Kenneth* and Mary Martin.* Taught at Leicester College of Art, in the mid-1960s. Group exhibitions include 'Geometric Environment' at the AIA, 1962 and 'Construction England', an Arts Council Touring Exhibition, 1963. Works in relief in a geometrical manner.

JONES, David   1895-1974

Painter and poet. Born Brockley, Kent. Studied at Camberwell School of Art, 1910-14. Served on the Western Front with the Royal Welch Fusiliers. Studied at Westminster School of Art, 1919-21. Received into the Catholic church in 1921 and began a friendship with Eric Gill.* Began to learn wood-engraving; in 1925 the Golden Cockerel Press published *Gulliver's Travels* with his wood-engravings and in 1927 *The Chester Play of the Deluge*. 1927 joint exhibition held at St. George's Gallery with Eric Gill. 1928-33 showed with the 7 & 5 Society. 1928 began to write his poem about the First World War, entitled *In Parenthesis* (published 1937). 1942 started to make inscriptions. 1932 and 1947 suffered nervous breakdowns. 1947 moved to Harrow and stayed there until his death. 1952 another long poem, *The Anathemata*, was published. 1974 created CH. 1981 retrospective exhibition at the Tate Gallery. (Plate 9, p.27.)

Bibl: Paul Hills, *David Jones*, Tate Gallery, 1981; Nicolete Gray, *The Paintings of David Jones*, John Taylor/Lund Humphries, London, 1989.

JONES, Deborah

Painter. Born Cardiff, Wales. Worked in films and the London theatre as a scenic artist. Designed *Richard III* with Laurence Olivier. Showed paintings with the RA, the ROI, the Aviation Artists, and the RBA. Solo exhibition at the Wells Gallery, Wells, Somerset, 1963.

JONES, Eric   1904-1963

Printmaker. Studied at Camberwell School of Art and then the RCA, from 1925. 1928 won Rome Scholarship for Engraving for two years study there. In that year the V & A and the British Museum bought prints by him. 1930-60 taught life drawing and etching at Sheffield College of Art. Memorial exhibition held at Graves Art Gallery, Sheffield, 1964.

JONES, Fred Cecil   1891-1956

Painter and printmaker. Born Bradford, Yorkshire, the son of an artist. Studied at Bradford College of Art, 1915-16 and part-time at Leeds College of Art, 1930-5. From 1931 showed at the RA. Work bought for the Chantrey Bequest. Elected RBA, 1940. Memorial exhibition at Bradford, 1956 and at Keighley, 1957.

JONES, Gareth   b.1941

Sculptor and light artist. Born Wales. Studied at the RCA, 1963-6. Taught at St. Martin's and the Central School of Art. 1971 included in mixed exhibitions, e.g. at the Serpentine Gallery. 1973 showed light drawings at the Whitechapel Art Gallery. 1976 showed sculpture at Art Net Gallery.

JONES, Garry A.   b.1943

Painter. Born Malvern, Worcestershire. Studied at Stourbridge College of Art and the RCA. Taught at Winchester School of Art and then worked as a design consultant until 1969; has since devoted himself to his art. Solo exhibition at the Woodstock Gallery, 1971.

HAROLD JONES, b.1904. *'The Steadfast Tin Soldier'*
(Hans Christian Andersen). Pen and ink. 8in. x 6in.
Sally Hunter Fine Art.

JONES, Glyn   b.1930
Painter. Born Cumberland. Studied at Tully House School
of Art, Carlisle. After the war resumed his art studies in
London and Paris. Travelled and worked in South and
North America, and became an American citizen. Won
Grand Prix for painting in the second Hispano-American
Biennale. Now lives in Spain. Solo exhibition at the Alwin
Gallery, 1978.

JONES, Glyn   b.1936
Painter. Born Tynewydd, Rhondda Valley, Wales. Studied
at Cardiff College of Art, 1953-7 and the Slade School,
1957-60. Lecturer at Mid-Warwickshire School of Art,
1961-5, and at Coventry School of Art, 1965-71, and made
Head of the Fine Art Department, Cardiff College of Art,
1972. Member of 56 Group Wales. 1975 awarded a Major
Bursary from the Welsh Arts Council. From 1958-75
showed at the Royal National Eisteddfod of Wales. 1976
exhibition of new work held at University College, Cardiff.

JONES, Harold   b.1904
Painter and illustrator. Born East London. On leaving
school he worked on a farm near Stratford-upon-Avon,

when he was profoundly influenced by his experience of
landscape and the natural world. He abandoned the idea of
becoming a farmer and studied at Goldsmiths' College,
afterwards supporting himself with a job as a clerk while
continuing his studies in evening classes at Camberwell
School of Art. There he won a scholarship to RCA where he
studied, 1924-8. Through Barnet Freedman,* was introduced into the publishing world and illustrated the last
three books written by H.G. Wells. During the war he
served in the cartographic section of the Royal Engineers.
1945-58 taught part-time at Chelsea College of Art. He
wrote several books for children, including *The Enchanted
Night* (1947). Exhibited at the RA, with the NEAC and
elsewhere, and in 1981 held a retrospective at the Langton
Gallery, London. Represented in the V & A, the Tate
Gallery and elsewhere.

JONES, Ian   b.1947
Painter. Born Birmingham, West Midlands. Worked as a
toolmaker, 1963-75. Studied art at Birmingham Polytechnic, 1975-8, and at the RCA, 1979-82. From 1975
included in mixed exhibitions. 1984 solo exhibition at
Chapter, Cardiff. 1986 Artist in Residence, Stratford-
upon-Avon School for Girls. Further solo exhibitions at
Camden Art Centre, London, 1988, and Anderson O'Day
Gallery, London, 1989.

JONES, Jean   b.1927
Painter. Studied at St. Martin's School of Art, then stopped
painting and attended Cambridge University. In the early
1960s read the letters of Van Gogh and began to make
drawings. Took up painting again and has worked from the
landscape in Oxford and Devon; is married to John Jones,
formerly Professor of Poetry at Oxford University. Solo
exhibition at the Ashmolean Museum, Oxford, 1980.

JONES, Jo
Painter. Exhibited often in Paris and London, beginning
at Wildensteins Gallery, 1938. Solo exhibitions at the
Zborowski Gallery, Paris, the Wolfberg Gallery, Zurich
and the O'Hana Gallery. Friend of both Augustus John*
and Matthew Smith.* Painted the gypsies of Granada for
six years. Works of this kind are in the Gypsy Museum at
the University of Leeds. Her work was used to illustrate
The Gypsies of Granada, published in 1969. Solo
exhibition at the Fieldbourne Gallery, 1981.

JONES, John   b.1926
Painter. Born Gloucestershire. Studied at West of
England College of Art, Bristol, 1942-4 and 1948-52, and
at the Slade, 1952-4. Taught in Argentina, 1956-9 and
Leeds, 1959-62. Exhibitions in Buenos Aires, London and
Leeds. Made films on Oldenburg and Matisse. Solo
exhibition at Park Square Gallery, Leeds, 1974.

JONES, Jonah   b.1919
Sculptor. Born East Bolden, Tyne and Wear. National
Service from 1940-6. Worked in Eric Gill's* workshops,
1949. Set up his own workshop in Gwynedd, Wales, 1951
and still lives and works in Wales. First solo exhibition at
Tegfryn Gallery, Menai Bridge, 1967; most recent at Oriel
Gallery, Powys, 1990. Executed many lettered inscriptions
and has undertaken major commissions for Welsh
institutions, e.g. Mold Law Courts, Harlech College and
Bangor Cathedral.

JONES, Justin

IAN JONES, b.1947. *'Hey Banana Jacket'*, 1988. 59¼ in. x 48in. Private Collection.

JONES, Justin   b.1961
Painter. Studied art at Leeds Polytechnic, 1981-4, and St. Martin's School of Art, 1986-7. Went to Poland to study at the Academy of Fine Art, Warsaw, 1988. 1983 first solo exhibition at Settle Gallery, London, followed by a series of solo exhibitions in 1987 and 1988. Included in the collection of The National Trust.

JONES, C. Kingsley   b.1926
Painter. Born London. Served in the paratroopers during the war; when demobbed studied at Central School, 1948-51. Inspired by the landscape of South Devon. Solo exhibition at Woodstock Gallery, 1971.

JONES, Lucy   b.1955
Painter. Born London. Studied at Byam Shaw School of Drawing and Painting, 1975-7, Camberwell School of Art, 1977-9, and RCA, 1979-82. Rome Scholar in Painting, 1983-4. First solo exhibition held at Spitalfields Health Centre, in association with the Whitechapel Art Gallery; that same year she began exhibiting at the Angela Flowers Gallery, with which she is still associated. First caught attention with her richly coloured scenes centred on the banks of the Thames in central London, their vistas punctuated and structured by bridges, pathways, lamp posts and tree trunks. Has also produced a remarkable series of self portraits. (Plate 61, p.259.)

Bibl: *Lucy Jones,* with an introduction by Marina Vaizey, Angela Flowers Gallery, 1989.

JONES, Mark   b.1942
Painter. Born Haverfordwest, Wales. Studied at Edinburgh College of Art, 1960-4. First solo exhibition at 57 Gallery, Edinburgh, 1967. Held a variety of teaching jobs in Edinburgh. Included in group exhibitions, at SSA and 57 Gallery.

JONES, Mary Lloyd   b.1934
Painter. Born Devil's Bridge, Cardigan, Wales. Studied at Cardiff College of Art, 1951-6. Member of 56 Group Wales. 1966 first solo exhibition at Aberystwyth University Gallery. Visiting Lecturer at Dyfed and Aberystwyth. 1974 won prize at Royal National Eisteddfod of Wales, Camarthen. 1975 exhibition at Oriel Gallery, Cardiff.

JONES, Patrick   b.1948
Painter. Studied at Birmingham College of Art, 1971-1, Maryland Institute, Baltimore, USA, 1973-5. Since 1971 included in mixed exhibitions at the Hayward, the Tolly Cobbold exhibition and at Nicola Jacobs Gallery. From 1981 held John Brinckley Fellowship in Painting at Norwich School of Art. 1981 solo exhibition at Nicola Jacobs Gallery.

JONES, Peter   b.1917
Painter and sculptor. Born London. Studied at Richmond School of Art. During Second World War he engaged in engineering and flying. Included in group shows, e.g. RA, RSA, V & A, RBA. Member of the Society of Mural Painters. Solo exhibitions at the Chichester Festival, 1962, Molton Gallery, 1965.

JONES, Peter Lloyd   b.1932
Painter. Studied science at London and Cambridge Universities, then art at the Slade School. Studied Old Master techniques at the Courtauld Institute of Art, 1959. From 1959 exhibited figurative paintings in group shows at the New Art Centre. 1969 became co-editor of the journal *Leonardo.* 1970 abstract paintings based on Indian musical scales shown at Richard Demarco Gallery, Edinburgh.

JONES, Philip   b.1933
Painter. Born London. Studied at the Slade School, 1953-6. Worked as art officer for the Welsh Arts Council and the Arts Council, 1956-61. 1962 first solo exhibition at Stone Gallery, Newcastle. 1962-72 travelled to the Mediterranean Islands and Tenerife for painting purposes. 1973 moved to live and work in Norfolk. Work in the collection of the CAS, the Nuffield Foundation, Newport and Plymouth Art Galleries. Exhibition at Louise Hallet Gallery, 1987. Specialises in paintings of the Breckland landscape.

JONES, Ray   b.1949
Painter. Born London. Studied at Chelsea School of Art, 1966-71, the RCA, 1971-4 and the University of Reading, 1974-5. Taught at Carlisle College of Art, 1975-6 and Halifax School of Art, 1976-7. From 1971 included in mixed exhibitions in London. 1979 exhibition at Battersea Arts Centre.

JONES, Susan
Painter and printmaker. Studied at Winchester School of Art and Brighton Polytechnic. Moved to the North East, 1972. Taught at Sunderland Polytechnic, 1972-4 and then set up and ran the printmaking workshop at Sunderland Arts Centre until 1980. 1979 prizewinner in the Cleveland

International Drawing Biennale. 1976 solo exhibition at Teesside College of Art Gallery. 1982 took part in artists' exchange programme to St. Louis, USA.

JONES, Trevor   b.1945
Painter. Born Stourbridge, West Midlands. Studied at Stourbridge College of Art, 1960-3, Birmingham College of Art, 1963-5 and the RCA, 1965-8. Visiting lecturer at Birmingham College of Art. From 1967 included in mixed exhibitions; first solo exhibition at New Art Centre, 1969.

JONES, Tim
Painter and printmaker. Studied at St. Martin's School of Art, 1969-72 and the RCA, 1977-80. From 1979 included in mixed exhibitions. 1980 won Mark Rothko travel award to USA and was a prizewinner at the John Moores Liverpool exhibition the same year. 1982 Artist in Residence for the London Borough of Lewisham.

JONES, Timothy Emlyn   b.1948
Painter and performance artist. Born London. Studied at Gloucestershire College of Art, 1965-6, Hornsey College of Art, 1966-9, the RCA, 1969-71, and University College, Cardiff, 1979-80. 1970 first solo exhibition at Howard Roberts Gallery, Cardiff. 1972 performances commenced with work 'Kontrapunkt' in Wroclaw, Poland, and continue to the present. 1984 exhibition at Sunderland Arts Centre.

JONES, William   b.1923
Painter. Born Liverpool, Merseyside. Studied at Liverpool School of Art. From 1951 lived in New Zealand, exhibiting widely there, with five one-man shows. 1967 returned to England and had a show in that year at the Bluecoat Gallery, Liverpool. 1972 exhibition at the Woodstock Gallery. Now lives in London.

JONES, Wynn   b.1939
Painter. Born Aberystwyth, Wales. Studied at Cardiff College of Art, 1957-62. Jubilee Fellow at Byam Shaw School of Art, 1963. From 1974 included in mixed exhibitions of figurative, narrative paintings. 1974 first solo exhibition at University of Wales. Work in the collection of the Arts Council, the Department of the Environment and Rugby Library. The dramas and transactions contrived for his figures are always unspecific. In the early 1980s, however, he turned to subject matter related to the nuclear threat. 1983 exhibition of recent work held at Artspace Galleries, Aberdeen, with catalogue introduction by Timothy Hyman.*

JONLEIGH, Leonie   d.1974
Painter. Born London. Trained as a ballet dancer; no art school training. Included in mixed exhibitions, e.g. London Group, RA, Leicester Galleries, Royal Society of British Artists. 1962-5 served on council of Royal Society of British Artists. 1959 first solo exhibition at Zwemmer Gallery. Set up a studio near Guildford, Surrey, and has offered it to other artists for exhibitions. Her work has been described as seeing the extraordinary in the ordinary.

JONZEN, Basil   b.1914
Painter. Recorder of Spanish topography, especially around Tenerife. Decorated the Petit Salon in San Fernando, Tenerife. Solo exhibitions at Redfern Gallery, 1937 and 1938.

KARIN JONZEN, b.1914. 'Camp Idealist'. Stoneware. 26in. high. Private Collection.

JONZEN, Karin   b.1914
Sculptor. Born London of Swedish parents. Studied at Slade School, 1933-7 and at the Royal Academy, Stockholm, 1939. Won Prix de Rome, 1939. Exhibited at the RA, RBA, with the NEAC and London Group. Elected RBA, 1948. Work commissioned from 1950 onwards from a variety of clients including the Arts Council, schools in Hertford, Leicestershire and Cardiff, churches, Guildford Cathedral, WHO, City of London Corporation, etc. Works in terracotta, carves and casts in bronze. Work in the collection of Glasgow Art Gallery, Bradford, Brighton and Southend Art Galleries, and the V & A. Has executed portrait busts of well-known figures, including Malcolm Muggeridge and Dame Ninette de Valois. Exhibition at Fieldbourne Galleries, 1974.

JOSEPH, Jane   b.1942
Painter. Born Surrey. Studied at Camberwell School of Art, 1961-5. First solo exhibition at Morley Gallery, London, 1973. 1987 exhibition at Angela Flowers Gallery. Group exhibitions since 1975. Work in the collection of the Welsh Arts Council, the Government Picture Collection, and Castle Museum, Norwich. Likes to paint deserted places, with signs of transitory human presence.

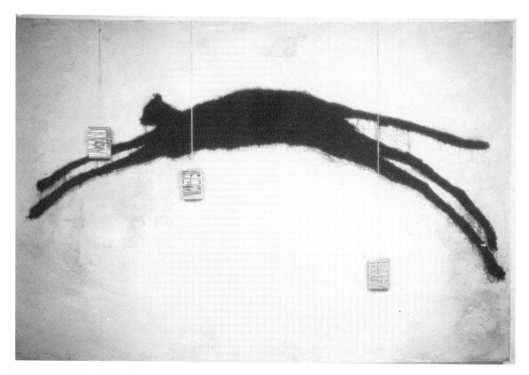

TAM JOSEPH, b.1947. *'Timespan'*, 1987. Acrylic medium, sand, pigment on canvas. 65 ½ in. x 98 ¾ in. Private Collection.

JOSEPH, Lily Delissa   1863-1940
Painter. Born London, the sister of the painter Solomon J. Solomon. Studied at the RCA and the Ridley School of Art. Married the architect Delissa Joseph. Exhibited with the RA, the RBA and the NEAC. Painted portraits, interiors and landscapes. Urbanscape painting in the Tate Gallery collection.

JOSEPH, Peter   b.1929
Painter. Born London. Self-taught. Spent two periods abroad living in Italy and Majorca, otherwise has lived and worked in London. In 1966 at Signals Gallery showed a painting 32ft. long, and produced other large scale work with an intention towards public art. Solo exhibitions at the Lisson Gallery from 1969 to the present. Work in the collections of the Tate Gallery, the Arts Council, the British Council, the CAS and in public galleries in the USA, Australia and Switzerland. His paintings usually consist of only two colours and take the format of a framed door or window. Interested in wholeness, clarity and colour.

JOSEPH, Tam   b.1947
Painter and sculptor. Born Dominica (Antilles). Studied at Central School of Art, 1967, and Slade School, 1968. Lives and works in London and deals in his art, often humorously, with the struggle for African identity. Organised and funded his own Barbican Gallery foyer exhibition, 1985. Work included in the 'From Two Worlds' exhibition at the Whitechapel Gallery, 1986. Solo exhibitions at St. Pancras Library and Shaw Theatre Foyer, 1986, and at Bedford Hill Gallery, 1988. Works in

the collections of Arts Council, CAS, Sheffield City Art Gallery, Camden Library and Bradford City Museum.

JOWETT, Percy Hague   1882-1955
Painter. Born Halifax, Yorkshire. Studied at Leeds School of Art and the RCA, winning the Prix de Rome there. Extensive travels in Italy, 1910-11. Served with the Royal Garrison Artillery during the First World War. 1918 taught at Beckenham School of Art, 1927 Head of the Chelsea Polytechnic, 1929 Principal of the Central School and 1935 Principal of the RCA, a post held until 1947. Gave Henry Moore* his first job. 1907-26 showed with the RA. 1923, 25, 27 and 29 solo exhibitions at St. George's Gallery. Member of the NEAC. 1920 one of the founder members of the 7 & 5 Society. A shy retiring figure, who liked to paint in watercolour. A most sympathetic teacher.

JOY, Steve   b.1952
Painter. Born Plymouth, Devon. Served in the RAF, 1968-75. Studied at Cardiff College of Art, 1975-6, Exeter College of Art, 1976-9 and Chelsea School of Art, 1979-80. 1978 first solo exhibition at Riverside Studios. 1981 travelled to Japan. 1981-2 lived and worked in southern Norway. 1982 exhibition held at Air Gallery.

JUN, Xi Juan   b.1962
Painter. Born China. Studied ceramics and painting at Central Academy of Art and Design, Beijing, 1982-6. First exhibited in a group show at the Autumn Gallery, Beijing, 1983. 1988 first exhibited in Great Britain in 'Contemporary Chinese Painting' at the Royal Festival Hall, London. 1988 awarded Residency at Delfina Studios Trust.

KAHN, Erich F.W.   1904-1980
Painter. Born Stuttgart, Germany. Studied under Scheidler at the School of Arts and Crafts, Stuttgart. 1926 studied with Léger in Paris. 1936 took part in the National Exhibition of Jewish Artists in the Jewish Museum, Berlin. 1938 was arrested and sent to a prison camp. 1939 fled to London, becoming a member of the FDKB (Free German League of Culture). An expressionist, influenced by Kokoschka, he led a withdrawn, modest life.

KALVELAGE, Franka Anna Maria   b.1958
Painter. Born Germany. Studied at Berliner Hochschule der Kunste and Middlesex Polytechnic. Has exhibited at the Kunststudenten Stellan aus Exhibition, Bonn, and Whitechapel Open Exhibitions, London, among other group exhibitions.

KANE, Martin   b.1958
Painter. Graduated from Edinburgh College of Art, 1987. First solo exhibition at the Angela Flowers Gallery, London, 1988. Is keenly aware of his environment and sensitive to contemporary social history, thus his landscapes provide an insight into industrial decline in the modern world.

KANIA, Stasia
Painter. Born Poland. Originally trained as an exterior designer and did not start painting until 1969. Her first solo exhibition was at the PUSK Gallery, 1978, her second at Leighton House Art Gallery. Member of the International Association of Art, Free Painters and Sculptors and the Association of Polish Artists in Great Britain.

KAPOOR, Anish   b.1954
Sculptor. Born Bombay, India. Moved to London, 1971. Studied at Hornsey School of Art, 1973-7, and Chelsea School of Art, 1977-8. 1980 first solo exhibition held at Galerie Patrice Alexandre, Paris. Others at Coracle Press, 1981, and Lisson Gallery, 1988. Work in the Tate Gallery collection. First became renowned for sculpture, in part reminiscent of Indian culture, which was covered with a loose layer of powder paint. Represented Britain at the Venice Biennale, 1990.

KAPP, Edmond Xavier   1890-1978
Portrait-caricaturist. Born London. Studied at Berlin University and Cambridge University. Read for a Medieval and Modern Language Tripos, but spent more time writing and drawing. Began publishing caricatures in *Granta* and *Cambridge Magazine*. Was given his first one-artist show at the Fitzwilliam Museum, Cambridge. On coming down he took a studio, and earned his living by selling caricatures to periodicals. During the First World War served in the Royal Sussex Regiment and in the Intelligence, GHQ. Studied for short periods at home and abroad and had a solo exhibition at the Leicester Galleries, London, 1922; this, like all his first ten solo exhibitions, consisted entirely of drawings. 1940-1 worked as an offical war artist on drawings of 'Life under London'. 1946-7 invited by Unesco to go to Paris and make twenty portrait-drawings of leading delegates to its first international congress. At the end of his life he experimented passionately with abstract painting.

Bibl: *Edmund Kapp: a retrospective exhibition of paintings and drawings, 1911-1961*, Whitechapel Art Gallery, London, 1961.

KARDIA, Caroline   b.1951
Painter. Born London. Studied at St. Martin's School of Art, 1970-3, and RCA, 1974-7. First solo exhibition held at Felicity Samuel Gallery, 1977.

KARLOWSKA, Stanislawa de   1876-1952
Painter. Born Poland. Studied art in Paris and met Robert Bevan* whom she married. Founder member of the London Group. Solo exhibition at the Adams Gallery, London, 1934. Memorial exhibition at the Adams Gallery, London, 1954. She specialised in London squares, West Country scenes and portraits.

KASHDAN, John   b.1917
Painter and printmaker. Born London of a Russian father and English mother. Studied at RA Schools, 1936-9. Lived in Cambridge during the early 1940s and met Henry Moore* who, with others, was to have an important influence upon him. 1945 first solo exhibition at Redfern Gallery, London. Met Jankel Adler* and through him Colquhoun* and MacBryde.* 1946 moved to Devon and set up an art department at the Royal Naval College, Dartmouth. Continued to exhibit in London and America until 1950 when he decided to withdraw from public exhibitions. Worked privately and taught at Guildford School of Art.

KAUFFER, E. McKnight   1890-1954
Painter and designer. Born and educated in USA. Travelled in Europe and came to England, 1914. At the suggestion of the poster artist John Hassall* he took his ideas to Frank Pick at the Underground Railway Company and in 1915 was given two commissions. 1921 gave up painting entirely for commercial art. 1925 held a retrospective exhibition at 60 Gower Street, London. Worked for the London Transport Board, Shell-Mex and BP Limited, the Great Western Railway, the Empire Marketing Board, the Orient Line, the GPO, the Gas, Light and Coke Company, and others. An outstanding poster designer, who used an Art Deco style and made a significant impact on sales.

KAY, Jill   b.1959
Painter. Born Malton, Yorkshire. Studied at Hull College of Higher Education, 1979-82. 1982 became a studio member of Hull Artists Association and began exhibiting regularly in group shows. 1986 first solo exhibition held at Posterngate Gallery, Hull. 1988 first London solo exhibition held at the Last Gallery. Claims the subject of her work is 'the significant or expressive moments, gestures or glimpses of everyday experience'.

KEANE, John   b.1954
Painter. Born Hertfordshire. Studied at Camberwell School of Art, 1972-6. First solo exhibition held at Minsky's Gallery, London, and since 1985 has been represented by Angela Flowers. 1985-6 artist-in-residence, Whitefield School, London. 1987 travelled to Nicaragua for six weeks in summer, and exhibited paintings related to this experience at the Angela Flowers Gallery, 1988.

KEARNEY, Joseph   b.1939
Printmaker. Born Glasgow, Scotland. Studied at Glasgow School of Art. Has had several solo exhibitions in Glasgow, including one at the Glasgow Art Club, 1977, and in London has shown at the RP.

KEATES, John   b.1915
Painter. Born Birkenhead, Cheshire. Studied at Liverpool College of Art. Influenced by French art. During the Second World War he spent five years in India and Burma, as a Captain in the Royal Artillery. Retrained in the evenings at Central School of Art and taught at Guildford

KEATS, Helen

College of Art. Retrospective exhibition held at Atkinson Art Gallery, Southport, 1988.

KEATS, Helen b.1947
Painter. Studied at Wimbledon School of Art, 1979-84. 1985 Fellow of Printmakers Council. 1985 first solo exhibition held at New Art Gallery, London; another at Ben Uri Art Gallery, 1987. A watercolourist and print-maker of scenic views.

KEENE, Arthur b.1930
Painter. Studied at Coventry School of Art and Birmingham School of Art. Began painting during his National Service, which was spent painting the history of Radar for the Royal Artillery, murals for the mess and executing officers' portraits. Studied in Italy, where he worked in a circus, the source of the recurring theme of *commedia del'arte* in his work. Solo exhibition at the Sue Rankin Gallery, London, 1989.

KEIGHTLEY, Moy
Painter. Studied at Chelsea School of Art and was awarded the Morland Lewis Travelling Scholarship. Has exhibited with the London Group, at the Leicester Galleries, Roland, Browse and Delbanco and at the RA. Solo exhibitions include two at the New Grafton Gallery, 1979 and 1982.

KELLY, Barbara b.1951
Painter. Born Newport. Studied at Luton Art College, Lanchester Polytechnic and Birmingham Polytechnic. Married the sculptor Aidan Francis Kelly. Solo exhibition at Derby Art Gallery, 1980. Traditional artist with a particular interest in the technical problems of rendering light.

KELLY, Felix b.1917
Painter. Born Auckland, New Zealand. Came to London shortly before the war. Joined the RAF and began to paint in his spare time. Held his first solo exhibition at the Lefevre Gallery, 1943, and was commissioned to do six paintings to illustrate Herbert Read's novel, *The Green Child.* Other solo exhibitions include several in the USA, three at the Arthur Jeffress Gallery, London, 1952-62, and four shows at Tooth's, London, 1965-74. Has also produced book illustrations, murals and theatrical décor.

KELLY, Francis b.1927
Painter. Born California, USA. Studied at Los Angeles Art School, the Académie de la Grande Chaumière, Paris, 1951-2 and University of Hawaii, 1953. Awarded a Fulbright Grant, 1955 and moved to London. Studied conservation at the Courtauld Institute and the V & A. In 1967 he was sent by the Italian Art and Archives Fund to Florence to restore flood damaged paintings. Regular solo exhibitions at the John Whibley Gallery, London.

KELLY, Sir Gerald 1879-1972
Painter. Born London of Irish parents. Studied at Trinity Hall, Cambridge and in Paris. 1904 member of the Salon d'Automne, Paris. 1907 founder-member of the Modern Portrait Painters Society. 1908 elected associate of the Royal Hibernian Academy and full member, 1914. 1910 founder-member of the National Portrait Society. 1924 travelled to New York to undertake several American commissions. 1938-43 member of the Royal Fine Art Commission. 1945 knighted. 1922 elected ARA, and 1930 RA. 1949-54 President of the RA. 1955 invested Knight Commander of the Royal Victorian Order. Painted

portraits with panache but is more charming in his small oils which admit a debt to Whistler.

Bibl: Derek Hudson, *For Love of Painting: The Life of Sir Gerald Kelly,* Peter Davies, London, 1975.

KELLY, Mary b.1941
Mixed media artist. Born Minnesota, USA. Studied at Pius XII Institute, Florence, 1963-5, and St. Martin's School of Art, 1968-70. Winner of an Arts Council Award, 1977, and on editorial board of *Screen Magazine,* 1979-81. Best known for her *Post-Partum Document,* a serial piece involving words, psychoanalytical thought and remnants of her own child's early years, which outraged visitors to the Hayward Annual, 1978. Artist-in-residence at New Hall and Kettle's Yard, Cambridge, 1985-6.

Bibl: *Mary Kelly: Interim,* The Fruitmarket Gallery, Edinburgh, 1986.

KELLY, Mick b.1949
Painter. Born Wallasey, Cheshire. Studied at Camberwell School of Art, 1969-71, and Goldsmiths' College, 1976-7. Solo exhibition at Woodlands Art Gallery, 1981.

KELLY, Robert Talbot 1861-1935
Painter. Born Birkenhead, Cheshire. Travelled widely, in Spain, Morocco, Algiers and Egypt, maintaining a home in Birkenhead and a studio in Liverpool until 1902, when he removed to London. Exhibited at Liverpool Autumn Exhibition from 1882, and occasionally at the RA from 1888. Published books on Egypt and Burma. Received the Order of the Medjidish from the Kedive of Egypt.

KEMP, David b.1945
Sculptor. Born Walthamstow, Essex. Studied navigation and was a merchant seaman, 1963-7. Studied at Farnham College of Art, 1967-9, and Wimbledon School of Art, 1969-72. Moved to West Cornwall, 1973, where he now lives and works. Solo exhibitions include one at Ashgate Gallery, Farnham, 1980, and another at Manchester City Art Galleries, 1987. Works with found objects, broken machinery or electronic equipment and refashions it into animals and totemic figures. His largest public commission to date can be found in Hay's Galleries, London.

KEMPSELL, Jake b.1940
Sculptor. Born Dumfries, Scotland. Studied at Edinburgh College of Art where he became a lecturer in 1965. 1975 became Head of Sculpture at Duncan of Jordanstone College of Art. 1978 founder member of Scottish Sculpture Trust. 1970 first solo exhibition held at Richard Demarco Gallery, Edinburgh. His sculpture includes the represent-ation of the ephemeral (clouds) in stone, slate and cement.

KEMP-WELCH, Lucy 1969-1958
Painter. Born Bournemouth, Hampshire. Studied under Sir Hubert Herkomer at Bushey, from 1891. 1894 began exhibiting at the RA. 1902-10 member of the RBA. Lived in Bushey for many years and took over Herkomer's school, 1905-26. Specialises in animal subjects, chiefly horses.

Bibl: David Messum, *Lucy Kemp-Welch,* Antique Collectors' Club, Woodbridge, 1976.

KENDALL, Richard b.1946
Painter. Spent his childhood in China and East Africa. Studied at Manchester School of Art, 1965-6, Central School of Art and Design, 1966-9 and Courtauld Institute of Art, 1969-71 (MA in Art History). Teaches at Manchester

Polytechnic. Solo exhibition at the Cylinder Gallery, London, 1983, where he showed a series of works based on images by Degas.

KENDRY, Alistair Carl   b.1957
Painter. Born Wiltshire. Studied at Royal Worcester Porcelain Co. Ltd., 1975-7, Herefordshire College of Art and Design, 1979-80, Bath Academy of Art, 1980-3, and at the Slade School of Fine Art, 1986-8. Awards include Waltham Forest Arts Council Award, 1986; Southern Arts Award, 1987 and Barclays Bank 'Young Painters Award', 1988. He has regularly exhibited in Great Britain since 1977 when he contributed to Dyson Perrins Museum, Worcester. Exhibited with Sue Williams, London, 1990.

KENNEDY, Alistair   b.1957
Painter. Studied at Hereford College of Art, 1979-80, Bath Academy of Art, 1980-3, and at the Slade School of Fine Art, 1986-8. First exhibited at the Whitworth Art Gallery, Manchester, 1981. Awards include the Southern Arts, 1987 and the Barclays Bank, 1988.

KENNEDY, Cedric   1898-1968
Painter. Born Exeter, Devon, the son of a major. The family moved to various army postings during his childhood. Studied at London School of Art, Florence School of Art and RA Schools. Taught art at Rugby School, 1926-8, and then moved to Painswick, Gloucestershire, with his mother. Taught art at Cheltenham College, 1935-6, and Dean Close School, 1938-9. Liked Savile Row suits, cars, scooters, watches and unconventional art. He lost an eye in 1952, by accident, whilst protecting his hostess at a party from an attack by an epileptic. Represented in the V & A.

KENNERLEY, George   b.1908
Painter. Born London. Began painting in 1945 and worked with a number of well-known British artists. Has exhibited at the RA, the Leicester Gallery, Crane Kalman Gallery and with the Arts Council. His paintings are represented in the Walker Art Gallery, Liverpool, Birkenhead Art Gallery and elsewhere.

KENNETT, Lady Kathleen   1878-1947
Sculptor. Born Carlton-in-Lindrick, Nottinghamshire. Studied at the Slade School and in Paris at the Atelier Colarossi, 1901-6, and under Rodin. 1908 married Captain Robert Falcon Scott who died in the Antarctic, 1912. Remarried in 1922 to Sir Edward Hilton Young, created Baron Kennett. Exhibited at RA from 1913. Elected ARBS, 1928, and FRBS, 1946. Specialised in bust portraiture and figure subjects and executed several memorial statues. Mother of Sir Peter Scott, the naturalist.

KENNETHSON, George   b.1910
Sculptor. Born Richmond, Surrey. Married the painter Eileen Guthrie. Studied painting at RA Schools but in the mid-1930s became interested in stone carving. Lives and works at Oundle, Northants. A practitioner of direct carving, who achieves harmonised relationships of planes, mass, weight and proportion, in both abstract and figurative work.

KENNINGTON, Eric   1888-1960
Painter and sculptor. Son of Thomas Benjamin Kennington.* Studied at Lambeth School of Art. 1904-5 spent several months with relatives in St. Petersburg, Russia. Joined the Artists' Rifles during the first week of the First World War. 1915 invalided home and painted 'The Kensingtons at Laventie' (Imperial War Museum) a large shell-torn scene, the whole painted in reverse on the back of plate glass. At an exhibition of his war pictures he met T.E. Lawrence, whose influence dominated the rest of his life. Became art editor of Lawrence's *Seven Pillars of Wisdom*. The Arab portraits which he drew in Bedouin encampments in 1921 became some of his best-known works. Turned to sculpture in the mid-1920s. Intensely patriotic, he became an official war artist again in 1939 and embarked on a long series of highly coloured pastel portraits. 1951 elected ARA and RA, 1959. An exhibition of his work was held at the Imperial War Museum, 1980.

KENNINGTON, Thomas Benjamin   1856-1916
Painter. Born Grimsby, Lincolnshire. Studied at Liverpool School of Art. A founder member of the NEAC and performed as its honorary secretary in 1886 and 1887. His subject pictures dwell on the pathos of the London poor. Became President of the ROI.

KENNY, Michael   b.1941
Sculptor. Born Liverpool, Merseyside. Studied at Liverpool College of Art, 1959-61 and the Slade, 1961-4. Has taught at Goldsmiths' College of Art since 1966. 1964 first one-person show at the Bear Lane Gallery, Oxford. 1975, 1977 and 1980 received Arts Council Major Awards. 1987 exhibition at the RA. Represented in the collections of the Arts Council, British Council, CAS, the British Museum, Tate Gallery and V & A.

KER, Angela   b.1933
Painter. Born Scotland. Studied at Glasgow School of Art and British School in Rome. 1957 won Torrance Memorial Award in Glasgow. Began painting commissioned portraits. 1962 worked in Morocco. 1958 first solo exhibition held at Blythswood Gallery, Glasgow.

KER, Dorian   b.1948
Painter. Born Rome, Italy. Studied at Central School of Art and Design for a short time but is largely self-taught. Inspired by North European art of the fifteenth century and by early Italian craftsmanship. 1975 first solo exhibition held at Roy Miles Gallery, London; another in 1977.

KERMA, Ingrid   b.1942
Painter. Born Berlin, Germany. Studied at Reading University, 1972-6. Worked at Butler's Wharf Studios, London, 1976-80. 1978 first solo exhibition held at Penwith Gallery, St. Ives, another at the AIR Gallery, London, 1979. Represented in Arts Council Collection and elsewhere.

KESSEL, Mary   b.1910
Painter. Born London. Studied at Clapham School of Art and Central School of Art and Crafts. Began painting, 1939. Executed Judith and Holofernes mural at Westminster Hospital during the Second World War. 1945 as an official war artist visited Belsen and Berlin. 1946 extracts from her *German Diary* were published in *The Cornhill Magazine*. Solo exhibitions at the Leicester Galleries, 1950, 1957, 1960, and 1964, and at the New Grafton Gallery, 1969. Represented in Imperial War Museum, Tate Gallery and elsewhere.

KESTELMAN, Morris

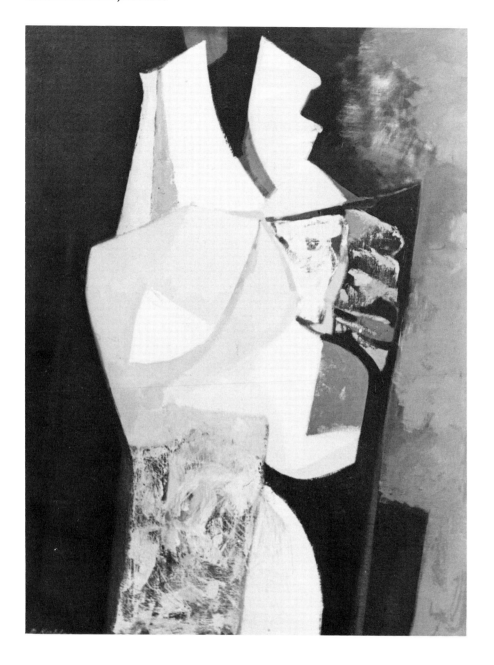

MORRIS KESTELMAN, b.1905.
'Greys on Black'. 48in. x 36in.
Private Collection.

KESTELMAN, Morris   b.1905
Painter. Studied at Central School of Art and Design,
1922-5 and RCA, 1926-9. An early interest in and
commissions for stage design led to an involvement with
mural painting and two large murals for the *Britain Can
Make It* exhibition at the V & A, 1946. Became Head of
Fine Art, Central School of Art and Design, and retired in
1973. His painting evolved from a figurative to a non-
figurative approach from the late 1950s onwards.

Bibl: Bryan Robertson, *Morris Kestleman*, Cork Street Gallery,
London, 1969.

KEY, Geoffrey   b.1941
Painter. Born Manchester, Lancashire. Studied at
Manchester Regional College of Art. Became a council
member of the Manchester Academy of Fine Arts. First
solo exhibition held at Salford Art Gallery, 1966.
Represented in Bolton City Art Gallery, Manchester City
Art Gallery and elsewhere. Stylised figurative artist who
uses strong colour.

KIDD, Richard   b.1952
Painter. Born Newcastle upon Tyne, Tyne and Wear.
Studied at Newcastle University, 1970-4, and the British
School in Rome, 1974-5. Since 1976 winner of several
awards and prizes and lectures at Newcastle University.
1977 first solo exhibition held at Rowan Gallery, London.

KIDNER, Michael   b.1917
Painter. Born Kettering, Northants. Studied at Cambridge
University (History and Anthropology), 1936-9, and Ohio
State University (Landscape Architecture), 1940-1. 1941-6
saw war service in the Canadian Army. 1946 entered
Goldsmiths' College of Art to study art but, dissatisfied
with the teaching, soon left. Did not begin full-time
painting until 1953, when he lived in Paris for two years

280

intermittently attending André L'Hôte's atelier. 1956 spent five or six months in St. Ives meeting its artists. 1957 moved to London and fell under the influence of American Abstract Expressionism. His ideas on colour were taken further by Harry Thubron* whose course at Leeds Kidner attended. 1963-7 he made interference pattern, stripe and wave paintings with the main emphasis on colour. Later became involved in 'systems' games and kinetic art. Exhibited with the Systems Group during the 1970s. Solo exhibitions include one at Serpentine Gallery, London, 1984.

Bibl: *Michael Kidner. Painting, drawing, sculpture, 1959-84,* Arts Council, 1984.

KIFF, Ken   b.1935
Painter. Born Dagenham, Essex. Studied at Hornsey School of Art, 1955-61. For many years he taught part-time in comprehensive and ESN schools and subsequently at art colleges including Chelsea School of Art and RCA. 1977 illustrated *Folk Tales of the British Isles,* edited by Michael Foss. 1981 painted at the Artist's Camp at Kasauli, North India. Has held several solo exhibitions since his first at the Gardner Centre Gallery, University of Sussex, 1979, including one at the Serpentine Gallery, London, 1986 and Fischer Fine Art, London, 1988. Has work in Tate Gallery, Arts Council and British Council collections and in public collections in America. Began painting from imagination in the 1960s, drawing upon imaginative and psychological processes which we all encounter. During 1960-9 he underwent psychotherapy which had a lasting influence on his choice of subject.

Bibl: *Ken Kiff. Paintings 1965-85,* Arts Council, 1986.

KILBOURN, Oliver   b.1904
Painter. Born Ashington, Northumberland, the son of a pitman. Worked in Ashington Colliery from the age of thirteen and then at Ellington Colliery. Was a miner for all his working life. In between shifts played football and went to WEA classes. 1934 took an eight year WEA class in Art Appreciation. This led to the founding of the Ashington Group of Painters, which still exists today. 1977 solo exhibition at the Midland Group Gallery, Nottingham.

KILLEEN, Bruce   b.1926
Painter. Studied English Literature at Oxford. Self-taught as a painter. Settled in Gloucestershire and became committed to painting in 1959. 1959-64 exhibited widely in the West Country. Member of the RWA, Bristol. 1964 also showed at the AIA New Members exhibition. Best known for his landscapes.

KILLPACK, Mona
Painter. Born Brighton, Sussex. Studied at Brighton School of Art and in Paris for several years. Held her first solo exhibition at the John Whibley Gallery, London, 1963. Others followed, reflecting her interest in place, atmosphere and figures.

KIMPTON, John   b.1961
Painter. Born Manchester, Lancashire. Exhibited locally around Manchester until 1980 when he entered Manchester Polytechnic to do a foundation course; left five months later. 1981 exhibited with the Manchester Academy. 1982 first solo exhibition held at the Ginnel Gallery, Manchester. Works also as an illustrator, publisher and printmaker.

KING, Caroline
Painter. Born London. Studied at Westminster and St. Martin's Schools of Art. Has taught art at the Working Men's College, Camden Town, and held a solo exhibition at the Woodstock Gallery, London, 1968.

KING, Dave   b.1946
Sculptor. Born West Midlands. Studied at Leeds College of Art, 1965-8 and Slade School of Art, 1968-70. 1972 awarded a Boise travelling scholarship. 1974 artist-in-residence, University of Sussex. 1970 first solo exhibition held at Serpentine Gallery, London. Since 1978 represented by Angela Flowers Gallery, London. Admires the work of William Tucker,* an artist with whom he shares many affinities.

KING, Dorothy
Painter. Studied at Hornsey School of Art and Slade School of Art. During the war she worked as a Welfare Officer. 1947 elected a member of RBA and in 1961 she was appointed Keeper of the South London Art Gallery. She continued to give art classes at the Southwark Art Centre and held a retrospective at the South London Art Gallery, in 1974, the year she retired.

KING, Jessie M.   1875-1949
Painter and illustrator. Born New Kilpatrick, Scotland. Revealed a precocious talent for drawing and illustration. Studied at Glasgow School of Art. Her subjects for illustration tended to be romantic or exotic. Was regularly illustrated in *The Studio.* Worked for the Bodley Head, illustrating *The High History of the Holy Grail* and *Defence of Guenevere* by William Morris. 1911 and 1912 divided her time between Scotland and Paris, not only illustrating books but also writing them, working also in batik, watercolours, china painting and design of all kinds.

Bibl: *Jessie M. King, 1875-1949,* The Scottish Arts Council, 1971.

KING, Phillip   b.1934
Sculptor. Born Kheredine, North Africa. 1946 came to England. National Service, 1952-4, in the Royal Signal Corps. Read modern languages at Cambridge University, 1954-7. 1957 studied under Anthony Caro* at St. Martin's School of Art. 1958-9 worked as assistant to Henry Moore.* 1959 began teaching at St. Martin's School of Art and won Boise Scholarship to Greece for three months. 1964 took a three months teaching post at Bennington College, Vermont, USA. 1964 first one-person exhibition at Rowan Gallery, London. Has continued to exhibit at the Rowan Gallery and in 1968 represented Britain with Bridget Riley* at the Venice Biennale. Trustee of the Tate Gallery, 1967-9. 1974 received CBE. 1977 elected ARA. 1980 appointed Professor of Sculpture at RCA. Major retrospective at Hayward Gallery, London, 1981.

KINGSBURY, Alan   b.1960
Painter. Born London. In 1988 exhibited a series of paintings based on Venice and the Lido at Jonathan Cooper's Park Walk Gallery, London.

KINLEY, Peter   1926-1988
Painter. Born Vienna, Austria. Arrived in England, 1938. Volunteered for the Young Soldiers' Battalion, 1944, afterwards moving into intelligence. After he was demobbed he was promised a place at St. Martin's School of Art a year hence, and so organised himself a year at the

KINNAIRD, John

Dusseldorf Academy. Exhibited abstract work whilst a student, but became known for his dense, rich figurative pictures, shown at Gimpel Fils in London and Rosenberg's in New York. In 1965 he hid in his studio and produced work secretly, emerging again with greater abundance. Continued to exhibit, at Tooth's, Waddington's and Knoedler's. A close friend of Howard Hodgkin,* he, like Hodgkin, tries to recapture experience through painting. His thinly painted, apparently simply but iconic pictures only received the attention they deserved in the 1980s. A retrospective was held at MOMA, Oxford.

KINNAIRD, John   b.1939
Painter. Born Gateshead, Co. Durham. Studied at University of Newcastle upon Tyne, 1958 onwards. 1963 awarded a travelling scholarship. 1965 began lecturing at the University of Leeds. Since 1963 has had regular exhibitions in Leeds, Hull and London.

KINNEAR, Leslie Gordon   1901-1976
Painter. Educated in Dundee and Bordeaux. In 1921 joined the commercial firm, D. Pirie and Co., but with increasing deafness decided to devote his life to painting. Studied at Dundee and Glasgow Colleges of Art where he became chiefly known for his watercolour landscapes. Exhibited at RSA and elsewhere. Made frequent visits to Italy and held exhibitions in Arezzo.

KIRBY, John   b.1949
Painter. Born Liverpool, Merseyside. Worked as a shipping clerk, 1965-7, and as a Catholic Bookshop salesman, 1967-9; other jobs followed. Studied art at St. Martin's School of Art, 1982-5, and RCA, 1986-8. 1988 first solo exhibition 'Other People's Lives', held at Angela Flowers (Ireland), Rosscarbery, Ireland.

KIRK, Barry   b.1933
Painter. Born Deal, Kent. Studied at Canterbury College of Art, then print-making and also design for television at the RCA. Became Head of the Department of History and Complementary Studies at Canterbury College of Art and eventually its Vice-Principal. Held regular solo exhibitions at the Alwin Gallery in London, of relief paintings.

KIRK, Eve   1900-1969
Painter. Studied at Slade School of Art. Painted scenes drawn from Provence, Italy and London and held three solo exhibitions at Wm. B. Paterson Galleries, Bond Street, 1930, and at Arthur Tooth and Sons, London, 1932 and 1935. Work in the Tate Gallery collection.

KIRK, Joanna   b.1963
Painter and pastellist. Born Cheshire. Studied at Goldsmiths' College, 1981-4. First solo exhibition held at Third Eye Centre, Glasgow, 1987; another at Nicola Jacobs Gallery, London, in the same year, and a third in 1989. Represented in 'The British Art Show' at the Hayward Gallery, 1990.

KIRKWOOD, John   b.1947
Mixed media artist. Born Edinburgh, Scotland. Studied at Dundee College of Art, 1965-70. First solo exhibition at the New 57 Gallery, Edinburgh in 1971. Has regularly held solo exhibitions at the gallery since this date. Elected as a professional member of the SSA, 1972.

KITAJ, R.B.   b.1932
Painter. Born Ronald Brooks in Cleveland, Ohio, of Russian-Jewish and Viennese descent. Signed on as a merchant seaman, making several voyages to the Caribbean and South America, before receiving formal art training at the Cooper Union, New York. Also studied in Vienna and travelled extensively in Europe. 1956-7 served in US Army. Continued his art education in England, on a GI grant, first at the Ruskin School, Oxford, and then at the RCA, 1960-2. His wide reading and breadth of experience made him an influence on his fellow artists and though his work least deserves the label 'pop', he acted as a catalyst on a number of artists associated with that movement, notably David Hockney.* His own brand of figuration brought together, with magpie-like wizardry, a complex mix of source and method that broke all stylistic conventions. 1962 he met the screenprinter Chris Prater and embarked on a long involvement with collage print. 1963 held first solo exhibition at Los Angeles County Museum of Art. Having taught at various London art colleges, he accepted a Guest Professorship at the University of California, Berkeley, 1967-8, during which time he became close friends with the Black Mountain poets, Robert Creeley and Robert Duncan. After the death of his first wife, he married the American painter, Sandra Fisher.* 1975 visited Paris and inspired by Degas' use of pastel began to use this medium for a significant proportion of his work. His recent work has shown an increased preoccupation with Jewish history and identity and with the history of revolutionary struggle. Has also been influential in the promotion of a return to figurative art, through his 1976 Hayward Gallery exhibition, 'The Human Clay', and in other ways. 1981 a major retrospective of his work was held in Washington, Cleveland and Düsseldorf. 1984 elected ARA. (Plate 15, p.39.)

Bibl: Marco Livingstone, *R.B. Kitaj,* Phaidon Press, Oxford, 1985.

KITCHIN, Roy   b.1926
Sculptor. Born Peterborough, Cambridgeshire. Studied at Birmingham School of Art, 1952-4. Worked as an architectural sculptor, 1954-60. 1961-71 was lecturer in Sculpture at Wolverhampton School of Art. 1971-80s Lecturer in Sculpture at Newcastle University. Works in steel, aluminium and wood. 1980 solo exhibition at Wolverhampton Art Gallery.

KITCHING, Arthur   b.1912
Painter. Born Sheffield, Yorkshire. Went into a steelworks as a clerk at age of sixteen and began painting two years later. Spent a year at Sheffield College of Art but is otherwise self-taught. Spent the next twenty years painting for six months and working in any available job for the next six. This ended in 1950 when he went to work for Essex County Council making 'artist's impressions' and arranging exhibitions concerned with the development of new satellite towns. 1961 returned to Yorkshire and became the first curator of Ilkley's Manor House Museum and Art Gallery. 1977 given retrospective at Cartwright Hall, Bradford. Painted regularly at Scarborough using bright colours.

KITE, Roger   b.1947
Painter. Born Bath, Avon. Studied at Hornsey College of Art, 1970-4, and Chelsea School of Art, 1974-5. Lecturer at Trent Polytechnic from 1977 onwards. Included in mixed exhibitions in the 1970s and '80s, e.g. Athena Art Awards

and the John Moores Liverpool Exhibition. Recent solo exhibitions include 'Death' at Kettle's Yard Gallery, Cambridge, 1988 and one at the Café Gallery, London, 1989.

KITSON, Linda   b.1945
Painter and illustrator. Studied at St. Martin's School of Art, 1964-7, and RCA, 1967-70. 1982 official war artist with the Falklands Islands Task Force.

Bibl: Linda Kitson, *The Falklands War, a Visual Diary,* Mitchell Beazley, London, 1983.

KLIMOWSKI, Andrzej   b.1949
Painter. Studied at St. Martin's School of Art, 1973 and at Warsaw Academy of Fine Arts, 1973-5. First solo exhibition at Galeria Wielka, Poznan, Poland, 1980. Solo exhibition at Vanessa Devereux Gallery, London, 1986. Included in the collections of National Museum, Warsaw; National Museum, Poznan; Stedilijk Museum, Amsterdam, Netherlands; California Museum of Science and Technology, Los Angeles, USA.

KLINGHOFER, Clara   1900-1970
Painter. Born Lemberg, Germany. Came to England aged two. Studied at the Slade School, 1918-19. First solo exhibition in London aged nineteen. Showed in group exhibitions, e.g. NEAC, Venice Biennale, Carnegie Institute, Pittsburgh, and the RA. 1939 went to New York. Well known for her portraits of famous people, e.g. Albert Schweitzer, Sir Winston Churchill, Vivien Leigh. The CAS bought a portrait of Torquato Simoncell, an old troubadour, which they presented to the Tate Gallery.

KNEALE, Bryan   b.1930
Sculptor. Born Isle of Man. Studied at Douglas School of Art and the RA Schools. Worked as a painter until 1959 and began making steel sculpture, 1960. 1965 held first solo exhibition at the Redfern Gallery, London. 1965 began teaching at the RCA. Represented in the collections of the Tate Gallery, Arts Council, the Manx Museum and Leicestershire Education Authority.

KNIGHT, Charles   1901-1990
Painter. Born Hove, Sussex. Studied at Brighton Art School and the RA Schools where he learned from Charles Sims* the technique of painting in oil over a tempera base. Won the gold medal, the Landseer scholarship and a portrait drawing prize. Taught at Brighton College of Art from 1925, returning after the war and retired in the mid-1960s. Also worked for an architectural firm, J.L. Denman of Brighton, detailing perspective drawings. Did forty drawings for the Pilgrim Trust's *Recording Britain* project in 1940 and was paid £5 each. Also decorated railway carriages with panel paintings of Lancashire scenes. His landscape style was more influenced by great artists of the past, such as Cotman, than any impressionist or post-impressionist development. Best known for his watercolours which with their strong sense of design, earned him the soubriquet 'the twentieth century Cotman'. Elected ROI, 1933, ARWS, 1933 and RWS, 1935; Vice President of RWS, 1961. Represented in several public collections, including Sheffield, Hull, Brighton, Eastbourne and Worthing.

KNIGHT, Harold   1874-1961
Painter. Born Nottingham, the son of William Knight, an architect and amateur painter. Studied at Nottingham School of Art, and in Paris, 1893-4, and at the Académie Julian. Met Laura Johnson, a fellow student at Nottingham School of Art, and married her, 1903. First exhibited at the RA, 1896 and had his first joint exhibition with his wife at the Leicester Galleries, 1906. Lived and worked at Staithes in Yorkshire; also made several working trips to Holland painting at the artists' colony of Laren. Moved to Newlyn, Cornwall, 1908 and joined the artists' colony there. 1909 embarked on a series of paintings of women in interiors, a subject dear to him all his life. Was a conscientious objector during the First World War. After the war, the Knights moved to London where Harold received a steady flow of commissions for portraits from figures in public life. Exhibited regularly at the RA and the RP. Elected ARA, 1928, and RA, 1937, each time a year after his wife.

KNIGHT, Dame Laura   1877-1970
Painter. Born Laura Johnson, at Long Eaton, Derbyshire. Took private lessons in art from her mother, then attended Nottingham School of Art aged thirteen. In 1903 had a painting accepted at the RA, and persuaded a fellow art student, Harold Knight,* to marry her; they then painted at Staithes in Yorkshire. Moved to Newlyn in Cornwall and joined the art colony there. 1919 elected associate of the RWS, 1927 associate of the RA, 1928 full member of the RWS. 1932 member of the RE. 1936 became full member of the RA. 1929 created DBE. Loved to draw and paint the circus, ballet and the theatre. Worked in oils, watercolours, etching, engraving and drypoint. Became an Official War Artist during the Second World War and painted the Nuremburg Trials. 1965 was given a retrospective exhibition at the RA, the first woman artist to be thus honoured. Wrote two autobiographical volumes, *Oil Paint and Grease Paint,* 1936, and *The Magic of a Line,* 1965. (Plate 62, p.318.)

Bibl: Caroline Fox, *Dame Laura Knight,* Phaidon Press, Oxford, 1988.

KNIGHT, Robert   b.1921
Sculptor. Born Leicester. Studied at Leicester College of Art, 1936-7. Worked in a small commercial studio, 1937-40. Served with the Royal Artillery, 1940-5. Studied at the RA Schools, 1946-50. Worked as a gardener, handyman, painter and decorator, 1950-70. First solo exhibition at Nicholas Treadwell Gallery, 1970. Included in mixed shows from 1968. Makes painted fibreglass reliefs of parts of imperfect bodies.

KNIGHTS, Winifred   1899-1947
Painter. Born London. Studied at the Slade School, 1915-19, winning the Slade Scholarship, and in 1920 the Rome Scholarship in Decorative painting, the first woman to do so. Studied at the British School in Rome, 1920-4, and in 1924 married Thomas Monnington,* a fellow student there. 1922 an Italian landscape view was bought by the Tate Gallery. 1927-31 exhibited at the Imperial College Gallery of Art, London. 1925-37 lived and worked in London when the Monningtons moved to Tunbridge Wells. 1934 her son John was born, the same year she painted a work for the Milner Memorial Chapel at Canterbury Cathedral. A slow and meticulous worker, she had an admiration for early Italian art. Work in the collections of the Slade School, the Tate Gallery and National Art Gallery, New Zealand.

EARDLEY KNOLLYS, b.1902. *'Hampshire Cornfield'*, 1982. 28in. x 36in. Private Collection.

KNOLLYS, Eardley   b.1902

Painter. Born Hampshire. Interested in the theatre while at Oxford. Lived and worked in Hollywood, 1927-8. Bought Storran Gallery, Knightsbridge, London, 1935, owned it until 1939 and showed the work of Modigliani, Soutine, Utrillo and the Euston Road painters. After the war he often travelled to France to paint. Close friend of the painters Edward Le Bas,* Vanessa Bell* and Duncan Grant.* Worked part-time for the National Trust in South West England. Served on the Education committee of the CAS, 1949-64. Included in group shows, e.g. the RA, Leicester Galleries, Redfern Gallery. His most recent solo exhibition was shown at the Michael Parkin Gallery, London.

KNOTT, George   1893-1969

Painter. Born Manchester. Went to sea aged sixteen. Took several jobs in the USA and Canada. Served with the Canadian Regiment in the First World War. Started painting in his forties, when living in Rockport, Massachusetts. Period of study at Boston College of Art. Arrived by boat in Liverpool in the mid-1950s. Memorial exhibition held at the Bluecoat Gallery, Liverpool, 1969.

KNOWLAND, Denis   1918-1985

Painter. Studied at Camberwell School of Art, 1946-9, after war service. Adopted a method close in style to that of William Coldstream* and was skilled at finding patterned relationships within ordinary views and events. 1949-72 worked as an examiner for London University. Also taught, and only painted at weekends until his retirement in 1972 when he began painting full-time. Also illustrated books and painted murals. A memorial exhibition of his work was held at the Central Library, Oxford, 1987.

KNOWLES, Justin   b.1935

Painter and sculptor. Born Exeter, Devon. No formal art training. Worked in industry until 1965. Travelled in West, Central and East Africa. Fellow of the Royal Anthropological Society. 1966-70 visiting lecturer at Bath Academy of Art, Corsham. First solo exhibition at Galleria Cadario, Milan. 1966 won a prize in the Open Painting exhibition, Arts Council of Northern Ireland. 1969 sculpture commissioned for School and Community Centre, Ilfracombe, Devon. 1970 commissioned to make a sculpture for Stirling University.

GHISHA KOENIG, b.1921. *'Tent Makers IV'*, 1981. Terracotta relief. 32in. x 38in. Private Collection.

KOENIG, Ghisha   b.1921
Sculptor. Studied at Hornsey School of Art, 1939-42, then served for four years in the army. 1947 resumed her studies, under Henry Moore* at Chelsea and for one year at the Slade School. Spent a period in Mexico, learning how terracotta is used there. Takes as her subject 'Man at Work'. Has drawn most of her subjects from factory life. A retrospective was held at the Serpentine Gallery, London, 1986. Work in the Tate Gallery.

KOKOSCHKA, Oskar   1886-1980
Painter. Born Pochlarn, Lower Austria. From 1905-9 he studied at Vienna School of Applied Arts and came under the influence of Klimt and Van Gogh. Established contact with 'Der Sturm' in Berlin, but returned to Vienna, 1911. Served in the First World War and was severely wounded. 1920-4 taught at Dresden Academy and afterwards embarked on extensive travels. 1931-4 lived in Vienna, and Prague 1934-38. 1938 arrived in England and in 1947 acquired British nationality. 1954 settled in Villeneuve on Lake Geneva.

KONDRACKI, Henry   b.1953
Painter. Born Edinburgh, Scotland. Studied at the Byam Shaw School of Fine Art, London, 1981-2, and at the Slade School of Art, 1982-6. First solo exhibition at Traverse Theatre Club, Edinburgh, 1979. Solo exhibition at the Vanessa Devereux Gallery, London, 1989, in which comic-book characters were used to explore emotions and memories connected with his past. Included in the

collections of the Granada Foundation, Manchester, and the British Arts Council.

KOPS, Adam   b.1956
Sculptor. Studied at Wimbledon School of Art, 1982-3 and at St. Martin's School of Art, 1984-7. First solo exhibition at Kingsgate Gallery, London, 1988.

KORDA, Henry   b.1957
Painter. Born London. Spent childhood in France and England. Studied at the City and Guilds, 1975-9 and the RA, 1979-81. Travelled in Africa, 1981-2. Solo exhibition at The Cylinder Gallery, 1983.

KORN, Halina   1902-1978
Painter. Born Halina Julia Korngold in Poland. Trained as a singer. All her family were killed by the Germans in the war. She survived because she was on holiday in France when war broke out. Married the painter Marek Zulawski* in 1948 and lived and worked in London. Included in many mixed exhibitions, e.g. RA, London Group, AIA, WIAC. 1948 first solo exhibition at the Mayor Gallery; 1968 at the BWA Gallery, Katowice, Poland, and another in 1981 at the Camden Arts Centre.

KOSSOFF, Leon   b.1926
Painter. Born London. Studied at St. Martin's School of Art and the Borough Polytechnic, 1949-53 and the RCA, 1953-6. 1957-64 had six solo exhibitions at the Beaux Arts Gallery. Further solo exhibitions include Fischer Fine Art, 1979 and 1984, Hirsch and Alder Modern, New York,

KOWALSKY, Elaine

1983 and L.A. Louver Gallery, Venice, California, 1984. Also exhibits with Anthony d'Offay, London. Like Auerbach,* with whom he studied under Bomberg* at the Borough Polytechnic, he has repeatedly reworked certain subjects, allowing the flow or sudden halt of the brushmarks to play an emotive role. Unsurpassed in his portrayal of London's East End, its shuddering sprawl, energy and decay. Work in the collection of the Tate Gallery.

Bibl: *Leon Kossoff: Paintings from a Decade 1970-80,* Museum of Modern Art, Oxford, 1981.

KOWALSKY, Elaine   b.1948

Printmaker. Born Winnipeg, Canada. Studied at University of Manitoba School of Art, 1967-71, St. Martin's School of Art, 1973-4, Brighton Polytechnic, 1974-5. First solo exhibition at Axix Gallery, Brighton, 1976. Included in mixed exhibitions from 1970. Lecturer in Printmaking techniques, Camberwell School of Art, 1979-83. Chairperson, Printmakers Council of Great Britain, 1984-5. 1985 on board of Directors, Design and Artists Copyright Society. 1986 won GLAA award. 1987-8 Henry Moore Printmaking Fellow at Leeds Polytechnic. 1988 exhibition of new work 'Hearts and Vessels' held at Leeds City Art Gallery.

KRAAY, Pauline

Painter. Born London, the daughter of a fashion artist. Studied at Slade School and at Dartington, Devon. Worked on props for the Old Vic Theatre. Studied the ancient craft of glass painting in Austria with the painter, Jupp Donhauser. 1970 solo exhibition of this technique held at Marjorie Parr Gallery, London.

KRAMER, Jacob   1892-1962

Painter. Born Klincy, in the Ukraine. Moved with his family to England and settled in Leeds, Yorkshire. Ran away to sea for six months and worked in a variety of jobs before returning to Leeds where he attended the Leeds School of Art. With financial assistance from others, he moved to the Slade in 1912. 1915 first solo exhibition held in Bradford. He also exhibited at the NEAC and with the Vorticists, applying their clipped, semi-abstract style to Jewish subjects, emphasising the anonymity of the individual within the communal act of devotion. Also developed a gift for portraiture which, after his return to Leeds, was utilised by local businessmen and other professionals and their wives. Became a local figure of significance, founding with others the Yorkshire Luncheon Group and in 1959 became President of the Leeds Fine Arts Club. He also taught at the Leeds Branch College which, following his death, was renamed after him. Retrospectives of his work include one at Ben Uri Art Gallery, London, 1984. (Plate 8, p.26.)

Bibl: *Jacob Kramer: A Memorial Volume,* compiled by Millie Kramer, E.J. Arnold and Son, London, 1969.

KRATOCHWIL, Marian   b.1906

Painter. Born Kosow, eastern Poland. Studied under the painter Batowski, 1926-9 and read philosophy at the University of Lwow. Lived and painted in the eastern province of Podole. 1937 solo exhibition at the Warsaw Academy of Art. After the war lived and painted in Scotland and then London. From 1956 made frequent visits to Spain for painting purposes. 1961 founded a school of painting in London. Work in the British Museum, the V & A, and the Scottish National Gallery of Modern Art, Edinburgh.

KRAVITZ, Roberta   b.1944

Painter and performance artist. Born New Jersey, USA. Moved to England, 1954. Originally studied philosophy before art training at City and Guilds and the Slade School. Her first public art activity was a performanc at David Medella's Fitzrovia Cultural Centre, 1977. Since then she has performed solo and with others. Currently a member of the Artists Placement Group and now paints, pursuing 'impulse as directly as I can'.

KREMER, Abi   b.1955

Painter. Born London. Studied at Harrow School of Art, 1973-4, Bournemouth College of Art, 1974-7. Since 1978 included in mixed exhibitions. 1987 solo exhibition at Poole Arts Centre. Paints large atmospheric canvases.

KROON, Rineke   b.1945

Painter. Born Hoogezand, Holland. Studied at the Jan van Eyck Academy, Maastricht, 1969-72. Moved to Scotland, 1976. Travelled around Scotland and the Orkney Islands. Lives and works in Scotland for a period every year. 1976 first exhibited at the Haagse Kunstkring, The Hague. 1980 first exhibited in Scotland at the Pier Arts Centre, Stromness.

Bibl: *Rineke Kroon,* Inverness Museum and Art Gallery, 1982.

KRIKHAAR, Anthony   b.1940

Painter. Born in Almelo, Holland. Came to Great Britain, 1959. Studied at St. Martin's School of Art, London. First solo exhibition at Gallery 10, London, 1987. Has exhibited regularly in Europe and London since this date. Represented in the collections of British Rail and London Brick Company Ltd.

KRUT, Ansel   b.1959

Painter. Born Cape Town, South Africa. Studied at RCA, 1983-6. Awarded Prix de Rome, 1986-7. First solo exhibition at Fischer Fine Art, 1989. Represented in group exhibitions since 1984, included in a touring exhibition which opened at Artsite Gallery, Bath, closing at Fischer Fine Arts, London, 1988. Represented in the collections of the Arts Council of Great Britain and the British Council.

KULICK, Barbara

Sculptor. Works in bronze, stone and alabaster. Portraits exhibited at the Royal Society of Portrait Sculptors exhibitions. Solo exhibition at the Drian Galleries, 1973.

KUHFELD, Peter   b.1952

Painter. Born Cheltenham, Gloucestershire. Studied at Leicester Polytechnic, 1972-6 and the RA Schools, 1977-80. Taught painting at Rugby School of Art, 1976-8. Created a Freeman of the Worshipful Company of Painters and Stainers, 1978. Won many awards including the Royal College of Surgeons Dooley Prize for Anatomical Drawing, 1980. First solo exhibition at the Highgate Gallery, 1983. Has shown with the RA since 1978.

KUBRICK, Christine   b.1932

Painter. Born Germany. Studied at UCLA, California, Art Students' League, New York and St. Martin's School of Art. Lives and works in Hertfordshire. Included in group exhibitions, e.g. RA, London Group, Women's International Art Club. Solo exhibitions held in New York, in Canada and at the Drian and Grosvenor Galleries, London; one at the Mercury Gallery, 1980.

LACK, Henry Martyn   b.1909
Etcher. Studied at Leicester College of Art and RCA, where he received his diploma, 1933. Exhibited at RA, in the provinces and abroad. Elected ARE 1934 and RE 1948. Tutor in the Engraving School, RCA, 1947-53 and then on the staff of Hastings School of Art.

LACEY, Bruce   b.1927
Painter, maker of assemblages. Born London. Studied at Hornsey School of Art, 1948-51, and RCA, 1951-4. Won Abbey Minor Travelling Scholarship, 1954. Began to exhibit in The Young Contemporaries show, 1954. First one-person show at Gimpel Fils, London, 1955. Retrospective exhibitions in 1975 at the Whitechapel Art Gallery, London and the Scottish Arts Council Gallery, Edinburgh. Collaborated on installations with Jill Bruce, 1980-1. Work in the collections of H.M. The Queen, Graves Art Gallery, Sheffield and Tate Gallery.

LA DELL, Edwin   1919-1970
Painter and lithographer. Studied at the RCA, under John Nash* and Percy Horton.* During the Second World War was stationed at the Camouflage Directorate in Leamington Spa. Commissioned by the War Artists Advisory Council to work on public murals and camouflage. Commissioned by Lyons for their three lithograph series, displayed in the tea shops nationwide, and for the Guinness sets which were intended to enhance canteens, bars and pubs. As a member of the Senefelder Club, he set up a Print Club to enable the public to buy original lithographs produced by leading artists. As Head of Printmaking at the RCA he organised schemes such as the 'Coronation Suite', 'Wapping to Windsor' and the 'Shakespeare Centenary'. He also illustrated books for the Folio Society, Faber & Faber and John Mills. Included in the collections of the Tate Gallery, V & A, and the Imperial War Museum.

LAMB, Henry   1883-1960
Painter. Born Adelaide, Australia. His family returned to Manchester in 1886. Obtained a Manchester University Scholarship to study medicine before absconding to London with Nina Forrest, whom he renamed Euphemia. 1906 enrolled at Chelsea Art School, run by Augustus John* and William Orpen.* 1907 visited Paris with the John family and studied at L'Ecole de la Palette. Married Euphemia, began to exhibit at NEAC and became emotionally involved, first with Dorelia John, then with Lady Ottoline Morrell. Having affiliated himself with Augustus John, he responded to Gauguin's influence during the summers of 1910 and 1911 when he stayed in Brittany. 1914 painted a famous portrait of Lytton Strachey (Tate Gallery), the same year that he befriended Stanley Spencer* whose style influenced Lamb's paintings of his wartime experience in Salonica. 1928 he married Lady Pansy Pakenham and put his more *mouvementé* life behind him. His skill at drawing is comparable with that of Augustus John but as a painter Lamb lacks artistic individuality, his style variously reflects that of the artists with whom he associated.

Bibl: *Henry Lamb 1883-1960,* Manchester City Art Galleries, 1984.

LAMB, Lynton   1907-1977
Painter. Born India. Studied at Central School of Arts and Crafts. For a period he shared a studio with Victor Pasmore* and attended the Euston Road School. Exhibited at the RA, RBA and with the London Group. Taught at the Slade School, 1950-71, and also part time at the RCA. His publications included *The Purpose of Painting* (1936) and *Preparation for Painting,* 1954. He designed several postage stamps.

LAMBERT, Alison   b.1957
Painter. Born Kingston, Surrey. Worked with horses, 1975-8. Studied at Leek School of Art and Design, 1978-9 and at Lanchester Polytechnic, Coventry, 1981-4. She worked and travelled abroad, 1979-81. Classical art and mythology have become the base from which she explores representations of humans and animals. First solo exhibition at Creaser Gallery, London, 1988.

LAMBERT, Maurice   1901-1964
Sculptor. Born Paris, France. Apprenticed for five years from the age of seventeen to Francis Derwent Wood,* RA. Attended life classes at Chelsea Polytechnic, 1919-27. First solo exhibition at the Claridge Gallery, London, 1927. Elected a member of the National Society of Painters, Sculptors, Engravers and Potters and of the London Group, 1930. Enlisted with the Welsh Fusiliers during the Second World War. Carried out commissions for the Cunard ships, the *Queen Mary* and *Queen Elizabeth.* Elected as an associate member of the RA, 1941 and to the Royal Society of British Sculptors, 1949. Became master of sculpture at the RA Schools, 1950, where he remained until 1958. Elected a Royal Academician, 1952. Produced a range of experimental abstract and figurative pieces as well as portrait busts. He experimented with every sort of marble, wood, stone, and metal, with cast iron, concrete and glass.

Bibl: E.G. Underwood, *A Short History of English Sculpture,* Faber & Faber, 1933.

LAMBOURN, George   1900-1977
Painter. Studied at Goldsmiths' College and the RA Schools. Settled in Cornwall, 1938. His first one-artist exhibition was at the Matthiessen Gallery, 1936. Acted as a war artist during the Second World War. Subsequently exhibited frequently and carried out numerous portrait commissions. Has work in the Imperial War Museum and the Tate Gallery.

LANCASTER, Mark   b.1938
Painter. Born Holmfirth, Yorkshire. Studied and taught at the Department of Fine Art, University of Newcastle upon Tyne, 1961-5. 1966-9 taught at Bath Academy of Art. 1969-70 Artist in Residence, King's College, Cambridge. 1972 moved to New York. Frequented Andy Warhol's Loft and took part in some of his films. Through Warhol met many American artists and for a period worked as assistant to Jasper Johns. 1975-84 designer and artistic advisor to the Merce Cunningham Dance Company, New York. 1985-9 lived and worked in Sandgate, Kent. Now lives in Argyll, Scotland. Solo exhibitions include two at the Mayor Rowan Gallery, London, 1980 and 1988.

LANGTON, John

LANGTON, John   b.1932

Painter. Born York. Studied at York School of Art, 1949-52, and Guildford School of Art, 1952-3. 1978-9 Artist Fellow at University of York. Has contributed articles on art and art theory to various magazines and newspapers. Public commissions include large panel paintings for York and Durham Universities, as well as collaborative work with the potter David Lloyd-Jones for Sussex University and Goole Town Hall. First solo exhibition held at Austin Hayes Gallery, York, 1961. Since 1974 has also exhibited regularly in Germany. Recent solo exhibitions include one at the Ergon Gallery, London, 1990.

LANYON, Peter   1918-1964

Painter. Born St. Ives, Cornwall. 1936 received tuition from Borlase Smart, a local landscape painter. 1937 studied at the Penzance School of Art. This same year he also met Adrian Stokes* who advised him to go to the Euston Road School which he attended for a few months. 1939 met Ben Nicholson,* the Russian Constructivist Naum Gabo, and Barbara Hepworth* in St. Ives, and under their influence the direction of his work changed. Began making constructions, many as preparatory ideas for paintings. Gabo's merging of internal and external shape helped Lanyon conceive of landscapes viewed from many angles and made visible the mine shafts buried into

JOHN LANGTON, b.1932. *'Poet's Walk, Clevedon'*, 1981. Charcoal and crayon drawing on paper. 36in. x 54in. Private Collection.

the earth. Liberated from mimetic representation, he evolved a kind of lyrical abstraction. Aware, earlier than most of his compatriots, of American Abstract Expressionism.

PETER LANYON, 1918-1964. *Untitled,* 1963. Gouache on paper. 22in. x 30in. Austin/Desmond Fine Art.

HENRY HERBERT LA THANGUE, 1859-1929. *'Gathering Oranges'*, 29in. x 32½in. Nottingham Castle Museum and Art Gallery.

Held a solo exhibition in New York, 1957 and made friends with several American painters. 1959 took up gliding and based many of his paintings on this experience. Died following a gliding accident. 1968 a posthumous retrospective was held at the Tate Gallery.

Bibl: *Peter Lanyon. Paintings, drawings and constructions 1937-64*, with an essay by Andrew Causey, Whitworth Art Gallery, Manchester, 1978.

LASSALLE, Harriet   b.1958
Painter. Born London. Studied at City and Guilds of London Art School, 1975-9. Began exhibiting at RA summer exhibitions, 1981. Solo exhibition at the Fieldbourne Galleries, London, 1983.

LAST, Marie Walker
Painter. Studied at Chelsea School of Art. Solo exhibitions include one at the New Vision Gallery, London, 1960, and another at the Camden Arts Centre, 1980. Represented in Bradford City Art Gallery, York University and elsewhere.

LATHAM, John   b.1921
Sculptor. Born Northern Rhodesia. Served in the Royal Navy, 1940-6. Studied at various London art colleges, 1946-51. 1951 married Barbara Steveni with whom he convened the Artist Placement Group from 1965. 1958 began making books as material for sculpture. 1961-2 visited New York and Washington. 1965-7 taught at St. Martin's School of Art. 1966-7 staged an event where

students and teachers were invited to chew a library copy of Clement Greenberg's *Art and Culture* and spit out the remains which were then distilled. Has since then worked variously with books and their destruction, in performances and installations. Solo exhibition held at Tate Gallery, 1976, and another, 'John Latham Decades Decoded', held at the Riverside Studios, London, 1990.

Bibl: *John Latham: Early Works,* with essay by Richard Hamilton, Lisson Gallery, London, 1987.

LATHAM, William   b.1961
Computer artist. Studied at Ruskin School of Drawing and Fine Art, Oxford, 1979-82, RCA, 1982-3 and the City of London Polytechnic, 1984-5. 1987 July-October visiting Fellow at the IBM UK Scientific Centre, Winchester. First solo exhibition held at The Picture Gallery, Christ Church, Oxford, 1986; another, entitled 'The Conquest of Form' at the Arnolfini Gallery, Bristol, 1989.

LA THANGUE, Henry Herbert   1859-1929
Painter. Born Croydon, Surrey. Studied at Lambeth School of Art and RA Schools, 1874-7, where he was a Gold Medallist. Also attended Ecole des Beaux-Arts under Gerome. Joined NEAC, but his attempt to alter its status failed, and he resigned. Painted with the broad square brush, a technique learnt in France, and displayed great skills in his presentation of *plein air* scenes. Has work in many public collections, including Cartwright Hall, Bradford and Laing Art Gallery, Newcastle.

SIR JOHN LAVERY, 1856-1941.
*'La Mort du Cygne: Anna
Pavlova',* 1911. 78in. x 57¾in.
The Tate Gallery.

LAVENSTEIN, Cyril   b.1891
Painter. Born Aston, Birmingham, the son of a tailor of
German descent. Studied at Birmingham Municipal School
of Art. Called up for military service in 1915 and served in
Salonika. Afterwards taught at Kidderminster School of
Art until his retirement in 1954. Exhibited with the Royal
Birmingham Society of Artists, at the NEAC and RA.

LAVERY, Sir John   1856-1941
Painter. Born Belfast, Northern Ireland. Studied at the
Haldane Academy in Glasgow and in Paris at the
Académie Julian. Influenced by Bastien-Lepage, he
worked in the painters' colony at Grèz-sur-Loing. On his
return to Glasgow he became one of the leaders of the
Glasgow School. 1912 commissioned to paint the Royal
Family for the National Portrait Gallery. 1917 appointed

Official War Artist. 1918 knighted. During the 1920s he
travelled widely and executed many 'portrait interiors' of
the rich and famous.

Bibl: *Sir John Lavery,* Ulster Museum, Belfast, and Fine Arts
Society, London, 1984.

LAW, Bob   b.1934
Painter. Born Brentford, Middlesex. Self-taught. 1957
moved to St. Ives, Cornwall, where he painted and made
pots. 1959 made his first 'field' drawings and paintings,
charting his position in time and space. Exhibited in the
two 'Situation' exhibitions of abstract art, 1960 and 1961.
Held first solo exhibition at the Grabowski Gallery,
London, 1962; others include a retrospective held at the
Whitechapel Art Gallery, 1978. 1975 he began the 'Castle'
series of painting in which a border is formed by a biro or

pencil line around the edge of the canvas and layers of white acrylic paint are applied to its surface. These works were inspired by Kafka.

Bibl: *Bob Law, Paintings and Drawings 1959-78,* Whitechapel Art Gallery, London, 1978.

LAW, John   b.1941
Sculptor. Studied at Corsham College of Art, and later at The Hague under the constructivist artist Joost Baljeu. Designed sets for the Netherlands Dance Theatre. Taught at Leeds College of Art in the 1960s. Included in mixed exhibitions, e.g. 'Unit Series Progression' organised by the Arts Council, 1967.

LAWLOR, Putrisha   b.1959
Painter. Born London. Studied at Middlesex Polytechnic, 1979-82, and at RCA, 1983-6. Awarded Scholarship to RCA Paris Studio, 1985. Awarded Chase/Taliani Scholarship to Venice, 1986-7. First exhibited at 'Hayward Annual: British Drawing', Hayward Gallery, London, 1982.

LAWMAN, Peter   b.1951
Painter. Born Wales. Studied painting and sculpture at Newport College of Art, 1970-4. He paints highly detailed landscapes, often with figures wearing medieval costume, accompanied by strange creatures and objects that endow his work with an enigmatic quality. Exhibits with the Portal Gallery, London.

LAWRENCE, David Herbert   1885-1930
Writer and painter. Born Eastwood, Nottinghamshire. Attended Nottingham University. Although primarily known as a writer, he was also an amateur painter with a wide knowledge of Italian Renaissance art. 1903-14 he painted still lifes and landscapes, learning by copying the work of other artists. 1926-8 painted twenty-five canvases, mostly of nude figure groups, for his first solo exhibition at the Warren Gallery, London, 1929. The Police closed the exhibition down and removed thirteen paintings to a police court where they were tried for obscenity; Augustus John* and William Rothenstein* testified on behalf of the paintings but lost. At the time he was painting Lawrence was writing *Lady Chatterley's Lover,* privately printed in 1928.

Paintings of D.H. Lawrence, edited by Mervyn Levy, Cory, Adams & Mackay, London, 1964.

LAWRENCE, Eileen   b.1946
Artist and scroll maker. Born Leith, Scotland. Studied at Edinburgh College of Art, 1963-8. 1969-72 lived and worked in London. 1972-3 lived and worked in Wuppertal, West Germany. 1973 summer tour of America. 1977 awarded Scottish Arts Council Major Bursary. Lives and works in Edinburgh. 1969 first solo exhibition held at Gallery 57, Edinburgh; others include one at Fischer Fine Art, London, 1980. Maker of scrolls and 'prayer-sticks' in which her interest in birds is combined with an ancient symbolism in which the bird symbolises the migration of the soul to God. Represented in the collections of the Department of the Environment, London, the Scottish Arts Council, Edinburgh and in the Scottish National Gallery of Modern Art, Edinburgh.

LAWRENCE, John   b.1934
Painter. Born London. Studied at Bromley School of Art. Obsessed by the sea and rivers and passionately interested in jazz. Solo exhibition at the Trefford Gallery, London, 1970.

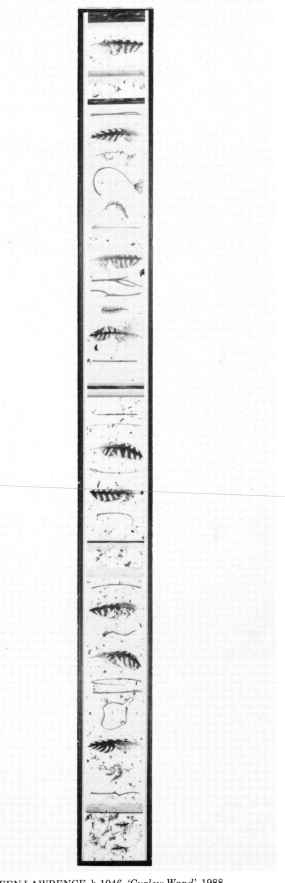

EILEEN LAWRENCE, b.1946. *'Curlew Wand',* 1988. Watercolour. 71⅝in. x 5in. Fischer Fine Art Limited, London.

GILBERT LEDWARD, 1888-1960. *'Study for the Bronze Relief Panel on the Rear of the Guards' Memorial'*, 1923. Pen and ink.
5 ½ in. x 9in. The Fine Art Society, London.

LAWRENCE, Mary
Plaque-maker and painter. Studied at Central School of
Arts and Crafts. Was for many years a member of the
Women's International Arts Club and also exhibited
several times .in London Group exhibitions. Solo
exhibition at Woodstock Gallery, London, 1968.

LAWSON, Fred   1888-1963
Painter. Born Yeadon, near Leeds, Yorkshire. In 1910 he
settled in Wensleydale in the heart of North Yorkshire
and, apart from occasional painting trips to the Continent,
remained in the area for the rest of his life. Has a fluid and
spontaneous naturalistic style. Has also illustrated
several books and contributed to *The Dalesman* from its
first issue.

LAWSON, Sonia   b.1934
Painter. Born Darlington, Co. Durham. Studied at
Worthing College of Art, Doncaster School of Art and
Royal College of Art, 1956-60. Elected ARA 1982; elected
Associate, RWS 1984. Thirteen one-artist shows since
1960, including a retrospective held at Mappin Art
Gallery, Sheffield, and elsewhere, 1982-3. Work in various
public collections including the Arts Council Collection.
Vigorous figurative painter, who makes imaginative use
of childhood memories of animals and landscapes.

LAWSON, Stephen   b.1942
Photographer and sculptor. Born Glasgow, Scotland.
Studied at Edinburgh College of Art, 1961-7, and University
of Colorado, Boulder, USA, 1968-70. Has exhibited regularly
since 1970 and is represented in the Glasgow Museum and
Art Gallery at Kelvingrove and elsewhere.

LEAPMAN, Edwina   b.1934
Painter. Born Hampshire. Studied at Slade School and
Central School of Arts and Crafts. Won Arts Council
Awards in 1976 and 1979. Solo exhibitions include one at
the New Art Centre, London, 1974 and another at Juda
Rowan Gallery, London, 1987. An abstract painter who
works solely with hand-painted stripes in monochrome.

LE BAS, Edward   1904-1966
Painter. Born London of Anglo-French descent. Studied
architecture at Cambridge University and later painting
at the RCA. Member of the London Group. His *intimiste*
interiors owe much to Vuillard but his style was also
influenced by the example of his friend, Duncan Grant.*
One of eleven artists whose work was sent to Australia by
the British Council, 1949. Elected ARA, 1943 and RA,
1954. He amassed a major collection of twentieth century
British art which was shown at the RA, 1963. Represented
in the collections of the Tate Gallery and the Arts Council.

LE BAS, Philip   b.1925
Painter. Born Bordeaux, France. Moved to London in 1934. Following RAF service during the war he studied at Regent Street Polytechnic and Brighton College of Art. 1977 gave up teaching to become a full-time painter. Regular exhibitor at the Portal Gallery, London, since 1968. Has an especial interest in greenhouses and railway stations, his detailed style gaining in richness through the use of enamel paint.

LE BROCQUY, Louis   b.1916
Painter. Born Dublin, Ireland. 1938 began teaching himself painting in museums in London, Paris and Geneva. 1946 first solo exhibition held at Gimpel Fils, London. 1957 entered upon his 'white period'. 1963 began his series of images based on the human head, with portraits of James Joyce, Yeats, Garcia Lorca, Samuel Beckett and others. Solo exhibitions include a retrospective at Dublin Municipal Gallery, 1966-67, and another at the Palais des Beaux Arts, Charleroi, 1982. Represented in major public collections around the world.

LEBRUN, Christopher   b.1951
Painter. Born Portsmouth, Hampshire. Studied at the Slade School of Fine Art, 1970-4, and Chelsea School of Art, 1974-5. Began exhibiting at Nigel Greenwood, London, 1980. His admiration for past art, especially the work of Tiepolo, Giorgione, Richard Wilson and Turner, has enabled him to blend modern abstract art with allusions to the Old Masters.

LE CLAIRE, Mark   b.1957
Painter. Born Peterborough, Cambridgeshire. Trained at Stourbridge College of Art. Has exhibited at Albion Studios, London, 1986, and elsewhere, and has work in private and public collections, including the Museum voor Schone Kunster, Ostend.

LEDGER, Janet
Painter. Born Northampton. Studied at Northampton College of Art. Exhibited 'London '77' in Somerset House, 1977; the proceeds of the sales were donated to Dockland settlements.

LEDWARD, Gilbert   1888-1960
Sculptor. Born Chelsea, London. Studied at RA Schools and was awarded the 'blue riband', the first Rome Scholarship in Sculpture. Served in the Artillery on the Italian Front, 1916-19, and later used the studies of soldiers that he made as the basis for his memorials. Professor of Sculpture at RCA, 1926-9; elected ARA 1937, and RA, 1937. 1954-6 was President of the Royal Society of British Sculptors. Work in the collections of the RA and the Tate Gallery.

LEE, Dick   b.1923
Painter. Studied at Camberwell School of Art 1947-50. Awarded Abbey Major Scholarship, 1951. Taught at Camberwell, 1953-82. First solo exhibition at Galerie de Seine, London, 1958. Further exhibitions at New Grafton Gallery, Gillian Jason Gallery and elsewhere. Primarily a landscape painter, his sensitivity to light allows him to combine an ordered tonality with a loose touch. Works purchased by Arts Council, Trinity College, Cambridge and elsewhere.

LEE, Rosie   b.1935
Painter. Born Rotterdam, Holland, of English parents.

TERRY LEE, b.1935. 'Visitor'. 32in. x 28in. Private Collection.

Studied at Sheffield College of Art, 1953-5, and Slade School of Art, 1955-8. A landscape artist with a touch of the magical and macabre, she has exhibited in Switzerland, Germany and Belgium and shows regularly with the Piccadilly Gallery, London.

LEE, Sarah   b.1961
Painter. Born London. Studied at St. Martin's School of Art, London, 1980-3 and RCA, 1984-7. Represented in group exhibitions since 1983, when she exhibited at the RA.

LEE, Sydney   1866-1949
Painter and printmaker. Born Manchester. Studied at Manchester School of Art, and at Atelier Colarossi, Paris. Developed his love there for topographical landscapes and architectural subjects. Began exhibiting at the NEAC, 1903, and at the RA, 1905. Elected ARA, 1922. Treasurer of the RA, 1932-40 and narrowly missed becoming its President in 1938, losing to Sir Edwin Lutyens. Solo exhibitions of prints and drawings held at Colnaghi's, 1937, 1939 and 1945.

LEE, Terry   b.1935
Painter. Born Sheffield, Yorkshire. Studied at Sheffield College of Art and the Slade School of Art. Became Head of Painting at Sheffield City Polytechnic until he took early retirement, 1984. Lives and paints in a Derbyshire cottage on the Chatsworth estate and in Spain, in a restored house in a mountain village. Solo exhibitions include four at the New Art Centre, London, 1960, 1961, 1963 and 1965, and at Thos. Agnew and Sons, London, 1973, 1976 and 1978. Represented in the Walker Art Gallery, Liverpool, the Graves Art Gallery, Sheffield and elsewhere.

DERWENT LEES, 1885-1931. *'Lyndra by the Pool'*, 1914. Oil on panel. 20¹⁄₁₆in. x 15¾in. Manchester City Art Galleries.

LEE, Thomas Stirling   1857-1916
Painter. Studied at RA Schools, 1878-80, winning a gold medal and travelling scholarship to Paris where he studied further at the Ecole des Beaux-Arts, 1880-1, and then in Rome, 1881-3. A member of the NEAC.

LEE-HANKEY, William   1869-1952
Painter. Born Chester, Cheshire. On leaving school he worked as a designer, studying art in the evenings at Chester School of Art. 1894 began exhibiting in London. 1899 became a member of the RI. 1902-4 President of London Sketch Club. 1904 first solo exhibition at the Leicester Galleries. He also built a house in Le Touquet and a studio in Etaples and from this time spent long periods in France. 1914-19 served in the Artists' Rifles. 1936 became member of the RWS and acted as its Vice-President, 1947-50.

LEES, Derwent **1885-1931**
Born Brisbane, Australia. Studied in Paris and at Melbourne University. Lost a foot in a riding accident. 1905-7 studied at the Slade where he met J.D. Innes.* 1908-18 worked as a teacher of drawing at the Slade and travelled widely in vacations through Europe. 1912 took a cottage at Ffestiniog, North Wales, and, under the influence of Innes, imitated his lyrical method of notation, attaining a similar intensity of colour and mood. Mental illness confined him to an asylum from 1918 until his death.

LEET, Gerald **b.1913**
Painter. Born London. Studied at Goldsmiths' College, 1929-34, at RCA, 1934-7, and at Goldsmiths' College and the Courtauld Institute, 1937-8. A friend of Denton Welch.* After war service he was appointed official war artist at the Viceroy's House, New Delhi, 1945-6. Occupied various teaching positions and in 1948 was commissioned by the Queen to do some portrait drawings. Has held solo exhibitions at Eton Art Gallery and the Isobar Gallery, Hampstead.

LE GRICE, Jeremy **b.1936**
Painter. Studied at Guildford School of Art, St. Peter's Loft, St. Ives, and Slade School of Art. Settled in St. Just-in-Penwith, Cornwall and held his first solo London exhibition at the Hannet Gallery, 1970.

LEHMANN, Olga
Painter and designer. Studied at Slade School of Art. A little recorded artist of fine calibre, who received early notice as a theatrical designer and during the Second World War executed a series of murals for British canteens and restaurants. Much of her work is 'surreal' and requires more attention than it has so far received. Has exhibited with the RBA and the Society of Women Artists.

LEIGH, Roger **b.1925**
Sculptor. Born Bradwell, Gloucestershire. Served in RAF during the war and for two years afterwards. 1947-52 studied architecture at Liverpool University. 1953-4 worked for Barbara Hepworth* in St. Ives and became a member of the Penwith Society of Arts. Solo exhibition at Queen's Square, Leeds, 1966. Abstract sculptor who works mostly in wood.

LEMAN, Martin **b.1934**
Painter. Born London. Educated at the Royal Masonic School. Trained and worked as a typographer. Began painting in 1969. First one-artist exhibition at the Portal Gallery, London, 1971.

LE MARCHANT, Francis **b.1939**
Painter. Born Mungerton, Lincolnshire. Studied at Byam Shaw School of Drawing and Painting, 1959-62, and RA Schools, 1962-6, where he was taught by Charles Mahoney* and Peter Greenham.* 1968 spent four months at Hornsey College of Art studying tapestry design. Has held five solo exhibitions at Agnew's, London, 1969, 1970, 1971, 1972 and 1978, and others elsewhere. Primarily a landscape painter with a talent for rendering atmospheric effects.

LEMON, Liz **b.1949**
Sculptor. Born Glenavy, Northern Ireland. Studied at West Surrey College of Art and Design, 1979-80 and at Birmingham Polytechnic, 1980-4. Prizewinner in the Maquette for Tacbloc Sculpture Competition, 1983, and prizewinner in the Maquette for Becker Paint Ltd Competition, 1984. First exhibited in Whitworth Young Contemporaries, Whitworth Art Gallery, Manchester.

LENAGHAN, Brenda **b.1941**
Painter. Born Galashiels, Scotland. Studied at Glasgow School of Art, graduating 1963. For a time she worked as a textile designer. Since 1973 she has painted full-time. Exhibits regularly at the RSA, the RA, the GI and the Scottish Society of Women Artists' Annual Exhibition in Edinburgh. Elected RSW, 1984. An enthusiastic traveller and painter in watercolour and gouache.

LENNON, Ciaran **b.1947**
Painter. Born Dublin, Ireland. Studied at the National College of Art and Design, Dublin, 1963-7. Awards include the Young Irish Foundation Award, 1968, Carroll Award, Irish Exhibition of Living Art, 1974, the Arts Council Bursary, 1980 and the Clare Morris Annual Exhibition, 1988. First solo exhibition at Project Arts Centre, Dublin, 1972. Recent solo exhibitions include two at Annely Juda Fine Art, 1987 and 1989. Minimalist.

LEONARD, Keith **b.1921**
Sculptor. Born London. Studied at the Slade School of Art. Worked as an assistant to both Ossip Zadkine in Paris, and Barbara Hepworth* in St. Ives, Cornwall. Taught sculpture at Sunderland College of Art and the West Surrey College of Art.

LEONARD, Michael **b.1933**
Painter. Born Bangalore, India. Studied at St. Martin's School of Art, 1954-7. 1957 onwards worked as a freelance illustrator. Since 1969 has devoted progressively more time to painting and gradually relinquished illustration. First solo exhibition held at Fischer Fine Art, London, 1974, followed by others in 1977, 1980, 1983 and 1988. Views himself as a realist in the classical tradition and brings a high degree of finesse to his paintings of the male and female nude.

Bibl: *Michael Leonard: Paintings,* with Edward Lucie-Smith in conversation with the artist, GMP Publishers, London, 1985.

LERMAN, Beryl **b.1948**
Painter. Born London. Studied at Wimbledon School of Art, 1966-70. Has travelled extensively in Israel and moved there after her first solo exhibition in London, at the Woodstock Gallery, 1970.

LESSORE, Helen **b.1907**
Painter. Born Helen Brook, London. Studied at the Slade School, 1924-8, where she won prizes for head, figure and composition painting. Became an assistant at her husband Frederick Lessore's gallery, the Beaux Arts, 1931; directed it alone from his death in 1951 until its closure in 1965. Resumed her painting in the early 1960s. An exhibition, 'Helen Lessore and the Beaux Arts Gallery', was held at Marlborough Fine Art, London, 1968. Elected a Senior Academician, 1987. An Eightieth Birthday Tribute exhibition was held at the Fine Art Society, 1987. Her paintings are often about retrieval, a recording of places or people she has known. Wrote *A Partial Testament,* published 1986.

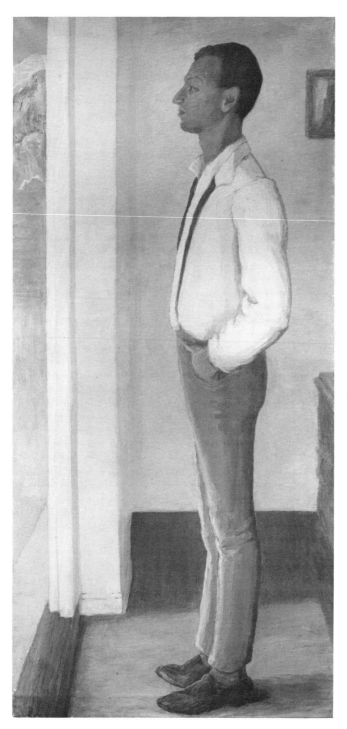

HELEN LESSORE, b.1907. *'Portrait of a Young Man'*.
54in. x 26in. Private Collection.

JOHN LESSORE, b.1939. *'Paule with Eclipse I'*, 1987.
59¾in. x 59¾in. Nigel Greenwood Gallery.

LESSORE, John   b.1939

Painter. Born London. Studied at Slade School, 1957-61.
First solo exhibition at Beaux Arts Gallery, London, 1965.
Recent solo exhibitions include two at Stoppenbach and
Delestre, London, 1983 and 1985. Son of Helen Lessore*
and nephew of Walter Sickert.* Included in the Tate
Gallery's 'The Hard Won Image', 1984. Represented in
Tate Gallery, RA, Westminster Hospital and elsewhere.

LETT-HAINES, Arthur   1894-1978

Painter and sculptor. Widowed in 1912, remarried and
was part of a London artistic circle including the D.H.
Lawrences, the Sitwells, Wyndham Lewis, Katharine
Mansfield and Middleton Murry. Met the painter Cedric
Morris* in 1918 and lived with him until his death. Lived
in Cornwall and then Paris, 1919-26. 1923 worked in the
studio of Brancusi. 1937 he and Morris founded the East
Anglian School of Painting and Drawing at Dedham,
Essex. 1940 moved the school to Benton End, Hadleigh,
Suffolk; pupils included Maggi Hambling* and Lucian
Freud.* Retrospective exhibition at Redfern Gallery,
1984.

LEVENE, Ben   b.1938

Painter. Born London. Studied at Slade School of Art,
1956-61 and awarded a Boise Scholarship. 1961-2 lived in
Spain. 1975 elected ARA. Solo exhibitions at the
Thackeray Gallery, 1973, 1975 and 1978. Represented in
Guildhall Art Gallery and elsewhere.

LEVENTIS, Michael   b.1944

Painter. Born Accra, Ghana. Studied agriculture at
California State College, from 1963. Worked for Leventis
family firm, 1968-9. Transferred to Lagos, Nigeria,
1970-2. Returned to England to begin career as a painter,
1972. Lived in Greece, farming in the Peloponnese and
painting in Athens, 1974-8. Gave up painting, 1978-80 and
farmed full-time in Greece. Encouraged by Francis
Bacon* to begin painting again in 1980, he returned to
England to paint full-time, 1982. First solo exhibition at
Solomon Gallery, London, 1988. His paintings encompass
a wide number of subjects, such as animals in motion,
portraiture and still life. References to reality are fused
with abstract application of paint, creating a tension
between the medium and the image depicted.

LEVY, Emmanuel   1900-1986
Painter. Studied art in Manchester, London and Paris. Held his first solo exhibition in Manchester, 1925 and afterwards exhibited regularly, holding a retrospective in Salford City Art Gallery, 1948. Liked to give public demonstrations in portrait painting. Also acted as art critic for *Manchester City News* and *Evening News*.

LEWIS, Anthea   b.1948
Painter. Born London. Studied at Edinburgh College of Art, 1966-70. Elected member of Society of Scottish Artists, 1973 and RSW, 1977. Joined Glasgow League of Artists, 1978. First solo exhibition held at New 57 Gallery, Edinburgh, 1971. Others include one at the Compass Gallery, Glasgow, 1979.

LEWIS, David   b.1955
Painter. Born Wigan, Lancashire. Trained at Manchester Polytechnic, 1973-4 and Leeds Polytechnic, 1974-7. First solo exhibition held at Bridge Arts Centre, Widnes, 1980. Exhibited at Christopher Hull Gallery, London, 1985 and 1988. Work in Sunderland Art Gallery, Huddersfield Art Gallery and other public collections.

LEWIS, Edward Morland   1903-1943
Painter. Studied at St. John's Wood School of Art and RA Schools where he met Sickert.* Left RA Schools to work under Sickert as his pupil and assistant. 1930 joined the London Artists' Association and exhibited with the group until it disbanded in 1934. Like Sickert, he tended to paint in patchwork areas of colour laid over warm under-painting. He concentrated on seaside towns, Irish scenes and ports at home and abroad, and often used photographs as the basis of his painting. The only large exhibition he had was at Picture Hire Limited, Brook Street, 1938. Died in North Africa while on active service as a camouflage officer.

LEWIS, Kit   b.1911
Painter. Born Kathleen Godfrey-Fausset-Osborne in Lichfield, Staffordshire. Spent four years in India in her early twenties and on her return home went to Chelsea School of Art where she was taught by Graham Sutherland* and Morland Lewis.* Married Morland Lewis, who died in 1943. Later married Sir James Richards, the architectural writer and editor. 1943 elected member of the London Group. 1953 first solo exhibition at Leicester Galleries. Continued to show there inter-mittently until they closed in the 1970s. 1988 exhibited with Roy Spencer* at Sally Hunter Fine Art, London. Represented in Arts Council Collection, National Museum of Wales and Carlisle City Art Gallery.

LEWIS, Michael   b.1943
Painter. Born Plymouth, Devon. Studied at Plymouth College of Art, 1962-5, and Hornsey College of Art, 1965-6. Taught art for two years in London before moving back to Devon. Taught in Newton Abbot for four years until July 1972. Since then has been painting full-time. Solo exhibition at Crane Arts, London, 1973.

LEWIS, Peter   b.1939
Sculptor. Born Cheshire. 1947 moved to Dyfed, Wales. Studied at Carmarthen School of Art, 1955-7, St. Martin's School of Art, 1957-9, and RCA, 1961-4. 1965-8 Fellowship in Fine Art at Nottingham University. 1968-70 Harkness Foundation Fellowship in United States. Has exhibited

ARTHUR LETT-HAINES, 1894-1978. *'The Steps, Paris 1921'*. Black chalk. 16¼ in. x 10¼ in. Private Collection.

regularly since 1965, including a solo show at the Serpentine Gallery, London, 1977.

LEWIS, Simon   b.1945
Painter. Born Okehampton, Dorset. Studied sculpture at Bath Academy of Art, Corsham, 1964-8, and did post-graduate work at the University of Reading, 1970-2. Has taught at art colleges in Chelsea, Newport, Hull and at the North East London Polytechnic. Has exhibited regularly since 1966. Solo exhibition at University College, Cardiff, 1980.

LEWIS, Stephen   b.1959
Sculptor. Born Lancashire. Graduated from Manchester Polytechnic, 1980. Began exhibiting in 1979 and has shown in Manchester, at the John Holden Gallery, and in Maastricht, the Netherlands. Solo exhibition at Francis Graham-Dixon Gallery, London, 1990. An abstract sculptor who works primarily in mild steel but sometimes incorporates found and prefabricated materials. Also sometimes paints his steel elements, playing off colour and outline in work that can encompass complexity without losing the clarity of the image.

LEWISOHN, Michael J.R.   b.1959
Painter. Studied at Epsom School of Art, 1978-82, and at
the Camden Institute, 1983-5. Awarded a scholarship to
study at the Royal Academy of Art, Copenhagen, 1985-6.
Travelled extensively in Europe, 1981-7 and in Asia,
1982-3. Visited New York and Boston, 1988. Commissioned
by Continental Waterways to design and paint the
exterior of a barge, by CND to design a poster, by City
Limits Magazine for a print, by Alternative Art to paint a
canvas mural at Convent Garden, London, and by
Amnesty International for a T-shirt and card. First solo
exhibition at the Radskaelderen, Charlottenburg,
Copenhagen, 1986. Exhibited with Sue Williams, London,
1988 and 1990.

LEWORTHY, Roger
Painter. Studied at Camberwell School of Art and the
Slade School of Art. Solo exhibition of drawings at
Christchurch Mansion, Ipswich, 1988.

LEWTY, Simon   b.1941
Painter. Born Sutton Coldfield, West Midlands. Studied at
Mid-Warwickshire School of Art, 1958-60 and Hornsey
College of Art, 1961-3. First solo exhibition held at
Woodstock Gallery, London, 1968. Other solo exhibitions
include a show at the Serpentine Gallery, London, 1985,
and at Anne Berthoud Gallery, London, 1987.

LIGHTFOOT, Maxwell Gordon   1886-1911
Painter. Born Liverpool, Merseyside. Studied at Chester
School of Art. Was apprenticed to a chromolithographer in
Liverpool and attended art classes at Sandon Terrace
Studios run by Gerard Chowne.* First exhibited at
Liverpool Autumn Exhibition, 1907. Studied at Slade
School, 1907-9 where he won various prizes. Produced
lyrical landscapes as well as near-macabre pen drawings
at this time. Joined Camden Town Group, 1911. Though
he responded to some extent to French Post-Impressionism,
he remained a sombre colourist. His considerable promise
was cut short by suicide brought on by personal problems.
He is said to have destroyed much of his work. Represented
in Walker Art Gallery, Liverpool.

LINES, Vincent   1909-1968
Painter and printmaker. Born Dulwich, London. Studied
at Central School of Arts and Crafts and at RCA. Close
friend of Thomas Hennell.* Principal of Horsham School
of Art and later of the Hastings School. Exhibited RA,
RWS, NEAC and in the provinces. Elected ARWS 1939,
RWS 1945, NEAC 1946 and RWA 1957. Primarily a
landscape and architectural painter, he travelled widely
in Britain and France and is represented in several public
collections.

LINKE, Simon   b.1958
Painter. Born Australia. Studied at St. Martin's School of
Art, the RCA and at Goldsmiths' College. Since 1968 has
exhibited widely in Europe and the USA, holding solo
exhibitions in London, New York and Nagoya, Japan.
Since 1986 has made and exhibited paintings of *Artforum*
advertisements; in these the contrast between rich, hand-
painted surfaces and the slick, anonymous typography of
the magazine creates an unexpected tension. In a recent
series of paintings exhibited at the Lisson Gallery,
London, 1990, he pursued further his enquiry into the
nature of contemporary art and its relationship to
commerce.

LIPTON, Laurie   b.1953
Graphic artist. Born New York, USA. Studied at
Carnegie-Mellon University, Pittsburgh. Works with
pencil and paper, producing drawings that reflect her
personal history as well as addressing contemporary
issues. Now lives in London and exhibited at Waterman's
Art Centre, Brentford, 1987.

LLEWELLYN, Sir William H. Samuel   1858-1941
Painter. Born Cirencester, Gloucestershire. Studied at
South Kensington under Poynter, and in Paris with
Lefebvre. Upon his return to England he was taught the
square brush technique by La Thangue* when they both
had studios in Manresa Road. A member of the NEAC, he
served as the President, 1928-38. Knighted c.1918.

LLOYD, Elizabeth Jane   b.1928
Painter. Born London. Studied painting at Chelsea School
of Art from 1946, then mural design at the RCA. Has had
several solo exhibitions, at the Barbican Centre and
elsewhere, and has also worked as a muralist undertaking
both public and private commissions. She also executed
some scene painting for the films *Flash Gordon* and
Chariots of Fire. Represented in the collections of the
Gulbenkian Trust and the Nuffield Foundation. Has
exhibited regularly at the RA since 1953. Solo exhibition
at Austin/Desmond Gallery, London, 1990.

LLOYD, James   1906-1974
Painter. Born Alsager, Cheshire. No formal training; a
farmer's son who worked first on the farm, then as
policeman, gasworks stoker and lamplighter. After war
service he settled in a small Yorkshire village and started
painting in 1948. First one-artist exhibition at Arthur
Jeffress Gallery, London, 1956. He was the subject of a
Ken Russell television film in 1964.

LOCKWOOD, Dorothy   b.1903
Painter and illustrator. Like her twin sister Marjorie
Sinclair, she studied at Birmingham Art School under
Bernard Fleetwood-Walker.* Began working for
advertising companies and became Head of Design at
Cadbury Brothers. With her sister she wrote and
illustrated children's books. Exhibited at the RA, RBA,
RWS and with the NEAC. 1969 elected ARWS and 1974 a
full member.

LOKER, John   b.1938
Painter. Born Leeds, Yorkshire. Studied at Bradford
College of Art, 1954-8, and RCA, 1960-3. First one-person
show entitled 'Horizontals and Drawings' at Angela
Flowers Gallery, and the ICA, London, 1970.
Commissions for paintings from Essex General Hospital,
and Watmoughs Holdings, Bradford. Publications:
Thriding and *Littered Ways* — a suite of six woodblocks
with a poem. Work in public collections includes Arts
Council, British Council, Tate Gallery, V & A, CAS,
Department of the Environment, Bradford, Dudley, Hull,
Glasgow, Leeds, Manchester, Rugby, Wakefield and
Worcester City Art Galleries.

LONG, Richard   b.1945
Sculptor. Born Bristol, Avon. Studied at West of England
College of Art, Bristol, 1962-6, and St. Martin's School of
Art, 1966-8. 1964 made his first work involving
landscapes. In 1967 his work began to show his concern
with distance and place. That same year he added the

dimension of time, making sculptures by walking, cycling or hitch-hiking, recorded in maps and photographs. 1969 began to travel the world, making landscape artworks in Europe, the Americas, Africa, Nepal, Australia and Japan. Many of these were impermanent but recorded by photography. 1976 represented Britain at the Venice Biennale. Solo exhibitions at the Anthony d'Offay Gallery, London, 1981, 1983, 1984, 1985, 1986 and 1990. 1989 winner of the Turner Prize.

Bibl: *Richard Long: Selected Works 1979-82,* National Gallery of Canada, Ottawa, 1983; *Richard Long,* Thames and Hudson, London, 1986.

LORD, Andrew   b.1950

Sculptor. Born Rochdale, Lancashire. Studied ceramics at the Central School of Art. Moved to Holland in 1975 and to New York in 1980. His sculpture takes as its starting point a limited range of domestic shapes. Solo exhibition at the Anthony d'Offay Gallery, 1990.

LOTT, Penelope   b.1957

Painter. Studied at Northampton School of Art and Leeds University. Lived in West Germany for two years. First solo exhibition at Tubingen, West Germany, 1983. First solo exhibition in Great Britain at York Racecourse, 1984.

LOUDEN, Albert   b.1942

Painter. Spent twenty-five years working as a lorry driver until he took up painting full-time. Solo exhibition at the Serpentine Gallery, 1985. Afterwards, he participated in exhibitions in Europe and America, followed by a two-person exhibition at the Boundary Gallery, London, 1990. His works are derived from his daily experiences of the urban environment.

LOVELL, Margaret   b.1939

Sculptor. Studied at the Slade School of Art. Member of the RBA. Retrospective exhibition at Plymouth City Art Gallery, 1972. Lives and works in Bath. Work in the Arts Council collection.

LOW, Sarah   b.1964

Sculptor. Studied at Torquay Technical College, 1980-2, Kingston Polytechnic, 1982-6, and at the RA Schools, 1987-9. Awarded the Landseer Scholarship, 1988. First exhibited at the City Artists Gallery, London, 1986.

LOWE, Jeff   b.1952

Sculptor. Born Lancashire. Studied at Leicester College of Art, 1970-1, and at St. Martin's School of Art, 1971-5. Began by making large, almost architectural, scaled steel constructions, then changed to smaller steel and stone works. 1974 first solo show at the Leicester Galleries. 1977 worked in Mermer Stone Quarry, Danilougrad, Yugoslavia. 1981 held solo shows at the Nicola Jacobs Gallery. Work in the Arts Council collection.

LOWE, Peter   b.1938

Painter and constructivist. Born London. Studied at Goldsmiths' College of Art under Kenneth* and Mary Martin.* 1960 started to make reliefs. From 1957 included in mixed exhibitions. 1974 first solo exhibition at the Gardner Centre, University of Sussex; more recent one at the Galerie Renée Ziegler, Zurich, 1981. Lives and works in London. Work in the Arts Council collection.

LOWNDES, Allan   1921-1979

Painter. Born Stockport, Cheshire. Left school at fourteen and was apprenticed to a decorator. Served in the Cheshire Regiment during the Second World War. Resumed work as a decorator, 1945, and attended evening classes at Stockport School of Art. Turned to painting full-time in the 1950s. Exhibited with the Crane Kalman Gallery, London, where he had had regular shows from 1957. Specialised in the northern industrial landscape, and has work in a number of public collections.

Bibl: John Willett, *Allan Lowndes, Paintings 1948-72,* Stockport Art Gallery, 1972.

LOWRY, Laurence Stephen   1887-1976

Painter. Born Manchester, Lancashire. Took private classes with the painter William Fitz before working as a clerk in a firm of chartered accountants in 1904. 1905-15 studied at the Municipal College of Art, Manchester. 1909 moved from Rusholme to Pendlebury in Salford. 1910 began to work as a rent collector. 1915-20 studied at Salford School of Art, and began to take an interest in city scenes. 1931 illustrated *A Cotswold Book* by Harold Timperley. 1932 began to exhibit at RA, and 1939 at the Lefevre Gallery where he thereafter exhibited regularly. Until 1952 continued to work for the Pall Mall Property Company, and rose from the post of rent collector to that of chief cashier. In 1948 moved from Salford to Mottram-in-Longendale in Cheshire. Became greatly honoured in his own lifetime, but never lost a certain dourness of character. 'Had I not been lonely', he told the critic Edward Mullins, 'none of my work would have happened. I should not have done what I've done, or seen the way I saw things. I work because there's nothing else to do.' His early paintings often focused on accidents and misfortune. He had a strong sense of humour and supported talent whenever he happened upon it, becoming an especial friend and supporter of Sheila Fell.*

LUKIE, Jelena   b.1962

Sculptor. Studied at Cambridge College of Arts and Technology, 1982-3, Hull College of Art, 1983-4, Sheffield Polytechnic, 1984-6, and at RA, 1988. Also worked at the Pixley Street Studio, 1986-7. Awarded the Bolton House Investment Prize, 1988.

LYDIAT, Anne   b.1947

Sculptor. Born Manchester, Lancashire. Studied Fine Art at Sheffield and Manchester Polytechnics, 1978-82. Included in mixed exhibitions from 1980, including 'New Contemporaries' at the ICA. Awarded Henry Moore Sculpture Fellowship at Birmingham Polytechnic, 1985-7. First one-person show at the Concourse Gallery, Birmingham, 1986. Visiting Artist Placement at Smethwick Hall Girls' High School, 1986.

LYDON, Tommy   b.1955

Painter. Born Glasgow, Scotland. Studied at Glasgow School of Art, 1972-7. Finalist, Athena Art Awards, 1980. Lydon's strategy as a representational painter is to place the everyday in a larger holistic context in order to politicise the familiar. Solo exhibition held at Todd Gallery, London, 1989.

LYNE, Michael   1912-1989

Painter. Studied for a short spell at Cheltenham School of Art. His interest lay in field sports in which he regularly took part and depicted. For many years he worked solely in watercolours, until the late 1940s when he found oil paints more suitable for the theme. This change led him to

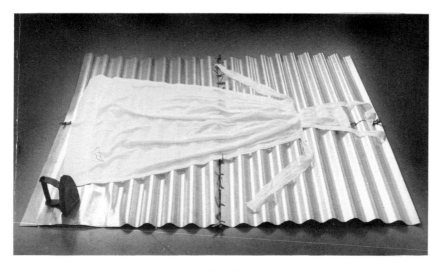

ANNE LYDIAT, b.1947. *'Ironing out the Wrinkles'*, 1987.
Corrugated steel, cotton and cast iron. 72in. x 72in.

MICHAEL LYONS, b.1943. *'Ocean'*, 1987. Mild steel. Yorkshire Sculpture Park.
Copyright Marks and Spencer. Photograph Don Williams.

produce original hunting scenes, rich in colour, which
culminated in a series he produced on the Grand National
in the late 1970s. Later, he returned to working in
watercolour, producing scenes in far greater detail. He
also produced illustrations for his own books, such as
*Horse, Hounds and Country, A Parson's Son, The Michael
Lyne Sketchbook,* and as commissions for other authors.

LYONS, Elizabeth
Painter. Born London. Attended evening classes in life
drawing and painting while running a company making
and designing horse-drawn carriages. Studied at
Falmouth School of Art. Paints in a style descended from
the teaching of David Bomberg.* One-artist exhibitions at
Art Space Gallery, Islington, 1986 and 1987. Her
paintings with their gestural use of strong colour, take
their inspiration from both myth and reality.

LYONS, Michael   b.1943
Sculptor. Born Bilston, Staffordshire. Studied at Wolverhampton College of Art, 1959-63, Hornsey College of Art,
1963-4 and the University of Newcastle upon Tyne,
1971-4. 1972 first solo show at Park Square Gallery, Leeds.
From 1977 lecturer in sculpture at Manchester Polytechnic.
Likes to make architectural type works that are sited out
of doors. Work in the collections of the Arts Council,
Bradford City Art Galleries and Ferens Art Gallery, Hull.

LYSYCIA, Anthony   b.1959
Sculptor and printmaker. Born Chorley, Lancashire. Attended
Preston Polytechnic, 1978-9; studied printmaking at the
Royal College of Art, 1981-4. 1984 awarded Prix de Rome,
British School in Rome. 1985-6 took a ten month painting
and drawing tour, travelling through Italy, Greece and
Turkey. Included in mixed exhibitions since 1977, including
'The Human Touch' at Fischer Fine Art, July 1986.

MABBUTT, Mary   b.1951
Painter. Born Luton, Befordshire. Studied at Lough-borough College of Art and Design, 1971-4 and at RA Schools, 1975-8. Represented in group exhibitions since 1976 when she exhibited in the Royal Academy Summer Show, London. First solo exhibition held at the New Grafton Gallery, London, 1980. Since 1985 she has regularly exhibited at the Paton Gallery, London. (Plate 63, p.319.)

McBEY, James   1883-1959
Watercolourist and etcher. Born Newburgh, Scotland. Began a career in banking and at the age of twenty-six became a full-time artist. Self-taught, he produced his first prints of any importance in 1910 and from that date on travelled widely, first to Europe, then to North Africa and America. After 1930 he turned increasingly to water-colour. Lived in America for some years, and became an American citizen, 1942.

MacBRYDE, Robert   1913-1966
Painter. Born Maybole, Scotland. Studied at Glasgow School of Art, 1932-7, where he became inseparable from Robert Colquhoun* with whom he was from then on associated. The two Roberts, as they were called, received support from the arts patron, Peter Watson, and moved to London where they shared a studio in Bedford Gardens with John Minton.* Influenced by Jankel Adler,* he developed a figurative expressionism that emphasised the organic relationship between the parts and the whole. First solo exhibition held at the Lefevre Gallery, 1943. Also produced lithographs and monotypes for the Miller's Press at Lewes. 1948 collaborated with Colquhoun on designs for Massine's ballet, *Donald of the Burthens.* Lived with Colquhoun for a period at Tilty Mill in Essex, a house belonging to the writer Ruthven Todd, but rented to the poet Elizabeth Smart. Is associated chiefly, however, with Soho, where the two Roberts cut a legend. Devastated by Colquhoun's death in 1962, he moved to Dublin and was run over by a car and killed.

MacCABE, Gladys   b.1918
Painter. Born Randalstown, Northern Ireland. Studied fashion, design and sculpture at Belfast College of Art, 1934-8, and taught herself painting. Has exhibited at RSA, ROI, SWA and elsewhere. Member of the Water-colour Society of Ireland and of the ROI. Founded the Ulster Society of Women Painters in 1957 and acted as its President on two occasions. Also works as an art critic and broadcaster. Awarded an honorary degree of Master of Arts by Queen's University, 1980, for services to the Arts. Also a fellow of the Royal Society of Arts and of the International Institute of Arts and Letters. Represented in the Imperial War Museum, and elsewhere.

MacCABE, Max   b.1917
Painter. Educated at the Royal Belfast Academical Institution. Has exhibited in London, America, Canada, Scotland, Belfast and Dublin. Represented in the Ulster Museum. Fellow of the International Institute of Arts and Letters.

McCALL, Charles   1907-1989
Painter. Born Edinburgh, Scotland. Began life as a lawyer but on winning a scholarship in 1933 he studied at

ROBERT MacBRYDE, 1913-1966. *'Woman with Cantaloupe',* c.1945. 49⅝in. x 24⁷⁄₁₆in. Manchester City Art Galleries.

Edinburgh College of Art under S.J. Peploe,* then in Paris at the Académie Colarossi. 1938 he returned to Britain when he was made a fellow of Edinburgh College of Art. In the same year he began exhibiting at the RA, with the NEAC and the London Group. He regularly held solo exhibitions in Britain, at the Leicester and Belgrave Galleries and elsewhere. He also exhibited in the USA, Canada and Ireland. His best work is often intimate in scale and deals with domestic interiors and the urban scene.

McCANCE, William

WILLIAM McCANCE, 1894-1970.
'Mediterranean Hill Town', 1923.
36in. x 24in.
Dundee Art Galleries and
Museums.

McCANCE, William   1894-1970

Painter and illustrator. Born Cambuslang, near Glasgow.
Studied at Glasgow School of Art and married a fellow
student, Agnes Miller Parker,* moving with her to
London in 1920. Worked as an illustrator and teacher, but
also produced paintings, sculpture and drawings close to
the style of Wyndham Lewis and the Vorticists; these near
abstract works are unrivalled in Scottish art of that
period. 1923-6 art critic of *The Spectator,* contributing also
to other journals. Began exhibiting in London and St.
Andrews. 1930-3 lived in Montgomeryshire where he
designed and illustrated books for the Gregynog Press.
Continued writing on art and in 1943 took over from

Robert Gibbings* as lecturer in typography and book
production at Reading University. 1960 first exhibition
held at Reading Art Gallery. 1975 a major retrospective,
shown at Dundee, Glasgow and Edinburgh, finally
redeemed him from obscurity and made better known his
originality.

Bibl: *William McCance (1894-1970),* City Art Gallery, Dundee,
1975.

McCLURE, Daphne

Painter. Born Helston, Cornwall. Studied at Hornsey
College of Art after the war and completed her studies at

Central School of Art and Crafts. Employed for many years in the Production Department of the Royal Opera House as a costume and set designer. 1976 returned to her native Cornwall, to live at Porthleven which she often paints. Member of the Newlyn Society of Artists.

McCLURE, David   b.1926
Painter. Born Lochwinnoch, Scotland. Studied at Edinburgh College of Art, 1947-52. Lecturer in painting at Duncan of Jordanstone College of Art, Dundee, 1957-83, and Head of the school, 1983-5. Elected ARSA 1963, and RSA 1971. First solo exhibition at the Circolo de Cultura, Palermo, 1957. Most recent at the Thackeray Gallery, London, 1986.

MacCOLL, Dugald Sutherland   1859-1948
Painter and art critic. Born Glasgow. Studied at University College, London, and Lincoln College, Oxford, 1876-84. Studied art at Westminster School of Art and at the Slade School, 1884-92. Became a member of the NEAC in 1896 and a spokesman for the kind of impressionism associated with the club; also wrote a book on one of its key figures, Philip Wilson Steer.* Art critic from 1890 of *The Spectator* and later of the *Saturday Review*. Became a History of Art lecturer at University College, London; also Keeper of Tate Gallery, 1906-11. His watercolours owe much to the example of Steer.

McCOMB, Leonard   b.1930
Painter and sculptor. Born Glasgow, Scotland. Studied at Manchester School of Art, 1954-6, and Slade School of Art, 1956-9. His work first received notice in the exhibition 'Human Clay' selected by R.B. Kitaj* and shown at the Hayward Gallery, 1976. 1979 first solo exhibition 'Blossoms and Flowers' held at Coracle Press. Since then he has exhibited regularly and in 1983 the Arts Council mounted a touring exhibition of his paintings and sculpture which was shown at the Museum of Modern Art, Oxford, and elsewhere. His drawings and paintings are built up with repeated lines and transparent washes of colour which weave their way around forms, emphasising their structure but at the same time conveying a visionary sense. He insists on direct experience and knowledge of nature, and works within a long-standing pictorial tradition which combines observation with spirituality. His recent work includes landscapes and still lifes that pay homage to the light and splendour of Provence. Recent solo exhibitions include one at Gillian Jason Gallery, London, 1989.

Bibl: *Leonard McComb, Drawings, Paintings and Sculpture*, Arts Council, London, 1983.

McCROSSAN, Mary   c.1864-1934
Painter. Born Liverpool, Merseyside. Studied at Liverpool School of Art where she won gold and silver medals and a travelling scholarship; also studied at the Académie Delacluze, Paris, and under Julius Olsson* and St. Ives. Lived in Liverpool, London, then St. Ives. Exhibited at the RA, IS, RE, in Liverpool and with the NEAC. Specialised in landscape and was much praised for her watercolours.

McCURDY, Matt   b.1959
Painter. Born Glasgow, Scotland. Studied at Glasgow School of Art, 1981-5. First solo exhibition held at Main Fine Art, Glasgow, 1986, the second at Thumb Gallery, London, 1988.

MacDONALD, Frances   1873-1921
Painter and designer. Born Kidsgrove, Staffordshire. Moved to Glasgow in 1890. With her eldest sister, Margaret, she attended Glasgow School of Art; married Herbert MacNair, the designer (the three, with C.R. Mackintosh,* formed an influential group known as 'The Glasgow Four'). Taught embroidery at the Liverpool Art Sheds, 1900-9. Exhibited in the International Exhibition of Modern Decorative Art, Turin, 1902. Taught embroidery and the design of metal and enamelwork at Glasgow until 1911. Collaborated with MacNair on silverware, jewellery and furniture design. After a cerebral haemorrhage caused her death, her distraught husband destroyed most of her work.

MacDONALD, Frances   b.1914
Painter. Born Wallasey, Cheshire. Studied at Wallasey School of Art, 1930-4, and the RCA, 1934-8. Official War Artist, 1940-6. Held first solo exhibition at Wildenstein, London, 1947. Painted London street scenes and also worked in Wales and the South of France. Married Leonard Appelbee.* Represented in several public collections.

McDONNELL, Hector   b.1947
Painter. Born Belfast, Northern Ireland. Educated at Eton and Oxford. Studied in Munich and Vienna, 1965-6. Lives and paints in both London and Northern Ireland. First one-person show at the Hamet Gallery, London. Recent one-person show at Fischer Fine Art, London, 1988.

McEVOY, Ambrose   1878-1927
Painter. Born Crudwell, Wiltshire. As a boy, was encouraged by Whistler and entered Slade School at the age of fifteen. Became a friend of Augustus John* and shared with Gwen John* his interest in Old Master techniques. Worked with Augustus John and Sickert* in Dieppe. Is also known for his Dutch influenced interiors. From 1900 exhibited with the NEAC. 1924 elected ARA and 1926 ARWS. Turned more and more to portraiture, mostly of female sitters.

McEVOY, Mary   1870-1941
Painter. Born Freshford, Somerset, née Edwards. Studied at Slade School. Exhibited with NEAC, 1900-6. Married Ambrose McEvoy* in 1902 and more or less gave up painting until after his death in 1927. Exhibited at the RA, 1928-37.

McEWAN, Rory   1932-1982
Painter and sculptor. Born Polwarth, Scotland. Studied at Cambridge and for five years worked as a professional musician. Became a full-time painter, 1951. Solo exhibitions at Durlacher Bros, New York, 1962 and 1964. After the second show he produced a series of abstract paintings in acrylics and by 1965 had begun painting directly on to glass and acrylic sheets. These led to free-standing sculptures incorporating glass, perspex, metal and sometimes polarised light, in coloured box constructions. Also had an interest in botanical illustration and held a retrospective of his paintings of flora and fauna was held at Inverleith House, Edinburgh, 1988.

McFADYEN, Jock

Painter. Born Paisley, Scotland. Studied at Chelsea School of Art, 1973-7. 1982 Artist-in-Residence at the National Gallery, London. Draws his subject matter from the East End of London, where he lives. Also deals bitingly with contemporary issues. Recent solo exhibitions include one at the Scottish Gallery, London, 1989.

Bibl: *Jock McFadyen: Paintings,* with essay by Lonis Biggs, Northern Centre for Contemporary Art, Sunderland, 1987.

McFALL, David   1919-1988

Sculptor. Born Glasgow, Scotland. Studied at Junior School of Arts and Crafts, Birmingham, 1931-4, Birmingham College of Art, 1934-9, RCA, 1940-1, and the Kennington School of Art, 1941-5. Worked with Jacob Epstein,* 1944-c.1958. Exhibited at the RA from 1943, ARA 1955 and RA 1963. Taught at Kennington School of Art from 1956. His commissions include the statue of Sir Winston Churchill at Woodford Green, portrait busts of Prince Charles and figures of St.Paul and St. Bride in St. Bride's, Fleet Street. His last major work, 'Christ', for Canterbury Cathedral, was completed just before his death and unveiled later in 1988. Represented in the Tate Gallery.

MacFARLANE, John   b.1948

Painter and designer. Born Glasgow, Scotland. Studied at Glasgow School of Art, 1966-70. First exhibition of drawings held at Gallery 'La Colonna', Milan, 1972; first exhibition of paintings at Galerie Ariadne, Vienna, 1975-6. Has exhibited widely in Europe and Great Britain since this date. Creates costume and set designs for dance and opera which include the Royal Opera House, London, Ballet Rambert, London and Cologne Opera House. First exhibition of stage designs held at Marina Henderson Gallery, London, 1986, followed by another there in 1988. Represented in the collections of the Welsh Arts Council, the Contemporary Arts Society, Wales and in Albertina, Vienna.

McGHIE, Kirsty   b.1959

Sculptor. Born Edinburgh, Scotland. Studied at Glasgow School of Art, 1980-5. 1985 travelled to Japan on a scholarship. Since 1983 has exhibited at numerous venues in Scotland, a solo exhibition at the Collective Gallery, Edinburgh, 1985. Uses a range of materials, including plastics, wax, resin, and wire netting.

MacGREGOR, W.Y.   1855-1923

Painter. Born Finnart, Scotland. Studied in Glasgow under Greenlees and Docharty and at the Slade School under Legros. Met James Paterson, 1878 and was, with him, one of the founders of the 'Glasgow School'. From 1875 exhibited at the RSA. Elected ARSA, 1898, and RSA, 1921. Member of the RSWS and exhibited at the RA twice. 1886-90 travelled on the Continent.

McGUINNESS, Norah   b.1903

Painter and illustrator. Born Derry, Northern Ireland. Studied at the Dublin Metropolitan School of Art, and Chelsea Polytechnic and in Paris. Exhibited in London, Ireland and abroad. Illustrated several books including Sterne's *Sentimental Journey.* Represented in several public collections.

MACH, David   b.1956

Sculptor. Born Methil, Scotland. Studied at Duncan of Jordanstone College of Art, 1974-9, and at the RCA, 1979-82, where he built his first works out of mass-produced items, namely books. At a well-known second-hand bookshop at Hay-on-Wye, he built a Rolls-Royce car out of thousands of books, layered one on top of another. This process has been repeated using various materials. In 1983, for the Hayward Annual, he built a *Polaris Submarine* out of old car tyres. One of his largest works was *Fuel for the Fire,* exhibited at the Riverside Studios, London, which used 30 tons of magazines and furniture. Each work is carefully planned, and can take three weeks to build with the aid of a team of helpers. His work also belongs to the realm of Performance Art in that the audience is invited to watch its construction. His use of waste products is a comment on today's erastz culture.

Bibl: *David Mach: 101 Dalmations,* Tate Gallery, London, 1988.

MACHIN, Arnold   b.1911

Sculptor. Born Trent Vale, Stoke-on-Trent, Staffordshire, of a family of potters. Studied at Stoke School of Art and then worked for Minton China Works. Studied sculpture at Derby School of Art, 1934-7 and at the RCA, 1937-40. Adviser to Wedgwoods from 1940. Exhibited at the RA from 1940. Elected ARA 1947 and RA 1956, ARBS 1953. Represented in the Tate Gallery.

McHUGH, Frank   b.1954

Painter. Studied at Stafford College of Art, Manchester Polytechnic and Chelsea School of Art. First solo exhibition held at Senate House, Liverpool University, 1977; subsequent ones include Margam Country Park, 1984 and Horsham Arts Centre, 1985.

MacILRAITH, William   b.1961

Painter. Born London. Studied at Camberwell School of Art. Awarded a Fellowship to Syracuse University, 1986-8. First exhibition held at Sanders Gallery, Syracuse University, 1988. In the same year he held a second exhibition at Connaught Brown, London. Abstract painter who explores man's relationship with the urban environment.

McINTYRE, Donald   b.1923

Painter. Studied in the studio of James Wright, RSW, and was much influenced by S.J. Peploe.* Also received instruction from the Canadian Impressionist, Gyrth Russell. Represented in the collections of Birkenhead Art Gallery, Newport Art Gallery, Merthyr Tydfil Gallery and the Welsh Contemporary Art Society. Specialises in landscape.

McINTYRE, Keith   b.1959

Painter. Born Edinburgh, Scotland. Studied at Duncan of Jordanstone College of Art, Dundee, 1978-82. Visual director for 'Jock Tamson's Bairns' at the Tramway Theatre, Glasgow, 1989-90. A solo exhibition of the images he produced on canvas for the play were shown at the RAAB Gallery, Glasgow, 1990. Figurative artist, with a vivid imagination and pronounced feelings about his identity as a Scot.

MACK, Alistair   b.1955

Printmaker. Born Edinburgh, Scotland. Studied at Edinburgh College of Art, 1983-8. Awards include the RSA Major Printmaking Award, Student Exhibition and the RSA Keith Prize, Annual Exhibition. 1987 first exhibited at the RSA. 1988 became a council member of Edinburgh Printmakers Workshop. Included in the collections of Edinburgh College of Art, Heriot-Watt University, The City of Edinburgh (Jean F. Watson Bequest), Queen Margaret College, Edinburgh, The Borders and Aberdeen Hospitals and The Arts in Fife.

McKEEVER, Ian   b.1946

Painter. Born Withernsea, East Yorkshire. Studied at

Avery Hill College of Education, London. Artist in Residence at Bridewell Studios, Liverpool, 1980-1. Artist in Residence, Nuremberg, West Germany, 1981. First solo show at Cardiff Arts Centre, 1971. Several one-man shows in the 1970s and '80s in Britain, Germany, Poland and Italy. McKeever examines the conventions of landscape painting and makes diptychs that measure the difference between what was seen and what remembered.

McKENNA, Stephen   b.1939
Painter. Born London. Studied at the Slade School, 1959-64. First solo exhibition at Galerie Olaf Hudtwalcker, Frankfurt, 1964. Visiting Lecturer at various art colleges in England, 1963-73. 1971-8 lived and worked in Bonn, West Germany. 1979 moved to Brussels and London. Now lives and works in Donegal and Rome. Shortlisted for the Tate Gallery Turner Prize, 1986. Paints ambiguous perspectival vistas and metaphysical still lifes.

Bibl: R.H. Fuchs, *Stephen McKenna,* Museum of Modern Art, Oxford, 1983.

MacKENNA, Tracy   b.1963
Sculptor. Born Oban, Scotland. Studied at Glasgow School of Art, 1981-6. 1986-7 lived and worked in Hungary as a guest of the Artists' Collective Studio, Budapest. Since 1987 has exhibited widely, holding a solo exhibition at the Collective Gallery, Edinburgh, 1986, another at the Young Artists' Club, Budapest, 1987, and a third at the Glasgow Print Studio, 1989. Uses waste and manufactured materials, reassembled and recently, mounted not on the floor, but the wall. Director of Glasgow Sculpture Studios.

MacKENNAL, Sir Bertrum   1863-1931
Sculptor. Born Melbourne, Australia, the son of the sculptor, J.S. MacKennal. Studied under his father and then at Melbourne School of Art. Came to London, 1882, and entered the RA Schools, but soon left for Paris. From 1886 exhibited at the RA. Spent 1889-92 in Australia, having won the competition for the decoration of Government House, Victoria. Elected ARA, 1909, RA, 1922, knighted, 1921. First solo exhibition held at Fine Art Society, London, 1932. Commissions include decorations for Government House, Melbourne, 1899, war memorials for Eton and the House of Commons, and the Edward VII Memorial, St. George's Chapel, Windsor.

Bibl: W.K. West, 'The Sculpture of Bertram MacKennal', *The Studio,* September, 1908.

MacKENZIE, Esmie   1887-1965
Painter. Spent her formative years singing and dancing. During the 1920s she met Claude Flight* and, greatly influenced by him and his work, began to paint in earnest. She also experimented successfully with lino-cuts. Exhibited with the NEAC, at the RBA and with the Redfern Gallery.

MacKENZIE, Robert Tait   1867-1938
Sculptor. Born Almonte, Ontario, Canada. Studied medicine; became demonstrator, then Lecturer in Anatomy at McGill University, 1894-1904. From 1907 exhibited sculpture of athletes at the RA. Held three exhibitions at the Fine Art Society, London, 1920, 1927 and 1930. Commissions include the Scottish American War Memorial, Princes Street Gardens, Edinburgh and the memorial to sixty years of confederation, Parliament Buildings, Ottawa.

MACKEOWN, James   b.1961
Painter. Grandson of Tom Carr,* a member of the Euston Road Group. First solo exhibition held in Haverfordwest, Dyfed, 1978; others include one at the Phoenix Galleries, Lavenham, 1989. Naturalist painter of domestic subjects and landscapes.

MacKIE, Charles U.   1862-1920
Painter. Born Aldershot, Hampshire. Studied at the RSA Schools. Exhibited at leading London exhibition venues from 1889 and still more prominently in Scotland. Chairman of the SSA, 1900-1. Elected RSW, 1902, ARSA, 1902, and RSA, 1917. Received a gold medal at the Amsterdam exhibition of 1912.

MacKIE, George   b.1920
Painter, designer and illustrator. Born Cupar, Scotland. Studied at Dundee College of Art, 1937-40, and Edinburgh College of Art, 1946-8. Exhibited at the RSA, RSW and SSA. Represented in several Scottish public collections. Became Head of Design at Grays School of Art, Aberdeen.

MACKINLEY, Elizabeth   b.1965
Sculptor. Born Middlesbrough, Cleveland. Studied at Chelsea School of Art, 1983-7, and at the RA, 1988. First exhibited at Southampton Art Gallery, 1988.

MacKINNON, Sine   b.1901
Painter. Born Newcastle, County Down, Northern Ireland. Studied at Slade School under Tonks,* 1918-20, 1921-4, winning many prizes. Went to Paris where she had two exhibitions before returning to London. First solo exhibition in London at the Goupil Gallery, 1928. Lived mostly in France. Specialised in landscapes.

MACKINTOSH, Charles Rennie   1868-1928
Painter and architect. Born Glasgow, Scotland. Whilst apprenticed to the architect, John Hutchinson, he began attending evening classes in architecture at Glasgow School of Art where he won many prizes and a travelling scholarship to Italy, France and Belgium. On his return to Glasgow he met the two sisters Frances and Margaret* MacDonald, and married the latter in 1900. Together with Herbert MacNair they formed the Glasgow Four group and created a specifically Scottish variant of European Art Nouveau. One of the Mackintosh's most famous buildings is the Glasgow School of Art. In 1904 he became a partner in the firm of Honeyman and Keppie, and that same year saw the opening of the Willow Tea Rooms, Glasgow, for which he had designed furnishings and fittings. Aside from his enormous influence as an architect and designer, he also painted in watercolour, with great precision and sensitivity, in Suffolk and the South of France.

Bibl: Roger Billcliffe, *Mackintosh Watercolours,* London, 1978.

MACKINTOSH, Margaret
Painter and stained-glass artist. Born Staffordshire, née MacDonald. Studied at Glasgow School of Art where she met and married Charles Rennie Mackintosh.* Exhibited widely on the Continent and received the Diploma of Honour at the Turin International Exhibition, 1902. Elected RSW, 1980.

MACLAGAN, Philip D.   1901-1972
Painter. Born North China; his family returned to Scotland in 1905. Studied at St. John's Wood Art School, 1918-19 and then the RA Schools. Exhibited with the RA, 1921-41. Taught art at City of London School, 1929-37. Served with RAF in North Africa and Italy, 1941-5.

MACLAREN, Donald

Retired from teaching in 1967 and moved to Totnes, Devon, where he died. Retrospective exhibition held at Clarges Gallery, London, 1976.

MACLAREN, Donald   1886-1917
Painter. Born Kensington, London, the son of an architect and nephew of D.S. MacColl.* Studied at Slade School, 1903-8, winning several prizes for figure compositions. From 1907 exhibited at the NEAC and with the Friday Club. Specialised in portraits and landscapes and taught art at Liverpool Technical School. Served in the First World War and was killed in action.

MACLAREN, Peter   b.1964
Painter. Studied at Edinburgh College of Art, 1982-7. Included in mixed shows from 1985. Solo exhibition at the Compass Gallery, Glasgow, 1988. Work in Scottish collections, e.g. City Arts Centre, Edinburgh, RSA, Edinburgh, Bank of Scotland. Likes to work in watercolour.

MACLAURIN, Robert   b.1961
Painter. Born Yorkshire. Studied at Edinburgh College of Art, 1979-83. 1984-5 spent a year in Istanbul on a Turkish government scholarship. Since then has visited Turkey annually and in his art has been much influenced by its colours and landscape. Began to exhibit in 1983, and held his first solo exhibition at Edinburgh University Staff Club, 1984. Recent solo exhibitions include ones at the 369 Gallery, Edinburgh, and Turbeville Smith, London, 1989. His work, which often shows a lone figure against a dramatic landscape backdrop, deals with the vulnerability of the individual.

McLEAN, Bruce   b.1944
Painter, sculptor, ceramicist and performance artist. Born Glasgow. Studied at Glasgow School of Art, 1961-3 and at St. Martin's School of Art, 1963-6. In reaction against the precepts of his teachers, Anthony Caro* and Phillip King,* began to execute work that questioned the permanence of sculpture. His gift for satire led him into performance and in 1971 he set up 'Nice Style — The World's First Pose Band' which mocked various social habits and professional practices. In 1972, at the age of twenty-seven, he was offered a retrospective at the Tate Gallery. He opted for one lasting only one day, entitled it 'King for a Day' and in this and other ways satirised the retrospective as a validating mechanism. Began to paint on photographic paper in the mid-1970s, as a means of notation for live works. His paintings developed increased autonomy while in West Berlin in 1981, on a DAAD Fellowship. 1985 awarded John Moores Painting Prize, 1986 began working with ceramics. Has also produced costume and set designs for the Ballet Rambert and continues to elude categorisation with his quick changes of media and ideas.

Bibl: *Bruce McLean: New Works and Performance/Actions/Positions,* Third Eye Centre, Glasgow, 1980; Mel Gooding, *Bruce McLean,* Phaidon Press, London, 1990.

McLEAN, John   b.1939
Painter. Born Liverpool, of Scottish parents. Studied at St. Andrews University, 1957-62 and the Courtauld Institute of Art, 1963-6. Self-taught as a painter. From 1971 included in mixed exhibitions. 1975 first solo exhibition held at the Talbot Rice Art Centre, Edinburgh. Recent solo exhibitions include two at the Frances Graham-Dixon Gallery, London, 1988 and 1989. Painter of abstract pictures composed of bands of colour arranged in a balanced sequence. (Plate 64, p.319.)

McLEAN, Talbert
Painter. Born Dundee, Scotland. Solo exhibitions at Talbot Rice Art Centre, Edinburgh, 1973 and 1976, and at Compass Gallery, Glasgow, 1980. Abstract painter. Work in public collections at Gallery of Modern Art, Edinburgh, Scottish Arts Council, CAS, Dundee and Arbroath Art Galleries.

MACLEAN, Will   b.1941
Painter and sculptor. Born Inverness, Scotland. Studied at Grays School of Art, Aberdeen, 1961-7, and the British School in Rome, 1967, where he had his first solo exhibition. Since 1969 included in mixed exhibitions in Scotland. 1978 elected ARSA. 1979-80 won Scottish Arts Council Award. From 1980 taught at Duncan of Jordanstone College of Art, Dundee. Fishermen and boats often form the basis of his subject matter. Since 1974 he has worked on sculptures and constructions composed of driftwood, found objects and sculpted elements, all fitted into box-like frames and painted.

Bibl: *Will Maclean: Sculptures and Box Constructions 1974-1987: A Catalogue Raisonné,* Claus Runkel Fine Art Ltd., London, 1987.

MACLENNAN, Alastair   b.1943
Performance artist. Born Blair Athol, Scotland. Studied at Duncan of Jordanstone College of Art, Dundee, 1960-5 and at the Art Institute in Chicago, 1966-8. 1973-4 studied Zen in Vancouver and in Los Angeles. 1971-5 created over 40 outdoor performances in Canada. Committed to the concept of 'art as healing'. 1975 settled in Belfast, Northern Ireland.

Bibl: *Alastair MacLennan: Is No: 1975-1988,* Arnolfini Gallery, Bristol, 1988.

McLURE, Emma   b.1962
Painter. Born London. Studied at Falmouth School of Art, 1980-1, Winchester School of Art, 1981-4, and Chelsea School of Art, 1984-5. Began exhibiting in 1985. Solo exhibitions at the Vanessa Devereaux Gallery, 1986 and at Wolf at the Door Gallery, Penzance, 1989.

McMAHON, Tommy   b.1945
Painter. Born Glasgow, Scotland. First solo exhibition at the House Gallery, London, 1981. Has also exhibited in USA, Holland and West Germany. A figurative expressionist.

MACMIADHACHAIN, Padraig   b.1929
Painter. Born Ireland. Studied at the National College of Art, Dublin and Belfast College of Art. First solo exhibition in Belfast, 1951; one in Madrid, 1955 and at the Woodstock Gallery, London, 1958.

McMILLAN, Ian Douglas   b.1946
Maker of relief constructions. Studied at Glasgow School of Art, 1964-8. From 1972 included in mixed exhibitions in Scotland. 1975 first solo exhibition at New 57 Gallery, Edinburgh. Work in the collections of Fife County Council and the Scottish Arts Council.

McMILLAN, William   b.1887
Sculptor. Born Aberdeen, Scotland. Studied at Gray's School of Art, Aberdeen, and the RCA, 1908-12. From 1917 exhibited at RA. Designed war memorials at Aberdeen and Manchester, 1918. Elected ARA, 1925, RA, 1935. Master of the RA Sculpture School, 1929-40. Other works include statues of George V at Calcutta, George VI in The Mall and Raleigh in Whitehall. Represented in the Tate Gallery.

MACNAB, Iain   1890-1967

Painter and printmaker. Born Philippines. Arrived in Scotland in 1894. Studied at Glasgow School of Art, 1917, Heatherley School of Fine Art, London, 1918, and in Paris, 1919. 1925 founded his own art school, the Grosvenor School of Modern Art, where he taught wood engraving and kept the school open until 1940. Until 1953 Director of Studies at Heatherley School of Art. Fellow of the RE and President of the ROI. 1959 became a governor of the Federation of British Artists. Memorial exhibition at the FBA Galleries, London, 1969. Best known for his stylised wood engravings of Spain, Corsica and the South of France, and for his book illustrations.

Bibl: *Iain MacNab and his Circle*, Blond Fine Art, London, 1979.

McNAIRN, Caroline   b.1955

Painter. Born Selkirk, Scotland. Studied Fine Art at Edinburgh University, 1972-8. First solo exhibition at Calton Studios, Edinburgh, 1980, most recent at the 369 Gallery, Edinburgh, 1987. From 1977 included in group exhibitions. Work in collections of Derby Art Gallery, Dundee Art Gallery, Hong Kong, Shangai Bank, Scottish Provident. Uses bold oppositions of shape, colour and texture in paintings expressive of the city dweller and of the Edinburgh inhabitant in particular.

MACNAUGHTON, Iris Carruthers

Painter. Studied at the Slade School of Fine Art, Westminster School of Art and Edinburgh College of Art. Regular exhibitor at RA, RSA, SSA and Society of Scottish Women Artists. Her work is in the collection of British Rail. Solo exhibition at Douglas and Foulis Art Gallery, Edinburgh, 1962.

MACNEICE, Corinna

Painter. Born near London. Studied at the Slade School, 1962-7. Since 1968 has taught painting at Croydon College of Art. 1970 first solo exhibition, of drawings, at the English Speaking Union, Oxford. 1973 solo show of paintings and drawings at the Arts Council Gallery, Cambridge.

MACPHERSON, George A.   b.1935

Painter. Born Invershin, Scotland. Studied at Edinburgh College of Art, 1954-8 and was awarded a travelling scholarship from the college, 1959-60. First solo exhibition at the '57 Gallery, Edinburgh and included in mixed Scottish exhibitions. Teaches at Edinburgh College of Art. Recent solo exhibition at the Scottish Gallery, Edinburgh, 1981.

MACPHERSON, Neil   b.1954

Painter. Born Glasgow, Scotland. Trained at Glasgow School of Art and in 1983 won Royal Scottish Academy's Young Artists Award. First one-artist show 1986. Included in 'Artists at Work' exhibition, Edinburgh International Festival, 1986. Lives in an isolated croft in Caithness and is steeped in the Celtic folklore that is reflected in his work.

MACPHERSON, Sophie   b.1957

Painter. Born London. Studied at St. Martin's and Camberwell Schools of Art. Produces urban and industrial landscapes and is to some extent influenced by English 'Romantic' painters. She has also been influenced by New York. Combines a precise method of drawing with a painterly technique. Often works with details of objects, seen close-up.

MACTAGGART, Sir William   1903-1981

Painter. Born Loanhead, Scotland, grandson of the

SIR WILLIAM MACTAGGART, 1903-1981. *'Poppies Against the Night Sky'*, c.1962. Oil on hardboard. 30in. x 25in. Scottish National Gallery of Modern Art.

painter William MacTaggart (1835-1910). Studied part-time at Edinburgh College of Art, 1918-21. Began annual painting visits to South of France, 1922. 1924 first solo exhibition in the hall of St. Andrews Church, Cannes. 1929 first solo Scottish exhibition at Aitken Dott and Son, Edinburgh. 1933-6 President of the Society of Scottish Artists. 1959-69 President of the Royal Scottish Academy. 1960 Trustee of the National Museum of Antiquities. 1962 knighted; 1965 made Freeman of the Burgh of Loanhead and 1968 ARA. His Post-Impressionist landscape style owed much to the Scottish Colourists. Later, in the 1930s, his style became more expressionistic under the influence of German and Norwegian art. His work developed further after he saw the 1952 Rouault exhibition in Paris, the forms within his pictures merging into masses of glowing colour. Work in most Scottish public galleries and in the Arts Council and Tate Gallery collections.

Bibl: H. Harvey Wood, *W. MacTaggart*, Edinburgh, 1974.

McWHIRTER, Ishbel   b.1927

Painter. Born London. From 1946 was taught by the painter Oskar Kokoschka* for several years. Travelled extensively in Europe, Africa and the Near East. First solo exhibition at the Arcade Gallery, London, 1945; another at Waddington Galleries, Dublin, 1952.

McWILLIAM, F.E.   b.1909

Sculptor. Born Banbridge, Northern Ireland. Studied at Belfast College of Art, the Slade School, and was awarded

CONROY MADDOX, b.1912.
'The Enchanted Day', 1952.
46in. x 32in. Private Collection.

Robert Ross Leaving Scholarship, 1928-31. 1931-2 worked in Paris. 1938 joined the British Surrealist Group. 1939 first solo exhibition at London Gallery, Cork Street. 1940 served with RAF. Since 1945 much of his sculpture has reflected situations of horror and atrocity in Belfast. 1953 won an award in the unknown Political Prisoner competition. 1959 ARA. 1964 received Honorary Doctorate of Letters from Queen's University, Belfast. Commissions include the Four Seasons Group for the Festival of Britain, 1951. 1989 retrospective exhibition at the Tate Gallery. Represented in the collections of the Tate, the Arts Council, the V & A, MOMA, New York and galleries in Leeds, Oldham, Coventry and Belfast.

Bibl: *F.E. McWilliam: Sculpture 1932-1989*, Tate Gallery, London, 1989.

MADDEN, Anne   b.1932
Painter and sculptor. Born London. Lived in Chile until 1936 and then in England and Ireland. 1958 married the painter Louis le Brocquy* and went to live in France. From 1951 included in mixed exhibitions. 1959 first solo exhibition at the Leicester Galleries, London. 1974 one at

the New Art Centre, London. 1970 awarded sculpture commission for Technical College, Dundalk, Ireland. 1970 mural commission for the Art Centre, University College, Dublin.

MADDEN, Charles   b.1906
Painter. Born into a distinguished naval family, he joined the navy aged fourteen and was educated at Royal Naval Colleges. Painted in watercolours throughout his naval career, with tuition from W.L. Wyllie,* RA, and part-time tuition at the Grosvenor School of Modern Art, London and Portsmouth Technical College. 1965 retired from the navy with rank of Admiral. Solo exhibitions at City Art Gallery, Plymouth, 1961, Upper Grosvenor Galleries, London, 1967 and 1970.

MADDOX, Conroy   b.1912
Painter. Born Ledbury, Herefordshire. 1937 worked in Paris with various members of the Surrealist Group of painters. 1940 joined the English Surrealist Group. 1945 lecturer in Modern Art at Birmingham University. 1946 contributor to *le Savoir Vivre* published by Belgian Surrealists. 1963 retrospective exhibition at the Grabowski Gallery, London. 1967 collaborated with the artist E.L.T. Mesens on collages. 1970 associated with the Chicago Surrealist Group and their publication *Arsenal.* 1972 retrospective exhibition at the Hamet Gallery, London.

Bibl: *Double Exhibition: Paintings by Conroy Maddox, and Surrealism Unlimited, 1968-78,* Camden Arts Centre, London, 1978.

MADGETT, Diana   b.1928
Painter. Studied at Hornsey College of Art, 1946-52. Studied the Chinese language and calligraphy while living in the Far East, 1952-6. Paints in a calligraphic manner. Taught art in the late 1950s at the Nigerian College at Zana. 1959 first solo show at the New Vision Centre Gallery, London.

MADGWICK, Clive   b.1934
Painter. Born London. Studied at Epsom College of Art and London University. 1972 took up painting. 1975 first exhibition at Haste Gallery, Ipswich, and has exhibited there regularly since. Commissioned by Calor Gas, Abbey National and Mann and Co., to produce paintings. Represented in the collection of H.M. The Queen.

MAECKLBERGHE, Margo   b.1932
Painter. Born Penzance, Cornwall. Studied at Bath Academy of Art, 1949-56. Lived and worked in Gibraltar, 1956-9, returned to Cornwall, 1959. 1960 first solo exhibition at Newlyn Art Gallery; most recent at Peter Hyde Fine Art, London, 1968.

MAFÉ, Daniel   b.1957
Painter. Born London. Studied at City and Guilds School of Art, 1980-3 and at RA Schools, 1983-6. Exhibits with London Group and RA. Works intuitively, producing paintings often about houses and rooms. 1987 solo exhibition at Oxford Gallery, Oxford.

MAGILL, Elizabeth   b.1959
Painter. Born Ontario, Canada. Studied at Belfast College of Art, 1979-82, and Slade School of Fine Art, 1982-4. First solo exhibition held at Kerlin Gallery, Belfast, 1987. Represented in 'The British Art Show' at the Hayward Gallery, London, 1990.

MAHONEY, Charles Cyril   1903-1968
Painter. Born Lambeth, London. Studied at Beckenham School of Art and RCA, 1922-6. Served first as assistant and later tutor at RCA, 1928-53. Collaborated with Bawden* and Ravilious* on the Morley College murals, 1928-30, painting a large decoration, *The Pleasures of Life,* which, like the rest, was destroyed by a bomb in the Second World War. Afterwards received many other commissions. Conscientious and hard-working, as a painter and teacher, he upheld academic discipline. Occasionally painted religious themes, but was equally fascinated with the ordinary and mundane. 1937 wrote *Gardens Choice,* illustrated by Evelyn Dunbar.* 1954-63 taught at Byam Shaw School of Art and 1961-8 at the RA Schools. Known as an outstanding teacher. Painted a mural in the Lady Chapel of Campion Hall, Oxford. 1961 elected ARA and 1968 RA.

Bibl: Robert Woolf, *The Artist as Evacuee,* The Wordsworth Trust, Grasmere, 1987.

MAINE, John   b.1942
Sculptor. Born Bristol, Somerset. Studied at West of England College of Art, 1960-4, and RCA, 1964-7. Held a fellowship at Gloucestershire College of Art, 1967-9, and at Yorkshire Sculpture Park, 1979-80. Held his first solo exhibition at the Serpentine Gallery, 1972. Has received many awards and been given public commissions. His work is in the Arts Council collection and elsewhere.

Bibl: *John Maine,* Arts Council of Great Britain/Bretton Hall College, 1980.

MAISTRE, Roy de   b.1894
Painter. Used the family form of his name, Roi de Mestre, until 1930. Born Bowral, New South Wales, Australia. Studied painting at the Royal Art Society of New South Wales and then at Sydney Art School. Exhibited with the Society of Arts, Sydney, 1916-29, and the Royal Art Society of New South Wales, 1917-18. Won Society of Artists travelling scholarship, 1923 and went to Paris, exhibiting at the Paris Salon, 1924. 1926 represented in the Australian section of the Venice Biennale. First solo exhibition in London held at the Beaux Arts Gallery, 1930. In the 1920s worked in France and Australia. In the 1930s divided his time between Paris and London. Opened a school of painting in London with Martin Bloch,* 1934. Retrospective exhibition held at Whitechapel Art Gallery, 1960. Created CBE, 1962. Represented in the Tate Gallery.

MAITLAND, Paul   1863-1909
Painter. Born Chatham, Kent. Studied at RCA and later under Theodore Roussel.* Much influenced by Whistler in his use of restrained tonality. Exhibited internationally and became Art Examiner for the Board of Education, 1893-1908. Owing to a spinal disability he led a restricted life and most of his paintings are confined to scenes of London's parks and gardens. They are small in scale, tonally exquisite and tinged with a wistful melancholy. (Plate 5, p.19.)

MAJOR, Julie C.   b.1964
Sculptor. Born London. Studied at Croydon College of Art and Design, 1980-2, Kingston Polytechnic, 1983-6, and at RA Schools, 1987. Took a course in printmaking, 1982-3. Awards include the Stanley Picker Travelling Scholarship to Italy, 1985 and the Bolton House Investment Award, 1988. First exhibited at the City Artists Gallery, London, 1986.

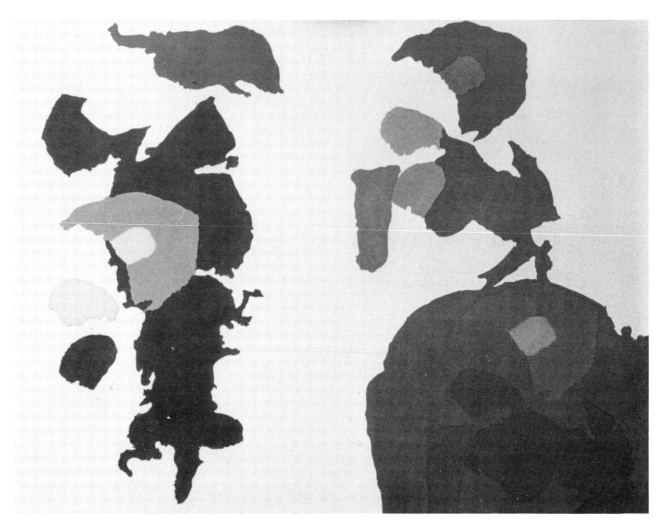

ERIC MALTHOUSE, b.1914. *'Step Off'*. 40in. x 50in. Private Collection.

MALET, Guy Seymour   1900-1973
Printmaker. Studied at the London School of Art, 1924-6, the Regent Street Polytechnic, 1926-7, and was taught wood-engraving by Iain Macnab* at the Grosvenor School of Art, 1927.

MALIN, Suzi   b.1950
Painter and sculptor. Born Leeds, Yorkshire. Studied at Slade School of Art, 1969-74. From 1970 included in group exhibitions. 1977 first solo exhibition at JPL Fine Art, London. Work in the collection of the National Portrait Gallery, London. Obsessed with painting the human head. Her style is remarkable for its clarity of definition.

MALTBY, Sally   b.1943
Painter of architectural subjects. Born Farringdon, Hampshire. Studied at Farnham School of Art and the Central School of Art, where she won an RSA travel bursary and used this to visit the USA and Mexico. Worked for a while as a textile designer. Produces prints of National Trust properties. First solo exhibition at Christopher Wood Gallery, London, 1987.

MALTHOUSE, Eric   b.1914
Painter and printmaker. Born Erdington, Birmingham, West Midlands. Studied at Birmingham College of Arts and Crafts, 1931-7. Taught art at Salt High Schools, Saltaire, Yorkshire, 1938-9. Served in the Royal Armoured Corps, 1940-2. 1938 first solo exhibition at Civic Playhouse, Bradford. 1944-73 Lecturer at Cardiff College of Art. 1959 ten year retrospective exhibition at Turner House, Penarth, Wales. 1956, founder member of 56 Group Wales, exhibited with the Society until 1970. 1973 moved to Cornwall. Most recent exhibition of paintings and prints at Oriel Gallery, Cardiff, 1981.

MAN, Maurice   b.1921
Painter. Born London. Studied at Willesden School of Art, 1934-8, then at St. Martin's School of Art and the Académie Grand Chaumière, Paris. During the Second World War he worked on government poster campaigns and designed propoganda material. 1949 started working exclusively in pastel. 1958 first solo exhibition at Kensington Art Gallery; another at Mount Gallery, London, 1964.

MANLEY, Edna   d.1990
Sculptor. Exhibition of carved wooden sculptures at The French Gallery, London, 1937. A wooden figure is in the collection of the Graves Art Gallery, Sheffield.

MANN, Alexander   1953-1908
Painter. Born Glasgow, Scotland. Studied in Paris under

Carolus Duran where he acquired an assured grasp of tone. Exhibited at principal London galleries from 1883, mainly at the RA. Painted in Italy, France and Morocco.

MANN, Allan R.   b.1949
Painter and printmaker. Born Ayrshire, Scotland. Studied textile design at Glasgow School of Art, 1969-73. Lecturer in printmaking and textiles at Duncan of Jordanstone College of Art, Dundee, 1973-6. First solo exhibition at Compass Gallery, Glasgow, 1979. Work in Scottish Arts Council collection.

MANN, Cathleen   1896-1959
Painter. Born London, daughter of Harrington Mann,* the portrait painter. Studied at the Slade School in Paris. Member of the RP and the National Society of Portrait Painters. Works bought by the French Government and Glasgow Art Gallery. Painter of flowers, landscapes and portraits. Solo exhibitions at Arthur Tooth Gallery, 1932, the Leicester Galleries, 1937, Reid and Lefevre Gallery, 1938 and 1954. Retrospective exhibition at the O'Hana Gallery, London, 1960.

MANN, Edna   b.1928
Painter. Born London. Studied at the RCA, 1945-8, under the painter David Bomberg.* Founder member, with Bomberg, of the Borough Group, 1947, and exhibited with fellow members. Also wrote radio plays, the first of which was broadcast 1965. Married to the sculptor Don Baldwin. First solo exhibition at Drian Galleries, London, 1966.

MANN, Harrington   1864-1937
Painter. Born Glasgow, Scotland. Studied at Glasgow School of Art and at the Slade School of Art under Alphonse Legros. From 1890 to 1900 lived in Glasgow and then moved to London. From 1885 exhibited at the RA. 1885 elected RE (resigned in 1891). Specialised in portraiture and attained a large reputation. Spent several seasons in America, where he maintained a home, painting portraits. Represented in many public collections. Father of Cathleen Mann.*

MANN, James Scrimgeour   1883-1946
Painter. Born Dundee, Scotland. Studied at Liverpool School of Art. Specialised in marine subjects and exhibited at the RA, with the RI and elsewhere. Elected RI, 1932.

MANNOCCI, Lino   b.1945
Painter. Born Viareggio, Italy. Moved to London in 1968 where he studied at Camberwell School of Art, 1971-4 and the Slade School of Art, 1974-6. Has exhibited in numerous shows in Britain, on the Continent and in the USA, and for a number of years has exhibited with a group of artists under the name 'La Metacosa', a term expressing their concern with the perception of profound thought through aspects of the ordinary world.

Bibl: *Lino Mannocci*, Curwen Gallery, London, 1988, with essay by Sarah Kent.

MANSFIELD, Andrew   b.1954
Painter. Born Leicester. Studied at Loughborough College of Art and Design, 1970-3 and Portsmouth Polytechnic, 1976-9. Solo exhibitions at Spacex Gallery, Exeter, 1984, Winchester Gallery, 1985, Midland Group, Nottingham, 1985, Anthony Reynolds Gallery, London, 1986.

MANSON, James Bolivar   1879-1945
Painter. Born London. Studied at Heatherley's, Lambeth

School of Art and in Paris under J.P. Laurens at the Académie Julian. 1911 founder-member and secretary of the Camden Town Group. 1914 founder-member of the London Group. From 1915 also exhibited with the NEAC, became a member 1927. A close friend of Lucien Pissarro* with whom he formed the Monarro Group in 1920 aimed at promoting the Impressionist tradition. 1923 first solo exhibition held at Leicester Galleries. 1917 joined the staff of the Tate Gallery and became its Director in 1930 for the next eight years. 1939 began exhibiting at the RA. Also wrote several books on art.

MARKS, Derek   b.1960
Painter. Born Stratford, London. Studied at Chelsea College of Art, 1978-9 and Goldsmiths' College of Art, 1979-82. Mural artist on Newham Community Murals Projects, 1978. First one-person show at East Ham Town Hall, Newham, London, 1978. Included in group exhibitions since 1980.

MARR, Leslie   b.1922
Painter. Born Durham City. Started painting in Israel during the Second World War and after release from the RAF joined David Bomberg's* classes. Became a founder member and secretary of the Borough Group created by Bomberg in 1949. Also exhibited with the Borough Bottega Group, at the Archer Gallery, the Arcade Gallery, at Braesnose College, Oxford, with the London Group, the Paris Salon and in the provinces. Solo exhibitions include those held at the Everyman Gallery, Hampstead, 1959 and 1962, the Drian Gallery, 1963 and the Laing Art Gallery, Newcastle, 1965. His most recent exhibition was held at the Catto Gallery, Hampstead, 1990. Now lives and works on the Isle of Arran.

MARRIOTT, Alan   b.1952
Painter. Born Reading, Berkshire. Studied at University of Newcastle upon Tyne, 1970-4 and Chelsea School of Art, 1975-6. Has exhibited at a number of group shows in London.

MARRIOTT, Frederick   1860-1941
Painter and etcher. Born Stoke-on-Trent, Staffordshire. Studied at the School of Art, Coalbrookdale and at the age of fourteen he went to work as a pottery painter in a factory. 1879 entered the RCA on a National Scholarship; after three years there he worked as a designer and illustrator to Marcus Ward & Co. Later became chief designer with the publishers, Eyre and Spottiswood. Also practised repoussé work, wood carving, enamelling and modelling with glass. Exhibited at RA, RE, the Paris Salon and elsewhere. 1895-1925 he occupied various trading positions and became a member of the Arts and Crafts Society. Elected ARE, 1909, and RE, 1924. Specialised in portraits, landscapes and architectural subjects.

MARSHALL, David Scott   b.1942
Constructivist. Born Edinburgh, Scotland. Has travelled in South America and Canada. Took a 'Non-ferrous metal course' at British Oxygen School, 1965. First solo exhibition at the Woodstock Gallery, London, 1972.

MARTIN, Gina   b.1957
Sculptor. Born Portsmouth, Hampshire. Studied at Portsmouth School of Art and Design, 1976-7 and Falmouth School of Art, 1977-80. Worked as assistant to the sculptor Anthony Caro,* 1981-3, then further study at the Royal College of Art, 1983-5. Artist-in-Residence, Liverpool International Garden Festival, 1984, and then Artist-in-Residence at the Salisbury Festival, 1987.

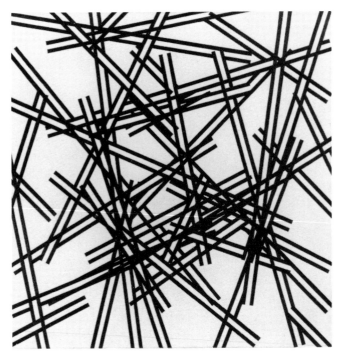

KENNETH MARTIN, 1905-1984. *'Chance and Order 18 (black)'*, 1974. 36in. x 36in. Annely Juda Fine Art.

Teaches at Lanchester Polytechnic and West Sussex College of Design. Solo exhibitions at the Benjamin Rhodes Gallery, 1987 and 1989.

MARTIN, Kenneth   1905-1984

Painter and constructionist. Trained at Sheffield School of Art, 1921-3, and 1927-9. Freelance graphic artist, 1923-9. Studied at RCA, 1929-32. In the 1930s painted landscapes in a naturalistic mode, but during the 1940s his forms became increasingly abstract. His first completely abstract paintings date from 1948 to 1949. In 1951 he began to produce geometrically abstract sculptures, built mainly in metal 'from a nucleus outwards'. He also continued to produce paintings, and was with others, including Mary Martin* his wife, at the forefront of the Constructionist movement in Britain in the 1950s. Retrospective at Tate Gallery, 1975 and Serpentine Gallery, 1985. Honorary Doctorate, RCA, 1976.

Bibl: *Kenneth & Mary Martin*, Annely Juda Fine Art, London, 1987.

MARTIN, Mary   1907-1969

Constructionist and relief maker. Studied at Goldsmiths' College, 1925-9 and RCA, 1929-32. Married the artist Kenneth Martin,* 1930. Her pre-war work consisted of boldly coloured landscapes and still lifes. During the 1940s she moved towards geometric abstraction and in 1950 created her first abstract painting. In 1951 she started producing metal, wood and perspex reliefs, making the cube sliced diagonally in two, her chosen unit. In many of her reliefs its hypotenuse is covered with stainless steel. The reflections this creates confuses the mathematically ordered arrangement of the relief and creates a challenging image, as in *Cross* (Walker Art Gallery, Liverpool). Became a leading figure within the British Constructionist movement in the 1950s and '60s.

Bibl: *Mary Martin*, Tate Gallery, London, 1984; *Kenneth & Mary Martin*, Annely Juda Fine Art, London, 1987.

MARTIN, Phillip   b.1927

Painter. Born East Anglia. Served in the navy from 1946-8. 1948-9 was a lay-brother in the Franciscan brotherhood; left the order in 1949 and devoted himself to painting. In 1951 lived on a yacht run aground on the Thames. First solo show at Fiama Vigo Gallery in Florence. Lived in Paris in 1952 and then Positano in Italy. First exhibition in USA at Pierre Matisse Gallery, New York, 1955.

MARTIN, William Alison   1878/9-1936

Painter. Born Liverpool, Merseyside. Trained at Liverpool School of Art from 1876 and under Augustus John* at the Liverpool University School. Won a travelling scholarship and worked in Paris and Italy. Member of the Liverpool Academy. Early work included mural decorations (Toxteth Branch Library, 1904). Was for a time influenced by Monticelli. Represented in Walker Art Gallery, Liverpool.

MARX, Enid   b.1902

Painter and designer. Born London (distantly related to Karl Marx). Educated at Roedean, Central School of Art and RCA. On leaving the college she joined Baron & Larcher, the Hampstead studio of textile painters, and in 1927 started her own workshop. Executed wood engravings for book covers, fabric designs for London Passenger Transport Board and many other commissions; also wrote and illustrated several children's books. Much interested in English popular decoration and craftwork, she wrote *English Popular and Traditional Art*, 1946, and *English Popular Art*, 1951. Also painted and drew. In 1979 the Camden Art Centre mounted a major exhibition of her work. (Plate 65, p.322.)

MASI, Dennis   b.1942

Sculptor. Born West Virginia, USA. Studied at Seton Hall University, New Jersey, 1960-4 and Brera Academy of Fine Arts, Milan, 1964-6. Lived and worked in Paris, 1966-7, and was a student at S.W. Hayter's* Atelier 17. First solo exhibition at Galleria Il Genobbia, Milan, 1966. 1967 moved to London and studied at the Slade School for a year. During the 1970s and '80s taught at Bradford College of Art and Croydon School of Art. Was the first Artist in Residence at the Imperial War Museum, 1984. Works with environments which usually include stuffed animals, tables, chairs and dramatic lighting in order to create a tense, nihilistic realm. Major touring exhibition, 1987-8, which started at the Third Eye Centre, Glasgow.

MASON, Arnold Henry   1885-1963

Painter. Born Birkenhead, Cheshire. Studied at Macclesfield School of Art, the RCA, the Slade School of Art and in Paris and Rome. Joined the Artists' Rifles in 1915. Exhibited at the RA from 1919 onwards. Elected ARA, 1940, and RA, 1951. Worked extensively in Provence.

MASON, Raymond   b.1922

Relief maker. Born Birmingham, West Midlands. Studied at Birmingham College of Arts and Crafts, 1937-9. Served in the Royal Navy, 1939-41, and was invalided out in 1942. Studied at RCA, 1942-3, and Ruskin School of Drawing and the Slade School of Fine Art, 1943-6. In 1952 produced the sculpture, *Man in the Street,* which he now considers the true beginning of his career. 1953 moved to Paris. 1960 with his wife opened Galerie Janine Hao, Paris. 1962-5 executed a series of street scenes, culminating in *The Crowd* (relief with 99 figures). 1989 held a retrospective at Birmingham Museum and Art Gallery, afterwards at

MARY MARTIN, 1907-1969.
'Grey Relief', 1952.
Painted balsa wood on plywood.
24in. x 24in. x 4½in.
Annely Juda Fine Art.

Manchester City Art Gallery. Works with polyester resin and acrylic relief, creating painted reliefs.

Bibl: *Raymond Mason: Painted Sculptures and Bronzes, 1952-82,* Marlborough Gallery, New York, 1985.

MASON, Robert   b.1946
Painter and sculptor. Born Leeds, Yorkshire. Studied sculpture at Harrogate School of Art and Hornsey College of Art. Awarded Italian Government Scholarship to study at the British School in Rome, 1968-70. First solo exhibitions at Galleria d'Arte, Rovigo, Italy, and Galerie Asinus, Hamburg, West Germany, 1970. Regularly exhibits in Europe and the USA. Solo exhibitions at the Anne Berthoud Gallery, London, and the Katzen Brown Gallery, New York, 1988. Painter of abstracts and near abstracts with nightmarish connotations. Included in the collections of the Arts Council of Great Britain; British Council; Leicester, Rugby and Wakefield City Art Galleries and Fitzwilliam Museum, Cambridge. An exhibition of his paintings based on the building of the new Broadgate office and shopping complex in the City of London was shown at the Yale Center for British Art, New Haven, Connecticut, USA, 1990.

MASON, William   b.1906
Painter. Born Newport, Gwent, Wales. Studied at Newport College of Art, 1923-7, and the RCA, 1927-31. Taught at Scarborough School of Art, 1932-7, and at St. Albans School of Art from 1945. Exhibits at the RA.

MATHEWS, Denis   b.1913
Painter. Born Hampstead, London, son of Richard George Mathews, a Canadian artist. Studied at Slade School of Art. Held first solo exhibition at the Leicester Galleries, London, 1947. Also exhibited with the London Group and 1946 was secretary of the Contemporary Art Society. Travelled extensively.

MATTHEWS, Anthony   b.1925
Painter. Born Cheltenham, Gloucestershire. Studied at Cheltenham College of Art, the RCA and at the University of Reading. Taught at Flintshire Technical College and became Head of Rugby School of Art, 1965. Member of the Royal Cambrian Academy. Solo exhibitions include one at the Gordon Waller Gallery, Coventry, 1971.

MATTHEWS, Philip   1916-1984
Painter. Studied at Maidenhead School of Art and the Euston Road School. Exhibited at the RA and with the NEAC and the London Group. 1946 joined the staff of Camberwell School of Arts and Crafts and eventually became Head of the Fine Art Department. Specialised in portraits and landscapes.

MAUDE-ROXBY, Alice
Painter. Studied at Brighton Polytechnic, 1981-2 and Newcastle upon Tyne Polytechnic, 1982-5. 1986-7 guest student at Kunstakademiet, in Trondheim, Norway. First solo exhibition held at Trondheim City Fort, as part of the

MICHAEL MAYER, b.1932.
'Tic-Toc', 1972. Acrylic.
60in. x 60in.
Gimpel Fils Gallery.

Scandinavian Arts Festival, Norway. Another was held at Sandra Higgins Fine Arts, London, 1990.

MAW, Peter   b.1954
Painter. Born Yorkshire. Studied art at schools in Preston and Cheltenham. Solo exhibitions of his comic figurative paintings include one at Cork Street Fine Arts, London, 1983.

MAXWELL, Donald   1877-1936
Painter and illustrator. Born London. Studied at RCA and the Slade School. Exhibited at the RA from 1906. Acted as Naval artist-correspondent to *The Graphic* for twenty years and during the First World War was official war artist to the Admiralty, visiting Palestine and Mesopotamia. Accompanied the Prince of Wales on his tour of India and illustrated *The Prince of Wales' Eastern Book*. He wrote and illustrated many books on travel and topography, including *A Painter in Palestine* and *Unknown Sussex*. Also illustrated books by Kipling, Hardy and Belloc.

MAXWELL, Hamilton   1830-1923
Painter. Born Glasgow, Scotland. Trained for a business career and lived in Australia, 1852-6 where he dug for gold. On returning to England he worked for two years in Derbyshire and then left for Bombay where he was Sheriff and Chairman of the Bank of Bombay. 1881 returned to Scotland and began painting full-time. Exhibited mostly in Scotland and became President of the Glasgow Art Club, 1909. Painted regularly on the Continent and kept a studio in Paris, 1893-1908.

MAXWELL, John   1905-1962
Painter. Born Dalbeattie, Scotland. Studied at Edinburgh College of Art, 1921-6. 1927 travelled to Italy and Spain and also studied in Paris at the Académie Moderne under Léger and Ozenfant, whose influence was negligible, Maxwell having more interest in the *faux-naïf* art of Klee or Christopher Wood.* On his return to Scotland he joined the staff of Edinburgh College of Art and began painting murals, not uninfluenced by certain Italian Renaissance examples. His oils with their rich impasto, have a dream-like quality closer to the work of Chagall. Elected ARSA, 1945, and RSA, 1949. Having retired from teaching in 1943 he was invited to return to Edinburgh College of Art in 1955, by his close friend William Gillies.* A retrospective was held at the Scottish National Gallery of Modern Art, 1963.

Bibl: David McClure, *John Maxwell*, University Press, Edinburgh, 1975.

MAYER, Michael   b.1932
Painter. Born Kent. Studied at Exeter College of Art, 1955-8. Taught at Exeter College of Art, 1965-89. Included in 'British Painting '74' at Hayward Gallery, 1974. Solo exhibitions at Gimpel Fils, London, 1978, 1981 and 1984. Abstract artist, working with systematic patterning.

MAYERSON, Anna
Painter. Born Australia, educated in Switzerland. Studied at Zurich Museum Art School and at the Vienna Academy. 1938 came to London. 1949-59 lived in Taormina, after-

FRED MAYOR, 1865-1916. *'The Harbour at Cassis'*, c.1908. Watercolour. 12in. x 16in. Mayor Gallery.

wards returning to London. First solo exhibition held at Leger Gallery, London, 1940. Others include one at Annely Juda Fine Art, London, 1972.

MAYFIELD, Andrew   b.1950
Painter. Born Hampshire. Studied at Winchester School of Art, 1968-9 and Goldsmiths' College, 1969-77. Solo exhibitions include one at Posterngate Gallery, Hull, 1985.

MAYNARD, Alister   b.1903
Painter. Born London. Studied briefly at Chelsea School of Art. Painter of murals and allegorical self-portraits. Served for ten years as a soldier in the Middle East, Africa and India. Solo exhibition at Arthur Tooth & Sons, London, 1966.

MAYOR, Fred   1865-1916
Painter. Born near Ripon, Yorkshire. Studied at RCA under Frank Brangwyn* and at the Académie Julian in Paris. Lived in France, 1902-10. From 1908 exhibited at NEAC and at the Leicester Galleries. 1916 member of the International Society. Practised realist genre scenes, close

in style to those of the Newlyn School. Also famous for his spontaneous rendering of beach and market scenes. His son (also called Fred), founded the Mayor Gallery in London.

MAZE, Paul   1887-1979
Painter. Born Le Havre of French parentage. During the First World War, having first attempted to fight with the French Army, he served with the British, afterwards writing *A Frenchman in Khaki*. Became a close friend of Winston Churchill, having made his home in England after the war. A direct, spontaneous painter whose subjects were drawn from whatever he found around him. Represented in the Tate Gallery.

Bibl: *A Tribute to Paul Maze — The Painter and His Time*, Marlborough Gallery, London, 1967.

MEAD, Philip   b.1948
Painter. Born Lincoln, Lincolnshire. Studied at Gloucester College of Art and Technology, 1979-82, and Birmingham Polytechnic, 1983-4. 1987-8 artist-in-residence at National Gallery, London. Has held solo exhibitions at Worcester

ROBERT MEDLEY, b.1905. *'The Butcher's Shop'*, 1937. 28in. x 36in. Louise Hallett Gallery.

City Art Gallery and Bury City Art Gallery. 1979 first solo exhibition held at Gloucester City Art Gallery; another, entitled 'Touch the Earth' at the Winchester Gallery, Winchester, 1988. 1986 was awarded a Greek Government Scholarship and spent ten months in Greece.

MEADOWS, Bernard   b.1915
Born Norwich, Norfolk. Studied at the Norwich School of Art, 1934-6, RCA, 1938-40, and 1948. Studio assistant to Henry Moore,* 1936-9. Served in the RAF, 1941-6. 1956 awarded an Italian state scholarship. 1957 first one-person show at Gimpel Fils. 1948-60 taught at Chelsea School of Art. 1960-79 Professor of Sculpture at RCA. Represented in the collections of the Tate Gallery, the Arts Council, MOMA, New York, The Solomon Guggenheim Museum, New York, among others.

Bibl: *Bernard Meadows at the Royal College of Art, 1960-80,* Fitzwilliam Museum, Cambridge, 1980.

MEDLEY, Robert   b.1905
Painter. Born London. Studied at the Byam Shaw School, 1923-4, the RA Schools, the Slade School of Art, and in Paris, 1926-8. From 1929 exhibited with the London Group, 1937 became a member. 1935-9 worked as a designer for the Group Theatre. Served in the Middle East during the Second World War, also became an official war artist. Occupied various teaching posts after the war, and in 1958 became Head of the Fine Art Department at Camberwell School of Arts and Crafts. Held a retrospective at the Whitechapel Art Gallery, London, 1965, and another at Oxford and elsewhere, 1984.

Bibl: *Robert Medley, Paintings, 1928-1984,* Museum of Modern Art, Oxford and elsewhere, 1984; Robert Medley, *Drawn from the Life: a memoir,* Faber & Faber, London, 1983.

MEDNIKOFF, Reuben   1906-1976
Painter. Born London. Studied at St. Martin's School of Art, 1920. 1923-35 worked in advertising until invited by Grace Pailthorpe* to join her in research into the psychology of art. 1936 contributed to the International Surrealist Exhibition, and to other subsequent Surrealist manifestations. With Grace Pailthorpe, spent the Second World War in America and Canada, pursuing their research and returning to England, 1946.

MEIDNER, Else   b.1901
Painter. Born and studied in Berlin, Germany. Held her first solo exhibition in Berlin, 1932. Came to England in 1939 and became a British subject. Exhibited at the Ben Uri Gallery, London, 1949, and at the Matthiesen Gallery, London, 1956.

MELLAND, Sylvia   b.1929
Painter. Born Cheshire. Studied at art schools in Manchester and London and then went to South Africa for two years. After her return to London she exhibited various mixed exhibitions and in 1932 had her first solo exhibition at the Wertheim Gallery, Manchester. Lived for a period in France but returned to England and attended the Euston Road School. During the 1950s began to concentrate chiefly on printmaking but returned to painting in the mid-1980s. Represented in the following collections: British Museum, South London Art Gallery, New York City Public Library, Leeds City Art Gallery and elsewhere.

MELLIS, Margaret   b.1914
Painter and collagist. Born in Win-Kung-Fu, China, to Scottish parents and came to Britain at the age of one. Studied at Edinburgh College of Art, 1929-33, and won a travelling scholarship which enabled her to study for a year in Paris under André L'Hôte. Held a Fellowship at Edinburgh College of Art, 1935-7; 1938 moved to London and briefly attended the Euston Road School, where she met Adrian Stokes* whom she married. They moved to St. Ives, Cornwall, in 1939, and became central figures in the St. Ives group. Under the influence of Ben Nicholson* and Barbara Hepworth,* who for a period at the start of the war lodged in the Stokes's house, she adopted a Constructivist idiom, in part also inspired by the example of Naum Gabo, who also lived in Cornwall during the war. Following her divorce from Adrian Stokes, she married Francis Davidson;* after a period in France they returned to England. She took up painting again after the war and gradually moved through a series of flower paintings into abstraction. In 1976 she moved to Southwold in Suffolk where found driftwood, often coloured, revived her interest in the making of constructions. (Plate 66, p.322.)

Bibl: *Margaret Mellis Restrospective, 1940-1987,* Redfern Gallery, London, 1987.

MELLON, Campbell A.   1876-1955
Painter. Born Sandhurst, Berkshire. Spent his early days in Nottingham. Not until the end of the First World War, when he was over forty, did he retire from business and devote himself to painting. Moved to Gorleston on Sea, Norfolk, and took painting lessons from Sir John Arnesby Brown* who lived nearby at Haddiscoe. 1924 first exhibited at the RA and showed regularly in its Summer Exhibitions from then on. At Gorleston he painted the beach, its crowds and jetty. Also painted along the Yare below Great Yarmouth and at Walberswick, Breydon, Bradwell, Bungay and Burgh Castle, as well as in Kent and South Wales.

MELVILLE, Arthur   1855-1904
Painter. Born Loanhead-of-Guthrie, Scotland. Studied at the RSA Schools, Edinburgh. First exhibited at the RSA, 1875. 1878 went to Paris and studied for three years at the Académie Julian, afterwards travelling to Egypt, Aden, India and Persia. After two years he returned to Scotland and came into contact with the Glasgow School upon which he had a crucial influence. Began painting with blob-like touches of watercolour which emphasise the decorative nature of the picture. 1899 moved to London; continued to travel, visiting Spain, Morocco and Italy, countries that inspired some of his most original work. Elected ARWS, 1888, and RWS, 1900. Is best known for his paintings of crowd scenes, at Henley Regatta or at Spanish bullfights.

MELVILLE, John   1902-1986
Painter and sculptor. Born London. In 1913 his family moved to Birmingham. Largely self-taught and held his first solo exhibition at the Crescent Theatre, Birmingham, 1932. A Birmingham civil servant, Enoch Lockett, began to buy his paintings in 1934 and guaranteed him a livelihood. 1938 he joined the Surrealist Group and had work illustrated in *London Bulletin.* Continued to exhibit in London and the West Midlands. Brother of Robert Melville, the writer on art.

Bibl: *John Melville 1902-1986. A Memorial Exhibition,* Gothick Dream Fine Art, London, 1987.

MENINSKY, Bernard   1891-1950
Painter. Born in the Ukraine, Russia. His family moved to England soon after his birth. Studied at Liverpool School of Art. Visited Paris 1911. Studied at Slade School of Art, 1912-13. 1914-18 Official War Artist. Exhibited with the NEAC of which he became a member, 1923. Also exhibited with the London Group, joining it in 1919. Taught at Central School of Arts and Crafts, and from 1920 at Westminster School of Art. First solo exhibition held at Goupil Gallery, London, 1919.

Bibl: *Bernard Meninsky,* Arts Council of Great Britain, 1951.

MENINSKY, Philip
Painter. Born London. Became interested in painting while studying accountancy. Began painting seriously in a Japanese POW camp and was selected to make graphic records for war criminal trials. Solo exhibitions at the Citizens Theatre Gallery, Glasgow, 1962 and 1965.

MENPES, Mortimer   1855-1938
Painter. Born Adelaide, Australia. Menpes was a close protégé of Whistler in the 1880s and helped print his master's Venice etchings. In 1888 he visited Japan which influenced his art. He travelled widely in Europe, visiting also India and the Far East. Exhibited at the RA from 1880. Elected RE, 1887, and RI, 1897. In 1900 acted as war artist in South Africa for the *Black and White.*

MENSFORTH, Charlotte   b.1936
Painter. Born Twickenham, Middlesex. Studied at Central School of Arts and Crafts where her teacher was William Roberts.* Began exhibiting with the NEAC, then decided to leave London and work abroad. Has worked as a painter all over Europe, specialising in colour which is rich and subtle.

METEYARD, Sidney Harold   1869-1947
Painter and stained-glass designer. Studied at Birmingham School of Art. Influenced by the Pre-Raphaelites in his love of strong colour and dramatic narrative subjects, and sustained a late development of their style well into the 20th century. Exhibited at the RA, RBA and at the Paris Salon. Elected ARBA, 1902, and RBA, 1908.

METHUEN, Lord (Paul Ayshford)   b.1886
Painter. Born Corsham, Wiltshire. Educated at New College, Oxford. Studied art under Sir Charles Holmes* and subsequently Walter Sickert.* Worked in South Africa, 1910-14. Served in France in the Scots Guards in

Plate 62. LAURA KNIGHT, 1877-1970. *'The Edge of the Cliff'*. 22½in. x 27in. David Messum Fine Paintings, London.

Plate 63. MARY MABBUTT,
b.1951. *'By the Sea'*, 1988.
13in. x 15in.
Paton Gallery, London.

Plate 64. JOHN McLEAN, b.1939. *'Fire Box'*, 1989. Acrylic on canvas. 54½in. x 86in. Francis Graham-Dixon Gallery, London.

MIDDLEDITCH, Edward

the First World War. First solo exhibition held at the Warren Gallery, London, 1928. Elected RBA, 1939, ARWS, 1944, ARA, 1951, RWS, 1952 and RA, 1959. From 1939 President of the RWA.

MIDDLEDITCH, Edward   1923-1987
Painter. Born Chelmsford, Essex. Served in the army, 1942-7, and was awarded the Military Cross. Studied at Regent Street Polytechnic, 1948, and RCA, 1949-52. Emerged from the RCA as one of the realists who became known as the 'Kitchen Sink School'. 1954 first solo exhibition at Beaux Arts Gallery, London, and he continued to show there throughout the 1950s and early 1960s. Occupied various teaching posts and became Head of Fine Art at Norwich School of Art, 1964, a post he retained until his retirement, 1984. His early work dramatised the ordinary — cow parsley, pigeons flapping in a pavement gully, bed springs or an upturned chair — and used a drained, near monochromatic palette to enhance their stark drama. Later, an interest in photography as source material fostered the duality in his art between image and abstract mark. An interest in flux, which first appeared in his paintings of water, reappeared in his late work, in elegiac drawings of cornfields.

Bibl: *Edward Middleditch,* with an essay by Helen Lessore, South Bank Centre, London, 1987.

MIERS, Christopher
Painter. Was a regular soldier until 1986 when he became secretary of the Arts Club, 40 Dover Street. During his time in the army he held several exhibitions, and in 1973 acted as war artist for the army in Northern Ireland. Elected to the RSBA and its council, 1986. Represented in Imperial War Museum.

MILLARD, Patrick   1902-1919
Painter. Born Aspatria, Cumberland. Received early encouragement from W.G. Collingwood, secretary to Ruskin, and studied at Liverpool School of Art and the RA Schools, 1921-5; also studied in Paris, Rome and Madrid where he developed a passion for the then little regarded artist, El Greco. Shared a studio with John Piper* in the 1930s and in 1933 took over the St. John's Wood Art School where he proved an inspiration to many of his students, including John Minton.* Moved on in 1938 and occupied various educational roles, as Headmaster of the Regent Street Polytechnic and finally Principal of Goldsmiths' College. His most original work was done in watercolour which he used with an expressive vigour that preceded John Piper's similar use of this medium. He also excelled at animal drawings.

MILLER, Alain   b.1961
Painter. Studied at Maidenhead School of Art, 1979-80, Brighton Polytechnic, 1981-4, Chelsea School of Art, 1984-5 and Goldsmiths' College, 1985-7. Has exhibited at Anthony Reynolds Gallery, London, 1985, AIR Gallery, London, 1986 and Hansard Gallery, Southampton, 1986.

MILLER, Alan   b.1941
Painter. Studied at Bath Academy of Art, 1959-63 and the Slade School of Art, 1963-5. From 1971 included in mixed exhibitions, e.g. Arts Council and British Council, the Tolly Cobbold and John Moores exhibitions. 1984 major solo exhibition of paintings from 1974-84 held at Ikon Gallery, Birmingham. Work in public collections, e.g. Arts Council, V & A, Edmonton Museum, Unilever, Guardian Newspapers Ltd., Wakefield City Art Gallery.

MILLER, Archibald Elliot Haswell   b.1887
Painter and illustrator. Born Glasgow, Scotland. Studied at Glasgow School of Art, 1906-9, and also in Munich, Berlin, Vienna and Paris. Exhibited at the RA, RSA and elsewhere. Elected RSW, 1924. Became assistant professor at Glasgow School of Art, 1910-14, 1919-30 and then became Keeper and Deputy Director of the National Galleries of Scotland, 1930-52. Specialised in landscapes, portraits and architectural subjects. Also illustrated books.

MILLER, Colin   b.1943
Sculptor. Has been sculpting full-time since 1966 after travelling for two years around the world. First solo exhibition in Norwich, 1969. Worked predominantly in bronze until 1976 when he moved to Paros, the Cyclades, Greece. While there he worked in white Parian marble and olive wood. He returned to live in England, 1984. Executed a commission for J. Lyons & Co., 1987-8.

MILLER, Jack   b.1945
Painter and printmaker. Born Edinburgh, Scotland. Studied at Hornsey College of Art, 1968-9, Brighton College of Art, 1969-72 and the Slade School, 1972-4. From 1970 included in group exhibitions. 1973 first solo exhibition 'Portraits of J.L. Borges' held at Jordan Gallery, London. Most recent 'Six Themes in Pastel' at Thumb Gallery, London, 1984. Work in many public collections, including British Council, V & A, Tate Gallery, Sheffield, Dundee, Perth, Aberdeen and Dudley City Art Galleries.

MILLER, John
Painter. Specialises in watery scenes of the Thames and Venice. Lives at Land's End, Cornwall; member of the Newlyn School of Artists. Elected Fellow of the RBA, 1964. Most recent solo exhibition at the Brotherton Gallery, London, 1979.

MILLER, Norman   b.1926
Painter. Born Leeds, Yorkshire. Studied at Leeds and Bradford Colleges of Art. Four solo exhibitions, one of recent paintings at John Whibley Gallery, London, 1972.

MILLER, Peter   b.1939
Painter. Born Colne, Lancashire. Since 1958 included in mixed shows, e.g. the RA, Free Painters and Sculptors, Northern Young Artists. Makes paintings inspired by Victorian and Edwardian photographs. Major retrospective exhibitions at Billingham Art Gallery and the Haworth Art Gallery. Seven solo shows at the Alwin Gallery, London, the most recent in 1979.

MILLICHIP, Paul   b.1929
Painter. Born Harrow. Studied at Leeds and Brighton College of Art. Included in group exhibitions from 1954. First solo exhibition at Gallery One, London, 1956; a more recent show was held at the Thames Gallery, Eton, 1965. Commissioned by London Transport to make paintings for posters, 1957-8; also received poster commissions from GPO, Shell and National Coal Board. Work in the V & A and the London Transport collection.

MILLS, Russell   b.1952
Mixed media artist and graphic designer. Born Ripon, Yorkshire. Studied at Canterbury College of Art, 1970-1, Maidstone College of Art, 1971-4, RCA, 1974-7. Awarded RCA travelling scholarship to Berlin, 1976. Has exhibited in group shows and held three one-artist exhibitions, the most recent at the Curwen Gallery, 1986. From 1977

included in group shows in London, Paris, USA, Canada, Holland, Australia and Bulgaria. 1980 solo exhibition at Thumb Gallery entitled 'Mixed Media Interpretations of the lyrics and music of Brian Eno'. His interest in texture encourages a wide use of materials, including nail-varnish and liquid boot polish. Represented in V & A Museum.

MILLS, William   b.1923
Painter. Served in RAF during Second World War. Studied at Goldsmiths' College. Solo exhibitions include shows at Leeds and Newcastle Universities, 1955, AIR Gallery, London, 1981, Woodlands Art Gallery, 1986, and the Boundary Gallery, London, 1988, among others. Began as an abstract artist, becoming fiercely expressionist after a visit to Southern Spain transformed his vision. Influenced by David Bomberg.*

MILNE, John   b.1931
Sculptor. Born Eccles, Lancashire. Studied at Salford School of Art, 1945-51, then a year at the Académie de la Grande Chaumière, Paris. 1951 visited Greece and studied at the British School of Archaeology in Athens. 1952 returned to England, settled in St. Ives and became an assistant to Barbara Hepworth. Travelled extensively in Morocco, Persia, Turkey and North Africa. Works in wood, stone, bronze, fibreglass. First solo exhibition with Alan Lowndes,* at Crane Gallery, Manchester, 1959. Most recent large solo exhibition at Louisville, Kentucky, USA, 1977.

MILNE, Malcolm   1887-1954
Painter. Born Cheadle, Cheshire. Articled to a Manchester firm of architects in 1900 but turned to painting instead. Studied at Slade School of Art and Westminster School of Art, 1908-11. First work exhibited with the NEAC, 1912 and was a frequent exhibitor with that society; became a member 1919. 1915 enrolled in First British Ambulance Unit and served in Italy. Painted often in Italy. Spent 1925 in Paris. 1926 left London and went to live at Dykes, Sussex. Painted and travelled in Syria, Turkey, Egypt, France, Switzerland, Sicily. 1937 solo exhibition at Galleries of Picture Hue Ltd., London. 1943 Converted to Roman Catholicism. Left unfinished at his death *Stations of the Cross* for the Church at North Balornock, Glasgow.

MILNER, Marion   b.1900
Painter and writer. Born London. Trained as a Freudian psycho-analyst after taking a science degree. Studied with the painters Cedric Morris* and Arthur Lett-Haines* at their summer school in Essex, 1947. 1953 attended for four years, at weekends, the painting classes of the exiled University of Vilmo in London. Studied under the artist Harry Thubron* at his summer courses. First solo exhibition at Drian Galleries, London in 1971.

MILNER, Peter   b.1951
Pen and ink artist. Born England. Studied at Stourbridge College of Art, 1970-1 and at Dyfed College of Art, 1976-9. First exhibited in a group show at Avon Open Exhibition, Arnolfini, Bristol, 1983.

MILNES, Jennifer   b.1936
Painter. Daughter of the painter Margaret Milnes.* Trained as a teacher at the Froebel Institute, Roehampton, Surrey, and then began to paint when she moved to London in 1958, studying with James Burr at the City Literary Institute. First solo exhibition at University College, Oxford, 1961 and more recently at the Ditchling Gallery, Ditchling, Sussex, 1967.

MILNES, Margaret   b.1908
Painter. Born London, into a family of painters, on her

KEITH MILOW, b.1945. *'Drawing 89/24/94/D'*. Oil on lead and copper. 18in. x 14in. Nigel Greenwood Gallery.

father's side. Her great grandfather was the Victorian landscape artist George Chester. Studied at Regent Street Polytechnic, London, 1926-30, then married and had two daughters, which limited her work until 1945. 1945-55 worked at free lance book illustrations. From 1955 concentrated on portrait painting. Exhibited at the RA, The Paris Salon, the RBA. Solo exhibition at her own gallery, the Ditchling Gallery in Ditchling, Sussex, 1961, and at the Hove Museum of Art.

MILNES-SMITH, John   b.1912
Painter. Born Middlesex. Trained as an architect at the Architectural Association, specialising in historic buildings. During the Second World War he spent three years in the Far East. Began as a representational painter in the 1940s but moved towards abstraction and was represented in 'British Abstract Art' at Gimpel Fils, London, 1951. Became a member of the London Group, 1952; also took part in the 'Metavisual, Tachiste and Abstract' exhibition at the Redfern Gallery, London, 1957. In the 1960s he began his long association with the Drian Galleries; also began working with collage in the 1960s. A retrospective was held at Austin/Desmond Fine Art, London, 1990.

MILOW, Keith   b.1945
Sculptor and printmaker. Born London. Studied at Camberwell School of Art, 1962-7, RCA, 1967-8. 1968 did experimental work at Royal Court Theatre. 1968-70 taught at Ealing School of Art. 1970 Gregory Fellow at Leeds University. 1970 first solo exhibition at Nigel Greenwood Gallery, London.

Plate 65. ENID MARX, b.1902. *'Self-Portrait'*, c.1925.
15¾in. x 13in. Sally Hunter Fine Art.

Plate 66. MARGARET MELLIS, b.1914. *'Number Thirtyfive'*, 1983-4. Relief construction in wood. 20¾in. x 28½in.
Tate Gallery.

Plate 67. LISA MILROY, b.1959. *'Greek Vases'*, 1989. 80in. x 112in. Nicola Jacobs Gallery, London.

Plate 68. ALEXANDER MOFFAT, b.1943. *'Berliners 2'*, 1977. 60¼in. x 78in. Private Collection.

MILROY, Jack   b.1938
Painter and printmaker. Born Glasgow, Scotland. Studied at Scarborough School of Art, 1956-60, University of London, Institute of Education, 1960-1. Since 1961 has lived and worked in London. 1977 first solo exhibition called 'Anagraphs' at Hester van Royan Gallery, London.

Bibl: *'Portraits of the Queen', the Stamp Collages of Jack Milroy,* Somesuch Press, Dallas, Texas, 1979.

MILROY, Lisa   b.1959
Painter. Born Vancouver, Canada. Studied at the Sorbonne, Paris, 1977-8, St. Martin's School of Art, 1978-9 and Goldsmiths' College, 1979-82. First solo exhibition at Nicola Jacobs Gallery, 1984. Since has held further solo shows in Paris, London and San Francisco. Her paintings offer collections of a single object — lightbulbs, shoes, tyres, stamps, Greek vases — which are ordered across the canvas in flat patterns which themselves carry allusions to other representational systems — grids, aerial photography or the organisation of cities, for example. Represented in the Saatchi Collection, London, and elsewhere. 1989 won First Prize, John Moores Liverpool Exhibition 16. (Plate 67, p.323.)

MILWARD, Frith   b.1906
Painter. Born at Worcester Park, Surrey. Studied at Wimbledon Art School, Kingston Art School and RCA, 1933-5. Taught at Abbotsholme and Denstone before joining the staff at Stoke-on-Trent College of Art. Married Peggy Lydia Rogenhagen, also a painter. Exhibited with the London Group, Manchester Art Club and elsewhere. Represented in Stoke-on-Trent Art Gallery.

MINTON, John   1917-1957
Painter and illustrator. Born Great Shelford, Cambridgeshire. Studied at St. John's Wood Art School, 1935-8, under P.F. Millard.* 1938-9 spent eight months in Paris, visiting Les Baux in Provence with Michael Ayrton* and Michael Middleton. Adopted many of the devices employed by the French neo-romantics. 1940 registered as a conscientious objector but in 1941 entered the Pioneer Corps. 1943 was released from the army and for the next three years shared a studio with Robert Colquhoun* and Robert MacBryde.* During this period the influence of Graham Sutherland* gave way to a Picasso-inspired stylisation. Taught at Camberwell, then Central School of Art and finally the Royal College of Art. 1945 held his first solo exhibition at Roland, Browse and Delbanco in London, but afterwards moved to the Lefevre Gallery, holding solo exhibitions there, 1945, 1949, 1950, 1953 and 1956. Also executed theatre designs and a mass of illustrative work for magazines and books, notably for the publishing houses owned by John Lehmann and Paul Elek. Was associated with Soho and was renowned, not only as an artist, but also for his profligate generosity and wit. An innate melancholy, combined with his troubled personal life, led him to take his own life at the age of forty.

Bibl: Frances Spalding, *Dance Till the Stars Come Down: A Biography of John Minton,* John Curtis, London, 1991.

MISTRY, Dhruva   b.1957
Sculptor. Born Kaujari, India. Studied at the Faculty of Fine Arts, University of Baroda, 1974-81, then at the RCA, 1981-3, on a British Council scholarship. From 1976 included in group exhibitions in India. 1981 first solo exhibition at Art Heritage, New Delhi. 1984-5 artist-in-residence at Churchill College and Kettles Yard Gallery, Cambridge. 1985 large touring exhibition of sculptures and drawings opened at Kettles Yard.

MITCHELL, Denis   b.1912
Sculptor. Born Wealdstone, Middlesex. 1930 moved to St. Ives with his brother to start a market garden and then began as a painter. Self-taught. 1949 founder member of the Penwith Society of Arts. 1949-60 worked as assistant to Barbara Hepworth* in St. Ives and during this period began to make his own sculptures. 1957 first one-person exhibition at the AIA Gallery. 1958 joined Waddington Galleries and showed with them, 1961. Represented in the following collections: Tate Gallery, Arts Council, Walker Art Gallery, Liverpool, National Gallery of New South Wales, Australia, National Gallery of Wellington, New Zealand.

MITCHELL, John   b.1942
Painter. Born Surrey. Studied at Kingston College of Art, 1959-64. Taught painting at Lanchester Polytechnic, 1964-71, then at Stourbridge College of Art. Solo exhibition at Camden Arts Centre, London, 1972.

MITZMAN, Richard   b.1945
Sculptor. Born London. Graduated in dentistry at University College Hospital, 1967. His interest in sculpture was kindled during his doctoral studies at the University of Southern California, primarily due to the sculptural approach to dental restorative work he encountered there. As a dentist he is renowned for his carving in amalgam. 1971 began making sculpture. Met Henry Moore* and became his dentist. 1987 abandoned dentistry for full-time work as a sculptor and spent a year at Pietrasanta. Has moved from abstract work to more figurative modes of expression, concentrating exclusively on the female form. First solo exhibition held at Boundary Gallery, London, 1990.

MOFFAT, Alexander   b.1943
Painter. Born Dunfermline, Scotland. Studied at Edinburgh College of Art, 1960-4. 1964-6 worked in an engineering factory in Edinburgh, 1966-74 as a photographer. 1963 he and John Bellany* exhibited their paintings in the open air at Castle Terrace, Edinburgh, and the following two years he showed work outside the RSA. 1968-78 chairman of the 57 Gallery, Edinburgh. Influenced by the German artist, Max Beckman, whose high-keyed colour and sharp black contours he employs. Moffat is chiefly a portraitist. Has also been influenced by R.B. Kitaj.* An exhibition of his portraits was held at the Scottish National Portrait Gallery, 1973. Since 1979 he has taught at Glasgow School of Art where he has been influential on a new generation of Glasgow painters. Has also written on art and selected several exhibitions. (Plate 68, p.323.)

Bibl: *Seven Poets: an Exhibition of Paintings and Drawings by Alexander Moffat,* Third Eye Centre, Glasgow, 1981.

MOIRA, Gerald   1867-1959
Painter. Born London, of Portuguese origin. Studied at RA Schools, 1887-9, and in Paris. From 1891 exhibited at the RA and from 1899 member of the National Portrait Society. 1911 founder member of the National Portrait Society. 1917 elected ARWS, and 1932, RWS. Professor at the RCA, 1900-22. Principal of Edinburgh College of Art, 1924-32. Also painted murals, for the Trocadero Restaurant, the Central Criminal Court and Lloyd's of London.

DRUVA MISTRY, b.1957.
'The Object', 1987. Plaster.
47in. x 28½in. x 28½in.
Nigel Greenwood Gallery.

MOLINS, Lorraine   b.1953
Painter. Studied at Chelsea School of Art, 1971-5, then at Goldsmiths' College, University of London, 1975-6. Won an Arts Council Award, 1977. First one-person exhibition at Swale Arts Festival, Kent, 1977, followed by another at AIR Gallery, London, 1981 and the Ikon Gallery, Birmingham, 1982. Paints on a large scale in an abstract manner.

MONKS, John   b.1954
Painter. Born Manchester, Lancashire. Studied at Liverpool College of Art, 1972-5, and at RCA, 1977-80.

Awarded the John Moores' Scholarship, 1975-6. 1981 first solo exhibition at Hull College of Art, followed by solo exhibitions at the Paton Gallery, 1982 and 1985. Represented in group exhibitions since 1973 when he exhibited in 'Northern Young Contemporaries' Manchester. Represented in the collections of the Contemporary Art Society, London, Metropolitan Museum of Art, New York and the Cleveland Gallery, Middlesbrough.

MONNINGTON, Sir Thomas   1902-1976
Painter. Born London. Studied at Slade School of Art, 1918-22 where he studied decorative painting. Won

Plate 69. CEDRIC MORRIS, 1889-1982. *'Flowers'*, 1927. 24in. x 20in. Private Collection.

Plate 70. WINIFRED NICHOLSON, 1893-1981. *'Candlemass'*, 1951. 25in. x 30in. Private Collection.

MONRO, Nicholas

scholarship to British School at Rome and spent years 1922-5 in Italy. 1924 married the painter Winifred Knights* in Rome. Painted a mural for St. Stephen's Hall in the Palace of Westminster. 1929-31 member of NEAC. 1928-37 worked on a decorative scheme at the Bank of England. 1931 elected ARA and 1938 RA. 1939 joined the design team of the Ministry of Camouflage. Taught at the RA Schools, Camberwell School of Art and the Slade. 1953-5 painted the ceiling of the new Council House, Bristol. 1960s produced abstract paintings. 1966 elected President of RA.

Bibl: *Drawings and Paintings by Sir Thomas Monnington, PRA,* with essays by Judy Egerton and Lawrence Gowing, Royal Academy, London, 1977.

MONRO, Nicholas   b.1936
Sculptor. Born London. Studied at Chelsea School of Art, 1958-62. 1963 taught at Swindon School of Art, then at Chelsea School of Art. 1968 first one-person show at the Robert Fraser Gallery, London. Produces humorous figurative sculpture, life-size.

MOODIE, Donald   1892-1963
Painter. Studied at Edinburgh College of Art. Exhibited at the RSA and was elected ARSA, 1943, and RSA, 1952. President of the SSA, 1937-41. Received the Guthrie Award, 1924, and taught at Edinburgh College of Art, 1919-55.

MOODY, Eric   b.1946
Construction maker. Born Sedgefield, Co. Durham. Studied at Sunderland College of Art, 1964-7, University of London, 1967-8 and 1974-5. Solo exhibitions include one of coloured constructions at AIR Gallery, London.

MOON, Jeremy   1934-1973
Painter. Born Cheshire. Read Law at Christ's College, Cambridge, 1954-7. Studied at Central School of Art, 1961. Taught at St. Martin's School of Art, 1963-8, and Chelsea School of Art, 1967-73. Solo exhibitions held at Rowan Gallery, London, 1963-73, followed by a memorial exhibition, 1974. Represented in Tate Gallery, Fitzwilliam Museum, Cambridge and elsewhere. Hard-edge abstract painter.

Bibl: *Jeremy Moon: paintings and drawings 1962-1973,* Arts Council, London, 1976.

MOON, Mick   b.1937
Painter. Born Edinburgh, Scotland. National Service in Germany, 1956-8. Studied at Chelsea School of Fine Art, 1958-62, and RCA, 1962-3. 1980-1 travelled in India. 1982 artist-in-residence, Prahan College of Further Education, Melbourne, Australia. Solo exhibitions at Waddington Galleries, London, 1970, 1972, 1978 and 1983 and elsewhere. 1986 had an exhibition of monotype at Waddington Graphics.

MOORE, Henry   1898-1986
Sculptor, Born Castleford, Yorkshire, the son of a coalmining engineer. Served in Civil Service Rifles in First World War. Studied at Leeds School of Art, 1919-21, and RCA. In London began visiting the British Museum; also read Roger Fry's* *Vision and Design* and became interested in non-European cultures. Helped sustain the return to direct carving which Jacob Epstein* had instigated. 1928 first solo exhibition held at Warren Gallery, London. 1930 became a member of the Seven and Five Society. 1933 helped Paul Nash* form the avant-garde group, Unit One. Lived in a Hampstead studio, next door to Barbara Hepworth,* and Ben Nicholson.* 1936 took part in the International Surrealist Exhibition. Although he experimented with abstract and biomorphic art during the mid-1930s, his abiding concern has been with the human figure. Reached a wider audience during the war with his 'Shelter' drawings, and in 1943 executed a *Madonna and Child* for St. Matthew's Church, Northampton. 1948 won the International Prize for sculpture at the Venice Biennale. From then on he was an artist of international stature who executed a great many public commissions including a *Reclining Figure* for the UNESCO headquarters in Paris. Received the Order of Merit, 1951 and made a Companion of Honour, 1953. Held numerous exhibitions at home and abroad, including two retrospectives at the Tate Gallery, 1951 and 1968. (Plate 12, p.34.)

Bibl: Roger Berthoud, *Henry Moore,* Faber & Faber, London, 1987.

MOORE, Leslie   1913-1976
Painter. Studied at Cardiff School of Art, 1931-5, under Ceri Richards.* Won a scholarship to the Slade but as his parents could not afford to make up the money needed for the rest of the fees he taught in local grammar schools instead. He served with the Artillery during the war and saw action in the Middle East and Italy. After demobilisation he returned to his post at Whitechurch Grammar School until 1950 when he became, for the next twenty-five years, Art Adviser to Glamorgan Education Authority. Had numerous solo exhibitions in Wales and was for some years chairman of the South Wales Group. A television film on his work was shown on Welsh television in February 1973. Represented in the collections of the National Museum of Wales, the Glynn Vivian Art Gallery at Swansea and elsewhere. A memorial exhibition was held at the National Museum of Wales, Cardiff, 1977.

MOORE, Nicholas   b.1858
Painter. Began exhibiting whilst still at school and has been shown in mixed exhibitions at home and abroad. Two solo exhibitions at Christopher Hull Gallery, London, 1986 and 1988, have demonstrated his fascination with Crete.

MOORE, Percival   1886-1964
Painter. Born Oakworth, Yorkshire. Studied at RCA, 1906-11. Exhibited at the RA and elsewhere. Became Principal of Wakefield School of Art, 1920-7, and of Southampton School of Art, 1927-44.

MOORE, Sally   b.1962
Painter. Born Cardiff, Wales. Studied at Ruskin School of Drawing and Fine Art, Oxford University, 1981-4 and at City of Birmingham Polytechnic, 1986-7. Worked at 'Association of Artists and Designers in Wales' Studios, Cardiff, 1984-6. First solo exhibition at Somerville College, 1982-3, followed by an exhibition at Viriamn Jones Gallery, University College, Cardiff. Since 1983 represented in group exhibitions and included in 'Welsh Group: Travelling Exhibitions'. Represented in the collections of the Contemporary Art Society, and the Sunderland Art Gallery.

MORE-GORDON, Harry
Painter. Born Scotland. Studied at Edinburgh College of Art, and then lectured during the 1960s in the Design Department. Now paints full time, undertaking many portrait commissions. Third solo exhibition at the Scottish Gallery, Edinburgh, 1989.

MORAND C. Morey de   b.1944
Painter. Born Paris, France. Studied at Queen's University, Kingston, Ontario, Canada. Has had several solo exhibitions in London. Her paintings operate on a knife edge between representation and abstraction. She exhibited with Jeffrey Dellow* and James Faure Walker* at Todd Gallery, London, 1988.

MORETON, Eleanor   b.1956
Painter. Born London. Studied at St. Martin's School of Art, 1974-5 and Exeter College of Art and Design, 1975-9. First solo exhibition held at South Hill Park Arts Centre and Wilde Theatre, Bracknell.

MORETON, Vic   b.1951
Painter. Born Bristol, Somerset. Studied at Gloucestershire College of Art and Design, 1969-73, Meadows School of Art, Dallas, Texas, USA, then Gloucestershire College of Art and Design, 1977-8. First solo exhibition at King Street Gallery, Bristol, 1982. Has exhibited regularly in group shows in the United Kingdom and the United States.

MORGAN, Arthur   b.1944
Painter. Born India and came to England, 1954. Studied at Canterbury College of Art and at Kingston College of Art, which he left in 1967. Solo exhibition at the Arnolfini Gallery, Bristol, 1968.

MORGAN, Glyn   b.1926
Painter. Born at Pontypridd, Wales. Studied at Cardiff School of Art, 1942-4 and 1947-8, Camberwell School of Art, 1947, and at East Anglian School of Painting and Drawing every summer since 1945. Lived in Paris, 1951. Regular solo exhibitions since 1947, including one at The Minories, Colchester, 1971.

MORGAN, Howard   b.1949
Painter. Born North Wales. Studied at Newcastle upon Tyne University, 1967-73. 1974 moved to London to set up as a portrait painter. 1978 painted Lord Home of the Hirsel for the Carlton Club. 1983 first solo exhibition at Anthony Mould Limited. 1986 elected to the Royal Society of Portrait Painters. Several of his works are in the National Portrait Gallery.

MORLAND, Francis   b.1934
Sculptor. Born Mundesley, Norfolk. Studied at Central School of Art, 1951-2. National Service, 1952-4. Slade School of Fine Art, 1954-7. 1957-62 travelled and worked in South America. 1963 began teaching at St. Martin's School of Art. 1963 solo exhibitions at New Vision Gallery, and Axiom Gallery, 1969, both in London. Represented in Arts Council Collection.

MORLEY, Harry   1881-1943
Etcher and painter. Born Leicester, Leicestershire. Studied at Leicestershire School of Art from 1897, gained a scholarship to the RCA in 1900 and studied architecture before travels in Italy inspired him to paint. Studied in Paris as a painter in 1908 before settling in London. Elected ARWS, 1927, ARE, 1929, RE and RWS, 1931, ARA, 1936 and acted as Vice-President of the RWS, 1937-41.

Bibl: *Harry Morley 1881-1943: painter, etcher, engraver,* Leicester Museum and Art Gallery, 1981.

MORLEY, John   b.1942
Painter. Born Beckenham, Kent. Studied at Beckenham School of Art, 1957-62, Ravensbourne College of Art, 1962-3, and RA Schools, 1963-6. 1965-6 David Murray Landscape scholarship. 1982 winner of the Royal Academy 'A Christmas Card Competition'. Exhibits with the Piccadilly Gallery, London. Became associated with the Brotherhood of Ruralists and exhibited with them during the 1980s.

MORLEY, Malcolm   b.1931
Painter. Born London. Worked on ships, spent a year in Borstal, then three years in prison; there he became interested in painting and took a correspondence course in art. Studied at Camberwell School of Arts and Crafts, 1952-8 and RCA, 1954-7. After seeing the Tate Gallery's 1956 exhibition, 'Modern Art in the United States' he immediately visited America and emigrated there in 1958, initially supporting himself by working evenings and weekends as a waiter. In this way met Barnett Newman, the Abstract Expressionist painter, who gave him encouragement. Moved from abstract art to the painting of ships, often based on postcards or travel brochures and surrounded by a large white border to enhance their artifice. Taught at various schools in America and in 1977 spent seven months in Berlin. A major exhibition of his work toured Europe and America, 1983-4. 1984 became the first recipient of the Turner Prize awarded by the Patrons of New Art at the Tate Gallery.

Bibl: *Malcolm Morley: Paintings 1965-82,* Whitechapel Art Gallery, London, 1983.

MORRIS, Anthony   b.1938
Painter. Born Headington Quarry, near Oxford. Studied at Oxford School of Art and the RA Schools, where he was taught by Peter Greenham.* Won the David Murray Scholarship for Landscape Painting, 1960. A regular exhibitor at the RA. A fine portraitist, elected RP, he works mostly with low, subdued colour and sensitive handling of tone. Most of his portraits are in private collections. Represented by the RP.

MORRIS, Sir Cedric, Bt.   1889-1982
Painter. Born in Glamorgan, Wales. Studied at the Académie Delacluse, Paris. 1914 joined the Artists Rifles but was later discharged as medically unfit. 1917 painted in Cornwall. 1918 began a life-long friendship with Arthur Lett-Haines* and with him took a cottage overlooking Newlyn Harbour. Moved to Paris in 1921 and attended the Académie Moderne, working under Friesz, L'Hôte and Léger. During 1920s he engaged in friendships with Frances Hodgkins* and Christopher Wood* and may have influenced the latter. 1927 moved back to London and exhibited with the 7 & 5 Society. 1935 moved to Suffolk and, with Lett-Haines, founded the East Anglian School of Painting and Drawing, based first at Dedham, then at Hadleigh. 1950-3 lectured in design at RCA. Continued to travel, teach, paint and garden, developing an especial love of irises. The strength of his paintings lies in their

Plate 71. JULIAN OPIE, b.1958. *'G'*, 1987. Glass, aluminium, stainless steel, foam, PVC, wood, cellulose paint. 25in. x 71½in. x 34in. Lisson Gallery, London.

Plate 72. THERESE OULTON, b.1953. *'Pearl One'*, 1987. 94in. x 84in. Marlborough Fine Art (London) Ltd.

Plate 73. MARGARET PULLEE, b.1910. *'Merrion Street, Leeds'*. Gouache. 22½in. x 30½in. Private Collection.

MORRIS, Desmond

SIR CEDRIC MORRIS,
1889-1982. 'Self portrait', c.1930.
28⅝ in. x 19¼ in.
National Portrait Gallery,
London.

directness and honesty, the unhesitant use of thick paint and undisguised brushmarks to build up a solid tapestry of colour. (Plate 69, p.326.)

Bibl: Richard Morphet, *Cedric Morris*, Tate Gallery, London, 1984.

MORRIS, Desmond   b.1928
Painter. Born Wiltshire. First solo exhibition in Wiltshire, 1948. 1962 he published the *Biology of Art*, followed by *The Naked Ape,* 1968, which became an international best-seller. His biographical work *The Secret Surrealist: The Paintings of Desmond Morris* was published in 1987 to coincide with his solo exhibition at the Mayor Gallery, London. He exhibited there again in 1989. He has also held solo exhibitions in Europe and the USA.

MORRIS, Gerard   b.1955
Painter. Born Glasgow, Scotland. Studied at Glasgow School of Art and after graduating in 1978 worked as a painting and drawing tutor at Glasgow College of Commerce for five years. Spent two years printmaking at Glasgow College of Building and Printing before deciding to move to London to concentrate solely on painting. Has shown in group exhibitions at Warwick Arts Trust, Boundary Gallery and Compass Gallery. His first solo show at Francis Graham-Dixon Gallery, London, 1988, included paintings inspired by St. Brendan's Voyage.

MORRIS, Mali   b.1945
Painter. Travelled in Cyprus, Spain and Canada. First

solo exhibition at the Ikon Gallery, London, 1979, followed by a second solo exhibition at the Nicola Jacobs Gallery, London, 1980. Her work was included in the 'The Tree of Life', South Bank Touring Exhibition, 1989. Solo exhibition at Francis Graham-Dixon Gallery, London, 1990.

MORRISEY, Sean b.1943
Sculptor. Born West of Ireland. Began as a painter, exhibiting in galleries in London, Paris and Dublin. Began to experiment with three-dimensional reliefs and mobiles for the Signals Gallery in Wigmore Street. Then moved into sculpture, working mainly in aluminium and bronze.

MORRISON, James b.1932
Painter and landscape artist. Born Glasgow, Scotland. Studied at Glasgow School of Art, 1950-4. 1957 elected member of SSA, and council member, 1964-7. 1968 won Arts Council Travelling Scholarship to Greece. 1970 elected to Royal Scottish Water Colour Society. 1986 received doctorate from Stirling University. 1989 solo exhibition 'Pen Marc and Marc: From Assyria to Angus' at Scottish Gallery, London.

MORROCCO, Alberto b.1917
Painter. Born Aberdeen, Scotland, of Italian parents. Studied at Gray's School of Art, Aberdeen, 1932-8. 1939 travelled in France and Switzerland. 1940-6 army service. 1950 appointed Head of Painting, Duncan of Jordanstone College of Art, Dundee. 1951 elected Associate of RSA. 1965 elected member of Royal Scottish Society of Painters in Watercolours. 1977 elected member of Royal Glasgow Institute. Regular solo exhibitions since 1949. Represented in all major Scottish collections.

MORTON, Alastair 1910-1963
Constructivist. Born Carlisle, Cumbria. Studied at Edinburgh University and Balliol College, Oxford. 1931 entered family business as Art Director to Edinburgh Weavers. 1936 began to paint and continued until 1962. 1937-8 adapted designs of painters and sculptors to fabrics. Launched 'Constructivist fabrics' at Edinburgh Weavers' New Bond Street showroom. 1939-45 studied hand-loom weaving under Ethel Mairet. Exhibited regularly in group shows, mostly abstracts.

Bibl: Jocelyn Morton, *Three Generations of a Family Textile Firm,* London, 1971.

MORTON, Katy
Painter. Born Leighton Buzzard, Bedfordshire. Studied at Wimbledon School of Art. Travelled in Hong Kong, Singapore, Malaysia and Thailand, and after returning to England utilised her memories of South East Asia in her art. Also sketched plants at Kew Gardens and exhibited these at Leighton Buzzard Library and Arts Centre, 1988.

MOSLIN, Helen b.1956
Painter. Born Manchester, Lancashire. Studied at Liverpool Polytechnic, 1974-9. Exhibited in Serpentine Summer Show 2, 1981. Held a solo exhibition at the Original Picture Shop, London, 1985.

MOSS, Colin William b.1914
Painter. Studied at Plymouth Art School, 1930-4, and RCA, where he received tuition from Gilbert Spencer,* Charles Mahoney* and Percy Horton.* 1938 executed murals for the British Pavilion at the New York World Fair. During the war he worked first as a camouflage

designer and then saw active service in the Middle East. Shortly after demobilisation he took up a teaching position at Ipswich School of Art from which he retired in 1979. Has held numerous solo exhibitions, including a retrospective at Christchurch Mansion, Ipswich. Also exhibits at RA and RWS. Founder-member of the Ipswich Art Group and for a brief period in the early 1960s he studied under Kokoschka* in Salzburg. Represented in the Imperial War Museum.

MOSS, Marlow 1890-1958
Painter and sculptor. Born Marjorie Sewell Moss in Richmond, Surrey. Began studying music. Studied art at St. John's Wood School of Art and then the Slade. Became aware of Cubism and in 1919 moved to a small house in Cornwall. Returned to London and spent much time in the British Museum reading room; Nietzsche's *The Joyful Wisdom* became her bible. 1927 settled in Paris and there met Mondrian. Became a pupil of Léger and Ozenfant and became an abstract artist and one of the founder-members of Abstraction-Création. 1940 returned to England and from 1941 until her death lived in a small, rented house in Penzance. The last two years of her life were a period of intense activity, but she never received the attention she deserved. Represented in the Tate Gallery collection.

Bibl: *Marlow Moss, 1890-1958: Bilder, Konstruktionen, Zeichnungen,* Gimpel and Hanover Galerie, Zürich, 1974.

MOTESICZKY, Marie-Louise von b.1906
Painter. Born Vienna, Austria. Studied at art schools in The Hague, Vienna and Paris, 1922-6, then became a pupil of Max Beckmann in Frankfurt. Moved to England, 1939. First solo exhibition in The Hague, 1938, then others at The Hague and Amsterdam, 1952, Munich, 1954 and a large show at the Beaux Arts Gallery, London, 1960. In 1986 she showed a remarkable series of portraits of her aged and bedridden mother at the Goethe Institute Gallery, London, one of which was purchased by the Tate Gallery. Work also in the collection of the Stedelijk Museum, Amsterdam.

MOUNT, Paul b.1922
Sculptor. Born Newton Abbot, Devon. Studied at Paignton School of Art and the RCA. After war service taught at Winchester School of Art. 1955 founded and directed the Art Department at Yaba Technical Institute in Nigeria. 1962 returned to Britain and settled in Cornwall. Commissioned work for the British Steel Building, London, and for the Swiss Embassy, the Chase Manhattan Bank and Ibadan University, all in Nigeria.

MOURAD, Joumana b.1954
Painter. Born Manchester, Lancashire. Studied at Heatherley School of Art, 1980-1 and Byam Shaw School of Art, London, 1985-6. Included in mixed exhibitions from 1986. First one-person show at Raab Gallery, London, 1988.

MOYNIHAN, Rodrigo b.1910
Painter. Began studying art in Florence and Rome before entering the Slade, 1928-31. Experimented with abstraction in 1930s, exhibiting with others as an 'Objective Abstractionist'. Like others during the late 1930s, he returned to a sober and traditional representation close in spirit to the painting associated with the Euston Road School, to which he never belonged. Served in the Royal Artillery, 1940-3, and as an Official War Artist, 1943-4. His skills as a portraitist developed during and after the

MUIR, Douglas

war. Became Professor of Painting at RCA, 1948, a post he held until 1957. CBE, 1953. Elected ARA, 1944, and RA, 1954. Since 1957 has retained a studio in London but spends much of his time in France. 1968-71 also had a studio in New York.

Bibl: *Rodrigo Moynihan: A Retrospective Exhibition,* Royal Academy of Art, London, 1978; John Ashbery and Richard Shone, *Rodrigo Moynihan,* Thames & Hudson, London, 1988.

MUIR, Douglas   b.1937
Painter. Born Edinburgh, Scotland. Studied at Edinburgh College of Art, 1954-8. Has taught at Birmingham College of Art, 1964-74, and Hull College of Higher Education, 1974-86. One-artist shows include two at the Posterngate Gallery, Hull, 1979 and 1987.

MULDER, Nanny   b.1948
Painter. Born in Leiden, Holland. Studied at Gerrit Rietveld Academy, Amsterdam, 1967-72 and 1973-4. Won a scholarship to study the mezzotint at Academi Sztuk Pienknych, Krakow, Poland, 1972-3. 1976 moved to Edinburgh. 1982-7 lived and taught art in Dublin, Ireland. 1987 returned to Edinburgh and started the Buccleuch School of Drawing and Painting. 1985 first solo exhibition at The Grafton Gallery, Dublin. Represented in the collections of the Aberdeen Art Gallery, Scottish Arts Council and the Arts Council of The Netherlands.

MULLAN, Colette   b.1961
Painter. Born Dungannon, County Tyrone, Northern Ireland. Studied at Ulster Polytechnic, 1979-83. First exhibited at the Octagon Gallery, Belfast.

MUNDY, Henry   b.1919
Painter. Born Birkenhead, Merseyside. Studied at Laird School of Art, Birkenhead, 1933-7 and Camberwell School of Art, 1946-50. First solo show at Hanover Gallery, London, 1960; more recnet one at Kasmin Gallery, London, 1972. Won First Prize at John Moores Liverpool Exhibition in 1961. Taught at Bath Academy of Art in the 1960s. Work in the collections of the Tate Gallery, the CAS, Arts Council, Brooklyn Museum, Bristol Art Gallery and the Carnegie Institute, Pittsburgh. Creates ambiguous canvases with rubbed lines and layered washes.

MUNCASTER, Claude Grahame   1903-1974
Painter. Born West Chiltington, Sussex, the son of Oliver Hall. In November 1945 he adopted the name Muncaster by deed poll, but had exhibited under that name since 1923 and previously as Grahame Hall. Exhibited at RA from 1919. First solo exhibition held 1926 at the Fine Art Society, London. Elected ARWS 1931, RWS 1936, SMA 1929, RBA 1946 and ROI 1948. 1946-7 commissioned to do a series of watercolours of royal presidents. President of RWS, 1951-60 and of SMA 1958. Wrote several books on art. Represented in Tate Gallery, RA, and Royal Collections at Sandringham, Balmoral and Windsor.

MUNNINGS, Alfred   1878-1959
Painter. Born Mendham, Suffolk. Apprenticed to the Norwich lithographers, Page Bros. & Co. Studied at Norwich School of Art and the Académie Julian in Paris. Served in the Canadian Cavalry Brigade in France, 1917-18, and painted 45 war pictures for the Canadian Government. His early gift was for landscape, rural life, gypsies, fairs, cattle and horses. In 1919 began to specialise in equestrian portraits which from then on dominated his output. Settled in Dedham, Suffolk, but during the Second World War kept a stable at Withypool,

Exmoor. Knighted in 1944 and for the next five years served as President of the RA. He also wrote a three-volume autobiography, rich in detail, and became famous for his outspoken criticism of abstraction and other forms of modern art.

MURFIN, Michael   b.1954
Painter. Born St. Neots, Cambridgeshire. Studied at Leicester Polytechnic, 1972-3, Trent Polytechnic, 1973-6, and at Birmingham Polytechnic, 1976-7. Participated in several 'Artist in School' schemes for Bedfordshire, Hertfordshire and Cambridgeshire, 1980-8. First solo exhibition at Huntingdon Public Library in 1978. Regularly exhibited at the Piccadilly Gallery, London, since 1983, and a solo exhibition there in 1988. Commissioned by Imperial College of Science and Technology, London to paint the portrait of Professor Abdus Salam, Nobel Laureate, 1987-8. A realist painter of the unexpected conjunction, gesture or situation. Included in the collections of CAS; Arts Council of Great Britain; Government Art Collection; British Council; Leeds City Art Galleries; Eastern Arts Association; Bedfordshire, Leicestershire and Yorkshire Education Authorities.

MURPHY, John   b.1945
Painter. Has held numerous solo exhibitions since 1971 and has been represented by the Lisson Gallery, London, since the early 1980s. Much of his work has concerned the relationship between texts and images. Both pictorial and verbal elements in each work are often fragments culled from historical sources.

MURPHY, Peter   b.1942
Sculptor. Born Goole, Yorkshire. Studied at Leeds College of Art, 1961-6. Took part in a British Council visit to Soviet Art Schools and Artists, 1980. First solo exhibition at Festival Gallery, Bath, 1979.

MURRAY, Charles   1894-1954
Printmaker and painter. Born Aberdeen, Scotland. Studied at Glasgow School of Art, c.1908-11. 1918-20 served with the White Army in Russia. Returned to Glasgow and won a Prix de Rome for etching, 1922. He studied at the British School in Rome, 1922-5. His use of attenuated, mannerist forms, curved lines and dynamic compositions gave his prints of the late 1920s an unusual intensity. These traits and his interest in the drama of a subject were passed on to one of his students, Ian Fleming.* A breakdown in his health in 1930 temporarily ended his etching career. In 1935, following his marriage and a move to Pinner, he began painting again, landscapes and religious subjects. First solo exhibition held at Leicester Galleries, London, 1946; another followed at Batley Art Gallery, 1950. A memorial exhibition was held at Temple Newsam, Leeds, 1955.

Bibl: Sir John Rothenstein, *Charles Murray 1894-1954,* The Merchant Company Hall, 1977.

MYUUS, Andrew   b.1935
Sculptor. Born London. National Service in the Royal Navy, 1955. Studied agriculture in Edinburgh, 1958-60. Attended Camberwell School of Art and the Slade School of Art, 1960-4. 1964-7 designed and manufactured racing cars. 1967 set up two sculpture studios, one in London and one in Fife. 1978 formed the Scottish Sculpture Trust and started the Sculpture Park at Carrbridge, Invernessshire. First one-person show at Gallery West, Los Angeles, 1968.

JOHN NAPPER, b.1916. *'Jesse'*, 1989. 25in. x 31in. Albemarle Gallery.

NAPPER, John   b.1916
Painter. Born London, the son of John Napper, illustrator. Studied at Dundee School of Art, 1930-3, then the RA schools 1933-4, and finally under Gerald Kelly,* 1936-8. During the Second World War, served as a war artist to the Ceylon Command, 1943-4. First solo exhibition at the Leicester Galleries, 1949. Taught life painting at St. Martin's School of Art, 1949-57. Lived in Paris and painted there, 1957-68. Visiting professor, University of Southern Illinois, USA, 1968-9. Has executed mural decorations in many private homes, and portraits of distinguished sitters including HM The Queen, 1953, and Lady Churchill, 1954. Represented in many public collections, including Walker Gallery, Liverpool, Tel Aviv Museum of Art, Musée d'Art Moderne, Paris, Brighton Art Gallery and Museum.

NASH, David   b.1945
Sculptor. Born Surrey. Trained at Kingston and Chelsea Schools of Art and has lived and worked in Blaenau Ffestiniog, North Wales, since 1967. Has exhibited sculpture and drawings in many parts of the world and in 1978 was the subject of an Arts Council film, *Woodman.*

1981-2 held a fellowship at the Yorkshire Sculpture Park. Responds to the natural environment and to the forces inherent within it, often wittily translating natural forms into a new context. Recent solo exhibitions include one at the Serpentine Gallery, London, 1990.

NASH, John   1893-1977
Painter, wood engraver and illustrator. Born London. Self taught, but encouraged by his brother, Paul Nash,* to make watercolours and comic drawings. First exhibited with his brother at the Dorien Leigh Galleries, 1913. Began to paint in oils in 1914. Served with the Artists Rifles, 1916-18; became Official War Artist, 1918. First art critic for the magazine *London Mercury,* 1919. First solo exhibition at the Goupil Gallery, 1921. Taught art at the Ruskin School, Oxford, 1922-7, and at the RCA, 1934-40, and 1945-57. Joined Observer Corps, 1939, and was an Official War Artist, 1940-4. 1944 went to live at Wormingford in Essex. 1954 retrospective exhibition held at the Leicester Galleries. Better known as a water-colourist than an oil painter, he is associated chiefly with landscape; also a prolific book illustrator, with a specialist interest in botanical works. The best known of these

NASH, Paul

DAVID NASH, b.1945.
'Three Ubus', Spring 1989.
Beech. 114in. high.
Annely Juda Fine Art.

include R. Gathorne-Hardy's *Wild Flowers in Britain*, 1938, and Gilbert White's *The Natural History of Selborne*, 1951 edition.

Bibl: Sir John Rothenstein, *John Nash*, Macdonald, London, 1983.

NASH, Paul   1889-1946
Painter. Born London, but brought up in Buckinghamshire. Studied at Chelsea Polytechnic and Slade School. Originally painted and drew in a Pre-Raphaelite style and, in his landscapes with great feeling for the *genus loci*. His perspective on landscape altered radically after his experience at the Front, where he served in the Artists' Rifles. Eventually made an Official War Artist and produced a memorable record of the war-torn landscape he had witnessed in France. Suffered a breakdown in 1923 and recovered at Dymchurch, Kent, where he painted and drew the sea and the sea wall. 1929 became interested in photography, in its own right and as a tool for painting. (Some of his photographs were published posthumously by his wife as *Fertile Images,* 1951.) To some extent he was influenced by Surrealism in the mid-1930s and exhibited in some of the major Surrealist exhibitions; also founded Unit One in 1933, an avant-garde exhibiting group which folded after a year. Supplemented his income as a painter by writing art criticism. His first love remained landscape. Became interested in prehistoric burial mounds and the equinoxes and read Sir James Frazer's *The Golden Bough*. Reappointed Official War Artist, 1940.

Bibl: Andrew Causey, *Paul Nash,* Oxford University Press, 1980.

NASH, Tom   b.1931
Painter. Born Ammanford, Wales. Studied at Swansea College of Art, 1950-4. His painting developed from naturalistic to abstract while working in the slate quarries of North Wales. Worked in Paris and Provence, 1963. Solo exhibition at Vandyck Theatre, University of Bristol, 1969. Now lives in Dyfed. Represented in the collections of the National Museum of Wales, Arts Council, CAS, Glynn Vivian Gallery, Swansea, and Clare College, Pembroke College, and Churchill College, Cambridge.

NATHAN, Janet   b.1938
Mixed media artist. Born London. Studied at St. Martin's School of Art, 1953-7. First solo exhibition held at Newcastle Polytechnic Art Gallery, 1979. Others held at Riverside Studios, London, 1983, Windsor Old Court, Windsor, 1986 and Warwick Arts Trust, London, 1988. Uses wood, resin and other materials to create abstract reliefs evocative of place, the movement of water and weather.

Bibl: *Janet Nathan: Coloured Constructions 1978-1988,* Warwick Arts Trust, 1988.

NAVIASKY, Philip   1894-
Painter. Born Leeds, Yorkshire. Studied at Leeds School of Art and the RCA. Exhibited at principal London exhibiting venues and in the provinces. Lived for a period in London, but returned to Leeds.

NAWAISKY, Mechtild   b.1906
Painter. Born Prague, Czechoslavakia. Spent her child-

hood in Austria and emigrated to London, 1935. Became Picture Editor of *Picture Post* and *Lilliput* in the 1940s, later moving to the *Observer*. She first made her reputation as a cartoonist and then turned to painting. Also involved herself with mysticism, mythology and self-healing, influences demonstrated in her work. 1964 began teaching at the RA Schools where her eccentricity made her a figure of note. Various solo exhibitions, in London, from 1940 onwards. Has work in the National Portrait Gallery, British Museum and Courtauld Institute Galleries.

NAYLOR, Martin   b.1944

Sculptor and painter. Born Morley, near Leeds, Yorkshire. Attended Dewsbury and Batley Technical and Art School, 1961-3, and Leeds College of Art, 1963. 1966 art adviser to the Psychology Dept., Leeds University, RCA, 1967-70, Gregory Fellow in Sculpture, Leeds University, 1973-4. First solo exhibition in 1966 and has since shown widely in UK, Western Europe and North and South America. 1972 one-person show at the Serpentine Gallery, London. 1974-6 tutor at the RCA and part-time lecturer at Hornsea College of Art and Chelsea School of Art. 1976 visiting Professor at the Ecole Nationale des Beaux Arts, Bourges. 1977 Head of Sculpture, Hornsey College of Art and Tutor in Sculpture at the RCA. 1987 retrospective held at Serpentine Gallery.

NEAGU, Paul   b.1938

Sculptor. Born Bucharest, Romania. Studied at Institute 'N Grigorescu', 1959-65. Settled in London, 1969 and in 1976 became a British subject. 1970s taught at Hornsey College of Art and Chelsea School of Art. 1969 first one-person show at the Amphora Gallery, Bucharest, and has held thirty solo exhibitions since, including 'Nine Catalytic Stations' at the Serpentine Gallery, 1987.

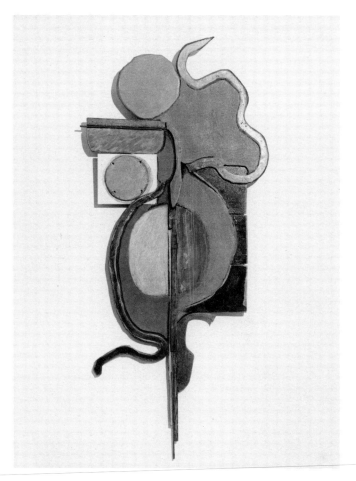

JANET NATHAN, b.1938. *'Manaus Waters'*, 1987. Mixed media on wood and resin. 39in. x 20in. Walker Art Gallery, Liverpool.

MARTIN NAYLOR, b.1944. *'Discarded Sweater'*, 1973. Mixed media. 86in. x 81in. x 32½in. Mayor Rowan Gallery.

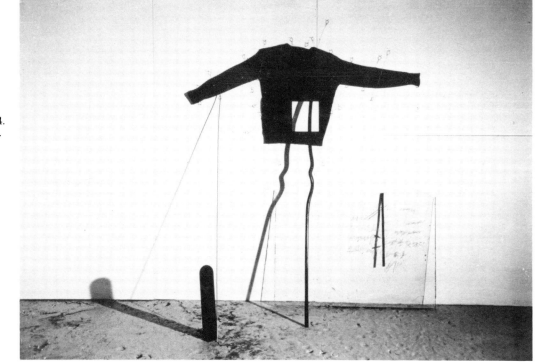

PAUL NEAGU, b.1938.
'Hyphen', 1986. Stainless steel.
40 ¼ in. x 73 ¼ in. x 41in.
Private Collection.

NEAL, Arthur   b.1951
Painter and printmaker. Studied at Camberwell School of
Arts, 1969-73. Published *Eight Poems,* a bound limited
edition of fourteen etchings illustrating poems by Edward
Thomas. He also contributed etchings for a book
celebrating Edward Thomas's centenary. In 1985 he won
second prize at the John Player Portrait Exhibition held at
the National Portrait Gallery.

NEAL, James
Painter. Born London. Studied at St. Martin's School of
Art and at RCA. First solo exhibition at Trafford Gallery,
London, 1955, and others at Wildensteins Gallery,
London, 1958, and the University of Hull, 1973. Included
in mixed exhibitions, including the RA Summer shows.

NEILAND, Brendan   b.1941
Painter and printmaker. Born Lichfield, Staffordshire.
Studied at Birmingham College of Art, 1962-6, and RCA,
1966-9; won the John Minton Scholarship, 1969. From
1969 included in mixed shows. 1971 first solo exhibition at
Angela Flowers Gallery, London. Interested in painting
reflections, and finds his subject matter in the glass and
metal office blocks of modern cities.

NELSON, Steven   b.1961
Painter. Born Whiston. Studied at St. Helen's College of
Art, 1979-80, and at Cardiff College of Art, 1980-3.
Awarded Travel Scholarship Exchange to Nantes, France,
and a Junior Fellowship in Painting, Cheltenham, 1984-5.
First exhibited at Coleg Harlech, Harlech Arts Centre, Wales.

NESSLER, Walter   b.1912
Sculptor. Born Leipzig, Germany. Studied in Dresden and came to London, 1937. Served with the British Army, 1940-7. Studied sculpture at St. Martin's School of Art. Started to make 'relief pictures' in polyester, and first showed these at the Molton Gallery, London, 1961. Work in public collections, including the CAS, Leicester and Lincoln City Art Galleries, and in Israel.

NEVIN, Pete   b.1952
Painter. Born Cheltenham, Gloucestershire. Studied at Mid-Cheshire College of Art, 1978-9, Leeds Polytechnic, 1979-82 and the RCA, 1982-5. 1985 Artist in Residence at Rank Xerox, and 1986 at Canterbury College of Art. 1986 first solo exhibition at Vanessa Devereux Gallery, London; 1987 and 1989 held solo exhibitions at the same gallery. A painter of colourful, figurative and dreamlike compositions that express a magical quality. Included in the collections of Leeds City Art Gallery and Huddersfield Art Gallery.

NEVINSON, Christopher R.W.   1889-1946
Painter and printmaker. Born London, son of Henry Nevinson, author and war correspondent. Studied at St. John's Wood School of Art, 1907-8, and the Slade School of Art, 1908-12. 1912-13 studied in Paris at the Académie Julian, and shared a studio with Modigliani. March 1914 he became a founder member of the London Group, and in June 1914 issued a manifesto *Vital English Art*, along with the Italian futurist painter Marinetti. During the First World War he served in Flanders and France as an ambulance driver, and with the RAMC. 1916 invalided out of the army and 1917 appointed an Official War Artist. 1916 first solo exhibition at Leicester Galleries, London. 1918, second solo exhibition at Leicester Galleries, opened by Lord Beaverbrook. 1919 visited Paris and New York. Wrote *Paint and Prejudice*, published London 1937. Created Chevalier of Legion d'Honneur in 1938 and an ARA in 1939.

Bibl: C.R.W. Nevinson, *Paint and Prejudice,* Methuen, London, 1937.

NEWBERY, Francis   1855-1946
Painter. Born Membury, Devon. Studied at Bridport Art School and the RCA. From 1884 exhibited at principal London galleries. In 1885 he was appointed Director of Glasgow School of Art where he left the imprint of his personality and thought. Later lived at Corfe Castle in Dorset.

NEWBERRY, John Coverdale   b.1934
Painter. Born Horsham, Sussex. Read architecture at Cambridge, 1955-7, and Fine Art at King's College, Newcastle, 1958-60, under Victor Pasmore.* From 1963 taught at Ruskin School of Drawing, Oxford. From 1963 annual exhibitions of watercolours held at Sanders Gallery, Oxford. 1975 retrospective exhibition held at Russell Coates Gallery, Bournemouth. Represented in the collection of the Ashmolean Museum. Elected ARWS, 1990.

NEWLING, John   b.1952
Sculptor. Studied at North Staffordshire Polytechnic, 1971-4, Chelsea School of Art, 1974-5, and Wolverhampton Polytechnic, 1975. Won the Sainsbury Award of Fine Art and an Arts Council award, 1980. Has declared his sculptures to be 'about the relationship between the natural and the measured'.

NEWMAN, Abraham   b.1907
Painter and sculptor. Born Bootle, Lancashire. Studied at Liverpool School of Art, 1927-32 and the RCA, 1932-5. 1936-9 studied law at Liverpool University and became a solicitor. Included in group exhibitions in and around Liverpool from 1928 to the 1970s. First solo show held at Galèrie Mouffe, Paris, 1969; more recent at the Serpentine Gallery, 1978. Chooses subject matter from opera and ballet. Work in the Arts Council collection.

NEWMAN, Avis   b.1946
Painter. Born and works in London. First solo exhibition at Matt's Gallery, London, 1982; most recent, entitled 'Earth of Paradise', at Arnolfini Gallery, Bristol, 1990. Included in mixed exhibitions since 1982. Work in the Tate Gallery.

NEWMAN, Gerald   b.1945
Performance artist. Born Marlborough, Wiltshire. Studied at Salisbury College of Art, 1963-4, Slade School of Art, 1964-70, then won a travelling scholarship to West Germany, 1970. Included in mixed shows from 1970. First solo show at Lisson Gallery, London, 1970. The leitmotif of the sea occurs in his work, which utilises sound. Works presented at the Tate Gallery, 1982.

NEWSOME, Victor   b.1935
Painter and sculptor. Born Leeds, Yorkshire. Studied at Leeds College of Art, 1953-5, and 1957-60, and was Rome Scholar in Painting, 1962-3. Received a Peter Stuyvesant Travel Bursary, 1966. Has taught painting and sculpture in various art colleges and lives in London. His figures and heads are subjected to a mathematical ordering of form into something calm, immaculate and enigmatic.

NEWTON, Algernon   1880-1968
Painter. Born Hampstead, London, and educated at Clare College, Cambridge. Studied under Calderon, the animal painter, at the Slade and at the London School of Art. Also studied the work of Canaletto and Richard Wilson in the National Gallery. 1923 began to paint architectural views of London, conveying great stillness with his precise and meticulous style. Specialised mostly in evening scenes, with the low light enhancing the melancholy sense of place, especially that found in his paintings of canal backwaters.

NICHOLLS, Bertram   1883-1974
Painter. Born Didsbury, Manchester. Studied at Slade School, 1901-4, and in Madrid, Italy and France. From 1912 exhibited at the RA. 1921-31 President of the Manchester Academy of Fine Arts, and 1931-47 PRBA. Frequently visited the Continent in order to paint, but is also associated with Sussex where he lived from 1912. Represented in many public collections, including the Tate Gallery.

NICHOLSON, Ben   1894-1982
Painter and relief-maker. Born Denham, Buckinghamshire. Studied at Slade, 1910-11. Lived abroad, 1912-18. Married Winifred Dacre, 1920. During the 1920s made regular visits to Paris. 1930 first solo exhibition at Lefevre Gallery, London. With Barbara Hepworth,* whom he later married, he joined the Association Abstraction-Création, exhibited at the 7 & 5 Society and was a member of Unit One. 1937 co-edited *Circle,* a compendium of constructivist art. 1939-58 lived in Cornwall. After his

NICHOLSON, E.Q.

SIR WILLIAM NICHOLSON, 1872-1949.
'Whitestone Pond, Hampstead', 1908. 15in. x 11in.
City of Bristol Museum and Art Gallery.

marriage to Hepworth was dissolved he married the photographer Felicitas Vogler and lived in Switzerland. Throughout his long and distinguished career he never surpassed the intensity and concision of his white reliefs, produced during the second half of the 1930s. (Plate 11, p.31.)

Bibl: *Ben Nicholson. Paintings, Reliefs, Drawings,* with an introduction by Herbert Read, Lund Humphries, London, 1948.

NICHOLSON, E.Q.   b.1908
Painter and designer. In 1926 learnt the art of batik in Paris, and then worked, the following year, for the designer Marion Dorn in London. Married the architect Kit Nicholson (brother of Ben Nicholson*), 1931. In the 1930s she continued to design and print fabrics, using batik methods and lino blocks. During the Second World War she taught herself to paint, and in 1945 began to design fabrics for machine printing for Edinburgh Weavers; also designed wallpaper in the 1950s. First solo show of paintings at the Hanover Gallery, 1950; most recent held at Michael Parkin Gallery, London, 1989.

Bibl: *E.Q. Nicholson, designer and painter,* with an introduction by Richard Morphet, The Cygnet Press, London, 1990.

NICHOLSON, Kate   b.1929
Painter. Born Bankshead, Cumbria, only daughter of Ben* and Winifred* Nicholson. Studied at Bath Academy of Art, 1949-54. Taught art at Totnes High School, 1954-6. Went to live in St. Ives, 1956. Became a member of the Penwith Society, 1957. First solo exhibition at Waddington Galleries, 1959; most recent at LYC Gallery, Banks, Brampton, Cumbria, 1981. Included in mixed exhibitions from 1956. She made annual painting visits with her mother to Greece in the 1960s.

NICHOLSON, Simon   1934-1990
Sculptor and designer. Born London, one of triplets born to Barbara Hepworth* and Ben Nicholson.* Studied sculpture at the RCA, 1953-4, then archaeology and anthropology at Trinity College, Cambridge, 1954-8. Lived in St. Ives in the early 1960s. First solo exhibition at McRoberts and Tunnard Gallery, London, 1964. Visiting Professor of Sculpture, Moore College of Art, Philadelphia, 1964-5; tutor, Sculpture Department, University of California, Berkeley, 1965-71. Tutor in practical arts, Open University from 1971. Recent solo exhibition held at York University, 1978.

NICHOLSON, Sir William   1872-1949
Painter. Studied under Herkomer and at the Académie Julian in Paris, where he met James Pryde* and married his sister Mabel. With Pryde he began to produce theatrical posters under the name 'The Beggarstaff Brothers' in the 1890s. After the commercial failure of these posters, Nicholson turned to woodcuts in colour, which were published by Heinemann. As a painter, specialising in portraits, landscapes and still lifes, he was a quintessential Edwardian in his fluid handling of muted tonalities. Also designed for the theatre including the original setting for *Peter Pan.* A dandy and aesthete, he set a standard of elegance which his son, Ben Nicholson,* rebelled against.

Bibl: Lilian Browse, *Sir William Nicholson,* Rupert Hart-Davis, London, 1956.

NICHOLSON, Winifred   1893-1981
(also used the name Winifred Dacre)
Painter. Born Oxford. Studied at Byam Shaw School of Art, London. 1920 married Ben Nicholson* and lived with him in Switzerland, spending part of each year in England. 1925 first solo exhibition at Mayor Gallery. 1926-35 member of 7 & 5 Society and exhibited with them. 1931 separated from Ben Nicholson. 1931-8 lived in Paris. Friendship with members of the Abstract-Création Group, including Hélion, Mondrian and Hartung. From 1939 lived in Cumbria, also painting in France, Hebrides, Greece and Morocco. Solo exhibitions at Leicester Galleries, Reid & Lefèvre and Crane Kalman Galleries. 1987 retrospective exhibition held at Tate Gallery. A colourist, whose influence on Ben Nicholson and other artists is not yet fully assessed. (Plate 70, p.327.)

Bibl: *Unknown Colour: Paintings, Letters, Writings by Winifred Nicholson,* Faber & Faber, London, 1987; *Winifred Nicholson,* Tate Gallery, London, 1987.

NIGHTINGALE, Paula
Painter. Studied at Beckenham Art School and RCA. Awarded Scholarship to Akademie der Bildenden Kunst where she studied etching; later awarded a travelling scholarship to France; has travelled since in Spain and Italy. Has executed two murals in Wandsworth Children's Hospital. First solo exhibition at Gallery 273, Queen Mary College, London, 1972.

NIMPTSCH, Uli   1897-1977
Sculptor. Born Berlin, Germany. Studied at the Applied

Art School, Berlin, 1915-17 and the Academy, Berlin, 1919-26. Travelled to Switzerland and Italy, 1931. Remained in Rome, 1931-8, and then lived in Paris 1939, after which he settled in Britain. First solo exhibition at the Redfern Gallery, London, 1942. Exhibited at the RA from 1957. Elected ARA 1958 and RA 1967. Commissioned to sculpt a statue of Lloyd George for the House of Commons in 1961, which was completed in 1963. Included in the collections of the Tate Gallery, galleries in Liverpool, Manchester, Leeds and Bremen and the Arts Council. Produced figurative sculptures, predominantly in bronze, in a classical humanist tradition.

NIVEN, Margaret Graeme   b.1906
Painter. Studied at Winchester School of Art, Heatherly's School of Fine Art and later under Bernard Adams.* Has exhibited with Cooling's, Wildenstein's and the Leicester Galleries in London and with the RP, the RBA and the RA. Member of the RBA and the RA. Member of the ROI and the National Society of Painters, Sculptors and Print-makers. Has work in the Government Art Collection and Homerton College, Cambridge.

NOAKES, Michael   b.1933
Painter. Studied at RA Schools. Married to the writer Vivien Noakes. Currently President of the ROI. Specialises in portraiture and has painted some of the most outstanding figures of the day, including Lord Denning, Sir Alec Guiness, Lord Mountbatten, Sir Ralph Richardson, Archbishop Runcie, Rt. Hon. Margaret Thatcher and many others. Has also painted many portraits of the Royal Family. Represented by the RP.

NOAKES, Roy
Sculptor. First solo exhibition at Mill Farmhouse, Nr. Saffron Walden, Essex, 1964. Produces portraits and experimental figurative work suggesting the influence of Henry Moore* and George Fullard.*

NOBLE, Guy   b.1959
Painter. Born Margate, Kent. Studied at Medway College of Art, 1976-7 and at the Byam Shaw School of Drawing and Painting, 1977-80. Awarded the British Institute Travelling Scholarship, 1979, taken in France. 1981-2 travelled in Spain and Italy. 1982 Artist-in-Residence, Byam Shaw School of Art. Award winner at National Portrait Gallery, 1981 and 1984 John Player Award. 1987 first solo exhibition held at Jablonski Gallery, London.

Bibl: *Guy Noble,* Jablonski Gallery, London, 1987.

NOBLE, James   b.1919
Painter. While working in family business of building and decorating studied art at evening classes in London under Iain MacNab.* During the Second World War as an assault engineer in the Infantry, he continued to draw. First solo exhibition at Bond Street Gallery, London, 1957. Painted predominantly still lifes and flowers, inspired by Dutch 17th century painters.

NOBLE, Peter   b.1953
Sculptor. Born Hemel Hempstead, Hertfordshire. Studied at St. Martin's School of Art, 1971-6 and at RCA, 1977-80. Spent 1980-1 at Kingston Polytechnic on a Stanley Picker Fellowship, then became Sculptor-in-Residence at Prior Weston School. 1980 awarded RCA travelling award, and 1982 won an award from the Calouste Gulbenkian Foundation and Westminster Arts Council. 1980 first solo

ULI NIMPTSCH, 1897-1977. *'Marietta'*, 1936. Bronze. 60in. high. Leeds City Art Galleries.

341

NORDEN, Gerald

exhibition at Islington Library Gallery, London. Produced experimental work in mixed-media.

NORDEN, Gerald

Painter. Studied at RCA, graduated 1937. First solo exhibition at Trafford Gallery, London, 1969. Regular exhibitor there and at RA. Has written a number of art manuals including *Practical Guide to Perspective* (Pitman). Has a special affinity for still life painting.

NORMAN, Anne   b.1937

Painter. Born London. Studied at Heatherly's and Académie Julian, Paris, 1953-4, and at the Slade, 1954-8. First exhibited at the Serpentine Gallery, London, 1982.

NORMAN, Margaret   1908-1976

Painter. Born Australia. Came to England with her family, 1926. Studied at the West of England College of Art and at the Slade School of Fine Art, 1929-33. First solo exhibition at Royal West of England Academy, Bristol, 1980.

NORRIS, Jane   b.1960

Sculptor, Born Nanuki, Kenya. Lived in Australia, 1962-6. Studied at Bournemouth and Poole College of Art, 1978-9, and at Newport College of Art, 1979-82. 1982-3 she joined the Minstead Lodge Christian Community helping to work a blacksmith's forge. Studied at Birmingham Polytechnic, 1983-4. First exhibited at the ICA, London, 1980.

NORRIS, Norman   b.1932

Painter. Born London. Studied at the Slade School of Art, 1953-6. Awarded Rome Scholarship in painting, 1956-8. Taught at West of England College of Art, 1958-62, then at Chelsea and Camberwell Schools of Art. Work in the Arts Council collection.

NORTON, Margaret

Painter. Born London. Began oil painting in 1959 under the tuition of Kit Barker.* 1966 held her first solo exhibition at The Grange, Rottingdean. Finds many of her subjects in Brighton and its architecture.

NORWICH, Anne   b.1929

Painter. Studied at RCA, 1954, continuing her studies at Belgrade Art School, Yugoslavia, until 1957, later at the American University of Beirut, Lebanon. Returned to England, 1960. First solo exhibition at the AIA Gallery, London, 1967. Commissioned to produce a silk screen poster for Turret Books, 1970. She has also produced etchings and aquatints for Christie's Contemporary Art. Included in the collections of Arts Council of Great Britain, the Contemporary Arts Society and the De Beers Collection of Contemporary Art. Solo exhibitions include one at the Patrick Seale Gallery, London, 1982.

NORWOOD, Peter   b.1929

Painter and sculptor. Studied ceramics at Camberwell School of Art, but turned to painting and sculpture. Exhibited at the Woodstock Gallery, London, 1973.

OAKLEY, Alfred J.   1878-1959
Sculptor. Born High Wycombe, Bucks. His father was an artist-craftsman in furniture. Studied at the City and Guilds School of Art, 1903-8 and in 1910. Served in the RAMC, 1915-18. Exhibited at the RA from 1922. Principally made wooden and bronze sculptures for churches. Represented in the Tate Gallery.

OAKLEY, Charles   b.1925
Painter. Born Manchester, Lancashire. Studied at Slade School of Art, 1948-52. Has taught painting in Belfast and Newcastle, now lives and works in Cumbria. First solo exhibition held at Crane Kalman Gallery, Manchester, 1957. Others include one at the Pyms Gallery, London, 1989. Also exhibits at RA, NEAC and elsewhere. Produces many paintings and *trompe-l'oeil* tableaux which are often based on famous images from the past. Represented in Brighton Art Gallery, Wadham College, Oxford, Salford Art Gallery, Carlisle Art Gallery, the Arts Council of Northern Ireland and Ulster Museum.

O'BRIEN, William Dermod   1865-1945
Painter. Born Foynes, Ireland. Educated at Trinity College, Cambridge. Studied art at the Antwerp Academy under Verlat, 1887, and then at the Académie Julian, Paris, and finally at the Slade School. Lived in London 1893-1901 but spent most of his life in Dublin. Exhibited at the RA but chiefly at the Royal Hibernian Academy of which he became President, 1910.

O'CASEY, Breon   b.1928
Painter and jeweller. Born London. Studied for three years at the Anglo French Art Centre, London. Moved to St. Ives. Assistant to Barbara Hepworth* from 1959-62 and to the sculptor Denis Mitchell.* First solo show of paintings at Somerville College, Oxford, 1954. Often exhibited with the Penwith Society. Turned to making jewellery in precious metals and has also exhibited this widely. Paintings in the collections of Kettles Yard, Cambridge, Leeds and Plymouth City Art Galleries.

OCEAN, Humphrey   b.1951
Painter. Studied at Tunbridge Wells, Brighton and Canterbury Schools of Art, 1967-73. Also a bass player and in 1976 toured the USA as Artist in Residence with Paul McCartney's group Wings. Has painted portrait commissions for the NPG — the poet Philip Larkin — and the Imperial War Museum. Regular exhibitor at the RA and in the annual John Player portrait exhibitions at the NPG. 1982 winner of the Imperial Tobacco Portait Award. 1985 appointed to Artistic Records Committee, Imperial War Museum. Solo exhibition held at the Ferens Art Gallery, Hull, 1986, with subsequent tour.

O'CONNELL, Eilis   b.1953
Sculptor. Born Derry, Northern Ireland. First solo exhibition at Hendricks Gallery, Dublin, 1981, followed by exhibitions at the gallery in 1983 and 1987. Awarded Residency at Delfina Studios Trust for two years, 1988.

O'CONNOR, John   b.1913
Painter. Studied at Leicester College of Art, 1931-4 and at RCA, 1934-7. In the RAF, 1941-7. Elected RE and senior member of the RWS. First solo exhibition at the Zwemmer Gallery, 1955. Exhibited regularly there until 1968. Since 1955 a regular exhibitor at the RA. Works in the collections of the Tate Gallery, RA, British Museum Print Room, the Contemporary Art Society, Oslo Museum and Zurich Museum.

O'CONNOR, Marcel   b.1958
Painter. Born Northern Ireland. Studied at Liverpool and Brighton Polytechnics. 1985-6 he was the arts co-ordinator of the Wester Hailes Festival Association. First solo exhibition at the 369 Gallery, Edinburgh, 1988.

O'CONNOR, Michael   b.1944
Sculptor. Born Seven Kings, Essex. Studied at Shoreditch College of Education, 1963-6. 1968 elected to the Royal Society of British Sculptors. 1968 won an award for a major piece of sculpture for the new Public Library, Balcon, Chester. 1968 first exhibited at Alwin Gallery, London; exhibited there regularly until 1973.

O'CONOR, Roderic   1860-1940
Painter. Born County Roscommon, Ireland. Studied at Metropolitan School of Art, Dublin and subsequently Antwerp before moving to Paris. Influenced by Pissarro, Sisley and by Gauguin with whom he worked at Pont Aven, developing a highly characteristic use of divisionist 'striped' colour. Exhibited chiefly in France.

O'DONNELL, Ron   b.1952
Installation artist and photographer. Born Stirling, Scotland. 1970-6 trainee photographer at Stirling University. 1976 began work as a technical photographer at Edinburgh University. During the 1970s and early 1980s he photographed interiors of old-fashioned shops and slum dwellings. Around 1984 he began making alterations to the interiors of disused buildings, for instance, painting Egyptian frescos over the peeling wallpaper in a tenement building, in this way giving the setting a surreal quality. Much of his work has been a reflection on the political life of Britain and the north-south divide. First solo exhibition held at Stills Gallery, Edinburgh, 1985.

Bibl: *Constructed Narratives: Photographs by Calum Colvin and Ron O'Donnell,* The Photographers Gallery, London, 1986.

O'DONOGHUE, Bernadette   b.1958
Printmaker. Born Greenwich, London. Studied at Wolverhampton Polytechnic, 1979-82 and at Camberwell School of Art, 1983-4. First exhibited in 1982 in the Humberside Print Making Competition.

O'DONAGHUE, Hughie   b.1953
Painter. Born Manchester, Lancashire. Graduated from Goldsmiths' College, 1982. 1977-9 awards from Lincolnshire and Humberside Arts Association. 1979 first one-person show at Ferens Art Gallery, Hull. 1983 Artist-in-Industry Fellowship, Yorkshire Arts Association. 1984 Artist-in-Residence, National Gallery, London. Work in the collections of Arts Council, National Gallery, Ferens Art Gallery, Hull and Huddersfield Art Gallery.

Bibl: *Hughie O'Donoghue, Paintings and Drawings 1983-86,* William Park and Michael Phillipson, Fabian Carlsson Gallery, London, 1986.

O'DRISCOLL, Suzanne   b.1955
Painter. Studied at Central College of Art and Design, London, 1974-7 and at Slade School of Fine Art, 1977-9.

OELMAN, Michael

1980 won the Boise Travelling Scholarship, which enabled her to visit Mexico and Guatemala. 1984 first solo exhibition at the Air Gallery, followed by two solo exhibitions in 1987 at South Hill Park Gallery, Bracknell, Berkshire and at the Anderson O'Day Gallery, London. Represented in the collections of The Southern Arts, British Rail and the John Radcliffe Hospital, Oxford.

OELMAN, Michael   b.1941

Printmaker. Born Llandudno, Wales. Studied at Reading University, 1960-4 and at Central and Slade Schools of Art, 1964-5. 1966 won a French Government Scholarship and 1969 travelled to the Far East. 1970 first exhibited at the Stedlijk Museum, Amsterdam, followed by an exhibition at the Blue Coat Gallery, Liverpool in the same year.

OGDEN, Geoff   b.1929

Painter. Born Ashton-under-Lyne, Lancashire. Studied for a limited period at Manchester School of Art. First solo exhibition at Fieldborne Galleries, London. Represented in the collection of Liverpool University and in the museums of Doncaster, Southport and Oldham.

OGILVIE, Elizabeth   b.1946

Painter and collagist. Born Aberdeen, Scotland. Studied at Edinburgh College of Art, 1964-70. Spent her last year there as a post-graduate working on white plaster reliefs. The constraints of this medium led her towards two-dimensional work and her favoured medium, monochromatic drawing. First solo exhibition held at 57 Gallery, Edinburgh, 1974. That year she discovered, with Robert Callendar,* the Point of Stoer in Sutherland, where the bleak emptiness of the seascape became a major source of inspiration. Sea images were the subject of a solo exhibition, held at the New 57 Gallery, 1976. The sea has remained her subject ever since. 1984 she began to incorporate seaweed into her work, as a metaphor for the moving surface of the sea. Since then she has added to her work coloured wash, collaged handmade paper and scrim. 1981-3 President of the SSA.

Bibl: *Sea Sanctuary,* Talbot Rice Art Centre, University of Edinburgh, 1988.

OKO, Yuji   b.1949

Painter. Born Tokyo, Japan. Studied Political Science at Jeiji University, Tokyo, graduating 1973. 1976 moved to London. Studied at the Byam Shaw School of Art, winning the Painting Prize, 1981. Included in mixed shows since 1981 including the Northern Young Contemporaries. 1986 first one-person show at the Curwen Gallery, London.

OLIVER, Cordelia

Painter and art critic. Born Glasgow, Scotland. Studied at Glasgow School of Art. Since 1960 she has written extensively about art, theatre and dance in *The Guardian* and elsewhere. A deep interest in the theatre led her to make drawings of theatrical groups on stage. 1955-65 works published in *The Glasgow Herald.* 1985 first exhibited at Mac Roberts Arts Centre Art Gallery, Stirling, Scotland.

OLIVER, Ken   b.1948

Painter. Born Yorkshire. Studied at Sheffield College of Art, 1967-71 and at Royal College of Art, 1971-4. 1977 first solo exhibition at the AIR Gallery, London. Included in the

collections of the V & A Museum, Arts Council of Great Britain, Sheffield City Art Galleries and in collections in Europe. 1977 received an Arts Council award. His work has moved in and out of abstraction and reveals a fascination with structure, framing devices and process.

OLIVER, Madge   1874-1924

Painter. Born Harrogate, Yorkshire. Studied at Slade School of Art. Mainly painted in France, settling there in 1910, in Cassis near Marseilles. 1924 exhibited at Druet Galleries, Paris. 1935 memorial exhibition at J. Leger & Son, London.

OLIVER, Maureen   b.1947

Painter. Born Lewisham, London. Studied at Camberwell School of Art, 1964-8. 1972 first solo exhibition at Wandsworth Libraries, London.

OLIVER, Patrick   b.1933

Painter. Born Leeds, Yorkshire. Studied at Leeds College of Art and Design, and St. Peter's Loft, St. Ives, under Peter Lanyon. First solo exhibition at Queen Square Gallery, Leeds, 1966. Represented in Wakefield City Art Gallery.

OLIVER, Peter   b.1927

Painter. Born Jersey, Channel Islands. First solo exhibition at the Redfern Gallery, London, 1955. Exhibited regularly there until 1963. Represented in the Lytton Foundation, California, USA, CAS and Leicestershire Education Authority.

OLSSON, Julius   1864-1942

Painter. Born London. Studied in London and abroad. Exhibited at the RA from 1890. Elected a member of the NEAC in 1891, ARA, 1914, PROI, 1919 and RA, 1920. Lived at St. Ives where he established a school for painters, and is best known for his seascapes, many of them seen at night. Represented in many public collections.

O'MALLEY, Tony   b.1913

Painter. Born Callan, Co. Kilkenny, Ireland. Began painting in 1948, in hospital during a long illness. Settled in St. Ives in 1955. Regularly exhibits with the Penwith Society of which he is a member. Member of Newlyn Society of Artists. Paints abstract paintings as well as figurative drawings and watercolours. Represented in the Contemporary Arts Society.

O'NEILL, Daniel   1920-1974

Painter. Born Belfast, Northern Ireland. Self-taught artist who worked as an electrician and painted in his spare time. Began painting full-time in 1948. First solo exhibition in 1948 at the Waddington Galleries, Dublin. Exhibited regularly at the Galleries until 1955. Produces romantic figurative and landscape paintings. Represented in The Municipal Gallery, Dublin, the Arts Council, Dublin, the Ulster Museum, The Municipal Gallery, Cork, the National Gallery, Melbourne, Australia and in the Arts Council, Wales.

O'NEILL, Shirley   b.1947

Painter. Born Warwickshire. Studied at Walthamstow College of Art, 1966-9 and at RA Schools, 1969-72. First solo exhibition at Francis Graham-Dixon Gallery, London, 1989.

BRYAN ORGAN, b.1935. *'Charles, Prince of Wales'*, 1980. Acrylic on canvas. 70in. x 70⅛ in.
National Portrait Gallery, London.

ONWIN, Glen b.1947

Mixed media artist. Born Edinburgh, Scotland. Studied painting at Edinburgh College of Art, 1966-71. Towards the end of his time there he began incorporating natural chemical substances into his work, including salt. 1973 he discovered a vast salt marsh on the east coast of Scotland, near Dunbar, consisting of hundreds of pools of evaporating salt water. Made a series of photographs of the site and transferred the natural decay it evoked into drawings and constructions on to which he added a variety of materials; he saw in salt a symbol, both life giving and destroying. He has subsequently developed the theme of elemental decomposition. In the 1980s he has introduced a great variety of natural substances such as leaves, sulphur, ash and earth into his work. First solo exhibition 'Saltmarsh' held at Scottish Arts Council Gallery, Edinburgh, 1975; others include 'Revenges of Nature' held at the Fruitmarket Gallery, Edinburgh, 1988. Represented in Glasgow City Art Gallery and elsewhere.

Bibl: Glen Onwin, *The Recovery of Dissolved Substances*, Arnolfini Gallery, Bristol, 1978.

OPIE, Julian b.1958

Sculptor. Born London. Studied at Goldsmiths' College, 1979-82. First solo exhibition held at Lisson Gallery, London, 1983. Exhibited at Kolnischer, Kunstverein, Cologne, West Germany, 1984, and has since then enjoyed an international reputation. Began working with steel sheets, which are cut and painted to create subjects, both familiar and humourous, and which often refer to tools, consumer goods or famous paintings. Recent work has involved transparent and opaque partitions that create spaces reminiscent of airport architecture. (Plate 71, p.330.)

OPPENHEIM, Duncan b.1904

Painter. Born Lancashire. Has lived and worked in London since 1929; since retirement in 1974 he has painted full-time. 1971 first solo exhibition at the Upper Grosvenor Gallery, London. 1957-83 exhibited regularly at RA Summer Exhibitions.

O'RAWE, Anne b.1955

Painter. Born Belfast, Northern Ireland. Graduated from RCA, 1981. Represented in group exhibitions at RCA since 1982. Represented in the Leicestershire Collection for Schools and Colleges and the Unilever Collection.

ORGAN, Bryan b.1935

Painter. Born Leicester. Studied at Loughborough College of Art, 1951-5 and at RA Schools, 1955-9. Awarded David Murray Travelling Scholarships to Malta and Italy, 1957-9. First solo exhibition at Leicester City Art Gallery, 1958. Has established himself as a leading portraitist, his subjects including Prince Charles (National Portrait Gallery), Princess of Wales and President Mitterand.

SIR WILLIAM ORPEN,
1878-1931. *'Self portrait'*, 1912.
24in. x 19¾in.
Peter Nahum Ltd.

ORGAN, Margaret   b.1946
Mixed media artist. Born Rochdale, Lancashire. Studied at Brighton Polytechnic, 1975-8 and at Chelsea School of Art, 1978-9. 1978 first exhibited in 'Making the Grade' at Arnolfini Gallery, Bristol. 1980 won the Southern Arts Association Award.

ORLICK, Henry   b.1947
Painter. Studied at Gloucestershire College of Art and Brighton College of Art. Lived in NY, 1981-4. First solo exhibition at the Acoris Surrealist Art Centre, 1972. His paintings develop out of his interest in the motion of the brush and how this expresses the force and essence of the form it conjures forth.

OROVIDA — see PISSARRO, Orovida Camille

ORPEN, William   1878-1931
Painter. Born County Dublin, Ireland. Studied at Metropolitan School of Art, Dublin, 1890-7, and Slade School of Fine Art, 1897-9. 1902 opened a School of Art in Flood Street, Chelsea with Augustus John.* 1904 elected associate of the RHA. 1908 began to exhibit regularly at RA. 1917 appointed Official War Artist. 1921 published his war memoirs as *An Onlooker in France.* Enjoyed a hugely successful career. Founder member of the National Portrait Society. Elected ARA, 1919, and RA, 1921. Knighted 1918. By the 1920s he was England's most fashionable portrait painter.

Bibl: Bruce Arnold, *Mirror to an Age,* Jonathan Cape, London, 1982.

ORR, Chris   b.1943

Printmaker. Born London. Studied at Ravensbourne College of Art, 1959-63, Hornsey College of Art, 1963-4 and RCA, 1964-7. Has taught at RCA and elsewhere. His prints are humorous and rich in incident. 1971 first solo exhibition at Serpentine Gallery, London. Since 1978 has exhibited regularly at the Thumb Gallery, London. Represented in the Arts Council of Great Britain, V & A, Welsh Arts Council, British Council, Ulster Museum, London Museum, Bradford Museum and Art Gallery and the National Museum of Wales.

Bibl: 'Arena' BBC TV, *The Swish of the Curtain,* 1980.

OSBORNE, Malcolm   1880-1963

Etcher and engraver of figures and landscapes. Born Frome, Somerset. Studied at Bristol School of Art and at the RCA under Lethaby and Short. Exhibited regularly with the RA and RE. Elected ARA, 1905, RE, 1909, ARA, 1918, RA, 1926, and PRE, 1938. Solo exhibition of etchings at the Rembrandt Gallery, London, 1929. Professor of Engraving at the RCA. Created CBE, 1948.

OSCAR, A.   b.1919

Painter. Born Sheldon Williams in Cork, Ireland, but changed his name when a fellow student at art school said he had just been to Sheldon Williams' memorial show. Studied at Central School of Arts and Crafts and abroad. 1936 first solo exhibition held at Galerie Zak, Paris; many others followed, including one at Windsor Arts Centre, 1986.

OULESS, Walter William   1848-1933

Painter. Born St. Helier, Jersey, son of the marine painter, P.J. Ouless. Studied at RA Schools, 1865-9. From 1869 exhibited at RA, 1877 elected ARA, and 1881, RA. Won gold and silver medals at Berlin, Munich and Paris. Began as a genre painter but later turned to portraiture, with great success.

OULTON, Thérèse   b.1953

Painter. Born Shrewsbury, Shropshire. Attended St. Martin's School of Art, 1979-83 and then the RCA. From 1982 included in mixed media exhibitions, beginning with the John Moores Liverpool show of that year. 1984 first one-person show at Gimpel Fils Gallery, London. 1987 shortlisted for the Tate Gallery's Turner Prize. An abstract artist in whose work critics have found a further extension of the romantic landscape tradition. Has developed a highly personal technique whereby small touches of paint are built into ridges and declivities that expand and diminish with rhythmic effect. In some instances musical titles have been applied to her pictures. Others have evoked an underwater world. Represented by Marlborough Fine Art. Work in the collections of Arts Council, British Council, Metropolitan Museum of Art, New York, Unilever, Harris Museum and Art Gallery, Preston, Walker Art Gallery, Liverpool. (Plate 72, p.330.)

Bibl: *Thérèse Oulton: recent paintings,* Marlborough Fine Art, London, 1990.

OVENDEN, Graham   b.1943

Painter. Born Arlesford, Hampshire. Studied at the RCA, 1965-8. Became a founder-member of the Brotherhood of Ruralists and has been a key figure within this group. He has written, illustrated or edited a number of books for Academy Editions, including several on the subject of early photography. Was commissioned to illustrated Emily Bronte's *Wuthering Heights* in 1981 by Carl Bertelsman, Gütersloh, Germany. Has exhibited regularly with the Piccadilly Gallery, London, and in all the Brotherhood of Ruralists exhibitions, the most significant of which was that held in 1981 at the Arnolfini Gallery, Bristol and elsewhere.

OWEN, Jane   b.1965

Painter. Born London. Studied at Central School of Art, 1983-4, and Canterbury College of Art, 1984-7. 1987 began exhibiting, and held her first solo exhibition at Merz Contemporary Art, London, 1990. Her paintings are vibrantly coloured and deal with human situations, often tense or ambiguous.

OXTOBY, David   b.1938

Painter and printmaker. Born Horseforth, Yorkshire. Studied at Bradford Regional Art School and at the RA Schools, 1960-4. Made his chosen subject contemporary music and musicians and throughout his career has celebrated the leading pop singers of the 1950s, '60s and '70s. 1964 became Visiting Professor at Minneapolis College of Art, Minnesota, USA. 1966-72 taught at Maidstone College of Art whilst nightclubbing and painting in London. His friend, Norman Stevens,* introduced him to etching and in 1974 he produced forty etchings within nine months. 1977 exhibited 'Oxtoby's Rockers' at the Redfern Gallery, London, where another exhibition was held, 1981; this was followed by a period of retreat and reassessment, then a return to his former interests in a more post-modernist mode. 'Oxtoby's Oxtoby's' was held at the Cartwright Hall, Bradford, 1990.

PACHECO, Ana M.   b.1943
Sculptor. Born Brazil. Studied at University of Goias, Brazil. British Council Scholarship, Slade School of Arts, 1973-5. 1970 held first solo exhibition at Cultural Foundation Brasilia, Brazil; another at Blackheath Gallery, London, 1979. Until recently Head of Sculpture at Norwich School of Art.

PACKENHAM, Jack   b.1938
Painter. Born Dublin, Ireland. Studied languages and philosophy at Queen's University, Belfast. Spent the winter of 1959-60 writing and painting in the island of Ibiza and later lived in Dorset. Recent solo exhibitions include one at the Hendriks Gallery, Dublin, 1987.

PAICE, Philip Stuart   1884-1940
Painter. Settled in Merseyside from Canada and USA, c.1920. Art master at the Birkenhead Institute. Member and President of the Liver Sketching Club. Exhibited in London and Liverpool.

PAILTHORPE, Grace W.   1883-1971
Painter. Born St. Leonards-on-Sea, Sussex. Served in the First World War as a surgeon. Travelled extensively abroad and did medical work in Western Australia, 1918-22. Returned to England, 1922, and became a Freudian analyst. Started research into criminal psychology, 1923, later publishing books on the psychology of delinquency, also founding the Institute for the Scientific Treatment of Deliquency (now known as the Portman Clinic). Met Reuben Mednikoff,* 1935, and with him embarked on research into the psychology of art. Contributed to the International Surrealist Exhibition where her work was admired by André Breton, 1936; also contributed to the *London Bulletin* as well as to other Surrealist exhibitions. Continued her research in America and Canada, 1939-46, returning to Britain, 1946.

PALLISER, Herbert William   1883-1963
Sculptor. Born Northallerton, Yorkshire. Served pupilage with an architect in Harrogate before going to the Central School of Arts and Crafts, 1906-11, and then at the Slade School, 1911-14, where he studied under J. Harvard Thomas. From 1921 exhibited at the RA. Taught at the Royal College of Art. Commissions include Calcutta War Memorial, 1924, two pediments on Victoria House, Bloomsbury Square, 1929, and Roosevelt Memorial, Westminster Abbey, 1946, among others.

PALMER, Alfred   1877-1951
Painter. Born London. Entered Clapham School of Art, 1895, the RA Schools, 1898, and afterwards, on John Singer Sargent's* advice, enrolled at the Académie Julian in Paris. Travelled extensively and exhibited at the Paris Salon. During the First World War he worked for British Intelligence, then for the Corps of Interpreters and was sent to sketch German prisoners in a POW camp. 1922 elected a member of ROI. Visited Africa and painted the Zulu and Bantu peoples. 1953 major retrospective exhibition held at RBA Galleries, London.

PALMER, Eugene
Painter. Born Kingston, Jamaica. Moved to Britain, 1965. Studied art and worked on various inner city art projects with young people in London. 1988 solo exhibition at Commonwealth Institute, London.

PALMER, Garrick   b.1933
Painter. Born Portsmouth, Hampshire. Studied at Portsmouth College of Art and RA Schools. Awarded David Murray Landscape Scholarships, 1955, 1956 and 1957. 1958 won the RA Gold Medal and the Edward Stott travelling scholarship. Exhibits regularly at RA and elsewhere.

PALMER, Lilli
Painter. Worked in the theatre. Explored a semi-figurative approach and held her first solo exhibition at Tooth's, 1965; others include one at the same gallery, 1972.

PALMER, Roger   b.1946
Painter. Born Portsmouth, Hampshire. Studied at Portsmouth College of Art, 1964-8, and Chelsea School of Art, 1968-9. 1970 first solo exhibition held at Warwick University; others include one at Angela Flowers Gallery, London, 1976.

PALTENGHI, Julian   b.1955
Painter and sculptor. Studied at Loughborough College of Art, 1976-80. Painted the backdrop for *Cession* by André du Bouchet, staged at the Pompidou Centre, Paris, 1981. First solo exhibition at the William Maler Gallery, Ludlow, Shropshire.

PANCHAL, Shanti   b.1951
Painter. Born Gujarat, India. Studied at Sir J.J. School of Art, Bombay, 1971-7 and Byam Shaw School of Art, London, 1978-80. 1985 executed an anti-racist mural at Lowood Street, East London, commissioned by the GLC. Has also occupied various artist-in-residency schemes in East London. His figurative paintings have an especial poignancy owing to their stillness, gentleness and poise. Has held several solo exhibitions in London and in 1986 won a GLC Spirit of London award.

Bibl: *Earthen Shades: Paintings by Shanti Panchal,* Bradford Art Galleries and Museums, 1988.

PANKHURST, Sylvia   1882-1960
Painter and suffragette. Born Manchester, Lancashire. Studied at RCA. After her mother, Emmeline Pankhurst, founded the Women's Social and Political Union, much of Sylvia's artistic energy went into the making of banners and other paraphernalia to support the Women's Cause. In 1907 she left London to canvass for the WSPU and to paint working conditions in industry and agriculture. Broke away from the WSPU when it became actively militant and sought to find a more broadly based movement. She was regularly imprisoned and endured hunger strikes and force feeding. Fired by anti-fascist convictions she continued to lead a life dominated by politics and for twenty years edited the *New Times and Ethiopia News.* In 1956 she moved to Addis Ababa where she founded and edited the monthly *Ethiopia Observer.* She died in Ethiopia.

Bibl: Richard Pankhurst, *Sylvia Pankhurst — Artist and Crusader,* Paddington Press, London, 1979.

PANTING, John   1940-1974
Sculptor. Born New Zealand. Studied at Canterbury University, New Zealand, 1959-62, and RCA, London, 1964-7. Taught at the RCA and Central School of Art and Design. Worked mostly in steel and fibreglass, producing abstact sculpture often very subtle in conception. Solo exhibitions include two at Galerie Swart, Amsterdam, 1967 and 1968 and another at West of England Academy, Bristol, 1971. Work in the collections of the Arts Council and the Tate Gallery.

SIR EDUARDO PAOLOZZI,
CBE, RA, b.1924.
'Study for Self-Portrait', 1988.
Bronze 34in. x 8in. x 11½ in.
Private Collection.

PAOLOZZI, Eduardo   b.1924

Sculptor. Born Leith, Scotland. Studied at Edinburgh
College of Art and at the Slade. 1947 went to live in Paris,
where he met Giacometti, among others, and was
considerably influenced by Dada and Surrealism.
Developed the approach of a collagist in two and three
dimensions. 1949 returned to London and in 1952 founded,
with others, the Independent Group. At its first meeting at
the ICA, Paolozzi projected numerous images of
advertisements, comic strips, industrial machinery, etc.,
in random order and with no verbal commentary — a
'lecture' — which became a landmark in the history of
British Pop Art. He also took part in the 1956 exhibition,
'This is Tomorrow' at the Whitechapel Art Gallery. His
sculptures of the 1950s combined mechanical, biological
and totemic features. In the 1960s he worked mostly in
aluminium, sometimes brightly painted, chromed or
polished. He also produced collage-based prints, including
the series *As Is When,* based on the life and work of Ludwig
Wittgenstein. 1960 retrospective at the Venice Biennale;
1971 at the Tate Gallery, followed by another at the
Nationalgalerie, West Berlin, 1975. 1977 print
retrospective at the V & A. 1979 was commissioned to
decorate Tottenham Court Road Underground Station
with brightly coloured mosaics (installed 1983-5). 1984
retrospective at Royal Scottish Academy, Edinburgh,
which travelled to Germany, France and Ireland. 1985
arranged the exhibition 'Lost Magic Kingdoms' at the
Museum of Mankind, London, in which 'primitive'
exhibits were shown alongside modern art. Taught at
RCA, 1968-89, and was Professor of Sculpture at Academy
of Fine Art in Munich for nine years. 1986 Her Majesty's
Sculptor in Ordinary for Scotland. 1988 knighted. Will be
doing the major sculpture for the new British Library
forecourt — a seated figure of Sir Isaac Newton.

Bibl: *Eduardo Paolozzi. Sculpture, Drawings, Collages and
Graphics,* Arts Council, London, 1976.

PARK, Alistair

PARK, Alistair   1930-1984
Painter. Born Edinburgh, Scotland. Studied at Edinburgh College of Art, 1949-52. National Service, 1953-5, then taught part-time at Edinburgh College of Art, and was art teacher in an Edinburgh secondary school, 1957-63. 1963 joined the staff of Bradford College of Art, moved from there to Newcastle upon Tyne College of Art, 1967, where he remained until his death. His first solo exhibitions were held at the 57 Gallery, Edinburgh, 1957 and 1958. During the 1960s he exhibited extensively throughout Britain. He continued to exhibit at the Richard Demarco Gallery, Edinburgh, with his last solo exhibition in 1983. Moved from an interest in elemental paintings of the human figure into non-figurative art.

PARK, Emma   b.1950
Sculptor. Born Yorkshire. Studied at Chelsea School of Art, 1968-72, and at Slade School of Art, 1972-4. 1974 awarded the Boise Travelling Scholarship and 1979 the Greater London Arts Association Major Award. 1980 first solo exhibition at the South East Gallery. Works mostly with wood, using simple geometrical units.

PARK, Gerald   b.1937
Painter. Born Cleckheaton, Yorkshire. Studied at Batley College of Art, Yorkshire and Liverpool College of Art, 1954-9, and Slade School of Art, 1959-61. Visiting tutor at South Devon College of Art, 1961-6. Lecturer in Painting, Manchester College of Art, 1966-9. Visiting Professor in Art, University of Wisconsin, USA, 1974-5. Showed in group exhibitions from 1959. First solo exhibition held at New Art Centre, London, 1966; more recent at Park Square Gallery, Leeds, 1978 and the New Art Centre, 1979. Work in the Arts Council collection and the Universities of Newcastle, Leeds and Leicester.

PARK, John   1880-1962
Painter. Born Preston, Lancashire. Studied under Julius Olsson,* who was so impressed by Park's ability that he refused payment for tuition. Travelled widely and exhibited at the Paris Salon, where he was awarded a Gold Medal, 1924. Helped form the St. Ives Society of Artists. Exhibited regularly at the RA. 1923 elected to the ROI and 1932 the RBA. Skilful naturalist, capturing the perpetual movement of light on water with a few deft stokes. Patrick Heron,* writing in the *New Statesman,* compared Park's work favourably with that of Duncan Grant.* Represented in the Tate Gallery.

PARKER, Agnes Miller   1895-1980
Wood engraver. Born Irvine, Scotland. Studied at Glasgow School of Art and also under two wood engravers, Gertrude Hermes* and Blair Hughes-Stanton.* Most of her work has been for private press books, and is therefore relatively little known. Her most famous works are the illustrations to the Gregynog Press edition of *Aesop's Fables,* 1931. She was much influenced by Northern European copper engravings of the late fifteenth and early sixteenth centuries. Married William McCance.* 1933 became a member of the Society of Wood Engravers.

PARKER, Constance Anne
Sculptor. Studied at the RA Schools, winning four silver and two bronze medals for her painting. Studied sculpture in the evenings at the Polytechnic School of Art. 1958 became assistant librarian at the RA (part-time). 1952-76 she was Hon. Treasurer of the Reynolds Club (the RA

Schools Old Students Society) and went on to become its chairman. 1971 published *Mr. Stubbs the Horsepainter.* 1974 was appointed librarian at RA. 1977 a retrospective exhibition of her sculpture was held at the Belgrave Gallery, London.

PARKIN, A.M.   b.1943
Painter. Born Kemsing, Kent. First solo exhibition held at Bakehouse Gallery, Sevenoaks, Kent, 1972. A retrospective was held at University College, Swansea, 1982.

PARKIN, Sally   b.1944
Printmaker. Born Hull, Yorkshire. Studied at Leeds College of Art and RCA. 1966 began exhibiting; 1968 first solo exhibition held at Phoenix Theatre, Leicester, another at Arnolfini Gallery, Bristol, 1969.

PARKINSON, Gerald   b.1926
Painter. Born Shipley, Yorkshire. Studied at Bradford College of Art, 1951-4. Served in the Royal Navy for three years, mainly in the Far East. Solo exhibitions in Stockholm, Bologna and London. Exhibits at the RA, the RWEA, in Sussex and York. Represented in Glasgow Art Gallery, Brighton Art Gallery and elsewhere.

PARSONS, Alfred   1847-1920
Painter. Born Beckington, Somerset. Worked as a clerk in the Savings Bank Department of the Post Office, 1865-7, before becoming a full-time painter. 1886-94 exhibited at the NEAC, but was more loyal to the RA to which he was elected a full member, 1911.

PARSONS, Elizabeth   b.1953
Painter. Born Cheltenham, Gloucestershire. Studied in Florence under Signorina Simi. First painted horses, but moved to portraits and landscapes. Her work has been shown at the RP, the NEAC and the Society of Equestrian Artists as well as in Florence. 1988 held a solo exhibition at the Richmond Gallery, London.

PARTRIDGE, Josh   b.1942
Painter. Studied at Bath Academy of Art, Corsham, 1959-63, and post-graduate studies at the Slade School of Art, 1963-5. 1965-75 she travelled extensively, visiting Japan, Australia and the USA. 1966-7 studied wood-block printing in Kyoto, Japan. Since 1975 has been teaching in Britain in Central and North London Polytechnics Architectural Departments. 1973 first one-person show at Waterhouse Gallery, London. Regular solo exhibitions, including two at Curwen Gallery, London, 1985 and 1988, and Maghi Bettini Gallery, Amsterdam, 1986. Work in public collections at home and abroad, including British Museum and Montreal Visual Arts Association. Imbued in her work is her childhood experience of the Pembrokeshire coast.

PARTRIDGE, M.W.   1913-1973
Painter and chemist. Born Lincoln. Studied pharmacy at University College, Nottingham. Graduated 1936, then transferred to the School of Chemistry. Various appointments followed. 1947 became a lecturer in chemistry, eventually becoming Lord Trent Professor of Pharmaceutical Chemistry. Self-taught as a painter, but influenced by Harold Cohen* whilst he was Fellow in Fine Art at Nottingham University, 1956-9.

Bibl: *M.W. Partridge: Memorial Exhibition,* University of Nottingham, 1973.

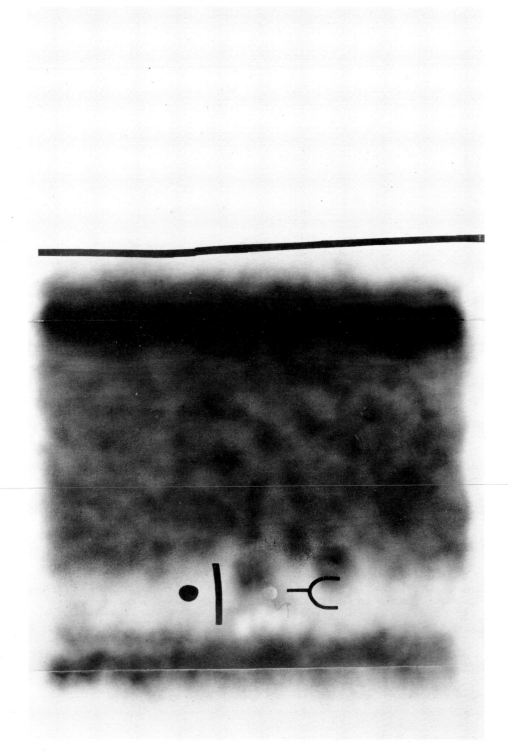

VICTOR PASMORE, b.1908.
'A Metaphysical Harmony',
1987-8. 76in. x 48in.
Marlborough Fine Art
(London) Ltd.

PASCOE, Jane   b.1955
Painter and sculptor. Studied at Bristol Polytechnic,
1973-7. Began exhibiting at the RWEA in 1974 and was
elected associate member in 1981, full member in 1987;
Also member of the Bath Society of Artists. Exhibits at
RWA annual exhibitions.

PASMORE, Victor   b.1908
Painter and relief-maker. Born Chelsham, Surrey. Owing
to the death of his father he went straight into employment on leaving school, as clerk in the head office of the
London County Council. Painted in his spare time and
studied the Impressionists, and Cotman and Turner,
among others, in the national collections. 1932 elected
into the London Artists' Association and 1934 into the
London Group. Attracted the attention of Kenneth Clark
whose financial assistance allowed him to become a full-
time painter. Experimentation with Fauvism gave way to
the quiet realism associated with the Euston Road School
which he helped found in 1937. 1942 moved to Chiswick

JAMES McINTOSH PATRICK, b.1907. *'The Stackyard, Benvie'*. 22in. x 30in. The Fine Art Society, London.

Mall where he painted river scenes partly inspired by Turner and Whistler. His post-war garden, river and park scenes are less romantic and reveal his search for an underlying geometry. 1948 experimented with pure abstraction, first with collage, then paint and finally abandoned painting temporarily to work solely with reliefs. Became a major figure in the 1950s and as the leader of the English Constructionists. Occupied various teaching posts, at Camberwell, Central School and, finally, King's College, Durham, where he became an exponent of Basic Form. In 1966 bought a house and studio in Malta. During the 1960s he returned to painting, still in an abstract style but used forms that evoke associations with nature.

Bibl: *Victor Pasmore,* with introduction by Alistair Grieve, Arts Council, London, 1980.

PASMORE, Wendy   b.1915
Painter. Born Dublin, Ireland, née Blood. Studied at Chelmsford School of Art, 1933-4. Married Victor Pasmore,* 1940. Member of the Women's International Art Club, 1955. From 1956 exhibited with the London Group, becoming a member in 1958. Taught at Sunderland College of Art, 1955-8, and afterwards at Leeds College of

Art. Represented in several public collections. Lives in Malta.

PASS, Douglas   b.1930
Painter. Born Cheshire. Studied at Stoke-on-Trent College of Art, 1947-51 and RA Schools, 1951-4. 1958 first solo exhibition held at Drian Gallery, London; others include two at the Mansard Art Gallery, Heal's, 1965 and 1966.

PATEL, Goswami   b.1925
Painter. Born India. Gained a scholarship to the Calcutta Government School of Art and was awarded a diploma, 1949. Worked in East Africa and India until 1967 when he settled in Coventry and became increasingly influenced by Western theories of modern art. Also writes and illustrates animal folk tales. 1968 solo exhibition at Herbert Art Gallery, Coventry.

PATEL, Sunil   b.1959
Painter. Born Nairobi, Kenya. Moved to Britain, 1975. Studied at the Slade School of Art, 1982-6. Awarded the Boise Travelling Scholarship to India, 1986-7. First solo exhibition at the Vanessa Devereux Gallery, London, 1986.

JANET PATTERSON, b.1941. *'Pinnacles — double figure'*, 1987. Acrylic on paper. 59in. x 94in. Private Collection.

PATERSON, James   1854-1932

Painter. Born Glasgow, Scotland. Studied at Glasgow School of Art, 1871-4. Spent two periods in Paris, 1877-9 under Jacquesson de la Chevreuse, and 1879-83 under Jean-Paul Laurens. He returned to Glasgow and associated with the Glasgow School, attending classes in the studio of his former school friend, W.Y. MacGregor, who encouraged artists to reject anecdotal subjects and to use a freer technique and bold colour. After his marriage in 1884 Paterson moved near the Dumfries village of Moniaive, where he applied the unified tonality that he had learnt in France to the village and its surrounding landscape. His style is smoother, more atmospheric and less experimental than others of the Glasgow School.

PATRICK, James McIntosh   b.1907

Painter. Born Dundee, Scotland. Showed a great dexterity as an artist from an early age. Studied at Glasgow School of Art where he began as he was to continue, with minutely detailed, panoramic views of landscape. His early talent was for etching. When the print market slumped in the 1930s he diversified, teaching part-time at Dundee College of Art, making illustrations for postcards and journals and turning to oil painting. From 1928 exhibited at RA, and in 1934 the Fine Art Society began selling his work. Most of his crisply painted scenes are of the countryside within a twenty-mile radius of his Dundee home. Did not paint *en plein air* till after the Second World

War but retained his desire for meticulous detail. Elected ARSA, 1949, and RSA, 1957. Major exhibitions of his work were held in Dundee in 1967 and in Dundee, Aberdeen and Liverpool in 1987.

Bibl: Roger Billcliffe, *James McIntosh Patrick,* Fine Art Society, London, 1987.

PATTERSON, Dorothea

Painter. Studied at Slade School of Fine Art and St. Martin's School of Art. Exhibits at RA, RWS and with the RE. Primarily a watercolourist and printmaker.

PATTERSON, Doug   b.1945

Painter. Studied at Nottingham College of Art and Design, 1967-8, Hornsey College of Art and Design, 1968-9, and RCA, 1969-72. Obtained a diploma in architecture at the Architectural Association, 1972-4. Travelled extensively in Central and South America, 1976-7. Runs an architectural and design consultancy and paints in his spare time.

PATTERSON, Janet   b.1941

Painter. Born Edinburgh, Scotland. Studied at Slade School of Fine Art, 1960-4. 1964-5 won French Government Scholarship to Aix-en-Provence. 1968 returned to Edinburgh. 1977 first solo exhibition held at Peter Potter Gallery, Haddington; others include three at the Scottish Gallery in Edinburgh, 1980, 1982 and 1988. 1987 selected

PAWLE, John

for British-Australia Bicentennial Programme and for five months was artist-in-residence in various Australian institutions. Her paintings are often symptomatic of the tensions and worries inherent in 20th century life; they also explore surfaces, signs, symbols and colour relationships. Represented in the Scottish Arts Council Collection, Sheffield City Art Galleries, Maclaurin Art Gallery, Ayr and elsewhere. Recent solo exhibitions include one at Queensland House, London, 1990.

PAWLE, John   b.1915
Studied under Mark Gertler* at Westminster School of Art. Painted on a purely amateur basis until he retired from the City in 1979. Since then has exhibited in England, France and America. Specialises in *intimiste* domestic subjects and subjects taken from his immediate environment.

PEACOCK, Brian   b.1934
Painter. Born London. Studied at Bromley College of Art, 1956-8, and RCA, 1958-61. Awarded a Silver Medal and won the Prix de Rome, 1961. 1961-2 worked in Italy. Taught at Manchester School of Art, and Sheffield Polytechnic, where he became Head of Painting. Solo exhibitions at the Piccadilly Gallery, London, 1963, 1964 and 1966.

PEACOCK, Clarisse Loxton
Painter. Born Budapest, Hungary. Studied at Chelsea School of Art, St. Martin's and Central School of Art. Exhibits at RA and Paris Salon. Solo exhibitions include one at Wylma Wayne Fine Art, London, 1982.

PEACOCK, Percy   b.1953
Ceramic sculptor. Born York. Studied ceramics at Bristol Polytechnic, 1972-5, and the RCA, 1975-7. Taught at the Fine Art Departments of Portsmouth and Sheffield Polytechnics, 1977-80, then became Ceramics Fellow at Hull College of Further Education, 1908-82. First solo show 'Objects and Artifacts' at Midland Group Gallery, Nottingham, 1978; a more recent one held at Ferens Art Gallery, Hull, 1982. His work now has a strong narrative and theatrical quality.

PEACOCK, Ralph   1868-1946
Portrait and landscape painter. Born London. Studied at the RA Schools, where he won a gold medal and the Creswick Prize, 1887. Exhibited at the RA, 1888-1934. Won a bronze medal at the Paris Universal Exhibition, 1900. Work in the Tate Gallery collection.

PEAKE, Mervyn   1911-1968
Illustrator and writer. Born in Southern China, the son of a missionary doctor. Some Chinese influence can be detected in his early work and his fictional Gormenghast is not unlike Peking. He had considerable success with *Titus Groan* and became known as 'the greatest living illustrator'. Also worked as a theatre designer. Contracted Parkinson's disease after a long and fruitful career.

PEARCE, Ashley   b.1962
Painter. Born London. Moved to Manchester in 1975 and attended first the High School and then Manchester Polytechnic, 1983-6. Began exhibiting in 1984 and held a solo exhibition at Garden Gallery, London, 1987. A figurative artist, influenced by Spanish art, his paintings

reveal an interest in indeterminate emotional states and divergent moods. Solo exhibitions at Sue Williams, London, 1989.

PEARCE, Bryan   b.1929
Painter. Born St. Ives, Cornwall. Began drawing and painting in 1953. Studied at St. Ives School of Painting, 1954-7. Painted only in watercolour until 1957. 1959 first solo exhibition held at Newlyn Gallery; others include three at the New Art Centre, London, 1966, 1968 and 1973. Suffered as a child from phenylketonuria — a rare genetic anomaly that causes damage to the brain — and was left handicapped. His paintings are less genuinely naïve than those of Alfred Wallis,* but they have a similar matter-of-fact freshness, with everything seen with a sharp singularity.

PEARCE, Charles Maresco   1874-1964
Painter. Born London, son of Maresco Pearce, artist and solicitor. Apprenticed to the architect Sir Ernest George, then studied at Chelsea School of Art under Augustus John* and William Orpen,* in Paris under J.E. Blanche and back in London under W.R. Sickert.* First solo show of watercolours at Carfax Gallery, London, 1910. Elected NEAC, 1912. Uses oils and watercolours to paint architectural subjects.

PEARSALL, Phyllis   b.1906
Painter. Born London. Studied at the Sorbonne, Paris, 1923, while teaching English at a French girls' school. Travelled widely in Europe. Returned to London in 1926 where she began painting and writing full-time. Produced the first A-Z street map. Throughout the 1930s she exhibited in Great Britain and the United States. During the Second World War she worked for the Ministry of Information, where she produced over a hundred drawings of women at war, with a descriptive text, in advance of the conscription of women, which were never published. After the war she was temporarily based in Holland. First solo exhibition held 1967, with thirteen solo exhibitions since then, including one at Sally Hunter Fine Art, London, 1989.

PEARSON, Dave   b.1937
Painter and printmaker. Born London. Studied at St. Martin's School of Art and RA Schools. Began exhibiting in 1960. Solo exhibitions include one at the Bede Gallery, Jarrow, 1983. Represented in the Arts Council collection.

PELLEW-HARVEY, Claughton   b.1890
Painter. Born Redruth, Cornwall, but brought up in Blackheath, London. Studied at the Slade School where he was a contemporary of Paul Nash* who admired Pellew-Harvey's 'searching intensity both in thought and execution'. Nash also credits this artist for having opened his mind to nature. Exhibited at the NEAC and elsewhere. Became increasingly drawn to Roman Catholicism and became a Catholic convert, 1914. Months later he became a conscientious objector and endured great hardship in so-called Home Office Work Centres which were in fact prisons. His wartime experience may explain his permanent sense of isolation and his decision to settle in a remote area of Norfolk. His reputation was revived by an exhibition at the Michael Parkin Gallery, London, 1990. Represented in Hove Museum of Art.

PEMBERTON, Alexander   b.1957
Painter. Born Shrewsbury, Shropshire. Studied at Camberwell School of Art, 1977-8, and at Chelsea School of Art, 1978-81. Awarded British Council Scholarship to work in Seville, Spain, 1981-2, and then the Elizabeth Greenshields Foundation Grant to paint in Bolivia and Mexico, 1983-4. First solo exhibition at Novo Ltd., Newcastle upon Tyne.

PENDER, Jack   b.1918
Painter. Born Mousehole, Cornwall, where his family has lived for centuries. Began painting in 1936. Studied at Penzance School of Art, 1938-9. War service with Duke of Cornwall's Light Infantry, 1939-46. Studied at Athens School of Art, 1945-6, Exeter School of Art, 1946-9, and West of England College of Art at Bristol, 1949-50. First solo exhibition held at the Arnolfini Gallery, Bristol, 1963. 1965 made a Bard of the Cornish Gorsedd. Enjoyed a friendship with other St. Ives artists, notably Frost,* Lanyon* and Hilton,* and has been the subject of a BBC film. Recent solo exhibitions include one at the Belgravia Gallery, London, 1990.

PENDLE, Joseph   b.1933
Painter and relief maker. Exhibited at New Vision Centre Gallery, London, 1956 (summer and winter exhibitions), and a solo show, 1959. Exhibited at Galerie V, Reutlingen, Germany, 1957. Worked for a period with aluminium, for its lightness, reflectivity and malleability.

PENN, John   b.1921
Painter and abstract artist. Educated at Trinity College, Cambridge. Served in the army in North Africa and Italy during the war. 1949 qualified as an architect, 1952 worked in California for Richard Neutra. 1952-6 lived in California and New York. 1964 solo exhibition at Drian Galleries, London.

PENN, William Charles   1877-1968
Painter. Born South London. Trained at Lambeth and the City and Guilds School of Art from 1895 where he won medals and scholarship to the RA Schools, 1900-5. Also studied at the Académie Julian, Paris, and in Holland and Belgium. Exhibited at RA, 1905-35 and at the Liverpool Autumn Exhibition from 1904.

PENNELL, Joseph   1858-1926
Etcher and lithographer. Born and educated in Philadelphia, USA. Specialised in architectural subjects and worked widely in Europe, illustrating many books some of which he wrote himself. Publications include *A Canterbury Pilgrimage*, 1885, *Our Sentimental Journey Through France and Italy*, 1888, *To Gipsyland*, 1893, and *The Work of Charles Keane*, 1897. Became a close friend of J.M. Whistler towards the end of his life and wrote a two-volume life of this artist, 1907. Became the first President of the Senefelder Club. Died in Brooklyn, New York.

PENNIE, Michael   b.1936
Sculptor. Born Wallasley, Cheshire. Studied at Sunderland College of Art and RCA. Rome scholar, 1961, Sir James Knott scholar, 1961. First solo exhibition held at ICA, London, 1965. Others include one at Angela Flowers, London, 1981. Represented in the V & A and Arts Council collection.

PENNY, Christopher   b.1947
Printmaker. Born Dorset. Studied at Bournemouth College of Art, 1964-8. Began exhibiting in 1969 and in 1971 became Head of Printmaking at Byam Shaw School of Art.

PENROSE, Roland   1900-1984
Painter, collagist and entrepreneur. Studied at Queen's College, Cambridge. 1922 went to France. First solo exhibition held at Galerie Van Leer, Paris. 1935 returned to England and the following year organised the International Surrealist Exhibition in London. 1937 opened the London Gallery in Cork Street as an outlet for Surrealist art and assisted with the publication of the *London Bulletin*. 1938 published *The Road is Wider than Long*. 1940-5 saw war service as a camouflage instructor. Married twice, first the poet Valentina Boué, then the photographer, Lee Miller. 1958 published a monograph on his friend, Picasso. 1969-76 President of the ICA. 1980 Arts Council retrospective exhibition held at ICA and elsewhere. Amassed a major collection of 20th century art, examples of which now reside in the Tate Gallery collection.

Bibl: Roland Penrose, *Scrapbook 1980-1981*, Thames & Hudson, London, 1981.

PEPLOE, Denis   b.1914
Painter. Son of S.J. Peploe,* Studied at Edinburgh College of Art and with André L'Hôte. War service, 1940-6. Elected ARSA, 1956 and RSA, 1966. Exhibited at the Scottish Gallery, Edinburgh, 1947, 1948, 1950, 1954, 1984 and 1988, and elsewhere. Represented in several major Scottish public collections, including the Glasgow Art Gallery.

PEPLOE, Samuel John   1871-1935
Painter. Born Edinburgh, Scotland. Studied at Edinburgh School of Art and at the Académie Julian in Paris. On his return to Scotland, he painted in the Hebrides on the island of Barra, producing seascapes, mostly small in scale and low in tone. Continued to paint out of doors during summer visits to France but also specialised in still lifes, using frank oppositions of full, rich colour, in a manner indebted to the example of the Fauves. In 1910 he married Margaret Mackay and took up residence in Paris, mixing with an Anglo-American circle of artists and writers that included J.D. Fergusson,* Anne Estelle Rice, Katherine Mansfield and J. Middleton Murry. In 1914 he returned to Scotland where he was found unfit for military service. In 1920 was taken by F.C.B. Cadell* to Iona and made repeated return visits over the next ten years, painting the north shore of the island under all weather conditions. Elected RSA, 1927, and had a solo exhibition at Krauschaar Gallery, New York, 1928.

Bibl: Stanley Cursiter, *Peploe: An Intimate Memoir of an Artist and of His Work*, London, 1947.

PEPLOE, William Watson   1869-1933
Painter. Brother of S.J. Peploe* whose career over-shadowed that of his elder brother. Became bank manager with the Commercial Bank of Scotland in Stockbridge, Edinburgh. In the mid-1890s he began painting with his brother and others on Barra. He published a volume of poetry dedicated to his brother and also produced drawings that satirised the Aubrey Beardsley school and the fashion for Japanese art. In 1918 he produced two tiny abstracts which were perhaps no more than another manifestation of his playfulness.

PEPPERCORN, Arthur Douglas   1847-1924
Painter. Born Deptford, London. Studied at the Ecole des Beaux Arts, Paris, under Gerome, 1870. Specialised in landscape and was much influenced by Corot and the Barbizon painters. Was often referred to as 'our English Corot'. Exhibited at the RA from 1869 and with the NEAC. Memorial exhibition held at the Leicester Galleries, London, 1924.

PERCEVAL, Matthew   b.1945
Painter. Born Melbourne, where he received early training in pottery and painting under his father, John Perceval. 1962 settled in London, 1967 moved to the South of France. 1969 solo exhibition at Clytie Jessop Gallery, London.

PERCIVAL, Maurice   1906-1987
Painter. Studied at Central School of Art and RCA. For the greater part of his life he taught at Malvern, Eton, Downside and Marlborough schools. 1945-54 was in charge of the art school at Harrow; whilst there he became a close friend of David Jones,* sharing a house with him for seven years. 1983 solo exhibition held at New Grafton Gallery, London.

PERERA, Ed
Painter. Studied at Central School of Arts and Crafts and London College of Printing. From 1967 onwards he exhibited regularly in group exhibitions in London and the Midlands, with a solo exhibition at the Erica Bourne Gallery, London, 1974.

PERI, Peter   1899-1967
Sculptor. Born Budapest, Hungary. Lived in Berlin 1920-33, when he moved to London. Retained the role of exile, and closely resembled the hero of his friend, John Berger's novel, *A Painter of Our Time*. Executed many commissions for schools. A social realist whose figurative sculptures were always dominated by human concerns. Pioneered the use of modelled concrete as a medium for sculpture. Represented in the Tate Gallery, the British Museum and elsewhere.

PERKINS, Brenda   b.1934
Painter. Born Ilford, Essex. Studied at Winchester School of Art and RA Schools. Awarded the David Murray landscape scholarship, 1954, 1955, 1957 and 1958. Exhibits regularly in London and the provinces.

PERKINS, Peter   b.1928
Painter. Born Southampton, Hampshire. Studied at Regent Street Polytechnic and the Architectural Association. Began exhibiting in 1959 and has exhibited regularly at the Upper Grosvenor Galleries, London, and elsewhere.

PERR, Simon   b.1962
Sculptor. Born London. Studied at Chelsea School of Art, 1982-4, and at RA Schools 1984-7. 1987 awarded Prix de Rome Scholarship in sculpture. 1988 first solo exhibition at Nicola Jacobs Gallery, London. Represented in group exhibitions since 1983.

PERRY, Ernest   b.1908
Painter. Born Belfast, Northern Ireland. Studied at Heatherley's and the RA Schools. Exhibited at the RA, with the NEAC and the London Group. Became joint principal of the St. John's Wood Art School in 1933 with Patrick Millard,* but is chiefly remembered as the sleeping partner. A fine draughtsman and portrait painter.

PERRYMAN, Margot   b.1938
Painter of abstracts. Interested in the types of space that a painting can conjure up. First solo exhibition held at Richard Demarco Gallery, Edinburgh, 1970. Work in the Tate Gallery and Arts Council collections.

PERSEY, Robert   b.1951
Sculptor. Born London. Studied at Bulmershe College, Reading, 1971-5, and at St. Martin's School of Art, 1976-7. First exhibited at the RA, 1977. In his work he highlights movement by focusing on particular structural elements of the human form. Included in the collection of Berkshire Education Authority.

PESKETT, Stan   b.1937
Painter. Born Epsom, Surrey. Worked as a jazz musician, 1956-8. Studied at Guildford College of Art, 1958-60 and RCA, 1960-3. 1963 won a travelling scholarship. 1963-4 took a post-graduate scholarship at Bradford. 1965 solo exhibitions at Bradford City Art Gallery, and at Queen Square Gallery, Leeds.

PETHERBRIDGE, Deanna   b.1939
Painter and sculptor. Born Pretoria, South Africa. Studied at University of Witwatersrand, 1956-60. Left South Africa in 1960 and travelled, via Italy, to England. Lived in England until 1966; 1967-72 she lived in Greece and travelled extensively in the Middle East, the Balkans and North Africa. From the mid-1960s she began experimenting with shaped canvases and sculpture in a variety of media. Began drawing extensively during the same period, producing a variety of abstract, mathematical drawings, and later a series of architectural projections. 1973 first solo exhibition at the Angela Flowers Gallery, London. 1973 and 1975 won Arts Council Minor Awards. 1975 began writing on art and architecture for art journals. 1979 travelled to India, where she executed a related series of drawings. 1981 won the Greater London Arts Association Award. 1982 Artist-in-Residence at City Art Gallery, Manchester. Included in the collections of the Arts Council of Great Britain, Basildon Arts Trust and City Art Gallery, Manchester.

Bibl: Timothy Clifford and Bryan Robertson, *Deanna Petherbridge: Drawings 1968-82*, Manchester City Art Galleries, 1982.

PETLEY, Roy   b.1950
Painter. Regularly exhibits in Norfolk. Specialises in British landscape painting.

PETO, Rosemary   b.1916
Painter. Studied drawing at Westminster School of Art, 1931-2, and later at RCA, 1953-6. First solo exhibition in London at Sally Hunter and Patrick Seale Fine Art, 1985.

PETTERSON, Melvyn   b.1947
Painter and etcher. Born Grimsby, Humberside. Studied at Grimsby School of Art and Camberwell. 1987 was elected an Associate of the RE.

PHILIPSON, Robin   b.1916
Painter. Born Broughton in Furness, Lancashire. Attended Edinburgh College of Art, 1936-40. 1940-6 served with King's Own Scottish Borderers in India. 1947

TOM PHILLIPS, b.1937.
'Samuel Beckett at The Riverside Studios 1984'. Lithograph.
10½ in. x 14⅝ in. Tom Phillips.

joined staff of Edinburgh College of Art and in 1960 appointed Head of School of Drawing and Painting there. 1959 won third prize, John Moores Exhibition, Liverpool. 1954 first one-person show at the Scottish Gallery, Edinburgh. 1966 mural for Glasgow Airport; 1977 mural for Dundee College of Education. 1976 knighted for services to the arts in Scotland. 1977 retrospective exhibition at McRobert Centre, Stirling University. 1982 retired from Edinburgh College of Art. Early influences on his painting included the Edinburgh painters, Gillies* and Maxwell,* but after the war Kokoscka's expressionist calligraphy greatly affected his work. Cock-fighting became one of his major themes. His work is distinguished by a love of sudden, explosively handled knots of interest, rich colour and a tendency towards abstraction.

Bibl: Maurice Lindsay, *Robin Philipson*, Edinburgh, 1976.

PHILLIPS, Aubrey
Painter. Member of the Royal West of England Academy, the Pastel Society, Watercolour Society of Wales and Armed Forces Art Society. Gold medallist at the Paris Salon. First solo exhibition at the National Library of Wales.

PHILLIPS, Harry   b.1911
Sculptor. Born London. Initially worked as a woodcarver, furniture maker, blacksmith and potter. In the 1930s he worked for Eric Gill* for a short period. From 1951 exhibited at RA. 1958 awarded the Herbert Baker Travelling Scholarship for sculpture. 1976 first solo exhibition at Stable Court Exhibition Galleries, Leeds.

PHILLIPS, Peter

GLYN PHILPOT, 1884-1937.
'Head of a Young Man', c.1930-5.
Charcoal on paper.
11⅛in. x 8⅜in.
Private Collection.

PHILLIPS, Peter   b.1939
Painter. Born Birmingham, West Midlands. Studied at Birmingham College of Art, 1955-9, and RCA, 1959-62. 1964-6 lived in New York City and travelled North America by car with Allen Jones.* 1976 first solo exhibition in London held at Waddington Galleries. 1982-3 a travelling retrospective opened at the Walker Art Gallery, Liverpool. A pop artist, who uses fragmented imagery and glossy, often photo-realistic techniques.

Bibl: Marco Livingstone, *Retrovision: Peter Phillips: Paintings 1960-1982,* Walker Art Gallery, Liverpool, 1982.

PHILLIPS, Tom   b.1937
Painter and translator. Born Clapham, London. Studied Anglo-Saxon literature at Oxford University and then art at Camberwell School of Art. His love of literature is made manifest in his art. He is also a great collector of postcards.

In 1966 he purchased a Victorian novel — W.H. Mallock's *A Human Document* — and reworked the pages isolating various words. This became a new book/art work entitled *A Humument,* a project on which he is still working. 1965 first solo exhibition at the AIA Gallery. 1969 prizewinner in the John Moores Liverpool exhibition. Translator and illustrator of Dante's *Inferno* (published 1985). Shows in the last few years include a solo at the Angela Flowers Gallery and a portrait exhibition at the National Portrait Gallery, 1989.

Bibl: *Tom Phillips, Works — Texts — to 1974,* Hansjorg Mayer, London, 1975.

PHILLIPS, Winifred   1882-1958
Painter. Studied at the Liverpool Art Sheds, 1902-5, after taking her degree at Liverpool University in 1902, and was tutored by, among others, Augustus John.* Studied at

the Slade, 1906-9, during which time she was a friend of Ida John, wife of Augustus. Won the Slade painting competition in 1908. Exhibited with the NEAC, 1909-15. During the First World War she joined the VAD and served in France and Egypt.

PHILPOT, Glyn   1884-1937

Painter and sculptor. Born Clapham, London. Studied at Lambeth School of Art. Began exhibiting at the RA, 1904. 1912 elected a member of the International Society. 1915 elected ARA. 1917 invalided out of the army. 1921 visited USA for portrait commissions. Elected ARA, 1923. 1926 painted a portrait of the Prime Minister, Stanley Baldwin. 1927 painted a mural in St. Stephen's Hall, Westminster. By the late 1920s he became dissatisfied with the Edwardian aesthetic ideals, still largely demanded in official art circles, and in the early 1930s he moved to Paris. There his style changed dramatically, owing to the influence of contemporary French art. His modern style lost him his former clientele, but, undeterred, he went on to produce some of his best pictures in the last five years of his life. He is especially known for his paintings of negroes, most based on Henry Thomas, a young Jamaican whom Philpot's godfather, Oliver Messel, had found wandering in the National Gallery. He became Philpot's housekeeper and devoted friend, living in his house until his death.

Bibl: A.C. Sewter, *Glyn Philpot 1884-1937*, B.T. Batsford, London, 1951; Robin Gibson, *Glyn Philpot 1884-1937, Edwardian Aesthete to Thirties Modernist*, National Portrait Gallery, London, 1985.

PICHÉ, Roland   b.1938

Sculptor. Born London. Studied at Hornsey College of Art, 1956-60. 1960 worked in Montreal with the sculptor Gaudia. 1960-4 studied sculpture at the Royal College of Art. 1962-3 worked as part-time assistant to Henry Moore. 1964 began teaching at Maidstone School of Art. 1967 first one-person show at the Marlborough New London Gallery. Work in the collection of the Tate Gallery and the Arts Council.

PICKING, John   b.1939

Painter. Born Lancashire. Studied at Wigan School of Art, 1956-60, where he was awarded the Governors' medal and a scholarship to Paris. 1960-3 continued his study at Edinburgh College of Art. 1963-4 awarded Andrew Grant Scholarship to Spain. 1967 first solo exhibition at New 57 Gallery, Edinburgh. 1969 studied in Italy; returned to Sicily, 1971 and 1974-81, to paint.

PIETSCH, Heinz-Dieter   b.1944

Painter. Born Glogau, Silesia, Poland. Studied at State Academy of Fine Art, Stuttgart, West Germany, State Academy of Fine Art, Karlsruhe, West Germany and at Stuttgart University, 1966-71. First solo exhibition at die galerie, Ulm, West Germany, 1972. Awarded scholarship by German Academic Exchange Service to study in London, 1974. This led him to study at St. Martin's School of Art, 1974-5 and at RCA, 1975-7. Painting Fellow at Gloucestershire College of Art and Design, 1977-8.

PIGHILLS, Joseph   1902-1984

Painter. Born near Haworth Moor, Yorkshire. Worked as an engineering pattern maker until he took early retirement and began to paint seriously from the mid-1960s. Briefly studied at Keighley School of Art. First solo exhibition at Cliffe Castle Museum and Art Gallery, 1961. Specialised in landscape painting.

PIPER, Edward   1938-1990

Painter and photographer. Son of John Piper.* Studied at Bath Academy of Art, Corsham, studying drawing under Howard Hodgkin,* and afterwards spent four years at the Slade. Began as a hard-edge pop artist, but gradually developed a fascination with life drawing, meanwhile working as a photographer, for Shell guides among other commissions, and as a graphic designer. First solo exhibition held at Marjorie Parr Gallery, London, 1975. His fourteenth solo exhibition was held at the Catto Gallery, Hampstead, 1987. His paintings share certain characteristics with the work of his father, in particular his use of a strong line and bold washes of colour.

PIPER, John   b.1903

Painter and theatre designer. Born Epsom, Surrey. Studied law in his father's office and wrote poetry, 1921-6. Studied at Richmond School of Art, 1926-8, under Raymond Coxon* through whom he met Henry Moore,* 1927. Studied at RCA. 1933 met Braque who encouraged him to experiment with collage. 1934 member of 7 & 5 Society. 1935 collaborated with Myfanwy Evans on the magazine, *Axis*. Mixed with the avant-garde in England and Paris, but in the late 1930s abandoned abstract art for a romantic portrayal of buildings and places, at a time when England's architectural heritage was under threat. During the war he painted the after-effects of the Baedeker raids, as well as a series of paintings based on Renishaw, the Sitwell family home, which were used as illustrations in Osbert Sitwell's autobiography. Frequent exhibitions in England and abroad. Has worked also in stained glass, at Coventry Cathedral and elsewhere. Friendship with Benjamin Britten led to his designs for opera. 1983 was given a Tate Gallery retrospective.

Bibl: Richard Ingram and John Piper, *Piper's Places. John Piper in England and Wales*, Chatto and Windus, London, 1983.

PISSARRO, Lucien   1863-1944

Painter, wood engraver and book designer. Born Paris, son of the great Impressionist Camille Pissarro, and father of Orovida Pissarro.* Studied under his father and exhibited at the last Impressionist exhibition, held in 1886; also influenced by the Neo-Impressionist, Seurat. Settled in London in 1890 and adopted British nationality, 1916. In 1893 he moved to Epping where he ran the Eragny Press, 1894-1914. Exhibited with the NEAC from 1904, becoming a member in 1906. Founder-member of the Camden Town Group, 1911 and of the Monarro Group, 1919. First solo exhibition held at the Carfax Gallery, London, 1913. Exhibited at the RA from 1934. Maintained an impressionist approach to landscape to the end of his life, albeit with less excitement than this movement had originally inspired.

PISSARRO, Orovida Camille   1893-1968

Painter. Born Epping, Essex, daughter of Lucien* and Esther Pissarro. Received an art education from her family. First exhibited in London, 1919. She exhibited regularly at the RA, the NEAC, the RBA and the Women's International Art Club. Represented in the collections of the British Museum, the V & A, the Ashmolean Museum, Oxford, New York Public Library, USA, the Rijks Museum, Amsterdam, the Stockholm Art Museum and the Contemporary Art Society.

PITCHFORTH, R. Vivian   1895-1982

Painter. Born Wakefield, Yorkshire. Studied at Leeds

JOHN PIPER, b.1903. *'Llawhaden'*, 1986. Chalk, Indian ink, watercolour and gouache on paper. 27 ½ in. x 37 in. James Kirkman, Limited.

School of Art, 1914-15 and 1919-21, and RCA, 1922-5. Served with the Wakefield Battery Royal Garrison Artillery, 1915-19. 1937-9 taught at RCA. 1940 Official War Artist. Membership of the London Artists' Association in the 1930s helped establish him as a painter, influenced by French artists, notably Cézanne. Also excelled at watercolour and concentrated, in his later years, on landscapes, seascapes and atmospheric effects. Elected ARA, 1942, and RA, 1953.

Bibl: Adrian Bury, *R. Vivian Pitchforth, RA, RWS*, Old Watercolour Society, 43rd Annual Vol., 1968.

PITMAN, P.V.
Painter. Studied at Exeter College of Art under James Sparks. Has regularly exhibited in Exeter. Her work was included in *Exeter Blitz*, published 1942. Became a member of the Society of Graphic Artists, 1953. Included in the collection of Royal Albert Memorial Museum, Exeter.

PITT, Ursula   b.1935
Painter. Born Zambia, Africa. Studied at Chelsea School of Art, 1953-6 and at Institute of Education, 1957. First solo exhibition at the Woodstock Gallery, London, 1972.

PITTUCK, Douglas   b.1911
Painter. Born London. Studied at Ruskin School of Drawing, Oxford, part-time. Military service, 1941-6; later returned to Ruskin School, under Albert Rutherston* and Percy Horton,* from where he graduated, 1948. Solo exhibition at Laing Art Gallery, Newcastle upon Tyne, 1963. Included in the collection of the Ashmolean Museum, Oxford and the Bowes Museum, Barnard Castle.

PLACKMAN, Carl   b.1943
Sculptor. Born Huddersfield, Yorkshire. Studied at West of England College of Art, Bristol, 1962-7 and at RCA, 1967-70. Worked for a while as assistant to Lynn Chadwick.* Has taught part-time at Goldsmiths' and Ravensbourne. First one-artist exhibition at Serpentine Gallery, 1972.

PLANT, Mary   b.1943
Painter. Born Cyprus. Studied at Chelsea School of Art, 1976-80. Included in 'Critics' Space 4' at AIR Gallery, London, 1987.

PLATT, John b.1886
Painter, also woodcut artist and designer of stained glass. Born Leek, Staffordshire. Studied at the RCA, 1905-8. Head of Leek School of Art, 1910-19, Harrogate School of Art, 1919, Derby School of Art, 1920, Head of Department of Applied Art, Edinburgh College of Art, 1920-3, and Leicester School of Art, 1923-9. Exhibited at RA from 1913, and NEAC from 1917. Published *Colour Woodcuts*, 1939-53. President of the Society of Graver Printers in Colour, 1939-53. Official War Artist to Ministry of Transport, 1939-45. Contributed murals and stained glass for All Saints Church, Leek.

PLUMB, John b.1927
Painter of abstracts. Born Luton, Bedfordshire. Studied at Luton School of Art, 1942-5, Byam Shaw School, 1948-50, and the Central School, 1952-4, under Anthony Gross,* Victor Pasmore,* William Turnbull* and Keith Vaughan.* Has taught at the Central School, Maidstone College of Art and Luton College of Technology. Showed in the AIA abstract exhibitions, 1953 and 1957 and the Situation exhibitions, 1960 and 1961. First solo exhibition at Gallery One, London, 1957. Work in the Tate Gallery collection.

PLUMMER, Alan b.1931
Painter. Born Leicester. Studied at Leicester College of Art, 1947-50 and at RCA, 1951-4. First exhibited at the Ikon Gallery, 1966.

PLUMMER, Brian b.1934
Painter. Born London. Studied at Hornsey College of Art and RA Schools. First solo exhibition at Manor House Gallery, Ilkley, 1969. Has since exhibited in England and abroad. Represented in the Abbot Hall Gallery, Kendal, and elsewhere.

PLUMMER, Robin b.1931
Painter. Born London. Studied at RCA. Lived in Italy, 1958-9. First exhibited in Italy at Galleria Trastevere, Rome, and in Great Britain at the New Vision Centre, London. Became Head of Fine Art at Brighton Polytechnic. Work in the Arts Council collection.

POLLOCK, Fred b.1937
Painter. Born Glasgow, Scotland. Studied at Glasgow School of Art, 1955-9. Guest artist at Triangle Art Workshop, New York, USA, 1984. First solo exhibition held at New Charing Cross Gallery, Glasgow, 1963. Exhibited with the Vanessa Devereux Gallery, London, 1988. Abstract painter preoccupied with colour and colour relationships.

POLLOCK, Ian b.1950
Painter and illustrator. Born Cheshire. Studied illustration at Manchester Polytechnic, 1969-73, and at the RCA, 1973-6. Was presented in 'The Best of British Illustration' at the Mall Galleries, London, 1979. Continues to earn his living as an illustrator, with work for books and magazines, but also produces paintings of drop-outs, drunks and drug addicts, drawn in London, New York and Amsterdam.

POLOVIN, Vladimir 1880-1957
Painter and theatre designer. Born Moscow, Russia. Studied in St. Petersburg, Munich and Paris. Settled in London immediately prior to the First World War and taught stage design at the Slade School.

POMERANCE, Fay b.1912
Painter. Studied at Birmingham College of Art, 1928-33. First solo exhibition at the Walker Gallery, Liverpool, 1949. Has exhibited over many years in London and the provinces. Several of her solo exhibitions have been on the theme of Lucifer. Her friendship with Michael Ayrton* has had a dominant influence on her work. Represented in the collections of Staffordshire and Hull Education Committees, Batley Art Gallery and the Museums of Israel.

POOLE, George b.1915
Painter. Studied in Wales and London. Exhibitions sponsored by the Miners' Union and the Coal Board in 1940s and 1950s. Held solo exhibitions in London and Europe.

POOLE, Henry 1873-1928
Sculptor. Born London, son of the sculptor Samuel Poole. Studied at Lambeth School of Art and RA Schools, 1892-7. Worked as an apprentice with Harry Bates, RA and then for G.F. Watts. Served in the Camouflage School, 1915-18. 1920 elected ARA; 1927 RA; 1927 Trustee of the Tate Gallery. 1929 memorial exhibition at the Leicester Galleries. Works include the memorial statue of Edward VII and the fountains at Bristol, the wooden St. George in the Chapel of St. Michael and St. George, St. Paul's Cathedral, and the memorial plaque for William Blake, in the crypt of St. Paul's. Represented in the Tate Gallery.

POOLEY, Vanessa b.1954
Sculptor. Born Norwich, Norfolk. Studied at Norwich School of Art, 1978-81, and at the City and Guilds of London Art School, 1981-2. First solo exhibition at Southwark Cathedral in 1985. Influenced by Brancusi, Zadkine and others, her work makes witty, playful use of the human figure. Recent solo exhibitions include one at the Orangery, Holland Park, London, 1989.

POPE, Nicholas b.1949
Sculptor. Studied at Bath Academy of Art, 1970-3. 1974-5 awarded the Romanian Government Exchange Scholarship, and 1974 the Southern Arts Association Bursary; 1976 awarded Calouste Gulbenkian Foundation Award. 1976 first solo exhibition at Garage Gallery Limited. Included in the collections of the Arts Council of Great Britain, Contemporary Arts Society, Calouste Gulbenkian Foundation, Portsmouth Museum and Art Gallery and the Tate Gallery. Solo exhibitions include one at City of Portsmouth Museum and Art Gallery, 1976.

POPE, Terence b.1941
Sculptor. Started making constructions in 1958. Studied at Bath Academy of Art, 1959-62, Royal Netherlands Academy, 1962-3. Included in group exhibitions from 1962. First solo show 'Space Constructions' at Lucy Milton Galley, London, 1974. Taught in Fine Art Department, Reading University in the 1970s. Work in the Arts Council collection.

PORTER, Frederick J. 1883-1944
Painter. Born New Zealand. Studied at Auckland, Melbourne and the Académie Julian, Paris. Afterwards worked both in France and England. Exhibited in group exhibitions from 1916, e.g. the London Group; became its Vice-President, 1925-35. Member of the London Artists' Association, 1925, a Bloomsbury oriented exhibiting society. First solo exhibition with the London Artists' Association

PORTER, Michael

VANESSA POOLEY, b.1954.
'*Sweet Pea*', 1989. Bronze.
11in. x 16in. x 19in.
Private Collection.

at the Cooling Galleries, 1930. Taught at the Central School, 1924-44. Work in the Tate Gallery collections.

PORTER, Michael   b.1948
Painter. Born Holbrook, Derbyshire. Studied at Derby College of Art and at Chelsea School of Art. Awarded Biddulph Scholarship, Chelsea School of Art and a Fellowship in Fine Art, Gloucestershire College of Art. First solo exhibition at Acme Gallery, London, 1976.

PORTWAY, Douglas   b.1922
Painter, abstract artist. Lived in St. Ives, Cornwall. First solo exhibition at the Drian Galleries, 1959. Has exhibited regularly in Europe since 1959 and in South Africa since

1962. Included in the collections of the V & A, Scottish National Museum of Modern Art, Glasgow, Musée des Beaux-Arts, Ostend, Belgium and in many public collections in South Africa.

POSTGATE, Stephen   b.1959
Painter and film maker. Born London. Studied at Medway College of Design, 1977. 1984 first solo exhibition at Hope Theatre Gallery, Bristol. 1985 first film, *Science*, screened at Canterbury Festival. 1987 solo exhibition at the October Gallery, London.

POTTER, Helen Beatrix   1866-1943
Painter, illustrator and author of children's books. Born

MARY POTTER, 1900-1981. *'Cygnet'*, 1963. 29½ in. x 31½ in. New Art Centre.

Kensington, London. Self-taught, but modelled her early style on the work of Randolph Caldecott. The first of her thirty books was *The Tale of Peter Rabbit,* privately printed in 1900, then reprinted by Frederick Warne, 1902. 1905 she bought Hill Top Farm at Sawrey, in the Lake District, which became the setting for many books. Married a solicitor, William Heelis, 1913 and from then on devoted herself mainly to farming and the preservation of the Lake District. Bequeathed her house and land at her death to the National Trust. Major retrospective of her illustrations held at the Tate Gallery, 1987.

POTTER, Mary   1900-1981
Painter. Born Beckenham, Kent (neé Attenborough). Studied at Beckenham School of Art and at the Slade under Professor Tonks.* Taught for a year at Eastbourne College of Art and at first earned her living from portrait

paintings. Joined the 7 & 5 Society soon after it was founded but resigned after two years. 1927 married Stephen Potter, author, humorist and BBC producer. Lived at Chiswick during the 1930s where she painted views of the river. During the war she was obliged to travel round the country with her husband; afterwards they lived in Harley Street, not far from Regent's Park which she painted in the light, muted colour harmonies that became her hallmark. In 1951 the Potters moved to the Red House, Aldeburgh, which, after her marriage was dissolved, Mary Potter exchanged with Benjamin Britten and Peter Pears for Crag House on the sea front. Later she moved into a studio, built for her in the grounds of her former house. She worked there in relative isolation, concentrating on the Suffolk landscape, using a delicacy and suggestiveness partly inspired by Paul Klee and by Oriental art. Her work began to explore the interface between abstraction and representation and continued to display her preference for light colours, unexpected shapes and abrupt, cursory marks.

Bibl: *Mary Potter,* with essays by Frances Spalding, Julian Potter and others, Oriel 31 cat., Newtown and Welshpool, 1989.

POTTER, Michael   b.1951
Painter and silk screen printer. Born London. Studied Renaissance art in Florence, 1969, followed by a photography diploma at Ealing School of Art. Afterwards worked as fashion and travel photographer. Later, studied silk screen printing. Commissioned by London Transport and Holiday Inn Group to produce silk screens for advertising. Has also completed commissions for Christie's Contemporary Art in London and New York. 1979 first exhibited at the Moreton Gallery, London. 1984 held an exhibition entitled 'Eating Places' at The Cadogan Gallery, London.

POTTS, Ian   b.1936
Painter. Studied at Sunderland College of Art and the RA Schools. Has produced a whole series of work based on the Carrara quarries in Italy and the Acropolis in Athens. Lives in Lewes and teaches at Brighton Polytechnic.

POULTNEY, Tony   b.1938
Painter. Studied at Camberwell School of Arts and Crafts, 1951-8, and studied music during same period. Travelled round the world playing music on leaving college. Commissioned to paint murals when in Yokohama and San Francisco. First solo exhibition at Woodstock Gallery, London, 1968.

POULTON, Yvonne
Painter. Born Berkshire. Studied Fine Art at Reading University. Toured Phillippines, Hong Kong and Japan, 1964. First solo exhibition at Madden Galleries, London, 1964, followed by a second solo exhibition in Japan in the same year. Makes pictures in coloured sands, silicon carbides and aluminium oxides.

POVEY, Ray   b.1947
Painter. Studied at Ruskin School of Drawing and Fine Art, Oxford, 1972-5. First solo exhibition at St. Catherine's College, Oxford, 1972. Another held at Zebra One, London, 1978. Represented in the Ashmolean Museum, Oxford.

POWELL, Virginia
Painter and printmaker. Studied at Chelsea School of Art during the early 1960s under Fred Brill.* 1967 first exhibited in Great Britain at the Traverse Theatre, Edinburgh. 1989 held her fourth solo exhibition at the Michael Parkin Gallery, London.

POWER, Caroline   b.1955
Painter. Born in Hertfordshire. Studied at Cambridge College of Arts and Technology, 1973-4 and the Byam Shaw School of Art, 1974-7. 1978 moved to live and work in the Pyrenees. 1981 began to show in RA summer exhibitions,. 1982 first solo show at the Brotherton Gallery; more recent one at the Thackeray Gallery, 1989.

POWER, Cyril   1872-1951
Architect, designer and printmaker. Born London.

Articled to an architect, 1890. Elected Associate member of RIBA, 1902. Worked as an architect at the Ministry of Works, 1905. Lecturer in Architectural Design and History, University College, London, 1908-16. Commissioned into the Royal Flying Corps, 1916. Continued in architectural practice after the war and began to produce watercolours and drypoints. Helped Iain Macnab* and Claude Flight* to set up the Grosvenor School of Modern Art, London, 1925. Claude Flight taught the art of linocutting which Power learnt from him there. Joint exhibition, with Sybil Andrews, of linocuts and monotypes at Redfern Gallery, London, 1933.

Bibl: *The Linocuts of Cyril Edward Power,* 1872-1951, Redfern Gallery, 1989.

POWER, James   b.1944
Painter. Studied at Hornsey College of Art, 1961-6. Teaches art in a comprehensive school.

POYNTER, Edward   1836-1919
Painter. Born Paris. Studied in Paris under Gleyre, 1856-9. Exhibited at RA from 1861. Elected ARA, 1868, RA, 1861 and was President of the RA, 1896-1918. Slade Professor, 1871-5 and Principal of the National Art Training School, South Kensington, 1876-91. Director of the National Gallery, 1894-1905. After his years in Paris, where with Whistler and others, he led a Bohemian life, became a pinnacle of respectability. His stilted grasp of the female nude troubled his allegories but, like Alma-Tadema,* he excelled at domestic scenes set in ancient Greece and Rome.

POYNTER, Malcolm   b.1946
Sculptor. Studied graphics at Goldsmiths' College and sculpture at RCA. First solo exhibition at Nicholas Treadwell Gallery, London, 1976. His three-dimensional figurative sculptures are half-humorous, half-grotesque. Recently his work for outlandish restaurants in Tokyo has brought him cult status in Japan.

PRATT, Brian   b.1934
Painter. Studied at Wimbledon School of Art and Slade School of Fine Art. Spent two years National Service in the Far East. First solo exhibition at the Woodstock Gallery, London, 1965. After a period as an abstract artist he returned to representional subjects.

PREECE, Lawrence   b.1942
Painter. Born Shepton Mallet, Somerset. Studied ceramics at Brighton College of Art, 1958-63. 1970 first solo exhibition at the Redfern Gallery, and has shown there regularly since, most recently in 1988. 1977 won Linbury Trust award for travels in Mexico and Guatemala, followed by a trip to Israel in 1979 with the British Council. 1977 he was commissioned by the British Museum to produce a painting for a poster. Included in the collections of York City Art Gallery, Birmingham Museum and Hull University.

PREECE, Patricia   1900-1971
Painter. Studied at the Slade School of Art and at the Académie André L'Hôte, Paris. Moved to Cookham, Berkshire, with her painter friend Doroth Hepworth, where she met the painter, Stanley Spencer,* 1929.

Although married to Hilda Carline,* Spencer courted Preece, 1932-7, when they were married in Maidenhead Town Hall, his divorce by then made absolute. First solo show of paintings at Reid and Lefevre Gallery, London, 1936, with catalogue preface by Duncan Grant.* Another solo show at Leger Galleries, London, 1938, with catalogue preface by Clive Bell.

PRENDERGAST, Peter   b.1946
Painter. Born South Wales. Studied at Cardiff College of Art, the Slade School, where in 1967 he won the Nettleship prize for painting, and Reading University. Since 1970 has lived in Bethesda, North Wales, and has found his source material from the dramatic landscapes near to hand. Solo exhibition of recent paintings of Wales at Bluecoat Gallery, Liverpool, 1973; more recent one, 'Heart Land' at Artsite Gallery, Bath, 1987. A major retrospective exhibition of work from 1960-82 was toured by the Mostyn Art Gallery, Llandudno, 1983. Work in the Tate Gallery collections.

PRENTICE, David   b.1936
Painter. Born Solihull, West Midlands. Studied at Birmingham College of Art and Design under Fleetwood-Walker.* Director of the Ikon Gallery. Has regularly exhibited in Great Britain. Included in the collections of the Arts Council, Birmingham Museum and Art Gallery, University of Birmingham and the Albright Knox Gallery, Buffalo, USA. Abstract artist who works with geometric grids. Represented in several public collections.

PRESTON, Edward Carter   1884-1965
Sculptor, painter and medallist. Born Liverpool, Merseyside. Apprenticed to a firm of glass decorators and studied in the School of Applied Art at Liverpool University. On its amalgamation with Liverpool School of Art, 1905, he joined the rival Sandon Terrace Studios where Gerard Chowne* was his chief mentor. Began as a painter but turned to sculpture after the First World War and gained national repute as a medallist. Also executed statues for Liverpool Cathedral.

PRICE, Richard
Sculptor. Read history and art at Culham College, Abingdon, Oxford, 1965-8. First solo exhibition at Woodstock Gallery, London, 1969.

PRIEST, Margaret   b.1944
Painter. Born Tyringham, Buckinghamshire. Studied at Maidstone College of Art, 1964-72, and at RCA, 1967-70. First solo exhibition at the Arnolfini Gallery, Bristol, 1970. Work held in the collections of Arts Council of Great Britain, British Council, Tate Gallery, London, Dallas County Museum, Texas, USA, and Art Gallery of Brant, Brantford, Ontario, Canada. Produces disciplined, detailed and precise renderings of architectural interiors in which the human presence, although absent, is always implied.

PRIESTMAN, Bertram RA   1868-1951
Painter. Born Bradford, Yorkshire. Visited Italy, Egypt and Israel after leaving school. Studied at the Slade School of Fine Art and worked in the studios of William Llewellyn. First exhibited at the RA, 1889; elected RA, 1923. He painted predominantly landscapes and rural scenes, with a zestful feeling for atmosphere. His East Anglian scenes made him a mentor for Edward Seago.*

PRIESTNER, Wilton   b.1934
Painter. Born Bolton, Lancashire. Studied at Bolton College of Art and at RCA, 1957-60. First solo exhibition at the Lane Gallery, Bradford, 1966. Painter of landscapes employing more than one kind of perspective.

PRINGLE, John Quinton   1864-1926
Painter. Born Glasgow, Scotland. Began painting at an early age. Was apprenticed to an optician, but in his own time studied art, using the *Art Journal* and the *Magazine of Art* as his tutors. He adopted the square brushstrokes employed by the French artist, Bastien-Lepage and by the Glasgow Boys. Attended an evening school 1883-5 and won a bursary which allowed him to attend evening classes at Glasgow School of Art, 1886-95, where he was an outstanding pupil. After setting up shop as an optician in 1896, he continued to paint in a back room. Around 1908 he began working in a style akin to Neo-Impressionism. After 1911, when his sister who had kept house for him died, he mostly painted in watercolour. A retrospective exhibition of his work was held at Glasgow School of Art in 1922, after which he was persuaded to give up his shop in order to concentrate on painting.

Bibl: *John Quinton Pringle 1864-1926*, with essays by James Meldrum and David Brown, Scottish Arts Council, 1981.

PROCTER, Dod   1891-1972
Painter. Born London. Moved to Cornwall, 1907, and began study at Stanhope Forbes School at Newlyn, where she met Ernest Procter.* Studied with him at Atelier Colarossi, Paris, 1910-11, then married him, 1912. Joint exhibition of watercolours, with Ernest Procter, at the Fine Art Society, London, 1913. Decorated the Kokine Palace, Rangoon, Burma, 1919-20. Showed 'Morning' at the RA, 1927, where it was dubbed Picture of the Year and bought for the nation by the *Daily Mail*. This and other paintings by Dod and Ernest toured Britain, 1927-8. Elected ARA, 1934, and RA, 1942. Travelled a lot after her husband's death, to Tenerife, Jamaica, South Africa, and painted dark-skinned children, for which she was famed. Continued to live in Newlyn until her death, where she remained a local celebrity.

Bibl: Elizabeth Knowles, *Dod Procter RA*, Laing Art Gallery, Newcastle, in collaboration with Newlyn Orion, Penzance, 1990.

PROCTER, Ernest   1886-1935
Painter and designer. Born Tynemouth, Northumberland. Moved to Cornwall, 1907 and studied at Stanhope Forbes School at Newlyn. Studied at the Atelier Colarossi, Paris, 1910-11. Married Dod Shaw, a painter, 1912. First joint show, with Dod Procter,* of watercolours at the Fine Art Society, London, 1913. Decorated, with his wife, the Kokine Palace, Rangoon, Burma, 1919-20. Elected member of the International Society, 1925. Touring exhibition, throughout Britain, of recent paintings by Ernest and Dod Procter, 1927-8. Elected member of NEAC, 1929. Solo exhibition of 'Diaphenicons', glazed and illuminated painted decorations, at the Leicester Galleries, 1931. Appointed Director of Studies in Design and Craft, Glasgow School of Art, 1934.

PROKOFIEV, Oleg
Painter and sculptor. Born in Paris. Moved to Russia at the age of seven with his parents, and studied at an Art School in Moscow. Studied painting in the studio of the painter, R. Falk. 1971 he moved to England and became a full-time

JOHN QUINTON PRINGLE, 1864-1925. *'Poultry yard, Gartcosh'*, 1906. 24 ½ in. x 29 ¾ in. National Galleries of Scotland.

artist. 1972-4 awarded the Gregory Fellowship in painting at Fine Art Department, Leeds University. 1979 he turned to sculpture, mainly using wood. 1974 first solo exhibition at Leeds City Art Gallery, followed by solo exhibitions in Europe and the United States.

PROUT, Margaret Fisher   1875-1963
Painter of landscapes, flowers and figures. Born London, the daughter of Mark Fisher, the painter. Studied with him and at the Slade School, 1894-7. Exhibited at the NEAC from 1906; became a member, 1925. Married John Prout, 1908. Taught drawing at Hammersmith School of Arts and Crafts before 1914, a notable early example of a woman holding such a post. First solo exhibition at the Beaux Arts Gallery, 1922. Exhibited at the RA from 1921. Elected RWS, 1945, and ARA, 1948. Work in the Tate Gallery collection.

PRYDE, James   1866-1941
Painter. Born Edinburgh, Scotland. Studied at the Royal Scottish Academy, and in Bouguereau's studio in Paris for three months. Moved to London, 1890. Mabel Pryde, his sister, had earlier moved to London to study painting and there she married William Nicholson.* 1894-6 James Pryde and Nicholson collaborated under the name of the 'Beggarstaff Brothers', producing highly successful posters. Their partnership lasted until around 1898. Their novel technique of using cut-out paper silhouettes effected a revolution in poster design. Pryde temporarily took to the stage after 1896, acting in touring productions. In the early 1900s he began producing portraits of figures such as Ellen Terry, Henry Irving and Lady Ottoline Morrell. He also began a series on celebrated criminals, which was not completed. 1905-25 he began producing large theatrical paintings which recall the work of Velasquez, Piranesi

and Hogarth, and highlight his preoccupation with horror and decay. 1930 was commissioned to design the sets for Paul Robeson's *Othello* at the Savoy. 1933 first retrospective exhibition at the Leicester Galleries, London. By then his health was ruined by alcohol and he was unable to be present at the private view.

Bibl: Derek Hudson, *James Pryde 1866-1941,* Constable, London, 1949.

PRYDE, Mabel   1871-1918
Painter. Born Edinburgh, the sister of the painter, James Pryde.* Studied at Hubert Herkomber's private art school at Bushey, where she met William Nicholson,* a close colleague of her brother. Married William Nicholson, 1893. Mother of Ben Nicholson.* Along with her husband, Mabel Pryde had a love of the theatre and costumes and often painted her children in various period clothes. Solo exhibition held at Chenil Gallery, 1911. Posthumous retrospective exhibition held at the Goupil Gallery, London, 1920.

PRYSE, Fitzgerald Spencer   b.1880
Painter of imperial subjects. Born France. Educated at Eton then studied painting at various art schools in London. Included in Venice exhibition, 1907. Served with distinction during the First World War, winning the MC and the Croix de Guerre. Illustrated the Pageant of Empire Souvenir of the Wembley exhibition, 1924. Visited Nigeria and the Gold Coast for the Empire Marketing Board, 1928. Patronised by King George V. Author of *Through the Lines to Abd El Karim's stronghold in the Riffs,* (no date). Works in the V & A, British Museum, Tate Gallery, and the galleries of Liverpool, Manchester and Birmingham.

PULHAM, Peter Rose   1910-1956
Painter and photographer. Born London. Studied at the AA School of Architecture, 1927-8, and then at Worcester College, Oxford. Worked as a photographer on Harper's Bazaar, but gave this up for painting , 1938. Worked in a Surrealist manner and knew painters of that style in Paris and London. Lived in Paris during the 1930s and returned there, 1944-5. First solo exhibition held at the Redfern Gallery, 1947; another at the Hanover Gallery, 1950. Died in France. Work in the Tate Gallery collection.

PULLEE, Margaret   b.1910
Painter. Born in USA. Studied at Chelsea School of Art, 1927-9, and RCA, 1928-31. Has exhibited at the RA, with the NEAC and in the provinces. Represented in Leeds City Art Gallery, as well as in public and private collections in America. (Plate 73, p.331.)

PURSER, Keith   b.1944
Painter and collagist. Born Bromley, Kent. He attended Sidcup School of Art, 1960-2. After leaving art school he travelled frequently in Europe, the Middle East and Scandinavia, funding the trips with a variety of temporary jobs, always painting but not exhibiting until 1978 and a move to Sussex, where he received encouragement to do so from Rye Art Gallery and the Rye Society of Artists of which he is still a member. Early work was mainly abstract (paintings, collages, reliefs) but after moving to Cornwall in 1983 his output became more and more directly influenced by landscape; other interests and influences include classical music and literature. He now lives in Lincolnshire.

PYE, William   b.1938
Sculptor. Born London. National Service, 1956-8, then attended Wimbledon School of Art, 1958-61. Studied sculpture at the Royal College of Art. 1972 visiting Professor at California State University. 1966 first one-person show at the Redfern Gallery, London. Best known for his abstract sculptures in stainless steel.

QUAY, Russell   b.1922
Painter. Studied at Beckenham Art School and Brighton College of Art. Travelled in Africa. First solo exhibition at the AIA Gallery, London, 1951.

QUICK, Bob   b.1939
Painter. Studied at Croydon College of Art, and Brighton College of Art. First solo exhibition at Pavilions in the Park, 1969. Travelled to Prague, Czechoslovakia for the British Council, 1971. Exhibited at the Grabowski Gallery, London, 1972, his work then attempting to express popular imagery in its most concentrated and skeletonic form.

QUICK, Charles   b.1957
Sculptor. Studied at Leeds Polytechnic, 1977-80. 1982 won Yorkshire Arts Association Award. 1984-5 studio member, Leeds Art Space Society, East Street Studios, followed by a position as Sculptor-in-Residence at the Henry Moore Centre for the Study of Sculpture, Leeds City Art Gallery, 1985. 1980 first solo exhibition at the Breadline Gallery, Rodley, Leeds, followed by a second exhibition there, 1981.

QUIGLEY, Peter   b.1925
Painter. Born Stockport, Cheshire. Graduated from Manchester College of Art, 1953, with an Associationship of the College and a travelling scholarship, spent in France. First solo exhibition in Manchester, 1960. Attracted to Eastbourne as a place to live and work owing to the coast and the downland landscape.

QUILTER, Roger   b.1921
Painter and constructionist. Born Stroud, Gloucestershire. Studied at Royal West of England College of Art. During the Second World War he was engaged with photographic and film work for the Royal Navy and joined a photographic agency at the end of the war. Renewed his interest in painting and began to make three-dimensional constructions; also became scenic designer for Southampton Student Players. First solo exhibition at the Hamwic Gallery, Southampton.

QUINTON, Marcelle
Sculptor. Born Berlin, Germany. Emigrated to New York with her family. Studied at Bryn Mawr College, USA, and at St. Hilda's College, Oxford, England. First exhibited at the O'Hana Gallery, London. Works in stone and plaster. Specialises in animals, human faces and figures.

CHARLES QUICK, b.1957. 'A Light Wave' (detail), 1988. Sculpture at Wakefield Westgate Station, West Yorkshire. Wood, steel light and electronics. 13ft. 8in. x 13ft. 8in. x 196ft. 8in. Photograph by Graham Sykes.

RABIN, Sam   b.1903
Sculptor and painter. Born Cheetham, North Manchester. Studied at Manchester School of Art and Slade, 1921-4. 1925 visited Paris and attended the studio of Charles Despiau. 1928 worked on 'The Four Winds', a sculptural decoration for the new London Underground headquarters. Admired Jacob Epstein* and pursued a career as a professional wrestler to finance his art. Also sang, and toured army camps during the Second World War. 1949 appointed Teacher of Drawing at Goldsmiths' College School of Art; his pupils included Bridget Riley* and Tom Keating. 1965 moved to Bournemouth College of Art. 1985 moved to Poole Art Centre, Dorset.

RACKHAM, Arthur   1867-1939
Illustrator and painter. Attended evening classes at Lambeth School of Art, where he enrolled in 1884. 1884-96 he worked on illustrations for magazines in his spare time. 1884 travelled to Australia. 1898 illustrated *The Ingoldsby Legends,* followed by *Gulliver's Travels* and in 1900 *Grimm's Fairy Tales.* 1890s-1930s visited Europe, mainly Germany, Switzerland and Italy and produced many watercolours while on these trips. 1902 elected ARSW. 1905 first solo exhibition of illustrations at Leicester Galleries, London. He exhibited there regularly thereafter. His last commission, in 1936, was for illustrations to *Wind in the Willows.* His illustrations are often ghoulishly supernatural, and were in part inspired by his admiration for Dürer.

RAE, Henrietta   1859-1928
Painter. Born London. Entered Queen's Square School of Art at the age of thirteen and went on to study at Heatherley's. After several attempts she was accepted into the RA schools, 1877. Exhibited at the RA from 1881, specialising in genre and classical subjects and was much berated for painting the female nude. Married the painter Ernest Normand in 1884. Won medals at the Paris Salon and at Chicago Universal exhibitions.

RAINEY, Clifford   b.1948
Sculptor. Born Whitehead, Co. Antrim, Northern Ireland. 1965-8 worked as a linen damask designer with William Ewart & Son Ltd., Belfast. Spent four months crewing with a trawler off Iceland, 1968. Travelled extensively and painted in America and Canada, 1969. Studied at Hornsey College of Art, 1968-9, and North East Polytechnic, 1963-71, in the Sculpture Department. After a period in Denmark and Norway, studied at RCA, 1971-3. First solo exhibition held at Arnolfini Gallery, Bristol, 1974. Exhibits regularly and also travels extensively. Represented by the Piccadilly Gallery, London.

RAMOS, Adrian   b.1956
Painter. Born London. Familiarly known as 'Tod' Ramos. Studied at Brighton College of Art, 1975-6, Gloucester College of Art and Design, 1976-9, and RA Schools, 1979-82. First solo exhibition at Richmond Gallery, London, 1985. He regularly depicts horse racing scenes, the result of a life-long involvement in horse racing and training.

RAMPLING, Madeleine   b.1941
Painter. Born Kent. Studied in Florence, 1958, under Signorina Simi, at Chelsea Polytechnic, London, 1959-60 and at Heatherleys Art School, London, 1962-3. She completed her studies in Florence, 1966-8. First solo exhibition at Casa Di Dante, Florence, Italy, 1967. Another held at the New Art Gallery, Birmingham, 1978.

RAMSAY, Lady Patricia   1886-1974
Painter. Daughter of the Duke and Duchess of Connaught and Strathearn and granddaughter of Queen Victoria. 1919 married Admiral The Hon. Sir Alexander Ramsay and by royal permission renounced the style and title of 'HRH' and 'Princess'. First solo exhibition held at the Goupil Gallery, London, 1928. Elected member of the NEAC, 1931, and an associate of the RSPW, 1940. Worked for a time in Ceylon and Bermuda.

RAMSBOTHAM, Meredith   b.1943
Painter. Born Palestine and later moved to Melbourne. Educated in England and entered the Slade School of Fine Art, 1965. Marriage and a family reduced her opportunity to paint, but, encouraged by the glass-engraver, Laurence Whistler, she took up glass-engraving for a period, afterwards returning to painting. Has held two solo exhibitions at the New Art Centre, London, and another at Sally Hunter Fine Art, 1990.

RAMSDEN, Michael   b.1947
Painter. Born New South Wales, Australia. Moved to London, 1968. First solo exhibition at Clytie Jessop Gallery, London, 1970.

RAMSEY, Alma
Sculptor. Studied at RCA, 1927-30 under Gilbert Ledward* and Henry Moore* and was much influenced by their emphasis upon direct carving in wood and stone. First solo exhibition at Peter Dingley, Stratford-upon-Avon, 1966. Included in the collections of Herbert Art Gallery, Coventry, Oxford City and County Museum, and Nottingham and Worcester Education Departments. Commissioned to do the First Coventry Crib at Coventry Cathedral.

RANCE, Victoria   b.1959
Sculptor. Born Wallingford, Oxon. Studied at North Oxon Technical College, Banbury, 1978-9 and at Newcastle University, 1979-83. Spent a year sculpting in Mexico and Bolivia. First exhibited at the Hatton Gallery, Newcastle upon Tyne, 1980. Works with mild steel using the traditional blacksmiths' technique, producing semi-abstract sculptures based on human and animal forms.

RAPHAEL, Sarah   b.1960
Painter. Studied at Camberwell School of Art, 1977-81. Began exhibiting with Agnew's, London, 1984. First solo exhibition held at Christopher Hull Gallery, London, 1985. Another held at Agnew's in 1989 had a series of paintings based on the theme of the scapegoat. Represented in a group exhibition at the National Portrait Gallery, 1983, and the 'Sunday Times Mother and Child Exhibition' at the Lefevre Gallery, 1988. Included in the collection of Metropolitan Art Gallery, New York, USA. Her paintings are often allegorical.

RAPHAEL, Wendy
Painter. Studied at the Regional College of Art, Manchester and at the Manchester College of Education. First solo exhibition at the Ginnel Gallery, Manchester, 1984. Member of Manchester Graphics Club and the Manchester Artists Studio Association. Has also designed

SARAH RAPHAEL, b.1960.
'The Marriage'. Pencil on paper.
6in. x 8in. Thomas Agnew and
Sons Ltd., London.

covers for the books of the Czech poet, V.J. Sverak, *One Day in the Life of Gabriel Sludkovic* and *The World Through Other Eyes*.

RASMUSSEN, Roy   b.1919
Sculptor. Born London. First solo exhibition at John Whibley Gallery, London, 1969.

RATCLIFF, John   b.1914
Painter and architect. Born Mirfield, Yorkshire. Studied architecture at the Architectural Association, London, 1932-7. First solo exhibition at the Drian Gallery, London, 1959. Fellow of the Free Painters Group. Exhibits at the RA and is represented in the British Council collection.

RATCLIFF, Sonia   b.1939
Painter. Born Oldham, Lancashire. Started a career in journalism. Turned to painting after the birth of four children, 1971. First solo exhibition at the Clarendon Gallery, Manchester, 1974, followed by a second exhibition there, 1975. Returned to full-time journalism in 1980 but continues to paint and exhibit.

RATCLIFFE, Andrew   b.1948
Painter. Born Colne, Lancashire. Studied at Burnley College of Art, 1964-6 and at Canterbury College of Art, 1966-9. First solo exhibition at Oldham Art Gallery, 1981.

RATCLIFFE, William   1870-1955
Painter. Born Churchwater, near King's Lynn, Norfolk.

WILLIAM RATCLIFFE, 1870-1955. *'Winter Scene, Sweden'*. 24¼ in. x 30³⁄₁₆ in. Manchester City Art Galleries.

Attended evening classes at Manchester School of Art under Walter Crane, whilst working as a pattern designer for the Wallpaper Combine. 1906 moved to Letchworth. 1908 produced artwork for the Garden City engagement calendar, and postcard views of the city in the same year. After 1907 he took up oil painting under the influence of Harold Gilman* who moved to Letchworth, 1908. 1910 took up painting full-time; the same year he moved to London and studied at the Slade part-time; 1910-11 also attended the Saturday afternoon Fitzroy Street meetings. 1911 became a member of the Camden Town Group and first exhibited in its June 1911 show. Also a founder member of the London Group, set up in 1914. 1946 first solo exhibition at Roland Browse and Delbanco Galleries, London. Included in the collections of Tate Gallery, Southampton Art Gallery, Letchworth Museum and Art Gallery and Plymouth Museum and Art Gallery.

RATHMELL, Lilian   b.1909
Painter and costume designer. Studied at Liverpool College of Art and Cardiff College of Art. Exhibited at the Playhouse Gallery, London, 1981. Has taught both Dress Design and Fine Art at Newport College of Art. Included in the collections of Welsh Arts Council and Newport Museum and Art Gallery.

RATHMELL, Thomas   b.1912
Painter. Born Wallasey, Cheshire. Studied at Liverpool School of Art and RCA. During the Second World War he worked in industrial and Naval camouflage. Has regularly held solo exhibitions in South Wales. 1969 commissioned to produce a commemorative painting of the Investiture of the Prince of Wales for the Welsh Office, and in 1978 produced a mural for the Welsh Rugby Union. Represented in public art galleries in Cardiff, Newport and Swansea.

RAVEN-HILL, Leonard   1867-1942

Illustrator and cartoonist. Born Bath, Avon. Studied first at City & Guilds School of Art, London, where he was a friend of Charles Ricketts* and Charles Shannon,* and then at Académie Julian, Paris. Exhibited at the Paris Salon from 1886, at the NEAC from 1888 and at the RA 1889-1913. Founder of the magazine *The Butterfly,* 1893. Contributor of illustrations to *Punch,* 1895-1935. Author of *An Indian Sketchbook,* 1903. Work in the Tate Gallery collections.

RAVERAT, Gwen   1885-1957

Painter and wood engraver. Granddaughter of Sir Charles Darwin. Studied at Slade School of Art. Her Cambridge childhood is described in her autobiography, *Period Piece.* 1911 married the French painter, Jacques Raverat, and with him emigrated to Vence in France in 1920 where they stayed until his death in 1925. Founder-member of the Society of Wood Engravers. 1928 settled in the Old Rectory at Harlton, Cambridgeshire, and from then on was constantly in demand as an illustrator; also continued to paint. Became a regular art critic for *Time and Tide.* 1987 a comprehensive exhibition of her work was shown at the Manor Gallery, Royston, Herts. Examples of her wood engravings can be found in the Fitzwilliam Museum, Cambridge.

RAVILIOUS, Eric   1903-1943

Painter, wood engraver and illustrator. Born London but brought up in Eastbourne, Sussex, where his father had an antiques shop and where he first saw examples of English watercolours. Studied at Eastbourne School of Art, 1919-22, and RCA where he entered the Design School. Befriended Edward Bawden,* with whom he was from then on closely associated, and was taught by Paul Nash,* whose use of the 'starved' brush informed Ravilious's own watercolour technique. 1926 won a travelling scholarship to Italy and was impressed by the work of the Italian Primitives. 1928 executed, with Bawden, a mural decoration for Morley College, London (now destroyed), and the following year they took a joint-rent on Brick House in Great Bardfield, Essex. At first used as a weekend retreat, it then became their permanent home until 1935 when Ravilious and his wife moved to Castle Hedingham, Essex. His output was prolific, both as a watercolourist and wood engraver. 1936 was commissioned by Wedgwood to execute designs for pottery and china which enjoyed wide success. 1940 appointed Official War Artist, first with the Royal Marines, then with the Royal Air Force. Was killed in an aeroplane accident. (Plate 10, p.27.)

Bibl: Helen Binyon, *Eric Ravilious: Memoir of an Artist,* Lutterworth Press, Guildford and London, 1983.

RAWLINS, Darsie   b.1912

Sculptor. Born Kentmere, Cumbria. Studied at RCA. Exhibits at RA and in the provinces. Commissions include sculpture for Denbighshire Technical College, Wrexham, Hampshire County Offices, Tewkesbury Abbey and elsewhere, including many churches.

RAYBOULD, Howard   b.1946

Woodworker. Born in England. Studied at Ravensbourne College of Art and Design, 1966-9. 1978 first solo exhibition at Crafts Advisory Committee, London. Since 1982 represented regularly in group and solo exhibitions at the Thumb Gallery, London. Author of *The Woodwork Book* published by Pan Books.

REA, Betty   1904-1965

Sculptor. Born London (Dr. Barnardo was her great uncle). Studied painting and sculpture at the Regent Street Polytechnic, 1922-4 and then at RCA, where Henry Moore* was a student teacher. Married in 1926. 1934-6 she was the secretary of the AIA. 1949-64 taught sculpture at Homerton College, Cambridge. A figure group of hers is at Hockerill College, Bishop's Stortford. 1960 solo exhibition at Zwemmer Gallery, and a retrospective at the same gallery, 1965.

READ, Simon   b.1949

Painter, sculptor and photographer. Born Bristol, Avon. Studied at Somerset College of Art, 1968-9, Leeds University, 1969-73 and Chelsea School of Art, 1973-5. 1970s taught at Middlesex Polytechnic. 1976 first one-person show at the Acme Gallery, London. 1979 studio at Butlers Wharf, London Docks, destroyed by fire. 1980 bought a Dutch cargo barge, which he uses as a studio, moored at Woodbridge, Suffolk. Teaches part-time at various art colleges, e.g. Corsham and Chelsea. 1976 first solo exhibition 'Twelve Stern Presences', at Acme Gallery. 1984 first Canadian exhibition 'Landmarks' at Mendel Art Gallery, Saskatoon.

REASON, Cyril   b.1931

Painter and printmaker. Born London. Studied at St. Albans School of Art, 1951 and RCA, 1951-4. Fellow in Fine Art at Nottingham University, 1959-62. First solo exhibition at the Beaux Arts Gallery, 1958. Has taught at various art colleges, including Brighton, and RCA, and was Director of Art at Morley College, 1972-9. Recent major exhibition at Brighton Museum and Art Gallery, 1986. Many of his paintings stem from literary sources.

REAY, John   b.1947

Painter. Born London. After working in a variety of jobs, he studied at Brighton and Norwich Schools of Art, 1969-73. 1974 moved to Lowestoft to live near the sea, where he paints the East Coast in light colours. 1978 first solo exhibition held at Alwyn Gallery. Solo exhibition held at the Piccadilly Gallery and has also exhibited at the Phoenix Gallery, Lavenham, Suffolk, 1988.

REDDAWAY, Jean (née Brett)   b.1923

Painter. Studied at Slade School of Art, 1940-4. Taught art at Impington Village School, Cambridge, 1944. Exhibited work at the RA, and had solo shows in Beirut, Khartoum and in Poland. Her husband was British Ambassador to Poland, 1974-8 and she painted many Polish scenes. 1979 awarded OBE for services to Anglo-Polish relations. 1979 solo exhibition of Polish paintings at the Polish Culture Institute, London.

REDDICK, Peter   b.1924

Painter and printmaker. Born Essex. Studied at the South East Essex Technical College, 1941-2, Cardiff School of Art, 1947-8 and the Slade School, 1948-51. Taught at Regent St. Polytechnic, 1951-6 and has held many teaching posts since, e.g. in Glasgow and currently in Brighton. Has provided the word engravings for numerous books from 1964 onwards, including several novels by Trollope for the Folio Society. 1979-80 Gregynog Fellow in wood engraving and 1980 given a touring show of this work by the Welsh Arts Council.

REDFERN, David   b.1947
Painter and printmaker. Born Burton-on-Trent, Stafford-shire. Studied Fine Art at Reading University, 1965-9, and at the Slade School, 1969-71. 1971-83 worked as a gallery assistant at the Serpentine Gallery. From 1977 included in mixed exhibitions. 1984 large exhibition held at Wolverhampton Art Gallery. Paints the overlooked corners of urban life. Work in the collections of the Arts Council and the British Council.

REDFERN, June   b.1951
Painter. Born Fife, Scotland. Studied at Edinburgh College of Art, 1968-73. 1976 first solo exhibition at the Scottish Arts Council Gallery, Edinburgh. 1982-3 taught at Preston Polytechnic and Cardiff College of Art. 1985-6 Artist-in-Residence at the National Gallery, London, with a show there, 1986. 1987 touring exhibition, of recent work, in Edinburgh, Bradford, Aberdeen and Eastbourne. 1987 illustrated *Blood and Ice* by Liz Lochhead. Her dramatic paintings employ bold expressionist brushwork and strong colour.

REDPATH, Anne   1895-1965
Painter. Daughter of a tweed designer of Galashiels ('I do with a spot of red or yellow in harmony of grey, what my father did in his tweed'). 1913 entered Edinburgh College of Art and in 1917 qualified as an art teacher. 1919 was awarded a travelling scholarship and visited, among other places, Siena, where she admired the Italian Primitives. 1920 married an architect working for the War Graves Commission in France, where they lived and had three sons. 1934 returned to Scotland and for the next fifteen years painted mostly still lifes and landscapes of the Borders and Skye, then began to travel regularly, to France, Corsica, Portugal, Spain, the Canary Isles and Italy. Her colours grew richer and freer, and in her late paintings, especially of church interiors, took on a searing intensity. Elected RSA, 1952, ARA, 1960, and ARWS, 1962. (Plate 74, p.422.)

Bibl: *Anne Redpath: A Memorial Exhibition*, Arts Council of Great Britain, Scottish Committee, 1965-6; Patrick Bourne, *Anne Redpath 1895-1965: Her life and work*, Bourne Fine Art, 1989.

REED, Denis William   1917-1979
Painter. Born Bristol, Avon. Studied at West of England College of Art, 1934-8, after which he moved to the RCA where his studies were interrupted by war. Entered the Army, but was found unfit for overseas service. Appointed Art Advisor to the London District of Army Education. One of several artists represented in the 'After Duty' exhibition presented by the AIA towards the end of the war. Demobbed 1946 and resumed his studies at RCA. Exhibited at the RA, RBA, RWEA, with the NEAC and elsewhere. Elected associate, and then full member of the Royal West of England Academy. Appointed to Lough-borough College of Art, he was soon obliged to resign, owing to ill-health. Thereafter he suffered recurring bouts of illness. Returned to Bristol and painted many local landscapes.

REES, John Bromfield Gay   1912-1965
Painter. Born Llanelly, South Wales. Was often confined at home as a child after developing serious eczema, and began to draw and paint. Awarded first prize in the junior section of the National Eisteddfod, when aged thirteen. Studied at the School of Art and Craft, Llanelly, 1926-31. First exhibited in the annual exhibition at the Swansea Art Galleries, 1930. Studied at the RA Schools, 1932-9.

Began suffering from a nervous disorder in 1935, and regularly needed constant supervision. 1939-44 he produced larger watercolour drawings, in which he cast aside the descriptive realism which was prevalent in his early work. 1948 visited Paris, where he was influenced by a George Braque exhibition. Owing to increasing bad health after 1951 his output lessened. 1989 retrospective exhibition held at Michael Parkin Fine Art Ltd., London.

REES, Sir Richard   1900-1970
Painter. Born Oxford, son of Sir J.D. Rees, MP. Educated at Trinity College, Cambridge. Studied watercolour painting under Fred Lawson* in Yorkshire, 1936, also at St. John's Wood Art School, 1937, and at Camberwell School of Art and Crafts, 1945-6. Exhibited at the RA, RBA, RSA and with the London Group.

REGO, Paula   b.1935
Painter. Born Lisbon, Portugal. Studied at Slade School of Art, 1952-6. 1957-63 lived in Ericeira, Portugal, with her husband the painter, Victor Willing.* 1963-75 lived in London and Portugal. 1976, settled permanently in London. 1988 retrospective held at the Gulbenkian Foundation, Lisbon, and the Serpentine Gallery, London. Her discovery of Dubuffet in the 1950s first began her pursuit of childhood experience. She gradually moved into a near-Surrealist style, collaging biomorphic shapes on to her canvas. In the early 1980s she began using cartoon-like animals to express her interest in human behaviour. When humans replaced animals in her work, it became more obvious that her interest lay with undercover emotions, 'cheating, lying, the half-sins, the mediocre ones', as she has admitted. Though her subject matter is never explicit, it hints at the appalling, and generates sinister unease. Her etchings based on nursery rhymes, exhibited at Marlborough Fine Art, London, 1989, were the most original illustrations to be produced since David Hockney's* designs for the Brothers Grimm. Work in the collections of the Arts Council, British Council and the Tate Gallery.

Bibl: *Paula Rego*, Serpentine Gallery, London, 1988.

REID, Norman   b.1915
Painter and art administrator. Born Scotland. Studied at Edinburgh College of Art. Served in the Argyll and Sutherland Highlanders during the Second World War. Joined the staff of the Tate Gallery, 1946, becoming Deputy Director, 1954. Keeper, 1959 and Director, 1964-79. While an employee of the Tate Gallery, he painted mostly in his summer holidays. Sent work to RA summer exhibitions. Work in the Tate Gallery collections. Knighted 1970.

REINGANUM, Victor   b.1907
Painter. Born London. Studied at Heatherley's School of Art and the Académie Julian, Paris, 1925-8, also privately under Fernard Léger. Art director at Elstree Studios, 1928-9. Made his first abstract paintings, 1929; also worked as a freelance illustrator. Exhibited with 'pandemonium' Group, 1930-2. Taught graphic design at Croydon College of Art, 1961. Solo exhibition held at Blond Fine Art, London, 1984.

REMINGTON, Mary   b.1920
Painter. Born Reigate, Surrey. Studied at Redhill School

of Art and was awarded a scholarship to the RCA. Afterwards studied at the Académie de la Grande Chaumière, Paris. Exhibits at the RA, ROI, RBA and with the NEAC. Represented in the collections of Brighton Art Gallery and Museum, Kensington Public Library and elsewhere.

REYNOLDS, Alan   b.1926
Painter. Born Newmarket, Suffolk. Left school at the age of fourteen and did various jobs. During the war he served with the Suffolk Regiment and the Highland Light Infantry in France, Belgium, Holland and Germany. After demobilisation in 1947 he studied at Woolwich Polytechnic, 1948-52. First solo exhibition held at Redfern Gallery, 1952. Studied at RCA, 1952-3. After this he exhibited regularly at the Redfern Gallery and also abroad, in New York, Rome and Paris. His early work displayed careful attention to nature which in his oils often become transformed into a slightly eery world of stylised, semi-abstract shapes. Even in these much emphasis was placed on the horizontal and vertical. In 1958 he became dissatisfied with this style and moved into pure abstraction, using simple geometric forms that reflected his admiration for equilibrium in abstract terms.

Bibl: J.P. Hodin, *Alan Reynolds,* The Redfern Artists Series, London, 1962.

REYNOLDS, Bernard Robert   b.1915
Sculptor. Studied at Norwich School of Art, 1932-7, and at Westminster School of Art, 1937-8. Became a lecturer in sculpture at Ipswich School of Art and exhibited at the RA.

REYNOLDS, Frank   1876-1953
Painter and illustrator. Born London. Studied at Heatherley's. Exhibited at the RA, RI and was elected RI in 1903. His name is associated with *The Illustrated London News, The Sketch,* and *Punch.* Also illustrated books, including the works of Dickens.

REYNOLDS, Ruth   b.1915
Sculptor and painter. Born India. Studied at Guildford School of Art, in Budapest and at Wycombe School of Art. Solo exhibitions include one at Halifax House, Oxford University Graduate Centre, 1965, and another at the Century Galleries, Henley-on-Thames, 1987. Represented in Stoke Mandeville Hospital, Aylesbury, in Lambeth Palace Garden and elsewhere.

REYNOLDS-STEPHENS, William   1862-1943
Sculptor. Born Detroit, USA, of British parents. Studied at the RA Schools, winning prizes for both painting and sculpture. Exhibited at the RA, 1886-1942, with sculpture only from 1894. Maker of numerous memorials, e.g. Archbishop Davidson in the courtyard of Lambeth Palace and William Quiller Orchardson in St. Paul's Cathedral. 1904 designed the screen, reredos and other fittings for St. Mary the Virgin, Great Warley, Essex. Elected FRBS 1904, PRBS 1921-33. Awarded RBS gold medal, 1928. Knighted 1931. Work in the Tate Gallery.

RHOADES, Geoffrey   b.1898
Painter and engraver. Born London. Studied at Clapham School of Art and the Slade School, 1919-24. Taught art part-time at Working Men's College, London, 1928-36, and at Bishop's Stortford College, 1930-45. Assistant at the Ruskin School of Drawing, Oxford in the 1950s. Solo

exhibition at Wye College, Ashford, Kent, 1956. Work in the Tate Gallery collections.

RICE, Anne Estelle   1879-1959
Painter and illustrator. Born Philadelphia, USA. Studied at Philadelphia Academy of Fine Arts. Travelled to France in 1906 to make illustrations of the social and fashion scene. Member of Societaire de Salon d'Automne, then jury member, 1910. First solo show at the Baillie Gallery, London, 1910. Contributed to J.D. Fergusson's* magazine *Rhythm,* 1911-13. Married the critic Raymond Drey, 1913 and thereafter divided her time between London and Paris. Her portrait of her friend, the writer Katherine Mansfield, is in the collection of the National Gallery of New Zealand, Wellington.

RICH, Alfred   1856-1921
Painter. Born Gravely, near Lindfield, Sussex. 1871-90 worked as an heraldic draughtsman. Studied at Westminster School of Art and the Slade School, 1890-6. As a landscape painter he was much influenced by Dutch examples, particularly Peter de Wint. Exhibited with the NEAC from 1896 and was elected a member, 1898. Represented in many public collections. Author of *Watercolour Painting,* published 1918.

RICHARDS, Albert   1919-1945
Painter. Born Liverpool, but moved to Wallasey, Cheshire, as a child. Studied at Wallasey School of Art and RCA. April 1940 called up for war service. Posted as private in the Royal Engineers. Painted in every spare moment and his pictures were bought by the War Artists Advisory Committee. In Spring 1943 he transferred to a parachute squadron. March 1944 confirmed as an Official War Artist with rank of Captain. Parachuted into Europe on D-Day with his old regiment and served with distinction. Killed whilst preparing to paint a night attack near the river Maas. His style showed a synthesis of then current stylistics and was informed by careful observation and the immediacy of his first-hand experience. Represented in Imperial War Museum and Walker Art Gallery, Liverpool.

RICHARDS, Ceri   1903-1971
Painter and relief maker. Born near Swansea, Wales. Studied at Swansea School of Art, 1921-4 and RCA, 1924-7. First solo exhibition held 1930 at the Glynn Vivian Art Gallery, Swansea. In the late 1930s began making relief constructions and assemblages in a Surrealist vein. 1937 became a member of the London Group. His mature work reveals his lifelong love of music and poetry as well as his interest in biomorphic imagery. Also designed costumes and sets for opera and murals for churches. Taught at RCA, 1956-61. Represented Britain at Venice Biennale, 1962.

Bibl: *Ceri Richards,* Tate Gallery, London, 1981.

RICHARDS, Frances   b.1903
Painter, illustrator and pottery designer. Born Burslem, Stoke-on-Trent, the daughter of a pottery artist. Studied at Burslem School of Art, 1919-24, and worked as a pottery designer before winning a scholarship to the RCA, 1924-7. Married the painter Ceri Richards,* 1929. Illustrated *The Book of Revelation,* published London and New York, 1931. First solo exhibition at Redfern Gallery, 1945.

RICHARDS, Paul   b.1949

Painter. Studied at St. Martin's School of Art and Maidstone School of Art. First solo exhibition at the Robert Self Gallery, London, 1967. Regularly exhibits in London, Europe and the USA. Solo exhibition at Connaught Brown, London, 1988. Painter of passion, questioning the conflicts of human relationships and man's relationship with nature, through his vigorous brushwork and use of colour.

RICHES, Lizzie   b.1950

Painter. Studied at Goldsmiths' College. Her paintings are mostly of gardens and wild animals. Her concern for endangered species and the plight of the rain forests has led her to paint a series of works depicting animals and birds at risk. Commissioned by London Underground to design a poster on 'Inner City Farms'. Regularly exhibits with the Portal Gallery, London, where she first showed her work in 1975. 1987 first solo exhibition at Portal Gallery; in 1988 she took part in a group exhibition arranged by the same gallery in Chicago.

RICHMOND, Oliffe   1919-1977

Sculptor. Born Tasmania, Australia. Studied sculpture in Sydney. Worked as an assistant to Henry Moore,* 1949-50. Taught sculpture at Chelsea School of Art. Represented in the collections of the Arts Council, Kroller-Müller Museum, Otterlo, Holland and elsewhere.

RICHMOND, Robin   b.1951

Painter. Born in USA but spent her childhood and early teens in Rome. Studied at Chelsea School of Art where she obtained a BA in Fine Art and an MA in art history. An exhibition at the Boundary Gallery, London, 1987, represented her seventh solo show. An interest in Mexico is reflected in both her painting and teaching of art history. Her paintings are poetic evocations of places observed and experienced. Has also exhibited in various group shows.

RICHMOND, William Blake   1842-1921

Painter and sculptor. Born London, the son of the painter George Richmond who was a friend of Blake. Studied at the RA schools from 1857. Exhibited at the RA from 1861. Elected ARA, 1888, and RA, 1895. An opponent of Post-Impressionism, he became a leading portrait painter; his subjects included Gladstone and Bismarck; he also painted classical subjects. Slade Professor at Oxford, 1878-83. Knighted, 1897. Worked for some while in Italy, Greece and Egypt. Executed mosaics for the dome of St. Paul's Cathedral, which were much criticised.

RICKETTS, Charles   1866-1931

Painter, sculptor and wood-engraver. Born Geneva, of English and French parentage. Spent his childhood in France and Italy. Studied at Lambeth School of Art from 1882 where he met Charles Shannon* with whom he was from then on associated and with whom he founded The Vale Press, 1896-1904. Interested in reviving Old Master techniques, his paintings combine Pre-Raphaelite imagery with symbolism. Elected ARA, 1922, and RA, 1928.

Bibl: J.G.P. Delaney, *Charles Ricketts: A Biography,* Clarendon Press, Oxford, 1990.

RIDEAL, Liz   b.1954

Multimedia artist. Born Buckinghamshire. Studied at Brighton College of Art, 1972-3 and Exeter College of Art

GEOFFREY RIGDEN, b.1943. *'Samsat *1',* 1989. Acrylic and oil on board. 11in. x 12¼in. Francis Graham-Dixon Gallery, London. Photograph by John Riddy.

and Design, 1973-6, and studied English literature at Exeter University at the same time. 1981 first solo show at Exe Gallery, Exeter; 1989 most recent solo exhibition at Cornerhouse Gallery, Manchester. 1990 commissioned to make a mural for the Newcastle Garden Festival Exhibition. Pioneered the use of photo-booth photography as an art form. Work in the collections of the Arts Council and the National Portrait Gallery.

RIDGEWELL, John   b.1937

Painter. Born Halstead, Essex. Studied at Colchester School of Art, 1954-8 and RCA, 1958-61. Taught painting at Scarborough School of Art, 1961-6. Now lives and works in Suffolk. Paints in detail aspects of the countryside under threat from modern urban life. 1974 first solo exhibition at Fischer Fine Art; others at same gallery, 1976 and 1979.

RIGBY, Harold Ainsworth   1879-1938

Painter. Born Preston, Lancashire. Studied at RCA in the Design School. Taught at various schools, including Christ's Hospital, Horsham, Sussex, where he revolutionised the art department with such success that it was recognised as the first in the country and many came to consult him on his methods. Exhibited at RA.

RIGDEN, Geoffrey   b.1943

Painter. Born Cheltenham, Gloucestershire. Studied at Somerset College of Art and RCA. He has exhibited regularly since 1965 when he was a prizewinner at John Moores Liverpool exhibition. His love of jazz is reflected in the shapes and motifs found in his work. He has also made a series of constructions, consisting of rough and improvisory materials. They were partly inspired by his visits to Cyprus and Turkey, and were exhibited at the Francis Graham-Dixon Gallery, London, 1990.

RILEY, Bridget   b.1931

Painter. Born London. Studied at Goldsmiths' College of Art, 1949-52, and RCA, 1952-5. She first established her independence through her study of Neo-Impressionism

ERIC RIMMINGTON, b.1926. *'Alomissos',* 1988. 20in. x 30in. Mercury Gallery Ltd., London.

and through copying Seurat's *Pont de Courbevoire;* broken dots of colour, enlarged into autonomous units, led into her early Op Art works. Her first solo exhibition at Gallery One, London, in 1962, was followed by a second in 1963, for which Anton Ehrenzweig wrote the catalogue foreword. He also prepared a major critical essay on her art for *Art International* which helped secure her reputation. Op Art rests on the realisation that certain image formations, though stationary on the canvas, move within the eye's retina. Riley manipulated these effects with dazzling intensity, working first solely with black and white introducing colour in 1966. 1968 she won the International Prize for Painting at the 34th Venice Biennale and in the same year, with Peter Sedgeley,* helped set up SPACE, a scheme for organising artists' studios which came into operation in 1969. 1970-1 travelled to Hanover, Berne, Düsseldorf and Prague, whilst another major show of her work was exhibited at the Hayward Gallery, London, 1971. Since then she has exhibited widely in numerous shows. She has also travelled extensively, a visit to Egypt having an important impact on the development of her use of colour.

Bibl: *Bridget Riley, Selected Works 1963-1984,* London, Goldsmiths' College Gallery, 1985.

RILEY, Harold   b.1934
Painter. Born Salford, Lancashire. L.S. Lowry* saw Riley's work when he was still at school and persuaded the director of Salford City Art Gallery to buy a small painting of a local mill. Studied at the Slade School of Art and then returned to live and work in Salford, where he renewed his friendship with Lowry. Solo exhibition of recent work at Salford Museum and Art Gallery, 1969. Has painted portraits of three Popes, three Presidents of the USA and members of the Royal Family.

RILEY, Paul   b.1944
Painter. Studied at Kingston College of Art. First exhibited at the age of sixteen at the RA, 1960. First solo exhibition held at Richmond Art Gallery. 1970-9 worked in architecture and carried out various commissions, including murals for Battle Hospital, Reading, Firth Brown Steelworks, Sheffield, and St. Frehmund's Church, Dunstable. 1979 moved to Devon and in 1984 opened Coombe Farm Studios, an arts centre for the teaching of art and crafts. His many solo exhibitions include one at Chris Beetles, London, 1990.

RILEY, Richard   b.1950
Painter and printmaker. Born Halifax, Yorkshire. Studied printmaking at Bradford College of Art, 1969-70 and worked for one year as a commercial screen printer. 1979-84 co-Director of the Manchester Print Workshop. 1983 worked for two months with an eminent Chinese artist/lithographer in Manchester. 1984 travelled in China and in 1985 worked there for three months. 1980 solo exhibition at Salford Art Gallery; most recent at the Ikon Gallery, 1985.

RIMMINGTON, Edith   b.1902
Painter. Born Leicester. Studied at Brighton Art School, 1919-22. Joined the Surrealists at the Surrealist Objects

exhibition at the London Gallery, 1937. Exhibited with the Surrealists and contributed to *London Bulletin,* 1940-7. Contributed to the International Surrealist Exhibition at the Galerie Maeght, Paris, 1947. Best known for her weird figures, which often combine human and animal parts, found in dream-like settings.

RIMMINGTON, Eric   b.1926
Painter. Studied at the Slade School of Art, 1949-52. Taught at Scarborough College of Art, 1952-8 and Bradford College of Art, 1958-66, then at Birmingham and Wolverhampton until 1982. 1963 first solo exhibition at the Lane Gallery, Bradford; 1989 most recent at the Mercury Gallery, London. Paints sumptuous small pictures using strong colour and much detail.

RINTOOL, Katherine   1890-1970
Painter. Born Clifton, Bristol. Studied at the Slade School of Art, 1909-12 where her peers were Stanley Spencer,* Mark Gertler,* Dora Carrington* and Edward Wadsworth.* Taught art at various girls schools beginning in 1914 and from 1928, for a while, with Marion Richardson, a pioneering art teacher at Benendon School. Last appointment was at the West of England College of Art. Painter of people and places. Memorial exhibition at Royal West of England Academy, Bristol, 1972.

RIPPON, Peter   b.1950
Painter. Born Essex. Studied at Colchester School of Art, 1967-9, St. Martin's School of Art, 1969-72 and RA Schools, 1972-5. From 1973 included in mixed exhibitions. 1977 first solo exhibition 'Recent Drawing' at Christchurch Gallery, Oxford; most recent at the Nicola Jacobs Gallery, 1980. 1975-6 commissioned to make paintings and drawings for the Albany Conference Rooms, Birmingham. His pictures often use collaged strips of canvas.

RIVIERE, Briton   1840-1920
Painter. Born London, son of William Riviere, a genre and portrait painter. Educated at Cheltenham College, where his father was drawing master, and at St. Mary Hall, Oxford. Produced illustrations for several English and American magazines. From 1858 exhibited at the RA and is best known for his animal pictures though he also painted classical and genre subjects. Elected ARA, 1878, and RA, 1881.

RIZVI, Jacqueline   b.1944
Painter. Born Dewsbury, Yorkshire. Studied at Chelsea School of Art, 1963-6. Works chiefly as a watercolourist and exhibits at RA, RWS and NEAC. Also holds solo exhibitions in various London galleries. Specialises in still lifes, landscapes, interiors, urban and genre scenes, and is also a sensitive portrait painter.

ROBB, Brian   b.1913
Painter and illustrator. Born Scarborough, Yorkshire. Studied at Chelsea School of Art, 1930-4, and Slade School of Fine Art, 1935-6. Published *My Middle East Campaigns,* 1945. Solo exhibitions include one at the Arthur Jeffress Gallery, London, 1962, and another at the Thames Gallery, Windsor, 1963. Represented in Arts Council collection, in Southampton and Leicester Art Galleries and elsewhere.

ROBB, Carole   b.1943
Painter. Born Renfrewshire, Scotland. Studied at Glasgow School of Art and University of Reading. First solo exhibition held at Collectors' Gallery, London, 1966. Others include one at the Compass Gallery, Glasgow, 1981, which included a series of paintings based on her experience of Greek cinema. Another solo exhibition held at the Forum Gallery, New York, 1982.

ROBB, Tom   b.1933
Painter. Born Edinburgh, Scotland. Studied at Carlisle College of Art, 1948-53 and RCA, 1955-8. Solo exhibition of landscapes held John Whibley Gallery, London, 1971 and 1973.

ROBBINS, Helen   b.1949
Printmaker. Born London. Studied at Huddersfield Polytechnic, 1966-7, Darlington College of Arts, 1969-71, Rolle College of Education, Exmouth, 1971-2 and Brighton Polytechnic (printmaking course) 1977-9. 1980 first solo exhibition held at Dryden Street Gallery, London; another at the Burstow Gallery, Brighton, 1983.

ROBBINS, Richard   b.1927
Painter and sculptor. Studied at New College, Oxford, afterwards studying painting at the Slade and Ruskin Schools and, part-time, at Goldsmiths' College. Has taught at Camberwell and Hornsey Schools of Art and at Middlesex Polytechnic. Solo exhibitions include two at Highgate Gallery, London, 1984 and 1986. Also shows at the Phoenix Gallery, Lavenham, Suffolk.

ROBERTS, Bert   b.1928
Painter and sculptor. Born Wirral, Cheshire. First trained as a sculptor at Liverpool Regional College of Art. Has taught art in various schools and exhibits in the North. Solo exhibition held at the Chandler Gallery, Leyburn, Yorkshire, 1988.

ROBERTS, Derek   b.1947
Painter. Born Berwick upon Tweed, Northumberland. Studied at Edinburgh College of Art, graduated 1971. 1974 and 1976 received Scottish Arts Council Awards. Exhibited in mixed exhibitions at the 57 Gallery, Edinburgh, and 1977 at a mixed exhibition at the Air Gallery, London. 1980 solo exhibition at the Talbot Rice Art Centre, Edinburgh University, and 1988 at the Laing Art Gallery, Newcastle. His paintings explore his reactions to the landscape around him within an abstract tradition, developing complete and balanced structures of interlocking colours, shapes and patterns.

Bibl: *Four Seasons. Paintings by Derek Roberts,* Laing Art Gallery, Newcastle, 1988.

ROBERTS, Keith   b.1958
Painter. Born Birkenhead, Cheshire. Studied at Wirral College of Art and Design, 1976-7 and the Polytechnic, Wolverhampton, 1977-80. 1981-2 research fellowship at Exeter College of Art and Frankfurt Akademie. 1984 solo exhibition at Sunderland Arts Centre.

ROBERTS, Marcus Rees   b.1951
Printmaker. Studied English at Cambridge University, 1970-3, film studies at the Slade, 1973-5 and did a postgraduate in printmaking, 1975-7. Since 1980 lecturer at Edinburgh College of Art. 1981 solo exhibition held at Printmakers Workshop Ltd., Edinburgh.

ROBERTS, Perry
Minimalist painter. Solo exhibitions held at Goldsmiths' MA Project Space, London, 1988 and at Laure Genillard Gallery, London, 1989.

ROBERTS, Simon   b.1946
Painter. Born St. Helier, Jersey, Channel Islands. Studied at Studio Simi, Florence, 1963-4, Sir John Cass College, 1964-5 and Ruskin School of Drawing and Fine Art, 1966-9. Has lived and worked abroad but is now based in Dorset. 1988 solo exhibition at the Patricia Wells Gallery, Thornbury.

ROBERTS, Will
Painter. Born Ruabon, North Wales. 1962 won the Byng-Stamper Award, in a competition judged by Sir Kenneth Clark. 1969 solo exhibitions at Roland, Browse and Delbanco, London and at Howard Roberts Gallery, Cardiff. Paints the scarred Glamorgan landscape, often depicting the ordinary people of South Wales. 'Man', he says, 'is never absent from my pictures, even though he is not always seen.' Exhibits frequently at the Tegfryn Art Gallery, Menai Bridge, Anglesey.

ROBERTS, William   1895-1980
Painter. Born Hackney, London. 1909 was apprenticed to an advertising firm and attended art classes in the evenings at St. Martin's School of Art. 1910 won a scholarship to the Slade where he remained until 1913, meeting fellow-student Jacob Kramer,* whose sister, Sarah, he later married. Became an English Cubist, eventually joining the Vorticists and exhibiting at the Vorticists Exhibition of 1915; in that year he also joined the London Group. 1916-18 served with the Royal Field Artillery in France. Returned to England as an Official War Artist for the Canadian War Records Office and the Ministry of Information. 1920 exhibited in Wyndham Lewis's* Group X exhibition and in 1923 held his first solo exhibition at the Chenil Gallery. Taught part-time at Central School of Arts and Crafts, 1925-60. 1927-34 exhibited with the London Artists' Association and after the Second World War showed regularly at the RA. 1958 elected ARA and 1966, RA. The brittle rhythmic elegance of his Vorticist style gave way to heavier rhythms and a blunter method of drawing, well suited to his love of everyday subjects based on crowded scenes, which, in his paintings, take on the ritual of a formal dance. 1965 a major retrospective of his work was held at the Tate Gallery. (Plate 75, p.422.)

Bibl: *William Roberts. An artist and his family,* National Portrait Gallery, London, 1984.

ROBERTS-JONES, Ivor   b.1913
Sculptor. Born Oswestry, Shropshire. Studied at Goldsmiths' College and RA Schools. 1939-46 served in Royal Artillery. From 1946 taught sculpture at Goldsmiths', becoming Head of Sculpture, 1964. 1968 elected ARA, and RA, 1973. 1954 and 1978 had solo exhibitions at the Beaux Arts Gallery, London, and at Oriel, Cardiff. Interested in portraiture and regards sculpture as a form of still life in which objects are isolated and grouped together. Portrait commissions include HRH, The Duke of Edinburgh, HRH, The Prince of Wales, Yehudi Menuhin, Geraint Evans and others.

ROBERTSON, Alexander   1927-1978
Painter and scientist. Born Scotland and left to become a Forestry Officer in Malaya and Hong Kong, 1946-59. Had attended evening classes at Edinburgh College of Art while at University. After leaving Hong Kong he attended the Academie di Belle Arte, Florence, and began painting full-time in the Trossachs, 1960. 1964 first solo exhibition at the Glasgow Citizens' Theatre. 1965 moved to Norfolk to set up a community of artists. 1968 began creating environmental installations. 1971 participated in the group show, 'Electric Theatre', at the ICA. Also moved into the field of sculpture with painted wooden constructions.

ROBERTSON, Barbara   b.1945
Painter. Born Broughty Ferry, Scotland. Studied printmaking and illustration at Duncan of Jordanstone College of Art, Dundee. Exhibits at RSA and elsewhere. 1980 first solo exhibition held at Cornerstone Gallery, Dunblane; another at the Compass Gallery, Glasgow, 1981. Represented in Glasgow Art Gallery, Aberdeen Art Gallery and elsewhere.

ROBERTSON, Eric   1887-1941
Painter. Born Dumfries, Scotland. Studied architecture in Edinburgh, moving from this to painting and drawing. Was regarded as a decadent symbolist as a student and on one occasion had his drawings removed from an exhibition at Edinburgh College of Art. Married the daughter of the painter E.A. Walton. 1913 formed the Edinburgh Group. 1917-18 served in the Friends Ambulance Service. After the war his work became more austere. When his marriage failed he moved to Ormskirk, then Liverpool. Married again, but suffered financial difficulties and contracted tuberculosis. Influenced by the Pre-Raphaelites, Gustave Moreau and William Blake.

ROBERTSON, Graham   1866-1948
Painter and illustrator. Born London. Studied under the late Victorian painter, Albert Moore. Moved in prominent artistic circles, a friend of Whistler, Burne-Jones, Sargent* and others. Painted landscapes and subject pictures in a Pre-Raphaelite style. During the 1890s he enjoyed some success as a theatre designer, and also wrote fairy stories, children's verse and plays. 1891 elected member of NEAC, 1896 the RBA, 1910 the ROI and 1912 the RP. Sometimes signed his work W. Graham Robertson.

Bibl: Graham Robertson, *Time Was,* Hamish Hamilton, London, 1931.

ROBERTSON, Henry   1848-1930
Painter. Born Liverpool, Merseyside. Wanted to go to sea but was prevented from doing so by weak eyesight. 1886 became associate member of the RE. Exhibited at RA, and elsewhere, chiefly with the Ipswich Art Society. Sketched extensively on site but also made use of photographs as source material. Painted watercolours of shops and harbours, not uninfluenced by J.M.W. Turner. His etchings are more wide-ranging in subject.

Bibl: *Henry Robertson, ARE, 1848-1930,* Reading Museum and Art Gallery, 1987.

ROBERTSON, Ian   b.1949
Maker of painted constructions. Born Glasgow, Scotland. Studied at University of Reading, 1968-72, and Chelsea School of Art, 1972-3. Appeared in group exhibitions from 1969 onwards.

ROBERTSON, James   b.1931
Painter. Born Cowdenbeath, Scotland. Studied at Glasgow School of Art, 1950-6. 1961 first solo exhibition at Douglis and Foulis Gallery, Edinburgh. 1962 elected RSW, ARSA, 1974 and RGA, 1980. Since 1967 has taught at Glasgow

School of Art. Represented in Glasgow Art Galleries and Museums, the Scottish Arts Council and the collections of HRH The Queen Mother and the Duke of Edinburgh.

ROBINS, Brian   b.1928
Kinetic artist. Born Ammanford, Wales. Left school at fourteen and worked in a coal mine and did other manual jobs. Self-taught artist since 1958. First exhibited kinetic structures at the Grosvenor Gallery, London, 1965. Represented in Arts Council collection and elsewhere.

ROBINSON, Barbara   b.1928
Painter. Studied at Slade School of Art and Ruskin Schools, London, 1943-5. 1954-5 lived in Japan, and 1957 settled in France. 1959-74 exhibited regularly at the New Art Centre, London.

ROBINSON, Bob   b.1951
Painter. Born Newton Stewart, Co.Tyrone, Northern Ireland. Served three years as a drawing office apprentice with Rolls-Royce, 1968-71, then studied at North East London and Trent Polytechnics. First solo exhibition held at Derby Museum and Art Gallery, 1980. Paints in a dead-pan, near photo-realist style, with great attention to contemporary detail.

ROBINSON, Carl   b.1958
Painter. Born Nelson, Lancashire. Studied at Trent Polytechnic, 1976-9. 1980 held first solo exhibition at Trent Polytechnic; 1981 his second, 'Painting for Hatred', at Midland Group Arts Centre, Nottingham. His figurative paintings often focus on a state of mind or activity that allows him to reflect on the political atmosphere or events of the day.

ROBINSON, Frederick Cayley   1862-1927
Painter. Born Middlesex. Studied at St. John's Wood School of Art, RA Schools, and at the Académie Julian in Paris, 1891-4. 1898-1902 lived in Florence, studying the technique of tempera painting. 1904 first solo exhibition held at the Baillie Gallery, London. Member of RBA and ROI. Also worked as theatre designer and illustrator. 1910-11 painted four panels for the entrance hall of Middlesex Hospital. 1912 elected member of NEAC. Appointed Professor of Figure Composition and Decoration at Glasgow University. 1921 elected ARA. His pictures are almost always of people set in a frozen, timeless world. They contain symbolic allusions yet have no precise narrative intent. Represented in Tate Gallery and elsewhere.

Bibl: *Frederick Cayley Robinson, ARA*, Fine Art Society, London, 1977.

ROBINSON, Geoffrey
Painter. Son of a book illustrator. Landscape artist concerned to catch 'the moment of eternity', a mood of exultation similar to that found in Thomas Traherne's *Centuries of Meditations,* a book this artist admires. Exhibited at the Mall Galleries in London, 1976 and 1978.

ROBINSON, William Heath   1872-1944
Illustrator. Born into a family with a tradition of illustration and engraving. Studied at Islington Art School and RA Schools. Although he originally set out to become a landscape painter, he was diverted to illustration by the many demands that soon reached him for work from his pen. Worked for a variety of publishers, his early illustrations sharing Dulac's fascination with the exotic and the macabre. Another skill in his repertoire was humorous drawings, but these did not come to the fore

until the First World War when, with incisive humour, he ridiculed in cartoons many aspects of the enemy's military behaviour. He repeated this success during the Second World War, and between the wars he satirised all things purely mechanical as well as the middle-class suburban scene.

Bibl: John Lewis, *Heath Robinson: Artist and Comic Genius,* Constable, London, 1973.

ROBOZ, Zsuzsi   b.1939
Painter. Born Budapest, Hungary. Came to England in 1947. Studied at RA Schools with Peter Greenham* and in Florence with Pietro Annigoni. Best known for her portraits of leading figures in the creative and performing arts. Her interest in the backstage world of theatre and ballet originated from her Hungarian childhood. Solo exhibitions at the André Weil Gallery, Paris, the Curwen, Hamilton and Patrick Seale Galleries in London. Exhibits at RA, RBA and elsewhere.

ROBSON, Gavin   b.1950
Painter. Born Edinburgh, Scotland. Studied at University of Edinburgh, 1968-73 and Edinburgh College of Art, 1968-74. 1974-5 travelled in France on a scholarship. 1975 appointed Fellow in Fine Art, University of Nottingham. 1975 solo exhibitions held at University of Nottingham, and 1983 at the Talbot Rice Art Centre, Edinburgh.

ROBSON, John   1931-1987
Sculptor. Studied at Kingston School of Art and RCA. Worked as an assistant to Henry Moore,* 1958-1961. Senior lecturer in Fine Art at Kingston Polytechnic, 1970-87.

ROBSON, William   1868-1952
Painter. Born Edinburgh, Scotland. Studied at Edinburgh School of Art and Académie Julian in Paris. 1888 left for Italy and settled in Capri where he became part of an international coterie of artists. 1900 returned to Edinburgh and became President of the Scottish Society of Artists, exhibiting regularly at the RSA, the RA and the Royal Glasgow Institute.

ROCHE, Alexander Ignatius   1861-1921
Painter. Born Glasgow, Scotland. Studied at Glasgow School of Art and in Paris. Exhibited at major London exhibiting venues, but more regularly in Scotland. Won medals at Munich and Dresden and received an Hon. Mention at the Paris Salon in 1892. Portrait commissions resulted in him spending time in America but he lived mostly in Scotland. Represented in most major Scottish public collections.

ROCKE, Basil   1904-1966
Painter. Studied at the Euston Road School. Included in an exhibition, organised by the Contemporary Arts Society, of the Members of the Euston Road Group at the Ashmolean Museum, 1948. His work was also included in the Euston Road School touring exhibition in the same year.

ROGERS, Charles   b.1930
Painter. Born Gateshead, Tyne and Wear. After National Service, 1948-50, he studied in night classes at King's College, Newcastle. Joined the Gateshead Art Society in the mid-1960s. First solo exhibition at Biddick Farm Arts Centre, Tyne and Wear, 1978. His paintings are derived from everyday life in northern towns.

ROGERS, Claude   1907-1979
Painter. Born London. Studied at Slade, 1925-8. Exhibited with London Group and London Artists' Association. 1937 founder member of the Euston Road School. 1940 held his first one-artist show at Leicester Galleries. 1941 entered Royal Engineers and was invalided out in 1943. 1945-8 taught at Camberwell School of Art, and 1948-63 at the Slade. 1952-5 President of the London Group. 1959 made OBE. 1963-72 Professor of Fine Art, University of Reading. The rigorous scrutiny of appearances encouraged by the Euston Road School later gave way to a more broadly handled, striking naturalism.

Bibl: *Claude Rogers: Paintings and Drawings 1927-1973,* introduction by Andrew Forge, Whitechapel Art Gallery, London, and elsewhere, 1973.

ROGERS, Edward   b.1911
Painter. Born Wisbech, Cambridgeshire. Self-taught as a painter. Served in the RAF, 1940-5. He has travelled widely in Europe and India and Asia. 1966 first solo exhibition at the Drian Galleries, London. Originally a landscape painter and portraitist, in 1947 he made his first abstract painting, and in 1948 his first constructions and reliefs, whilst earning his living as a stockbroker.

ROGERS, Howard   b.1946
Painter and sculptor. Born London. Studied at Manchester College of Art, 1965-8 and at Chelsea School of Art, 1968-9. First solo exhibition at the Museum of Modern Art, Oxford, in 1973. Others include one at Moira Kelly, Fine Art, London, 1981.

ROGERS, Martin   b.1951
Sculptor. Born Surrey. Studied at Bath Academy of Art, 1969-73, and Brighton Polytechnic, 1973-4. From the late 1970s included in mixed exhibitions. 1979 one-person exhibition at Coracle Press, London, entitled 'Instruments for Outdoor Use'. Creates sculpture that makes sounds.

ROGERS, Peter   b.1933
Painter. Born London. Studied at St. Martin's School of Art, 1954-6. 1957-60 member of RBA. 1962-3 lived in Majorca and Almeria, Spain. 1960 first solo exhibition in the Crypt of St. Mary-Le-Bow, London. Religious painter who concentrates mostly on incidents from the life of Christ. 1966 had a solo exhibition of these at Arthur Tooth and Sons.

ROGOCKI, Jozefa   b.1957
Mixed media artist. Studied at Brighton Polytechnic, 1976-9 and at Chelsea School of Art, 1979-80. First exhibited in a group show at the Roundhouse Gallery, London, 1980.

ROLFE, Nigel   b.1950
Sculptor, video and performance artist. Born Isle of Wight. Since 1975 has lived and worked in Dublin. First performance work, 'Bird, Dog, Tree', presented in Boston and Toronto, 1974. First solo exhibition, 'Balance Structures', at the Project Arts Centre, Dublin, 1976; most recent at Dolan/Maxwell Gallery, New York, and the Orchard Gallery, Derry, both in 1990. Performance artist-in-residence, Newcastle Polytechnic, 1989.

ROLT, David   b.1915
Painter. Born Yorkshire. Lived in Cape Town, South Africa, 1919-24. Studied at Chelsea Polytechnic and Central School of Arts and Crafts, 1932-3 and at the Slade School, 1933-5. 1937 first solo exhibition in Cape Town. 1947 first solo exhibition in Britain at the Razlitt Gallery, London; others include one at the Adams Gallery, 1957.

RONAY, Emma   b.1961
Painter. Born London. Studied at West Surrey College of Art and Design, 1980-3, and at Slade School of Art, 1986-8. 1984 first represented in an exhibition at Plymouth Art Centre, followed in 1985 by a touring exhibition which began at Plymouth Art Centre, Devon.

ROOKE, Noel   1881-1953
Painter and engraver. Born London, son of T.M. Rooke.* Studied at the Slade School, 1899-1900. Employed by William Richard Lethaby in 1899 to make drawings of the Chapter House at Westminster Abbey. From 1900 studied at Central School, under Edward Johnston and Lethaby, specialising in writing and illumination. For six years he spent every summer studying in various galleries and libraries in Europe. 1912-46 taught wood engraving at Central School. Elected ARE, 1920. 1984 retrospective exhibition held at Christ Church Picture Gallery, Oxford.

Bibl: *Noel Rooke 1881-1953,* Christ Church Picture Gallery, Oxford, 1984.

ROOKE, Thomas Matthew   1842-1942
Painter. Born London. Studied at the National School of Design and at the RA Schools in the 1860s. At the age of twenty-nine he became Burne-Jones's assistant, until his death in 1895. His influence is evident in Rooke's figurative and decorative work. He produced gesso panels, stained glass and mural designs. He also worked for the firm Collinson and Loche which produced painted furniture during the 1870s. He was held in high regard by John Ruskin who sent him to make drawings of ancient cathedrals and monuments on the Continent, 1878-93. These drawings were made with great detail, and a feeling for the idiosyncracies of individual buildings. Elected ARWS, 1891 and RWS, 1903. An exhibition of his work was held at the Martyn Gregory Gallery, London, 1975.

ROONEY, Mick   b.1944
Painter. Born Epsom, Surrey. Studied at Sutton School of Art, 1959-62, Wimbledon School of Art, 1962-4 and RCA, 1964-7, British School at Rome, 1967-8. 1968-82 taught part-time in various art colleges. 1983 artist-in-residence at Towner Art Gallery, Eastbourne. 1965 solo exhibitions began at the Fulham Gallery, London, and have continued in London and Holland. 1989 a retrospective of his work was held at the Metropole Arts Centre, Folkestone, Kent. Recurring elements in his work include the ritual of food, literature, social gatherings and humour. His paintings are not realistic, more like haunted apparitions in a world of greed, avarice and mediocrity. Works in the collections of the Hove Museum and Art Gallery, the Towner Museum and Art Gallery, Eastbourne, and the Rye Art Gallery, Sussex. Elected ARA, 1990.

Bibl: *Paintings by Mick Rooney 1978-1988,* Metropole Arts Centre, Folkestone, 1989.

ROPER, Geoffrey   b.1942
Painter. Born Nottingham. Studied at Nottingham College of Art, 1958-60 and at Edinburgh College of Art, 1960-2. He was awarded the Andrew Grant Scholarship, 1963. First exhibited at William Street Gallery, Edinburgh, 1964. Included in the collections of Civic Art

Gallery, Middlesbrough, the New University of Ulster, Coleraine, and Edinburgh New Towns Conservative Committee. Recent solo exhibitions include one at the Fine Art Society, Edinburgh, 1988.

ROSE, Colin   b.1945
Painter. Born Kent. First solo exhibition held in Sunderland, 1969. His many solo exhibitions include one at Huddersfield Art Gallery, 1986. Has attempted to integrate the techniques of serial music into a purely graphic medium. Included in the collections of the Arts Council, Northern Arts, Abbot Hall Art Gallery, Lowich House Trust and British Rail.

ROSE, Emma   b.1962
Printmaker. Born Taplow, Buckinghamshire. Studied at Leeds Polytechnic, 1981-4 and at Chelsea School of Art, 1985-6. Since 1984 represented in group exhibitions when she exhibited in a two-person exhibition at Leeds Polytechnic Gallery. 1987 awarded Lloyd's Bank Printmaker's Prize, Royal Academy.

ROSE, Sir Francis   1909-1979
Painter, illustrator and stage designer. Born Moor Park, Hertfordshire. 1925-9 travelled in France, Italy and Austria. 1929-36 studied with Francis Picabia and for a short time with Jose Sert. 1928 visited Morocco and North Africa. 1929 designed sets for Diaghilev and painted with Christopher Wood* in Brittany. 1931 met Gertrude Stein who promoted his work. Exhibited in London and Paris and was given a retrospective by the French government at the Petit Palais, Paris, 1938. Continued to travel and exhibit, holding another retrospective at the South London Art Gallery, 1966.

Bibl: *Sir Francis Rose 1909-1979. A Retrospective,* with essays by Bryan Robertson and others, England & Co., London, 1988.

ROSE, Kate   b.1948
Painter. Born Nottingham. Studied at Birmingham College of Art, 1967-70 and at RCA, 1970-1. First solo exhibition at the Gallery Upstairs, Mappin Art Gallery, Sheffield, 1980, followed by a second exhibition in the same year at the Thumb Gallery, London. Exhibits also at RA. Everyday objects, doors, hairdryers and views through a window become edgily atmospheric in her drawings and paintings.

ROSE, Rose   b.1946
Painter. Born London. Trained as a graphic designer and worked as such before going to Exeter University to take a BA in Painting and Literature and, later, at Bretton Hall, Yorkshire, a post-graduate certificate in Fine Art Education. Her paintings are often concerned with broad themes related to patterns of human experience.

ROSE, Tim   b.1953
Painter. Born London. Studied at Watford School of Art, 1971-2, and Sheffield Polytechnic, 1972-5. Lives in Sheffield and paints views of Derbyshire houses and gardens, mostly in watercolour.

ROSEN, Frank
Painter. Studied at Central School of Arts and Crafts, 1955-8. Exhibited at the John Whibley Gallery, London, 1963. Travels extensively and evolves fantasies around the places and people he sees.

SIR FRANCIS ROSE, 1909-1979. *'Christian Berard: The Death Mask',* 1948. Ink and gouache on paper. 81 ½ in. x 58in. England and Co., London.

ROSEN, Ismond   b.1924
Sculptor. Born South Africa. Began practising sculpture as a child. Studied at the Ecole des Beaux-Arts and the Académie Julian, Paris, 1955. 1959 elected to Portrait Sculptors Society. 1972 first solo exhibition at John Whibley Gallery, London. His central concern is the human condition, expressed in his art through symbols and a play upon the interface between abstraction and realism.

ROSENBERG, Isaac   1890-1918
Painter and poet. Born Bristol, Avon. When he was seven his parents moved to Whitechapel, London, where he went to school and spent most of his life. Apprenticed as a photographic process etcher. Studied at Slade School of Art, 1911-13, where his peers were Mark Gertler,* Stanley Spencer* and David Bomberg.* 1915 joined the army and was killed in France.

Bibl: *Word and Image VI: Isaac Rosenberg 1890-1918,* National Book League, 1975; Joseph Cohen, *Journey to the Trenches: The Life of Isaac Rosenberg,* Robson Books, London, 1975.

ROSOMAN, Leonard

LEONARD ROSOMAN, b.1913. *'Self-portrait drawing the River Arno, Florence'*, 1989. Acrylic. 40in. x 50in. Private Collection.

ROSOMAN, Leonard   b.1913
Painter. Born London. Studied at Durham University, RA Schools and Central School of Arts and Crafts. 1943 appointed Official War Artist to the Admiralty. Has taught at various art schools, including the RCA and Edinburgh College of Art. 1960 elected ARA, and 1970 RA. Distinguished muralist but is best known for his paintings of people in interiors. Claims he is not a portrait painter in the conventional sense, and attempts 'to enter and comment on people's lives rather than remove them and examine them. They are as much to do with environment, situation and emotion. . .' An exhibition of his war work was held at the Imperial War Museum, 1989.

ROSS, Charles   b.1924
Painter. First solo exhibition at the Doctors' Restaurant, 19 New Cavendish Street, London, 1965. Travelled extensively and drew the subject matter for his paintings from his experience of the Far East.

ROSS, David   b.1941
Painter. Born Perivale, Middlesex. Studied at Hammersmith and Hornsey Schools of Art, 1957-9. First solo exhibition at the Lisson Gallery, London, 1967.

ROSS, Stuart   b.1949
Painter. Born London. Studied at the Central School of Art and Design, 1967-8, Hull College of Art, 1968-71 and at Leeds Polytechnic, 1971-2. Travelled in USA throughout 1979. First solo exhibition at Leeds Polytechnic Gallery, 1978.

ROSSBERG, Sara   b.1952
Painter. Born Recklinghausen, West Germany. Studied at Academy of Fine Art, Frankfurt, 1971-6 and at Camberwell School of Art, 1976-8. Awarded German Scholarship Foundation, 1973-7 and a Travel Scholarship, 1977-8. First solo exhibition at International Art Fair, Basle, Switzerland, 1986.

WILLIAM ROTHENSTEIN, 1872-1945. *'Reading the Book of Esther'*, 1907. 34¼ in. x 41¹⁵/₁₆ in. Manchester City Art Galleries.

ROSSER, John   b.1931
Painter. Studied at Regent Street Polytechnic and Watford School of Art, which he left in 1952. First solo exhibition at the Hallam Gallery, London, 1989. Represented in group exhibitions at the RA Summer Show and the RBA. Represented at Watford Museum.

ROSSI, Mario   b.1958
Painter and sculptor. Born Glasgow, Scotland. Studied at the Glasgow School of Art, 1975-7, and at the RCA, 1979-81. Awards include the Gulbenkian Rome Scholarship, British School of Rome, 1982-3. Artist-in-Residence at Trinity College, Cambridge, 1988-9. 1984 first solo exhibition at the Demarco Gallery, City Arts Centre, Edinburgh, followed by a second solo exhibition in the same year at L'Escargot, London. 1990 solo exhibition at Anderson O'Day Fine Art, London. He produced images for *Night and Day* (1984), a limited edition book made for Riverside Studios with Gerard de Thame.* Unlike his fellow Scots, he abandoned colour and figuration in favour of a more oblique approach, in colouring effects of rust, iron and gold. His imagery frequently derives from classical sources. Included in the collections of CAS, London, V & A, Gallery of Modern Art, Edinburgh, and Unilever.

ROSSITER, Anthony   b.1926
Painter and writer. Studied at Chelsea Polytechnic, 1947-51. 1962 published his autobiography, *The Pendulum.* 1967 won Art Council award for *The Pendulum,* followed by an award in 1970 for *The Golden Chain.* 1959 first solo exhibition at Galerie de Seine, Paris. Included in the collections of the V & A, Bristol City Art Gallery, Reading Art Gallery, Smithsonian Institute, Washington DC, USA, Royal West of England Academy, and Ashmolean Museum, Oxford.

ROTHENSTEIN, Michael   b.1908
Painter and printmaker. Born London, the younger son of Sir William Rothenstein.* Studied at Chelsea School of Art, 1923 and Central School, 1924-7. First solo exhibition at Matthieson Gallery, London, 1938. Sufered from debilitating illness from mid-1920s to 1940. 1940-3 worked for the Pilgrim Trust in the Recording Britain project. Published *Looking at Paintings,* 1947, *Linocuts and Woodcuts,* 1962, *Relief Printing,* 1970. ARA, 1977, RA, 1980. Elected Hon. Fellow of RE.

Bibl: Mel Gooding, *Michael Rothenstein: The Retrospective,* Stoke-on-Trent Art Gallery, 1989.

ROTHENSTEIN, William   1872-1945
Painter. Born Bradford, Yorkshire. Trained at Slade, 1888-9, and Académie Julian, Paris, 1889-93. Official War Artist, 1917-18. 1920 became Principal of RCA and transformed it into a leading art school; in particular he encouraged the revival of mural painting as a public art. 1931 knighted. 1939-43 unofficial war artist with RAF. 1972 centenary exhibition at Bradford City Art Gallery. His intense though conservative paintings comprise

mainly landscape, domestic interiors and portraits of artists and intellectuals. His three-volume memoirs *Men and Memories* remain indispensible to the history of this period. Represented in many public collections, including the Tate Gallery.

Bibl: Robert Speight, *William Rothenstein*, Eyre and Spottiswoode, London, 1962.

ROTHMER, Dorothy
Painter. Studied at Santa Monica College, California, USA and in Manchester, England. First solo exhibition at the Woodstock Gallery, London, 1969. The theme of most of her art is based on patterns created by elements in our everyday surroundings.

ROUSSEL, Theodore   1847-1926
Painter and etcher. Born Lorient, Brittany, France. Educated at the Collège Henri Quatre in Paris. After two years spent in Rome, owing to ill-health, he returned to Paris and fought in the Franco-Prussian War in 1870, after which he left the Army and devoted himself to art. Settled in Chelsea and became a friend of Whistler. Also developed a new technique of colour etching. Exhibited at several leading London exhibiting venues from 1886. Elected ARE, 1921.

ROWLETT, George   b.1941
Painter. Born Troon, Scotland. Studied at Camberwell School of Art, 1962-5, and RA Schools, 1965-8. Winner of many awards, including two David Murray travelling Scholarships. Since 1961 his work has been shown in numerous mixed exhibitions and at the RA. Principally a landscape painter who employs an impasto approach that has an affinity with the work of Kossoff* and Auerbach.* Solo exhibition at the Albemarle Gallery, 1990.

ROWNTREE, Kenneth   b.1915
Painter. Born Scarborough, Yorkshire. Studied at Ruskin School of Drawing, Oxford, 1930-4, and the Slade School, 1934-5. First solo exhibition held 1946 at the Leicester Galleries, London. 1949 became a tutor at RCA, a post he held until 1958. 1959 became Professor of Fine Arts, University of Newcastle upon Tyne. 1980 held a retrospective exhibition at Newcastle University. Represented in several public collections.

Bibl: *Paintings and Drawings by Kenneth Rowntree*, Hexham Abbey Festival Catalogue, 1987.

ROYDS, Mabel   1874-1941
Painter and printmaker. Born Bedfordshire. 1889 won a scholarship to the RA Schools but preferred instead to enrol at the Slade School of Art. In Paris at the turn of the century she worked alongside Sickert,* sometimes even on his paintings. After several years in Canada she settled in Edinburgh, joining the staff of Edinburgh College of Art. 1913 married the etcher and portrait painter, E.S. Lumsden. 1914-17 travelled widely, and afterwards returned to Edinburgh. Painted a ceiling for the Episcopal Church in Hamilton, Lanarkshire, but is best known for her colour woodcuts. Exhibited regularly at the SSA, and with the Society of Artist Printmakers and Graveur Painters in Colour. Her subjects include scenes of India and Tibet, flower pieces, religious scenes, children and ducks.

ROYLE, David   b.1947
Painter. Born Manchester. Studied at Central School of Art and Design, 1966-9. 1969 began teaching at Winchester School of Art and held a solo exhibition there, 1971. Continued to teach and exhibit. 1975 held solo exhibition

at the New 57 Gallery, Edinburgh, and completed a large painting and a suite of ten etchings for the Albany Hotel, Birmingham. Represented in the Arts Council collection.

ROYLE, Herbert F.   1870-1958
Landscape painter. Born Lancashire. Trained at Harris Institute, Preston and School of Art, Southport and subsequently moved to Yorkshire. Member of the Manchester Academy of Fine Arts, the Liverpool Academy of Art and Sandon Studios Society. From 1893 exhibited in London and at the Liverpool Autumn Exhibition.

ROYLE, Stanley   1888-1961
Painter. Born in Stalybridge, Lancashire, son of a station master. Attended Sheffield School of Art, winning bronze and silver medals for lithography. Began to attract attention at exhibitions in the 1920s, at the RA and the Paris Salon. Member of the Sheffield Society of Artists and the RBA. 1931 travelled to Nova Scotia, Canada, and by 1937 had become Director of the Art Gallery and College of Arts associated with Mount Allison University at New Brunswick. Returned to England shortly before the Second World War and settled at Worksop, Nottinghamshire. A provincial impressionist, he had a liking for pure colour and specialised in snow scenes, taking himself around Derbyshire on a two-stroke motorbicycle. Represented in Sheffield City Art Galleries.

Bibl: *Stanley Royle. A Memorial Exhibition,* Graves Art Gallery, Sheffield, 1962.

RUBENSTEIN, Gerda   b.1931
Sculptor. Born in Berlin, Germany. Moved to Amsterdam, the Netherlands, 1933. Studied in Wessel Couzijn's studio, Amsterdam, 1948 and then at the Rijks Academy, Amsterdam, followed by the Grande Chaumière, Paris, 1949-53. Won Prix Jeune Sculpture. 1959 moved to London. 1983 first solo exhibition at South London Gallery. Regularly exhibits in Amsterdam and in Britain.

RUSHBURY, Henry   1889-1968
Painter and etcher. Born Harborne, near Birmingham, West Midlands. Studied stained glass design and mural decoration at Birmingham College of Art, 1903-9, later working as assistant to Henry Payne, RWS. 1912 settled in London and specialised in architectural subjects. 1921 first solo exhibition held at the Grosvenor Gallery, London. 1917 became a member of the NEAC. 1921 elected ARE, 1924, RE, 1926, RWS, 1927, ARA, and 1936, RA. 1944 Vice-President of the RWS. Worked in London but also travelled abroad in search of other architectural scenes. 1955 created CVO, 1960, CBE, and 1964 was knighted.

RUSHTON, George   1868-1948
Painter, muralist and stained glass designer. Born Birmingham, West Midlands. Studied art in Birmingham and London. Moved to Newcastle upon Tyne around 1897 where he taught art and worked as a stained glass designer. Left Newcastle in 1906 and moved to Berkshire, painting mostly landscapes, his colours having a luminous richness not unlike that found in stained glass. He also painted in East Anglia and for a period lived in Ipswich. Elected RBA, 1922. Is said to have had a genius for discovering creativity in others and was the first to recognise the talent of Leonard Squirrel.*

RUSSELL, Bruce   b.1946
Painter. Studied at Chelsea School of Art, 1964-9. Awards include Young Contemporaries Prizewinner, 1968; Arts Council Award, 1975 and an Arts Council Major Award,

VERONICA RYAN, b.1956. *'Defined Place'*.
42in. x 33in. x 13in.
Kettle's Yard, Cambridge.

1978. First solo exhibition at the Hoya Gallery, London, 1976. He regularly exhibits in the USA and Europe. Solo exhibition with the Benjamin Rhodes Gallery, London, 1989. Included in the collections of the Arts Council of Great Britain, British Council, CAS, Kettles Yard, Leicestershire Education Authority, Newcastle Polytechnic, Whitworth Art Gallery, Manchester, and University of Texas, Dallas.

RUTHERSTON, Albert   1881-1953
Painter. Born Bradford, Yorkshire, younger brother of William Rothenstein.* Studied at Slade School, 1898-1902. From 1901 exhibited with the NEAC, becoming a member, 1905. 1910 first solo exhibition held at the Carfax Gallery, London. 1914 changed his name to Rutherston, to avoid anti-German feeling. Served in Palestine, 1916-19. Acted as Ruskin Master of Drawing, Oxford University, 1929-48. Elected ARWS, 1934, and RWS, 1942. A less weighty figure than his brother, his charm as a painter lies precisely in its light decorative manner. He was especially adept at designs for fans.

RYAN, Adrian   b.1920
Painter. Born Hampstead, London. Studied at Slade School of Art, 1939. Associated with the St. Ives School, he first visited Cornwall in 1943 and 1944 when he spent the summers painting in Padstow. Lived in Cornwall, 1945-51 and 1959-65. Taught at Goldsmiths' College, 1948-83. 1943-52 held several solo exhibitions of Cornish paintings and still lifes at the Redfern Gallery, London. 1956 held a solo exhibition at Tooth's, London. In 1959 he returned to Mousehole where he lived until 1965, when he returned to London. Exhibits at the RA and elsewhere. Represented in the Tate Gallery, V & A, Belfast Art Gallery, Manchester City Art Gallery and elsewhere.

RYAN, Paul   b.1955
Painter. Born Burslem, Staffordshire. Studied at Crewe and Alsager College, Cheshire, 1973-6, North Staffordshire Polytechnic, 1976-9, and Manchester Polytechnic, 1979-80. First solo exhibitions held at Rochdale Art Gallery and Curwen Gallery, London, 1981. Recent ones include a joint exhibition with Jim Unsworth* at Winchester Gallery, 1989. Often works with coloured paper pulp.

Also makes boxed constructions and screen prints.

RYAN, Thomas   b.1929
Painter. Studied at Dublin Academy of Art under Jack Yeats,* among others. Has exhibited at all major exhibiting institutions including the RA, NEAC, RBA, and the RHA, becoming president of the latter. He is also an Hon. Member of the RA and the RSA.

RYAN, Veronica   b.1956
Sculptor. Born Montserrat, West Indies. Attended St. Albans College of Art, 1974-5, Bath Academy of Art, 1975-8 and the Slade School, 1978-80. Studied at the School of Oriental and African Studies, London University, 1981-3. 1983 winner of the Cleveland International Drawing Biennale. 1985 first one-person show, an installation, at the ICA, London. 1986 won an award from the Henry Moore Foundation. 1987-8 Kettles Yard Arts Council Fellow, and artist-in-residence at Jesus College, Cambridge. Her sculptures and drawings reveal the influence of her West Indian origins and draw inspiration from the structure of pods and shells.

RYDER, Sophie   b.1963
Sculptor. Studied painting at RA Schools, 1981-4, and whilst there began to realise the potential of wire as a medium with which to model sculpture. Deals exclusively with animals for her subject matter. 1986 sculptor-in-residence, first at Yorkshire Sculpture Park, then in Grizedale Forest, Cumbria. 1988 solo exhibition at St. Paul's Gallery, Leeds; another held at Berkeley Square Gallery, London, 1989.

RYLAND, Adolphine Mary   1903-1983
Sculptor and printmaker. Born Windsor, Berkshire. Studied at Heatherley's, 1922-4, and the Grosvenor School, where under the influence of Iain McNab,* the Principal, and Claude Flight,* she developed an interest in the woodcut and linocut, as well as sculpture and drawing. During the 1930s she worked for the London County Council, executing low reliefs in public places. She exhibited regularly, her work attaining an unusual mixture of modernity and traditional craftsmanship. Work in the Tate Gallery collection.

SADIQ b.1950
Sculptor. Born Delhi, India. Studied at the Delhi College of Art. Awarded a National Cultural Scholarship by the Government of India, 1975-7, which was followed by a British Council Scholarship to the Slade. His sculpture is derived from his preoccupation with philosophical and religious concerns, expressed in animal forms that are inspired by Hindu and Buddhist art and archaeology. Solo exhibition at The New Art Centre, London.

SAGMAN, Gail b.1957
Painter. Born Glasgow, Scotland. Studied at Sir John Cass School of Art, London, 1975-6, and St. Martin's School of Art, London, 1976-9. First solo exhibition at Benjamin Rhodes Gallery, London, 1985, followed by a second exhibition at the same gallery, 1986. Solo exhibition at Sue Williams, London, 1990.

SALMON, Tabitha b.1955
Painter. Studied at Brighton Art College, graduating in 1977. After two years post-graduate work began part-time teaching. Held an exhibition based on life in Moscow in 1987, at the National Theatre, London, and elsewhere. In 1989 exhibited 'Paintings of Naples' at Leighton House, London. Has worked mostly with oil pastels, using bold colour and a lively calligraphic style.

SANDEMAN, Margot b.1922
Painter. Born Glasgow, Scotland. Studied at Glasgow School of Art and became a friend of Joan Eardley.* Won the Guthrie Award in 1964 and the Anne Redpath Award, 1970, both at the RSA. Has exhibited at the Richard Demarco Gallery, Edinburgh, and at the Compass Gallery, Glasgow, 1978. Has collaborated with Ian Hamilton Finlay* on still life paintings which incorporate poetic or philosophical texts. Represented in Glasgow Museum and Art Gallery, the Scottish Arts Council Collection and elsewhere.

SANDERS, Peter b.1940
Painter. Studied at Camberwell School of Art and Crafts, 1957-61, afterwards winning a scholarship to the Slade. Won Slade School Painting Prize, 1963. Later taught at Norwich Art School. Has exhibited widely with solo exhibitions at the AIR Gallery, London, and at Corpus Christi College, Oxford.

SANDERSON, Christopher b.1939
Sculptor. Born Jerusalem. Came to England in 1948. Studied painting at Leeds College of Art, 1955-60, and at the Slade School of Art, 1960-2, turning to the sculpture department, 1961. 1962-4 worked in Rome and travelled in France, Italy and Switzerland. 1964-5 taught at Leeds College of Art. 1965 visited New York for three months. 1966-7 taught at the Royal College of Art and Ravensbourne College of Art. 1967 first one person show at the Axiom Gallery, London.

SANDLE, Michael b.1936
Sculptor. Born Weymouth, Dorset. Moved to Douglas, Isle of Man, 1936. Studied at Douglas School of Art, 1951-7 and the Slade School of Art, 1957-9. 1960 was awarded a French Government Scholarship. 1961-4 taught print-making at Leicester College of Art and the Slade School of Art. 1961 founded the Leicester Group of Artists. 1963 first one-person show at the Drian Galleries, London. 1964 lectured at Coventry College of Art. 1964-8 acted as

MICHAEL SANDLE, b.1936. '*Maquette for the Drummer*', 1989. Bronze: edition of 8. 12½ in. high.
Fischer Fine Art Limited, London.

Visiting Professor, University of Calgary. 1970 travelled in Canada. 1978 moved to Germany and lives and works there to the present day. Has exhibited in several major group shows, including a Hayward Annual, and has solo exhibitions at Fischer Fine Art, London. Has specialised in the theme of memorials, occasionally using the figure of Mickey Mouse to represent American civilisation.

SANDS, Ethel 1873-1962
Painter. Born Newport, Rhode Island, USA. Studied in Paris under Eugene Carrière, 1896-1900. Settled in England in 1900 with the painter Nan Hudson, sharing with her a house at Garsington in Oxford and then one in London. Owing to her friendship with Walter Sickert* she became a member of the Fitzroy Group, 1907, and of the London Group, 1913. Her paintings are rare and admit a debt to Vuillard in their handling and choice of subject. Later moved to a small chateau at Offranville, near Dieppe, where she commissioned Vanessa Bell* and

ETHEL SANDS, 1873-1962.
'The Mantelpiece, Auppegard, Near Dieppe', 1923. 21in. x 17in.
Michael Parkin Fine Art Ltd.,
London.

Duncan Grant* to decorate the summer house. Her friendship with many artists and writers of the day makes her an interesting, if minor, figure within the art world during the first decades of this century.

Bibl: Wendy Baron, *Miss Ethel Sands and Her Circle*, Peter Owen, London, 1977.

SARGEANT, Gary   b.1939
Painter. Born Wales. Taught by Austin Spear,* Nelly Lapwood, mosaics by Boris Anrep* and engraving by Ecob. He also trained in the workshops of the theatrical designer Edward Delaney. First solo exhibition at the Edinburgh Festival, 1961. Has travelled widely in Europe. His street scenes are based on actual experience but in their intricate layering build up a Kafkaesque maze. Neither imaginative nor realistic, they distill the essence of industrial England.

SARGENT, John Singer   1856-1925
Painter. Born Florence, Italy, of American parents, who encouraged his early efforts at painting and he studied first at the Academy in Florence. In 1874 he met Whistler in Venice and later became a pupil of Carolus-Duran in

Paris, 1874-9. Moved to England, 1885-6 and joined NEAC, to which he sent some Monet-influenced landscapes. He specialised in portraits, gradually gaining acceptance as the most dazzling, nonchalant and effective portrait painter of the plutocracy and aristocracy. He became so tired of painting 'mugs' that after 1907 he tried to refuse commissions and concentrated instead on watercolour painting. During the First World War he produced the large oil *Gassed* for the Ministry of Information and after the war worked on murals for Boston Public Library, USA.

Bibl: Stanley Olsen, *John Singer Sargent*, Macmillan, London, 1986; Richard Ormonde, *John Singer Sargent*, Phaidon, Oxford, 1970.

SATCHWELL, Eric   b.1926
Painter. Born Northampton. Studied in Northampton and London. Included in the collections of Manchester City Art Gallery and Salford City Art Gallery.

SAUNDERS, Anne   b.1955
Painter. Born Edinburgh, Scotland. Studied at Duncan of Jordanstone College of Art, Dundee, 1973-7. 1977 went to

SAUNDERS, David

JOHN SINGER SARGENT, 1856-1925. 'Henry James', 1913. 33½ in. x 26½ in. National Portrait Gallery, London.

Australia where she lived and worked at Darling Downs Institute of Advanced Education, Toowoomba. 1975 first exhibited at 'Impress', Aberdeen Art Gallery. Became a member of the Australian Print Council and of the Association of Illustrators, London, 1979.

SAUNDERS, David   b.1936
Painter and sculptor. Studied at St. Martin's School of Art and the RA Schools. First solo exhibition at Greenwich Theatre Art Gallery, London, 1969. Included in the collections of the Arts Councils of Great Britain and Wales, Contemporary Arts Council for Wales and University College, Aberystwyth. Often works with repeated shapes exploring notions of transition, transformation, contingency and phasing.

SAUNDERS, Helen   1885-1963
Painter. Born Croydon, Surrey. Studied at Central School of Arts and Crafts and at the Slade School, 1906-7. Became associated with Wyndham Lewis* and the Vorticists and was one of first in Britain to work in a non-figurative

abstract vein. Represented in the exhibition of Twentieth Century Art held at the Whitechapel in 1914 and in the Vorticist exhibition held the following year. Also worked with Lewis on murals for the Eiffel Tower restaurant in London. Signed the Vorticist Manifesto, 1915, but after 1920 returned, as did Lewis and others, to the use of representation.

SAWICKA, Magda
Painter, engraver and lithographer. Born Poland. Moved to England, 1940. Studied at the School of Photo-Engraving and Lithography, London, and at the USB School of Painting, London. First exhibited at the RBA Gallery, London, 1949. Member of the Association of Polish Artists in Great Britain.

SAWTELL, Jeff   b.1946
Painter. Born Ellesmere Port, Cheshire. Studied at London College of Printing, 1962-4, and St. Martin's School of Art, 1965-9, and at RCA, 1969-72. First solo exhibition at the Pentonville Gallery, London, 1983, entitled 'Doves: A Tribute to the Peace Movement'.

SAXTON, Colin   b.1927
Painter. Born Mirfield, Yorkshire. Studied at Batley School of Arts and Crafts, 1942-5 and at the Slade School, 1945-8. First solo exhibition at the Manor House, Ilkley. Included in the collections of Wakefield City Art Gallery, Abbot Hall, Art Gallery, Kendal, West Riding Art Collection and Granada TV. Abstract artist inspired by nature and atmospheric effects.

SCALES, Terence   b.1932
Painter. Born Bermondsey, London. Studied at Camberwell School of Art, 1946-52. First exhibited in 'British Realists', Ikon Gallery, Birmingham, 1976. Fluent landscape artist, with a taste for romantic buildings in odd places. Inspired also by poets and, at times, by his own fantasies.

SCANLON, Claire   b.1962
Painter. Studied at Brighton Polytechnic, 1980-4, and at Goldsmiths' College, 1987-9. Exhibited at Goldsmiths' Gallery, London, 1989, followed by two more exhibitions at the Mall and Todd Galleries, London, in the same year.

SCARBOROUGH, Joe   b.1938
Painter. Born Pitsmoor, Sheffield, Yorkshire. First solo exhibition at Mappin Art Gallery, Sheffield, 1975. His paintings focus on local subjects painted in bright colours and a near-cartoon style. Has exhibited in London, at the Portal Gallery, but his reputation is mostly confined to Yorkshire.

SCARFE, Herbert   b.1920
Painter. Born Bradford, Yorkshire. Studied art in the West Riding. During the Second World War served as architectural draughtsman and camouflage specialist. First solo exhibition in Bradford, 1948. Strongly influenced by the coastal environment, producing works based on the theme of seabirds, rocks and sea.

SCHILSKY, Eric   1898-1974
Sculptor. Born Southampton, Hampshire. Studied at Slade School and married the artist Victorine Foot.* Taught at Central School of Arts and Crafts and became Head of Sculpture at Edinburgh College of Art, 1946-69. Elected ARSA, 1952, RSA, 1956, and ARA, 1957.

SCHOTZ, Benno   1891-1984
Sculptor. Born Arensburg, Estonia. 1911 went to Darmstadt in Germany to study engineering, moved on to Glasgow (where he had relatives) in 1912, and attended Glasgow Technical College. Began working as a draughtsman for the Clydesdale shipping firm of John Brown & Co., while in the evenings attending Glasgow School of Art. After visiting the Ivan Mestrovic exhibition at the V & A, London, 1915, he decided to become a sculptor. Modelled portrait busts in the evenings after work and began exhibiting these, 1917. 1920 elected President of the Society of Painters and Sculptors, Glasgow, and in 1923 became a full-time sculptor. Exhibited both in London and Scotland. Elected ARSA, 1933, and RSA, 1937, and appointed Head of Sculpture and Ceramics at Glasgow School of Art, 1938. Influenced by Rodin and Epstein.* During the 1940s also produced several stylised wood-carvings which are more modernist than his bust portraits. 1949 executed a series of *Stations of the Cross* for St. Matthew's Church, Glasgow, and in 1958 made a large altar cross for St. Paul's Church in Glenrothes. Retired from teaching, 1961. Major Schotz

exhibitions include one at Glasgow Art Gallery and Museum, 1971.

Bibl: Benno Schotz, *Bronze in My Blood*, Gordon Wright, Edinburgh, 1981.

SCHMOLLE, Stella   b.1908
Lithographer. Exhibited at the RA, 1938-40.

SCHWABE, Randolph   1885-1948
Painter, printmaker, theatre designer and illustrator. Born Manchester. Studied for a short while at the RCA, at the Slade School, 1900-5, and in Paris at the Académie Julian. Exhibited with the London Group, 1915 and became a member, 1917. Official war artist, 1914-18. Elected ARWS, 1938, and RWS, 1942. From 1930 Drawing Master at the RCA and Professor at the Slade School.

SCOBIE, Gavin   b.1940
Sculptor. Born Edinburgh, Scotland. Studied painting at Edinburgh College of Art, 1958-62. Taught in a school at Edinburgh, 1963-74. First one-person show at the Richard Demarco Gallery in Edinburgh, 1972. His earliest sculptures date from 1966 and are minimalist in style. 1972 won the Invergordon Sculpture Prize and in 1974 left his teaching job to become a full-time sculptor. Began working with aluminium and Cor-ten steel, a material which develops a natural rust patina. Solo exhibition at Inverness Art Gallery, 1977. This same year he began a series of bronze 'books' which open to reveal sculptural elements enclosed within. Since 1983 has worked principally with terracotta. A major retrospective was held at Talbot Rice Art Centre, Edinburgh University, 1984.

Bibl: Duncan MacMillan, *Gavin Scobie*, John Donald, Edinburgh, 1984.

SCOTT, Bill   b.1935
Sculptor. Born Scotland. Studied at Edinburgh College of Art and at the Ecole des Beaux-Arts, Paris. First solo exhibition at the John Whibley Gallery, London, 1972. Began making studies of male figures and of family groups but moved into more abstract work in the 1970s. Taught at Edinburgh College of Art, 1961-80.

SCOTT, Colin   b.1941
Painter. Born Sunderland, Tyne and Wear. Studied at Sunderland College of Art. Began painting full-time in 1974, has since had numerous solo exhibitions throughout England and Northern Europe. A figurative artist, interested in the relationships between people and in the underlying pressures that also keep them apart.

SCOTT, David   b.1945
Painter. Born Edinburgh, Scotland. Studied at the Byam Shaw School of Art, 1963-6 and at the RA Schools, 1966-7. First solo exhibition at Rutland Gallery, London, 1973. Included in the collections of Dublin Art Museum and Thameside Council.

SCOTT, Eric   b.1945
Painter. Born Sunderland, Tyne and Wear. Won the Northern Young Painters Competition, 1964, when he first exhibited his work.

SCOTT, Ian   b.1940
Sculptor. Born North Ronaldsay, Orkney. Studied at Gray's School of Art, Aberdeen under Leo A. Glegg. 1962

WILLIAM SCOTT, b.1913. *'Yellow Still Life'*, 1958. 40¼in. x 50in. Gimpel Fils Gallery.

first solo exhibition at the Orkney County Library. 1965 won the Latimer Award, RSA, 1966 the Benno Schotz* Prize, RSA, and 1969 the Scottish Arts Council Bursary Award. 1969 took a research trip to Shetland to study rock formations for his sculpture, followed by research trips to Iceland, 1970 and to Yorkshire, 1973. 1969 elected as Associate Member of the Society of British Sculptors and, 1972, as a fellow. In the collections of the Scottish Arts Council, Linacre College, Oxford, Faroese Art Society, Faroe Islands and Oxford University Art Society. Produces abstract sculptures with landscape connotations, not uninfluenced by Henry Moore.*

SCOTT, Kathleen (Lady Kennet)   1878-1947
Sculptor. Born Carlton-in-Lindrick, Nottinghamshire. Studied at the Slade School, and then at the Académie Colarossi in Paris, 1901-6. Married Captain R.F. Scott (Scott of the Antarctic) 1908, and secondly (in 1922) Hilton Young, later Lord Kennet. Exhibited at the RA from 1913. Solo exhibition at the Fine Art Society, London, 1934. Commissions include First World War memorials for Huntingdon, 1923, and Oundle School, the Captain Scott memorial, Waterloo Place and Lord Northcliffe, Fleet Street, 1929-30.

SCOTT, Kevin   b.1952
Painter. Born Hillsdale, New Jersey, USA. Studied at Ridgewood College of Art, the Art Students League, and at the Cooper Union, New York, USA. Moved to London in 1974, when he joined the Royal Opera House as a technical draughtsman and model maker, which led to him working on a number of operas and ballets with Marco Marelli. First solo exhibition of paintings at Chastenet European Arts Centre, 1980. Produces abstract compositions in oil on canvas and paper, influenced by late Monet.

SCOTT, Michael   b.1954
Painter. Born Lisburn, Northern Ireland. Studied at Chelsea School of Art, 1977-81. Awarded a Northern Ireland Arts Council Bursary for travel in Portugal, 1984. Exhibited in John Moores, 1982 and 1987.

SCOTT, Pamela   b.1937
Painter. Born London. Studied at Reading University, 1957-60. Awarded David Murray Landscape Scholarship, 1961. First solo exhibition at Halifax House, Oxford, 1961.

ELLIOTT SEABROOKE, 1886-1950. 'A Bank of Trees', 1929. Oil on board. 17⅝in. x 24⅝in. Harris Museum and Art Gallery, Preston.

SCOTT, Patrick   b.1921
Painter. Born Kilbrittain, Co. Cork, Ireland. Qualified as an architect, but he now paints full-time. First solo exhibition at the White Stag Gallery, Dublin, 1944. One of Ireland's leading abstract artists with an international reputation. Represented in MOMA, New York, the Ulster Museum, Belfast and elsewhere. Works mostly with cool colours as well as gold, in spare, semi-Eastern designs.

SCOTT, Tim   b.1937
Sculptor. Born London. Studied architecture at the Architectural Association, 1954-9, and sculpture at St. Martin's under Anthony Caro,* 1955-9. Worked in Paris, 1959-61. First solo exhibition at Waddington Galleries, London, 1966. One of the New Generation artists who dominated interest in sculpture in the 1960s, he worked then with a variety of materials including wood, fibreglass, steel tubing and acrylic sheets.

SCOTT, William   1913-1989
Painter. Born Greenock, Scotland. Moved to Enniskillen, Northern Ireland, 1924. Studied at Belfast College of Art, 1928-31 and at the RA Schools, 1931. 1937 travelled and lived in France. 1942 first solo exhibition at the Leger Gallery, London. Represented Britain in the Venice Biennale, 1958. 1959 awarded first prize at the 2nd John

Moores Exhibition, Liverpool. 1963-5 Ford Foundation artist-in-residence in Berlin. 1977 elected to the RA. His paintings of still lifes in the late 1940s and early 1950s led on to a brief experimentation with pure abstraction. This was later discarded for a spare arrangement of simple shapes on a flat ground which are reminiscent of pots, pans and other household items. Also painted nudes.

Bibl: Alan Bowness, *William Scott: Paintings,* Lund Humphries, London, 1964.

SEABROOKE, Elliott   1886-1950
Painter. Born Upton Park, Essex. Studied at Slade School, under Henry Tonks,* 1906-11. 1921 first solo exhibition at the Carfax Gallery, London. 1914-18, served with the British Red Cross and then became official war artist on the Italian Front. 1920 became a member of the London Group, having exhibited with them in 1919. 1943-8 President of London Group, and 1949-50 Vice President. Primarily a landscape artist, his work variously admits the influence of Cézanne and Seurat. His reputation has yet to be reassessed.

SEAGER, Harry   b.1931
Sculptor. Born Birmingham, West Midlands. Studied at Birmingham College of Art. National Service spent in

SEAGO, Edward

RONALD SEARLE, b.1920.
*'The Wonderful World of Wine:
Abbreviated course of wine-
tasting chez the Borgias',* 1987.
Pen, watercolour and coloured
pencil. 17 ¼ in. x 12 ¾ in.
Private Collection.

Hong Kong and Far East, 1956-7. First solo exhibition at Gimpel Fils, London, 1965. Works with glass with light-catching effects.

SEAGO, Edward   1910-1974

Painter. Born Norwich, Norfolk. Spent his childhood in Norfolk, mostly confined to his bed with a heart complaint which troubled him throughout his life. A self-taught artist who began his artistic career in opposition to his parents' wishes, he received some tuition on landscape painting from Bertram Priestman.* 1929 held his first solo exhibition in London. Spent several years touring with circuses throughout Europe and related his experiences in *Circus Company,* 1933, and *Sons of Sawdust,* 1934. Also became interested in ballet and enjoyed an association with John Masefield. Served with the Royal Engineers during the Second World War working on camouflage and designed the insignia and colours for the Airborne Forces. Invalided out of the army in 1944, but was invited to Italy by General Alexander to record the Italian Campaign. In 1945 Colnaghi's exhibited his war paintings and showed his work annually from that time on. He enjoyed unprecedented success, with queues forming outside the gallery long before the doors opened: every exhibition sold out within an hour of opening. 1946 elected RBA, 1957 ARWS, and 1959 RWS. Exhibited at RA and Paris Salon and had several solo exhibitions abroad. 1953 appointed one of the official artists for the Coronation and in 1956 was invited by the Duke of Edinburgh to join the Royal yacht, *Britannia,* on a round-the-world tour. He painted many scenes in Antarctica. He died of a massive brain tumour. (Plate 76, p.423.)

Bibl: Edward Seago, *With Capricorn to Paris,* Collins, London, 1956; Jean Goodman, *Edward Seago,* Collins, London, 1978.

SEARLE, Ronald   b.1920
Illustrator. Born Cambridge. Studied at the Cambridge School of Art. First drawings published in *Cambridge Daily News,* 1935. Prisoner of war in Siam and Malaysia, 1942-5. His drawings appeared in *Punch, Tribune, Sunday Express, News Chronicle* and *Life,* 1946; in the same year he invented 'The Girls of St. Trinians'. Settled in Paris in 1957 and produced a series of travel books. *Cats* published in London, 1967, since when he has produced and illustrated many children's books. Included in the collections of the British Museum, the V & A and Kunsthalk Museum, Bremen, among others. His humour, gleeful and macabre, is matched by a drawing style that combines great panache with elegant precision.

Bibl: Ronald Searle, *To the Kwai — and back: War drawings, 1939-45,* Collins, London, 1986, published on the occasion of an exhibition held at the Imperial War Museum, 1986; *Ronald Searle,* with an introduction by Henning Bock and an essay by Pierre Dehaye, André Deutsch, London, 1978.

SEDDON, Richard   b.1915
Painter. Born Sheffield, Yorkshire. Studied at RCA, 1936-9. Served in France during the Second World War and painted war subjects. Became director of Sheffield City Art Galleries, but continued to paint. Also wrote occasional art criticism for *The Guardian* and elsewhere. Has exhibited at the RCA, the RBA and with the NEAC.

Bibl: Richard Seddon, *A Hand Uplifted: a fragment of autobiography,* Frederick Muller Ltd., London, 1963.

SEDGELEY, Peter   b.1930
Painter. Studied architecture, 1944. Military service in Egypt, 1948-50. Founded a Co-operative of Associated Technicians, concerned with design and construction, 1958. Began painting, 1963. Founder member of SPACE, 1968. First solo exhibition at McRoberts and Tunnard Gallery, London, 1965. Second solo exhibition in the same year at Howard Wise Gallery, New York, USA. His work took direction after his meeting with Bridget Riley* and passed, like hers, through a monochromatic period into experiments with a controlled chromatic scale. The optical effects he achieved invite an analogy with music in their use of rhythm and variation.

SEKALSKI, Jozef   1904-1972
Painter and printmaker. Born Turek, Poland. After studying medicine for three years, he enrolled in the Faculty of Fine Art at Wilno University, 1929-34. After graduating he spent three years painting church murals. 1937 became head of an artists' and designers' studio in Lodz. 1940 escaped from German-occupied Poland to Hungary. In Budapest he held a solo exhibition of prints based on his experience of the burning of Warsaw and which sold out within a day. On the proceeds he travelled on to France and enlisted in the Polish Army. Was captured, escaped, and finally reached Britain in 1942, joining the remnants of the Polish army near Dundee. Towards the end of the war he settled in St. Andrews where he became one of an important group of wood-engravers. 1949 elected ARE and in 1950, SSA. Exhibited paintings and wood-engravings at the RA and RSA. From 1957 lectured in printmaking at Duncan of Jordanstone College of Art, Dundee.

SELF, Colin   1941
Painter. Born Norwich, Norfolk. Studied at the Slade

DEREK SELLARS, b.1935. *'Signpost to Spidean Mialach',* 1984. Wood, marble, glass, resin and Hoptonwood stone. 75in. high. Photograph Ken Phillip.

School of Art. Visited the USA and Canada, 1962 and 1965. First solo exhibition at the Piccadilly Gallery, London, 1965. He has also exhibited widely in Europe.

SELF, Lawrence   b.1924
Painter. Born Sutton, Surrey. War service, 1944-7. Studied at the RCA 1949-52. First solo exhibition at East Anglian Gallery, Ipswich.

SELLARS, Derek   b.1935
Sculptor. Born Sheffield, Yorkshire. Studied at Sheffield College of Art, 1951-6, and at the RCA, 1958-61. First solo exhibition at Sheffield University, 1963. Works with strong simple abstract shapes that yet arouse reminiscences of landscape experience.

EMMA SERGEANT, b.1959.
'Awancia'. Watercolour.
28in. x 21in.
Thomas Agnew and Sons Ltd.,
London.

SELLARS, Terry   b.1934
Painter. Born Buckinghamshire. Went to Australia, 1963.
First solo exhibition in Sydney, 1967.

SELWAY, John   b.1938
Painter. Born Askern, near Doncaster, Yorkshire.
Studied at Newport College of Art, 1953-7. National
Service, 1957-9. Studied at the RCA, 1959-62. 1962 won
the Boise Scholarship Award, and travelled to Portugal.
1964 first solo exhibition at Roland, Browse and Delbanco,
London. Included in the collections of Arts Council of
Great Britain, National Museum of Wales, CAS of Wales,
Ferens Art Gallery, Johannesburg Art Gallery, CAS,
Glynn Vivian Art Gallery, Swansea and the Welsh Arts
Council.

SELWOOD, Cordelia   b.1920
Painter. Born Manchester. Originally trained for décor
and costume design in the theatre and television, but
continued painting and drawing. First solo exhibition in
London, 1964.

SEMMENCE, John   b.1930
Painter. Born Kincardine O'Neil, Scotland. Studied at
Gray's School of Art, Aberdeen. After, he was awarded a
travelling scholarship to study in Europe. He remained to
live in Paris for four years, returning to England, 1957.
First solo exhibition at Federation of British Artists,
Suffolk Street, London, 1965. Also exhibits at the RSA and
with the NEAC.

SEMPLE, Pat
Painter. Studied at Edinburgh College of Art, 1958-63.
First solo exhibition at Stirling Gallery, Stirling, 1980.
Elected as a professional member of SSA. In the collections
of the Universities of Aberdeen, Edinburgh, Aberdeen Art
Gallery and the Scottish Arts Council.

SENFT, Nadin
Sculptor. Born London. Studied design at Leicester College of Art and Technology. Spent some years in industry, returning to sculpture when she later attended the City and Guilds of London Art School. First solo exhibition at the Alwin Gallery, London, 1969. Produced a bronze sculpture for sitting on for Guildhall Square, Portsmouth.

SENIOR, Bryan   b.1935
Painter. Born Bolton, Lancashire. Studied at Clifton College, Bristol, where he began painting before taking a language degree at Cambridge University. Spent a short time at Chelsea School of Art. First exhibited at the Heffer Gallery, Cambridge, 1957. Included in the collections of Bolton Art Gallery, Nuffield Foundation and the Contemporary Art Society of Wales. Solo exhibition at the Crane Kalman Gallery, London, 1971.

SERGEANT, Emma   b.1959
Painter. Born London. Studied at Camberwell School of Arts and Crafts and at the Slade. Winner of the Imperial Tobacco Award for Portrait Exhibition, held at the National Portrait Gallery, 1980. First solo exhibition at Agnew's, London, 1984.

SERGEANT, John   b.1937
Painter. Born London. Studied at Canterbury College of Art, 1954-7. National Service, 1957-9. He continued his studies at RA Schools, 1959-62. First exhibited at the RA. Also a book illustrator of *Oliver Twist*, E.M. Almedingen's *I Remember St. Petersburg* and Richard Church's *Portrait of Canterbury*. His watercolours owe much to the example of William Russell Flint.*

SETCH, Terry   b.1936
Painter. Born Lewisham, London. Studied at Sutton and Cheam School of Art, 1950-4. National Service, 1954-6. Continued at Slade School of Art, 1956-60. 1964 moved to Cardiff and since then has taught at Cardiff College of Art. 1975 elected member of the Artists Association of Wales, after being a member of the 56 Group, 1966. 1967 first solo exhibition at the Grabowski Gallery, London. Since then has exhibited regularly in London and Cardiff as well as abroad. 1968 awarded Welsh Arts Council Commission for large scale hoarding poster print for Royal National Eisteddfod. 1971 won the Welsh Arts Council Painting Award and 1978 the Welsh Arts Council Major Artist Award. Since 1975 a member of 'Artists and Designers in Wales'. Included in the collections of Arts Council of Great Britain, Welsh Arts Council, V & A, CAS for Wales and the Museum of Modern Art, Lodz, Poland. His recent work has continued his fascination with detritus strewn beaches, car wrecks and pollution. He works on large scale, using often unstretched, unframed canvas.

SHACKLETON, Elizabeth   b.1951
Painter. Born Midgley, near Halifax, Yorkshire. Studied at Percival Whitley School of Art, 1967-9, and at Bradford College of Art, 1969. First solo exhibition at Ginnel Gallery, Manchester, 1980.

SHACKLETON, Judith
Painter. Studied at Southampton School of Art and at the RCA. First exhibited at Liverpool Academy, 1955. Included in the collections of the Universities of Leeds, Liverpool and Durham.

DUNCAN SHANKS, b.1937. *'The Glen Burn'*, c.1986. 76in. x 58in. Talbot Rice Gallery, Edinburgh.

SHACKLETON, Peter   b.1933
Painter. Born Harwood, Lancashire. Studied at Accrington School of Art and Liverpool College of Art. First exhibited in Gibb's Bookshop, Manchester, 1956. Solo exhibition held at Crane Kalman Gallery, London, 1959. Represented in Blackburn Art Gallery.

SHACKLETON, William   1872-1933
Painter. Born Bradford, Yorkshire. Studied at Bradford Technical College. With a British Institute Scholarship in 1896, he travelled to France and Italy. On returning to London he took a studio with Philip Connard* and Oliver Onions in Chelsea and generally spent the summers in Amberley, Sussex. After 1914 he moved to Malham, Yorkshire, which became the subject of his later landscapes. Exhibited at the RA and with the NEAC. Included in the collections of Bradford Art Galleries and Museum, Rochdale Art Gallery, Harris Museum and Art Gallery, Preston, Atkinson Art Gallery, Southport, Manchester City Art Gallery, and York Art Gallery. His mystical view of the world inclined him towards images, soft-centred and cinematic, which were given such titles as *The Island of Dreams*.

SHANKS, Duncan   b.1937
Painter. Born Airdrie, Scotland. Studied at Glasgow School of Art. Awarded travelling scholarship to Italy. First solo exhibition at Stirling University. Won Scottish

SHANNON, Charles

Arts Council Award, and the Latimer Award and MacAulay Prize, RSA. 1988 held a solo exhibition at the Talbot Rice Gallery, University of Edinburgh, taking for its subject the Falls of the Clyde and the burns that run into it. Works in the collections of Scottish Arts Council, Arts Council of Great Britain, Glasgow Art Gallery, Dundee Art Gallery, Lillie Art Gallery, Milngavie and the Universities of Glasgow, Edinburgh and Stirling.

SHANNON, Charles   1863-1937
Painter and lithographer. Born Sleaford, Lincolnshire. Studied at Lambeth School of Art, 1882, where he met his lifelong friend Charles Ricketts* with whom he ran the Vale Press, 1896-1904 and founded *The Dial* magazine, 1889-97. He exhibited a the RA, IS and at the Grosvenor Gallery, London. First solo exhibition held at Leicester Galleries, London, 1907. Elected ARE, 1891, ARA, 1911, and RA, 1920. Greatly interested in Venetian art, he tried in his own paintings to revive their techniques and use of rich, glowing colour. As a result his classical and figure subjects have the air of Old Masters but not always the conviction.

SHANNON, James Jebusa   1862-1923
Painter. Born Auburn, New York, USA, of Irish parents. Came to London in 1878 and studied at South Kensington School of Art, 1878-81. He was taught the square brush technique by La Thangue and used it for his early portraits. Became a founder member of the NEAC. Exhibited at the RA from 1881. Elected ARA, 1897, and RA, 1909.

SHARIFFE, Hussein   b.1937
Painter. Born Omdurman, Sudan. Studied at the Slade School of Fine Arts. 1958 first solo exhibition at Gallery One, London. 1961 prize winner, John Moores Liverpool Exhibition. 1963 third solo exhibition held at Gallery One, London.

SHARP, Dorothea   1874-1955
Painter. Studied at Regent Street Polytechnic and in Paris. Exhibited at the RA, abroad and in the provinces. Elected RBA, 1907, and ROI, 1922. Lived in London, also in Berkshire and for a period at St. Ives, Cornwall. Interest in her work has recently revived owing to saleroom demand for her pleasant, if untaxing, impressionism.

SHARP, Nancy   b.1909
Painter. Born Cornwall. Studied at Slade School of Art, 1928-31. Showed her work at several London galleries during the 1930s, also with the London Group. Married William Coldstream.* 1945-77 taught art in various schools. Represented in the Ashmolean Museum and the Government Art Collection.

SHARPE, Charles William   1881-1955
Painter. Born Liverpool, grandson of an engraver. Studied at Liverpool School of Art. Held various teaching posts and from 1930 was Principal of the Laird School of Art, Birkenhead. Member and Hon. Secretary of the Royal Cambrian Academy. Also member of Ulster Academy of Arts, Liverpool Academy and Sandon Studios Society. Exhibited London, Liverpool and internationally. Represented in the Walker Art Gallery, Liverpool.

SHARRATT, Leo
Painter. Born Durham, Co. Durham. Studied at Durham

University under Sir Lawrence Gowing* and Victor Pasmore.* Served his National Service in Cyprus and Germany. Returned to study at the Slade, 1958-9; later he travelled widely in Turkey, Iran, Pakistan, Afghanistan and Europe. Regularly exhibits at the Westgate Gallery, Newcastle.

SHAVE, Terry   b.1952
Painter. Born Suffolk. Studied at Ipswich School of Art, 1971-2, Loughborough College, 1972-5 and the Slade, 1975-7. 1983 won prize in the 4th Tolly Cobbold Eastern Arts National Exhibition and in same year had solo exhibitions at North Staffordshire Polytechnic Gallery and Morley Gallery, London. 1986 solo show at Ikon Gallery, Birmingham. Senior lecturer in painting at North Staffordshire Polytechnic. His expressionistic drawings and paintings are often based on ceremonies and rituals.

SHAW, David   b.1952
Painter. Born Kent. Studied at Canterbury College of Art, 1970-3. First solo exhibition at Aberbach Fine Art, London, 1977, followed by a second exhibition at the same gallery, 1978, and a third, 1980.

SHAW, John Byam   1872-1919
Painter. Born Madras, India. Came to England in 1878. Studied at St. John's Wood School of Art from 1889. 1893 began exhibiting at the RA. His paintings, in their choice of subject matter and use of rich colour, contributed to a late revival of Pre-Raphaelitism which continued well into the 20th century. 1898 elected RI. Illustrated several books, including works by Robert Browning and Edgar Allen Poe. Became a partner with Rex Vicat Cole* in The Byam Shaw and Vicat Cole School of Art, Kensington.

SHAW, Susan   b.1938
Painter. Born Sussex. Studied at St. Martin's School of Art and the RCA. First solo exhibition at Heal's Mansard Gallery, London, 1969.

SHELLEY, John
Painter. Studied at Wimbledon School of Art and the Slade. He was awarded the British Institute Fund Prize and the David Murray Landscape Prize. First solo exhibition at the Trafford Gallery, London, 1973. Works in the collections of the Tate Gallery and CAS. Also a dedicated musician, playing the trombone in various jazz groups.

SHELTON, Harold   b.1913
Etcher. Born St. Helen's, Lancashire. Studied at Wallasey School of Art, 1934-6, and at the RCA, 1936-9. Exhibited at major venues in London, including the RA and the RE. Elected ARE, 1940. Became Principal of Carlisle School of Art and then Principal of Hornsey College of Art.

SHELTON, John   b.1923
Painter. Studied at Burslem School of Art, 1937-40, and at Stoke-on-Trent Art School before winning a scholarship to the Slade, 1944. Whilst there he met Robert MacBryde* from whom he learnt much and whom he got to know well. Exhibited wih the London Group and returned to the Potteries where he became a designer of Staffordshire china. 1957 began teaching at Newcastle Art School and retired from there in 1983. Represented in Stoke-on-Trent Art Gallery and elsewhere.

SHEMILT, Elaine b.1954
Printmaker and sculptor. Born Edinburgh, Scotland. Moved to Northern Ireland, 1960. Studied at Winchester School of Art, 1973-6, and at RCA, 1976-9. 1980-2 Artist in Residence, South Hill Park Arts Centre, Bracknell, Berkshire. 1982 awarded Printmaking Fellowship at Winchester School of Art. 1982 first solo exhibition at Main Gallery, South Hill Park Arts Centre. Figurative artist, working primarily with the head and the female body to explore notions of bondage and the split personality.

SHEPARD, E.H. 1879-1976
Illustrator and cartoonist. Born London. Studied at Heatherley's School, 1896-7, and won a scholarship to the RA, 1897-1901. Won a Landseer Scholarship and a British Institution Prize. 1901 first exhibited at the RA Summer Exhibition. Published his first book illustrations in 1900 and in 1906 had his first cartoon accepted by *Punch*. 1915-18 commissioned as a gunner officer; awarded the MC. 1921 joined the staff of *Punch*. 1924 began collaborating with A.A. Milne, initially on Milne's book of verses, *When We Were Young*. After this he stamped the image of Christopher Robin and his friends in popular imagination with his illustrations for *Winnie the Pooh*. 1928 illustrated *The House at Pooh Corner* and in 1931 Kenneth Grahame's *The Wind in the Willows*. 1945 became senior political cartoonist of *Punch*. 1957 wrote and illustrated his autobiography, *Drawn from Memory*, 1957, and *Drawn from Life*, 1961. 1974 reworked his original drawings for *The House at Pooh Corner* in colour. Received the OBE, 1972. 1988 retrospective exhibition held at Sally Hunter Fine Art, London.

SHEPHARD, Rupert b.1909
Painter. Born London. Studied at the Slade School of Art, 1926-9. 1939 first solo exhibition at Calman Gallery. Since 1929 represented in group exhibitions with the London Group at the Wertheim Gallery and Coolings Gallery. During the 1930s he often painted in music halls, pubs and streets. 1937-9 exhibited with William Coldsteam,* Claude Rogers* and Victor Pasmore* at the Storran Gallery, while continuing to exhibit with the London Group. 1940-3 worked as a draughtsman in industry. 1945 appointed official War Artist to the Ministry of Transport. 1945 elected to NEAC. 1948 moved to South Africa to become Professor of Fine Art in the University of Cape Town. 1963 returned to England and became a full-time painter. 1972 elected to RP. Represented in the collections of the National Portrait Gallery, Imperial War Museum and the British Museum Print Room.

SHEPHERD, David b.1931
Painter. Studied in Chelsea under Robin Goodwin. Solo exhibitions include one at the Parson's Gallery, London, 1955, and several others at the Tryon Gallery, London. Through colour reproductions of his work, sold in Boots and elsewhere, he has reached a wide public, and, though critically disregarded, is one of the best loved artists working in Britain today. His two main interests are trains and animals, both of which appear in his paintings. Has set up the David Shepherd Charitable Foundation to assist with Wild Life Conservation and in 1979 was awarded the OBE for his work in this area. Has published two volumes of autobiography, *The Man who loves Giants. An Artist among Elephants and Engines,* 1975, and *David Shepherd. The Man and His Paintings, 1985.*

SHEPHERD, David b.1944
Painter and sculptor. Born Wigan, Lancashire. Studied at Wigan School of Art, 1961-5 and at University of London Goldsmith's College, 1965-6. 1968 first solo exhibition at Compendium Gallery, Birmingham. 1972-80 member of 56 Group, Wales. 1975 won Welsh Arts Council Artist Award, with his linear, repeated-pattern wood installations.

SHEPHERD, Horne b.1909
Painter. Born Dundee, Scotland. Studied at Dundee School of Art, 1924-6 and at Glasgow School of Art, 1926-7. 1927 won a travelling scholarship. 1932 first solo exhibition in Dundee, Scotland. Included in the collections of Melbourne Art Gallery, Australia, the Arts Council, and the V & A. Works mainly with translucent colour circumscribed by dark outlines.

SHEPPARD, Clive b.1930
Sculptor. Born London. Initially studied architecture, 1946-53, but began studying sculpture in 1953, at St. Martin's College of Art. Became assistant to Henry Moore,* 1960. First exhibited at the New Vision Centre Gallery, London. Included in the collection of the Arts Council of Great Britain. Abstract sculptor, who works mainly with wood.

SHEPPARD, Maurice b.1947
Painter. Studied at Kingston College of Art and the RCA. 1965 awarded scholarship to Eisteddfod, Maldwyd. 1970 won the British Institution Award and 1971 the David Murray Landscape Award. 1973 awarded Geoffrey Crawshay memorial Travelling Scholarship. 1978 elected Vice-President of RWS. 1979 first solo exhibition at the New Grafton Gallery, London. A skilled landscape artist, who captures both detail and momentary effects.

SHEPPARD, Stephen
Painter. Studied at L'Ecole des Beaux-Arts, Paris, 1946-8 and at Camberwell School of Arts and Crafts, 1949-52. First solo exhibition at the Court Lodge Gallery, Kent, 1972. Painter of nudes, figure subjects, still lifes and landscapes.

SHEPPERSON, Patricia b.1929
Painter. Born London. Studied at Heatherley's School of Art and at Sir John Cass School of Art, 1959-67. 1978 elected member of United Society of Artists. 1978 solo exhibition at Woodlands Art Gallery, London, of animals and birds drawn in pastel.

SHERINGHAM, George 1884-1937
Painter, interior and theatre designer. Studied at the Slade, 1899-1901 and under Harry Becker, 1901-4. 1905-6 lived in Paris. 1908 travelled to Algeria, Portugal, Belgium and Brittany. 1908 first solo exhibition at the Brook Street Gallery, London. 1910 first solo exhibition of his decorative work — fans and silk panels — at the Ryder Gallery, London, which led to a commission to paint panels for Judge Evans at Illington Manor. His decorative work was influenced by Eastern art, examples of which he saw at the Musée Guimet, when living in Paris. 1912 joined the Pastel Society. 1915 executed his first book illustrations for Max Beerbohm's *The Happy Hypocrite*. 1917 he also produced his first theatre designs for the Plough Club. 1920 began writing articles for *The Studio*. 1924 he began a long association with Nigel Playfair at the Lyric

GEORGE SHERINGHAM, 1884-1937. *'Corner in my Studio'*. Gouache on board. 12⅝in. 16in.
Nottingham Castle Museum and Art Gallery.

Theatre, Hammersmith, producing set designs, which led to many commissions from other theatres. 1932 produced a chocolate box design for a Cadbury's commission for the Bourneville 'Artists Series'. After 1932 ill health led him to concentrate on still life painting.

SHERLOCK, Marjorie   1879-1973
Painter. Born Wanstead, Essex. Studied at Slade School and at Westminster School of Art under Walter Sickert* and Harold Gilman* during the First World War. First exhibited at the RA, 1917. Later she returned to study etching at the RCA, 1926. 1938 studied in Paris with André L'Hôte and Segonzac. Moved to Axminster, Devon, during the Second World War, where, in 1947, she was a founder member of the Axminster Art Society. 1973 a retrospective was held at the Maltzahn Gallery, London. She was a close friend of Orovida Pissarro* who paid for their occasional visits abroad. Sherlock excelled at etching, bringing a subtle control of tone to such complex scenes as that presented by Waterloo Station.

SHETLAND, Llric   b.1947
Painter. Born London. Studied at Goldsmiths' College,

1964-6 and at Hornsey College of Art, 1966-9. 1974 first solo exhibition at Gamstyl, Brussels. 1977 first solo exhibition in Great Britain at Patrick Seale Gallery, London. Skilled draughtsman who achieves camera-like effects in images that often play upon illusion.

SHIELDS, Dennis   b.1947
Sculptor. Born Liverpool, Merseyside. Studied at Liverpool College of Art, 1960-2. Emigrated to Canada, 1964. Studied at Ontario College of Art, 1970-3. 1973 awarded 'The Lieutenant Governor General of Ontario' Medal; returned to England in the same year. 1981 first solo exhibition at the Compass Gallery, Glasgow. Works with recycled materials which he reclaims for unexpected purposes.

SHIRAISHY, Yuko   b.1956
Painter and printmaker. Born Tokyo, Japan. Lived in Canada, 1974-6. Studied at Chelsea School of Art, 1978-82. First solo exhibition held at Curwen Gallery, London, 1984. Most recent solo exhibition held at Edward Totah Gallery, London, and Artsite Gallery, Bath, 1990. Paints abstracts with complex colour combinations: 'I want painting to be like the sea — you soak in it, like swimming.'

SHORT, Frank   1857-1945
Painter and engraver. Born Stourbridge, Worcestershire. Trained as an engineer but abandoned this career for art. Studied at South Kensington and Westminster Schools of Art. From 1874 exhibited at leading London galleries, mainly at the RA, RI, RBA and RE. 1889 and 1900 won gold medals at the Paris Salon, both for engraving. 1891 appointed Director of Engraving at the RCA, becoming Professor, 1913 and remained in this influential position until his retirement, 1924. Elected RE, 1885, ARA, 1906, PRE, 1910-38, RE, 1911, RI, 1917. Became Treasurer of the RA, 1919-32, as well as Master of the Art Workers' Guild. Knighted 1911. Was one of the leading figures in the field of etching and engraving during the early years of this century. A dedicated craftsman and confirmed traditionalist, his etchings often admitted a debt to past masters.

SICKERT, Bernard   c.1863-1932
Painter. Born Munich, Germany, the brother of Walter Sickert.* Came to England in 1868 with his family but did not devote himself to painting until around 1885. 1888 elected a member of the NEAC. 1895 exhibited with his brother, Walter, at the Dutch Gallery, London. His work is sensitive and rare, less confident than that of his brother, and often tellingly influenced by Whistler. Often worked in Dieppe, and also visited Holland, Italy and France.

SICKERT, Walter Richard   1860-1942
Painter and etcher. Born Munich, Germany, son of a painter. The family moved to England in 1868. After a brief career as an actor in a repertory company, Sickert studied at the Slade, 1881-2, and afterwards worked as an assistant to Whistler. Degas was to prove a more crucial influence, and Sickert became obsessed, less with style, than with method and the construction of a picture. His cosmopolitan background and desire to teach made him an influential figure and after periods abroad, in Venice and Dieppe, he returned to London and founded the Fitzroy Street Group which in 1911 changed its name to the Camden Town Group. Sickert believed that poetry and beauty could be found in the overlooked and often grimy corners of London, in lodging house interiors and the back streets of Camden. He placed great emphasis on drawing and though he aimed in his paintings at, in his words, 'the sensation of a page torn from the book of life', he was highly professional in his method of working, building up his pictures with layers of paint, achieving dingy tonal harmonies of often extraordinary richness. He was particulary fond of music halls and the working-class culture they upheld, but he was as much interested in the pale faces hanging over the balustrade in the gods as he was in the antics on the stage. He was made ARA, 1924 and RA, 1934, from which he resigned, 1935. His late work made startling use of photography for its subject matter. He also revamped trite scenes drawn from Victorian illustrations. In his dress, manner and art he knew how to surprise. A book of his art writings, *A Free House!*, edited by Osbert Sitwell, was published in 1947. (Plate 2, p.14.)

Bibl: Wendy Baron, *Sickert*, Scolar Press, London, 1973; Richard Stone, *Walter Sickert*, Phaidon, Oxford, 1989.

SILVERMAN, Howard   b.1946
Painter. Born New York, USA. Studied at New York High School of Music and Art and San Francisco Art Institute. Since 1972 he has lived and exhibited in Britain, with solo exhibitions at Bath University, 1982, Woodlands, Greenwich, 1986 and Bath Festival Gallery, 1987.

SIMCOCK, Jack   b.1929
Painter. Born Biddulph, Staffordshire. First solo exhibition at Piccadilly Gallery, London, 1957, followed by a second solo exhibition there, 1958. Included in the collections of Stoke-on-Trent Art Gallery and the Education Authorities of Leicestershire, Yorkshire, Essex, Nottinghamshire, Hertfordshire, Surrey and Durham. He is also represented in many universities in Great Britain.

SIMMONDS, Stanley   b.1917
Painter. Studied at the RCA. First solo exhibition at the Bear Lane Gallery, Oxford, 1958, followed by a second exhibition there, 1959. Included in the collections of Oxford Education Committee, Coventry Education Committee and University College, Oxford.

SIMMONDS, William   1876-1968
Painter and carver. Born Instanbul, Turkey. Studied at the RCA, under Walter Crane, 1893-9 and at the RA Schools, 1899-1904. 1906-10 worked as assistant to the painter and illustrator, Edwin Austen Abbey.* 1914-18 worked as a precision draughtsman on tank and aircraft design. 1912 married Eveline Peart, who became known for her embroidery. Took up carving. Regularly exhibited at the Arts and Crafts Exhibition Society and at the RA. 1966 a retrospective of his work was held at Painswick, Gloucestershire. Included in the collections of the Tate Gallery, Gloucester City Museum, Museum of Rural Life, University of Reading and Cheltenham Art Gallery and Museum.

SIMON, Edith
Painter and sculptor. Studied at the Slade and Central School of Arts and Crafts, after which she worked as a writer and historian. She has published seventeen fiction and non-fiction books and was at one time a contributor to *Time-Life Magazine* and the *Encyclopaedia Britannica.* Returned to full-time work as a painter and sculptor in 1972, holding many exhibitions in Britain and abroad. Her most original works are her paper-cuts which are bas-reliefs in which the effects of painting are achieved by cutting shapes out of layers of variously coloured papers with a scalpel, with intricate results.

SIMON, Keith   b.1922
Painter. Born Honduras, Central America. When young he travelled to the West Indies, Canada and the USA. Grew up and was educated in the USA. 1952 first solo exhibition at the 44th Gallery, New York, and moved to London. 1953 second solo exhibition at the Archer Gallery, London.

SIMON, Robert Scott   b.1926
Sculptor. Born Birmingham, West Midlands. Qualified as a mechanical engineer, 1945. 1961 founded a workshop where he began exploring precision engineering techniques relative to sculpture. 1970 first exhibited at the Marjorie Parr Gallery, London. Has worked on, among other things, special commissions for sculpture-based clocks. These include his designs for Essex County Newspapers and for the British Steel Corporation Headquarters.

SIMPSON, Audrey   b.1946
Painter. Born Tufnell Park, London. Studied at South Essex School of Art, Walthamstow, London, 1962-4, at Wimbledon School of Art, 1975-8 and at Goldsmiths' College, 1979-81. First solo exhibition at Everyman Theatre, Liverpool.

JOHN SKELTON, b.1923. *'Two turning torsos'*, 1989. Ancaster weatherbed stone. 72in. x 48in. x 36in. Private Collection.

SIMPSON, Henry   1853-1921
Painter. Born Cumberland. Studied at Slade School, where he was an intimate friend of Whistler. 1910 first solo exhibition at the Leicester Galleries, London. Until 1914 travelled and lived in Cairo, Alexandria and Paris, then mainly painted in the Isle of Wight, Scotland and Suffolk.

SIMPSON, John   b.1944
Painter. Born Fraserburgh, Scotland. Studied at the Slade in the mid-1960s. First solo exhibition at the New 57 Gallery, Ediburgh, 1969; others include two at the Galeria Picasso, Spain, 1987 and 1988. His paintings focus on the natural environment from which he derives near abstract images, rich in colour and surface texture.

SIMPSON, Michael   B.1940
Painter. Born Dorset. Studied at Bournemouth College of Art, 1959-60 and at RCA, 1960-3. 1960 won scholarship to the Soviet Union. 1964 first solo exhibition at Piccadilly Gallery, London, followed by a second solo exhibition in the same year at Southampton University. Included in the collections of Arts Council of Great Britain, Arts Council of Northern Ireland, Carlisle Art Gallery and Museum, Leicestershire Education Authority and the RCA.

SIMPSON, Ruth   889-1964
Painter. Née Alison. Studied at Newlyn, Cornwall, under Elizabeth* and Stanhope* Forbes. Married the artist Charles Simpson* in 1913 and lived at Newlyn, moving briefly to Lamorna and then St. Ives, c.1916, where they ran a painting school. 1924 they moved to London but returned in 1931 to Cornwall. Specialised in figure and portrait painting.

SIMS, Charles   1873-1928
Painter. Born Islington, London. Studied at the RCA, 1890, and in Paris at the Académie Julian, 1891, and at the

RA Schools, 1892-5, where he received the Landseer Scholarship. 1894 began exhibiting at the RA. 1906 first solo exhibition held at the Leicester Galleries. Elected ARA, 1908, ARWS, 1911, RWS, 1914, and RA, 1916. 1918 became Official War Artist. 1920-6 Keeper of the RA. In the 1920s he began to suffer from hallucinations and mental illness and eventually committed suicide.

SIMS, Ronald   b.1944
Painter. Studied at Manchester College of Art and Design, 1965-6, and at RA Schools, 1967-70. 1968 won the *Connoisseur* Magazine Prize for painting and 1970-1 the Gloucestershire Fellowship. 1971 first solo exhibition at 'Minories', Colchester. Specialises in heads created out of geometric components.

SINNOTT, Kevin   b.1947
Painter. Born Wales. Studied at Cardiff College of Art and Design, 1967-8, Gloucester College of Art and Design, 1968-71 and RCA, 1971-4. 1978 first solo exhibition held in Thetford, Norfolk. Recent solo shows include two at Bernard Jacobson Gallery in London, 1986, and in New York, 1987.

SKEAPING, John   1901-1980
Sculptor. Born South Woodford, Essex, son of the painter Kenneth Matheison Skeaping. Studied at Goldsmiths' College School, at the Central School of Arts and Crafts, 1917-19, and the RA Schools, 1919-20. 1924 awarded the Prix de Rome. In Italy met and married Barbara Hepworth.* Both learnt to carve from a master carver and for a brief period there was a close affinity between their work, both in its subject matter and handling. Their marriage was dissolved, 1933. First solo exhibition, with Hepworth, held at Alex Reid and Lefevre, Glasgow, 1928. Became a member of the London Group, 1928 and of the 7 & 5 Society, 1932. 1940-5 Official War Artist. 1949-50 worked in Mexico. Elected ARA, 1950, and RA, 1960. From 1953 Professor of Sculpture at the RCA.

SKELTON, John   b.1923
Sculptor and letter-cutter. Born Glasgow, Scotland. Studied architecture at Coventry School of Art, 1939-40. Apprenticed to Eric Gill,* 1940, but only served three months owing to Gill's death. 1941-2 apprentice to Joseph Cribb at Ditchling. Served in Royal Artillery in India, Burma and Malaya, during Second World War. 1950 set up own workshop in Sussex. 1953 began exhibiting at the RA. 1963 first one-person exhibition at Chichester Museum. 1965 retrospective exhibition at Herbert Art Gallery, Coventry. 1966 invited to Yugoslavia to contribute a large work to the UN Pavilion. 1970 exhibition in Norwich Cathedral Cloisters, and Hereford Cathedral Crypt, 1976. Shows work at his own workshop at Street in Sussex. 1984 one-person exhibition at the Bright Festival. Numerous major public commissions for lettered panels, coats of arms, memorials and a bishop's chair for Chelmsford Cathedral. Works in the collections of Toledo Museum of Art, USA, Shakespeare Centre, Stratford-upon-Avon, The British Museum, HM The Queen, Chichester City Museum, Plymouth Art Gallery, Coventry Art Gallery.

SKELTON, Pam   b.1949
Painter. Born Harrogate, Yorkshire. Studied at Southport School of Arts and Crafts, 1967-9, and at Camberwell School of Arts and Crafts, 1969-72. 1977 first solo

exhibition at Northcott Theatre Gallery, Exeter. 1984 commissioned to paint a mural for Bilston Community College and to work with the Public Art Collective on Mazzoni Gardens Mural, Birmingham. 1986 finalist, Athena Art Award. 1989 Artist in Residence, Birmingham City Art Gallery. Regularly exhibits with the Benjamin Rhodes Gallery. Solo exhibition held at the Ikon Gallery, Birmingham, 1989-90. Included in the Birmingham City Museum and Art Gallery collection. Uses elements of archaeology and anthropology in richly coloured and textured paintings.

SKINNER, John   b.1953
Painter. Born Chatham, Kent. Since 1976 included in mixed exhibitions. 1977 worked at the Summer School at Pahpos, Cyprus. 1980 first solo exhibition at the New Gallery, Haringey Park, London; another at the Woodlands Art Gallery, Blackheath, 1982.

SKIOLD, Birgit   1923-1982
Printmaker. Born Stockholm, Sweden, and studied there. 1948 settled in England. Studied at the Anglo-French Centre, London, the Regent Street Polytechnic and the Académie Grande Chaumière, Paris. 1957 started the Print Workshop in London to provide printmaking facilities for artists. Taught at Bradford, Hammersmith and Wolverhampton Colleges of Art and at the University of Wisconsin, 1964. Work in many public collections, including Tate Gallery, V & A, Leeds, Hull, Oldham, Eastbourne and Portsmouth City Art Galleries.

SLEEMAN, Keith   b.1922
Painter. Born Bristol, Somerset. Studied at Willesden School of Art and at Hornsey School of Art. First solo exhibition, 1961; another at the Woodstock Gallery, 1966. Painter of broad abstract works.

SLINGER, Penelope   b.1947
Sculptor. Born London. Studied at Farnham School of Art, 1964-6 and Chelsea School of Art, 1966-9. 1970-1 worked with experimental theatre groups and film-makers. 1973 first solo exhibition at Angela Flowers Gallery. Maker of mixed-media constructions, using tables, food, life casts of bodies, wax fruit, and other objects, which reflect upon the human condition.

SLOAN, Bob   b.1940
Painter and sculptor. Born Belfast, Northern Ireland. Studied at Belfast College of Art. Since 1965 included in mixed exhibitions in Dublin, Belfast and Cork. 1982 first solo exhibition at the Caldwell Gallery, Belfast. 1979 commissioned to make a public sculpture for Downpatrick and in 1984 to make trophies for the Northern Ireland Tourist Board. 1982 began to make figurative and landscape hand-made paper works, which were shown at the Octagon Gallery, Belfast, 1985. Currently lectures at the University of Ulster.

SLOAN, Victor   b.1945
Painter and photographer. Born Dungannon, Co. Tyrone, Northern Ireland. Studied at Belfast College of Art, 1964-8 and Leeds College of Art, 1968-9. Lives and works in Portadown, Co. Armagh. 1981 first solo exhibition 'The Brownlow Series', at Pinebank House, Craigaron. Takes photographs of typically Irish subjects, prints them up very large and works on them with toner and watercolour. 1985-7 included in the New Irish Art exhibition which toured the USA and Canada.

ELINOR BELLINGHAM-SMITH, 1906-1988. *'Figures in an East Anglian Marsh'*, c.1960s. Private Collection.

SMART, Anthony   b.1949
Sculptor. Born Yorkshire. Studied at Hull College of Art, 1967-70, and at St. Martin's School of Art, 1970-3. 1972 first exhibited at the Museum of Modern Art, Oxford. Works from the human body. Included in the collections of the Arts Council of Great Britain and Robinson College, Cambridge.

SMART, R. Borlase   1881-1947
Painter, etcher and poster-designer. Born Kingsbridge, South Devon. Studied under Julius Olsson* at St.Ives. Exhibited at the RA, RSA, the Paris Salon and elsewhere. In 1919 settled permanently in St. Ives. Became Secretary of the St. Ives Arts Club and acted as art critic for the *Western Morning News*. Is chiefly associated with seascapes and architectural views.

SMITH, Arthur Reginald   1871-1934
Painter. Born Skipton-in-Craven, Yorkshire. Studied at Keighley School of Art and taught there for several years. Also studied at the RCA, 1901-4. 1905 studied in Italy on a

scholarship. Exhibited at the RA, other leading London galleries, in the provinces and abroad. Elected ARWS, 1917, RWS, 1923, and RSW, 1926. Drowned in the River Wharfe, near Bolton Abbey.

SMITH, Claire   b.1949
Painter. Born Bristol, Somerset. Studied at Reading University, 1967-71 and at Chelsea School of Art, 1972-3. 1976 first solo exhibition at the Acme Gallery, London, followed by one in the same year at the Gardner Centre, Brighton.

SMITH, Colin   b.1953
Painter. Born Hertfordshire. Studied at Falmouth School of Art, 1972-5, and at the RCA, 1976-9. 1982 first solo exhibition at the Nicola Jacobs Gallery, where she has regularly exhibited since 1979. 1983 awarded the Harkness Fellowship, which led him to live in New York for several years. 1990 solo exhibition at Anderson O'Day Fine Art, London. Included in the collections of Galerie de

IAN McKENZIE SMITH, b.1935. *'Mulberry Gate'*. Aberdeen Art Gallery and Museums, Aberdeen City Arts Department. Private Collection.

Beerenburght, Holland, Unilever, London and Arts Council of Great Britain.

Bibl: Marjorie Allthorpe-Guyton, 'Colin Smith', *Flash Art,* May 1987, no.134.

SMITH, Elinor Bellingham   1906-1988
Painter. Studied at Slade School of Art. 1931 married Rodrigo Moynihan,* and lived near Regent's Park, which she often painted. Produced fashion magazine drawings and illustrations and also exhibited paintings with the London Group and at the Leicester Galleries. During the 1950s lived in Chelsea and Soho, at the centre of an artistic and literary world. In 1957, after separating from Moynihan, she moved to Boxted, Suffolk, and began to concentrate on landscapes and on the Fens in winter. 1989 memorial exhibition held at the New Grafton Gallery, Barnes. A retrospective was held at the RA in 1990.

SMITH, George Grainger   1892-1961
Painter and engraver. Born Hull, Yorkshire. Moved to Liverpool, 1895. Studied at Liverpool School of Art. Became Art Master at Liverpool College. Exhibited in London, Liverpool and elsewhere. Member of the Liverpool Academy. Member and President of the Royal Cambrian Academy. Retired to Wales.

SMITH, Ian McKenzie   b.1935
Painter. Born Montrose, Scotland. Studied at Gray's

School of Art, Aberdeen, 1953-8; also attended courses at Hospitalfield School of Art, Arbroath, 1957 and 1958, winning a travelling scholarship, 1958. He visited Paris and was especially attracted to the Egyptian and Japanese sections in the Louvre. Though his abstracts of the early 1960s imitate American Abstract Expressionism, during the 1970s an Oriental sense of finesse and balance took over. 1968 he was appointed Director of Aberdeen Art Gallery and in this role acquired many additions for its outstanding collection of 20th century British art. Since the late 1960s his own abstracts have been more muted and occasionally make subtle references to language. Has held several solo exhibitions, at the 57 Gallery, Edinburgh, 1959 and 1963, and at the Scottish Gallery, 1965 and 1971. Elected ARSA, 1973, and RSA, 1987. President of the RSW, 1988.

SMITH, Ivy   b.1945
Painter. Studied at Chelsea School of Art and the RA Schools. First solo exhibition at Royal Leamington Spa Gallery, 1974. Commissioned by the National Portrait Gallery to paint a double portrait of Sir Richard and Sir David Attenborough. Included in the collections of Graves Art Gallery, Sheffield, Royal Leamington Spa Art Gallery, The National Trust, Castle Museum, Norwich, Sheffield University, Sussex University and Coventry Polytechnic.

SMITH, Jack   b.1928
Painter. Born Sheffield, Yorkshire. Studied at Sheffield College of Art, 1944-6, St. Martin's School of Art, 1948-50, and RCA, 1950-3. First solo exhibition held at the Beaux Arts Gallery, 1953. With John Bratby,* Derrick Greaves* and Edward Middleditch,* he became associated with 'Kitchen Sink' painting which took its subject matter from the texture of everyday life. Though Smith was the one who actually painted a kitchen sink (and the child being bathed in it), he later more or less repudiated his realist work and instead developed an abstract style in which the rhythm and movement of notational marks have a musical effect. Solo exhibitions include one at Flowers East, London, 1990.

SMITH, Keir   b.1950
Sculptor. Born Kent. Studied at the University of Newcastle upon Tyne, 1969-73 and Chelsea School of Art, 1973-5. Junior Fellow at Cardiff College of Art, 1975-6. From 1980 senior lecturer in sculpture at Birmingham Polytechnic. Has shown in many mixed exhibitions, including 'Sculpture in the Close' at Jesus College, Cambridge.

SMITH, Lance   b.1950
Painter. Born Bournemouth, Dorset. Studied at Camberwell School of Arts and Crafts, 1969-73 and at the Royal Academy Schools, 1973-6. 1980 gained Arts Council Minor Award. Won First Prize in the 5th Tolly Cobbold Eastern Arts Exhibition. 1986 first one-person exhibition at the Fabian Carlsson Gallery, London. Work included in the collection of the Fitzwilliam Museum, Cambridge.

SMITH, Matthew   1879-1959
Painter. Born Halifax, Yorkshire. Worked in industry before studying at Manchester School of Art. Moved to London at the age of twenty-six and attended the Slade School. For health reasons he spent a year in Brittany, then settled in Paris where he attended Matisse's school. 1912 returned to England and married ex-Slade student Gwen Salmond. With her, he returned to France and spent several months at Grèz-sur-Loing, an artists' colony, before setting up house in Kensington and taking a studio in Fitzroy Street. 1916 joined the Artists' Rifles and two years later was wounded. Recuperated in his Fitzroy Street studio painting watercolours based on Delacroix's illustrations to *Faust,* and shunning society. 1920 spent a period in Cornwall in a state of nervous tension, staying with his wife (from whom he separated in 1922) and two sons, at St. Austell and moving to St. Columb Major after his family returned to London. There he painted the Cornish landscape in strangely livid harmonies employing reds, greens, purples and blacks. During the 1920s and early 1930s he divided his time between London and Paris and painted full fleshed nudes and still lifes in hot colours. 1933 settled at Aix-en-Provence and thereafter lived a migratory existence between London and Provence, using in his work curved forms and high-keyed but more naturalistic colours. A retrospective exhibition was held at the Tate Gallery, 1953, and a memorial show, at the RA, 1960. A large bequest of his work was donated to the Barbican Art Gallery which mounted a major retrospective, 1983.

Bibl: Philip Hendy, *Matthew Smith,* Penguin Modern Painters, London, 1944; Francis Halliday and John Russell, *Matthew Smith,* George Allen and Unwin, London, 1962.

SMITH, Ralph Maynard   1904-1964
Painter. Studied architecture in London in the mid-'twenties. Later he worked on many projects such as the Bank of England building, Debden and the Shell Centre. He began to paint seriously in 1926.

SMITH, Ray   b.1949
Painter. Born Harrow, Middlesex. Studied at Trinity Hall, Cambridge, 1968-71. 1970 first solo exhibition held at Cambridge. 1978-81 he was Fine Art Fellow at the University of Southampton. Solo exhibitions in London, Southampton, Bristol, Birmingham and Llandudno.

SNOOK, Harry   b.1944
Sculptor. Born Gower, South Wales. From 1961 studied at Hornsey College of Art. From 1968 taught at Bradford, Watford and Exeter Schools of Art. 1980 taught at Birmingham Polytechnic. 1969 first one-person show at the Edinburgh Gallery West in Los Angeles, USA.

SNOW, Peter   b.1927
Painter. Born London. Saw military service, 1946-8. Studied at the Slade School of Art, 1948-53. Awarded Malcolm Scholarship in Decorative Painting and Theatre Design. 1953 his first stage design was *Love's Labours Lost* for Southwark Shakespeare Festival, followed by the design for *The Beggar's Opera,* 1954. 1958 first solo exhibition at Beaux Arts Gallery, London. Since this date he has continued to design many stage sets for the theatre and ballet, while exhibiting in group and solo exhibitions.

SOMERVILLE, Peggy   1918-1975
Painter. Born Margaret Scott Somerville at Ashford, Middlesex. Both her father and her elder brother were artists and her training came from watching them paint. An infant prodigy, she held her first solo exhibition at the age of ten, which was loudly acclaimed and sold out. She relied heavily on instinct, declaring: 'I see the picture in my mind and then just paint it'. This distillation of memory and imagination was to remain her practice all her life. At the age of twenty-one she entered the RA Schools but soon left to work in the Women's Land Army. She continued all her life to exhibit, even after her name lost its youthful novelty. She maintained a light, spontaneous touch and a love of vibrant colour. A major collection of her work can be found in Norwich Castle Museum.

SOMERVILLE, Stuart Scott   b.1908
Painter. Born at·Arksey, Yorkshire, brother of Peggy Somerville.* Studied art under his father, the painter Charles Somerville. At the age of twenty-three he went to Africa with an Oxford and Cambridge Expedition to record the visit in paint. Exhibited at ROI, RA, and in the provinces.

SONNABEND, Yolanda   b.1935
Painter. Born Rhodesia. Studied at Académie des Beaux Arts, Geneva, and Slade School of Fine Art. 1956 began exhibiting with the London Group. 1960 awarded a Boise travelling scholarship. Has worked both as a painter and as a stage designer. 1975 solo exhibitions held at Whitechapel Art Gallery and at Serpentine Gallery, London, 1985-6. Represented in Arts Council and British Council Collections, National Portrait Gallery and elsewhere. 1988 began lecturing at the Slade.

SORRELL, Alan   **1904-1974**
Painter and illustrator. Born Tooting, London, son of a master jeweller and watchmaker. Studied at Southend Municipal School of Art. Worked as a commercial designer in the City, and then went to the RCA. 1928 won the Prix de Rome in painting and spent two years in Rome. 1933-6 taught at RCA and painted murals for Southend Municipal Library. 1935 travelled to Iceland and then held an exhibition at Walker's Galleries in Bond Street, London. 1936 recorded the archaeological excavations of the Roman Forum at Leicester and in 1937 these were published in *The Illustrated London News*. Dr. Mortimer Wheeler asked for similar reconstructions of Maiden Castle, Dorset, which he was excavating and these, too, were published in *The Illustrated London News*. Continued to work on archaeological reconstructions and was a camouflage officer during the Second World War.

SOUKOUP, Willi   **b.1907**
Sculptor. Born Vienna, Austria. Studied at Academy of Fine Art, Vienna, 1928-34. 1934-40 taught sculpture at Dartington Hall. 1935 began exhibiting at RA. In 1949 and 1950 exhibited in 'Sculpture in the Open Air' in Battersea Park. 1952-75 member of Faculty of Sculpture, British School at Rome. 1963 elected ARA, and RA, 1969. Recent solo exhibitions include one at the Yehudi Menuhin School, Cobham, 1979.

SOUTER, Camille   **b.1929**
Painter. Born Northampton, moved to Ireland, 1930. Trained as a nurse in London and did not begin painting again until 1950. 1951 returned to Ireland. 1956 began exhibiting in Dublin restaurants and London galleries. 1958 won an Italian Government scholarship and worked for a year in Italy. Has produced series of paintings on a variety of themes, including the circus, slaughterhouses, docks and canals. Often regarded as Ireland's best woman painter. A retrospective was held at the Douglas Hyde Gallery, Dublin, 1986.

Bibl: *Camille Souter,* The Douglas Hyde Gallery and Trinity College, Dublin, 1980.

SOUTER, John Bulloch   **1890-1972**
Painter. Born Aberdeen, Scotland. Studied at Gray's School of Art, Aberdeen and the Alan Fraser School of Art, Arbroath. 1914 began exhibiting at the RA and continued to do so almost every year until 1952. 1939-45 served as a non-combatant in the Royal Army Medical Corps and shortly after the war married and moved to London. Portraiture became a major source of income and he had a gift for establishing a rapport with his sellers. Said to be 'gentle and unpretentious' in person, he worked with traditional styles and subjects yet was capable of the unexpected view and a refreshing boldness of touch.

SOUTHALL, Joseph Edward   **1861-1944**
Painter. Born Nottingham. 1878 articled to a major firm of Birmingham architects and a year later began attending art classes in the evening. 1881 saw some Arundel Society prints in a shop window, including one of the Wilton Diptych. This 'opened my eyes', as he said, to the beauty of medieval art and decoration; he subsequently read Ruskin and visited Italy. After seeing Carpaccio's *Life of St. Ursula* in Venice, he decided to paint in tempera, seeking advice from Charles Eastlake's *Materials for a History of Oil Painting*. Attended the Birmingham School of Art

where he met Arthur Gaskin who shared his interests. 1901 became a founder-member of the Society of Painters in Tempera. Gave informal lessons on this medium in his home to Maxwell Armfield,* Ethelbert White* and others. 1906 toured Italy with Charles Gere* and his sister. With them, Arthur Gaskin, Bernard Sleigh and others formed the Birmingham Group of Artist-Craftsmen which exhibited for the first time in 1907 at the Fine Art Society, London. 1914 acted as Chairman of the Birmingham branch of the Independent Labour Party. Became a conscientious objector during the First World War. Sought to build up his pictures with 'spaces of bright colour', delicately but firmly outlined. He abandoned the use of shadow and often used an underpaint of raw sienna to create a golden tone throughout.

Bibl: *Joseph Southall 1861-1944. Artist-Craftsman,* Birmingham City Museum and Art Gallery, 1980.

SOUTHGATE, Frank   **1872-1916**
Painter. Born Hunstanton, Norfolk. Specialised in paintings of birds and spent many hours observing them in their natural habitat in Norfolk. Studied in Cambridge, Perth, the Slade School, and under Arthur Cope.* His early pictures of birds appear to have been done in the studio, from stuffed birds or from photographs. But as his work developed he combined skilled handling of pigment with a naturalistic precision. His fascination with birds did not prevent him also from becoming a fine sportsman with the gun. Became a regular contributer to *The Illustrated Sporting and Dramatic News*. He also collaborated on several natural history and travel books. 1905 elected RSBA. 1914 joined the Sportsman's Battalion of the Royal Fusiliers and two years later was killed in action.

SOUTTAR, Margaret   **B.1914**
Painter. Born Scotland. Won a Royal Exhibition to the RCA, 1935. Whilst working for her diploma she executed some stage designs which led to an invitation from Michael St. Denis to work with the London Studio Theatre. Has also produced prints and altar panels and murals for several churches in the south of England. 1959 held her first solo exhibition at the Zwemmer Gallery.

SOUZA, F.N.   **b.1924**
Painter. Born Goa. 1940 joined Sir J.J. School of Art, Bombay and was expelled five years later. In Bombay he founded a progressive artists' group. 1948 represented in the exhibition of Indian Art held at Burlington House, London. 1949 moved to London. Continued to exhibit regularly in London and Paris and in 1958 represented Great Britain in the Guggenheim International Award. His forceful paintings often have a frenzied insistence on sensuality and sin.

SPACKMAN, Sarah   **b.1958**
Painter. Born Reading, Berkshire. Studied at Byam Shaw School of Art, 1977-8, and at Camberwell School of Art, 1978-81. 1982 first solo exhibition at Henley Exhibition Centre. 1986 awarded the Winsor & Newton Young Artist Award. 1986 travelled in Italy. The subjects of her paintings are taken from objects, people and places she daily comes into contact with and are built up through angular nodes of colour.

HAROLD SPEED, 1872-1957.
'View from the Artist's home.
Camden Square'.
Private Collection.

SPALDING, Anne   b.1911
Painter. Born London. Studied at Ruskin School of
Drawing, 1929-33. 1939 moved to London, but was soon
recalled to Oxford to look after her parents' large house
and to provide for lodgers, the author Charles Williams,
the sociologist Barbara Ward and the nephew of the
Victorian poet, Gerry Hopkins. Revisited the Ruskin one
day a week in order to learn lithography. 1949 first solo
exhibition held at the Paul Alexander Gallery, London.
(Plate 77, p.426.)

Bibl: *Anne Spalding,* Sally Hunter Fine Art, London, 1988.

SPARE, Austin Osman   1888-1956
Painter and lithographer. Born Smithfield, London. Had
one of his drawings exhibited at the RA at the age of
fourteen. Studied at Lambeth School of Art and RCA. John
Singer Sargent* is said to have acclaimed him a genius at
the age of seventeen and he became a keen dabbler in the
spiritual world before he was twenty. Employed undulating,
sinewy lines adapted from natural forms and shapes. By
1912 his mood intensified and surface decoration gave way
to a powerful, fantastic rendering of swirling masses,
floating bodies and areas of dark shadow. 1916-17
appointed editor of *Form,* a magazine intended as a
successor to *The Yellow Book.* Wrote some twenty books on
the occult. Lived alone in Brixton towards the end of his
life, drawing Lambeth and Southwark local types and
holding exhibitions in pubs in the working class districts
of London. Painted portraits and figure compositions, also
etched and drew. His esoteric symbolism and grotesque
imagery make him a minor cult figure. During the Second
World War he was injured by a bomb blast and lost the use
of both arms.

SPEAR, Ruskin   1911-1990
Painter. Born Hammersmith, London. Won scholarships
to Hammersmith School of Art, 1926 and the RCA, 1931-5.
Influenced by Sickert* and the Euston Road School, Spear
developed a line in flamboyant and satirical portraits,
some based on photojournalism. 1944 elected ARA, and
RA, 1954. 1948-75 tutor at RCA. 1949 President of the
London Group. 1979 CBE. 1980 retrospective at RA.
Commissioned portraits include Sir Laurence Olivier, Sir

ROBERT SPEIGHT, b.1947.
'Street Scene'.
Charcoal and pastel.
23 ¾ in. x 19 ¾ in.
Boundary Gallery, London.

Ralph Richardson, Harold Wilson, Lord Butler and Francis Bacon.*

Bibl: Mervyn Levy, *Ruskin Spear,* Weidenfeld and Nicolson, London, 1985.

SPEARS, Frank   b.1906
Painter. Born Staffordshire. Studied art, music and drama in Birmingham and later in London. Held his first solo exhibition, 1935. Moved to South Africa and worked as a broadcaster but continued to exhibit in Johannesburg and in London.

SPEED, Harold   1872-1957
Painter. Born London. Studied at the National Art Training School (later the RCA) and the RA Schools where he won a travelling scholarship and spent a year in Italy. First solo exhibition held at Leicester Galleries, London, 1907. Became an excellent academic painter, producing landscapes and many portraits, and was a popular choice for presentation portraits. Executed mural decorations in the RA refreshment room and at Wesley House. Taught for many years at Goldsmiths' College. He was always interested in craftsmanship and in 1916 was elected Master of the Art Workers' Guild.

SPEIGHT, Robert   b.1947
Painter. Born South Wales. His father's work took him and his family to many parts of Africa and the Middle East. Trained and practised as a general practitioner. Hesitated for some years between art and medicine, but after training at St. Martin's and Central School of Art, 1975-8, has opted in favour of art. Though he paints landscapes and still lifes, the human figure, in relation to others, remains an important factor in his work. Solo exhibition at the Boundary Gallery, London, 1986.

SPENCE   b.1932
Painter. Born Morecambe, Lancashire. Studied at Lancaster and Morecambe College of Art. Member of Lancaster Art Group. Worked as an industrial designer. In the 1960s painted scenes influenced by the strong Riviera sunlight, of fishing ports, rocks and sea. Exhibited at the Woodstock Gallery, London, 1964 and 1966.

GILBERT SPENCER, 1892-1979. *'A Cotswold Farm'*, 1930-1. 55 ½ in. x 72 ½ in. The Tate Gallery.

SPENCE, John   b.1918
Painter. Born London. Studied at the South West Essex School of Art. During the war served in the Royal Navy on convoys to Russia and Malta. After the war he travelled extensively in Canada and America. Has exhibited at RA, ROI, RWA and other places.

SPENCER, Doris
Painter. Born London. Studied at RCA. Exhibited at the RA, the RP, the NEAC and in the provinces. Became a war widow with a young son to support and so took to teaching, first in London Grammar Schools, then, when she decided to move to the country, at Leighton Buzzard, Bedfordshire. Held a retrospective at The Grange, Rottingdean, Sussex, 1965. Favoured flowers and children as her subjects.

SPENCER, Gilbert   1892-1979
Painter. Studied at Ruskin School, Maidenhead, 1909-10, Camberwell, 1910-11 and South Kensington, c.1912-14; also part-time at the Slade, 1913-20. 1915-18 served in the Army. 1930 joined the RCA teaching staff, becoming Professor of Painting, 1933-48. 1948-50 Head of Painting, Glasgow School of Art, and 1950-7 Head of Painting at Camberwell. Elected ARWS, 1943, RWS, 1949, ARA, 1950 and RA, 1960. The talented younger brother of Stanley Spencer* whose style he imitated, often with more gentle, less claustrophobic effect.

Bibl: Gilbert Spencer, *Memoirs of a Painter,* Chatto & Windus, London, 1974.

SPENCER, Jean   b.1942
Relief-maker. Studied at Bath Academy of Art, 1960-3. Has taught at Loughborough College of Art and at Bulmershe College, Reading. 1965 first solo exhibition held at Bear Lane Gallery, Oxford; another at the University of Sussex, 1969. Works with cubes in reliefs that involve mathematical procedures but which are determined by intuition. 1967 prize-winner John Moores, Liverpool. Represented in Arts Council Collection and elsewhere.

SPENCER, John   b.1925
Painter. Studied at Wimbledon School of Art and Reading University. Solo exhibition at the Woodstock Gallery, London, 1965 and 1966.

SPENCER, John
Painter. Originally trained as a sculptor, at Camberwell School of Art, 1949-53. Moved abroad, living first at Arles, in France, then in Italy for four or five years. 1964 solo exhibition of icons and paintings held at the Portal Gallery, London.

SPENCER, Roy   b.1918
Painter. Born Gloucestershire. Studied architecture for three years before joining up in 1939. Served in Royal Engineers as an architect and exhibited paintings in Siena and Cairo. 1946 entered the Chelsea School of Art and was taught by Ceri Richards* and Henry Moore.* Became a lecturer at Chelsea School of Art. Recent exhibitions include one with Kit Lewis* at Sally Hunter Fine Art, London, 1988.

SPENCER, Stanley   1891-1959
Painter. Born Cookham, Berkshire, the eighth child of an organist and piano teacher. Studied at Maidenhead Technical Institute and the Slade School, and was to a limited extent influenced by the arrival of the French Post-Impressionists in England. His early paintings concentrated on the mystical experience he had of walking in an earthly paradise: the village of Cookham became the setting for biblical stories. 1915 he enlisted in the Royal Army Medical Corps and was eventually sent to Macedonia with an ambulance brigade. His war-time experiences formed the basis for his decoration of the Burghclere Chapel, 1923-32. His skill at organising multi-figure compositions can also be seen in his paintings of the Resurrection and in those of Lithgow's shipyard at Port Glasgow which he created during the Second World War. As his career developed the intensity of his early visionary years diminished and was replaced by an element of *faux-naïf* eccentricity. His colours became dryer and paler, his compositions more claustrophobic. Often he turned to landscape for commercial reasons, but even so brought to these a Pre-Raphaelite attention to detail and superb compositional control. He married twice, first to Hilda Carline,* then to Patricia Preece,* but continued to write love letters to his first wife, even after her death.

Bibl: *Stanley Spencer*, Royal Academy, London, 1980, with essays by Duncan Robinson and Richard Carline.

SPENCER, Vera
Painter and abstract artist. Has been described as a 'product of the Slade plus a dash of the Central School of Textile Design'. Has exhibited with leading artists in both London and in Brussels and has held solo exhibitions in Paris.

SPENDER, Humphrey   b.1910
Painter, photographer, architect, designer and mural painter. Initially studied architecture before training as a photographer and working freelance, for a number of magazines, including *Picture Post* as a photo-journalist. During the war, after a period in the Tank Corps, he was made War Office Official Photographer. After the war he continued to paint and make documentary photographs. 1956-76 tutor in Textile Department, RCA. His numerous solo exhibitions include several at the Redfern Gallery, London. His fame as a photographer has tended to obscure his originality as a painter. Has also designed carpets, plastics, wallpapers and textiles and has won several Council of Industrial Design Awards. (Plate 78, p.426.)

SPENDER, Matthew   b.1945
Painter. Born London, eldest son of the writer Stephen Spender and his wife Natasha. Read Modern History at New College, Oxford. 1967 married the painter Maro Gorky and a year later moved to Tuscany where they have lived ever since. Painter of complex figure compositions, but has also recently moved into the making of wooden reliefs and terracotta figurines.

SPIERDIJK, Renée   b.1957
Painter. Born Amsterdam, The Netherlands. Moved to Great Britain, 1977. Studied at the Byam Shaw School of Art, 1979-83 and at Goldsmiths' College, London, 1987. 1984 first solo exhibition held at Kingsgate Gallery, London. Has exhibited regularly at the Kingsgate Gallery since this date.

SPRADBERY, Walter   1889-1969
Painter. Born East Dulwich, London. From 1903 he attended Walthamstow School of Arts and Crafts. From 1905 became a student teacher at the same art school. Began to make a name for himself when he produced, c.1911, his first poster designs for the London Underground and the General Bus Company. Served as a Sergeant in the Royal Army Medical Corps in First World War and was awarded the DCM. From 1921-64 taught watercolour painting at Walthamstow Educational Settlement. 1936 initiated the Brangwyn Gift to the Borough of Walthamstow and helped to bring about the formation of the William Morris Gallery there in 1950. Designed posters for the London Underground until 1944, and also for the Southern and Great Western Railways. Exhibited regularly at the RA. 1970 memorial exhibition at the William Morris Gallery.

SPRAWSON, Derek   b.1955
Painter. Born Liverpool, Merseyside. Studied at Liverpool Polytechnic, Newport College of Art and Design and at Reading University. First solo exhibition at the Axiom Gallery, Cheltenham, 1983. Others include one at Clifford Street Fine Art, London, 1988.

SQUIRRELL, Leonard   1893-1979
Printmaker. Born Ipswich. Studied at Ipswich School of Art and at the Slade. An etcher and illustrator whose orderly style sometimes recalls that of J.S. Cotman, for, though he suffered from deafness, a speech impediment and nervousness, his hand rarely faltered, his topographical views of Ipswich having a remarkable firmness and clarity of definition. From 1912 he exhibited annually at the RA, also at the RWS, RI and RE. Elected ARE, 1917, RE, 1919, RI, 1933, ARWS, 1935, RWS, 1941. Published *Landscape Painting in Pastel*, 1938, and *Practice in Watercolour*, 1950. Founder member of the Ipswich Art Club. Renowned for his aquatints and etchings of beauty spots and architecture in East Anglia, the Lake District and Scotland.

Bibl: Josephine Walpole, *Leonard Squirrell, RWS, RE: A biographical scrapbook*, Baron Publishing, Woodbridge, 1982.

STAFFORD-BAKER, Julius   1904-1988
Painter. Born Leigh on Sea, Essex. Studied as a graphic artist under his father, the originator of the *Tiger Tim* comic strip in *The Rainbow*. He was self taught as a painter. Served in the RAF during Second World War in North Africa, Europe and Japan, where he regularly

STAFFORD-BAKER, Philip

painted, and sold his work to the War Artists' Advisory Committee. While in Japan he learnt to paint Japanese theatre portraits. Later he spent eighteen months painting in the Shetlands to recover from his war experiences. First exhibited before the war, and then after the war annually at the RA Summer Exhibitions. He continued to produce *Tiger Tim* and other comic strips for children. 1950 he was awarded a Giles Bequest Prize for printmaking. 1989 a joint exhibition was held with his brother, Philip Stafford-Baker* at Sally Hunter Fine Art, London. Included in the collections of the Imperial War Museum, the British Museum, the V & A, the City Art Gallery, Glasgow, Manchester City Art Gallery, the Cabinet Office, Whitehall, and the National Museum of Modern Art, Poland.

STAFFORD-BAKER, Philip   1908-1955
Painter. Born Leigh on Sea, Essex. Studied at the Southend-on-Sea Art School. After he had completed his studies he suffered a serious illness which left him an invalid for the rest of his life, and painting became his only activity. He never attempted to exhibit in his lifetime but his work was shown in a joint exhibition with that of his brother, Julius Stafford-Baker,* at Sally Hunter Fine Art, London, 1988.

STAHL, Andrew   b.1954
Painter. Born London. Studied at Slade School of Art, London, 1973-9. Awarded Abbey Major Rome Scholarship, 1979-81. 1981 first solo exhibition at the Air Gallery, London. Since 1982 has frequently shown in group exhibitions, including ones organised by the British Council in Europe, the Far East and Australia. Has an obsession with fountains and on a visit to Thailand in 1986 was impressed by the golden buddhas he saw there; both were combined in his solo exhibition at the Paton Gallery, 1988. Represented in the Arts Council, British Council and the Contemporary Arts Society collections.

STANYER, Peter   b.1952
Painter. Born Stoke-on-Trent, Staffordshire. Studied at North Staffordshire Polytechnic, 1969-74. 1977-9 worked as a dustman. 1979-82 took a post-graduate MA in painting at RCA. 1981 first solo exhibition held in the Queen's Elm Pub, Chelsea; another held at Stoke-on-Trent Museum and Art Gallery, 1982. A vigorous and imaginative and sometimes allegorical figure painter.

STAPLETON, Judy
Painter. Born Manchester. Studied in London. First solo exhibition held at Avgarde Gallery, Manchester, 1960. Others include one at the University of Sussex, 1969.

STARR, Sydney   1857-1925
Painter. Born Hull, Yorkshire. Studied at Slade School. Met Whistler in 1882 and joined his circle of admirers. Elected to membership of the Society of British Artists, 1886. Began to explore pastel as a medium and low-life subjects. 1892 left London for New York to escape scandal. Little is known of his career thereafter.

STARSZAKOWNA, Norma   b.1945
Batik artist. Studied printed textiles and printmaking at Duncan of Jordanstone College of Art, Dundee, 1962-6. Held first solo exhibition at the Compass Gallery, Glasgow, 1971. Has continued to exhibit regularly ever since. Represented in Scottish Arts Council collection and elsewhere.

STARTUP, Peter   1921-1976
Sculptor. Born London. A heart condition precluded him from military service. Studied at Hammersmith School of Art, 1935-9, the Central School of Art, 1943-4, the Ruskin School of Drawing, Oxford, 1944-5, and the Slade School of Art, 1945-8. 1965-76 taught at Wimbledon School of Art. 1964 awarded Second Prize in the Littlewoods Sculpture Competition. Worked mainly in wood. 1977 retrospective exhibition at the Serpentine Gallery. He used all kinds of found bits of furniture, Formica off-cuts, paper flongs, as well as wood and plaster, to explore the strange within the familiar. Represented in the Tate Gallery and Arts Council collections.

STEELE, Jeffrey   b.1931
Painter and systems artist of black and white paintings and white reliefs. Born Cardiff, Wales. 1959 awarded French Government Scholarship and lived and worked in Paris. 1969 co-founded the Systems group of artists who work with programmed abstract structures. 1961 first solo exhibition at the ICA. 1973 solo exhibition at Lucy Milton Gallery.

STEELE-MORGAN, Tony   b.1931
Painter. Born Montreal, Canada, of Welsh parents. 1935 his family returned to Wales. 1949-67 worked as a librarian. 1867-71 studied at Newport College of Art and Design. Has lectured at Ware College, Hertfordshire, but since 1974 has been a full-time painter. 1978 solo exhibition at Oriel, Cardiff.

STEER, Philip Wilson   1860-1942
Painter. Born Birkenhead, Cheshire. Studied at Gloucester School of Art, 1878-81, at Julian's in Paris, 1882-3, and at the Ecole des Beaux-Arts, 1883-7. A founder-member of the NEAC, 1886. First solo exhibition held at the Goupil Galley, London, 1894. His impressionist-influenced land and seascapes did not find favour with the conservative factions. For a period his art was amongst the most avant-garde in its use of chromatic divisionism, but after the reverberations caused by the Oscar Wilde trial, he returned to English traditions, painting scenes associated with Turner in a style indebted, not to foreign influence but to Constable. He also excelled as a watercolourist and was for many years painting tutor at the Slade. 1931 awarded OM. Represented in many public collections, including the Tate Gallery.

Bibl: Bruce Laughton, *Philip Wilson Steer,* Oxford University Press, Oxford, 1971.

STEGGLES, Harold
Painter of landscapes. Showed at London galleries in the 1930s. Solo exhibition, with W.J. Steggles,* at Reid and Lefevre Gallery, 1938.

STEGGLES, Walter J.   b.1902
Painter of landscapes. Showed at London galleries in the 1930s. Solo exhibition, with Harold Steggles,* at Reid and Lefevre Gallery, 1938.

STEPHENSON, Cecil   1889-1965
Painter. Born Bishop Auckland, Co. Durham. Studied at Darlington Technical College, 1906-8, Leeds School of Art, 1908-14, RCA, 1914-18, and Slade, 1918. 1915-18 did war

IAN STEPHENSON.
'Giustichrome', 1962.
40in. x 36in. Private Collection.

work making tools. 1919 took 6 Mall Studios, off Parkhill Road, Hampstead, from Sickert,* where he was later joined by Herbert Read, Barbara Hepworth* and Henry Moore.* 1922-55 Head of Art Teaching in the Architectural Department, Northern Polytechnic, Holloway Road. 1932-3 began making his first abstract works, exhibiting during the next decade in many abstract and constructive shows in England, France and the USA. 1942 returned to figurative work, making paintings of the Blitz. 1950 returned to abstraction. 1951 made 10ft. x 30ft. fluorescent paint mural for the Festival of Britain; also began working with plyglass for murals. 1958 suffered three strokes which left him unable to move or talk.

Bibl: *Cecil Stephenson 1889-1965,* Fischer Fine Art, London, 1976.

STEPHENSON, Chaim   b.1926
Sculptor. Born Liverpool, the fifth child of immigrant Russian parents. Emigrated to Palestine aged twenty-one, where he formed a kibbutz and fought with the Communists, then worked as a shepherd when he began to carve in wood and stone. In 1959 the kibbutz gave him a year's leave to study sculpture in England. 1969 solo exhibition in Tel Aviv. Since 1971 has lived and worked in England. 1972 solo exhibition at New Grafton Gallery, London.

STEPHENSON, George V.   b.1926
Sculptor. Son of the sculptor George Stephenson. Has shown in mixed exhibitions, with the RBA, AIA, London Group, NEAC and Group 13. First solo exhibition at St. Martin's Gallery, 1963. Member of the AIA. Lecturer in the 1960s at Rochdale College of Art.

STEPHENSON, Ian   b.1934
Painter. Born near Meadowfield, Co. Durham. Studied at King's College, Newcastle, 1951-6, where he later assisted with the Basic Design Course taught by Victore Pasmore* and Richard Hamilton.* 1958-9 travelled in Italy on a Boise Scholarship. Has since then taught in both Newcastle and London, at Chelsea School of Art, and has exhibited his abstract paintings regularly, holding solo exhibitions at the New Art Centre, London. Elected ARA, 1975. Retrospective exhibitions at the Laing Art Gallery, Newcastle, 1970, the Hayward Gallery, London, 1977, and Birmingham City Art Gallery, 1978. Represented in the Hayward Annual, 1980.

STERN, Bernard

STERN, Bernard b.1920
Painter. Born Brussels, Belgium, of a Russian father and an English mother. Studied at the Académie Royale des Beaux-Arts in Brussels and at the Academy in Antwerp. Came to England in 1940 and studied at St. Martin's School of Art. 1970 first large solo exhibition at the Archer Gallery, London; another at the John Whibley Gallery, 1973. Paints humans in a mix of dreamlike and real situations.

Bibl: J.P. Hodin, *Bernard Stern*, Drian Galleries, London, 1972.

STERN, Catharini b.1925
Sculptor. Born Hampshire. Studied at Chelmsford Art School and the RA Schools. Won the Feodora Gleichen Award for Sculpture, 1952, then taught part-time at Bournemouth College of Art while working, 1955-60, in her studio at Maldon, Essex. 1962 first solo exhibition at the Whibley Gallery; solo shows there every two years until the gallery closed in 1975. Carved wooden madonnas for Totnes Church, Devon, and for Willesden Parish Church. 1986 retrospective exhibition at The Minories, Colchester.

STERN, Deborah b.1938
Painter and sculptor. Born Germany. 1962 studied painting under Adrian Heath.* Studied sculpture at the Camden Arts Centre, 1973. Included in mixed exhibitions from 1974 onwards, chiefly at the RA and RSA but also at Nathan Silberberg and Alex Rosenberg Galleries in New York. First solo exhibition at the Demarco Gallery, Edinburgh, 1975; most recent at Christie's Contemporary Art, 1987. Work included in private and corporate collections in Europe, USA and Japan.

STERN, Deborah b.1948
Painter, sculptor and printmaker. Born in New York, USA. Studied at the Slade School, 1966-71. Makes abstract sculptures from clay and plaster which are cast into bronze, and which imitate the forms and rhythms of nature. Member of Printmakers Council. 1972 first solo exhibition of drawings and etchings at Woodstock Gallery, London, 1972.

STEVENS, Chris b.1956
Painter. Born Basingstoke, Hampshire. Studied at the University of Reading, 1974-8. Worked as a scenic artist for ATV Birmingham, 1978-9, and as a community artist, 1979-81. 1981-3 Director of Cheltenham Arts Centre, where he designed sets for *Cossi fan Tutte* and *A Journey through Unemployment* for the Cheltenham Fringe Festival. 1983-4 Arts Council residency at Sunderland Football Club. 1984-5 Artist in Residence at Birmingham International Airport. 1986 commissioned by Mercury Films, Los Angeles, USA, to work on a series of paintings. Artist in Residence at North Street Films, Los Angeles, on the set of *Scenes from the Class Struggle in Beverly Hills*. Awards include George Rowney sponsorship for a series of paintings based on Arsenal Football Club, 1986. 1975 first solo exhibition at the Willis Gallery, Basingstoke. Regularly exhibits in Great Britain and the USA. 1989 solo exhibition at Sue Williams Gallery, and at the Black Bull Gallery, London. Included in the collections of Calouste Gulbenkian Foundation, London, National Gallery of Wales and University of Durham.

STEVENS, Christopher b.1961
Painter. Born Staines, Middlesex. Studied at Somerset College of Arts, 1976-8, Brighton Polytechnic, 1978-81 and postgraduate painting at the Central School of Art, 1981-2. From 1981 included in mixed exhibitions. 1986 first solo exhibition at the Piccadilly Gallery. 1985 prizewinner in John Moores Liverpool Exhibition 14.

STEVENS, Elsie E.
Painter. Born Brighton, Sussex. Began painting in 1962. Studied art privately in London with Professor Marian Bohusz. Solo exhibitions at the Woodstock Gallery, Alwin Gallery, the Polish Centre, London and in Brighton, Eastbourne, Dublin and Durham, most recent at the Gardner Centre for the Arts, Brighton, 1973.

STEVENS, Norman b.1937
Painter and printmaker. Born Yorkshire. Studied at Bradford College of Art, 1952-7 and the RCA, 1957-60. From 1966 included in mixed exhibitions. 1974-5 Gregory Fellow at the University of Leeds. 1979 and 1982 prizewinner at British International Print Biennale at Bradford. 1983 elected ARA. In his work he has long been attracted to formal gardens, with their paths, alleys, sculptured hedges and sense of enclosure. Represented in many public collections, including the V & A, Leeds Art Gallery and the Tate Gallery.

STEVENS, Philip b.1953
Painter. Studied at Wimbledon School of Art, 1973-6 and at RCA, 1977-80. 1987 first solo exhibition at the Paton Gallery, London. Since 1981 he has regularly exhibited at the Paton Gallery in group exhibitions.

STEVENSON, Robert Macaulay 1854-1952
Painter. Born Glasgow, Scotland. Studied at Glasgow School of Art. Began exhibiting at the RA, 1884, but showed mainly in Scotland. Lived for a period in France.

STEVENSON, Stansmore Dean 1866-1944
Painter. Born Glasgow, Scotland. Studied at Glasgow School of Art and was awarded a travelling scholarship, then studied in Paris under August Courtois. 1894 first exhibited at the Glasgow Institute, and then regularly until 1910, and 1928-32; she also exhibited in London, Liverpool and Edinburgh. Married the Glasgow artist Robert Macaulay Stevenson,* they moved to France in 1910 and did not return until 1926. She used muted tones as a firm foundation of drawing.

Bibl: *Stansmore Dean Stevenson 1866-1944*, Lillie Art Gallery, Milngavie, 1984.

STEWART, Dorothy b.1905
Painter. Born Sydney, Australia. Studied botany at Melbourne University. 1931 married and came to England. 1950 began studying painting at the Hampstead Artists' Council Studio. 1962 first solo exhibition held at Hampstead Art Cellar. Became a member of the Free Painters' Group.

STEWART, Robert
Painter. Studied textile design at Glasgow School of Art. 1947 won a travelling scholarship. 1949 appointed Head of Printed Textiles, Glasgow School of Art. 1951-6 Designer

to Edinburgh Tapestry Company. 1957-64 formed his own company, producing ceramic kitchenware. 1968 began exhibiting his paintings. Solo exhibitions include one at the Compass Gallery, Glasgow, 1978. 1978 appointed Head of Design School, Glasgow School of Art.

STEWART, W.A.   1882-1953
Painter. Born Ilkley, Yorkshire. Studied at RCA under Augustus John,* afterwards returning to Yorkshire to find employment in the design department of a mill. Continued to paint in his leisure time and became a member of the Bradford Arts Club. Emigrated to the Middle East in his late twenties and became an Inspector of Arts and Crafts in the Egyptian Ministry of Education. Helped set up the Cairo School of Arts and Crafts and became its first Principal. After the First World War he was seconded to Palestine to advise, with C.R. Ashbee, on crafts and small industries damaged by war. Other activities over the next years included the reorganisation of the Bezalel School of Art in Jerusalem. After the Second World War he was deeply saddened by the Arab-Jewish rift. He returned in 1948 to High Wycombe, Buckinghamshire, where he concentrated on his painting.

STEYN, Carole   b.1938
Relief-maker. Born Manchester. Studied at Académie Julian, Paris, and St. Martin's School of Art. 1971 first solo exhibition held Drian Galleries, London. Works in nylon bonded clay and with polyester resin.

STOCKHAM, Alf   b.1933
Painter. Born London. Served with the Royal Navy, 1950-6. Studied at Camberwell School of Art, 1960-3 and at RCA, 1963-6. 1966-7 he was awarded a Rome Scholarship. 1967-8 won a Granada Arts Fellowship at University of York. 1974 first solo exhibition at the Festival Gallery, Bath, and a second solo exhibition, 1975. He regularly exhibits at the Neville Gallery, Bath.

STOKES, Adrian   1854-1935
Painter. Born Southport, Lancashire. Studied at RA Schools, 1872-5, and with Dagnan-Bouveret in Paris, 1885-6. From 1876 he made regular sketching trips to France, especially to Barbizon. He was a member of the NEAC. Also exhibited at the RA from 1876. Elected ARA, 1910, RA, 1919, ARWS, 1920 and RWS, 1926. Vice President of the RWS, 1932-5. Became highly renowned as a landscape artist, working in a naturalistic style untroubled by modern developments. Published *Landscape Painting*, 1925

STOKES, Adrian   1902-1972
Painter and writer. Born London. Read Modern Greek at Magdalen College, 1920-3, and afterwards travelled in Italy, studying the Quattro Cento and meeting the poet Ezra Pound whose *Cantos* influenced him. Began publishing on art and also read Freud intensively after suffering periods of depression. Met Melanie Klein and in 1930 entered into seven years of analysis with her. Began writing intensively on art, both that of the Italian Renaissance, and the work of his contemporaries. His books include *The Stones of Rimini*, 1934, *Colour and Form*, 1937, *Cézanne*, 1946, and *Paintings and the Inner World*, 1963. Began painting in 1936, and in 1938 married Margaret Mellis.* Briefly attended the Euston Road School in London in the late 1930s before moving to Carbis Bay, Cornwall, where he gave hospitality to Barbara

Hepworth* and Ben Nicholson* and their triplets, after the outbreak of war. In 1947, after the break-up of his marriage, he married his first wife's sister, Ann Mellis. In the 1950s, his aesthetic of carving and modelling, which he applied both to painting and sculpture, became incorporated into a psychoanalytic dualism derived from Melanie Klein. The heavy use of psychoanalytical theory in his later writings lost him the support of many in the art world and limited his audience. Continued to write profusely and towards the end of his life he became a prolific poet. Painted up until two days before his death. His paintings, hazy and subdued, glow with gentle light and colour, the forms often deliquescent.

Bibl: *Adrian Stokes 1902-72 — A Retrospective,* Serpentine Gallery, London, 1982.

STOKES, Marianne   1855-1927
Painter. Born Austria, née Preindlsberger. Studied art in Munich for five years and then in Paris. Painted in Brittany where she met her future husband, Adrian Stokes,* whom she married in 1884. Came to England and exhibited at leading London galleries from 1883. In the 1890s she lived and worked in St. Ives. 1923 elected ARWS.

STONE, Edward   b.1940
Painter. Born Berkshire. Studied at Hammersmith College of Art, London. 1988 first solo exhibition at the Francis Kyle Gallery, London.

STONE, Geoffrey   b.1931
Painter. Born King's Langley, Hertfordshire. Became interested in painting when, aged sixteen, he suffered a prolonged illness. Studied zoology, then recommenced painting and has since had several solo exhibitions. Specialises in street scenes of the period 1890-1920 when horse-drawn vehicles were still the common form of transport; also paints canal scenes of the inland waterways.

STONE, Jacqueline
Painter. Born Hull, Yorkshire. Qualified as a physical educationalist before studying art at Camberwell Art School, 1961. Paints figures in athletic actions or performances. 1966 first solo exhibition at the Woodstock Gallery.

STONE, Marcus   1840-1921
Painter. Born the son of the painter, Frank Stone, ARA. Exhibited at the RA from 1858. Elected ARA, 1877, and RA, 1887; also won medals at international exhibitions in Paris, Berlin, Vienna, Philadelphia, Chicago and Melbourne. Illustrated several books including works by Dickens and Trollope. Adapted well to the changing artistic climate, as story-telling became less morally elevating and more anecdotal. Occasionally used Regency dress in courtship scenes and earned a fortune through the sale of prints based on his paintings. Taught at the RA Schools.

STONES, Alan   b.1947
Painter. Born Manchester. Studied at St. Martin's School of Art, 1967-71. Has worked as a self-employed artist since that date. 1982 Artist in School with Bedfordshire Education Authority and 1983 Artist in Industry Fellow at a Doncaster bakery. Recently recorded the work of the farm labourers in Cumbria.

PAUL STOREY, b.1957. *'Isotta, No.3 (with Thrones)'*. Acrylic on canvas. 96in. x 84in. Private Collection.

STOREY, Paul   b.1957

Painter. Born London. Studied at Birmingham Polytechnic, 1979-82 and at RCA, 1984-7. 1985 first exhibited at Oriel Gallery, Cardiff. 1986 represented in a group exhibition, 'Fresh Art' at the Barbican, London. Recent solo exhibitions include one at Fischer Fine Art, London, 1989. His paintings are filled with a conscious confusion of strangely distorted figures and architectural details.

STOTT, Edward   1859-1918

Painter. Born Rochdale, Lancashire. Studied art in Manchester, also in Paris under Carolus Duran and at the Ecole des Beaux-Arts. Influenced by Bastien Lepage, he adopted the square-brush method and painted rural subjects *en plein air*. Founder member of the NEAC, 1886. Elected ARA, 1906.

STRACHEY, Rosemary

Painter. Studied at Slade School of Art and at Andre L'Hôte's summer school near Montélimar, France. In the mid-1950s moved to the South of Spain and has consistently painted the landscape of Andalusia. 1984 exhibited at Mackinnon and Strachey, London.

STRANG, Ian   1886-1952

Painter. Born London, elder son of William Strang.* Studied at Slade School, 1902-6, and at the Académie Julian, Paris, 1906-8. Also travelled and studied in France, Belgium, Italy, Sicily and Spain. 1914 enlisted in the Middlesex Regiment. Held solo exhibitions at the Goupil, Chenil and Lefevre, and Leicester Galleries in London. Exhibited at the RA from 1923 and with the NEAC from 1919. Elected ARE, 1926, and RE, 1930. 1937 published *The Students' Book of Etching*. Represented in British Museum, Tate Gallery, Imperial War Museum, V & A and elsewhere.

STRANG, William   1859-1921

Painter, etcher and engraver. Born Dumbarton, Scotland. Moved to London in 1875 and studied at the Slade School under Legros. His outgoing character gave hospitality to various artistic and literary figures and encouraged in his

TREVOR STUBLEY, b.1932. *'Cliff'*, c.1985. Watercolour. 42in. x 42in. Collection of Kirklees Leisure Service.

art a forthright statement of appearances and a love of bold colour oppositions. Elected RE, 1881. He produced a large number of prints and in 1889 was awarded a silver medal for etching at the Paris International Exhibition. As a painter he produced some startling figure subjects, as well as memorable portraits of John Masefield, Vita Sackville-West and others. Exhibited at the RA from 1883. Elected ARA, 1906, and RA, 1921. President of the IS from 1918. Represented in many public collections, including the Tate Gallery.

STREET, Evelyn
Painter. Taught at South Devon College of Art. Produced abstract paintings with references to geological strata, rocks and hillsides. Solo exhibition held at Drian Galleries, London, 1965.

STREET, Peter   b.1951
Painter. Self-taught. His work caught the attention of R.G. Pilkington of the Piccadilly Gallery. He uses a geometry of black lines to shadow and shape his view of nature, his style semi-cubist and semi-impressionist. Solo show held at Exhibition Gallery, S.E.15, 1968.

STRIDE, Jeffrey   b.1946
Painter. Born Southampton, Hampshire. Studied at Camberwell School of Arts and Crafts. Since 1980 has exhibited regularly in Paris, London and New York.

STRIDE, Sally
Painter. Brought up in North Wales. Studied painting at the Froebel Institute, London. Married the artist Jeffrey Stride* and moved to France. Has exhibited in France, Switzerland, America and London.

STRINDBERG, Madeleine
Painter. Studied at the Byam Shaw School of Art and at the RCA. She has exhibited at the ICA, the Riverside Open and the Warwick Arts Trust. She was Artist in Residence at the National Gallery, October 1988 to March 1989.

STRINGER, Simon   b.1960
Sculptor. Born Bovey Tracey, South Devon. Studied at RA Schools. Has exhibited at the RA and elsewhere. Was brought up in Africa which he feels gives him a different perspective on middle-class England. His humane themes often focus on human cruelty. Solo exhibition at the Pentonville Gallery, 1987.

STUBBING, Tony   b.1921
Painter. Born London. 1939-46 served in the Royal Artillery (Kent Yeomanry), 1946-7 in 654 Squadron, RAF. 1944 held first solo exhibition at the British Institute, Famagusta, Cyprus. Has exhibited regularly since in New York, Italy, London, Spain and Munich.

STUBLEY, Trevor   b.1932
Painter. Born Leeds, Yorkshire. Studied at Leeds College

ROWLAND SUDDABY, 1912-1972. *'Fallen elm and pond'*. Pen, ink and watercolour. 18in. x 22in.
Austin/Desmond Fine Art.

of Art, 1947-9, and Edinburgh College of Art, 1949-53. A
vigorous landscapist who also specialises in portraits. Has
exhibited in London, Edinburgh, Sheffield, Leeds, Bologna,
Bratislava, Wichita Falls, USA, and elsewhere.

STUDHAM, Lynn   b.1936
Collagist. Born Stanley, Co. Durham. Studied at Sunder-
land College of Art and the Royal Academy of Fine Art,
Copenhagen, Denmark, 1958-9. 1960 emigrated to Canada.
1968 solo exhibition at the Compendium Gallery,
Birmingham.

SUDDABY, Rowland   1912-1972
Painter. Born Kimberworth, Yorkshire. Studied at
Sheffield College of Art and also worked, as a young man,
in the steel industry. 1931 moved to London and worked
ornamenting the titles of black and white films for a firm
in Wardour Street. 1935 first solo exhibition at the
Wertheim Gallery, followed by more solo shows at the
Redfern Gallery in the '40s and '50s. 1940 worked for the
Pilgrim Trust on the Recording Britain project. After the
war, began to exhibit at the RA. Moved to Suffolk, 1939.
1946 became a founder member of the Colchester Arts
Society. Remained active as a landscape painter in Suffolk
until his death, while holding the appropriate post of
Curator of Gainsborough's Sudbury home. The freshness
and joyfulness of his work makes it akin to that of Dufy or
Segonzac.

SUFF, David   b.1955
Painter. Born Essex, Devon. Studied at the University of
Leeds, 1973-7 and at RCA, 1978-81. Awards include the
Anstruther Award for Drawing, 1980 and the Pimms
Award for Drawing or Watercolour, 1987. 1978 first solo
exhibition at the Parkinson Gallery, London. Since 1983
he has regularly exhibited at the Piccadilly Gallery,
London, and held a solo show there, 1989. His fascination
with gardens and his detailed, near miniaturist technique
give his art an affinity with that of the Ruralists.

SUJO, Glenn   ·b.1952
Painter. Born Buenos Aires, Argentina. Studied at the
Slade, 1972-5, before taking a post-graduate degree in
History of Art at the Courtauld Institute. 1981 gave up
teaching in order to paint full-time; 1982 and 1983 solo
exhibitions at Bluecoat Gallery, Liverpool, and Anne
Berthoud. Also exhibits in Caracas, Venezuela, which he
regularly visits. His figurative paintings enact memories
of his childhood circumstances, combined with fantasies,
desires and fears. Born into a Jewish family in a
predominantly Catholic society, his ethics and cultural
background were at odds with his surroundings and this
sense of displacement frequently surfaces in his work.

SUKIENNICKA, Halina   b.1906
Painter. Born Poland. Graduated from Wilno University.
Obtained a doctorate in Political Science and Economics at

Paris University. Published *International Organisation of Labour* and *Fédéralisme en Europe Orientale*. Employed as a barrister in Poland before the war; after the war she joined her husband in London and has lived there ever since. Studied painting at the Polish School of Painting and has exhibited in London, Munich, Hamburg and Los Angeles.

SULLIVAN, John   b.1940
Painter. Born London. Studied at St. Martin's School of Art, 1958-62 and Hornsey College of Art, 1962-3. 1961 first solo exhibition held at Architectural Association, London. In the 1960s, like many of his generation, was influenced by American art and 1964-75 made several visits to America. Later moved away from abstract art back to a representation indebted to a European expressionist tradition.

SULLIVAN, P.J.   b.1940
Painter. Born London of Irish parents. Studied at Carlisle College of Art, 1956-60, and RA Schools. 1964 first solo exhibition held in Lewes, Sussex. 1969 solo exhibition at Woodstock Gallery, London. Has taught in London, Sheffield and Winchester.

SULLY, Frank   b.1898
Painter. Born London. Studied at Hammersmith School of Art and the Académie Julian, Paris. 1920 moved to Cornwall, and 1923 returned to London. Exhibited widely in the provinces.

SUMMERS, Leslie   b.1919
Sculptor. Studied at Chelsea School of Art. 1965 exhibited at the RA for the first time. Has since exhibited at home and abroad. Produces abstract work in acrylic (Perspex and Oroglas) as well as figurative bronzes. Represented in the National Museum of Wales and elsewhere.

SUMMERSGILL, Derek H.   b.1940
Painter. Born York. Studied at York School of Art until 1962. 1962-9 occupied with part-time lecturing and some painting commissions, e.g. portraits. Included in mixed exhibitions during this period. Taught art in Bootle and Skelmersdale, 1970-6. First solo exhibition at Bootle Art Gallery, 1976, another at Atkinson Art Gallery, Southport, 1978.

SUMRAY, Maurice   b.1920
Painter. Born London. 1935-40 studied and practised engraving, and painted in sporadic bursts. 1940-6 saw war service with the Ministry of Economic Warfare. 1942-6 was an active member of the 'Hogarth Group' in Fitzroy Street. 1946-9 he established a studio called Sunray Textiles, specialising in hand-painted cottons. 1949-53 won scholarship to Goldsmiths' College. 1953 ceased painting and destroyed all the work in his possession. 1953-68 established an engraving studio in Fitzroy Street. 1968 moved to St. Ives and returned to painting. 1980 elected member of Penwith Society of Arts. 1981 elected member of Newlyn Society of Artists.

SUNLIGHT, Ben   b.1935
Painter. Born Brighton, Sussex. Studied at Magdalene College, Cambridge. Served with the Royal Engineers in Egypt, 1953-5. 1962 gained a Diploma in Mural Painting from Central School of Arts. Fellow and Vice Chairman of Free Painters and Sculptors. 1958 first solo exhibition held at Heffer Gallery, Cambridge; others include one entitled 'Human Situations' at the Drian Galleries, London, 1967.

SUTCLIFFE, Geoffrey   b.1929
Painter. Studied at Leicester College of Art. After service in the army in Germany he taught in secondary and art schools in Birmingham, and elsewhere. Exhibited widely in London and the provinces and held his first solo exhibition at Brook House, Chandlers Ford, Hampshire, 1960.

SUTCLIFFE, Stuart   1940-1962
Painter. Born Edinburgh, Scotland. Studied at Liverpool College of Art. Left in 1960 to play bass guitar with the Beatles in a Hamburg night club. April 1961-March 1962 he was a pupil under Eduardo Paolozzi* at Hamburg State High School (Art School) while playing with the Beatles every night. Most of his work was concentrated into these months. He died of a brain tumour. Represented in the Walker Art Gallery, Liverpool.

SUTHERLAND, Carol Ann   b.1952
Painter. Born Greenock, Scotland. Studied at Glasgow School of Art, 1969-73. Travelled in Italy, 1972-3. 1974-80 taught as peripatetic art adviser in the Highlands. 1983 first solo exhibition held at Mercury Gallery, London, followed by others, in 1985, 1987 and 1989. Works in mixed media on paper, employing a child-like vision.

SUTHERLAND, David McBeth   1883-1973
Painter. Born Wick, Scotland. Studied at the Royal Institution School of Art in Edinburgh and subsequently at the Royal Scottish Academy Life Class. 1911 awarded the Carnegie travelling scholarship and went to Paris, then Spain. Began exhibiting regularly at the RSA. Served in the 16th Battalion during the First World War and was awarded the Military Cross; was wounded and invalided home. A founder member of the Royal Scots Club. 1919 resumed teaching at Edinburgh College of Art. 1922 elected associate of RSA and became member of the Society of Scottish Artists. 1930 executed murals in the Royal Navy Officers' mess in Plymouth (destroyed during the Second World War). 1933 appointed Head of Gray's School of Art, Aberdeen. 1936 elected RSA. 1940 Official War Artist. 1948 retired as Head of Gray's School of Art.

SUTHERLAND, Graham   1903-1980
Painter. Born London. Originally intended for a career in engineering, in 1920 he was apprenticed at the Midland Railway Works at Derby. Studied at Goldsmiths' School of Art, 1921-6, where he specialised in etching in a style indebted to Samuel Palmer. 1925 elected an associate-member of the RE. 1926 converted to Roman Catholicism. The sudden collapse of the print market after the Wall Street Crash in 1929 obliged him to earn money by designing for posters, china, glass and fabric. He also took up painting. 1934 he made his first visit to Pembrokeshire which he revisited every summer until the outbreak of war. There his earlier interest in Samuel Palmer combined with his sense of 'encompassing disquiet' to produce visionary drawings and paintings that had an important influence on the neo-romantic artists of the 1940s. 1940-5 worked as an official war artist, drawing scenes of devastation, blast furnaces, tin mining and quarrying. After the war he spent part of each year in the South of France which affected his appreciation of colour. 1952 he was commissioned to design a vast tapestry for the new Coventry Cathedral. He also began to paint portraits; these further enhanced his reputation which, in Britain, was at its height in the 1950s. Although honours and awards continued to be bestowed on him, he received more

LINDA SUTTON, b.1947.
'Rhinoceros with Sun Face'.
Mixed media. 17in. x 24in.
Austin/Desmond Fine Art.

critical acclaim in Italy than in Britain during his last
twenty years.

Bibl: John Hayes, *Graham Sutherland,* Phaidon Press, Oxford, 1983.

SUTTON, Clive
Constructionist. Born Sussex. Studied at Croydon, West
Surrey, Newport College of Art and Glasgow School of Art.
Has had solo exhibitions in Glasgow and Edinburgh,
including one at the Third Eye Centre, Glasgow, 1978, at
which he exhibited constructions made out of paper, then
rods, glue and varnish. Has a studio at the Glasgow Print
Studio in Ingram Street.

SUTTON, John   b.1935
Painter. Born near Great Yarmouth, Norfolk. Studied at
art schools in Norwich and Brighton. Has exhibited in
London and the provinces. He works on his landscapes in a
large studio in an old rectory in North Norfolk. 1978 solo
exhibition held at Weston Gallery, Norwich. Untroubled
traditionalist.

SUTTON, Linda   b.1947
Painter. Studied at Southend College of Technology,
Winchester School of Art and RCA. 1971 first solo
exhibition held Galerij de Zwarte Panter, Antwerp,
Belgium. Has also exhibited in London, Milan and the RA.
The personal mythology she has created in her paintings
has in part been inspired by reading. Her paintings are
never pure illustration, but juggle ideas and conjure up
complex, and at times near chaotic, imagery.

SUTTON, Philip   b.1928
Painter. Born Poole, Dorset. Studied at Slade School of
Art. 1956 elected member of the London Group. Travelled
to Fiji to paint for two years. Since 1953 has held regular
solo exhibitions at Roland, Browse and Delbanco, and now
Browse and Derby. Represented in many provincial public
art galleries. His work is characterised by strong, bright
colour and an expansive drawing style. Represented in the
Tate Gallery.

SUTTON, Trevor   b.1948
Painter. Born Romford, Essex. Studied at Hornsey College
of Art, 1967-71, and Birmingham Polytechnic, 1971-2.
1981 solo exhibition at the South East Gallery, London. A
severely geometric abstract artist.

SWALE, Suzan   b.1946
Painter. Born Nottingham. Studied at Bristol Polytechnic,
1966-9 and at the RCA, 1969-72. 1969 first solo exhibition
at the Bristol Arts Centre; others include one at the
Atlantis Gallery, London 1983, and another at the Pentonville Gallery, London, 1985.

SWAN, Douglas   b.1935
Painter. Born New Britain, Connecticut, USA. In 1936 his
family moved to Scotland. Studied at Dundee College of
Art and with the artist William Scott* in London and
Bath; also studied at Trinity College of Music, Dublin.
1986 was awarded the Kunststipendium des Stadt, Bonn
and now divides his time between Scotland and Bonn. Solo

exhibitions began in 1957 at St. Hilda's College, Oxford. Recent ones include one at the Galerie Hennemann, Bonn, 1985-6. His paintings blend influences from Cy Twombly, Jasper Jones and William Scott.

SWAN, Peter   b.1935
Painter. Studied at Somerset College of Art and at St. Martin's School of Art. First solo exhibition at the Arnolfini Gallery, Bristol. For a period his abstract paintings evolved out of his preoccupation with the seaons of the year.

SWANWICK, Betty   1915-1989
Painter, writer and illustrator. Born Scilly Isles. Studied at Goldsmiths' College of Art where she learned to create imaginative compositions and befriended the artist and writer Denton Welch.* Returned to Goldsmiths' to reach drawing, succeeding Edward Bawden.* When aged nineteen, she was asked by Frank Pick to design a poster for London Transport. Author and illustrator of three imaginative books: *The Cross Purposes,* 1945, *Hoodwinked,* 1957, and *Beauty and the Burglar,* 1958. Regular exhibitor at the RA, 1965-89. ARA, 1973, RA, 1980. Worked mainly in pencil with watercolour washes and chose subjects with biblical associations.

SWANWICK, Joseph Harold   1866-1929
Painter. Born Middlewich, Cheshire. Studied art in Liverpool, at the Slade School and in Paris at the Académie Julian. Exhibited at the RA from 1889, also at the RBA, the RI, in the provinces and abroad.

SWEET, David   b.1945
Painter. Born Hull, Humberside. Studied at Hull College of Art, 1961-5, and RCA, 1966-9. Has taught at various art institutions and is now Head of Painting at Manchester Polytechnic. First began exhibiting, 1969, in the 'Conservative Abstraction' exhibition, held at RCA Gallery, London, and in the 1970s was closely associated with the magazine *Artscribe* for which he wrote several articles.

SWIMMER, Tom   b.1932
Painter. Born France. Studied at the RCA. Awarded the Gold Medal and a Travelling Scholarship which he spent painting in Italy. 1960 first solo exhibition at the Trafford Gallery, London.

SWINBURNE, John   b.1939
Painter. Born York, Yorkshire. Studied at the School of Art, York, 1956-60. He has travelled extensively in Europe, studying art. First solo exhibition at the Austen Hayes Collection, York; others include one at the Woodstock Gallery, 1964.

SWYNNERTON, Annie   1844-1933
Painter. Born Kersal, near Manchester, née Robinson. Studied at Manchester School of Art, in Paris and in Rome where she met and married the Manx sculptor, Joseph Swynnerton in 1883. With Isabel Dacre* she formed the Manchester Society of Women Painters. Exhibited at the RA from 1879, also at the Grosvenor and New Galleries, specialising in allegorical subjects that suggest the influence of the Victorian artist, G.F. Watts. Lived in Rome until her husband died in 1910 and then returned to England. 1922 elected ARA, the first woman to receive this honour since 1768.

SYDDALL, Joseph   1864-1942
Painter and sculptor. Born Whittington. Studied at Bushey Art School, under Sir Hubert von Herkomer during the 1890s. During the 1920s he designed the Four Crown War Memorial at Old Whittington and the Stone Soldier Monument at Dronfield to commemorate the First World War. 1985 retrospective exhibition held at the Lecture Hall, Chesterfield.

SYDNEY, Berenice   1944-1983
Painter and etcher. Born Esher, Surrey. Studied at the Central School of Art. First solo exhibition at the Drian Galleries, London, 1968. In her colourful abstracts geometric shapes alternate with amorphous forms. She also experimented with etching and screen painting. Included in the collections of V & A, British Council, British Museum, Tate Gallery, Ashmolean Museum and Fitzwilliam Museum.

SYKES, Caroline
Painter and graphic designer. Studied at St. Martin's School of Art, 1967-71 and at Goldsmiths' College. First solo exhibition at the White Elephant Club, London, 1977. She draws her subject from Devon which she frequently visits. Has exhibited at the RA and at 'The British Artists Show', Chelsea, 1981.

SYKES, John Gutteridge   1866-1941
Watercolour painter. Born Sheffield, Yorkshire. Studied at Sheffield Art School. 1903 visited Staithes and met Harold* and Laura* Knight. Moved to Newlyn, and lived in a house found for him by Frank Dobson.* Exhibited widely, in London and elsewhere.

SYKES, Sandy   b.1944
Painter and printmaker. Born Wakefield, Yorkshire. Studied at Leeds College of Art, 1962-6, Middlesex Polytechnic, 1966-7 and Wimbledon College of Art, 1962-6. First solo exhibition at Brunel University, 1981. Works with woodcuts and linocuts and also makes monotypes, on top of which she often paints or draws. Her subjects often allude to social and political issues, through the use of motifs or symbols that have historical and universal significance. Represented in the V & A, Wakefield Art Gallery and elsewhere.

SYMONS, Mark   1886-1935
Painter. Studied at the Slade, 1905-9. Had a deep religious faith and initially hoped to enter the Carthusian Order, but after 1924 he devoted himself to painting. 1927 first exhibited at the RA. 1979 solo exhibition of his work at Reading Museum and Art Gallery. He painted many religious subjects, taken from the life of Christ, as well as figurative paintings derived from fantasies. His paintings teem with secret gardens, mysterious forests, mountains, waterfalls, fairies, nymphs, children and dreamers. His vision encompassed both the Christian war of good and evil as well as a pagan celebration of the seasons. At times his work is akin to that of Richard Dadd.

SYMONS, Patrick   b.1925
Painter. Born Bromley, Kent. Studied at Camberwell School of Arts and Crafts, 1946-50. First solo exhibition at the New Arts Centre, London, 1960. An underlying sense of geometry informs his natural scenes, so that they become at once a flat patterned tapestry and a space-creating image. His attentively precise attitude towards landscape painting invites comparison with Euan Uglow's* approach to the nude. Represented by Browse and Darby, London.

T

TABNER, Len   b.1946
Painter. Born South Bank, near Middlesbrough, Cleveland. Studied painting at Middlesbrough College of Art, 1964-5, Bath Academy of Art, 1965-8 and Reading University, 1968-70. 1974 received the Northern Arts Production Award and 1976 the Trident TV Fellowship in Fine Art. 1982 solo exhibition at Moira Kelly Fine Art; another at Sunderland Museum and Art Gallery, 1987, in which he showed paintings and drawings made underground in a potash mine near his home in East Cleveland.

TABORN, David   b.1947
Painter. Born Smethwick, West Midlands. Studied at Birmingham College of Art, 1966-70 and the Slade School, 1970-2. From 1969 included in mixed exhibitions. 1973 first solo exhibition at Greenwich Theatre Art Gallery; another at Nottingham University Art Gallery, 1979, whilst Fellow in Fine Art at Nottingham University. Paints colourful, complex, layered abstract paintings.

TAGG, Robert   b.1942
Painter. Born Leicester. Studied at Loughborough College of Art, 1958-61, Manchester College of Art, 1961-4 and Birmingham College of Art, 1964-5. Since 1965 has taught at Oldham, Manchester and Loughborough Colleges of Art. 1981 won Portrait Award at the National Portrait Gallery. 1982 solo exhibition at Bletchley Leisure Centre.

TAGGART, David   b.1937
Painter. Born London. Studied at the Regent Street Polytechnic, 1954-7 and the Central School, 1957-60. Solo show at the Rowan Gallery, 1963 and 1965.

TAIN, Michael   b.1927
Painter. Born Glasgow, Scotland. Studied at Glasgow School of Art and then in London under Ruskin Spear.* Three solo exhibitions at the John Whibley Gallery, 1962, 1963 and 1965, and one at the Madden Galleries, 1968. Solo shows in Australia and Vienna, 1967.

TALBOT, Mary
Painter. Born Melbourne, Australia. 1958 arrived in England. 1959 first solo exhibition at the New Art Centre and 1961 the Arthur Jeffress Gallery. 1962 and 1963 she exhibited in Australia and Paris. 1964 she painted a series of portrait commissions in Melbourne and travelled in the Far East. 1964, 1966 and 1969 three solo exhibitions held at the Trafford Gallery.

TALBOT, Richard   b.1956
Sculptor. Studied at Goldsmiths' College, 1976-9, Chelsea School of Art, 1979-80 and the British School in Rome, 1980-2. 1980 Rome scholar in sculpture. From 1978 included in mixed exhibitions. 1980 won a prize at the New Contemporaries. 1983 first solo exhibition at LYC Gallery, Cumbria and showed recent 'perspectival' drawings at the Bakehouse Gallery, Blackheath, London; others include one at Wolfson College, Oxford, 1987.

TALMAGE, Algernon   1871-1939
Painter. Born Fifield, Oxfordshire, the son of a clergyman. Studied under Herkomer at Bushey, and in St. Ives, Cornwall. Became a painter of landscape and animals. Around 1900 he ran an art school in St. Ives. Moved to London, 1907 and held his first solo exhibition at the Goupil Gallery, London, 1909. During the First World War he became an official war artist to the Canadian Government. Elected ARA, 1922, and RA, 1929. Took up etching in 1927, and at the height of the etching boom. Represented in several public collections including the Victoria Art Gallery, Bath.

TANDY, John   1905-1982
Painter and engraver. Born London. Studied architecture at the Architectural Association and then painting and engraving at Leon Underwood's* School, 1923-5. Worked as a painter and engraver in Paris and Provence, 1929-36. 1928 first solo exhibition at Cottars Studio Gallery. 1936 worked as interior decorator with Duncan Miller; 1937-8 designed carpets for Alistair Morton of Edinburgh Weavers. 1939 worked on camouflage with Roland Penrose* and S.W. Hayter.* 1952 founded Tandy Halford Mills group, specialising in corporate design. 1984 exhibition of work from the 1920s and '30s held at the Redfern Gallery.

TANNER, Anne
Painter and sculptor. Partly self-taught. Born Manchester. Studied music at the Royal College of Music, Manchester. Worked with sculptors and attended part-time courses in art to give her a grounding in painting and sculpture. Makes painted sculptural reliefs from aluminium. 1978 first solo exhibition at Aberbach Fine Art; another at same gallery, 1980.

TANNER, Arthur   fl.c.1908-1915
Very little is known about this artist except that he lived in Lamorna, Cornwall, and painted landscapes of that area. He was a friend of Lamorna Birch* and Henry Tuke* and used to travel abroad regularly. He disappeared during the First World War.

TANNER, Noel   b.1941
Painter. Studied at Croydon College of Art, 1958-64, then taught at Leeds School of Art, 1965-6. From 1963 included in group exhibitions. Member of the AIA. 1969 solo exhibition at the Woodstock Gallery.

TANNER, Robin   1904-1988
Etcher. Born Bristol, Avon. Studied at Goldsmiths' College, 1922-4. Taught art in Deptford, 1924-8, whilst studying etching under Stanley Anderson* in the evenings. In 1928 moved to Wiltshire. Whilst at Goldsmiths' took part in a revival of interest in etching and in the work of Samuel Palmer. Became a teacher in art and in 1935 was appointed as H.M. Inspector of Schools, a post he held until 1964. During the Second World War his book, *Lettering for Children,* introduced a whole generation to the pleasures of 'manuscript writing' in Indian ink. Also wrote a number of books around his etchings, some in collaboration with his wife, Heather. Is best known for his images of mysterious, romantic, rural England. 1969 wrote *Adventures in Education.* 1980 presented impressions of all his etchings to Bristol Museum and Art Gallery. Large retrospective exhibitions at Bristol Museum and Art Gallery, 1980, Devizes Museum, 1986, and at Garton & Co., 1988.

Bibl: Robin Tanner, *Double Harness,* Impact Books, London, 1987; *Robin Tanner: The Etchings,* Garton & Co., London, 1988.

TANSEY, Francis   b.1959
Painter. Born Dublin, Ireland. Studied at National College of Art and Design, Dublin, 1978-83, during which time he worked in the theatre as a set designer. 1905-6

Artist-in-residence at Butler Gallery, Kilkenny Castle. 1986 solo exhibition at the Solomon Gallery.

TARR, James   b.1905
Painter. Born Oystermouth, Wales. Studied at Cheltenham School of Art, 1922-5, and at the RCA, 1925-9. Exhibited at the RA and in the provinces. His work has an affinity with that of Gilbert Spencer.* Was Principal, successively, of Lydney School of Art, 1936-8, High Wycombe School of Art, 1938-46, and Cardiff College of Art, 1946-70.

TARRANT, Margaret   1888-1959
Painter. Born Margate, Kent, the daughter of Percy Tarrant, the landscape painter. Studied art at Clapham Art School and Heatherley's and then for a while taught art. From 1910 she lived in Gomshall, then Penslake in Surrey. Painter of Christian scenes and of fairies and pixies. Worked as a book illustrator for, among other titles, Charles Kingsley's *Water Babies,* for J.M. Dent. 1921 the Medici Society published her picture, 'Peter's Friends', which became one of her best known works; from then on most of her work was published by the Medici Society. In the 1940s she went to Palestine to see and sketch the Holy places. 1961 memorial exhibition held at the Medici Gallery, London.

TARRANT, Peter   b.1943
Painter. Born Morville, Shropshire. Studied at Shrewsbury Art School. Took various odd jobs in order to keep himself while painting. His main themes are the countryman and his environment. 1969 first solo exhibition at Compendium Galleries, Birmingham; most recent at the Silk Top Hat Gallery, Ludlow, 1981.

TATE, Elizabeth   b.1948
Sculptor. Studied at Sunderland College of Art, 1967-71 and Manchester University, 1971-2. From 1971 included in group exhibitions. 1976 first solo exhibition entitled 'Shades' at the Bede Gallery, Jarrow, with another at the LYC Gallery, Brampton, Cumbria.

TATE, Nairne
Painter. Born Denbigh, North Wales. Studied drawing privately. Painted in France, Spain, California and Corfu. Has exhibited at the RA and in the Paris Salon. Wife of Sir Henry Tate, whose great-grandfather gave the Tate Gallery to the nation. Solo exhibition of 'Recent Paintings' at Tooth & Sons Ltd., 1970.

TAYLER, Albert Chevallier   1862-1925
Painter. Studied at Slade and in Paris. Exhibited at the RA from 1884 and at the NEAC from 1886 onwards. Won a medal at the Paris Salon, 1891. He spent twelve years in Newlyn, Cornwall, and then moved to London, and is best known for his interior scenes. Specialised in portraits, genre, historical and religious scenes.

TAYLOR, Bruce   b.1921
Sculptor. Born Yorkshire. Served in the RAF, 1941-6. Became Assistant Director, Natural History Museum, Halifax, then studied at Bath Academy of Art, 1950-2. Taught art in Hertfordshire and then in Cornwall. Lives in Towednack, St. Ives. Member of the Penwith Society of Arts. 1958 first solo exhibition at Drian Galleries; another at the Arnolfini Gallery, Bristol, 1966.

TAYLOR, Charles William   1878-1960
Etcher and engraver. Born Wolverhampton, West Midlands. Studied at Wolverhampton School of Art and the RCA. Originally trained with a firm of commercial engravers. Taught art at Southend and exhibited at RA. His print-making came to the attention of the public in the mid-1920s and over the next ten years he produced a small but interesting number of works, mostly wood-engravings of unspoilt rural areas in the south and east of England. Elected ARA, 1922, and RE, 1930.

TAYLOR, Christine
Painter. Studied at the Slade School, 1956-60. Included in group exhibitions in London, Bristol and Belfast. First solo exhibition at the Woodstock Gallery, 1965.

TAYLOR, Dawn
Painter. Trained as a beautician and a hairdresser. Works in charcoal, chalk and acrylics. Member of the Jenako Visual Arts Collective. First solo exhibition at Wood Green Library, 1985; others include those at the Black Art Gallery, Finsbury Park, 1987 and Brent Art Gallery, Neasden, 1988.

TAYLOR, Donald   b.1945
Painter. Born Bury, Lancashire. Studied at Bolton College of Art, 1963-4, Newport College of Art, 1964-8, the Slade School, 1968-70 and was Rome Scholar in Painting, 1970-2. Worked for a while as keeper of fine art at Salford Art Gallery. Has a studio at Sunderland Point, on the Lune estuary in Lancashire. 1974 first solo exhibition at the ICA; another at Bolton Museum and Art Gallery, 1981.

TAYLOR, Eric   b.1909
Painter and printmaker. Born London. Studied at RCA, 1932-5. 1935 awarded prize for best print at International Print Exhibition, Chicago, USA. 1939-45 soldier and war artist. Between 1936 and 1949 he taught at Camberwell, Willesden and Central Schools of Art. Elected ARE, 1935, and RE, 1948. 1949-56 Head of Leeds School of Design; 1956-69 Principal of Leeds College of Art; 1969-71 Assistant Director of Leeds Polytechnic. 1949 bought a lithography press from Jacob Kramer* when he arrived in Leeds, and has used it for printmaking workshops since then. 1972 retrospective exhibition of prints at Goosewell Gallery, Menston, Yorkshire.

TAYLOR, Eric Alan   b.1924
Painter. Born England, brought up in Canada. Gained Art Teacher's Certificate from Culham College, Oxford. 1955 first exhibited in group exhibitions at Daily Express Young Artists Exhibition. Abstract painter by the 1960s. 1963 solo exhibition at the Woodstock Gallery.

TAYLOR, Fraser   b.1960
Painter and printmaker. Born Luton, Bedfordshire. Studied at Glasgow School of Art, 1977-81 and the RCA, 1981-3. 1983 set up 'The Cloth' Studio, specialising in textile designs. From 1982 included in group exhibitions. 1984 first solo exhibition at L'Escargot, London. 1984 won a prize in Lloyds Young Printmakers' competition. Painted a mural for the Braganza Restaurant, London. 1987 most recent solo show at the Thumb Gallery.

TAYLOR, Jack   b.1930
Painter. Born East End of London. Left school aged fourteen and took a variety of manual jobs. Self-taught as a painter. 1954, whilst cleaning builders' rubble from near the Redfern Gallery, he took some of his paintings in and

Plate 74. ANNE REDPATH, 1895-1965. *'Still life with Lemons',* 1937. Oil on board. 24in. x 20in. Mercury Gallery, London.

Plate 75. WILLIAM ROBERTS, 1895-1980. *'The Rhine Boat',* 1928. 20in. x 16in. Scottish National Gallery of Modern Art.

Plate 76. EDWARD SEAGO, 1910-1974. *'Norfolk Cottage'*. 26in. x 36in. Spink & Son Ltd., London.

WALTER TAYLOR, 1860-1943.
'Regency Square, Brighton',
c.1930. 20in. x 16in.
Michael Parkin Fine Art Ltd.

was given his first solo exhibition that year. Produced designs for the ballet *Café des Sports* at Sadlers Wells. Took up sculpture as well and had a show of paintings and sculpture at the Mercury Gallery, 1965.

TAYLOR, Jim   b.1937
Painter. Born Edinburgh, Scotland. Studied at Edinburgh College of Art, 1963-7. From 1965 included in group shows, e.g. at the Edinburgh Festival and the SSA. 1971 solo exhibition at the New 57 Gallery.

TAYLOR, John   b.1936
Painter. Born Darvel, Scotland. Studied at Glasgow School of Art, 1954-9 and at Birmingham Polytechnic, 1972-3. Works mostly in watercolour. 1966 first solo exhibition at the New Charing Cross Gallery, Glasgow, showing both paintings and ceramics. 1987 most recent

exhibition, 'The View from the Bunker', at the Compass Gallery, Glasgow.

TAYLOR, John   b.1952
Sculptor. Studied at Batley Art College, 1971-3, at Jacob Kramer School of Art, 1983-4, Leeds Polytechnic, 1984-7, and at the RA Schools, from 1987. Awards include a travelling Scholarship, 1977, from Leeds Polytechnic and the '88 Henfield Award, Premiums Show, at the RA, 1988. Included in the collection of Leeds City Art Gallery.

TAYLOR, Leonard Campbell   1874-1969
Painter. Born Oxford. Studied at Ruskin School, Oxford, at the St. John's Wood School of Art and the RA Schools. From 1899 exhibited at the RA. Elected ROI, 1905, RP, 1909, ARA, 1923 and RA, 1931. Is best known for his paintings of interiors often inhabited by single women.

Owing to his use of an uninflected style, and illusionistic method, his paintings have the calmness of a Vermeer, if not the profundity. His work entered many homes, in the form of reproduction prints, and he was for a period one of the most popular artists of his day.

TAYLOR, Linda   b.1959
Mixed media artist. Born Stranraer, Scotland. Studied at Edinburgh College of Art, 1976-80. Since graduating has worked primarily as a sculptor. Solo exhibition held at the Collective Gallery, Edinburgh, 1985; another at the Graeme Murray Gallery, Edinburgh, 1987. A large sculpture, *Unseen Currents,* was shown at the Glasgow Garden Festival, 1988.

TAYLOR, Lulu
Painter. Born Sarawak, North Borneo, where she taught art until her first exhibition in 1966. 1971 moved to Britain, after exhibitions in Singapore and Kuala Lumpur. Likes to work with batik techniques. 1971-6 included in many mixed exhibitions in London. 1977 solo exhibition at the Commonwealth Art Gallery.

TAYLOR, Marigold   b.1922
Painter. Born Sussex. Studied for three years at Wimbledon School of Art, then took up theatrical design. For most of the war she was occupied in designing and painting large murals for the RAF dining halls. 1946-56 worked as a painter and a scenic designer. 1956 married and painted less for a while, but 1965 resumed painting. 1969 solo exhibition entitled 'Space Probes' at the Arts Centre, Basildon, Essex.

TAYLOR, Roderick   b.1937
Painter. Born Manchester. Studied at Manchester College of Art, 1955-61. 1963 first solo exhibition at the Central Library, Manchester; another in 1968 at the Peterloo Gallery, Manchester. Interested in painting windows, curtains and views through them to the landsape beyond.

TAYLOR, Walter   1860-1943
Painter. Born Leeds, Yorkshire. Initially trained as an architect and later took up painting. Became a friend of Walter Sickert* and painted with him in Dieppe, France; also worked extensively in Italy. First solo exhibition held at the Grafton Gallery, London, 1911. Founder member of the London Group, 1913.

TAYLOR, Wendy   b.1945
Sculptor and printmaker. Born Stamford, Lincolnshire. Studied at St. Martin's School of Art, 1961-6, winning three awards during her years there. 1970 first solo exhibition at Axiom Gallery, London. From 1964 included in group exhibitions. 1971 executed commissions for Somerville College, Oxford, and 1973 the Tower Hotel, St. Katherine's Dock, London. 1976 exhibition at the Oliver Dowling Gallery, Dublin. Likes to make sculpture from industrial materials that gives the illusion of defying gravity.

TAYLOR, W.S.   b.1920
Painter. Born Sheffield, Yorkshire. Studied at Sheffield College of Art, 1936-9, and the RCA, 1939-43. 1940s-76 taught art at Sheffield, Chesterfield and Rotherham. 1964-70 wrote weekly art reviews in the *Sheffield Telegraph.* 1943-55 exhibited widely in group shows. 1979 made a film *What Treatment* for Sheffield Hospitals Board. 1980 retrospective exhibition held at Philip Francis Gallery, Sheffield.

TCHEREPNINE, Jessica   b.1938
Flower painter. Born Sussex. Studied drawing privately in Florence, Italy. Since 1968 has lived in New York, and has turned from English flowers to those of the tropics. Group shows held in London and New York. 1982 first solo exhibition at the Clarges Gallery.

TEASDALE, Anna
Painter and printmaker. Born East Molesey, Surrey. Studied painting at Hastings School of Art and at St. Martin's School of Art and etching at the Central School. Lived in Bath. From 1960 included in group shows. 1976 solo exhibition at the Festival Gallery, Bath.

TEBBY, Susan   b.1944
Sculptor. Born Wakefield, Yorkshire. Studied at Goldsmiths' College, London, 1962-6, and Chelsea School of Art, 1966-7. From 1967 taught sculpture at Leicester Polytechnic. 1971 first solo exhibition in the East Gallery of the Serpentine Gallery, and 1981 at the Sally East Gallery, Camberwell.

TEED, Shirley   b.1933
Painter. Born Bristol, Avon. Studied at the West of England College of Art, 1949-54. 1955-8 resident in Australia, where her work was influenced by John Brock, Head of the Art Department of Melbourne Grammar School (who later became Director of the Victoria National Gallery). 1959 returned to England and later moved to Yorkshire. 1959-64 was her productive period when she lived in Wallington and exhibited regularly at the RA, the RSBA and the RSA. From 1965 lived in Goole, Yorkshire. Many solo exhibitions including Usher Gallery, Lincoln, 1975 and 1983, University of Exeter, 1978, Falmouth Art Gallery, 1981, Leeds Playhouse, 1984 and the Patricia Wells Gallery, Thornbury, near Bristol, 1987. Primarily a landscape artist with an interest in geological formations.

TEGETMEIER, Dennis   1895-1987
Painter and illustrator. Born Hampstead, London. Apprenticed to an advertising agency, 1912. Served with the Royal Field Artillery, 1914-18. Studied art at the Central School, 1919-22. From the 1920s was a friend of Eric Gill,* and 1930 married his daughter Petra. 1928 moved to Pigotts, High Wycombe, to be part of Gill's group of craftsmen. Produced many book illustrations, among which are *The Seven Deadly Virtues* (his own book), *The Mysteriousness of Marriage* by Jeremy Taylor, *Money and Morals* by Eric Gill, *A Sentimental Journey* by Laurence Sterne, *Unholy Trinity* by Gill and Tegetmeier. Until 1962 lived at Pigotts, when moved to Wardour, Wiltshire. His creative period of oil paintings on gesso were done during his Wiltshire period. 1977 a large exhibition of work held at Studio One Gallery, Oxford.

TEH, Hock-Aun   b.1950
Painter. Born Malaysia. Studied at the Tan Guan-Hi Painting School there before arriving at Glasgow School of Art, 1970; studied there until 1974. First Chinese recipient of a Diploma in Painting and Drawing from Glasgow. 1977-9 lectured in Chinese Painting and Calligraphy at Glasgow School of Art. From 1973 included in many group exhibitions. 1977 first solo exhibition at Loudon Hall, Ayr. 1988 retrospective exhibition at 369 Gallery, Edinburgh. Paints in an abstract manner which fuses both oriental and western styles.

Plate 77. ANNE SPALDING, b.1911. *'The Mantelpiece'*, 1951. 12¼in. x 16¼in. Sally Hunter Fine Art, London.

Plate 78. HUMPHREY SPENDER, b.1910. *'Flowers in a Goblet on a Terrace'*, 1945. Oil on board. 24in. x 18in. Private Collection. Photograph: Sandra Lummis Fine Art

Plate 79. MARGARET THOMAS, b.1916. *'Still Life with Narcissus'*, 1988. Oil on board. Sally Hunter Fine Art, London.

Plate 80. WILLIAM TILLYER, b.1938. *'Untitled English Landscape Painting'*, 1989. Acrylic on canvas. 72in. x 60in. Bernard Jacobson Gallery, London.

TELEPNEFF, Andrew   b.1927
Painter. Studied at St. Martin's School of Art and the RA Schools, and gained a Leverhulme Scholarship. Taught for a while at Bournemouth School of Art. Included in mixed exhibitions, e.g. the RA, the London Group and the RP. Solo exhibitions at the Woodstock Gallery, 1966 and the Hamwic Gallery, Southampton, 1967.

TENNANT, Dorothy   1855-1926
Painter. Born London. Studied at the Slade School and in Paris. From 1886 exhibited at the RA, and at the New Gallery and the Grosvenor Gallery, London, the Fine Art Society, Glasgow, and in the Autumn Exhibitions held in Manchester and Liverpool. Married the explorer, H.M. Stanley, 1890. After his death, she completed and published his autobiography. 1907 married Dr. Henry Curtis. A portrait painter and illustrator, she also specialised in studies of London urchins. Her 'Street Arabs at Play' was bought by Lord Leverhulme with a view to using it as an advertisement for soap.

TENNANT, Stephen   1906-1986
Painter and illustrator. The youngest son of Lord Glenconner, his mother, Pamela Wyndham, was one of the three sisters in Sargent's* painting 'The Wyndham Sisters'. Studied painting at the Slade School, and also studied ballet, dancing before Diaghilev. 1925 illustrated his mother's book *A Vein in the Marble*. 1938 wrote and illustrated *Leaves from a Missionary's Notebook*. Travelled widely, but then lived the life of a recluse in his later years at his house at Wilsford, near Salisbury. Solo exhibitions at the Redfern Gallery, Alexander Iolas Gallery, New York, and in 1976, at Anthony d'Offay Gallery.

Bibl: Philip Hoare, *Serious Pleasures: The Life of Stephen Tennant,* Hamish Hamilton, London, 1990.

TENNANT, Trevor   b.1906
Sculptor. Born London. Studied at Goldsmiths' College of Art and the RA Schools. Solo exhibitions at the French Gallery, 1933, the Leger Gallery, 1934 and the Leicester Galleries, 1938. From c.1939 has been involved in numerous sculptural commissions, in Coventry, Bournemouth, LCC Estate, Stepney, London, Shopping Centre, Bracknell New Town, Queen Elizabeth II Hospital, Welwyn Garden City and the British Embassy extension at Washington, USA.

TENNENT, John   b.1926
Painter of birds and printmaker. Spent sixteen years as a Civil Servant, ten years in Kenya and six years in the Diplomatic Service. His interest in painting grew during these years and he had his first solo exhibition in Cairo, 1967. 1968 he became a full-time artist, resigning from the Foreign Office. Member of the Society of Wildlife Artists. Numerous solo exhibitions, including two at Clarges Gallery, 1972 and 1977, Cornell University, 1979 and the Patricia Wells Gallery, Thornbury, near Bristol, 1984. 1973 he was commissioned by the Wildlife Conservation Society to paint in Zambia.

THOMAS, Margaret   b.1916
Painter. Born London. Studied at Sidcup Art School. Won a scholarship to the Slade but left after two years for the RA Schools where she studied under Thomas Monnington* and Ernest Jackson.* 1949 first solo exhibition held at Leicester Gallery; recent solo exhibitions include one at Sally Hunter Fine Art, London, 1988. Member of the NEAC, RBA and Royal West of England Academy.

THELWELL, Norman   b.1923
Painter and illustrator. Born Birkenhead, Cheshire. Served in Britain and India during the Second World War, then studied at Liverpool College of Art, 1947-50. Taught at Wolverhampton College of Art and began sending cartoons to *Punch,* c.1952, then worked for that magazine for the next twenty-five years. 1956 gave up teaching and took up illustration full time; his first girl and pony cartoon appeared in 1953. Illustrated over thirty books beginning with *Angels on Horseback,* 1957. 1986 published *Wrestling with a Pencil* (Methuen, London). 1989 held a large exhibition of illustrations and topographical watercolours at Chris Beetles Ltd.

THEMERSON, Franciszka   1907-1988
Painter. Born Warsaw, Poland. Studied painting and graphic arts at the Academy of Fine Arts, Warsaw, 1924-31. 1931-7 worked on films, paintings and book illustrations. 1937 moved to Paris and 1940 to London, where her husband, Stefan Themerson, joined her in 1942. With him she founded the Gaberbocchus Press, 1948. 1951 first solo exhibition at Watergate Theatre Club Gallery, London. 1963 retrospective exhibition of work from 1943-63 held at the Drian Galleries. Other solo exhibitions include one at the Whitechapel Art Gallery, London, 1975.

THESIGER, Ernest   1879-1961
Painter. Born London. Studied at Slade School. Exhibited at RA and in the provinces. Held two solo exhibitions of flower paintings at the Fine Art Society, 1936 and 1938. Also acted, first appearing on the stage in 1909 and giving many performances. Published his autobiography, *Practically True,* 1927.

THISTLETHWAITE, Morvenna
Painter. Studied at Leamington and Birmingham Schools of Art. Likes to paint still lifes. Has exhibited in mixed exhibitions at the RA and Roland, Browse and Delbanco, London. 1973 first solo exhibition at Andsell Gallery; others in Canada, 1975 and 1977, New Grafton Gallery, 1980 and the Newlyn Art Gallery, Cornwall, 1982.

THOMAS, Brenda   b.1950
Painter and sculptor. Born Swansea, Wales. Studied at Swansea College of Art, Leicester Polytechnic and Goldsmiths' College, London. From 1972 included in group exhibitions. 1975 first solo exhibition at Oriel, Cardiff. Commissioned to make a sculpture of a rhinoceros and a dinosaur for Ringo Starr.

THOMAS, Chris   b.1957
Painter. Born Merthyr Tydfil, Wales. Studied at Cardiff College of Art, 1975-6, and Birmingham Polytechnic, 1976-9 and 1982-3. 1983-5 employed as a relief teacher in Birmingham. 1980 first solo exhibition at Worcester Arts Workshop; more recent one entitled 'Under the Heavens' at the Tettenhall Gallery, Wolverhampton, 1985.

THOMAS, Colin   b.1912
Painter. Born Edinburgh, Scotland. Studied at Grays School of Art, Aberdeen and taught there, 1951-77. 1966 first solo exhibition at the Scottish Gallery, Edinburgh; most recent at the Pier Arts Centre, Stromness, Orkney in 1987. Works in public collections, e.g. Scottish Arts Council, Aberdeen and Kirkaldy Art Galleries, Edinburgh City Arts Centre.

THOMAS, Gareth   b.1955
Painter. Born Swansea, Wales. Studied at Trinity College,

Carmarthen, 1975-8 and began to paint full time in 1979. 1983 elected member of Welsh Watercolour Society. From 1982 included in group exhibitions; 1981 first solo School of Art exhibition at the Grand Theatre, Swansea. 1986 exhibition of recent landscapes at the Glynn Vivian Art Gallery, Swansea.

THOMAS, George Havard   1893-1933
Sculptor. Born Sorrento, Italy, son of James Havard Thomas.* Studied under his father at the Slade School, 1914-15, and 1919-20. From 1919 exhibited at the RA. Became a teacher of sculpture at the Slade, 1920. Specialised in portraits and figure subjects.

THOMAS, Ivor   1928-1980
Painter and sculptor. Born South Wales. Served a welding apprenticeship. A self taught artist, he started painting after seeing a Van Gogh exhibition in London, and in 1957 held his first solo painting exhibition at the Leicester Gallery. Later turned to sculpture and in 1961 held his first solo sculpture exhibition at the Lincoln School of Art Gallery. From the 1960s on he produced many sculpture commissions, and liked to work in steel. 1986 retrospective exhibition at Ashford Library Gallery, Kent.

THOMAS, James Havard   1854-1921
Sculptor. Born Bristol, Avon. Studied at Bristol School of Art, winning a scholarship to the RCA. Afterwards studied at the Ecole des Beaux Arts in Paris. Worked in Italy near Naples, 1889-1906, and was much influenced by the vogue for Tanagra statuettes. From 1872 exhibited at the RA. First solo exhibition held at the Carfax Gallery, London, 1909. Began teaching at the Slade, 1911 and was made Professor of Sculpture, 1915. Represented in several public collections including Sheffield City Art Galleries. Father of George Havard Thomas.*

THOMAS, Margaret   b.1916
Painter. Born London. Studied at Sidcup Art School, the Slade School for two years and then the RA Schools under W.T. Monnington.* Regular exhibitor in the group exhibitions of the RA and RSA. Member of the NEAC and RBA. 1949 first solo exhibition at the Leicester Galleries. 1982 retrospective exhibitions at Aitken Dott, Edinburgh. 1988 recent exhibition at Sally Hunter Fine Art. (Plate 79, p.427.)

THOMAS, Oliver   b.1919
Painter. Began to be interested in painting at Eton with Robert Drumm as his art master. Studied at Chelsea School of Art, 1937-9. Prisoner of war in Singapore during the Second World War. Brief spell as student teacher at the art school of King's College, Newcastle; 1949 joined the staff at Eton as a member of the Drawing Schools staff. 1972 left Eton in order to spend more time painting. From 1947 included in group exhibitions, e.g. at the RA. 1980 solo exhibition at Eton College, Windsor and Bury St. Edmunds Art Gallery; 1987 at Dunelm House, Durham.

THOMAS, Roy
Painter. Self taught, and started to paint in 1969, while working as a priest in Wapping, East London. Painted the changing skyline there as the Docklands underwent commercial development, then studied painting part-time at the Sir John Cass School of Art. Is currently Team Rector of Wickford and Runwell in Essex. 1984 first solo exhibition at Colchester Arts Centre.

THOMAS, Simon   b.1960
Sculptor. Born Portsmouth, Hampshire. Studied at Plymouth College of Art and Design, 1978-9, at Ravensbourne College of Art of Design, 1979-82, and at RCA, 1985-8. Assistant to John Maine, 1983-4, when he assisted in carving Portland stone for *Arena* on the South Bank, London. 1984 became an assistant to Phillip King on the Docklands Sculpture Project at Canary Wharf. Commissions include *New Milestones* for Common Ground coastal walk at Durdle Door, Dorset, 1986, and three large woodcarvings for the London Wildlife Trust, 1986. 1988 won Madame Tussaud's Award for figurative art. 1989 first solo exhibition at the Albermarle Gallery, London.

THOMPSON, Brian   b.1950
Sculptor. Born Morley, Yorkshire. Studied fine art at Newcastle University, 1969-73. From 1973 lecturer in sculpture at Sheffield Polytechnic, Teeside College of Art and the Fine Art Department, Newcastle University. 1975 first one-person exhibition at the Usher Art Gallery, Lincoln.

THOMPSON, Ernest Heber   1891-1971
Painter and etcher. Born Dunedin, New Zealand. Began as a freelance black-and-white artist in Dunedin and then served with the New Zealand Expeditionary Force, 1915-17, in Egypt and France. After the war he studied at the Slade School and at the RCA under Frank Short.* Exhibited at leading London venues. Elected ARA, 1924, and RE, 1939.

THOMS, Colin   b.1912
Painter. Born Edinburgh, Scotland. Encouraged and taught in his youth by S.J. Peploe* and through him inherited many of the characteristics associated with the Scottish Colourists. Wartime experience in North Africa led to his appreciation of the work of Paul Klee. Has also drawn inspiration from Miró. Exhibits regularly with the RSA and in 1949 was elected President of the SSA. Regular solo exhibitions in Scotland, also one at England & Co., London, 1989. Represented in several Scottish public collections.

THOMSEN, Marjorie
Painter and printmaker. Born London. Studied full-time at St. Albans School of Art, and part-time at the Central School. Joined the Central Office of Information as a graphic designer. First solo exhibition, of watercolours, at the Questors Theatre, Ealing, 1975; another at the Brunswick Gallery, 1978.

THOMSON, Alfred R.   b.1894
Painter. Born Bangalore, India. Attended the Royal School for the Deaf and Dumb, Margate. Studied at the London Art School, Kensington. Exhibited at the RA from 1920. Elected ARA, 1938, RA, 1945. Official War Artist to the RAF, 1940-4. Work in the Tate Gallery and the Imperial War Museum.

THOMSON, George   1860-1939
Painter. Born Towie, Scotland. Trained as an architect in Glasgow. Studied at the RA Schools and exhibited at the RA, 1886-1934. Member of the NEAC, 1891. Art critic for the *Pall Mall Gazette* and the *Westminster Gazette*. Lecturer in perspective, Slade School, 1895-1914. Moved to France, 1914 and subsequently died there. Liked to paint

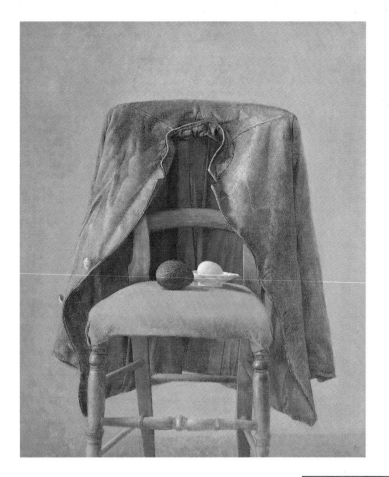

Plate 81. DAVID TINDLE, b.1932. *'Jacket'*, 1987-8.
Egg tempera on canvas. 28in. x 24in.
Fischer Fine Art Ltd., London.

Plate 82. JULIAN TREVELYAN, 1910-1988.
'Newhaven', 1985. 24in. x 20in. Private Collection.

430

Plate 83. LEON UNDERWOOD, 1890-1975. *'Icelandic Fisherfolk'*, c.1923. 25in. x 25in. Private Collection.
Photograph: Sandra Lummis Fine Art.

VALERIE THORNTON. *'King David and his musicians, Ripoll'*, 1978. Etching in colour. 15in. x 24½in. Private Collection.

architectural subjects. Retrospective exhibition held at Colnaghi's Gallery, London, 1927. Work in the Tate Gallery.

THORNEYCROFT, William Hamo   1850-1925
Sculptor. Born London, the son of the sculptors Thomas and Mary Thorneycroft. Studied under his father at the RA Schools, 1869. From 1872 exhibited at the RA. Elected ARA, 1881, and RA, 1888. Taught at the RA Schools, 1882-1914. Commissions include General Gordon, Trafalgar Square (now moved to Embankment Gardens), 1888, Oliver Cromwell, Westminster Hall, 1899 and Gladstone, The Strand, 1905.

Bibl: Elfrida Manning, *Marble and Bronze: The Art and Life of Hamo Thorneycroft*, 1982.

THORNTON, Alfred   1863-1939
Painter. Born Delhi, India. Educated at Trinity College, Cambridge. Studied art at the Slade School, 1888-9, and at Westminster School of Art, 1890-2, winning prizes for landscape painting. He also taught there as an assistant to Walter Sickert,* 1893-4. Became a member of the NEAC, 1895, and its Hon. Secretary from 1928. Became a member of the London Group, 1924. Wrote *The Diary of an Art Student of the Nineties,* published 1938, which remains a useful source of information on the various issues and factions shaping the period.

THORNTON, Valerie   b.1931
Painter and etcher. Born London. Studied at Byam Shaw School and Regent Street Polytechnic, 1950-3, then spent eight months in 1954 at S.W. Hayter's* Atelier 17 in Paris, studying etching and engraving techniques. On her return to England she bought her own press and began making prints, mostly of architectural subjects. Very experimental and adventurous in her techniques. 1960 spent a year in USA and worked at Pratt Graphic Art Centre. First solo exhibition at The Minories, Colchester, 1960; recent show of paintings and new prints at the Albermarle Gallery, London, 1990. Work in most regional galleries throughout the UK and many in the USA. Regular exhibitor at the RA and the RE. Married to the artist Michael Chase.*

THUBRON, Harry   1915-1985
Relief-maker and collagist. Studied at Sunderland School of Art, 1933-8, and RCA, 1938-40. Began making reliefs out of wood, spun copper, brass and resins, before turning to collages made from humble materials, including corrugated paper, which, although abstract, contain references to human activity and human geography. Some were also influenced by the textures of Mexico and southern Spain. 1950-5 had a distinguished career as a teacher at Sunderland College of Art, Leeds College of Art, 1955-64, and Leicester College of Art, 1966-8. Solo exhibitions include Serpentine Gallery, 1976, Goldsmiths' College Gallery, London, 1986 and Gray City Art Gallery, Hartlepool, 1987.

TIBBLE, Geoffrey   1909-1952
Painter. Born Reading, Berkshire. Studied at Reading School of Art, 1925-7; early influences included Stanley Spencer* and the French painter André Derain. Studied at Slade School of Art where he associated with Rodrigo Moynihan,* William Townsend* and William Coldstream.* Briefly flirted with abstraction and exhibited with the 'Objective Abstractionists' at the Zwemmer Gallery, 1934. Began exhibiting with the London Group, 1935 and was elected a member, 1944. Became interested in Surrealism in the mid-1930s but afterwards returned to a more realistic style and became associated with the Euston Road School of painters, particularly Graham Bell.* Solo exhibitions include one at the Lefevre Gallery, London, 1942, and two at Arthur Tooth, London, 1946 and 1949. He is chiefly associated with paintings of women, bathing or dressing, as well as with genre scenes.

TILLYER, William   b.1938
Painter, printmaker and watercolourist. Born Middlesbrough, North Yorkshire. Studied at Middlesbrough College of Art, 1956-9 and the Slade, 1960-2. Awarded French Government Scholarship and studied printmaking at Atelier 17, Paris, 1963. Taught drawing and lithography at Central School of Art, 1964-70. Taught etching at the Bath Academy of Art, 1964-72. Taught printmaking at Watford School of Art, 1970-3. Also visiting lecturer at various institutions, including Rhode Island School of Design, USA, and Reading University. 1981 awarded British Council Travel Grant; 1981-2 Artist in Residence at Melbourne University, Australia. 1983 and 1984 travelled extensively in Europe, and in California, Arizona and New Mexico, USA. Since 1959 he has exhibited in group exhibitions and one man shows throughout Europe, USA and Australia. Lives and paints in North Yorkshire. Likes to paint the English landscape in atmospheric watercolours. Recent show at Bernard Jacobson Gallery, 1990. (Plate 80, p.427.)

Bibl: Richard Mabey, 'William Tillyer: Painting Beyond Landscape', *Modern Painters*, Vol.2 No.3, Autumn 1988.

TILMOUTH, Sheila   b.1949
Painter. Studied at Hornsey College of Art, 1969-72. She continued her studies at the Finnish Academy, Helsinki, at the Byam Shaw School of Drawing and Painting and at Middlesex Polytechnic. First exhibited in 1978 at Fischer Fine Art, London and at the RA Summer Exhibition; has exhibited regularly there since this date.

TILSON, Joe   b.1928
Mixed-media artist. Born London. Worked as a cabinet maker and carpenter, 1944-6, and served in the RAF, 1946-9. Studied at St. Martin's School of Art, 1949-52 and RCA, 1952-5. Became associated with the Pop Art movement, chiefly through 'Young Contemporaries' exhibitions. 1962 held first solo exhibition, since when he has exhibited regularly in London (Marlborough Galleries), New York and throughout Europe. 1984 was awarded a prize in the Bradford International Print Biennale and the Grand Prix at the Zjubljana Biennale, 1985. Has work in many public collections, including the Walker Art Gallery, Liverpool and Tate Gallery.

Bibl: Arturo Carlo Quintavalle, *Tilson*, Pre-Art, Milan, 1977.

TIMMIS, Robert   1886-1960
Painter. Born Leek, Staffordshire. Studied at Allan Fraser Art College, Arbroath. Art Master at Liverpool College of Art. Exhibited in London, the provinces and abroad. Represented in Walker Art Gallery, Liverpool.

TINDLE, David   b.1932
Painter. Born Huddersfield, Yorkshire. Studied at Coventry School of Art, 1945-7. Whilst working as a commercial artist in Soho he became friendly with John Minton,* and other artists associated with the area. 1952 first solo exhibitions held at Archer Gallery, Notting Hill. 1954-83 represented by Piccadilly Gallery, and since 1985 has been with Fischer Fine Art, London. Ruskin Master of Drawing, University of Oxford, and Professional Fellowship at St. Edmund Hall, Oxford. Paints with egg tempera. Elected ARA, 1973, and RA, 1979. Taught at RCA, 1972-83. (Plate 81, p.430.)

TIRR, Willy   b.1915
Painter. Born Berlin, Germany. Settled in England, 1938. Self-taught. Became Head of the Fine Art Department at Leeds Polytechnic. Began exhibiting in 1957 and has shown in Bradford, Leeds, Basel, Manchester, Washington, D.C. and London. From 1966, as well as working in watercolour, he has concentrated on shaped canvases.

TISDALL, Hans   b.1910
Painter. Born Munich, Germany. Studied at Academy of Fine Art, Munich, 1928-9. 1929 lived in Paris and Ascona. Moved to London, 1930 and took up a full-time career as a painter after three days' work in an advertising agency. 1931-5 designed fabrics. His early paintings were inspired by marine subjects, then his work became increasingly abstracted. Has concerned himself with mural painting, mosaics and tapestry designs for universities, offices and municipal buildings throughout the UK. First solo show at the Leger Galleries, London, 1945. His wife Isabel ran the Edinburgh Weavers, for whom he created textile designs from 1956 on. Taught at the Central School, 1948-1980s. Retrospective exhibition with catalogue held at the Pride Gallery, London, 1987. Work in the Tate Gallery.

TOD, Murray   1909-1974
Painter and printmaker. Studied at Glasgow School of Art, 1927-31, and was a contemporary of Ian Fleming.* Won a scholarship to the British School in Rome. Became a frequent exhibitor at the RSA. Specialised in Scottish, Italian and Spanish landscapes. Elected ARE, 1947, and RE, 1953. From the late 1940s he suffered from muscular dystrophy.

TODD, A.R. Middleton   1891-1966
Painter. Born Helston, Cornwall. Studied under Stanhope Forbes,* at the Central School of Arts and Crafts and, after service in the Army, at the Slade School, 1920-1. Began exhibiting at the RA, 1918. On leaving the Slade he spent time in France, Italy and Holland. Elected ARE, 1923, ARWS, 1929, RE, 1930, RWS, 1937, ARA, 1939, and RA, 1949. Became a member of the NEAC, 1945. Occupied various teaching posts in Leicester, at Regent Street Polytechnic, at the RA Schools and at City and Guilds School, Kennington. An admirer of Degas, he excelled at pastels. A posthumous exhibition of work from his studio was held at the Fosse Gallery, Stow-on-the-Wold, Gloucestershire, 1985.

TODD, Daphne   b.1947
Painter. Born York. Studied at the Slade School of Fine Art, 1965-71. Visiting Tutor at Byam Shaw School of Art,

Plate 84. ALLAN WALTON, 1892-1948. *'Statue of Queen Victoria, Southend'*, exh. 1933. 30¼in. x 25¼in. Sally Hunter Fine Art, London.

Plate 85. BILLIE WATERS, 1896-1979. *'Still Life with Flowers and Shells'*. Oil on board. 19in. x 15½in. Sandra Lummis Fine Art, London.

434

Plate 86. TOM WOOD, b.1955. *'HRH The Prince of Wales'*, 1989. Oil on panel. 60in. x 62in. Smith Settle Fine Arts.

Plate 87. DORIS ZINKEISEN, b.1898. *'Wall Decoration for the Vestibule of the Royal Academy'*, c.1920. Oil on board. 11in. x 24in. Private Collection.

TOFT, Albert

1971-5. Director of Studies, Heatherley School of Art, 1980-6. 1984 elected member of the NEAC. 1985 elected RP. Has won many awards and exhibited in several group shows. A skilful portraitist with a fine grasp of subtle effects of light. Represented in the National Portrait Gallery, Royal Holloway Museum and Art Gallery and various university colleges. Her sitters include Dame Janet Baker. Represented by the RP.

TOFT, Albert   1862-1949

Sculptor. Born Birmingham, West Midlands. Studied at evening classes at Hanley School of Art and at Newcastle under Lyme School of Art. Apprenticed to Josiah Wedgwood and Sons. Moved to London and studied at South Kensington Schools, 1880-5. From 1885 exhibited at the RA. Commissions include the Boer War Memorial, Birmingham, 1905; statues of Queen Victoria for Leamington, Nottingham and South Shields, and war memorials, including the Royal Fusiliers, Holborn, 1922-4. Published *Modelling and Sculpture,* 1911.

TOLANSKY, Ottilie   1912-1977

Painter. Born Vienna, Austria. Studied at Reinmann Schule and the Berlin Academy of Fine Arts. 1933 moved to England, and began studying at Manchester Municipal School. She continued studying after the war at Hammersmith Art School. She regularly exhibited at the RA, with the NEAC and throughout the UK. 1979 the Mall Galleries held a major retrospective of her work; another retrospective was held at the Hurlingham Gallery, London. Painter of nudes, still lifes and flower pieces.

TOMBS, Sarah   b.1961

Sculptor. Studied at Wimbledon School of Art, 1981-4, Chelsea School of Art, 1984-5, and at the RCA, 1985-7, where he was awarded the Henry Moore Bursary. 1981 first exhibited at Cannizaro Park, Wimbledon, where she exhibited regularly until 1986. 1986 appointed Artist-in-Residence by British Steel, and 1988 by Nicholas Chamberlaine Comprehensive School.

TOMKINS, Ridnan   b.1941

Painter. Born Weymouth, Dorset. Studied at Poole School of Art, 1958-60, West of England College of Art, Bristol, 1960-2, Wimbledon School of Art, 1964-5, and RA, 1965-8. 1972 first solo exhibition at the Greenwich Theatre. 1979 exhibition of recent paintings held at the Whitechapel Art Gallery. Paints colour-field paintings which allude to landscape spaces.

TOMLIN, Stephen   1901-1937

Sculptor. Born London. Studied at New College, Oxford, for a short time before taking up sculpture. Apprenticed for two years to Frank Dobson.* He specialised in portrait busts and owing to his association with Bloomsbury made memorable likenesses of Virginia Woolf and Lytton Strachey, casts of which are both now in the National Portrait Gallery.

TONKS, Henry   1862-1937

Painter, teacher, surgeon. Born Solihull, West Midlands. Began to study medicine, 1880, and in 1888 was appointed Senior Medical Officer at Royal Free Hospital, London. Also began to study painting with Fred Brown* at the Westminster Art School in his spare time. 1891 began to exhibit with the NEAC and continued until 1930. 1892

appointed Assistant Professor at the Slade School of Art. 1905 first solo exhibition at the Carfax Gallery. 1910 published *Elementary Propositions in Painting and Drawing.* 1911 moved to Vale Avenue, Chelsea where he lived for the rest of his life. Worked on the development of plastic surgery during the First World War, as well as receiving the appointment of an Official War Artist. 1918 appointed Slade Professor. Wrote *Wander Years* (published 1929). 1930 retired from the Slade. 1936 retrospective exhibition held at the Tate Gallery. Maintained an imposing presence at the Slade for many years and is mentioned in almost every artists' memoir of that period.

Bibl: Joseph Hone, *The Life of Henry Tonks,* Wm. Heinemann, London, 1939.

TOPOLSKI, Feliks   1907-1989

Painter and draughtsman. Born Warsaw, Poland. Studied at the Academy of Art, Warsaw, 1925-30, also in Italy and Paris, 1938. Settled in England, 1935. Official Polish war artist, 1940-5; painted air-raid subjects in London and also worked with the armies in Russia. Became a naturalised British subject, 1947. Developed a habit of working at speed, in an expressionist style, his drawings often having the quality of something seen and immediately reported. His studio, under Hungerford Bridge, became a meeting place for friends and associates. It was there he painted his portrait of Edith Sitwell, now in the collection of the University of Texas at Austin. Exhibited internationally and was widely acclaimed for his vivid rendering of the passing scene. 1949-50 travelled around the world collecting material about people, to be used in his work. 1951 Cavalcade of Commonwealth mural shown at Festival of Britain exhibition, South Bank, London. 1953 started *Topolski's Chronicle,* a global publication, which was displayed throughout the world. 1958-60 painted 'The Coronation of Elizabeth II' for Buckingham Palace. 1961-2 painted twenty portraits of English writers for the University of Texas.

TOREN, Amikam   b.1945

Sculptor. Born Israel. Lives and works in London. 1973 first solo exhibition at Annely Juda Fine Art. 1979 published *Replacing* to coincide with an exhibition at the ICA. 1990 retrospective exhibition to tour Israel and Britain.

TORMEY, Richard   b.1959

Sculptor. Studied at Cleveland College of Art, 1982-3, Norwich School of Art, 1983-6, and at the RA Schools, 1986-9. Awards include: the Norwich County Council Award for Sculpture, 1984, and the De Segonzac Travelling Scholarship to Peru, 1989. First exhibited at the Norwich School of Art Gallery, 1984.

TOROK, Karl   b.1950

Painter. Born Bradford, Yorkshire. Studied at Bradford College of Art, 1968-72. 1973 first solo exhibition at New Lane Gallery, Bradford. 1979 exhibition entitled 'In a Summer Garden' held at Cartwright Hall, Bradford. Became part of the Yorkshire-based group, the New Arcadians. Works mostly in watercolour and has made topiary gardens his major subject.

TOWNER, Donald   1903-1985

Painter. Born Eastbourne, Sussex. His great uncle bequeathed the money to found the Towner Art Gallery there which opened in 1923. Studied at Eastbourne School of Art, 1919-23, then the RCA, 1923-6. From the 1920s he began to exhibit in mixed London exhibitions. In recent years he has become a ceramic historian of repute. 1979 published his autobiography *Reflections,* in America. 1982 solo exhibition of Sussex Paintings held at Towner Art Gallery, Eastbourne. Represented in RA collection.

TOWNSEND, Patricia   b.1926
Painter. Born in England but began her painting career in Mexico. Has exhibited her work in New York. First solo exhibition in England at the Trafford Gallery, 1962.

TOWNSEND, William   1909-1973
Painter. Born London. Studied at the Slade School, 1926-9. 1931 first solo exhibition at the Bloomsbury Gallery. 1940-6 saw war service as a battery officer in the Royal Artillery. 1946-9 taught part time at Camberwell School of Art, then joined the teaching staff at Slade. 1957 appointed senior lecturer. During 1960s, he broadcast on BBC on townscapes, and was occupied with journalism. 1966 Head of Painting, Banff Summer School, Canada. 1968 Professor, University College, London, responsible for running the post-graduate department at the Slade School. 1976 retrospective exhibition at Tate Gallery and published *The Townsend Journals,* extracts from diaries. 1978 a further retrospective exhibition held at Royal West of England Academy, Bristol.

TOYNBEE, Lawrence   b.1922
Painter. Youngest son of Arnold Toynbee, the historian. Studied at the Ruskin School of Drawing, Oxford, and then taught art, firstly at the Ruskin School, Oxford School of Art, and Bradford. Solo exhibitions at the Leicester Galleries, 1961, 1963, 1965 and 1967. Executed several mural paintings, notably for the Duke of Norfolk. Likes to paint sporting events, such as cricket, rugby and football.

TRAHERNE, Margaret
Painter who also works with fabric collages and stained glass. Studied at the RCA and later at the Central School of Art. Designed stained glass windows for Coventry Cathedral, the Roman Catholic Cathedral in Liverpool and Manchester Cathedral. From the 1960s included in group exhibitions in Oxford, London and Edinburgh. 1967 solo exhibition at the Bear Lane Gallery, Oxford.

TRAPP, George   b.1948
Painter and sculptor. Born Trowbridge, Wiltshire. Studied at Hammersmith College of Art, 1968-72. 1972 first solo exhibition at Redcliffe Road, London. 1970s worked in the graphics business and as a model maker in the 1980s. 1983 solo exhibition of boxes at the Cylinder Gallery, entitled 'In Case of Art Break Glass'.

TREMLETT, David   b.1945
Sculptor. Born Cornwall. Studied at Falmouth College of Art, 1962-3, Birmingham College of Art, 1963-6, and the RCA, 1966-9. Included in mixed exhibitions from 1969, which was also the year of his first solo show at the Grabowski Gallery, London. Most recent major exhibition at the Serpentine Gallery, 1989. His work has progressed from object sculpture, through line drawings to monumental coloured wall drawings. Simplifies into graphic imagery and symbols things seen while undertaking long travels. Work in the Tate Gallery.

TREVELYAN, Julian   1910-1988
Painter and etcher. Born Dorking, Surrey. Educated at Cambridge and became a member of a group known as 'Experiments' and contributed to its magazine a text devoted to dreams. Later, he rented a studio in Montparnasse, Paris, while attending the Académie Moderne and S.W. Hayter's* school, Atelier 17, 1931-4, where he learnt printmaking. 1934 returned to England and exhibited surrealist works at the Bloomsbury Gallery. In his own paintings he ran through a variety of experiments. 1936 Roland Penrose selected three of his works for the International Surrealist Exhibition and he was one of twenty British artists represented there. 1938 he left the British Surrealist Movement and became involved with 'Mass Observation'. One of its projects was based in Bolton and attempted to record the daily lives of individuals. Other artists involved were Humphrey Spender,* William Coldstream,* Graham Bell* and Humphrey Jennings.* When war broke out he became involved in camouflage work. After the war he moved into Durham Wharf, Hammersmith, where his boat race parties became famous events. After the break-up of his marriage to the potter, Ursula Darwin, he married the painter, Mary Fedden.* He never lost his enthusiasm for the dreamlike and fantastic or for the use of such unconventional materials as flotsam and jetsam. Elected RA. Published *Indigo Days,* 1957, *The Artist and His World,* 1960, *Etching,* 1963, and *A Place, a State,* 1975. 1988 a retrospective was held at Waterman's Art Centre, Brentford. (Plate 82, p.430.)

TRIVICK, Henry Houghton   fl. from c.1940
Painter and lithographer. A friend of Stanley Spencer* and, like him, came from Cookham. Taught lithography at Regent Street Polytechnic. Exhibited at leading London galleries. Chairman of the Senefelder Group. Represented in the V & A, Ashmolean and Imperial War Museums.

TROOSTWYK, David   b.1929
Sculptor. Born London. Studied at St. Albans College of Art and the RCA. Included in group exhibitions from 1955. First solo show at Southampton Art Gallery, 1966. Worked with PVC in the 1960s, then made sign paintings and sound works with tape cassettes. Prizewinner, John Moores Liverpool exhibition, 1969. Showed at Matts Gallery, London, 1979. Work in the Tate Gallery.

TROTTER, Josephine   b.1940
Painter. Born Peshawar, India (now in Pakistan). Came to England and was taught painting privately by Maurice Field, then studied at St. Alban's School of Art, 1957-9, and Chelsea School of Art, 1959-61. Married and had five children, but continued to paint, exhibiting regularly in the 1970s. Her most recent solo exhibition was held at the New Grafton Gallery, 1987.

TRYON, Wyndham   1883-1942
Painter. Born London. Studied at Slade School, 1906-11. In 1911 and 1914 he visited Spain in the company of Darsie Japp* and made many return visits thereafter. First solo exhibition held at the XXI Gallery, London, 1919. Became a member of the NEAC, 1920.

TUCKER, William   b.1935
Sculptor. Born Cairo, Egypt. Studied History at Oxford University, 1955-8. Studied art at Central School of Art and Crafts and St. Martin's School of Art. Awarded Peter

WILLIAM TUCKER, b.1935.
'Horse IV', 1986. Bronze edition
of six. 35in. x 16in. x 26in.
Annely Juda Fine Art.

Stuyvesant Foundation travel bursary, 1965. Appointed Gregory Fellow at Leeds University, 1968. Since 1976 has occupied various teaching posts in Canada and America. Came to the fore in the 1960s as one of the New Generation sculptors, working with clear, simple shapes influenced by his interest in gestalt psychology. An influential teacher and theoretician, he selected 'The Condition of Sculpture' exhibition held at the Hayward Gallery, 1975. He also published *The Language of Sculpture,* 1974 (retitled *Early Modern Sculpture* for the American edition).

TUKE, Henry Scott   1858-1929

Painter. Born York. Studied at Slade, 1875-9, and visited France, 1878, returning to study under Jean-Paul Laurens in Paris, 1881. 1882 he met Bastien-Lepage. A founder-member of the NEAC and associated with the Newlyn School. Exhibited at the RA from 1879 and elected RA, 1914. His favourite subject was nude boys disporting themselves in boats and water.

TUNNARD, John   1900-1971

Painter. Born Sandy, Bedfordshire. Studied textile design at RCA, 1919-23. During the 1920s he worked as a designer in the textile industry and played jazz on a semi-professional basis. 1929 started painting and came under the influence of Surrealism in the mid-1930s. Settled in Cornwall in 1930 where he established a hand-blocked silk printing business. Solo exhibition held at the Redfern Gallery, London, 1933. Served as a coastguard in Cornwall, 1940-5. Taught design at Penzance School of Art, 1948-64. The natural world remained his starting point, though music and mathematics were also important sources. His paintings of the late 1940s and '50s, in which landscape motifs reappear, are more readily legible than his pre-war work.

Bibl: *John Tunnard,* Arts Council, London, 1977.

JOHN TUNNARD, 1900-1971. *'French Boats, Newlyn'*, 1933. 16in. x 20in. Michael Parkin Fine Art Ltd.

TURNBULL, Alison   b.1956
Painter. Born Bogota, Colombia. Studied at Academia Arjona, Madrid, 1975-7, West Surrey College of Art, 1977-8, and Bath Academy of Art, Corsham, 1978-81. Awarded a Greater London Arts Award, 1988. First solo exhibition at the Anne Berthoud Gallery, London, 1989. Painter of geometric abstracts in cool colours.

TURNBULL, Michael   b.1950
Painter. Born Gosforth, Northumberland. Trained at Sunderland Art College and RCA. Since 1976 has taught in Gateshead where currently he is Head of Art at St. Edmund Campion School.

TURNBULL, William   b.1922
Painter and sculptor. Born Dundee, Scotland. Left school at fifteen and worked as illustrator for the D.C. Thompson publishing house, attending classes at art school in the evenings. Served in RAF during the Second World War and then studied at Slade School of Fine Art, 1946-8. Lived in Paris, 1948-50, seeing much of fellow Slade student, Eduardo Paolozzi* and meeting several leading French artists. First exhibited sculpture at the Hanover Gallery, London, 1950 (with Paolozzi) and showed sculpture and paintings there, 1952. In the same year was represented in 'New Aspects of British Sculpture' at the Venice Biennale. Founder member of the Independent Group at the ICA and contributed to the 'This is Tomorrow' exhibition at the Whitechapel Art Gallery, 1956. On executive committee of the 'Situation' exhibition, RBA Galleries, London,

1960, and thereafter associated with a minimalist approach to both sculpture and painting. Has occupied various teaching positions, in England and America. Was given a retrospective exhibition at the Tate Gallery, 1973. Married to the artist, Kim Lim,* and is represented by Waddington's, London.

TURNELL, Kenneth   b.1948
Sculptor. Born Sheffield, Yorkshire. Studied at Hornsey School of Art, Maidstone School of Art and Chelsea School of Art. 1978 sculptor at Grizedale Forest. Works with rough-hewn segments of wood in abstract configurations that yet suggest the human figure. Represented in the Arts Council collection.

TURNER, Alfred   1874-1940
Sculptor. Born London, son of the sculptor Charles Halsey Turner. Studied at South London Technical Art School, Lambeth and the RA Schools, 1895-8. Worked in the studio of Harry Bates.* Exhibited at the RA, 1898-1937. 1902 commissioned to make two figures for Fishmongers' Hall, London. 1901-2 commissioned to make three monuments to Queen Victoria; for Delhi, Tynemouth and Sheffield. Made a figural group for the façade of the Old Bailey, 1905-6 and designed some metalwork there. 1907-34 taught at the Central School of Art. 1912 made a statue of Owain Glyndwr for the Welsh Heroes series at Cardiff City Hall. Greatly occupied with war memorials from 1919 on. Elected ARA, 1922, RA, 1931. 1937-8 Head of Department of Painted and Architectural Decoration at Central School of Art. Work in the Tate Gallery.

TURNER, Donald Chisholm 1903-1985
Painter. Studied at Royal College of Art under William Rothenstein,* 1923-7. Exhibited at RA, NEAC and held several solo exhibitions. Taught at Christ's Hospital during the Second World War. An accomplished flautist. Lived in Hampstead after the war. Represented in RA collection, Sheffield City Art Galleries and elsewhere. Primarily a landscape artist, who wrote several scholarly volumes on eighteenth century cream-coloured earthenware and was for many years secretary of the English Ceramics Circle and for some twenty years editor of *Transactions*.

TURNER, Jacquie b.1959
Painter. Born Kent. Studied at Winchester School of Art, 1979-81, under the direction of Gillian Ayres.* After working part-time in arts administration, she became a full-time painter, 1987. Works predominantly with still life and exhibits at Cadogan Contemporary, London.

TURNER, Winifred 1903-1983
Sculptor. Born London, the daughter of Alfred Turner.* Studied at Central School, 1921-4 and the RA Schools, 1924-9. Exhibited at the RA, 1924-62. Her work in the 1920s was indebted to archaic Greek ideals. Unlike her father, she was primarily a modeller rather than a carver. FRBS, 1930. Taught at the Central School in the 1930s and early 1940s. Married the sculptor Humphrey Thomas Paget, 1942. Work in the Tate Gallery.

TUTE, Sophie b.1960
Painter. Studied at Wimbledon College of Art, 1980-1, Ruskin School of Fine Art and Drawing, Oxford, 1981-4, and RCA, 1984-7. Exhibited with Graham Giles, at Cadogan Contemporary, London, 1988.

TWEED, John 1869-1933
Sculptor. Born Glasgow, Scotland. Studied at Glasgow School of Art, then Lambeth School of Art and the RA Schools. 1893 went to Paris to see Rodin and worked with the French sculptor Falguiere. Executed commissions for Cecil Rhodes from 1893. Exhibited at the RA from 1894. Introduced Rodin to the British public, 1902. Executed many war memorials after 1919. Memorial exhibition held at the Imperial Institute, London, 1934. Work in the Tate Gallery.

Bibl: Lendal Tweed, *John Tweed: Sculptor,* London, 1936.

TYE, Roderick b.1958
Sculptor. Studied at Coventry Art School, 1977-8, Ravensbourne College of Art, 1978-9, Leeds Polytechnic, 1979-81, and Slade School of Fine Art, 1982-4. Since 1982 included in mixed exhibitions. 1984-5 Gulbenkian Rome Scholar in Sculpture. First solo exhibition, 'The Promised Land and the Possible', held at Atlantis Gallery, London; others include 'Il Fume e Rosso', at Anna Bornholt Gallery, London, 1989.

TYRWHITT, Ursula 1878-1966
Painter. Born Nazeing, Essex. Studied at the Slade School, 1893-4, where she became a friend of Gwen John,* and with her, studied in Paris at the Atelier Colarossi. Also studied in Rome at the British Academy and returned to the Slade, 1911-12. Became a member of the NEAC, 1914 and of the Oxford Art Society, 1917. Did not exhibit very regularly and is best known for her sensitive flower pictures. Lived for a time at Puerto de la Cruz, Tenerife.

TYSON, Ian b.1933
Painter, sculptor and printmaker. Born Wallasey, Cheshire. Studied at Birkenhead School of Art and the RA Schools. First solo show at Ashgate Gallery, Farnham, 1961. First prize at Welsh Arts Council St. David's exhibition, 1964. Included in major group exhibitions in Britain and Europe from the 1960s on. Interested in the relationship between text and image and the ambiguity of surface. Work in many public collections in the UK and the USA.

TYZACK, Michael b.1933
Painter. Born Sheffield, Yorkshire. Studied at Sheffield College of Art, 1950-2, Slade School, 1952-6, and won a French Government Scholarship, 1956-7. 1964-8 Lecturer, Cardiff College of Art. 1965 prizewinner, John Moores Liverpool exhibition. 1966 first solo exhibition held at Axiom Gallery, London. 1969 Welsh Arts Council Commission award. Interested in chromatic situations in terms of the painting's surface and the external shape of the canvas. 1971-6 Visiting Artist at the University of Iowa, USA. 1976 Professor of Fine Arts, College of Charleston, Iowa. Exhibited at Francis Aronson Gallery, Atlanta, Georgia, 1978.

EUAN UGLOW, b.1932. *'Zagi'*,
1981-2. 58 ½ in. x 41 ½ in.
Browse & Darby Ltd.

UDDIN, Shafique   b.1962
Painter. Born Borodari, Bangladesh, where he spent his
childhood. No formal art training. Paints from memory,
scenes from his childhood or things seen in London where
he now lives. First solo exhibition held at the Whitechapel
Art Gallery, London, 1979; others include one at the
Salvatore Ala Gallery, New York. Has received recognition
by the art establishment, and was included in the 'British
Art Show' held at the Hayward Gallery and elsewhere,
1990, but has also been included in 'Outsider' shows,
including 'In Another World', at Hayward Gallery,
1987-8.

UGLOW, Euan   b.1932
Painter. Born London. Studied at Camberwell School of
Art and Crafts, 1948-51. Awarded State Scholarship to
Slade School of Art, 1951 and Spanish State Scholarship to
Spain, 1952. 1953 awarded Abbey Minor Scholarship and
travelled to France, Holland, Belgium and Italy. 1961 first
one-artist exhibition at Beaux Arts Gallery. Teaches part-
time at Slade and Camberwell, in both schools associated
with a method of painting descended from the Euston Road
School and which Uglow upholds.

UHLMAN, Fred   b.1901
Painter. Born Stuttgart, West Germany. Initially studied
law and became a barrister, 1927-33. Began painting in
1934 and was self taught. First exhibited at Galleries Le
Niveau and Jeanne Castel, Paris, 1936. Settled in London
in the late 1930s and did much to assist refugees to Britain.
Also collected primitive carvings, eventually donating his
collection to the University of Newcastle upon Tyne.

UNDERHILL, Liz

Included in the collections of Musée de Grenoble, French Government, National Gallery, Sydney, National Gallery of New Zealand, National Gallery of Wales, British Museum, CAS of Wales, V & A, and Fitzwilliam Museum, Cambridge.

UNDERHILL, Liz   b.1948

Painter. Born Worthing, Sussex. Studied at Gloucestershire College of Art, 1966-7, and at Portsmouth College of Art, 1967-70. First solo exhibition at the Stamford Gallery, Stamford, 1975, followed by a second solo exhibition in the same year at South Holland Centre, Spalding, Lincolnshire.

UNDERWOOD, Leon   1890-1975

Painter and sculptor. Studied at Regent Street Polytechnic, 1907-10, and at the RCA, 1910-12. Served in the Artillery, 1914-18. Returned to study at the Slade, 1918-19. 1920 opened Brook Green School of Art and began to practise sculpture; in the same year he was awarded the Prix de Rome which led him to travel to Paris and Iceland, 1923. 1925-6 travelled to USA, where he illustrated books, published his own book of verse and prose, and engraved and painted. 1927 sent to Mexico, where he studied Aztec and Mayan art and illustrated *Red Tiger*. 1931 founded *The Island,* which ran for four issues. 1934 republished *Art for Heaven's Sake.* 1939-45 worked in the camouflage unit. During 1944 he travelled in West Africa, collecting and studying African art, which led him to publish *Figures in Wood of West Africa,* 1947, *Masks of West Africa,* 1948, and *Bronzes of West Africa,* 1949. 1955 commissioned to produce a stained glass window and reredos for the Church of St. Michael and All Angels, New Marston, Oxfordshire. 1958 published *Bronze Age Technology in Western Asia and Northern Europe.* 1961 elected Honorary member of the Society of British Sculptors. 1921 first solo exhibition at the Chenil Gallery, London. Underwood's travels in Mexico and West Africa had a profound influence on his work, and formed the inspiration for many of his paintings, engravings and colour prints. (Plate 83, p.431.)

Bibl: Christopher Neve, *Leon Underwood,* Thames & Hudson, London, 1974.

UNSWORTH, Jim   b.1958

Sculptor. Born Wigan, Lancashire. Studied at Reading University, 1976-80. First solo exhibitions held at Dan Sullivan's Gallery, Bedford, and AIR Gallery, London, 1984. Recent shows include a joint exhibition with Paul Ryan* at Winchester Gallery, 1989. His abstract steel assemblages are usually slightly larger in height than the average person and have an animated appearance. Titles, such as *The Travelling Trombonist* or *The Travelling Waiter,* further enhance the expressive, jokey and wayward nature of his work. Inspired to some extent by the American sculptor, David Smith, and possibly also by African masks, his art is formally complex yet defies the more usual expectations that accompany abstract steel sculpture.

UNSWORTH, Peter   b.1937

Painter. Born Co. Durham. Studied at Middlesbrough School of Art and St. Martin's School of Art. He lives and paints in Ibiza and London. First solo exhibition at the Piccadilly Gallery, London, 1963. Recent solo exhibitions include one at the Piccadilly Gallery, 1987.

UNWIN, Francis   1885-1925

Lithographer and etcher. Born Stalbridge, Dorset. Studied at Winchester School of Art and at the Slade, 1902-5. 1907-8 travelled in Europe; in 1908 he made drawings of the interiors of tombs in Egypt for an American archaeological publication. 1912-13 travelled in Italy. Member of the NEAC to which he regularly contributed. One of the founder members of the Society of Print-makers. 1920 and 1921 due to illness, he travelled to the Alps, where he made many studies of the mountains. 1924 first solo exhibition at St. George's Gallery, London. Included in the collection of the British Museum. 1926 memorial exhibition held at St. George's Gallery, London.

UPTON, Michael   b.1938

Painter. Born Birmingham, West Midlands. Studied at Birmingham College of Art, 1954-8, and at the RA Schools, 1958-62. Awards include Leverhulme Scholarship, 1960; Abbey Scholarship, Rome Scholarship to Italy, 1962; Cassandra Foundation Award, New York, 1971 and South West Arts Major Award, 1981. First solo exhibition at the Piccadilly Gallery, London, 1966. Regularly exhibits with the Anne Berthoud Gallery, London, in group and solo exhibitions; he held a solo exhibition at this gallery, 1989. Uses close toned pastel colours to reinforce the two-dimensional design within his figurative and still life compositions. Included in the collections of Arts Council of Great Britain, British Council and Government Art Collection.

Bibl: *Michael Upton, Paintings 1977-87,* Yale Center for British Art, 1987.

UPWARD, Peter   b.1932

Painter. Born Melbourne, Australia. Studied in Melbourne, and under John Passmore in Sydney. 1958 first solo exhibition at the Museum of Modern Art, Melbourne. 1962 came to England and held first solo exhibition at the Rowan Gallery, London. Other solo exhibitions include one at the Rowan Gallery, 1964.

URIE, Joseph   b.1947

Painter. Born Glasgow, Scotland. Studied at Duncan of Jordanstone College of Art, Dundee, 1977-81, and at the RA Schools, 1981-4. Awards include the Chalmer-Jervis Prize and the British Institute Prize, 1980, Farquhar Reid Travelling Scholarship, 1981, Vincent Harris Prize, 1982, the Dorothy M. Morgan Prize, 1983, and the J. Van Bueren Wittman Prize, 1984. First solo exhibition at Howard Gardens Gallery, Cardiff, 1984. Recent solo exhibitions include one at the Roger Francis Gallery, London, 1985. Included in the collections of Duncan of Jordanstone College of Art and Sir John Sainsbury Company Collection.

KEITH VAUGHAN, 1912-1976. *'Fishermen and bathers'*, 1951. 30in. x 50in. Private Collection.

VALENTINE, Tony   b.1939
Painter. Studied at Edinburgh College of Art, 1958-9 and 1963-4, and at Glasgow College of Art, 1959-63. He moved to live and work in France, 1967. First solo exhibition at the Gardner Centre Gallery, Brighton, 1970.

VALETTE, Adolphe   1876-1942
Painter. Born St. Etiénne, France. Worked as a painter and engraver, while studying in Lyon. Attended evening classes at the Ecole des Arts Décoratifs, 1900-3. 1903 won travelling scholarship to Japan. 1904 travelled to England and studied at the Birkbeck Institute, London. 1905 moved to Manchester and attended evening classes at the Muncipal School of Art. He also worked for a printing firm, designing calendars and piece tickets to go on velvet goods destined for the Far East. 1906 became an Art Master at the Manchester School of Art. 1912 Founder Member of the Society of Modern Artists, with Rowley Smart and Margaret Nicholls. 1918 first solo exhibition at Finnigan's Showroom. 1908-22 he painted many scenes of Manchester, catching this city under grey atmospheric conditions which reflect his interest in Impressionism. His portraits were executed in a more academic style with a brighter palette. 1928 he retired to France. Included in the collections of Manchester City Art Gallery and Musée St. Etienne. He was a teacher of L.S. Lowry,* who paid a large tribute to Valette's influence.

VALLEY, John   b.1941
Painter. Born Armagh, Northern Ireland. Studied at Belfast College of Art, 1959-60, and at Edinburgh College of Art, 1961-3. Awards include Edinburgh College of Art travelling scholarship, 1963, Andrew Grant Bequest Minor and Major Travelling Scholarships, and the Clason-Harvie Bequest Travelling Scholarship, 1964. Travelled widely in southern Europe and Morocco. 1963 first solo exhibition at Studio 25, followed by a second solo exhibition there, 1964. Derives inspiration for his paintings from traditional Irish music and Irish mythology. Included in the collections of the Arts Council of Northern Ireland and the Young Irish Artists' foundation.

VAN DER HEIDE, Bé   b.1933
Painter. Born Enschede, The Netherlands. Studied at Academy of Fine Arts, Enschede, 1956-60. From 1960 lived in Montreal and Toronto, Canada, and Istanbul, Turkey. Studied in Canada, 1975-80, followed by travel in the Middle East and Africa. 1982 moved to London. 1978 first solo exhibition at the Powerhouse Gallery, Montreal, Quebec, Canada. 1987 first solo exhibition in Great Britain at the Showroom Gallery, London. Included in the collections of City of Enschede, Bibliothèque National de Quebec, the National Library of Canada, Ottawa, Ontario, Carlton University, Ottawa, Ontario and the Quebec Government.

VAN DE WAL, Ineke   b.1954
Painter. Born Ophemert, The Netherlands. Moved to Great Britain, 1972. Studied Art History at University of Wales, Bangor, 1972-3. Won South West Arts Award, 1987. First exhibited at Double Vision Galleries, Exeter.

Bibl: Jenny Pery, 'Ineke van der Wal', *Women Artists Slide Library Journal,* October/November, 1987.

VAN INGEN, Jennifer   b.1942
Painter. Born Whitley, Surrey. Studied at Ealing School of Art, 1959-62. Travelled extensively in Europe, and took a studio in Paris, 1963. First solo exhibition at the Drian Galleries, London, 1969.

VAN RIEL, Christa   b.1963
Painter. Born The Hague, The Netherlands. Moved to Great Britain in the late 1960s. Studied at Wimbledon School of Art, 1981-3. 1983-7 worked with the mentally ill and disabled, teaching art in residential care. 1984 first exhibited in '8 young painters', Chertsey, Surrey. Since 1987 has also worked as a scene painter on productions such as *The Hooded Fang* at the Unicorn, London and on the set for *Prince Lovesexy* Concert, Oslo, Norway, 1988.

VAN WIECK, Nigel   b.1947
Painter and pastellist. Born Bexley, Kent. Studied at Hornsey College of Art, 1968-71. 1971 first solo exhibition held at Marjorie Parr Gallery, London. Since has had regular exhibitions, at home and in New York. 1988 held a solo exhibition, 'Working Girls', at the Lefevre Gallery: narrative pastels mostly set in Manhattan's night clubs, bars and bedrooms, juxtaposing naked or semi-naked women with clothed, often predatory men. The viewpoint, however, is less harsh than sentimental, less critical than seductive.

VAUGHAN, Keith   1912-1976
Painter. Born Selsey Bill, Sussex. Worked for Lintas, an advertising agency, 1931-9 when, with the prospect of war ahead, decided to paint for a year and did so at Shere, in Surrey. Registered as conscientious objector, but later joined the Pioneer Corps. He was placed in a prisoner of war camp in Yorkshire, until demobilisation in 1946, as a clerk and assistant German interpreter. 1942 exhibited drawings at the Lefevre Gallery, London, and paintings, in his first solo exhibition, at the same gallery, 1946. 1946-52 shared a flat with John Minton,* then moved to Belsize Park. 1952 he made his first 'Assembly of Figures', a theme that became a major, recurring one in his work. Travelled widely. Held a retrospective at Royal West of England Academy, Bristol, and another at the Whitechapel Gallery, London, 1962. He first began keeping journals in 1939 and returned to them intermittently; an illustrated selection was first published in 1966 and another, unillustrated, 1989 (John Murray). Vaughan's interest in the human figure — formalised and ceremonial — is married to a formal control, inspired by De Staël and Cézanne, among others. He is the subject of a forthcoming monograph by Malcolm Yorke.

VAUGHAN, Michael   b.1938
Painter. Born Shipley, Yorkshire. Studied at Bradford Regional College of Art, 1956-60, and RA Schools, 1960-3. 1963-4 Fellowship in Painting at Manchester College of Art. Has taught at both Manchester and Hornsey Colleges of Art. First exhibited at a 'New Generation' show at the Whitechapel Art Gallery, 1964. Was included in the 'British Painting '74' held at the Hayward Gallery, London, 1974. After a period of depression when he worked only in black and white, he returned to the use of colour, recreating family photographs in terms of paint.

VAUX, Marc   b.1932
Painter. Born Swindon, Wiltshire. Studied at Swindon School of Art, 1954-7, and at the Slade, 1957-60. 1960 awarded Boise Scholarship. Travelled in Italy and in 1961 worked in the Lithographic Studio of Jean Pons, Paris. 1963 first solo exhibition at the Grabowski Gallery, London. Included in the collections of the Arts Council of Great Britain, V & A, City Art Gallery, Bradford, City Art Gallery, Leeds, CAS, Tate Gallery, York Art Gallery, Graves Art Gallery, Sheffield, Museum of Modern Art, Belgrade. Recent solo exhibitions include one at the Park Gallery, Cheltenham, 1989.

VELLACOTT, Elizabeth   b.1905
Painter. Born Grays, Essex. 1908 her family moved to Highgate, its woods leaving their imprint on the artist's memory. 1912 the family moved to Cambridge and then back to London, 1920. Studied at Willesden School of Art, 1922-5, and RCA, 1925-9. Whilst at the RCA she reacted against the academic styles of her day and found stimulus in the decorative art in the V & A Museum. 1931 became assistant scene painter at the Old Vic. 1933 returned to Cambridge, designing sets for the Cambridge University Musical Society. Began to paint again during the war. Her paintings place figures in landscapes or interiors by use of pure linear contour and the minimum of modelling. Her figurative scenes are mostly imaginative though based on experience. Bryan Robertson has drawn a parallel between her imaginative scenes and certain aspects of Iris Murdoch's novels. 1954 founder-member of Cambridge Society of Painters and Sculptors. Around 1960 began to form her concept of 'inside and outside' form and the way they can be related through the portrayal of doors and windows. 1963 abandoned the use of canvas and began to paint consistently on wood panels. Exhibits regularly at the New Art Centre, London, and had a retrospective at Kettle's Yard, Cambridge and the Warwick Arts Trust, London, 1981.

Bibl: *Elizabeth Vellacott. Paintings and Drawings 1942-81,* Kettle's Yard, Cambridge, 1981.

VENTON, Patrick
Painter. Studied at Birmingham College of Art, 1946-50. Held solo exhibition at the Ikon Gallery, Birmingham in the 1960s. Represented in Birmingham, Bradford and Liverpool City Art Galleries.

VERITY, Charlotte   b.1954
Painter. Studied at Slade School of Art, 1973-7. Awarded Boise Travelling Scholarship to Italy, 1978. Married to Christopher Le Brun.* First solo exhibition at the Anne Berthoud Gallery, London, 1984, and a second exhibition at the same gallery, 1988. Included in the collections of the Eastern Arts Association and the Arts Council of Great Britain.

VERNEY, Sir John   b.1913
Painter. Born London. Studied at the Ruskin School of Art and the Architectural Association. Served in the Army during the Second World War and was awarded the MC. Put his war experience into book form in *Going to the Wars* and *A Dinner of Herbs*. Divides his time between painting, writing and illustrating. Showed at the Redfern, Leicester, Zwemmers and AIA Galleries. Solo exhibitions at the Ashgate Gallery, Farnham, 1962 and 1964. Inherited his title, 1949.

VERREN, Angela   b.1930
Painter. Born Hampstead, London. Studied at King's College, London University. Has exhibited in Cambridge

ELIZABETH VELLACOTT, b.1905. 'Adam and Eve after Uccello', 1985. 25 ½ in. x 50in. New Art Centre, London.

and London and held a solo exhibition at the Crane Kalman Gallery, 1978. Her interest in texture grounds and in forms abstracted from nature and objects reflects the influence of Ben Nicholson.*

VEZELAY, Paule   1892-1984
Painter, sculptor, printmaker and fabric designer. Born Marjorie Watson-Williams at Clifton, Bristol. Studied at Bristol School of Art and London School of Art under George Belcher,* also lithography at Chelsea Polytechnic. The influence of Aubrey Beardsley upon her work gave way to French Post-Impressionism after her first visit to Paris, 1920. Member of the London Group, 1922-32. 1926 settled in Paris and adopted the name Paule Vezelay. Closely associated with André Masson, Jean Arp and Sophie Tauber-Arp, among others. Experimented with abstraction, making her first non-referential works, 1928-9. 1934 joined Société Abstraction-Création in Paris

and shared its commitment to international abstract art. 1936 began using wire for boxed constructions and free-standing sculptures called 'Lines in Space'. Her career was interrupted by the war. Returned to England and spent second half of her life working in isolation in London, making reliefs, painting and designing non-figurative textiles. 1983 was given a small retrospective at the Tate Gallery.

Bibl: *Paule Vezelay,* Tate Gallery, London, 1983; Interview with Germaine Greer in *Women of Our Century,* ed. Leonie Caldecott, 1984.

VILAINCOUR, Leon   b.1923
Painter and printmaker. Born Cracow, Poland, of French-Polish parentage, his childhood was spent mostly between Poland and France. 1940 he came to England and volunteered for the army. 1945-7 he gained an ex-service scholarship to Central School of Art. First solo exhibition

VIRGILS, Katherine

held at New Art Centre, London, 1964. Another held at the Serpentine Gallery, London, 1983. Exhibits at the RA.

Bibl: *Leon Vilaincour: Paintings 1968-83,* Serpentine Gallery, London, 1983, with an interview with Nick Wadley.

VIRGILS, Katherine   b.1954
Painter. Born Houston, Texas, USA. Studied at Brighton College of Art, 1974-5, Ravensbourne College of Art, 1976-9, and RCA, 1979-81. 1983, Oxford Arts Council, Artist-in-Residence. 1987, Artist-in-Residence, the Burren Project, Ireland. First solo exhibition, 'Heads, Faces and Elevations', held at Camden Arts Centre, London, 1983; also exhibits at Thumb Gallery, London.

VIRTUE, John   b.1947
Draughtsman and painter. Born Accrington, Lancashire. 1964 won first prize *Sunday Mirror* painting exhibition. Studied at Slade School of Fine Art, 1965-9, where he was taught by Frank Auerbach.* 1966 won Walter Neurath prize for painting awarded by Thames & Hudson publishers. 1970-7 taught part-time then began painting full-time. Has concentrated as an artist singlemindedly on Green Haworth, a small village on the edge of the Pennine moorland, to which he moved in 1971. Eventually rejected paint in favour of a dense network of lines drawn with pen and ink. Worked as a postman for seven years and deliberately removed himself from contact with the world of art. 1980 began laying his drawings on hardboard in monumental grid formations. 1981 received an Arts Council Major Award and in 1983 was a major prizewinner in the 4th Tolly Cobbold exhibition. Solo exhibitions at Lisson Gallery, London, 1985, 1986 and 1990. Included in 'Six Painters' at Max Protetch Gallery, New York, 1986.

Bibl: *John Virtue: Green Haworth 1978-1988,* with an essay by Richard Cork, Lisson Gallery, London, 1988.

VIVIAN, Timothy   b.1926
Painter. Studied at St. Martin's School of Art and Brighton College of Art. Became Director of Art at King's School, Worcester, 1957. First solo exhibition held at John Whibley Gallery, London, 1968.

VIVIS, Geoffrey   b.1944
Painter. Born Sleaford, Lincolnshire. Studied at High Wycombe College of Art, 1959-63, and RCA, 1963-7. Exhibited at RA in the 1960s and elsewhere. First solo exhibition held at Cross Keys Gallery, Beaconsfield, 1968.

VOLLEY, Jo   b.1953
Painter. Born Grimsby, Lincolnshire. Studied at the Slade, 1972-7. Awards include Stowells Trophy Silver Medal, 1976, the Henry Tonks Drawing Prize and a Boise Travelling Scholarship to Italy, 1977. First exhibited at the RA Diploma Galleries, London, 1976. Included in the collections of University College, London, London University Picture Club and Leicestershire Education Authority.

VULLIAMY, Edward   1876-1962
Painter. Born of French parentage. Educated at King's College, Cambridge, where he studied classics and modern languages. Later lectured in languages in Cambridge and was made Hon. Keeper of the Pictures, Fitzwilliam Museum. Painted in his spare time and exhibited with the NEAC and elsewhere.

EDWARD WADSWORTH, 1889-1949. *'Harbour Still Life'*. Ivor Braka Limited, London.

WADDELL, C.G.

Painter. Born Carrickfergus, Northern Ireland. Lives and works in Coventry. First solo exhibition at the Molesworth Galleries, Dublin, 1966; another held at the Woodstock Gallery, 1974.

WADE, Dorothy

Painter. Studied at Leeds and Bradford Colleges of Art. Travelled to Venice, Italy, Turkey and France. First solo exhibition at the Beaux Art Gallery, London. A visit to Venice, the mosaics at Ravenna and Istanbul and the stained glass at Chartres, have all fed her interest in colour.

WADE, Maurice   b.1917

Painter. Born near Stoke-on-Trent, Staffordshire. Apart from the war years, has lived and worked there ever since. Three solo exhibitions at the Thackeray Gallery, London, the last in 1974. Records the industrial heritage of the Potteries.

WADSWORTH, Edward   1889-1949

Painter. Born Cleckheaton, Yorkshire. On leaving school he started engraving for one year in Munich, spending his spare time at the Knirr Art School. Studied at Bradford School of Art and the Slade. Participated briefly in the Omega Workshops, then broke away from it with Wyndham Lewis* and took part in The Rebel Art Centre. His knowledge of German enabled him to contribute a translation of Kandinsky's *Uber das Geistige in der Kunst* to *Blast No 1*, 1914. He also signed the Vorticist Manifesto and helped pioneer an abstract style. During the First World War he served as an intelligence officer in the Navy and was invalided out in 1917, when he spent a year working on dazzle camouflage for ships in Liverpool and Bristol; this experience also provided the subject for one of his monumental war paintings. During the 1920s he returned to a more straightforward representational style, helped pioneer a revival of tempera as a medium, and travelled much abroad. 1934 founder member of Unit One. 1940 represented Britain at the Venice Biennale. 1943 elected ARA. A meticulous craftsman, Wadsworth at times comes close to surrealism in his use of unexpected juxtapositioning and hyper-real clarity. 1951 a memorial exhibition was held at the Tate Gallery. A retrospective was held at the Camden Arts Centre, London, 1990.

Bibl: *A Genius of Industrial England: Edward Wadsworth 1889-1949*, edited by Jeremy Lewison, The Arkwright Arts Trust, London, 1990.

WAIN, Louis   1860-1939

Cat painter. Born London. Studied at West London School

WAINWRIGHT, Albert

of Art, 1877-80, and taught there, 1881-2. Began to draw cats, 1883. Joined the staff of *The Illustrated Sporting and Dramatic News,* 1882, and *The Illustrated London News,* 1886. Soon made his name as a humorous cat artist and became immensely popular. In the words of H.G. Wells he 'invented a cat style, a cat society, a whole cat world'. 1902-14 he produced 600 cat pictures a year for his famous *Louis Wain Annuals.* After 1918 he suffered a mental decline, becoming a schizophrenic, as his work clearly revealed. His cats became frenzied and jagged, sometimes disappearing into kaleidoscopic shapes. When, in 1925, he was found in a pauper's lunatic asylum, an appeal was launched on his behalf and he was transferred to a comfortable room with his paints in the Royal Bethlem Hospital.

Bibl: Michael Parkin, *Louis Wain's Cats,* Thames and Hudson, London, 1983.

WAINWRIGHT, Albert   1898-1943
Painter and illustrator. Born Castleford, Yorkshire, where like his school-fellow, Henry Moore,* he was taught at school by Alice Gostick. Studied at Leeds College of Art, 1914-17, then joined the Royal Flying Corps until 1919. 1920 first exhibited work in public at Leeds City Art Gallery, and 1923 in London at the Goupil Gallery, which later became the sole agent for his work. Showed regularly at the West Riding Artists exhibitions. Produced designs for theatres in Leeds and Castleford. 1927-39 visited Germany and Austria every year. During the Second World War he painted murals in army camp canteens and helped with theatrical entertainments. 1943 appointed art master at Bridlington School, a post terminated by his early death. 1986 retrospective exhibition held at Michael Parkin Gallery.

WAKEFIELD, Larry   b.1925
Painter. Trained as a town-planner at Cheltenham School of Art and at the Royal West of England Academy, Bristol. First solo exhibition of paintings at University of Southampton, 1960. Abstract artist who works with brick-like slabs of colour.

WAKEFORD, Edward   1914-1973
Painter. Born Isle of Man. Studied at Chelsea School of Art and at the RCA. Served in the army in the Middle East, 1939-45. 1944 first exhibited at the British Council, Jerusalem. 1971 won the Lord Mayor's Award. 1968 elected ARA. 1971 won the Edwin Austin Abbey Award. Included in the collections of the Tate Gallery, Royal Academy, Borough of Camden, Royal Chelsea Hospital, Education Authorities of Leicestershire, West Riding of Yorkshire, Hertfordshire, Gloucestersire and Kent. Painted landscapes and cityscapes with a sense of moments snatched in time.

Bibl: Edward Wakeford, *Autobiography: A Prize for Art,* Macmillan, 1961.

WALCOT, William   1874-1943
Etcher. Born Odessa, Russia. Travelled in Europe and South America. Began studying architecture at St. Petersburg, Russia, but transferred to the Ecole des Beaux-Arts, Paris. Afterwards he studied at the Atelier Redan. Began practising architecture in Moscow, but a commission brought him to London. While in London he began to draw buildings as works of art rather than technical plans, which led to a commission from the Fine

Art Society to visit Venice and Rome. 1912 first solo exhibition at the Fine Art Society Gallery, London. 1912 studied etching. Most of his etchings produced 1913-24 were published in London by H.C. Dickens, who had encouraged him to study the medium. Exhibited at the RA, RBA, RE, in the provinces and abroad. Elected ARE, 1918, and RE, 1920. Represented in several public collections.

Bibl: William Walcot, 'Modern Masters of Etching No.16', *The Studio,* 1927.

WALDRON, Peter   b.1941
Painter. Born Swindon, Wiltshire. Took an engineering apprenticeship, 1956-62. Studied at Swindon and Chelsea Schools of Art, 1962-7. Painting fellowship at Gloucester College of Art, 1968-9. First solo exhibition at University of Nottingham Gallery, 1969.

WALES, Geoffrey   1912-1990
Printmaker. Studied at Royal College of Art, graduating 1936. Taught at Norwich School of Art and exhibited with the Norwich 20 Group and elsewhere. Elected ARE, 1948, and RE, 1961. An admirer of Thomas Bewick, Paul Nash,* Samuel Palmer and William Blake, he brought to this visionary tradition a crisp, modern sense of design. His small, poetic but formally taut abstracts take their patterns and textures from nature.

WALKE, Anne   c.1888-1965
Painter. Born Anne Fearon. Studied at Chelsea School of Art and at the London School of Art under Augustus John* and William Orpen.* Moved to Fowey in Cornwall after her marriage to a curate, Bernard Walke. With him moved to St. Hilary in 1912 and was closely associated with the nearby Newlyn artists; the church at St. Hilary became famous for her decorations. Her *Crucifixion* can be found in the Jesus Chapel, Truro Cathedral. Exhibited London, Paris and in the provinces.

WALKER, C. Edward   b.1931
Painter and calligrapher. Studied at Lincoln School of Art, the Central School of Art and Reading University. First solo exhibition at the University of Hull, 1967.

WALKER, Darryl   b.1950
Painter. Born Shrewsbury, Shropshire. Studied at the Art College of Shrewsbury, 1968-70, and at Canterbury Art College, 1970-3. 1973 won the RA Landscape Prize, David Murray Fund. 1973 first solo exhibition at Shrewsbury Art Centre. 1974 travelled in Morocco.

WALKER, Eric George   1907-1985
Painter. Born Heston, Northumberland. Lived and worked in Birmingham. Believed to have exhibited at the Royal Society of Artists in Birmingham, at the Dudley Gallery and the Dudley New Gallery.

WALKER, Ethel   1861-1951
Painter. Born Edinburgh, Scotland. Studied at Putney Art School, 1893 and at Westminster School of Art under Fred Brown.* She transferred to the Slade when Brown began teaching there. She also attended classes with Walter Sickert.* 1900 elected member of the NEAC. 1912-13 and 1916-19 she resumed her studies at the Slade; 1916-19 she also studied sculpture under James Harvard Thomas.* 1921-2 returned to study at the Slade. 1927 first solo

ETHEL WALKER,
1861-1951. *'Flower Piece'*,
c.1930. 30in. x 25in.
Courtauld Institute Galleries,
London.

exhibition at the Redfern Gallery, London. 1929 became a member of the 7 and 5 Society and 1936 of the London Group. 1938 awarded the CBE. 1940 elected ARA. 1948 awarded DBE. Represented in the Tate Gallery, the Courtauld Institute and elsewhere. Specialised in portraits, flower pieces, landscapes and seascapes, but also produced large allegorical figure paintings, inspired by the example of Gauguin. A dominant personality, she exerted considerable presence in her day, but her reputation now languishes and has yet to be reassessed.

WALKER, Frances   b.1930
Painter. Born Kirkcaldy, Scotland. Studied at Edinburgh College of Art, 1949-54. 1954 awarded travelling scholarship. 1957 first solo exhibition at the 57 Gallery, Edinburgh. Exhibited regularly with the RSA, SSA, and AAS. 1970 solo exhibition at the Richard Demarco Gallery, Edinburgh. Lives and teaches in Aberdeen.

WALKER, Heather   b.1959
Sculptor. Born Dunfermline, Scotland. Studied at Grays School of Art, Aberdeen, 1981-4, and at Chelsea School of Art, 1984-5. First represented in group exhibitions at Edinburgh Festival Exhibition, Hunter Gallery, Edinburgh, followed by an exhibition of British Young Artists which toured Australia, 1982. 1981 awarded the Carnegie Commission for Public Sculpture, Falkirk Park, Scotland.

WALKER, James Faure   b.1948
Born London. Studied at St. Martin's School of Art, 1966-70 and the RCA, 1970-2. 1972-85 taught art history and painting at a wide variety of regional art schools. 1976 joint founder of *Artscribe* magazine and editor of this journal until 1983. From 1969 included in mixed exhibitions. Has exhibited in major group shows such as the Hayward Annual, the Whitechapel Open, the John Moores and in a Serpentine Summer Show. He has also had numerous solo shows at the Whitworth Art Gallery, Manchester and elsewhere. Was influential in the revival of interest in painting after a period of conceptualism.

MARIE WALKER LAST, b.1917. *'Sentinel Rock'*, 1977. Gouache. 14¼ in. x 18in. Private Collection

WALKER, John   b.1939
Painter. Born Birmingham, West Midlands. Studied at Birmingham College of Art, 1956-60 and at the Académie de la Grande Chaumière, Paris 1961-3. 1964-70 lived in London, then moved to New York. 1967 first solo exhibition held at Axiom Gallery, London. Has held various teaching positions in America and Australia. 1972 represented Britain in the Venice Biennale. Walker first came to fame in the mid to late 1960s with a series of shaped canvases which were abstract in content. By the mid-1970s he had begun collaging pieces of canvas on to his paintings, also caking their surface with chalk dust thrown into wet paint. Since then his paintings have often contained references to Old Masters, notably Goya's *Duchess of Alba,* though in appearance they retain a predominantly abstract aspect.

Bibl: *John Walker: Paintings from the Alba and Oceans Series 1979-84,* Arts Council, London, 1985.

WALKER, Judith   b.1955
Painter. Born Leeds, Yorkshire. Studied at Jacob Kramer School of Art, Leeds, Central School of Art and Crafts and at New Mexico State University, New Mexico, USA. 1986 first solo exhibition at the Broker Restaurant, London; in the same year she also had solo exhibitions at The Original Picture Shop, London and at Waterman's Art Centre, Brentford. Included in the collections of New Mexico State University Art Gallery and the Bureau of Art Exhibitions, Poland.

WALKER, Raymond   b.1945
Painter. Born Liverpool, Merseyside. Studied at Liverpool College of Art, 1961-5 and the RCA, 1966-9. From 1968 onwards included in mixed exhibitions. 1970 first solo exhibition at the Clytie Jessop Gallery. Paints pictures which mix realism with fantasy.

WALKER, Richard   b.1954
Painter. Born Yorkshire. Studied at Camberwell School of Art, 1973-6 and at Chelsea School of Art, 1976-7. 1978 first solo exhibition at Minsky's Gallery, London. Has received commissions from *Time Out, Radio Times, Tatler, New Style, City Limits* and Virgin Airways. Included in the collections of the British Council and Sheffield City Art Gallery.

WALKER, Richard   b.1955
Painter. Born Cumbernauld, Scotland. Studied at Glasgow School of Art, 1973-7. Solo exhibitions at Glasgow Arts Centre, 1983, Transmission Gallery, Glasgow, 1986. Awarded first prize at Inverclyde Bienniale, 1986.

WALKER, Roger   b.1942
Painter. Born Birmingham, West Midlands. First solo exhibition at Elisabeth Gallery, Coventry, 1965. A graphic artist whose illustrative work has appeared in the *Tatler, Radio Times, Time Out* and other magazines. Exhibits at the Thumb Gallery, London.

WALKER-LAST, Marie   b.1917
Painter. Studied at Chelsea School of Art in the 1950s. First solo exhibition at the New Vision Gallery, London, 1960. Member of the AIA, the Free Painters Group and the Womens International Art Club. Abstract painter using golden hues, but recently moved into landscape. Solo exhibitions include one at the Manor House Museum and Art Gallery, Ilkley, 1985; another held at Leeds University, 1987. Winner of the Constable Prize at the Camden Arts Centre, 1989. Retrospective at the Dean Clough Contemporary Art Gallery, Halifax, 1990. Included in the collections of York University, Bradford University, Bradford City Art Gallery and the Open University.

WALL, Brian   b.1931
Sculptor. Born London. Worked as a glass-blower, 1945-50. Studied painting, 1950-2. Lived in Paris, 1952-3. 1954-9 lived in St. Ives, working part-time as an assistant to Barbara Hepworth.* Moved to London and became Head of Sculpture at the Central School of Art. Has also taught at Ealing College of Art, and the University of California where he has been Assistant Professor since 1975. First one-person show at the School of Architecture, 1957. His commissions include work for the University of Texas, 1978. Represented in the collections of the Tate, the Arts Council of Great Britain, the British Council, the CAS, the Whitworth Art Gallery, Manchester, the Leicestershire Education Authority and Art Gallery of New South Wales, Sydney. Works with painted steel.

WALL, George   1930-1974
Painter. Born Co. Durham. Studied at King's College, Newcastle, 1949-54 and at the Slade, 1954-6. First solo exhibition of his work held at the Herbert Art Gallery, Coventry, 1976. An abstract artist with a rigorous aesthetic sensibility.

WALLACE, Anne Paterson
Painter. Studied at Chelsea School of Art. Ran her own art gallery, 1967-75. First solo exhibition at The Old Fire Engine House, Ely, 1970. Granddaughter of one of the 'Glasgow Boys', James Paterson, she has asserted her originality chiefly through the medium of watercolour. Paints the Suffolk coast and countryside.

WALLACE, Laurence   b.1952
Painter. Studied at Hornsey College of Art, 1971-5, and at RCA, 1975-8. First solo exhibition at the RCA, 1977, and exhibits regularly at the Thumb and Piccadilly Galleries. Paints architectural exteriors with dead-pan but disquieting realism.

WALLER, Jonathan   b.1956
Painter. Born Stratford-upon-Avon, Warwickshire. Studied at Lanchester Polytechnic, 1980-3, and Chelsea School of Art, 1984-5. 1984 first solo exhibition held at Nene College, Northampton, followed by others in London and Coventry. 1985-6 held the Junior Painting Fellowship at Cardiff. Most recent solo exhibition held at Flowers East, London, 1990. An ambitious figurative artist, painting images of industrial labour on a grand scale.

WALLINGER, Mark   b.1959
Painter. Born Chigwell, Essex. Studied at Loughton College, Essex, 1977-8, Chelsea School of Art, 1978-81 and Goldsmiths' College, 1985-6. First solo exhibition held at The Minories, Colchester, 1983, followed by others in London and mixed exhibitions abroad. Borrows details from Old Master paintings, using the past to comment satirically on the present.

WALLIS, Alfred   1855-1942
Painter. The facts concerning his life are uncertain but he is thought to have been entirely uneducated. Born Davenport, near Plymouth, Devon, and brought up in the Scilly Isles. He claimed he went to sea at the age of nine, first as a cabin boy, later as an ordinary seaman in Atlantic schooners and windjammers. Around 1880 he abandoned deep-sea fishing for local fishing with the Newlyn and Mousehole fleets, at a time when the Cornish fishing industry was at its zenith. Later joined his younger brother in the rag-and-bone trade. Gradually withdrew into himself, keeping company only with his wife, his newspapers and his Bible. Took up painting at the age of seventy in 1922, after his wife's death. Painted on pieces of old card mostly obtained from a nearby greengrocer. Ignored all artistic conventions in his attempt to express his nostalgia for the boats and harbours as they were when the fishing industry was at its height. His unconventional style had a liberating influence on Ben Nicholson* and Christopher Wood* when they discovered his work in 1928.

Bibl: Sven Berlin, *Alfred Wallis, Primitive,* Nicholson & Watson, London, 1949; Edwin Mullins, *Alfred Wallis: Cornish Primitive Painter,* Macdonald, London, 1967.

WALLIS, Colin   b.1937
Painter. Studied at Colchester School of Art and at the RCA, 1959-62. First solo exhibition at 'Art at The Minories', Colchester, 1984. Has produced paintings on the theme of the body-builder, an image which he regards as a metaphor for the self-centredness of Western civilisation. His paintings are large and striking.

WALNE, Kathleen   b.1915
Painter. Born Suffolk. Studied at Ipswich Art School, 1930-4. 1935 first exhibited at Salford Art Gallery. Member of the 20s Group. 1986 first solo exhibition at Salford Art Gallery. Included in the collections of the Towner Gallery, Eastbourne and Auckland City Art Gallery, New Zealand. Painted still lifes and domestic subjects with clear washes of watercolour, fluently handled.

WALSH, Alexander   b.1947
Painter. Born Boston, Massachusetts, USA. Studied at Rhode Island School of Design, Providence, Rhode Island, USA, 1965-7, and at Hammersmith College of Art, 1971-3. Completed three-piece commissions for Germaine Monteil Cosmetiques, New York, 1974. First solo exhibition at James Hunt Barker Gallery, London, 1975.

WALSH, David   b.1927
Painter. Born India. Studied at Anglo-French Art Centre, 1947-9 and at the RCA. 1954 moved to Ibiza. 1964 first exhibited at the Madden Galleries, London. Romantic artist, who works with the human figure in tempera.

WALSH, Samuel   b.1951
Painter and abstract artist. Born London. Resident in Limerick, Ireland, since 1968. Studied at Limerick School of Art, 1969-74. 1978 first solo exhibition at Kevin Cummins Gallery, Limerick. 1986 produced a tapestry for P.J. Carroll & Co. Ltd., Dundalk. 1988 overall winner at Irish Exhibition of Living Art, Dublin. 1988-90 studied Philosophy at Mary Immaculate College of Education, Limerick.

WALTON, Allan   1892-1948
Painter and textile designer. Born Cheadle Hulme, Cheshire. Studied at the Slade and the Académie de la Grande Chaumière, Paris, then went to Westminster School of Art, London, 1918-19. 1925 elected to the London Group. In the same year he designed Marcel Boulestin's first restaurant in Leicester Square and founded the firm of Allan Walton Textiles with his brother. 1932 first exhibition of Walton fabrics at Cooling Galleries, London. 1932 designed an anteroom as part of Fortnum and Mason's decorative department; in this year he became a member of the Council of the Society of Industrial Artists. 1933 first solo exhibition of his paintings at Tooth's Gallery, London. 1936 became a member of the Faculty of Royal Designer for Industry, set up by RSA. 1944 founder member of the Council of Industrial Design and member of the Council of the RCA. Influenced by Sickert* and Duncan Grant,* bringing also to his handling of oil paint a sensitive panache. (Plate 84, p.434.)

WALTON, Edward Arthur   1860-1922
Painter. Born Renfrewshire, Scotland. Studied at Glasgow School of Art and Düsseldorf Academy. His early landscapes betray the influence of Bastien-Lepage and of Barbizon painting. By the end of the 1880s, however, like other members of the Glasgow School, he had revised his style towards that of Whistler. Took a leading role in the formation of the International Society, 1898. By then he had moved to London, but in 1900 returned to Glasgow to execute a decorative panel for the Corporation's Banqueting Hall.

WALTON, Ian   b.1943
Architect and painter. Born Canada. Moved to England. Trained as an architect, which led to work in England and abroad. Became a set designer at BBC TV Centre. He began painting full-time, 1971. First solo exhibition at the Cheyne Gallery, London.

WALTON, Ian   b.1950
Painter. Born Colnbrook, Buckinghamshire. Studied at Newcastle upon Tyne College of Art, 1969-70, and at Canterbury College of Art, 1970-3. First solo exhibition at Greenwich Theatre, 1978.

WALTON, John
Painter. Studied at the Ruskin School of Drawing, Oxford, and Slade School of Fine Art, winning the Melville Nettleship Prize for Figure Composition, 1948. Elected RP, 1978. Became Principal of the Heatherley School of Fine Art, 1947. Elected RP, 1978. Became Governor of the Federation of British Artists, 1982. Represented by the RP.

WAPLINGTON, Paul   b.1938
Painter. Left school at fifteen and began work as a lace designer and draughtsman. Started to paint in oils five years later, whilst still working as a lace designer in Nottingham. Made his reputation with paintings of coal miners and of the city of Nottingham. His perspective is often bent so that the roads curve, as do the cliff-face flats. This helps pull the spectator in and creates the feel of streets that are lived and walked in. Working-class life, its dignity and degradation, is his subject.

WARBURTON, Joan   b.1920
Painter. Born Edinburgh, Scotland. Studied in the studio of Oswald Poreau, Belgium and at the East Anglian School of Painting, Dedham, Essex, after she had returned to England in 1937. Spent the Second World War in the WRENS and in an arms factory. She also worked in the Red Cross as an ambulance driver. First exhibited at Women's International Art Club. Remained a close associate of Cedric Morris* and Lett Haines.* Solo exhibition at the Michael Parkin Gallery, London, 1984.

WARD, Cynthia   b.1944
Painter. Born East Retford, Nottinghamshire. Studied at Hull College of Higher Education, 1980-3. First solo exhibition held at Posterngate Gallery, Hull, 1987. Paints her local environment, using distortion to make a personal statement. A regular contributor to Winter Exhibitions at the Ferens Art Gallery, Hull.

WARD, David   b.1951
Painter, photographer and performance artist. Born Wolverhampton, West Midlands. Studied at Wolverhampton College of Art, 1968-9, and at Winchester School of Art, 1969-73. First solo exhibition at Angela Flowers Gallery, London, 1981. Collaborates with Bruce McLean on performances. Worked with him on 'The Invention of Tradition' for the opening of the Tate Gallery, Liverpool, 1988. Represented in the collections of the CAS, Leeds City Art Galleries, Arts Council, National Portrait Gallery, Goethe Institute, Van Reekummuseum, Apeldoorn, Netherlands, Cleveland Art Gallery and Castle Museum and Art Gallery, Haverford West.

WARD, Dick   b.1937
Painter. Born London. Studied at Chelsea School of Art. Junior Prizewinner, John Moores Exhibition. 1972 first solo exhibition at the Serpentine Gallery, London, followed by an exhibition at the New Art Centre, London, in the same year. Included in the collections of Sussex University, Mid-Northumberland Arts Group and the Arts Council of Great Britain.

WARD, Francis   b.1926
Painter. First solo exhibition at the Woodstock Gallery,

London, 1973, where he exhibited drawings based on recollections of faces seen in restaurants, in films and on the streets.

WARD, James   1851-1924
Painter and author. Born Belfast, Northern Ireland, son of James Ward, a decorative artist. Educated in Belfast and was a National Scholar at the RCA, 1873-6. Became assistant to Lord Leighton, PRA, 1878-86. Exhibited at the RA and published several books on art, including *Floral Subjects for Decorative Design*, 1901, *Fresco Painting: Its Art and Technique*, 1909, and *Colour Decoration of Architecture*, 1913. 1907 was made Headmaster of the Dublin Metropolitan School of Art.

WARD, John   b.1917
Painter and illustrator. Born Hereford. Studied at the RCA, 1936-9, returning to study there in 1946 after the Second World War, to complete his studies. Awarded a travelling scholarship. He then worked for *Vogue* for four years producing many fashion illustrations. After 1940 he travelled in Europe, India, Hong Kong, Turkey and the USA. 1954 first exhibited at Wildenstein's. 1956 elected to the RA; executed a mural in Challock Church, Kent, in the same year. He also began illustrating books for R.E. Church, H.E. Bates and Laurie Lee. 1981 commissioned to paint the wedding of the Prince and Princess of Wales; he has also made some drawings of the Queen at Balmoral Castle. 1984 he executed a triple portrait of the Cabinet Secretaries for the National Portrait Gallery. Included in the collections of the National Portrait Gallery, University of London and the Royal Museum and Art Gallery, Canterbury. Has also specialised in academic portraits and work by him can be found in many Oxford and Cambridge colleges. A retrospective was held at Agnew's, London, 1990.

WARD, Leslie   1888-
Painter and etcher. Born Worcester. Studied at Bournemouth Art School, 1903. He won Gold Medals in National Competitions, 1909-10. First solo exhibition in Bournemouth, 1930. Elected ARE, 1916, and RE, 1936. Included in the collections of Bournemouth Art Gallery, Southampton Art Gallery, Cheltenham Art Gallery and Oldham Art Gallery.

WARD, Martin   b.1944
Painter. Born Bexley, Kent. Studied at Bromley College of Art, 1960-2, Ravensbourne College of Art, 1962-4 and at the Slade, 1965-7. First exhibited in 'Young Contemporaries at the Tate', Tate Gallery, 1967.

WARD, Ray   b.1960
Painter. Born Leicester. Studied at Leicester Polytechnic, 1979-80, and Trent Polytechnic, 1980-3. First solo exhibition at the Young Vic, London, 1985. Regularly exhibits with the Vanessa Devereux Gallery.

WARD, Richard   b.1937
Painter. Born Kingsbury. Studied at Regent Street Polytechnic and Chelsea School of Art, 1962-7. First solo exhibition at the New Art Centre, London, 1973. Included in the collection of Sussex University and the Arts Council of Great Britain. Abstract artist using letters and words in patterned arrangements.

WARREN, Michael   b.1950
Sculptor. Born Gorey, County Wexford, Northern Ireland. Studied at Bath Academy of Art, Wiltshire, 1969-70, and under Frank Morris, sculptor, 1970. Studied at Academia de Brera, Milan, under Luciano Minguizzi, 1971-5. 1978 executed a commission from Radio Telfis, Dublin. 1979 awarded the Alice Berger Hammerschlag Scholarship and the Macaulay Fellowship for Sculpture. 1980 first solo exhibition at 'Letalin', Gorey; in the same year he received his second commission, from Dublin Port and Docks Board and won the Mont Kavanagh Award for Environmental Art. Included in the collections of University College, Galway, and the Arts Council of Ireland.

WARRINGTON, Richard William   1868-1953
Painter and stained glass designer. Taught stained glass design at Liverpool University, Department of Design, 1900-5, under Herbert McNair, and drew in the evening classes. Transferred to Liverpool School of Art. Many of his drawings are in the collections of the Walker Art Gallery, Liverpool.

WATERHOUSE, John William   1849-1917
Painter. Brought up in Italy. Studied at RA Schools. Began exhibiting at the RA, 1874, in a style not dissimilar to that of Alma-Tadema whose domestic scenes in classical settings he imitated. After seeing the Millais retrospective held at the Grosvenor Gallery, 1886, he attempted to marry Pre-Raphaelite subject matter with the broader methods of painting that by the late 1880s had infiltrated England from France. He became a leading exponent of medieval romanticism up to and around the turn of the century. Elected ARA, 1885, and RA, 1895.

WATERLOW, Ernest Albert   1850-1919
Painter. Born London. Studied in Lausanne and Heidelberg, and at the RA Schools from 1872. Won the Turner Gold Medal, 1873. Exhibited at the RA and RWS, 1872-1919. Influenced by the Etruscans, especially George Heming Mason, and the Barbizon painters. Elected ARWS, 1880, ARA, 1890, RWS, 1894, and RA, 1903. President of the RWS, 1897-1914. Knighted 1902. As a landscapist, he travelled widely, at home and abroad.

WATERS, Billie   1896-1979
Painter. Born Richmond, Surrey. Studied at Heatherley's and Chelsea School of Art and at the Grosvenor School. Spent five years at Newlyn, 1926-31, where she studied under Ernest Proctor* and Harold Harvey.* Became interested in fresco techniques. 1928 began exhibiting at RA, showing there annually thereafter, also at the RI and NEAC. Continued to visit Cornwall regularly. 1933 first one-artist exhibition held at Leicester Galleries. Frequently travelled to France and Italy. 1934 she was commissioned to execute a mural for the Knightsbridge Grill. Exhibited at RA, NEAC, the Society of Women Artists and elsewhere. Briefly experimented with abstract art after meeting Ben Nicholson,* but is better known as a representational painter with a studied sense of design. (Plate 85, p.434.)

WATKINS, Darton   b.1928
Painter. Studied modern history at Oxford University, 1951. Largely self-taught as a painter. 1960-1 lived in Spain and Portugal. 1961 first solo exhibitions in Portugal. 1965 first solo exhibition in Britain at the Bear Lane Gallery, Oxford. Included in the collection of Liverpool University. His abstracts sometimes take the form of reliefs in which oil is mixed with other substances to give textured effects and into which lines can be incised.

WATKINS, Frank   b.1951
Painter. Born Glanaman, Wales. Studied at Carmarthen

HARRY WATSON, 1871-1936. *'Holidays'*, 1922. 40½ in. x 61 in. The Bridgeman Art Library, City of Bristol Museum and Art Gallery.

School of Art, 1969-70, at Newport College of Art, 1970-3, and at Cardiff College of Art, 1973-4. Awards include Leslie Moore Award, Welsh Arts Council, 1967-7 and an Elephant Trust Scholarship which enabled him to study at the Miró Foundation, Barcelona, Spain, 1985. First solo exhibition held at West Wales Arts, Carmarthen, 1974. His work incorporates discarded materials from the urban environment in order to evoke the fragility of the human condition.

WATKINS, Jesse
Sculptor. Began life at sea and sailed in coasters, square-riggers, and ocean-going liners. Entered the Royal Navy during the war and ended his service days as a Commodore of Convoys. He always painted and drew, and did spells at Goldsmiths' and Chelsea Art Schools. His life ashore was spent building and running a factory and designing tiles. 1960 began sculpting full-time, working in welded steel and then aluminium. Member of the Free Painters and Sculptors, and of the Hampstead Artists Council.

WATKINSON, Bob   b.1914
Painter. Born Wigan, Lancashire. Self taught as a painter. Engineering draughtsman for seventeen years, until in 1946 he moved into commercial art full-time. 1971 first solo exhibition at the Woodstock Gallery, London. His abstracts are based on curvilinear forms which are, in part, a reaction against the straight lines which dominate modern architecture.

WATKISS, Gill   b.1938
Painter. Studied at South West Essex School of Art. Won 'The Small Picture Lives Again' at Wills Lane Gallery, 1972. First solo exhibition at Exeter University, 1975. Included in the collections of East and West Riding of Yorkshire, Leicester Education Committee, Birmingham University and Vassar College, New York, USA. Her paintings are mostly based on the life of West Penwith in Cornwall, and reflect some influence of Edvard Munch.

WATSON, Alan   b.1957
Painter. Born St. Andrews, Scotland. Studied at Duncan of Jordanstone College of Art, Dundee, 1976-81. Awards include Royal Scottish Academy Carnegie Travelling Scholarship, and Scottish Education Department Major Travelling Scholarship, 1981, followed by a Scottish Arts Council Young Artists Bursary, 1983 and the Royal Scottish Academy Latimer Award, 1985. First solo exhibition at 369 Gallery, Edinburgh, 1982, and has exhibited there regularly since. His most recent work concentrates on the history of whaling from the east coast of Scotland in the 19th century. His figures demonstrate the physical extremities to which fishermen were subjected when at work.

WATSON, Arthur   b.1951
Sculptor and screenprinter. Born in Aberdeen, Scotland. Studied at Gray's School of Art. Founder member of Peacock Printmakers Workshop, 1975. Awarded Scottish

454

Arts Council grant, 1976. First solo exhibition at Edinburgh Print Workshop, 1979. Included in the collections of Leeds Education Department, Scottish Arts Council, Hunterian Museum, Glasgow, Tayside Regional Council, Inverness Art Gallery and Aberdeen Art Gallery.

WATSON, Derek

Painter. Born Smallbridge, Devon. Worked at Rochdale Wallpaper Printing Company, where he served apprentice-ships in colour mixing and wallpaper printing. Paints part-time. First solo exhibition at Rochdale Art Gallery, Rochdale, 1988. His paintings highlight the changes that have taken place in Lancashire since the industrial revolution to the 1950s.

WATSON, Fred   b.1937

Sculptor. Born Gateshead, Co. Durham. Studied at King's College, Durham University. First solo exhibition at Nevill Gallery, Llanelli Festival, 1980. Won the Northern Arts Production Award twice and the Hatton Scholarship.

WATSON, George Spencer   1869-1934

Painter. Born London. Studied at St. John's Wood School of Art, then the RA, which he began attending in 1889. 1891 first exhibited at the RA. 1891 awarded a silver medal for drawing, and 1892 the Landseer Scholarship. 1897 admitted to the Arts Club and 1900 the Art Workers' Guild. Until 1914 exhibited regularly at the Salon in Paris. 1920 first solo exhibition at Hampstead Gallery, London. Elected ARA, 1923, and RA, 1932. 1934 memorial exhibition held at the Fine Art Society, London. Though he produced some landscape and subject paintings, he concentrated mainly on portraits, with close attention to detail.

Bibl: Michael Compton, 'Introduction', *George Spencer Watson RA (1869-1934)*, Southampton Art Gallery, 1988.

WATSON, Harry   1871-1936

Painter. Born Scarborough, Yorkshire. Lived in Canada, 1881-3. Studied at Scarborough School of Art, 1884-8, at the RCA and Lambeth School of Art. While studying he won many medals in gold, silver and bronze, and a travelling Scholarship to Rome. 1915 elected to the RWS, 1928 the Royal Western Academy, and 1932 the ROI. 1896 first exhibited at the RA. 1938 memorial exhibition at Leamington Spa Art Gallery. He worked chiefly in Wales, Scotland and France, and from 1913 taught at the Regent Street Polytechnic. A fluent naturalist with a fondness for painting figures in open-air settings. (Plate 6, p.22.)

WATSON, Hilary   b.1946

Painter and sculptor. Born Glasgow, Scotland. Studied at Epsom School of Art, 1964-9, and at Byam Shaw School, 1969-70. First solo exhibition University of Strathclyde, 1975, at which she exhibited a series of reliefs made out of interchangeable prefabricated tetrahedral units made out of cast resin.

WATSON, Lyall

Painter. Solo exhibition at the Woodstock Gallery, London. Founder of the Free Painters Group. Director of the Wood-stock Gallery, also a teacher, muralist and stage designer.

WATSON, Mary Spencer   b.1913

Sculptor. Born London, daughter of George Spencer Watson.* Studied at Bournemouth Municipal College, 1929-30, Slade School of Sculpture, 1930-1, RA Schools, 1931-4, and at Central School under John Skeaping,* 1934; she also attended his lectures at London Zoo. Later,

she studied in Paris under Ossip Zadkine while making a tour of French cathedrals. 1937 first solo exhibition at Heals Mansard Gallery, London. Her works reflect her inspiration, derived from archaic Greek sculpture. Terse stylisation, and a concern to retain the sense of wholeness originating from the original block of stone, often gives her work a formal integrity and strength. She has also executed a number of commissions for architects, including a pair of limewood angels for Guildford Cathedral. 1988 solo exhibition held at Pelter/Sands Art Gallery, Bristol.

WATSON, William   b.1946

Sculptor. Born Homes Chapel, Cheshire. Studied at Birmingham College of Art and Design, 1965-6, and at Bath Academy of Art, 1966-9. 1978 won an Arts Council Award, and held first solo exhibition at the Project Gallery, Dublin. His sculptures are abstract, but frequently incorporate real objects such as chairs and trestle tables.

WATT, Alison   b.1965

Painter. Studied at Glasgow School of Art, 1983-8. First exhibited at the RSA Student Competition, Glasgow, 1986; later in the same year she exhibited at the RA. First solo exhibition at the Scottish Gallery, London, 1990. Awards include First Prize, John Player Portrait Prize, National Portrait Gallery and Armour prize for still life painting, Glasgow School of Art, 1987. Commissions include a portrait of HM Queen Elizabeth the Queen Mother, by the National Portrait Gallery, unveiled in 1989. Realist painter with an original vision and a fascination with the self-portrait. Included in the collections of the BBC and the National Portrait Gallery.

WATTS, Charles   b.1953

Painter. Born Edinburgh, Scotland. Studied at Gloucester-shire College of Art and Design, 1979-82, and RCA, 1983-6. Awarded RCA travel scholarships to Berlin, 1984 and Madrid, 1985. Represented in Cheltenham Art Gallery and Museum.

WATTS, E.B.

Painter. Born New York, USA. Spent her childhood in Great Britain and New Jersey, USA. Studied at Sarah Lawrence College, USA, and at the Italian Academy, Rome. 1962 first exhibited at the Spook Farm Gallery, New Jersey, and in 1970 at Crane Arts, London, followed by two others, 1973 and 1979.

WATTS, Ken   b.1932

Painter. Born London. Became a joiner, 1946, followed by National Service, 1950-5. 1966 began painting; 1970 first solo exhibition at Epinay, France; 1971 first solo exhibition in Britain at Jarrow Festival. Has also been involved in schemes for murals in Sunderland's East End.

WAUGH, Eric   b.1929

Painter. Studied at Croydon School of Art, 1946-50, and at the RCA, 1950-3. First solo exhibition in Manchester, 1963. Included in the collection of the Ferens Art Gallery, Hull. Has also exhibited at Roland, Browse and Delbanco, London, and with the London Group.

WAYMAN, Kathryn   b.1962

Sculptor. Studied at Kingston Polytechnic, 1980-5, and at the RA Schools, 1986-9. Awards include the Stanley Picker Travelling Scholarship to Italy, 1983, the Bolton House Trust Award, 1987 and the Landseer Scholarship, 1988. First exhibited at the Darlington Arts Centre, 1985.

WEATHERHEAD, Tim   b.1964
Painter. Born Redhill, Surrey. Studied at West Sussex College of Art, 1982-3, and West Surrey College of Art and Design, 1983-7. 1987 took up an ICI award scholarship to Rome. 1987 exhibited at John Moores.

WEBB, Anthony   b.1932
Painter. Born Sheffield, Yorkshire. Studied at Sheffield College of Art. First solo exhibitions at the Lantern Theatre, where he also designed the settings for some productions and directed and acted in plays. 1968 exhibited a series of gouaches at the Woodstock Gallery, London, based on the music of Stravinsky.

WEBB, Boyd   b.1947
Conceptual artist and photograper. Studied at RCA, 1972-5. First solo exhibition held at Robert Self, London, 1976. Others include shows at Anthony d'Offay, London and a retrospective at the Whitechapel Art Gallery, London, 1987. His photographs look like contemporary moral tales, but they deliver no point, no graspable narrative, and resist any single meaning.

Bibl: *Boyd Webb,* 1987, with essay by Stuart Morgan, Whitechapel Art Gallery, 1987.

WEBB, Clifford   1895-1972
Wood engraver. Born London. Apprenticed to a London firm of lithographers, 1913, while he studied evening classes at Camberwell School of Arts and Crafts. Served in the army, 1914-19. Returned to study at Westminster School of Art, 1919-22. 1923-6 associated with the Artist Craftsmen's Group, and the Modern Group. 1926 first solo exhibition at the Ruskin Galleries, Birmingham. 1935 elected a member of the Society of Wood Engravers, 1936 the RBA, and 1948 the RE. 1937-54 illustrated books for the Golden Cockerel Press.

WEBB, Joseph   1908-1962
Painter and printmaker. Studied at Hospital Fields Art College, Arbroath, Scotland. 1930 elected RE. 1933 solo exhibitions at Colnaghi's, and 1934 at Ryman's in Oxford. 1929-47 exhibited at RA, also in Paris salons, the Scottish Academy and elsewhere; also worked as a portrait painter and muralist. 1930s taught at Chiswick Art School, and in 1940s at the Hammersmith School of Art. 1977 solo exhibition at the David Cross Gallery, Bristol.

WEBB, Kenneth   b.1927
Painter. Born London. Studied at the University of Wales. Commissioned to paint the Bangor Abbey Mural, 1960. First solo exhibition in Dublin. He works with translucent coloured glazes and wax emulsion to give his paintings textures not always available with conventional painting techniques.

WEBB, Mary   b.1939
Painter. Born London. Studied at University of Newcastle, 1958-63, and at Chelsea School of Art, 1963-4. Awarded Hatton Scholarship, 1962-3. 1971 first solo exhibition held at the School of Art Gallery, Norwich. Recent exhibitions of her abstract paintings, collages and prints include one at The Showroom, Bethnal Green, London, 1984. Included in the collections of Newcastle and East Anglia Universities, Lincolnshire, Northern and Eastern Arts Associations, Leicestershire, Suffolk and Norfolk Education Authorities, Nottingham Castle Museum and Kettles Yard, Cambridge.

WEBB, Richard   b.1963
Painter. Studied at Camberwell School of Art, 1982-5, and at the RCA, 1986-8. First exhibited at the South London Gallery, 1985.

WEBB, Richard Kenton   b.1959
Painter. Studied at Chelsea College of Art, 1977-8, Slade School of Art, 1978-82, RCA, 1982-3 and at Cité International des Arts, Paris, 1985. Awards include Nettleship Prize, Slade School of Art, and a Boise Travelling Scholarship, 1982; Paris Studio Scholarship, 1985 and a Painting Fellowship, Gloucester College of Art, 1986-7. First solo exhibition at Chichester Assembly Rooms, Chichester, 1982, followed by a second exhibition at the same gallery, 1983. Solo exhibition at the Benjamin Rhodes Gallery, London, 1989.

WEBBE, Diana
Painter. Born London. Studied at Camberwell Art School. Awarded a State Scholarship to study at the Slade. First solo exhibition at the Woodstock Gallery, London, 1961. Her abstract paintings take their titles and inspiration from music.

WEBSTER, Harry   b.1921
Painter. Studied at Birmingham College of Art, 1946-51. First solo exhibition at the Woodstock Gallery, London, 1966. Represented in Birmingham Museum and Art Gallery, and elsewhere. Has incorporated Phoenician, Kufic and Chinese letter forms into his abstract paintings.

WEBSTER, Norman   b.1924
Printmaker. Born Southend-on-Sea, Essex. Studied at Tunbridge Wells School of Art, 1940-3, and RCA, 1946-9. Served in the Royal Navy, 1943-6. Has had solo exhibitions in Leeds and at Southampton University and has been represented in numerous group shows. His aim has been to 'draw from a thorough knowledge of tradition the reasoned and free sense of my own individuality'. Has taught at Leeds Polytechnic. Represented in the V & A, the Ashmolean Museum, Oxford, and in Leeds and Wakefield City Art Galleries.

WEDGBURY, David
Painter. Born London. Studied at Gravesend School of Art. First solo exhibition at Clytie Jessop Gallery, London, 1970. Included in the collections of City of Manchester Art Gallery and University of London. Recent solo exhibitions include one at the Woodlands Art Gallery, London, 1979.

WEDGE, Martin
Painter. Studied at Art and Design Centre, Belfast, 1977-82. Held first solo exhibition at the Octagon Gallery, Belfast, 1981. Uses a highly emotional figurative style with ideas derived from Freudian and Jungian psychology.

Bibl: *Martin Wedge,* Arts Council of Northern Ireland, Belfast, 1989.

WEDGWOOD, Geoffrey Heath   b.1900
Engraver and etcher. Born Leek, Staffordshire. Studied at Liverpool School of Art, 1919-21, and at the RCA. 1923 first exhibited at the RA. 1925 awarded Rome Prize, which led him to live and travel in Italy. 1929 he returned to Liverpool. 1935 became a member of the RE. He produces realistic scenes, and admires Meryon, Piranesi and David Strang. Included in the collections of the V & A, British Museum, Manchester City Art Gallery, Walker Art Gallery, University of Liverpool, Liverpool City Libraries,

CAREL WEIGHT, b.1908. *'Woman taken in Adultery'*, 1955. Oil on board. 20¼ in. x 44¾ in. Bernard Jacobson Gallery, London.

Art Institute of Chicago, USA, and Boston Museum of Fine Arts, USA.

WEIGHT, Carel   b.1908
Painter. Born London. Studied at Hammersmith School of Art and Goldsmiths' College. First showed at the RA, 1931 and has stayed loyal to this institution. Became a war artist during the Second World War, afterwards joining the painting staff at the RCA; became Head of Painting, 1957 and resigned, 1973. Influenced by Edvard Munch and Stanley Spencer,* he often paints everyday scenes that have a spiritual or religious content, with demons occurring in everyday streets, and angels in Battersea Park. The terrain in his paintings is usually that of South London where he lives, its shops and terraced streets, railway stations, parks and back gardens. A sense of drama pervades all he paints: even when his figures merely go about their daily lives, Weight leaves the impression that this is a world on edge. For many years he has been regarded with affectionate esteem, but around the time of his eightieth birthday critical opinion of his work suddenly escalated, as did the prices paid for his work.

Bibl: *Carel Weight, RA: A Retrospective*, Royal Academy of Arts, London, 1982.

WEINBERGER, Harry   b.1924
Painter. Born Germany. Studied at Chelsea School of Art, and privately with Martin Bloch.* Influenced by Van Gogh and the Fauves, his representional paintings are built up out of unmodulated patches of pure colour and have a charged, noumenal atmosphere. Recent solo exhibitions include one at Duncan Campbell Fine Art, London, 1988.

WELCH, Denton   1915-1948
Painter and writer. Born Shanghai, China. His mother died when he was nine and he was brought up by his grandfather. After a return visit to Shanghai he enrolled at Goldsmiths' College, 1933. 1938 he had a serious road accident which fractured his spine and thereafter he led an increasingly cloistered life despite periods of respite from recurrent pain and ill health. First caught attention as a writer with an article on Walter Sickert,* published in *Horizon*, 1942. Wrote and illustrated novels and short stories, publishing *Maiden Voyage, In Youth is Pleasure* and *Brave and Cruel* in his lifetime. Three novels, two collections of short stories and poems published after his death, were all written during the last eight years of his life. Between 1942 and 1948 he kept a journal, first published in heavily abridged form in 1952. An exhibition of his work was shown at the Leicester Galleries, 1954.

Bibl: *The Journals of Denton Welch*, ed. Michael De-la-Noy, Allison & Busby, London, 1984.

WELLINGTON, Hubert   1879-1967
Painter. Born Gloucester. Studied at Gloucester School of Art, 1895-7, at Birmingham School of Art, 1898-9, and at Slade School, 1899-1900. Served in the army, 1916-18. Lecturer at the National Gallery, 1919-23. Registrar and lecturer at the RCA, 1923-32; Principal, Edinburgh College of Art, 1932-42, and lecturer at the Slade, 1946-9. His paintings, rendered in an impressionistic manner, are influenced by the members of the Camden Town Group, and Walter Sickert,* with whom he worked closely in the early years of the century. A retrospective of his work was held at Thos. Agnew and Sons, London, 1963. Wrote books on William Rothenstein* and Jacob Epstein.* Represented in the Tate Gallery.

WELLS, Denys   1881-1973
Painter. Born Bedford. Studied at the Slade, 1897-1903, and in Monmartre, Paris. Elected a member of the RBA, 1906. Awarded the de Laszlo Medal twice. Served in the Artists' Rifles, 1914-18. He exhibited regularly at the RA and with the RBA and NEAC. Included in the collections of Sunderland Art Gallery, Municipal Art Gallery, Oldham, the Imperial War Museum, and the Museum of London. Was commissioned by Queen Mary to paint a picture for the Queen's Dolls House at Windsor.

KARL WESCHKE, b.1925.
'Leda and the Swan', 1985-6.
72in. x 54in.
Redfern Gallery, London.

WELLS, Donald
Sculptor. Born Newcastle upon Tyne, Tyne and Wear. First solo exhibition at the AIA Gallery, London, 1962. Others include an exhibition of reliefs at the Drian Galleries, London, 1967.

WELLS, John   b.1907
Painter. Born London. Qualified as a doctor, 1930. Has had many solo exhibitions in London and New York. He moved to Newlyn in 1945 and was influenced by Naum Gabo whilst he was living in Cornwall. His abstract paintings and reliefs associate him with the St. Ives School. Included in the collections of the Tate Gallery, Wakefield City Art Gallery, Gothenberg Museum, USA, Arts Council, British Council, CAS, Birmingham Museum, Plymouth Art Gallery and Ulster Museum.

WENTWORTH, Richard   b.1947
Sculptor. Born Samoa. Studied at Hornsey College of Art, and RCA. Uses everyday objects, altered and recombined in such a way as to suggest disruption and displacement.

WERNER, Michael   b.1912
Sculptor. Born London. Studied art in Paris. First solo exhibition at the Twenty Brook Street Gallery, 1949. Commissioned to make a bust of George Bernard Shaw for the Royal Court Theatre. Retrospective exhibition at Bradford City Art Gallery, 1965, and another 1982. Included in the collections of the Smithsonian Institute, Washington DC, USA, County Museum of Modern Art, Los Angeles USA, The Stellenbosch Museum, South Africa and New English Library, Oxford. Exhibits with Annely Juda Fine Art, London.

WESCHKE, Karl b.1925
Painter. Born Thuringen, Germany. Moved to England in 1948. Lived in Spain, 1953 and in Sweden, 1944-5. Awards include Art Council of Great Britain Major Award, 1976, and the South West Arts Major Award, 1978. First solo exhibition at the New Vision Centre Gallery, London, 1958. Included in the collections of the Tate Gallery, Arts Council of Great Britain, CAS, Ministry for the Environment, National Museum of Wales, City Galleries in Bristol and Plymouth, National Gallery of Victoria, Melbourne, and Museum of Modern Art New York. Recent solo exhibitions include one at the Redfern Gallery, London, 1985.

WESS, Glenys
Painter. Studied at Liverpool College of Art, 1952-7. First solo exhibition at Lane Gallery, Bradford, 1967. Included in the collection of Leeds University. Originally taught art in schools, then worked as a freelance fabric designer, before turning to painting in 1964.

WESS, Jim b.1933
Sculptor. Born Kirkby, Liverpool. Studied at Liverpool College of Art. First solo exhibition at the Manor House, Ilkley, 1966. Affiliated to the Constructionists and is best known for his wall sculptures.

WESSON, Edward b.1910
Painter. Born Blackheath, London. Self-taught as an artist. Elected to Royal Institute of Painters in Water-colour, 1952, and to Royal Society of Marine Painters, 1957. Solo exhibition at Arundel Arts Centre Ltd., West Sussex, 1983.

WEST, David b.1939
Painter and modelmaker. Born London. Studied at Sutton and Cheam School of Art, 1956-8, and at Camberwell School of Art and Crafts, 1958-60. First solo exhibition at Fisher Fine Art Ltd., London, 1985. He produces scaled down models of buildings such as houses, shops and theatre sets, as well as making imaginative and experimental models.

WEST, Francis b.1936
Painter. Born Scotland. Did National Service in the Far East, 1955-7. Studied at Chelsea School of Art, 1957-60. Lived in Turkey, 1966-7. First solo exhibition at the Hamet Gallery, London, 1978; others followed, at the Michael Parkin Gallery and Edward Totah Gallery, London.

WESTLEY, Ann b.1948
Sculptor and printmaker. Born Kettering, Northants. Studied at Northampton School of Art, 1965-7, at Bristol Polytechnic, 1967-70, and had a studio in the British School, Rome, 1970-1. Awards include Northampton Travel Award, 1967, which led her to visit Italy, the Gulbenkian Foundation Rome Scholarship in Sculpture, 1970, a Gulbenkian Printmakers Prize, 1982, and a British Council Grant, 1988. First solo exhibition at Ferens Art Gallery, Hull, 1973. Her prints portray violent scenes, drawn from mythological and other sources. Included in the collections of the Eastern Arts Association, the Gulbenkian Foundation, Bolton City Art Gallery, Essex University, Thameside Borough Metropolitan Council, and Leicestershire and Suffolk Schools Associations.

WESTWOOD, Dennis b.1928
Sculptor. Born Westcliff on Sea, Essex. Graduated from the RCA, 1955. He spent many years living in the Lake District, which provided the inspiration for his sculpture; his vocabulary of abstract forms has evolved from his response to the land and sea. Has regularly held solo exhibitions in Britain.

WHAITE, Gillian b.1934
Painter and printmaker. Born London. Studied at the Slade and the RA Schools. First solo exhibition at the South London Art Gallery, London, 1979. Included in the collections of St. Gabriel's College and Carnegie-Mellon University, Pittsburgh, USA.

WHALEN, Thomas 1903-1975
Sculptor. Born Leith, Scotland. Worked as a shipwright during the First World War, carving in his spare time with left-over bits of wood. Continued to carve during the 1920s whilst unemployed. His carvings were noticed and a scholarship obtained for him at Edinburgh College of Art, where he won the first Andrew Grant Fellowship. From 1930 exhibited at the RSA. Elected ARSA, 1940, and RSA, 1953. Commissions included a Mother and Child for the 1951 Festival of Britain.

WHARTON, Michael b.1933
Painter. Studied at the Slade, 1955-9. First solo exhibition in North East England in 1976; another held at the Gilbert Parr Gallery, London, 1978. An abstract painter, who uses swirls of colour which create structure out of the suggestion of movement through light and space.

WHEATLEY, Grace 1888-1970
Painter and sculptor. Born London, née Wolfe. Studied at Slade School, 1906-8, and in Paris at the Atelier Colarossi. Married John Wheatley,* 1912. Elected a member of the NEAC, 1921. Went to South Africa with her husband and lectured in Fine Art at the University of Cape Town, 1925-37. Returned to England, 1937 and settled in Sheffield. Elected ARWS, 1945, and RWS, 1952.

WHEATLEY, John 1892-1955
Painter and printmaker. Born Abergavenny, Wales. Studied under Stanhope Forbes,* Walter Sickert* and at the Slade School, 1912-13. Married Grace Wolfe (Wheatley*), 1912. Became a member of the NEAC, 1917. Official war artist, 1918-20. Assistant teacher at the Slade, 1920-5. Went to South Africa with his wife and was appointed Director of the National Gallery of South Africa and Michaelis Professor of Fine Art, University of Cape Town, 1925-37. Returned to England, 1937 and was appointed Director of Sheffield City Art Galleries, 1938-47. Curator of the National Gallery of British Sports and Pastimes, 1948-50. Elected ARWS, 1943, ARA, 1945, and RWS, 1947.

WHEELER, Charles 1892-1974
Sculptor. Born Codsall, Staffordshire. Studied at Wolverhampton College of Art, 1908-12 and the RCA, 1912-17 under Lanteri. From 1914 exhibited at the RA. 1926 elected ARBS, 1935, FRBS. 1934 elected ARA, 1940 RA. 1942-9 Trustee of the Tate Gallery. 1946 member of the Royal Fine Art Commission. 1948 awarded CBE. 1965 President of the RA. 1930 made reliefs and figures for the Bank of England, and the fountains in Trafalgar

ETHELBERT WHITE, 1891-1972. *'The Piggeries'*. Watercolour. 11in. x 14in. The Fine Art Society, London.

Square. Published his autobiography, *High Relief,* 1968. 1949 received the RBS Gold Medal for Distinguished Services to Sculpture. Knighted 1958. Represented in the Tate Gallery.

WHEELWRIGHT, Rowland   1870-1955
Painter and illustrator. Born Queensland, Australia. Moved to England and studied at Hubert Herkomer's School at Bushey, Hertfordshire. Painted historical and classical subjects, and executed black and white illustrations. Elected member of the RBA, 1906.

WHISHAW, Anthony   b.1930
Painter. Born London. Trained at Chelsea School of Art, 1948-52, and RCA, 1952-6. 1979 member of the London Group. 1980 elected ARA. Has won various prizes and scholarships, and has work in many public collections including the Tate Gallery, and National Gallery of Wales. Since 1957 he has had some twenty one-artist exhibitions, the most recent at Nicola Jacobs Gallery, London. A figurative artist who turned abstract in the late 1960s, but whose work retains allusions to landscape. In

the mid-1980s reintroduced the human figure in a series based on Velasquez's *Las Meninas,* and which were exhibited at the RA, 1987.

WHISTLER, Rex   1905-1944
Painter, illustrator and muralist. Born Eltham, Kent, brother of the glass engraver, Laurence Whistler. Studied at RA Schools and the Slade School of Fine Art. 1926 was invited to design and paint mural decorations in the Tate Gallery Refreshment Room (now the restaurant). His architectural fantasy, inspired in part by the gardens and monuments at Stowe and Wilton, epitomised his love of pastiche. The success of these murals ensured his success, and he became a prolific illustrator and designer. His illustrations to *Gulliver's Travels* (Cresset Press, 1935) make it one of the greatest illustrated books of this century. Also worked as a designer for theatre, ballet and opera. 1940 volunteered for the Welsh Guards, and was killed on active service.

Bibl: Laurence Whistler, *The Laughter and the Urn: The Life of Rex Whistler,* Weidenfeld and Nicolson, London, 1985.

WHITE, Caroline   b.1952
Painter and sculptor. Born London. Studied at St. Martin's School of Art, 1969-70, at Bristol Polytechnic, Faculty of Art and Design, 1970-3, and at Chelsea School of Art, 1973-4. 1975 first solo exhibition held at Bristol City Museum and Art Gallery, followed by many others, including one at Pelter/Sands Gallery, Bristol, 1990. 1976 won a South West Arts Minor Award, followed by South West Arts Major Awards, 1979 and 1981. Included in the collections of the Department of the Environment, the De Beer Collection, Eastern Arts, Bristol City Museum and Art Gallery and South West Arts.

WHITE, Ernest Howard   1908-83
Painter. Apprenticed as a lithographic artist and designer at Ratands Ltd., 1922. He also studied in evening classes at Hanley School of Art, 1922-30. 1970 became a member of the Society of Staffordshire Artists. 1978 first solo exhibition at Stafford Art Gallery. He painted many scenes of Hanley as it was in the early 20th century. Concentrating mostly on the 1920s, he has provided a view of the potteries that is nostalgic, but not sentimental. 1983 exhibited 'Old Hanley Retrospectives and Local Landscapes' at Stoke-on-Trent City Museum and Art Gallery.

WHITE, Ethelbert   1891-1972
Painter, wood engraver, poster designer and book illustrator. Born Isleworth, Middlesex. Studied at St. John's Wood School of Art, 1911-12. 1921 first solo exhibition held at Carfax Gallery. 1915 elected to the London Group, 1921 the NEAC, 1933 ARWS, 1934 RSW, and 1939 RWS. He produced many illustrations for books, among them Herbert Read's *Eclogues*, 1919, and Cyril Beaumont's monographs on ballets, *The Three Cornered Hat, L'Oiseau de Fen,* and *Tamar*. Regularly exhibited at the RA. 1979 memorial exhibition held at the Fine Art Society, London. Visited Spain, Italy, France, Belgium and Ireland, but worked mainly in England, finding his inspiration chiefly in the countryside. As watercolour became his dominant mode of expression in the 1920s, his style became freer, in contrast with the tighter handling evident in his engravings and early paintings. Represented in many British public collections.

Bibl: *Ethelbert White 1891-1972: A Memorial Exhibition,* Fine Art Society, London, 1979, with introduction by Peyton Skipwith.

WHITE, Gabriel   b.1902
Painter and etcher. Born Rome, Italy. Moved to Switzerland, 1906, and then to England, 1911. Studied at Westminster School of Art under Meninsky,* 1926-9, and at Central School of Art under Fred Porter,* 1928-30. He also exhibited with the London Group. 1930 held first solo exhibition at the Mayor Gallery, London. 1939-45 served in the Camouflage Organisation. 1945 became assistant director of the Arts Council, 1958 appointed director. In the 1950s he studied etching at the Slade School of Art under Anthony Gross.* After he retired from the Arts Council in 1970 he devoted himself to painting and etching full-time. Had several solo exhibitions at Sally Hunter Fine Art, London, during the 1980s, followed by a retrospective exhibition, 1989.

WHITE, Harry   b.1938
Sculptor. Born Newcastle upon Tyne, Tyne and Wear. Studied mechanical engineering, and worked as a designer in industry until 1960. 1960-1 National Service, and later studied at Sunderland College of Art. 1970 first solo exhibition at City Art Gallery, Plymouth.

WHITE, Kathleen
Painter. Studied at Lancaster School of Art, and under Theodore Major. First solo exhibition at Tib Lane Gallery, Manchester. Included in the collections of Salford and Lichfield City Art Galleries, Abbot Hall Art Gallery, Kendal, Bradford Education Committee, and Fitzwilliam College, Cambridge. Other solo exhibitions include one at the Goosewell Gallery, Manchester, 1972.

WHITE, Noel   b.1938
Painter. Born London. Studied at the West of England College of Art, and at the University of Aarhus, Denmark. He also studied privately with the philosopher, E.H. Visiak, and the Danish artist, M.J. Lange. First solo exhibition at Towner Art Gallery, Eastbourne, 1981, of paintings and drawings on the theme of Babylon.

WHITELEY, Alfred   b.1928
Painter. Studied at Chesterfield College of Art and RCA. 1957-83 taught at the Glyn Grammar School, Ewell. Has exhibited at the RA since 1980. Solo exhibitions include on at the Odette Gilbert Gallery, London, 1985.

WHITEFORD, Kate   b.1952
Painter, sculptor and printmaker. Born Glasgow, Scotland. Studied painting at Glasgow School of Art, 1969-73. Studied History of Art at Glasgow University, 1974-6. Whilst on a British Council Scholarship to Rome in 1976, she visited Pompeii and Herculaneum and the frescos she saw there influenced her paintings. First solo exhibition held at Stirling Art Gallery in 1978. Her early work was minimal and non-figurative, but from around 1980 she began incorporating classical lettering and archaeological imagery into her work. Her interest in ancient, runic symbolism is part of an attempt to tap a collective cultural consciousness. Moved to London, 1978. 1982-3 was artist-in-residence at St. Andrews University. 1984-5 artist-in-residence at the Whitechapel Art Gallery, London. Has held solo exhibitions at the Third Eye Centre, Glasgow, 1984, Riverside Studios, London, 1986, and the Frith Street Gallery, London, 1989. In 1987 she produced three vast land-works on Calton Hill, Edinburgh, using white stone chippings in shallow trenches describing fish and spiral motifs. She and two others represented Scotland at the Venice Biennale, 1990.

Bibl: *Puja: Ritual Offerings to the Gods,* Riverside Studios, London, 1986.

WHITTAKER, Edward   b.1948
Sculptor. Born Manchester. Studied at Slade School of Art, 1971-3. Has won several awards and taught in various art establishments. In the 1970s he assembled wall constructions out of wood, steel, felt, canvas, paint and other materials in an attempt to 'ventilate' the section of the wall that they covered. Included in the Arts Council touring exhibition, 'Style in the Seventies', 1979.

WHYMPER, Charles   1853-1941
Painter and wood engraver. Born London into a family of artists. Studied with the animal painter, Joseph Wolf. Painted landscapes, sporting subjects and animal pictures. Also practised as a wood engraver, etcher and illustrator in line, half-tone and full colour. The periodicals to which he contributed include *Good Words* and *The Illustrated London News.*

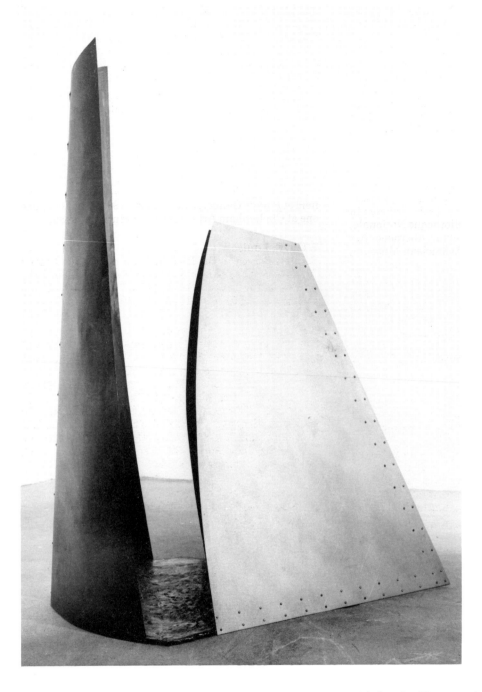

ALISON WILDING, b.1948.
'Stormy Weather', 1987.
Galvanised steel and bronze.
88½ in. x 45½ in. x 33½ in.
The Weltkunst Foundation
Collection. Photograph Karsten
Schubert Ltd.

WICKHAM, Mabel   b.1901
Painter. Born Fleet, Hampshire. Studied at Clapham High School, 1919-22. Later studied landscape painting under St. Clair Marston, every summer for fourteen years. 1936 elected to the Society of Women Artists, and 1938 to the RI. Early retirement from teaching in 1953 enabled her to devote more time to painting and travel. 1988 first solo exhibition at Chesil Gallery, Chiswell. Primarily a landscape painter, who portrays her local community with close attention to detail.

WIENER, Martin
Painter and printmaker. Born USA. Whilst making his career as a scriptwriter in Hollywood he began drawing. Travelled to Paris, 1961, where he studied printmaking with Stanley Hayter at Atelier 17. Moved to London when he was offered a research fellowship in Stained Glass at the RCA. Solo exhibition at the Boundary Gallery, London, 1987. A favourite image is the human profile, set against abstract patterns and shapes.

WIFFEN, Alfred K.   1896-1968
Painter. Born Eastwood, Nottinghamshire. After serving in the First World War and for a period farming in Nottinghamshire, he studied at Nottingham Art School. 1928 moved to Liverpool to teach Graphic Arts at Liverpool School of Art. Retired 1961. Subsequently President of Deeside Art Group. Member of Royal Cambrian Academy. Exhibited in London and Liverpool. Represented in Walker Art Gallery, Liverpool.

WIGG, Charles Mayes   1889-1969
Painter. Born Nottingham. Painted during childhood
visits to Florence and studied at Norwich School of Art.
Served in the army during the First World War, but was
invalided out after being wounded at Gaza. Produced
firmly drawn and coloured paintings as well as etchings in
which wherries are usually predominant. His career was
abruptly terminated in 1952 when he married his
mother's nurse who prevented him painting and even
broke his brushes. Much of his work was put on to a
bonfire. Not until he became a widower was he able to
resume his career.

WIGHT, Dorothea   b.1944
Printmaker. Born Devon. Studied at Dartington School of
Art, 1963-4, and at the Slade, 1964-8. First solo exhibition
at Edinburgh Festival King's Theatre, 1969. Included in
the collections of British Council, Bibliotheque Nationale,
Paris, University of British Columbia, Aberdeen Art
Galleries and Museums, Scotland, Ashmolean Museum,
Oxford, and Bedford County Council.

WIGLEY, John   b.1962
Sculptor. Studied at Reading University, 1980-4, and the
RCA, 1986-8. 1985 awarded a Boise Travelling Scholar-
ship. 1988 Rome Scholar in Sculpture. First solo exhibition,
'Landlocked and Overboard', held at St. David's Hall,
Cardiff. Others include 'Occasional Tables' at the Berkeley
Square Gallery, London, 1990.

WILBOURN, Colin   b.1956
Sculptor. Born Hertfordshire. Studied at Hertfordshire
College of Art, 1974-5, Newcastle upon Tyne Polytechnic,
1975-8, and at Newcastle upon Tyne University, 1978-80.
1983 awarded Fellowship from Yorkshire Arts as 'Artist
in Industry'. 1986-7 Artist in Residence at Durham
Cathedral. 1981 first solo exhibition at the Spectro
Gallery, Newcastle upon Tyne. Included in the collections
of Northern Arts, Rowntree Mackintosh, York, and
Durham Cathedral.

WILD, Chris   b.1945
Painter. Born Birmingham, West Midlands. Studied at
Birmingham School of Art. Solo exhibition at Omell
Galleries, London, 1986. His paintings are naturalistic,
generally depicting dilapidated and decaying cottages and
farm buildings which are his favourite subjects.

WILDE, David   b.1931
Painter. Born Burnley, Lancashire. Studied at Burnley
Municipal School of Art, the Slade and the British School
in Rome. First solo exhibition at the Tib Lane Gallery,
Manchester. Included in the collections of the Walker Art
Gallery, Liverpool; Bolton, Blackburn, Manchester City
and Salford Art Galleries and Granada TV, Manchester.

WILDE, Fred
Painter. Studied at Hyde Art School and Manchester
Municipal. Freelance textile designer, 1929-39. Head
textile designer for John Colt and Co., 1946-70. During
this time he made many trips to West Africa. First solo
exhibition at Liverpool Academy Gallery, 1973.

WILDE, Gerald   1905-1986
Painter. Born London. Studied at Chelsea School of Art,
1926-35. First solo exhibition at the Hanover Gallery,
London, 1948. Included in the collections of the Arts
Council of Great Britain, Fitzwilliam Museum, Magdalen
and Pembroke Colleges, Oxford, and the Tate Gallery.
Wilde was associated with Fitzrovia in the 1940s. In 1954
he spent some time in a mental hospital and after that date
painted only sporadically. Solo exhibition at the
Serpentine Gallery, London, 1977. Memorial exhibition
held at the October Gallery, London, 1988.

Bibl: *Gerald Wilde, 1905-1986,* ed. Chili Hawes, October Gallery,
London, and Synergetic Press, Oracle, Arizona, 1988.

WILDE, Helen   b.1954
Printmaker. Studied at Gloucester College of Art and
Design, 1974-80, and RCA, 1980-3. Rome Scholar in
Printmaking, 1983-5. 1986 Brinkley Fellowship in
Printmaking, Norwich School of Art. First solo exhibition
held at Parade Gallery, Cheltenham, 1982; others include
one at Cheltenham Art Gallery and Museum, 1985.

WILDE, Louise
Painter. Served in the RAF in India during the Second
World War. Entered Leeds College of Art, 1951. Founder
member of the 'Sevens' Group, 1954. First solo exhibition
at Chiltern Art Gallery, London, 1959.

WILDING, Alison   b.1948
Sculptor. Born Blackburn, Lancashire. Studied at Ravensbourne College of Art, 1967-70 and the RCA, 1970-3. First
solo exhibition at Kettle's Yard Gallery, Cambridge,
1982, with further ones at Salvatore Ala Gallery, Milan,
and the Serpentine Gallery, 1985, Salvatore Ala Gallery,
New York, 1983 and 1986, Karsten Schubert Ltd., and the
projects Gallery at MOMA, New York, 1987. Her work is
in several public collections, e.g. the British Council, the
Tate Gallery. She works with cast metals, rubber, wood,
wax and often colours her work.

WILDING, Noel   1903-1966
Painter. Born Sutton, Surrey. Studied at Richmond Art
School. Continued to paint whilst working as a journalist.
Served in the RNVR during the Second World War.
1952-65 lived in the South of France. 1960 first solo
exhibition at Galerie Tedesco, Paris; others include one at
the Furneaux Galleries, London, 1966.

WILENSKI, Reginald Howard   1887-1975
Painter and critic. Studied at Frank Brangwyn's* London
School of Art, where he dressed in a Bohemian fashion. He
became better known as an author and critic, his art
criticism promoting the modern movement and the
'architectural' qualities in painting.

WILKINSON, Norman   1878-1971
Painter and illustrator. Born Cambridge. In 1895 his
family moved to Southsea, Hampshire, where he attended
the Portsmouth and Southsea School of Art. Dr. Conan
Doyle introduced him to Jerome K. Jerome, the author and
publisher of *Idler* and *Today.* Began to work as an
illustrator, for *The Illustrated London News* and
elsewhere. Studied painting at St. Ives and in Paris.
Travelled widely as an illustrator, reporting on the Russo-
Japanese war for *The Illustrated London News,* and also
gained fame as a painter of ships and became an
innovative poster artist with the work he produced for the
London North West Region Company. 1915 served in the
navy and did on-the-spot drawings for his book, *The
Dardenelles,* published that year. 1917 invented dazzle

GLYNN WILLIAMS, b.1939.
'Cat's Cradle', 1988.
Ancaster stone. 10in. x 7in. x 6in.
Bernard Jacobson Gallery.

camouflage and in 1939 camouflaged airfields for the RAF. Painted 56 pictures of Second World War naval actions, now in the National Maritime Museum.

WILLATS, Stephen   b.1943
Mixed media artist and community artist. Born London. Lectured at Ipswich School of Art, 1965-7, Nottingham College of Art, 1968-72. 1972-3 organised Centre for Behavioural Art, Gallery House, London. 1978 awarded Fellowship for 1979 by the DAAD, Berlin. Has worked on various community projects on housing estates and elsewhere. Has also lectured widely and published many writings and statements.

Bibl: *Stephen Willats: Concerning our Present Way Of Living*, Whitechapel Art Gallery, 1979.

WILCOX, Ted
Embroiderer. Born Brentford, Middlesex. Served in the RAF during the Second World War. Wounded in 1943 and during convalescence he began to practise embroidery. From this date he has specialised in embroidering images of women. First solo exhibition at the Portal Gallery, London. His embroidered images are based on magazine illustrations and have earned him the praise of Peter Blake.*

WILLIAMS, Andrew   b.1954
Painter. Born Barry, South Wales. Studied at Edinburgh University and Edinburgh College of Art, 1972-7. 1979-80 lived in France, and 1984 worked in New York. Awards include the Scottish Council Young Artists Bursary, 1983.

1979 first solo exhibition held at the 369 Gallery, Edinburgh. He has exhibited here regularly since this date in group and solo exhibitions. Uses an expressionistic style and dissonant colour, and paints male figures, often in movement.

Bibl: *Andrew Williams,* 369 Gallery, Edinburgh, 1979.

WILLIAMS, Aubrey   1926-1990
Painter. Born Guyana, South America. Worked in the civil service in Guyana and trained under De Winter and Burrowes. Participated in 'Working Peoples' Art Group. 1952 moved to Britain and studied at St. Martin's School of Art; later travelled widely in Europe. 1955 held first solo exhibition at the Archer Gallery, London. Thereafter exhibited at the New Vision Centre Gallery, London. 1965 won the Commonwealth Prize for painting. 1966 founder-member of the Caribbean Artists Movement. Throughout 1970s and 1980s worked and exhibited as much in the Caribbean as in London. A major solo exhibition was held at the Commonwealth Institute, London, 1985.

WILLIAMS, Chester   b.1921
Painter. Born Lewiston, Idaho, USA. Studied at Academia di Belliarti, Venice, 1949-53, and at the Courtauld Institute, London, 1954. First solo exhibition at the Drian Galleries, London, 1964. Included in the collections of the Italian Government, New College, Oxford, Aberdeen Art Gallery, National Gallery of Poland, Eastern Arts Association and Unilever.

WILLIAMS, Christopher   1873-1934
Painter. Born Maesteg, South Wales. Studied at the Technical Institute, Neath, 1892-3, and at the RCA, 1893-6, for which he was awarded a scholarship. 1896-1901 studied at the RA, where he was awarded a Landseer scholarship for two years. 1902 first exhibited at the RA. 1904 travelled in Italy and 1914 in Spain and Morocco. 1906 elected a member of the RBA. 1935 a memorial exhibition of his work was held at The Palser Gallery, London. Painted mostly portraits and landscapes.

WILLIAMS, David   b.1934
Painter. Born Torquay, Devon. Studied at Devon College of Art, 1959-64, and at Hornsey College of Art, 1965-7. First solo exhibition held at Battersea Arts Centre. His abstract paintings are derived from architecture, graphs, mass production and computer print-outs.

WILLIAMS, Emrys   b.1958
Painter. Born Liverpool, Merseyside. Studied at Slade School of Art, 1976-8. Awards include Boise Travelling Scholarship, 1980 and Stewart Powell Bowen Fellowship; Artist in Residence, Mostyn Art Galley, Llandudno, 1983; Artist in Residence, South Hill Park Arts Centre and Wild Theatre, Bracknell, 1985; and Welsh Arts Council Award for Travel in Normandy, France, 1988. First solo exhibitions at the Andrew Knight Gallery, Cardiff, and Wrexham Arts Centre, 1984. Exhibited with the Benjamin Rhodes Gallery, 1989. Included in the Government Art Collection.

WILLIAMS, Evelyn   b.1929
Painter and sculptor. Studied at St. Martin's School of Art, 1944-7, RCA, 1947-50. 1958 first solo exhibition held at Woodstock Gallery, London. 1972 retrospective exhibition held at Whitechapel Art Gallery. Recent solo exhibitions include one at the Ikon Gallery, Birmingham, 1985. Much of her painting has been about the conflict between the demands of family life and artistic creation. She began to use papier mâché in reliefs, afterwards turning to clay, then wax and finally modelling material for her three-dimensional works. Has continued her dedication to the human figure, often found in simple timeless relationships or in the depths of despair. Recent solo exhibitions include one at the Riverside Studios, 1986. Represented in Arts Council collection, Rugby Art Gallery, Leicestershire Museums and Art Galleries, Nuffield Foundation, Department of the Environment and Graves Art Gallery, Sheffield.

WILLIAMS, Fred   1930-1985
Painter. Born Manchester. Began his career as an apprentice in engineering, later becoming a draughtsman, Outward Bound Instructor and art teacher. He became a professional artist, 1976. Founder member of the Yorkshire Watercolour Society, a member of the Fylingdales Group and a Fellow of Architectural Illustrators. First solo exhibition at Whitby, 1981.

WILLIAMS, Glynn   b.1939
Sculptor. Born Shrewsbury, Shropshire. Studied at Wolverhampton College of Art, 1955-61, and at the British School in Rome, 1961-3. 1967 first solo exhibition held ICA Gallery, London. A dozen others followed including one at Bernard Jacobson Gallery, London, 1988. Began as an abstract sculptor, but then turned to figuration, working in a style that updates that of Eric Gill.*

WILLIAMS, Haydon   b.1942
Textile designer and painter. Studied at Loughborough College of Art, 1958-62, and at the RCA, 1962-5. 1965-6 lived and worked in New York as a freelance textile and wallpaper designer. Awards include Council of Industrial Design Award for printed fabric, 1968, and 1st prize in an International Carpet Design competition, organised by 'Gilt Edge' Carpets Ltd., 1969. In the same year he held his first solo exhibition for paintings and collages at the Drian Gallery, London.

WILLIAMS, Jacqueline   b.1962
Painter. Studied at Gloucester College of Art, 1982-5, and at the RA, 1985-8. Awards include Antique Collectors' Prize 1987, and the de Segonzac Travel Scholarship and Elizabeth Greenshields Award, 1988. First solo exhibition held at the New Grafton Gallery, London, 1989.

WILLIAMS, Kit   b.1946
Painter and craftsman. His work has become well known since the success of his book *Masquerade.* His works are highly detailed, juxtaposing the fantastic with the everyday. In addition to painting he regularly works with silver, gold, precious stones and marquetry. Commissioned to make a clock for the City of Cheltenham. Since 1970 has exhibited with the Portal Gallery, London; he has also exhibited in Japan, Germany and the USA. Published *Masquerade* (1979); *The Bee on the Comb* (1984); *Out of One Eye* (1986).

WILLIAMS, Kyffin   b.1918
Painter. Born Llangefni, Anglesey, North Wales. Studied at Slade School of Art, 1941-4. Solo exhibitions at Leicester Galleries, London, 1951, 1953, 1956, 1960, 1966 and 1970. 1970 elected ARA, and 1974 RA. 1968 was awarded the Winston Churchill Fellowship to record the Welsh in Patagonia, and 1969 was elected President of the Royal

WILLIAMS, Michael

Cambrian Academy. 1982 awarded OBE. 1985 became Deputy Lieutenant for the county of Gwynedd. Recent solo exhibitions include a retrospective held at the Mortyn Art Gallery, Wales, 1987. His landscapes are mostly bleak, pared down, the shapes made still more abrupt by the use of thick impasto laid on with the palette knife.

Bibl: Kyffin Williams, *Across the Straits* (autobiography), Duckworth, London, 1973

WILLIAMS, Michael   b.1936

Painter. Born Patna, India. Read Modern History at Oxford University, afterwards studying art history and painting in Paris. Lectured in art history at St. Martin's School of Art, 1962-71, then moved to Goldsmiths' College, but in 1980 reduced his teaching commitments to concentrate on painting. 1981-4 active in the Association of Artists and Designers in Wales as editor of *Link*. 1988 solo exhibition held at Austin/Desmond Fine Art, with a catalogue introduction by Peter Fuller who praised his 'unfashionable fidelity to the evidence which presents itself to the eye'.

WILLIAMS-ELLIS, David   b.1959

Sculptor. Born Ireland. Studied in Florence with Signorina Nerina Simi and as a part-time apprentice with Florentine woodcarvers, 1977-8. 1979-80 awarded the Elizabeth T. Greenshield Foundation Scholarship, which enabled him to study with marble carvers in Pietra Santa and Carrara, Italy. 1981-2 he studied part-time at the Sir John Cass School of Art. 1987 first solo exhibition at the Otter Gallery, Belfast. His portraits and figurative pieces maintain a traditional, humanist approach.

WILLIAMSON, Harold   1898-1972

Painter. Born Manchester. Studied in evening classes at Manchester School of Art, 1913-16. Served in the Royal Navy Volunteer Reserve, 1916-19. Later, he returned to study at Manchester School of Art with a scholarship, 1919-22. He regularly exhibited at the RA and with the NEAC. 1979 solo exhibition at the Belgrave Gallery, London. Included in the collections of Southampton, Manchester, Southport and Bournemouth Art Galleries.

WILLIAMSON, Harold Sandys   b.1892

Painter and poster designer. Born Leeds, Yorkshire. Studied at Leeds School of Art, 1911-14, and the RA Schools, 1914-15, where he received the Turner Gold Medal. Served with the King's Royal Rifle Corps during the First World War. Exhibited at the RA, with the NEAC and the London Group, he became headmaster of Chelsea Polytechnic, 1930-58. Designed posters for the Empire Marketing Board, the GPO and the Council for the Encouragement of Music and the Arts. Throughout his career he retained a documentary style, making vivid use of detail. Represented in the Imperial War Museum.

WILLIAMSON, Jane   b.1921

Painter. Born Yorkshire. Served in the WAAF during the Second World War. Moved to Uganda after she married in 1948, and later returned to England after her husband's death. Studied under Patricia Willis in 1960, at the Byam Shaw School of Art and Drawing and at Heatherley's. First solo exhibition at the Cassel Gallery, London.

WILLING, Victor   1928-1988

Painter. Born Alexandria, Egypt. Moved to England, 1932. Studied at Slade School of Fine Art, 1949-54. 1955 first solo exhibition held at Hanover Gallery, London. 1957-74 lived in Portugal. 1974 returned to London. 1980 received the Thorne Scholarship. 1982 Artist-in-Residence, Corpus Christi College and Kettle's Yard, Cambridge. His paintings were based on the workings of the subconscious which began to obsess him when he fell ill with multiple sclerosis. He married the artist, Paula Rego.*

Bibl: *Victor Willing: A Retrospective Exhibition, 1952-85*, Whitechapel Art Gallery, 1986.

WILLIS, Lucy   b.1954

Painter. Studied at Ruskin School of Drawing and Fine Art, Oxford, 1972-5. 1976 moved to Greece and set up an etching workshop in affiliation with the Aegean School of Fine Art. 1978 returned to England and 1980 set up the Moorland House Workshop, Somerset. 1978 first solo exhibition held at Market Print Gallery, Exeter. She has regularly exhibited at Chris Beetles, London, where she first held a solo exhibition, 1986, followed by two more exhibitions, 1988 and 1989. Her works are naturalistic, loosely rendering the detail of domestic subjects in Britain and Greece.

WILLIS, Victor

Painter. Studied at Camberwell School of Art, City and Guilds of London Art School and Sir John Cass College. First solo exhibition at Woodlands Art Gallery, London, 1983. His austere, somewhat quirky pictures are often based on myths.

WILLOUGHBY, Trevor   b.1926

Painter. Studied at Hull Regional College of Art, 1947-50, and at the London School of Painting. Worked at S.H. Benson Advertising Agency, 1952, and then freelanced as an illustrator, working for leading magazines. First exhibited at the RA and RP, 1956. Elected RP, 1967. Has had eight solo exhibitions and has participated in many group shows. Represented by RP.

WILLSHER, Brian   b.1930

Sculptor. Born Catford, London. Studied engineering at Woolwich Polytechnic, afterwards doing a variety of jobs and finally qualifying as a dental technician. Turned to creative work in the mid-1950s and at first applied his interest in sculpture to the making of wooden bases for lamps. He exhibited regularly in the second half of the 1960s, but then held back from public exhibitions for twenty years, until 1990, when he exhibited at the Boundary and the Belgrave Galleries, London.

WILLSON, Graeme   b.1951

Painter. Born North Yorkshire. Studied at Reading University, 1969-73. Began painting full-time, 1975. Solo exhibitions include one at Sloane Street Gallery, London, 1977 and one at Cartwright Hall, Bradford, 1980. Has produced a number of religious pictures for churches and schools.

WILLSON, Terry   b.1948

Printmaker. Studied at Bradford Regional College of Art, 1966-7, at Stourbridge College of Art, 1970-3, and at the Slade, 1973-5. 1975-6 awarded the Prix de Rome Scholarship in Etching and Engraving, Rome, Italy. 1978-82 set up Palm Tree Editions, where he published his own and other artists' work. 1974 first solo exhibition held at Perrins Art Gallery, London. Included in the collections of the Tate Gallery, V & A, and in many other city and regional galleries in Great Britain, Europe and the USA.

WILSON, Arthur   b.1929

Sculptor. Born London. Studied at Chelsea School of Art.

VICTOR WILLING, 1928-1988.
'Mask drawing', 1984.
Pastel and charcoal.
11in. x 15in.
Bernard Jacobson Gallery.

Later he studied air wave forms while an air radar fitter in the RAF. Elected a member of the London Group, 1968. First solo exhibition at the Arnolfini Gallery, Bristol, 1966, when he showed a series of constructions based on the theme of the sea.

WILSON, Avray   b.1914
Painter. Studied Natural Sciences at Cambridge University and became a full-time painter, 1947. First solo exhibition held in England, 1960; he has exhibited widely throughout Europe and the USA. His abstract paintings derive inspiration from the urban and industrial environment.

WILSON, Cyril   b.1911
Painter. Born High Wycombe, Buckinghamshire. Studied at Reading College of Art. 1941-7 President of the Forces Art Club, Cairo. 1948 moved to live in Dumfries, Scotland; after 1959 he regularly visited Ibiza. 1954-8 President of

Dumfries and Galloway Fine Arts Society. 1955 elected a professional member of the Society of Scottish Artists. Included in the collections of Scottish National Gallery of Modern Art, Museum of Modern Art, Cairo, Scottish Arts Council, Dundee Art Gallery and Gracefield Art Gallery, Dumfries.

WILSON, David Forrester   1873-1950
Painter and muralist. Born Glasgow, Scotland, son of John Wilson, a lithographer. Exhibited at the RSA, the Royal Glasgow Institute of Fine Arts, in Liverpool and America. Commissioned by Glasgow Corporation to paint one of a series of decorative panels in the Banqueting Hall in Glasgow Municipal Buildings. Represented in several public collections.

WILSON, Douglas   b.1936
Painter. Studied at Ruskin School, Oxford, under Percy

WILSON, Elaine

Horton.* Elected a Royal Cambrian Academician. First solo exhibition at the Bluecoat Gallery, Liverpool; others include two at King Street Galleries, London, 1983 and 1986, and the Phoenix Gallery, Kingston-upon-Thames, 1987. He lives and works in Shropshire. His main interest and inspiration is derived from the English countryside from which he seeks to capture a timeless quality.

WILSON, Elaine   b.1959

Sculptor. Born Kilmarnock, Scotland. Studied at Duncan of Jordonstone College of Art, 1977-81, and RA Schools, 1981-4. Has won several scholarships and awards. 1984-6 travelled and worked in Italy. Began exhibiting at the 369 Gallery, Edinburgh, 1981, which gave her a solo exhibition, 1987.

WILSON, Franklyn   b.1941

Sculptor. Born Fazakerly, Lancashire. Studied at Liverpool College of Art, 1960-3, and the RCA, 1964-7. 1963-4 awarded a City Travelling Scholarship, which he spent travelling in France and Italy. 1967 first solo exhibition at 346 Kings Road, London. Included in the collection of the Arts Council of Great Britain.

WILSON, Helen   b.1954

Painter. Born Paisley, Scotland. Studied at Glasgow School of Art and Hospitalfield, 1974-6. Awards include Governor's Prize, Glasgow School of Art and the Robert Hart Bursary, 1974, a Cargill Travelling Scholarship to Colonsay and Italy, 1976-7, and Lauder Award, Glasgow Society of Women Artists, 1979. Travelled in Italy and Yugoslavia, 1975. First solo exhibition at the Glasgow School of Art, 1978. Included in the collections of Glasgow Art Gallery and Museums, the Scottish Arts Council, the Glasgow School of Art, the Royal Society of Physicians and Surgeons, the Bank of Scotland, and Arthur Anderson & Co.

WILSON, Lyons   b.1892

Painter. Born Leeds, Yorkshire. Since 1925 has exhibited regularly at the RA. Held a solo exhibition at the Rimmel Gallery, London.

WILSON, Ross   b.1959

Painter. Born Co. Antrim, Northern Ireland. Studied at Ulster Polytechnic, 1978-9, the College of Art and Design, Belfast, 1979-82, and Chelsea School of Art, 1982-3. Commissions include six drawings for BBC Northern Ireland, 1982, and a portrait for Ulster Museum, Belfast, 1983. In the same year the Arts Council of Northern Ireland commissioned him to produce a limited edition of prints. 1983-4 Artist in Residence at Harmony Hill Art Centre, Lisburn. 1980 first solo exhibition at Queen's University, Belfast. In his work naturalistic images are juxtaposed with abstract shapes and patterns. Included in the collections of the Department of the Environment, the Arts Council of Northern Ireland, Queen's University of Belfast, the Ulster Museum, Belfast, the County Museum, Enniskillen, and the Northern Ireland Housing Executive.

WILSON, Scottie   1889-1972

Painter. Born Glasgow, Scotland, of working-class parents. Had a scant formal education. 1906 enlisted in the army and served in India, South Africa and France. Around 1930 he went to Canada and opened a junk shop in Toronto. He collected old fountain pens in order to salvage the gold nibs and with one of these he began to draw; using closely hatched black lines and coloured crayons, he created totemic images of birds, flowers, castles, trees, streams and the eerie faces of his 'Greedies' and 'Evils'. Held his first solo exhibition at the Picture Loan Society, Toronto, 1943. 1945 moved to London and exhibited in several London galleries, as well as in Paris, Basle and New York, though his preferred exhibition venue was an old bus. His work was admired by the Surrealists, and in 1952 he went to Paris to meet Dubuffet who had shown his work in his 1949 *Art Brut* exhibition. 1964 the Royal Worcester Porcelain Company commissioned him to design some plates; also did tapestry designs for the Aubusson factory in France and the Edinburgh Tapestry Company, as well as a mural for a bank in Zurich.

George Melly, *'It's all writ out for you'. The Life and Work of Scottie Wilson,* Thames & Hudson, London, 1986.

WILSON, William   1905-1972

Printmaker. Born Edinburgh, Scotland. Served an apprenticeship in the stained glass studio of James Ballantine, Edinburgh. Studied etching and engraving at Edinburgh College of Art and in 1932 won a travelling scholarship to France, Germany, Spain and Italy. Further scholarships enabled him to move to study engraving at the RCA and contemporary stained glass in Germany. His prints reflect an admiration for Mantegna and Italian Primitive art; they gradually became more dramatic and darkly expressive. 1937 he opened his own stained glass studio in Edinburgh and established a wide reputation through his work for cathedrals and churches in Britain and overseas. Has been acclaimed by his fellow etcher, Ian Fleming,* as the master of Scottish 20th century print making. A large collection of his graphic work can be found in the Scottish National Gallery of Modern Art, Edinburgh. Elected SSA, 1930, ARSA, 1939, RSW, 1946 and RSA, 1949. Lost his sight, 1961.

WINGATE, James Lawton   1846-1924

Painter. Born Glasgow, Scotland. Received no formal art training and did not take up painting seriously until the age of twenty-six. From 1880 exhibited at the RA, but was a more regular contributor to the RSA. Elected ARSA, 1879, RSA, 1886 and became President of the RSA, 1919. His initial interest in Scottish genre subjects gave way to a concern purely with landscape. Knighted.

WINGRAVE, Mark   b.1957

Painter. Studied at Portsmouth College of Art and Design, 1974-7, Bath Academy of Art, 1978-81, and Chelsea School of Art, 1981-2. 1982-4 Abbey Major Scholarship in Painting, British School at Rome. First solo exhibition held at Centro di Sarro, Rome, 1985; others include one at Galerie Rudolf Mangisch, Zurich, 1990.

WINTER, William Tatton   1855-1928

Painter. Born Ashton-under-Lyne, Lancashire. Initially began work in a Manchester business, studying art in the evenings at Manchester Academy of Fine Arts. When he began painting full-time he visited Holland and Belgium and studied under Verlat at the Antwerp Academy. From 1889 exhibited at the RA, also at the Paris Salon and in Munich. 1902 elected a member of the London Sketch Club. Specialised in landscape, especially that of south east England.

EDWARD WOLFE, 1897-1981.
'Charlotte Haldene', 1932.
40in. x 30in.
Odette Gilbert Gallery.

WISZNIEWSKI, Adrian   b.1958

Painter. Born Glasgow, Scotland, of Polish extraction. Studied at the Mackintosh School of Architecture, Glasgow, 1975-9, and Glasgow School of Art, 1979-83. Won several scholarships and held his first solo exhibition at the Compass Gallery, Glasgow, and at the AIR Gallery, London, 1984. 1986-7 artist-in-residence at the Walker Art Gallery, Liverpool, where he held another solo exhibition, 1987. His paintings depict an Arcadian world populated by young men, many of whom are covert self-portraits. Much of his early work was confined to charcoal on paper but since 1985-6 he has concentrated on large scale oil paintings. If his work has become less densely patterned, the arcane symbolism, suggestive of suppressed sexual desire, is still in evidence. Often there are allusions to the work of other artists, to Van Gogh, de Chirico and the Surrealists.

Bibl: *Adrian Wiszniewski,* Walker Art Gallery, Liverpool, 1987.

WITKIN, Isaac   b.1936

Born Johannesburg, South Africa, where he worked as an apprentice to a sculptor. Came to England, 1956. Studied at St. Martin's School of Art, 1957-60. 1960 worked part-time for Anthony Caro.* 1961-4 assistant to Henry Moore.* Became associated with the New Generation sculptors of the 1960s and held his first solo exhibition at the Rowan Gallery, 1963. 1963-6 taught at St. Martin's School of Art. 1966 taught at Bennington College, Vermont, USA. Represented in the collections of the Tate Gallery and the Arts Council.

WOLFE, Edward   1897-1981

Painter. Born Johannesburg, South Africa. Became a child actor before emigrating to England where he studied art at Regent Street Polytechnic, 1916, and the Slade School of Fine Art 1917-18. Introduced by Nina Hamnett*

WOLLAND, Peter

to Roger Fry's* Omega Workshops. 1919 fell ill with Spanish influenza and returned to South Africa to recuperate; also travelled to France, Italy, Morocco, Spain, America and Mexico and became known as 'England's Matisse', owing to his use of strong colour. Member of the London Group, the 7 & 5 Society, and the London Artists' Association. 1967 elected ARA, and 1972 RA.

WOLLAND, Peter   b.1961
Painter. Studied at Reading University, 1979-83, and University of Newcastle upon Tyne, 1985-7. 1987 awarded British Academy Travel Grant and visited Washington and New York. 1987-8 Rome Scholar in Painting. First solo exhibition held at University of Newcastle upon Tyne, Long Gallery, 1987; another held at Newcastle upon Tyne Polytechnic, 1990.

WOLMARK, Alfred   1877-1961
Painter. Born Warsaw, Poland. Came to England, 1883. From 1895 studied at the RA Schools and won a silver medal. From 1901 exhibited at the RA and held his first solo show at the Bruton Galleries, London, 1905. He lived and worked at Concarneau in Brittany, 1910-12, where he developed a Post-Impressionist style using slabs of colour and simplified design. Returned to London and was a friend of David Bomberg* and others. Represented in the Tate Gallery, the Cartwright Hall, Bradford and other public collections.

WOLSELEY, Garnet   1884-1969
Painter. Trained at the School of Painting, Bushey, Hertfordshire, and at the Slade where he won a scholarship. Was associated with Newlyn during the pre-1914 period. During the First World War he served in the navy and painted watercolours of ships and aeroplanes in his spare time. After the war, he took a studio in Chelsea and became a fashionable portrait painter. Associate of the Royal West of England Academy.

WONNACOTT, John   b.1940
Painter. Born London. Studied at Slade School of Fine Art, 1958-63. Has taught at Reading and Norwich Schools of Art. Solo exhibitions include one at The Minories, Colchester, 1977, Rochdale Art Gallery, 1978 and one at Marlborough Fine Art, London, 1981. All his paintings stay close to direct observation and render period detail in timeless fashion.

WOOD, Alan   b.1935
Painter. Born Widnes, Lancashire. Studied at Liverpool College of Art, 1956-9. Has taught in Devon and Leeds. 1964 commissioned to paint a large mural for Bodington Head, University of Leeds Hall of Residence. Solo exhibition at New Art Centre, 1964.

WOOD, Andrew   b.1947
Painter. Born Porlock, Somerset. Studied at Croydon College of Art, 1966-8 and Newport College of Art, 1968-70. First solo exhibition held at Westgate Gallery, Winchester, 1979. Member of the RI. Recent solo exhibitions include one at the Thackeray Gallery, London, 1981.

WOOD, Christopher   1901-1930
Painter. Born Knowsley, near Liverpool. After initial attempts at studying medicine and architecture, in 1921 he went to Paris and enrolled at the Académie Julian. Became a friend of Jose Antonio de Gandarillas and with

JOHN WONNACOTT, b.1940. 'The Grandfather', 1965-9. 93in. x 48in. Thomas Agnew & Sons Ltd., London.

him travelled through Europe, and North Africa and Greece. Returning to France he enjoyed friendships with Picasso and Cocteau. 1924 exhibited at Heals, in London, and 1925 at the Redfern Gallery, with Paul Nash.* 1926 met Ben* and Winifred Nicholson* and painted with them in St. Ives, Cornwall. 1928 visited Cumberland with the Nicholsons, and Cornwall, where he met Alfred Wallis* whom he befriended. Became a member of the 7 & 5 Society and practised the *faux-naïf* style associated with this exhibiting group. His paintings, especially those produced in Brittany during the last few months of his life, combine a remarkable directness of touch with a lyrical sense of colour.

Bibl: *Christopher Wood*, with introduction by William Mason, Arts Council Catalogue, 1979.

ANDREW WOOD, b.1947. *'Tea with Piet'*. Acrylic. 14in. x 18in. Private Collection.

CHRISTOPHER WOOD, 1901-1930. *'Sleeping Fisherman, Ploare. Brittany'*, 1930. 14⅞in. x 28⅝in. Tyne & Wear County Council Museum.

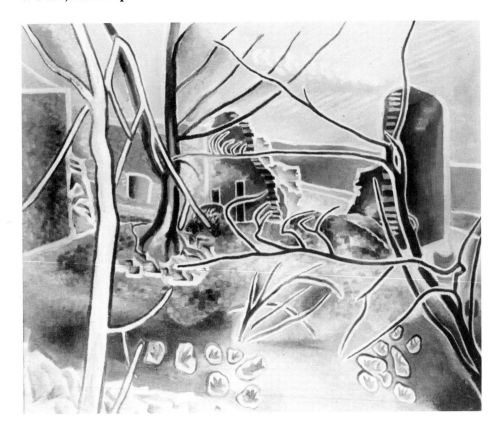

JAMES WOOD, 1889-1975.
'Sharples Ruin', 1945.
Blond Fine Art Limited.

WOOD, Christopher P.   b.1961

Painter and printer. Born Leeds, Yorkshire. Studied at Jacob Kramer College of Art, Leeds, 1980-1, Leeds Polytechnic, 1981-4, and at Chelsea College of Art, 1985-6. Printmaker in Residence at Leeds Polytechnic, January-February, 1987, followed by a residency at Oldham Art Gallery in February, 1987. First solo exhibition at Sue Williams, London, 1989; he held a second exhibition at the same gallery, 1990. Included in the collections of Oldham Art Gallery and Leeds City Art Gallery.

WOOD, David   b.1944

Painter. Born Rochdale, Lancashire. Studied at Rochdale College of Art, Manchester College of Art and Design and RCA. Awarded David Murray Landscape Scholarship and other prizes. First solo exhibition held at Goosewell Gallery, Menston, 1970.

WOOD, Flora   b.1910

Painter. Born Portobello, near Edinburgh, Scotland. Studied in Florence and for a short period in Paris under André L'Hôte. Entered the Edinburgh School of Art, 1930, afterwards spent two terms at Glasgow School of Art. Exhibited in mixed exhibitions from the 1940s onwards, at the RSA, the Royal Glasgow Institute of the Fine Arts, Scottish Society of Women Artists and Glasgow Society of Women Artists. Solo exhibitions include one at the Lillie Art Gallery, Milngavie, Glasgow, 1979 and another at England and Co., London, 1989. A figurative artist who has painted in a number of styles, but frequently displays a bias towards the geometric rather than the organic.

WOOD, Francis   1871-1926

Sculptor. Born Keswick, Cumbria. Educated in Switzerland and Germany. Studied art at Karlsruhe, Germany, returning to England, 1889; also studied at the RCA and the Slade School, 1890-2, and finally entered the RA Schools where he won a travelling scholarship, 1895. Became assistant to Sir Thomas Brock, RA, 1894-5. From 1895 exhibited at the RA. Modelling Master at Glasgow School of Art, 1897-1901, after which he returned to London. Enlisted in the RAMC, 1915. Elected ARA, 1910, and RA, 1920. Professor of Sculpture at the RCA, 1918-23.

WOOD, Harold   b.1918

Painter. Born Preston, Lancashire. On leaving school he worked for a paint company, learning gilding, graining and other decorative arts. After six years of war service in the Army, he turned to commercial art and spent six months in Fleet Street drawing strip cartoons. 1946 decided to become a painter and returned to Lancashire. 1953 returned south and began executing murals; for three years worked solely for Wolf Mankowitz. Solo exhibitions include one at the Beaux Arts Gallery, London, 1956.

WOOD, James   1889-1975

Painter. Born Southport, Lancashire. Studied history at Jesus College, Cambridge, 1908-11. 1911-14 visited Paris, and became a pupil of the etcher Bracquemond; also studied at Tudor Hart's School of Art, and visited Munich. 1914-18 saw war service in the Royal Field Artillery and Royal Flying Corps. 1922 wrote *The Foundation of Aesthetics* with C.K. Ogden and I.A. Richards. 1926 published *New World Vistas* — 'autobiographical tales'. Impressed by an exhibition of Persian art at the RA, he studied Persian poetry, literature and art, later becoming art adviser to the Persian Government. Exhibited at the Zwemmer Gallery. Erudite, literary and an admirer of Kandinsky, he experimented boldly in his paintings but

OWEN WOOD, b.1939. *'Gentleman's Relish'*, 1980. Silk screen print. 12½ in. x 10in. Private Collection.

never evolved any definite artistic personality. A retrospective exhibition was held at Blond Fine Art, 1980.

WOOD, John Glyn
Sculptor. Born Liverpool, Merseyside. Studied at Sheffield Polytechnic, 1973-7 and Liverpool Polytechnic, 1977-8. Co-founder of the Yorkshire Art Space Society. 1982-3 held a Sculpture fellowship at Humberside College of Higher Education. Transfers ideas and feelings about landscapes into three-dimensional pieces using wood, perspex, resin, sail cloth, plaster and paper.

WOOD, Julie   b.1953
Painter. Studied at Bristol Polytechnic, 1971-2, Exeter College of Art, 1972-5, and RCA, 1975-8. Solo exhibition at the ICA, London, 1984, at which her paintings, of figures and heads, travelled across the walls and corridors in 'An Adventure in the Interior', as the show was called.

WOOD, Owen   b.1939
Painter and illustrator. Studied at Camberwell School of Art, 1945-8, under John Minton* who became a friend. National Service, 1948-9. Worked for the Civil Service, 1950-2. A versatile painter and illustrator who has executed a great variety of commissions, ranging from illustrations to Edward Lear to bank notes for Clydeside Bank of Scotland.

WOOD, Ron b.1922
Painter. Born London. Apprenticed as an engineer, 1936-41. Served in Royal Navy, 1941-6, 1946-66 pursued a career in nuclear engineering, whilst also studying at St. Martin's School of Art, London, 1953-5. 1966 moved to Cornwall to concentrate on painting and sculpture. Much of his work is based on the chequerboard theme.

WOOD, Tom b.1955
Painter. Born Dar es Salaam, East Africa. Moved to England, 1960. Studied at Batley School of Art, 1975-6, Leeds Polytechnic, transfering in mid-course to Sheffield School of Art, 1976-8. 1981 held an Artist in Industry Fellowship, working at Redfern National Glass, Barnsley. His *trompe-l'oeil* fidelity has proved effective in portraiture; in 1985 he was a second prizewinner in the John Player Portrait Award and in 1989 painted HRH the Prince of Wales. Has also produced 'Dream' pictures which deal with the political situation in South Africa. (Plate 86, p.435.)

WOOD, Veronica
Sculptor. Studied at St. Helen's College of Art, Liverpool Polytechnic and Goldsmiths' College. First exhibited at the Ikon Gallery, Birmingham, 1984.

WOOD, William Thomas 1877-1958
Painter. Born Ipswich, Suffolk, son of Thomas Wood, an artist. Studied at the Regent Street Polytechnic and in Italy. Exhibited at leading London galleries and in the provinces, holding solo exhibitions mostly with the Leicester Galleries. Elected ARWS, 1913, RWS, 1918 and became Vice-President of the RWS, 1923-6. Represented in several public collections.

WOOD, Wilfred R. 1888-1976
Painter and printmaker. Born Cheadle Hulme, Manchester. Studied at Central School of Art. Enlisted in the Artists Rifles during the First World War. 1918 entered Slade School of Art. Member of Manchester Academy of Fine Arts, serving as Vice-President for over ten years. Favoured watercolour as a medium and was a master of detail and architectural perspective. Left the residue of his estate to Manchester City Art Gallery, a gift that has enabled the gallery to acquire major works by Bridget Riley,* Francis Bacon,* and others.

WOODCOCK, John b.1927
Printer and painter. Born London. Studied as a printer's apprentice in Devonshire. Following National Service in the RAF he attended drama school at the Bristol Old Vic. First solo exhibition at the Coventry Post Office Club, 1960. This was followed by a second solo exhibition at the Coventry Umbrella Club, 1962. 1963 exhibited relief panels made out of miscellaneous materials at the Tower Gallery, Christ Church, Newgate, London.

WOODFORD, David b.1938
Painter. Born Rawmarsh, Yorkshire. Studied at West Sussex College of Art and RA Schools. 1968 moved to North Wales, to live and paint in a remote chapel house near Bethesda, in the heart of Snowdonia. His paintings, in style and approach, follow Constable's example and exhibit both an impressive craft and a profound knowledge of landscape and transitory effects. A major retrospective exhibition of his work, 'Moments of Light', was held at the Mostyn Art Gallery, Llandudno, 1981.

WOODFORD, James 1893-1976
Sculptor. Born Nottingham, the son of a lace designer. Studied at Nottingham School of Art prior to the First World War, returning after service with the 11th Sherwood Foresters, before going on to the RCA where he was awarded the Prix de Rome for sculpture. From 1926 exhibited at the RA. Elected ARA, 1937, and RA, 1945. Commissions include stone figures and panels for Huddersfield Library and Art Gallery, 1935, and Queen's Beasts for Westminster Abbey, 1953 (now housed at Kew). Awarded the OBE, 1953.

WOODHALL, Mary 1901-1988
Painter and art historian. Studied history at Somerville College, Oxford, afterwards studying painting and drawing privately under Franklin White. Later she attended the Slade and studied in Rome. Took a Ph.D. at Courtauld Institute of Art on Gainsborough's landscape drawings. After the war she became Keeper, then Director of Birmingham Art Gallery, 1956-65. In her retirement she returned to drawing and painting, exhibiting at the Ashmolean Museum, Oxford, 1978.

WOODINGTON, Walter b.1916
Painter. Born London. Studied at Woolwich Polytechnic School of Art and City and Guilds of London School where he was taught by A.R. Middleton-Todd.* Curator of the RA Schools, 1961-84. Exhibits regularly at the RA, RBA and elsewhere. Elected RP and RBA. Has painted portraits for the Royal College of Physicians, various hospitals and the Government of Zambia. Represented by the RP.

WOODLEY, Gary b.1953
Sculptor. Born London. Studied at Berkshire College of Art and Design, 1970-3, Camberwell School of Art and Crafts, 1973-6, and at Chelsea School of Art, 1977-8. First solo exhibition at South East Gallery, London, 1981. His works are often based on grid formations.

WOODROW, Bill b.1948
Sculptor. Born Henley, Oxfordshire. Studied at Winchester School of Art, 1967-8, St. Martin's School of Art, 1968-71 and Chelsea School of Art, 1971-2. First solo exhibition held at Whitechapel Art Gallery, 1972. Since 1980 has held regular exhibitions in London, at the Lisson Gallery, and abroad, including one at the Kunsthalle, Basle, Switzerland. Working with found objects and debris, Woodrow transforms one object into another, a washing machine into a guitar, for instance, the end result a humorous metaphor for the pathos inherent in the shifting values of our fast-changing society.

Bibl: *Bill Woodrow: Sculpture 1980-86,* The Fruitmarket Gallery, Edinburgh, 1986.

WOODS, Henry 1846-1921
Painter. Born Warrington, Lancashire. Studied at Warrington School of Art and the RCA. Worked as a magazine illustrator and was one of the original staff members of *The Graphic.* From 1869 exhibited at the RA and was elected ARA, 1882, and RA, 1893. Visited Venice in 1876 and settled there. Represented in many public collections.

WOODS, S. John b.1915
Painter. Born London. Before 1939 showed in exhibitions of abstract art at home and abroad and wrote extensively

BILL WOODROW, b.1948.
'First Chair', 1989.
Cardboard into bronze.
49 ½ in. x 24 ½ in. x 23 ½ in.
Lisson Gallery, London.
Photograph Sue Ormerod.

on the subject. Solo exhibitions at Roland, Browse and Delbanco, 1946, Taverty Brook Street, 1949 and Beaux Arts Gallery, 1954. Published *John Piper, Paintings, Drawings and Theatre Designs 1932-1954*, 1955. Worked as Advertising Director of Ealing Studios, 1943-55, involving a number of artists in designs for film posters, and afterwards worked in television for Unilever.

WOODWARD, Derek   b.1923
Painter. Born Oxford. Studied at Southern College of Art, Portsmouth, and St. Martin's School of Art. Solo exhibition of abstracts at the New Vision Gallery, London, 1964.

WOODWARD, Eric   b.1926
Painter. Born Heswall, Cheshire. Worked for his father in

a butcher's shop, 1942-4. National Service, 1944-7. Studied at Liverpool College of Art, 1948-53. 1951 founder member of the Wirral Arts Society. 1953-6 regularly exhibited at the Liverpool Academy. He stopped painting after this period until 1973. 1981 first solo exhibition at Wakefield Art Gallery. 1978 was awarded the MBE for his services to education as organiser of the West Riding School Museum Service.

WOODWARD, Malcolm   b.1943
Sculptor. Born Doncaster, Yorkshire. Studied at Doncaster and Leicester Colleges of Art and the RCA. Worked for a period as Henry Moore's* assistant and taught at Camden Arts Centre. 1978 solo exhibition at the Alpine Gallery, London. 1983 executed *Stations of the Cross,* eleven

WOOLF, Hal

sculptures for holograms commissioned by Coventry Cathedral. 1983 major retrospective held at Leeds City Art Gallery.

WOOLF, Hal   1902-1962
Painter. Born London. Studied engineering at London University before moving to Chelsea School of Art. Became chiefly a landscape painter, travelling in Europe and the Middle East. Exhibited widely during the inter-war years and after. Served in the Royal Engineers during the war. Lived by his art until 1953 when, unable to follow the latest trends, he took on various jobs, becoming the last employed lamplighter in the Postal Department of London University. Was reported missing seven days before his death, which took place in a Wimbledon hospital without friends or relatives.

WOOTTON, Frank   b.1911
Painter. Born Milford, Hampshire. Studied at Eastbourne School of Art. Exhibited at the RA, the ROI and in the provinces and abroad. Worked as a war artist for the RAF during the Second World War, in France, India and Burma. A meticulously technical artist, he brought to his work a specialist knowledge of aircraft and the same serious scrutiny of weather as a meteorologist. Also painted advertisements for de Havilland. President of the Guild of Aviation Artists.

Bibl: Alan Ross, *Colours of War: War Art 1939-45,* Jonathan Cape, London, 1983.

WOROPAY, Vincent   b.1951
Sculptor. Studied at Portsmouth School of Art and Design, 1973-4, Brighton Polytechnic, 1974-7, and Slade School of Fine Art, 1977-9. Rome Scholar in Sculpture, 1979-81. First solo exhibition held at the Drawing Schools Gallery, Eton, 1983; others include 'Supra Limum' at Fabian Carlsson Gallery, London, 1988.

WORTH, Leslie   b.1923
Painter. Born Bideford, Devon. Studied at Bideford and Plymouth Schools of Art and at the RCA. Awards include the de Laszlo Silver Medal for Painting, 1983. He is Vice-President of the RWS and a Trustee member of the RBA. He has exhibited regularly at the RA and at Agnew's where he has held five solo exhibitions, including one in 1985. Works in the collections of public galleries at Aberdeen, Brighton, Dundee, Guildford, Rochdale, Southport, Wakefield; National Gallery of New Zealand; the Department of the Environment and the RA, London.

WRAGG, Gary   b.1946
Painter. Studied at High Wycombe School of Art, 1962-6, Camberwell School of Art and Crafts, 1966-9, and Slade School of Fine Art, 1969-71. 1972 visited America and Mexico on a Boise Travelling Scholarship. During the 1970s did various teaching jobs at Camberwell School of Art and Crafts, Portsmouth Polytechnic and St. Martin's School of Art. First solo exhibition held at the Acme Gallery, London, 1976, where he held another, 1979. Wragg's abstract paintings, at times as garish and chaotic as Bank Holiday Brighton (which has inspired some of his paintings), have been described as 'a continuous autobiography of subconscious feelings'. When he first came to the fore in the 1970s his hectic, multi-coloured canvases seemed to generate a raw energy comparable with that found in punk music. Recent solo exhibition at Goldsmiths Gallery, London, 1990.

Bibl: *Gary Wragg: Paintings 1977/1978,* with essay by Bryan Robertson, The Acme Gallery, London, 1979.

WRIGHT, Austin   b.1911
Sculptor. Born Chester, Cheshire. Brought up in Cardiff. Studied languages at Oxford. Began working as a sculptor in 1955. Has lived and worked most of his life in Upper Poppleton, near York. Inspired by the underlying structure in natural forms. 1961-4 a held Gregory Fellow-ship in Sculpture, Leeds University. Works in steel and has exhibited widely. Represented in the V & A, the Arts Council Collection and in various private and public collections throughout the world.

WRIGHT, Brian   b.1937
Painter. Born London. Studied at Chelsea School of Art, 1955-9, and RCA, 1959-62. Solo exhibitions include one at the Grabowski Gallery, London, 1965.

WRIGHT, Charles   b.1931
Painter. Born Hull, Yorkshire, and has rarely left it. Studied at Hull College of Art, 1949-54. After his National Service he worked as a commercial artist for three years, after which he combined painting with art teaching at a local school. First solo exhibition held at University of Hull, 1964.

WRIGHT, Edward   b.1912
Painter, relief-maker and collagist. At first studied to be an architect at London University. Though born in England, his family was South American and in the mid-1930s he went to Equador and Chile where he worked as an architect. He returned to this country as a volunteer at the beginning of the war. Began to paint seriously, also worked as a designer and typographer. Solo exhibitions include one at the Mayor Gallery, London, 1959.

WRIGHT, Gerry   b.1931
Painter. Born Maidstone, Kent. Studied at Maidstone Art School, 1951-3. Began exhibiting, 1955. Moved from London to Wiltshire, 1968. His early paintings were in a style appropriate to the *Boy's Own Paper*. Developed a less naïve but still very personal style, concentrating on English landscape and cricket. Recent solo exhibitions include one at the Cleveland Gallery, Bath, 1984.

WRIGHT, John   b.1931
Painter. Born London. Won an Arts Council Purchase Prize, 1955, and 1961 held his first solo exhibition at the Howard Roberts Gallery, London. 1965 appointed Principal to Newport College of Art; also makes radio and television broadcasts.

WRIGHT, John   b.1932
Painter. Trained in Wales and London. Began exhibiting in 1954 and since then has shown in Wales, London, Europe and America. 1957 he won a Phoenix Literary Award and he has published short stories in various periodicals. 1960 exhibited at New Art Centre, London, and that year won the Llandaff Festival Cover Design Competition. Represented in Arts Council Collection, National Museum of Wales and elsewhere.

JOHN BUCKLAND WRIGHT,
1897-1954. *'Baignade'*, 1932.
Wood engraving. 8in. x 6in.
Blond Fine Art Limited.

WRIGHT, John Buckland   1897-1954
Painter and printmaker. Born New Zealand. 1905 his
family moved to England. 1916 joined Scottish ambulance
unit attached to the French Army. Served at Verdun,
awarded Croix de Guerre. 1918 went up to Oxford to read
History. 1921-2 turned to architecture and graduated as
an architect from the Bartlett School of Architecture,
London University. 1924 abandoned architecture, visited
Paris and Italy and settled in Brussels where he taught
himself engraving. 1929-39 lived in Paris and joined
William Hayter's Atelier 17. Exhibited in London and
Paris and returned to England at the outbreak of war.
Worked as Censor in Charge with Reuters. 1940, one of
three engravers representing Britain at the Venice
Biennale. From 1948 taught at various art schools. 1953
published *Etching and Engraving: Techniques and the
Modern Trend.*

Bibl: *John Buckland Wright 1897-1954, Paintings, Drawings and
Prints,* Blond Fine Art Ltd., 1981.

WRIGHT, Liz   b.1950
Painter. Born Wembley, Middlesex. Studied at St.
Martin's School of Art, 1968-9, and West of England
College, Bristol, 1969-72. Began exhibiting, 1977. Solo
exhibitions include one at Austin/Desmond in Ascot,
1987. Occasionally ransacks past art for images often
humorously used, her works having a *faux naïveté* which is
both playful and sharp. She has called her work
'Surruralist', an elision of 'Surrealism' and 'Ruralism'.

WRIGHT, Paul   b.1946
Painter. Born Lancashire. Studied at Southport Art
College, 1961-3. Worked as a stage designer for ten years
in repertory theatres around Britain. Returned to
painting and held a solo exhibition at the Grabowski
Gallery, London, 1974.

WRIGHT, Peter   b.1932
Painter. Studied at St. Martin's School of Art, 1949-55.

WRIGHT, William

First solo exhibition held at Woodstock Gallery, London, 1963. Numerous shows followed including one at Reading Museum and Art Gallery, 1979. His paintings reflect the influence of the Norwich School of landscape painters and the dominating impact of the horizon on the East Anglian countryside.

WRIGHT, William   b.1938
Painter. Born Sydney, Australia. Attended National Art School of Australia, 1954-8. Studied in Florence, 1959-62. 1962 arrived London and studied graphic techniques at Central School of Arts and Crafts. 1966 first solo exhibition held at the Traverse Art Gallery, London.

WYATT, Anthony   b.1927
Painter. Born Brentford, Middlesex. Studied at St. Martin's School of Art, 1953-6. First solo exhibition at the Beaux Arts Gallery, London, 1961.

WYETH, Paul   b.1920
Painter. Born London. Studied at Hammersmith College of Art and at the RCA. Member of the RBA, the RP and the Salon des Beaux Arts. Awards include the Paris Salon Medaille d'Argent, 1976, Medaille d'Or, 1977 and 1979, and the de Laszlo award, 1978. Exhibited regularly in Britain and Europe, including the RA and the RP. Solo exhibition at the Mall Galleries, 1980. Works in the collections of the Municipal Galleries in Melbourne, Boston, Massachusetts, and Birmingham.

WYLLIE, Charles William   1859-1923
Painter. Born London, younger brother of W.L. Wyllie.* Studied at Leigh's School of Art and the RA Schools. Exhibited at the RA from 1872. Represented in the Tate Gallery.

WYLLIE, Harold   1880-1973
Painter. Born London, son of the marine painter W.L. Wyllie.* Took up art after failing to gain entrance to the Navy. 1898 went to New York as special artist to *The Graphic.* Fought in the Boer War. At various intervals studied painting under his father, Sir T. Graeme Jackson, E.A. Abbey* and Frank Short.* Exhibited at the RA, RI and in the provinces. Served in the Royal Flying Corps in the First World War. 1934 appointed Hon. Marine Painter to the Royal Yacht Squadron. Became Vice-President of the Royal Society of Marine Artists, 1958. Represented in several public collections.

WYLLIE, William Lionel   1851-1931
Painter. Born London, son of William Morrison Wyllie, a genre painter and brother of C.W. Wyllie.* Studied at Heatherley's, 1865, and the RA Schools, 1866-9, winning the Turner Medal in 1869. Exhibited at the RA from 1868. Elected RI, 1882-94 (re-elected 1917), ARA, 1889, ARE, 1903, RE, 1904, and RA, 1907. Wrote books on Turner and Norway and published *Marine Painting and Water-colour,* 1901. Father of Harold Wyllie.* Worked for twenty years for *The Graphic* from its inception in 1870; his last drawing was of the sinking of HMS *Victoria* after its collision with *Camperdown. Toil, Glitter, Grime, and Wealth, on a Flowing Tide* was a Chantrey Bequest purchase for the Tate Gallery in 1883. A painter all his life of 'ships and sea and atmosphere', he also etched for Robert Dunthorne who ran the Rembrandt Gallery, made posters for the Orient Company and in 1930 completed a panorama of the Battle of Trafalgar for the *Victory Museum* at Portsmouth.

WYNDHAM, Nicholas   b.1944
Sculptor. Born Oxfordshire. Studied at Ealing School of Art and the Universities of Paris, Oxford and Reading, 1962-9. Worked as a lecturer in art, translator, crafts instructor and civil servant. First solo show at the Serpentine Gallery, 1971. Works in the collections of the Arts Council and the Ferens Art Gallery, Hull.

WYNNE, David   b.1926
Born Hampshire. Educated at Trinity College, Cambridge. Served with the RNVR in minesweepers during the war. Became a sculptor in 1949. Had no formal art training. Studied with the sculptor Georg Ehrlich* and worked as a stone mason in Paris, 1951. Art master at Langford Grove School for Girls, 1953-7. First one person show at the Leicester Galleries, 1955. Has completed many outdoor public sculpture commissions, including a black marble figure of Guy the Gorilla at Crystal Palace Park and the marble Genesis column at BOC Headquarters, Hammersmith. 1983 carved the statue of God for one west front of Wells Cathedral. Critical appreciation of his work has never equalled its popular demand.

Bibl: T.S.R. Boase, *The Sculpture of David Wynne, 1949-1967,* Michael Joseph, London, 1968.

WYNNE-JONES, Nancy   b.1922
Painter. Born Dolgellau, Wales. Studied at Heatherley's and at Chelsea School of Art. Later, in 1956, studied under Peter Lanyon* in St. Ives. First solo exhibition held at New Vision Centre, London, 1962. Recent solo shows include one at Taylor Galleries, Dublin, 1990. Married to Basil Blackshaw.* Earlier work was often abstract, but now she mostly paints small, warmly coloured landscapes of Ireland, France and Crete.

WYNNE-MORGAN, John   b.1906
Painter. Born Yorkshire. He regularly exhibited in Britain, including a solo exhibition at the Upper Grosvenor Gallery, London. He wrote a number of books on the practice of painting and had a studio in Hampstead where he taught pupils. He favours an impressionist technique, using small touches of unmixed colour and an impasto technique.

WYNTER, Bryan   1915-1975
Painter. Born London. Studied at the Slade, 1938-40. Co-founder of the Crypt Group, St. Ives, which later became the Penwith Society of Arts. First solo exhibition at the Redfern Gallery, London, 1947, where he exhibited regularly until 1957. He began as a landscape painter in a neo-romantic vein. After 1956 he moved from figurative to abstract painting, using highly complex grids, the rapid brush marks creating semi-transparent veils of colour. In 1962, after suffering the first of several heart attacks, he began making constructions which he called IMOOS (Images Moving Out Onto Space). He would hang pairs of painted shapes, which contrasted with each other, in front of a parabolic mirror leaving them to rotate freely. As they did so their reflections reversed and became enlarged and appeared to move in opposite directions. A memorial exhibition of his work was held at the Hayward Gallery, London, 1976, followed by two more exhibitions in 1981 and 1982 at the New Art Centre, London.

Bibl: *Bryan Wynter: A Selection of Work from 1951 to 1975,* with introduction by Tom Cross, Penwith Galleries, St. Ives, 1982.

YALE, Brian   b.1936
Painter. Born Staffordshire. Studied at Stourbridge School of Art, 1952-6, and at the RCA, 1958-62. 1965-71 founder member of Group One Four. 1966 first solo exhibition at the Axiom Gallery, London. 1979 invited to paint in Israel. His work from the trip was shown in a group exhibition, 'Israel Observed', in Israel and London, 1980-1. In 1980 he also held a solo exhibition at Dudley Museum and Art Gallery, followed in 1984 by a solo exhibition devoted to his paintings of the battlefields of the First World War. His paintings are figurative, recording landscapes and people with close attention to detail. Included in the collections of the Tate Gallery, Arts Council of Great Britain, Welsh Arts Council, Manchester City Art Gallery, Library and Museum, Dudley, Girton and Magdalene Colleges, Cambridge.

Bibl: *No Man's Land; Paintings of the battlefields of the First World War,* Imperial War Museum, London, 1984.

YARDLEY, John   b.1933
Painter. Born Beverley, Yorkshire. He began painting following his National Service with the Royal Sussex Regiment. He exhibits regularly at the Royal Institute galleries, London, and is a member of the Armed Forces Art Society. First solo exhibition at the Hampton Hill Gallery, Middlesex, 1981. He specialises in watercolour, painting landscapes in a relaxed, spontaneous, traditional style.

YATES, Fred   b.1922
Painter. Born Manchester. Studied at Art College, 1946-51, following National Service as a Grenadier Guardsman, 1941-5. He has painted full-time since 1969. First solo exhibition at the Reynolds Gallery, Plymouth, 1976, followed by a second exhibition at the same gallery, 1980. He regularly exhibits at the RA and in other group exhibitions in London. He paints scenes of leisure, focusing on fairs and parks where diminutive figures are depicted in relation to the expanse of their environment. Included in the collections of Dewsbury City Art Gallery, Russell Coates Gallery, Bournemouth, Torquay Art Gallery and the collections of Leicestershire, Gloucestershire, Sussex and Buckinghamshire County Councils.

YATES, Harold   b.1916
Painter. Studied at Portsmouth School of Art, 1930-1, later joined a commercial studio as a figure painter. His disillusionment with commercial art led him to explore abstraction. Works from this period were shown at the Artists International Association. First solo exhibition at Foyles Art Gallery, London, 1935. In the late 1930s he moved away from abstraction to a personal symbolism. During this period, when he was serving in the army, he also made studies of his fellow soldiers which were often humorous and satirical. On leaving the army he continued to paint part-time while working in an advertising agency. He later became a free-lance artist. A solo exhibition of his work was held at The Belgrave Gallery, London, 1989. Included in the collection of the Imperial War Museum.

YATES, Peter   b.1920
Architect and painter. Born London. 1936 became a commercial artist, working for international exhibitions in Paris and Glasgow. 1938 studied architecture under Sir Hugh Bennet, Peter Moro and Robin Day. 1941 he became a fireman on the St. Paul's Watch and made paintings and drawings of the fires in London. 1942 volunteered for the RAF. He was posted to North Wales where he made many drawings of the Snowdonia Range. 1943 posted to Versailles Palace, where he met artists and collectors living in Paris, such as Le Corbusier, Gertrude Stein and Alice Toklas. 1945 worked in Ove Arup's office on industrial and architectural designs. 1950 moved to Paris to run a commercial art firm. 1953 moved to Newcastle where he worked as an architect with Gordon Ryder. 1975 first solo exhibition at the Colbert Gallery, Durham, which was followed by a second exhibition at the same gallery, 1976. A retrospective was held of his paintings at the Hatton Gallery, Newcastle upon Tyne, 1980.

YEADON, Richard   b.1896
Painter. Born Brierfield, Lancashire. Studied at the Allen Technical School, Kendal. Exhibited at the RA and in the provinces. Specialised in Lake District scenes, in oil and watercolour. Signed his work 'Dick Yeadon'.

YEATS, Jack Butler   1871-1957
Painter. Born London, son of the painter, John Butler Yeats and brother of the poet, William Yeats. Studied under Fred Brown* at Westminster School of Art. Held his first solo exhibition in Dublin, 1899. Illustrated books by J.M. Synge and worked for the Cuala Press. Had five paintings included in the Armoury Show, New York, 1913. Exhibited at the Royal Hibernian Academy of which he was elected an associate, 1914 and full member, 1915. Best known for his scenes of Dublin and Irish life. Published *Life in the West of Ireland* (1912), *Sligo* (1930) and other works. Has been the subject of several retrospectives, including one held at York City Art Gallery, 1960. Represented in several major public collections.

YEO, Wendy
Painter. Born Hong Kong. Studied at the Slade School of Fine Art, 1955-9. Awards include a Young Contemporaries Arts Council Prize and a travelling scholarship. Solo exhibition at the Commonwealth Art Gallery, London, 1975. Included in the collections of the Ashmolean Museum, University College, London, and Hong Kong City Hall Museum.

YEOMANS, Geoffrey   b.1934
Painter. Studied at Laird School of Art, Birkenhead, 1951-4, Liverpool College of Art, 1955-6 and at Birmingham Polytechnic, 1976-7. First solo exhibition at the Burton Galleries, Wirral, 1969. He has exhibited throughout Britain, including a solo exhibition at the Montpelier Studio, London, 1980, which was followed by a second exhibition in the same year at the Williamson Art Gallery and Museum, Birkenhead. Included in the collections of the Walker Art Gallery, Liverpool, Liverpool School loans collection, Williamson Art Gallery, Birkenhead, the Granada Collection, Manchester, The Stanley Picker Trust, London, and Leicestershire County Council.

YHAP, Laetitia   b.1941
Painter. Born St. Albans, Hertfordshire. Studied at Camberwell School of Art, 1958-62 and the Slade School of Art, 1963-5. Included in mixed exhibitions since 1965. Awards include the Thames & Hudson Award and the Anne M. Berry Award, 1962; 1962-3 Leverhulme travelling scholarship, which she spent in Italy. 1964 first solo exhibition at Norwich Art School; second solo exhibition 1968 at the Piccadilly Gallery, London. Married the painter Jeffrey Camp* and has produced

JACK BUTLER YEATS, 1871-1957. *'Queen Maeve Walked Upon this Strand'*, 1950. 36in. x 48⅛ in.
Scottish National Gallery of Modern Art.

NAN YOUNGMAN, b.1906. *'Path to the Sea'*, 1976. 15in. x 23in. Collection Barbara Todd.

many paintings based on Lowestoft and Hastings and their fishermen. A touring exhibition was held at the Camden Arts Centre, London and elsewhere, 1989. Works on shaped canvases, which are part of the composition of the painting.

YOUNG, Alfred   b.1936
Painter. Studied at London School of Printing, 1958-9 and RCA, 1959-63. Has taught at Berkshire, Kingston and Maidstone Colleges of Art. Solo exhibition of abstract paintings held at Molton Gallery, London, 1965.

YOUNG, Donald   b.1924
Painter. Studied at Chelsea School of Art, 1940-2 and 1944-7. 1949 taught life drawing at Loughborough College of Art. His figurative drawings and paintings are painted in a child-like style. Solo exhibition at the Drian Galleries, London, 1966; various others followed, including one at Southwark Cathedral, 1971, as well as three in West Germany.

YOUNGMAN, Nan   b.1906
Painter. Born Maidstone, Kent. Studied at Slade School of Art, 1924-7. 1927-8 taught and painted in South Africa. 1928-9 attended London Day Training College, studying for an art teacher's diploma under Marion Richardson. 1931 organised a large exhibition of paintings by children at the Wertheim Gallery, London. 1936 joined the Artists International Association. 1944 appointed part-time Art Adviser to Cambridgeshire Education Committee under Henry Morris. 1947 organised first 'Pictures for Schools' exhibition at the V & A. 1953 solo exhibition at Leicester Galleries, London, and began to paint full-time. Various exhibitions followed, including four at the Old Engine House, Ely. Painter of landscapes and industrial scenes, some of her best work has been inspired by the Rhondda Valley.

Bibl: *Nan Youngman: Paintings, Drawings, Prints 1924-1983,* Kettle's Yard, Cambridge, 1987.

YUDKIN, Cicely
Painter. Studied at St. Martin's School of Art, 1948-50, the Art School at Postliano, Italy, 1952-5, and with Josef Herman,* 1956-60. Held a solo exhibition at Hampstead Artists Council, 1961; another held at the John Whibley Gallery, 1970.

YULE, Ainslie   b.1941
Sculptor. Born North Berwick, Scotland. Studied at Edinburgh College of Art, 1959-64. 1964 travelling scholarship to New York. 1974-5 Gregory Fellow in Sculpture at Leeds University. 1969 first solo exhibition, of paintings and lithographs, held at New '57 Gallery, Edinburgh; others include one at Aberdeen Art Gallery, 1977. His sculpture challenges perceived notions as to what sculpture should be, using materials that are often essentially two-dimensional and apparently flimsy. Carefully constructed, they yet look ephemeral and are often situated on the floor, not a pedestal. His pictorial sculpture is indebted to the example of Picasso, Schwitters and the Russian Constructivists.

ZARONI, Murray   b.1947
Painter and illustrator. Born Australia. Studied at the Gordon Institute of Technology in Melbourne. Has lived in London since 1972. A topographical draughtsman who has produced extensive portfolios of work on a wide range of places and subjects. Exhibits regularly at the Thumb Gallery, London.

ZIEGLER, Archibald   b.1903
Painter. Born Plaistow, East London. Studied at Central School of Arts and Crafts, the RA Schools and the RCA. Responsible for the mural decorations in the Lecture Hall, Toynbee Hall, 1932. Visiting lecturer at St. Martin's School of Art from 1938 until his retirement. 1963-70 exhibited at the RA. Held a solo exhibition at Kenwood House, June 1971 and died the following month. 1973 a retrospective was held at the Passmore Edwards Museum, Stratford.

ZINKEISEN, Anna   1901-1976
Painter. Born Kilcreggan, Scotland. Decided to become an artist at the age of eleven and entered a technical school to study drawing and anatomy. Entered the RA Schools at the age of fifteen and stayed five years. Whilst there studied sculpture, at the suggestion of Sir William Orpen* and received her first commission from Messrs Wedgwood for some plaques which were sent to the Exposition des Art Décoratifs in Paris where they were awarded a Silver Medal. Gave up sculpture for painting, specialising in portraits and mural decoration. Executed designs with her sister, Doris Zinkeisen,* for the *Queen Mary* and the *Queen Elizabeth*. During the war worked as Medical Artist at St. Mary's Hospital, Paddington; also made drawings of war injuries for the Royal College of Surgeons. Became Vice-President of the ROI.

ZINKEISEN, Doris   b.1898
Painter and stage designer. Born Gairloch, Scotland. Studied at RA Schools. Exhibited at the RA, the Paris Salon, with the RBA and ROI and in the provinces. Specialised in portraiture and theatre design. Sister of Anna Zinkeisen.* Lives and works in Badingham, Suffolk. (Plate 87, p.435.)

ZABOLE, Ernest   b.1927
Painter. Born in the Rhondda Valley, Wales. Studied at Cardiff College of Art. First solo exhibition held at Piccadilly Gallery, London, 1964; others include one at Newport Museum and Art Gallery, 1976. His paintings reflect his commitment to the Rhondda Valley and the life lived within it. Represented in the National Museum of Wales, the Welsh Arts Council collection, Clare College, Cambridge and elsewhere.

ZYCH, Anthony
Painter. Born Richmond. Studied at Camberwell School of Art and Crafts, 1977-8. Student of philosophy at St. Andrews University, 1979-80. Studied at Slade School of Art, 1980-4. Has travelled extensively in Europe, Africa

ANNA ZINKEISEN, 1901-1976. *'The Dark Lady'*, 1938. 24in. x 20in. Nottingham Castle Museum & Art Gallery.

and America. Held his first solo exhibition at the Bernard Jacobson Gallery, London, 1985; recent solo exhibitions include one at the Albemarle Gallery, London, 1989. Painter of landscapes that are representative less of place than states of mind.

ZYW, Adam   b.1948
Sculptor. Born Edinburgh, Scotland. 1973 graduated from the Architectural Association. 1976 graduated in Landscape Architecture. First solo exhibition held at the 369 Gallery, Edinburgh, 1982, where he held another, 1987. Has received public commissions from the Royal Fine Art Commission for Scotland, the Scottish National Gallery of Modern Art and Podere Fonte Ferrata Castagneto Carducci, Italy.

ZYW, Akksander   b.1905
Painter. Born Licla, Poland. Studied at Warsaw Academy of Fine Arts, 1926-32, also in Athens, Rome and Paris. Settled in Britain in 1940. First solo exhibition held at Scottish Gallery, Edinburgh, 1945. Specialised in landscapes and figurative compositions.